Koren Talmud Bavli
THE NOÉ EDITION

BAVA BATRA

Steinsaltz Center

KOREN

תלמוד בבלי

KOREN TALMUD BAVLI

THE NOÉ EDITION

בבא בתרא

BAVA BATRA

Daf 2a through Daf 27b

COMMENTARY BY

Rabbi Adin Even-Israel Steinsaltz

EDITOR-IN-CHIEF

Rabbi Dr Tzvi Hersh Weinreb

SENIOR CONTENT EDITOR

Rabbi Dr Shalom Z Berger

EXECUTIVE EDITOR

Rabbi Joshua Schreier

•

STEINSALTZ CENTER

KOREN PUBLISHERS JERUSALEM

Supported by the Matanel Foundation

Koren Talmud Bavli, The Noe Edition
Vol. 23a: Tractate Bava Batra, Daf 2a through Daf 27b
Paperback, ISBN, 978-965-7766-08-8

First Hebrew/English paperback edition, 2021

Koren Publishers Jerusalem Ltd.
PO Box 4044, Jerusalem 91040, ISRAEL
PO Box 8531, New Milford, CT 06776, USA
www.korenpub.com

Steinsaltz Center

Steinsaltz Center is the parent organization of institutions established by Rabbi Adin Even-Israel Steinsaltz

PO Box 45187, Jerusalem 91450 ISRAEL
Telephone: +972 2 646 0900, Fax +972 2 624 9454
www.steinsaltz-center.org

This book was published in cooperation with the Israel Institute for Talmudic Publications.

הִנֵּה יָמִים בָּאִים, נְאֻם אֲדֹנָי יֱהֹוִה, וְהִשְׁלַחְתִּי רָעָב בָּאָרֶץ,
לֹא־רָעָב לַלֶּחֶם וְלֹא־צָמָא לַמַּיִם, כִּי אִם־לִשְׁמֹעַ אֵת דִּבְרֵי יהוה.

Behold, days are coming – says the Lord God – I will send a hunger to the land, not a hunger for bread nor a thirst for water, but to hear the words of the Lord. (AMOS 8:11)

The Noé edition of the Koren Talmud Bavli
with the commentary of Rabbi Adin Even-Israel Steinsaltz
is dedicated to all those who open its covers
to quench their thirst for Jewish Knowledge,
in our generation of Torah renaissance.

This beautiful edition is for the young, the aged,
the novice and the savant alike,
as it unites the depth of Torah knowledge
with the best of academic scholarship.

Within its exquisite and vibrant pages,
words become worlds.

It will claim its place in the library of classics,
in the bookcases of the Beit Midrash,
the classrooms of our schools,
and in the offices of professionals and business people
who carve out precious time to grapple with its timeless wisdom.

For the Student and the Scholar

DEDICATED BY LEO AND SUE NOÉ

Steinsaltz Center

Executive Director, Steinsaltz Center

Rabbi Meni Even-Israel

Managing Editor

Rabbi Jason Rappoport

Senior Content Editor

Rabbi Dr. Shalom Z. Berger

Editors

Rabbi Dr. Joshua Amaru, *Coordinating Editor*
Rabbi Yehoshua Duker, *Final Editor*
Rabbi Avishai Magence, *Content Curator*
Yedidya Naveh, *Content Curator*
Tal Avrahami
Menucha Chwat
Rabbi Adin Krohn
Betzalel Philip Edwards
Rabbi Yonatan Shai Freedman
Raphael Friedman
Rabbi Ayal Geffon
Rabbi Uri Goldstein
Nechama Greenberg
Rabbi Tzvi Chaim Kaye
Rabbi Yonatan Kohn
Catriel Lev
Elisha Loewenstern
Adina Luber
Rabbi Simcha Mirvis
Rabbi Jonathan Mishkin
Rabbi David Sedley
Avi Steinhart
Rabbi David Strauss
Rabbi Yitzchak Twersky

Copy Editors

Aliza Israel, *Coordinator*
Ita Olesker
Debbie Ismailoff
Shira Finson
Ilana Sobel
Deena Nataf
Eliana Kurlantzick Yorav
Erica Hirsch Edvi
Nava Wieder
Sara Henna Dahan
Shalom Dinerstein

Language Consultants

Dr. Stephanie E. Binder, *Greek & Latin*
Rabbi Yaakov Hoffman, *Arabic*
Dr. Shai Secunda, *Persian*
Shira Shmidman, *Aramaic*

KOREN

Design & Typesetting

Dena Landowne Bailey, *Typesetting*
Tani Bayer, *Jacket Design*
Raphaël Freeman, *Design & Typography*

Images

Eliahu Misgav, *Illustration & Image Acquisition*
Daniel Gdalevich, *Illustration & Image Acquisition*

Introduction by the Publisher

The Talmud has sustained and inspired Jews for thousands of years. Throughout Jewish history, an elite cadre of scholars has absorbed its learning and passed it on to succeeding generations. The Talmud has been the fundamental text of our people.

Beginning in the 1960s, Rabbi Adin Even-Israel Steinsaltz שליט״א created a revolution in the history of Talmud study. His translation of the Talmud, first into modern Hebrew and then into other languages, as well the practical learning aids he added to the text, have enabled millions of people around the world to access and master the complexity and context of the world of Talmud.

It is thus a privilege to present the *Koren Talmud Bavli*, an English translation of the talmudic text with the brilliant elucidation of Rabbi Steinsaltz. The depth and breadth of his knowledge are unique in our time. His rootedness in the tradition and his reach into the world beyond it are inspirational.

Working with Rabbi Steinsaltz on this remarkable project has been not only an honor, but a great pleasure. Never shy to express an opinion, with wisdom and humor, Rabbi Steinsaltz sparkles in conversation, demonstrating his knowledge (both sacred and worldly), sharing his wide-ranging interests, and, above all, radiating his passion. I am grateful for the unique opportunity to work closely with him, and I wish him many more years of writing and teaching.

Our intentions in publishing this new edition of the Talmud are threefold. First, we seek to fully clarify the talmudic page to the reader – textually, intellectually, and graphically. Second, we seek to utilize today's most sophisticated technologies, both in print and electronic formats, to provide the reader with a comprehensive set of study tools. And third, we seek to help readers advance in their process of Talmud study.

To achieve these goals, the *Koren Talmud Bavli* is unique in a number of ways:

- The classic *tzurat hadaf* of Vilna, used by scholars since the 1800s, has been reset for great clarity, and opens from the Hebrew "front" of the book. Full *nikkud* has been added to both the talmudic text and Rashi's commentary, allowing for a more fluent reading with the correct pronunciation; the commentaries of *Tosafot* have been punctuated. Upon the advice of many English-speaking teachers of Talmud, we have separated these core pages from the translation, thereby enabling the advanced student to approach the text without the distraction of the translation. This also reduces the number of volumes in the set. At the bottom of each *daf*, there is a reference to the corresponding English pages. In addition, the Vilna edition was read against other manuscripts and older print editions, so that texts which had been removed by non-Jewish censors have been restored to their rightful place.

- The English translation, which starts on the English "front" of the book, reproduces the *menukad* Talmud text alongside the English translation (in bold) and commentary and explanation (in a lighter font). The Hebrew and Aramaic text is presented in logical paragraphs. This allows for a fluent reading of the text for the non-Hebrew or non-Aramaic reader. It also allows for the Hebrew reader to refer easily to the text alongside. Where the original text features dialogue or poetry, the English text is laid out in a manner appropriate to the genre. Each page refers to the relevant *daf*.

- Critical contextual tools surround the text and translation: personality notes, providing short biographies of the Sages; language notes, explaining foreign terms borrowed from Greek, Latin, Persian, or Arabic; and background notes, giving information essential to the understanding of the text, including history, geography, botany, archaeology, zoology, astronomy, and aspects of daily life in the talmudic era.
- Halakhic summaries provide references to the authoritative legal decisions made over the centuries by the rabbis. They explain the reasons behind each halakhic decision as well as the ruling's close connection to the Talmud and its various interpreters.
- Photographs, drawings, and other illustrations have been added throughout the text – in full color in the Standard and Electronic editions, and in black and white in the Daf Yomi edition – to visually elucidate the text.

This is not an exhaustive list of features of this edition, it merely presents an overview for the English-speaking reader who may not be familiar with the "total approach" to Talmud pioneered by Rabbi Steinsaltz.

Several professionals have helped bring this vast collaborative project to fruition. My many colleagues are noted on the Acknowledgments page, and the leadership of this project has been exceptional.

RABBI MENACHEM EVEN-ISRAEL, DIRECTOR OF THE STEINSALTZ CENTER, was the driving force behind this enterprise. With enthusiasm and energy, he formed the happy alliance with Koren and established close relationships among all involved in the work.

RABBI DR. TZVI HERSH WEINREB שליט"א, EDITOR-IN-CHIEF, brought to this project his profound knowledge of Torah, intellectual literacy of Talmud, and erudition of Western literature. It is to him that the text owes its very high standard, both in form and content, and the logical manner in which the beauty of the Talmud is presented.

RABBI JOSHUA SCHREIER, EXECUTIVE EDITOR, assembled an outstanding group of scholars, translators, editors, and proofreaders, whose standards and discipline enabled this project to proceed in a timely and highly professional manner.

RABBI MEIR HANEGBI, EDITOR OF THE HEBREW EDITION OF THE STEINSALTZ TALMUD, lent his invaluable assistance throughout the work process, supervising the reproduction of the Vilna pages.

RAPHAËL FREEMAN, EXECUTIVE EDITOR OF KOREN, created this Talmud's unique typographic design which, true to the Koren approach, is both elegant and user friendly.

It has been an enriching experience for all of us at Koren Publishers Jerusalem to work with the Steinsaltz Center to develop and produce the *Koren Talmud Bavli*. We pray that this publication will be a source of great learning and, ultimately, greater *avodat Hashem* for all Jews.

Matthew Miller, Publisher
Koren Publishers Jerusalem
Jerusalem 5772

Contents

For the vocalized Vilna Shas layout, please open as a Hebrew book.

Introduction to **Bava Batra**

Tractate *Bava Batra* was originally part of a large tractate called *Nezikin*, meaning damages, which was composed of what are now the first three tractates in the Order of *Nezikin*. *Bava Batra* was the third and last section of the super-tractate; from this placement it derived its name, which means the last gate. The first two parts of the original tractate *Nezikin* were tractate *Bava Kamma*, meaning the first gate, and tractate *Bava Metzia*, the middle gate. Each of these three parts has its own central topic.

Bava Batra differs from *Bava Kamma* and *Bava Metzia* in two major ways. These first two parts examine *halakhot* that at least in part relate to prohibitions, whereas *Bava Batra* is primarily occupied with civil law, including the *halakhot* of contracts, property, and estates. Furthermore, much of what is recorded in *Bava Kamma* and *Bava Metzia* is based on biblical verses and their rabbinic interpretations, whereas the *halakhot* discussed in *Bava Batra* are mostly rabbinic ordinances based on the Sages' understanding of human nature, societal conventions, and the need to establish limits and guidelines to regulate business relationships.

The regulations established by the Sages are, of course, based on the fundamental principles underlying monetary law: The prohibition against taking what belongs to another person: "You shall not steal" (Leviticus 19:11), "You shall not defraud your neighbor, neither rob him" (Leviticus 19:13); the prohibition against deceiving one's neighbor or causing him any type of pain: "You shall not deal falsely, neither lie one to another" (Leviticus 19:11), "You shall not exploit one another" (Leviticus 25:17); and the principles that guide all of the Sages' enactments: "And you shall do that which is right and good in the sight of the Lord" (Deuteronomy 6:18), "You shall put the evil away from the midst of you" (Deuteronomy 13:6). By themselves, these principles do not create a basis for organizing economic and social life. The Sages, therefore, instituted a system of rules, on the basis of which the practical solutions to real-life problems can be established.

Since this tractate deals primarily with monetary law and monetary relationships, the principles governing these issues differ in their very essence from those governing ritual matters, or the *halakhot* and judgments of the Torah in general. One of the central components is the enormous authority granted to courts to ordain laws and enactments. By power of the principle that property declared ownerless by a court is ownerless, a court is authorized to declare one's property ownerless or grant it to another person. Therefore, whatever is done by power of the court, and in great measure also that which is done by the community's leaders, has the force of *halakha*, even when not explicitly stated in the Torah.

Another difference between Jewish monetary law and Jewish ritual law follows from the fact that one may give away his money or waive rights granted to him by *halakha*. For this reason, many of the laws and enactments in this tractate are directives for deciding the *halakha* when no agreement has been reached between the parties. But when the parties are prepared to reach an agreement, they can decide monetary matters between them as they see fit.

Tractate *Bava Batra* addresses four principal issues: Relations between neighbors, the *halakhot* of presumption of ownership and deeds, the *halakhot* of sales, and the *halakhot* of inheritance.

Most of these *halakhot* are based on *ḥazaka*, a concept that has multiple meanings, some of which are clarified in this tractate in a comprehensive and profound manner.

In its most general sense, a *ḥazaka* is a presumption with regard to the nature of reality, and in the special context of this tractate it is a presumption with regard to the nature and behavior of human beings, i.e., how an ordinary person behaves in a particular situation, and how an ordinary person understands and formulates agreements. With regard to the details, there is, of course, room for disagreement: Does one suffer when another can see into his property, and to what extent does he suffer? Is a foul odor or excessive noise beyond what an ordinary person is prepared to accept? At what point does one protest when an unauthorized person uses his property? How long does the average person hold on to written records?

Similar questions arise with regard to the *halakhot* of sales. When one buys or sells property, whether by way of a written or an oral agreement, how are his intentions to be understood? Of course, a precise and detailed contract prevents misunderstandings and disagreements. But in the absence of a clear contract, such matters must at times be decided by a court. This tractate provides the definition of certain items, e.g., house, vineyard, boat, and the like. What does each of these terms include, and what is not included? If one buys an item that turns out to be defective or deficient, can he cancel the transaction or demand compensation? When is it said that a defect is insignificant and no reasonable person would raise objections about it?

Another fundamental issue in commercial transactions relates to *gemirut da'at*, final intention or making up of the mind of the parties to a transaction. Here too, the matter is decided in accordance with normal human behavior: When is an action performed under compulsion considered void, and when does it have legal force?

Since the *halakhot* in these areas are not established according to objective criteria dictated by Torah law, they enjoy considerable flexibility. Much depends on regional custom and the manner in which the people of a particular place conduct their affairs. The principle that everything is in accordance with the regional custom is important with regard to these *halakhot*, because general agreement can establish the *halakha* in a particular place, whether it was reached through a formal decision of the local residents or expresses the general consensus without any explicit decision ever having been reached. Similarly, many of the matters discussed in this tractate are decided in practice in accordance with the discretion of the judges, who must take into account the circumstances of the time and place, and the particular parties.

The *halakhot* of inheritance differ slightly from the rest of the topics discussed in the tractate, because they are based on what is written in the Torah, and for this reason they do not depend solely on the intentions of the deceased and the heir. While the *halakhot* of inheritance are by Torah law and are not subject to change, they can be circumvented in various ways, e.g., through a deed of gift or through a deathbed declaration. The requirement that the marriage contract to a widow or a divorcée be paid, and the complex conditions attached to it with regard to providing for the needs of the widow and those of the sons and daughters of the deceased, create an additional factor that must be addressed. Some of the discussions in the tractate come to resolve the problems, and occasionally the contradictions, stemming from this additional consideration.

The printed editions of tractate *Bava Batra* are longer than any other tractate in the Babylonian Talmud because most of the commentary to the tractate was written not by Rashi, whose writing is a shining example of brevity, but by his grandson and disciple Rabbeinu Shmuel ben Meir, the Rashbam,[1] whose detailed and expansive style lies somewhere between that of Rashi and that of *Tosafot*.

Tractate *Bava Batra* is composed of ten chapters, the first five of which are printed in the present volume. While issues occasionally extend from one chapter to another, in general each chapter deals with a particular and well-defined set of problems.

Chapter One addresses the *halakhot* governing the division of jointly owned property, especially land.

Chapter Two delineates the actions one may not perform on his own property when they involve causing damage to his neighbor or to the public.

Chapter Three discusses the *halakhot* of presumptive status and proof of ownership, especially with regard to land.

Chapter Four explores sale agreements concerning land, houses, courtyards, fields, and cities.

Chapter Five deals with various aspects of the sale of movable property, ordinary sale agreements, leasing contracts, and appropriate business practices.

Tractate *Bava Batra* also contains sections of *aggada* that are connected to issues mentioned in the tractate. They are found primarily in the first and the fifth chapters.

1 Various scholars, including Rabbi Raphael Natan Rabinowitz in *Dikdukei Soferim*, maintain that from 87a to 89b, and again from 130b to 131b, the commentary attributed to Rashbam was not written by him. They prove this by comparing quotes of the Rashbam as found in some early commentaries to the commentary attributed to the Rashbam, which reveals significant discrepancies. In light of this claim, the publisher of the classic Vilna edition printed an extra commentary on the page believed to be the authentic commentary of Rashbam, calling it *Peirush HaRashbam HaIkari*, the primary commentary of the Rashbam. This commentary will be referred to in this volume as Rashbam Commentary. Plain references to Rashbam refer to the commentary attributed to Rashbam.

Introduction to **Perek I**

People generally live in a society, and therefore their personal properties are located one next to the other. This is true of houses in a courtyard, of courtyards in an alleyway, and of parcels of land in an expanse of fields. In many cases, properties are jointly owned by more than one person. Sometimes it is more convenient for people to live side by side with other people without marking a boundary between them; at other times people prefer to divide up jointly owned property and erect a barrier between them and their neighbors.

This chapter addresses issues concerning the division of jointly owned property and the erection of barriers. One series of questions relates to the separating wall: Are there fixed *halakhot* concerning the height or thickness of the wall, or the materials of which the wall must be constructed? Where exactly is the wall erected, and who enjoys the rights to the wall, both the right to use it and the right to possess the materials from which it is constructed, should it one day collapse?

When the two co-owners agree to build a barrier, the matter is relatively simple. But what is the *halakha* when only one of the co-owners wishes to divide the property and erect a barrier? Can one compel the other to contribute to the construction costs? There are even more basic questions: Can one party insist that jointly owned property be divided? Are all properties subject to the *halakha* of division, or are there certain properties that cannot be divided, whether the division is made unilaterally by one of the parties or with the consent of both parties?

These questions are to a certain degree connected to the issue of damage caused by sight, that is, whether the invasion of one's privacy when he is exposed to the gaze of others is considered actual damage, or merely a matter of personal sensitivity.

Over and beyond the discussion of the division of jointly owned property and the preservation of privacy, a general question arises: What can neighbors, in a house, a courtyard, an alleyway, or a city, compel each other to do for the sake of their jointly owned property, or for the sake of the other neighbors?

These are the basic issues that are addressed in this chapter.

מתני׳ הַשּׁוּתָּפִין שֶׁרָצוּ לַעֲשׂוֹת מְחִיצָה בֶּחָצֵר – בּוֹנִין אֶת הַכּוֹתֶל בָּאֶמְצַע. מָקוֹם שֶׁנָּהֲגוּ לִבְנוֹת גְּוִיל, גָּזִית, כְּפִיסִין, לְבֵינִין – בּוֹנִין, הַכֹּל כְּמִנְהַג הַמְּדִינָה.

MISHNA **Partners who wished to make a partition** [*meḥitza*][H] **in a** jointly owned **courtyard build the wall** for the partition **in the middle** of the courtyard. What is this wall fashioned from? In **a place where it is customary to build** such a wall **with non-chiseled stone** [*gevil*], **or chiseled stone** [*gazit*], **or small bricks** [*kefisin*], **or large bricks** [*leveinim*], **they must build** the wall with that material. **Everything is in accordance with the regional custom.**[NH]

גְּוִיל – זֶה נוֹתֵן שְׁלֹשָׁה טְפָחִים וְזֶה נוֹתֵן שְׁלֹשָׁה טְפָחִים; בְּגָזִית – זֶה נוֹתֵן טְפָחַיִים וּמֶחֱצָה וְזֶה נוֹתֵן טְפָחַיִים וּמֶחֱצָה; בִּכְפִיסִין – זֶה נוֹתֵן טְפָחַיִים וְזֶה נוֹתֵן טְפָחַיִים; בִּלְבֵינִין – זֶה נוֹתֵן טֶפַח וּמֶחֱצָה וְזֶה נוֹתֵן טֶפַח וּמֶחֱצָה. לְפִיכָךְ, אִם נָפַל הַכּוֹתֶל – הַמָּקוֹם וְהָאֲבָנִים שֶׁל שְׁנֵיהֶם.

If they build the wall with **non-chiseled stone, this** partner **provides**[H] **three handbreadths** of his portion of the courtyard **and that** partner **provides three handbreadths,** since the thickness of such a wall is six handbreadths. If they build the wall with **chiseled stone, this** partner **provides two and a half handbreadths and that** partner **provides two and a half handbreadths,** since such a wall is five handbreadths thick. If they build the wall **with small bricks, this** one **provides two handbreadths and that** one **provides two handbreadths,** since the thickness of such a wall is four handbreadths. If they build **with large bricks,**[N] **this** one **provides one and a half handbreadths and that** one **provides one and a half handbreadths,** since the thickness of such a wall is three handbreadths. **Therefore, if the wall** later **falls,**[H] the assumption is that **the space** where the wall stood **and the stones belong to both of them,** to be divided equally.

וְכֵן בַּגִּינָּה, מָקוֹם שֶׁנָּהֲגוּ לִגְדּוֹר – מְחַיְּיבִין אוֹתוֹ; אֲבָל בַּבִּקְעָה, מָקוֹם שֶׁנָּהֲגוּ שֶׁלֹּא לִגְדּוֹר – אֵין מְחַיְּיבִין אוֹתוֹ,

And similarly with regard to a garden,[H] in **a place where it is customary to build a partition** in the middle of a garden jointly owned by two people, and one of them wishes to build such a partition, the court **obligates** his neighbor to join in building the partition. **But with regard to** an expanse of **fields** [*babbika*],[HL] **in a place where it is customary not to build a partition** between two people's fields, and one person wishes to build a partition between his field and that of his neighbor, the court **does not obligate** his neighbor to build such a partition.

NOTES

Everything is in accordance with the regional custom – הַכֹּל כְּמִנְהַג הַמְּדִינָה: The Ramban explains this phrase to mean: According to the way that people in a given city build their homes and walls. The Rashba asks: If the purpose of the wall is to ensure privacy between the neighbors, why must it be so thick? He explains that regional custom means: According to how people in that region construct partitions in jointly owned courtyards. The Ramah and Rabbeinu Yona concur.

Large bricks, etc. – לְבֵינִין וכו׳: According to the Rashba, the rulings of the mishna all apply in a place where there is an accepted regional custom. But in a new town which has no defined practices any sort of barrier may be erected, even one made out of branches, provided that it serves its purpose.

LANGUAGE

Expanse of fields [*bika*] – בִּקְעָה: In mishnaic Hebrew, and perhaps in biblical Hebrew as well (see, e.g., Isaiah 40:4), the term *bika* refers to a plain, an expanse of grain fields, or the like. In the Torah, the word is used in reference to the land of Babylonia (Genesis 11:2).

HALAKHA

Partners who wished to make a partition – הַשּׁוּתָּפִין שֶׁרָצוּ לַעֲשׂוֹת מְחִיצָה: If a courtyard is legally subject to the *halakha* of division, or if its joint owners wished to divide it although it is not subject to the *halakha* of division, each partner can compel the other to contribute to the construction of a wall. This is the *halakha* even if the courtyard stood for an extended period of time without any sort of partition; at any point, one partner can force the other to share in the building of the wall. The Rema writes that even if the local custom is not to make a partition, or if one of the two partners claims that the other waived his privacy rights or sold them to him, the partner about whom it is claimed that he waived or sold his rights can still compel the other partner to participate in the building of the wall, unless the other partner can prove that the latter waived his rights. This applies even if no act of acquisition was performed to formalize their agreement (Rambam *Sefer Kinyan*, *Hilkhot Shekhenim* 2:14; *Shulḥan Arukh*, *Ḥoshen Mishpat* 157:1, and *Sma* there).

Everything is in accordance with the regional custom – הַכֹּל כְּמִנְהַג הַמְּדִינָה: Regional custom dictates the thickness of the partition built between neighbors as well as the materials to be used (*Mishne LaMelekh*; see Gra). If the local custom is to make the partition out of reeds that is how it should be built, provided the reeds prevent people from seeing through the barrier. The Rema, citing the Mordekhai, writes that regional custom is ignored if it tolerates anything less substantial than a barrier made of reeds (Rambam *Sefer Kinyan*, *Hilkhot Shekhenim* 2:15; *Shulḥan Arukh*, *Ḥoshen Mishpat* 157:4).

This partner provides, etc. – זֶה נוֹתֵן וכו׳: If the partners build the partition with non-chiseled stone each must provide three handbreadths of his portion of the courtyard. If chiseled stone is used, they must each provide two and a half handbreadths; for small bricks, two handbreadths; and for large bricks, one and a half handbreadths. These measures include the mortar and lime on the two sides of the wall. This is all in accordance with local custom. The costs are shared equally, even when one person's area is larger than that of the other person (Rambam *Sefer Kinyan*, *Hilkhot Shekhenim* 2:18; *Shulḥan Arukh*, *Ḥoshen Mishpat* 157:3).

If the wall falls – אִם נָפַל הַכּוֹתֶל: Since the wall dividing a jointly owned courtyard presumably belongs to both owners, if it later falls the space where the wall stood and the stones belong to both of them, to be divided equally. This is the *halakha* even if the wall fell mostly onto one person's property, or if the stones were cleared into his area. Some commentaries claim that the stones are divided equally only if there are witnesses who can testify that the stones being divided had been part of the wall (Rambam *Sefer Kinyan*, *Hilkhot Shekhenim* 2:18; *Shulḥan Arukh*, *Ḥoshen Mishpat* 157:5, and see *Shakh*).

And similarly with regard to a garden – וְכֵן בַּגִּינָּה: The *halakha* governing a garden is the same as the *halakha* governing a courtyard. If the joint owners divide the area and one wishes to build a partition, the other is obligated to join in its construction. Regional custom is followed where the custom is not to build a partition in a garden (Rambam *Sefer Kinyan*, *Hilkhot Shekhenim* 2:16; *Shulḥan Arukh*, *Ḥoshen Mishpat* 158:1).

With regard to an expanse of fields – בַּבִּקְעָה: A partition is built in a grain field only if both owners agree to it or if that is the regional custom. If only one of the two wishes to build the partition he constructs it on his property with his own funds. He then makes a border mark on the outside of the wall to indicate that he paid for it. If both parties agree to build a partition, they divide the area, share the construction costs, and make a border mark on both sides of the wall. In this case, if the wall later falls, both the space where the wall stood and the stones belong to both of them (Rambam *Sefer Kinyan*, *Hilkhot Shekhenim* 2:16; *Shulḥan Arukh*, *Ḥoshen Mishpat* 158:1, 4).

אֶלָּא אִם רָצָה, כּוֹנֵס לְתוֹךְ שֶׁלּוֹ וּבוֹנֶה וְעוֹשֶׂה חָזִית מִבַּחוּץ. לְפִיכָךְ, אִם נָפַל הַכּוֹתֶל – הַמָּקוֹם וְהָאֲבָנִים שֶׁלּוֹ.

Rather, if one person **wishes** to erect a partition, **he must withdraw into his own** field **and build** the partition there. **And he makes** a border **mark on the outer side** of the barrier facing his neighbor's property, indicating that he built the entire structure of his own materials and on his own land. **Therefore, if the wall** later **falls,** the assumption is that **the space** where the wall stood **and the stones** belong only **to him,** as is indicated by the mark on the wall.

אִם עָשׂוּ מִדַּעַת שְׁנֵיהֶם – בּוֹנִין אֶת הַכּוֹתֶל בָּאֶמְצַע וְעוֹשִׂין חָזִית מִכָּאן וּמִכָּאן. לְפִיכָךְ, אִם נָפַל הַכּוֹתֶל – הַמָּקוֹם וְהָאֲבָנִים שֶׁל שְׁנֵיהֶם.

Nevertheless, in a place where it is not customary to build a partition between two people's fields, **if they made** such a partition **with the agreement of the two of them, they build it in the middle,** i.e., on the property line, **and make** a border **mark on the one** side **and on the other** side. **Therefore, if the wall** later **falls,** the assumption is that **the space** where the wall stood **and the stones** belong **to both of them,** to be divided equally.

גמ׳ סַבְרוּהָ מַאי מְחִיצָה? גּוּדָא, כִּדְתַנְיָא: מְחִיצַת הַכֶּרֶם שֶׁנִּפְרְצָה – אוֹמֵר לוֹ ״גְּדוֹר״, חָזְרָה וְנִפְרְצָה – אוֹמֵר לוֹ ״גְּדוֹר״,

GEMARA The Sages initially **assumed: What** is the meaning of the term ***meḥitza*** mentioned in the mishna? It means **a partition, as it is taught in a** *baraita*: Consider the case where **a partition of** [*meḥitzat*] **a vineyard**[H] which separates the vineyard from a field of grain **was breached,** resulting, if the situation is not rectified, in the grain and grapes becoming items from which deriving benefit is prohibited due to the prohibition of diverse kinds planted in a vineyard. The owner of the field of grain may **say to** the owner of the vineyard: **Build a partition**[N] between the vineyard and the field of grain. If the owner of the vineyard did so, and the partition **was breached again,** the owner of the field of grain may **say to him**[N] again: **Build a partition.**

HALAKHA

A partition of a vineyard – מְחִיצַת הַכֶּרֶם: If a partition that separated a vineyard from a grain field was breached, the owner of the vineyard is admonished to repair the breach; if necessary, he is reminded a second time (Mahari Kurkus). As long as he is occupied in building the partition, the prohibition of diverse kinds planted in a vineyard does not apply. But if he decides not to build the partition, and the grain increases by 0.5 percent over its prior amount, the grain and grapes become forbidden (Rambam *Sefer Zera'im*, *Hilkhot Kilayim* 7:17; *Shulḥan Arukh*, *Yoreh De'a* 296:47).

NOTES

Build a partition – גְּדוֹר: The owner of the vineyard is seen as causing damage to the owner of the grain, even though the prohibition applies equally to the produce of both, because in the absence of a partition the vineyard owner must remove his vines to a distance of four cubits from the boundary between the two properties to work the vineyard (Rashi; Rid). Furthermore, it is his responsibility to build the partition (Rabbeinu Yona). Some commentaries explain that the roots of the vine spread toward the grain crop rather than the other way around (see Rashba; Rid).

If it was breached again the owner of the field of grain may say to him – חָזְרָה וְנִפְרְצָה אוֹמֵר לוֹ: *Tosafot*, citing Rabbeinu Yitzḥak of Dampierre, writes that this repetition teaches that there is an obligation to warn the vineyard owner each time in order to make him responsible for the damage. By contrast, Rabbeinu Tam understands that the repetition teaches that the amounts of growth of the crops during each period following a breach do not combine to reach the minimum measure for the prohibition. The Ramban disagrees, stating that it is learned from here that the two periods of growth are combined.

Perek **I**
Daf **2** Amud **b**

נִתְיָאֵשׁ הֵימֶנָּה וְלֹא גְּדָרָהּ – הֲרֵי זֶה קִידֵּשׁ וְחַיָּיב בְּאַחֲרָיוּתָהּ;

If the owner of the vineyard **neglected**[N] to make the necessary repairs **and did not** properly **build a partition** between the fields, the grain and grapes are **rendered forbidden**[NB] due to the prohibition of diverse kinds planted in a vineyard, **and he is liable for the** monetary **loss.** He must compensate the owner of the grain for the damage suffered, as it is the vineyard owner's fault that deriving benefit from the grain is now prohibited.

טַעֲמָא דִּרְצוּ, הָא לֹא רָצוּ – אֵין מְחַיְּיבִין אוֹתוֹ, אַלְמָא: הֶיזֵּק רְאִיָּה לָאו שְׁמֵיהּ הֶיזֵּק.

According to the understanding that the term *meḥitza* means a partition, one can infer: **The reason** that they build a wall **is that they** both **wished** to make a partition in their jointly owned courtyard. **But if they did not** both **wish** to do so, the court **does not obligate** the reluctant partner to build such a wall, although his neighbor objects to the fact that the partner can see what he is doing in his courtyard. **Apparently,** it may be concluded that **damage** caused **by sight,** that is, the discomfort suffered by someone because he is exposed to the gaze of others while he is in his own private domain, **is not called damage.**

וְאֵימָא: מְחִיצָה – פְּלוּגְתָּא, כִּדְכְתִיב: ״וַתְּהִי מֶחֱצַת הָעֵדָה״, וְכֵיוָן דִּרְצוּ – בּוֹנִין אֶת הַכּוֹתֶל בְּעַל כָּרְחוֹ, אַלְמָא: הֶיזֵּק רְאִיָּה שְׁמֵיהּ הֶיזֵּק!

The Gemara objects to this conclusion: **But say** that the term ***meḥitza*** used in the mishna means **a division, as it is written: "And the division of** [*meḥetzat*] **the congregation was"** (Numbers 31:43), referring to the half of the spoil that belonged to the entire congregation. According to this interpretation the mishna means: **Since they wished** to divide the jointly owned courtyard, **they build** a proper **wall** in the center even **against the will** of one of the partners. **Apparently,** it may be concluded that **damage** caused by **sight is called damage.**

NOTES

He neglected – נִתְיָאֵשׁ הֵימֶנָּה: That is, it is apparent that he is making no effort to repair the breach. *Tosafot* write that this teaches that as long as the vineyard owner is occupied in repairing the barrier, the crop is not forbidden. This is so even if while the barrier was breached the grain increased by 0.5 percent, the minimum amount of growth that creates a prohibition.

Rendered forbidden [*kiddesh*] – קִידֵּשׁ: Rashi explains that the term *kiddesh* means forbidden, as in the phrase: "Lest the yield be forbidden [*tikdash*]" (Deuteronomy 22:9). This teaches that products of diverse kinds planted or maintained in a vineyard may neither be eaten nor utilized for any benefit; rather, they must be burned (see *Kiddushin* 56b). This prohibition applies to the grain once it grows by 0.5 percent in a forbidden fashion.

The early commentaries address the issue of how one person can render another person's property forbidden. They also discuss whether the grain is forbidden by Torah law or by rabbinic decree (see Rid).

BACKGROUND

Rendered forbidden – קִידֵּשׁ: It is prohibited to plant or maintain any grain in a vineyard (see Deuteronomy 22:9). The produce of such a mixture may not be eaten or used, and must be burned. By contrast, the penalties for planting or maintaining diverse kinds of grain, fruit, or vegetables are less stringent.

אִי הָכִי, הַאי ״שֶׁרָצוּ לַעֲשׂוֹת מְחִיצָּה״, ״שֶׁרָצוּ לַחֲצוֹת״ מִבָּעֵי לֵיהּ! אֶלָּא מַאי, גּוּדָא? ״בּוֹנִין אֶת הַכּוֹתֶל״, ״בּוֹנִין אוֹתוֹ״ מִבָּעֵי לֵיהּ! אִי תְּנָא ״אוֹתוֹ״, הֲוָה אָמִינָא בִּמְסֵיפָס בְּעָלְמָא, קָא מַשְׁמַע לָן: כּוֹתֶל.

The Gemara rejects this line of reasoning: **If** it is **so** that the term *meḥitza* means a division, the words: **Who wished to make a division,** are imprecise, as the *tanna* **should have said: Who wished to divide. Rather, what** is the meaning of the term *meḥitza*? **A partition.** The Gemara retorts: If so, the words: **They build the wall,** are imprecise, as the *tanna* **should have said: They build it,** since the wall and the partition are one and the same. The Gemara responds: **Had** the *tanna* **taught:** They build **it, I would say that a mere partition of pegs** [***bimseifas***][NL] would suffice. He therefore **teaches us** that they build an actual **wall,** all in accordance with the regional custom.

״בּוֹנִין אֶת הַכּוֹתֶל בָּאֶמְצַע״ וכו׳. פְּשִׁיטָא!

The mishna teaches: Partners who wished to make a partition in a jointly owned courtyard **build the wall** for the partition **in the middle** of the courtyard. The Gemara asks: Isn't it **obvious** that if they agree to build a wall it should be built in the middle? Why should one of them contribute more than the other?

לָא צְרִיכָא, דְּקָדֵים חַד וְרַצְיֵיהּ לְחַבְרֵיהּ; מַהוּ דְּתֵימָא מָצֵי אָמַר לֵיהּ: כִּי אִיתְרַצַּאי לָךְ – בַּאֲוִירָא, בְּתַשְׁמִישְׁתָּא לָא אִיתְרַצַּאי לָךְ, קָא מַשְׁמַע לָן.

The Gemara answers: **No,** it is **necessary** to state this *halakha* in a case **where one** of the partners **went ahead**[H] **and convinced the other** that they should build a partition. **Lest you say** that the second **can** later **say to** the first when the latter comes to begin construction: **When I was persuaded by you** to build a partition, it was **with regard to the airspace.**[N] I agreed to the erection of a minimal barrier that would result in a loss of open space in the courtyard. **But I was not persuaded by you with regard to the use** of the courtyard. I did not agree to forfeit any usable space on the ground in my share of the courtyard for the building of a wall. To counter this, the mishna **teaches us** that since they agreed to make a partition, they must each contribute a part of the courtyard for the building of the wall.

וְהֶיזֵּק רְאִיָּה לָאו שְׁמֵיהּ הֶיזֵּק? (סִימָן: גִּינָּה כּוֹתֶל כּוֹפִין וְחוֹלְקִין חַלּוֹנוֹת דְּרַב נַחְמָן).

§ After having determined that the wording of the mishna is unproblematic only if the term *meḥitza* means a wall, it follows that damage caused by sight is not called damage. The Gemara asks: **And is damage** caused by **sight** in fact **not called damage?** The Gemara provides **a mnemonic**[B] for the proofs, which follow, that challenge this assumption: **Garden, wall, compels, and they divide, windows, as Rav Naḥman.**

תָּא שְׁמַע: וְכֵן בַּגִּינָּה!

The Gemara suggests: **Come** and **hear** that which the mishna teaches: **And similarly with regard to a garden,**[N] in a place where it is customary to build a partition in the middle of a garden jointly owned by two people, and one of them wishes to build such a partition, the court obligates his neighbor to join in building the partition. This indicates that invading one's privacy by looking at him while he is in his private domain is called damage.

גִּינָּה שָׁאנֵי, כִּדְרַבִּי אַבָּא, דְּאָמַר רַבִּי אַבָּא אָמַר רַב הוּנָא אָמַר רַב: אָסוּר לְאָדָם לַעֲמוֹד בִּשְׂדֵה חֲבֵירוֹ בְּשָׁעָה שֶׁהִיא עוֹמֶדֶת בְּקָמוֹתֶיהָ.

The Gemara answers: **A garden is different**[N] with regard to the *halakha* governing invasion of privacy, **in accordance with** the statement **of Rabbi Abba, as Rabbi Abba says** that **Rav Huna says** that **Rav says:** It is **prohibited for a person to stand**[NH] **in another's field** and look at his crop **while** the grain **is standing,** because he casts an evil eye upon it and thereby causes him damage, and the same is true for a garden. Since the issue in this case is damage resulting from the evil eye, no proof can be brought with regard to the matter of damage caused by sight.

וְהָא ״וְכֵן״ קָתָנֵי! אַגְּוִיל וְגָזִית.

The Gemara objects: **But** the mishna **teaches: And similarly** with regard to a garden, which suggests that a garden and a courtyard are governed by the same rationale. The Gemara answers: The term: And similarly, is stated not with regard to the reason for the obligation to construct a wall, but **with regard to** the *halakha* concerning **non-chiseled and chiseled stones.** A partition in a garden is built with the same materials used for the building of a wall in a courtyard, in accordance with regional custom.

NOTES

A mere partition of pegs [*meseifas*] – מְסֵיפָס בְּעָלְמָא: Rashi explains that a *meseifas* is constructed out of short wooden pegs that are stuck into the ground, whereas Rabbeinu Gershom defines it as a temporary barrier of reeds. Rabbeinu Ḥananel and most of the early commentaries explain that the term signifies an actual wall constructed from windows.

It was with regard to the airspace – בַּאֲוִירָא: According to the opinion of Rashi, the second partner agreed to a thin partition which would limit his usage of the courtyard's airspace, but he was not persuaded to give up land that would reduce the ground area available for his use. Rabbeinu Yona writes that he agreed to share in the expenses of the partition's construction, but was not prepared to sacrifice land for the project.

And similarly with regard to a garden – וְכֵן בַּגִּינָּה: The language of the mishna itself is no proof; rather, the proof is based on Rava's understanding of the mishna (4a), according to which a partition should be built in every garden, unless the customary practice is not to do so, in order to prevent an invasion of privacy (*Tosafot*; Rashba; Maharam).

A garden is different – גִּינָּה שָׁאנֵי: *Tosafot* ask: If there is a concern about the effect of the evil eye with regard to looking at somebody's crop, why aren't people forced to construct a partition in a grain field as well? They answer that a grain field yields one crop per year, so the concern is limited to the time of its harvest. Therefore, the demand is placed upon others not to gaze at the field at that time. By contrast, a garden yields produce throughout the year, so a partition is built to prevent people from gazing at the grown produce (see Rabbeinu Yehonatan).

It is prohibited for a person to stand – אָסוּר לְאָדָם לַעֲמוֹד: In a responsum, the Rambam explains that this is not a matter of *halakha* but an act of piety. In his opinion the prohibition is not based on the fact that looking causes damage. Rather, when one gazes at another person's crops, he harms himself because he becomes envious.

LANGUAGE

Partition of pegs [*meseifas*] – מְסֵיפָס: The early commentaries struggle to define this term, but there is no consensus with regard to its origins except that it is a foreign term. Some claim that the word is derived from the Greek μεσοπόρος, *mesoporos*, meaning something hollow through the middle of which something can pass, which fits the geonic understanding that it refers to a wall of windows. Others suggest that the word comes from the Latin sepes, or saepes, meaning a fence or a barrier, or from the Greek ψῆφος, *psēfos*, meaning a small round stone or pebble. It might be related to the Greek word μέσος, *mesos*, meaning center or something that stands in the middle.

HALAKHA

It is necessary where one went ahead – צְרִיכָא דְּקָדֵים חַד: One of the joint owners of a courtyard that is not governed by the *halakha* of division cannot claim that he agreed to build a partition only on condition that the other owner would provide the space for the wall and pay for the materials. Rather, both parties must contribute equally (*Shulḥan Arukh, Ḥoshen Mishpat* 157:3).

It is prohibited for a person to stand – אָסוּר לְאָדָם לַעֲמוֹד: It is prohibited for one to stand in another's field and look at his crop while it is fully grown, as his very gazing is likely to cause damage. This is certainly forbidden when the onlooker's presence prevents the owner from performing his work (*Shulḥan Arukh, Ḥoshen Mishpat* 378:5).

BACKGROUND

Mnemonic – סִימָן: Because the Talmud was studied orally for many generations, mnemonic devices became necessary to enable students to remember a series of cases in the order in which they were taught.

HALAKHA

A wall in a courtyard that fell – כּוֹתֶל חָצֵר שֶׁנָּפַל: If a dividing wall in a jointly owned courtyard collapsed, each party can compel the other to contribute to the reconstruction of the wall up to a height of four cubits. The parties cannot be compelled to build it higher than that even if the height of the wall had been more than four cubits (Rambam *Sefer Kinyan*, *Hilkhot Shekhenim* 3:1; *Shulḥan Arukh*, *Ḥoshen Mishpat* 157:10, 13).

NOTES

Fell is different – נָפַל שָׁאנֵי: Rashi and others explain that since there was a wall there in the past the court compels the owners to rebuild it, as the assumption is that having a wall there was an established norm concerning this courtyard. *Tosafot* and others explain that since there was a wall there, the residents became accustomed to engage in private matters in the courtyard.

And he who asked the question – וּדְקָאָרֵי לַהּ: Rashi and most of the commentaries explain: Why did the questioner, who believes that invasion of privacy is called damage, pose this question? Clearly there is a difference if there was a wall there at the outset. On the contrary, the fact that the mishna states its ruling specifically in a case where the wall had fallen proves that in an ordinary situation there would be no obligation to build a wall (*Tosafot*). The Ri Migash explains that the question is asked concerning the *tanna* himself: The requirement to rebuild the wall after it had fallen is so obvious that it need not be stated.

It was necessary to teach the latter clause – סֵיפָא אִיצְטְרִיכָא לֵיהּ: Rashi explains that according to the opinion that invasion of privacy is called damage, the latter clause of the mishna proves that the wall is not rebuilt to restore the status quo but to prevent invasion of privacy. The Ri Migash explains that the novelty of the ruling of the latter clause is that the wall can be rebuilt only to a height of four cubits, and that the neighbor cannot maintain he is prepared to contribute to the rebuilding of the wall only if it is returned to its prior state (see Rabbeinu Gershom).

Damage in one's house is different – הֶיזֵּיקָא דְּבֵית שָׁאנֵי: It is obvious that people engage in private actions in a house, and it is clear that damage will be caused if outsiders can look inside. Therefore, a ruling with regard to a house proves nothing with regard to a courtyard, which is an open space and therefore a place where it is less likely that people will engage in private acts.

תָּא שְׁמַע: כּוֹתֶל חָצֵר שֶׁנָּפַל – מְחַיְּיבִין אוֹתוֹ לִבְנוֹת עַד אַרְבַּע אַמּוֹת! נָפַל שָׁאנֵי.

The Gemara suggests: **Come** and **hear** a proof from a mishna (5a): In the case of a dividing **wall** in a jointly owned **courtyard that fell,**[H] if one of the owners wishes to rebuild the wall, the court **obligates** the other owner **to build** the wall with him again **up to** a height of **four cubits.** This indicates that damage caused by sight is called damage. The Gemara rejects this proof: The case of a wall that **fell is different;**[N] since a wall had already stood there, the court compels the owners to rebuild it as it was.

וּדְקָאָרֵי לַהּ מַאי קָאָרֵי לַהּ? סֵיפָא אִיצְטְרִיכָא לֵיהּ: מֵאַרְבַּע אַמּוֹת וּלְמַעְלָה – אֵין מְחַיְּיבִין אוֹתוֹ.

The Gemara expresses its astonishment: **And he who asked** the question,[N] **why did he ask it** at all? The mishna is clearly referring to a wall that has fallen, which means that the joint owners have already agreed in the past to build a partition between their respective portions. The Gemara answers: He who asked the question maintains that the joint owners can be compelled to build a wall even in a case where a wall had not stood there before, to prevent any invasion of privacy. And the mishna does not address the case of a wall that fell to teach that only in such a case is there an obligation to build a wall. Rather, **it was necessary** to teach **the latter clause,**[N] which states that even in a case where there had previously been a high wall the court **does not obligate him** to rebuild it **higher than four cubits,** because once there is a wall of four cubits there is no further invasion of privacy.

תָּא שְׁמַע: כּוֹפִין אוֹתוֹ לִבְנוֹת בֵּית שַׁעַר וְדֶלֶת לֶחָצֵר; שְׁמַע מִינַּהּ: הֶיזֵּק רְאִיָּה שְׁמֵיהּ הֶיזֵּק! הֶיזֵּיקָא דְּרַבִּים שָׁאנֵי.

The Gemara suggests: **Come** and **hear** an additional proof that damage caused by sight is called damage, from what is taught in a mishna (7b): The residents of a courtyard **can compel** each inhabitant of that courtyard **to** financially participate in the **building of a gatehouse and a door to the** jointly owned **courtyard,** so that the courtyard not be open to the eyes of those standing in the public domain. **Learn from it** that **damage** caused by **sight is called damage.** The Gemara answers: This is not a proof to the *halakha* in the case of two neighbors, as the **damage** of being exposed to the gaze **of** the general **public,** which has unimpeded sight of what is happening in the courtyard, **is different** and certainly called damage.

וּדְיָחִיד לָא? תָּא שְׁמַע: אֵין חוֹלְקִין אֶת הֶחָצֵר עַד שֶׁיְּהֵא בָּהּ אַרְבַּע אַמּוֹת לָזֶה וְאַרְבַּע אַמּוֹת לָזֶה; הָא יֵשׁ בָּהּ כְּדֵי לָזֶה וּכְדֵי לָזֶה – חוֹלְקִין, מַאי לָאו בְּכוֹתֶל? לָא, בִּמְסִיפָס בְּעָלְמָא.

The Gemara asks: **And is** exposure to the sight of **an individual not** considered damage? **Come** and **hear** a proof that it is called damage from what is taught in a mishna (11a): **One divides a courtyard** at the request of one of the co-owners **only** if its area is sufficient so **that there will be in it four** by four **cubits for this one and four** by four **cubits for that one,** that is, the same minimal dimensions for each of the co-owners. This means that **if there is enough for this** one **and enough for that** one, **they do divide** the courtyard at the request of one of the owners. **What, is it not** so that the courtyard must be divided **with a wall** that will prevent one neighbor from seeing the other? The Gemara answers: **No,** perhaps it is divided **with a mere partition of pegs** through which one can still see.

תָּא שְׁמַע: הַחַלּוֹנוֹת, בֵּין מִלְמַעְלָה בֵּין מִלְּמַטָּה וּבֵין מִכְּנֶגְדָּן – אַרְבַּע אַמּוֹת; וְתָנֵי עֲלַהּ: מִלְמַעְלָן – כְּדֵי שֶׁלֹּא יָצִיץ וְיִרְאֶה, מִלְּמַטָּן – כְּדֵי שֶׁלֹּא יַעֲמוֹד וְיִרְאֶה, מִכְּנֶגְדָּן – כְּדֵי שֶׁלֹּא יַאֲפִיל!

The Gemara further suggests: **Come** and **hear** another proof that damage caused by sight is called damage from what is taught in a mishna (22a): One who desires to build a wall opposite **the windows** of a neighbor's house must distance the wall **four cubits** from the windows, **whether above, below, or opposite. And** a *baraita* **is taught with regard to** that mishna: Concerning the requirement of a distance **above,** the wall must be high **enough so that one cannot peer** into the window **and see** into the window; concerning the requirement of a distance **below,** the wall must be low **so that he will not** be able to **stand** on top of it **and see** into the window; **and** concerning the requirement of a distance **opposite,** one must distance the wall from the windows **so that it will not darken** his neighbor's house by blocking the light that enters the house through the window. This indicates that there is a concern about the damage caused by exposure to the gaze of others.

הֶיזֵּיקָא דְּבֵית שָׁאנֵי.

The Gemara rejects this argument: The **damage** of being exposed to the sight of others while **in one's own house is different,**[N] as people engage in activities in their homes that they do not want others to see. By contrast, a courtyard is out in the open and it is possible that the residents are indifferent to being observed.

תָּא שְׁמַע, דְּאָמַר רַב נַחְמָן אָמַר שְׁמוּאֵל: גַּג הַסָּמוּךְ לַחֲצַר חֲבֵירוֹ – עוֹשִׂין לוֹ מַעֲקֶה גָּבוֹהַּ אַרְבַּע אַמּוֹת! שָׁאנֵי הָתָם, דְּאָמַר לֵיהּ בַּעַל הֶחָצֵר לְבַעַל הַגַּג: לְדִידִי קְבִיעָה לִי תַּשְׁמִישִׁי, לְדִידָךְ לָא קְבִיעָה לָךְ תַּשְׁמִישְׁתָּךְ, וְלָא יָדַעְנָא בְּהֵי עִידָּנָא סָלֵיקְא וְאָתֵית

The Gemara challenges this distinction: **Come and hear** a proof, as **Rav Naḥman says that Shmuel says:** If one's **roof is adjacent to another's courtyard,**[H] **he must make a parapet** around the roof **four cubits high** so that he will not be able to see into his neighbor's courtyard. This indicates that the damage of being exposed to the eyes of others even in a courtyard is called damage. The Gemara refutes this proof: The situation **is different there, as the owner of the courtyard can say to the owner of the roof: I** make **use of my** courtyard **on a regular** basis. **You,** by contrast, **do not** make **use of your** roof **on a regular** basis, but only infrequently. Consequently, **I do not know when you will go up** to the roof,

HALAKHA

If one's roof is adjacent to another's courtyard – גַּג הַסָּמוּךְ לַחֲצַר חֲבֵירוֹ: If one's roof is adjacent to his neighbor's courtyard, the owner of the roof must build a parapet on his roof to a height of four cubits to avoid an invasion of privacy from the roof to the courtyard. The owner of the courtyard must contribute funds for ten handbreadths of the wall. The *Baḥ* writes that this *halakha* applies to an ordinary roof that is not regularly used. If the roof is regularly used, it is treated like a courtyard and both residents must contribute equally to the wall's construction (Rambam *Sefer Kinyan, Hilkhot Shekhenim* 3:6; *Shulḥan Arukh, Ḥoshen Mishpat* 159:2, 160:1).

דְּאִיצְטְנַע מִינָּךְ.

so that I can hide from you at that time and avoid coming under your gaze.

לִישָּׁנָא אַחֲרִינָא אָמְרִי לַהּ: סְבוּרוּהָ, מַאי מְחִיצָה? פְּלוּגְתָּא, דִּכְתִיב: ״וַתְּהִי מֶחֱצַת הָעֵדָה״, וְכֵיוָן דְּרָצוּ – בּוֹנִין אֶת הַכּוֹתֶל בְּעַל כּוֹרְחָן, אַלְמָא: הֶיזֵּק רְאִיָּה שְׁמֵיהּ הֶיזֵּק.

§ The Gemara has so far presented one version of the discussion of the mishna. **A different version relates** the discussion as follows: The Sages initially **assumed: What** is the meaning of the term *meḥitza* mentioned in the mishna? **A division,** not a partition, **as it is written: "And the division of [*meḥetzat*] the congregation was"** (Numbers 31:43). According to this interpretation, the mishna means to say: **Since they wished** to divide the jointly owned courtyard, **they build**[H] a proper **wall** in the center even **against the will** of one of the partners. **Apparently,** it may be concluded that **damage** caused by **sight is called damage.**

HALAKHA

Since they wished to divide the jointly owned courtyard, they build – כֵּיוָן דְּרָצוּ בּוֹנִין: In the case of a jointly owned courtyard that is subject to the *halakha* of division where one party compels the other to divide the area, or in the case of a courtyard that is not subject to the *halakha* of division but where the two parties agree to divide the area (see *Sma*), each party can compel the other to build a proper wall, in accordance with regional custom (Rambam *Sefer Kinyan, Hilkhot Shekhenim* 2:14; *Shulḥan Arukh, Ḥoshen Mishpat* 157:1).

אֵימָא: מַאי מְחִיצָה? גּוּדָא, דִּתְנַן: מְחִיצַת הַכֶּרֶם שֶׁנִּפְרְצָה – אוֹמֵר לוֹ ״גְּדוֹר״, נִפְרְצָה – אוֹמֵר לוֹ ״גְּדוֹר״. נִתְיָאֵשׁ הֵימֶנָּה וְלֹא גְּדָרָהּ – הֲרֵי זֶה קִידֵּשׁ וְחַיָּיב בְּאַחֲרָיוּתָהּ;

The Gemara objects to this conclusion: **But** why not **say: What** is the meaning of the term *meḥitza* mentioned in the mishna? It means **a partition.** This usage would be **as we learned** in a *baraita*: Consider the case where **a partition of [*meḥitzat*] a vineyard** which separates the vineyard from a field of grain **was breached,** resulting, if the situation is not rectified, in the grain and grapes becoming items from which deriving benefit is prohibited. The owner of the field of grain may **say to** the owner of the vineyard: **Build a partition** between the vineyard and the field of grain. If the owner of the vineyard did so, and the partition **was breached again,** the owner of the field of grain may **say to him** again: **Build a partition.** If the owner of the vineyard **neglected** to make the necessary repairs **and did not** properly **build a partition** between the fields, the grain and grapes are **rendered forbidden** due to the prohibition of diverse kinds planted in a vineyard, **and he is liable for the** monetary **loss.**

וְטַעְמָא דְּרָצוּ, הָא לֹא רָצוּ – אֵין מְחַיְּיבִין אוֹתוֹ, אַלְמָא: הֶיזֵּק רְאִיָּה לָאו שְׁמֵיהּ הֶיזֵּק!

The Gemara concludes stating the objection: **And** according to the understanding that the term *meḥitza* means a partition, one can infer: **The reason** that they build a wall is **that they** both **wished** to make a partition in their jointly owned courtyard. **But if they did not** both **wish** to do so, the court **does not obligate** the reluctant partner to build such a wall, although his neighbor objects to the fact that the partner can see what he is doing in his courtyard. **Apparently,** it may be concluded that **damage** caused by **sight is not called damage.**

אִי הָכִי, ״בּוֹנִין אֶת הַכּוֹתֶל״, ״בּוֹנִין אוֹתוֹ״ מִבְּעֵי לֵיהּ! אֶלָּא מַאי, פְּלוּגְתָּא? אִי הָכִי, ״שֶׁרָצוּ לַעֲשׂוֹת מְחִיצָה״, ״שֶׁרָצוּ לַחֲצוֹת״ מִבְּעֵי לֵיהּ! כִּדְאָמְרִי אֱינָשֵׁי: ״תָּא נַעֲבֵיד פְּלוּגְתָּא״.

The Gemara rejects this argument: **If so,** the words: **They build the wall,** are imprecise, as the *tanna* **should have said: They build it,** since the wall and the partition are one and the same. The Gemara retorts: **Rather, what** is the meaning of the term *meḥitza*? **A division. If** it is **so** that the term *meḥitza* means a division, the words: **Who wished to make a division,** are imprecise, as the *tanna* **should have said: Who wished to divide.** The Gemara answers: The phrasing of the mishna is **as people** commonly **say: Come, let us make a division.** Consequently, the mishna can also be understood as referring to two people who wished to divide a jointly owned area.

וְאִי הֶיזֵּק רְאִיָּה שְׁמֵיהּ הֶיזֵּק, מַאי אִירְיָא רָצוּ? אֲפִילּוּ לֹא רָצוּ נַמִי! אָמַר רַבִּי אַסִּי אָמַר רַבִּי יוֹחָנָן: מִשְׁנָתֵנוּ – כְּשֶׁאֵין בָּהּ דִּין חֲלוּקָּה, וְהוּא דְּרָצוּ.

The Gemara asks, according to the understanding that *meḥitza* means division: **But if damage** caused by **sight is called damage, why** does the *tanna* **specifically** teach that **if they wish,** they build a wall? **Even if they did not** both **wish** to do so, it should **also** be possible to compel the reluctant party to build a wall between them. **Rabbi Asi said** that **Rabbi Yoḥanan said: Our mishna** is referring to a courtyard **that is not subject to the *halakha* of division.** Joint owners of a courtyard cannot be compelled to divide the courtyard unless each party will receive at least four square cubits of the courtyard. **And** therefore, **this** ruling of the mishna applies only in the case **where they** both **wished** to divide the courtyard.

מַאי קָא מַשְׁמַע לָן? דְּכִי לֵית בֵּיהּ דִּין חֲלוּקָּה כִּי רָצוּ פְּלִיגִי? תְּנֵינָא: אֵימָתַי – בִּזְמַן שֶׁאֵין שְׁנֵיהֶם רוֹצִים, אֲבָל בִּזְמַן שֶׁשְּׁנֵיהֶם רוֹצִים – אֲפִילּוּ פָּחוֹת מִכָּאן חוֹלְקִין! אִי מֵהָתָם, הֲוָה אָמֵינָא: אֲפִילּוּ פָּחוֹת מִכָּאן – בִּמְסֵיפָס בְּעָלְמָא, קָא מַשְׁמַע לָן הָכָא: כּוֹתֶל.

The Gemara asks: According to this understanding, **what is** the *tanna* **teaching us?** Is he teaching us **that when** a courtyard **is not subject to the *halakha* of division, if they** nevertheless **wished** to do so, **they divide** it? But **we** already **learned** this in the latter clause of a different mishna (11a): **When** do they not divide the courtyard because it is not large enough to compel division? **When** the joint owners **do not both wish** to divide it. **But when both of them wish** to divide it, **they divide** it **even** if it is **smaller than this,** i.e., smaller than four square cubits for each party. The Gemara answers: **If** we had learned this *halakha* only **from there, I would say** that they divide the courtyard **even** if it is **smaller than this by** constructing **a mere partition of pegs,** which does not prevent invasion of privacy. Therefore, the *tanna* **teaches us here** in this mishna that if they wish to divide the courtyard they can be compelled to build a proper **wall.**

וְלִיתְנֵי הָא וְלָא לִיתְנֵי הָךְ! סֵיפָא אִיצְטְרִיכָא לֵיהּ: וְכִתְבֵי הַקֹּדֶשׁ, אַף עַל פִּי שֶׁשְּׁנֵיהֶם רוֹצִים – לֹא יַחֲלוֹקוּ.

The Gemara asks: If so, **let** the *tanna* **teach this** mishna **and not teach that** other mishna, as this mishna teaches more details than the later one. The Gemara answers: **It was necessary for** the *tanna* to teach the other mishna to introduce **the last clause** of that mishna, which states: **And** jointly owned **sacred writings** that are contained in a single scroll **should not be divided even if both** owners **wish** to do so.

(לִישָּׁנָא אַחֲרִינָא: וְכִי רָצוּ מַאי הָוֵי? לִיהֲדַר בֵּיהּ! אָמַר רַב אַסִּי אָמַר רַבִּי יוֹחָנָן: בְּשֶׁקָּנוּ מִיָּדוֹ כו׳.

The Gemara brings **a different version** of the previous discussion: **And if they wished** to divide the courtyard, **what of it?** What forces them to build the wall? If one of the parties does not wish to build a wall, **let him retract. Rav Asi said** that **Rabbi Yoḥanan said** that the mishna is not discussing a case where they merely reached a verbal agreement to divide the courtyard, but rather with a case where each party **performed** an act of **acquisition with** the other, confirming their respective commitments. Therefore, neither side can retract.

אַדְּאַשְׁמְעִינַן בְּשֶׁאֵין בָּהּ דִּין חֲלוּקָּה וְהוּא דְּרָצוּ, לִישְׁמְעִינַן בְּיֵשׁ בָּהּ דִּין חֲלוּקָּה וְאַף עַל גַּב דְּלָא רָצוּ! אִי אַשְׁמְעִינַן בְּיֵשׁ בָּהּ דִּין חֲלוּקָּה וְאַף עַל גַּב דְּלָא רָצוּ, הֲוָה אָמֵינָא: שֶׁאֵין בָּהּ דִּין חֲלוּקָּה אֲפִילּוּ רָצוּ נַמִי לָא, קָא מַשְׁמַע לָן.

The Gemara asks: **Rather than teaching us** a case **where** the courtyard **is not subject to the *halakha* of division, but** nevertheless **they wished** to divide it, **let** the mishna **teach us** a case **where** the courtyard **is subject to the *halakha* of division, even if they did not** both **wish** to divide it. The Gemara answers: **Had it taught us** only a case **where** the courtyard **is subject to the *halakha* of division** that applies **even if they did not** both **wish** to divide it, **I would say** that in a case where the courtyard **is not subject to the *halakha* of division** then **even if they** both **wished** to divide it, if one of the parties does not wish to build a proper wall he **cannot** be compelled to do so. Therefore, the mishna **teaches us** that he is compelled to participate.

וּמִי מָצֵית אָמְרַתְּ הָכִי? וְהָא קָתָנֵי סֵיפָא: אֵימָתַי? בִּזְמַן שֶׁאֵין שְׁנֵיהֶם רוֹצִים, אֲבָל בִּזְמַן שֶׁשְּׁנֵיהֶם רוֹצִים – יַחֲלוֹקוּ; מַאי לָאו אַכּוֹתֶל? לָא, אַמְּסֵיפָס בְּעָלְמָא.

The Gemara asks: **But how can you say this? Doesn't the latter clause** of the mishna (11a) **teach: When** do they not divide the courtyard because it is not large enough to compel division? **When the** joint owners **do not both wish** to divide it. **But when both of them wish** to divide it, **they divide** it even if it is smaller than this. **What,** is this clause of the mishna **not** referring **to** the fact that either one can force the other to build a proper **wall?** The Gemara answers: **No,** it is referring to **a mere partition of pegs** and not to an actual wall.

לִיתְנֵי הַאי וְלָא לִיתְנֵי הַאי! סֵיפָא אִיצְטְרִיכָא לֵיהּ: וּבְכִתְבֵי הַקֹּדֶשׁ, אַף עַל פִּי שֶׁשְּׁנֵיהֶם רוֹצִים – לֹא יַחֲלוֹקוּ).

The Gemara asks: If so, **let the** *tanna* **teach this** mishna **and not teach that** other mishna, as this mishna teaches more details than the later one. The Gemara answers: **It was necessary** to teach the other mishna for **the last clause** of that mishna, which states: **And** jointly owned **sacred writings** that are contained in a single scroll **should not be divided even if both** owners **wish** to do so. This concludes the alternative version of the discussion.

בְּמַאי אוֹקִימְתָּא לְמַתְנִיתִין – בְּשֶׁאֵין בָּהּ דִּין חֲלוּקָה, אִי בְּשֶׁאֵין בָּהּ דִּין חֲלוּקָה, כִּי רָצוּ מַאי הָוֵי? נֶהְדְּרוּ בְּהוּ! אֲמַר רַבִּי אַסִּי אֲמַר רַבִּי יוֹחָנָן: שֶׁקָּנוּ מִיָּדָן.

The Gemara continues its analysis of the mishna: **To what** case **did you interpret the mishna** to be referring? To a case **where the** courtyard **is not subject to the** *halakha* **of division. But if there is no** *halakha* **of division,** then **if they wished** to divide the courtyard, **what of it;** how can either one force the other to build a wall? If the parties no longer want to build a wall, **let them retract. Rabbi Asi said** that **Rabbi Yoḥanan said:** It is referring to a case where each party **performed** an act of **acquisition with** the other, confirming their respective commitments. Therefore, neither party can retract.

וְכִי קָנוּ מִיָּדָן מַאי הָוֵי? קִנְיַן דְּבָרִים בְּעָלְמָא הוּא! בְּשֶׁקָּנוּ מִיָּדָן בְּרוּחוֹת. רַב אַשִׁי אֲמַר: כְּגוֹן שֶׁהָלַךְ זֶה בְּתוֹךְ שֶׁלּוֹ וְהֶחֱזִיק, וְזֶה בְּתוֹךְ שֶׁלּוֹ וְהֶחֱזִיק.

The Gemara asks: **But** even **if** each party **performed** an act of **acquisition with** the other, **what of it?**[NH] **It is merely a verbal acquisition,** meaning there was no actual transfer of property, but only a verbal agreement to act in a certain manner in the future and not a true act of acquisition. The Gemara answers: **They performed** an act of **acquisition with** the other **with regard to directions,** i.e., not only did they verbally agree to divide the courtyard, they also determined which of them would get which part of the courtyard. Consequently, the acquisition related to actual property, a particular plot of land. **Rav Ashi said: For example, this one walked**[N] **through his** designated portion and **performed an act demonstrating ownership**[B] there, **and that one walked through his** designated portion **and performed an act demonstrating ownership** there.

"מָקוֹם שֶׁנָּהֲגוּ לִבְנוֹת" כו׳. "גְּוִיל" – אַבְנֵי דְּלָא מְשַׁפְּיָא; "גָּזִית" – אַבְנֵי דִּמְשַׁפְּיָא, דִּכְתִיב: "כׇּל אֵלֶּה אֲבָנִים יְקָרוֹת כְּמִדּוֹת גָּזִית" (וגו׳); "כְּפִיסִין" – אָרְחֵי; "לְבֵינִין" – לִיבְנֵי.

§ The mishna teaches: In **a place where it is customary to build** such a wall with non-chiseled stone [*gevil*], or chiseled stone [*gazit*], or small bricks [*kefisin*], or large bricks [*leveinim*], they must build the wall with that material. The Gemara identifies the various building materials: ***Gevil***[L] refers to **stones that are not planed.** ***Gazit***[L] means **stones that are planed, as it is written: "All these were of costly stones, according to the measures of chiseled stones [*gazit*],** sawed with saws, within and without" (I Kings 7:9). This teaches that chiseled stones are those that have been planed and smoothened. ***Kefisin*** refers to **small bricks.** ***Leveinim*** means **large bricks.**

אֲמַר לֵיהּ רַבָּה בְּרֵיהּ דְּרָבָא לְרַב אַשִׁי: מִמַּאי דִּגְוִיל – אַבְנֵי דְּלָא מְשַׁפְּיָא נִינְהוּ, וְהַאי טֶפַח יְתֵירָא לְמוּרְשָׁא דְּקַרְנָתָא? דִּילְמָא פַּלְגָּא דְּגָזִית הוּא, וְהַאי טֶפַח יְתֵירָא לְבֵינֵי אוּרְבֵּי הוּא,

Rabba, the son of Rava, said to Rav Ashi: From where do you know **that** ***gevil*** refers to **stones that are not planed, and this extra handbreadth** that a wall of *gevil* has compared to what a wall of *gazit* has is **for the protruding edges?** That is, a wall of *gevil* is six handbreadths thick because the stones have not been planed and smoothened, and therefore protrude somewhat outward. **Perhaps** *gevil* refers to planed stones that **are half** the thickness **of** ***gazit,*** namely, just two and a half handbreadths, as compared to *gazit*, which is five handbreadths thick; **and this extra handbreadth** in a wall of *gevil* **is** for the space **between the** two **rows** [***urbei***].[BL] That is, a wall of *gevil* is actually two walls of planed stones that are each two and a half handbreadths thick; and the two walls are separated by one handbreadth, which is later filled in with mortar for added strength.

NOTES

But even if each party performed an act of acquisition with the other, what of it – **וְכִי קָנוּ מִיָּדָן מַאי הָוֵי**: Most commentaries explain that this question, unlike the previous question, was asked according to the opinion that *meḥitza* means a division. According to the opinion that *meḥitza* means wall, the act of acquisition is performed with regard to something concrete, i.e., the materials that will be used to build the wall (*Tosafot*).

For example this one walked – **כְּגוֹן שֶׁהָלַךְ זֶה**: He went to his designated portion and performed some type of act demonstrating ownership, e.g., hoeing (Rashi).

HALAKHA

But even if each party performed an act of acquisition with the other, what of it – **וְכִי קָנוּ מִיָּדָן מַאי הָוֵי**: In the case of a jointly owned courtyard that is not subject to the *halakha* of division but the two parties agree to divide the area, either one can later change his mind even if an act of acquisition had been performed, since the act is merely a verbal acquisition. But if the two parties determined their respective parts of the courtyard and an act of acquisition was performed, they cannot retract. Even if an act of acquisition was not performed, but each party went and took possession of his part, they cannot retract.

Some authorities suggest that even if only one party went and took possession of his part, the other party acquires the other part. The *Haggahot Maimoniyyot* writes that the second party acquires his part only if the first party performed a proper act of taking possession. But if he merely walked the length and breadth of the area as a sign of ownership, the second party acquires his part only if he acts in similar fashion (Rambam *Sefer Kinyan, Hilkhot Shekhenim* 3:10; *Shulḥan Arukh, Ḥoshen Mishpat* 157:2).

BACKGROUND

Performed an act demonstrating ownership [*heḥezik*] – **הֶחֱזִיק**: The term *ḥazaka* can be used in different senses: With regard to legal claims it refers to unchallenged possession of property. The physical possession of an item for a period of time enjoyed by someone, varying according to the nature of the item, serves as proof that the person in possession is, as he claims, the legal owner. One who is able to prove uninterrupted possession for the necessary period is no longer required to produce documentary evidence of his legal title to the item.

With regard to the transfer of ownership of immovable property, the term *ḥazaka* refers to the performance of an action that demonstrates ownership. The performance of that action constitutes the formal mode of acquisition through which one formally acquires property received as a gift or purchased from another person.

Space between the rows – **בֵּינֵי אוּרְבֵּי**: The standard way of building with bricks involves filling the space between rows of bricks with a different material, such as mortar or stones, which creates a thick, strong wall and also adds insulation.

Double-layered wall

LANGUAGE

Gevil – **גְּוִיל**: The source of this word is unclear, but the term means something that remains in its natural state without any noticeable change. Accordingly, *gevil* stones are non-chiseled and not planed. The same term is also used to describe hides which have not been processed to become parchment and remain in their original state.

Planed stones [*gazit*] – **גָּזִית**: From the root *gimmel, zayin, zayin*, meaning stones that have been planed so that their sides are straight and smooth.

Rows [*urbei*] – **אוּרְבֵּי**: Some versions of the text read *orkhei*, which derives from the Greek term ὄρχος, *orkhos*, referring to a row of grapevines. Here the Gemara is describing a wall built of thin bricks constructed next to another similar wall, with the space between the two walls filled with various materials to add to its strength and insulation.

כִּדְקָאָמְרִינַן: כְּפִיסִין – אָרְחֵי, לְבֵינִין – לִיבְנֵי, וְהַאי טֶפַח יְתֵירָא לְבֵינֵי אוּרְבֵּי!

A proof for this explanation can be brought from **what we say,** i.e., that *kefisin* are **small bricks,** whereas *leveinim* are **large bricks,** twice the thickness of small bricks. **And this extra handbreadth** of thickness that a wall of *kefisin* has compared to what a wall of *levinim* has is for the space **between the** two **rows** of small bricks.

אֲמַר לֵיהּ: וְלִיטַעֲמִיךְ, כְּפִיסִין – אָרְחֵי מְנָלַן? אֶלָּא גְּמָרָא גְּמִירִי לַהּ, גְּוִיל נַמִי אַבְנֵי דְּלָא מְשַׁפְּיָא – גְּמָרָא גְּמִירִי לַהּ.

Rav Ashi **said to him: And according to your reasoning, from where do we** derive that *kefisin* are **small bricks?**[N] **Rather,** the Sages **learned this as a tradition. And so too, they learned as a tradition** that *gevil* **refers to non-planed stones.**

אִיכָּא דְּאָמְרִי, אֲמַר לֵיהּ רַב אַחָא בְּרֵיהּ דְּרַב אָוְיָא לְרַב אַשִׁי: מִמַּאי דְּהַאי כְּפִיסִין – אָרְחֵי נִינְהוּ, וְהַאי טֶפַח יְתֵירָא לְבֵינֵי אוּרְבֵּי? דִּילְמָא מַאי כְּפִיסִין – אַבְנֵי דְּלָא מְשַׁפְּיָין, וְהַאי טֶפַח יְתֵירָא לְמוּרְשָׁא דְּקַרְנָתָא, כִּדְקָאָמְרִינַן: גְּוִיל – אַבְנֵי דְּלָא מְשַׁפְּיָין, גָּזִית – אַבְנֵי דִּמְשַׁפְּיָין, וְהַאי טֶפַח יְתֵירָא לְמוּרְשָׁא דְּקַרְנָתָא!

The Gemara presents a different version of the discussion. **There are those who say that Rav Aḥa, son of Rav Avya, said to Rav Ashi: From where** do you know **that** *kefisin* **are small bricks,** one-half the width of large bricks, **and this extra handbreadth** of thickness that a wall of *kefisin* has compared to what a wall of *leveinim* has covers the space **between the** two **rows** of *kefisin*? **Perhaps** you should say **what are** *kefisin*? **Stones that** are **not planed, and this extra handbreadth** of thickness that a wall of *kefisin* has in comparison to what a wall of *leveinim* has **is for the protruding edges.** And proof for this explanation can be brought from **what we say,** i.e., that *gevil* refers to **stones that** are **not planed,** whereas *gazit* means **planed stones, and this extra handbreadth** of thickness that a wall of *gevil* has compared to what a wall of *gazit* has **is for the protruding edges.**

אֲמַר לֵיהּ: וְלִיטַעֲמִיךְ, גְּוִיל – אַבְנֵי דְּלָא מְשַׁפְּיָין מְנָלַן? אֶלָּא גְּמָרָא גְּמִירִי לַהּ, הָכָא נַמִי גְּמָרָא גְּמִירִי לַהּ.

Rav Ashi **said to him: And according to your reasoning, from where do we** derive that *gevil* **are stones that** are **not planed? Rather,** the Sages **learned** this **as a tradition. Here too, they learned as a tradition** that *kefisin* are small bricks.

אֲמַר אַבַּיֵי, שְׁמַע מִינַּהּ: כָּל בֵּינֵי אוּרְבֵּי – טֶפַח. הָנֵי מִילֵּי בְּטִינָא, אֲבָל בְּרִיכְסָא בָּעֵי טְפֵי. וְאִיכָּא דְּאָמְרִי: הָנֵי מִילֵּי בְּרִיכְסָא, אֲבָל בְּטִינָא לָא בָּעֵי כּוּלֵּי הַאי.

Abaye said: Learn from it[N] that the space left **between the** two **rows** of a wall **is always a handbreadth.** The Gemara comments: **This matter** applies only when the two rows of the wall are filled in **with mortar. But** when they are filled in **with gravel** [*berikhsa*],[L] **more** space **is required. And there are** those **who say** that **this matter** applies only when the two rows of the wall are filled in **with gravel. But when mortar** is used to fill in the space, **not as much** space **is required,** and less than a handbreadth suffices.

לְמֵימְרָא, דִּבְגָזִית דְּכָל אַרְבַּע אַמּוֹת גּוֹבַהּ, אִי הָוֵי פּוּתְיָא חַמְשָׁא – קָאֵי, אִי לָא – לָא קָאֵי? וְהָא אַמָּה טְרַקְסִין דַּהֲוַאי גְּבוֹהַּ תְּלָתִין אַמְּתָא, וְלָא הֲוָה פּוּתְיָא אֶלָּא שִׁית פּוּשְׁכֵי, וְקָם! כֵּיוָן דְּאִיכָּא טֶפַח יְתֵירָא קָאֵי.

§ The Gemara asks: Is this **to say that** in the case of a wall of **chiseled stone, if for every four cubits of height there are five** handbreadths **of thickness** the wall **will stand,** and **if not it will not stand,** as this is the required ratio between a wall's height and its thickness? **But wasn't there** the **one-cubit-thick wall separating the Holy of Holies from the Sanctuary of the Temple** [*amah teraksin*][LB] separating the Holy of Holies from the Sanctuary, **which was thirty cubits high and its thickness was only six handbreadths and** nevertheless **stood?** The Gemara answers: **Since there was an extra handbreadth**[N] of thickness, it was able to **stand** even to such a great height.

וּבְמִקְדָּשׁ שֵׁנִי מַאי טַעְמָא לָא עֲבוּד אַמָּה טְרַקְסִין? כִּי קָאֵי – בִּתְלָתִין קָאֵי, טְפֵי לָא קָאֵי.

The Gemara asks: **And what is the reason** that **in the Second Temple they did not fashion an** *amah teraksin* to separate between the Holy of Holies and the Sanctuary, as they had done in the First Temple? The Gemara answers: **When** a partition **stands** even though it is only six handbreadths thick, **it is** able to remain standing up to **thirty** cubits in height. But **it will not** be able to **stand** if it is **more** than that height. The Second Temple was taller than the First Temple, and therefore the partition separating the Holy of Holies from the Sanctuary also had to be higher.

וּמְנָלַן דַּהֲוָה גָּבוֹהַּ טְפֵי? דִּכְתִיב: ״גָּדוֹל יִהְיֶה כְּבוֹד הַבַּיִת הַזֶּה הָאַחֲרוֹן מִן הָרִאשׁוֹן״ – רַב וּשְׁמוּאֵל, וְאָמְרִי לַהּ רַבִּי יוֹחָנָן וְרַבִּי אֶלְעָזָר, חַד אֲמַר: בְּבִנְיָן, וְחַד אֲמַר:

The Gemara comments: **And from where do we** derive **that** the Second Temple **was taller** than the First Temple? **As it is written: "The glory of this latter house shall be greater than that of the former"** (Haggai 2:9). **Rav and Shmuel** disagree about the meaning of this verse, **and some say** it was **Rabbi Yoḥanan and Rabbi Elazar** who disagreed as to its meaning. **One** of them **said** that it means that the Second Temple will be greater **in** the size of its **structure,**[N] i.e., taller. **And one** of them **said**

NOTES

Kefisin are small bricks – כְּפִיסִין אָרְחֵי: Each small brick is one and a half handbreadths wide, one-half the size of a large brick. When a wall is built with small bricks, two rows of such bricks are laid, and mortar is placed between them to a thickness of one handbreadth to hold the rows in place.

Learn from it – שְׁמַע מִינַּהּ: The halakhic relevance of this statement is that if one person stipulated with another that he would build him a wall of chiseled or non-chiseled stone, he must follow the measurements listed here (Rashi).

An extra handbreadth – טֶפַח יְתֵירָא: *Tosafot* point out that the Gemara (3b) provides a different solution, namely that the one-cubit partition between the Holy of Holies and the rest of the Sanctuary stood because of the stable manner in which it was attached to the ceiling.

In the structure – בְּבִנְיָן: The height of the Sanctuary in the Second Temple was one hundred cubits, much greater than that of the First Temple (Rashi). In the opinion of *Tosefot Yom Tov* (*Yoma* 5:1), the Second Temple was forty cubits in height.

LANGUAGE

Gravel [*rikhsa*] – רִיכְסָא: Apparently from the word *rekhes*, meaning a knot. Here it refers to the small stones that are used to bind and strengthen the mortar.

Wall [*teraksin*] – טְרַקְסִין: Many attempts have been made to uncover the origin of this term and its precise meaning in this context. *Tosafot*, for example, offer two suggestions. Some authorities link the word to the Greek τοῖχος, *toikhos*, meaning a wall, and specifically an external wall upon which the capstone is placed. Others connect it to the Greek τηρέω, *tēreo*, meaning to protect, guard, or take care of something that is inside. Various other suggestions based on Greek words have also been proposed.

BACKGROUND

One-cubit-thick wall – אַמָּה טְרַקְסִין: The biblical sources indicate that in the First Temple a cubit-thick wall separated the Sanctuary from the Holy of Holies. This wall had an opening, which allowed entrance into the Holy of Holies. In the Second Temple this wall was replaced by two curtains separated by one cubit.

בְּשָׁנִים, וְאִיתָא לְהָא וְאִיתָא לְהָא.

that it will be greater **in years,** meaning that the Second Temple will stand for a longer period of time than the First Temple. **And** the Gemara comments that **this is** true **and that is** true, meaning that the Second Temple was taller than the First Temple and also stood for a longer period of time.

וְנִיעַבְדוּ תְּלָתִין אַמִּין בְּבִנְיָן, וְאִידָךְ נִיעֲבֵיד פָּרוֹכֶת! כִּי קָאֵי תְּלָתִין אַמְּהָתָא נַמִי – אַגַּב תִּקְרָה וּמַעֲזִיבָה הֲוָה קָאֵי, בְּלָא תִּקְרָה וּמַעֲזִיבָה לָא הֲוָה קָאֵי.

The Gemara asks: If so, if the Second Temple building was taller, then to separate between the Holy of Holies and the Sanctuary in the Second Temple **they should have made a wall thirty cubits** high **and** then **made a curtain** for **the rest** of the height, the seventy-cubit difference in height between the First and Second Temples. The Gemara answers: This would have been impossible, as **even when a thirty-cubit** wall that is six handbreadths thick **stands, it is due to the ceiling and plaster** which attaches it to the ceiling that **it stands.** But **without a ceiling and plaster** holding it in place, **it does not stand.**

וְלִיעֲבֵיד מַה דְּאֶפְשָׁר בְּבִנְיָן, וְלִיעֲבֵיד אִידָךְ פָּרוֹכֶת! אָמַר אַבָּיֵי, גְּמִירִי: אִי כּוּלְּהוּ בְּבִנְיָן אִי כּוּלְּהוּ בְּפָרוֹכֶת; אִי כּוּלְּהוּ בְּבִנְיָן – מִמִּקְדָּשׁ, אִי כּוּלְּהוּ בְּפָרוֹכֶת – מִמִּשְׁכָּן.

The Gemara continues: **But they should have made a wall** as high as can **possibly** stand by itself, **and** then should have **made a curtain** for **the rest** of the height. **Abaye said:** The Sages **learned** as a tradition that the partition separating the Holy of Holies from the Sanctuary should be built **either entirely as a wall or entirely as a curtain.** It should be built **either entirely as a wall,** as is learned **from** the First **Temple, or** it should be built **entirely as a curtain,** as is learned **from** the **Tabernacle.** At no time, however, was there a partition that combined a wall and a curtain.

אִיבַּעְיָא לְהוּ: הֵן וְסִידָן, אוֹ דִּילְמָא הֵן בְּלֹא סִידָן? אָמַר רַב נַחְמָן בַּר יִצְחָק: מִסְתַּבְּרָא הֵן וְסִידָן, דְּאִי סָלְקָא דַּעְתָּךְ הֵן בְּלֹא סִידָן, לִיתְנְיֵיהּ לְשִׁיעוּרֵיהּ! אֶלָּא לָאו שְׁמַע מִינַּהּ: הֵן וְסִידָן. לָא, לְעוֹלָם אֵימָא לָךְ: הֵן בְּלֹא סִידָן, וְכֵיוָן דְּלָא הָוֵי טֶפַח לָא תָּנֵי.

§ **A dilemma was raised before** the Sages: Do the measurements given in the mishna apply to **them,** the thickness of the materials themselves, **and the plaster**[H] with which the materials were coated, **or perhaps** just to **them without their plaster? Rav Naḥman bar Yitzḥak said: It is reasonable** to say the measurements refer to **them and their plaster, as, if** it should **enter your mind** to say they refer to **them without their plaster,** then the *tanna* **should have taught the measurements** of the plaster as well. **Rather, isn't it** correct to **conclude from here** that the measurements refer to **them and their plaster?** The Gemara rejects this conclusion: **No, actually I** could **say to you** that they apply to **them without their plaster, and since** the plaster **does not have** the thickness of **one handbreadth** the *tanna* **did not teach** such a small measurement.

וְהָא קָתָנֵי: בִּלְבֵינִין – זֶה נוֹתֵן טֶפַח וּמֶחֱצָה וְזֶה נוֹתֵן טֶפַח וּמֶחֱצָה! הָתָם חֲזֵי לְאִיצְטָרוּפֵי.

The Gemara asks: **But doesn't** the *tanna* **teach with regard to bricks** that **this one provides one and a half handbreadths, and that** one **provides one and a half handbreadths?** Evidently, the *tanna* lists even an amount less than one handbreadth. The Gemara answers: **There** mention is made of half-handbreadths because **they are fit to be combined** into a full handbreadth.

תָּא שְׁמַע: הַקּוֹרָה שֶׁאָמְרוּ – רְחָבָה כְּדֵי לְקַבֵּל אָרִיחַ, וְהָאָרִיחַ – חֲצִי לְבֵינָה שֶׁל שְׁלֹשָׁה טְפָחִים!

The Gemara suggests: **Come** and **hear** a solution to the question, from a mishna (*Eiruvin* 13b) in which it is taught: **The** cross **beam,**[N] **which** the Sages **stated**[H] may be used to render an alleyway fit for one to carry within it on Shabbat, must be **wide enough to receive** and hold **a small brick. And** this **small brick is half a large brick,** the width **of** which is **three handbreadths.** That mishna is referring to a brick without the plaster.

הָתָם בְּרַבְרְבָתָא. דַּיְקָא נַמִי, דְּקָתָנֵי: שֶׁל שְׁלֹשָׁה טְפָחִים, מִכְּלָל דְּאִיכָּא זוּטְרָא, שְׁמַע מִינַּהּ.

The Gemara answers: **There,** the mishna in *Eiruvin* is referring to **large bricks** that measure three full handbreadths, whereas here the mishna is referring to bricks that measure slightly less than three handbreadths, and the measurement of three handbreadths includes the plaster with which they are coated. The Gemara comments: The language of the mishna there **is also precise, as it teaches** about a brick **of three handbreadths,** from which one can conclude **by inference that there exists** also **a smaller**-sized brick. The Gemara affirms: **Learn from here** that the mishna there is referring to large bricks.

HALAKHA

Them and the plaster – **הֵן וְסִידָן:** All of the measurements given for building a barrier include the thickness of the plaster (Rambam *Sefer Kinyan, Hilkhot Shekhenim* 2:18).

The beam which they stated – **הַקּוֹרָה שֶׁאָמְרוּ:** A cross beam that is placed across an open alleyway for the sake of an *eiruv* must be at least one handbreadth in width, but any amount in thickness. It must be strong enough to hold a small brick, i.e., one-half of a three-handbreadth brick (Rambam *Sefer Zemanim, Hilkhot Shabbat* 17:13; *Shulḥan Arukh, Oraḥ Ḥayyim* 363:17).

NOTES

The beam – **הַקּוֹרָה:** The Gemara in tractate *Eiruvin* explains that a beam placed across the width of the entrance to an alleyway is considered a partition, which turns the alleyway into a private domain.

אָמַר רַב חִסְדָּא: לָא לִיסְתּוֹר אִינִישׁ בֵּי כְנִישְׁתָּא עַד דְּבָנֵי בֵּי כְנִישְׁתָּא אַחֲרִיתִי. אִיכָּא דְּאָמְרִי: מִשּׁוּם פְּשִׁיעוּתָא, וְאִיכָּא דְּאָמְרִי: מִשּׁוּם צַלּוּיֵי.

§ **Rav Ḥisda says: A person may not demolish**[N] **a synagogue**[H] **until he** first **builds another synagogue** to take its place. **There are** those **who say** that the reason for this *halakha* is **due to** potential **negligence,**[N] lest he fail to build a new structure after the old one has been razed. **And there are** those **who say** that the reason for this *halakha* is **due to** the disruption of **prayer,** for in the meantime there will be nowhere to pray.

מַאי בֵּינַיְיהוּ? אִיכָּא בֵּינַיְיהוּ, דְּאִיכָּא בֵּי כְנִישְׁתָּא אַחֲרִיתִי. מָרֵימָר וּמָר זוּטְרָא סָתְרִי וּבָנוּ בֵּי קַיְיטָא בְּסִיתְוָוא, וּבָנוּ בֵּי סִיתְוָוא בְּקַיְיטָא.

The Gemara asks: **What is** the practical difference **between** these two explanations? The Gemara answers that **there is** a difference **between them** in a situation **where there is another synagogue.** Even though the community has an alternative place to pray there is still a concern that the new synagogue will never get built. It is related that **Mareimar and Mar Zutra**[N] **demolished and built a summer synagogue in the winter, and,** in like manner, **they built a winter synagogue in the summer,**[B] so that the community would never be left without a synagogue.

אֲמַר לֵיהּ רָבִינָא לְרַב אַשִׁי: גְּבוּ זוּזֵי וּמַחְתִּי, מַאי? אֲמַר לֵיהּ: דִּילְמָא מִיתְרַמֵּי לְהוּ פִּדְיוֹן שְׁבוּיִים וְיָהֲבִי לְהוּ.

Ravina said to Rav Ashi: What is the *halakha* if **money** for the construction of a new synagogue **has** already **been collected and it rests** before us for that purpose? Is it then permitted to demolish the old synagogue before building the new one? Rav Ashi **said to him:** Even if the money has been collected there is still concern that **perhaps** an opportunity for **redeeming captives**[H] **will present itself, and they will hand over** the money for that urgent requirement, and the community will be left without a synagogue.

שְׁרִיגִי לִיבְנֵי וְהַדְרִי הוּדְרֵי וּמַחְתִּי כָּשׁוּרֵי, מַאי? אֲמַר לֵיהּ: זִמְנִין דְּמִתְרַמֵּי לְהוּ פִּדְיוֹן שְׁבוּיִים, מְזַבְּנִי וְיָהֲבִי לְהוּ. אִי הָכִי, אֲפִילּוּ בָּנוּ נַמִי! אֲמַר לֵיהּ: דִּירָתֵיהּ דֶּאֱינָשֵׁי לָא מְזַבְּנִי.

Ravina continues: **What** is the *halakha* if **the bricks** to be used for the construction of the new synagogue **are piled up, the boards are prepared, and the beams are ready?** Is it permitted to demolish the old synagogue before building the new one? Rav Ashi **said to him:** Even so, **sometimes** an opportunity for **redeeming captives will present itself, and they will sell** the building materials **and hand over** the proceeds for this purpose. Ravina raises an objection: **If so,** that is, if you are concerned that they will sell the materials to redeem captives, then **even** in a case where **they** already **built**[N] the synagogue there should be a concern that they might come to sell the structure for that purpose, and therefore one should never be permitted to destroy an old synagogue. Rav Ashi **said to him: People do not sell their residences,** and certainly not their synagogues.

וְלָא אֲמַרַן אֶלָּא דְּלָא חָזֵי בָּהּ תִּיוּהָא, אֲבָל חָזֵי בָּהּ תִּיוּהָא – סָתְרִי וּבָנֵי; כִּי הָא דְּרַב אַשִׁי חֲזָא בָּהּ תִּיוּהָא בִּכְנִישְׁתָּא דְּמָתָא מְחַסְיָא, סַתְרֵיהּ וַעֲיֵיל לְפוּרְיֵיהּ לְהָתָם, וְלָא אַפְּקֵיהּ עַד דְּמַתְקִין לֵיהּ שְׁפִיכֵי.

The Gemara comments: **And we said** that an old synagogue must not be razed before its replacement is built **only** in a case **where cracks are not seen** in the old synagogue. **But if cracks are seen**[H] they may first **demolish** the old synagogue **and** then **build** the new one. **This is like** the incident involving **Rav Ashi,** who **saw cracks in the synagogue** in his town **of Mata Meḥasya** and immediately **demolished it. He** then **brought his bed in there,** to the building site, so that there should be no delays in the construction, as he himself required shelter from the rain, **and he did not remove** his bed from there **until they** finished building the synagogue and even **affixed drainpipes** to the structure.

NOTES

May not demolish – לָא לִיסְתּוֹר: This passage is not apparently connected to the previous discussion. The *Torat Ḥayyim* suggests that since the Gemara mentioned that the Second Temple was bigger than the First Temple, it wished to note that Herod's Temple was also more beautiful than that which preceded it. Such a discussion had to be prefaced with Rav Ḥisda's ruling about destroying a synagogue.

Due to negligence – מִשּׁוּם פְּשִׁיעוּתָא: Rashi explains that the concern is that the destroyed synagogue will never be rebuilt. The Rashba explains that the fear is simply that the project will be delayed. This disagreement has certain halakhic ramifications.

Mareimar and Mar Zutra – מָרֵימָר וּמָר זוּטְרָא: Rabbeinu Yona maintains that Mareimar and Mar Zutra assumed the prohibition is due to the disruption of prayer, as they destroyed the old synagogue and were not concerned that a new one might not be built to replace it. The Rashba and Ramah suggest the opposite: Mareimar and Mar Zutra relied on the winter synagogue in order to destroy the other synagogue, as in such a case there is no concern about negligence.

Even where they built – אֲפִילּוּ בָּנוּ נַמִי: *Tosafot* and other early commentaries point out that this means that even if the structure is complete, it lacks the sanctity of a synagogue until it has actually been used for prayer; mere designation is not considered binding. Consequently, the building can be sold for the mitzva of redeeming captives. Rabbeinu Yona writes that the building can be sold for that purpose even after it has been used for prayer, but it is not customary for people to do so.

BACKGROUND

Summer synagogue and winter synagogue – בֵּי קַיְיטָא וּבֵי סִיתְוָוא: Babylonia is marked by a typical continental climate, with a great disparity between summer and winter temperatures. In the summer, the temperature can rise well above 40°C, or 100°F, whereas in the winter it usually hovers between 10°C and 15°C, which would be 50–60°F, occasionally dropping below 0°C, or 32°F. For this reason, Jews in Babylonia built one type of synagogue, providing good ventilation, for the summer, and another type, offering enhanced protection from the rain and cold, for the winter.

HALAKHA

One may not demolish a synagogue – לָא לִיסְתּוֹר אִינִישׁ בֵּי כְנִישְׁתָּא: A synagogue may not be demolished in order to build a new one in its place. Rather, the new one must be built first and only then may the old one be demolished, even if there is an alternative synagogue that can be used temporarily. This prohibition is based on our concern that due to negligence the new building will not be constructed. The *Taz* states that the old synagogue can be destroyed first if there exists an alternative synagogue that can be used on a permanent basis (Rambam *Sefer Ahava, Hilkhot Tefilla* 11:12; *Shulḥan Arukh, Oraḥ Ḥayyim* 152:1).

Redeeming captives – פִּדְיוֹן שְׁבוּיִים: If money was collected for the construction of a new synagogue, it can be reassigned for any other mitzva. Even stones and wood that were set aside for a new synagogue may be sold for the redemption of captives. A synagogue that has already been built may not be sold for such a purpose; instead, new money must be collected from the community. If the building was not completed, it may be sold (Rambam *Sefer Zera'im, Hilkhot Mattenot Aniyyim* 8:11; *Shulḥan Arukh, Yoreh De'a* 252:1).

But if cracks are seen – אֲבָל חָזֵי בָּהּ תִּיוּהָא: If an old synagogue was found to have cracks it may be demolished immediately, even before a new one is built. The community must work day and night to construct the new synagogue. One should place his bed at the construction site so that he may work diligently to finish the project (Rambam *Sefer Ahava, Hilkhot Tefilla* 11:13; *Shulḥan Arukh, Oraḥ Ḥayyim* 152).

וּבָבָא בֶּן בּוּטָא הֵיכִי אַסְבֵּיהּ לֵיהּ עֵצָה לְהוֹרְדוֹס לְמִיסְתְּרֵיהּ לְבֵית הַמִּקְדָּשׁ? וְהָאָמַר רַב חִסְדָּא: לָא לִיסְתּוֹר אִינִישׁ בֵּי כְנִישְׁתָּא עַד דְּבָנֵי בֵּי כְנִישְׁתָּא אַחֲרִיתָא! אִי בָּעֵית אֵימָא: תִּיוּהָא חֲזָא בֵּיהּ; אִיבָּעֵית אֵימָא: מַלְכוּתָא שָׁאנֵי, דְּלָא הָדְרָא בֵּיהּ. דְּאָמַר שְׁמוּאֵל: אִי אָמַר מַלְכוּתָא ״עָקַרְנָא טוּרֵי״ – עָקַר טוּרֵי וְלָא הָדַר בֵּיהּ.

The Gemara asks: **How could Bava ben Buta**[P] **have advised Herod**[P] **to raze the Temple** and build another in its place, as will be described later? **But doesn't Rav Ḥisda say** that **a person must not demolish a synagogue unless he** first **builds another synagogue** to take its place? The Gemara answers: **If you wish, say** that **he saw cracks in** the old Temple structure. **And if you wish, say** that actions taken by **the government are different,** as the government **does not go back** on its decisions. Therefore, there is no need to be concerned about negligence, as there is in the case of ordinary people. **As Shmuel says: If the government says** it will **uproot mountains, it will uproot mountains and not retract** its word.

הוֹרְדוֹס עַבְדָּא דְּבֵית חַשְׁמוֹנַאי הֲוָה, נָתַן עֵינָיו בְּאוֹתָהּ תִּינוֹקֶת. יוֹמָא חַד שְׁמַע הַהוּא גַּבְרָא בַּת קָלָא דְּאָמַר: כָּל עַבְדָּא דְּמָרֵיד הַשְׁתָּא מַצְלַח, קָם קַטְלִינְהוּ לְכוּלְּהוּ מָרְוָתֵיהּ וְשַׁיְּירָהּ לְהַהִיא יְנוּקְתָּא. כִּי חֲזַת הַהִיא יְנוּקְתָּא דְּקָא בָּעֵי לְמִינְסְבָהּ, סְלִיקָא לְאִיגְּרָא וּרְמָא קָלָא, אֲמַרָה: כָּל מַאן דְּאָתֵי וְאָמַר מִבֵּית חַשְׁמוֹנַאי קָאָתִינָא – עַבְדָּא הוּא, דְּלָא אִישְׁתַּיְּירָא מִינַּיְיהוּ אֶלָּא הַהִיא יְנוּקְתָּא, וְהַהִיא יְנוּקְתָּא נָפְלָה מֵאִיגְּרָא לְאַרְעָא.

§ The Gemara elaborates on the episode involving Bava ben Buta. **Herod was a slave in the house of the Hasmoneans. He set his eyes upon a certain young girl** from the house of the Hasmoneans. **One day that man,** Herod, **heard a Divine Voice**[B] **that said: Any slave who rebels now will succeed. He rose up** and **killed all his masters, but spared that girl. When that girl saw that he wanted to marry her, she went up to the roof and raised her voice,** and **said: Whoever comes and says: I come from the house of the Hasmoneans, is a slave, since only that girl,** i.e., I, **remained from them. And that girl fell from the roof to the ground** and died.

טְמָנָהּ שְׁבַע שְׁנִין בְּדוּבְשָׁא. אִיכָּא דְּאָמְרִי: בָּא עָלֶיהָ, אִיכָּא דְּאָמְרִי: לֹא בָּא עָלֶיהָ. דְּאָמְרִי לָהּ בָּא עָלֶיהָ, הָא דִּטְמָנָהּ – לְיַתּוּבֵיהּ לְיִצְרֵיהּ; וּדְאָמְרִי לָהּ לֹא בָּא עָלֶיהָ, הַאי דִּטְמָנָהּ – כִּי הֵיכִי דְּנֶאמְרוּ: בַּת מֶלֶךְ נְסַב.

It is related that Herod **preserved** the girl's body **in honey for seven years** to prevent it from decaying. **There are** those **who say** that **he engaged in necrophilia with her** corpse and **there are those who say he did not engage in necrophilia with her** corpse. According to those **who say he engaged in necrophilia with her** corpse, the reason **that he preserved her** body was **to gratify his** carnal **desires. And** according to those **who say he did not engage in necrophilia with her** corpse, the reason **that he preserved her** body was **so that** people **would say he married a king's daughter.**

אֲמַר: מַאן דָּרֵישׁ ״מִקֶּרֶב אַחֶיךָ תָּשִׂים עָלֶיךָ מֶלֶךְ״? רַבָּנַן, קָם קַטְלִינְהוּ לְכוּלְּהוּ רַבָּנַן, שַׁבְקֵיהּ לְבָבָא בֶּן בּוּטָא לְמִשְׁקַל עֵצָה מִינֵּיהּ.

Herod **said** to himself: **Who expounds** the verse: **"One from among your brothers you shall set as king over you"** (Deuteronomy 17:15)[H] as meaning that he who is appointed as king must come from a Jewish family and cannot be an emancipated slave or a convert? It is **the Sages** who expound the verse in this manner, insisting that a king must have Jewish roots. **He** then **rose up and killed all the Sages,** but **spared Bava ben Buta in order to take counsel with him.**

BACKGROUND

Divine Voice [*bat kala*] – בַּת קָלָא: This term has been explained in various ways. Some expound that a Divine Voice is a subcategory of prophecy; although true prophecy had ceased before this time, this lower form of it remained (see *Ge'onim*; *Tosafot*). Others suggest that a Divine Voice is a type of echo or sound whose source cannot be placed, e.g., a conversation about something that resolves another's difficulty that happens to be overheard. Such cases are found in the Jerusalem Talmud (Maharatz Ḥayyut). Another possibility is that the word *bat* refers here to the biblical liquid-volume measure of that name; accordingly, the phrase connotes a voice for those who measure up, i.e., a voice heard only by those who are worthy (Rosh; see *Sefer HaNitzaḥon*).

HALAKHA

One from among your brothers you shall set as king over you – מִקֶּרֶב אַחֶיךָ תָּשִׂים עָלֶיךָ מֶלֶךְ: A convert may not be appointed as king. Nor may his descendant be appointed king, even several generations after the conversion of his ancestor, unless he has a Jewish mother. And certainly only someone who was born a Jew can be appointed as a judge or a *nasi* (Rambam *Sefer Shofetim*, *Hilkhot Melakhim* 1:4).

PERSONALITIES

Bava ben Buta – בָּבָא בֶּן בּוּטָא: One of the most important sages of his generation, Bava ben Buta was among Shammai's greatest students. Nevertheless, he ruled according to the opinions of Beit Hillel on various important halakhic matters. Bava ben Buta was well known for his righteousness and wisdom. Many stories are told about his deep modesty, and how he waived his own honor for the sake of domestic peace or the glory of God. Known for his worldly knowledge, Bava ben Buta appears to have been a judge in Jerusalem. In Josephus' opinion, Shammai predicted that Herod would rise to prominence. This might have been an additional reason why Herod spared Bava ben Buta.

Herod – הוֹרְדוֹס: Appointed to his position by the Roman senate, Herod ruled as king over Judea during the first century BCE, bringing to an end the Hasmonean dynasty. He was known for his excessive brutality; he executed those who stood in the way of his maintaining power, including members of his own family.

Yet under Herod's rule Judea prospered economically and benefited from his preoccupation with and investment in elaborate architectural projects. These include the port city of Caesarea, his summer palace at Herodium, and the fortress at Masada. His greatest achievement in this regard was the rebuilding of the Temple. The Sages of the Talmud report that Herod's Temple was one of the most beautiful buildings ever constructed (see *Sukka* 51b). Herod employed thousands of workers, insisting that only priests who were ritually pure work on the inner areas of the Temple complex. Much of the information about Herod's life is learned from the writings of Josephus. Herod died in 4 BCE.

אהדר ליה כלילא דיילי, נקרינהו לעיניה. יומא חד אתא ויתיב קמיה, אמר: חזי מר האי עבדא בישא מאי קא עביד! אמר ליה: מאי אעביד ליה? אמר ליה: נלטייה מר! אמר ליה, כתיב: "גם במדעך מלך אל תקלל". אמר ליה: האי לאו מלך הוא! אמר ליה: וליהוי עשיר בעלמא, וכתיב: "ובחדרי משכבך אל תקלל עשיר". ולא יהא אלא נשיא, וכתיב: "ונשיא בעמך לא תאר".

Herod **placed a garland** made **of porcupine**[B] hide **on** Bava ben Buta's head, which **pricked his eyes out. One day** Herod **came and sat before him** without identifying himself in order to test him. **He,** Herod, **said: See, Master, what this evil slave** Herod **is doing.** Bava ben Buta **said to him: What should I do to him?** Herod **said to him:** The **Master should curse him.** Bava ben Buta **said to him:** But **it is written: "Do not curse the king, not even in your thoughts"** (Ecclesiastes 10:20). Herod **said to him: He is not a king,** since he rules illegally. Bava ben Buta **said to him: And even if he were merely a rich man** I would not curse him, as **it is written: "And do not curse a rich person in your bedchamber"** (Ecclesiastes 10:20). **And** even **were he only a leader** I would not curse him, as **it is written: "And you shall not curse**[H] **a leader among your people"** (Exodus 22:27).

אמר ליה: בעושה מעשה עמך, והאי לאו עושה מעשה עמך! אמר ליה: מסתפינא מיניה. אמר ליה: ליכא איניש דאזיל דלימא ליה, דאנא ואת יתיבנא. אמר ליה, כתיב: "כי עוף השמים יוליך את הקול ובעל כנפים יגיד דבר".

Herod **said to him:** That *halakha* stated **with regard to** "a leader among your people," that is, to a fit Jew who **acts as a** member of **your people,** i.e., in accordance with Torah law, **and this one does not do the deeds of your people.** Bava ben Buta **said to him:** Nevertheless, **I am afraid of him.** Herod **said to him: There is nobody who will go and tell him, since you and I are sitting** here alone. Bava ben Buta **said to him:** Nevertheless, **it is written: "For a bird of the sky shall carry the sound, and that which has wings shall tell the matter"** (Ecclesiastes 10:20).

אמר ליה: אנא הוא, אי הואי ידענא דזהירי רבנן כולי האי לא הוה קטילנא להו, השתא מאי תקנתיה דההוא גברא? אמר ליה: הוא כבה אורו של עולם, דכתיב: "כי נר מצוה ותורה אור", ילך ויעסוק באורו של עולם, דכתיב: "ונהרו אליו כל הגוים". איכא דאמרי, הכי אמר ליה: הוא סימא עינו של עולם, דכתיב: "והיה אם מעיני העדה", ילך ויתעסק בעינו של עולם, דכתיב: "הנני מחלל את מקדשי גאון עזכם מחמד עיניכם".

Herod **said to him: I am he. Had I known that the Sages were so cautious I would not have killed them. Now, what is that man's remedy,** i.e., what can I do to repent for my sinful actions? Bava ben Buta **said to him: He** who **extinguished the light of the world** by killing the Torah Sages, **as it is written: "For the mitzva is a lamp, and the Torah is light"** (Proverbs 6:23), **should go and occupy himself with the light of the world,** the Temple, **as it is written** with regard to the Temple: **"And all the nations shall flow [*venaharu*] unto it"** (Isaiah 2:2), the word *venaharu* alluding to light [*nehora*]. **There are** those **who say** that **this** is what **he said to him: He** who **blinded the eye of the world, as it is written** in reference to the Sages: **"And if** it be committed through ignorance **by the eyes of the congregation"** (Numbers 15:24), **should go and occupy himself with the eye of the world,** the Temple, **as it is written: "I will desecrate my Temple, the pride of your strength, the delight of your eyes"** (Ezekiel 24:21).

אמר ליה: מסתפינא ממלכותא. אמר ליה: שדר שליחא, וליזיל שתא וליעכב שתא ולהדר שתא, אדהכי והכי סתרית [ליה] ובניית [ליה]. עבד הכי. שלחו ליה: אם לא סתרתה אל תסתור, ואם סתרתה אל תבני, ואם סתרתה ובנית, עבדי בישא בתר דעבדין מתמלכין, אם זיינך עלך ספרך כאן, לא רכא ולא בר רכא, הורדוס [עבדא] קלניא מתעביד.

Herod **said to him: I am afraid of the** Roman **government,** that they will not permit me to make changes in the Temple. Bava ben Buta **said to him: Send a messenger** who will **travel** there for a **year, and remain** there for another **year, and** take yet another **year** to **return. In the meantime, you can demolish** the Temple **and rebuild it. He did so.** Eventually, **they sent** a message **to** Herod from Rome: **If you have not** yet **demolished it, do not demolish it; and if you have** already **demolished it, do not rebuild it; and if you have demolished it and** already **rebuilt it,** you shall be counted among **those who act wickedly, seeking counsel** only **after they have** already **acted.** Even **if you are armed** and in command of a military force, **your book,** i.e., your genealogical record, **is here.** You are **neither a king** [*reikha*][L] **nor the son of a king,** but rather **Herod the slave who has made himself a freeman** [***kelonya***].[L]

מאי רכא? מלכותא, דכתיב: "אנכי היום רך ומשוח מלך". ואי בעית אימא, מהכא: "ויקראו לפניו אברך".

The Gemara explains: **What** is the meaning of the word ***reikha***? It denotes **royalty, as it is written: "I am today a tender [*rakh*] and anointed king"** (II Samuel 3:39). **And if you wish, say** that the meaning of the word is learned **from here,** from the term describing Joseph after he was appointed viceroy to the king: **"And they cried before him, *Avrekh*"** (Genesis 41:43).[N]

BACKGROUND

Porcupine – **יילי:** This creature has not been definitively identified. Rashi and other commentaries claim it is a porcupine. The *Arukh* suggests that the reference here is to leeches, which Herod placed around Bava ben Buta's head, and which sucked out the blood of his eyes, thereby blinding him.

HALAKHA

You shall not curse – **לא תאר:** Whoever curses a fellow Jew using the name of God or one of His appellations transgresses a negative mitzva and is liable to receive lashes, provided he has been forewarned and there are witnesses to his deed, even if he curses himself or curses somebody who cannot hear him. If one curses the king or the head of the Sanhedrin he is also liable to receive two sets of lashes for violating the prohibition: "You shall not curse a leader among your people." Some maintain that such an individual does not receive two sets of lashes (*Sma*, citing *Tur*).

If the offender was not forewarned, or if he uttered the curse without using the name of God, or if the curse was indirect, he is not liable to receive lashes, even though all these actions are prohibited (Rambam *Sefer Shofetim, Hilkhot Sanhedrin* 26:1; *Shulḥan Arukh, Ḥoshen Mishpat* 27).

LANGUAGE

King [*reikha*] – **רכא:** From the Latin rex, meaning king.

Freeman [*kelonya*] – **קלניא:** From the Latin colonia, meaning a settlement of decommissioned Roman soldiers. Since those living in such areas were exempt from paying taxes, the term came to denote a state of freedom or exemption.

NOTES

And they cried before him *Avrekh* – **ויקראו לפניו אברך:** The Ri Migash explains that this proof is based on the Aramaic translation of the verse, which renders the word *avrekh* as: This is the father of the king, indicating that the term *rekh* in the compound *av-rekh* means king.

אָמְרִי: מִי שֶׁלֹּא רָאָה בִּנְיַן הוֹרְדוֹס, לֹא רָאָה בִּנְיָן נָאֶה [מִיָּמָיו]. בְּמַאי בְּנָיֵיהּ? אֲמַר רַבָּה: בְּאַבְנֵי שֵׁישָׁא וּמַרְמָרָא. אִיכָּא דְּאָמְרִי: בְּאַבְנֵי כּוּחְלָא, שֵׁישָׁא וּמַרְמָרָא. אַפֵּיק שָׁפָה וְעָיֵיל שָׁפָה, כִּי הֵיכִי דְּנְקַבֵּיל סִידָא. סָבַר לְמִשְׁעֵייהּ בְּדַהֲבָא, אֲמַרוּ לֵיהּ רַבָּנַן: שַׁבְקֵיהּ, דְּהָכִי שַׁפִּיר טְפֵי, דְּמֶיחֱזֵי כִּי אִידְוָותָא דְּיַמָּא.

The Sages say: **One who has not seen Herod's building has never seen a beautiful building in his life.** The Gemara asks: **With what did he build it? Rabba said: With stones of white and green marble** [*umarmara*].[L] **There are those who say** that he built it **with stones of blue, white, and green marble.** Alternate rows of stones **sent out an edge** a bit **and drew in an edge** a bit, **so that they would** better **receive** and hold **the plaster. He considered covering it with gold, but the Rabbis said to him: Leave it,** and do not cover it, **since it is more beautiful this** way, **as it looks like the waves of the sea.**

וּבָבָא בַּר בּוּטָא הֵיכִי עֲבַד הָכִי? וְהָאָמַר רַב יְהוּדָה אָמַר רַב, וְאִיתֵּימָא רַבִּי יְהוֹשֻׁעַ בֶּן לֵוִי: מִפְּנֵי מָה נֶעֱנַשׁ דָּנִיֵּאל? מִפְּנֵי שֶׁהִשִּׂיא עֵצָה לִנְבוּכַדְנֶצַּר, שֶׁנֶּאֱמַר: ״לָהֵן מַלְכָּא מִלְכִּי יִשְׁפַּר עֲלָךְ וַחֲטָאָךְ בְּצִדְקָה פְרֻק וַעֲוָיָתָךְ בְּמִחַן עֲנָיִן הֵן תֶּהֱוֵי אַרְכָא לִשְׁלֵוְתָךְ״ וגו׳, וּכְתִיב: ״כֹּלָּא מְטָא עַל נְבוּכַדְנֶצַּר מַלְכָּא״, וּכְתִיב: ״וְלִקְצָת יַרְחִין תְּרֵי עֲשַׂר״ וגו׳!

The Gemara asks: **And how did Bava ben Buta do this,** i.e., give advice to Herod the wicked? **But doesn't Rav Yehuda say** that **Rav says, and some say** it was **Rabbi Yehoshua ben Levi** who says: **For what reason was Daniel punished?**[H] **Because he offered advice**[N] **to Nebuchadnezzar,** as after sharing a harsh prophecy with him, **it is stated: "Therefore, O king, let my counsel be acceptable to you, redeem your sins with charity and your iniquities with graciousness to the poor, that there may be a lengthening of your prosperity"** (Daniel 4:24). **And it is written: "All this came upon King Nebuchadnezzar"** (Daniel 4:25). **And it is written: "And at the end of twelve months"** (Daniel 4:26). Only after a year was the prophecy fulfilled but not before that, apparently because Nebuchadnezzar heeded Daniel's advice.

אִיבָּעֵית אֵימָא: שָׁאנֵי עַבְדָּא, דְּאִיחַיַּיב בְּמִצְוֹת. וְאִיבָּעֵית אֵימָא: שָׁאנֵי בֵּית הַמִּקְדָּשׁ, דְּאִי לָא מַלְכוּת לָא מִתְבְּנֵי.

The Gemara answers: **If you wish, say** that **a slave** like Herod **is different since he is obligated in the mitzvot,** and therefore Bava ben Buta had to help him repent. **And if you wish, say the Temple is different, as without** the help of **the government it would not have been built.**

וְדָנִיֵּאל מְנָלַן דְּאִיעֲנַשׁ? אִילֵימָא מִשּׁוּם דִּכְתִיב: ״וַתִּקְרָא אֶסְתֵּר לַהֲתָךְ״, וְאָמַר רַב: הֲתָךְ – זֶה דָּנִיֵּאל? הָנִיחָא לְמַאן דְּאָמַר: שֶׁחֲתָכוּהוּ מִגְּדוּלָּתוֹ, אֶלָּא לְמַאן דְּאָמַר: שֶׁכָּל דִּבְרֵי מַלְכוּת נֶחְתָּכִין עַל פִּיו, מַאי אִיכָּא לְמֵימַר? דְּשַׁדְיוּהוּ לְגוּבָּא דְאַרְיָוָותָא.

The Gemara asks: **And from where do we** derive **that Daniel was punished? If we say** we know this **because it is written: "And Esther called for Hatach,** one of the king's chamberlains, whom he had appointed to attend upon her" (Esther 4:5), **and Rav said: Hatach is Daniel. This works out well according to the one who says** Daniel was called Hatach because **they cut him down** [*ḥatakh*] **from his greatness** and turned him into a minor attendant. **But according to the one who says** he was called Hatach **because all governmental matters were determined** [*ḥatakh*] **according to his word, what is there to say?** What punishment did he receive? The Gemara answers: His punishment was **that they threw him into the den of lions.**

״הַכֹּל כְּמִנְהַג הַמְּדִינָה״. ״הַכֹּל״ לְאַתּוּיֵי מַאי? לְאַתּוּיֵי אַתְרָא דִּנְהִיגִי בְּהוּצָא וְדַפְנָא.

§ The mishna teaches: In a place where it is customary to build a wall of non-chiseled stone, or chiseled stone, or small bricks, or large bricks, they must build the partition with that material. **Everything is in accordance with the regional custom.** The Gemara asks: **What** does the word **everything** serve **to add?** The Gemara answers: It serves **to add a place where it is customary** to build a partition **out of palm and laurel branches.**[HN] In such a place, the partition is built from those materials.

״לְפִיכָךְ, אִם נָפַל הַכּוֹתֶל – הַמָּקוֹם וְהָאֲבָנִים שֶׁל שְׁנֵיהֶם״. פְּשִׁיטָא! לָא צְרִיכָא, דִּנְפַל לִרְשׁוּתָא דְּחַד מִינַּיְיהוּ, אִי נַמִי דְּפָנִינְהוּ חַד לִרְשׁוּתָא דִּידֵיהּ; מַהוּ דְּתֵימָא: נֶיהֱוֵי אִידָךְ הַמּוֹצִיא מֵחֲבֵירוֹ עָלָיו הָרְאָיָה, קָא מַשְׁמַע לָן.

The mishna teaches: **Therefore, if the wall** later **falls,** the assumption is that **the space** where the wall stood **and the stones belong to both of them,** to be divided equally. The Gemara questions the need for this ruling: Isn't it **obvious** that this is the case, since both neighbors participated in the construction of the wall? The Gemara answers: **No,** it is **necessary** to teach this *halakha* for a case **where** the entire wall **fell into the domain of one of them.**[H] **Alternatively,** it is necessary in a case **where one of them** already **cleared**[N] all the stones **into his own domain. Lest you say** that **the other** party **should be** governed by the principle that **the burden of proof rests upon the claimant,** that is, if the other party should have to prove that he had been a partner in the construction of the wall, the mishna **teaches us** that they are presumed to have been partners in the building of the wall, and neither requires further proof.

LANGUAGE

Green marble [*marmara*] – מַרְמָרָא: From the Greek μάρμαρος, *marmaros*, meaning marble or gleaming marble.

HALAKHA

For what reason was Daniel punished – מִפְּנֵי מָה נֶעֱנַשׁ דָּנִיֵּאל: It is prohibited to offer sound advice to a wicked gentile or slave. It is even prohibited to counsel him to observe a mitzva as long as he perseveres in his wickedness. Daniel was punished only because he advised Nebuchadnezzar to give charity (Rambam *Sefer Nezikin, Hilkhot Rotze'aḥ UShmirat HaNefesh* 12:15).

Palm and laurel branches – הוּצָא וְדַפְנָא: In a place where it is customary to erect a partition between neighbors that is made of reeds, the partition may be built from this material provided that one cannot see through it and breach the other's privacy. The Rema, citing the *Tur*, writes that some say that a less substantial barrier should be avoided even in communities where such a partition is customary. In locations where there is no fixed custom the partition should be built in accordance with the judge's discretion. In any event the wall should not be narrower than the narrowest partition described in the mishna (Rambam *Sefer Kinyan, Hilkhot Shekhenim* 2:15; *Shulḥan Arukh, Ḥoshen Mishpat* 157:4).

Where it fell into the domain of one of them – דִּנְפַל לִרְשׁוּתָא דְּחַד: If a wall separating the properties of neighbors collapsed into the domain of one of them, the materials and the space are divided equally. Such apportionment also applies where one of the neighbors cleared all the material into his own space, arguing that he had acquired it from his neighbor or that it had always belonged to him (*Sma*). The Shakh writes that the stones are divided equally only if witnesses attest that the stones were among those that had been jointly owned by the two of them (Rambam *Sefer Kinyan, Hilkhot Shekhenim* 2:18; *Shulḥan Arukh, Ḥoshen Mishpat* 157:5).

NOTES

Because he offered advice – מִפְּנֵי שֶׁהִשִּׂיא עֵצָה: The Rambam and the Maharal seem to say that one should not offer advice to someone who acts wickedly, because even the mitzvot that he observes are not performed for pure motives. The Ramah understands that the prohibition applies specifically to gentiles who harass Jews, lest they take the advice and grow in power. The Meiri explains that people should act as God does when He prevents excessively wicked people from repenting and punishes them by allowing them to stumble in sin. This is how God treated Pharaoh. Similarly, one is not required to assist a known sinner but rather should allow him to wallow in his wickedness.

Where it is customary to build out of palm and laurel branches – דִּנְהִיגִי בְּהוּצָא וְדַפְנָא: Some commentaries hold that even if people use a more transparent barrier than palm and laurel branches, that is an acceptable custom (Ramban). But Rabbeinu Tam maintains that anything less than palm and laurel branches is a foolish custom and should not be tolerated even in a place where people do so.

Where one of them cleared – דְּפָנִינְהוּ: The reference here is to a case where the one who cleared the stones into his own domain claims that he purchased them from the neighbor. Consequently, the mishna teaches that this claim is ignored unless it is substantiated with proof.

״וְכֵן בַּגִּינָּה, מָקוֹם שֶׁנָּהֲגוּ לִגְדּוֹר – מְחַיְּיבִין אוֹתוֹ״. הָא גּוּפָא קַשְׁיָא, אָמְרַתְּ: וְכֵן בַּגִּינָּה, מָקוֹם שֶׁנָּהֲגוּ לִגְדּוֹר – מְחַיְּיבִין אוֹתוֹ, הָא סְתָמָא – אֵין מְחַיְּיבִין אוֹתוֹ;

§ The mishna continues: **And similarly with regard to a garden,** in **a place where it is customary to build a partition** in the middle of a garden jointly owned by two people, and one of them wishes to build such a partition, the court **obligates** his neighbor to join in building the partition. The Gemara comments: **This** matter **itself** is **difficult.** On the one hand, **you said: And similarly with regard to a garden,** in **a place where it is customary to build a partition** in the middle of a garden jointly owned by two people, and one of them wishes to build such a partition, the court **obligates** his neighbor to join in building the partition. One can infer **that ordinarily,** where there is no custom, the court **does not obligate him** to build a partition.

אֵימָא סֵיפָא: אֲבָל בִּקְעָה, מָקוֹם שֶׁנָּהֲגוּ שֶׁלֹּא לִגְדּוֹר – אֵין מְחַיְּיבִין אוֹתוֹ, הָא סְתָמָא – מְחַיְּיבִין אוֹתוֹ; הַשְׁתָּא סְתַם גִּינָּה אָמְרַתְּ לָא, סְתַם בִּקְעָה מִיבַּעְיָא?

But **say the latter clause** of the mishna: **But** with regard to an expanse of **fields,** in **a place where it is customary not to build a partition** between two people's fields, and one person wishes to build a partition between his field and that of his neighbor, the court **does not obligate** his neighbor to build such a partition. One can infer **that ordinarily,** where there is no custom, the court **obligates him** to build a partition. The Gemara explains the difficulty: **Now** that **you said** by inference that in **an ordinary garden** the court **does not** obligate him to build a partition, **is it necessary** to say that the court does not obligate him to build a partition in **an ordinary field?** Clearly in a field there is less of a need for a partition, as there is less damage caused by exposure to the gaze of others.

אָמַר אַבָּיֵי, הָכִי קָאָמַר: וְכֵן סְתַם גִּינָּה, וּבְמָקוֹם שֶׁנָּהֲגוּ לִגְדּוֹר בַּבִּקְעָה – מְחַיְּיבִין אוֹתוֹ. אֲמַר לֵיהּ רָבָא: אִם כֵּן, מַאי ״אֲבָל״? אֶלָּא אֲמַר רָבָא, הָכִי קָתָנֵי: וְכֵן סְתַם גִּינָּה כְּמָקוֹם שֶׁנָּהֲגוּ לִגְדּוֹר דָּמֵי, וּמְחַיְּיבִין אוֹתוֹ; אֲבָל סְתַם בִּקְעָה כְּמָקוֹם שֶׁלֹּא נָהֲגוּ דָּמֵי, וְאֵין מְחַיְּיבִין אוֹתוֹ.

Abaye said that **this** is what the *tanna* **is saying: And similarly** with regard to **an ordinary garden, and** also **in a place where it is customary to build a partition in** an expanse of **fields,** the court **obligates him** to build a partition. **Rava said to him: If so, what** is the point of the word: **But,** mentioned afterward in connection with an expanse of fields, which seems to indicate that the issue of fields had not yet been addressed? **Rather, Rava said** that **this** is what the *tanna* is **teaching: And similarly an ordinary garden** is treated **like a place where it is customary to build a partition, and** therefore the court **obligates him** to build a partition. **But an ordinary** expanse of **fields**[H] is treated **like a place where it is customary not** to build a partition, **and** therefore the court **does not obligate him** to build one.

״אֶלָּא אִם רָצָה, כּוֹנֵס לְתוֹךְ שֶׁלּוֹ וּבוֹנֶה וְעוֹשֶׂה חָזִית״. מַאי חָזִית? אֲמַר רַב הוּנָא: אַכְפֵּיהּ לֵיהּ לְקַרְנָא לְבַר. וְנַעֲבֵיד מִלְּגָיו! עָבֵיד חַבְרֵיהּ נַמִי מִלְּבַר, וְאָמַר: דִּידִי וְדִידֵיהּ הוּא. אִי הָכִי, הַשְׁתָּא נַמִי גָּיֵיז לֵיהּ חַבְרֵיהּ, וְאָמַר: דִּידִי וְדִידֵיהּ הוּא! גִּיזּוּזָא מֵידַע יְדִיעַ.

§ The mishna teaches: **Rather, if** one person **wishes** to erect a partition, **he must withdraw into his own** field **and build** the partition there. **And he makes** a border **mark**[N] **on the outer side** of the barrier facing his neighbor's property, indicating that he built the entire structure of his own materials and on his own land. The Gemara asks: **What** is the meaning of a border **mark? Rav Huna said: He bends the edge** of the wall **toward the outside.**[N] The Gemara suggests: **Let him make it on the inside.** The Gemara explains: In that case, **his neighbor might also make** a mark **on the outside,** that is, on the side facing his own property, **and say:** The wall **is** both **mine and his.** The Gemara responds: **If so,** that is, there is a concern about such deception, **now also** when the person who builds the wall makes a border mark on the outer side of the wall, **his neighbor might cut it off and say:** The wall **is** both **mine and his.** The Gemara answers: Such **a cut is noticeable** and the deception will not work.

אִיכָּא דְּאָמְרִי, אֲמַר רַב הוּנָא: מִיכְפָּא לְקַרְנָא מִלְּגָיו. וְנֶיעְבַּד מִלְּבַר! גָּיֵיז לֵיהּ חַבְרֵיהּ, וְאָמַר: דִּידִי וְדִידֵיהּ הוּא. אִי הָכִי, הַשְׁתָּא נַמִי לָיֵיף לֵיהּ חַבְרֵיהּ, וְאָמַר: דִּידִי וְדִידֵיהּ הוּא! לִיפּוּפָא מֵידַע יְדִיעַ. וְהָא ״מִבַּחוּץ״ קָתָנֵי! קַשְׁיָא.

There are those **who say** that in answer to the question: What is the meaning of a border mark, **Rav Huna said: He bends the edge** of the wall **toward the inside.** The Gemara suggests: **Let him make it on the outside.** The Gemara explains: In that case, **his neighbor might cut it off and say:** The wall **is** both **mine and his.** The Gemara asks: **If so,** that is, there is a concern for such deception, **now also** when the person who builds the wall makes a border mark toward the inside, **his neighbor might add** a border mark on his own side **and say:** The wall **is** both **mine and his.** The Gemara answers: **An addition is noticeable** and the deception will not work. The Gemara asks: **But doesn't** the mishna **teach** that he makes the border mark **on the outside** and not on the inside? The Gemara comments: This is **a difficulty.**

רַבִּי יוֹחָנָן אֲמַר:

Rabbi Yoḥanan said:

HALAKHA

An ordinary garden and an ordinary expanse of fields – סְתַם גִּינָּה וּסְתַם בִּקְעָה: An ordinary garden is treated like an area where it is customary to construct a partition. Therefore, if the joint owners of a garden wish to divide the area, each one can compel the other to erect a partition, even if there is no local custom to do so. If there is a definitive custom not to build such a partition, one cannot compel the other to build one (*Sma*, citing *Tur*). This barrier is not required to measure four cubits in height, as a partition of ten handbreadths suffices; the Ra'avad and the Ramban maintain that four cubits are necessary. As for an ordinary expanse of fields, the parties can be compelled to build a wall only if that is the local custom (Rambam *Sefer Kinyan*, *Hilkhot Shekhenim* 2:16–17; *Shulḥan Arukh*, *Ḥoshen Mishpat* 158:1).

NOTES

Mark – חָזִית: Rashi explains that according to the opinion of Rav Huna, this term means an edge or protrusion. The *Arukh* renders it a face or surface.

He bends the edge toward the outside – אַכְפֵּיהּ לֵיהּ לְקַרְנָא: Rashi explains that he should add stones and mortar so that the corner of the wall will protrude toward the neighbor's yard, thereby indicating that he built the barrier. According to the opinion of Rabbeinu Gershom, he should stick reeds into the top of the wall and bend them outward. The latter understanding is more in keeping with the wording of the Gemara.

Wall with protruding edge

נִשְׁעֲיֵיהּ בְּאַמְּתָא מִלְּבַר. וְנֶיעֱבַד מִלְּגָיו! עָבֵיד חַבְרֵיהּ מִלְּבַר, וְאָמַר: דִּידִי וְדִידֵיהּ הוּא. אִי הָכִי, הָשְׁתָּא נַמִי דְּקָפֵיל לֵיהּ חַבְרֵיהּ, וְאָמַר: דִּידִי וְדִידֵיהּ הוּא! קִילּוּפָא מֵידַע יְדִיעַ.

The party who builds the wall **should smear it**[N] with clay **up to a cubit**[H] at the top of the wall **on the outside.**[N] The Gemara suggests: **Let him do** this **on the inside.** The Gemara explains: In that case, **his neighbor might** also **do it on the outside,** that is, on the side facing his own property, **and say:** The wall is both **mine and his.** The Gemara responds: **If so,** that is, if there is a concern for such deception, **now also** when the person who builds the wall smears it with clay on the outside, **his neighbor can peel it off and say:** The wall **is** both **mine and his.** The Gemara explains: **Peeling** clay **is noticeable** and the deception will not succeed.

הוּצָא – אֲמַר רַב נַחְמָן: סִינּוּפֵי יְרִיכֵי מִלְּבַר. וְנֶיעֱבַד מִלְּגָיו! עָבֵיד נַמִי חַבְרֵיהּ מִלְּבַר, וְאָמַר: דִּידִי וְדִידֵיהּ הוּא. אִי הָכִי, הָשְׁתָּא נַמִי גָּיֵיז וְשָׁדֵי לֵיהּ, וְאָמַר: דִּידִי וְדִידֵיהּ הוּא! מַשְׁרֵיק לֵיהּ טִינָא. הָשְׁתָּא נַמִי אָתֵי חַבְרֵיהּ וְקָלֵיף לֵיהּ! קִילּוּפָא מֵידַע יְדִיעַ.

The Gemara asks: If he builds a partition of **palm branches,** how does he make a border mark? **Rav Naḥman said: He directs the tips of the branches**[N] **to the outside.**[BH] The Gemara suggests: **Let him do** this **to the inside.** The Gemara states: If he so directs the branches, **his neighbor might also do** the same **to the outside,** that is, to the side facing his own property, **and say:** The partition **is** both **mine and his.** The Gemara objects: **If so,** that is, if there is concern for such deception, **now also** when the one who builds the partition directs the tips of the branches to the outside, the neighbor **can cut off** the tips **and throw** them away, **and say:** The partition **is** both **mine and his.** The Gemara counsels: **He should smear** the tips of the palm branches **with clay.** The Gemara comments: **Now also, the neighbor might come and peel** the clay off. The Gemara answers: **Peeling is noticeable.**

אַבַּיֵי אֲמַר: הוּצָא לֵית לֵיהּ תַּקַּנְתָּא אֶלָּא בִּשְׁטָרָא.

Abaye said: One who builds a partition of **palm branches has no remedy**[N] to prove who erected it, **except with** a written **document.** The neighbor should draw up a document stating that he has no claim to the space or to the partition, because they belong exclusively to the other neighbor.

״אֲבָל אִם עָשׂוּ מִדַּעַת שְׁנֵיהֶם״. אֲמַר לֵיהּ רָבָא מִפַּרְזִיקָא לְרַב אַשִׁי: לֹא יַעֲשׂוּ לֹא זֶה וְלֹא זֶה! אֲמַר לֵיהּ: לָא צְרִיכָא, דְּקָדֵים חַד מִנַּיְיהוּ וַעֲבַד דִּידֵיהּ, וְאִי לָא עָבֵיד חַבְרֵיהּ – אָמַר: דִּידֵיהּ הוּא.

§ The mishna teaches: Nevertheless, in a place where it is not customary to build a partition between two people's fields, **if they made** such a partition **with the agreement of the two of them,** they build it in the middle, i.e., on the property line, and make a border mark on the one side and on the other side. Therefore, if the wall later falls, the assumption is that the space where the wall stood and the stones belong to both of them, to be divided equally. **Rava from Parzika said to Rav Ashi: Neither this one nor that one should make a** border mark.[H] Rav Ashi **said to him: No,** this ruling **is necessary** in a case **where one of them went ahead and made** a border mark **for himself,** so that **if his neighbor does not make** one as well, the first one **will say** that **it is** entirely **his.**

NOTES

Should smear it – נִשְׁעֲיֵיהּ: In the opinion of most early commentaries, Rabbi Yoḥanan and Rav Huna disagree as to the nature of the mark. Rabbeinu Yona and others maintain that there is no dispute; each propose a different way to make the border mark.

Up to a cubit on the outside – בְּאַמְּתָא מִלְּבַר: The mark should not be less than a cubit, because then the mark would not be noticeable.

The tips of the branches – סִינּוּפֵי יְרִיכֵי: Rashi explains that this refers to the tips of the palm branches, which should be turned toward the neighbor's yard to serve as a border mark. Rabbeinu Ḥananel maintains that the reeds placed to support the barrier should be put on the outside. Some commentaries explain that the reference here is to the ropes used to tie the palm branches, which should be tied on the outside as a mark (Rabbeinu Gershom; Ra'avad).

A partition of palm branches has no remedy – הוּצָא לֵית לֵיהּ תַּקַּנְתָּא: According to the opinion of Abaye, peeling of the branches will not be noticed on such a partition; the clay might peel off unintentionally, or the neighbor might peel it off without the owner taking notice. Therefore, a written document should be drawn up definitively stating who built the partition and upon whose land it stands.

BACKGROUND

The tips of the branches to the outside – סִינּוּפֵי יְרִיכֵי מִלְּבַר: This partition is made of woven palm branches. The border mark is fashioned by directing the tips of the branches to the outer side of the partition.

Fence with protruding branches

HALAKHA

He should smear it up to a cubit – נִשְׁעֲיֵיהּ בְּאַמְּתָא: If one wishes to build a partition between his stretch of fields and that of his neighbor, he must build it on his property and with his own materials. He should then make a mark, using lime or mortar, on the outside of the wall that is one square cubit in area, thereby indicating that the wall is his. According to the opinion of the Rema, in accordance with the opinion of Rabbi Yoḥanan, other types of marks that are used locally are also acceptable. In the event that the wall collapses, the materials and ground where the partition stood belong to the one who built it (Rambam *Sefer Kinyan, Hilkhot Shekhenim* 2:16; *Shulḥan Arukh, Ḥoshen Mishpat* 158:4, and *Sma* there).

He directs the tips of the branches to the outside – סִינּוּפֵי יְרִיכֵי מִלְּבַר: If one wishes to build a partition out of palm branches between his stretch of fields and that of his neighbor he should direct the tips of the branches toward his neighbor, as this signals that he built the wall on his own. If the wall later collapses, the material and the ground where the partition stood belong to the one who built it. This is in accordance with the opinion of Rav Naḥman (*Tur, Ḥoshen Mishpat* 158:4).

Neither this one nor that one should make a border mark – לֹא יַעֲשׂוּ לֹא זֶה וְלֹא זֶה: If both owners of neighboring fields contribute land and materials for the construction of a partition, neither one should make a border mark. According to the opinion of Rashi, the materials with which the partition was built belong to both of them, even if it collapsed into the property of one of them. Rabbeinu Yona rules that in such a situation the materials belong to the owner of the property into which the partition collapsed (*Shulḥan Arukh, Ḥoshen Mishpat* 158:5).

וְתַנָּא, תַּקַּנְתָּא לְרַמָּאֵי קָא מַשְׁמַע לַן? אֲמַר לֵיהּ: וְרֵישָׁא לָאו תַּקַּנְתָּא לְרַמָּאֵי הוּא?

Rava from Parzika asked him: **And is the *tanna* of the mishna teaching us a remedy** to be used **against a swindler?** Rav Ashi **said to him: But isn't the former clause** of the mishna's ruling also **a remedy** to be used **against a swindler?** That clause teaches that one who builds a wall should make a border mark to indicate that the wall is his.

אֲמַר לֵיהּ: בִּשְׁלָמָא רֵישָׁא תְּנָא דִּינָא, וּמִשּׁוּם דִּינָא תְּנָא תַּקַּנְתָּא, אֶלָּא סֵיפָא דִּינָא קָתָנֵי, דְּקָתָנֵי תַּקַּנְתָּא? אֲמַר רָבִינָא: הָכָא בְּהוּצֵי עָסְקִינַן, לְאַפּוֹקֵי מִדְּאַבָּיֵי דְּאָמַר: הוּצָא לֵית לֵיהּ תַּקַּנְתָּא אֶלָּא בִּשְׁטָרָא, קָא מַשְׁמַע לַן דִּבְחָזִית סַגְיָא.

Rava from Parzika **said to him: Granted,** in **the former clause** the *tanna* **taught the *halakha*** that if one wishes to build a partition between his own field and that of his neighbor, he does so at his own expense and on his own land, **and due to** the need to teach that ***halakha* he** also **taught a remedy** to be used against a swindler. **But does he teach a *halakha*** in **the latter clause,** so **that he** also **teaches a remedy** to be used against a swindler? **Ravina said: Here,** in the latter clause, **we are dealing with** a barrier made of **palm branches.** This is **to the exclusion** of the opinion **of Abaye, who said:** One who builds a partition of **palm branches has no remedy** to prove who erected it, **except with** a written **document. He teaches us that** a border **mark suffices.**

מתני׳ הַמַּקִּיף אֶת חֲבֵירוֹ מִשָּׁלֹשׁ רוּחוֹתָיו, וְגָדַר אֶת הָרִאשׁוֹנָה וְאֶת הַשְּׁנִיָּה וְאֶת הַשְּׁלִישִׁית – אֵין מְחַיְּיבִין אוֹתוֹ; רַבִּי יוֹסֵי אוֹמֵר: אִם עָמַד וְגָדַר אֶת הָרְבִיעִית – מְגַלְגְּלִין עָלָיו אֶת הַכֹּל.

MISHNA With regard to **one who surrounds another**[NH] **on three sides,** that is, he owns parcels of land on three sides of the other person's field, **and he built a partition** on **the first, the second, and the third** sides, the court **does not obligate**[N] the neighbor who owns the inner field to contribute to the construction of the partition if he does not wish to do so. **Rabbi Yosei says: If he arose and built a partition** on **the fourth** side of the field, the court **imposes upon** the owner of the inner field the responsibility to pay his share for **all** of the partitions.[B]

גמ׳ אָמַר רַב יְהוּדָה אָמַר שְׁמוּאֵל: הֲלָכָה כְּרַבִּי יוֹסֵי, דְּאָמַר: אִם עָמַד וְגָדַר אֶת הָרְבִיעִית – מְגַלְגְּלִין עָלָיו אֶת הַכֹּל, לֹא שְׁנָא עָמַד נִיקָּף, לֹא שְׁנָא עָמַד מַקִּיף.

GEMARA Rav Yehuda says that **Shmuel says:** The ***halakha*** is **in accordance with** the opinion of **Rabbi Yosei, who says** that **if he arose and built a partition** on **the fourth** side of the field, the court **imposes upon** the owner of the inner field the responsibility to pay his share for **all** of the partitions. The Gemara comments: It **is no different** if it was the owner of the **surrounded** field who **arose** and built a partition on the fourth side, and it **is no different** if it was the owner of the **surrounding** field who **arose** and built a partition on the fourth side. The *halakha* is the same in both cases.

אִיתְּמַר, רַב הוּנָא אָמַר: הַכֹּל – לְפִי מַה שֶּׁגָּדַר; חִיָּיא בַּר רַב אָמַר: הַכֹּל – לְפִי דְּמֵי קָנִים בְּזוֹל.

It was stated that the *amora'im* disagreed with regard to the following point. **Rav Huna says** that when Rabbi Yosei said the court obligates the owner of the inner field to pay his share for **all** of the partitions, he pays **in accordance with what** the other person actually spent when he **built the partitions.**[NH] That is, the owner of the inner field must contribute his share according to the cost of the partition his neighbor built. **Ḥiyya bar Rav says:** He must pay his share for **all** of the partitions **in accordance with a reduced** assessment of the **price of reeds,**[N] and no more. The owner of the surrounded field can claim he had no desire for a more substantial partition.

NOTES

One who surrounds another – הַמַּקִּיף אֶת חֲבֵירוֹ: There are various opinions with regard to the meaning of this mishna. The Meiri lists four possibilities. According to Rashi and the Rambam, Shimon's field is surrounded on all sides by the fields of his neighbor Reuven. These fields are located in a place where it is not customary for neighbors to build partitions between their respective fields, but Reuven built partitions to separate his land from Shimon's land. The Ba'al HaMaor understands that these fields are found in a place where it is customary for neighbors to build partitions, but until the partitions are complete the owner of the inner field is not required to pay anything. The Ri Migash and Rabbeinu Yona put forward a third opinion, according to which the mishna is not referring to a partition separating the inner field from the outer fields. Rather, Reuven builds a partition on three of the outer borders of his fields to separate his property from the public domain, and that partition also protects the inner field owned by Shimon, leaving only one side open.

According to the opinion of the Meiri, these three opinions all address the function of the partition as a barrier against invasion of privacy, whether by the neighbor or by the people passing in the public domain. By contrast, according to the opinion of the Ra'avad, the mishna is not dealing with invasion of privacy but is discussing a low partition intended to prevent animals from entering the fields. He agrees with the Ri Migash that the mishna is describing the construction of a partition on the outer borders of Reuven's fields, but he understands that Reuven, the owner of the outer fields, owns land on only three sides of Shimon's property and he builds a partition only on those three sides. If a fourth partition were built it would be for the benefit of Shimon alone.

The court does not obligate him – אֵין מְחַיְּיבִין אוֹתוֹ: Rashi provides two explanations for this. First, the court does not obligate the owner of the inner field because according to *halakha* there is no obligation to erect a partition, and this owner claims he has no desire for one. Second, he can maintain that as long as the fourth side remains open the partitions do not help him at all.

In accordance with what he spent when he built the partition – לְפִי מַה שֶּׁגָּדַר: This too has limitations, because if the owner of the inner field built a partition on the fourth side with less expensive material than what the neighbor had used to construct the other three partitions, the owner of the inner field cannot be forced to pay his full share in those partitions. His share is based only on the cost of the materials that he himself used for the partitions he built (see Ramban).

A reduced assessment of the price of reeds – דְּמֵי קָנִים בְּזוֹל: The Rashbam comments (146b) that the Sages use the term reduced to indicate a price one-third less than what is usually paid, since this is the usual amount of a large discount. Some commentaries challenge this generalization.

BACKGROUND

The surrounding field and the surrounded field – מַקִּיף וְנִיקָּף: If Reuven wishes to construct a partition between his field and the field of his neighbor Shimon, he cannot force Shimon to pay for the partition even if he builds a partition on three sides. But if Shimon erects a partition on the fourth side, he must contribute his share of the cost of the entire partition.

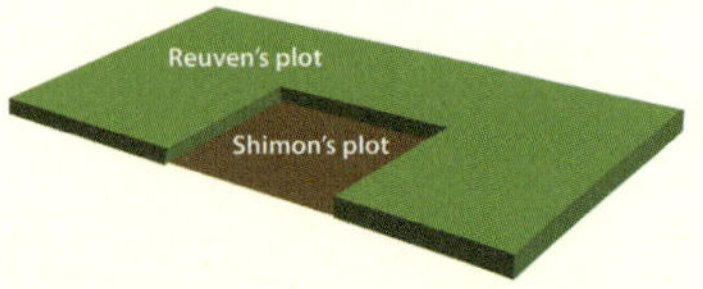

Plot of land surrounded on three sides by another's plot

HALAKHA

One who surrounds another – הַמַּקִּיף אֶת חֲבֵירוֹ: If one's field or garden is surrounded on all sides by another person's fields or gardens, and the owner of the outer property builds a partition on the first, second, and third sides, the owner of the inner property is not obligated to contribute to the construction costs. If the latter builds a partition on the fourth side, he must pay half the cost of the entire partition to a height of four cubits, or ten handbreadths in the case of a field. This is in accordance with the opinion of Shmuel.

This ruling applies only when the land upon which the partition was built belongs to both neighbors. If it belongs solely to the owner of the outer fields, the owner of the inner field must pay only a small amount, based on the judge's discretion. If the owner of the outer property builds a partition around the fields on the outside, while the inner border between the fields remains open, the owner of the inner field is not required to pay anything even if the partition surrounds his fourth side (Rambam *Sefer Kinyan*, *Hilkhot Shekhenim* 3:3; *Shulḥan Arukh*, *Ḥoshen Mishpat* 158:6).

In accordance with what he spent when he built the partition – לְפִי מַה שֶּׁגָּדַר: The owner of the inner field must pay half the cost of the partition, in accordance with the opinion of Rav Huna. The Ramban writes that if either of the neighbors builds the partition on the fourth side solely out of reeds, the owner of the inner field is required to pay only his share of the cost of that type of partition for all four sides, even if the other three partitions were constructed out of stone (*Shulḥan Arukh*, *Ḥoshen Mishpat* 158:7).

תְּנַן: הַמַּקִּיף אֶת חֲבֵירוֹ מִשָּׁלֹשׁ רוּחוֹתָיו, וְגָדַר אֶת הָרִאשׁוֹנָה וְאֶת הַשְּׁנִיָּה וְאֶת הַשְּׁלִישִׁית – אֵין מְחַיְּיבִין אוֹתוֹ; הָא רְבִיעִית – מְחַיְּיבִין אוֹתוֹ. אֵימָא סֵיפָא, רַבִּי יוֹסֵי אוֹמֵר: אִם עָמַד וְגָדַר אֶת הָרְבִיעִית – מְגַלְגְּלִין עָלָיו אֶת הַכֹּל;

The Gemara attempts to bring a proof from what **we learned** in the mishna: With regard to **one who surrounds another on three sides,** that is, he owns parcels of land on three sides of the other person's field, **and he built a partition** on **the first, the second, and the third** sides, the court **does not obligate** the neighbor who owns the inner field to contribute to the construction of the partition. By inference, if he also built a partition on the **fourth** side of the field, the court **does obligate** the owner of the inner field to contribute to the building of the partition. The Gemara continues with its proof: **Say the latter clause** of the mishna: **Rabbi Yosei says: If he arose and built a partition** on **the fourth** side of the field, the court **imposes upon** the owner of the inner field the responsibility to pay his share for **all** of the partitions. The first *tanna* and Rabbi Yosei seem to be stating the same ruling.

בִּשְׁלָמָא לְרַב הוּנָא דְּאָמַר: הַכֹּל לְפִי מַה שֶּׁגָּדַר בָּהּ, הַיְינוּ דְּאִיכָּא בֵּין תַּנָּא קַמָּא וְרַבִּי יוֹסֵי, תַּנָּא קַמָּא סָבַר: הַכֹּל לְפִי דְּמֵי קָנִים בְּזוֹל אִין, וּמַה שֶּׁגָּדַר לָא, וְרַבִּי יוֹסֵי סָבַר: הַכֹּל לְפִי מַה שֶּׁגָּדַר;

Granted, according to Rav Huna, who says that the owner of the inner field pays for **all** of the partitions **in accordance with what** the other person actually spent when he **built the partitions, this is** the difference **between the first *tanna* and Rabbi Yosei: The first *tanna* maintains** that **yes,** he pays his share for **all** of the partitions **in accordance with a reduced** assessment of the **price of reeds, but not** a larger sum in accordance with **what** the other person actually spent when he **built the partitions. And Rabbi Yosei maintains** that he pays his share for **all** of the partitions **in accordance with what** the other person actually spent when he **built the partitions.**

אֶלָּא לְחִיָּיא בַּר רַב דְּאָמַר: הַכֹּל לְפִי דְּמֵי קָנִים בְּזוֹל, מַאי אִיכָּא בֵּין תַּנָּא קַמָּא לְרַבִּי יוֹסֵי? אִי דְּמֵי קָנִים בְּזוֹל לָא קָיָהֵיב לֵיהּ, מַאי קָיָהֵיב לֵיהּ?

But according to Ḥiyya bar Rav, who says he pays his share for **all** of the partitions **in accordance with the value of** a partition fashioned from **inexpensive reeds, what** difference **is there between the first *tanna* and Rabbi Yosei? If** according to the first *tanna* **he does not give him** his share for all of the partitions in accordance with **a reduced** assessment of the **price of reeds, what does he give him?**

אִי בָּעֵית אֵימָא: אֲגַר נְטִירָא אִיכָּא בֵּינַיְיהוּ, תַּנָּא קַמָּא סָבַר: אֲגַר נְטִירָא אִין, דְּמֵי קָנִים בְּזוֹל לָא, וְרַבִּי יוֹסֵי סָבַר: דְּמֵי קָנִים בְּזוֹל.

The Gemara answers: **If you wish, say there is** a practical difference **between them** with regard to **the wage of a watchman.**[N] **The first *tanna* maintains** that **yes,** since his field is safeguarded by the partition which surrounds it, the one who built the partition can demand payment of **the wage of a watchman.** He cannot, however, demand the cost of building the partition, **not** even the other's share for all of the partitions in accordance with **a reduced** assessment of the **price of reeds. And Rabbi Yosei maintains** that he can demand the other's share for all of the partitions in accordance with **a reduced** assessment of the **price of reeds.**

וְאִי בָּעֵית אֵימָא: רִאשׁוֹנָה שְׁנִיָּה וּשְׁלִישִׁית אִיכָּא בֵּינַיְיהוּ, תַּנָּא קַמָּא סָבַר: רְבִיעִית הוּא דְּיָהֵיב לֵיהּ, אֲבָל רִאשׁוֹנָה שְׁנִיָּה וּשְׁלִישִׁית – לָא יָהֵיב לֵיהּ, וְרַבִּי יוֹסֵי סָבַר: רִאשׁוֹנָה שְׁנִיָּיה וּשְׁלִישִׁית נַמִי יָהֵיב לֵיהּ.

And if you wish, say there is a practical difference **between them** with regard to the partitions built on the **first, second, and third** sides of the inner field. **The first *tanna* maintains** that the owner of the inner field must **give to** his neighbor money for the partition built on the **fourth** side, **but** he is **not** required to **give him** money for the partitions built on the **first, second, and third** sides. **And Rabbi Yosei maintains** that **he** must **also give him** money **for** the partitions built on **the first, the second, and the third** sides.

אִיבָּעֵית אֵימָא: מַקִּיף וְנִיקָּף אִיכָּא בֵּינַיְיהוּ, דְּתַנָּא קַמָּא סוֹבֵר: טַעְמָא דְּעָמַד נִיקָּף דִּמְגַלְגְּלִין עָלָיו אֶת הַכֹּל, אֲבָל עָמַד מַקִּיף – אֵינוֹ נוֹתֵן לוֹ אֶלָּא דְּמֵי רְבִיעִית;

The Gemara suggests another difference between the two opinions: **If you wish, say there is** a practical difference **between them** with regard to the issue of whether the partition on the fourth side was built by the owner of the **surrounding** field **or** by the owner of the **surrounded** field. This is **because the first *tanna* maintains** that **the reason** the owner of the **surrounded** field must contribute his share of the entire expense is **that he arose** and built a partition on the fourth side of his field. Therefore, the court **imposes upon him** the responsibility to pay his share for **all** of the partitions, because his actions demonstrate that he wants the partition between their fields. **But** if the owner of the **surrounding** field **arose** and built a partition on the fourth side of the field, the owner of the surrounded field **must give him only** his share of **the value of** the partition of the **fourth** side.

NOTES

The wage of a watchman – אֲגַר נְטִירָא: This refers to the minimum wage paid to a watchman to prevent animals from entering a field and eating the crops. The cost of such protection is even less than that of a partition fashioned from reeds.

וְרַבִּי יוֹסֵי סָבַר: לָא שְׁנָא נִיקָּף וְלָא שְׁנָא מַקִּיף, אִם עָמַד וְגָדַר – מְגַלְגְּלִין עָלָיו אֶת הַכֹּל.

And Rabbi Yosei maintains that it is **no different** if it was the owner of the **surrounded** field who arose and built a partition on the fourth side, **and** it is **no different** if it was the owner of the **surrounding** field who arose and built a partition on the fourth side. **If** either one **arose and built a partition** on the fourth side, the court **imposes upon** the owner of the inner field the obligation to pay his share for **all** of the partitions.

לִישָּׁנָא אַחֲרִינָא: מַקִּיף וְנִיקָּף אִיכָּא בֵּינַיְיהוּ, תַּנָּא קַמָּא סָבַר: אִם גָּדַר מַקִּיף אֶת הָרְבִיעִית נַמִּי יָהֵיב לֵיהּ, וְרַבִּי יוֹסֵי סָבַר: אִם עָמַד נִיקָּף וְגָדַר אֶת הָרְבִיעִית הוּא דְּיָהֵיב לֵיהּ, דְּגַלֵּי דַּעְתֵּיהּ דְּנִיחָא לֵיהּ, אֲבָל אִם גָּדַר מַקִּיף – לָא יָהֵיב לֵיהּ מִידֵּי.

The Gemara reports **another version** of this last answer: **There is** a practical difference **between them** with regard to the issue of whether the partition on the fourth side was built by the owner of the **surrounding** field **or** by the owner of the **surrounded** field. **The first *tanna* maintains** that even **if** the owner of the **surrounding** field **built a partition** on **the fourth** side, the owner of the surrounded field **also gives him** his share of the cost of the partitions. **And Rabbi Yosei maintains** that only **if** the owner of the **surrounded** field **arose** and **built a partition** on **the fourth** side **does he give** the owner of the surrounding field his share of the cost of the partitions. Why is that? **Because he reveals that he is pleased** with the partitions. **But if** the owner of the **surrounding** field **built a partition** on the fourth side, the owner of the surrounded field **does not give him anything,** as he can continue to claim that he has no interest in the partitions.

Perek **I**
Daf **5** Amud **a**

רוֹנְיָא, אַקְפֵיהּ רָבִינָא מֵאַרְבַּע רוּחוֹתָיו. אֲמַר לֵיהּ: ״הַב לִי כַּמָּה דְּגָדְרִי״, לָא יָהֵיב לֵיהּ. ״הַב לִי לְפִי קָנִים בְּזוֹל״, לָא יָהֵיב לֵיהּ. ״הַב לִי אֲגַר נְטִירוּתָא״, לָא יָהֵיב לֵיהּ.

It is related that a man named **Ronya** had a field that **was surrounded by** fields belonging to **Ravina on all four sides.** Ravina built partitions around his fields and **said to him: Give me** your share of the expense **in accordance with what I** actually spent when I **built the partitions,** i.e., half the cost of the partitions. Ronya **did not give** it **to him.** Ravina said to him: **Give me** then at least your share of the expense **in accordance with a reduced** assessment of the **price of reeds.** Ronya **did not give** it **to him.** Ravina said to him: **Give me** then at least **the wage of a watchman.** But **he did not give** even this **to him.**

יוֹמָא חַד הֲוָה קָא גָּדַר דִּיקְלֵי, אֲמַר לֵיהּ לַאֲרִיסֵיהּ: זִיל שְׁקוֹל מִנֵּיהּ קִיבּוּרָא דַּאֲהִינֵי. אֲזַל לְאַתּוּיֵי, רְמָא בֵּיהּ קָלָא. אֲמַר לֵיהּ: גַּלֵּית דַּעְתָּךְ דְּמֵינַח נִיחָא לָךְ, לָא יְהֵא אֶלָּא עִיזָּא בְּעָלְמָא, מִי לָא בָּעֵי נְטִירוּתָא? אֲמַר לֵיהּ: עִיזָּא בְּעָלְמָא לָאו לְאַכְלוּיֵי בָּעֲיָא? אֲמַר לֵיהּ: וְלָא גַּבְרָא בָּעֵית דְּמִיכְלֵי לָהּ?

One day, Ronya **was harvesting dates.** Ravina **said to his sharecropper: Go take a cluster** [*kibbura*][L] **of dates from him.** The sharecropper **went to bring them,** but Ronya **raised his voice at him** in protest, whereupon Ravina **said to him: You have revealed that you are pleased** with the partitions and the protection that they provide you. Even **if it were only a goat** that entered your field, **wouldn't** the field **need safeguarding,** to prevent the goat from eating the dates? Ronya **said to him:** If it were **only a goat, doesn't** one **need** merely **to chase it away** [*le'akhluyei*]?[L] No partition is required. Ravina **said to him: But wouldn't you need a man to chase** the goat **away?** Pay me then at least the wage of a watchman.

אֲתָא לְקַמֵּיהּ דְּרָבָא, אֲמַר לֵיהּ: זִיל פַּיְיסֵיהּ בְּמַאי דְּאִיפַּיֵּיס, וְאִי לָא – דָּאֵינְנָא לָךְ דִּינָא כְּרַב הוּנָא אַלִּיבָּא דְּרַבִּי יוֹסֵי.

Ravina **came before Rava** to adjudicate the matter. Rava **said to** Ronya: **Go appease** Ravina **with what he** expressed his willingness to be **appeased with,** namely, the wage of a watchman. **And if not, I will judge you in accordance with** the ruling of **Rav Huna in accordance with** the opinion of **Rabbi Yosei,** and you will be required to pay half the cost of the partition based on what Ravina actually spent on it.

LANGUAGE

Cluster [*kibbura*] – קִיבּוּרָא: From the Aramaic, meaning tuber. The word has been appropriated to describe a large cluster of dates that resembles a tuber.

To chase it away [*le'akhluyei*] – לְאַכְלוּיֵי: Based on the Aramaic translation of the Prophets and the Writings, some commentaries understand this to mean shout (see Rashi and Rabbeinu Ḥananel). That is, one could raise one's voice and thereby prevent the goat from entering the field. Others suggest that the word denotes removal or preventing something from arriving, as in the *kala orev* which kept birds away from the Temple (*Arukh*; Ri Migash); *le'akhluyei* and *kala* share the same root.

רוֹנְיָא זְבַן אַרְעָא אַמִּיצְרָא דְּרָבִינָא, סְבַר רָבִינָא לְסַלּוֹקֵי מִשּׁוּם דִּינָא דְּבַר מִצְרָא; אֲמַר לֵיהּ רַב סָפְרָא בְּרֵיהּ דְּרַב יֵיבָא לְרָבִינָא, אָמְרִי אֱינָשֵׁי: אַרְבְּעָה לְצַלָּא, אַרְבְּעָה לְצַלָּלָא.

Incidental to that episode, the Gemara relates another encounter between Ravina and Ronya. **Ronya** once **bought land adjoining** property belonging to **Ravina. Ravina considered removing him due to the *halakha* of one** whose field **borders** the field of his neighbor. When land is up for sale, the owners of the adjoining fields have the right of first refusal. If one of the neighbors is willing to match the highest price being offered to the seller, that neighbor has the preemptive right to purchase the property, and if somebody else buys it, that buyer can be removed. Since Ravina owned the adjacent property, he thought that he enjoyed the right of first refusal. **Rav Safra, son of Rav Yeiva, said to Ravina: People say: Four** dinars **for a large hide [*tzalla*],**[N] **four for a small hide [*tzelala*].** Since Ronya also owned land bordering the desired parcel, you cannot remove him even though his plot of land is smaller than yours.

מתני׳ כּוֹתֶל חָצֵר שֶׁנָּפַל – מְחַיְּיבִין אוֹתוֹ לִבְנוֹתוֹ עַד אַרְבַּע אַמּוֹת; בְּחֶזְקַת שֶׁנָּתַן, עַד שֶׁיָּבִיא רְאָיָה שֶׁלֹּא נָתַן.

MISHNA In the case of a dividing **wall** in a jointly owned **courtyard that fell,**[H] if one of the owners wishes to rebuild the wall, the court **obligates** the other owner **to build** the wall with him **up to** a height of **four cubits.**[H] If after the wall was built one of the neighbors claims he alone constructed it and the other did not participate in its building, the latter is nevertheless **presumed to have given**[N] his share of the money, **unless** the claimant **brings proof that** the other **did not give** his part.

מֵאַרְבַּע אַמּוֹת וּלְמַעְלָן – אֵין מְחַיְּיבִין אוֹתוֹ. סָמַךְ לוֹ כּוֹתֶל אַחֵר, אַף עַל פִּי שֶׁלֹּא נָתַן עָלָיו אֶת הַתִּקְרָה – מְגַלְגְּלִין עָלָיו אֶת הַכֹּל; בְּחֶזְקַת שֶׁלֹּא נָתַן, עַד שֶׁיָּבִיא רְאָיָה שֶׁנָּתַן.

The court **does not obligate** the reluctant neighbor to contribute to the building of the wall **higher than four cubits.**[HN] But if the reluctant neighbor **built another wall close** to the wall that had been built higher than four cubits, in order to set a roof over the room that was thereby created, the court **imposes upon him** the responsibility to pay his share for **all** of the rebuilt wall, **even though he has not** yet **set a roof over it.** Since he has demonstrated his desire to make use of what his neighbor built, he must participate in the cost of its construction. If the builder of the first wall later claims that he did not receive payment from his neighbor, the neighbor **is presumed not to have given** his share of the money, **unless he brings proof that he did** in fact **give** money for the building of the wall.

גמ׳ אָמַר רֵישׁ לָקִישׁ: הַקּוֹבֵעַ זְמַן לַחֲבֵירוֹ, וְאָמַר לוֹ ״פְּרַעְתִּיךָ בְּתוֹךְ זְמַנִּי״ – אֵינוֹ נֶאֱמָן, וּלְוַאי שֶׁיִּפְרַע בִּזְמַנּוֹ. אַבָּיֵי וְרָבָא דְּאָמְרִי תַּרְוַיְיהוּ: עָבֵיד אִינִישׁ דְּפָרַע בְּגוֹ זִמְנֵיהּ, זִימְנִין דְּמִתְרְמוּ לֵיהּ זוּזֵי, אָמַר: אֵיזִיל אִיפְרְעֵיהּ,

GEMARA **Reish Lakish says:** If a lender **set a time for another** to repay the loan that he had extended to him **and** when the debt came due the borrower **said** to the lender: **I** already **repaid you within the time, he is not deemed credible,**[N] as people do not ordinarily repay their debts before they are due. The lender would be happy **if** the borrower **would only repay** his debt **on time. Abaye and Rava** disagree with Reish Lakish, **as they both say: A person is apt to repay** his debt **within its time,** i.e., before it is due. This is because **sometimes he happens to have money** and the borrower **says** to himself: **I will go and repay** my debt

NOTES

Four for a large hide [*tzalla*], etc. – אַרְבְּעָה לְצַלָּא וכו׳: Several explanations have been given for this statement of Rav Safra. Rashi cites an explanation that the term *tzalla* refers to a poor leatherworker and the term *tzelala* refers to a wealthy leatherworker. Rav Safra was stating that both a poor leatherworker and a wealthy leatherworker require the same amount of food to sustain their families, i.e., four loaves of bread per day. Therefore, although Ravina was justified in claiming that he had the right of one whose field borders the field of his neighbor, nevertheless, since the basis for that *halakha*, as explained in *Bava Metzia* 108a, is the verse: "And you shall do that which is right and good in the eyes of the Lord" (Deuteronomy 6:18), Ravina should also do what is right and good and forgo his claim, enabling Ronya, who was poor, to purchase the field.

Rashi offers a second explanation: *Tzalla* is a hide and *tzelala* is a leatherworker, and Ronya himself was a shoemaker. Rav Safra was telling Ravina that Ronya's profession does not provide a sufficient livelihood, as shoemakers have a lot of expenses such as paying for the leather and paying the leatherworker to process it. Therefore, Ravina should act beyond the letter of the law and allow Ronya to purchase the field.

The Ri Migash and the Ramah both explain that the term *tzalla* refers to a poor leatherworker and the term *tzelala* refers to a wealthy leatherworker, but explain Rav Safra's statement in a different manner entirely. The four in question alludes to the four cubits of a grave. Rav Safra was telling Ravina that since everyone is destined for the grave, he should not insist upon exercising his rights in order to increase his wealth but should allow Ronya to purchase the field.

The commonality among these three explanations is that Rav Safra was not issuing a halakhic ruling that Ronya has the right to purchase the field, but was recommending to Ravina that he act beyond the letter of the law and allow Ronya to purchase it.

Tosafot, citing Rabbeinu Tam, explain that Rav Safra was issuing a halakhic ruling. The case was that Ravina bordered the seller on three sides, while Ronya bordered the seller on only one side. Ravina was of the opinion that he alone would have the right of one whose field borders the field of his neighbor, as his fields bordered the seller's field on more sides than Ravina's did. Rav Safra explained to him that one pays a leatherworker four dinars to process a large piece of leather [*tzalla*] and one pays the leatherworker the same four dinars to process a small piece of leather [*tzelala*], thereby alluding to him that it is immaterial whether one's fields border the seller's fields on many sides or one side. Either neighbor has the right of one whose field borders the field of his neighbor, so Ronya's purchase of the field stands.

He is presumed to have given – בְּחֶזְקַת שֶׁנָּתַן: Since everybody is familiar with the *halakha* that the cost of the wall must be shared between the two neighbors, it is clear that one would not have built the entire wall at his own expense without demanding money from the other. But not everybody is familiar with the *halakha* concerning raising the wall, and therefore it can be assumed that the neighbor did not pay to raise the wall above four cubits (see Rashi and *Tosafot*).

Higher than four cubits – מֵאַרְבַּע אַמּוֹת וּלְמַעְלָן: Above four cubits there is no longer any fear of invasion of privacy because a four-cubit-high wall is higher than a person's height.

He is not deemed credible – אֵינוֹ נֶאֱמָן: This applies when there are witnesses both to the loan and to the setting of a date on which the loan is due, as in that case the borrower cannot claim that he never borrowed money from the creditor.

HALAKHA

A wall in a courtyard that fell – כּוֹתֶל חָצֵר שֶׁנָּפַל: If a wall in a jointly owned courtyard fell, each party can compel the other to rebuild the wall up to a height of four cubits even if the previous wall was higher than that (*Sma*). Either party can subsequently raise the height at his own expense. If one neighbor built the dividing wall higher than four cubits and afterward the other built another wall next to it in order to set a roof over the room that was thereby created, the latter can be compelled to contribute to the cost of the additional height of the first wall (Rambam *Sefer Kinyan*, *Hilkhot Shekhenim* 3:1; *Shulḥan Arukh*, *Ḥoshen Mishpat* 157:10).

Up to four cubits – עַד אַרְבַּע אַמּוֹת: If a wall divides a jointly owned courtyard, it may be assumed that both parties contributed to its construction costs. Even if it is known that one neighbor laid out the expenses for the wall and now claims that the other did not compensate him for the project, the latter can take an oath that he paid and then be absolved, unless witnesses testify that he really did not share in the costs of the wall (Rambam *Sefer Kinyan*, *Hilkhot Shekhenim* 3:2; *Shulḥan Arukh*, *Ḥoshen Mishpat* 157:8).

Higher than four cubits – מֵאַרְבַּע אַמּוֹת וּלְמַעְלָן: If one built a dividing wall higher than four cubits, and then his neighbor built another wall close to it that is also higher than four cubits, and they disagree about whether the second person paid for the additional height of the first wall, the second person is not deemed credible. The first person can take an oath that he received no money, and then collect payment, even if he lacks further proof. The *Tur* cites the Ramah and the Ramban, who say that he can collect the money even without taking an oath (Rambam *Sefer Kinyan*, *Hilkhot Shekhenim* 3:2; *Shulḥan Arukh*, *Ḥoshen Mishpat* 157:11, and see *Sma* and *Shakh* there).

NOTES

Each and every row – כָּל שָׁפָא וְשָׁפָא: The *Arukh* has a version of the text that reads *safa*, meaning a row. The Rif and the Ri Migash have a version of the text that reads *sha'a*, meaning that each one owes the money at each step throughout the construction.

Even from orphans – אֲפִילּוּ מִיַּתְמֵי: Rashi explains that if the borrower died before the loan became due, the lender can collect the debt from his orphans, and there is no concern that the father might have paid back the debt before its time. Rabbeinu Gershom explains that before he died, the borrower claimed that he repaid the debt prematurely and the orphans as well state that this is what their father told them.

HALAKHA

Because the time to pay is upon the completion of each and every row – דְּכָל שָׁפָא וְשָׁפָא זִימְנֵיהּ הוּא: If one neighbor in a jointly owned courtyard claims that the other neighbor did not pay his share of the cost of building the wall separating their properties, while the other claims he paid his share before the wall was completed, or he paid it even before the construction began, he is deemed credible and is exempt from paying after he takes an oath (*Shulḥan Arukh*, *Ḥoshen Mishpat* 157:8 and *Sma* there).

And the *halakha* is in accordance with Reish Lakish – וְהִלְכְתָא כְּרֵישׁ לָקִישׁ: If one lends a person money and sets a date when the debt must be repaid, and then attempts to collect the money before the due date, and the borrower asserts that he already repaid the debt or that the debt was forgiven (Rema), the borrower is not deemed credible. The lender can collect his money without taking an oath. If the borrower died the lender can collect the debt even from the borrower's minor orphans as long as the debt is substantiated with a document or if there were witnesses to the loan and to the setting of a time. The Rema writes that this *halakha* applies both to loans and to wages. By contrast, a bailee safeguarding a deposit can claim that he returned it before its time (Rambam *Sefer Mishpatim*, *Hilkhot Malve VeLoveh* 14:1; *Shulḥan Arukh*, *Ḥoshen Mishpat* 78:1).

One who comes to collect from the property of orphans – הַבָּא לִיפָּרַע מִנִּכְסֵי יְתוֹמִים: One can collect a debt from orphans, even if they are adults, only after taking an oath. If the borrower died before the debt was due, or if he admitted at the time of death that he still owed money, or if he had been placed under a ban to force him to pay a debt and he died while still under the ban, the debt can be collected from the heirs even without taking an oath (Rambam *Sefer Mishpatim*, *Hilkhot Malve VeLoveh* 14:1; *Shulḥan Arukh*, *Ḥoshen Mishpat* 108:1, 17).

BACKGROUND

Presumption – חֲזָקָה: This halakhic term connotes different meanings depending on the context. Most often, it refers to an accepted presumption based on facts, circumstances, custom, or behavioral tendencies of people. For example, there is an accepted presumption that an agent carries out his agency, or that children who are treated as family members are, in fact, their parents' offspring. Unless the facts prove otherwise these presumptions are accepted as truth, to the extent that they may even serve as the basis for administering corporal punishment.

כִּי הֵיכִי דְּלָא לִיטַרְדַּן.

so that he will not trouble me later by constantly demanding the money.

תְּנַן: בְּחֶזְקַת שֶׁנָּתַן, עַד שֶׁיָּבִיא רְאָיָה שֶׁלֹּא נָתַן;

The Gemara attempts to bring a proof in support of the opinion of Abaye and Rava from what **we learned** in the mishna (5a): If after the wall was built one of the neighbors claims he alone constructed it and the other did not participate in its building, the latter is nevertheless **presumed to have given** his share of the money, **unless** the claimant **brings proof that** the other **did not give** his part.

הֵיכִי דָּמֵי? אִילֵימָא דְּאָמַר לֵיהּ: ״פְּרַעְתִּיךָ בִּזְמַנִּי״ – פְּשִׁיטָא בְּחֶזְקַת שֶׁנָּתַן! אֶלָּא לָאו דְּאָמַר לֵיהּ: ״פְּרַעְתִּיךָ בְּתוֹךְ זְמַנִּי״; אַלְמָא עָבֵיד אִינִישׁ דְּפָרַע בְּתוֹךְ זְמַנֵּיהּ! שָׁאנֵי הָכָא, דְּכָל שָׁפָא וְשָׁפָא זִימְנֵיהּ הוּא.

The Gemara clarifies the matter: **What are the circumstances** of the case under discussion? **If we say** that **he said to him: I paid you at the time** when the payment became due, when the wall was completed, it is **obvious** that **he is presumed to have given** his part. **Rather, is it not that he said to him: I paid you within the time** before the payment became due, while the wall was still under construction? And with regard to such a case the mishna states that he is presumed to have given his share. **Apparently, a person is apt to repay** his debt **within its time,** in accordance with the opinion of Abaye and Rava. The Gemara rejects this proof: **Here** it **is different, because the time** to pay is upon the completion of **each and every row.**[NH] Payment does not become due specifically at the completion of the entire wall.

תָּא שְׁמַע: בְּחֶזְקַת שֶׁלֹּא נָתַן, עַד שֶׁיָּבִיא רְאָיָה שֶׁנָּתַן;

The Gemara further suggests: **Come** and **hear** a proof in support of the opinion of Reish Lakish from the continuation of the mishna (5a): The court does not obligate the reluctant neighbor to contribute to the building of the wall higher than four cubits. But if the reluctant neighbor built another wall close to the wall that had been built higher than four cubits, in order to set a roof over the room that was thereby created, the court imposes upon him the responsibility to pay his share for all of the rebuilt wall, even though he has not yet set a roof over it. If the builder of the first wall later claims he did not receive payment from his neighbor, the neighbor **is presumed not to have given** his share of the money, **unless he brings proof that he did** in fact **give** money for the building of the wall.

הֵיכִי דָּמֵי? אִילֵימָא דְּאָמַר לֵיהּ: ״פְּרַעְתִּיךָ בִּזְמַנִּי״, אַמַּאי לָא? אֶלָּא לָאו דְּאָמַר לֵיהּ: ״פְּרַעְתִּיךָ בְּתוֹךְ זְמַנִּי״; אַלְמָא לָא עָבֵיד אִינִישׁ דְּפָרַע בְּגוֹ זִימְנֵיהּ! שָׁאנֵי הָכָא, דְּאָמַר: מִי יֵימַר דִּמְחַיְּיבוּ לִי רַבָּנַן.

The Gemara clarifies the matter: **What are the circumstances** of the case under discussion? **If we say** that **he said to him: I paid you at the time** that the payment became due, when the wall was completed, **why** is he **not** deemed credible? **Rather,** is it **not that he said to him: I paid you within the time** before the payment became due, and therefore he is not deemed credible? **Apparently, a person is not apt to repay** his debt **within its time,** in accordance with the opinion of Reish Lakish. The Gemara rejects this proof: **Here** it **is different, since** the reluctant neighbor **says: Who says that the Rabbis will obligate me** to pay for this wall? In such a case he certainly does not pay before the payment becomes due.

רַב פַּפָּא וְרַב הוּנָא בְּרֵיהּ דְּרַב יְהוֹשֻׁעַ עָבְדִי כְּאַבַּיֵי וְרָבָא. מָר בַּר רַב אַשִׁי עֲבַד כְּרֵישׁ לָקִישׁ. וְהִלְכְתָא כְּרֵישׁ לָקִישׁ, וַאֲפִילּוּ מִיַּתְמֵי; וְאַף עַל גַּב דְּאָמַר מָר: הַבָּא לִיפָּרַע מִנִּכְסֵי יְתוֹמִים לֹא יִפָּרַע אֶלָּא בִּשְׁבוּעָה, חֲזָקָה לָא עָבֵיד אִינִישׁ דְּפָרַע בְּגוֹ זִימְנֵיהּ.

Rav Pappa and Rav Huna, son of Rav Yehoshua, acted in such a case **in accordance with** the opinion of **Abaye and Rava. Mar bar Rav Ashi acted in accordance with** the opinion of **Reish Lakish.** The Gemara concludes: **And the *halakha* is in accordance with** the opinion of **Reish Lakish**[H] that one is not deemed credible when he says that he repaid a loan before it became due. **And** if the debtor dies, the court collects payment **even from** his **orphans**[N] based on this assumption. **And even though the Master said** that **one who comes to collect** money **from the property of orphans**[H] **cannot collect unless** he first takes **an oath** that he did not already collect the debt from the deceased, here he can collect without taking an oath because there is a **presumption**[B] that **a person is not apt to repay** his debt **within its time.**

אִיבַּעְיָא לְהוּ: תְּבָעוֹ לְאַחַר זְמַן, וְאָמַר לוֹ "פְּרַעְתִּיךָ בְּתוֹךְ זְמַנִּי", מַהוּ? מִי אָמְרִינַן: בִּמְקוֹם חֲזָקָה אָמְרִינַן "מָה לִי לְשַׁקֵּר",

A dilemma was raised before the Sages: **What is** the *halakha* if the lender stipulated a time with the borrower for repayment of the debt, and **he demanded** payment of the money **after the time**[H] that the payment became due had passed, **and** the borrower **said to him: I** already **repaid you within the time** before the payment became due? **Do we say** that even **where there is a presumption** against someone's claim, as in this case where there is a presumption that people do not pay their debts before they become due, **we say** that the borrower can claim: **Why would I lie?** If one of the litigants could have advanced a claim more advantageous to his cause than the one he actually did, the assumption is that he is telling the truth. Consequently, in this case had the borrower wished to lie, he could have said that he repaid his debt when it became due, and he would have been deemed credible. Therefore, when he claims that he repaid it before it came due he should also be deemed credible.

HALAKHA

He demanded payment after the time – תְּבָעוֹ לְאַחַר זְמַן: If one claims a debt recorded in a document after its due date has passed and the debtor disputes the claim, insisting that he paid the debt before it was due or when it came due, the creditor can collect his money only after taking an oath. If the loan was not recorded in a document, the debtor takes an oath and is exempt from payment (Rambam *Sefer Mishpatim, Hilkhot Malve VeLoveh* 14:1; *Shulḥan Arukh, Ḥoshen Mishpat* 78:5).

Perek **I**
Daf **6** Amud **a**

אוֹ דִילְמָא בִּמְקוֹם חֲזָקָה לָא אָמְרִינַן "מָה לִי לְשַׁקֵּר"? תָּא שְׁמַע: בְּחֶזְקַת שֶׁנָּתַן, עַד שֶׁיָּבִיא רְאָיָה שֶׁלֹּא נָתַן;

Or perhaps where there is a presumption against a person's claim, **we do not say** that the borrower can claim: **Why would I lie?** The Gemara suggests: **Come** and **hear** a proof from the mishna: If after the wall was built one of the neighbors claims he alone constructed it and the other did not participate in its building, the latter is nevertheless **presumed to have given** his share of the money, **unless** the claimant **brings proof that** the other **did not give** his share.

הֵיכִי דָמֵי? אִילֵימָא שֶׁתְּבָעוֹ לְאַחַר זְמַן, וְאָמַר לוֹ: "פְּרַעְתִּיךָ בִּזְמַנִּי" – פְּשִׁיטָא! אֶלָּא לָאו דְּאָמַר לֵיהּ: "פְּרַעְתִּיךָ בְּתוֹךְ זְמַנִּי"; אַלְמָא אֲפִילּוּ בִּמְקוֹם חֲזָקָה אָמְרִינַן "מָה לִי לְשַׁקֵּר"! שָׁאנֵי הָכָא, דְּכׇל שָׁפָא וְשָׁפָא זִמְנֵיהּ הוּא.

The Gemara clarifies the matter: **What are the circumstances** of the case? **If we say that** one partner **demanded** that the other party pay the money **after the time** that the payment became due, i.e., after the wall was rebuilt, **and** the other partner **said to him: I paid you at the time** that the payment became due, it is **obvious** that he is presumed to have given him the money. **Rather, is it not** a case **where he said to him: I paid you within the time,** i.e., before the payment became due? **Apparently, even where there is a presumption** against a person's claim, **we say** that the defendant can claim: **Why would I lie?** The Gemara rejects this proof: **Here** it is **different, because the time** to pay is upon the completion of **each and every row.** Therefore, it is as if he said: I paid you at the time that the payment became due.

תָּא שְׁמַע: מֵאַרְבַּע אַמּוֹת וּלְמַעְלָה – אֵין מְחַיְּיבִין אוֹתוֹ; סָמַךְ לוֹ כּוֹתֶל אַחֵר כּוּ' עַד שֶׁיָּבִיא רְאָיָה שֶׁנָּתַן;

The Gemara suggests: **Come** and **hear** another proof from the continuation of the mishna. The court **does not obligate** the reluctant neighbor to contribute to the building of the part of the wall that is **above four cubits.** But if the reluctant neighbor **built another wall close to** the wall that was built higher than four cubits, in order to set a roof over the room that was thereby created, the court imposes upon him the responsibility to pay his share for all of the rebuilt wall, even though he has not yet set a roof over it. If the builder of the first wall later claims that he did not receive payment from his neighbor, the neighbor is presumed not to have given his share of the money, **unless he brings proof that he did** in fact **give** money for the building of the wall.

הֵיכִי דָמֵי? אִילֵימָא שֶׁתְּבָעוֹ לְאַחַר זְמַנּוֹ, וְאָמַר לוֹ: "פְּרַעְתִּיךָ בִּזְמַנִּי", אַמַּאי לָא? אֶלָּא לָאו דְּאָמַר: "פְּרַעְתִּיךָ בְּתוֹךְ זְמַנִּי"; אַלְמָא בִּמְקוֹם חֲזָקָה לָא אָמְרִינַן "מָה לִי לְשַׁקֵּר". שָׁאנֵי הָכָא, דְּאָמַר: מִי יֵימַר דִּמְחַיְּיבִי לִי רַבָּנַן.

The Gemara clarifies: **What are the circumstances** of the case? **If we say that** one partner **demanded** that the other party pay the money **after the time** that the payment became due, **and he,** the latter, **said to him: I paid you at the time** that the payment became due, **why** is he **not** deemed credible? **Rather, is it not that he said: I paid you within the time,** before the payment became due? And with regard to this case, the mishna states that he is not deemed credible. **Apparently, where there is a presumption** against a person's claim, **we do not say** that the defendant can claim: **Why would I lie?** The Gemara rejects this proof: **Here** it is **different, since** the reluctant neighbor **says: Who says that the Rabbis will obligate me** to pay for this additional part of the wall? In such a case he certainly does not pay before the payment becomes due. The mishna does not provide a proof one way or the other.

אֲמַר לֵיהּ רַב אַחָא בְּרֵיהּ דְּרָבָא לְרַב אַשִׁי, תָּא שְׁמַע: ״מָנֶה לִי בְּיָדְךָ״, אָמַר לוֹ: ״הֵין״. לְמָחָר אָמַר לוֹ: ״תְּנֵהוּ לִי״, אִם אָמַר ״נְתַתִּיו לְךָ״ – פָּטוּר, ״אֵין לְךָ בְּיָדִי״ – חַיָּיב;

Rav Aḥa, son of Rava, said to Rav Ashi: Come and **hear** a proof from what is taught in a mishna (*Shevuot* 38b): If one said to another: I have **one hundred dinars in your possession,**[H] and the other one **said to him** in the presence of witnesses: **Yes,** that is so; and **the next day** the lender **said to** the borrower: **Give me** the money that you owe me, the *halakha* is as follows: **If** the borrower **said: I** already **gave it to you,** he is **exempt.** But if he said: **Nothing** of **yours** is **in my possession,** he is **liable.**

מַאי לָאו ״נְתַתִּיו לְךָ״ – דְּאָמַר לֵיהּ: ״פְּרַעְתִּיךָ בִּזְמַנִּי״, ״אֵין לְךָ בְּיָדִי״ – דְּאָמַר לֵיהּ: ״פְּרַעְתִּיךָ בְּתוֹךְ זְמַנִּי״, וְקָתָנֵי: חַיָּיב; אַלְמָא בִּמְקוֹם חֲזָקָה לָא אָמְרִינַן ״מָה לִי לְשַׁקֵּר״. לָא, מַאי ״אֵין לְךָ בְּיָדִי״? לֹא הָיוּ דְּבָרִים מֵעוֹלָם, דְּאָמַר מָר: כׇּל הָאוֹמֵר ״לֹא לָוִיתִי״, כְּאוֹמֵר ״לֹא פָּרַעְתִּי״ דָּמֵי.

The Gemara clarifies the matter: **What, is it not** that when he says: I already **gave it to you, he is saying to him: I repaid you at the time** that the payment became due; and when he says: **Nothing** of **yours** is **in my possession, he is saying to him: I repaid you within the time,** before the payment became due? **And** yet, the mishna **teaches** with regard to the latter case that he is **liable. Apparently, where there is a presumption** against a person's claim, **we do not say** that the borrower can claim: **Why would I lie?** The Gemara rejects this proof: **No, what** does he mean when he says: **Nothing** of **yours** is **in my possession?** He is saying: **There were never such matters;** i.e., the purported loan never occurred. **As the Master says: Anyone who says: I did not borrow,**[H] is treated **as one who says: I did not repay,** and since it is known by his own admission that he borrowed money, he is liable to pay.

״סָמַךְ לוֹ כּוֹתֶל אַחֵר – מְגַלְגְּלִין עָלָיו אֶת הַכֹּל״ כו׳. אָמַר רַב הוּנָא: סָמַךְ לְפַלְגָּא סָמַךְ לְכוּלַּהּ; וְרַב נַחְמָן אָמַר: לְמַאי דִּסְמַךְ – סְמַךְ, לְמַאי דְּלָא סְמַךְ – לָא סְמַךְ.

§ The mishna teaches: But if the reluctant neighbor **built another wall close to** the wall that was built higher than four cubits, in order to set a roof over the room that was thereby created, the court **imposes upon him** the responsibility to pay his share for **all** of the rebuilt wall. **Rav Huna says:** If **he built** another wall **close to** the first wall that was **half** the length or the height of the wall that was built higher than four cubits, it is as if **he built** it **close to** the height and length of **the entire** wall.[B] Since he can easily add to his wall so that it will be equal in length or height to the wall the neighbor rebuilt, he must therefore pay half the cost of the entire rebuilt wall. **And Rav Naḥman says:** With regard to **that which he built close, he built** it **close;**[H] with regard to **that which he did not build close, he did not** yet **build** it **close.** Accordingly, he is required to pay an additional share only for the part of the wall corresponding to the new wall he built.

HALAKHA

I have one hundred dinars in your possession – מָנֶה לִי בְּיָדְךָ: If one claims money from another individual who admits to the debt before witnesses or a court (*Sma*) and the next day the creditor demands the money, at which time the debtor says that he already has paid it after he admitted owing it (*Netivot HaMishpat*), the latter can take an oath and is then exempt from paying. If he said that he never owed the money, he is confirmed as a liar, and the creditor can collect from him even without taking an oath (Rambam *Sefer Mishpatim, Hilkhot To'en VeNitan* 6:6; *Shulḥan Arukh, Ḥoshen Mishpat* 79:10).

Anyone who says, I did not borrow – כׇּל הָאוֹמֵר לֹא לָוִיתִי: If an individual demands money that he lent to another and the latter denies having borrowed any money from him, and subsequently witnesses come and testify that he did indeed borrow money but repaid it, the debtor must pay, because if one claims that he did not borrow money, he is treated as if he said that he did not repay anything (Rambam *Sefer Mishpatim, Hilkhot To'en VeNitan* 6:3; *Shulḥan Arukh, Ḥoshen Mishpat* 79:1).

With regard to that which he built close, he built it close – לְמַאי דִּסְמַךְ סְמַךְ: If the wall between two neighbors in a courtyard fell and one of them rebuilt the wall, extending it higher than four cubits, and the other one subsequently built another wall close by whose height or length was less than that of the rebuilt wall, the latter is obligated to contribute to the costs of the first wall only to the height or length of the second wall (Rambam *Sefer Kinyan, Hilkhot Shekhenim* 3:1; *Shulḥan Arukh, Ḥoshen Mishpat* 157:10).

BACKGROUND

If he built close to half the wall he built close to the entire wall – סָמַךְ לְפַלְגָּא סָמַךְ לְכוּלַּהּ: In these three diagrams, the rear wall has been built on the boundary between the properties by one neighbor. The front wall is built by the second neighbor on his own property, close to the boundary wall. By building a new wall close to the original, the second neighbor has created a space bounded by the two walls that he can enclose, thus making use of all or part of the wall built by the first neighbor.

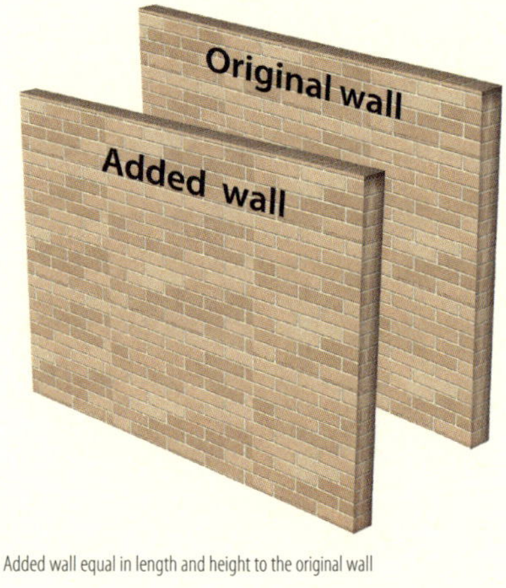

Added wall equal in length and height to the original wall

Added wall half the length of the original wall

Added wall half the height of the original wall

וּמוֹדֶה רַב הוּנָא בְּקַרְנָא וְלוּפְתָּא. וּמוֹדֶה רַב נַחְמָן בְּאַפְרִיזָא וּבְקַבַּעְתָּא דִּכְשׁוּרֵי.

And Rav Huna concedes with regard to an attachment to the corner[N] of his house that he is not required to pay half the cost of the entire rebuilt wall. If he built the extension of his house in this manner, it is not considered as if he built it close to the entire wall, as it is unlikely that he will add to it. **And Rav Naḥman concedes** that **in** a case in which he places a heavy **beam** [*be'afriza*][NL] on the wall that can support a roof, **or** carves into the wall **indentations to fix beams in place,**[BH] then even if he has not yet made use of the entire height of the wall, he has demonstrated his desire to do so in the future, and therefore he must pay half the cost of the entire wall.

אָמַר רַב הוּנָא: בֵּי כַּוֵּי לָא הָוֵי חֲזָקָה, וְאַף עַל גַּב דַּעֲבַד לֵיהּ הִימַלְטֵי, דְּאָמַר לֵיהּ: אָמֵינָא, לְכִי פַּיְיסַת לִי לָא לִיתְרַע אֲשִׁיתַאי.

§ The mishna teaches that if the builder of the first wall later claims that he did not receive payment from his neighbor, the neighbor is presumed not to have given his share of the money, unless he brings proof that he did in fact give money for the building of the wall. **Rav Huna says:** Even if **openings in the wall** were built on the side facing the reluctant partner and these openings are suited to serve as beam rests, this does **not** create **a presumption**[H] that the reluctant partner contributed his share to the building of the wall. **And** this is the *halakha* **even if** the builder of the wall **made sills**[N] for these openings. As the builder of the wall can **say to** his neighbor: **I said** to myself that **when you will appease me** and pay me for the construction of the wall, you might want to attach beams to it, and I do **not** want **the foundations of my wall to be damaged** by your fashioning new openings in it. Therefore, from the outset, I built the wall with these openings.

אָמַר רַב נַחְמָן: אַחְזֵיק לְהוּרְדֵי לָא אַחְזֵיק לִכְשׁוּרֵי, לִכְשׁוּרֵי – אַחְזֵיק לְהוּרְדֵי; רַב יוֹסֵף אָמַר: אַחְזֵיק לְהוּרְדֵי אַחְזֵיק לִכְשׁוּרֵי.

With regard to the use of a neighbor's wall, **Rav Naḥman says:** If one **acquired the privilege to** place **thin beams**[NH] on his neighbor's wall, i.e., if one had used the wall in that manner in the past and the owner did not protest, so the one using it can maintain that he had acquired from the owner the right to do so, **he has not acquired the privilege to** place **thick beams** there. But if he acquired the privilege **to** place **thick beams** on the wall, **he has acquired the privilege to** place **thin beams** there. **Rav Yosef says: If he acquired the privilege to** place **thin beams, he** also **has acquired the privilege to** place **thick beams.**

BACKGROUND

Indentations to fix beams in place – קַבַּעְתָּא דִּכְשׁוּרֵי:

Wall with sockets to hold beams

LANGUAGE

Beam [*afriza*] – אַפְרִיזָא: The origin of this word is not clear, although it seems to derive from Middle Persian and is probably related to the term frasp, meaning beam.

Afriza on a wall, supporting beams

HALAKHA

In a case in which he places a beam or carves indentations to fix beams in place – בְּאַפְרִיזָא וּבְקַבַּעְתָּא דִּכְשׁוּרֵי: If the neighbor did not build another wall close to the partition wall but rather made grooves in that wall for the purpose of placing beams there, or a single groove for a large beam the length of the wall, thereby demonstrating that he is pleased with the construction of the wall, he must pay half the cost of the entire wall above the height of four cubits. Similarly, if he built another wall close to the partition wall and made grooves at its top, he must contribute to the construction of the entire partition wall (*Tur*; *Sma*). The Rema adds that the *halakha* is the same if he demonstrated in any way that he is pleased with the entire length or height of the partition wall (Rambam *Sefer Kinyan*, *Hilkhot Shekhenim* 3:1; *Shulḥan Arukh*, *Ḥoshen Mishpat* 157:10).

Openings in the wall do not create a presumption – בֵּי כַּוֵּי לָא הָוֵי חֲזָקָה: If one extended his wall beyond a height of four cubits and placed beams on it pointing in the direction of his courtyard, and in the direction of his neighbor he prepared grooves for the placement of beams, which might be construed as an indication that the neighbor contributed toward the construction of the wall, the neighbor has no share in the extension of the wall beyond four cubits. The first one can claim that he made the grooves to protect the wall in case the other decided to later contribute to its construction and use it (Rambam *Sefer Kinyan*, *Hilkhot Shekhenim* 8:9; *Shulḥan Arukh*, *Ḥoshen Mishpat* 153:19).

If one acquired the privilege to place thin beams – אַחְזֵיק לְהוּרְדֵי: If one of the neighbors built the partition wall by himself and the second neighbor made a groove in it and placed a beam there and the first neighbor did not protest, the second neighbor has acquired the privilege to place the beam there. It is even permitted for him to replace it with a thicker beam. Some disagree and say that he acquires the privilege only if the beams remained there for three years (Rema, citing Rosh and Rabbeinu Yona). This is in accordance with the opinion of Rav Yosef and the second version of Rav Naḥman's statement (Rambam *Sefer Kinyan*, *Hilkhot Shekhenim* 8:7; *Shulḥan Arukh*, *Ḥoshen Mishpat* 153:16).

NOTES

With regard to an attachment to the corner – בְּקַרְנָא וְלוּפְתָּא: Rashi interprets these words as a single concept, an addition to a house that is attached [*lufta*] to the house's wall at the corner [*karna*], where it is evident from the construction that he wishes merely to juxtapose the corner with the neighbor's wall. Other commentaries understand these words as referring to two different elements. *Tosafot*, citing Rabbeinu Tam, explain that *karna* signifies an angle he creates at the end of the wall to indicate that he has no intention of extending the wall any further. *Lufta* denotes an indicator that he leaves near the top of the wall, e.g., a tapering toward the top that shows that he does not intend to make the wall any higher. Rabbeinu Ḥananel and the Ri Migash propose additional interpretations.

Beam – אַפְרִיזָא: Most commentaries explain that this word relates to the height of the wall. Rashi writes that this is the large beam that supports the ceiling beams. The *ge'onim* maintain that the word denotes a projection beneath the ceiling beams. Rabbeinu Yehonatan defines it as a beam, part of which rests on the wall and part of which protrudes from it to support other beams. By contrast, *Tosafot* write that the term refers to the length of the wall, the stones at the end of which are not left even; rather, some of them are left jutting out, suggesting that the owner intends to continue building it further.

Sills – הִימַלְטֵי: Rashi explains that the builder of the wall inserts small boards into the openings to protect the beams. Some commentaries explain that he constructs a small structure of bricks around the hole (*Ge'onim*; Rabbeinu Gershom). Others write that the term denotes mortar, which is put into the opening (*Ge'onim*; *Arukh*). The Ramah maintains that the term is referring to a beam upon which other beams are placed.

Acquired the privilege to place thin beams – אַחְזֵיק לְהוּרְדֵי: The early commentaries disagree about this privilege. Rashi and many other early commentaries explain that this privilege does not relate to a shared wall but to the right of one individual to use another's wall. The fact that the owner failed to protest indicates that he granted his neighbor the right to use the wall, either because he paid him for that privilege or simply persuaded him to grant it to him. Rabbeinu Yona and other early commentaries understand that this right is like other rights, and therefore the claimant must maintain that he had acquired the right and prove that he enjoyed the right for three full years.

Some explain that it relates to the mishna, which is discussing a jointly owned wall, and that the placement of thin beams on a wall higher than four cubits indicates that the neighbor paid his share of the construction of the entire wall, including additional height. For this reason, he is allowed to use it even for thick beams (Ramban, citing Rabbeinu Tam; Ramah).

NOTES

Let water drip [*natfei*] – נָטְפֵי: The *ge'onim* and the Ri Migash explain that *natfei* refers to water dripping from the shingles in various places along the length of the roof and falling to the courtyard, whereas *shafkhei* refers to water draining off from a gutter and drainpipe onto one area of the courtyard.

A hut whose roof is composed of willow branches – צְרִיפָא דְאוּרְבָנֵי: Rashi explains that this term refers to a *sukka*-like structure covered with willow branches. In such a case, the water does not drip down in isolated places, but rather along the entire length of the wall. Others expound that since the structure is not covered with shingles that absorb some of the water but rather with willow branches that release all the water, the neighbor might not give his consent (Rabbeinu Gershom; Responsa of the *Ge'onim*). The Ramah explains that a roof covered with willow branches drips water for an extended period of time. Most early commentaries contend that the Gemara is describing a structure with a slanted roof that allows rainwater to run off in a relatively strong stream.

HALAKHA

Acquired the privilege to let water pour – אַחְזִיק לְשָׁפְכֵי: If one acquired the privilege to let water drip from his house through a drainpipe into his neighbor's courtyard, he has the privilege to let water drip to there from his roof. The *Shulḥan Arukh* states that this privilege is acquired immediately, whereas the Rema says that it is acquired by doing this for three years. He can even increase the strength of the flow by increasing the slope of his roof, provided that this does not cause greater damage to the courtyard (Rambam *Sefer Kinyan*, *Hilkhot Shekhenim* 8:6; *Shulḥan Arukh*, *Ḥoshen Mishpat* 153:10).

אִיכָּא דְּאָמְרִי אָמַר רַב נַחְמָן: אַחְזִיק לְהוּרְדֵי אַחְזִיק לְכְשׁוּרֵי, לִכְשׁוּרֵי – אַחְזִיק לְהוּרְדֵי.

There are those who say that Rav Naḥman says: If one **acquired the privilege to** place **thin beams** on his neighbor's wall, **he has acquired the privilege to** place **thick beams** there; and if he acquired the privilege **to** place **thick beams, he has acquired the privilege to** place **thin beams.** This version of Rav Naḥman's statement accords with the statement of Rav Yosef.

אָמַר רַב נַחְמָן: אַחְזִיק לְנָטְפֵי אַחְזִיק לְשָׁפְכֵי, אַחְזִיק לְשָׁפְכֵי לָא אַחְזִיק לְנָטְפֵי; וְרַב יוֹסֵף אָמַר: אֲפִילּוּ אַחְזִיק לְשָׁפְכֵי אַחְזִיק לְנָטְפֵי.

With regard to a similar matter, **Rav Naḥman says:** If one **acquired the privilege to** let **water drip**[N] from his roof into his neighbor's courtyard, **he has acquired the privilege to** let the **water pour** there though a drainpipe. If the neighbor did not protest about the water dripping from the roof into his courtyard, he would certainly allow him to build a drainpipe, which would limit the water to a single place. But if **he acquired the privilege to** let the **water pour** through a drainpipe into his neighbor's courtyard, **he has not acquired the privilege** to let **water drip** there from his roof. **And Rav Yosef says: Even if he acquired the privilege to** let **water pour** there through a drainpipe, **he** also **has acquired the privilege to let water drip** there from his roof.

אִיכָּא דְּאָמְרִי, אָמַר רַב נַחְמָן: אַחְזִיק לְשָׁפְכֵי אַחְזִיק לְנָטְפֵי, לְנָטְפֵי – אַחְזִיק לְשָׁפְכֵי, אֲבָל לִצְרִיפָא דְאוּרְבָנֵי לָא; רַב יוֹסֵף אָמַר: אֲפִילּוּ צְרִיפָא דְאוּרְבָנֵי. עֲבַד רַב יוֹסֵף עוּבְדָא בִּצְרִיפָא דְאוּרְבָנֵי.

There are those who say that Rav Naḥman said: If one **acquired the privilege to** let **water pour**[H] through a drainpipe into his neighbor's courtyard, **he has acquired the privilege to** let **water drip** there from his roof; and **if he acquired the privilege to** let **water drip** from his roof into his neighbor's courtyard, **he has acquired the privilege to** let **water pour** there through a drainpipe. **But** he has **not** acquired the privilege **to** let water drip from **a hut** whose roof is composed **of willow branches**[N] into his neighbor's courtyard. **Rav Yosef said:** He has acquired the privilege to let water drip there **even** from **a hut** whose roof is composed **of willow branches.** The Gemara comments: **Rav Yosef performed an action,** i.e., issued a practical ruling, **with regard to a hut** whose roof is composed **of willow branches,** allowing the neighbor to let water drip from there after he had acquired the privilege to use a drainpipe.

אָמַר רַב נַחְמָן אָמַר רַבָּה בַּר אֲבוּהּ: הַמַּשְׂכִּיר בַּיִת לַחֲבֵירוֹ

Rav Naḥman says that Rabba bar Avuh says: If one rents a room to another

Perek **I**
Daf **6** Amud **b**

HALAKHA

He may make use of the projections – מִשְׁתַּמֵּשׁ בְּזִיזִיָּה: If one rents a room in another's house, he may use the outer sides of the building's walls and the projections from those walls up to a distance of four cubits from the room he rented. He may also use the garden in the courtyard; the *Sma* states that he may use only the walls of the garden. He may also use the yard at the back of the house (Rambam *Sefer Mishpatim*, *Hilkhot Sekhirut* 6:1; *Shulḥan Arukh*, *Ḥoshen Mishpat* 313:1).

LANGUAGE

Garden [*tarbatz*] – תַּרְבָּץ: This word, meaning courtyard or garden, is most likely of Semitic origin, in the form of the Akkadian word tarbāṣu.

בְּבִירָה גְּדוֹלָה, מִשְׁתַּמֵּשׁ בְּזִיזִיָּה וּבִכְתָלֶיהָ עַד אַרְבַּע אַמּוֹת, וּבְעוֹבִי הַכּוֹתֶל בְּמָקוֹם שֶׁנָּהֲגוּ, אֲבָל בְּתַרְבָּץ אַפַּדְנֵי לָא; וְרַב נַחְמָן דִּידֵיהּ אָמַר: אֲפִילּוּ בְּתַרְבָּץ אַפַּדְנֵי, אֲבָל רְחָבָה שֶׁאֲחוֹרֵי הַבָּתִּים לָא; וְרָבָא אָמַר: אֲפִילּוּ רְחָבָה שֶׁאֲחוֹרֵי הַבָּתִּים.

in a large building with many residences, the renter **may make use of the** building's **projections**[HN] **and of the** cavities in its external **walls up to** a distance of **four cubits** from his room, **and** he may make use **of the thickness of the wall**[N] **in a place where it is customary**[N] to do so. **But** as for making use **of the** building's front **garden** [***betarbatz***],[LN] he may **not** do so. **And Rav Naḥman himself said:** He may make use **of even the building's** front **garden. But** he may **not** use **the yard that is at the back of the house. And Rava said:** He may use **even the yard that is at the back of the house.**

NOTES

Of the projections – בְּזִיזִיָּה: He may use the projections protruding from the wall to hang items on them even if they are four cubits from his apartment (Rashi).

And of the thickness of the wall – וּבְעוֹבִי הַכּוֹתֶל: Rashi explains that this means that he can use the top surface of the wall if his apartment is on the upper story. Other commentaries expound that he can place items in the window openings of the wall as long as he does not damage it (Rabbeinu Ḥananel; Ra'avad).

Where it is customary – בְּמָקוֹם שֶׁנָּהֲגוּ: The meaning is, where it is the custom of owners to use the thickness of the walls, since it would be unnecessary to say this if it were referring to the custom of renters (Rabbeinu Yona, citing Rabbi Shlomo min HaHar).

The building's garden – תַּרְבָּץ אַפַּדְנֵי: Rashi notes that this refers to a small ornamental garden that even the owner of the apartment does not ordinarily enter; therefore, it is prohibited for the renter to use it. The Ra'avad states that the term does not refer to use of the garden itself, which was certainly not included in the rental, but to the use of the walls of the garden.

אָמַר רָבִינָא: הַאי כְּשׁוּרָא דִּמְטַלַּלְתָּא – עַד תְּלָתִין יוֹמִין לָא הָוֵי חֲזָקָה, בָּתַר תְּלָתִין יוֹמִין הָוֵי חֲזָקָה; וְאִי סוּכָּה דְּמִצְוָה הִיא – עַד שִׁבְעָה יוֹמִין לָא הָוֵי חֲזָקָה, בָּתַר שִׁבְעָה יוֹמִין הָוֵי חֲזָקָה; וְאִי חַבְּרֵיהּ בְּטִינָא – לְאַלְתַּר הָוֵי חֲזָקָה.

Apropos the use of a wall between neighbors, **Ravina says:** If one's **beam** supporting a covering **for shade**[H] was resting on his neighbor's wall **for up to thirty**[N] **days, there is no acquired privilege** for him to continue using it, since the neighbor can claim that he had assumed that the beam was there only temporarily and for that reason he did not protest. But **after thirty days, there is an acquired privilege. And if it was for a *sukka*** that was being used **for the mitzva**[N] on the festival of *Sukkot*, **for up to seven days there is no acquired privilege** for him to continue using it, since it is assumed that it is there for the mitzva and that after the Festival it will be removed. But if **after seven days** the neighbor did not protest, **there is an acquired privilege** for him to continue using it. **And if** the one using the beam **attached it with clay, there is immediately** such **an acquired privilege.**

אָמַר אַבַּיֵי: שְׁנֵי בָתִּים בִּשְׁנֵי צִדֵּי רְשׁוּת הָרַבִּים – זֶה עוֹשֶׂה מַעֲקֶה לַחֲצִי גַּגּוֹ וְזֶה עוֹשֶׂה מַעֲקֶה לַחֲצִי גַּגּוֹ, זֶה שֶׁלֹּא כְּנֶגֶד זֶה, וּמַעֲדִיף.

§ **Abaye says:** If there were **two houses**[H] **on two sides of a public domain,**[BN] **this** one, the owner of one of the houses, must **build a fence for half his roof, and that** one, the owner of the other house, must **build a fence for half his roof.** They must position the fences so that **one** fence **is not opposite the other** fence, **and** each one must **add** to his fence a little beyond the midway point, so that each one should not be able to see the activity on the other's roof.

מַאי אִירְיָא בִּרְשׁוּת הָרַבִּים? אֲפִילּוּ רְשׁוּת הַיָּחִיד נַמִי! רְשׁוּת הָרַבִּים אִיצְטְרִיכָא לֵיהּ; מַהוּ דְּתֵימָא נֵימָא לֵיהּ: סוֹף סוֹף הָא בָּעֵית לְאִצְטַנּוּעֵי מִבְּנֵי רְשׁוּת הָרַבִּים,

The Gemara asks: **Why** discuss **specifically** the case of two houses on opposite sides of **a public domain,** considering that the same *halakha* should apply **even** if the two houses are separated by **a private domain?** The Gemara answers: **It was necessary for** Abaye to mention **a public domain, lest you say** that one neighbor can **say to** the other: **Ultimately, you need to conceal** yourself **from people in the public domain.** Since in any event you have to build a fence across your entire roof, you cannot compel me to build a fence on my roof.

קָא מַשְׁמַע לָן דְּאָמַר לֵיהּ: רַבִּים – בִּימָמָא חָזוּ לִי, בְּלֵילְיָא לָא חָזוּ לִי, אַתְּ – בֵּין בִּימָמָא בֵּין בְּלֵילְיָא חָזֵית לִי; אִי נַמִי, רַבִּים – כִּי קָאֵימְנָא חָזוּ לִי, כִּי יָתֵיבְנָא לָא חָזוּ לִי, אַתְּ חָזֵית לִי בֵּין כִּי קָאֵימְנָא בֵּין כִּי יָתֵיבְנָא; רַבִּים – כִּי מְעַיְּינוּ חָזוּ לִי, כִּי לָא מְעַיְּינוּ לָא חָזוּ לִי, אַתְּ מִמֵּילָא נַמִי חָזֵית לִי.

To counter this, Abaye **teaches us** that this is not so, because the second homeowner **can say to** the first in response: **The public can see me** only **during the day,** when pedestrians pass by, **but they cannot see me at night. You,** by contrast, **can see me both during the day and at night. Alternatively,** he can say: **The public can see me** from the street only **when I am standing,** but **they cannot see me when I am sitting. You,** by contrast, **can see me both when I am standing and when I am sitting.** And furthermore, **the public can see me** only **when they look** specifically at me, **but they cannot see me when they do not look** specifically at me, since the average pedestrian does not look up to see what is happening on the roofs. **You,** by contrast, **can see me in any case,** because you live opposite me.

אָמַר מָר: זֶה עוֹשֶׂה מַעֲקֶה לַחֲצִי גַּגּוֹ וְזֶה עוֹשֶׂה מַעֲקֶה לַחֲצִי גַּגּוֹ, זֶה שֶׁלֹּא כְּנֶגֶד זֶה וּמַעֲדִיף. פְּשִׁיטָא!

The Master, i.e., Abaye, **said** above: **This** one, the owner of one of the houses, must **build a fence for half his roof, and that** one, the owner of the other house, must **build a fence for half his roof.** They must position the fences so that **one** fence **is not opposite the other** fence, **and** each one must **add** to his fence a little beyond the midway point. The Gemara asks: Isn't it **obvious** that each one must make a fence for half his roof?

BACKGROUND

Two houses on two sides of a public domain – שְׁנֵי בָתִּים בִּשְׁנֵי צִדֵּי רְשׁוּת הָרַבִּים: The section of the fence that is indicated with the broken lines is the supplement that each party must add to his fence beyond the midway point.

Two houses on two sides of a public domain

HALAKHA

Beam for shade – כְּשׁוּרָא דִּמְטַלַּלְתָּא: If one of the neighbors places a beam with a covering for shade on top of the wall that divides two neighbors' courtyards, during the first thirty days he does not acquire the privilege to leave the beam there because the other neighbor can claim that he thought that the beam had been placed there temporarily. But after thirty days, he acquires the privilege to leave it there because it is no longer considered temporary. This is so even before three years have passed, and even without the claim of a formal acquisition or gift (*Sma*). Similarly, if a *sukka* is erected for the Festival, during the first seven days there is no presumption that the neighbor granted any privilege to use his wall in that manner. Once those seven days have passed, there is such a presumption. According to some (*Haggahot Asheri*; Ra'avad), the one using it for thirty days before the Festival does not acquire the privilege to continue using it until seven days after the Festival have passed (Rambam *Sefer Kinyan*, *Hilkhot Shekhenim* 8:7; *Shulḥan Arukh*, *Ḥoshen Mishpat* 153:17).

Two houses – שְׁנֵי בָתִּים: If there were two houses of equal height (*Sma*) on opposite sides of a public domain, whose rooftops are used, the residents of each house must build a fence four cubits high along slightly more than half the length of the roof. The two fences must not be aligned directly opposite each other. The *Tur*, citing Rabbeinu Yona, writes that if the roofs were low enough for passersby to see onto them, there is no privacy issue with regard to the neighbor (Rambam *Sefer Kinyan*, *Hilkhot Shekhenim* 3:5; *Shulḥan Arukh*, *Ḥoshen Mishpat* 159:1).

NOTES

Up to thirty – עַד תְּלָתִין: Until that point, the homeowner remains indifferent and does not protest, believing that the beam was placed there temporarily and will soon be removed. *Tosafot*, citing Rabbeinu Tam, write that the discussion here relates to the mishna, where it is unclear whether or not a neighbor paid his share of a joint wall. Consequently, if he places the beam on the wall, the presumption is that he did pay for the wall and has full partnership in it. This explains why this passage appears here and not in the third chapter of this tractate, which addresses presumptions of usage. Other commentaries explain that here too the issue is presumption of usage.

If it was a *sukka* for the mitzva – וְאִי סוּכָּה דְּמִצְוָה: The early commentaries ask why thirty days are allotted for a beam that is used to provide shade, whereas only seven days are allotted for a *sukka* that is used for the mitzva. Rabbeinu Yona holds that thirty days is the standard grace period, but since a *sukka* is usually taken down immediately after the Festival, any further delay would indicate the intention to leave it up indefinitely. Similarly, Rashi states that neglecting to take down the *sukka* shows one's intention to use the same booth year after year to fulfill his mitzva. The Ramah and the Ra'avad explain that in the case of an ordinary *sukka* there is an acquired privilege established by usage of thirty days. But if the festival of *Sukkot* occurs at the end of the thirty-day period, there is no acquired privilege until seven days have passed from the end of the Festival.

On two sides of a public domain – בִּשְׁנֵי צִדֵּי רְשׁוּת הָרַבִּים: *Tosafot* and Rabbeinu Yona write that this passage refers to a situation where the houses are a distance apart, on two sides of a public domain. In this case, one owner may make use of his roof without being aware that the other is observing him. But if the houses are adjacent, and each individual is aware if the other is observing him while he makes use of the roof, this concern does not apply. The Ri Migash understands that the case is one of rooftops that are used on a regular basis like a courtyard.

LANGUAGE

Expenditure [*uzinka*] – אוּזִינְקָא: Apparently derived from the Middle Iranian term uzenak, meaning a price or expense.

NOTES

He can give an excuse – מָצֵי מִשְׁתַּמֵּיט: He can give the excuse that he dropped an item in the other's property (Rashi), or that owing to the insignificance of the barrier he did not realize that it was a boundary marker (Rabbeinu Gershom), or that he simply did not pay attention and entered the area inadvertently.

He was stretching himself [*mamtzurei*] – מַמְצוּרֵי: The *ge'onim* and the *Arukh* explain that the neighbor claims that all he did was stretch his body, but it looked as if he had entered the other's property. Rashi (*Avoda Zara* 70b) interprets the word *mamtzurei* in the sense of measurement; the neighbor claims that he had to measure something and therefore momentarily entered the other's space. Others explain the term *mamtzurei* as connected to the word *meitzar*; he was checking his boundaries.

He is not required to attend to it – אֵין נִזְקָקִין לוֹ: The owner of the courtyard is not obligated make a partition since the rooftop is used infrequently and there is no constant invasion of privacy (Rashi).

לָא צְרִיכָא, דְּקָדֵים חַד מִנַּיְיהוּ וַעֲבַד; מַהוּ דְּתֵימָא, נֵימָא לֵיהּ אִידָךְ: שְׁקוֹל אוּזִינְקָא וַעֲבְדֵיהּ אַתְּ כּוּלֵּיהּ, קָא מַשְׁמַע לָן דְּאָמַר לֵיהּ: אַתְּ מַאי טַעֲמָא לָא עָבְדַתְּ? מִשּׁוּם דְּמִיתְרַע אֲשִׁיתָךְ, אֲנָא נַמִי מִיתְרַע לֵיהּ אֲשִׁיתַאי.

The Gemara answers: **No,** it is **necessary** in a case where **one of them went ahead** on his own and **constructed**[H] a fence on half his roof, **lest you say** that **the other can say to him: Take** from me compensation for **the expenditure** [*uzinka*],[L] **and you build the entire** fence, and in that way we will not invade one another's privacy. Therefore, Abaye **teaches us** that the neighbor who built the fence for half his roof **can say to him: What is the reason you do not** want to **build** a fence? It is **because** the added weight **will damage your house's foundation. My foundation too will be damaged** if I continue to build on my roof.

אָמַר רַב נַחְמָן אָמַר שְׁמוּאֵל: גַּג הַסָּמוּךְ לַחֲצַר חֲבֵירוֹ – עוֹשֶׂה לוֹ מַעֲקֶה גָּבוֹהַּ אַרְבַּע אַמּוֹת, אֲבָל בֵּין גַּג לְגַג לֹא; וְרַב נַחְמָן דִּידֵיהּ אָמַר: אֵינוֹ זָקוּק לְאַרְבַּע אַמּוֹת, אֲבָל זָקוּק לִמְחִיצַּת עֲשָׂרָה.

Rav Naḥman says that **Shmuel says:** If one's **roof is adjacent to his neighbor's courtyard,**[H] **he must build a fence** on the roof **four cubits high,** so that he will not be able to see into his neighbor's courtyard, **but** he is **not** required to build a fence **between** one **roof and** another **roof. And Rav Naḥman himself says: He is not required to** build a fence **four cubits** high on the roof, **but he is required to** build **a partition** that is **ten** handbreadths[H] high.

לְמַאי? אִי לְהֶיזֵּק רְאִיָּה – אַרְבַּע אַמּוֹת בָּעֵינַן, אִי לְנִתְפָּס עָלָיו כְּגַנָּב – בִּמְסֵיפָס בְּעָלְמָא סַגְיָא, אִי לִגְדָיִים וּטְלָאִים – בִּכְדֵי שֶׁלֹּא יִזְדַּקֵּר בְּבַת רֹאשׁ סַגִּי! לְעוֹלָם לְנִתְפָּס עָלָיו כְּגַנָּב; בִּמְסֵיפָס מָצֵי מִשְׁתַּמֵּיט לֵיהּ [אָמַר: מַמְצוּרֵי קָמְמַצֵּירְנָא], בִּמְחִיצַּת עֲשָׂרָה לָא מָצֵי מִשְׁתַּמֵּיט לֵיהּ.

The Gemara asks: **For what** purpose, according to Rav Naḥman, does the neighbor have to build such a partition? **If** it is **to** prevent **damage** caused by exposure to the **sight** of others, **we require** a partition of **four cubits. If** it is **to catch** the neighbor **as a thief,** i.e., to set a boundary between the two properties so that any trespass will be construed as attempted theft, **a mere partition of pegs suffices.** And **if** it is to prevent **kid goats and lambs** from crossing from one roof to the other, a low partition that is high **enough so that** the goat or lamb **will not** be able to **leap headlong** from one roof to the other **suffices.** The Gemara answers: **Actually,** it is built **to catch** the neighbor **as a thief. With a partition of pegs he can give an excuse**[N] **and say** that **he was** merely **stretching himself,**[N] but **with a partition of ten** handbreadths **he cannot give** such **an excuse.**

מֵיתִיבֵי: אִם הָיָה חֲצֵרוֹ לְמַעְלָה מִגַּגּוֹ שֶׁל חֲבֵירוֹ – אֵין נִזְקָקִין לוֹ; מַאי לָאו אֵין נִזְקָקִין לוֹ כְּלָל? לָא, אֵין נִזְקָקִין לְאַרְבַּע אַמּוֹת, אֲבָל נִזְקָקִין לִמְחִיצַּת עֲשָׂרָה.

The Gemara **raises an objection** to the opinion of Rav Naḥman from a *baraita*: **If his courtyard was higher than the other's roof,**[H] **he is not required to attend to it.**[NH] **What, is it not** teaching **that he is not required to attend to it at all,** i.e., that he need not build any type of fence? The Gemara answers: **No,** it means that **he is not required to attend** to building a partition **of four cubits, but he must attend** to building **a partition of ten** handbreadths, as maintained by Rav Naḥman.

HALAKHA

Where one of them went ahead and constructed – דְּקָדֵים חַד מִנַּיְיהוּ וַעֲבַד: If one neighbor waited until the other built the fence on half of his roof, the former cannot compel the latter to complete the construction to the end of the roof, even if he pays him (*Shulḥan Arukh*, *Ḥoshen Mishpat* 159:3).

If one's roof is adjacent to his neighbor's courtyard – גַּג הַסָּמוּךְ לַחֲצַר חֲבֵירוֹ: If one's roof is adjacent to his neighbor's courtyard and is not regularly used, the owner of the roof must construct a fence of four cubits on his roof to avoid damage by sight. The owner of the courtyard must contribute to the costs of the fence up to ten handbreadths (Rambam *Sefer Kinyan*, *Hilkhot Shekhenim* 3:6; *Shulḥan Arukh*, *Ḥoshen Mishpat* 159:2).

But he is required to build a partition that is ten handbreadths – אֲבָל זָקוּק לִמְחִיצַּת עֲשָׂרָה: There is no requirement to build a partition between two adjacent roofs of the same height if they are not used. Rav Naḥman states that a ten-handbreadth-high barrier is sufficient to mark the boundary between them so that if one of the neighbors crosses the line he will be considered a thief. The Rema states that this applies only to adjacent roofs, even when they are occupied, but not to roofs that are distant from each other, which require proper four-cubit-high fences (Rambam *Sefer Kinyan*, *Hilkhot Shekhenim* 3:6; *Shulḥan Arukh*, *Ḥoshen Mishpat* 159:2).

If his courtyard was higher than the other's roof – חֲצֵרוֹ לְמַעְלָה מִגַּגּוֹ שֶׁל חֲבֵירוֹ: If one's courtyard is higher than his neighbor's roof, the owner of the roof must build a wall on it that is four cubits higher than the ground of the courtyard. If the roof is at least four cubits lower than the courtyard, some say that the owner of the roof must still build a wall four cubits higher than the ground. Others say that he is not required to build a wall at all (*Shulḥan Arukh*, *Ḥoshen Mishpat* 160:1).

He is not required to attend to it – אֵין נִזְקָקִין לוֹ: The Rambam states that if a one's courtyard is higher than his neighbor's roof, the owner of the courtyard is not required to assist the other in the construction of the wall. Some maintain that if the courtyard is less than ten handbreadths higher than the roof, its owner must contribute to the construction of the wall up to ten handbreadths from ground level. The Gra holds that the Rambam agrees with this (Rambam *Sefer Kinyan*, *Hilkhot Shekhenim* 3:7; *Shulḥan Arukh*, *Ḥoshen Mishpat* 160:2).

אִיתְּמַר: שְׁתֵּי חֲצֵירוֹת זוֹ לְמַעְלָה מִזּוֹ – אָמַר רַב הוּנָא: תַּחְתּוֹן בּוֹנֶה מִכְּנֶגְדּוֹ וְעוֹלֶה, וְעֶלְיוֹן בּוֹנֶה מִכְּנֶגְדּוֹ וְעוֹלֶה; וְרַב חִסְדָּא אָמַר: עֶלְיוֹן מְסַיֵּיעַ מִלְּמַטָּה וּבוֹנֶה.

It was stated that *amora'im* disagree about the following case: If there are **two** adjoining **courtyards,**[N] **one higher than the other,**[HB] **Rav Huna says** that the owner of **the lower** courtyard **builds** the wall separating the courtyards **from his level and upward, and** the owner of **the upper** courtyard **builds** the wall **from his level and upward. And Rav Ḥisda says:** The owner of **the upper** courtyard **assists** the owner of the lower courtyard **and builds**[N] **from below,** even including that part of the wall which is opposite the lower courtyard.

תַּנְיָא כְּוָותֵיהּ דְּרַב חִסְדָּא: שְׁתֵּי חֲצֵירוֹת זוֹ לְמַעְלָה מִזּוֹ, לֹא יֹאמַר הָעֶלְיוֹן: ״הֲרֵינִי בּוֹנֶה מִכְּנֶגְדִּי וְעוֹלֶה״, אֶלָּא מְסַיֵּיעַ מִלְּמַטָּה וּבוֹנֶה. וְאִם הָיְתָה חֲצֵרוֹ לְמַעְלָה מִגַּגּוֹ שֶׁל חֲבֵירוֹ – אֵינוֹ זָקוּק לוֹ.

The Gemara notes that **it is taught** in a *baraita* **in accordance with** the opinion **of Rav Ḥisda:** If there were **two** adjoining **courtyards, one higher than the other,** the owner of **the upper** courtyard **cannot say: I will build from my level and upward, but** rather **he assists** the owner of the lower courtyard **and builds from below. And if his courtyard is higher than the roof of his neighbor, he is not required to attend to it.** The owner of the upper courtyard need not build a partition because people do not ordinarily use their roofs.

הָנְהוּ בֵּי תְּרֵי דְּהָווּ דָּיְירִי, חַד הֲוָה דָּיֵיר עִילַּאי וְחַד הֲוָה דָּיֵיר תַּתַּאי. אִיתְּבַר תַּתַּאי, אֲמַר לֵיהּ תַּתַּאי לְעִילַּאי: תָּא וְנִבְנְיֵיהּ, אֲמַר לֵיהּ: אֲנָא שַׁפִּיר קָא דָּאֵירְנָא.

§ It is related that **two** people **were living** in a two-story building; **one was living in the upper** story, **and one was living in the lower** one. **The lower** story began to **collapse,** its walls sinking into the ground to the point that it was no longer fit for dwelling. The owner of **the lower** story **said to** the owner of **the upper** story: **Come and let us** demolish the whole building and **rebuild it** together. The owner of the upper story **said to him: I am living comfortably** and am under no obligation to rebuild your residence.

NOTES

Two courtyards – שְׁתֵּי חֲצֵירוֹת: The commentaries agree that this case relates to the issue of invasion of privacy rather than the issue of use of the wall. Consequently, most commentaries maintain that the upper courtyard is not four cubits higher than the lower one, and therefore activity in the upper area can be seen from the lower area. Similarly, the *ge'onim* write that in a case where the ground level of the upper courtyard is four cubits higher than that of the lower courtyard, the owner of the lower one is not required to participate in any costs. By contrast, the Ramah explains that the passage does not concern the issue of invasion of privacy. Rather, the neighbor with the lower courtyard benefits from the construction of the wall because he can use it and because it prevents items from falling into his courtyard from above. For these reasons, he is required to participate in the costs.

The upper one assists the lower one and builds – עֶלְיוֹן מְסַיֵּיעַ מִלְּמַטָּה וּבוֹנֶה: Rashi explains that the owner of the lower courtyard must also assist in building the part of the wall that is opposite the upper courtyard. But most early commentaries maintain that he is required to contribute only to the height of four cubits above his own courtyard. The owner of the upper courtyard alone pays for any additional construction (see Rambam).

BACKGROUND

Two courtyards one higher than the other – שְׁתֵּי חֲצֵירוֹת זוֹ לְמַעְלָה מִזּוֹ: Rashi states that the owner of the lower courtyard builds wall A at his own expense and contributes to the construction of wall B, which he builds together with the owner of the upper courtyard on top of wall A.

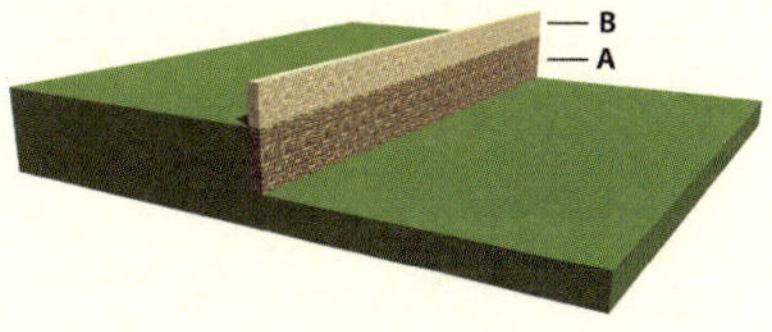

Two adjoining courtyards, one higher than the other

HALAKHA

Two courtyards one higher than the other – שְׁתֵּי חֲצֵירוֹת זוֹ לְמַעְלָה מִזּוֹ: If there are two adjacent courtyards, one higher than the other, the two owners must jointly pay for the construction of a partition wall. Earth must be removed from the ground of the upper courtyard to the thickness of half a handbreadth, so that the wall will be built on land belonging to both of them. The wall is built to a height of four cubits above the ground of the upper courtyard, in accordance with the opinion of Rav Ḥisda. The Rema, citing Rabbeinu Yona, writes that there is no fixed measure and that the neighbor with the lower courtyard must pay only until the point of the wall's height at which he can no longer see into the upper courtyard of his neighbor (Rambam *Sefer Kinyan, Hilkhot Shekhenim* 3:7; *Shulḥan Arukh, Ḥoshen Mishpat* 160:3).

Perek **I**
Daf **7** Amud **a**

אֲמַר לֵיהּ: אֶיסְתְּרֵיהּ אֲנָא וְאֶבְנְיֵיהּ, אֲמַר: לֵית לִי דּוּכְתָּא לְמֵידַר בָּהּ. אֲמַר לֵיהּ: אֲנָא אוֹגַר לָךְ דּוּכְתָּא, אֲמַר לֵיהּ: לָא טָרַחְנָא. לָא קָא מִתְדַּר לִי. שׁוּף אַכְּרֵיסָךְ וְעוּל, וְשׁוּף אַכְּרֵיסָךְ וּפוּק.

The owner of the lower story **said to him: I will dismantle** the structure **and rebuild it.** The owner of the upper story **said:** But then **I** will **have no place to live** while you are renovating. The owner of the lower story **said to him: I will rent a place for you** to live for the duration. The owner of the upper story **said to him: I** do not want **to bother** with moving. The owner of the lower story said to him: But **I cannot live** in my apartment in this condition, as the walls have sunk into the ground. The owner of the upper story said to him: That is not my problem. **Crawl on your stomach to go in, and crawl on your stomach to go out.**

אֲמַר רַב חָמָא: בְּדִינָא קָא מְעַכֵּב. וְהָנֵי מִילֵּי דְּלָא מָטוּ כְּשׁוּרֵי לְמַטָּה מֵעֲשָׂרָה, אֲבָל מָטוּ כְּשׁוּרֵי לְמַטָּה מֵעֲשָׂרָה, מָצֵי אֲמַר לֵיהּ: לְמַטָּה מֵעֲשָׂרָה רְשׁוּתָא דִּידִי הוּא וְלָא מְשַׁעְבַּד לָךְ.

Rav Ḥama said: By law, the owner of the upper story **can prevent**[H] his downstairs neighbor from rebuilding. The Gemara comments: **And this statement** applies **only when the beams** supporting the second story **have not reached lower than ten** handbreadths from the ground. **But if** those **beams have reached lower than ten** handbreadths from the ground, the owner of the lower story **can say to** the owner of the upper story: **Below ten** handbreadths **is my domain and** my domain **is not bound to you** to support your residence.

HALAKHA

By law the neighbor can prevent – בְּדִינָא קָא מְעַכֵּב: If two people are living in a two-story building, one in the upper story and one in the lower one, and the beams supporting the upper story begin to sink, the owner of the lower story cannot force his upstairs neighbor to demolish the whole building and rebuild it, even if he offers to pay for the entire project and cover the rent of his neighbor during the time of reconstruction. This *halakha* applies even if the upstairs neighbor is not living in the upper story but rather using it to store wood or straw. It applies only if the beams did not sink more than ten handbreadths below the ground; but if they sink more than ten handbreadths, the owner of the lower story can demolish the structure and rebuild it at his own expense. According to the Rema, if the house sinks into the ground, so that the height of the lower story is less than ten handbreadths, the owner of the lower story can force his upstairs neighbor to vacate the building so that it can be rebuilt, and he can also require him to contribute to the construction costs (Rambam *Sefer Kinyan, Hilkhot Shekhenim* 4:6; *Shulḥan Arukh, Ḥoshen Mishpat* 164:2).

וְהָנֵי מִילֵּי דְּלָא אַתְנוּ גַּבֵּי הֲדָדֵי, אֲבָל אַתְנוּ גַּבֵּי הֲדָדֵי – סָתְרִי וּבָנוּ.

The Gemara further comments: **And this statement,** that the owner of the upper story can prevent his downstairs neighbor from rebuilding, applies **only** when **they did not stipulate with each other** that if the house sinks they will rebuild the house anew. **But if they made** such **a stipulation with each other,**[H] **they must dismantle** the house **and rebuild it.**

וְכִי אַתְנוּ בַּהֲדֵי הֲדָדֵי עַד כַּמָּה? אֲמַרוּ רַבָּנַן קַמֵּיהּ דְּרַבָּה מִשְּׁמֵיהּ דְּמָר זוּטְרָא בְּרֵיהּ דְּרַב נַחְמָן, דַּאֲמַר מִשְּׁמֵיהּ דְּרַב נַחְמָן: כְּאוֹתָהּ שֶׁשָּׁנִינוּ: רוּמוֹ כַּחֲצִי אָרְכּוֹ וְכַחֲצִי רָחְבּוֹ. אֲמַר לְהוּ רַבָּה, לָאו אָמִינָא לְכוּ: לָא תִּיתְלוּ בֵּיהּ בּוּקֵי סְרִיקֵי בְּרַב נַחְמָן? הָכִי אֲמַר רַב נַחְמָן: כִּי דְּדָיְירִי אֱינָשֵׁי. וְכַמָּה? אֲמַר רַב הוּנָא בְּרֵיהּ דְּרַב יְהוֹשֻׁעַ: כִּי הֵיכִי דְּעָיְילִי אִיסּוּרְיָתָא דִּמְחוֹזָא וְהָדַר.

The Gemara asks: **And if they made** such **a stipulation with each other, to what extent**[N] must the ceiling of the lower story drop before they implement the stipulation? **The Sages said before Rabba in the name of Mar Zutra, son of Rav Naḥman, who said in the name of Rav Naḥman: Like that which we learned** in a mishna (98b): If one takes upon himself to build a house for another person, without stipulating its dimensions, **its height** must be equal to the sum of **half its length and half its width. Rabba said to them: Did I not tell you not to hang empty pitchers on Rav Naḥman,** meaning not to attribute foolish opinions to him? Rather, **this is what Rav Naḥman said: As people normally live,** and no more. **And how much** space is that? **Rav Huna, son of Rav Yehoshua, said:** The ceiling of the lower story must be high enough **so that one could bring in bundles** of reeds **of** the type made in **Meḥoza**[N] **and** be able to **turn around.**

הַהוּא גַּבְרָא דַּהֲוָה בָּנֵי אֲשִׁיתָא אֲחוֹרֵי כַּוֵּי דְּחַבְרֵיהּ, אֲמַר לֵיהּ: קָא מַאֲפְלַתְּ עֲלַי, אֲמַר לֵיהּ: סָכַרְנָא לָךְ הָכָא וְעָבֵידְנָא לָךְ כַּוֵּי לְעֵיל מֵאֲשִׁיתַאי. אֲמַר לֵיהּ: קָא מַרְעַתְּ לֵיהּ לַאֲשִׁיתַאי, אֲמַר לֵיהּ: סָתַרְנָא לָךְ לַאֲשִׁיתָךְ עַד דּוּכְתָּא דְּכַוֵּי, וּבָנֵינָא לָהּ וְעָבֵידְנָא לָךְ כַּוֵּי בְּבִנְיָנָא לְעֵיל מֵאֲשִׁיתַאי. אֲמַר לֵיהּ: אֲשִׁיתָא מִתַּתָּאָה עַתִּיקָא וּמִלְּעֵיל חֲדַתָּא לָא קַיְימָא.

It is further related that **a certain man built a wall outside the windows of his neighbor.**[H] The neighbor **said to him: You are** blocking the light with your wall and **darkening my** house. The one who built the wall **said to him: I will seal** your windows **here and make** new **windows for you** in your wall **above the wall** that I am building. The neighbor **said to him:** By doing so **you will damage my wall.** The one who built the wall **said to him: I will demolish your wall until the level of the windows and rebuild it, and then I will make windows for you in** the new part of **the building above my wall.** The neighbor **said to him: A wall that is old at the bottom and new at the top will not endure.**

אֲמַר לֵיהּ: סָתַרְנָא לָהּ עַד לְאַרְעָא, וּבָנֵינָא לָהּ וְעָבֵידְנָא לָךְ כַּוֵּי בְּגַוַּהּ. אֲמַר לֵיהּ: חֲדָא אֲשִׁיתָא חֲדַתָּא בְּכוּלֵּיהּ בֵּיתָא עַתִּיקָא לָא קַיְימָא, אֲמַר לֵיהּ: סָתַרְנָא לָהּ לְכוּלֵּיהּ בֵּיתָא, וּבָנֵינָא לָךְ כַּוֵּי בְּבִנְיָנָא. אֲמַר לֵיהּ: לֵית לִי דּוּכְתָּא לְמֵידַר בָּהּ. אֲמַר לֵיהּ: אָגֵירְנָא לָךְ דּוּכְתָּא, אֲמַר לֵיהּ: לָא טָרַחְנָא. אֲמַר רַב חָמָא: בְּדִין קָא מְעַכֵּב.

The one who built the wall **said to him: I will demolish** the wall **until the ground and** entirely **rebuild it, and** then **I will make windows for you in it** above my wall. The neighbor **said to him: One new wall**[B] **in an old house will not endure.** The one who built the wall **said to him: I will demolish your entire house and put windows in the** new **building** that I will erect in its place. The neighbor **said to him:** But in the meantime **I will have no place to live.** The one who built the wall **said to him: I will rent a place for you** to live. The neighbor **said to him: I do not** want **to bother** with moving. **Rav Ḥama said: By law,** the neighbor **can prevent** him[N] from building the wall.

הַיְינוּ הַךְ, וְהָא תּוּ לָמָּה לִי? הָא קָא מַשְׁמַע לַן, דְּאַף עַל גַּב דְּלָא מִשְׁתַּמֵּשׁ אֶלָּא תִּיבְנָא וּבֵי צִיבֵי בְּעָלְמָא.

The Gemara asks: **This** case **is** identical to **that** case; this case is very similar to the previous case of the owner of the upper story who can prevent the owner of the lower story from rebuilding. **Why do I need this additional** case? The Gemara answers: **This teaches us that even if he uses** the house **only for** storing **straw and wood,** he can still maintain that blocking the light causes him damage and can prevent the neighbor from erecting the wall.

HALAKHA

If they made a stipulation with each other – אַתְנוּ גַּבֵּי הֲדָדֵי: If the owners of the two stories stipulated with each other from the outset that should the beams supporting the upper story sink they would rebuild the house, and the ceiling of the lower story sunk to such an extent that one could no longer bring in a medium-sized bundle of reeds on his head, they must dismantle the house and rebuild it. This is in accordance with the opinions of Rav Naḥman and Rav Huna, son of Rav Yehoshua (Rambam *Sefer Kinyan, Hilkhot Shekhenim* 4:7; *Shulḥan Arukh, Ḥoshen Mishpat* 164:2).

He built a wall outside the windows of his neighbor – בָּנֵי אֲשִׁיתָא אֲחוֹרֵי כַּוֵּי דְּחַבְרֵיהּ: One who has windows in his wall can prevent his neighbor from building a wall in front of them. This is so even if the neighbor promises to make him new windows higher up on his wall, to build the whole wall anew, or even to rebuild his entire house. Furthermore, this *halakha* holds even if the structure is used only to store straw or wood, but only if it would present a hardship to the owner of the windows to move out during the period of construction. Otherwise, he must accede to his neighbor (Rambam *Sefer Kinyan, Hilkhot Shekhenim* 7:8; *Shulḥan Arukh, Ḥoshen Mishpat* 154:13).

BACKGROUND

One new wall – חֲדָא אֲשִׁיתָא: Rashi explains that the new mortar on the new part of the wall does not adhere well to the old mortar. Furthermore, over time the stones of an old wall begin to slant in accordance with the weight of the stones resting on top of them and the type of ground on which the wall stands. Consequently, a new section of wall does not join well with older sections, and the entire structure becomes unstable.

NOTES

To what extent – עַד כַּמָּה: If neighbors agree that if their house sinks into the ground they will both contribute to its reconstruction, how much must the house sink before the resident of the upper story is required to pay? Presumably, a minor shift in the house is not that bothersome and could be ignored. The height of a room must be the sum of half the length and half the width (Rashi). Rabbeinu Gershom explains that the Gemara is asking to what height the resident of the lower story can demand that the house be raised.

Bundles of reeds of Meḥoza – אִיסּוּרְיָתָא דִּמְחוֹזָא: The Ramah writes that this measurement was specific to the location where the statement was performed, and that every place has to base the measurement on large items that are ordinarily carried into homes.

By law the neighbor can prevent him – בְּדִין קָא מְעַכֵּב: The early commentaries state that this *halakha* applies only when the party preventing the building has a good reason for doing so. But if the structure being blocked by the wall was empty and unused, the owner of the structure cannot protest, without stating a cogent reason, if his neighbor offers to completely rebuild it. Such behavior is termed conduct characteristic of Sodom and we compel people to refrain from such conduct (Ramah). By contrast, the Ra'ah writes that an individual can never be compelled to have his structure destroyed.

הָנְהוּ בֵּי תְּרֵי אַחֵי דְּפָלְגִי בַּהֲדֵי הֲדָדֵי, חַד מְטָיֵיהּ אַסְפְּלִידָא וְחַד מְטָיֵיהּ תַּרְבִּיצָא, אֲזַל הַהוּא דְּמְטָיֵיהּ תַּרְבִּיצָא וְקָא בָּנֵי אֲשִׁיתָא אַפּוּמָא דְּאַסְפְּלִידָא. אֲמַר לֵיהּ: קָא מַאַפְלַתְּ עָלַי, אֲמַר לֵיהּ: בְּדִידִי קָא בָּנֵינָא. אֲמַר רַב חָמָא: בְּדִין קָאָמַר לֵיהּ.

The Gemara further relates: **There were two brothers who divided** their father's estate **between them. One received a hall** [*aspelida*][NL] in his share **and one received a garden. The one who received the garden went and built a wall in front of the opening of the hall.** His brother **said to him: You are** blocking the light with your wall and **darkening my** house.[N] The one who received the garden **said to him: I am building on my** property.[H] **Rav Ḥama said: By right he said** that **to him,** as it is permitted for him to build there.

אֲמַר לֵיהּ רָבִינָא לְרַב אַשִׁי, מַאי שְׁנָא מֵהָא דְּתַנְיָא: שְׁנֵי אַחִין שֶׁחָלְקוּ, אֶחָד מֵהֶן נָטַל שְׂדֵה כֶּרֶם וְאֶחָד מֵהֶן נָטַל שְׂדֵה לָבָן – יֵשׁ לוֹ לְבַעַל הַכֶּרֶם אַרְבַּע אַמּוֹת בִּשְׂדֵה לָבָן, שֶׁעַל מְנָת כֵּן חָלְקוּ?

Ravina said to Rav Ashi: In what way is this **different from that which is taught** in a *baraita*: If **two brothers divided** their father's estate between them, **one of them taking a vineyard**[H] and the other **one taking a grain field, the owner of the vineyard has** the right to an area **four cubits** wide **in the grain field**[N] for the purpose of working the vineyard, **since it was on that condition** that **they divided** the estate. Why in this case does the owner of the hall not have the right to make use of the light coming in from the garden?

אֲמַר לֵיהּ: הָתָם דְּעָלוּ לַהֲדָדֵי. אֲבָל הָכָא מַאי, דְּלָא עָלוּ לַהֲדָדֵי? וְכִי בְּשׁוּפְטָנֵי עָסְקִינַן, דְּהַאי שָׁקֵיל אַסְפְּלִידָא וְהַאי שָׁקֵיל תַּרְבִּיצָא וְלָא עָלוּ לַהֲדָדֵי? אֲמַר לֵיהּ: נְהִי דְּעָלוּ לַהֲדָדֵי דְּמֵי לִיבְנֵי כְּשׁוּרֵי וְהוּדְרֵי, דְּמֵי אֲוִירָא לָא עָלוּ לַהֲדָדֵי.

Rav Ashi **said to him: There,** the reason is that **they made an assessment with each other** with regard to the value of the fields, arranging for compensation if one received more than the other, and they took the work area into account. Ravina asked: **But what** did they do **here? Did they not make an assessment with each other? Are we dealing with fools, that this one took the** valuable **hall and the** other **one took** the much less valuable **garden without making an assessment with each other? Rav Ashi said to him: Although they assessed with each other the value of the bricks, the beams, and the boards,**[N] **they did not assess with each other the value of the airspace.** With regard to that, each one retained full rights to his respective airspace.

וְלֵימָא לֵיהּ: מֵעִיקָּרָא אַסְפְּלִידָא פְּלַגְתְּ לִי, הָשְׁתָּא מְשַׁוֵּית לִי אִידְרוֹנָא! אֲמַר רַב שִׁימִי בַּר אַשִׁי: שְׁמָא בְּעָלְמָא פְּלַג לֵיהּ;

The Gemara says: **And let** the one who received the hall **say to** the other: **Initially, you gave me** a well-lit **hall; now you are making it** into **a small** dark **room** [*idrona*].[L] **Rav Shimi bar Ashi said: He gave him only** a place that is called a hall **by name,**[B] that is, a place that is called a hall even though it is no longer used that way.

מִי לָא תַּנְיָא: הָאוֹמֵר: "בֵּית כּוֹר עָפָר אֲנִי מוֹכֵר לְךָ", אַף עַל פִּי שֶׁאֵינוֹ אֶלָּא לֶתֶךְ – הִגִּיעוֹ, שֶׁלֹּא מָכַר לוֹ אֶלָּא שְׁמָא, וְהוּא דְּמִיתְקְרֵי בֵּית כּוֹר; "פַּרְדֵּס אֲנִי מוֹכֵר לְךָ", אַף עַל פִּי שֶׁאֵין בּוֹ רִמּוֹנִים – הִגִּיעוֹ, שֶׁלֹּא מָכַר לוֹ אֶלָּא שְׁמָא, וְהוּא דְּמִיתְקְרֵי פַּרְדֵּס; "כֶּרֶם אֲנִי מוֹכֵר לְךָ", אַף עַל פִּי שֶׁאֵין בּוֹ גְּפָנִים – הִגִּיעוֹ, שֶׁלֹּא מָכַר לוֹ אֶלָּא שְׁמָא, וְהוּא דְּמִיתְקְרֵי כַּרְמָא!

Rav Ashi continues: **Isn't it taught** in a *baraita*: In the case of **one who says** to another: **I am selling you a** ***beit kor***[B] **of dirt,**[H] **it becomes his even if it is only a** ***letekh***,[L] i.e., a half-*kor*, and the sale is not void, **because he sold him only** a place that is called a *beit kor* **by name.** The Gemara comments: **And this** ruling applies only as long as the land he is selling him **is actually called**[N] **a** ***beit kor***. Similarly, if he says to him: **I am selling you an orchard, it becomes his even if it lacks pomegranates, because he sold him only** a place that is called an orchard **by name.** The Gemara comments: **And this** applies only as long as the land he is selling **is** actually **called an orchard.** And similarly, if he says to him: **I am selling you a vineyard, it becomes his even if it lacks grapevines, because he sold him only** a place that is called a vineyard **by name.** The Gemara comments: **And this** applies only as long as the land he is selling **is** actually **called a vineyard.**

NOTES

A hall – אַסְפְּלִידָא: Rashi explains that this refers to a beautiful hall. The *Arukh* says it is a cave. Many early commentaries maintain that the structure under discussion is a well-lit portico that is completely open on one side.

You are darkening my house – קָא מַאַפְלַתְּ עָלַי: *Tosafot* state that the wall does not completely block the light but leaves the place much darker than it had been before the wall was built. Rabbeinu Tam maintains that the issue here is not the blocking of light but of the hall owner's field of vision (see *Tosafot*).

Four cubits in the grain field – אַרְבַּע אַמּוֹת בִּשְׂדֵה לָבָן: These four cubits are for the animals and tools needed to work the vineyard, so that the owner can easily enter and plow the area (Rabbeinu Gershom; Rashi). The Ritva writes that this does not mean that he receives an extra four cubits, but that he is entitled to use these four cubits for his work.

They assessed with each other the value of the bricks, the beams, and the boards – דְּעָלוּ לַהֲדָדֵי דְּמֵי לִיבְנֵי כְּשׁוּרֵי וְהוּדְרֵי: If they made a general assessment, they certainly considered the airspace in the evaluation, and rights to the space cannot be denied him (Rabbeinu Yona; Ra'ah).

And this applies as long as the land he is selling him is actually called – וְהוּא דְּמִיתְקְרֵי: *Tosafot* add two restrictions to the matter. One is that the buyer has to know that the seller has a place called by this name. If he does not, the purchase is considered as having been made in error. Another is that the price has to be reasonable and based on the size and quality of the land. Others add that the seller has to have said: This *beit kor*; but if he said: A *beit kor*, the buyer can demand that measure of land.

LANGUAGE

Hall [*aspelida*] – אַסְפְּלִידָא: Some link this term to the Greek σπηλάδιον, *spēladion*, meaning a small cave. Others suggest it is connected to ψαλίς, *psalis*, or the genitive form ψαλίδος, *psalidos*, meaning a store, a booth, or a place under a vault.

Small room [*idrona*] – אִידְרוֹנָא: Apparently related to the Persian term andarōn, which refers to the inside of a room. This is the source of the Aramaic term for an inner chamber.

Letekh – לֶתֶךְ: This word is already found in the Bible (Hosea 3:2) although its meaning there is uncertain. A *letekh* is a dry measure of fifteen *se'a*, or a half-*kor*. As a measurement of land, it refers to the area in which a *letekh* of seed is planted. A *beit letekh* has a fixed measure: Approximately 37,500 square cubits, a cubit being about half a meter.

BACKGROUND

Name – שְׁמָא: That is to say, when the seller does not specify the item he is selling but uses the name that people commonly use, the buyer cannot claim that he did not receive what had been agreed upon. Parcels of land or buildings are usually called by such names, because at some point in the past they had larger dimensions or had been used in a particular way. Even if over time the names no longer corresponded to reality, they were nevertheless kept. In our times as well, people call their homes or property by certain names despite the fact that the name no longer accurately describes the property.

Beit kor – בֵּית כּוֹר: A *beit kor* is the space needed for the sowing of a *kor*, or 30 *se'a*, of grain. The space required for the sowing of a *se'a* is 2,500 square cubits. A *beit kor* is therefore an area of 75,000 square cubits, which is approximately 18,750 sq m.

HALAKHA

I am building on my property – בְּדִידִי קָא בָּנֵינָא: If brothers divided a courtyard that they received as an inheritance and assessed the value of the building and the trees in each portion but not that of the open space, and one brother received the garden and the other a portico, it is permitted for the one who received the garden to build a wall in front of the other's portico even though it will block the sunlight, according to the opinion of Rav Ḥama. If they made a general assessment without specifying any particular values, it presumably includes the value of using the open space in the courtyard; therefore, the one who received the garden may not build a wall in front of his brother's portico (Rambam *Sefer Kinyan*, *Hilkhot Shekhenim* 7:10; *Shulḥan Arukh*, *Ḥoshen Mishpat* 154:27, and *Shakh* there).

One of them taking a vineyard – אֶחָד מֵהֶם נָטַל שְׂדֵה כֶּרֶם: If two brothers divided an inheritance, one receiving an orchard and the other a field of grain, the one who inherited the orchard receives four cubits in the grain field alongside his orchard. This need not be stated explicitly, as it is something that is well known (Rambam *Sefer Kinyan*, *Hilkhot Mekhira* 24:10; *Shulḥan Arukh*, *Ḥoshen Mishpat* 173:4).

A *beit kor* of dirt – בֵּית כּוֹר עָפָר: If one says to his fellow: I am selling you a *beit kor* of dirt, the sale is valid even if the parcel of land is smaller than that, provided that the seller can prove that the parcel in question is actually called a *beit kor*. Similarly, if one sells a vineyard, the sale is valid even if it lacks grapevines, as long as the seller can prove that the place is actually called a vineyard. Similarly, if one sells an orchard, the sale is valid even if it lacks pomegranates, provided that the seller can prove that the place is actually called an orchard (Rambam *Sefer Kinyan*, *Hilkhot Mekhira* 28:14; *Shulḥan Arukh*, *Ḥoshen Mishpat* 218:17–18).

מִי דָּמֵי? הָתָם מָצֵי אָמַר לֵיהּ מוֹכֵר לַלּוֹקֵחַ: שְׁמָא זַבֵּינִי לָךְ, הָכָא מָצֵי אָמַר לֵיהּ: אַדַּעְתָּא דְּהָכִי פְּלַגִי, דְּדָאֵירְנָא בֵּיהּ כִּי הֵיכִי דְּדָרוּ אֲבָהָתָן.

The Gemara rejects this argument: **Are these** cases **comparable? There, the seller can say to the buyer: I sold you** only a place that is called that **by name; here,** the one who received the hall **can say to** his brother: **I took** this portion **as my share on condition that I would live there the way our fathers lived** there, and that you would not change that by blocking the light entering through the windows.

אֲמַרוּ לֵיהּ

With regard to Rav Ḥama's ruling that it is permitted for the brother who received the garden to build a wall in front of the hall, **they said to him,**

Perek **I**
Daf **7** Amud **b**

מָר יְנוּקָא וּמָר קַשִּׁישָׁא בְּרֵיהּ דְּרַב חִסְדָּא לְרַב אַשִׁי: נְהַרְדְּעֵי לְטַעֲמַיְיהוּ, דְּאָמַר רַב נַחְמָן אָמַר שְׁמוּאֵל: הָאַחִין שֶׁחָלְקוּ – אֵין לָהֶן לֹא דֶּרֶךְ זֶה עַל זֶה,

i.e., **Mar Yenuka and Mar Kashisha, sons of Rav Ḥisda,** said **to Rav Ashi:** The Sages **of Neharde'a follow their** usual line of **reasoning,** as Rav Ḥama, who was from Neharde'a, issued his ruling in accordance with the opinion of Shmuel, who was also from that city. **As Rav Naḥman says** that **Shmuel says:** In the case of **brothers who divided**[H] their father's estate, **they do not have** a right-of-**way against each other.** Although the father would traverse the outer field from the inner field to access the public domain, the brother who received the inner field as an inheritance does not have the right to traverse his brother's outer field.

וְלֹא חַלּוֹנוֹת זֶה עַל זֶה, וְלֹא סוּלָּמוֹת זֶה עַל זֶה, וְלֹא אַמַּת הַמַּיִם זֶה עַל זֶה, וְהִזָּהֲרוּ בָּהֶן שֶׁהֲלָכוֹת קְבוּעוֹת הֵן; וְרָבָא אָמַר: יֵשׁ לָהֶן.

Shmuel continues: **Nor** do they have the right of **windows**[N] **against each other,** i.e., the right to prevent the other from building a wall facing his windows; **nor** do they have the right of **ladders**[N] **against each other,** i.e., the right to set up a ladder in the other's property in order to get to his own; **nor** do they have the right of **a water channel**[N] **against each other,** i.e., the right to pass a water channel through the other's property. **And be careful with these, since they are established *halakhot*. Rava says:** The brothers **do have** all of the aforementioned rights. Rav Ḥama agrees with Shmuel's opinion, that each brother can do as he pleases on his own property without the other one preventing him from doing so.

הַהוּא שְׁטָרָא דְּיַתְמֵי דִּנְפֵיק עֲלֵיהּ תַּבְרָא, אָמַר רַב חָמָא: אַגְבּוּיֵי לָא מַגְבִּינַן לֵיהּ וּמִיקְרַע לָא קָרְעִינַן לֵיהּ; אַגְבּוּיֵי לָא מַגְבִּינַן לֵיהּ – דִּנְפַק תַּבְרָא עֲלֵיהּ; מִיקְרַע לָא קָרְעִינַן לֵיהּ – דְּכִי גָּדְלִי יַתְמֵי דִּילְמָא מַיְיתוּ רְאָיָה וּמַרְעֵי לֵיהּ.

Since Rav Ḥama's rulings were mentioned, the Gemara cites another halakhic ruling in his name. There was **a certain promissory note** inherited **by orphans** from their father, stating that somebody owed them money, **against which a receipt was produced**[H] by the borrower, stating that the debt was already paid. **Rav Ḥama said: We cannot** use the note to **collect** the debt on behalf of the orphans, **nor can we tear it up.** The Gemara explains: **We cannot collect** with the note because **a receipt against it was produced** by the borrower; and **we cannot tear** the note **up because perhaps when the orphans grow up they will bring proof** that the receipt was forged **and undermine it.**

אֲמַר לֵיהּ רַב אַחָא בְּרֵיהּ דְּרָבָא לְרָבִינָא: הִלְכְתָא מַאי? אֲמַר לֵיהּ: בְּכוּלְּהוּ הִלְכְתָא כְּרַב חָמָא, לְבַר מִתַּבְרָא, דְּסָהֲדֵי בְּשַׁקְרֵי לָא מַחְזְקִינַן.

Rav Aḥa, son of Rava, said to Ravina: What is the *halakha*? Ravina **said to him: In all** the cases in this discussion, **the *halakha* is in accordance with** the opinion of **Rav Ḥama, except for** the case of **the receipt, because we do not presume that the witnesses are liars.** Since witnesses signed the receipt, the court trusts that the debt was paid and they tear up the promissory note.

מָר זוּטְרָא בְּרֵיהּ דְּרַב מָרִי אָמַר: בְּהָא נָמֵי הִלְכְתָא כְּרַב חָמָא, דְּאִם אִיתָא דְּתַבְרָא מְעַלְּיָא הוּא – אִיבְּעֵי לֵיהּ לְאַפּוּקֵי בְּחַיֵּי אֲבוּהוֹן, וּמִדְּלָא אַפְּקֵיהּ, שְׁמַע מִינָּהּ זַיּוֹפֵי זַיְּיפֵיהּ.

Mar Zutra, son of Rav Mari, said: In this case **as well, the *halakha* is in accordance with** the opinion **of Rav Ḥama,** because the validity of the receipt is in doubt. **As, if it is so that** it is **a valid receipt,** the borrower **should have produced it during their father's lifetime. And since he did not produce it** at the proper time, **we learn from this that he** may have **forged it.** Even though this is not an absolute proof, it is sufficient reason not to tear up the promissory note.

HALAKHA

Brothers who divided – הָאַחִין שֶׁחָלְקוּ: If two brothers divided their father's estate and neither paid anything in order to receive his share (*Sma*), neither retains a right-of-way through the other's property, nor the right to erect a ladder, nor the right to pass an irrigation channel, even if such was the arrangement when the father was still alive, in accordance with the opinion of Shmuel (Rambam *Sefer Kinyan, Hilkhot Shekhenim* 2:12; *Shulḥan Arukh, Ḥoshen Mishpat* 173:3).

A promissory note by orphans against which a receipt was produced – שְׁטָרָא דְּיַתְמֵי דִּנְפֵיק עֲלֵיהּ תַּבְרָא: If orphans inherited a promissory note from their father, and the debtor produced a receipt against the note, the orphans cannot collect the debt since there is a receipt. The note itself is not torn up because upon reaching adulthood, the orphans might be able to bring proof that the receipt was forged. Because the receipt was not produced during the father's lifetime, the court suspects it is a forgery. This is in accordance with the opinion of Rav Ḥama and Mar Zutra, son of Rav Mari. The early commentaries disagree as to whether this *halakha* applies only when the debt became due during the father's lifetime and witnesses attest that the father demanded his money, but if the debt did not become due during the father's lifetime, the note is torn up immediately (Ramah; Shakh); or whether it applies even if the father died before the debt became due (Rambam *Sefer Mishpatim, Hilkhot Malve VeLoveh* 17:8; *Shulḥan Arukh, Ḥoshen Mishpat* 108:16).

NOTES

Nor windows – וְלֹא חַלּוֹנוֹת: They cannot challenge each other about a wall blocking light in front of a window (Rashi). Some commentaries explain that this does not refer to the blocking of light, but is stating that they are treated like two people who jointly buy a courtyard and are thereby subject to all of the *halakhot* governing invasion of privacy. Therefore, they must block windows that infringe on the other's privacy.

Ladders – סוּלָּמוֹת: If one of them inherits an upper story, he may not stand a ladder in the other's courtyard in order to reach his dwelling (Rashi). Rabbeinu Yona explains that he may not do so even for temporary use. *Tosafot* maintain that this would be the same point stated earlier, that neither one has the right-of-way to the other's dwelling. Consequently, *Tosafot* explain this clause to mean that one may not lean a ladder against the other's wall even though it stands on his own property. The Meiri explains that the brother who inherits the lower story is entitled to build around the ladder even though it impinges on the other's ability to ascend to his dwelling.

Water channel – אַמַּת הַמַּיִם: If the water channel irrigating one brother's field flows through the other's property, the latter can block it (Rashi).

מתני׳ כּוֹפִין אוֹתוֹ לִבְנוֹת בֵּית שַׁעַר וְדֶלֶת לֶחָצֵר; רַבָּן שִׁמְעוֹן בֶּן גַּמְלִיאֵל אוֹמֵר: לֹא כׇּל הַחֲצֵרוֹת רְאוּיוֹת לְבֵית שַׁעַר. כּוֹפִין אוֹתוֹ לִבְנוֹת לָעִיר חוֹמָה וּדְלָתַיִם וּבְרִיחַ; רַבָּן שִׁמְעוֹן בֶּן גַּמְלִיאֵל אוֹמֵר: לֹא כׇּל הָעֲיָירוֹת רְאוּיוֹת לְחוֹמָה.

MISHNA The residents of a courtyard **can compel** each inhabitant of that courtyard **to** financially participate in the **building of a gatehouse**[NB] **and a door to the** jointly owned **courtyard.**[H] **Rabban Shimon ben Gamliel** disagrees and **says: Not all courtyards require a gatehouse,** and each courtyard must be considered on its own in accordance with its specific needs. Similarly, the residents of a city **can compel** each inhabitant of that city **to** contribute to the **building of a wall, double doors, and a crossbar for the city.**[H] **Rabban Shimon ben Gamliel** disagrees and **says: Not all towns require a wall.**

כַּמָּה יְהֵא בָּעִיר וִיהֵא כְּאַנְשֵׁי הָעִיר? שְׁנֵים עָשָׂר חֹדֶשׁ. קָנָה בָּהּ בֵּית דִּירָה – הֲרֵי הוּא כְּאַנְשֵׁי הָעִיר מִיָּד.

With regard to this latter obligation, the mishna asks: **How long** must one live **in the city**[H] **to be** considered **like** one of **the people of the city** and therefore obligated to contribute to these expenses? **Twelve months.** But if he **bought** himself **a residence** in the city, **he is immediately** considered **like** one **of the people of the city.**

גמ׳ לְמֵימְרָא דְּבֵית שַׁעַר מְעַלְּיוּתָא הִיא? וְהָא הַהוּא חֲסִידָא דַּהֲוָה רָגִיל אֵלִיָּהוּ דַּהֲוָה מִשְׁתָּעֵי בַּהֲדֵיהּ, עֲבַד בֵּית שַׁעַר וְתוּ לָא מִשְׁתָּעֵי בַּהֲדֵיהּ! לָא קַשְׁיָא: הָא מִגַּוַּאי, הָא מִבַּרַאי.

GEMARA The Gemara asks: **Is this to say that** making **a gatehouse is beneficial? But** wasn't there **that pious man, with whom** the prophet **Elijah**[P] **was accustomed to speak,** who **built a gatehouse, and** afterward Elijah **did not speak with him again?** The objection to the building of a gatehouse is that the guard who mans it prevents the poor from entering and asking for charity. The Gemara answers: This is **not difficult: This,** the case presented in the mishna, is referring to a gatehouse built **on the inside**[N] of the courtyard, in which case the poor can at least reach the courtyard's entrance and be heard inside the courtyard; **that,** the story of the pious man and Elijah, involves a gatehouse that was built **on the outside** of the courtyard, completely blocking the poor's access to the courtyard's entrance.

וְאִי בָּעֵית אֵימָא: הָא וְהָא מִבַּרַאי, וְלָא קַשְׁיָא: הָא דְּאִית לֵיהּ דֶּלֶת, הָא דְּלֵית לֵיהּ דֶּלֶת. אִי בָּעֵית אֵימָא: הָא וְהָא דְּאִית לֵיהּ דֶּלֶת, וְלָא קַשְׁיָא: הָא דְּאִית לֵיהּ פּוֹתַחַת, הָא דְּלֵית לֵיהּ פּוֹתַחַת. אִי בָּעֵית אֵימָא: הָא וְהָא דְּאִית לֵיהּ פּוֹתַחַת, וְלָא קַשְׁיָא: הָא דְּפוֹתַחַת דִּידֵיהּ מִגַּוַּאי, הָא דְּפוֹתַחַת דִּידֵיהּ מִבַּרַאי.

And if you wish, say instead that in **both** cases the gatehouse was built **outside** the courtyard, **and** yet this is **not difficult:** In the one case, **there is a door** to the gatehouse, so that the poor cannot be heard inside the courtyard, while in the other case **there is no door. Or if you wish, say** that in **both** cases **there is a door, and** still this is **not difficult:** In the one case, **there is a key**[B] needed to open the door, and the key is not available to the poor people, whereas in the other case, **there is no key** needed. **Or if you wish, say** that in **both** cases **there is a key** needed, **and** even so this is **not difficult:** In the one case **the key is on the inside,** so that the poor cannot reach it, while in the other case of the mishna, **the key is on the outside.**

HALAKHA

Building a gatehouse and a door to the courtyard – לִבְנוֹת בֵּית שַׁעַר וְדֶלֶת לֶחָצֵר: The residents of a courtyard can compel each other to build a gatehouse for the courtyard and to build other items required for the courtyard or customarily found there. They cannot compel each other to pay for ornaments or other unnecessary items (Rambam *Sefer Kinyan*, *Hilkhot Shekhenim* 5:1; *Shulḥan Arukh*, *Ḥoshen Mishpat* 161:1).

Building of a wall…for the city – לִבְנוֹת לָעִיר חוֹמָה: The residents of a city can compel each to contribute to the building of a wall, double doors, and a crossbar for the city. Moreover, the minority can force the majority to do so (Rabbeinu Yeruḥam) even if the town is not on the border (*Sma*), in accordance with the opinion of the anonymous first *tanna* (Rambam *Sefer Kinyan*, *Hilkhot Shekhenim* 6:1; *Shulḥan Arukh*, *Ḥoshen Mishpat* 163:1).

How long must one live in the city – כַּמָּה יְהֵא בָּעִיר: If one lives in a city for twelve months or buys a house in a city, he is considered one of the residents of the city and can be compelled to contribute to all the municipal costs. The Rema adds that if one rents a house in a city and demonstrates that he wishes to live there permanently, or if he rents a house for twelve months in advance, he is immediately considered a resident. If he did not rent or buy a house in the city but received a dwelling as a gift or as an inheritance, he is not considered a resident until he demonstrates that he wishes to be one (Rambam *Sefer Kinyan*, *Hilkhot Shekhenim* 5:6; *Shulḥan Arukh*, *Ḥoshen Mishpat* 163:2 and *Sma* there).

NOTES

Gatehouse – בֵּית שַׁעַר: Rabbeinu Gershom, Rashi, and others explain that this structure houses a guard who prevents the public from entering the courtyard.

On the inside – מִגַּוַּאי: If the gatehouse is built outside the courtyard and the guard does not permit outsiders to enter, the cry of the poor will not be heard inside; but if the gatehouse is built inside, the poor can stand at the entrance and call out (Ri Migash; Ramah). Rabbeinu Gershom and Rashi understand this in the opposite manner: If the gatehouse is outside the courtyard, the poor person can pass through it to the entrance of the courtyard and call out; but if it is inside the courtyard, it muffles the sound of his voice. The Ra'avad proposes that if the gatehouse is outside, the poor person is not deterred from reaching the courtyard entrance since he knows it is only a gatehouse. If it is inside, it looks like a private house and he avoids going in.

BACKGROUND

Gatehouse – בֵּית שַׁעַר: A gatehouse is a small structure built at the entrance to a courtyard which forces people to stop before entering that area. It is generally open in front, with the gate to the courtyard forming the rear wall. If the courtyard has a guard, he often sits in the gatehouse.

Gatehouse of ancient palace in Amman, Jordan

Key – פּוֹתַחַת:

Key from the bar Kokheva period

PERSONALITIES

Elijah – אֵלִיָּהוּ: In many places in the Talmud and the midrash, Elijah the prophet appears to people, especially to the Sages, and resolves their dilemmas. As stated in II Kings 2:11, Elijah did not die, and he continues to serve as an emissary of God. On the one hand, he is the zealous angel of the covenant. On the other hand, he alleviates problems in the world.

"כּוֹפִין אוֹתוֹ לִבְנוֹת בֵּית שַׁעַר וְדֶלֶת לֶחָצֵר". תַּנְיָא, רַבָּן שִׁמְעוֹן בֶּן גַּמְלִיאֵל אוֹמֵר: לֹא כָּל חֲצֵרוֹת רְאוּיוֹת לְבֵית שַׁעַר, אֶלָּא, חָצֵר הַסְּמוּכָה לִרְשׁוּת הָרַבִּים – רְאוּיָה לְבֵית שַׁעַר, וְשֶׁאֵינָהּ סְמוּכָה לִרְשׁוּת הָרַבִּים – אֵינָהּ רְאוּיָה לְבֵית שַׁעַר. וְרַבָּנַן? זִימְנִין דְּדָחֲקִי בְּנֵי רְשׁוּת הָרַבִּים וְעָיְילוּ וְאָתוּ.

§ The mishna teaches that the residents of a courtyard **can compel** each inhabitant of that courtyard **to** financially participate in the **building of a gatehouse and a door to the** jointly owned **courtyard. It is taught** in a *baraita* that **Rabban Shimon ben Gamliel says: Not all courtyards require a gatehouse. Rather, a courtyard that adjoins the public domain requires a gatehouse** to prevent people from peering in. **But** a courtyard **that does not adjoin the public domain does not require a gatehouse.** The Gemara asks: **And** why don't **the Rabbis** make this distinction? The Gemara answers: Even if a courtyard does not adjoin the public domain, **people in the public domain sometimes are forced** toward the courtyard due to crowding in the public domain, **and come and enter** the courtyard.

"כּוֹפִין אוֹתוֹ לִבְנוֹת לָעִיר" כו׳. תָּנוּ רַבָּנַן: כּוֹפִין אוֹתוֹ לַעֲשׂוֹת לָעִיר דְּלָתַיִם וּבְרִיחַ. וְרַבָּן שִׁמְעוֹן בֶּן גַּמְלִיאֵל אוֹמֵר: לֹא כָּל הָעֲיָירוֹת רְאוּיוֹת לְחוֹמָה, אֶלָּא, עִיר הַסְּמוּכָה לַסְּפָר – רְאוּיָה לְחוֹמָה, וְשֶׁאֵינָהּ סְמוּכָה לַסְּפָר – אֵינָהּ רְאוּיָה לְחוֹמָה. וְרַבָּנַן? זִימְנִין דְּמִקְרוּ וְאָתֵי גַּיְיסָא.

§ The mishna teaches that the residents of a city **can compel** each inhabitant of that city **to** contribute to the **building** of a wall, double doors, and a crossbar **for the city. The Sages taught** in a *baraita*: The residents of a city **can compel** each inhabitant of that city **to build double doors and a crossbar for the city. And Rabban Shimon ben Gamliel says: Not all cities require a wall. Rather, a city that adjoins the** state **border requires a wall,** whereas a city **that does not adjoin the** state **border does not require a wall.** The Gemara asks: **And** why don't **the Rabbis** make this distinction? The Gemara answers: Even if a city does not adjoin the border, **it sometimes happens that** invading **troops come** into the area. Therefore, it is always good for a city to be protected by a wall.

בְּעָא מִינֵּיהּ רַבִּי אֶלְעָזָר מֵרַבִּי יוֹחָנָן: כְּשֶׁהֵן גּוֹבִין, לְפִי נְפָשׁוֹת גּוֹבִין, אוֹ דִּילְמָא לְפִי שְׁבַח מָמוֹן גּוֹבִין? אֲמַר לֵיהּ: לְפִי מָמוֹן גּוֹבִין, וְאֶלְעָזָר בְּנִי, קְבַע בָּהּ מַסְמְרוֹת.

With regard to this issue, **Rabbi Elazar**[P] **asked Rabbi Yoḥanan:**[P] **When** the residents of the city **collect** money to build a wall, **do they collect based on** the number of **people**[N] living in each house, **or perhaps they collect based on the** net **worth** of each person?[H] Rabbi Yoḥanan **said to him: They collect based on the** net **worth** of each person, **and Elazar, my son,** you shall **fix nails in this,** i.e., this is an established *halakha*, and you must not veer from it.

אִיכָּא דְּאָמְרִי, בְּעָא מִינֵּיהּ רַבִּי אֶלְעָזָר מֵרַבִּי יוֹחָנָן: כְּשֶׁהֵן גּוֹבִין, לְפִי קֵירוּב בָּתִּים הֵן גּוֹבִין, אוֹ דִּילְמָא לְפִי מָמוֹן גּוֹבִין? אֲמַר לֵיהּ: לְפִי קֵירוּב בָּתִּים הֵן גּוֹבִין, וְאֶלְעָזָר בְּנִי, קְבַע בָּהּ מַסְמְרוֹת.

There are those **who say that Rabbi Elazar asked Rabbi Yoḥanan: When they collect** money to build a wall, **do they collect based on the proximity of the houses**[N] to the wall, so that those people who live closer to the wall pay more? **Or perhaps they collect based on the** net **worth** of each person. Rabbi Yoḥanan **said to him: They collect based on the proximity of the houses** to the wall, **and Elazar, my son,** you shall **fix nails in this.**

NOTES

They collect based on the number of people – לְפִי נְפָשׁוֹת גּוֹבִין: The question here is whether the main concern with potential assaulters is that they might harm people, in which case they collect based on the number of people; or that they might loot, in which case they collect based on wealth (Ritva).

They collect based on the proximity of the houses – לְפִי קֵירוּב בָּתִּים: Most early commentaries explain that the invading troop that comes to loot stops first at the houses close to the wall. Consequently, the houses further away from the wall are less vulnerable. *Tosafot* explain that this does not mean that they collect based exclusively on proximity to the wall, as wealth is also taken into account. This is because an empty house near the wall will not be looted. The Ri Migash states that the collection is based primarily on wealth but that proximity is also a factor. The Ramah expresses an altogether different opinion. He concludes that those further away from the city center must pay more because their location demands the building of a longer wall to encompass their properties. Consequently, the residents who pay more are those who live further from the center and those with bigger homes.

HALAKHA

Based on what do they collect – לְפִי מַה גּוֹבִין: With regard to funds collected from the residents of a city for the building of a wall, some say that the collection is based on the proximity of the houses to the wall so that those people who live closer to the wall pay more, in accordance with the later version of Rabbi Yoḥanan's statement (Rif). The Ri Migash rules that the individual's worth is also taken into account. Consequently, if two homeowners are equally wealthy and live at equal distances from the wall, they pay the same amount of wall tax. If a poor person with no means lives near the wall and a wealthy person lives farther away, only the latter is required to pay. If two people are of equal means, but live at different distances from the wall, the one who lives closer pays more. This is in accordance with both versions of Rabbi Yoḥanan's statement (Rambam *Sefer Kinyan*, *Hilkhot Shekhenim* 5:4; *Shulḥan Arukh*, *Ḥoshen Mishpat* 163:3).

PERSONALITIES

Rabbi Elazar – רַבִּי אֶלְעָזָר: In the Gemara, citations of Rabbi Elazar with no patronymic refer to Rabbi Elazar ben Pedat, a second-generation *amora* in Eretz Yisrael. In many cases in the Gemara, he is referred to as Rabbi Eliezer, but this is probably a textual corruption. He was born in Babylonia, where he was a student of both Rav and Shmuel. In his youth, he immigrated to Eretz Yisrael, where he married and became one of Rabbi Yoḥanan's most important students. The connection between them was so close that at times the Gemara raises a contradiction between the statement of one and the statement of the other, under the assumption that it was unlikely that they would hold different opinions in matters of *halakha*. This relationship is reflected by Rabbi Yoḥanan's referring to Rabbi Elazar as: My son.

Rabbi Yoḥanan – רַבִּי יוֹחָנָן: Rabbi Yoḥanan bar Nappaḥa was one of the greatest *amora'im*. His statements are fundamental components of both the Jerusalem Talmud and the Babylonian Talmud. He resided in Tiberias and lived to an advanced age. Almost nothing is known of his family background. He was orphaned at a young age, and although his family apparently owned considerable property, he devoted virtually all of his resources to the study of Torah. He eventually became impoverished.

In Rabbi Yoḥanan's youth, he had the privilege of studying under Rabbi Yehuda HaNasi, the redactor of the Mishna, but most of his Torah study was accomplished under Rabbi Yehuda HaNasi's students: Ḥizkiyya ben Ḥiyya, Rabbi Oshaya, Rabbi Ḥanina, and Rabbi Yannai, who lavished praise upon him. In time, he became the head of the yeshiva in Tiberias, at which point his fame and influence increased greatly.

For a long time, Rabbi Yoḥanan was the leading rabbinic scholar in the Jewish world, in Eretz Yisrael as well as in Babylonia, where he was respected by the Babylonian Sages. Many of them came to Eretz Yisrael and became his outstanding students. He was a master of both *halakha* and *aggada*. In recognition of his intellectual and spiritual stature, the *halakha* follows his opinion in almost every case, even when Rav or Shmuel, the preeminent *amora'im* of Babylonia, whom he treated deferentially, disagreed with him. Only in disputes with his teachers in Eretz Yisrael, such as Rabbi Yannai and Rabbi Yehoshua ben Levi, does the *halakha* not follow his opinion.

רַבִּי יְהוּדָה נְשִׂיאָה רְמָא דְּשׁוּרָא אַדְּרַבָּנַן, אֲמַר רֵישׁ לָקִישׁ: רַבָּנַן לָא צְרִיכִי נְטִירוּתָא, דִּכְתִיב: ״אֶסְפְּרֵם מֵחוֹל יִרְבּוּן״, אֶסְפְּרֵם לְמַאן? אִילֵימָא לַצַּדִּיקִים דִּנְפִישִׁי מֵחָלָא, הַשְׁתָּא כּוּלְּהוּ יִשְׂרָאֵל כְּתִיב בְּהוּ: ״כַּחוֹל אֲשֶׁר עַל שְׂפַת הַיָּם״, צַדִּיקִים עַצְמָם מֵחוֹל יִרְבּוּן?!

§ It is related that **Rabbi Yehuda Nesia**[P] once **imposed** payment of the tax for **the wall even on the Sages. Reish Lakish said to him: The Sages do not require protection,**[H] **as it is written:** "How precious are your dear ones to me, O God… **If I should count them, they are more in number than the sand"** (Psalms 139:17–18). **If I should count whom? If we say** this is referring to **the righteous,** and the verse is saying **that they are greater in number than the** grains of **sand,** this is difficult. **Now if it is written about all of Israel: "As the sand which is upon the seashore"** (Genesis 22:17), can **the righteous themselves,** who are a part of Israel, **be greater in number than the** grains of **sand?** How can they possibly outnumber the grains of sand upon the seashore?

אֶלָּא הָכִי קָאָמַר: אֶסְפְּרֵם לְמַעֲשֵׂיהֶם שֶׁל צַדִּיקִים – מֵחוֹל יִרְבּוּן, וְקַל וָחוֹמֶר: וּמַה חוֹל שֶׁמּוּעָט – מֵגֵין עַל הַיָּם, מַעֲשֵׂיהֶם שֶׁל צַדִּיקִים שֶׁהֵם מְרוּבִּים – לֹא כׇּל שֶׁכֵּן שֶׁמְּגִינִּים עֲלֵיהֶם.

Rather, this is what the verse **is saying:** If I should count **the deeds of the righteous, they are greater in number than the** grains of **sand. And** it follows by an ***a fortiori*** inference: **If the** grains of **sand, which are fewer** in number, **protect** the shore from **the sea,** barring it from flowing inland (see Jeremiah 5:22), **do not all the more so the deeds of the righteous, which are greater** in number, **protect them?** Consequently the Sages do not need additional protection.

כִּי אֲתָא לְקַמֵּיהּ דְּרַבִּי יוֹחָנָן, אֲמַר לֵיהּ, מַאי טַעֲמָא לָא תֵּימָא לֵיהּ מֵהָא: ״אֲנִי חוֹמָה וְשָׁדַי כַּמִּגְדָּלוֹת״; ״אֲנִי חוֹמָה״ – זוֹ תּוֹרָה, ״וְשָׁדַי כַּמִּגְדָּלוֹת״

When Reish Lakish **came before Rabbi Yoḥanan** and reported the exchange to him, Rabbi Yoḥanan **said to him: What is the reason** that **you did not quote this** verse **to him: "I am a wall and my breasts are like towers"** (Song of Songs 8:10), which may be explained as follows: **"I am a wall"; this is referring to the Torah. "And my breasts are like towers";**

Perek **I**
Daf **8** Amud **a**

אֵלּוּ תַּלְמִידֵי חֲכָמִים? וְרֵישׁ לָקִישׁ סָבַר לַהּ כִּדְדָרֵשׁ רָבָא: ״אֲנִי חוֹמָה״ – זוֹ כְּנֶסֶת יִשְׂרָאֵל, ״וְשָׁדַי כַּמִּגְדָּלוֹת״ – אֵלּוּ בָּתֵּי כְנֵסִיּוֹת וּבָתֵּי מִדְרָשׁוֹת.

these are Torah scholars,[N] and towers do not require additional protection? The Gemara comments: **And Reish Lakish,** who did not cite this verse, **holds in accordance with** the way **that Rava expounded** the verse: **"I am a wall"; this is referring to the Congregation of Israel.**[N] **"And my breasts are like towers"; these are the synagogues and study halls.**

רַב נַחְמָן בַּר רַב חִסְדָּא רְמָא כַּרְגָּא אַרַבָּנַן, אֲמַר לֵיהּ רַב נַחְמָן בַּר יִצְחָק: עֲבַרְתְּ אַדְּאוֹרָיְיתָא וְאַדִּנְבִיאֵי וְאַדִּכְתוּבֵי.

It is similarly related that **Rav Naḥman bar Rav Ḥisda** once **imposed** payment of **the** poll **tax** [*karga*][L] even **on the Sages.**[H] **Rav Naḥman bar Yitzḥak said to him: You have transgressed** the words of **the Torah, the Prophets, and the Writings.**

אַדְּאוֹרָיְיתָא, דִּכְתִיב: ״אַף חֹבֵב עַמִּים כׇּל קְדֹשָׁיו בְּיָדֶךָ״, אָמַר מֹשֶׁה לִפְנֵי הַקָּדוֹשׁ בָּרוּךְ הוּא: רִבּוֹנוֹ שֶׁל עוֹלָם, אֲפִילּוּ בְּשָׁעָה שֶׁאַתָּה מְחַבֵּב עַמִּים – כׇּל קְדוֹשָׁיו יִהְיוּ בְּיָדֶךָ. ״וְהֵם תֻּכּוּ לְרַגְלֶךָ״ – תָּנֵי רַב יוֹסֵף: אֵלּוּ תַּלְמִידֵי חֲכָמִים, שֶׁמְּכַתְּתִים רַגְלֵיהֶם מֵעִיר לְעִיר וּמִמְּדִינָה לִמְדִינָה לִלְמוֹד תּוֹרָה, ״יִשָּׂא מִדַּבְּרוֹתֶיךָ״ – לִישָּׂא וְלִיתֵּן בְּדִבּוּרוֹתָיו שֶׁל מָקוֹם.

You have transgressed the words of **the Torah, as it is written: "Even when He loves the peoples, all His holy ones are in Your hand"** (Deuteronomy 33:3), which is understood to mean that **Moses said to the Holy One, Blessed be He: Master of the Universe, even when You hold the** other **nations dear** and grant them dominion over Israel, let **"all His holy ones,"** meaning the Torah scholars, **be** exclusively **in Your hand** and free from the authority of the nations, and therefore be exempt from paying taxes. The continuation of that verse can also be understood as referring to Torah scholars, as it states: **"And they sit [*tukku*] at Your feet,** receiving Your words" (Deuteronomy 33:3), and **Rav Yosef teaches: These are Torah scholars who pound [*mekhatetim*] their feet from city to city and from country to country to study Torah; "receiving [*yissa*] Your words," to discuss [*lissa velitten*] the utterances of God.**

PERSONALITIES

Rabbi Yehuda Nesia – רַבִּי יְהוּדָה נְשִׂיאָה: Based on the chronology of the generations, this name seems to refer to Rabbi Yehuda Nesia II, who was the grandson of Rabbi Yehuda Nesia I, the grandson of Rabbi Yehuda HaNasi, who redacted the Mishna. In the days of Rabbi Yehuda Nesia, the position of *Nasi* was merely a public office; the leading Torah authorities headed the academies and the courts. Rabbi Yehuda Nesia studied with Rabbi Yoḥanan and was subordinate to Rabbi Yoḥanan's students, Rabbi Abbahu and Rabbi Ami. Many anecdotes about Rabbi Yehuda Nesia are recorded in the Jerusalem and Babylonian Talmuds, including his meeting with the Roman emperor, Diocletian.

HALAKHA

The Sages do not require protection – רַבָּנַן לָא צְרִיכִי נְטִירוּתָא: Torah Sages are exempt from paying taxes to protect the city because their learning protects them (Rambam *Sefer Kinyan, Hilkhot Shekhenim* 5:6; *Shulḥan Arukh, Ḥoshen Mishpat* 163:4 and *Yoreh De'a* 243:2).

NOTES

These are Torah scholars – אֵלּוּ תַּלְמִידֵי חֲכָמִים: These people provide Torah to others as breasts nourish a baby (see Rabbeinu Gershom). The early commentaries disagree about the definition of a Torah scholar in this context: Does the term signify someone who occupies himself exclusively with Torah, or does it include somebody whose primary occupation is the study of Torah but who also devotes a minimal portion of his time to earning a living?

This is the Congregation of Israel – זוֹ כְּנֶסֶת יִשְׂרָאֵל: All of Israel are surrounded and protected, as it were, by a wall, and they do not assimilate among the nations (Rashi).

LANGUAGE

Tax [*karga*] – כַּרְגָּא: The origin of this term is the Persian yarak or arak, which also led to the Arabic خراج, *ḫarāj*. All these words mean a poll tax imposed on every resident of a country.

HALAKHA

Tax on the Sages – כַּרְגָּא אַדְּרַבָּנַן: Torah scholars are exempt from the taxes and duties imposed on the residents of a city. They pay neither their share of a tax levied on the city as a whole nor the head tax imposed on each individual. They are exempt from both ordinary taxes and extraordinary ones. There is no difference between a wealthy Torah scholar and a poor Torah scholar (Rambam *Sefer HaMadda, Hilkhot Talmud Torah* 6:10; *Shulḥan Arukh, Ḥoshen Mishpat* 163:5 and *Yoreh De'a* 243:2, and in the comment of Rema).

NOTES

This is referring to the head tax – זוֹ כֶּסֶף גּוּלְגַּלְתָּא: Many early commentaries explain that this tax exemption applies only in a situation where a tax is imposed on the entire community based on the number of its members, but scholars are not exempt when the tax is imposed directly upon each individual. The Ramah does not accept this distinction, asserting that a tax imposed directly upon each individual is the very definition of a head tax.

The digging of cisterns [*karya patya*] – כַּרְיָא פַּתְיָא: Rashi explains that *karya* refers to digging a cistern for drinking water, and *patya* means a clay utensil used for drinking water or for cooking. Others explain that this term describes the digging of an aqueduct (Rav Sherira Gaon), or even the paving of a town square (Rif; Ri Migash).

אַדִּנְבִיאֵי, דִּכְתִיב: "גַּם כִּי יִתְנוּ בַגּוֹיִם עַתָּה אֲקַבְּצֵם וַיָּחֵלּוּ מְעָט מִמַּשָּׂא מֶלֶךְ וְשָׂרִים", אָמַר עוּלָּא: פָּסוּק זֶה בִּלְשׁוֹן אֲרָמִית נֶאֱמַר; אִי תָּנוּ כּוּלְּהוּ – עַתָּה אֲקַבְּצֵם, וְאִם מְעַט מֵהֶם – יָחֵלּוּ מִמַּשָּׂא מֶלֶךְ וְשָׂרִים.

And you have transgressed the words of **the Prophets, as it is written: "Though they have hired lovers [*yitnu*] among the nations, now I will gather them, and they will begin to be diminished by reason of the burden of kings and princes"** (Hosea 8:10). With regard to this verse, **Ulla says:** Part of **this verse is stated in the Aramaic language;** the word *yitnu* should be understood here in its Aramaic sense: To learn. And the verse should be interpreted as follows: **If all** of Israel **learns** Torah, **I will gather them** already **now; and if** only **a few of them** learn Torah, **they will be excused from the burden** imposed **by kings and princes.** This indicates that those who study Torah should not be subject to paying taxes.

אַדִּכְתוּבֵי, דִּכְתִיב: "מִנְדָּה בְלוֹ וַהֲלָךְ לָא שַׁלִּיט לְמִרְמֵא עֲלֵיהֹם", וְאָמַר רַב יְהוּדָה: "מִנְדָּה" – זוֹ מִנַת הַמֶּלֶךְ, "בְּלוֹ" – זוֹ כֶּסֶף גּוּלְגַּלְתָּא, "וַהֲלָךְ" – זוֹ אַרְנוֹנָא.

And furthermore, you have transgressed the words of **the Writings, as it is written: "It shall not be lawful to impose tribute, impost or toll upon them"** (Ezra 7:24), i.e., upon the priests and Levites who serve in the Temple. This *halakha* would apply to Torah scholars as well. **And Rav Yehuda says: "Tribute"; this** is referring to **the king's portion,** a tax given to the king. **"Impost"; this** is referring to **the head tax.**[N] **"Toll"; this** is referring to **a tax [*arnona*]**[L] paid with property that was imposed from time to time.

רַב פַּפָּא רְמָא כַּרְיָא חֲדַתָּא אַיַּתְמֵי, אֲמַר לֵיהּ רַב שֵׁישָׁא בְּרֵיהּ דְּרַב אִידִי לְרַב פַּפָּא: וְדִילְמָא לָא מִידְוִיל! אֲמַר לֵיהּ: מִישְׁקַל שָׁקֵילְנָא מִנַּיְיהוּ, אִי מִידְוִיל – מִידְוִיל, וְאִי לָא – מַהֲדַרְנָא לְהוּ נִיהֲלַיְיהוּ.

It is related that **Rav Pappa** once **imposed** a tax for **the digging of a new** cistern even **on orphans.**[H] **Rav Sheisha, son of Rav Idi, said to Rav Pappa: Perhaps** they will dig, but in the end **they will not draw** any **water** from there, and it will turn out that the money will have been spent for nothing. The rest of the townspeople can relinquish their rights to their money, but orphans who are minors cannot do so. Rav Pappa **said to him: I shall collect** money **from** the orphans; **if they draw** water, **they** will **draw** water, **and if not, I will return** the money **to** the orphans.

אָמַר רַב יְהוּדָה: הַכֹּל לְאַגְלֵי גַּפָּא, אֲפִילּוּ מִיַּתְמֵי, אֲבָל רַבָּנַן לָא צְרִיכִי נְטִירוּתָא; הַכֹּל לְכַרְיָא פַּתְיָא, אֲפִילּוּ מֵרַבָּנַן. וְלָא אֲמַרַן אֶלָּא דְּלָא נָפְקִי בְּאַכְלוּזָא, אֲבָל נָפְקִי בְּאַכְלוּזָא, רַבָּנַן לָאו בְּנֵי מֵיפַּק בְּאַכְלוּזָא נִינְהוּ.

Rav Yehuda says: All of the city's residents must contribute **to** the building and upkeep of **the city gates [*le'aglei gappa*],**[LH] and for this purpose money is collected **even from orphans. But the Sages do not require protection** and are therefore exempt from this payment. **All** of the city's residents must contribute **to the digging of cisterns [*lekarya patya*],**[NLH] and for this purpose money is collected **even from the Sages,** since they too need water. The Gemara comments: **And we said** this **only when** the people are **not** required to **go out en masse [*be'akhluza*]**[L] and do the actual digging, but are obligated merely to contribute money for that purpose. **But if** the people are required to **go out en masse** and actually dig, **the Sages** are **not** expected to **go out** with them **en masse,** but rather they are exempt from such labor.

LANGUAGE

Tax [*arnona*] – אַרְנוֹנָא: From the Latin annona, which was a forced labor tax imposed by governments for public works or the army. Work animals were also seized, temporarily or permanently, for this purpose. A sizable portion of this tax was collected when troops passed from place to place, and the local residents had to provide them with food and assist them with their animals.

The city gates [*aglei gappa*] – אַגְלֵי גַּפָּא: *Aglei* is related to the word *gali*, which is derived from the Aramaic root *gimmel, lamed*, and means gate. *Gappa*, or *gafa*, means wall; another version reads *agfa*, meaning enclosure.

The digging of wells [*karya patya*] – כַּרְיָא פַּתְיָא: Some understand that the term *patya* derives from the Assyrian *pattu*, meaning a water channel. Consequently, this refers to the digging of a water channel to the city.

En masse [*akhluza*] – אַכְלוּזָא: Some commentaries read this as *okhlosa*, which comes from the Greek ὄχλος, *okhlos*, meaning the masses.

HALAKHA

A tax for the digging of a new cistern on orphans – כַּרְיָא חֲדַתָּא אַיַּתְמֵי: Money may be collected from orphans for the digging of cisterns or the channeling of rivers for the good of the town. If water is not discovered, their money is refunded (Rambam *Sefer Kinyan, Hilkhot Shekhenim* 6:7; *Shulḥan Arukh, Ḥoshen Mishpat* 163:4).

All contribute to the city gates – הַכֹּל לְאַגְלֵי גַּפָּא: Everyone, including orphans, is required to contribute funds for building walls and paying guards. Torah scholars, by contrast, are exempt, since their Torah study protects them (Rambam *Sefer Kinyan, Hilkhot Shekhenim* 6:6; *Shulḥan Arukh, Ḥoshen Mishpat* 163:4 and *Yoreh De'a* 243:2).

All contribute to the digging of cisterns – הַכֹּל לְכַרְיָא פַּתְיָא: Everyone, including Torah scholars and orphans, is required to contribute funds for repairing roads or water sources. But if the work is to be carried out by the residents themselves, Torah scholars are not obligated to participate in the efforts and are not required to pay others to do the work on their behalf (Rambam *Sefer Kinyan, Hilkhot Shekhenim* 6:6; *Shulḥan Arukh, Ḥoshen Mishpat* 163:4 and *Yoreh De'a* 243:2).

רַבִּי פָּתַח אוֹצָרוֹת בִּשְׁנֵי בַצּוֹרֶת, אָמַר: יִכָּנְסוּ בַּעֲלֵי מִקְרָא, בַּעֲלֵי מִשְׁנָה, בַּעֲלֵי תַלְמוּד, בַּעֲלֵי הֲלָכָה, בַּעֲלֵי הַגָּדָה, אֲבָל עַמֵּי הָאָרֶץ אַל יִכָּנְסוּ. דָּחַק רַבִּי יוֹנָתָן בֶּן עַמְרָם וְנִכְנַס, אָמַר לוֹ: רַבִּי, פַּרְנְסֵנִי! אָמַר לוֹ: בְּנִי, קָרִיתָ? אָמַר לוֹ: לָאו. שָׁנִיתָ? אָמַר לוֹ: לָאו. אִם כֵּן, בַּמֶּה אֲפַרְנֶסְךָ? [אָמַר לוֹ:] פַּרְנְסֵנִי כְּכֶלֶב וּכְעוֹרֵב. פַּרְנְסֵיהּ.

It is related that **Rabbi Yehuda HaNasi**[P] once **opened** his **storehouses** to distribute food **during years of drought. He said: Masters of Bible, masters of Mishna, masters of Talmud, masters of *halakha*, masters of *aggada* may enter** and receive food from me, **but ignoramuses should not enter.**[N] **Rabbi Yonatan ben Amram,**[P] whom Rabbi Yehuda HaNasi did not know, **pushed** his way in, **and entered,** and **said to him: Rabbi** Yehuda HaNasi, **sustain me.** Rabbi Yehuda HaNasi **said to him: My son, have you read** the Bible? Rabbi Yonatan ben Amram **said to him,** out of modesty: **No.** Rabbi Yehuda HaNasi continued: **Have you studied** Mishna? Once again, Rabbi Yonatan ben Amram **said to him: No.** Rabbi Yehuda HaNasi then asked him: **If so, by what** merit **should I sustain you?** Rabbi Yonatan ben Amram **said to him: Sustain me like a dog and like a raven,** who are given food even though they have not learned anything. Rabbi Yehuda HaNasi was moved by his words and **fed him.**

בָּתַר דִּנְפַק, יָתֵיב רַבִּי וְקָא מִצְטָעֵר וְאָמַר: אוֹי לִי שֶׁנָּתַתִּי פִּתִּי לְעַם הָאָרֶץ! אָמַר לְפָנָיו רַבִּי שִׁמְעוֹן בַּר רַבִּי: שֶׁמָּא יוֹנָתָן בֶּן עַמְרָם תַּלְמִידְךָ הוּא, שֶׁאֵינוֹ רוֹצֶה לֵיהָנוֹת מִכְּבוֹד תּוֹרָה מִיָּמָיו? בְּדַקוּ וְאַשְׁכַּח, אָמַר רַבִּי: יִכָּנְסוּ הַכֹּל.

After Rabbi Yonatan **left, Rabbi** Yehuda HaNasi **sat, and was distressed, and said: Woe is me, that I have given my bread to an ignoramus.**[H] His son, **Rabbi Shimon bar Rabbi** Yehuda HaNasi, **said to him: Perhaps he was your disciple Yonatan ben Amram, who never in his life wanted to** materially **benefit from the honor** shown to the **Torah? They investigated** the matter **and found** that such was the case. **Rabbi** Yehuda HaNasi then **said: Let everyone enter,**[N] as there may also be others who hide the fact that they are true Torah scholars.

רַבִּי לְטַעֲמֵיהּ, דְּאָמַר רַבִּי: אֵין פּוּרְעָנוּת בָּא לָעוֹלָם אֶלָּא בִּשְׁבִיל עַמֵּי הָאָרֶץ. כְּהַהוּא דְּמֵי כְּלִילָא דִּשְׁדוּ אַטְּבֶרְיָא, אָתוּ לְקַמֵּיהּ דְּרַבִּי וַאֲמַרוּ לֵיהּ: לֵיתְבוּ רַבָּנַן בַּהֲדַן, אֲמַר לְהוּ: לָא. אֲמַרוּ לֵיהּ: עֲרוֹקִינַן, [אֲמַר לְהוּ:] עֲרוֹקוּ. עֲרַקוּ פַּלְגֵיהוֹן, דָּלְיוּהּ פַּלְגָא.

Commenting on Rabbi Yehuda HaNasi's opinion, the Gemara notes that **Rabbi Yehuda HaNasi** conformed **to his** standard line of **reasoning,** as **Rabbi Yehuda HaNasi says: Suffering comes to the world only due to ignoramuses.** This is **like** the incident of **the crown tax** [*kelila*][L] **that was imposed on** the residents of the city of **Tiberias.** The heads of the city **came before Rabbi** Yehuda HaNasi **and said to him: The Sages should contribute** along **with us.** Rabbi Yehuda HaNasi **said to them: No,** the Sages are exempt. **They said to him:** Then **we will run away** and the entire burden will fall on the Torah scholars. Rabbi Yehuda HaNasi **said to them: Run away** as you please. **Half** of the city's residents **ran away.** The authorities then **waived half** the sum that they had initially imposed on the city.

אֲתוּ הָנְהוּ פַּלְגָא קַמֵּי דְּרַבִּי, אֲמַרוּ לֵיהּ: לֵיתְבוּ רַבָּנַן בַּהֲדַן, אֲמַר לְהוּ: לָא. עֲרוֹקִינַן, עֲרוֹקוּ. עֲרַקוּ כּוּלְּהוּ, פַּשׁ הַהוּא כּוֹבֵס, שַׁדְיוּהּ אַכּוֹבֵס. עֲרַק כּוֹבֵס, פְּקַע כְּלִילָא. אָמַר רַבִּי: רְאִיתֶם, שֶׁאֵין פּוּרְעָנוּת בָּא לָעוֹלָם אֶלָּא בִּשְׁבִיל עַמֵּי הָאָרֶץ.

The half of the population that remained in the city then **came before Rabbi** Yehuda HaNasi, and **said to him: The Sages should contribute** along **with us.** Rabbi Yehuda HaNasi **said to them: No,** the Sages are exempt. They said to him: Then **we** too **will run away.** Rabbi Yehuda HaNasi said to them: **Run away** as you please. **They all ran away,** so that only **one launderer was left** in the city. The authorities **imposed** the entire tax **on the launderer. The launderer** then **ran away** as well. **The crown tax** was then **canceled** in its entirety. **Rabbi Yehuda HaNasi said: You see** from this **that suffering comes to the world only due to ignoramuses,** for as soon as they all fled from the city, the crown tax was completely canceled.

NOTES

Ignoramuses should not enter – **עַמֵּי הָאָרֶץ אַל יִכָּנְסוּ:** The Ritva writes that this phrase does not refer to people who were starving, as in such a case it is obvious that all Jews would be provided for. In this case, the rest of the people could have found other ways to sustain themselves, and Rabbi Yehuda HaNasi wished to give an extra gift to the Torah scholars. The Ramah distinguishes between different levels of ignoramuses.

Let everyone enter – **יִכָּנְסוּ הַכֹּל:** This expression teaches that one should provide for poor people without checking their backgrounds (Ramah).

HALAKHA

Woe is me that I have given my bread to an ignoramus – **אוֹי לִי שֶׁנָּתַתִּי פִּתִּי לְעַם הָאָרֶץ:** Rabbi Yehuda HaNasi was distressed that he gave money to a poor ignoramus in a drought year because he might have deprived scholars of charity. When there is enough for everybody, ignoramuses must certainly be sustained as well. Similarly, if a poor person is dying of hunger, he is given food even if it means that a scholar might not receive what he needs (*Shulḥan Arukh*, *Yoreh De'a* 251:11).

LANGUAGE

Crown tax [*kelila*] – **כְּלִילָא:** *Kelila* means a crown. The term signifies a special tax referred to in Latin as aurum coronarium, gold of the crown. At first people of different cities or districts donated crowns of gold to the monarch. Over time this became an obligatory tax in every sense, even though it continued to be called crown tax.

PERSONALITIES

Rabbi Yehuda HaNasi – **רַבִּי יְהוּדָה הַנָּשִׂיא:** The period of *tanna'im* concluded with Rabbi Yehuda HaNasi's redaction of the Mishna. The son of Rabbi Shimon ben Gamliel II, Rabbi Yehuda HaNasi lived from 135 to 220 CE. When he was thirty years old, he was appointed *Nasi*, or prince, but due to his great scholarship the Talmud refers to him simply as Rabbi. Rabbi Yehuda HaNasi spoke Greek, which was the language of the elite in Eretz Yisrael, and he was friendly with the Roman emperor, Antoninus. Rabbi Yehuda HaNasi's knowledge of Hebrew was legendary, to the extent that the Sages learned the meaning of difficult words from servants who worked in his house. According to the Gemara (*Gittin* 59a) Rabbi Yehuda HaNasi combined the qualities of Torah scholarship and prominent leadership more than any other individual since the time of Moses. Rabbi Yehuda HaNasi's lifework was the collection of oral traditions and opinions that he wove into the Mishna, which serves as the basis for the Talmud that is studied to this day. Rabbi Yehuda HaNasi's students were the Sages of the first generation of *amora'im*, including Rabbi Yoḥanan, Rabbi Ḥiyya, bar Kappara, and Rav.

Rabbi Yonatan ben Amram – **רַבִּי יוֹנָתָן בֶּן עַמְרָם:** Rabbi Yonatan ben Amram belonged to the last generation of *tanna'im*. This episode describes his great modesty and refusal to derive any benefit from the honor of the Torah. A different source indicates that he was a student of Rabbi Ḥiyya. The Talmud cites only one *halakha* in the name of Rabbi Yonatan ben Amram.

״וְכַמָּה יְהֵא בָּעִיר וִיהֵא כְּאַנְשֵׁי הָעִיר״ וכו׳. וּרְמִינְהִי: הַחַמֶּרֶת וְהַגַּמֶּלֶת הָעוֹבֶרֶת מִמָּקוֹם לְמָקוֹם, וְלָנָה בְּתוֹכָהּ וְהוּדְּחָה עִמָּהֶן – הֵן בִּסְקִילָה וּמָמוֹנָן פָּלֵט,

§ The mishna teaches: **And how long** must one live **in the city to be** considered **like** one of **the people of the city?** Twelve months. **And we raise a contradiction** from what is taught in a *baraita*: In the case of a **donkey caravan or a camel caravan**[NH] **that was journeying from place to place, and it lodged inside** an idolatrous city, **and its** members **were led astray** along **with** the other residents of the city, and they too engaged in idol worship, **they,** the members of the caravan, are liable to death **by stoning** like ordinary individual idolaters, **and their property escapes** destruction, i.e., they are not treated like the residents of an idolatrous city, who are liable to death by the sword and whose property is destroyed.

וְאִם נִשְׁתַּהוּ שָׁם שְׁלֹשִׁים יוֹם – הֵן בְּסַיִיף וּמָמוֹנָן אָבֵד!

The *baraita* continues: **And if** the caravan members **had remained** in that city for **thirty days, they** are liable to death **by the sword and their property is destroyed,** just as it is for the rest of the residents of the city. This seems to indicate that once an individual has lived in a city for thirty days, he is already considered one of its residents.

אֲמַר רָבָא, לָא קַשְׁיָא: הָא לִבְנֵי מָתָא, הָא לְיָתוּבֵי מָתָא; כִּדְתַנְיָא: הַמּוּדָּר הֲנָאָה מֵאַנְשֵׁי הָעִיר, כָּל שֶׁנִּשְׁתַּהָא שָׁם שְׁנֵים עָשָׂר חֹדֶשׁ – אָסוּר לֵיהָנוֹת מִמֶּנּוּ, פָּחוֹת מִכָּאן – מוּתָּר; מִיּוֹשְׁבֵי הָעִיר, כָּל שֶׁנִּשְׁתַּהָא שָׁם שְׁלֹשִׁים יוֹם – אָסוּר לֵיהָנוֹת מִמֶּנּוּ, פָּחוֹת מִכָּאן – מוּתָּר לֵיהָנוֹת מִמֶּנּוּ.

Rava said: This is **not difficult. This** period, i.e., twelve months, is required in order to be considered one of the **members of the city;** and **that** period, i.e., thirty days, suffices in order to be considered one of the **residents of the city. As it is taught** in a *baraita*: **One who is prohibited by a vow from deriving benefit from the people of** a particular **city**[H] is **prohibited from deriving benefit from anyone who has stayed there** for **twelve months,** but it is permitted for him to derive benefit from anyone who has stayed there for **less** time **than that.** By contrast, if he prohibited himself by way of a vow from deriving benefit **from the residents of a** particular **city,** he is **prohibited from deriving benefit from anyone who has stayed there** for **thirty days,** but **it is permitted for him to derive benefit from** anyone who has stayed there for **less** time **than that.**

וּלְכָל מִילֵּי מִי בָּעֵינַן שְׁנֵים עָשָׂר חֹדֶשׁ? וְהָתַנְיָא: שְׁלֹשִׁים יוֹם – לְתַמְחוּי, שְׁלֹשָׁה חֳדָשִׁים – לְקוּפָּה, שִׁשָּׁה – לִכְסוּת, תִּשְׁעָה – לִקְבוּרָה, שְׁנֵים עָשָׂר – לְפַסֵּי הָעִיר! אֲמַר רַבִּי אַסִּי אֲמַר רַבִּי יוֹחָנָן: כִּי תְּנַן נַמִּי מַתְנִיתִין שְׁנֵים עָשָׂר חֹדֶשׁ – לְפַסֵּי הָעִיר תְּנַן.

The Gemara asks: **And do we require** that one live in a city for **twelve months for all matters? But isn't it taught** in a *baraita*: If one lives in city for **thirty days,** he must contribute **to** the **charity platter**[H] from which food is distributed to the poor. If he lives there for **three months,** he must contribute **to** the charity **box.** If he lives there for **six** months, he must contribute **to** the **clothing** fund. If he lives there for **nine** months, he must contribute **to** the **burial** fund. If he lives there for **twelve** months, he must contribute **to** the **columns of the city** [*lepassei ha'ir*],[L] i.e., for the construction of a security fence. **Rabbi Asi said** that **Rabbi Yoḥanan said: When we learned twelve months in the mishna, we learned** that with regard to contributing **to** the **columns of the city,** money used for protecting and strengthening the city, but not for other matters.

NOTES

A donkey caravan or a camel caravan – הַחַמֶּרֶת וְהַגַּמֶּלֶת: The *halakha* of an idolatrous city is described in Deuteronomy 13:13–19. If all the inhabitants of a city worship idolatry, they are put to death by the sword and their property is destroyed. The Gemara here considers people not included among the city's inhabitants, but who participated in the idol worship. If they are considered inhabitants of the city, they suffer the same fate as the other people of the city, but if not, they are treated as individuals who worshipped idolatry. The latter are liable to the more severe punishment of stoning, but their property is not destroyed. With regard to this matter, the Torah emphasizes "the residents of that city," which teaches that residency is the critical factor.

LANGUAGE

Columns of the city [*passei ha'ir*] – פַּסֵּי הָעִיר: The commentaries explain this term in various ways, each of which presents a certain difficulty. The term *pissin* refers to a specific tax. In the passage in the Gemara, it might signify the municipal taxes a resident would owe only after living in a city for twelve months.

HALAKHA

A donkey caravan or a camel caravan – הַחַמֶּרֶת וְהַגַּמֶּלֶת: Members of a traveling caravan who were led astray and worshipped idolatry along with the other residents of a city are considered residents of an idolatrous city if they had resided in the city for thirty days before the inhabitants were enticed into idol worship. If they had not been there that long, they are considered individual idolaters. If the majority of the city had been led astray, but the members of the caravan who had been there for thirty days had not been, they join the minority to form a majority and save the city (Rambam *Sefer HaMadda*, *Hilkhot Avoda Zara* 4:9, and *Kesef Mishne* and *Leḥem Mishne* there).

One who is prohibited by a vow from deriving benefit from the people of a city – הַמּוּדָּר הֲנָאָה מֵאַנְשֵׁי הָעִיר: If one is prohibited by a vow from deriving benefit from the people of a city, it is prohibited for him to derive benefit from anybody who has lived there for twelve months. If he is prohibited by a vow from deriving benefit from the residents, rather than people, of a city, he may not derive benefit from anybody who had been there for thirty days. If he prohibited himself from deriving benefit from people who live in the city, he may not benefit from somebody who is living there temporarily with his family even less than thirty days (Rambam *Sefer Hafla'a*, *Hilkhot Nedarim* 9:17; *Shulḥan Arukh*, *Yoreh De'a* 217:32, and in the comment of Rema).

Thirty days to the charity platter – שְׁלֹשִׁים יוֹם לְתַמְחוּי: Whoever lives in a city for thirty days is obligated to contribute to the communal charity box. If he lives there for three months, he must also contribute to the charity platter. If he lives there for six months, he must donate money to the clothing fund. If he lives there for nine months, he must provide funds for burying the poor. After twelve months, he is considered a resident of the town with regard to all taxes and obligations. This is in accordance with the version of the Gemara found before the Rif and the Rambam. These *halakhot* apply to an individual who upon his arrival in the city announces that he does not intend to stay there. But if he does intend to settle there, he is obligated at once. The Rema, citing the Maharik, writes that residents of a new city are obligated at once. He adds that according to some (*Smak*), in our times thirty days marks the start of all obligations to a city (Rambam *Sefer Zera'im*, *Hilkhot Mattenot Aniyyim* 9:12; *Shulḥan Arukh*, *Yoreh De'a* 256:5).

וְאָמַר רַבִּי אַסִּי אָמַר רַבִּי יוֹחָנָן: הַכֹּל לְפַסֵּי הָעִיר וַאֲפִילּוּ מִיַּתְמֵי, אֲבָל רַבָּנַן לָא, דְּרַבָּנַן לָא צְרִיכִי נְטִירוּתָא. אָמַר רַב פַּפָּא: לְשׁוּרָא וּלְפָרָשָׁה וּלְטַרְזִינָא – אֲפִילּוּ מִיַּתְמֵי, אֲבָל רַבָּנַן לָא צְרִיכִי נְטִירוּתָא. כְּלָלָא דְּמִילְּתָא: כֹּל מִילְּתָא דְּאִית לְהוּ הֲנָאָה מִינֵּיהּ – אֲפִילּוּ מִיַּתְמֵי.

And Rabbi Asi says that **Rabbi Yoḥanan says: All** are required to contribute **to the columns of the city, and** money is collected for that purpose **even from orphans. But the Sages are not** required to contribute, **since the Sages do not need protection. Rav Pappa said:** Money is collected **even from orphans for the** city **wall, for the** city **horseman, and for the guard** [*uletarzina*][L] of the city armory, **but the Sages do not require protection. The principle of the matter** is: Money is collected **even from orphans** for **anything from which they** derive **benefit.**

רַבָּה רְמָא צְדָקָה אַיַּתְמֵי דְּבֵי בַּר מַרְיוֹן, אָמַר לֵיהּ אַבַּיֵי, וְהָתָנֵי רַב שְׁמוּאֵל בַּר יְהוּדָה: אֵין פּוֹסְקִין צְדָקָה עַל הַיְּתוֹמִים אֲפִילּוּ לְפִדְיוֹן שְׁבוּיִם! אָמַר לֵיהּ: אֲנָא לְאַחְשׁוּבִינְהוּ קָא עֲבֵידְנָא.

It is reported that **Rabba imposed** a contribution to a certain **charity on the orphans of the house of bar Maryon. Abaye said to him: But didn't Rav Shmuel bar Yehuda teach: One does not impose a charity** obligation **on orphans**[H] **even for** the sake of **redeeming captives,** since they are minors and are not obligated in the mitzvot? Rabba **said to him: I did this to elevate them** in standing, i.e., so that people should honor them as generous benefactors; not in order that the poor should benefit.

אִיפְרָא הוּרְמִיז, אִימֵּיהּ דִּשְׁבוֹר מַלְכָּא, שְׁדַרָה אַרְנְקָא דְּדִינָרֵי לְקַמֵּיהּ דְּרַב יוֹסֵף, אָמְרָה: לֶיהֱוֵי לְמִצְוָה רַבָּה. יָתֵיב רַב יוֹסֵף וְקָא מְעַיֵּין בַּהּ: מַאי מִצְוָה רַבָּה? אָמַר לֵיהּ אַבַּיֵי, מִדְּתָנֵי רַב שְׁמוּאֵל בַּר יְהוּדָה: אֵין פּוֹסְקִין צְדָקָה עַל הַיְּתוֹמִים אֲפִילּוּ לְפִדְיוֹן שְׁבוּיִם, שְׁמַע מִינָּהּ

Incidental to this story, the Gemara relates that **Ifera Hurmiz,**[P] **the mother of King Shapur,** king of Persia, **sent a purse** [*arneka*][L] **full of dinars to Rav Yosef. She said** to him: **Let** the money be used **for a great mitzva. Rav Yosef sat and considered** the question: **What** did Ifera Hurmiz mean when she attached a condition to the gift, saying that it should be used for a **great mitzva? Abaye said to him: From what Rav Shmuel bar Yehuda taught,** that one **does not impose a charity** obligation **on orphans even for** the sake of **redeeming captives, learn from this**

LANGUAGE

Guard [*tarzina*] – טַרְזִינָא: This has been explained as a contraction of *neter zina*, meaning he who guards the weapons of a city.

Purse [*arneka*] – אַרְנְקָא: From the Greek ἀρνακίς, *arnakis*, which is a box or wallet for coins.

HALAKHA

One does not impose a charity obligation on orphans – אֵין פּוֹסְקִים צְדָקָה עַל הַיְּתוֹמִים: The court does not impose the obligation of charity on minor orphans even for the important mitzva of redeeming captives and even if the orphans are wealthy. But if the orphans do not have a good reputation and the judge wishes to improve their image, he may impose the obligation of charity upon them. This only applies if their steward does not object (Rambam *Sefer Zera'im, Hilkhot Mattenot Aniyyim* 7:12; *Shulḥan Arukh, Yoreh De'a* 248:3).

PERSONALITIES

Ifera Hurmiz – אִיפְרָא הוּרְמִיז: Ifera Hurmiz was the mother of Shapur II, king of Persia, who ruled between 309 and 379 CE. Because Shapur was crowned at birth, his mother had great influence over him for many years. Ifera Hurmiz is mentioned several times in the Talmud as an admirer of Judaism and the Sages of Israel.

Perek **I**
Daf **8** Amud **b**

פִּדְיוֹן שְׁבוּיִם מִצְוָה רַבָּה הִיא.

that **redeeming captives is a great mitzva.**[H]

אָמַר לֵיהּ רָבָא לְרַבָּה בַּר מָרִי: מְנָא הָא מִילְּתָא דְּאָמוּר רַבָּנַן דְּפִדְיוֹן שְׁבוּיִם מִצְוָה רַבָּה הִיא? אָמַר לֵיהּ, דִּכְתִיב: "וְהָיָה כִּי יֹאמְרוּ אֵלֶיךָ אָנָה נֵצֵא וְאָמַרְתָּ אֲלֵיהֶם כֹּה אָמַר ה' אֲשֶׁר לַמָּוֶת לַמָּוֶת וַאֲשֶׁר לַחֶרֶב לַחֶרֶב וַאֲשֶׁר לָרָעָב לָרָעָב וַאֲשֶׁר לַשְּׁבִי לַשֶּׁבִי", וְאָמַר רַבִּי יוֹחָנָן: כָּל הַמְאוּחָר בְּפָסוּק זֶה קָשֶׁה מֵחֲבֵירוֹ.

Rava said to Rabba bar Mari: Concerning **this matter that the Sages stated, that redeeming captives is a great mitzva, from where is** it derived? Rabba bar Mari **said to him: As it is written: "And it shall come to pass, when they say to you: To where shall we depart? Then you shall tell them: So says the Lord: Such as are for death, to death; and such as are for the sword, to the sword; and such as are for famine, to famine; and such as are for captivity, to captivity"** (Jeremiah 15:2). **And Rabbi Yoḥanan says: Whichever** punishment **is written later in this verse is more severe than the one** before it.

חֶרֶב קָשֶׁה מִמָּוֶת – אִי בָּעֵית אֵימָא קְרָא, וְאִי בָּעֵית אֵימָא סְבָרָא; אִי בָּעֵית אֵימָא סְבָרָא: הַאי קָא מִינַּוֵּול וְהַאי לָא קָא מִינַּוֵּול; וְאִיבָּעֵית אֵימָא קְרָא: "יָקָר בְּעֵינֵי ה' הַמָּוְתָה לַחֲסִידָיו".

Rabbi Yoḥanan explains: **The sword is worse than death. If you wish, say** that this is learned from **a verse; if you wish, say** instead that it is derived by way of **logical reasoning. If you wish, say** that this is derived by way of **logical reasoning: This** punishment, i.e., death by sword, **mutilates** the body, **but that** punishment, i.e., natural death, **does not mutilate** it. **And if you wish, say** that the fact that the sword is worse than death is learned from **a verse: "Precious in the sight of the Lord**[N] **is the death of His pious ones"** (Psalms 116:15).

רָעָב קָשֶׁה מֵחֶרֶב – אִיבָּעֵית אֵימָא סְבָרָא: הַאי קָא מִצְטַעֵר וְהַאי לָא קָא מִצְטַעֵר; אִיבָּעֵית אֵימָא קְרָא: "טוֹבִים הָיוּ חַלְלֵי חֶרֶב מֵחַלְלֵי רָעָב". שְׁבִי [קָשֶׁה מִכּוּלָּם], דְּכוּלְּהוּ אִיתְנְהוּ בֵּיהּ.

Famine is worse than the sword. If you wish, say that this is derived by way of **logical reasoning: This one,** who dies of famine, **suffers** greatly before departing from this world, **but that one,** who dies by the sword, **does not suffer. If you wish, say** instead that the fact that famine is worse than the sword is learned from **a verse: "More fortunate were the victims of the sword than the victims of famine"** (Lamentations 4:9). **And captivity is worse than all of them, as it includes all of them,** i.e., famine, the sword, and death.

HALAKHA

Redeeming captives is a great mitzva – פִּדְיוֹן שְׁבוּיִים מִצְוָה רַבָּה הִיא: Redeeming captives is a great mitzva, which takes precedence over sustaining the poor and providing them with clothing. Therefore, if the community has collected money for any particular cause, they may use that money to redeem captives (Rambam *Sefer Zera'im, Hilkhot Mattenot Aniyyim* 8:10; *Shulḥan Arukh, Yoreh De'a* 252:1).

NOTES

Precious in the sight of the Lord – יָקָר בְּעֵינֵי ה': In other words, God wants the righteous to die in an honorable fashion, rather than suffer a disgraceful death by the sword or famine (Ritva).

תָּנוּ רַבָּנַן: קוּפָּה שֶׁל צְדָקָה נִגְבֵּית בִּשְׁנַיִם וּמִתְחַלֶּקֶת בִּשְׁלֹשָׁה, נִגְבֵּית בִּשְׁנַיִם – שֶׁאֵין עוֹשִׂים שְׂרָרוּת עַל הַצִּבּוּר פָּחוֹת מִשְּׁנַיִם, וּמִתְחַלֶּקֶת בִּשְׁלֹשָׁה – כְּדִינֵי מָמוֹנוֹת;

§ In connection with the previous discussion concerning charity distribution, the Gemara cites a *baraita* in which **the Sages taught:** Money for **the charity fund**[H] **is collected by two** people **and distributed by three** people. **It is collected by two** people **because one does not appoint an authority over the community** composed **of fewer than two** people. **And it is distributed by three people, like** the number of judges needed in cases of **monetary law,**[N] since the distributors determine who receives money and who does not, as well as how much each person receives.

תַּמְחוּי נִגְבֵּית בִּשְׁלֹשָׁה וּמִתְחַלֶּקֶת בִּשְׁלֹשָׁה, שֶׁגְּבוּיָיהּ וְחִלּוּקָהּ שָׁוִים; תַּמְחוּי – בְּכָל יוֹם, קוּפָּה – מֵעֶרֶב שַׁבָּת לְעֶרֶב שַׁבָּת,

Food for **the charity platter**[H] **is collected by three** people **and distributed by three** people **because its collection and its distribution** take place on **the same** day.[N] Food for **the charity platter** is collected and distributed **every day,** and therefore a third individual must participate in the collection so that he will be available to take part in the distribution without delay; whereas the money of **the charity fund** is distributed only once a week, on **each Shabbat eve.**

תַּמְחוּי – לַעֲנִיֵּי עוֹלָם, קוּפָּה – לַעֲנִיֵּי הָעִיר; וְרַשָּׁאִים בְּנֵי הָעִיר לַעֲשׂוֹת קוּפָּה תַּמְחוּי וְתַמְחוּי קוּפָּה, וּלְשַׁנּוֹתָהּ לְכָל מַה שֶּׁיִּרְצוּ;

There are additional differences between these two types of charity operations: The food from **the charity platter** is distributed **to the poor of the world,** meaning, to any poor individual arriving in the city; the money of **the charity fund** is allocated exclusively **to the poor of the city. But it is permitted for the residents of the city to use** money that has been collected for **the charity fund** to purchase food for **the charity platter** to feed the poor; **and** similarly they may use food that had been collected for **the charity platter** for **the charity fund.** In general, it is permitted for them **to change** the purpose toward which charity will be used **to whatever they want,**[N] in accordance with the needs of the community.

וְרַשָּׁאִין בְּנֵי הָעִיר לְהַתְנוֹת עַל הַמִּדּוֹת וְעַל הַשְּׁעָרִים, וְעַל שְׂכַר פּוֹעֲלִים, וּלְהַסִּיעַ עַל קִיצָתָן.

Similarly, **it is permitted for the residents of the city to set the measures**[H] used in that city, **the prices** set for products sold there, **and the wages** paid **to its workers, and to fine** people **for violating their specifications,**[N] in order to enforce observance of these *halakhot*. This marks the end of the *baraita*, the details of which the Gemara proceeds to analyze.

אָמַר מָר: אֵין עוֹשִׂין שְׂרָרוּת עַל הַצִּבּוּר פָּחוֹת מִשְּׁנַיִם. מְנָא הָנֵי מִילֵּי? אָמַר רַב נַחְמָן, אָמַר קְרָא: ״וְהֵם יִקְחוּ אֶת הַזָּהָב״ וגו׳.

The Master said in the *baraita*: **One does not appoint an authority over the community** composed **of fewer than two** people. The Gemara asks: **From where are these matters** derived? **Rav Naḥman says** that this is derived from a verse referring to those engaged in building the Tabernacle and weaving the priestly vestments, who received the community's donations. **The verse states: "And they shall take the gold,** and the sky-blue wool, and the purple wool" (Exodus 28:5). The plural "they" indicates that the collection must be performed by two people.

HALAKHA

Charity fund – **קוּפָּה:** Money for the charity fund is collected by two people and distributed by three people. Food for the charity platter is collected by three people and distributed by three people (Rambam *Sefer Zera'im, Hilkhot Mattenot Aniyyim* 9:5; *Shulḥan Arukh, Yoreh De'a* 256:3).

Charity platter – **תַּמְחוּי:** Food for the charity platter is collected every day and distributed every day, while money for the charity fund is collected only once a week, on Shabbat eve. Food is distributed to all people, but money from the charity fund is given only to the poor of that city. It is permitted for the residents of a city to change the purpose toward which the charity will be used to whatever they want, in accordance with the needs of the community. This is so even if no condition had been stipulated from the outset to allow the change (Rambam *Sefer Zera'im, Hilkhot Mattenot Aniyyim* 9:6–7; *Shulḥan Arukh, Yoreh De'a* 256:4).

To set the measures – **לְהַתְנוֹת עַל הַמִּדּוֹת:** It is permitted for the residents of a city to set the measures and prices of all commodities, even food staples. It is permitted for the craftsmen in a city to establish regulations with regard to their work. Similarly, a city can institute fines for those who do not follow the municipal ordinances. If only a small number of artisans wish to establish regulations, they are ignored (Rambam *Sefer Kinyan, Hilkhot Mekhira* 14:9–10; *Shulḥan Arukh, Ḥoshen Mishpat* 231:27–28, and in the comment of Rema).

NOTES

And it is distributed by three people like in cases of monetary law – **וּמִתְחַלֶּקֶת בִּשְׁלֹשָׁה כְּדִינֵי מָמוֹנוֹת:** Three people are required for the distribution of charity because the distributors must examine each case and determine how much money the recipient is entitled to receive (Rashi). But three people are not required for the collection of charity because the amount that each person must give is fixed (Rabbeinu Gershom; Rabbeinu Ḥananel; *Tosafot*).

Its collection and its distribution on the same day – **שֶׁגְּבוּיָיהּ וְחִלּוּקָהּ שָׁוִים:** Rashi explains that both the collection and the distribution are performed on the same day, as is stated later in the *baraita*, as once food is collected it cannot be kept until Friday. And since the food is distributed every day, it is difficult to find a third person to participate in that distribution of the food platter. Some commentaries understand that there was no fixed amount collected for the charity platter, just as there was no fixed amount distributed from it, and therefore three people were required for the collection to determine how much each person should contribute (Rabbeinu Gershom; Rif).

To change to whatever they want – **וּלְשַׁנּוֹתָהּ לְכָל מַה שֶּׁיִּרְצוּ:** The early commentaries disagree about this point. Some explain that the charity collectors can change as they please the purpose toward which the charity will be used, as long as it remains as charity for the poor. They have the discretion to use the funds for any pressing needs of the poor (Rabbeinu Ḥananel; Ri Migash; Ramah). The Ramban and Rabbeinu Yona maintain that money collected for the poor can serve as emergency funds for the community for any communal need, as long as that money is replaced. *Tosafot* seem to say that the money does not even need to be replaced.

To fine [*lehassia*] people for violating their specifications – **וּלְהַסִּיעַ עַל קִיצָתָן:** While everyone agrees that the residents of a city can force its members to abide by the principles that they created using any means at their disposal, there is a dispute with regard to the meaning of this phrase. Rashi says it means that somebody can be fined for violating what has been fixed and established. The *Arukh* writes that *lehassia* means that principles can be altered occasionally. The Ri Migash and Ramah explain that the term is connected to assistance, meaning that they can support their enactments by force.

שְׂרָרוּת הוּא דְּלָא עָבְדִי, הָא הֵימוּנֵי מְהֵימַן; מְסַיַּיע לֵיהּ לְרַבִּי חֲנִינָא, דְּאָמַר רַבִּי חֲנִינָא: מַעֲשֶׂה וּמִינָּה רַבִּי שְׁנֵי אַחִין עַל הַקּוּפָּה.

The Gemara comments: The *baraita* indicates that **authority may not be exercised** by less than two people, **but** even a single individual **is trusted**[H] to be a treasurer. That is, money for the charity fund is collected by two people, not because a single individual is not trusted not to misappropriate the money, but rather because a single individual should not be given authority over the community. **This supports** the opinion **of Rabbi Ḥanina, as Rabbi Ḥanina says: There was an incident where Rabbi** Yehuda HaNasi **appointed two brothers to** administer **the charity fund.** Even though the brothers were relatives who are not trusted to testify against each other, Rabbi Yehuda HaNasi was not concerned and he appointed them.

מַאי שְׂרָרוּתָא? דְּאָמַר רַב נַחְמָן אָמַר רַבָּה בַּר אֲבוּהּ: לְפִי שֶׁמְּמַשְׁכְּנִין עַל הַצְּדָקָה וַאֲפִילּוּ בְּעֶרֶב שַׁבָּת. אִינִי? וְהָא כְּתִיב: "וּפָקַדְתִּי עַל כׇּל לֹחֲצָיו", וְאָמַר רַבִּי יִצְחָק בַּר שְׁמוּאֵל בַּר מָרְתָא מִשְּׁמֵיהּ דְּרַב: וַאֲפִילּוּ עַל גַּבָּאֵי צְדָקָה!

The Gemara asks: **What authority** is associated with collecting charity? The Gemara answers: **As Rav Naḥman says** that **Rabba bar Avuh says: Because they can seize collateral for the charity;**[H] i.e., they can collect charity by force, **and even on Shabbat eve,** when people are busy and might claim that they have no time or money. The Gemara objects: **Is that so? But isn't it written: "I will punish all that oppress them"** (Jeremiah 30:20),[H] **and Rabbi Yitzḥak bar Shmuel bar Marta says in the name of Rav: And** punishment will be meted out **even to charity collectors?** If charity collectors are permitted to force people to contribute charity, why are they counted among Israel's oppressors?

לָא קַשְׁיָא: הָא דַּאֲמִיד, הָא דְּלָא אֲמִיד. כִּי הָא דְּרָבָא אַכְפְּיֵהּ לְרַב נָתָן בַּר אַמִי, וְשָׁקֵיל מִינֵּיהּ אַרְבַּע מְאָה זוּזֵי לִצְדָקָה.

The Gemara answers: This is **not difficult. This,** Rabbi Naḥman's statement, applies **when** the contributor is **rich,** in which case the collectors may seize money from him even by force. **That,** Rabbi Yitzḥak's statement, applies **when** he is **not rich,** in which case the collectors who take money from him by force are termed oppressors of Israel. **This** right to force contributions from the rich **is like** what occurred in the incident in which **Rava compelled Rav Natan bar Ami and took four hundred dinars**[B] **from him for charity.**

"וְהַמַּשְׂכִּלִים יַזְהִרוּ כְּזֹהַר הָרָקִיעַ" וגו'. "הַמַּשְׂכִּלִים יַזְהִרוּ כְּזֹהַר הָרָקִיעַ" – זֶה דַּיָּין שֶׁדָּן דִּין אֱמֶת לַאֲמִתּוֹ, "וּמַצְדִּיקֵי הָרַבִּים כַּכּוֹכָבִים לְעוֹלָם וָעֶד" – אֵלּוּ גַּבָּאֵי צְדָקָה.

Having raised the issue of charity collection, the Gemara cites various rabbinic expositions with regard to the matter. The verse states: **"And they who are wise shall shine like the brightness of the firmament;** and they who turn many to righteousness like the stars for ever and ever" (Daniel 12:3). **"And they who are wise shall shine like the brightness of the firmament"; this is a judge who judges an absolutely true judgment,** as his wisdom and understanding lead him to a correct judgment. **"And they who turn many to righteousness**[H] **like the stars for ever and ever"; these are the charity collectors,** who facilitate the giving of charity.

בְּמַתְנִיתָא תָּנָא: "וְהַמַּשְׂכִּלִים יַזְהִרוּ כְּזֹהַר הָרָקִיעַ" – זֶה דַּיָּין שֶׁדָּן דִּין אֱמֶת לַאֲמִתּוֹ וְגַבָּאֵי צְדָקָה, "וּמַצְדִּיקֵי הָרַבִּים כַּכּוֹכָבִים לְעוֹלָם וָעֶד" – אֵלּוּ מְלַמְּדֵי תִּינוֹקוֹת. כְּגוֹן מַאן? אָמַר רַב: כְּגוֹן רַב שְׁמוּאֵל בַּר שִׁילַת. דְּרַב אַשְׁכְּחֵיהּ לְרַב שְׁמוּאֵל בַּר שִׁילַת דַּהֲוָה קָאֵי בְּגִינְּתָא, אֲמַר לֵיהּ: שַׁבְקְתֵּיהּ לְהֵימָנוּתָךְ? אֲמַר לֵיהּ: הָא תְּלֵיסַר שְׁנִין דְּלָא חַזְיָא לִי, וְהַשְׁתָּא נָמֵי דַּעְתַּאי עִלָּוַיְהוּ.

It was taught in a *baraita*: "And they who are wise shall shine like the brightness of the firmament"; this is a judge who judges an absolutely true judgment and also charity collectors.[N] **"And they who turn many to righteousness like the stars for ever and ever"; these are schoolteachers.** The Gemara asks: **Like whom?** Certainly not every schoolteacher is worthy of such accolades. **Rav said: For example, Rav Shmuel bar Sheilat.**[P] **As** it is told that **Rav** once **found Rav Shmuel bar Sheilat standing in a garden.** Rav **said to him: Have you abandoned your trust** and neglected your students? Rav Shmuel bar Sheilat **said to him: It has been thirteen years** now **that I have not seen** my garden, **and even now my thoughts are on** the children.

HALAKHA

But he is trusted – **הָא הֵימוּנֵי מְהֵימַן**: Even though authority may not be exercised by fewer than two people, this is not due to a lack of trust of one person. Therefore, after the money is collected a single individual may be appointed to serve as treasurer. Similarly, two brothers may be appointed to administer the charity fund (Rambam *Sefer Zera'im, Hilkhot Mattenot Aniyyim* 9:5; *Shulḥan Arukh, Yoreh De'a* 256:3).

They can seize collateral for the charity – **מְמַשְׁכְּנִין עַל הַצְּדָקָה**: The residents of a city can compel people to donate money for charity in accordance with their means. The residents can seize their property and impose physical punishment. They can seize collateral at any time, including on Shabbat eve (Rambam *Sefer Zera'im, Hilkhot Mattenot Aniyyim* 7:10; *Shulḥan Arukh, Yoreh De'a* 248:2).

I will punish all that oppress them – **וּפָקַדְתִּי עַל כׇּל לוֹחֲצָיו**: It is prohibited to demand charity from a generous person who gives more than he can afford, or from one who causes himself difficulty and gives charity in order to avoid embarrassment. Charity collectors who make such demands will suffer punishment in the future (Rambam *Sefer Zera'im, Hilkhot Mattenot Aniyyim* 7:11; *Shulḥan Arukh, Yoreh De'a* 248:7).

And they who turn many to righteousness – **וּמַצְדִּיקֵי הָרַבִּים**: One who causes others to donate charity receives a greater reward than the one who actually gives the charity (Rambam *Sefer Zera'im, Hilkhot Mattenot Aniyyim* 10:6).

BACKGROUND

Four hundred dinars – **אַרְבַּע מְאָה זוּזֵי**: The easiest way to appreciate the value of this sum is by quantifying its buying power: Four hundred dinars was approximately four months' salary.

NOTES

They who are wise…and charity collectors – **מַשְׂכִּילִים...וְגַבָּאֵי צְדָקָה**: Charity collectors must be wise so that they can determine what the poor person needs and how to supply it (Rashi).

PERSONALITIES

Rav Shmuel bar Sheilat – **רַב שְׁמוּאֵל בַּר שִׁילַת**: Rav Shmuel bar Sheilat was an *amora* of the second generation in Babylonia. He was a teacher of children who was greatly respected by Rav for his teaching methods. Rav also advised him on how to handle children. Rav Shmuel bar Sheilat was apparently wealthy despite the fact that he involved himself only in education and not in business. It seems that he was also a preacher in the city of Sura, and it is possible that he eulogized Rav after his death. The few statements cited in his name indicate that he was a leading disciple of Rav even though he also quotes statements of Rav's students. Rav Shmuel bar Sheilat's son, Rav Yehuda, was an important Sage of the next generation.

LANGUAGE

They exchange [*poretin*] – פּוֹרְטִין: This term is used in mishnaic Hebrew in opposite senses: Both for exchanging large coins for smaller ones, and for exchanging small coins for larger ones.

וְרַבָּנַן מַאי? אֲמַר רָבִינָא: ״וְאֹהֲבָיו כְּצֵאת הַשֶּׁמֶשׁ בִּגְבֻרָתוֹ״.

In light of the praises heaped upon judges, tax collectors, and schoolteachers, the Gemara asks: **And what** was said about **the Sages? Ravina said** that about them it is stated: **"But let them that love Him be as the sun when it comes out in its might"** (Judges 5:31).

תָּנוּ רַבָּנַן: גַּבָּאֵי צְדָקָה אֵינָן רַשָּׁאִין לִפְרוֹשׁ זֶה מִזֶּה, אֲבָל פּוֹרֵשׁ זֶה לַשַּׁעַר וְזֶה לֶחָנוּת; מָצָא מָעוֹת בַּשּׁוּק – לֹא יִתְּנֵם בְּתוֹךְ כִּיסוֹ, אֶלָּא נוֹתְנָן לְתוֹךְ אַרְנָקִי שֶׁל צְדָקָה, וְלִכְשֶׁיָּבֹא לְבֵיתוֹ יִטְּלֵם; כַּיּוֹצֵא בּוֹ, הָיָה נוֹשֶׁה בַּחֲבֵירוֹ מָנֶה וּפְרָעוֹ בַּשּׁוּק – לֹא יִתְּנֶנּוּ לְתוֹךְ כִּיסוֹ, אֶלָּא נוֹתְנָן לְתוֹךְ אַרְנָקִי שֶׁל צְדָקָה, וְלִכְשֶׁיָּבֹא לְבֵיתוֹ יִטְּלֵם.

The Gemara resumes its discussion of the *halakhot* of charity collection: **The Sages taught** in a *baraita*: **Charity collectors may not separate from each other,**[H] each one collecting in a different place; **but** in a place where the two can see each other, one collector **may separate** from the other, e.g., **this** one going **to the gate** of a house **and that** one going **to a store.** If a charity collector **found coins in the market,**[H] **he may not put them into his own pocket, but** rather **he must put them into the charity purse, and** then later **when he comes home, he may take them** from there. This is necessary so that people should not suspect him of taking charity money for himself. **Similarly,** if the charity collector **was owed one hundred dinars by another, and** the latter **repaid** his debt **in the market,** the collector **may not put** the money he received **into his own pocket, but** rather **he must put it into the charity purse, and** then later **when he comes home, he may take it.**

תָּנוּ רַבָּנַן: גַּבָּאֵי צְדָקָה שֶׁאֵין לָהֶם עֲנִיִּים לְחַלֵּק – פּוֹרְטִין לַאֲחֵרִים, וְאֵין פּוֹרְטִין לְעַצְמָן; גַּבָּאֵי תַּמְחוּי שֶׁאֵין לָהֶם עֲנִיִּים לְחַלֵּק – מוֹכְרִין לַאֲחֵרִים, וְאֵין מוֹכְרִין לְעַצְמָן; מָעוֹת שֶׁל צְדָקָה אֵין מוֹנִין אוֹתָן שְׁתַּיִם, אֶלָּא אַחַת אַחַת.

The Sages taught in a *baraita*: **Charity collectors who have no poor people to** whom they can **distribute** the money, **may exchange** [***poretin***][L] the money, i.e., exchange the copper coins, which tend to rust, for silver dinars, **with other** people,[H] **but they should not change it** by **themselves,** i.e., with their own coins, to avoid any suspicion of wrongdoing. Likewise, **collectors** of food **for the charity platter who do not have poor people** to whom **to distribute** the food **may sell** the food **to others, but they should not sell it to themselves,** for a similar reason. **Coins of charity are not counted two** by two,[H] **but rather one by one,** to avoid errors in tallying.

אֲמַר אַבַּיֵי: מֵרֵישׁ לָא הֲוָה יָתֵיב מָר אַצִּיפֵּי דְּבֵי כְנִישְׁתָּא, כֵּיוָן דִּשְׁמָעָהּ לְהָא דְּתַנְיָא: וּלְשַׁנּוֹתָהּ לְכָל מַה שֶּׁיִּרְצוּ, הֲוָה יָתֵיב. אֲמַר אַבַּיֵי: מֵרֵישׁ הֲוָה עָבֵיד מָר תְּרֵי כִּיסֵי, חַד לַעֲנִיֵּי דְּעָלְמָא וְחַד לַעֲנִיֵּי דְּמָתָא, כֵּיוָן דִּשְׁמָעָהּ לְהָא דַּאֲמַר לֵיהּ שְׁמוּאֵל לְרַב תַּחֲלִיפָא בַּר אַבְדִּימִי: עֲבֵיד חַד כִּיסָא

Abaye said: At first, my **Master,** Rabba, **would not sit on the mats in the synagogue**[N] because they had been purchased with charity funds. **Once he heard that which is taught** in a *baraita*, that it is permitted for the residents of a city **to change** the purpose toward which charity will be used **to whatever they want, he did sit** on them. **Abaye said: At first,** my **Master,** Rabba, **would make two purses, one for the poor of** the rest of **the world, and one for the poor of his city. Once he heard what Shmuel said to Rav Taḥalifa bar Avdimi: Make** only **one purse,**

HALAKHA

Charity collectors may not separate from each other – גַּבָּאֵי צְדָקָה אֵינָן רַשָּׁאִין לִפְרוֹשׁ: Charity collectors may not separate from each other while they are collecting funds unless they can still see each other. Consequently, one person may go to the gate of a courtyard while the other goes to an adjacent store. *Pitḥei Teshuva*, citing *Beit Ya'akov*, states that they may separate if the amount they are collecting is small (Rambam *Sefer Zera'im, Hilkhot Mattenot Aniyyim* 9:8; *Shulḥan Arukh, Yoreh De'a* 257:1).

If he found coins in the market – מָצָא מָעוֹת בַּשּׁוּק: If a charity collector finds coins in the market or if somebody repays a debt to the charity collector in the market, the charity collector must not put the money into his own pocket, so that he not place himself under suspicion. Instead, he must put the money into his charity purse and take back the sum in question only after he gets home (Rambam *Sefer Zera'im, Hilkhot Mattenot Aniyyim* 9:9; *Shulḥan Arukh, Yoreh De'a* 257:1).

They may change the money with other people – פּוֹרְטִין לַאֲחֵרִים: When a charity collector has no poor people to whom to give the money, he may exchange the coins for dinars, but only with the coins of another person and not with his own coins. Similarly, people who collect food for the charity platter may not buy leftover food for themselves, but must sell it to others (Rambam *Sefer Zera'im, Hilkhot Mattenot Aniyyim* 9:11; *Shulḥan Arukh, Yoreh De'a* 257:2).

Are not counted two by two – אֵין מוֹנִין אוֹתָן שְׁתַּיִם: Charity collectors should not count the coins two by two, but rather one by one, to avoid suspicion (Rambam *Sefer Zera'im, Hilkhot Mattenot Aniyyim* 9:10; *Shulḥan Arukh, Yoreh De'a* 257:1).

NOTES

Mats in the synagogue – אַצִּיפֵּי דְּבֵי כְנִישְׁתָּא: Some early commentaries maintain that the mats were bought with money collected for the charity fund, or specifically for the poor people to sleep on. Once Rabba heard that it was permitted for him to exchange charity funds for communal needs, he was prepared to sit on them (Rabbeinu Gershom; Rashi). Others write that these mats were provided for prayer, based on the *baraita* that permits exchanges. Rabba expounds that since the mats were given for communal needs, one is not obligated to be particular about which requirements are satisfied. Consequently, even though they were designated for prayer, one can still sit or learn on them (Rabbeinu Yona, citing Ri Migash; see Meiri).

וְאַתְנֵי עֲלַהּ, אִיהוּ נַמִּי עֲבַד חַד כִּיסָא וְאַתְנֵי עֲלַהּ. רַב אַשִׁי אֲמַר: אֲנָא אַתְנוּיֵי נַמִּי לָא צְרִיכְנָא, דְּכׇל דְּקָא אָתֵי אַדַּעְתָּא דִּידִי אָתֵי, וּלְמַאן דְּבָעֵינָא יָהֵיבְנָא לֵיהּ.

and stipulate about it with the people of your city that the money collected will be given to whomever needs it, **he too made** only **one purse and stipulated** with the people of his city **about it. Rav Ashi said: I do not even need to make a stipulation, as whoever comes** to donate to this charity fund **comes relying on my discretion and** understanding that **I will give** the funds **to whomever I want.**

הָנְהוּ בֵּי תְּרֵי טַבָּחֵי דַּעֲבְדִי עִנְיָינָא בַּהֲדֵי הֲדָדֵי, דְּכׇל מַאן דְּעָבֵיד בְּיוֹמָא דְּחַבְרֵיהּ נִקְרְעוּהּ לְמַשְׁכֵּיהּ. אֲזַל חַד מִנַּיְיהוּ עֲבַד בְּיוֹמָא דְּחַבְרֵיהּ, קְרַעוּ לְמַשְׁכֵּיהּ; אֲתוּ לְקַמֵּיהּ דְּרָבָא, חַיְּיבִינְהוּ רָבָא לְשַׁלּוּמֵי.

The Gemara relates: There were **these two butchers who made an agreement**[N] with each other that whichever one of them **worked on the day** assigned **to the other** according to their mutually agreed-upon schedule **would tear up the hide** of the animal that he slaughtered that day. **One of them went and worked on the other's day, and** the other butcher **tore up the hide** of the animal that he slaughtered. **They came before Rava** for judgment, and **Rava obligated him to pay** the butcher who slaughtered that animal.

אֵיתִיבֵיהּ רַב יֵימָר בַּר שְׁלַמְיָא לְרָבָא: וּלְהַסִּיעַ עַל קִיצָתָם! לָא אַהֲדַר לֵיהּ רָבָא. אֲמַר רַב פָּפָּא: שַׁפִּיר עֲבַד דְּלָא אַהֲדַר לֵיהּ מִידֵּי; הָנֵי מִילֵּי הֵיכָא דְּלֵיכָּא אָדָם חָשׁוּב, אֲבָל הֵיכָא דְּאִיכָּא אָדָם חָשׁוּב – לָאו כֹּל כְּמִינַּיְיהוּ דְּמַתְנוּ.

Rav Yeimar bar Shelamya raised an objection to Rava: Isn't it stated among actions that the residents of a city may take: **And to fine** people **for violating their** specifications, i.e., those ordinances that the residents passed? **Rava did not respond to him. Rav Pappa said: He did well that he did not respond to him,** as **this matter** applies only **where there is no important person**[H] in the city, in which case it is permitted for the residents of the city to draw up ordinances on their own. **But where there is an important person,**[N] **it is not** in the residents' **power to make stipulations,** i.e., regulations; rather, they are required to obtain the approval of the city's leading authority to give force to their regulations.

תָּנוּ רַבָּנַן: אֵין מְחַשְּׁבִין בִּצְדָקָה עִם גַּבָּאֵי צְדָקָה, וְלֹא בְּהֶקְדֵּשׁ עִם הַגִּזְבָּרִין, וְאַף עַל פִּי שֶׁאֵין רְאָיָה לַדָּבָר – זֵכֶר לַדָּבָר, שֶׁנֶּאֱמַר: "וְלֹא יְחַשְּׁבוּ אֶת הָאֲנָשִׁים אֲשֶׁר יִתְּנוּ אֶת הַכֶּסֶף עַל יָדָם לָתֵת לְעֹשֵׂי הַמְּלָאכָה כִּי בֶאֱמֻנָה הֵם עֹשִׂים".

§ **The Sages taught: One does not calculate** sums **with charity collectors**[H] **concerning** the money they collected **for charity,** to verify how much they received and how much they distributed, **nor** does one calculate sums **with the** Temple **treasurers concerning** the property **consecrated** to the Temple. **And even though there is no** explicit **proof of the matter**[N] from the Bible, there is nevertheless **an allusion to the matter, as it is stated: "And they did not reckon with the men into whose hand they delivered the money to pay out to the workmen; for they dealt in good faith"** (II Kings 12:16).

אָמַר רַבִּי אֶלְעָזָר: אַף עַל פִּי שֶׁיֵּשׁ לוֹ לְאָדָם גִּזְבָּר נֶאֱמָן בְּתוֹךְ בֵּיתוֹ – יָצוּר וְיִמְנֶה, שֶׁנֶּאֱמַר: "וַיָּצֻרוּ וַיִּמְנוּ".

Rabbi Elazar says: Even though a person has a trusted treasurer in his house like the aforementioned Temple treasurers, who were fully trusted, **he should** nevertheless **tie up** his money **and count it,**[N] **as it is stated:** "And the king's scribe and the High Priest came up, **and they tied** it in bags **and counted** the money… And they gave the money that was counted into the hands of them that did the work, that had the oversight of the House of the Lord" (II Kings 12:11–12).

NOTES

These two butchers who made an agreement, etc. – הָנְהוּ בֵּי תְּרֵי טַבָּחֵי דַּעֲבְדִי עִנְיָינָא וכו׳: According to the standard version of the text, this agreement was made between two specific butchers. One of the two of them violated the terms of the agreement, whereupon the other tore the hide of the slaughtered animal. Many commentaries note that restrictions on trade can be instituted only by all of the tradesman of a locale (see Ramban). These commentaries would prefer the version of the text presented by the Baḥ, also found in the Rif, which reads: These butchers who made an agreement. According to this version, all of the butchers of the town agreed to these restrictions, and when one of them violated the restrictions, the others tore the hide of the animal he slaughtered.

Where there is an important person – הֵיכָא דְּאִיכָּא אָדָם חָשׁוּב: The Ri Migash and the Ramah write that this term refers specifically to a case where the important personage is both a Torah scholar and a communal leader. If he lacks either of these criteria, the lack of his approval does not nullify the stipulation. The reason for the restriction of the ability of people to make these regulations is that it would be disrespectful to establish regulations without the approval of the local scholar. Additionally, this leader will ensure that the regulations are appropriate (Ritva).

There is no proof of the matter – אֵין רְאָיָה לַדָּבָר: This verse does not provide an absolute proof, because the Temple treasurers referred to were in charge of the complex task of Temple repairs. In such a situation it is difficult to keep track of the accounts (Rashi). *Tosafot* explain that this verse is no proof because the Temple treasurers were thoroughly righteous individuals, which is not necessarily the case with charity collectors.

Tie up and count it – יָצוּר וְיִמְנֶה: Some commentaries maintain that this teaches that although one does not calculate sums with charity collectors or the Temple treasurers concerning the money that they distribute, one does keep track of the amounts that they receive (Ramah).

HALAKHA

Where there is no important person – הֵיכָא דְּלֵיכָּא אָדָם חָשׁוּב: If the craftsmen or the residents of a city pass local ordinances, they have the authority to enforce them. But if they pass these ordinances in a place where there is a local Sage without consulting with that Sage, they cannot force them upon those who did not accept them. The Rema, citing the Ran, writes that if the ordinances do not cause anybody a financial loss, they may be established even without consulting with the Sage (Rambam *Sefer Kinyan, Hilkhot Mekhira* 14:9–11; *Shulḥan Arukh, Ḥoshen Mishpat* 231:27–28).

One does not calculate sums with charity collectors – אֵין מְחַשְּׁבִין בִּצְדָקָה עִם גַּבָּאֵי צְדָקָה: One does not calculate sums with the charity collectors or with the Temple treasurers. The Rema, citing the *Tur*, writes that it is nevertheless appropriate for the charity collectors to provide the community with a financial report. This applies to responsible charity collectors, but if they are irresponsible, even if they were appointed by the community (*Shakh*), or if they were appointed through violence and are suspected of having made inappropriate use of the funds, the community leaders are obligated to calculate sums with them (Rambam *Sefer Zera'im, Hilkhot Mattenot Aniyyim* 9:11; *Shulḥan Arukh, Yoreh De'a* 257:2).

HALAKHA

Charity collectors examine for food – בּוֹדְקִין לִמְזוֹנוֹת: If a poor person declares that he is hungry, he is given food without any examination. But if he asks for clothing, he must first be investigated to make sure he is in fact in need. If he is familiar to the community, he is immediately provided with clothing in accordance with his stature. This is in accordance with the opinion of Rav Yehuda (Rambam *Sefer Zera'im, Hilkhot Mattenot Aniyyim* 7:6; *Shulḥan Arukh, Yoreh De'a* 251:10).

One does not give a poor person…less – אֵין פּוֹחֲתִין לֶעָנִי: A poor person traveling from place to place begging for charity is given at least a loaf of bread worth a *pundeyon* when a *sela* buys four *se'a* of grain. If he stays overnight he is given a bed and a pillow. If he spends Shabbat in the town, he is given food for three meals, including lentils, fish, and vegetables. This is the way an unknown poor person is treated, but if the community is familiar with him he is given provisions in accordance with his stature (Rambam *Sefer Zera'im, Hilkhot Mattenot Aniyyim* 7:8; *Shulḥan Arukh, Yoreh De'a* 250:4).

One is not required to attend to him and give him a large gift – אֵין נִזְקָקִין לוֹ לְמַתָּנָה מְרוּבָּה: If a poor person who goes door to door collecting money requests money from the charity fund, the charity collector is not obligated to give him a large donation from the fund. Rather, he gives him a small donation and does not turn him away empty-handed (Rambam *Sefer Zera'im, Hilkhot Mattenot Aniyyim* 7:7; *Shulḥan Arukh, Yoreh De'a* 250:3).

NOTES

It is written with a *shin* – כְּתִיב פְּרֹשׁ: In the standard versions of the Bible the verse is not written this way. The Ramah apparently omits this sentence from the Gemara. This is cited as one of the instances where the talmudic Sages had a version that differs slightly from the Masoretic text.

Than a loaf worth a *pundeyon* – מִכִּכָּר בְּפוּנְדְּיוֹן: Rashi maintains that this refers to a loaf that weighs a quarter-*kav*, which suffices for two meals.

A pillow [*bei sadya*] – בֵּי סַדְיָא: Rashi explains that *bei sadya* signifies pillow, whereas Rabbeinu Ḥananel writes that the term includes all bedding.

LANGUAGE

***Pundeyon* – פּוּנְדְּיוֹן:** From the Latin dupondium. A *pundeyon* is a coin equal in value to two *issar*.

Pillow [*bei sadya*] – בֵּי סַדְיָא: Possibly related to *isdohi*, the Aramaic translation of the Hebrew *merashotav* (*Targum Onkelos* on Genesis 28:11), generally understood to mean: Under his head.

אָמַר רַב הוּנָא: בּוֹדְקִין לִמְזוֹנוֹת וְאֵין בּוֹדְקִין לִכְסוּת; אִי בָּעֵית אֵימָא קְרָא, וְאִי בָּעֵית אֵימָא סְבָרָא;

Rav Huna says: Charity collectors **examine** the level of poverty of one who asks **for food,**[H] **but they do not examine** the level of poverty of one who asks **for clothing.** If a person comes before the charity collectors in tattered clothes, he is given clothing without any questions being asked. **If you wish, say** that this distinction is derived from **a verse; if you wish, say** instead that it is derived via **logical reasoning.**

אִי בָּעֵית אֵימָא סְבָרָא: הַאי קָא מִבַּזֵּי וְהַאי לָא קָא מִבַּזֵּי; אִי בָּעֵית אֵימָא קְרָא: ״הֲלֹא פָּרֹשׂ לָרָעֵב לַחְמֶךָ״ בְּשִׁי״ן כְּתִיב – פְּרֹשׁ וַהֲדַר הַב לֵיהּ, וְהָתָם כְּתִיב: ״כִּי תִרְאֶה עָרֹם וְכִסִּיתוֹ״, ״כִּי תִרְאֶה״ – לְאַלְתַּר.

If you wish, **say** that this distinction is derived via **logical reasoning: This one** who stands before us in rags **is exposed to contempt, whereas that one** who is hungry **is not exposed to contempt. If you wish, say** instead that this distinction is derived from **a verse,** as it is written: **"Is it not to share [*paros*] your bread with the hungry?"** (Isaiah 58:7). The word *paros* **is written with a *shin*,**[N] alluding to the word *parosh*, meaning **examine** and investigate, **and** only **then** should you **give him. And there** in the same verse **it is written** with regard to clothing: **"When you see the naked, that you cover him,"** indicating that **"when you see"** him you should **immediately** cover him.

וְרַב יְהוּדָה אָמַר: בּוֹדְקִין לִכְסוּת וְאֵין בּוֹדְקִין לִמְזוֹנוֹת; אִי בָּעֵית אֵימָא סְבָרָא, וְאִי בָּעֵית אֵימָא קְרָא;

And Rav Yehuda says just the opposite: Charity collectors **examine** the level of poverty of one who asks **for clothing, but they do not examine** the level of poverty of one who asks **for food.** He too adduces supports for his opinion. **If you wish, say** that this distinction is derived via **logical reasoning; if you wish, say** instead that it is derived from **a verse.**

אִי בָּעֵית אֵימָא סְבָרָא: הַאי קָמְצַעֲרָא לֵיהּ וְהַאי לָא קָמְצַעֲרָא לֵיהּ; אִי בָּעֵית אֵימָא קְרָא: הָכָא כְּתִיב: ״הֲלֹא פָרֹס לָרָעֵב לַחְמֶךָ״ – פְּרוֹס לְאַלְתַּר, וְכִדְקָרֵינַן, וְהָתָם כְּתִיב: ״כִּי תִרְאֶה עָרֹם וְכִסִּיתוֹ״ – כְּשֶׁיֵּרָאֶה לְךָ. תַּנְיָא כְּוָותֵיהּ דְּרַב יְהוּדָה: אָמַר ״כַּסּוּנִי״ – בּוֹדְקִין אַחֲרָיו, ״פַּרְנְסוּנִי״ – אֵין בּוֹדְקִין.

If you wish, **say** that this distinction is derived via **logical reasoning: This one** who is hungry **suffers, whereas that one** who is in tattered clothing **does not suffer** in the same way. **And if you wish, say** instead that this distinction is derived from **a verse. Here, it is written: "Is it not to share [*paros*] your bread with the hungry?"** meaning, **share** it **immediately, just as** the word **is read.** Since the word is read with a *samekh*, Rav Yehuda does not understand it as alluding to examining the recipient. **And there, it is written: "When you see the naked, that you cover him,"** meaning, **when it will be** clearly **apparent to you,** after you have investigated the matter and found that the supplicant is deserving, then you shall cover him. The Gemara comments: **It is taught** in a *baraita* **in accordance with** the opinion **of Rav Yehuda:** If a poor person **said: Cover me** with clothing, the charity collectors **examine him;** but if he said: **Sustain me** with food, **they do not examine him.**

תְּנַן הָתָם: אֵין פּוֹחֲתִין לֶעָנִי הָעוֹבֵר מִמָּקוֹם לְמָקוֹם מִכִּכָּר בְּפוּנְדְּיוֹן, מֵאַרְבַּע סְאִין בְּסֶלַע; לָן – נוֹתְנִין לוֹ פַּרְנָסַת לִינָה. מַאי פַּרְנָסַת לִינָה? אָמַר רַב פָּפָּא: פּוּרְיָא וּבֵי סַדְיָא. שַׁבָּת – נוֹתְנִין לוֹ מְזוֹן שָׁלֹשׁ סְעוּדוֹת. תָּנָא: אִם הָיָה מַחֲזִיר עַל הַפְּתָחִים – אֵין נִזְקָקִין לוֹ.

We learned in a mishna **there** (*Pe'a* 8:7): **One does not give a poor person who is traveling from place to place** requesting charity **less**[H] **than a loaf** worth **a *pundeyon*,**[NL] one forty-eighth of a *sela*, when the standard price of grain is **four *se'a* for a *sela*.** If the poor person **sleeps** in that place, **one gives him provisions for lodging.** The Gemara asks: **What** is meant by **provisions for lodging? Rav Pappa said: A bed and a pillow [*bei sadya*].**[NL] And if he **spends Shabbat** in that place, **one gives him food for three meals.** A Sage **taught** in a *baraita*: **If a poor person was going door to door** asking for charity, one is **not** required to **attend to him** and give him money from the charity fund.

הַהוּא עַנְיָא דַּהֲוָה מַחֲזִיר עַל הַפְּתָחִים דַּאֲתָא לְקַמֵּיהּ דְּרַב פָּפָּא, לָא מִזְדַּקֵּיק לֵיהּ. אֲמַר לֵיהּ רַב סָמָא בְּרֵיהּ דְּרַב יֵיבָא לְרַב פָּפָּא: אִי מָר לָא מִזְדַּקֵּיק לֵיהּ, אֱינָשׁ אַחֲרִינָא לָא מִזְדַּקֵּיק לֵיהּ, לֵימוּת לֵיהּ? וְהָא תַּנְיָא: אִם הָיָה עָנִי הַמַּחֲזִיר עַל הַפְּתָחִים – אֵין נִזְקָקִין לוֹ! אֲמַר לֵיהּ: אֵין נִזְקָקִין לוֹ לְמַתָּנָה מְרוּבָּה, אֲבָל נִזְקָקִין לוֹ לְמַתָּנָה מוּעֶטֶת.

It is related that **a certain poor person who was going door to door** requesting charity **came before Rav Pappa,** the local charity collector, but Rav Pappa **did not attend to him. Rav Sama, son of Rav Yeiva, said to Rav Pappa: If the Master does not attend to him, nobody else will attend to him** either; **should he** be left to **die** of hunger? Rav Pappa said to him: **But isn't it taught** in a *baraita*: **If a poor person was going door to door** asking for charity, one is **not** required to **attend to him?** Rav Sama **said to him:** That *baraita* means to say that one is **not** required to **attend to him** and give him **a large gift,**[H] since he is already collecting money as he goes door to door, **but one does attend to him** and give him **a small gift.**

אָמַר רַב אַסִי: לְעוֹלָם אַל יִמְנַע אָדָם עַצְמוֹ [מִלָּתֵת] שְׁלִישִׁית הַשֶּׁקֶל בְּשָׁנָה, שֶׁנֶּאֱמַר: ״וְהֶעֱמַדְנוּ עָלֵינוּ מִצְוֹת לָתֵת עָלֵינוּ שְׁלִישִׁית הַשֶּׁקֶל בַּשָּׁנָה לַעֲבֹדַת בֵּית אֱלֹהֵינוּ״. וְאָמַר רַב אַסִי: שְׁקוּלָה צְדָקָה כְּנֶגֶד כָּל הַמִּצְוֹת, שֶׁנֶּאֱמַר: ״וְהֶעֱמַדְנוּ עָלֵינוּ מִצְוֹת״ וגו׳, ״מִצְוָה״ אֵין כְּתִיב כָּאן, אֶלָּא ״מִצְוֹת״.

Rav Asi says: A person should never prevent himself from giving at least **one-third of a shekel**[N] **a year**[H] in charity, **as it is stated: "And we also established mitzvot upon ourselves,**[N] **to charge ourselves yearly with the third part of a shekel for the service of the House of our God"** (Nehemiah 10:33). **And Rav Asi says: Charity is equivalent to all the** other **mitzvot** combined, **as it is stated** in that verse: **"We also established mitzvot upon ourselves." A mitzva is not written here, but** rather **mitzvot**, in the plural, thereby teaching that this mitzva is equivalent to all the other mitzvot.

(סִימָן: גָּדוֹל, מִקְדָּשׁ מֹשֶׁה) אָמַר רַבִּי אֶלְעָזָר: גָּדוֹל הַמְעַשֶּׂה יוֹתֵר מִן הָעוֹשֶׂה, שֶׁנֶּאֱמַר: ״וְהָיָה מַעֲשֵׂה הַצְּדָקָה שָׁלוֹם וַעֲבֹדַת הַצְּדָקָה הַשְׁקֵט וָבֶטַח עַד עוֹלָם״, זָכָה – ״הֲלֹא פָרֹשׂ לָרָעֵב לַחְמֶךָ״, לֹא זָכָה – ״וַעֲנִיִּים מְרוּדִים תָּבִיא בָיִת״.

The Gemara offers **a mnemonic** device for the following statements extolling the mitzva of charity: **Greater; Temple; Moses. Rabbi Elazar says: One who causes others to perform** [*me'aseh*] a meritorious act **is greater**[NH] **than one who performs** that act himself, **as it is stated: "And the causing** [*ma'aseh*] **of righteousness**[N] **shall be peace, and the work of righteousness, quietness, and assurance forever"** (Isaiah 32:17). If one **merits,** the following verse is applied to him: **"Is it not to share your bread with the hungry?"** (Isaiah 58:7), i.e., he will wholeheartedly give charity to the poor. If he **does not merit,** the latter clause of that verse is applied to him: **"You shall bring the poor that are cast out**[N] **to your house,"** i.e., he will be compelled by the government to billet soldiers in his house and sustain them against his will.

אֲמַר לְהוּ רָבָא לִבְנֵי מְחוֹזָא: בְּמָטוּתָא מִנַּייכוּ, עוּשׂוּ בַּהֲדֵי הֲדָדֵי, כִּי הֵיכִי דְּלֶיהֱוֵי לְכוּ שְׁלָמָא בְּמַלְכוּתָא. וְאָמַר רַבִּי אֶלְעָזָר: בִּזְמַן שֶׁבֵּית הַמִּקְדָּשׁ קַיָּים, אָדָם שׁוֹקֵל שִׁקְלוֹ וּמִתְכַּפֵּר לוֹ, עַכְשָׁיו שֶׁאֵין בֵּית הַמִּקְדָּשׁ קַיָּים, אִם עוֹשִׂין צְדָקָה – מוּטָב, וְאִם לָאו – בָּאִין אוּמּוֹת הָעוֹלָם וְנוֹטְלִין בִּזְרוֹעַ. וְאַף עַל פִּי כֵן נֶחְשָׁב לָהֶן לִצְדָקָה, שֶׁנֶּאֱמַר: ״וְנֹגְשַׂיִךְ צְדָקָה״.

Rava said to the people of Meḥoza: I beg of you, strive with each other to perform acts of charity and righteousness, **so that you will** live in **peace with the government,** since if you do not act charitably toward each other, you will end up paying fines to the government. **And Rabbi Elazar says: When the Temple is standing, a person contributes his shekel**[B] for the Temple service **and achieves atonement** for his sins. **Now that the Temple no longer stands, if** people **act charitably,** it will be **well** for them; **but if not, the nations of the world will come and take** their money **by force.** The Gemara comments: **And even so,** the money taken from them by force **is credited to them as** if they had freely given **charity,**[N] **as it is stated:** "And I will make **your oppressors charity"** (Isaiah 60:17).

אָמַר רָבָא: הַאי מִילְּתָא אִישְׁתַּעֵי לִי עוּלָּא

Rava said: This following **matter was told to me by the infant**

HALAKHA

From giving one-third of a shekel a year – מִלָּתֵת שְׁלִישִׁית הַשֶּׁקֶל בְּשָׁנָה: Every person must give charity in accordance with his financial capability and the needs of the poor. This applies even to the poor themselves, who survive on charity. One may give up to 20 percent of his assets. Even when there are none in great need of support, he must give at least one-third of a shekel a year in order to fulfill the mitzva of charity (Rambam *Sefer Zera'im, Hilkhot Mattenot Aniyyim* 7:5, and see Radbaz there; *Shulḥan Arukh, Yoreh De'a* 249:1–2).

One who causes others to perform is greater – גָּדוֹל הַמְעַשֶּׂה: One who causes others to give charity receives a greater reward than the person who actually gives the charity. The *Tur* states that both receive the same reward (Rambam *Sefer Zera'im, Hilkhot Mattenot Aniyyim* 10:6; *Shulḥan Arukh, Yoreh De'a* 249:5, and see *Taz* there).

BACKGROUND

Contributes his shekel – שׁוֹקֵל שִׁקְלוֹ: This is a reference to the obligation incumbent upon every Jewish male who is at least twenty years old to donate one-half of a biblical shekel to the Temple each year (Exodus 30:11–16). The money was used primarily for the purchase of communal sacrifices and was also used for maintenance of the Temple. This obligation is in force only when the Temple is standing. The details of this mitzva are enumerated in tractate *Shekalim*.

NOTES

From giving one-third of a shekel – מִלָּתֵת שְׁלִישִׁית הַשֶּׁקֶל: It is written in the *She'iltot deRav Aḥai Gaon* that this is the minimum amount a person can give to fulfill the mitzva of charity. Even one who is sustained by charity must give this amount to fulfill this positive mitzva.

And we also established mitzvot upon ourselves – וְהֶעֱמַדְנוּ עָלֵינוּ מִצְוֹת: Even though this text refers to donations to the Temple, giving charity is a greater mitzva; therefore, the matter can be derived through an *a fortiori* inference (*Tosafot*).

One who causes others to perform is greater – גָּדוֹל הַמְעַשֶּׂה: The Sages explain that such a person brings benefit to both the donor and the recipient. Furthermore, collecting charity from others often brings insult and embarrassment upon the collector, which can be more painful than the actual giving of money.

And the causing of righteousness – וְהָיָה מַעֲשֵׂה הַצְּדָקָה: Rashi and the *She'iltot deRav Aḥai Gaon* understand *ma'aseh* in the sense of *me'aseh*, causing others to act. The Ritva writes that Rabbi Elazar maintains that one who causes others to act righteously is greater because the verse uses the word peace, which denotes permanent tranquillity, about such a person, whereas in connection with righteousness itself the verse speaks of quietness, and assurance, which denote fleeting rest.

The poor that are cast out [*merudim*] – עֲנִיִּים מְרוּדִים: This is a reference to the gentile authorities, who are referred to as the poor because they constantly claim they have no money and are in need of funds, and therefore they scream and demand this money (Rashi). The Ramah explains that government officials are called poor because they have a paucity of mitzvot, and they are termed *merudim* because they rebel [*mordim*] against God.

It is credited to them as charity – נֶחְשָׁב לָהֶן לִצְדָקָה: Some commentaries write that charity given under duress is still considered charity. Others explain that when money is given to the government faithfully, it leads the authorities to sympathize with the poor and not to collect taxes from them. Alternatively, because a person suffers at the hands of the government due to the fact that he is a Jew, the act of giving is meritorious for him (Meiri).

מְשַׁגֵּשׁ אָרְחָתֵיה דְּאִימֵּיה, מִשְּׁמֵיהּ דְּרַבִּי אֶלְעָזָר, מַאי דִּכְתִיב: ״וַיִּלְבַּשׁ צְדָקָה כַּשִּׁרְיָן״? לוֹמַר לְךָ, מַה שִּׁרְיוֹן זֶה – כׇּל קְלִיפָּה וּקְלִיפָּה מִצְטָרֶפֶת לְשִׁרְיוֹן גָּדוֹל, אַף צְדָקָה – כׇּל פְּרוּטָה וּפְרוּטָה מִצְטָרֶפֶת לְחֶשְׁבּוֹן גָּדוֹל. רַבִּי חֲנִינָא אָמַר, מֵהָכָא: ״וּכְבֶגֶד עִדִּים כׇּל צִדְקֹתֵינוּ״, מַה בֶּגֶד זֶה – כׇּל נִימָא וְנִימָא מִצְטָרֶפֶת לְבֶגֶד גָּדוֹל, אַף צְדָקָה – כׇּל פְּרוּטָה וּפְרוּטָה מִצְטָרֶפֶת לְחֶשְׁבּוֹן גָּדוֹל.

who perverted[N] **the ways of his mother.** He said **in the name of Rabbi Elazar: What** is the meaning of that **which is written: "And He donned charity like a coat of mail"** (Isaiah 59:17)? This verse serves **to tell you** that **just as** with regard to **this coat of mail, each and every scale**[B] of which it is fashioned **combines to form one large coat of mail, so too** with regard to **charity,**[N] **each and every** *peruta* that one gives **combines to form a great sum. Rabbi Ḥanina says:** The same idea is derived **from here,** as it is stated: **"And all our charity is as a polluted garment"** (Isaiah 64:5). **Just as** with regard to **this garment, each and every thread** in it **combines to form one large garment, so too** with regard to **charity, each and every** *peruta* **combines to** form **a great sum.**

אַמַּאי קָרוּ לֵיהּ עוּלָּא מְשַׁגֵּשׁ אָרְחָתֵיה דְּאִימֵּיהּ? דִּבְעָא מִינֵּיהּ רַב אַחַדְבּוֹי בַּר אַמִי מֵרַב שֵׁשֶׁת: מִנַּיִן לִמְצוֹרָע בִּימֵי סְפוֹרוֹ שֶׁמְּטַמֵּא אָדָם? אָמַר לוֹ: הוֹאִיל וּמְטַמֵּא בְּגָדִים מְטַמֵּא אָדָם.

The Gemara comments: **Why was** this Sage **called the infant who perverted the ways of his mother?** It was because of the following incident: **Rav Aḥadvoi bar Ami asked Rav Sheshet: From where** is it derived **that a leper**[B] **renders a person impure** through contact **during his days of counting,**[HN] i.e., during the seven days that the leper must count from the start of his purification process, when he brings his birds, until he completes that process with the bringing of his sacrifices? Rav Sheshet **said to him: Since he renders** his **garments impure,** as it states that on the seventh day of his purification he must wash his clothes (see Leviticus 14:9), **he** also **renders people impure.**

אָמַר לֵיהּ: דִּילְמָא טוּמְאָה בְּחִבּוּרִים שָׁאנֵי, דְּהָא הֶסֵּיט נְבֵילָה דִּמְטַמֵּא בְּגָדִים וְאֵינוֹ מְטַמֵּא אָדָם!

Rav Aḥadvoi **said to him: Perhaps connected impurity is different,**[N] meaning perhaps he renders his garments impure because they are connected to the source of the impurity, but this does not mean that he renders impure a person whom he touches. A proof for this distinction may be brought from the fact **that** if **one moves an animal carcass,**[H] an action that renders him impure even if there was no actual contact with the carcass, **he renders** the **garments** that he is wearing **impure but does not render** another **person impure.**

BACKGROUND

Every scale – כׇּל קְלִיפָּה: The coat of mail referred to here is apparently one made by attaching scales of metal or some other hard material to leather. The leather foundation made the armor flexible and permitted movement, while the scales prevented penetration of arrows or swords. This type of armor was used even in antiquity and was common in Rome and Persia during the talmudic period. The Gemara may also be referring to chain mail, which was made by linking many small rings of metal to form one large piece of armor.

Armor scales found at Masada

Leper – מְצוֹרָע: The *halakhot* of *tzara'at*, traditionally rendered as leprosy but not necessarily identified medically with that illness, are recorded in the Torah in the book of Leviticus (chapters 13–14). They are detailed in tractate *Nega'im*, which examines exclusively the different types of leprosy. The *halakha* distinguishes between the impurity of a quarantined leper, i.e., a suspected leper, who is isolated for a period of up to two weeks until the matter is clarified, and that of a confirmed leper. A leper must let his hair grow, rend his garments, and cover his head in a particular way. He constitutes a particularly severe source of ritual impurity in that he, similar to a corpse, imparts ritual impurity to items found under the same roof as him.

HALAKHA

A leper…during his days of counting – מְצוֹרָע בִּימֵי סְפוֹרוֹ: After a leper has recovered and has brought the two birds, cedar wood, hyssop, and crimson thread, and shaved all his hair, he counts a further seven days. During this period an item or another person can contract impurity through contact with him (Rambam *Sefer Tahara, Hilkhot Tumat Tzara'at* 11:2).

Moving an animal carcass – הֶסֵּט נְבֵילָה: One who moves a piece of an animal carcass the volume of an olive-bulk renders his garments impure (Rambam *Sefer Tahara, Hilkhot She'ar Avot HaTumot* 1:5, 6:12–13).

NOTES

The infant who perverted – עוּלָּא מְשַׁגֵּשׁ: Rashi explains that Rava called Rav Sheshet by this sobriquet, as he understands the incident described later to be one where Rav Sheshet's mother debased herself for what her son did to Rav Aḥadvoi. Nevertheless, most commentaries, starting with Rabbeinu Ḥananel and Rabbeinu Gershom, state that the designation refers to Rav Aḥadvoi bar Ami and that he caused his mother to debase herself before Rav Sheshet.

So too charity – אַף צְדָקָה: Although one who gives another a larger sum of money all at once provides more assistance, giving charity little by little also helps. The money accumulates and increases the reward of the donor (*Torat Ḥayyim*; Maharal). Some commentaries write that Rabbi Elazar is saying that multiple donations of small amounts are preferable to one large donation, just as armor is more effective when it is made of scales rather than from a single piece (*Ḥatam Sofer*).

A leper…during his days of counting – מְצוֹרָע בִּימֵי סְפוֹרוֹ: The fact that a leper imparts impurity to a person through contact is stated in the mishna, but not in the biblical text. This is why Rav Aḥadvoi seeks the source in the Torah for this *halakha* (*Tosafot*). The leper's days of counting begin after his first purification ritual, which involves the bringing of two birds (see Leviticus 14:4). He counts seven days and is then completely purified with the bringing of his sacrifices. As long as the leper is impure, it is clear that he imparts impurity to another person. Although this is not stated explicitly in the Torah, there are many proofs to this point, e.g., that he is removed from the camp, that he must proclaim about himself that he is impure, and that he is compared in the text to a corpse. Even so, it might have been reasoned that during his days of counting, when he seems to be cured from the leprosy, his status is similar to one who lacks atonement.

Connected impurity is different – טוּמְאָה בְּחִבּוּרִין שָׁאנֵי: Rashi expounds that since the clothing he is wearing clings to him, it is connected to his body and therefore becomes impure. In similar fashion, he explains that one who carries an animal carcass or causes it to move transfers impurity to his garments because he is wearing them, but he does not transfer impurity to other clothes with which he comes into contact.

Many early commentaries (*Tosafot*) challenge Rashi's understanding, since the ensuing discussion with regard to the impurity of the carcass of a creeping animal is completely unrelated to this issue. *Tosafot* therefore comment that the impurity of garments is different. They explain that this leper renders garments and other items impure, because they can be rendered impure even by something that is not a primary source of impurity. But only a primary source of impurity can render a person impure.

Other early commentaries (Ramah; Ramban) explain the term: Connected impurity, differently. It does not refer specifically to the garments the individual is wearing but to those which he touches when he is connected to impurity, e.g., where he is holding a primary source of impurity in one hand and touching garments with the other. It is only in such circumstances that he renders garments, but not a person, impure. This is why the leper renders impure the clothes he is wearing during his days of counting when he himself is the source of impurity, but he does not render a person impure. This is like the *halakha* that one who moves an animal carcass renders garments impure, even those that he is not wearing, if he touches them while he is in contact with the carcass, but he does not render a person impure.

אמר ליה: ואלא שרץ דמטמא אדם מנלן, לאו משום דמטמא בגדים? אמר ליה: שרץ בהדיא כתיב ביה: "או איש אשר יגע בכל שרץ". אלא שכבת זרע דמטמא אדם מנלן, לאו משום דהואיל ומטמא בגדים מטמא אדם? אמר ליה: שכבת זרע נמי בהדיא כתיב ביה: "או איש" – לרבות את הנוגע.

Rav Sheshet **said to him: But from where do we** derive that the carcass of **a creeping animal renders a person impure?**[H] **Is it not because** we know **that it renders** his **garments impure?** Rav Aḥadvoi **said to him: It is written explicitly** with regard to the carcass of **a creeping animal: "Or a man who touches any creeping animal,** whereby he may be made unclean" (Leviticus 22:5). Rav Sheshet said to him: **But from where do we** derive that **semen renders a person impure?**[H] **Is it not because** we say that **since it renders** his **garments impure** (see Leviticus 15:17) **it** also **renders a person impure?** Rav Aḥadvoi **said to him: It is also written explicitly** with regard to **semen: "Or a man** from whom semen is expelled" (Leviticus 22:4), and the Sages expound the superfluous word "or" as serving **to include** as impure **one who touches** semen.

אהדר ליה בבדיחותא. חלש דעתיה דרב ששת, אישתיק רב אחדבוי בר אמי ואתיקר תלמודיה. אתיא אימיה וקא בכיא קמיה, צווחה צווחה ולא אשגח בה. אמרה ליה: חזי להני חדיי דמצית מינייהו! בעא רחמי עליה ואיתסי.

The Gemara relates that with each of his answers Rav Aḥadvoi **responded to** Rav Sheshet **in a mocking tone,** intimating that he doubted Rav Sheshet's grasp of Torah verses. **Rav Sheshet was deeply offended,** and as punishment, **Rav Aḥadvoi bar Ami became mute and forgot his learning.** Rav Aḥadvoi's **mother came and wept before** Rav Sheshet. **She cried and cried but he ignored her.** As she had once been Rav Sheshet's nursemaid, **she said to him: Look at these breasts of mine from which you suckled.** Upon hearing that, Rav Sheshet **prayed for mercy for** Rav Aḥadvoi, **and he was healed.** And since it was Rav Aḥadvoi whose behavior led to his mother's acting in this manner, he was referred to as the infant who perverted his mother's ways.

ודאתאן עלה, מנא לן? כדתניא, רבי שמעון בן יוחי אומר: נאמר כבוס בגדים בימי ספורו, ונאמר כבוס בגדים בימי חלוטו – מה להלן מטמא אדם, אף כאן מטמא אדם.

The Gemara comments: With regard to **that which we arrived at,** i.e., this particular subject, let us clarify the matter: **From where do we** derive that a leper renders impure a person with whom he comes into contact during his days of counting? **As it is taught** in a *baraita*: **Rabbi Shimon bar Yoḥai says: Washing garments is stated with respect to his days of counting, and washing garments is stated with respect to his days of confirmed** leprosy, after he has been declared conclusively impure by a priest. **Just as there,** when he is a confirmed leper **he renders a person impure,** as is explicitly stated in the Torah, **so too here,** during his days of counting **he renders a person impure.**

אמר רבי אלעזר: גדול העושה צדקה בסתר יותר ממשה רבינו, דאילו במשה רבינו כתיב: "כי יגרתי מפני האף והחמה", ואילו בעושה צדקה כתיב: "מתן בסתר יכפה אף [ושחד בחק חמה עזה]". ופליגא דרבי יצחק, דאמר רבי יצחק: אף כופה, חמה אינו כופה, שנאמר: "ושחד בחק חמה עזה", אף על פי ששוחד בחיק – חמה עזה. איכא דאמרי, אמר רבי יצחק: כל דיין שנוטל שחד – מביא חמה עזה לעולם, [שנאמר: "ושחד בחק" וגו'].

§ The Gemara resumes its discussion of the virtues of giving charity. **Rabbi Elazar said: One who performs** acts of **charity in secret is greater than Moses, our teacher. Whereas with regard to Moses, our teacher, it is written: "For I was afraid of the anger and the wrath"** (Deuteronomy 9:19), **with regard to one who performs** acts of **charity it is written: "A gift in secret pacifies anger, and a present in the bosom fierce wrath"** (Proverbs 21:14). The Gemara comments: **And this** statement **disagrees with** a statement **of Rabbi Yitzḥak, as Rabbi Yitzḥak says:** A secret gift **pacifies anger,** but it **does not pacify wrath, as it is stated: "And a present in the bosom fierce wrath,"** meaning that **although a present is in the bosom,** i.e., even if one gives charity in secret, nevertheless **fierce wrath** can still harm him. **There are those who say** that **Rabbi Yitzḥak says** as follows: **Any judge who accepts a bribe brings fierce wrath upon the world, as it is stated: "And a present in the bosom** fierce wrath."

ואמר רבי יצחק: כל הנותן פרוטה לעני מתברך בשש ברכות, והמפייסו בדברים – מתברך באחת עשרה ברכות. הנותן פרוטה לעני מתברך בשש ברכות, דכתיב: "הלא פרש וגו' ועניים מרודים תביא בית (וגו') כי תראה ערם" וגו';

And Rabbi Yitzḥak says: Anyone who gives a *peruta* **to a poor person receives six blessings, and whoever consoles him**[N] **with words**[H] of comfort and encouragement **receives eleven blessings.** The Gemara explains: **One who gives a** *peruta* **to a poor person receives six blessings, as it is written: "Is it not to share** your bread with the hungry, **and that you shall bring the poor that are cast out to your house? When you see the naked,** that you cover him" (Isaiah 58:7). And the next verses list six blessings: "Then shall your light break forth like the dawn, and your health shall spring forth speedily, and your righteousness shall go before you, the glory of the Lord shall be your rearguard. Then, shall you call, and the Lord shall answer; you shall cry, and He shall say: Here I am" (Isaiah 58:8–9).

HALAKHA

A creeping animal renders a person impure – שרץ דמטמא אדם: The carcass of a creeping animal is a primary source of ritual impurity, and renders impure people and items with which it comes into contact. This *halakha* applies to a carcass that is at least a lentil-bulk in volume (Rambam *Sefer Tahara, Hilkhot She'ar Avot HaTumot* 4:2).

Semen renders a person impure – שכבת זרע דמטמא אדם: Semen is a primary source of ritual impurity and renders impure people and items with which it comes into contact (Rambam *Sefer Tahara, Hilkhot She'ar Avot HaTumot* 5:1).

And whoever consoles him with words – והמפייסו בדברים: When one gives charity to a poor person, he should give it pleasantly and exhibit empathy. If one gives charity angrily and unpleasantly, he loses the merit he gained from his gift, even if he gives a large sum (*Shakh*). One who has no money to give should console the poor person with words (Rambam *Sefer Zera'im, Hilkhot Mattenot Aniyyim* 10:4–5; *Shulḥan Arukh, Yoreh De'a* 249:3–4).

NOTES

And whoever consoles him – והמפייסו: *Tosafot* and Rambam maintain that this phrase does not mean that words of consolation and an act of charity are offered together, in which case one's reward would certainly be great. Rather, it teaches that even a person who cannot give money should encourage the poor person and console him, and his reward will still be great.

וְהַמְפַיְּיסוֹ בִּדְבָרִים מִתְבָּרֵךְ בְּאַחַת עֶשְׂרֵה בְּרָכוֹת, שֶׁנֶּאֱמַר: ״וְתָפֵק לָרָעֵב נַפְשֶׁךָ וְנֶפֶשׁ נַעֲנָה תַּשְׂבִּיעַ וְזָרַח בַּחֹשֶׁךְ אוֹרֶךָ וַאֲפֵלָתְךָ כַּצָּהֳרָיִם. וְנָחֲךָ ה׳ תָּמִיד וְהִשְׂבִּיעַ בְּצַחְצָחוֹת נַפְשֶׁךָ וגו׳, וּבָנוּ מִמְּךָ חָרְבוֹת עוֹלָם מוֹסְדֵי דוֹר וָדוֹר תְּקוֹמֵם״ וגו׳.

And whoever consoles a poor person **with words** of comfort and encouragement **receives eleven blessings, as it is stated: "And if you draw out your soul to the hungry and satisfy the afflicted soul, then shall your light shine in darkness, and your gloom shall be as the noonday. And the Lord shall guide you continually, and satisfy your thirst in drought… And they that shall be of you shall build the old waste places, you shall raise up the foundations of many generations"** (Isaiah 58:10–12).

וְאָמַר רַבִּי יִצְחָק, מַאי דִּכְתִיב: ״רוֹדֵף צְדָקָה וָחֶסֶד יִמְצָא חַיִּים צְדָקָה וְכָבוֹד״? מִשּׁוּם דְּרוֹדֵף צְדָקָה יִמְצָא צְדָקָה? אֶלָּא לוֹמַר לְךָ: כָּל הָרוֹדֵף אַחַר צְדָקָה – הַקָּדוֹשׁ בָּרוּךְ הוּא מַמְצִיא לוֹ מָעוֹת וְעוֹשֶׂה בָּהֶן צְדָקָה.

And Rabbi Yitzḥak says: What is the meaning of that **which is written: "He who pursues charity and mercy finds life, charity, and honor"** (Proverbs 21:21)? Is this to say that **because one has pursued charity, he** himself **shall find charity?** That is, shall the reward of one who has always given charity be that he will eventually become poor and other people will act charitably toward him? **Rather,** the verse serves **to tell you** that with regard to **anyone who pursues charity,** giving to the poor and leading others to do so, **the Holy One, Blessed be He, furnishes him with money with which to perform** his acts of **charity.**

רַב נַחְמָן בַּר יִצְחָק אָמַר: הַקָּדוֹשׁ בָּרוּךְ הוּא מַמְצִיא לוֹ בְּנֵי אָדָם הַמְהוּגָּנִים לַעֲשׂוֹת לָהֶן צְדָקָה, כְּדֵי לְקַבֵּל עֲלֵיהֶם שְׂכָרוֹ. לְאַפּוּקֵי מַאי? לְאַפּוּקֵי מִדְּדָרַשׁ רַבָּה; דְּדָרַשׁ רַבָּה, מַאי דִּכְתִיב: ״וְיִהְיוּ מֻכְשָׁלִים לְפָנֶיךָ בְּעֵת אַפְּךָ עֲשֵׂה בָהֶם״? אָמַר יִרְמְיָה לִפְנֵי הַקָּדוֹשׁ בָּרוּךְ הוּא: רִבּוֹנוֹ שֶׁל עוֹלָם, [אֲפִילּוּ] בְּשָׁעָה שֶׁכּוֹפִין אֶת יִצְרָן וּמְבַקְשִׁין לַעֲשׂוֹת צְדָקָה לְפָנֶיךָ, הַכְשִׁילֵם בִּבְנֵי אָדָם שֶׁאֵינָן מְהוּגָּנִין, כְּדֵי שֶׁלֹּא יְקַבְּלוּ עֲלֵיהֶן שָׂכָר.

Rav Naḥman bar Yitzḥak says: The Holy One, Blessed be He, sends him people who are deserving of charity, so that he will reap his just **reward for** helping **them.** The Gemara comments: **What** does this statement serve **to exclude?** It serves **to exclude Rabba's homiletical interpretation** of a different verse, **as Rabba taught: What** is the meaning of that **which is written: "Let them be made to stumble before You; deal thus with them in the time of Your anger"** (Jeremiah 18:23)? The prophet **Jeremiah said before the Holy One, Blessed be He: Master of the Universe, even when** those wicked men who pursued me **subdue their inclinations and seek to perform** acts of **charity before You, cause them to stumble upon** dishonest **people who are not deserving** of charity, **so that they will not receive reward** for coming to their assistance.

רַבִּי יְהוֹשֻׁעַ בֶּן לֵוִי אָמַר: כָּל הָרָגִיל לַעֲשׂוֹת צְדָקָה – זוֹכֶה, הָוְיָין לוֹ בָּנִים בַּעֲלֵי חָכְמָה, בַּעֲלֵי עוֹשֶׁר, בַּעֲלֵי אַגָּדָה. בַּעֲלֵי חָכְמָה – דִּכְתִיב:

Rabbi Yehoshua ben Levi says: Anyone who is accustomed to performing acts of **charity merits** blessing; **he will have sons who are masters of wisdom, masters of wealth, and masters of *aggada*.** The Gemara explains: **Masters of wisdom, as it is written:**

Perek **I**
Daf **10** Amud **a**

״יִמְצָא חַיִּים״; בַּעֲלֵי עוֹשֶׁר – דִּכְתִיב ״צְדָקָה״; בַּעֲלֵי אַגָּדָה – דִּכְתִיב ״וְכָבוֹד״, כְּתִיב הָכָא ״וְכָבוֹד״, וּכְתִיב הָתָם: ״כָּבוֹד חֲכָמִים יִנְחָלוּ״.

"He who pursues charity and mercy, **finds life**" (Proverbs 21:21), and with regard to wisdom it is written: "He who finds Me, finds life" (Proverbs 8:35). **Masters of wealth, as it is written:** "He who pursues charity and mercy finds **charity,**" meaning he will be able to give charity. **Masters of *aggada*, as it is written:** "He who pursues charity and mercy, finds **honor.**"[N] And how do we know that this refers to masters of *aggada*? **It is written here "honor," and it is written there: "The wise shall inherit honor"** (Proverbs 3:35).

NOTES

Masters of *aggada*, as it is written honor – בַּעֲלֵי אַגָּדָה דִּכְתִיב וְכָבוֹד: Masters of *aggada* lecture in public to the masses who appreciate and enjoy their words; therefore, they are shown more honor than other Torah scholars.

תַּנְיָא: הָיָה רַבִּי מֵאִיר אוֹמֵר: יֵשׁ לוֹ לְבַעַל הַדִּין לְהָשִׁיבְךָ וְלוֹמַר לְךָ: אִם אֱלֹהֵיכֶם אוֹהֵב עֲנִיִּים הוּא, מִפְּנֵי מָה אֵינוֹ מְפַרְנְסָן? אֱמוֹר לוֹ: כְּדֵי שֶׁנִּיצּוֹל אָנוּ בָּהֶן מִדִּינָהּ שֶׁל גֵּיהִנָּם. וְזוֹ שְׁאֵלָה שָׁאַל טוּרְנוּסְרוּפוּס הָרָשָׁע אֶת רַבִּי עֲקִיבָא: אִם אֱלֹהֵיכֶם אוֹהֵב עֲנִיִּים הוּא, מִפְּנֵי מָה אֵינוֹ מְפַרְנְסָם? אָמַר לוֹ: כְּדֵי שֶׁנִּיצּוֹל אָנוּ בָּהֶן מִדִּינָהּ שֶׁל גֵּיהִנָּם.

§ **It is taught** in a *baraita*: **Rabbi Meir would say: An opponent may bring an argument against you and say to you: If your God loves the poor, for what** reason **does He not support them** Himself? In such a case, **say to him:** He commands us to act as His agents in sustaining the poor, **so that through them we will be** credited with the performance of mitzvot and therefore be **saved from the judgment of Gehenna. And this is the question that Turnus Rufus**[P] **the wicked asked Rabbi Akiva:**[P] **If your God loves the poor, for what** reason **does He not support them** Himself? Rabbi Akiva **said to him:** He commands us to sustain the poor, **so that through them** and the charity we give them **we will be saved from the judgment of Gehenna.**

אָמַר לוֹ: [אַדְּרַבָּה,] זוֹ שֶׁמְּחַיַּיבְתָּן לַגֵּיהִנָּם! אֶמְשׁוֹל לְךָ מָשָׁל, לְמָה הַדָּבָר דּוֹמֶה? לְמֶלֶךְ בָּשָׂר וָדָם שֶׁכָּעַס עַל עַבְדּוֹ וַחֲבָשׁוֹ בְּבֵית הָאֲסוּרִין, וְצִוָּה עָלָיו שֶׁלֹּא לְהַאֲכִילוֹ וְשֶׁלֹּא לְהַשְׁקוֹתוֹ, וְהָלַךְ אָדָם אֶחָד וְהֶאֱכִילוֹ וְהִשְׁקָהוּ, כְּשֶׁשָּׁמַע הַמֶּלֶךְ לֹא כּוֹעֵס עָלָיו? וְאַתֶּם קְרוּיִן עֲבָדִים, שֶׁנֶּאֱמַר: ״כִּי לִי בְנֵי יִשְׂרָאֵל עֲבָדִים״!

Turnus Rufus **said to** Rabbi Akiva: **On the contrary, it is this** charity **which condemns you,** the Jewish people, **to Gehenna** because you give it. **I will illustrate** this **to you with a parable. To what is this matter comparable?** It is comparable **to a king of flesh and blood who was angry with his slave and put him in prison and ordered that he should not be fed or given to drink. And one person went ahead and fed him and gave him to drink. If the king heard about this, would he not be angry with** that person? **And you,** after all, **are called slaves, as it is stated: "For the children of Israel are slaves to Me"** (Leviticus 25:55). If God decreed that a certain person should be impoverished, one who gives him charity defies the will of God.

אָמַר לוֹ רַבִּי עֲקִיבָא: אֶמְשׁוֹל לְךָ מָשָׁל, לְמָה הַדָּבָר דּוֹמֶה? לְמֶלֶךְ בָּשָׂר וָדָם שֶׁכָּעַס עַל בְּנוֹ וַחֲבָשׁוֹ בְּבֵית הָאֲסוּרִין, וְצִוָּה עָלָיו שֶׁלֹּא לְהַאֲכִילוֹ וְשֶׁלֹּא לְהַשְׁקוֹתוֹ, וְהָלַךְ אָדָם אֶחָד וְהֶאֱכִילוֹ וְהִשְׁקָהוּ, כְּשֶׁשָּׁמַע הַמֶּלֶךְ לֹא דּוֹרוֹן מְשַׁגֵּר לוֹ? וַאֲנַן קְרוּיִן בָּנִים, דִּכְתִיב: ״בָּנִים אַתֶּם לַה׳ אֱלֹהֵיכֶם״!

Rabbi Akiva said to Turnus Rufus: **I will illustrate** the opposite **to you with a** different **parable. To what is this matter comparable?** It is comparable **to a king of flesh and blood who was angry with his son and put him in prison and ordered that he should not be fed or given to drink. And one person went ahead and fed him and gave him to drink. If the king heard** about this once his anger abated, **would he not** react by **sending** that person **a gift? And we are called sons, as it is written: "You are sons of the Lord your God"** (Deuteronomy 14:1).

אָמַר לוֹ: אַתֶּם קְרוּיִם בָּנִים וּקְרוּיִן עֲבָדִים, בִּזְמַן שֶׁאַתֶּם עוֹשִׂין רְצוֹנוֹ שֶׁל מָקוֹם אַתֶּם קְרוּיִן בָּנִים, וּבִזְמַן שֶׁאֵין אַתֶּם עוֹשִׂין רְצוֹנוֹ שֶׁל מָקוֹם אַתֶּם קְרוּיִן עֲבָדִים, וְעַכְשָׁיו אֵין אַתֶּם עוֹשִׂים רְצוֹנוֹ שֶׁל מָקוֹם! אָמַר לוֹ, הֲרֵי הוּא אוֹמֵר: ״הֲלֹא פָרֹס לָרָעֵב לַחְמֶךָ וַעֲנִיִּים מְרוּדִים תָּבִיא בָיִת״, אֵימָתַי ״עֲנִיִּים מְרוּדִים תָּבִיא בָיִת״ – הָאִידָנָא, וְקָאָמַר: ״הֲלֹא פָרֹס לָרָעֵב לַחְמֶךָ״.

Turnus Rufus **said to him: You are called sons and you are called slaves. When you fulfill the will of the Omnipresent, you are called sons; when you do not fulfill the will of the Omnipresent, you are called slaves. And** since **now you do not fulfill the will of the Omnipresent,** the parable that I offered is more apt. Rabbi Akiva **said to him:** The verse **states: "Is it not to share your bread with the hungry, and that you shall bring the poor that are cast out to your house?"** (Isaiah 58:7). **When** do we **bring the poor that are cast out** into our **houses? Now,** when we have to billet the Roman soldiers in our homes; **and** about that very time, the verse **states: "Is it not to share your bread with the hungry?"**

PERSONALITIES

Turnus Rufus – טוּרְנוּסְרוּפוּס: This is the appellation assigned to the Roman consul Quintus Tineius Rufus, who ruled Judea during the bar Kokheva revolt. He suppressed the revolt with great cruelty. For this reason, he was dubbed Turnus Rufus, a deliberate distortion of his name alluding to the phonetically similar Greek word for tyrant, τύραννος, *turannos*. The midrash recounts his debates with Rabbi Akiva, whom he later commanded to be tortured and killed (*Midrash Tanḥuma*, *Tazria* 8). Tractate *Ta'anit* reports that Turnus Rufus ordered that the Temple Mount be plowed over to show its complete destruction.

Rabbi Akiva – רַבִּי עֲקִיבָא: Rabbi Akiva, who lived just after the destruction of the Second Temple, was one of the greatest of the *tanna'im*. Unlettered until the age of forty, Akiva was encouraged by his wife, Rachel, to devote himself to the study of Torah. After years of study under the tutelage of Rabbi Eliezer ben Hyrcanus, Yehoshua ben Ḥananya, and others, he acquired thousands of students and established his own academy in Bnei Brak. Rabbi Akiva arranged many oral traditions, and it was the tradition of Rabbi Akiva as received by his disciple, Rabbi Meir, that ultimately became the basis of the six orders of the Mishna.

Rabbi Akiva was the spiritual leader of the bar Kokheva revolt. Although he even proclaimed bar Kokheva the Messiah early in the struggle, he later retracted this opinion. Despite Roman decrees against disseminating Torah, the aged Rabbi Akiva continued to teach. Rabbi Akiva was arrested by the Romans, imprisoned, tried, and sentenced to death. He suffered a martyr's death at the hands of the Romans, and is listed as one of the ten martyrs whose execution by the Romans is described in liturgy. As the Romans were torturing him to death, he explained to his students that he now had the opportunity to fulfill the true meaning of loving God with all of one's soul (*Berakhot* 61b).

דָּרַשׁ רַבִּי יְהוּדָה בְּרַבִּי שָׁלוֹם: כְּשֵׁם שֶׁמְּזוֹנוֹתָיו שֶׁל אָדָם קְצוּבִין לוֹ מֵרֹאשׁ הַשָּׁנָה, כָּךְ חֶסְרוֹנוֹתָיו שֶׁל אָדָם קְצוּבִין לוֹ מֵרֹאשׁ הַשָּׁנָה, זָכָה – ״הֲלֹא פָרֹס לָרָעֵב לַחְמֶךָ״, לֹא זָכָה – ״וַעֲנִיִּים מְרוּדִים תָּבִיא בָיִת״.

Rabbi Yehuda, son of Rabbi Shalom taught: Just as a person's entire **livelihood**[N] **is allocated to him from Rosh HaShana,** when God issues His judgments for the entire year, **so too are a person's** monetary **losses allocated to him from Rosh HaShana.** If one **merits,** the following verse is applied to him: **"You shall share your bread with the hungry,"** i.e., he will spend the sum allocated to him on gifts of charity; and if **he does not merit,** the following verse is applied to him: **"You shall bring the poor that are cast out to your house,"** i.e., he will be compelled by the government to billet soldiers in his house and feed them against his will.

כִּי הָא דִּבְנֵי אַחְתֵּיהּ דְּרַבָּן יוֹחָנָן בֶּן זַכַּאי חֲזָא לְהוּ בְּחֶילְמָא דְּבָעוּ לְמֶיחְסַר שְׁבַע מְאָה דִּינָרֵי, עַשִּׂינְהוּ, שְׁקַל מִינַּיְיהוּ לִצְדָקָה, פּוּשׁ גַּבַּיְיהוּ שִׁיבְסַר דִּינָרֵי. כִּי מְטָא מַעֲלֵי יוֹמָא דְּכִיפּוּרֵי, שְׁדוּר דְּבֵי קֵיסָר נָקְטִינְהוּ.

It is **like this** incident **involving the nephews of Rabban Yoḥanan ben Zakkai,** who once **saw in a dream that** his nephews **were** destined **to lose seven hundred dinars** over the course of the year. **He encouraged them** and **took** money **from them for charity, and they were left with seventeen dinars** out of the seven hundred. **When Yom Kippur eve arrived, the government sent** messengers who came and **took** the remaining seventeen dinars.

אֲמַר לְהוּ רַבָּן יוֹחָנָן בֶּן זַכַּאי: לָא תִּדְחֲלוּן, שִׁיבְסַר דִּינָרֵי גַּבַּיְיכוּ שָׁקְלִינְהוּ מִינַּיְיכוּ. אָמְרִי לֵיהּ: מְנָא יָדְעַתְּ? אֲמַר לְהוּ: חֶלְמָא חֲזַאי לְכוּ. אֲמַרוּ לֵיהּ: וְאַמַּאי לָא אֲמַרְתְּ לָן [דְּנֵיתְבִינְהוּ]? אֲמַר לְהוּ: אָמִינָא, כִּי הֵיכִי דְּתַעַבְדוּ מִצְוָה לִשְׁמָהּ.

Rabban Yoḥanan ben Zakkai said to them: Do not fear that they will take even more from you; **they took from you** the **seventeen dinars** that were still **with you.** The nephews **said to him: How did you know?** Rabban Yoḥanan ben Zakkai **said to them: I saw a dream about you,** and he related his dream to them. **They said to him: And why did you not tell us** about the dream? Rabban Yoḥanan ben Zakkai **said to them: I said,** It is better **that they perform a mitzva for its own sake.** Had you known from the start that you were fated to lose that amount of money, the mitzva would not have been performed purely for its own sake.

רַב פַּפָּא הֲוָה סָלֵיק בְּדַרְגָּא, אִישְׁתַּמִּיט כַּרְעֵיהּ בָּעֵי לְמִיפַּל, אֲמַר: הַשְׁתָּא כֵּן אִיחַיַּיב מַאן דְּסָנֵי לָן כִּמְחַלְּלֵי שַׁבָּתוֹת וּכְעוֹבְדֵי עֲבוֹדָה זָרָה?! אֲמַר לֵיהּ חִיָּיא בַּר רַב מִדִּפְתִּי לְרַב פַּפָּא: שֶׁמָּא עָנִי בָּא לְיָדְךָ וְלֹא פִּרְנַסְתּוֹ.

The Gemara relates: **Rav Pappa was** once **climbing** up **a ladder** when **his foot slipped and he almost fell. He said: Now, is the one who hates us,** a euphemism for himself, **liable like Shabbat desecrators**[N] **and idol worshippers,** who are subject to death by stoning, which is similar to death by falling, the punishment that Rav Pappa narrowly escaped? **Ḥiyya bar Rav of Difti said to Rav Pappa: Perhaps a poor person** once **approached you and you did not sustain him,** and therefore you were given a glimpse of the punishment that you actually deserve.

דְּתַנְיָא, רַבִּי יְהוֹשֻׁעַ בֶּן קָרְחָה אוֹמֵר: כָּל הַמַּעֲלִים עֵינָיו מִן הַצְּדָקָה – כְּאִילּוּ עוֹבֵד עֲבוֹדָה זָרָה; כְּתִיב הָכָא: ״הִשָּׁמֶר לְךָ פֶּן יִהְיֶה דָבָר עִם לְבָבְךָ בְלִיַּעַל״, וּכְתִיב הָתָם: ״יָצְאוּ אֲנָשִׁים בְּנֵי בְלִיַּעַל״, מַה לְּהַלָּן עֲבוֹדָה זָרָה, אַף כָּאן עֲבוֹדָה זָרָה.

As it is taught in a *baraita*: **Rabbi Yehoshua ben Korḥa says: Anyone who turns his eyes away from** one seeking **charity**[H] **is** considered **as if he worships idols.** From where is this derived? **It is written here: "Beware that there be not a base thought in your heart…** and your eye be evil against your poor brother, and you give him nothing" (Deuteronomy 15:9). **And it is written there: "Certain base men have gone out…** and have drawn away the inhabitants of their city, saying, Let us go and serve other gods" (Deuteronomy 13:14). **Just as there,** the base men sin with **idolatry, so too here,** the base thought is treated like **idolatry.**

תַּנְיָא, אָמַר רַבִּי אֶלְעָזָר בְּרַבִּי יוֹסֵי: כָּל צְדָקָה וָחֶסֶד שֶׁיִּשְׂרָאֵל עוֹשִׂין בָּעוֹלָם הַזֶּה, שָׁלוֹם גָּדוֹל וּפְרַקְלִיטִין גְּדוֹלִין בֵּין יִשְׂרָאֵל לַאֲבִיהֶן שֶׁבַּשָּׁמַיִם, שֶׁנֶּאֱמַר: ״כֹּה אָמַר ה׳ אַל תָּבֹא בֵּית מַרְזֵחַ וְאַל תֵּלֵךְ לִסְפּוֹד וְאַל תָּנֹד לָהֶם כִּי אָסַפְתִּי אֶת שְׁלוֹמִי מֵאֵת הָעָם הַזֶּה וגו׳ [אֶת] הַחֶסֶד וְאֶת הָרַחֲמִים״, ״חֶסֶד״ – זוֹ גְּמִילוּת חֲסָדִים, ״רַחֲמִים״ – זוֹ צְדָקָה.

It is taught in a *baraita* that **Rabbi Elazar, son of Rabbi Yosei, said: All** acts of **charity and kindness that Jews perform in this world** make **great peace and** are **great intercessors between the Jewish people and their Father in Heaven, as it is stated: "So said the Lord, enter not into a house of mourning, neither go to lament nor bemoan them, for I have taken away My peace**[N] **from this people,** says the Lord, **both kindness and mercy"** (Jeremiah 16:5). **"Kindness"; this** is referring to **acts of kindness. "Mercy"; this** is referring to acts of **charity.** This indicates that when there is kindness and mercy, God is at peace with His people.

NOTES

Just as a person's livelihood – כְּשֵׁם שֶׁמְּזוֹנוֹתָיו: It is stated in tractate *Beitza* (16a) that on Rosh HaShana God apportions food and livelihood to all people for the year. Rabbi Yehuda, son of Rabbi Shalom, expounds that just as God determines how much income a person will earn during the year, so does He decree how much money a person will lose during the year.

Like Shabbat desecrators – כִּמְחַלְּלֵי שַׁבָּתוֹת: Violation of a Shabbat prohibition is punishable by stoning. As described in tractate *Sanhedrin*, a convicted criminal who is liable to be stoned is first hurled to the ground from a high place. Rashi explains this passage based on what is stated in tractate *Ketubot* (30b), that even though capital punishment is no longer administered by the courts, God still punishes those deserving of death in a way similar to the type of execution they would have received. This is how Rav Pappa understood his near-fatal fall from the ladder; he was being shown the death that he deserved.

I have taken away My peace – אָסַפְתִּי אֶת שְׁלוֹמִי: Rashi writes that peace is identified with kindness and mercy. Rabbeinu Gershom explains that God withdrew his peace from the people because they were not treating each other with kindness and mercy.

HALAKHA

Anyone who turns his eyes away from charity – כָּל הַמַּעֲלִים עֵינָיו מִן הַצְּדָקָה: It is a great mitzva for a person to give charity in accordance with his means, and one who turns his eyes from needy people transgresses several prohibitions and positive mitzvot. He is called a sinner and a wicked and base person, and he is likened to idolaters. One must be very careful not to avoid giving charity, lest the poor person be in great need and die if he is not sustained, rendering the person who ignored him like a murderer (Rambam *Sefer Zera'im*, *Hilkhot Mattenot Aniyyim* 10:3; *Shulḥan Arukh*, *Yoreh De'a* 247:1).

תניא, רבי יהודה אומר: גדולה צדקה שמקרבת את הגאולה, שנאמר: "כה אמר ה' שמרו משפט ועשו צדקה כי קרובה ישועתי לבא וצדקתי להגלות". הוא היה אומר, עשרה דברים קשים נבראו בעולם: הר קשה – ברזל מחתכו, ברזל קשה – אור מפעפעו, אור קשה – מים מכבין אותו, מים קשים – עבים סובלים אותן, עבים קשים – רוח מפזרתן, רוח קשה – גוף סובלו, גוף קשה – פחד שוברו, פחד קשה – יין מפיגו, יין קשה – שינה מפכחתו, ומיתה – קשה מכולם, [וצדקה – מצלת מן המיתה], דכתיב: "וצדקה תציל ממות".

It is taught in a *baraita* that **Rabbi Yehuda says: Great is charity in that it advances the redemption,**[H] **as it is stated: "So said the Lord, uphold justice and do charity, for My salvation is near to come, and My righteousness to be revealed"** (Isaiah 56:1). **He would say: Ten strong entities were created in the world,** one stronger than the other. **A mountain is strong,** but **iron,** which is stronger, **cleaves it. Iron is strong,** but **fire melts it. Fire is strong, but water extinguishes it. Water is strong,** but **clouds bear it. Clouds are strong,** but **wind disperses them. Wind is strong,** but the human **body withstands it.** The human **body is strong,** but **fear breaks it. Fear is strong,** but **wine dispels it. Wine is strong, but sleep drives it off. And death is stronger than them all,**[N] **but charity saves** a person **from death, as it is written: "And charity delivers from death"** (Proverbs 10:2, 11:4).

דרש רבי דוסתאי ברבי ינאי: בוא וראה, שלא כמדת הקדוש ברוך הוא מדת בשר ודם; מדת בשר ודם, אדם מביא דורון גדול למלך – ספק מקבלין אותו הימנו, ספק אין מקבלין אותו הימנו; [ואם תמצא לומר מקבלים אותו ממנו] ספק רואה פני המלך, ספק אינו רואה פני המלך. והקדוש ברוך הוא אינו כן, אדם נותן פרוטה לעני – זוכה ומקבל פני שכינה, שנאמר: "אני בצדק אחזה פניך אשבעה בהקיץ תמונתך".

Rabbi Dostai, son of Rabbi Yannai, taught: Come and see that the attribute of the Holy One, Blessed be He, is not like the attribute of flesh and blood. An illustration **of the attribute of flesh and blood** is that when **a person brings a great gift to the king, it is uncertain whether** the king **will accept it from him or will not accept it from him. And if you say that** the king **will accept it from him, it is uncertain whether** the person who brought the gift **will** eventually **see the face of the king, or will not see the face of the king. But the Holy One, Blessed be He, does not** act in **this way.** Even when **a person** gives a mere *peruta* **to a poor person, he merits to receive the Divine Presence, as it is stated: "As for me, I will behold Your face through charity; I will be satisfied, when I awake, with Your likeness"** (Psalms 17:15).

רבי אלעזר יהיב פרוטה לעני והדר מצלי, אמר, דכתיב: "אני בצדק אחזה פניך". מאי "אשבעה בהקיץ תמונתך"? אמר רב נחמן בר יצחק: אלו תלמידי חכמים שמנדדין שינה מעיניהם בעולם הזה, והקדוש ברוך הוא משביען מזיו השכינה לעולם הבא.

It is related that **Rabbi Elazar would** first **give a** *peruta* **to a poor person and** only **then** would he **pray.**[H] **He said:** As it is **written** in the same verse: **"I will behold Your face through charity."** The Gemara asks: **What** is the meaning of that which is written: **"I will be satisfied, when I awake, with your likeness"? Rav Naḥman bar Yitzḥak says: These are Torah scholars,** who in pursuit of their studies **banish sleep from their eyes**[H] **in this world, and the Holy One, Blessed be He, satiates them with the radiance of the Divine Presence in the World-to-Come.**

אמר רבי יוחנן, מאי דכתיב: "מלוה ה' חונן דל"? אלמלא מקרא כתוב אי אפשר לאומרו, כביכול "עבד לוה לאיש מלוה".

Rabbi Yoḥanan says: What is the meaning of that **which is written: "He that graciously gives to the poor makes a loan to the Lord,** and that which he has given, He will pay him back" (Proverbs 19:17)? How can it be that one is considered to have granted a loan to God? **Were it not** explicitly **written in the verse, it would be impossible to say this,** that somebody who is gracious to a poor person is seen as lending to God. It would be impertinent, since **"the borrower is servant to the lender"** (Proverbs 22:7), **as it were.**

אמר רבי חייא בר אבא, רבי יוחנן רמי, כתיב: "לא יועיל הון ביום עברה וצדקה תציל ממות", וכתיב: "לא יועילו אוצרות רשע וצדקה תציל ממות", שתי צדקות הללו למה? אחת שמצילתו ממיתה משונה, ואחת שמצילתו מדינה של גיהנם; ואי זו היא שמצילתו מדינה של גיהנם – ההוא דכתיב ביה "עברה", דכתיב: "יום עברה היום ההוא"; ואי זו היא שמצילתו ממיתה משונה

Rabbi Ḥiyya bar Abba says: Rabbi Yoḥanan raises a contradiction between two texts. In one place **it is written: "Riches profit not on the day of wrath, but charity delivers from death"** (Proverbs 11:4), **and** elsewhere **it is written: "Treasures of wickedness profit nothing, but charity delivers from death"** (Proverbs 10:2). **Why** is it necessary to have **these two** verses about **charity,** that it delivers from death? Rabbi Ḥiyya bar Abba continues: **One** verse serves to teach **that** charity **delivers from an unnatural death**[H] in this world, **and one** verse serves to teach **that** charity **delivers from the judgment of Gehenna** in the World-to-Come. **And in which** of the verses **is that** charity **which delivers from the judgment of Gehenna** mentioned? It is in **that** verse **in which "wrath" is written, as** with regard to the day of judgment **it is written: "That day is a day of wrath"** (Zephaniah 1:15). **And which** type of charity **is that which delivers from an unnatural death?**

HALAKHA

It advances the redemption – שמקרבת את הגאולה: The Jewish people will be redeemed only due to the merit of giving charity (Rambam *Sefer Zera'im, Hilkhot Mattenot Aniyyim* 10:1).

He would give a *peruta* to a poor person and then… pray – יהיב פרוטה לעני והדר מצלי: It is proper to give charity before praying, so that one's prayers will be accepted. This was the practice of Rabbi Elazar (Rambam *Sefer Zera'im, Hilkhot Mattenot Aniyyim* 10:15; *Shulḥan Arukh, Yoreh De'a* 249:14 and *Oraḥ Ḥayyim* 92:10).

They banish sleep from their eyes – שמנדדין שינה מעיניהם: One who wishes to merit the crown of Torah should be careful not to squander his nights in emptiness but to spend his time engaged in the study of Torah and words of wisdom. This is because most of one's knowledge is attained at night (Rambam *Sefer HaMadda, Hilkhot Talmud Torah* 3:13; *Shulḥan Arukh, Yoreh De'a* 246:23).

That it delivers from an unnatural death – שמצילתו ממיתה משונה: The mitzva of charity delivers a person from all types of decrees and deaths (*Shulḥan Arukh, Yoreh De'a* 247:4 and see *Shakh* there).

NOTES

And death is stronger than them all – ומיתה קשה מכולם: Because sleep is considered one-sixtieth of death, death is more severe than all of the matters listed here (Maharsha).

HALAKHA

One gives it without knowing – נוֹתְנָהּ וְאֵינוֹ יוֹדֵעַ: A high, though not the highest, level of giving charity is to give to the poor without knowing to whom one gave and without the poor person knowing from whom he received. A level slightly lower than this is to donate to a charity fund. A person should contribute to such a fund only if he is confident that its custodian is trustworthy. A still lower level of charity is achieved when the donor knows the identity of the recipient, but the poor person does not know the identity of the donor (Rambam *Sefer Zera'im*, *Hilkhot Mattenot Aniyyim* 10:8–10; *Shulḥan Arukh*, *Yoreh De'a* 249:7–9).

NOTES

Into the charity purse – לְאַרְנָקֵי שֶׁל צְדָקָה: Although one is ashamed when he feels indebted to a donor, when a poor person receives money from the charity collector he knows that the money does not come from him but from other people, and he therefore does not feel shame in taking it.

To have male offspring – וְיִהְיוּ לוֹ בָּנִים זְכָרִים: The connection between the mitzva of charity and male children is not explained. The Maharsha suggests that the association is perhaps based on: "His seed shall be mighty upon earth; the generation of the upright shall be blessed" (Psalms 112:2), and later in that same psalm: "He has distributed freely, he has given to the poor" (Psalms 112:9).

נוֹתְנָהּ וְאֵינוֹ יוֹדֵעַ לְמִי נוֹתְנָהּ, נוֹטְלָהּ וְאֵינוֹ יוֹדֵעַ מִמִּי נוֹטְלָהּ. נוֹתְנָהּ וְאֵינוֹ יוֹדֵעַ לְמִי נוֹתְנָהּ – לְאַפּוּקֵי מִדְּמָר עוּקְבָא; נוֹטְלָהּ וְאֵינוֹ יוֹדֵעַ מִמִּי נוֹטְלָהּ – לְאַפּוּקֵי מִדְּרַבִּי אַבָּא. וְאֶלָּא הֵיכִי לִיעֲבִיד? לֵיתִיב לְאַרְנָקֵי שֶׁל צְדָקָה.

It is the type in which **one gives** the charity **without knowing**[H] **to whom he gave it,** and the other **one takes it without knowing from whom he took it.** The Gemara explains: **One gives it without knowing to whom he gave it,** this serves **to exclude** the practice **of Mar Ukva,** who would personally give charity to poor people without their knowing he was the donor. The other one **takes it without knowing from whom he took it;** this serves **to exclude** the practice **of Rabbi Abba,** who would render his money ownerless, so that poor people would come and take it without his knowing whom he helped, although they would know from whom the money came. The Gemara asks: **Rather, how** then **should one act** to conceal his own identity and also remain ignorant of the identities of the recipients? The Gemara answers: The best method is **to put** the money **into the charity purse.**[N]

מֵיתִיבֵי: מַה יַּעֲשֶׂה אָדָם וְיִהְיוּ לוֹ בָּנִים זְכָרִים? רַבִּי אֱלִיעֶזֶר אוֹמֵר: יְפַזֵּר מְעוֹתָיו לַעֲנִיִּים; רַבִּי יְהוֹשֻׁעַ אוֹמֵר: יְשַׂמַּח אִשְׁתּוֹ לִדְבַר מִצְוָה; רַבִּי אֱלִיעֶזֶר בֶּן יַעֲקֹב אוֹמֵר: לֹא יִתֵּן אָדָם פְּרוּטָה לְאַרְנָקִי שֶׁל צְדָקָה אֶלָּא אִם כֵּן מְמוּנֶּה עָלֶיהָ כְּרַבִּי חֲנַנְיָא בֶּן תְּרַדְיוֹן! כִּי קָא אָמְרִינַן – דִּמְמַנֵּי עֲלַהּ כְּרַבִּי חֲנַנְיָא בֶּן תְּרַדְיוֹן.

The Gemara **raises an objection** from what is taught in a *baraita*: **What should a person do to have male offspring?**[N] **Rabbi Eliezer says: He should distribute his money liberally among the poor. Rabbi Yehoshua says: He should gladden his wife before** engaging in the **mitzva** of conjugal relations. **Rabbi Eliezer ben Ya'akov says: A person should not donate a *peruta* to the charity purse unless** a great and trusted individual **like Rabbi Ḥananya ben Teradyon**[P] **is appointed** as supervisor **over it.** This seems to indicate that putting money into the charity box is not always preferred. The Gemara answers: **When we say** that putting money into the charity box is the preferred way to give charity, this is referring to **when** a man **like Rabbi Ḥananya ben Teradyon is appointed** as supervisor **over it.**

אָמַר רַבִּי אַבָּהוּ, אָמַר מֹשֶׁה לִפְנֵי הַקָּדוֹשׁ בָּרוּךְ הוּא: רִבּוֹנוֹ שֶׁל עוֹלָם, בַּמֶּה תָּרוּם קֶרֶן יִשְׂרָאֵל? אָמַר לוֹ: בְּ״כִי תִשָּׂא״.

The Gemara discusses other matters concerning charity. **Rabbi Abbahu says: Moses said before the Holy One, Blessed be He: Master of the Universe, with what shall the horn of Israel be exalted? God said to him: With** the passage of **"When you raise,"** i.e., Israel will be exalted by way of the donations and charity that they will give, as it is stated: "When you raise the heads of the children of Israel…then shall they give" (Exodus 30:12).

וְאָמַר רַבִּי אַבָּהוּ, שָׁאֲלוּ אֶת שְׁלֹמֹה בֶּן דָּוִד: עַד הֵיכָן כֹּחָהּ שֶׁל צְדָקָה? אָמַר לָהֶן, צְאוּ וּרְאוּ מַה פֵּירַשׁ דָּוִד אַבָּא: ״פִּזַּר נָתַן לָאֶבְיוֹנִים צִדְקָתוֹ עוֹמֶדֶת לָעַד קַרְנוֹ תָּרוּם בְּכָבוֹד״. רַבִּי אַבָּא אָמַר, מֵהָכָא: ״הוּא מְרוֹמִים יִשְׁכֹּן מְצָדוֹת סְלָעִים מִשְׂגַּבּוֹ לַחְמוֹ נִתָּן מֵימָיו נֶאֱמָנִים״, מַה טַּעַם ״מְרוֹמִים יִשְׁכֹּן מְצָדוֹת סְלָעִים מִשְׂגַּבּוֹ״? מִשּׁוּם דְּ״לַחְמוֹ נִתָּן״ וּ״מֵימָיו נֶאֱמָנִים״.

And Rabbi Abbahu says: They asked King **Solomon, son of David: How far does the power of charity extend?** King Solomon **said to them: Go out and see what my father David explained: "He has distributed freely, he has given to the poor, his righteousness endures forever, his horn shall be exalted with honor"** (Psalms 112:9). **Rabbi Abba said:** It is derived **from here** how far the power of charity extends: **"He shall dwell on high, his place of defense shall be the fortress of rocks; his bread shall be given, his water shall be sure"** (Isaiah 33:16). **What is the reason** that **"He shall dwell on high, his place of defense shall be the fortress of rocks"? Because "his bread shall be given"** to the poor, **and "his water shall be sure,"** i.e., it shall be given faithfully and he can be trusted in the matter.

PERSONALITIES

Rabbi Ḥananya ben Teradyon – רַבִּי חֲנַנְיָא בֶּן תְּרַדְיוֹן: A fourth- and fifth-generation *tanna*, Rabbi Ḥananya lived in Sikhni in the Upper Galilee, where he apparently presided over a large yeshiva. Although few of his statements are preserved in the Mishna and other sources, it is clear from several sources that he was a charity collector and that he also gave charity liberally. Following the bar Kokheva revolt, he defied the decrees against teaching Torah in public despite the mortal danger of such activity. Rabbi Ḥananya was caught by the authorities and sentenced to death. The Romans wrapped him in a Torah and burned him along with it. He is listed in the midrash and liturgical poetry as one of the ten martyrs, the rabbis who were executed by the Romans in the period after the destruction of the Second Temple.

Rabbi Ḥananya's wife was executed as well. Of his children, one son was killed by the Roman authorities, and one daughter was sent to a brothel, though she was eventually rescued by her brother-in-law. Rabbi Ḥananya's daughter Berurya was a famous Torah scholar on par with the *tanna'im*, and she married the *tanna* Rabbi Meir.

וְאָמַר רַבִּי אַבָּהוּ, שָׁאֲלוּ אֶת שְׁלֹמֹה: אֵיזֶהוּ בֶּן הָעוֹלָם הַבָּא? אָמַר לָהֶם: כָּל שֶׁ״כְּנֶגֶד זְקֵנָיו כָּבוֹד״. כִּי הָא דְּיוֹסֵף בְּרֵיהּ דְּרַבִּי יְהוֹשֻׁעַ חֲלַשׁ, אִינְגִּיד. אֲמַר לֵיהּ אֲבוּהּ: מַאי חֲזֵית? אֲמַר לֵיהּ: עוֹלָם הָפוּךְ רָאִיתִי, עֶלְיוֹנִים לְמַטָּה וְתַחְתּוֹנִים לְמַעְלָה. אֲמַר לֵיהּ: עוֹלָם בָּרוּר רָאִיתָ. וַאֲנַן הֵיכִי חֲזִיתִינַן? [אֲמַר לֵיהּ:] כִּי הֵיכִי דַּחֲשִׁיבִינַן הָכָא חֲשִׁיבִינַן הָתָם.

And Rabbi Abbahu says: They asked King **Solomon: Who is one** who is destined **for the World-to-Come?** King Solomon **said to them: All** those about whom it is stated: **"And before His Elders will be His glory"** (Isaiah 24:23),[N] referring to those who are honored in this world due to their wisdom. This is **like** the incident involving **Yosef, son of Rabbi Yehoshua, who became ill** and **fainted.** When he returned to good health, **his father said to him: What did you see** when you were not conscious? Yosef **said to him: I saw an inverted world. Those above,** i.e., those who are considered important in this world, were **below,**[N] insignificant, while **those below,** i.e., those who are insignificant in this world, were **above.** Rabbi Yehoshua **said to him: You have seen a clear world.** The world you have seen is the true world, one in which one's spiritual and moral standing determines his true importance. Rabbi Yehoshua further asked him: **And how did you see us,** the Torah scholars, there? Yosef **said to him: Just as we are important here, we are important there.**

וְשָׁמַעְתִּי שֶׁהָיוּ אוֹמְרִים: אַשְׁרֵי מִי שֶׁבָּא לְכָאן וְתַלְמוּדוֹ בְּיָדוֹ. וְשָׁמַעְתִּי שֶׁהָיוּ אוֹמְרִים: הֲרוּגֵי מַלְכוּת – אֵין כָּל בְּרִיָּה יְכוֹלָה לַעֲמוֹד בִּמְחִיצָּתָן. מַאן נִינְהוּ? אִילֵימָא רַבִּי עֲקִיבָא וַחֲבֵרָיו – מִשּׁוּם הֲרוּגֵי מַלְכוּת וְתוּ לָא? פְּשִׁיטָא, בְּלָאו הָכִי נַמִי! אֶלָּא הֲרוּגֵי לוֹד.

Yosef added: **And I heard that they were saying** in that world: **Happy is the one who arrives with his studies in hand. And I** also **heard that they were saying: Those executed by the government** enjoy such exalted status that **no one can stand in their section.** The Gemara asks: **Who are these** martyrs to whom Yosef was referring? **If we say** that he was referring to **Rabbi Akiva and his colleagues,** who were killed by the Romans, this cannot be: Is their elevated status **due** only **to** the fact that **they were martyred by** the Roman **government and nothing more?** These men were exceptional in their piety and sanctity during their lives as well. Therefore **it** is **obvious that even without** their martyrdom they would be greater than other people. **Rather,** it is referring to those like **the martyrs of Lod,**[B] who died for the sanctification of God's name but were not Torah scholars.

תַּנְיָא, אָמַר לָהֶן רַבָּן יוֹחָנָן בֶּן זַכַּאי לְתַלְמִידָיו: בָּנַי, מַהוּ שֶׁאָמַר הַכָּתוּב ״צְדָקָה תְּרוֹמֵם גּוֹי וְחֶסֶד לְאֻמִּים חַטָּאת״? נַעֲנָה רַבִּי אֱלִיעֶזֶר וְאָמַר: ״צְדָקָה תְּרוֹמֵם גּוֹי״ – אֵלּוּ יִשְׂרָאֵל, דִּכְתִיב: ״וּמִי כְּעַמְּךָ יִשְׂרָאֵל גּוֹי אֶחָד בָּאָרֶץ״, ״וְחֶסֶד לְאֻמִּים חַטָּאת״ – כָּל צְדָקָה וָחֶסֶד שֶׁאוּמּוֹת הָעוֹלָם עוֹשִׂין, חֵטְא הוּא לָהֶן, שֶׁאֵינָם עוֹשִׂין אֶלָּא לְהִתְגַּדֵּל בּוֹ, כְּמוֹ שֶׁנֶּאֱמַר: ״דִּי לֶהֱוֹן מְהַקְרְבִין נִיחוֹחִין לֶאֱלָהּ שְׁמַיָּא וּמְצַלַּיִן לְחַיֵּי מַלְכָּא וּבְנוֹהִי״.

It is taught in a *baraita*: **Rabban Yoḥanan ben Zakkai said to his students: My sons, what is** the meaning of **that which the verse states: "Righteousness exalts a nation, but the kindness of the peoples is sin"** (Proverbs 14:34)? **Rabbi Eliezer answered and said: "Righteousness exalts a nation"; these are** the people **of Israel, as it is written: "And who is like your people Israel, one nation on the earth?"** (I Chronicles 17:21). **"But the kindness of the peoples is sin,"** meaning that **all the** acts of **charity and kindness that the nations of the world perform is** counted **as a sin for them, since they perform them only to elevate them**selves in prestige, **as it is stated: "That they may sacrifice offerings of pleasing aroma to the God of heaven, and pray for the life of the king and of his sons"** (Ezra 6:10). Even though they donated offerings, they did so only for their own benefit.

וּדְעָבֵיד הָכִי לָאו צְדָקָה גְּמוּרָה הִיא? וְהָתַנְיָא: הָאוֹמֵר ״סֶלַע זֶה לִצְדָקָה בִּשְׁבִיל שֶׁיִּחְיוּ בָּנַי, וּבִשְׁבִיל שֶׁאֶזְכֶּה לָעוֹלָם הַבָּא״ – הֲרֵי זֶה צַדִּיק גָּמוּר! לָא קַשְׁיָא: כָּאן בְּיִשְׂרָאֵל, כָּאן בְּגוֹי.

The Gemara asks: **And if one acts this way, is it not full-fledged charity? But isn't it taught** in a *baraita* that **one who says:** I am contributing **this** ***sela*** **to charity so that my sons will live, or** if he says: I am performing the mitzva **so that I will merit** a share in **the World-to-Come, this** person **is a full-fledged righteous person,** as far as that mitzva is concerned, even though he has his own welfare in mind? The Gemara answers: This is **not difficult. Here,** the statement that he is considered absolutely righteous is **with regard to a Jew;**[N] while **there,** the statement that such benefaction is not credited as charity is **with regard to a gentile.**

NOTES

And before His Elders will be His glory – **שֶׁכְּנֶגֶד זְקֵנָיו כָּבוֹד:** These words in the verse refer to one who merits honor due to his wisdom rather than his wealth or power (Rashi). The Meiri explains this in accordance with the statement that God is pleased with those individuals with whom other people are pleased (see *Avot* 3:13); one who is honored by his local elders in this world finds favor in the eyes of God as well.

Those above were below – **עֶלְיוֹנִים לְמַטָּה:** That is, those who were important in this world because of their wealth or power appear in a low position in the upper world. But those who were important here due to their wisdom are important there as well.

Here with regard to a Jew – **כָּאן בְּיִשְׂרָאֵל:** Jews do not donate money on condition; when they decide to contribute, they do so even if the desired benefit, e.g., that a son will live, is likely not to materialize. Gentiles, by contrast, make their donations conditional and regret their generosity if their reward is not forthcoming, as the verse states: "And it shall come to pass, that when they shall be hungry, they shall fret themselves, and curse their king and their god, and look upward" (Isaiah 8:21).

BACKGROUND

The martyrs of Lod – **הֲרוּגֵי לוֹד:** There are conflicting traditions with regard to the meritorious act of those who were martyred in Lod and the circumstances surrounding their execution. Some (Rabbeinu Ḥananel) identify the martyrs with Shemaya and his brother. Another tradition identifies these martyrs as Pappos and Luliyanos, two wealthy leaders of Israel who were killed in Ludkiya, also known as Lod. It is related that when the daughter of the Caesar was killed the Jews were blamed. In order to save the Jews Pappos and Luliyanos claimed responsibility for her death. They were subsequently executed for their confession. Due to their willingness to sacrifice their lives for the sake of the community their merits are so great that nobody can stand before them.

נענה רבי יהושע ואמר: "צדקה תרומם גוי" – אלו ישראל, דכתיב: "ומי כעמך ישראל גוי אחד", "וחסד לאמים חטאת" – כל צדקה וחסד שאומות העולם עושין, חטא הוא להן, שאין עושין אלא כדי שתמשך מלכותן, שנאמר: "להן מלכא מלכי ישפר עלך וחטיך בצדקה פרק ועויתך במחן ענין הן תהוי ארכא לשלותך" וגו׳.

Rabbi Yehoshua answered Rabban Yoḥanan ben Zakkai's challenge to interpret the verse **and said: "Righteousness exalts a nation"; these are** the people **of Israel, as it is written: "And who is like your people Israel, one nation** on the earth." **"But the kindness of the peoples is sin"** means that **all the acts of charity and kindness that the nations of the world perform** is counted **as a sin for them, since they perform them only to perpetuate their dominion, as it is stated** by Daniel to Nebuchadnezzar: **"Therefore, O king, let my counsel be acceptable to you, and break off your sins by charity, and your iniquities by showing mercy to the poor; that there may be an extension of your serenity"** (Daniel 4:24). Since this is the argument that persuaded Nebuchadnezzar, it would appear that his actual motive was his own benefit.

נענה רבן גמליאל ואמר: "צדקה תרומם גוי" – אלו ישראל, דכתיב: "ומי כעמך ישראל" [וגו׳], "וחסד לאמים חטאת" – כל צדקה וחסד שגויים עושין, חטא הוא להן, שאין עושין אלא להתיהר בו, וכל המתיהר נופל בגיהנם, שנאמר: "זד יהיר לץ שמו עושה בעברת זדון", ואין עברה אלא גיהנם, שנאמר: "יום עברה היום ההוא".

Rabban Gamliel answered and said: "Righteousness exalts a nation"; these are the people **of Israel, as it is written: "And who is like your people Israel,** one nation on the earth." **"But the kindness of the peoples is sin"** means that **all the acts of charity and kindness that the nations of the world perform is** counted as **a sin for them, since they perform them only in order to act haughtily through them, and whoever acts haughtily falls into Gehenna, as it is stated: "The proud and haughty one, scorner is his name, acts in arrogant wrath"** (Proverbs 21:24). **And wrath means nothing other than Gehenna, as it is stated: "That day is a day of wrath"** (Zephaniah 1:15).

אמר רבן גמליאל: עדיין אנו צריכין למודעי. רבי אליעזר המודעי אומר: "צדקה תרומם גוי" – אלו ישראל, דכתיב: "ומי כעמך ישראל גוי אחד", "וחסד לאמים חטאת" – כל צדקה וחסד שאומות העולם עושין, חטא הוא להן, שאין עושין אלא לחרף אותנו בו, שנאמר: "ויבא ויעש ה׳ כאשר דבר כי חטאתם לה׳ ולא שמעתם בקולו והיה לכם הדבר הזה".

Rabban Gamliel said: We still need to hear what **the Moda'i** has to say, as **Rabbi Eliezer HaModa'i**[P] **says: "Righteousness exalts a nation"; these are** the people **of Israel, as it is written: "And who is like your people Israel, one nation on the earth." "But the kindness of the peoples is sin"** means that **all the acts of charity and kindness that the nations of the world perform** is counted **as a sin for them, since they perform them only to taunt us with them, as it is stated** that the Babylonian officer Nebuzaradan said: **"The Lord has brought it, and done according as He has said; because you have sinned against the Lord and have not obeyed His voice, therefore this matter is come upon you"** (Jeremiah 40:3).

נענה רבי נחוניא בן הקנה ואמר: "צדקה תרומם גוי וחסד" – לישראל, ו"לאמים – חטאת". אמר להם רבן יוחנן בן זכאי לתלמידיו: נראין דברי רבי נחוניא בן הקנה מדברי ומדבריכם, לפי שהוא נותן צדקה וחסד לישראל, ולאומים חטאת. מכלל דהוא נמי אמר, מאי היא? דתניא, אמר להם רבן יוחנן בן זכאי: כשם שהחטאת מכפרת על ישראל, כך צדקה מכפרת על אומות העולם.

Rabbi Neḥunya ben HaKana answered and said: "Righteousness exalts a nation and kindness" is referring to **Israel; and** in addition, **"of the peoples is sin." Rabban Yoḥanan ben Zakkai said to his students: The statement of Rabbi Neḥunya ben HaKana appears** to be more precise **than** both **my statement and your statements, because he assigns** both **righteousness and kindness to Israel, and sin to the peoples** of the world. The Gemara asks: **By inference,** it appears **that he,** Rabban Yoḥanan ben Zakkai, **also offered** an interpretation of this verse. **What is it? As it is taught** in a *baraita*: **Rabban Yoḥanan ben Zakkai said to them** that the verse should be understood as follows: **Just as a sin-offering atones for Israel, so charity atones for the nations of the world.**

איפרא הורמיז, אימיה דשבור מלכא, שדרה ארבע מאה דינרי לקמיה דרבי אמי ולא קבלינהו; שדרינהו קמיה דרבא, וקבלינהו משום שלום מלכות. שמע רבי אמי איקפד, אמר: לית ליה "ביבש קצירה תשברנה נשים באות מאירות אותה"? ורבא, משום שלום מלכות.

It is related that **Ifera Hurmiz, the mother of King Shapur,** king of Persia, **sent four hundred dinars to Rabbi Ami, but he did not accept them.**[N] **She** then **sent them to Rava, and he accepted them for the sake of peace with the kingdom.**[H] **Rabbi Ami heard** what Rava had done **and was angry. He said: Does** Rava **not accept** the lesson of the verse: **"When the boughs are withered, they shall be broken off; the women shall come and set them on fire"** (Isaiah 27:11), meaning that when righteousness has ceased from a particular nation, it is time for its citizens to be punished, and therefore we should not help them perform any meritorious deeds, which would delay their punishment? The Gemara asks: **And** why did **Rava** accept the money? The Gemara answers: He did so **for the sake of peace with the kingdom.**

PERSONALITIES

Rabbi Eliezer HaModa'i – רבי אליעזר המודעי: Rabbi Eliezer HaModa'i was a Sage who lived after the destruction of the Temple and was apparently a young student of Rabban Yoḥanan ben Zakkai. Most of the quotations cited in his name are explications of verses. Rabban Gamliel often remarked: We still need the Moda'i. As his name indicates, this Sage was from the city of Modi'in. Rabbi Eliezer HaModa'i was bar Kokheva's maternal uncle, and he died during the siege of Beitar.

NOTES

But he did not accept them – ולא קבלינהו: This is because it is a disgrace to Jews when they are unable to take care of their own and are forced to accept charity from gentiles. An individual Jew who openly accepts charity from a gentile is despicable and even disqualified from serving as a witness.

HALAKHA

And he accepted them for the sake of peace with the kingdom – וקבלינהו משום שלום מלכות: A Jew should not accept charity from a gentile in public. If he is unable to survive without such charity, he should receive the money in private. Nevertheless, if a gentile king or officer donates money to the Jews for the poor, the money is accepted for the sake of peace with the kingdom. These funds are then given in secret to poor gentiles, as in the case involving Rava. The Rema writes that if the money was earmarked for distribution among the Jewish poor, it should be given to them and the donor should not be deceived. The money should be given to poor gentiles only if the official did not specify how it was to be used (Rambam *Sefer Zera'im, Hilkhot Mattenot Aniyyim* 8:9; *Shulḥan Arukh, Yoreh De'a* 254:1–2 and *Shakh* there).

ורבי אמי נמי, משום שלום מלכות – דאיבעי ליה למפלגינהו לעניי גויים. ורבא נמי, לעניי גויים יהבינהו. ורבי אמי דאיקפד הוא

The Gemara asks: **But** did **Rabbi Ami** not **also** see the importance of accepting the money **for the sake of peace with the kingdom?** The Gemara answers: Rabbi Ami maintains that Rava **should have distributed** the money **to the gentile poor** rather than to the Jewish poor, as it is a disgrace to the Jews to require the kindness of the nations of the world in order to support their poor. The Gemara comments: In fact, **Rava also gave** the money **to the gentile poor** and not to the Jewish poor. **And Rabbi Ami got angry** because

Perek **I**
Daf **11** Amud **a**

דלא סיימוה קמיה.

those who reported the story to him **did not conclude it before him;** consequently, Rav Ami was not informed that Rava had indeed given the money to the gentile poor.

תניא: אמרו עליו על בנימין הצדיק שהיה ממונה על קופה של צדקה, פעם אחת באתה אשה לפניו בשני בצורת, אמרה לו: רבי, פרנסני! אמר לה: העבודה, שאין בקופה של צדקה כלום! אמרה לו: רבי, אם אין אתה מפרנסני, הרי אשה ושבעה בניה מתים! עמד ופרנסה משלו. לימים חלה ונטה למות, אמרו מלאכי השרת לפני הקדוש ברוך הוא: רבונו של עולם, אתה אמרת: כל המקיים נפש אחת מישראל כאילו קיים עולם מלא, ובנימין הצדיק שהחיה אשה ושבעה בניה ימות בשנים מועטות הללו? מיד קרעו לו גזר דינו. תנא: הוסיפו לו עשרים ושתים שנה על שנותיו.

§ **It is taught** in a *baraita*: The following **was said about Binyamin the righteous,**[P] **who was appointed** supervisor **over the charity fund. Once, a woman came before him during years of drought** and **said to him: My master, sustain me. He said to her:** I swear **by the Temple service that there is nothing** left **in the charity fund. She said to him: My master, if you do not sustain me, a woman and her seven sons will die. He arose and sustained her with his own** funds. **After some time, he fell deathly ill. The ministering angels said to the Holy One, Blessed be He: Master of the Universe, You said** that **anyone who preserves**[H] **a single life in Israel is** regarded **as if he has preserved an entire world. Should** then **Binyamin the righteous, who saved a woman and her seven sons, die after these few years,** still in his youth? **They immediately tore up his sentence.** A Sage **taught: They added twenty-two years to his life.**

תנו רבנן: מעשה במונבז המלך שבזבז אוצרותיו ואוצרות אבותיו בשני בצורת, וחברו עליו אחיו ובית אביו ואמרו לו: אבותיך גנזו והוסיפו על של אבותם, ואתה מבזבזם! אמר להם: אבותי גנזו למטה, ואני גנזתי למעלה, שנאמר: "אמת מארץ תצמח וצדק משמים נשקף"; אבותי גנזו במקום שהיד שולטת בו, ואני גנזתי במקום שאין היד שולטת בו, שנאמר: "צדק ומשפט מכון כסאך";

The Sages taught: There was **an incident involving King Munbaz,**[P] **who liberally gave away his treasures and the treasures of his ancestors in the years of drought,** distributing the money to the poor. **His brothers and his father's household joined together against him** to protest against his actions, **and they said to him: Your ancestors stored up** money in their treasuries **and added to** the treasures **of their ancestors, and you are liberally distributing** it all to the poor. King Munbaz **said to them:** Not so, **my ancestors stored up below, whereas I am storing above, as it is stated: "Truth will spring out of the earth and righteousness will look down from heaven"** (Psalms 85:12), meaning that the righteous deeds that one has performed are stored up in heaven. **My ancestors stored up** treasures **in a place where the** human **hand can reach,** and so their treasures could have been robbed, **whereas I am storing up** treasures **in a place where the** human **hand cannot reach,** and so they are secure, **as it is stated: "Righteousness and justice are the foundation of Your throne"** (Psalms 89:15).

אבותי גנזו דבר שאין עושה פירות, ואני גנזתי דבר שעושה פירות, שנאמר: "אמרו צדיק כי טוב כי פרי מעלליהם יאכלו"; אבותי גנזו [אוצרות] ממון ואני גנזתי אוצרות נפשות, שנאמר: "פרי צדיק עץ חיים ולוקח נפשות חכם"; אבותי גנזו לאחרים, ואני גנזתי לעצמי, שנאמר: "ולך תהיה צדקה"; אבותי גנזו לעולם הזה, ואני גנזתי לעולם הבא, שנאמר: "והלך לפניך צדקך כבוד ה' יאספך".

My ancestors stored up something that does not generate profit, as money sitting in a treasury does not increase, **whereas I am storing up something that generates profit, as it is stated: "Say of the righteous, that it shall be well with them, for they shall eat the fruit of their doings"** (Isaiah 3:10). **My ancestors stored up treasures of money, whereas I am storing up treasures of souls, as it is stated: "The fruit of the righteous is a tree of life, and he that wins souls is wise"** (Proverbs 11:30). **My ancestors stored up for others,** for their sons and heirs, when they themselves would pass from this world, **whereas I am storing up for myself, as it is stated: "And it shall be as righteousness to you"** (Deuteronomy 24:13). **My ancestors stored up for this world, whereas I am storing up for the World-to-Come, as it is stated: "And your righteousness shall go before you, the glory of the Lord shall be your rearguard"** (Isaiah 58:8).

PERSONALITIES

Binyamin the righteous – בנימין הצדיק: This Binyamin appears to have lived during the amoraic period. Alternatively, he might be the *tanna* Rabbi Binyamin, student of Rabbi Akiva, or the *tanna* Abba Binyamin.

Munbaz – מונבז: Munbaz was the king of Adiabene at the end of the Second Temple period. This tiny principality was an independent kingdom in the Parthian empire located in northern Aram Naharaim in the area that today includes Kirkuk and Mosul. Members of the royal family of Adiabene and some of the military joined the rebels against Rome during the great rebellion before the destruction of the Temple. Munbaz's mother, Queen Helene, and his brother, Izats, called Zutus in the talmudic sources, converted to Judaism and scrupulously kept the mitzvot (see *Bereshit Rabba*, chapter 46, and *Nidda* 17a). Initially, Munbaz abdicated the throne for the sake of his brother but subsequently accepted the throne upon the latter's death. Josephus describes the history and conversion of this family in detail. Like the rest of his family, Munbaz appears to have been buried in the Tombs of the Kings in Jerusalem.

Sarcophagus of Queen Helene, mother of Munbaz

HALAKHA

Anyone who preserves – כל המקיים: Whoever preserves the life of single Jew is regarded as if he has saved the entire world (Rambam *Sefer Nezikin*, *Hilkhot Rotze'aḥ UShmirat Nefesh* 1:16 and *Sefer Shofetim*, *Hilkhot Sanhedrin* 12:3).

״וְאִם קָנָה בָּהּ בֵּית דִּירָה – הֲרֵי הוּא כְּאַנְשֵׁי הָעִיר״. מַתְנִיתִין דְּלָא כְּרַבָּן שִׁמְעוֹן בֶּן גַּמְלִיאֵל; דְּתַנְיָא, רַבָּן שִׁמְעוֹן בֶּן גַּמְלִיאֵל אוֹמֵר: אִם קָנָה בָּהּ קַרְקַע כָּל שֶׁהוּא – הֲרֵי הוּא כְּאַנְשֵׁי הָעִיר.

§ The Gemara resumes its analysis of the mishna, which taught that one must reside in a place for twelve months in order to be considered a resident for the purposes of issues such as paying taxes. But if he **bought** himself **a residence in** the city, **he is** immediately considered **like** one of **the people of the city.** The Gemara comments: **The mishna is not in accordance with** the opinion of **Rabban Shimon ben Gamliel, as it is taught** in a *baraita* that **Rabban Shimon ben Gamliel says: If he bought any amount of land in** the city, and not necessarily a residence, **he is** immediately considered **like** one of **the people of the city.**

וְהָא תַּנְיָא, רַבָּן שִׁמְעוֹן בֶּן גַּמְלִיאֵל אוֹמֵר: אִם קָנָה שָׁם קַרְקַע הָרְאוּיָה לְבֵית דִּירָה – הֲרֵי הוּא כְּאַנְשֵׁי הָעִיר! תְּרֵי תַּנָּאֵי וְאַלִּיבָּא דְּרַבָּן שִׁמְעוֹן בֶּן גַּמְלִיאֵל.

The Gemara asks: **But isn't it taught** otherwise in a different *baraita*: **Rabban Shimon ben Gamliel says: If** one **bought land that is suitable for a residence, he is** immediately considered **like** one of **the people of the city.** This contradicts the first *baraita*. The Gemara answers: This is a dispute between **two** *tanna'im* **and** they disagree **with regard to** the opinion **of Rabban Shimon ben Gamliel.**

מתני׳ אֵין חוֹלְקִין אֶת הֶחָצֵר – עַד שֶׁיְּהֵא אַרְבַּע אַמּוֹת לָזֶה וְאַרְבַּע אַמּוֹת לָזֶה. וְלֹא אֶת הַשָּׂדֶה – עַד שֶׁיְּהֵא בָּהּ תִּשְׁעָה קַבִּין לָזֶה וְתִשְׁעָה קַבִּין לָזֶה; רַבִּי יְהוּדָה אוֹמֵר: עַד שֶׁיְּהֵא בָּהּ תִּשְׁעַת חֲצָיֵי קַבִּין לָזֶה וְתִשְׁעַת חֲצָיֵי קַבִּין לָזֶה. וְלֹא אֶת הַגִּינָּה – עַד שֶׁיְּהֵא בָּהּ חֲצִי קַב לָזֶה וַחֲצִי קַב לָזֶה; רַבִּי עֲקִיבָא אוֹמֵר: בֵּית רוֹבַע.

MISHNA The court **does not divide**[H] **a courtyard** at the request of one of the joint owners **unless there will be** in it four by **four cubits for this one and** four by **four cubits for that one,** i.e., this minimum area for each of the joint owners. **And** the court does **not** divide **a** jointly owned **field unless there is** space **in it** to plant **nine** *kav*[B] of seed **for this one and nine** *kav* of seed **for that one. Rabbi Yehuda says:** The court does not divide a field **unless there is** space **in it** to plant **nine half-*kav*** of seed **for this one and nine half-*kav*** of seed **for that one. And** the court does **not** divide a jointly owned **garden unless there is** space **in it** to plant **a half-*kav*** of seed **for this one and a half-*kav*** of seed **for that one. Rabbi Akiva says** that half that amount is sufficient, i.e., the **area required for sowing a quarter-*kav*** **of seed** [*beit rova*].

וְלֹא אֶת הַטְּרַקְלִין, וְלֹא אֶת הַמּוֹרָן, וְלֹא אֶת הַשּׁוֹבָךְ, וְלֹא אֶת הַטַּלִּית, וְלֹא אֶת הַמֶּרְחָץ, וְלֹא אֶת בֵּית הַבַּד, וְלֹא אֶת בֵּית הַשְּׁלָחִין – עַד שֶׁיְּהֵא בָּהֶן כְּדֵי לָזֶה וּכְדֵי לָזֶה. זֶה הַכְּלָל: כָּל שֶׁיֵּחָלֵק וּשְׁמוֹ עָלָיו – חוֹלְקִין, וְאִם לָאו – אֵין חוֹלְקִין.

Similarly, the court does **not** divide **a hall** [*hateraklin*],[HL] **a drawing room, a dovecote,**[B] **a cloak, a bathhouse, an olive press, and an irrigated field**[N] **unless there is enough for this one** to use the property in the usual manner **and enough for that one** to use the property in the usual manner. **This is the principle: Anything** for **which** when it **is divided,** each of the parts is large enough to **retain the name** of the original item, the court **divides** it. **But if** the parts will **not** retain the original name, the court **does not divide** it.

אֵימָתַי? בִּזְמַן שֶׁאֵין שְׁנֵיהֶם רוֹצִים, אֲבָל בִּזְמַן שֶׁשְּׁנֵיהֶם רוֹצִים – אֲפִילּוּ פָּחוֹת מִכָּאן יַחֲלוֹקוּ. וְכִתְבֵי הַקֹּדֶשׁ, אַף עַל פִּי שֶׁשְּׁנֵיהֶם רוֹצִים – לֹא יַחֲלוֹקוּ.

When does this rule apply? It applies **when** the joint owners **do not both wish** to divide the item; when only one of the owners wishes to divide the property, he cannot force the other to do so. **But when both of them wish**[H] to divide the item, **they may divide** it, **even** if each of the owners will receive **less than** the amounts specified above. **But** in the case of **sacred writings,** i.e., a scroll of any of the twenty-four books of the Bible, that were inherited by two people, **they may not divide** them, **even if both of them wish** to do so, because it would be a show of disrespect to cut the scroll in half.

HALAKHA

The court does not divide – **אֵין חוֹלְקִין**: A jointly owned courtyard, field, or garden is divided only if each party will receive a portion that is large enough to be called by its original designation. Therefore, a courtyard is not divided unless each partner will receive an area of four by four cubits, in addition to the four cubits required for the entrances. A field is divided only if each party will receive a plot large enough to plant nine *kav* of seed in it. A garden is divided only if each party will receive a plot large enough to plant a half-*kav* of seed in it (Rambam *Sefer Kinyan*, *Hilkhot Shekhenim* 1:4, 2:1; *Shulḥan Arukh*, *Ḥoshen Mishpat* 171:3).

Hall, etc. – **טְרַקְלִין וכו׳**: One should not divide a hall, a drawing room, a dovecote, a bathhouse, or a garment unless each of the recipients will receive a portion that can be used in the same manner as the item was used when it was whole (Rambam *Sefer Kinyan*, *Hilkhot Shekhenim* 1:5).

When both of them wish – **בִּזְמַן שֶׁשְּׁנֵיהֶם רוֹצִים**: If partners agree to divide a jointly owned item that is otherwise not fit to be divided, they may divide it, even though the discrete portions will lack their original designation. The twenty-four books of the Bible may not be divided if bound together in a single scroll, even if the partners agree to do so (Rambam *Sefer Kinyan*, *Hilkhot Shekhenim* 2:9; *Shulḥan Arukh*, *Ḥoshen Mishpat* 173:1).

LANGUAGE

Hall [*teraklin*] – **טְרַקְלִין**: From the Greek τρικλίνιον, *triklinion*, which was a room with three couches. The term later came to refer to any large space for entertaining guests.

Roman triclinium

NOTES

Irrigated field – **בֵּית הַשְּׁלָחִין**: Some versions of the text omit these words since this is included under a field. By contrast, Rashi explains that an irrigated field is different; owing to its irrigation system, it is worthwhile to cultivate the field even if it is an area that requires less than nine *kav* of seed.

BACKGROUND

Nine *kav* – **תִּשְׁעָה קַבִּין**: Measurements of area in the Talmud are based on the amount of space required for the sowing of certain quantities of seed. A *beit se'a* is the space required in order to sow one *se'a* of seed and is equivalent to 2,500 square cubits. Accordingly, and in keeping with the different opinions as to the length of a cubit, the area of nine *kav* equals between 950 and 1,400 sq m. The area of a half-*kav* equals 50 to 80 sq m, and the area of a quarter-*kav* equals half of this.

Dovecote – **שׁוֹבָךְ**:

Dovecote

גמ׳ אָמַר רַבִּי אַסִּי אָמַר רַבִּי יוֹחָנָן: אַרְבַּע אַמּוֹת שֶׁאָמְרוּ, חוּץ מִשֶּׁל פְּתָחִים. תַּנְיָא נַמִּי הָכִי: אֵין חוֹלְקִים אֶת הֶחָצֵר – עַד שֶׁיְּהֵא בָּהּ שְׁמוֹנֶה אַמּוֹת לָזֶה וּשְׁמוֹנֶה אַמּוֹת לָזֶה; וְהָא אֲנַן תְּנַן: אַרְבַּע אַמּוֹת לָזֶה וְאַרְבַּע אַמּוֹת לָזֶה! אֶלָּא שְׁמַע מִינָּהּ כִּדְרַבִּי אַסִּי, שְׁמַע מִינָּהּ.

GEMARA **Rabbi Asi says** that **Rabbi Yoḥanan says: The four cubits** of the courtyard **which they said** each of the joint owners must receive is **in addition to** the space in front of **the entrances**[BH] to each of the houses that is assigned to the owner of the house for loading and unloading. That opinion **is also taught** in a *baraita*: The court **does not divide a courtyard unless** its area is sufficient so that **there will be in it eight cubits for this one and eight cubits for that one.** The Gemara asks: **But didn't we learn** in the mishna that it suffices that there be **four cubits for this one and four cubits for that one? Rather, conclude from it** that the *baraita* was taught **in accordance with the opinion of Rabbi Asi.** The Gemara affirms: **Conclude from it** that it is so.

וְאִיכָּא דְּרָמֵי לְהוּ מִירְמָא; תְּנַן: אֵין חוֹלְקִין אֶת הֶחָצֵר – עַד שֶׁיְּהֵא בָּהּ אַרְבַּע אַמּוֹת לָזֶה וְאַרְבַּע אַמּוֹת לָזֶה; וְהָתַנְיָא: שְׁמוֹנֶה אַמּוֹת לָזֶה וּשְׁמוֹנֶה אַמּוֹת לָזֶה! אֲמַר רַבִּי אַסִּי אֲמַר רַבִּי יוֹחָנָן: אַרְבַּע אַמּוֹת שֶׁאָמְרוּ, חוּץ מִשֶּׁל פְּתָחִים.

And there are those **who raise** the *baraita* as a contradiction to what is taught in the mishna and use the previously mentioned point to reconcile the two texts. **We learned** in the mishna: The court **does not divide a courtyard** at the request of one of the joint owners **unless there will be** in it four by **four cubits for this one and** four by **four cubits for that one. But isn't it taught** in a *baraita*: The court does not divide a courtyard unless there are **eight cubits for this one and eight cubits for that one?** About this **Rabbi Asi said** that **Rabbi Yoḥanan said: The four cubits** of the courtyard **which they said** each of the joint owners must receive is **in addition to** the space in front of **the entrances** to each of the houses.

אָמַר רַב הוּנָא: חָצֵר מִתְחַלֶּקֶת לְפִי פְּתָחֶיהָ; וְרַב חִסְדָּא אָמַר: נוֹתְנִין אַרְבַּע אַמּוֹת לְכָל פֶּתַח וּפֶתַח, וְהַשְּׁאָר חוֹלְקִין בְּשָׁוֶה.

Further with regard to the division of a courtyard, **Rav Huna says: A courtyard is divided according to its entrances.**[N] Each of the owners receives a share of the courtyard in proportion to the number of entrances that his house has opening onto the courtyard. **And Rav Ḥisda says: Four cubits are allotted** to each of the owners **for each and every entrance,**[H] **and the rest** of the courtyard **is** then **divided equally** between them.

תַּנְיָא כְּוָותֵיהּ דְּרַב חִסְדָּא: פְּתָחִים שֶׁבֶּחָצֵר יֵשׁ לָהֶן אַרְבַּע אַמּוֹת; הָיָה לָזֶה פֶּתַח אֶחָד וְלָזֶה שְׁנֵי פְתָחִים – זֶה שֶׁיֵּשׁ לוֹ פֶּתַח אֶחָד נוֹטֵל אַרְבַּע אַמּוֹת, וְזֶה שֶׁיֵּשׁ לוֹ שְׁנֵי פְתָחִים נוֹטֵל שְׁמוֹנֶה אַמּוֹת, וְהַשְּׁאָר חוֹלְקִין בְּשָׁוֶה; הָיָה לָזֶה פֶּתַח רָחָב שְׁמוֹנֶה אַמּוֹת – נוֹטֵל שְׁמוֹנֶה אַמּוֹת כְּנֶגֶד הַפֶּתַח וְאַרְבַּע אַמּוֹת בֶּחָצֵר. אַרְבַּע אַמּוֹת בֶּחָצֵר מַאי עֲבִידְתַּיְיהוּ? אֲמַר אַבָּיֵי, הָכִי קָאָמַר: נוֹטֵל שְׁמוֹנֶה אַמּוֹת בְּאוֹרֶךְ הֶחָצֵר וְאַרְבַּע אַמּוֹת בְּרוֹחַב הֶחָצֵר.

The Gemara comments: **It is taught** in a *baraita* **in accordance with** the opinion **of Rav Ḥisda:** Each of **the entrances** opening **to a courtyard** is allotted **four cubits. If this one has one entrance and that one has two entrances, the one who has one entrance takes four cubits, and the one who has two entrances takes eight cubits, and they divide the rest** of the courtyard **equally** between them. If **this one had an entrance eight cubits wide,** he **takes eight cubits adjacent to the entrance and four cubits in the courtyard.** The Gemara expresses surprise: **What are these four cubits in the courtyard doing here?** Doesn't it all depend on the size of the courtyard? **Abaye said: This** is what the *baraita* **is saying:** For the entrance **he takes eight cubits along the length of the courtyard and four cubits along the width of the courtyard.** In other words, he takes a strip four cubits wide along the entire length of his entrance.

אָמַר אַמֵּימָר: הַאי פֵּירָא דְּסוּפְלֵי – יֵשׁ לוֹ אַרְבַּע אַמּוֹת לְכָל רוּחַ וְרוּחַ. וְלָא אֲמַרַן אֶלָּא דְּלָא מְיַיחַד לֵיהּ פִּתְחָא,

Ameimar says: A pit for holding **animal food** [*peira desuflei*][NLH] **has four cubits on each and every side** so that there will be sufficient space for the animals to stand. The Gemara adds: **And we said** this **only when** the pit **has no special entrance**[N] to reach it, but rather it is accessed from all sides.

BACKGROUND

In addition to the entrances – חוּץ מִשֶּׁל פְּתָחִים: According to Rav Ḥisda, whose opinion was accepted as the *halakha*, a courtyard is divided equally between its joint owners, with the exception of an area of four cubits in front of each entrance to a house which is given to the owner of that house.

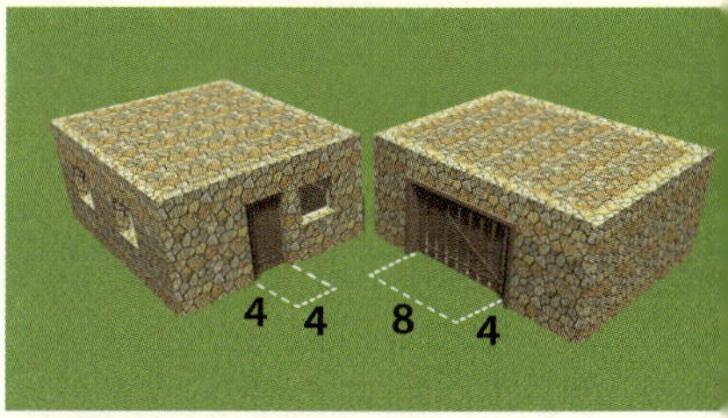

Space afforded each neighbor in front of his doorway

NOTES

A courtyard is divided according to its entrances – חָצֵר מִתְחַלֶּקֶת לְפִי פְּתָחֶיהָ: The commentaries and halakhic authorities agree that this term does not refer to a courtyard purchased by two people, as in such a case each party buys a specific area. Rather, it refers to a courtyard that was inherited, where the father left one son a house with a single entrance and the other a house with several entrances (Rashi). Alternatively, the Gemara is referring to houses that were constructed on ownerless land and subsequently surrounded by a partition that created a courtyard. In such a case, neither neighbor acquired ownership in the courtyard (Ri Migash).

A pit for animal food – פֵּירָא דְּסוּפְלֵי: Some commentaries explain that this passage refers to a father who left a courtyard to his sons and the portion that one received contained a pit for holding animal food (Rabbeinu Gershom). Others suggest that the Gemara is referring to a case where the co-owners of a courtyard wish to divide the courtyard between themselves, and one of the owners has a pit for animal food. Several explanations have been offered for the expression: Pit for animal food. Rashi and others claim the phrase signifies a hole in the ground into which people cast date pits that served as animal food. The *ge'onim* explain that the pit held the lees, leftover from date beer. The Ramah maintains this pit was used to store substances used in the tanning of hides, and the space required alongside it was for unloading the hides.

And we said this only when the pit has no special entrance – וְלָא אֲמַרַן אֶלָּא דְּלָא מְיַיחַד לֵיהּ פִּתְחָא: Rashi explains that the owner of the pit does not have a special opening in his house through which he casts his date pits. Rather, he uses his regular door to go out to the courtyard and from there he makes his way to the pit. Other early commentaries understand that this refers to an entrance to the pit itself. This entrance is constructed for loading and unloading the refuse.

LANGUAGE

Pit for animal food [*peira desuflei*] – פֵּירָא דְּסוּפְלֵי: *Peira* is derived from *pir*, meaning a pit or any other deep place. *Suflei* refers to the refuse of dates, i.e., date pits and skins, or the lees that remain after the dates are converted into beer. After being cast into a pit, this date refuse was used as animal feed.

HALAKHA

In addition to the entrances – חוּץ מִשֶּׁל פְּתָחִים: A jointly owned courtyard may be divided only if each partner will receive an area of four by four cubits, in addition to the four cubits required for the entrances (Rambam *Sefer Kinyan*, *Hilkhot Shekhenim* 2:1; *Shulḥan Arukh*, *Ḥoshen Mishpat* 171:3).

Four cubits are allotted for each and every entrance – נוֹתְנִין אַרְבַּע אַמּוֹת לְכָל פֶּתַח: Before a courtyard is divided, each entrance is granted four cubits in front of it for the entire length of the entrance. This is in accordance with the opinion of Rav Ḥisda, which is supported by the *baraita*. If the entrance is ten cubits wide, its owner receives forty square cubits along the length of the entrance. In any event, he receives an area at least four cubits long, so that if the entrance is less than four cubits wide, he receives additional space on either side of his entrance to complete the four cubits (Rambam *Sefer Kinyan*, *Hilkhot Shekhenim* 2:1; *Shulḥan Arukh*, *Ḥoshen Mishpat* 172:1).

A pit for animal food – פֵּירָא דְּסוּפְלֵי: If a house or any other place in which items are brought in or out has entrances on all sides, the owner is given four cubits for each entrance. But if the owner designated one entrance for bringing items in and out, he is given four cubits only adjacent to that entrance (Rambam *Sefer Kinyan*, *Hilkhot Shekhenim* 2:2; *Shulḥan Arukh*, *Ḥoshen Mishpat* 172:3).

אבל מייחד ליה פיתחא – אין לו אלא ארבע אמות לפני פתחו.

But if he designates an entrance leading to this pit and does not approach it from all sides, **he has four cubits only in front of his entrance.**

אמר רב הונא: אכסדרה אין לה ארבע אמות; טעמא מאי? משום פירוק משאו, הכא אפשר דעייל לגואי ומפרק. מתיב רב ששת: אחד שערי בתים ואחד שערי אכסדראות – יש להן ארבע אמות! כי תניא ההיא – באכסדרה דבי רב. אכסדרה דבי רב, פשיטא, אידרונא מעליא הוא! אלא, באכסדרה רומייתא.

Rav Huna says: A portico [*akhsadra*][LHBN] that opens onto a courtyard **does not have** the adjoining **four cubits.** The Gemara explains: **What is the reason** that four cubits were granted for each entrance? The four cubits were granted so that the owner would have room **for unloading** his animal of **its burden. Here he can go inside** the portico **and unload. Rav Sheshet raises an objection** from a *baraita*: **Both gates of houses and gates of porticos have** the adjoining **four cubits** for unloading. The Gemara answers: **When that** *baraita* **is taught, it is** specifically **with regard to the portico of a study hall,**[N] which is closed and is not used for unloading burdens. The Gemara expresses surprise at this answer: It is **obvious that** this is the *halakha* governing **the portico of a study hall, as it is a proper room. Rather,** the *baraita* is referring to **a Roman portico,**[N] which is more open than the portico of a study hall, but also not used for unloading.

תנו רבנן: בית שער, אכסדרה ומרפסת – יש להן ארבע אמות; היו חמשה בתים פתוחין למרפסת – אין להן אלא ארבע אמות בלבד. בעא מיניה רבי יוחנן מרבי ינאי: לול של תרנגולין, יש לו ארבע אמות או אין לו ארבע אמות? אמר ליה: טעמא מאי? משום פירוק משאו, הכא מטפס ועולה, מטפס ויורד.

The Sages taught in a *baraita*: **A gatehouse,**[HN] **a portico, and a balcony** with a staircase leading down to the courtyard **have** the adjoining **four cubits** for unloading. Even if **five houses open onto the balcony, they only have four cubits** in front of the entrance to the staircase that leads to the balcony. **Rabbi Yoḥanan asked Rabbi Yannai:** Does **a chicken coop**[H] that also has a staircase **have four cubits or does it not have four cubits?** Rabbi Yannai **said to him: What is the reason** that four cubits are granted? It is so that the owner will have room **for unloading** the **burden** of **his** animal. **Here** this space is not needed, as the chickens **climb up**[N] to get into the coop **and climb down** to get out. No additional place is required for the owner to stand alongside them.

בעא מיניה רבא מרב נחמן: בית חציו מקורה וחציו אינו מקורה, יש לו ארבע אמות או אין לו ארבע אמות? אמר ליה: אין לו ארבע אמות; לא מבעיא קירויו מלגיו, דאפשר דעייל לגואי ומפרק, אלא אפילו קירויו כלפי חוץ, אפשר דעייל לגואי ומפרק.

Rava asked Rav Naḥman: If **a house** is **half roofed**[H] **and half unroofed, does it have** the adjoining **four cubits or does it not have** the **four cubits?** Rav Naḥman **said to him: It does not have** the **four cubits.** The Gemara comments: It is **not necessary** to state this *halakha* when the house's **roofing is** over **the inside** portion of the house, **since it is possible** for the owner **to go inside and unload** his animal. **Rather, even** when the house's **roofing is** over **the outside** portion of the house, it is not given four cubits, as even in such a case **it is possible** for the owner **to go inside and unload** his animal there.

LANGUAGE

Portico [*akhsadra*] – אכסדרה: From the Greek ἐξέδρα, *exedra*, which refers to a covered entrance to a house.

HALAKHA

Portico – אכסדרה: If one can enter his portico with his load, he is not given four cubits for its entrance to the courtyard. If he cannot enter, he is granted the four cubits, provided that the portico itself is four square cubits in size (Rambam *Sefer Kinyan*, *Hilkhot Shekhenim* 2:3; *Shulḥan Arukh*, *Ḥoshen Mishpat* 172:4).

Gatehouse – בית שער: A gatehouse and a balcony are each given four cubits adjacent to the entrance. If several houses open to the balcony and the balcony has one entrance to the courtyard, only four cubits are given (Rambam *Sefer Kinyan*, *Hilkhot Shekhenim* 2:4; *Shulḥan Arukh*, *Ḥoshen Mishpat* 172:4).

Chicken coop – לול של תרנגולין: A chicken coop is not granted four cubits adjacent to its entrance (Rambam *Sefer Kinyan*, *Hilkhot Shekhenim* 2:5; *Shulḥan Arukh*, *Ḥoshen Mishpat* 172:5).

If a house is half roofed – בית חציו מקורה: If a building is half roofed and half unroofed, it is not given four cubits adjacent to its entrance, whether the roofed part is on the inside or on the outside. Rav Naḥman holds that four cubits are given if the unroofed area is less than four square cubits (Rambam *Sefer Kinyan*, *Hilkhot Shekhenim* 2:6; *Shulḥan Arukh*, *Ḥoshen Mishpat* 172:6).

BACKGROUND

Portico – אכסדרה:

Regular portico according to Rashi and Rabbeinu Gershom Meor HaGola

Portico of study hall according to Rashi

Roman portico according to Rashi

NOTES

Portico – אכסדרה: There are different opinions with regard to the nature of this construction. Rashi and Rabbeinu Gershom Meor HaGola describe a structure with a roof but no walls. Others say it is closed on three sides but completely open in the front.

Portico of a study hall – אכסדרה דבי רב: Rabbeinu Gershom explains that this term refers to a portico of a schoolhouse for children that has three full walls and a fourth that does not reach the ceiling. Rashi states that all the walls of this portico are formed of windows. The *Arukh* explains that in contrast to a regular portico in which the fourth side is completely open, this portico has very wide pillars on its fourth side. Rav Hai Gaon explains that the entrance to this portico is low and narrow.

Roman portico – אכסדרה רומייתא: Most commentaries understand that this type of portico is surrounded by pillars or low walls. Rav Hai Gaon explains that while the entrance to a portico of a study hall is both low and narrow, the Roman portico has a wide entrance but a low ceiling, so unloading would still be difficult.

Gatehouse – בית שער: Apparently this gatehouse does not belong to all of the courtyard's residents. Rather, one of the residents has a gatehouse which belongs solely to his house. Rabbeinu Gershom understands that the reference is to the gatehouse of a courtyard, which is given four cubits in the alleyway (see also Ramah and Meiri).

They climb up – מטפס ועולה: Rashi explains that four cubits are not required here since the chickens climb up to the coop. Others explain that even the owner of the coop does not require the space because when he feeds the chickens he climbs up and enters the coop (*Ge'onim*).

בְּעָא מִינֵּיהּ רַב הוּנָא מֵרַבִּי אַמִי: אֶחָד מִבְּנֵי מָבוֹי שֶׁבִּקֵּשׁ לְהַחֲזִיר פִּתְחוֹ לְמָבוֹי אַחֵר, בְּנֵי מָבוֹי מְעַכְּבִין עָלָיו אוֹ אֵין מְעַכְּבִין עָלָיו? אֲמַר לֵיהּ: בְּנֵי מָבוֹי מְעַכְּבִין עָלָיו.

§ **Rav Huna asked Rabbi Ami: If one of the residents of an alleyway** onto which several courtyards open **wishes to alter his entrance to a different alleyway,** i.e., to make an entrance to his courtyard that will open onto a different alleyway, can **the residents of the** other **alleyway prevent him**[N] from opening this entrance, **or can they not prevent him** from doing so? Rabbi Ami **said to him: The residents of** the other **alleyway can prevent him** from making the change.[H]

אַכְסַנְיָא, לְפִי בְּנֵי אָדָם מִתְחַלֶּקֶת אוֹ לְפִי פְּתָחִים מִתְחַלֶּקֶת? אֲמַר לֵיהּ: לְפִי בְּנֵי אָדָם מִתְחַלֶּקֶת. תַּנְיָא נַמִּי הָכִי: זֶבֶל שֶׁבֶּחָצֵר מִתְחַלֶּקֶת לְפִי פְּתָחִים, אַכְסַנְיָא – לְפִי בְּנֵי אָדָם.

Rav Huna further asked: When a king issues **a billeting** order to the residents of a courtyard, obligating them to house his soldiers in their homes, is the burden **divided according to** the number of **people**[N] in each household, **or** is it **divided according to** the number of **entrances** that each house has opening into the courtyard? Rabbi Ami **said to him: It is divided according to the** number of **people** in each household. The Gemara comments: **That** opinion **is also taught** in a *baraita*: **The dung in a courtyard**[N] which the residents wish to use **is divided** among them **according to** the number of **entrances** that open into the courtyard, whereas **billeting**[H] is divided **according to** the number of **people** in each household.

אָמַר רַב הוּנָא: אֶחָד מִבְּנֵי מָבוֹי שֶׁבִּקֵּשׁ לִסְתּוֹם כְּנֶגֶד פִּתְחוֹ – בְּנֵי מָבוֹי מְעַכְּבִין עָלָיו, שֶׁמַּרְבֶּה עֲלֵיהֶן אֶת הַדֶּרֶךְ.

Rav Huna says: If one of the residents of an alleyway wishes to close off an area **adjacent to his entrance,**[N] i.e., to build a structure in the alleyway adjacent to the entrance to his courtyard, **the residents of the alleyway can prevent him** from doing so. This is because **it will increase the way for them,** since they will have to circumvent the structure when going to and from their homes.

מֵיתִיבֵי: חָמֵשׁ חֲצֵרוֹת פְּתוּחוֹת לְמָבוֹי – כּוּלָּן מִשְׁתַּמְּשׁוֹת עִם הַחִיצוֹנָה, וְהַחִיצוֹנָה מִשְׁתַּמֶּשֶׁת לְעַצְמָהּ. וְהַשְּׁאָר מִשְׁתַּמְּשׁוֹת עִם הַשְּׁנִיָּה, וְהַשְּׁנִיָּה מִשְׁתַּמֶּשֶׁת לְעַצְמָהּ וּמִשְׁתַּמֶּשֶׁת עִם הַחִיצוֹנָה.

The Gemara **raises an objection** from a *baraita*: If **five courtyards open onto an alleyway,**[HB] **all** the residents of the alleyway may **use** that part of the alleyway that faces the entrance to **the outermost** courtyard, **and** the residents of **the outermost** courtyard may **use** only that part of the alleyway adjacent to **its own** entrance. **And** similarly, the residents of **the other** courtyards may **use** that part of the alleyway that faces **the second** courtyard, i.e., the one next to the outermost courtyard, **and** the residents of **the second** courtyard may **use** that part of the alleyway adjacent to **its own** entrance **and** they may **use** that part of the alleyway facing **the outermost** courtyard.

NOTES

Can the residents of the alleyway prevent him – בְּנֵי מָבוֹי מְעַכְּבִין עָלָיו: Many commentaries, including Rashi, explain that this is referring to residents of an alleyway onto which someone wishes to open a new entrance, and the question is whether they can prevent him from doing so because they do not want another individual to use the alleyway. The Ritva and others understand that the case in the Gemara is where one of the residents of the alleyway wishes to open an entrance to an additional alleyway, and the question is whether the residents that use the latter alleyway can object because they are concerned that residents of the first alleyway will pass through that person's courtyard and enter the second alleyway.

The Ra'avad writes that the two questions of Rav Huna, this one and the following one, are connected, and the issue is whether the residents of an alleyway can prevent one of their members from leaving the alleyway because his leaving would increase the burden on those who remain, in the event they have to billet soldiers. The Rambam appears to have a similar understanding, whereas the Ramban disagrees.

According to the people – לְפִי בְּנֵי אָדָם: Some suggest that this is referring to the relative wealth of the residents; i.e., the wealthier the residents or the larger their house, the greater the number of soldiers they must billet (Responsa *Tzemaḥ Tzedek*).

The dung in a courtyard – זֶבֶל שֶׁבֶּחָצֵר: The issue is how to divide the dung, which is used to fertilize the fields. The reason for dividing it according to the number of entrances is that the amounts of dung deposited in the courtyard are relative to the number of entrances, which correlates to the size of the courtyard. The *Sma* understands that according to the opinion of the Rambam the issue is how the residents are to divide the costs of removing the dung.

To close off adjacent to his entrance – לִסְתּוֹם כְּנֶגֶד פִּתְחוֹ: Rashi, Rabbeinu Gershom Meor HaGola, and the *ge'onim* understand that this is referring to one who wishes to build a structure around the entrance to his courtyard from the alleyway that only he will be able to use for loading or unloading. They reason that just as the entrance to a house is given four cubits in the courtyard, so the entrance to a courtyard is given four cubits in the alleyway. The question is whether the residents of the alleyway can claim that the structure interferes with their passing through the alleyway and makes the route longer for them.

Tosafot, as well as the Ri Migash and the Ramah, explain that the Gemara is referring to one whose courtyard opens onto an alleyway, near one end of the alleyway, and who wishes to expand his courtyard by sealing off his end of the alleyway and making it available to him alone. The other residents of the alleyway can protest that they were previously entitled to use the entire length of the alleyway and that sealing off the end of the alleyway will make the area available to them more congested.

HALAKHA

The residents of the alleyway can prevent him – בְּנֵי מָבוֹי מְעַכְּבִין עָלָיו: If one resident of an alleyway wishes to open an entrance to a different alleyway, some say that the residents of the first alleyway can prevent him from doing so because this would increase traffic in their alleyway (Maharam of Rothenburg). Even if he plans to seal his entrance to the alleyway and open an entrance to a different alleyway, the residents of the first alleyway can stop him, because his portion of the taxes levied on the alleyway will fall on the other residents of the alleyway. Consequently, if there is no such tax, they cannot prevent him from doing as he pleases. This ruling is in accordance with the version of the Gemara used by the Rif and the Rambam (Rambam *Sefer Kinyan*, *Hilkhot Shekhenim* 5:15; *Shulḥan Arukh*, *Ḥoshen Mishpat* 162:4, 6).

Dung…billeting [*akhsanya*] – זֶבֶל...אַכְסַנְיָא: The dung in a courtyard is divided among the residents according to the number of entrances. The burden of the king's *akhsanya* is divided according to the number of people in each household (see *Sma* and *Shakh*). Some claim that the term *akhsanya* refers to the dung left behind by the animals of the king's soldiers who are hosted; others say this term refers to the obligation to house soldiers (Rambam *Sefer Kinyan*, *Hilkhot Shekhenim* 2:8; *Shulḥan Arukh*, *Ḥoshen Mishpat* 172:9).

If five courtyards open onto an alleyway – חָמֵשׁ חֲצֵרוֹת פְּתוּחוֹת לְמָבוֹי: If five courtyards open onto an alleyway, the residents of the inner courtyards may use that part of the alleyway adjacent to the outer courtyards, but residents of the outer courtyards may not use that part of the alleyway adjacent to the inner courtyards, in accordance with the opinion of Rabbi Yehuda HaNasi. Therefore, if one built a bench adjacent to the entrance to his courtyard, the residents of the inner courtyards can object, because this forces them to walk around the bench, but the residents of the outer courtyards cannot protest (Rambam *Sefer Kinyan*, *Hilkhot Shekhenim* 5:16; *Shulḥan Arukh*, *Ḥoshen Mishpat* 162:7).

BACKGROUND

Five courtyards open onto an alleyway – חָמֵשׁ חֲצֵרוֹת פְּתוּחוֹת לְמָבוֹי:

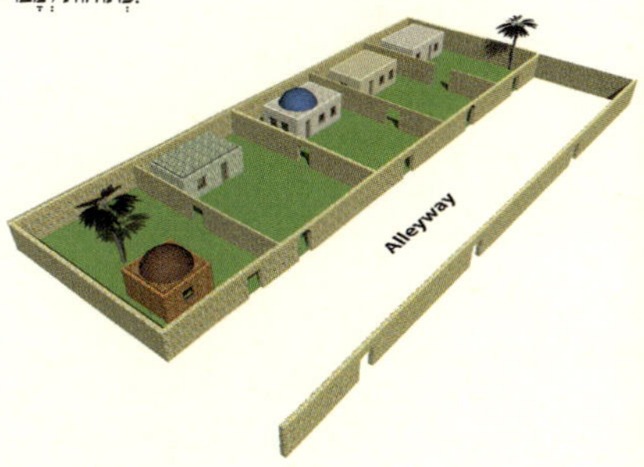

Five courtyards along an alleyway

נִמְצֵאת פְּנִימִית מִשְׁתַּמֶּשֶׁת לְעַצְמָהּ וּמִשְׁתַּמֶּשֶׁת עִם כׇּל אַחַת וְאַחַת!

The *baraita* continues: The **outcome** is that the residents of **the innermost** courtyard may **use** that part of the alleyway adjacent to **its own** entrance, **and** they may **use** that part of the alleyway facing **each and every** other courtyard as well. According to this analysis, it should be permitted for the owner of the innermost courtyard to close off the area in front of his courtyard, since he is the only one who has permission to use it.

תַּנָּאֵי הִיא; דְּתַנְיָא: אֶחָד מִבְּנֵי מָבוֹי שֶׁבִּיקֵּשׁ לְהַחֲזִיר פִּתְחוֹ לְמָבוֹי אַחֵר – בְּנֵי מָבוֹי מְעַכְּבִין עָלָיו. הָיָה סָתוּם וּבִיקֵּשׁ לְפוֹתְחוֹ – אֵין בְּנֵי מָבוֹי מְעַכְּבִין עָלָיו, דִּבְרֵי רַבִּי; רַבִּי שִׁמְעוֹן בֶּן אֶלְעָזָר אוֹמֵר: חָמֵשׁ חֲצֵרוֹת הַפְּתוּחוֹת לְמָבוֹי – כּוּלָּן מִשְׁתַּמְּשׁוֹת בַּמָּבוֹי זוֹ עִם זוֹ.

The Gemara answers: It **is a dispute between *tanna'im*, as it is taught** in a *baraita*: **If one of the residents of an alleyway wishes to alter his entrance to a different alleyway, the residents of the** other **alleyway can prevent him** from doing so. If **there had been** an entrance there beforehand which is now **sealed and he wishes to open it,**[H] **the residents of the** other **alleyway cannot prevent him** from doing so; this is **the statement of Rabbi** Yehuda HaNasi. **Rabbi Shimon ben Elazar says:** If there are **five courtyards which open onto an alleyway,** the residents of all the courtyards **may all use the alleyway with each other.**

חֲצֵרוֹת מַאן דְּכַר שְׁמַיְיהוּ? חַסּוֹרֵי מִחַסְּרָא וְהָכִי קָתָנֵי: וְכֵן חָמֵשׁ חֲצֵרוֹת הַפְּתוּחוֹת לְמָבוֹי – כּוּלָּן מִשְׁתַּמְּשׁוֹת עִם הַחִיצוֹנָה, וְהַחִיצוֹנָה מִשְׁתַּמֶּשֶׁת לְעַצְמָהּ וְכוּ׳, דִּבְרֵי רַבִּי; רַבִּי שִׁמְעוֹן בֶּן אֶלְעָזָר אוֹמֵר: חָמֵשׁ חֲצֵרוֹת הַפְּתוּחוֹת לְמָבוֹי – כּוּלָּם מִשְׁתַּמְּשׁוֹת בַּמָּבוֹי.

The Gemara expresses surprise about this last ruling: **Courtyards, who mentioned anything about them?** Why are they mentioned, considering that the *baraita* is not discussing the *halakhot* of courtyards? The Gemara answers: The *baraita* **is incomplete and this** is what **it is teaching:**[B] **Additionally,** if there are **five courtyards which open onto an alleyway,** the residents of all the courtyards **may all use** the area facing **the outermost** courtyard, **and the** residents of the **outermost one** may **use** only the area facing their **own** entrance; this is **the statement of Rabbi** Yehuda HaNasi. **Rabbi Shimon ben Elazar says:** If there are **five courtyards which open onto an alleyway,** the residents of all the courtyards **may all use the alleyway.**

אָמַר מָר: הָיָה סָתוּם וּבִיקֵּשׁ לְפוֹתְחוֹ – אֵין בְּנֵי מָבוֹי מְעַכְּבִין עָלָיו. אָמַר רָבָא: לֹא שָׁנוּ אֶלָּא שֶׁלֹּא פָּרַץ אֶת פְּצִימָיו, אֲבָל פָּרַץ אֶת פְּצִימָיו – בְּנֵי מָבוֹי מְעַכְּבִין עָלָיו. אֲמַר לֵיהּ אַבָּיֵי לְרָבָא, תַּנְיָא דִּמְסַיַּיע לָךְ.

The Gemara directs the discussion to the details mentioned in the *baraita*. **The Master said:** If **there had been** an entrance there beforehand that is now **sealed and he wishes to open it,**[B] **the residents of the** other **alleyway cannot prevent him** from doing so. **Rava says: This was taught only when he did not break its doorposts,** i.e., when the doorposts remained intact even after the entrance was sealed. **But if he** sealed the entrance and **broke its doorposts,** thereby demonstrating that the entrance had been completely negated, **the residents of the** other **alleyway can prevent him** from opening a new entrance. **Abaye said to Rava:** A *baraita* **is taught which supports you:**

HALAKHA

Sealed and he wishes to open it – סָתוּם וּבִיקֵּשׁ לְפוֹתְחוֹ: If one's home has an entrance that leads to an alleyway, and the entrance is currently sealed but witnesses confirm that at one point it had been open, he can open the entrance, and the other residents of the alleyway cannot prevent him from doing so. This applies only if the doorposts still exist; if the doorposts were destroyed, the residents can prevent him from reopening the entrance (Rambam *Sefer Kinyan, Hilkhot Shekhenim* 5:15; *Shulḥan Arukh, Ḥoshen Mishpat* 162:5).

BACKGROUND

It is incomplete and this is what it is teaching – חַסּוֹרֵי מִחַסְּרָא וְהָכִי קָתָנֵי: This method of explanation is often found in the Gemara. The addition introduced by the Gemara is an elaboration upon that which is written in the tannaitic source, based on various difficulties raised in the Gemara that render the source in its original form incoherent or inconsistent with another authoritative source. The addition provides the necessary clarification.

BACKGROUND

Sealed and he wishes to open it – סָתוּם וּבִיקֵּשׁ לְפוֹתְחוֹ:

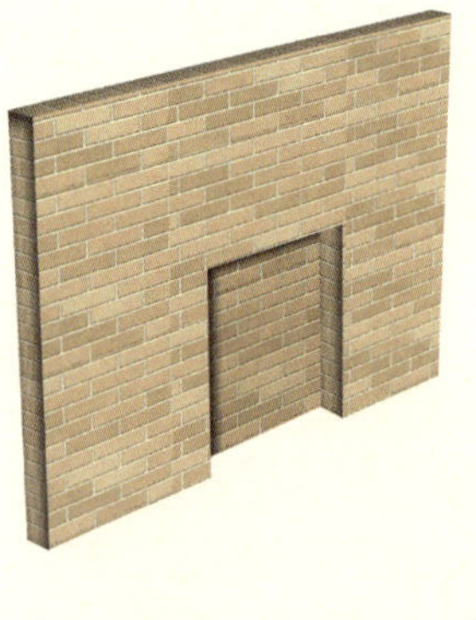

Sealed entrance with doorposts intact

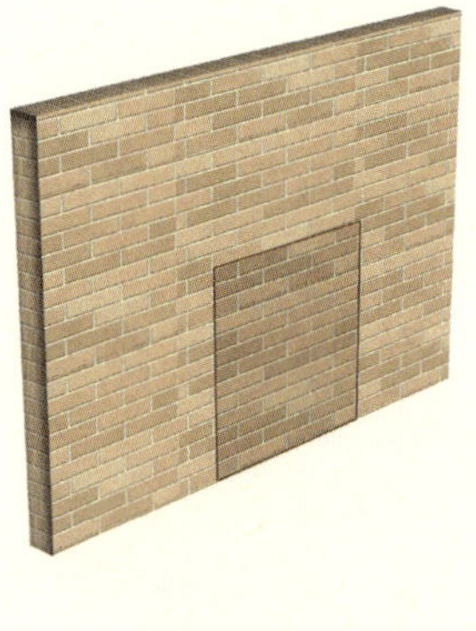

Sealed entrance with doorposts removed

בַּיִת סָתוּם – יֵשׁ לוֹ אַרְבַּע אַמּוֹת, פָּרַץ אֶת פְּצִימָיו – אֵין לוֹ אַרְבַּע אַמּוֹת;

A house that has **a sealed** entrance[H] still **has the four cubits** adjoining that entrance because the entrance can be reopened. If **one broke its doorposts** and sealed the entrance, the entrance is completely negated, and **it does not have** the **four cubits** adjoining it.

קֶבֶר שֶׁפִּתְחוֹ סָתוּם – אֵינוֹ מְטַמֵּא כׇּל סְבִיבָיו, פָּרַץ אֶת פְּצִימָיו וּסְתָמוֹ – מְטַמֵּא כׇּל סְבִיבָיו; בַּיִת סָתוּם – אֵינוֹ מְטַמֵּא כׇּל סְבִיבָיו, פָּרַץ אֶת פְּצִימָיו – מְטַמֵּא כׇּל סְבִיבָיו.

There is a similar distinction with regard to the *halakhot* of ritual impurity. There is a *halakha* that a house in which there is a corpse transmits ritual impurity only through its doorways. The *baraita* continues: **A grave whose entrance is sealed**[N] **does not render all its surroundings ritually impure;** the ritual impurity extends only to the area opposite the entrance. But if **one broke its doorposts and sealed it,** it is no longer considered an entrance, and the grave **renders all its surroundings ritually impure,** because impurity that has no egress bursts from all sides. Similarly, **a house** in which there is a corpse that has **a sealed** entrance **does not render all its surroundings ritually impure.**[NH] But if **one broke its doorposts,** it is no longer considered an entrance, and the corpse **renders all of its surroundings ritually impure.**

אָמַר רַבָּה בַּר בַּר חָנָה אָמַר רַבִּי יוֹחָנָן: מְבוֹאוֹת הַמְפוּלָּשׁוֹת לְעִיר אַחֶרֶת וּבִקְּשׁוּ בְּנֵי הָעִיר לְסוֹתְמָן – בְּנֵי אוֹתָהּ הָעִיר מְעַכְּבִין עֲלֵיהֶן; לָא מִיבָּעֵי כִּי לֵיכָּא דַּרְכָּא אַחֲרִינָא דִּמְעַכְּבִי, אֶלָּא אֲפִילּוּ כִּי אִיכָּא דַּרְכָּא אַחֲרִינָא נָמֵי מְעַכְּבִי,

Rabba bar bar Ḥana says that **Rabbi Yoḥanan says:** With regard to **alleyways that are open to another city,**[H] and through which one would ordinarily travel to reach that other city, if **the residents of the city** in which the alleyways are located **wished to block them** off, **the residents of the city** into which the alleyways open **can prevent them** from doing so, because they have a right to reach their city via those routes. The Gemara explains: **It is not necessary** to state **that they can prevent** them from blocking the alleyways **when there is no alternative route** to reach their town, **but they can prevent** them from blocking the alleyways **even when there is an alternative route.**

מִשּׁוּם דְּרַב יְהוּדָה אָמַר רַב, דְּאָמַר: מֵצַר שֶׁהֶחֱזִיקוּ בּוֹ רַבִּים – אָסוּר לְקַלְקְלוֹ. כִּדְרַב גִּידֵּל, דְּאָמַר רַב גִּידֵּל: רַבִּים שֶׁבָּרְרוּ דֶּרֶךְ לְעַצְמָן – מַה שֶּׁבָּרְרוּ בָּרְרוּ.

This is **due to** the reasoning that **Rav Yehuda says** that **Rav says. As Rav says:** One is **prohibited from ruining a path that the public has established**[NH] as a public thoroughfare, i.e., steps may not be taken to prevent people from using it. This is in accordance with the statement **of Rav Giddel, as Rav Giddel says:** If **the public has chosen a route for itself** and they walk on it, **what they have chosen is chosen,** and it cannot be taken away from them.

אָמַר רַב עָנָן אָמַר שְׁמוּאֵל: מְבוֹאוֹת הַמְפוּלָּשִׁין לִרְשׁוּת הָרַבִּים וּבִקְּשׁוּ בְּנֵי מְבוֹאוֹת לְהַעֲמִיד לָהֶן דְּלָתוֹת – בְּנֵי רְשׁוּת הָרַבִּים מְעַכְּבִין עֲלֵיהֶן.

Rav Anan says that **Shmuel says:** With regard to **alleyways that open onto a public thoroughfare,**[HB] **if the residents of the alleyways wished to put up doors** at the entrance to their alleyways, **the people** who use **the public thoroughfare can prevent them** from doing so.

NOTES

A grave whose entrance is sealed – קֶבֶר שֶׁפִּתְחוֹ סָתוּם: By Torah law, a person is rendered impure if he comes into contact with a grave unless the grave has an opening through which the impurity can exit. Rashi comments that the Sages ordained that the four cubits surrounding a grave impart impurity just as they ordained with regard to the area surrounding a corpse, so that people would distance themselves from a grave and avoid touching it. The passage here is difficult, as it is unclear what the entrance would be in the context of a grave. In fact, in the text before many of the early commentaries, this *halakha* concerning a grave does not appear.

A house that has a sealed entrance does not render all its surroundings ritually impure – בַּיִת סָתוּם אֵינוֹ מְטַמֵּא כׇּל סְבִיבָיו: A house that contains a corpse and has a sealed entrance renders impure only the area opposite the entrance. Rashi comments that the Sages decreed that a person present in the area opposite the entrance is rendered impure in order to keep people from approaching a house containing a corpse. Other early commentaries explain that this *halakha* is based on a mishna (*Oholot* 7:3; see *Beitza* 10a), which states that the impurity is considered to leave through the entrance. Therefore, only one who touches the sealed entrance (*Nimmukei Yosef*) or stands under the entrance (Rashi on *Beitza* 10a) is rendered impure.

A path that the public has established – מֵצַר שֶׁהֶחֱזִיקוּ בּוֹ רַבִּים: *Tosafot* explain that this *halakha* applies only when the owner of the property permitted people to walk there, in which case he may not retract that right by blocking the path. Nevertheless, if people troop through his property without permission, the owner can prevent them from doing so, even by force.

BACKGROUND

Alleyways that open onto a public thoroughfare – מְבוֹאוֹת הַמְפוּלָּשִׁין לִרְשׁוּת הָרַבִּים:

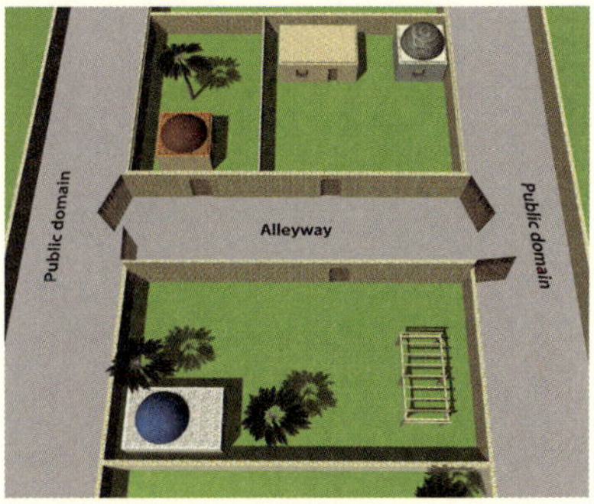

Alleyway open to the public domain on both sides

HALAKHA

A house that has a sealed entrance – בַּיִת סָתוּם: A house that has a sealed entrance is still entitled to four cubits in the courtyard opposite its entrance. But if the doorposts are broken and the entrance is sealed, the house is not entitled to those four cubits, though its owner still has rights in the courtyard (Rambam *Sefer Kinyan*, *Hilkhot Shekhenim* 2:7; *Shulḥan Arukh*, *Ḥoshen Mishpat* 172:7).

A house that has a sealed entrance does not render… impure – בַּיִת סָתוּם אֵינוֹ מְטַמֵּא: A corpse found in a sealed building, or in one that has an entrance but its doorposts are broken and it is sealed, renders all its surroundings ritually impure. By contrast, if the building has an entrance, even one that is sealed up, as long as its doorposts are not broken only the area in front of the entrance renders its surroundings impure (Rambam *Sefer Tahara*, *Hilkhot Tumat Met* 7:1).

Alleyways that are open to another city – מְבוֹאוֹת הַמְפוּלָּשׁוֹת לְעִיר אַחֶרֶת: With regard to alleyways that open to a road leading to a different city, the residents of that city can prevent the residents of the alleyway from blocking off the alleyway, since such obstruction would block the route to their city. According to the *Sma*, this is so even if there is an alternative route, but the route through the alleyway is closer (*Shulḥan Arukh*, *Ḥoshen Mishpat* 162:2).

A path that the public has established – מֵצַר שֶׁהֶחֱזִיקוּ בּוֹ רַבִּים: If a person granted the public the right to traverse his property, he cannot withdraw that right (Rambam *Sefer Nezikin*, *Hilkhot Nizkei Mamon* 13:24; *Shulḥan Arukh*, *Ḥoshen Mishpat* 377:1, 417:2).

Alleyways that open onto a public thoroughfare – מְבוֹאוֹת הַמְפוּלָּשִׁין לִרְשׁוּת הָרַבִּים: With regard to an alleyway that opens onto a public thoroughfare even if only on one side (*Sma*), if the residents of the alleyway wish to place doors at the entrance, the people who use the public thoroughfare can prevent them from doing so. This is because of the crowding in the public thoroughfare, which sometimes forces people to spill into the alleyway. The Rema, citing the *Tur*, comments that the residents of the alleyway cannot be prevented from erecting doors if there are already door frames at the entrance to the alleyway (Rambam *Sefer Kinyan*, *Hilkhot Shekhenim* 5:13; *Shulḥan Arukh*, *Ḥoshen Mishpat* 162:1).

סְבוּר מִינָּהּ: הָנֵי מִילֵּי בְּאַרְבַּע אַמּוֹת, כִּדְרַבִּי זֵירָא אָמַר רַב נַחְמָן, דְּאָמַר רַבִּי זֵירָא אָמַר רַב נַחְמָן: אַרְבַּע אַמּוֹת הַסְּמוּכוֹת לִרְשׁוּת הָרַבִּים כִּרְשׁוּת הָרַבִּים דָּמְיָין. וְלָא הִיא, הָתָם – לְעִנְיַן טוּמְאָה, אֲבָל הָכָא – זִימְנִין דְּדָחֲקִי בְּנֵי רְשׁוּת הָרַבִּים וְעָיְילִי טוּבָא.

Some Sages **understood from this** that **this statement** applies specifically to the area **within four cubits** of the public thoroughfare, **in accordance with** the statement **that Rabbi Zeira** says that **Rav Naḥman says, as Rabbi Zeira says** that **Rav Naḥman says: The four cubits** in an alleyway **that are adjacent to the public thoroughfare are considered like the public thoroughfare** itself. Consequently, this area has the *halakha* of a public thoroughfare. **But that is not so. There,** the ruling of Rav Naḥman was stated **with regard to the issue of ritual impurity,**[N] with regard to which only the first four cubits of the alleyway are considered like the public thoroughfare. **But here,** with regard to doors set up at the entrance to the alleyway, **sometimes the public thoroughfare becomes crowded with people and they enter far** into the alleyway, even farther than four cubits.

״וְלֹא אֶת הַשָּׂדֶה – עַד שֶׁיְּהֵא בָּהּ תִּשְׁעָה קַבִּין לָזֶה וְתִשְׁעָה קַבִּין לָזֶה״ כו׳. וְלָא פְּלִיגִי, מָר כִּי אַתְרֵיהּ וּמָר כִּי אַתְרֵיהּ.

§ The mishna teaches: **And** the court does **not** divide a jointly owned **field unless there is** space **in it** to plant **nine *kav*** of seed **for this one and nine *kav*** of seed **for that one.** Rabbi Yehuda says: The court does not divide a field unless there is space in it to plant nine half-*kav* of seed for this one and nine half-*kav* of seed for that one. The Gemara comments: **And** they **do not disagree** with regard to the fundamental *halakha*, as this **Sage** ruled **in accordance with** the custom of **his locale,**[N] **and** that **Sage** ruled **in accordance with** the custom of **his locale.** In Rabbi Yehuda's locale, even a smaller parcel of land was considered a viable field.

בְּבָבֶל מַאי? אֲמַר רַב יוֹסֵף: בֵּי רָדוּ יוֹמָא.

The Gemara asks: The mishna was taught in Eretz Yisrael; **what** practice should be followed **in Babylonia?**[N] **Rav Yosef said:** In Babylonia, a parcel of land the size of which is **the area of a day's plowing**[NH] is considered a field; if each of the parties will receive less than that, the field should not be divided.

מַאי בֵּי רָדוּ יוֹמָא? אִי יוֹמָא זַרְעָא – תְּרֵי יוֹמָא כְּרָבָא לָא הָוֵי, אִי יוֹמָא כְּרָבָא – יוֹמָא דְּזַרְעָא לָא הָוֵי!

The Gemara asks: **What** is meant by a parcel of land the size of which is **the area of a day's plowing? If** it means **a day's** plowing in **the planting** season, i.e., the winter, when it is easy to plow, since the earth has already been turned over at the end of the summer, the field will **not** require **two** full **days** of plowing in **the plowing** season, i.e., at the end of the summer, when it is more difficult to plow, since the earth is hard and dry. In that case, he will have to pay his summer plowman two days' wages for less than two days of work. And **if** it means a **day's** plowing in the **plowing** season, the field will **not** require a full **day** of plowing in the **planting** season. In that case, he will have to pay his winter plowman a full day's wages for less than a full day of work.

אִי בָּעֵית אֵימָא: יוֹמָא דִּכְרָבָא – דְּכָרֵיב וְתָנֵי; וְאִי בָּעֵית אֵימָא: יוֹמָא דְּזַרְעָא – בְּהָדוּרֵי.

The Gemara answers: **If you wish, say** it is referring to **a day's** plowing in the **plowing** season, and the field will still require a full day of plowing in the planting season **since he plows** once before he sows the seeds **and** then he **repeats**[N] the plowing after the seeds are sown. **And if you wish, say** instead that it is referring to **a day's** plowing in the **planting** season, and the field will in fact require two full days of plowing in the plowing season if it is **rocky ground,**[N] on which plowing takes longer.

דַּוְולָא – אֲמַר רַב נַחְמָן: בֵּי דָאלוּ יוֹמָא. פַּרְדֵּסָא – אָמַר אֲבוּהּ דִּשְׁמוּאֵל: בַּת שְׁלֹשֶׁת קַבִּין.

In connection with this discussion, the Gemara clarifies the conditions under which **a cistern,**[N] from which its joint owners draw their water, is divided. **Rav Naḥman said:** It should be divided only if each party will receive **the volume of** water needed for **a day's irrigation** work.[H] As for **an orchard, Shmuel's father says:** It should be divided only if each party will receive **an area** large enough to plant **three *kav*,** one-third of the measure required for a field.

NOTES

There, with regard to the issue of ritual impurity – הָתָם לְעִנְיַן טוּמְאָה: The reason for the difference in *halakha* between the two rulings is that in the case of any uncertainty concerning ritual impurity occurring in the public domain, it is deemed pure (Rabbeinu Gershom; see *Sota* 28b).

This Sage ruled in accordance with his locale – מָר כִּי אַתְרֵיהּ: The commentaries explain that the land in Rabbi Yehuda's area was of a higher quality; therefore, a plot large enough to plant nine half-*kav* was fit for cultivation (*Tosafot*), or was sufficient to provide a livelihood (Rabbeinu Ḥananel). Rabbeinu Gershom maintains that land in Rabbi Yehuda's region was much more expensive; consequently, even a small parcel was considered a distinct field. Other commentaries explain, by contrast, that in Rabbi Yehuda's area land was difficult to farm; as a result, even a small area of land required a great deal of labor (Ramah).

What practice in Babylonia – בְּבָבֶל מַאי: The commentaries disagree about this as well, in accordance with their opinions in the previous note. According to *Tosafot*, the land in Babylonia was not as fertile as that in Eretz Yisrael, and therefore was assigned a larger measure. Rabbeinu Gershom explains that the land in Babylonia was not as expensive as that in Eretz Yisrael. According to the Meiri, the land in Babylonia was flat, moist, and easier to plow; therefore, it required a measure of its own.

The area of a day's plowing – בֵּי רָדוּ יוֹמָא: This term signifies the size of land that can be plowed in a full day. It was not worthwhile for a person to buy a smaller plot of land or to receive a smaller parcel when jointly owned property was divided up, because the common practice was for the owner to hire workers and oxen for a full day of work in any event, even if their services were required for only a portion of the day (Ri Migash). Alternatively, it might be difficult to find a worker who would agree to work for less than a full day (Rabbeinu Gershom).

He plows and repeats – דְּכָרֵיב וְתָנֵי: The meaning of this expression varies according to the different versions of the Gemara. Some commentaries explain that in the hours of the day that remain after the field has been plowed, the worker returns and plows the field again. This second plowing, which is beneficial to the field, is easier and can be completed in the time left over from the first plowing. Other commentaries say that the expression refers to the plowing that is performed right before planting and that can be completed quickly. Consequently, it is possible to plow and plant in a single day a field whose first plowing had taken an entire day.

Rocky ground [*hadurei*] – הָדוּרֵי: Rashi explains this as a rocky, hilly field that is hard to work. According to *Tosafot*, the word *hadurei* is related to repetition, which means that he goes back and plows the field after it has been planted (see Maharsha and Rashash).

A cistern – דַּוְולָא: Rashi explains that this refers to the division of a well: How much water must it contain in order for it to be subject to the *halakha* of division? The Gemara answers that it must have enough water for each party to draw water all day on alternate days. Other commentaries (Rabbeinu Gershom Meor HaGola; Ri Migash; *Tosafot*, citing Rabbeinu Ḥananel) understand that this refers to the division of land that is watered with buckets. Accordingly, Rav Naḥman's response is a description of an area of land, not an amount of water.

HALAKHA

The area of a day's plowing – בֵּי רָדוּ יוֹמָא: A jointly owned field in Babylonia can be divided only if each party will receive a parcel of land in the area of a day's plowing (Rambam *Sefer Kinyan*, *Hilkhot Shekhenim* 1:4; *Shulḥan Arukh*, *Ḥoshen Mishpat* 171:3).

The volume of water needed for a day's irrigation work – בֵּי דָאלוּ יוֹמָא: A jointly owned field in Babylonia that is watered with buckets (Rabbeinu Ḥananel; see *Tosafot*) can be divided only if each party will receive a parcel of land in the area of a day's irrigation (Rambam *Sefer Kinyan*, *Hilkhot Shekhenim* 1:4; *Shulḥan Arukh*, *Ḥoshen Mishpat* 171:3).

תַּנְיָא נַמִּי הָכִי: הָאוֹמֵר לַחֲבֵירוֹ ״מְנָת בְּכֶרֶם אֲנִי מוֹכֵר לָךְ״ – סוּמָכוֹס אוֹמֵר: לֹא יִפְחוֹת מִשְּׁלֹשָׁה קַבִּין. אָמַר רַבִּי יוֹסֵי: אֵין אֵלּוּ אֶלָּא דִּבְרֵי נְבִיאוּת. בְּבָבֶל מַאי? אֲמַר רָבָא בַּר קִסְנָא: תְּלָת אַצְיָאתָה בְּנֵי תְּרֵיסַר גּוּפְנֵי, כִּי הֵיכִי דְּרָפֵיק גַּבְרָא בְּיוֹמָא.

That opinion **is also taught** in a *baraita*: With regard to **one who says to another: I am selling you part of a vineyard,** without specifying how much of the vineyard, **Sumakhos says: He may not** give him **less than an area** large enough to plant **three *kav*. Rabbi Yosei said: These are nothing other than words of prophecy,** i.e., I do not see the logic behind this statement, and it is as if based on prophecy and a heavenly decree, as the seller did not mention any area, but rather spoke in the most general of terms: Part of a vineyard. The Gemara asks: **What** is the measure with regard to this matter **in Babylonia? Rava bar Kisna said: Three rows [*atzyata*]**[L] **of twelve vines, which is** the area **a person can hoe in** a single **day.**

אָמַר רַבִּי אַבְדִּימִי דְּמִן חֵיפָה: מִיּוֹם שֶׁחָרַב בֵּית הַמִּקְדָּשׁ, נִיטְּלָה נְבוּאָה מִן הַנְּבִיאִים וְנִיתְּנָה לַחֲכָמִים. אַטּוּ חָכָם לָאו נָבִיא הוּא? הָכִי קָאָמַר: אַף עַל פִּי שֶׁנִּיטְּלָה מִן הַנְּבִיאִים, מִן הַחֲכָמִים לֹא נִיטְּלָה.

§ In connection with Rabbi Yosei's statement that Sumakhos's words are nothing but words of prophecy, the Gemara reports that **Rabbi Avdimi from Haifa says: From the day that the Temple was destroyed prophecy was taken from the prophets and given to the Sages.** The Gemara expresses astonishment: **Is that to say** that a **Sage is not** fit to be **a prophet?** Rabbi Avdimi seems to say that these are two distinct categories of people. The Gemara explains: **This is what** Rabbi Avdimi **is saying: Even though** prophecy **was taken from the prophets,**[N] **it was not taken from the Sages.**

אָמַר אַמֵימָר: וְחָכָם עָדִיף מִנָּבִיא, שֶׁנֶּאֱמַר: ״וְנָבִא לְבַב חָכְמָה״, מִי נִתְלֶה בְּמִי? הֱוֵי אוֹמֵר: קָטָן נִתְלֶה בְּגָדוֹל.

Ameimar said: And a Sage is greater than a prophet, as it is stated: "And a prophet has a heart of wisdom" (Psalms 90:12), i.e., he is wise. When comparisons are drawn, **who is compared to whom? You must say** that **the lesser is compared to the greater.** Here too, prophecy is compared to wisdom, thus indicating that wisdom is greater than prophecy.

אֲמַר אַבַּיֵי: תֵּדַע, דְּאָמַר גַּבְרָא רַבָּה מִילְּתָא, וּמִתְאַמְרָא מִשְּׁמֵיהּ דְּגַבְרָא רַבָּה אַחֲרִינָא כְּוָותֵיהּ. אֲמַר רָבָא: וּמַאי קוּשְׁיָא? וְדִילְמָא תַּרְוַיְיהוּ בְּנֵי חַד מַזָּלָא נִינְהוּ! אֶלָּא אֲמַר רָבָא: תֵּדַע, דְּאָמַר גַּבְרָא רַבָּה מִילְּתָא, וּמִתְאַמְרָא

Abaye said: Know that this is so, that the Sages still enjoy the prophetic gift, **as a great man makes a statement** with regard to a point of *halakha* **and** the same statement **is** then **cited in the name of a different great man in accordance with his** statement, indicating that the Sages makes their statements by way of prophecy. **Rava** disagreed and **said: And what is the difficulty** with explaining this? **Perhaps they were born under the same constellation,** and since they are similar in their traits, they reach the same conclusions. **Rather, Rava said: Know** that this is so, **as a great man makes a statement and** the same statement **is** then **cited**

Perek **I**
Daf **12** Amud **b**

מִשְּׁמֵיהּ דְּרַבִּי עֲקִיבָא בַּר יוֹסֵף כְּוָותֵיהּ. אֲמַר רַב אַשִׁי: וּמַאי קוּשְׁיָא? דִּלְמָא לְהָא מִילְּתָא בַּר מַזָּלֵיהּ הוּא!

in the name of the well-known *tanna* **Rabbi Akiva**[N] **bar Yosef in accordance with his** statement. It certainly cannot be maintained that the first Sage is similar in his nature to the illustrious Rabbi Akiva, so he must have arrived at his statement through prophecy. **Rav Ashi said: And what is the difficulty** with explaining this? **Perhaps** they were born under **the same constellation, and with regard to this issue** the first Sage has the same understanding as Rabbi Akiva.

אֶלָּא אֲמַר רַב אַשִׁי: תֵּדַע, דְּאָמַר גַּבְרָא רַבָּה מִילְּתָא, וּמִתְאַמְרָא הֲלָכָה לְמֹשֶׁה מִסִּינַי כְּוָותֵיהּ. וְדִלְמָא כְּסוּמָא בַּאֲרוּבָּה! וְלָאו טַעַם יָהֵיב?

Rather, Rav Ashi said: Know that this is so, **as a great man makes a statement and** the same statement **is** then **cited as a *halakha*** transmitted **to Moses from Sinai in accordance with his** statement. The Sage makes a statement that corresponds to words pronounced in Heaven, which, without prophecy, is beyond human capability. The Gemara states: **But perhaps** he arrived at this idea by chance, without the assistance of prophecy, **like a blind man** who makes his way **through a skylight.** A blind man cannot deliberately find a skylight; therefore, his finding it occurs by chance. The Gemara answers: **But does** the Sage **not offer a reason** for his statement? The fact that he demonstrates an understanding of the issue indicates that he does not arrive at his idea by chance, but rather by prophecy.

LANGUAGE

Rows [*atzyata*] – אַצְיָאתָה: The origin of this word is uncertain. Some commentaries suggest that it stems from *atzatz*, which is the Aramaic cognate of the root *ḥet*, *tzadi*, *tzadi*, meaning something erected as a barrier, like a row of trees or a furrow in a garden.

NOTES

Even though it was taken from the prophets – אַף עַל פִּי שֶׁנִּיטְּלָה: Rashi explains that prophecy was taken from those prophets who were not Sages, but it was not taken from those who were Sages. The Ramban finds this difficult, as it is clear from other sources that being a Sage was a prerequisite for receiving prophecy. The Ramban and the Ritva explain that prophetic power was taken away, but the Sages retained their divine inspiration.

NOTES

In the name of Rabbi Akiva – מִשְּׁמֵיהּ דְּרַבִּי עֲקִיבָא: It cannot be argued that the first Sage was similar in nature to Rabbi Akiva, since the latter was undoubtedly greater (Rashi). The Maharal maintains that the phrase: Under the same constellation, means that he was born at the same time, and Rabbi Akiva was certainly born at a different time from the other Sage.

אָמַר רַבִּי יוֹחָנָן: מִיּוֹם שֶׁחָרַב בֵּית הַמִּקְדָּשׁ, נִיטְּלָה נְבוּאָה מִן הַנְּבִיאִים וְנִיתְּנָה לַשּׁוֹטִים וְלַתִּינוֹקוֹת. לַשּׁוֹטִים – מַאי הִיא? כִּי הָא דְּמָר בַּר רַב אַשִׁי דַּהֲוָה קָאֵי בְּרִסְתְּקָא דִּמְחוֹזָא, שְׁמָעֵיהּ לְהַהוּא שׁוֹטֶה דְּקָאָמַר: רֵישׁ מְתִיבְתָּא דְּמָלֵיךְ בְּמָתָא מְחַסְיָא – "טַבְיוּמֵי" חָתֵים. אֲמַר: מַאן חָתֵים "טַבְיוּמֵי" בְּרַבָּנַן? אֲנָא, שְׁמַע מִינָּהּ לְדִידִי קַיְימָא לִי שַׁעְתָּא. קָם אֲתָא. אַדַּאֲתָא אִימְנוּ רַבָּנַן לְאוֹתְבֵיהּ לְרַב אַחָא מִדִּפְתִּי בְּרֵישָׁא.

Rabbi Yoḥanan said: From the day that the Temple was destroyed, prophecy was taken from the prophets and given to imbeciles and children. The Gemara explains: In what way was prophecy given to imbeciles? It was like this incident involving Mar bar Rav Ashi,[P] who was standing in the street [*beristeka*][L] of Meḥoza when he heard a certain imbecile say: The head of the yeshiva who will be appointed in Mata Meḥasya signs his name Tavyumei.[B] Mar bar Rav Ashi said to himself: Who among the Sages signs his name Tavyumei? Nobody but me. Conclude from the statement by the imbecile that my hour has arrived, and I will reap success in this matter. He arose and went to Mata Meḥasya. By the time he arrived, the Sages had already decided to appoint Rav Aḥa of Difti[P] as the head of the yeshiva.

כֵּיוָן דְּשָׁמְעִי דַּאֲתָא, שְׁדוּר זוּגָא דְּרַבָּנַן לְגַבֵּיהּ לְאִימְּלוֹכֵי בֵּיהּ, עַכְּבֵיהּ. הֲדַר שְׁדוּר זוּגָא דְּרַבָּנַן אַחֲרִינָא, עַכְּבֵיהּ גַּבֵּיהּ, עַד דְּמָלוּ בֵּי עַשְׂרָה. כֵּיוָן דְּמָלוּ בֵּי עַשְׂרָה, פְּתַח הוּא וּתְנָא וּדְרַשׁ, לְפִי שֶׁאֵין פּוֹתְחִין בְּכַלָּה פָּחוֹת מֵעֲשָׂרָה.

As soon as the Sages heard that Mar bar Rav Ashi had arrived, they determined not to proceed with their appointment without the approval of an important figure such as him. They sent a pair of Sages to him to consult with him, and he detained them. They again sent a pair of Sages to him, and he detained them as well. This continued until they completed a quorum of ten Sages. Once they reached ten men, Mar bar Rav Ashi opened his lecture, taught, and expounded. He did not speak earlier because one should not open a lecture during *kalla*, the gatherings for Torah study during the months of Elul and Adar, when less than ten men are present. He was then appointed as head of the yeshiva.

קָרֵי רַב אַחָא אַנַּפְשֵׁיהּ: כׇּל הַמְּרֵיעִין לוֹ – לֹא בִּמְהֵרָה מְטִיבִין לוֹ, וְכׇל הַמְּטִיבִין לוֹ – לֹא בִּמְהֵרָה מְרֵיעִין לוֹ.

Understanding that he had been passed over for the position, Rav Aḥa of Difti read about himself the rabbinic aphorism: Anyone who is treated poorly will not soon be treated well; and anyone who is treated well will not soon be treated poorly. Rav Aḥa understood that he had lost the chance to be appointed, whereas Mar bar Rav Ashi had the good fortune to be appointed, and would remain in his position.

תִּינוֹקוֹת – מַאי הִיא? כִּי הָא דְּבַת רַב חִסְדָּא הֲוָה יָתְבָה בְּכַנְפֵּיהּ דַּאֲבוּהּ, הָווּ יָתְבִי קַמֵּיהּ רָבָא וְרָמִי בַּר חָמָא. אֲמַר לָהּ: מַאן מִינַּיְיהוּ בָּעֵית? אֲמַרָה לֵיהּ: תַּרְוַיְיהוּ, אֲמַר רָבָא: וַאֲנָא בַּתְרָא.

And in what way was prophecy given to children? It was like this incident involving the daughter of Rav Ḥisda, who when she was a child was sitting on her father's lap while he sat and learned. Rava and Rami bar Ḥama were sitting before him. Rav Ḥisda jokingly said to his daughter: Which of them would you want as a husband? She said: I want both of them. Rava said: And I will be last. And this is what happened; first she married Rami bar Ḥama, and when he died she married Rava.

אָמַר רַבִּי אַבְדִּימִי דְּמִן חֵיפָה: קוֹדֶם שֶׁיֹּאכַל אָדָם וְיִשְׁתֶּה יֵשׁ לוֹ שְׁתֵּי לְבָבוֹת, לְאַחַר שֶׁאוֹכֵל וְשׁוֹתֶה – אֵין לוֹ אֶלָּא לֵב אֶחָד, שֶׁנֶּאֱמַר: "אִישׁ נָבוּב יִלָּבֵב", וּכְתִיב: "נְבוּב לֻחֹת", וּמְתַרְגְּמִינַן: חֲלִיל לוּחִין.

Having already cited one statement of Rabbi Avdimi from Haifa, the Gemara cites another statement in his name: Rabbi Avdimi from Haifa says: Before a person eats and drinks he has two hearts,[N] meaning his heart is unsettled because he is distracted by hunger. But after he eats and drinks he has only one heart, as it is stated: "A hollow [*nevuv*] man is two-hearted" (Job 11:12). How is it indicated that "*nevuv*" means hungry? As it is written concerning the altar: "*Nevuv luḥot*" (Exodus 27:8), which we translate into Aramaic as: Hollow with planks, meaning that a hollow person, i.e., one who has not yet eaten, is two-hearted.

אָמַר רַב הוּנָא בְּרֵיהּ דְּרַב יְהוֹשֻׁעַ: הָרָגִיל בְּיַיִן, אֲפִילּוּ לִבּוֹ אָטוּם כִּבְתוּלָה – יַיִן מְפַקְּחוֹ שֶׁנֶּאֱמַר: "וְתִירוֹשׁ יְנוֹבֵב בְּתֻלוֹת".

The Gemara continues to discuss the meaning of *nevuv*, Rav Huna, son of Rav Yehoshua, says: With regard to one who is accustomed to wine, although his heart, i.e., his mind, is closed like a virgin, wine opens it, as it is stated: "And new wine opens [*yenovev*] the virgins" (Zechariah 9:17). The word *yenovev* is used here in the sense of clearing out a space: Even if one's heart and mind are closed, wine will open them to understanding.

PERSONALITIES

Mar bar Rav Ashi – מָר בַּר רַב אַשִׁי: Mar bar Rav Ashi was a seventh-generation Babylonian *amora*, the son of the well-known *amora* Rav Ashi. While many understand that Tavyumei was a nickname, some believe that it was his actual name. His primary teacher was his father; while delivering a lecture he would quote his father with the phrase: My father, my master said, which his disseminator would change to: So said Rav Ashi (*Kiddushin* 31b). After the death of Rav Ashi, who was the head of the yeshiva in Mata Meḥasya, three other Sages served in his place; nevertheless, after twenty-eight years, Mar bar Rav Ashi finally assumed the position, which he held for thirteen years.

Rav Aḥa of Difti – רַב אַחָא מִדִּפְתִּי: Rav Aḥa of Difti was an *amora* of the fifth and sixth generations. A devoted student of Ravina, with whom he discussed many *halakhot*, Rav Aḥa was apparently the Sage in the Exilarch's house, and was certainly a leader of his generation. The Gemara relates that he and Mar bar Rav Ashi were colleagues who treated each other as equals.

LANGUAGE

Street [*risteka*] – רִסְתְּקָא: Apparently from the Middle Iranian term rastak, meaning a row of houses.

BACKGROUND

Signs his name Tavyumei – טַבְיוּמֵי חָתֵים: The word *Mar* often serves as a title, meaning master or teacher. It is also used as a term of address when speaking to an important person or as a title for certain sages, such as members of the Exilarch's family. There were also certain people whose given name was Mar. In any event, this episode demonstrates that Mar bar Rav Ashi was not named Mar, but rather that Mar was an honorary title given to him as the son of Rav Ashi, one of the generation's leading authorities. His given name was Tavyumei, which is cognate with the Hebrew name Yom Tov. It is clear that he used his true name when signing documents or letters.

NOTES

He has two hearts – יֵשׁ לוֹ שְׁתֵּי לְבָבוֹת: Rashi, Rabbeinu Gershom, and the Ramah explain that before a person eats, his heart is distracted due to his feeling of hunger; therefore, he is like a person with two hearts who thinks about food while thinking about something else at the same time. The Maharal offers the opposite explanation: Before a person eats, his heart is wide open as if he had two hearts, whereas after he eats his body is occupied with digestion and his attention suffers.

אָמַר רַב הוּנָא בְּרֵיהּ דְּרַב יְהוֹשֻׁעַ: פְּשִׁיטָא, חֵלֶק בְּכוֹר וְחֵלֶק פָּשׁוּט – יָהֲבִינַן לֵיהּ אַחַד מִצְרָא, יָבָם מַאי?

§ The Gemara resumes its discussion of the division of property. **Rav Huna, son of Rav Yehoshua, says:** It is **obvious** that if a person inherits **a portion** of his father's estate because he is the **firstborn, and** he also inherits **a portion** of that estate as **an ordinary** son,[H] like the rest of his brothers, **he is given** his two portions **along one boundary,** so that they are adjacent to one another and form a single property. The Gemara asks: **What** is the *halakha* with regard to **a** ***yavam*****,**[BH] a man whose brother died without children, who is obligated by Torah law to marry his deceased brother's widow or grant her *ḥalitza*? If he marries his brother's widow, the *halakha* dictates that he receive his brother's portion of their father's estate in addition to his own. Does he too receive the two portions along one boundary?

אֲמַר אַבַּיֵי: הִיא הִיא; מַאי טַעֲמָא? בְּכוֹר קָרְיֵיהּ רַחֲמָנָא. רָבָא אֲמַר, אָמַר קְרָא: "וְהָיָה הַבְּכוֹר", הֲוָיָיתוֹ כִּבְכוֹר וְאֵין חֲלוּקָתוֹ כִּבְכוֹר.

Abaye said: This case **is** equal to **that** case. **What is the reason** for this? **The Merciful One calls** the *yavam* **"firstborn"** (see *Yevamot* 24a) and therefore he is treated like a firstborn in all regards. He receives the two portions of his father's estate as a single parcel of land. But **Rava said: The verse states: "And it shall be, the firstborn"** (Deuteronomy 25:6). With regard to **his being,** i.e., his inheritance itself, he **is like a firstborn; but** as for **the distribution** of the estate, he **is not like a firstborn,**[N] and the brothers are not obligated to give him two adjacent portions.

הַהוּא דִּזְבַן אַרְעָא אַמֵּצְרָא דְּבֵי נָשְׁיֵיהּ, כִּי קָא פָּלְגוּ אֲמַר לְהוּ: פְּלִיגוּ לִי אַמִּצְרַאי; אֲמַר רַבָּה: כְּגוֹן זֶה כּוֹפִין עַל מִדַּת סְדוֹם.

It is reported that **a certain person bought land along the boundary of his father's property.**[N] After some time the father died. **When they** came to **divide** the estate, this person **said to** his brothers: **Give me my portion** of the estate **along my boundary.**[H] **Rabba said: In** a case **such as this,** the court **compels** people to refrain from **conduct** characteristic **of Sodom.** The court forces a person to waive his legal rights in order to prevent him from acting in a manner characteristic of the wicked city of Sodom. Since it makes no difference to the brothers which portion they receive since the parcels of land must be of equal value, whereas it matters to this brother that the area he receives should be adjacent to the land he already bought, the court forces the others to give this brother his portion along his boundary.

BACKGROUND

Yavam – יָבָם: A man whose brother died without children is obligated by Torah law to marry his deceased brother's widow or to free her by means of a *ḥalitza* ceremony (see Deuteronomy 25:5–10). As long as neither levirate marriage nor *ḥalitza* has taken place, it is prohibited for her to marry another man. By Torah law, levirate marriage is achieved by the act of sexual intercourse. The Sages, nevertheless, instituted the practice of *ma'amar*, in which the deceased husband's brother betroths the widow, even though this betrothal is not effective by Torah law without intercourse. Intercourse consummates the marriage between the deceased's brother and the widow, and she is thereafter considered his wife in all respects. A bill of divorce would be necessary to formalize a divorce between them. Nowadays, the brother-in-law is required to free his brother's widow through *ḥalitza*, and it is not permitted for him to marry her through levirate marriage.

NOTES

But as for the distribution he is not like a firstborn – וְאֵין חֲלוּקָתוֹ כִּבְכוֹר: The early commentaries explain that the verse states that a firstborn son receives "a double portion" (Deuteronomy 21:17) of his father's estate. Therefore, it is understood that he receives one contiguous parcel of land that is twice the size of those received by his brothers. By contrast, a *yavam* receives two independent portions. He inherits one portion as the son of his father, and also receives the portion that was to be inherited by the deceased brother. These are two distinct portions; therefore, the brothers are not obligated to give him two adjacent portions.

His father's property – בֵּי נָשְׁיֵיהּ: The usual meaning of this phrase is: His father-in-law's property, but Rashi explains here that it refers to his father's property. This is based on the continuation of the passage, where the brothers come and protest, indicating that they inherited along with him; such a protest can emerge only with regard to their father's estate. But most commentaries, including *Tosafot*, *Arukh*, and Ri Migash, explain that this refers to the case of a father-in-law who had only daughters, who in turn divided his estate among themselves.

HALAKHA

A portion of a firstborn and a portion of an ordinary son – חֵלֶק בְּכוֹר וְחֵלֶק פָּשׁוּט: A firstborn son who inherits a double portion is provided his two portions along one boundary, even when all the portions are not of equal quality and giving him two portions along one boundary results in his receiving higher-quality portions. In this case, he would have to compensate his brother for the difference in value between the respective portions (*Sma*). The Rema, citing the Rosh, disagrees and says that the *halakha* that a firstborn is provided his two portions along one boundary applies only when all the portions are of equal quality, but if not, the inheritance is divided by lottery (Rambam *Sefer Kinyan*, *Hilkhot Shekhenim* 12:2; *Shulḥan Arukh*, *Ḥoshen Mishpat* 174:2).

Yavam – יָבָם: With regard to a *yavam* who married his deceased brother's widow and therefore receives that brother's portion of their father's estate in addition to his own, if the portions of the estate are not of equal value, he is given the portion due to the deceased brother by lottery and cannot insist that he be given two adjacent portions. Nevertheless, if all the portions are of the same value, he can take two adjacent portions. The Rema, citing *Tur* and Rosh, writes that he cannot insist on two adjacent portions even when all the portions are of equal value (Rambam *Sefer Kinyan*, *Hilkhot Shekhenim* 12:2; *Shulḥan Arukh*, *Ḥoshen Mishpat* 174:2).

Give me my portion along my boundary – פְּלִיגוּ לִי אַמִּצְרַאי: When brothers divide their father's estate, in a case in which all the parcels of land are of equal quality and one brother asks that he receive a portion adjacent to a field that he already owns, his request is honored. Refusing his request in such a situation would be conduct characteristic of the people of Sodom. This is in accordance with the opinion of Rabba, following the Rambam's version of the text of the Gemara, which omits the words: And the *halakha* is in accordance with the opinion of Rav Yosef. The Rema writes that some authorities disagree and say that his request is not granted unless he agrees to pay for the privilege. Others rule that it is uncertain whether the *halakha* is in accordance with the opinion of Rava or Rav Yosef in this case, and therefore the estate is divided by lottery. Nevertheless, he cannot demand that a parcel superior in quality be given to him even if he owns the adjacent property, and even if he is prepared to receive a smaller portion, so that his portion be equal in value to the other portions (Rambam *Sefer Kinyan*, *Hilkhot Shekhenim* 12:1; *Shulḥan Arukh*, *Ḥoshen Mishpat* 174:1, and *Shakh* there).

NOTES

We assess this as valuable – מַעֲלִינַן לַהּ עִילּוּיָא: The early commentaries express two main explanations. According to the first explanation, there is a qualitative difference between the area along the boundary and the parcels the others are receiving. For example, that area might be superior in quality to the rest of the field. The Meiri writes that were the areas equal in value, even Rav Yosef would agree that the brothers could not deny the desired parcel along the boundary from their brother who already owned property there. According to the second explanation, all the areas are equal in value, but the other brothers insist on assigning the portions by lottery. If one of the brothers wants a particular portion for himself, that parcel is assigned a higher value so that if a different brother receives it in the lottery, he can sell it to him at a higher price (see Ramban and Rashba).

Like the property of the house of bar Maryon – כִּי נִכְסֵי דְּבֵי בַּר מָרְיוֹן: According to Rashi this land was of especially high value. *Tosafot* and others explain that these people were tremendously wealthy and would not sell their land for less than an exceedingly steep price.

Two parcels of land next to two channels – תְּרֵי אַרְעָתָא אַתְּרֵי נִגְרֵי: Rashi holds that in this case as well, one of the brothers owns land along the boundary, and therefore wishes to receive his portion of his father's estate next to it. His brother disagrees, maintaining that they should divide the land in such a manner that both fields are irrigated from both water channels. *Tosafot* understand that neither brother owns land along the boundary. Rather, one brother thinks they should divide the property so that each area has its own channel, whereas the other calls for a different arrangement. They explain the subsequent case of two parcels of land with one water channel in a similar fashion.

LANGUAGE

Channel [*nigra*] – נִיגְרָא: Based on the root *nun*, *gimmel*, *reish*, which denotes the drawing or flowing of water. Here and in other places, the word refers to a fixed water channel or a river (*Arukh*).

מַתְקִיף לַהּ רַב יוֹסֵף: אָמְרִי לֵיהּ אַחֵי: מַעֲלִינַן לֵיהּ עִלּוּיָא כִּי נִכְסֵי דְּבֵי בַּר מָרְיוֹן! וְהִלְכְתָא כְּרַב יוֹסֵף.

Rav Yosef objects to this, saying this is not a case involving conduct characteristic of Sodom, since the brothers can explain their refusal to grant the request. **The brothers** can **say to him: We assess this** field that you want for yourself as particularly **valuable,**[N] **like the property of the house of bar Maryon.**[N] The brothers can claim that the portion he wants is more desirable than the others, and for that reason they do not want to give it to him. The Gemara concludes: **And the *halakha* is in accordance with** the opinion of **Rav Yosef,** and the brothers can refuse the request.

תְּרֵי אַרְעָתָא אַתְּרֵי נִגְרֵי – אָמַר רַבָּה: כְּגוֹן זֶה כּוֹפִין עַל מִדַּת סְדוֹם. מַתְקִיף לַהּ רַב יוֹסֵף, זִמְנִין דְּהַאי מְדַוֵּיל וְהַאי לָא מְדַוֵּיל! וְהִלְכְתָא כְּרַב יוֹסֵף.

If a father leaves his two sons **two** parcels of **land next to two** water **channels** [*nigrei*],[NLB] and one brother requests the field that is next to a field that he already owns, **Rabba says: In** a case **such as this,** the court **compels** people to refrain from **conduct** characteristic **of Sodom** and allows that brother to receive the field adjoining his own. **Rav Yosef objects to this,** saying that if the other brother protests and wants that parcel of land, it is not a case involving conduct characteristic of Sodom because he may have a valid reason for objecting: **Sometimes this** water channel **continues running** well, **while this** second one **does not continue running** well; therefore, the second brother wants to receive land that adjoins a water channel on both sides. The Gemara concludes: **And the *halakha*** is **in accordance with** the opinion of **Rav Yosef.**

תַּרְתֵּי אַחַד נִגְרָא – אָמַר רַב יוֹסֵף: כְּגוֹן זֶה כּוֹפִין עַל מִדַּת סְדוֹם. מַתְקִיף לַהּ אַבַּיֵי, מָצֵי אָמַר: בָּעֵינָא דְּאַפֵּישׁ אֲרִיסֵי! וְהִלְכְתָא כְּרַב יוֹסֵף, אַפּוּשֵׁי לָאו מִילְּתָא הִיא.

If a father leaves his two sons **two** parcels of land **next to one channel**[B] and one of the brothers already owns a field next to one of those parcels of land, **Rav Yosef said: In** a case **such as this,** the court **compels** people to refrain from **conduct** characteristic **of Sodom** and allows that brother to receive the field adjoining his own. **Abaye objects to this,** saying that this is not a case involving conduct characteristic of Sodom because the other brother **can say** to him: **I want** the number of **sharecroppers to increase.** If my field is in the middle and you have fields on either side, you will need more sharecroppers to work them and my field will enjoy greater security. **And the *halakha*** is **in accordance with** the opinion of **Rav Yosef** because **the increase** of sharecroppers **is** considered as **nothing,** and this is therefore not a valid reason for objecting.

BACKGROUND

Two parcels of land next to two channels – תְּרֵי אַרְעָתָא אַתְּרֵי נִגְרֵי: The diagrams illustrate the opinions of the *amora'im* according to Rashi's interpretation. Here, the father has left two plots, Plot B and Plot C, to his two sons, one of whom already owns a third plot, Plot A, next to one of them. According to Rav Yosef, the second son may demand that the two plots be redivided lengthwise, such that while the first son still receives the plot adjacent to the one he already owns, both sons have equal access to each channel.

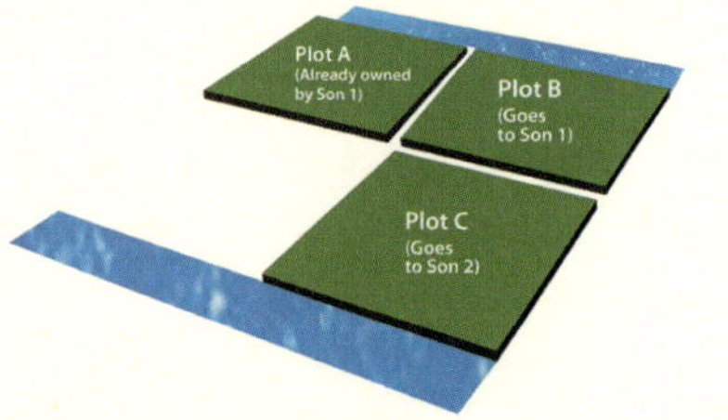

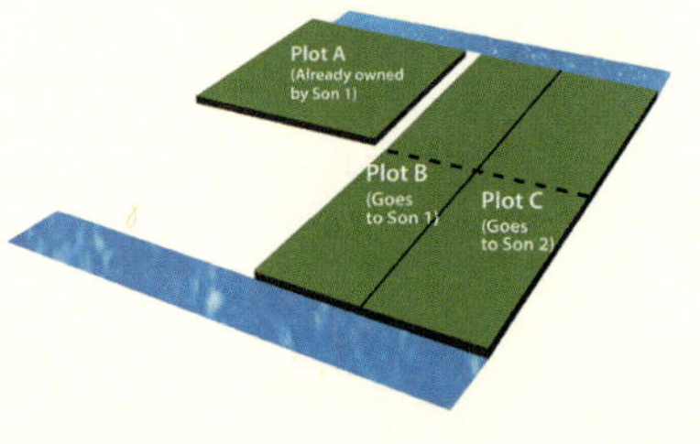

Above: Division of the plots according to Rabba

Right: Division of the plots according to Rav Yosef

Two parcels of land next to one channel – תַּרְתֵּי אַחַד נִגְרָא: Here, Rav Yosef concedes that the first son receives the plot adjacent to the one he already owns.

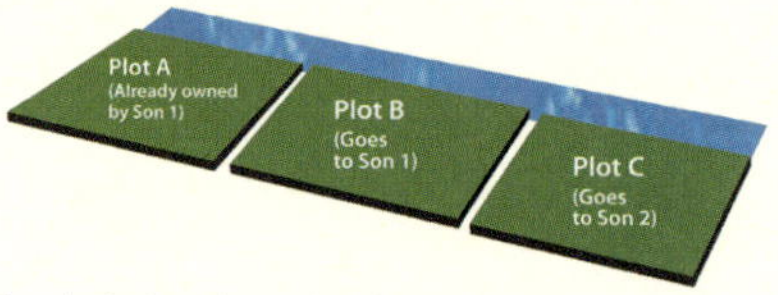

Three plots bordering the same channel

חַד גִּיסָא נַגְרָא וְחַד גִּיסָא נַהֲרָא – פָּלְגִין לָהּ בְּקַרְנָא זוֹל.

If there is a water **channel on one side**[H] of the field **and a river** on **the other side,**[N] the field **is divided diagonally** [*bekarna zol*][L] between the two brothers, so that they each receive land adjoining both the river and the water channel.

״וְלֹא אֶת הַטְּרַקְלִין״ כו׳. אֵין בָּהֶן כְּדֵי לָזֶה וּכְדֵי לָזֶה, מַהוּ? רַב יְהוּדָה אֲמַר: אִית דִּינָא דְּ״גּוֹד אוֹ אֲגוֹד״, רַב נַחְמָן אֲמַר: לֵית דִּינָא דְּ״גּוֹד אוֹ אֲגוֹד״.

§ The mishna teaches that **a hall,** a drawing room, and the like should **not** be divided unless the two parties will be able to use their respective portions in the same manner that they had previously used them. The Gemara asks: **What is the** ***halakha*** if **there is not enough for this one and that one?** What is to be done if one of the parties wishes to dissolve the partnership? **Rav Yehuda said: There is a** ***halakha*** of: Either **you set** a price **or I will set**[H] a price.[N] That is to say, one party can say to the other: Set a price you are willing to pay for my share, and I will sell my share to you or purchase your share from you at that price. **Rav Naḥman said: There is no** ***halakha*** of: Either **you set** a price **or I will set** a price; rather, the partnership continues.

אֲמַר לֵיהּ רָבָא לְרַב נַחְמָן, לְדִידָךְ דְּאָמְרַתְּ: לֵית דִּינָא דְּ״גּוֹד אוֹ אֲגוֹד״, בְּכוֹר וּפָשׁוּט שֶׁהִנִּיחַ לָהֶן אֲבִיהֶן עֶבֶד וּבְהֵמָה טְמֵאָה, כֵּיצַד עוֹשִׂין? אֲמַר לֵיהּ, שֶׁאֲנִי אוֹמֵר: עוֹבֵד לָזֶה יוֹם אֶחָד וְלָזֶה שְׁנֵי יָמִים.

Rava said to Rav Naḥman: According to you who say that **there is no** ***halakha*** of: Either **you set** a price **or I will set** a price, **what should they do** if there was **a firstborn** son **and an ordinary** brother **whose father left them a slave and a non-kosher animal** as an inheritance? How are they to be divided? Rav Naḥman **said to him: I say that they work for this one,** the ordinary brother, **one day, and for the other one,** the firstborn, **two days.**

מֵיתִיבֵי: מִי שֶׁחֶצְיוֹ עֶבֶד וְחֶצְיוֹ בֶּן חוֹרִין, עוֹבֵד אֶת רַבּוֹ יוֹם אֶחָד וְאֶת עַצְמוֹ יוֹם אֶחָד, דִּבְרֵי בֵּית הִלֵּל; בֵּית שַׁמַּאי אוֹמְרִים: תִּקַּנְתֶּם אֶת רַבּוֹ, אֶת עַצְמוֹ לֹא תִּקַּנְתֶּם, לִישָּׂא שִׁפְחָה אֵינוֹ יָכוֹל, לִישָּׂא בַּת חוֹרִין אֵינוֹ יָכוֹל, יִבָּטֵל? וַהֲלֹא לֹא נִבְרָא הָעוֹלָם אֶלָּא לִפְרִיָּה וּרְבִיָּה, שֶׁנֶּאֱמַר: ״לֹא תֹהוּ בְרָאָהּ לָשֶׁבֶת יְצָרָהּ״!

The Gemara **raises an objection** to Rav Yehuda's approach from what is taught in a mishna (*Gittin* 41a): **One who is half-slave**[H] **half-freeman,** e.g., a slave who had been jointly owned by two people, one of whom emancipated him, **serves his master one day and himself one day;** this is **the statement of Beit Hillel. Beit Shammai say: You have remedied** the situation **of his master,** who benefits fully from all his rights to the slave, but **you have not remedied his own** situation. **He cannot marry a maidservant,** since half of him is free, and a free Jew may not marry a Canaanite maidservant. **He is** also **not able to marry a free woman,** since half of him is a slave, and a Jewish woman may not marry a Canaanite slave. And if you say **he should be idle** and not marry, **but is it not** true that **the world was created only for procreation, as it is stated: "He did not create it to be a waste; He formed it to be inhabited"** (Isaiah 45:18)?

אֶלָּא כּוֹפִין אֶת רַבּוֹ וְעוֹשִׂין אוֹתוֹ בֶּן חוֹרִין, וְכוֹתְבִין שְׁטָר עַל חֲצִי דָּמָיו. וְחָזְרוּ בֵּית הִלֵּל לְהוֹרוֹת כְּדִבְרֵי בֵּית שַׁמַּאי!

Rather, the court **forces his master**[N] **to make him a freeman** by emancipating the half that he owns, **and** the court **writes a bill** in which the slave accepts responsibility to pay **half his value** to his master. This was the original version of the mishna. The ultimate version of the mishna records the retraction of Beit Hillel: **And Beit Hillel retracted** its opinion and **ruled in accordance with the statement of Beit Shammai.** This indicates that it is only in this case, where there is the particular consideration of procreation, that the court compels one of the parties to forfeit his portion and dissolve the partnership. But in other cases there is no *halakha* of: Either you set a price or I will set a price.

NOTES

A river on the other side – חַד גִּיסָא נַהֲרָא: The early commentaries disagree about the details of this case and about how the field is divided. Rashi explains that there is a river on one side of a field, e.g., the east side, and a water channel on an adjacent side, e.g., the north side. In order for the division to be equal, the field must be divided into eight parts so that each brother will receive an equal portion next to the river and next to the channel. Other commentaries explain that the river flows on two sides of the field, e.g., the east and the north sides, while the channel is situated on the other two sides, the west and the south sides. The field must be divided diagonally into two parts so that each portion borders on both the river and the water channel (Rabbeinu Ḥananel; Rif; Ri Migash).

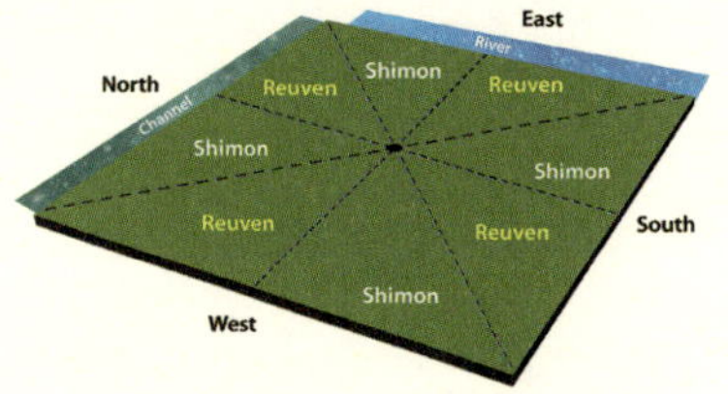

Division of the field according to Rashi

A *halakha* of you set or I will set a price – דִּינָא דְּגוֹד אוֹ אֲגוֹד: The commentaries disagree about the meaning of these words. Rashi holds that the word *gode* means to fix, to set: You fix the price and I will buy it, or I will fix the price and you will buy it. Rabbeinu Ḥananel explains the word *gode* to mean pull: You pull my part or I will pull your part. The Ritva understands that the disagreement extends beyond the precise meaning of the words and involves the question: Can either side suggest any price he wants for buying or selling the field, or is the true value of the land assessed and then each one offers the other the opportunity to buy or sell his share?

The court forces his master – כּוֹפִין אֶת רַבּוֹ: Even though there is a positive mitzva that states that *ab initio* it is prohibited for one to emancipate a Canaanite slave, the injunction of: "He did not create it to be a waste" (Isaiah 45:18), is so important that it overrides other positive mitzvot (*Tosafot*).

LANGUAGE

Diagonally [*karna zol*] – קַרְנָא זוֹל: The meaning of this term is uncertain. The accepted interpretation is: Go to the corners, which yields the Aramaic term for diagonal. Some, however, suggest that this is a foreign term for a line that does not extend straight but rather zigzags.

HALAKHA

A water channel on one side – חַד גִּיסָא נַגְרָא: A square field that has a river on two adjacent sides, e.g., on the north and on the east, and a path or a brook (*Sma*) on its other sides, in this case, on the south and on the west, is divided diagonally so that each portion borders on the river and on the path (Rambam *Sefer Kinyan*, *Hilkhot Shekhenim* 12:3; *Shulḥan Arukh*, *Ḥoshen Mishpat* 174:3).

There is a *halakha* of either you set or I will set – אִית דִּינָא דְּגוֹד אוֹ אֲגוֹד: If two partners own something that cannot be divided or is not subject to the *halakha* of division, one of the two can say to the other: Sell me your share at a certain price, even one that is higher than its market value, or buy my share, and the other partner can be compelled either to sell or to buy, following Rabbi Yehuda's opinion (Rambam *Sefer Kinyan*, *Hilkhot Shekhenim* 1:2; *Shulḥan Arukh*, *Ḥoshen Mishpat* 171:6).

One who is a half-slave – מִי שֶׁחֶצְיוֹ עֶבֶד: If a person is half-slave half-freeman, the court forces his master to emancipate him. The slave writes the master a promissory note stating that he owes him half his value. This *halakha* applies to a male slave, who is obligated to procreate. It does not apply to a woman who is half-maidservant and half-free woman, because she is not obligated in that mitzva. This is in accordance with the opinion of Beit Shammai, with whom Beit Hillel agree. If the woman was engaging in licentious behavior, the court forces her master to emancipate her so that she can marry, and she writes him a promissory note for what she owes him (Rambam *Sefer Kinyan*, *Hilkhot Avadim* 7:7; *Shulḥan Arukh*, *Yoreh De'a* 267:62).

שָׁאנֵי הָכָא, דְּ״אֲגוֹד״ אִיכָּא, ״גּוֹד״ לֵיכָּא.

The Gemara answers: **It is different here, because** the slave can say: **I will set**[N] a price, but he is **not** able to say: **You set** a price. In other words, the slave cannot offer to sell himself, because his Jewish side precludes him from selling himself as a Canaanite slave. Therefore, the court would not be able force the master to sell his share, were it not for the consideration of procreation. By contrast, in a situation where either side can buy or sell, one partner can compel the other to either buy his portion or sell his portion to him.

תָּא שְׁמַע: שְׁנֵי אַחִין, אֶחָד עָנִי וְאֶחָד עָשִׁיר, וְהִנִּיחַ לָהֶן אֲבִיהֶן מֶרְחָץ וּבֵית הַבַּד, עֲשָׂאָן לְשָׂכָר – הַשָּׂכָר לְאֶמְצַע, עֲשָׂאָן לְעַצְמוֹ – הֲרֵי עָשִׁיר אוֹמֵר לֶעָנִי:

The Gemara suggests: **Come and hear** a proof from what is taught in a mishna (172a): In a case where there are **two brothers, one poor**[H] **and one rich, and their father left them a bathhouse or an olive press** as an inheritance, if the father had **built** these facilities **for profit,** i.e., to charge others for using them, **the profit** that accrues after the father's death is **shared equally** by the two brothers. If the father had **built them for himself** and for the members of his household to use, the poor brother, who has little use for these amenities, cannot force the rich brother to convert the facilities to commercial use; rather, **the rich** brother can **say to the poor** brother:

NOTES

Because I will set – דַּאֲגוֹד אִיכָּא: This is because the slave can buy the master's share of himself and thereby go free, but the master cannot buy the free half of the slave, since there is no mechanism by which a Jew can sell himself to another Jew and thereby acquire the status of Canaanite slave (see Rashi and Rashba).

HALAKHA

Two brothers, one poor – שְׁנֵי אַחִין, אֶחָד עָנִי: In the case of two brothers, one of whom is poor and the other rich, and their father left them an inheritance of a bathhouse or an olive press, and the father had rented it out, they divide the rental fee between them. If the structure had been for the father's personal use, the poor brother cannot force the rich one to buy his share. Rather, the place continues to be used the way it had been by the father (see *Sma*). This is because when one brother cannot buy the other's share, he cannot force the other to sell his share. This is so unless the poor brother commits to borrowing money to buy out his brother's share, or if he tells his brother that he will buy his share and then sell the entire inheritance to others (Rambam *Sefer Kinyan*, *Hilkhot Shekhenim* 1:2; *Shulḥan Arukh*, *Ḥoshen Mishpat* 171:6).

Perek I
Daf 13 Amud b

״קַח לְךָ עֲבָדִים וְיִרְחֲצוּ בַּמֶּרְחָץ״, ״קַח לְךָ זֵיתִים וּבֹא וַעֲשֵׂה בְּבֵית הַבַּד״! הָתָם נַמִי ״גּוֹד״ אִיכָּא, ״אֲגוֹד״ לֵיכָּא.

Go **take servants for yourself,**[N] **and they will bathe in the bathhouse.** Or he can say: Go **take olives for yourself and come and transform** them into oil **in the olive press.** Evidently, the poor brother cannot say to him: Buy my share. The Gemara rejects this proof: **There too** the poor brother can say: **You set** a price and buy my share, as the rich brother has the means to buy his poor brother's portion; but he is **not** able to say: Or else **I will set** a price and buy your share, as the poor brother does not have the money to buy his brother out.

תָּא שְׁמַע: כֹּל שֶׁאִילּוּ יֵחָלֵק וּשְׁמוֹ עָלָיו – חוֹלְקִין, אִם לָאו – מַעֲלִין אוֹתוֹ בְּדָמִים! תַּנָּאֵי הִיא; דְּתַנְיָא: ״טוֹל אַתָּה שִׁיעוּר וַאֲנִי פָּחוֹת״ – שׁוֹמְעִין לוֹ. רַבָּן שִׁמְעוֹן בֶּן גַּמְלִיאֵל אוֹמֵר: אֵין שׁוֹמְעִין לוֹ;

The Gemara further proposes: **Come** and **hear** a proof from what is taught in a *baraita*: **Anything which,** even after it **is divided,**[H] each of the parts **retains the name** of the original item, **may be divided.** And **if** the parts will **not** retain the original name, the item should not be divided, but rather **its monetary** value **is assessed,** because one of the joint owners can say to the other: Either you set a price and buy it from me, or I will set a price and buy it from you. The Gemara explains: Actually, this matter **is** a dispute between ***tanna'im*****, as it is taught** in a *baraita*: If a courtyard or the like was not large enough to warrant division into two, and one of the co-owners said to the other: **You take** a minimum **measure** of the courtyard, e.g., four cubits, **and I will take less,**[NH] the court **listens to him. Rabban Shimon ben Gamliel says: They do not listen to him.**

הֵיכִי דָּמֵי? אִילֵימָא כִּדְתָנֵי, מַאי טַעֲמָא דְּרַבָּן שִׁמְעוֹן בֶּן גַּמְלִיאֵל? אֶלָּא לָאו חַסּוּרֵי מִחַסְּרָא וְהָכִי קָאָמַר: ״טוֹל אַתָּה שִׁיעוּר וַאֲנִי פָּחוֹת״ – שׁוֹמְעִין לוֹ, וְ״גּוֹד אוֹ אֲגוֹד״ – נַמִי שׁוֹמְעִין לוֹ, וְאָתָא רַבָּן שִׁמְעוֹן בֶּן גַּמְלִיאֵל לְמֵימַר: אֵין שׁוֹמְעִין לוֹ!

The Gemara clarifies the *baraita*: **What are the circumstances** of the case under discussion? **If we say it is exactly as it is taught, what is Rabban Shimon ben Gamliel's reasoning?** Why does he rule that the court ignores the party who is prepared to settle for less? **Rather, is it not that** the *baraita* **is incomplete and this** is what it **is saying:** If one of the co-owners said to the other: **You take** a minimum **measure** of the courtyard, **and I will take less,** all agree that the court **listens to him.** And the *tanna* of the *baraita* adds: **And** if one says: Either **you set** a price and buy it from me, **or I will set** a price and buy it from you, **they also listen to him. And Rabban Shimon ben Gamliel comes to say:** In the first case the court does listen to him, but **they do not listen to him** when he says: Either you set a price or I will set a price. Accordingly, this issue is the subject of a tannaitic dispute.

NOTES

Go take servants for yourself – קַח לְךָ עֲבָדִים: Rashi's version of the text seems not to have had the words: And let them wash you, because he explains: Take yourselves some servants and heat the water. In any event, the rich brother can say this even though he knows that his poor brother cannot afford to do so and will therefore be unable to make use of the bathhouse.

I will take less – וַאֲנִי פָּחוֹת: One of the co-owners can say to the other that since the courtyard cannot be divided so that both of us will receive a usable area, you take the minimal measure, i.e., four cubits of a courtyard that is seven cubits long, and I will take the rest, even though it is too small to be used in the usual manner.

HALAKHA

Anything which even after it is divided – כֹּל שֶׁאִילּוּ יֵחָלֵק: Items that retain their original name even after they are divided between partners are subject to the *halakha* of division. If the parts will not retain the original names, one partner cannot compel the other to divide the item. Rather one can say to the other: Buy my share or sell me yours, and he can compel the partner to comply (Rambam *Sefer Kinyan*, *Hilkhot Shekhenim* 1:4–5; *Shulḥan Arukh*, *Ḥoshen Mishpat* 171:3, 6–7).

You take a measure and I will take less – טוֹל אַתָּה שִׁיעוּר וַאֲנִי פָּחוֹת: If there was a plot of jointly owned land that was not large enough to warrant division, and one partner said to the other: You take the minimum measure, and I will take the rest even though it is less than the minimum measure, and you will compensate me with money for the difference, he cannot compel him to accept this arrangement. Even if he grants him the extra land as a gift, the partner can refuse to accept a gift. This is in accordance with the opinion of Rabban Shimon ben Gamliel. Some authorities rule that he can compel him to accept this arrangement, in accordance with the opinion of the first *tanna* (Rambam *Sefer Kinyan*, *Hilkhot Shekhenim* 1:5; *Shulḥan Arukh*, *Ḥoshen Mishpat* 171:10).

לָא, לְעוֹלָם כִּדְקָתָנֵי. וּדְקָאָמְרַתְּ: מַאי טַעֲמָא דְּרַבָּן שִׁמְעוֹן בֶּן גַּמְלִיאֵל? מִשּׁוּם דְּאָמַר לֵיהּ: אִי בְּדָמֵי – לֵית לִי דָּמֵי לְמֵיתַן לָךְ, בְּמַתָּנָה – לָא נִיחָא לִי, דִּכְתִיב: ״וְשׂוֹנֵא מַתָּנֹת יִחְיֶה״.

The Gemara rejects this interpretation of the *baraita*: **No,** the *baraita* should **actually** be understood exactly **as it is taught. And with regard to what you said: What is Rabban Shimon ben Gamliel's reasoning?** Why can't one of the parties say that they should divide the property and he will settle for less? It is **because** the second one **can say to him: If** you want me to compensate you with **money** for the difference between my share and your share, **I have no money to give you.** And if you wish to give it to me as **a gift, I am not at ease** with that, **as it is written: "But he who hates gifts shall live"** (Proverbs 15:27).[N] The *baraita* indicates that there is a *halakha* of: Either you set a price or I will set a price, in accordance with the opinion of Rav Yehuda.

אֲמַר לֵיהּ אַבַּיֵי לְרַב יוֹסֵף: הָא דְּרַב יְהוּדָה – דִּשְׁמוּאֵל הִיא, דִּתְנַן: וְכִתְבֵי הַקּוֹדֶשׁ, אַף עַל פִּי שֶׁשְּׁנֵיהֶם רוֹצִים – לֹא יַחֲלוֹקוּ; וַאֲמַר שְׁמוּאֵל: לֹא שָׁנוּ אֶלָּא בִּכְרֶךְ אֶחָד, אֲבָל בִּשְׁנֵי כְּרִיכוֹת – חוֹלְקִין; וְאִי סָלְקָא דַּעְתָּךְ לֵית דִּינָא דְּ״גּוֹד אוֹ אֲגוֹד״, מַאי אִירְיָא בִּכְרֶךְ אֶחָד? אֲפִילּוּ בִּשְׁנֵי כְּרִיכִין נַמִי!

As a continuation of this discussion, **Abaye said to Rav Yosef: That** statement **of Rav Yehuda is** actually the opinion **of Shmuel,**[N] his teacher, **as we learned** in the mishna (11a): **But** in the case of **sacred writings,** i.e., a scroll of any of the twenty-four books of the Bible, that were inherited by two people, **they may not divide** them, **even if both of them wish** to do so, because it would be a show of disrespect to cut the scroll in half. **And Shmuel said: They taught** that sacred writings should not be divided **only** if they are contained **in one scroll;**[NH] **but** when they are contained **in two scrolls, they may be divided. And if it should enter your mind** to say **that there is no** ***halakha*** **of:** Either **you set** a price **or I will set** a price, **why** does the *halakha* apply **specifically to one scroll? Even** if the sacred writings were contained **in two scrolls,** they should **also** not divide them, since the respective parts will not be even and one of the recipients will have to compensate the other.

תַּרְגְּמָא רַב שַׁלְמָן: בְּשֶׁשְּׁנֵיהֶן רוֹצִין.

Rav Shalman interpreted the mishna: It is referring to a case **where they both want** to divide the sacred writings; therefore, Shmuel said that they may do so when they are contained in two scrolls. But if just one of them wishes to divide them, there is no proof that he can compel the other one to accept the division.

אֲמַר אַמֵּימָר, הִלְכְתָא: אִית דִּינָא דְּ״גּוֹד אוֹ אֲגוֹד״. אֲמַר לֵיהּ רַב אַשִׁי לְאַמֵּימָר: הָא דְּרַב נַחְמָן מַאי? אֲמַר לֵיהּ: לָא שְׁמִיעָא לִי, כְּלוֹמַר לָא סְבִירָא לִי. וְלָא? וְהָא רָבִין בַּר חִינָּנָא וְרַב דִּימִי בַּר חִינָּנָא שְׁבַק לְהוּ אֲבוּהּ תַּרְתֵּי אַמְהָתָא, חֲדָא יָדְעָא אָפְיָא וּבַשּׁוּלֵי, וַחֲדָא יָדְעָא פִּילְכָא וְנַוּוֹלָא, וַאֲתוּ לְקַמֵּיהּ דְּרָבָא וַאֲמַר לְהוּ: לֵית דִּינָא דְּ״גּוֹד אוֹ אֲגוֹד״!

Ameimar said: The *halakha* is in accordance with the opinion of Rav Yehuda that **there is a *halakha* of:** Either **you set** a price **or I will set** a price. **Rav Ashi said to Ameimar: What** about **that** statement **of Rav Naḥman,** who disagrees with Rav Yehuda and says that there is no such *halakha*? Ameimar **said to him: I do not know** of it, **that is to say, I do not maintain** this opinion. The Gemara asks: **And is** the *halakha* **not** in accordance with the opinion of Rav Naḥman? **But** it happened that **the father of Ravin bar Ḥinnana and Rav Dimi bar Ḥinnana** died and **left them two maidservants, one** of whom **knew how to bake and to cook, and the other** of whom **knew how to spin and to weave.** One of the brothers suggested that each of them take one of the maidservants entirely for himself and forfeit his rights to the other maidservant. **They came before Rava and he said to them: There is no *halakha* of:** Either **you set** a price **or I will set** a price.

שָׁאנֵי הָתָם, דִּלְמָר מִיבָּעֵי לֵיהּ תַּרְוַיְיהוּ וּלְמָר מִיבָּעֵי לֵיהּ תַּרְוַיְיהוּ, כִּי קָאָמַר לֵיהּ: שְׁקוֹל אַתְּ חֲדָא וַאֲנָא חֲדָא – לָאו ״גּוֹד אוֹ אֲגוֹד״ הוּא. וְכִי לָא מָצֵי לְמֵימַר הָכִי? וְהָא כִּתְבֵי הַקֹּדֶשׁ דְּתַרְוַיְיהוּ מִיבָּעֵי לְהוּ, וְאָמַר שְׁמוּאֵל: לֹא שָׁנוּ אֶלָּא בִּכְרֶךְ אֶחָד, אֲבָל בִּשְׁנֵי כְּרִיכִין – חוֹלְקִין! הָא תַּרְגְּמָא רַב שַׁלְמָן: בְּשֶׁרָצוּ.

The Gemara answers: It is **different there, since this master wanted both of them**[H] **and the other master wanted both of them.** Therefore, **when** one of the brothers **said to** the other: **You take one and I** will take the other **one,**[N] **it is not** a case of: Either **you set** a price **or I will set** a price. The Gemara asks: **And can we not say so? But** there is the case of **sacred writings, which both of them** presumably **want, and Shmuel said: They taught** that sacred writings should not be divided **only** if they are contained **in one scroll; but** when they are contained **in two scrolls, they may be divided.** The Gemara answers: **Rav Shalman interpreted** the mishna: It is referring to a case **where they** both **want** to divide the sacred writings, and in such a case they may divide them, provided that they are in two scrolls.

NOTES

But he who hates gifts shall live – וְשׂוֹנֵא מַתָּנוֹת יִחְיֶה: The commentaries state that the Sages who disagree with Rabban Shimon ben Gamliel understand that the principle "But he who hates gifts shall live" does not apply here, because the co-owner who offers to take less is not set on giving a gift, but does so because he prefers any division of the property to joint ownership (Ramah).

That statement of Rav Yehuda is the opinion of Shmuel – הָא דְּרַב יְהוּדָה דִּשְׁמוּאֵל הִיא: For this reason the *halakha* is in accordance with the opinion of Rav Yehuda (Ritva).

In one scroll – בִּכְרֶךְ אֶחָד: It is disrespectful to cut the scroll itself, and sacred writings must not be treated in such a manner.

You take one and I will take one – שְׁקוֹל אַתְּ חֲדָא וַאֲנָא חֲדָא: The *halakha* of: Either you set a price or I will set a price, would apply here only if one of the brothers were to offer to buy or sell both maidservants. Since both of them are needed, they are considered a single unit and not two separate items.

HALAKHA

Sacred writings…in one scroll – כִּתְבֵי הַקּוֹדֶשׁ...בִּכְרֶךְ אֶחָד: Jointly owned sacred writings contained in a single scroll should not be divided, even if the two owners wish to do so. But if the writings are contained in two scrolls, they may be divided (Rambam *Sefer Kinyan*, *Hilkhot Shekhenim* 2:9; *Shulḥan Arukh*, *Ḥoshen Mishpat* 173:1).

This master wanted both of them – דִּלְמָר מִיבָּעֵי לֵיהּ תַּרְוַיְיהוּ: If two people co-owned two items that have different uses but are equally needed by both of them, neither one can force the other to divide the items between them, even if they are of equal value. This is also not a case of: Either you set a price or I will set a price (*Shulḥan Arukh*, *Ḥoshen Mishpat* 173:13, and see 173:1).

תָּנוּ רַבָּנַן: מְדַבִּיק אָדָם תּוֹרָה נְבִיאִים וּכְתוּבִים כְּאֶחָד, דִּבְרֵי רַבִּי מֵאִיר; רַבִּי יְהוּדָה אוֹמֵר: תּוֹרָה בִּפְנֵי עַצְמָהּ, נְבִיאִים בִּפְנֵי עַצְמָן, וּכְתוּבִים בִּפְנֵי עַצְמָן; וַחֲכָמִים אוֹמְרִים: כָּל אֶחָד וְאֶחָד בִּפְנֵי עַצְמוֹ.

§ The Gemara now begins a general discussion about sacred writings. **The Sages taught: A person may attach the Torah, the Prophets, and the Writings together**[H] as one scroll; this is **the statement of Rabbi Meir. Rabbi Yehuda says: The Torah** should be a scroll **by itself,**[N] the books of the **Prophets** a scroll **by themselves, and** the books of the **Writings** a scroll **by themselves. And the Sages say: Each one** of the books of the Prophets and the Writings should be a scroll **by itself.**

וְאָמַר רַבִּי יְהוּדָה: מַעֲשֶׂה בְּבַיְיתוֹס בֶּן זוּנִין שֶׁהָיוּ לוֹ שְׁמֹנָה נְבִיאִים מְדוּבָּקִין כְּאֶחָד, עַל פִּי רַבִּי אֶלְעָזָר בֶּן עֲזַרְיָה; וְיֵשׁ אוֹמְרִים: לֹא הָיוּ לוֹ אֶלָּא אֶחָד אֶחָד בִּפְנֵי עַצְמוֹ. אָמַר רַבִּי: מַעֲשֶׂה וְהֵבִיאוּ לְפָנֵינוּ תּוֹרָה נְבִיאִים וּכְתוּבִים מְדוּבָּקִים כְּאֶחָד, וְהִכְשַׁרְנוּם.

And Rabbi Yehuda said: There was **an incident involving Baitos ben Zunin,**[L] **who had eight** books **of the Prophets attached together as one** scroll, and he did this **with the approval of Rabbi Elazar ben Azarya.**[P] **And others say that** each and every **one** of the books was a scroll **by itself,** in accordance with the opinion of the Sages. **Rabbi** Yehuda HaNasi **said:** There was **an incident where they brought before us the Torah, the Prophets, and the Writings attached together as one** scroll **and we** ruled in accordance with the opinion of Rabbi Meir and **deemed them fit.**

בֵּין חוּמָּשׁ לְחוּמָּשׁ שֶׁל תּוֹרָה – אַרְבָּעָה שִׁיטִין, וְכֵן בֵּין כָּל נָבִיא לְנָבִיא, וּבְנָבִיא שֶׁל שְׁנֵים עָשָׂר – שָׁלֹשׁ שִׁיטִין. וּמְסַיֵּים מִלְּמַטָּה וּמַתְחִיל מִלְמַעְלָה.

The Gemara states: When different books are included in the same scroll, **four** empty **lines** of space should be left **between each book of the Torah,**[H] **and similarly between one** book of **the Prophets and another. But** between each of the books of **the Twelve Prophets** only **three** empty **lines** should be left, because they are considered one book. **And** the scribe may **finish** a book **at the bottom**[N] of one column **and begin** the next book **at the top** of the next column without leaving any empty space in between.

תָּנוּ רַבָּנַן: הָרוֹצֶה לְדַבֵּק תּוֹרָה נְבִיאִים וּכְתוּבִים כְּאֶחָד – מְדַבֵּק, וְעוֹשֶׂה בְּרֹאשׁוֹ כְּדֵי לָגוֹל עַמּוּד וּבְסוֹפוֹ כְּדֵי לָגוֹל הֶיקֵּף. וּמְסַיֵּים מִלְּמַטָּה וּמַתְחִיל מִלְמַעְלָה,

The Sages taught in a *baraita*: **One who wishes to attach the Torah, the Prophets, and the Writings together as one** scroll **may attach** them. **He should leave enough** empty parchment **at the beginning** of the scroll **for winding around the pole** to which the beginning of the scroll is fastened. **And at the end** of the scroll he should leave enough empty parchment **for winding around the** entire **circumference**[B] of the rolled-up scroll. **And he may finish** a book **at the bottom** of one column **and begin** the next book **at the top** of the next column without leaving any empty space between them.

HALAKHA

A person may attach the Torah, the Prophets, and the Writings together – מְדַבִּיק אָדָם תּוֹרָה נְבִיאִים וּכְתוּבִים: It is permitted to fasten the Torah, the Prophets, and the Writings together into one scroll. Such a scroll does not have the same level of sanctity as a Torah scroll; it has the sanctity of one of the five books of the Torah. This is in accordance with the opinion of Rabbi Meir (Rambam *Sefer Ahava, Hilkhot Tefillin UMezuza VeSefer Torah* 7:15; *Shulḥan Arukh, Yoreh De'a* 283:1).

Between each book of the Torah – בֵּין חוּמָּשׁ לְחוּמָּשׁ שֶׁל תּוֹרָה: A scribe must leave a space of four empty lines between one book of the Torah and another. Three lines must be left between one book of the Prophets and another, and between one book of the Twelve Prophets and another (Rambam *Sefer Ahava, Hilkhot Tefillin UMezuza VeSefer Torah* 7:15; *Shulḥan Arukh, Yoreh De'a* 273:1).

LANGUAGE

Baitos ben Zunin – בַּיְיתוֹס בֶּן זוּנִין: The name Baitos comes from the Greek word βoηθός, *boēthos*, meaning assistant. It might be a translation of the Hebrew name Ezra. Zunin is a form of the Greek name Ζήνων, *Zēnon*.

NOTES

The Torah by itself – תּוֹרָה בִּפְנֵי עַצְמָהּ: *Tosafot* write that the reason that the books of the Torah, Prophets, and Writings must be separated is not that one will occasionally rest the books of the Prophets on top of the Torah, as is suggested by Rabbeinu Ḥananel, because were that so, there would be no need to distinguish between the Prophets and the Writings. Rather, they should be separated so as not to appear like one book in which all sections have the same level of sanctity.

And he may finish at the bottom – וּמְסַיֵּים מִלְּמַטָּה: Rashi explains that should a scribe finish a book at the end of one column, he need not leave a space of four lines, but rather begins the next book at the top of the next page. The commentaries understand that this refers to the books of the Prophets, which may be separated, with the exception of those of the Twelve Prophets. Some commentaries maintain that *ab initio* each book should end at the bottom of a column and the next book should begin at the top of the next column. If a book ends in the middle of a column, the scribe should not continue on that column; rather, he should start the next book at the top of the next column so that it should be easy to divide up the books (Ri Migash).

Tosafot expound that it is permitted to end a book of the Prophets at the bottom of a column and to start at the top of the next column, but four empty lines must always be left even if the next book begins at the top of the column. This is not done in a Torah scroll, where each book must end in the middle of a column, with the next book beginning in the same column, four lines of empty space dividing between them. This is the way the Torah scroll should be arranged, so that the scroll not become divided.

The Meiri cites a version of this passage according to which no space need be left after any of the books of the Prophets, but rather one should start at the top of the column. The Ri Migash and others advance yet a another version: The scribe starts at the bottom and ends at the top, meaning that with respect to the Twelve Prophets and also the books of the Torah, one need not take care to start the next book at the top of a column. Rather, one continues with the next book after leaving the requisite space, even if it turns out that a book will end at the top of a column, or that a new book will begin in the middle of a column.

BACKGROUND

For winding around the pole…for winding around the circumference – לָגוֹל עַמּוּד...לָגוֹל הֶיקֵּף: The circumference of the entire scroll is significantly greater than the circumference of the pole around which it is wound.

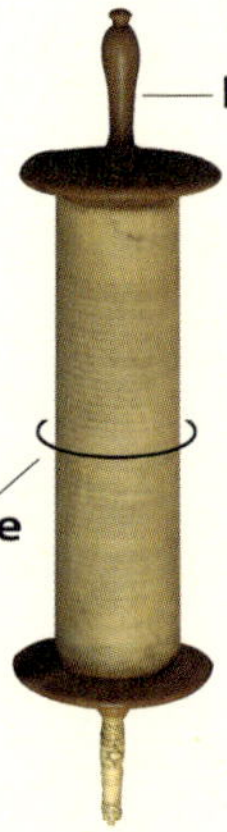

Above: Space left at the beginning and end of a scroll
Right: Circumference of the scroll and the pole around which it is wound

PERSONALITIES

Rabbi Elazar ben Azarya – רַבִּי אֶלְעָזָר בֶּן עֲזַרְיָה: One of the most important *tanna'im* in the generation following the destruction of the Second Temple, Rabbi Elazar ben Azarya descended from a wise, distinguished, and wealthy family. His father, Azarya, was a Torah scholar and an extremely wealthy man. Azarya supported his own brother, Shimon, enabling him to devote his time to Torah study; therefore, he is referred to as Shimon, brother of Azarya. Rabbi Elazar ben Azarya descended from a family of priests, which traced its lineage back to Ezra the Scribe, and there are traditions that describe the similarities between the two figures. The Gemara relates that due to Rabbi Elazar ben Azarya's knowledge, wealth, and lineage, he was the Sages' choice to replace Rabban Gamliel as *Nasi* when he was removed from his position of leadership after embarrassing Rabbi Yehoshua (*Berakhot* 27b).

וְאִם בָּא לַחֲתוֹךְ – חוֹתֵךְ. מַאי קָאָמַר? הָכִי קָאָמַר: שֶׁאִם בָּא לַחֲתוֹךְ – חוֹתֵךְ.

And if he wishes to cut[NH] the scroll, **he may cut** it. The Gemara is surprised at this: **What is the** *tanna* **saying?** Why is mention made here of cutting the scroll? The Gemara answers: **This is what** the *tanna* **is saying:** He arranges the text so that if he finishes a book at the bottom of one column, he begins the next book at the top of the next column without leaving any empty space, **so that if he wishes to cut** the scroll, **he may cut** it. If he does not begin the next book at the top of the next column, he will not be able to cut the scroll, because it is not fitting for a scroll to begin with an empty space.

וּרְמִינְהִי: תְּחִלַּת סֵפֶר וְסוֹפוֹ – כְּדֵי לָגוֹל; כְּדֵי לָגוֹל מַאי? אִי כְּדֵי לָגוֹל עַמּוּד – קַשְׁיָא הֵקֶף, אִי כְּדֵי לָגוֹל הֵקֶף – קַשְׁיָא עַמּוּד!

The Gemara **raises a contradiction** between this *baraita* and another *baraita* that teaches: **Enough** parchment should be left at **the beginning of the scroll and at its end**[H] **for winding.** The Gemara clarifies: **For winding** around **what? If** it means **for winding around the pole** to which the beginning of the scroll is fastened, this is **difficult** in light of what is taught in the first *baraita*, that at the end of the scroll enough parchment should be left for winding around the entire **circumference** of the scroll. And **if** it means **for winding around** the entire **circumference,** this is **difficult** in light of what is taught in the first *baraita* that at the beginning of the scroll enough parchment should be left for winding around the **pole.**

אָמַר רַב נַחְמָן בַּר יִצְחָק: לִצְדָדִין קָתָנֵי.

Rav Naḥman bar Yitzḥak said: The *tanna* **teaches** the *halakha* **disjunctively,** referring to two separate cases. He issues a general statement requiring that enough parchment be left for winding as needed: At the beginning of the pole, enough to wind around the pole, and at the end of the scroll, enough to wind around the circumference.

רַב אַשִׁי אָמַר: כִּי תַּנְיָא הַהִיא – בְּסֵפֶר תּוֹרָה; כִּדְתַנְיָא: כָּל הַסְּפָרִים נִגְלָלִים מִתְּחִלָּתָן לְסוֹפָן, וְסֵפֶר תּוֹרָה נִגְלָל לְאֶמְצָעִיתוֹ, וְעוֹשֶׂה לוֹ עַמּוּד אֵילָךְ וְאֵילָךְ. אָמַר רַבִּי אֱלִיעֶזֶר בְּרַבִּי צָדוֹק: כָּךְ הָיוּ כּוֹתְבֵי סְפָרִים שֶׁבִּירוּשָׁלַיִם עוֹשִׂין סִפְרֵיהֶם.

Rav Ashi said: When that second *baraita* **is taught,** indicating that the same measure of parchment is left at both the beginning and the end of the scroll, it was referring **to a Torah scroll, as it is taught** in a *baraita*: **All** other **scrolls are wound from the beginning to the end**[NH] around a single pole, **but a Torah scroll is wound** from both ends **to the middle**[N] around two **poles,** one of which **he attaches at this** end of the scroll **and** the other **at the other** end. **Rabbi Eliezer, son of Rabbi Tzadok, said: This is how the scribes in Jerusalem made their scrolls,** i.e., with poles at either end so that it could be rolled to the middle.

תָּנוּ רַבָּנַן: אֵין עוֹשִׂין סֵפֶר תּוֹרָה לֹא אׇרְכּוֹ יוֹתֵר עַל הֶקֵּיפוֹ וְלֹא הֶקֵּיפוֹ יוֹתֵר עַל אׇרְכּוֹ. שָׁאֲלוּ אֶת רַבִּי: שִׁיעוּר סֵפֶר תּוֹרָה בְּכַמָּה? אָמַר לָהֶן: בִּגְוִיל – שִׁשָּׁה. בִּקְלָף בְּכַמָּה? אֵינִי יוֹדֵעַ.

§ **The Sages taught: A Torah scroll should not be made** in such a manner **that its length,** i.e., its height, **is greater than its circumference**[H] when it is rolled up; **nor should its circumference be greater than its length. They asked Rabbi** Yehuda HaNasi: **What should the size of a Torah scroll be?** Rabbi Yehuda HaNasi **said to them:** If it was written **on a hide that was treated with gallnuts** [*gevil*] it should be **six** handbreadths[N] long. They asked him further: **How much** should it be if it was written **on** ordinary **parchment** [*kelaf*]?[B] Rabbi Yehuda HaNasi said to them: **I do not know.**

BACKGROUND

Gevil and *kelaf* – גְּוִיל וּקְלָף: *Gevil* is a whole animal hide that has been treated in the way crude leather is made fit for clothes, shoes, and the like. During the processing, the hair and flesh is removed, and the skin is smoothed out, shrunk, and treated to become more durable. The skin is smoothed until suitable for writing. This was the prevalent process for preparing Torah scrolls in ancient times.

In the talmudic period, the process of preparing the animal hides changed somewhat. After its initial treatment, the hide was cut into two layers. The outer layer of skin, which had been covered with hair, was called *kelaf*, while the inner layer facing the flesh was called *dukhsustos*. During the Middle Ages, particularly in France and Germany, a new practice developed, in which the hides, rather than being split, were stripped down on both sides by removing the hair and the layer immediately beneath it, as well as the inner layer. The exposed core of the hide was then used for writing. This core layer is subject to all the *halakhot* of a *kelaf* taught in the Gemara despite not being true *kelaf*. This type of parchment is still used today for writing Torah scrolls, phylacteries, and *mezuzot*.

NOTES

If he wishes to cut – אִם בָּא לַחֲתוֹךְ: This is surprising, as it was taught in the mishna that it is disrespectful to divide sacred writings. It may be suggested that while it is disrespectful to divide sacred writings as part of a division of assets, there is nothing wrong with dividing them when no monetary consideration is involved (*Tosafot*).

All scrolls are wound from the beginning to the end – כָּל הַסְּפָרִים נִגְלָלִים מִתְּחִלָּתָן לְסוֹפָן: This is Rashi's version of the text. Most of the early commentaries, by contrast, appear to understand this as: All scrolls are wound to their beginning. Tractate *Soferim* explicitly states that all scrolls, except for Torah scrolls, are rolled from their end to their beginning. The commentaries disagree about how to resolve the contradiction between this version of the text and the earlier *baraita* that states that enough empty parchment must be left at the beginning of the scroll to wind the scroll around a pole, and enough empty parchment must be left at the end of the scroll to wind it around the entire circumference of the rolled-up scroll, since this *baraita* indicates that the scrolls are rolled from their beginning to their end.

But a Torah scroll is wound to the middle – וְסֵפֶר תּוֹרָה נִגְלָל לְאֶמְצָעִיתוֹ: This does not mean literally to the middle, but rather to the spot where the previous reading had ended and the next reading will begin. The difference between a Torah scroll and other scrolls lies in the honor that must be shown to the community, that the people should not be kept waiting while the Torah is being rolled to the proper place from the beginning or from the end. It would be similarly disrespectful to the community if the Torah had to be rolled from the middle each time it was read (Ri Migash).

On *gevil* it should be six handbreadths – בִּגְוִיל שִׁשָּׁה: The *ge'onim*, citing Rav Yehudai Gaon, write that this measurement was chosen to correspond to the dimensions of the tablets of the covenant. Others write that that this is the measurement of the Torah that was in the Ark of the Covenant (Ya'avetz).

HALAKHA

If he wishes to cut – אִם בָּא לַחֲתוֹךְ: The empty lines that must be left between the books of the Torah and the books of the Prophets are intended to facilitate cutting of the scroll, should one desire to do so (Rambam *Sefer Ahava, Hilkhot Tefillin UMezuza VeSefer Torah* 7:15).

At the beginning of the scroll and at its end – תְּחִילַּת סֵפֶר וְסוֹפוֹ: An empty portion of parchment must be left at the beginning and at the end of a Torah scroll to facilitate winding the scroll around the poles. An additional two fingerbreadths must be left between the pole and the column of writing (Rambam *Sefer Ahava, Hilkhot Tefillin UMezuza VeSefer Torah* 9:2; *Shulḥan Arukh, Yoreh De'a* 273:1).

All scrolls are wound from the beginning to the end – כָּל הַסְּפָרִים נִגְלָלִים מִתְּחִלָּתָן לְסוֹפָן: All sacred scrolls are wound around a pole fastened to the end of the scroll. A Torah scroll is rolled from both ends to the middle around two poles fastened to either end. The parchment is sewn with sinews (Rambam *Sefer Ahava, Hilkhot Tefillin UMezuza VeSefer Torah* 9:2; *Shulḥan Arukh, Oraḥ Ḥayyim* 691:2 and *Yoreh De'a* 278:2).

Its length should not be greater than its circumference – לֹא אׇרְכּוֹ יוֹתֵר עַל הֶקֵּיפוֹ: A Torah scroll should be written in such a way that after it is sewn and rolled, its length equals its circumference. When the scroll is written on *gevil*, its length should be six handbreadths; when it is written on ordinary parchment, it can be more or less than that, provided that its length equals its circumference. Some authorities say that the thickness of the pole at the end of the scroll is included in the measurement of the circumference (Rambam *Sefer Ahava, Hilkhot Tefillin UMezuza VeSefer Torah* 9:1; *Shulḥan Arukh, Yoreh De'a* 272:1).

רַב הוּנָא כְּתַב שִׁבְעִין סִפְרֵי דְּאוֹרַיְיתָא, וְלָא אִיתְרְמֵי לֵיהּ אֶלָּא חַד. רַב אַחָא בַּר יַעֲקֹב כְּתַב חַד אַמַּשְׁכֵיהּ דְּעִיגְלֵי וְאִיתְרְמֵי לֵיהּ, יְהַבוּ בֵּיהּ רַבָּנַן עֵינַיְיהוּ וְנָח נַפְשֵׁיהּ.

It is related that **Rav Huna wrote seventy Torah scrolls** himself, **and it happened for him** only **once** that the length and the circumference were equal. **Rav Aḥa bar Ya'akov wrote one** Torah scroll **on calf hide and it happened** to have the same length and circumference. **The Sages looked at him** and his achievement with jealousy, **and he died** from their envious gaze.

אֲמַרוּ לֵיהּ רַבָּנַן לְרַב הַמְנוּנָא: כְּתַב רַבִּי אַמִּי אַרְבַּע מְאָה סִפְרֵי תוֹרָה. אֲמַר לְהוּ: דִּילְמָא "תּוֹרָה צִוָּה לָנוּ מֹשֶׁה" כְּתַב. אֲמַר לֵיהּ רָבָא לְרַבִּי זֵירָא: נְטַע רַבִּי יַנַּאי אַרְבַּע מְאָה כַּרְמֵי. אֲמַר לֵיהּ: דִּילְמָא שְׁתַּיִם כְּנֶגֶד שְׁתַּיִם וְאַחַת יוֹצֵא זָנָב.

The Sages said to Rav Hamnuna: Rabbi Ami wrote four hundred Torah scrolls. Rav Hamnuna **said to them: Perhaps he wrote** the verse: **"Moses commanded us the Torah"** (Deuteronomy 33:4)[N] four hundred times, rather than four hundred complete Torah scrolls, as it is difficult to say that he could have written so many, even over a lifetime. Similarly, **Rava said to Rabbi Zeira: Rabbi Yannai planted four hundred vineyards.**[N] Rava **said to him: Perhaps** he did not plant large vineyards, but only the smallest possible vineyards recognized by *halakha*, which are composed of **two** vines **facing** another **two** vines, with a fifth **one protruding** like **a tail,** extending out beyond the square.

מֵיתִיבֵי: אָרוֹן שֶׁעָשָׂה מֹשֶׁה, אַמָּתַיִם וָחֵצִי אָרְכּוֹ וְאַמָּה וָחֵצִי רׇחְבּוֹ וְאַמָּה וָחֵצִי קוֹמָתוֹ, בְּאַמָּה בַּת שִׁשָּׁה טְפָחִים.

The Gemara **raises an objection** to what is taught with regard to the length of a Torah scroll from a *baraita*: With regard to **the Ark** of the Covenant **that Moses fashioned,**[B] **its length was two and one-half cubits, its width was one and one-half cubits, and its height was one and one-half cubits** (see Exodus 25:10), **the cubit** used for these measurements **being six handbreadths.** Therefore, the Ark was fifteen handbreadths long, nine handbreadths wide, and nine handbreadths high.

וְהַלּוּחוֹת, אׇרְכָּן שִׁשָּׁה וְרׇחְבָּן שִׁשָּׁה וְעׇבְיָין שְׁלֹשָׁה, מוּנָּחוֹת כְּנֶגֶד אׇרְכּוֹ שֶׁל אָרוֹן. כַּמָּה לוּחוֹת אוֹכְלוֹת בָּאָרוֹן? שְׁנֵים עָשָׂר טְפָחִים, נִשְׁתַּיְּירוּ שָׁם שְׁלֹשָׁה טְפָחִים; צֵא מֵהֶן טֶפַח, חֶצְיוֹ לְכוֹתֶל זֶה וְחֶצְיוֹ לְכוֹתֶל זֶה – נִשְׁתַּיְּירוּ שָׁם שְׁנֵי טְפָחִים שֶׁבָּהֶן סֵפֶר תּוֹרָה מוּנָּח,

The *baraita* continues: **And** as for **the tablets, their length was six** handbreadths, **their width was six** handbreadths, **and their thickness was three** handbreadths. The tablets **were placed along the length of the Ark,** one next to the other. If so, **how much** space did **the tablets occupy** along the length **of the Ark? Twelve handbreadths,** as each tablet was six handbreadths long. **Three handbreadths were left there** along the length of the Ark, for a total of fifteen handbreadths. **Deduct a handbreadth from them: One-half** a handbreadth **for this wall,** namely, the thickness of the wooden Ark itself, **and one-half** a handbreadth **for the other wall.** Accordingly, **two handbreadths were left there, in which the Torah scroll** written by Moses **lay.**

NOTES

Perhaps he wrote, Moses commanded us the Torah – דִּילְמָא תּוֹרָה צִוָּה לָנוּ מֹשֶׁה כְּתַב: Some commentaries suggest that Rabbi Ami wrote this verse alone for himself four hundred times because in his opinion, writing this verse is like writing the entire Torah (Ri Migash; see Meiri). Nevertheless, most commentaries explain that four hundred Torah scrolls were brought to him; in each he wrote only that verse to complete the scrolls, and by completing the scrolls it was considered as if he had written the entire Torah each time (see *Menaḥot* 30a).

Four hundred vineyards – אַרְבַּע מְאָה כַּרְמֵי: He planted the vineyards due to his love for the land of Eretz Yisrael, which he wished to build up and plant with his own two hands (Ra'avad; Ritva; Meiri).

BACKGROUND

The Ark that Moses fashioned – אָרוֹן שֶׁעָשָׂה מֹשֶׁה:

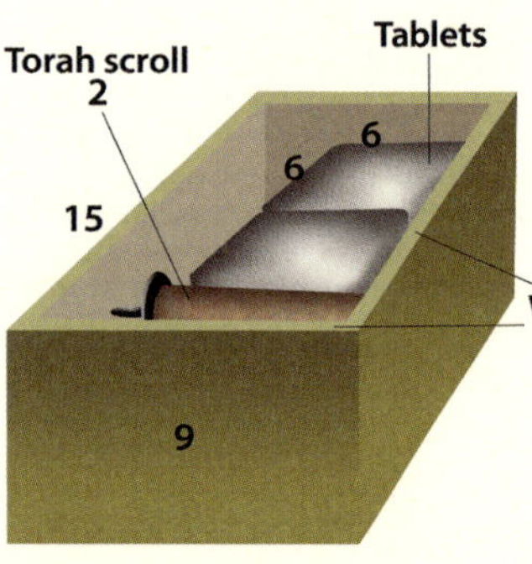

The Ark that Moses fashioned, according to Rabbi Meir

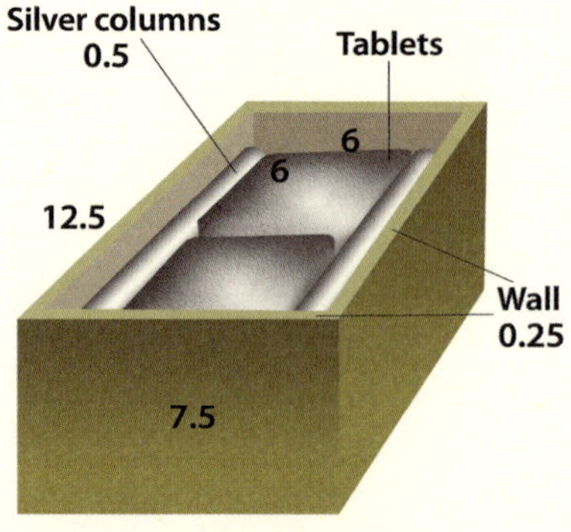

The Ark that Moses fashioned, according to Rabbi Yehuda

Summary of both opinions:

Length	Rabbi Meir	Rabbi Yehuda
Walls	1	0.5
Tablets	12	12
Torah Scroll	2	–
Total	**15**	**12.5**

Width	Rabbi Meir	Rabbi Yehuda
Walls	1	0.5
Tablets	6	6
Silver Columns	–	1
Empty Space	2	–
Total	**9**	**7.5**

שֶׁנֶּאֱמַר: ״אֵין בָּאָרוֹן רַק שְׁנֵי לֻחוֹת הָאֲבָנִים אֲשֶׁר הִנִּחַ שָׁם מֹשֶׁה״ [וגו׳]; מַאי ״אֵין בָּאָרוֹן רַק״? מִיעוּט אַחַר מִיעוּט, וְאֵין מִיעוּט אַחַר מִיעוּט אֶלָּא לְרַבּוֹת סֵפֶר תּוֹרָה שֶׁמּוּנָּח בָּאָרוֹן.

What biblical source indicates that a Torah scroll was placed there? **As it is stated: "There was nothing in the Ark except the two tablets of stone which Moses put there"** (I Kings 8:9). **What** does **"there was nothing in the Ark except"** mean? This is an example of **a restriction following a restriction,** as both terms, "nothing" and "except," indicate that the Ark was empty. **And** there is a hermeneutical principle that **a restriction following a restriction serves only to amplify** and include other matters. In this case, it serves **to include a Torah scroll that lies in the Ark.**

פִּירְנַסְתָּ אָרוֹן לְאׇרְכּוֹ, צֵא וּפַרְנֵס אָרוֹן לְרׇחְבּוֹ: כַּמָּה לוּחוֹת אוֹכְלוֹת בָּאָרוֹן? שִׁשָּׁה טְפָחִים, נִשְׁתַּיְּירוּ שָׁם שְׁלֹשָׁה טְפָחִים; צֵא מֵהֶן טֶפַח, חֶצְיוֹ לְכוֹתֶל זֶה וְחֶצְיוֹ לְכוֹתֶל זֶה – נִשְׁתַּיְּירוּ שָׁם שְׁנֵי טְפָחִים, שֶׁלֹּא יְהֵא סֵפֶר תּוֹרָה נִכְנָס וְיוֹצֵא כְּשֶׁהוּא דָּחוּק, דִּבְרֵי רַבִּי מֵאִיר.

The *baraita* continues: With this explanation **you have accounted for the** entire **length of the Ark; go** now **and account for the width of the Ark,** which was nine handbreadths. **How much** space did **the tablets occupy** of the width **of the Ark,** which was nine handbreadths wide? **Six handbreadths;** therefore, **three handbreadths were left there** along the width of the Ark. **Deduct a handbreadth from them: One-half** a handbreadth **for** the thickness of **this wall and one-half** a handbreadth **for** the thickness of **the other wall.** Accordingly, **two handbreadths were left there.** What was their purpose? These were necessary **so that the Torah scroll would be able to go in and out without being pressed;** this is **the statement of Rabbi Meir.**

רַבִּי יְהוּדָה אוֹמֵר: בְּאַמָּה בַּת חֲמִשָּׁה טְפָחִים. וְהַלּוּחוֹת, אׇרְכָּן שִׁשָּׁה וְרׇחְבָּן שִׁשָּׁה וְעׇבְיָין שְׁלֹשָׁה, מוּנָּחוֹת בְּאוֹרְכּוֹ שֶׁל אָרוֹן. כַּמָּה לוּחוֹת אוֹכְלוֹת בָּאָרוֹן? שְׁנֵים עָשָׂר טְפָחִים; נִשְׁתַּיֵּיר שָׁם חֲצִי טֶפַח, אֶצְבַּע לְכוֹתֶל זֶה וְאֶצְבַּע לְכוֹתֶל זֶה.

Rabbi Yehuda disagrees and **says:** The **cubit** used for all the measurements of the Ark **was five handbreadths** long. Therefore, the Ark was twelve and one-half handbreadths long, seven and one-half handbreadths wide, and seven and one-half handbreadths high. **And** as for **the tablets, their length was six** handbreadths, **their width was six** handbreadths, **and their thickness was three** handbreadths, and **they were placed along the length of the Ark,** one next to the other. If so, **how much** space did **the tablets occupy** along the length **of the Ark? Twelve handbreadths,** so that **one-half a handbreadth was left there,** which is two fingerbreadths. **One fingerbreadth** of those two was **for** the thickness of **this wall and one fingerbreadth** of those two was **for** the thickness of **the other wall.**

פִּירְנַסְתָּ אָרוֹן לְאׇרְכּוֹ, צֵא וּפַרְנֵס אָרוֹן לְרׇחְבּוֹ: כַּמָּה לוּחוֹת אוֹגְדוֹת בָּאָרוֹן? שִׁשָּׁה טְפָחִים, נִשְׁתַּיֵּיר שָׁם טֶפַח וּמֶחֱצָה; צֵא מֵהֶן חֲצִי טֶפַח, אֶצְבַּע וּמֶחֱצָה לְכוֹתֶל זֶה וְאֶצְבַּע וּמֶחֱצָה לְכוֹתֶל זֶה – נִשְׁתַּיֵּיר שָׁם טֶפַח שֶׁבּוֹ עַמּוּדִין עוֹמְדִין, שֶׁנֶּאֱמַר: ״אַפִּרְיוֹן עָשָׂה לוֹ הַמֶּלֶךְ שְׁלֹמֹה מֵעֲצֵי הַלְּבָנוֹן. עַמּוּדָיו עָשָׂה כֶסֶף רְפִידָתוֹ זָהָב מֶרְכָּבוֹ אַרְגָּמָן״ וגו׳;

With this explanation, **you have accounted** for **the** entire **length of the Ark; go** now **and account for the width of the Ark,** which was seven and one-half handbreadths. **How much** space did **the tablets occupy in the Ark? Six handbreadths,** meaning that **one and one-half handbreadths were left there** along the width of the Ark. **Deduct one-half a handbreadth, one and one-half fingerbreadths**[N] **for** the thickness of **this wall, and one and one-half fingerbreadths for** the thickness of **the other wall.** Accordingly, **one handbreadth was left there in which the** silver **columns**[N] **were placed** on either side of the tablets, **as it is stated: "King Solomon made himself a palanquin of the timbers of Lebanon; he made its columns of silver, its back of gold, its seat of purple"** (Song of Songs 3:9–10). This is understood as an allusion to the Ark of the Covenant.

וְאַרְגָּז שֶׁשִּׁיגְּרוּ בּוֹ פְּלִשְׁתִּים דּוֹרוֹן לֵאלֹהֵי יִשְׂרָאֵל מוּנָּח מִצִּדּוֹ, שֶׁנֶּאֱמַר: ״וְאֵת כְּלֵי הַזָּהָב אֲשֶׁר הֲשֵׁבֹתֶם לוֹ אָשָׁם תָּשִׂימוּ בָאַרְגַּז מִצִּדּוֹ וְשִׁלַּחְתֶּם אוֹתוֹ וְהָלָךְ״; וְעָלָיו סֵפֶר תּוֹרָה מוּנָּח, שֶׁנֶּאֱמַר: ״לָקֹחַ אֵת סֵפֶר הַתּוֹרָה הַזֶּה וְשַׂמְתֶּם אֹתוֹ מִצַּד אֲרוֹן בְּרִית ה׳״, מִצַּד הוּא מוּנָּח וְלֹא בְּתוֹכוֹ.

And the chest in which the Philistines sent the gift to the God of Israel was placed alongside the Ark, **as it is stated: "And put the golden devices which you are restoring to Him for a guilt-offering in a chest by the side of it, and send it away that it may go"** (I Samuel 6:8). **And upon** this chest **lay the Torah scroll, as it is stated: "Take this Torah scroll and put it at the side of the Ark of the Covenant of the Lord"** (Deuteronomy 31:26). This means that **it was placed at the side** of the Ark, **and not inside** it.

וּמָה אֲנִי מְקַיֵּים ״אֵין בָּאָרוֹן רַק״? לְרַבּוֹת

And accordingly, **how do I realize** the meaning of that which is stated: **"There was nothing in the Ark except** the two tablets of stone which Moses put there," which, according to the opinion of Rabbi Meir, teaches that something else was in the Ark besides the tablets themselves? It serves **to include**

NOTES

One and one-half fingerbreadths – **אֶצְבַּע וּמֶחֱצָה**: The version of the *baraita* found in many manuscripts is: One fingerbreadth. This would accord better with what had been stated previously in the *baraita* concerning the length of the Ark and tablets. According to the standard version of the text, it is possible that this clause of the *baraita* is referring to a narrower finger than the previous clause (see Rashi and *Tosafot*).

Columns – **עַמּוּדִין**: These columns are not mentioned in the description of the construction of the Ark either in the days of Moses or at the time of the building of the Temple. The nature of these columns is also unclear. Rashi explains that the tablets were placed between the columns, indicating that their purpose was to hold the tablets in place and prevent them from sliding around inside the Ark. The Ra'avad suggests that the Torah was wound around these columns when it was read. The Ritva proposes that these columns were used to support the Ark cover either from the inside or the outside.

LANGUAGE

Handbreadths [*pushkei*] – פּוּשְׁכֵּי: From the Aramaic *peshakh*, meaning a handbreadth. This term is found in several Aramaic translations of the Bible.

שִׁבְרֵי לוּחוֹת שֶׁמּוּנָּחִים בָּאָרוֹן; וְאִי סָלְקָא דַּעְתָּךְ סֵפֶר תּוֹרָה הֶקֵּיפוֹ שִׁשָּׁה טְפָחִים, מִכְּדִי כָּל שֶׁיֵּשׁ בְּהֶקֵּיפוֹ שְׁלֹשָׁה טְפָחִים יֵשׁ בּוֹ רוֹחַב טֶפַח, וְכֵיוָן דִּלְאֶמְצָעִיתוֹ נִגְלָל – נָפֵישׁ לֵיהּ מִתְּרֵי טִפְחָא רַוְוחָא דְּבֵינֵי בֵּינֵי, בִּתְרֵי פּוּשְׁכֵּי הֵיכִי יָתֵיב?

the broken pieces of the first set of **tablets, which were placed in the Ark.** Having cited the *baraita*, the Gemara now presents its objection to what was taught earlier with regard to the dimensions of a Torah scroll: **And if it should enter your mind** to say, as Rabbi Yehuda HaNasi held, that **the circumference of a Torah scroll is six handbreadths, now since any** cylindrical object **having a circumference of three handbreadths has a diameter of one handbreadth,**[N] a Torah scroll with a circumference of six handbreadths has a diameter of two handbreadths. **And since** a Torah scroll **is wound to the middle,** since it is rolled from both sides, **it** must take up **more than two handbreadths** due to **the space between** the sheets of parchment and the double rolling. According to Rabbi Meir, who says that the Torah scroll was placed inside the ark, **how did** the scroll **fit in** the remaining **two handbreadths** [*pushkei*][L] of space in the Ark?

אֲמַר רַב אַחָא בַּר יַעֲקֹב: סֵפֶר עֲזָרָה לִתְחִלָּתוֹ הוּא נִגְלָל. וְאַכַּתִּי תְּרֵי בִּתְרֵי הֵיכִי יָתֵיב? אֲמַר רַב אַשִׁי: דְּכָרֵיךְ בֵּיהּ פּוּרְתָּא וּכְרָכֵיהּ לְעֵיל.

Rav Aḥa bar Ya'akov said: The scroll of the Temple **courtyard,** which was kept in the Ark, **was wound to its beginning,** i.e., it had only a single pole, so that its circumference was only two handbreadths. The Gemara asks: **But still, how does** an item **that is two** handbreadths wide **fit into** a space that is precisely **two** handbreadths? It would be impossible to fit it in. **Rav Ashi said: A small section** of the scroll **was wound** separately **and** then **placed on top** of the scroll.

וְרַבִּי יְהוּדָה, מִקַּמֵּי דְּלֵיתֵי אַרְגָּז, סֵפֶר תּוֹרָה הֵיכִי הֲוָה יָתֵיב? דַּפָּא הֲוָה נָפֵיק מִינֵּיהּ וְיָתֵיב עִילָּוֵיהּ סֵפֶר תּוֹרָה. וְרַבִּי מֵאִיר, הַאי "מִצַּד אֲרוֹן" מַאי עָבֵיד לֵיהּ? הַהוּא מִיבָּעֵי לֵיהּ, דְּמַתְנַח לֵיהּ מִצַּד וְלָא מַתְנַח בֵּינֵי לוּחֵי, וּלְעוֹלָם בְּגַוֵּיהּ מִן הַצַּד.

Having concluded its current discussion, the Gemara now addresses the details of the aforementioned *baraita* and asks: **And** according to **Rabbi Yehuda,** who says that the Torah scroll rested on the chest that came from the Philistines, **where was the Torah scroll placed before the chest arrived?** The Gemara answers: **A shelf protruded from** the Ark **and the Torah scroll rested on it.** The Gemara asks: **And** according to **Rabbi Meir,** who says that the Torah scroll rested inside the Ark, **what does he do with this** verse: "Take this Torah scroll and put it **at the side of the Ark**" (Deuteronomy 31:26)? The Gemara answers: **He requires** that verse to teach **that** the Torah scroll **was placed at the side** of the tablets, **and that it was not placed between** the two **tablets, but** it was **actually** placed **inside** the Ark **at the side** of the tablets.

וְרַבִּי מֵאִיר, עַמּוּדִין הֵיכָא הָווּ קַיְימֵי? מִבָּרַאי. וְרַבִּי מֵאִיר, שִׁבְרֵי לוּחוֹת דְּמוּנָּחִין בָּאָרוֹן מְנָא לֵיהּ? נָפְקָא לֵיהּ מִדְּרַב הוּנָא; דְּאָמַר רַב הוּנָא, מַאי דִּכְתִיב: "אֲשֶׁר נִקְרָא שֵׁם שֵׁם ה׳ צְבָאוֹת יֹשֵׁב הַכְּרֻבִים עָלָיו"? מְלַמֵּד, שֶׁלּוּחוֹת וְשִׁבְרֵי לוּחוֹת מוּנָּחִים בָּאָרוֹן.

The Gemara asks: **And** according to **Rabbi Meir, where were the** silver **columns placed?** The Gemara answers: **Outside** the Ark. The Gemara further asks: **And from where does Rabbi Meir** derive that **the broken pieces of the** first set of **tablets were placed in the Ark,** as the verse from which Rabbi Yehuda learns this: "There was nothing in the Ark except" (I Kings 8:9), is needed by Rabbi Meir to teach that the Torah scroll was placed there? The Gemara answers: **He derives** this point **from what Rav Huna** expounded, **as Rav Huna says: What** is the meaning of that **which is written:** "The Ark of God, **whereupon is called the Name,**[N] **the name of the Lord of hosts that sits upon the cherubs**" (II Samuel 6:2)? The phrase "the name, the name of the Lord" **teaches that** both **the** second **tablets and the broken pieces of the** first set of **tablets were placed in the Ark.**

NOTES

Has a diameter of one handbreadth – יֵשׁ בּוֹ רוֹחַב טֶפַח: The Gemara states here and elsewhere that the ratio of the circumference of a circle to its diameter is precisely three to one, when in fact this number, known as pi, is closer to 3.14. Rambam's Commentary on the Mishna (*Eiruvin* 1:5) notes that since the true ratio can only be approximated, as it is an irrational number, the Sages expressed the ratio in terms of whole numbers. Others explain, based on a verse (see I Kings 7:23), that for halakhic purposes, the Sages had a tradition that the ratio should be considered three to one. See Tashbetz, who discusses whether this smaller ratio is applied only in cases where it results in a stringency, or even in cases where it results in a leniency.

Whereupon is called the Name – אֲשֶׁר נִקְרָא שֵׁם: In his introduction to the Torah, the Ramban explains at length that the entire Torah is constructed of the names of God. The term: Name, may therefore be understood as a reference to the essence of the Torah, the tablets of the covenant written by God and resting inside the Ark. The fact that the term appears twice in this verse teaches that the broken pieces of the first set of tablets, which were fashioned by God, were also placed in the Ark.

וְאִידָךְ? הַהוּא מִבָּעֵי לֵיהּ לְכִדְרַבִּי יוֹחָנָן, דְּאָמַר רַבִּי יוֹחָנָן אָמַר רַבִּי שִׁמְעוֹן בֶּן יוֹחַאי: מְלַמֵּד, שֶׁהַשֵּׁם וְכָל כִּינּוּיָו מוּנָּחִין בָּאָרוֹן.

The Gemara asks: **And** what does **the other** Sage, i.e., Rabbi Yehuda, derive from this verse? The Gemara responds: **He requires** that text **for** that **which Rabbi Yoḥanan** says, **as Rabbi Yoḥanan says** that **Rabbi Shimon ben Yoḥai says:** This **teaches that the** ineffable **name** of God **and all of His appellations were placed in the Ark.**

וְאִידָךְ נַמִּי מִיבָּעֵי לֵיהּ לְהָכִי! אִין הָכִי נַמִּי. אֶלָּא שִׁבְרֵי לוּחוֹת דְּמוּנָּחִין בָּאָרוֹן מְנָא לֵיהּ? נָפְקָא לֵיהּ מִדְּתָנֵי רַב יוֹסֵף, דְּתָנֵי רַב יוֹסֵף: "אֲשֶׁר שִׁבַּרְתָּ וְשַׂמְתָּם" – מְלַמֵּד, שֶׁהַלּוּחוֹת וְשִׁבְרֵי לוּחוֹת מוּנָּחִין בָּאָרוֹן.

The Gemara inquires: **And** doesn't **the other** Sage, Rabbi Meir, **also require it for that?** The Gemara answers: **Yes, it is indeed so. Rather, from where does he** derive that **the broken pieces of the** first set of **tablets were placed in the Ark?** The Gemara expounds: **He derives** this **from** that **which Rav Yosef taught, as Rav Yosef taught** a *baraita*: The verses state: "At that time the Lord said to me: Hew for yourself two tablets of stone like the first…and I will write on the tablets the words that were on the first tablets, **which you broke, and you shall put them**[N] in the Ark" (Deuteronomy 10:1–2). **This teaches that** both **the** second set of **tablets and the broken pieces of the** first set of **tablets were placed in the Ark.**

וְאִידָךְ? הַהוּא מִיבָּעֵי לֵיהּ לְכִדְרֵישׁ לָקִישׁ, דְּאָמַר רֵישׁ לָקִישׁ: "אֲשֶׁר שִׁבַּרְתָּ" – אָמַר לוֹ הַקָּדוֹשׁ בָּרוּךְ הוּא לְמֹשֶׁה: יִישַׁר כֹּחֲךָ שֶׁשִּׁבַּרְתָּ.

The Gemara asks: **And** what does **the other** one, Rabbi Yehuda, learn from this verse? The Gemara answers: **He requires it for** that **which Reish Lakish** teaches, **as Reish Lakish says:** What is the meaning of that which is stated: "The first tablets, **which you broke** [*asher shibbarta*]"? These words allude to the fact that God approved of Moses' action, as if **the Holy One, Blessed be He, said to Moses: May your strength be straight** [*yishar koḥakha*] **because you broke** them.

תָּנוּ רַבָּנַן, סִדְרָן שֶׁל נְבִיאִים: יְהוֹשֻׁעַ וְשׁוֹפְטִים, שְׁמוּאֵל וּמְלָכִים, יִרְמְיָה וִיחֶזְקֵאל, יְשַׁעְיָה וּשְׁנֵים עָשָׂר. מִכְּדִי הוֹשֵׁעַ קָדֵים, דִּכְתִיב: "תְּחִלַּת דִּבֶּר ה׳ בְּהוֹשֵׁעַ", וְכִי עִם הוֹשֵׁעַ דִּבֵּר תְּחִלָּה? וַהֲלֹא מִמֹּשֶׁה וְעַד הוֹשֵׁעַ כַּמָּה נְבִיאִים הָיוּ! וְאָמַר רַבִּי יוֹחָנָן: שֶׁהָיָה תְּחִלָּה לְאַרְבָּעָה נְבִיאִים שֶׁנִּתְנַבְּאוּ בְּאוֹתוֹ הַפֶּרֶק, וְאֵלּוּ הֵן: הוֹשֵׁעַ וִישַׁעְיָה, עָמוֹס וּמִיכָה. וְלִיקְדְּמֵיהּ לְהוֹשֵׁעַ בְּרֵישָׁא!

§ **The Sages taught: The order of the** books of the **Prophets**[NH] when they are attached together is as follows: **Joshua and Judges, Samuel and Kings, Jeremiah and Ezekiel,** and **Isaiah and the Twelve** Prophets. The Gemara asks: **Consider: Hosea preceded** some of the other prophets whose books are included in the Bible, **as it is written: "The Lord spoke first to Hosea"** (Hosea 1:2). At first glance this verse is difficult: **But did God speak first with Hosea,** and not with any other prophet before him? **Weren't there many prophets between Moses and Hosea? And Rabbi Yoḥanan says: He was the first of four prophets who prophesied in that period, and they were: Hosea and Isaiah, Amos and Micah.** Accordingly, Hosea preceded those three prophets; **and** the book of **Hosea** as well **should precede** the books of those prophets.

כֵּיוָן דִּכְתִיב נְבוּאָתֵיהּ גַּבֵּי חַגַּי זְכַרְיָה וּמַלְאָכִי, וְחַגַּי זְכַרְיָה וּמַלְאָכִי סוֹף נְבִיאִים הָווּ, חָשֵׁיב לֵיהּ בַּהֲדַיְיהוּ. וְלִיכְתְּבֵיהּ לְחוּדֵיהּ וְלִיקַדְּמֵיהּ! אַיְּידֵי דִּזוּטָר מִירְכַּס.

The Gemara answers: **Since his prophecy is written together with** those of **Haggai, Zechariah, and Malachi** in one book of the Twelve Prophets, **and Haggai, Zechariah, and Malachi were the last of the prophets, he is counted with them.** The Gemara inquires: **But let** the book of Hosea **be written separately and let it precede** the others. The Gemara answers: Were it written separately, **since it is small it would be lost.**

NOTES

Which you broke and you shall put them – אֲשֶׁר שִׁבַּרְתָּ וְשַׂמְתָּם: Rashi explains that the words "which you broke" are redundant and serve to teach, through juxtaposition, that the broken pieces of the first tablets were also subject to: "And you shall put them."

The order of the Prophets – סִדְרָן שֶׁל נְבִיאִים: This was the order that was followed in the Bible and, for example, is presented in the *Yalkut Shimoni*. Nevertheless, over time a more chronological order was adopted that was also followed in the versions of the Bible of gentiles.

HALAKHA

The order of the Prophets – סִדְרָן שֶׁל נְבִיאִים: The order of the books of the Prophets when they are bound together is: Joshua, Judges, Samuel, Kings, Jeremiah, Ezekiel, Isaiah, and the Twelve Prophets. Bibles printed today follow a different order (Rambam *Sefer Ahava, Hilkhot Tefillin UMezuza VeSefer Torah* 7:15; *Shulḥan Arukh, Yoreh De'a* 283:5).

HALAKHA

The order of the Writings – **סִדְרָן שֶׁל כְּתוּבִים**: The order of the books of the Writings is: Ruth, Psalms, Job, Proverbs, Ecclesiastes, Song of Songs, Lamentations, Daniel, Esther, Ezra and Nehemiah, and Chronicles. Bibles printed today follow a different order (Rambam *Sefer Ahava, Hilkhot Tefillin UMezuza VeSefer Torah* 7:15; *Shulḥan Arukh, Yoreh De'a* 283:5).

מִכְּדִי יְשַׁעְיָה קָדֵים מִיִּרְמְיָה וִיחֶזְקֵאל, לִיקְדְּמֵיהּ לִישַׁעְיָה בְּרֵישָׁא! כֵּיוָן דִּמְלָכִים סוֹפֵיהּ חוּרְבָּנָא, וְיִרְמְיָה כּוּלֵּיהּ חוּרְבָּנָא, וִיחֶזְקֵאל רֵישֵׁיהּ חוּרְבָּנָא וְסֵיפֵיהּ נֶחָמְתָא, וִישַׁעְיָה כּוּלֵּיהּ נֶחָמְתָא, סָמְכִינַן חוּרְבָּנָא לְחוּרְבָּנָא וְנֶחָמְתָא לְנֶחָמְתָא.

The Gemara further asks: **Consider: Isaiah preceded Jeremiah and Ezekiel; let** the book of **Isaiah precede** the books of those other prophets. The Gemara answers: **Since** the book of **Kings ends with the destruction** of the Temple, **and** the book of **Jeremiah** deals **entirely with** prophecies of **the destruction,**[N] **and** the book of **Ezekiel begins with the destruction** of the Temple **but ends with consolation** and the rebuilding of the Temple, **and Isaiah** deals **entirely with consolation,** as most of his prophecies refer to the redemption, **we juxtapose destruction to destruction and consolation to consolation.** This accounts for the order: Jeremiah, Ezekiel, and Isaiah.

סִידְרָן שֶׁל כְּתוּבִים: רוּת וְסֵפֶר תְּהִלִּים, וְאִיּוֹב וּמִשְׁלֵי, קֹהֶלֶת, שִׁיר הַשִּׁירִים וְקִינוֹת, דָּנִיֵּאל וּמְגִילַּת אֶסְתֵּר, עֶזְרָא וְדִבְרֵי הַיָּמִים. וּלְמַאן דְּאָמַר: אִיּוֹב בִּימֵי מֹשֶׁה הָיָה, לִיקְדְּמֵיהּ לְאִיּוֹב בְּרֵישָׁא! אַתְחוּלֵי בְּפוּרְעֲנוּתָא לָא מַתְחֲלִינַן. רוּת נַמִי פּוּרְעָנוּת הִיא! פּוּרְעָנוּת דְּאִית לֵיהּ אַחֲרִית; דְּאָמַר רַבִּי יוֹחָנָן: לָמָּה נִקְרָא שְׁמָהּ רוּת? שֶׁיָּצָא מִמֶּנָּה דָּוִד שֶׁרִיוָּהוּ לְהַקָּדוֹשׁ בָּרוּךְ הוּא בְּשִׁירוֹת וְתוּשְׁבָּחוֹת.

The *baraita* continues: **The order of the Writings**[H] is: **Ruth and the book of Psalms, and Job and Proverbs; Ecclesiastes, Song of Songs, and Lamentations; Daniel and the Scroll of Esther;** and **Ezra and Chronicles.** The Gemara asks: **And according to the one who says** that **Job** lived **in the time of Moses, let** the book of **Job precede** the others. The Gemara answers: **We do not begin with suffering,** i.e., it is inappropriate to start the Writings with a book that deals so extensively with suffering. The Gemara asks: But the book of **Ruth,** with which the Writings opens, **is also** about **suffering,** since it describes the tragedies that befell the family of Elimelech. The Gemara answers: This is **suffering which has a future**[N] of hope and redemption. **As Rabbi Yoḥanan says: Why was she named Ruth,** spelled *reish, vav, tav*? Because there **descended from her David who sated,** a word with the root *reish, vav, heh,* **the Holy One, Blessed be He, with songs and praises.**

וּמִי כְּתָבָן? מֹשֶׁה כָּתַב סִפְרוֹ וּפָרָשַׁת בִּלְעָם וְאִיּוֹב; יְהוֹשֻׁעַ כָּתַב סִפְרוֹ וּשְׁמוֹנָה פְּסוּקִים שֶׁבַּתּוֹרָה; שְׁמוּאֵל כָּתַב סִפְרוֹ וְשׁוֹפְטִים וְרוּת; דָּוִד כָּתַב סֵפֶר תְּהִלִּים עַל יְדֵי עֲשָׂרָה זְקֵנִים: עַל יְדֵי אָדָם הָרִאשׁוֹן, עַל יְדֵי מַלְכִּי צֶדֶק, וְעַל יְדֵי אַבְרָהָם, וְעַל יְדֵי מֹשֶׁה, וְעַל יְדֵי הֵימָן, וְעַל יְדֵי יְדוּתוּן, וְעַל יְדֵי אָסָף,

The *baraita* now considers the authors of the biblical books: **And who wrote** the books of the Bible? **Moses wrote his own book,** i.e., the Torah, **and the portion of Balaam**[N] in the Torah, **and** the book of **Job. Joshua wrote his own book and eight verses in the Torah,** which describe the death of Moses. **Samuel wrote his own book,** the book of **Judges, and** the book of **Ruth. David wrote the book of Psalms by means of ten elders**[N] of previous generations, assembling a collection that included compositions of others along with his own. He included psalms authored **by Adam the first** man, **by Melchizedek** king of Salem, **and by Abraham, and by Moses, and by Heman, and by Jeduthun, and by Asaph,**

NOTES

And Jeremiah deals entirely with the destruction – **וְיִרְמְיָה כּוּלֵּיהּ חוּרְבָּנָא**: To be precise, the book of Jeremiah also contains prophecies of consolation, and the book of Isaiah includes threats of punishment, but the statements here refer to the majority of the content in the respective books. The book of Jeremiah is composed chiefly of words of rebuke and suffering, whereas the book of Isaiah is composed mostly of prophecies of consolation (Maharsha).

Which has a future – **דְּאִית לֵיהּ אַחֲרִית**: The book of Job also ends on an optimistic note, with Job regaining what he had lost. Nevertheless, the happy ending in the book of Ruth relates not only to the family of Elimelech, but to all of the Jewish people, as the Davidic dynasty represents consolation and salvation to the entire nation. The benefits granted to Job, by contrast, were his alone (*Tosafot*).

Moses wrote his own book and the portion of Balaam – **מֹשֶׁה כָּתַב סִפְרוֹ וּפָרָשַׁת בִּלְעָם**: According to the Riaf, Moses' own book is a reference specifically to Deuteronomy.

The commentaries raise the question: If the passage of Balaam is part of the Torah, why then is it singled out for special mention? The Ritva writes that Moses wrote an entire book about Balaam, but it has been lost. The Maharal suggests that this statement is necessary because otherwise one might have thought that Balaam's words are his own prophecy and lack the sanctity of Torah. Therefore, the *baraita* teaches that Moses wrote these words as well, and that the passage of Balaam has a status equal in sanctity to that of every other passage in the Torah.

By means of ten elders – **עַל יְדֵי עֲשָׂרָה זְקֵנִים**: It has been suggested that Psalms, chapter 139 is attributed to Adam: "Your eyes did see my imperfect substance." Melchizedek is credited with the authorship of chapter 110, which states: "After the manner of Melchizedek." Chapter 89 is attributed to Abraham, as it says: "Maskil of Ethan the Ezrahite," who is identified with Abraham. Chapter 90 is explicitly introduced as: "A prayer of Moses," and many commentaries assume that the next ten chapters were composed by him as well. Heman wrote chapter 88; Jeduthun, chapter 39; and Asaph, chapters 50 and 73–83. The sons of Korah are credited with chapters 42, 44–49, 84, 85, 87, and 88.

וְעַל יְדֵי שְׁלֹשָׁה בְּנֵי קֹרַח;

and by the three sons of Korah.[N]

יִרְמְיָה כָּתַב סִפְרוֹ וְסֵפֶר מְלָכִים וְקִינוֹת; חִזְקִיָּה וְסִיעָתוֹ כָּתְבוּ (ימש״ק סִימָן) יְשַׁעְיָה, מִשְׁלֵי, שִׁיר הַשִּׁירִים וְקֹהֶלֶת; אַנְשֵׁי כְּנֶסֶת הַגְּדוֹלָה כָּתְבוּ (קנד״ג סִימָן) יְחֶזְקֵאל וּשְׁנֵים עָשָׂר, דָּנִיֵּאל וּמְגִילַּת אֶסְתֵּר; עֶזְרָא כָּתַב סִפְרוֹ וְיַחַס שֶׁל דִּבְרֵי הַיָּמִים עַד לוֹ.

Jeremiah wrote his own book, and the book of Kings, and Lamentations. Hezekiah and his colleagues[N] **wrote** the following, and a **mnemonic** to remember which books they wrote is ***yod, mem, shin, kuf*****: Isaiah** [*Yeshaya*]**, Proverbs** [*Mishlei*]**, Song of Songs** [*Shir HaShirim*]**, and Ecclesiastes** [*Kohelet*]**. The members of the Great Assembly wrote** the following, and a **mnemonic** to remember these books is *kuf, nun, dalet, gimmel*: **Ezekiel** [*Yeḥezkel*]**, and the Twelve Prophets** [*Sheneim Asar*],[N] **Daniel** [*Daniel*]**, and the Scroll of Esther** [*Megillat Ester*]**. Ezra wrote his own book and the genealogy** of the book of **Chronicles until his** period.

מְסַיְּיעָא לֵיהּ לְרַב, דְּאָמַר רַב יְהוּדָה אָמַר רַב: לֹא עָלָה עֶזְרָא מִבָּבֶל עַד שֶׁיִּחֵס עַצְמוֹ וְעָלָה. וּמַאן אַסְקֵיהּ? נְחֶמְיָה בֶּן חֲכַלְיָה.

The Gemara comments: This **supports Rav, as Rav Yehuda says** that **Rav says: Ezra did not ascend from Babylonia** to Eretz Yisrael **until he established his own genealogy, and after that he ascended.** This genealogy is what is written in the book of Chronicles. **And who completed** the book of Chronicles for the generations following Ezra? **Nehemiah, son of Hacaliah.**

אָמַר מָר: יְהוֹשֻׁעַ כָּתַב סִפְרוֹ וּשְׁמוֹנָה פְּסוּקִים שֶׁבַּתּוֹרָה. תַּנְיָא כְּמַאן דְּאָמַר: שְׁמוֹנָה פְּסוּקִים שֶׁבַּתּוֹרָה יְהוֹשֻׁעַ כְּתָבָן, דְּתַנְיָא: ״וַיָּמָת שָׁם מֹשֶׁה עֶבֶד ה׳״ – אֶפְשָׁר מֹשֶׁה מֵת וְכָתַב ״וַיָּמָת שָׁם מֹשֶׁה״? אֶלָּא, עַד כָּאן כָּתַב מֹשֶׁה, מִכָּאן וְאֵילָךְ כָּתַב יְהוֹשֻׁעַ, דִּבְרֵי רַבִּי יְהוּדָה, וְאָמְרִי לַהּ רַבִּי נְחֶמְיָה.

The Gemara elaborates on the particulars of this *baraita*: **The Master said** above that **Joshua wrote his own book and eight verses of the Torah.**[N] The Gemara comments: This *baraita* **is taught in accordance with the one who says that** it was **Joshua** who **wrote the** last **eight verses in the Torah.** This point is subject to a tannaitic dispute, **as it is taught** in another *baraita*: **"And Moses the servant of the Lord died there"** (Deuteronomy 34:5); **is it possible that** after **Moses died,** he himself **wrote "And Moses died there"? Rather, Moses wrote** the entire Torah **until this point,** and **Joshua wrote from this** point **forward;** this is **the statement of Rabbi Yehuda. And some say** that **Rabbi Neḥemya** stated this opinion.

אָמַר לוֹ רַבִּי שִׁמְעוֹן: אֶפְשָׁר סֵפֶר תּוֹרָה חָסֵר אוֹת אַחַת? וּכְתִיב: ״לָקֹחַ אֵת סֵפֶר הַתּוֹרָה הַזֶּה״! אֶלָּא, עַד כָּאן הַקָּדוֹשׁ בָּרוּךְ הוּא אוֹמֵר וּמֹשֶׁה אוֹמֵר וְכוֹתֵב, מִכָּאן וְאֵילָךְ הַקָּדוֹשׁ בָּרוּךְ הוּא אוֹמֵר וּמֹשֶׁה כּוֹתֵב בְּדֶמַע, כְּמוֹ שֶׁנֶּאֱמַר לְהַלָּן: ״וַיֹּאמֶר לָהֶם בָּרוּךְ מִפִּיו יִקְרָא אֵלַי אֵת כָּל הַדְּבָרִים הָאֵלֶּה וַאֲנִי כּוֹתֵב עַל הַסֵּפֶר בַּדְּיוֹ״.

Rabbi Shimon said to him: Is it possible that the **Torah scroll** was **missing a single letter? But it is written: "Take this Torah scroll"** (Deuteronomy 31:26), indicating that the Torah was complete as is and that nothing further would be added to it. **Rather, until this point the Holy One, Blessed be He, dictated and Moses repeated** after Him **and wrote**[N] the text. **From this** point **forward,** with respect to Moses' death, **the Holy One, Blessed be He, dictated and Moses wrote with tears.** The fact that the Torah was written by way of dictation can be seen **later, as it is stated** concerning the writing of the Prophets: **"And Baruch said to them: He dictated all these words to me, and I wrote them with ink in the scroll"** (Jeremiah 36:18).

כְּמַאן אָזְלָא הָא דְּאָמַר רַבִּי יְהוֹשֻׁעַ בַּר אַבָּא אָמַר רַב גִּידֵּל אָמַר רַב: שְׁמוֹנָה פְּסוּקִים שֶׁבַּתּוֹרָה יָחִיד קוֹרֵא אוֹתָן? לֵימָא, רַבִּי יְהוּדָה הִיא וּדְלָא כְּרַבִּי שִׁמְעוֹן? אֲפִילּוּ תֵּימָא רַבִּי שִׁמְעוֹן, הוֹאִיל וְאִשְׁתַּנּוּ אִשְׁתַּנּוּ.

The Gemara asks: **In accordance with whose** opinion **is that which Rabbi Yehoshua bar Abba says that Rav Giddel says that Rav says:** When the Torah is read publicly in the synagogue, **one person reads**[N] **the** last **eight verses**[H] **in the Torah,** and that section may not be divided between two readers? **Shall we say** that **this is** in accordance with the opinion of **Rabbi Yehuda and not in accordance with** the opinion of **Rabbi Shimon,** as according to Rabbi Shimon these verses are an integral part of the Torah, written by Moses just like the rest? The Gemara answers: **Even if you say** that this was said in accordance with the opinion of **Rabbi Shimon, since they differ** from the rest of the Torah in one way, as Moses wrote them with tears, **they differ** from the rest of the Torah in this way as well, i.e., they may not be divided between two readers.

NOTES

The three sons of Korah – **שְׁלֹשָׁה בְּנֵי קֹרַח**: *Tosafot* cite a version of this *baraita* that credits Solomon and the three sons of Korah, since there are also chapters in the book of Psalms that are attributed to Solomon (72, 127). *Tosafot* explain that there are variations to this *baraita*, one of which states that David and Solomon composed the book, and another which lists Abraham as a contributor distinct from Ethan the Ezrahite, who is identified as Jacob (see Rabbeinu Gershom and Maharsha; Rashi at the beginning of the book of Psalms).

Hezekiah and his colleagues – **חִזְקִיָּה וְסִיעָתוֹ**: The source for this assertion is: "These are the proverbs of Solomon which were copied by the colleagues of Hezekiah, king of Judea" (Proverbs 25:1).

Ezekiel and the Twelve Prophets – **יְחֶזְקֵאל וּשְׁנֵים עָשָׂר**: Rashi wonders why Ezekiel did not write his own book. He suggests that perhaps prophecies outside of Eretz Yisrael were not recorded outside Eretz Yisrael, but were written by prophets and the other members of the Great Assembly. Consequently, they wrote the books of Ezekiel, Daniel, and Esther, all of which refer to events that took place outside Eretz Yisrael. They themselves completed the record of their prophecies and combined the books of the twelve minor prophets into one book. *Tosafot* comment that Jeremiah went to Egypt but is said not to have returned, and yet it states that he wrote his own book. The Maharal takes a different approach, which resolves this difficulty: The members of the Great Assembly wrote the books of those who died during their era, such as Ezekiel and Daniel. This was not the case with Jeremiah and Ezra.

And eight verses of the Torah – **וּשְׁמוֹנָה פְּסוּקִים שֶׁבַּתּוֹרָה**: While most commentaries understand this to be a reference to the final eight verses in the Torah (Deuteronomy 34:5–12), it has also been explained to be referring to the eight verses beginning "and Moses ascended from the plains of Moab" (Deuteronomy 34:1) through the verse ending "so the days of weeping in the mourning for Moses were ended" (see Ibn Ezra and *Ḥatam Sofer*).

Moses repeated and wrote – **מֹשֶׁה אוֹמֵר וְכוֹתֵב**: Moses repeated after God so as not to err in his writing (Rashi on *Menaḥot* 30a), as this is the customary practice of scribes.

One person reads – **יָחִיד קוֹרֵא**: This ruling has been understood in several ways. Rashi explains that a single individual reads these verses without interruption. Another suggestion is that these verses must be read as a distinct passage without the previous text, so as not to combine this unique passage with the rest of the Torah (Ri Migash). The Ramah combines these two approaches. *Tosafot* cites Rabbeinu Meshullam as saying that one individual reads the verses rather than two, as is the practice in most places today where one person is called to the Torah while another actually reads from it. The Rambam maintains that one can read these verses even in the absence of a quorum of ten men. The Meiri and the Mordekhai explain that an important man must read these verses.

HALAKHA

Eight verses – **שְׁמוֹנָה פְּסוּקִים**: The last eight verses of the Torah may be read even in the absence of a quorum of ten men, i.e., where at first there are ten men and one steps out. According to the *Shulḥan Arukh*, these verses must be read by one person and may not be divided between two readers. The Rema, citing the Mordekhai, writes that these verses should be read by a Torah scholar (Rambam *Sefer Ahava*, *Hilkhot Tefilla* 13:6 and *Kesef Mishne* there; *Shulḥan Arukh*, *Oraḥ Ḥayyim* 428:7 and 669:1 in the comment of Rema).

יְהוֹשֻׁעַ כָּתַב סִפְרוֹ. וְהָכְתִיב: ״וַיָּמָת יְהוֹשֻׁעַ בִּן נוּן עֶבֶד ה׳״! דְּאַסְקֵיהּ אֶלְעָזָר. וְהָכְתִיב: ״וְאֶלְעָזָר בֶּן אַהֲרֹן מֵת״! דְּאַסְקֵיהּ פִּנְחָס.

It is stated in the *baraita* that **Joshua wrote his own book.** The Gemara asks: **But isn't it written** toward the end of the book: **"And Joshua, son of Nun, the servant of the Lord, died"** (Joshua 24:29)? Is it possible that Joshua wrote this? The Gemara answers: Aaron's son **Eleazar completed it.** The Gemara asks: **But isn't it** also **written: "And Eleazar, son of Aaron, died"** (Joshua 24:33)? The Gemara answers: **Pinehas completed it.**

שְׁמוּאֵל כָּתַב סִפְרוֹ. וְהָכְתִיב: ״וּשְׁמוּאֵל מֵת״! דְּאַסְקֵיהּ גָּד הַחוֹזֶה וְנָתָן הַנָּבִיא.

It is also stated in the *baraita* that **Samuel wrote his own book.** The Gemara asks: **But isn't it written: "And Samuel died"** (I Samuel 28:3)? The Gemara answers: **Gad the seer and Nathan the prophet finished it.**

דָּוִד כָּתַב סֵפֶר תְּהִלִּים עַל יְדֵי עֲשָׂרָה זְקֵנִים. וְלִיחְשׁוֹב נַמִּי אֵיתָן הָאֶזְרָחִי! אָמַר רַב: אֵיתָן הָאֶזְרָחִי זֶה הוּא אַבְרָהָם, כְּתִיב הָכָא: ״אֵיתָן הָאֶזְרָחִי״, וּכְתִיב הָתָם: ״מִי הֵעִיר מִמִּזְרָח צֶדֶק״ [וגו׳].

It is further stated that **David wrote the book of Psalms by means of ten elders,** whom the *baraita* proceeds to list. The Gemara asks: **But** then **let it also count Ethan the Ezrahite** among the contributors to the book of Psalms, as it is he who is credited with Psalms, chapter 89. **Rav says: Ethan the Ezrahite is** the same person as **Abraham.** Proof for this is the fact that **it is written here:** "A Maskil of **Ethan the Ezrahite"** (Psalms 89:1), **and it is written there: "Who raised up one from the east [*mizraḥ*], whom righteousness** met wherever he set his foot" (Isaiah 41:2). The latter verse is understood as referring to Abraham, who came from the east, and for that reason he is called Ethan the Ezrahite in the former verse.

קָא חָשֵׁיב מֹשֶׁה וְקָא חָשֵׁיב הֵימָן; וְהָאָמַר רַב: הֵימָן זֶה מֹשֶׁה, כְּתִיב הָכָא: הֵימָן, וּכְתִיב הָתָם: ״בְּכָל בֵּיתִי נֶאֱמָן הוּא״! תְּרֵי הֵימָן הָווּ.

The Gemara asks: The *baraita* **counts Moses** among the ten elders whose works are included in the book of Psalms, **and it** also **counts Heman. But doesn't Rav say:** The **Heman** mentioned in the Bible (I Kings 5:11) **is the same person as Moses?** This is proven by the fact that **it is written here: "Heman"** (Psalms 88:1), which is Aramaic for trusted, **and it is written there** about Moses: **"For he is the trusted one in all My house"** (Numbers 12:7). The Gemara answers: **There were two Hemans,** one of whom was Moses, and the other a Temple singer from among the descendants of Samuel.

מֹשֶׁה כָּתַב סִפְרוֹ וּפָרָשַׁת בִּלְעָם וְאִיּוֹב. מְסַיְּיעָא לֵיהּ לְרַבִּי לֵוִי בַּר לַחְמָא, דְּאָמַר רַבִּי לֵוִי בַּר לַחְמָא: אִיּוֹב בִּימֵי מֹשֶׁה הָיָה, כְּתִיב הָכָא: ״מִי יִתֵּן אֵפוֹא וְיִכָּתְבוּן מִלָּי״, וּכְתִיב הָתָם: ״וּבַמֶּה יִוָּדַע אֵפוֹא״.

The *baraita* further states that **Moses wrote his own book,** i.e., the Torah, **the portion of Balaam, and** the book of **Job. This supports Rabbi Levi bar Laḥma, as Rabbi Levi bar Laḥma says: Job** lived **in the time of Moses. It is written here** with regard to Job: **"Oh, that my words were written now [*eifo*]"** (Job 19:23), **and it is written there** in Moses' words to God: **"For in what shall it be known here [*eifo*]"** (Exodus 33:16). The unusual use of the word *eifo* in these two places indicates that Job and Moses lived in the same generation.

וְאֵימָא: בִּימֵי יִצְחָק, דִּכְתִיב: ״מִי אֵפוֹא הוּא הַצָּד צַיִד״! וְאֵימָא: בִּימֵי יַעֲקֹב, דִּכְתִיב: ״אִם כֵּן אֵפוֹא זֹאת עֲשׂוּ״! וְאֵימָא: בִּימֵי יוֹסֵף, דִּכְתִיב: ״אֵיפֹה הֵם רוֹעִים״!

The Gemara comments: **But** if that is the proof, **say** that Job lived **in the time of Isaac, as it is written** in connection with Isaac: **"Who then [*eifo*] is he that has taken venison"** (Genesis 27:33). **Or say** that he lived **in the time of Jacob, as it is written** with respect to Jacob: **"If it must be so now [*eifo*], do this"** (Genesis 43:11). **Or say** that he lived **in the time of Joseph, as it is written** with respect to Joseph: "Tell me, I pray you, **where [*eifo*] are they feeding their flocks?"** (Genesis 37:16).

לָא סָלְקָא דַּעְתָּךְ, דִּכְתִיב: ״מִי יִתֵּן בַּסֵּפֶר וְיֻחָקוּ״, וּמֹשֶׁה הוּא דְּאִיקְּרֵי מְחוֹקֵק, דִּכְתִיב: ״וַיַּרְא רֵאשִׁית לוֹ כִּי שָׁם חֶלְקַת מְחֹקֵק סָפוּן״.

The Gemara answers: It could **not enter your mind** to say this, **as it is written** in the continuation of the previously mentioned verse: **"Oh, that** my words **were inscribed [*veyuḥaku*] in a book"** (Job 19:23), **and it is Moses who is called the inscriber, as it is written** with regard to him: **"And he provided the first part for himself, for there was the inscriber's [*meḥokek*] portion reserved"** (Deuteronomy 33:21).

רָבָא אָמַר: אִיּוֹב בִּימֵי מְרַגְּלִים הָיָה, כְּתִיב הָכָא: ״אִישׁ הָיָה בְאֶרֶץ עוּץ אִיּוֹב שְׁמוֹ״, וּכְתִיב הָתָם: ״הֲיֵשׁ בָּהּ עֵץ״. מִי דָּמֵי? הָכָא ״עוּץ״, הָתָם ״עֵץ״! הָכִי קָאָמַר לְהוּ מֹשֶׁה לְיִשְׂרָאֵל: יֶשְׁנוֹ לְאוֹתוֹ אָדָם, שֶׁשְּׁנוֹתָיו אֲרוּכוֹת כָּעֵץ וּמֵגֵין עַל דּוֹרוֹ כָּעֵץ?

Rava says: Job lived **at the time of the spies** whom Moses sent to scout the land of Canaan. This is proven by the fact that **it is written here: "There was a man in the land of Utz, whose name was Job"** (Job 1:1), **and it is written there** in the account of the spies: **"Whether there are trees [*eitz*] in it"** (Numbers 13:20). The Gemara asks: **Is it comparable? Here** the word that is used is ***Utz***, whereas **there** the word is ***eitz***. The Gemara answers: **This is what Moses said to Israel,** i.e., to the spies: **Is that man** named Job still alive, **he whose years are as long as** the years **of a tree and who protects his generation like a tree?** This is why the allusion to him here is through the word *eitz*, rather than *Utz*.

יָתֵיב הַהוּא מֵרַבָּנַן קַמֵּיהּ דְּרַבִּי שְׁמוּאֵל בַּר נַחְמָנִי, וְיָתֵיב וְקָאָמַר: אִיּוֹב לֹא הָיָה וְלֹא נִבְרָא, אֶלָּא מָשָׁל הָיָה. אֲמַר לֵיהּ, עָלֶיךָ אָמַר קְרָא: ״אִישׁ הָיָה בְאֶרֶץ עוּץ אִיּוֹב שְׁמוֹ״.

The Gemara relates that **one of the Sages sat before Rabbi Shmuel bar Naḥmani and he sat and said: Job never existed and was never created;** there was never such a person as Job. **Rather,** his story **was a parable.** Rabbi Shmuel bar Naḥmani **said to him:** In rebuttal **to you, the verse states: "There was a man in the Land of Utz whose name was Job"** (Job 1:1), which indicates that such a man did indeed exist.

אֶלָּא מֵעַתָּה, ״וְלָרָשׁ אֵין כֹּל כִּי אִם כִּבְשָׂה אַחַת קְטַנָּה אֲשֶׁר קָנָה וַיְחַיֶּהָ״ וגו׳, מִי הֲוָה? אֶלָּא מָשָׁל בְּעָלְמָא, הָכָא נַמִי מָשָׁל בְּעָלְמָא. אִם כֵּן, שְׁמוֹ וְשֵׁם עִירוֹ לָמָּה?

The Gemara asks: **But if that is so,** that the words "there was" prove that Job existed, what shall we say about the parable that Natan the prophet presented to David: "There were two men in one city; the one rich and the other poor. The rich man had very many flocks and herds, **but the poor man had nothing except one little lamb, which he had bought and reared"** (II Samuel 12:3)? **Was there** really such a person? **Rather, it was merely a parable; here too it is merely a parable.** The Gemara answers: **If so,** that it is a parable, **why** state **his name and the name of his city?** Rather, Job was clearly a real person.

רַבִּי יוֹחָנָן וְרַבִּי אֶלְעָזָר דְּאָמְרִי תַּרְוַיְיהוּ: אִיּוֹב מֵעוֹלֵי גוֹלָה הָיָה, וּבֵית מִדְרָשׁוֹ בִּטְבֶרְיָא הָיָה. מֵיתִיבֵי: יְמֵי שְׁנוֹתָיו שֶׁל אִיּוֹב, מִשָּׁעָה שֶׁנִּכְנְסוּ יִשְׂרָאֵל לְמִצְרַיִם וְעַד שֶׁיָּצְאוּ!

The Gemara cites another opinion with regard to the time when Job lived. **Rabbi Yoḥanan and Rabbi Elazar both say: Job was among those who ascended from the exile** to Eretz Yisrael at the start of the Second Temple period, **and his house of study was in Tiberias.** The Gemara **raises an objection** from what is taught in a *baraita*: **The days of Job's life** extended **from when Israel entered Egypt until they left,** indicating that this is the period during which he lived and not, as suggested, in the early days of the Second Temple.

Perek **I**
Daf **15** Amud **b**

אֵימָא: כְּמִשָּׁעָה שֶׁנִּכְנְסוּ יִשְׂרָאֵל לְמִצְרַיִם וְעַד [שָׁעָה] שֶׁיָּצְאוּ.

The Gemara answers: **Say** that the *baraita* means that the duration of Job's life lasted as long **as from when Israel entered Egypt until when they left,** but not that he lived during that specific time frame.

מֵיתִיבֵי: שִׁבְעָה נְבִיאִים נִתְנַבְּאוּ לְאוּמּוֹת הָעוֹלָם, וְאֵלּוּ הֵן: בִּלְעָם וְאָבִיו, וְאִיּוֹב, אֱלִיפַז הַתֵּימָנִי, וּבִלְדַּד הַשּׁוּחִי, וְצוֹפַר הַנַּעֲמָתִי, וֶאֱלִיהוּא בֶּן בַּרַכְאֵל הַבּוּזִי! אֲמַר לֵיהּ: וְלִיטַעֲמִיךְ, אֱלִיהוּא בֶּן בַּרַכְאֵל לָאו מִיִּשְׂרָאֵל הֲוָה? וְהָא כְּתִיב ״מִמִּשְׁפַּחַת רָם״!

The Gemara **raises an objection** from another *baraita* against the notion that Job was a Jew: **Seven prophets prophesied to the nations of the world, and they are: Balaam and his father**[N] Beor, **and Job, Eliphaz the Temanite, and Bildad the Shuhite, and Zophar the Naamathite, and Elihu ben Barachel the Buzite,** which indicates that Job was not Jewish. **He said to him: And according to your reasoning** that Job could not have been Jewish because he prophesied to the nations of the world, **was Elihu ben Barachel not a Jew? Is it not written: "Of the family of Ram"** (Job 32:2), meaning Abraham?

אֶלָּא אִינַּבּוּי אִינַּבֵּי לְאוּמּוֹת הָעוֹלָם, הָכִי נַמִי אִיּוֹב אִינַּבּוּי אִינַּבֵּי [לְאוּמּוֹת הָעוֹלָם]. אַטּוּ כּוּלְּהוּ נְבִיאֵי מִי לָא אִינַּבּוּי לְאוּמּוֹת הָעוֹלָם? הָתָם עִיקַּר נְבִיאוּתַיְיהוּ לְיִשְׂרָאֵל, הָכָא עִיקַּר נְבִיאוּתַיְיהוּ לְאוּמּוֹת הָעוֹלָם.

Rather, one must explain that Elihu is included in this list because **he prophesied to the nations of the world;** and **so too** it may be maintained that **Job** is included in this list, even though he is Jewish, because he **prophesied to the nations of the world.** The Gemara asks: **But did not all the** other **prophets** also **prophesy to the nations of the world?** Why then are only these seven mentioned? The Gemara answers: **There,** with regard to the other prophets, **their main prophecies were** directed **to Israel,** whereas **here,** with regard to these seven prophets, **their main prophecies were** directed **to the nations of the world.**

מֵיתִיבֵי: חָסִיד הָיָה בְּאוּמּוֹת הָעוֹלָם וְאִיּוֹב שְׁמוֹ, וְלֹא בָּא לָעוֹלָם אֶלָּא כְּדֵי לְקַבֵּל שְׂכָרוֹ, הֵבִיא הַקָּדוֹשׁ בָּרוּךְ הוּא עָלָיו יִסּוּרִין, הִתְחִיל מְחָרֵף וּמְגַדֵּף, כָּפַל לוֹ הַקָּדוֹשׁ בָּרוּךְ הוּא שְׂכָרוֹ בָּעוֹלָם הַזֶּה [כְּדֵי] לְטָרְדוֹ מִן הָעוֹלָם הַבָּא!

The Gemara **raises an objection** from what is taught in a different *baraita*: **There was a certain pious man among the nations of the world and his name was Job, and he came into the world only to receive his reward. The Holy One, Blessed be He, brought afflictions upon him,** and **he began to blaspheme and curse. The Holy One, Blessed be He, doubled his reward in this world in order to expel him from the World-to-Come.** This *baraita* states that Job was not a Jew, but rather a gentile.

NOTES

Balaam and his father – בִּלְעָם וְאָבִיו: *Tosafot* explain that this phrase is based on the principle that whenever a prophet's father is named, it means that he too had prophetic abilities. Therefore, it can be understood that Balaam's father was also a prophet.

תַּנָּאֵי הִיא; דְּתַנְיָא, רַבִּי אֱלִיעֶזֶר אוֹמֵר: אִיּוֹב בִּימֵי שְׁפוֹט הַשּׁוֹפְטִים הָיָה, שֶׁנֶּאֱמַר: ״הֵן אַתֶּם כֻּלְּכֶם חֲזִיתֶם וְלָמָּה זֶּה הֶבֶל תֶּהְבָּלוּ״, אֵיזֶה דּוֹר שֶׁכּוּלּוֹ הֶבֶל? הֱוֵי אוֹמֵר: זֶה דּוֹרוֹ שֶׁל שְׁפוֹט הַשּׁוֹפְטִים.

The Gemara responds: The matter of whether or not Job was Jewish **is a dispute between** ***tanna'im*****, as it is taught** in a *baraita* with regard to the period during which Job lived: **Rabbi Elazar says: Job** lived **in the days of the judging of the Judges, as it is stated** in connection with Job: **"Behold, all you yourselves have seen it; why then have you become altogether vain?"** (Job 27:12). **Which generation was completely vain?**[N] **You must say it was the generation of the judging of the Judges,** when the people judged the Judges, as will be explained shortly.

רַבִּי יְהוֹשֻׁעַ בֶּן קָרְחָה אוֹמֵר: אִיּוֹב בִּימֵי אֲחַשְׁוֵרוֹשׁ הָיָה, שֶׁנֶּאֱמַר: ״וְלֹא נִמְצָא נָשִׁים יָפוֹת כִּבְנוֹת אִיּוֹב בְּכָל הָאָרֶץ״, אֵיזֶהוּ דּוֹר שֶׁנִּתְבַּקְּשׁוּ בּוֹ נָשִׁים יָפוֹת? הֱוֵי אוֹמֵר: זֶה דּוֹרוֹ שֶׁל אֲחַשְׁוֵרוֹשׁ. וְאֵימָא: בִּימֵי דָּוִד, דִּכְתִיב: ״וַיְבַקְשׁוּ נַעֲרָה יָפָה״! הָתָם בְּכָל גְּבוּל יִשְׂרָאֵל, הָכָא בְּכָל הָאָרֶץ.

Rabbi Yehoshua ben Korḥa says: Job lived **in the days of Ahasuerus, as it is stated: "And in all the world were no women found so beautiful as the daughters of Job"** (Job 42:15). **In which generation were beautiful women sought? You must say it was the generation of Ahasuerus** (Esther, chapter 2). The Gemara asks: **But** why not **say** it was **in the days of David, as it is written: "And they sought a beautiful maiden"** (I Kings 1:3)? The Gemara answers: **There,** in the time of David, they searched **"throughout the territory of Israel"** (I Kings 1:3), whereas **here,** in the time of **Ahasuerus,** they searched **throughout the world,** as is similarly stated with regard to Job's daughters.

רַבִּי נָתָן אוֹמֵר: אִיּוֹב בִּימֵי מַלְכוּת שְׁבָא הָיָה, שֶׁנֶּאֱמַר: ״וַתִּפֹּל שְׁבָא וַתִּקָּחֵם״. וַחֲכָמִים אוֹמְרִים: אִיּוֹב בִּימֵי כַּשְׂדִּים הָיָה, שֶׁנֶּאֱמַר: ״כַּשְׂדִּים שָׂמוּ שְׁלֹשָׁה רָאשִׁים״. וְיֵשׁ אוֹמְרִים: אִיּוֹב בִּימֵי יַעֲקֹב הָיָה, וְדִינָה בַּת יַעֲקֹב נָשָׂא, כְּתִיב הָכָא: ״כְּדַבֵּר אַחַת הַנְּבָלוֹת תְּדַבֵּרִי״, וּכְתִיב הָתָם: ״כִּי נְבָלָה עָשָׂה בְיִשְׂרָאֵל״. וְכוּלְּהוּ תַּנָּאֵי סְבִירָא לְהוּ דְּאִיּוֹב מִיִּשְׂרָאֵל הֲוָה, לְבַר מִ״יֵּשׁ אוֹמְרִים״,

Rabbi Natan says: Job lived **in the days of the kingdom of Sheba, as it is stated: "And Sheba fell upon them, and took them away"** (Job 1:15). **And the Rabbis say: Job** lived **in the days of** the kingdom of **the Chaldeans** in the time of Nebuchadnezzar, **as it is stated: "The Chaldeans formed three bands"** (Job 1:17). **And some say** that **Job** lived **in the days of Jacob** and that **he married Dina, the daughter of Jacob.** As **it is written here: "You speak as one of the loathsome women speaks"** (Job 2:10), **and it is written there** in the account of the incident involving Dina: **"He has done a loathsome act in Israel"** (Genesis 34:7). This concludes the text of the *baraita*. The Gemara comments: **And all these** ***tanna'im*** **hold that Job was a Jew except for** the opinion introduced with the phrase: **And some say,** according to which Job lived in the time of Jacob, and he was certainly not one of Jacob's sons.

דְּאִי סָלְקָא דַּעְתָּךְ מֵאוּמּוֹת הָעוֹלָם הֲוָה, בָּתַר דִּשְׁכִיב מֹשֶׁה מִי שַׁרְיָא שְׁכִינָה עַל אוּמּוֹת הָעוֹלָם? וְהָא אָמַר מָר: בִּקֵּשׁ מֹשֶׁה שֶׁלֹּא תִּשְׁרֶה שְׁכִינָה עַל אוּמּוֹת הָעוֹלָם, וְנִתַּן לוֹ, שֶׁנֶּאֱמַר: ״וְנִפְלֵינוּ אֲנִי וְעַמְּךָ״.

And what is the proof that all these *tanna'im* maintain that Job was Jewish? **As if it should enter your mind** to say that he came **from the nations of the world,** there is a difficulty: **After Moses died, did the Divine Presence rest** any longer **on the nations of the world? But doesn't the Master say: Moses requested that the Divine Presence not rest** again **on the nations of the world,** and his request **was granted to him, as it is stated: "That we shall be differentiated, I and Your people,** from all the people that are upon the face of the earth" (Exodus 33:16), and it is stated there that God acceded to his request.

אָמַר רַבִּי יוֹחָנָן: דּוֹרוֹ שֶׁל אִיּוֹב שָׁטוּף בְּזִמָּה הָיָה, שֶׁנֶּאֱמַר: ״הֵן אַתֶּם כּוּלְּכֶם חֲזִיתֶם וְלָמָּה זֶּה הֶבֶל תֶּהְבָּלוּ״, וּכְתִיב: ״שׁוּבִי שׁוּבִי הַשּׁוּלַמִּית שׁוּבִי שׁוּבִי וְנֶחֱזֶה בָּךְ״. אֵימָא: בִּנְבוּאָה, דִּכְתִיב: ״חֲזוֹן יְשַׁעְיָהוּ בֶן אָמוֹץ״! אִם כֵּן, ״לָמָּה זֶּה הֶבֶל תֶּהְבָּלוּ״ לָמָּה לִי?

Rabbi Yoḥanan says: The generation of Job was awash in licentiousness, as it is stated: "Behold, all of you yourselves have seen [*ḥazitem*] it; why then have you become altogether vain?" (Job 27:12), **and it is written: "Return, return, O Shulamite; return, return, that we may look [*veneḥeze*] upon you"** (Song of Songs 7:1), which teaches that the phrase "you have seen it" connotes a licentious gaze. The Gemara asks: But **say** that the phrase "you yourselves have seen it" signifies **prophecy, as it is written: "The vision [*ḥazon*] of Isaiah ben Amoz"** (Isaiah 1:1). The Gemara answers: **If so, why do I** need the words: **"Why then have you become altogether vain"?** Rather, the reference must be to inappropriate licentious gazing.

NOTES

Generation was completely vain – **דּוֹר שֶׁכּוּלּוֹ הֶבֶל**: This can be understood in light of what is stated subsequently: "In the days of the judging of the Judges" (Ruth 1:1), the generation judged its own judges, as they too were sinful. The Maharal writes that the generation's primary ruin lay in the absence of order and leadership: "Every man did what was right in his eyes" (see, e.g., Judges 17:6). Such a generation deserves to be called completely vain.

וְאָמַר רַבִּי יוֹחָנָן, מַאי דִּכְתִיב: ״וַיְהִי בִּימֵי שְׁפוֹט הַשּׁוֹפְטִים״? דּוֹר שֶׁשּׁוֹפֵט אֶת שׁוֹפְטָיו; אוֹמֵר לוֹ: טוֹל קֵיסָם מִבֵּין עֵינֶיךָ – אוֹמֵר לוֹ: טוֹל קוֹרָה מִבֵּין עֵינֶיךָ; אָמַר לוֹ: ״כַּסְפֵּךְ הָיָה לְסִיגִים״ – אָמַר לוֹ: ״סָבְאֵךְ מָהוּל בַּמָּיִם״.

And further, with regard to Rabbi Elazar's statement in the *baraita* that the generation of the judging of the Judges was one of vanity, **Rabbi Yoḥanan says: What** is the meaning of that **which is written: "And it happened in the days of the judging of the Judges"** (Ruth 1:1)? This indicates **a generation that judged its judges.** If a judge would **say to** the defendant standing before him: **Remove the splinter from between your eyes,** meaning rid yourself of some minor infraction, the defendant would **say to him: Remove the beam from between your eyes,** meaning you have committed far more severe sins. If the judge would **say to him: "Your silver is become dross"** (Isaiah 1:22), meaning your coins are counterfeit, the defendant would **say to him: "Your wine is mixed with water"** (Isaiah 1:22), meaning you yourself dilute your wine with water and sell it. Since nobody behaved in proper manner, the judges were unable to judge.

אָמַר רַבִּי שְׁמוּאֵל בַּר נַחְמָנִי אָמַר רַבִּי יוֹנָתָן: כָּל הָאוֹמֵר מַלְכַּת שְׁבָא אִשָּׁה הָיְתָה – אֵינוֹ אֶלָּא טוֹעֶה, מַאי ״מַלְכַּת שְׁבָא״? מַלְכוּתָא דִּשְׁבָא.

Rabbi Shmuel bar Naḥmani says that Rabbi Yonatan says: Anyone who says that the queen of Sheba [*malkat Sheva*][N] who came to visit King Solomon (see 1 Kings, chapter 10) **was a woman is nothing other than mistaken. What** is the meaning of ***malkat* Sheba? The kingdom [*malkhuta*] of Sheba,** as is mentioned in Job: "And Sheba fell on them and took them away" (Job 1:15).

״וַיְהִי הַיּוֹם וַיָּבֹאוּ בְּנֵי הָאֱלֹהִים לְהִתְיַצֵּב עַל ה׳ וַיָּבֹא גַם הַשָּׂטָן בְּתוֹכָם. וַיֹּאמֶר ה׳ אֶל הַשָּׂטָן מֵאַיִן תָּבֹא וַיַּעַן הַשָּׂטָן״ וגו׳ – אָמַר לְפָנָיו: רִבּוֹנוֹ שֶׁל עוֹלָם, שַׁטְתִּי בְּכָל הָעוֹלָם כּוּלּוֹ וְלֹא מָצָאתִי נֶאֱמָן כְּעַבְדְּךָ אַבְרָהָם, שֶׁאָמַרְתָּ לוֹ: ״קוּם הִתְהַלֵּךְ בָּאָרֶץ לְאׇרְכָּהּ וּלְרׇחְבָּהּ כִּי לְךָ אֶתְּנֶנָּה״, וַאֲפִילּוּ הָכִי בְּשָׁעָה שֶׁלֹּא מָצָא מָקוֹם לִקְבּוֹר אֶת שָׂרָה [עַד שֶׁקָּנָה בְּאַרְבַּע מֵאוֹת שֶׁקֶל כֶּסֶף] לֹא הִרְהֵר אַחַר מִדּוֹתֶיךָ.

§ Having mentioned the book of Job, the Gemara addresses several matters relating to it. It is stated: **"Now there was a day when the sons of God came to present themselves before the Lord, and the Satan came also among them. And the Lord said to the Satan: From where do you come? And the Satan answered** the Lord, and said: From going to and fro in the earth, and from walking through it" (Job 1:6–7). The Satan **said to** God: **Master of the Universe, I have gone to and fro throughout the entire world and I have not found anyone as faithful as Your servant Abraham, to whom You said: "Arise, walk through the land in the length of it and in the breadth of it; for I will give it to you"** (Genesis 13:17). **And even so, when he did not find a place to bury Sarah before he purchased** a burial site **for four hundred silver shekels, he did not find fault with Your ways** or complain about the fact that you had failed to fulfill Your promise.

״וַיֹּאמֶר ה׳ אֶל הַשָּׂטָן הֲשַׂמְתָּ לִבְּךָ אֶל עַבְדִּי אִיּוֹב כִּי אֵין כָּמֹהוּ בָּאָרֶץ״ וגו׳, אָמַר רַבִּי יוֹחָנָן: גָּדוֹל הַנֶּאֱמַר בְּאִיּוֹב יוֹתֵר מִמַּה שֶּׁנֶּאֱמַר בְּאַבְרָהָם, דְּאִילּוּ בְּאַבְרָהָם כְּתִיב: ״כִּי עַתָּה יָדַעְתִּי כִּי יְרֵא אֱלֹהִים אַתָּה״, וּבְאִיּוֹב כְּתִיב: ״אִישׁ תָּם וְיָשָׁר יְרֵא אֱלֹהִים [וְסָר מֵרָע]״.

"And the Lord said to the Satan: Have you considered My servant Job, that there is none like him on earth, a perfect and upright man, one who fears God and turns away from evil?" (Job 1:8). About this **Rabbi Yoḥanan says: That** which **is stated** about **Job is greater than that** which **is stated about Abraham. As** with **regard to Abraham it is written: "For now I know that you fear God"** (Genesis 22:12), **with regard to Job it is written: "A perfect and an upright man, one who fears God and turns away from evil"** (Job 1:8).

מַאי ״וְסָר מֵרָע״? אָמַר רַבִּי אַבָּא בַּר שְׁמוּאֵל: אִיּוֹב וַוְתְּרָן בְּמָמוֹנוֹ הָיָה; מִנְהָגוֹ שֶׁל עוֹלָם – נוֹתֵן חֲצִי פְּרוּטָה לַחֶנְוָנִי, אִיּוֹב וִיתְּרָהּ מִשֶּׁלּוֹ.

The Gemara clarifies the meaning of the aforementioned verse: **What** is meant by **"and turns away from evil"? Rabbi Abba bar Shmuel says: Job was forgiving with his money.** It is **the way of the world** that **one pays the storekeeper** for even **half-*peruta*** of merchandise purchased from him. But if somebody bought an item of such little value from **Job,** he **would forgive him** his half-*peruta*.

״וַיַּעַן הַשָּׂטָן אֶת ה׳ וַיֹּאמַר הַחִנָּם יָרֵא אִיּוֹב אֱלֹהִים. הֲלֹא אַתָּה שַׂכְתָּ בַעֲדוֹ וּבְעַד בֵּיתוֹ״ וגו׳ – מַאי ״מַעֲשֵׂה יָדָיו בֵּרַכְתָּ״? אָמַר רַבִּי שְׁמוּאֵל בַּר רַב יִצְחָק: כׇּל הַנּוֹטֵל פְּרוּטָה מֵאִיּוֹב מִתְבָּרֵךְ.

The Gemara continues to clarify the verses concerning Job. **"Then the Satan answered the Lord, and said: Does Job fear God for naught? Have You not made a hedge about him, and about his house,** and about all that he has on every side? You have blessed the work of his hands, and his cattle is increased in the land" (Job 1:9–10). **What is meant by: "You have blessed the work of his hands"? Rabbi Shmuel bar Rav Yitzḥak says: Anyone who took a *peruta* from Job was blessed.** Not only was Job's own handiwork blessed, but anybody who received anything from him was also blessed.

NOTES

Queen of Sheba [*malkat Sheva*] – מַלְכַּת שְׁבָא: The Maharsha explains that this term does not mean that the individual referred to was not a woman, since the entire text uses feminine language. Rather, the term signifies that the queen of Sheba was not merely the wife of the king who arrived accompanying her husband. On the contrary, she was the sovereign ruler of Sheba, which had a female monarch.

מַאי ״וּמִקְנֵהוּ פָּרַץ בָּאָרֶץ״? אָמַר רַבִּי יוֹסֵי בַּר חֲנִינָא: מִקְנֵהוּ שֶׁל אִיּוֹב פָּרְצוּ גְּדֵרוֹ שֶׁל עוֹלָם; מִנְהָגוֹ שֶׁל עוֹלָם – זְאֵבִים הוֹרְגִים הָעִזִּים, מִקְנֵהוּ שֶׁל אִיּוֹב – עִזִּים הוֹרְגִים אֶת הַזְּאֵבִים.

The Gemara continues with its explication of these verses. **What is meant by: "And his livestock is increased [*paratz*] in the land"** (Job 1:10)? **Rabbi Yosei bar Ḥanina says: Job's livestock breached [*paretzu*] the order of the world.** It is **the way of the world** that **wolves kill goats, but in the case of Job's livestock, the goats killed the wolves.**

״וְאוּלָם שְׁלַח נָא יָדְךָ וְגַע בְּכָל אֲשֶׁר לוֹ אִם לֹא עַל פָּנֶיךָ יְבָרְכֶךָּ. וַיֹּאמֶר ה׳ אֶל הַשָּׂטָן הִנֵּה כָל אֲשֶׁר לוֹ בְּיָדֶךָ רַק אֵלָיו אַל תִּשְׁלַח יָדֶךָ״ וגו׳. ״וַיְהִי הַיּוֹם וּבָנָיו וּבְנוֹתָיו אוֹכְלִים וְשׁוֹתִים יַיִן בְּבֵית אֲחִיהֶם הַבְּכוֹר. וּמַלְאָךְ בָּא אֶל אִיּוֹב וַיֹּאמַר הַבָּקָר הָיוּ חוֹרְשׁוֹת״ וגו׳ – מַאי ״הַבָּקָר הָיוּ חוֹרְשׁוֹת וְהָאֲתֹנוֹת רֹעוֹת עַל יְדֵיהֶם״? אָמַר רַבִּי יוֹחָנָן: מְלַמֵּד, שֶׁהִטְעִימוֹ הַקָּדוֹשׁ בָּרוּךְ הוּא לְאִיּוֹב

The Gemara continues to relate the Satan's challenge to God: **"But now put forth Your hand, and touch all that he has, and he will curse You to Your face. And the Lord said to the Satan: Behold, all that he has is in your power; only upon himself do not put forth your hand.** And the Satan went out from the presence of the Lord" (Job 1:11–12). The verses relate what then occurred: **"Now there was a day when his sons and his daughters were eating and drinking wine in their eldest brother's house, and there came a messenger to Job, and said: The oxen were plowing,** and the asses were feeding beside them" (Job 1:13–14). The Gemara asks: **What is meant by: "The oxen were plowing and the asses were feeding beside them"? Rabbi Yoḥanan says: This teaches that the Holy One, Blessed be He, gave Job a taste**

Perek **I**
Daf **16** Amud **a**

מֵעֵין הָעוֹלָם הַבָּא.

of the World-to-Come, when plowing and harvesting will take place at the same time. Here too, the oxen plowed and the donkeys grazed on the crops that grew from that effort.

״עוֹד זֶה מְדַבֵּר וְזֶה בָּא וַיֹּאמַר אֵשׁ אֱלֹהִים״ וגו׳. ״עוֹד זֶה מְדַבֵּר וְזֶה בָּא וַיֹּאמַר כַּשְׂדִּים שָׂמוּ שְׁלֹשָׁה רָאשִׁים וַיִּפְשְׁטוּ עַל הַגְּמַלִּים וַיִּקָּחוּם״ וגו׳. ״עוֹד זֶה מְדַבֵּר וְזֶה בָּא וַיֹּאמַר בָּנֶיךָ וּבְנוֹתֶיךָ אוֹכְלִים וְשׁוֹתִים יַיִן בְּבֵית אֲחִיהֶם הַבְּכוֹר. וְהִנֵּה רוּחַ גְּדוֹלָה בָּאָה מֵעֵבֶר הַמִּדְבָּר וַיִּגַּע בְּאַרְבַּע פִּנּוֹת הַבַּיִת וַיִּפֹּל עַל הַנְּעָרִים״ וגו׳. ״וַיָּקָם אִיּוֹב וַיִּקְרַע אֶת מְעִלוֹ וַיָּגָז אֶת רֹאשׁוֹ״ וגו׳, ״וַיֹּאמֶר עָרֹם יָצָאתִי מִבֶּטֶן אִמִּי וְעָרֹם אָשׁוּב שָׁמָּה ה׳ נָתַן וה׳ לָקָח יְהִי שֵׁם ה׳ מְבוֹרָךְ. בְּכָל זֹאת לֹא חָטָא אִיּוֹב וְלֹא נָתַן תִּפְלָה לֵאלֹהִים״.

The Gemara continues to interpret verses from the book of Job. **"While he was yet speaking, there came also another and said: The fire of God** has fallen from heaven, and has burned up the sheep, and the servants, and consumed them…**While he was yet speaking, there came also another and said: The Chaldeans formed three bands, and fell among the camels, and have carried them away,** and have slain the servants with the edge of the sword… **While he was yet speaking, there came also another and said: Your sons and your daughters were eating and drinking wine in their eldest brother's house; and, behold, there came a great wind from across the wilderness, and smote the four corners of the house, and it fell upon the young men,** and they are dead… **Then Job arose, and rent his coat, and shaved his head,** and fell down on the ground and prostrated himself. **And he said: I came naked out of my mother's womb, and naked I shall return there; the Lord gave, and the Lord has taken away, blessed be the name of the Lord. In all this Job sinned not, nor did he lay reproach on God"** (Job 1:16–22).

״וַיְהִי הַיּוֹם וַיָּבֹאוּ בְּנֵי הָאֱלֹהִים לְהִתְיַצֵּב״ וגו׳. ״וַיֹּאמֶר ה׳ אֶל הַשָּׂטָן אֵי מִזֶּה תָּבֹא וַיַּעַן הַשָּׂטָן אֶת ה׳ וַיֹּאמַר מִשֻּׁט בָּאָרֶץ״ [וגו׳]. אָמַר לְפָנָיו: רִבּוֹנוֹ שֶׁל עוֹלָם, שַׁטְתִּי בְּכָל הָעוֹלָם וְלֹא מָצָאתִי כְּעַבְדְּךָ אַבְרָהָם, שֶׁאָמַרְתָּ לוֹ: ״קוּם הִתְהַלֵּךְ בָּאָרֶץ לְאָרְכָּהּ וּלְרׇחְבָּהּ כִּי לְךָ אֶתְּנֶנָּה״, וּבְשָׁעָה שֶׁבִּקֵּשׁ לִקְבּוֹר שָׂרָה לֹא מָצָא מָקוֹם לְקוֹבְרָהּ, וְלֹא הִרְהֵר אַחַר מִדּוֹתֶיךָ.

"Again there was a day when the sons of God came to present themselves before the Lord, and the Satan came also among them to present himself before God. **And the Lord said to the Satan: From where do you come? And the Satan answered the Lord, and said: From going to and fro in the earth** and from walking up and down in it" (Job 2:1–2). The Satan **said before** God: **Master of the Universe, I have gone to and fro across the entire world and have not found anyone as faithful as your servant Abraham, to whom you said: "Arise, walk through the land in the length of it and in the breadth of it; for I will give it to you"** (Genesis 13:17). **And when he wanted to bury Sarah, he could not find a place to bury her, and yet he did not criticize Your ways,** or accuse You of having failed to keep Your promise.

״וַיֹּאמֶר ה׳ אֶל הַשָּׂטָן הֲשַׂמְתָּ לִבְּךָ אֶל עַבְדִּי אִיּוֹב כִּי אֵין כָּמֹהוּ בָּאָרֶץ״ וגו׳, ״וְעֹדֶנּוּ מַחֲזִיק בְּתֻמָּתוֹ וַתְּסִיתֵנִי בוֹ לְבַלְּעוֹ חִנָּם״

About this it says: **"And the Lord said to the Satan: Have you considered My servant Job, that there is none like him on earth,** a perfect and an upright man, one that fears God and turns away from evil? **And still he holds fast to his integrity, although you moved Me against him, to destroy him without cause"** (Job 2:3).

אָמַר רַבִּי יוֹחָנָן: אִלְמָלֵא מִקְרָא כָּתוּב אִי אֶפְשָׁר לְאוֹמְרוֹ, כְּאָדָם שֶׁמְּסִיתִין אוֹתוֹ וְנִיסָּת.

Rabbi Yoḥanan says: Were it not explicitly **written in the verse, it would be impossible to say this,**[N] as it would be insulting to God's honor. The verse states: "You moved Me against him," **like a person whom others persuade and** allows himself to be **persuaded,** as if God had not wanted to do anything, but allowed Himself to be persuaded to bring harm to Job.

בְּמַתְנִיתָא תָּנָא: יוֹרֵד וּמַתְעֶה וְעוֹלֶה וּמַרְגִּיז, נוֹטֵל רְשׁוּת וְנוֹטֵל נְשָׁמָה.

It was taught in a ***baraita*** with regard to the methods of the Satan: He **descends** to this world **and misleads** a person into sinning. He then **ascends** to Heaven, levels accusations against that very sinner, **and inflames** God's **anger** against him. He then **receives permission** to act **and takes away the** sinner's **soul** as punishment.

״וַיַּעַן הַשָּׂטָן אֶת ה׳ וַיֹּאמַר עוֹר בְּעַד עוֹר וְכֹל אֲשֶׁר לָאִישׁ יִתֵּן בְּעַד נַפְשׁוֹ. אוּלָם שְׁלַח נָא יָדְךָ וְגַע אֶל עַצְמוֹ וְאֶל בְּשָׂרוֹ אִם לֹא עַל פָּנֶיךָ יְבָרְכֶךָּ. וַיֹּאמֶר ה׳ אֶל הַשָּׂטָן הִנּוֹ בְיָדֶךָ אַךְ אֶת נַפְשׁוֹ שְׁמֹר. וַיֵּצֵא הַשָּׂטָן מֵאֵת פְּנֵי ה׳ וַיַּךְ אֶת אִיּוֹב״ וגו׳ – אָמַר רַבִּי יִצְחָק: קָשֶׁה צַעֲרוֹ שֶׁל שָׂטָן יוֹתֵר מִשֶּׁל אִיּוֹב; מָשָׁל לְעֶבֶד שֶׁאָמַר לוֹ רַבּוֹ: שְׁבוֹר חָבִית וּשְׁמוֹר אֶת יֵינָהּ.

The Gemara returns to discuss the text of the book of Job: **"And the Satan answered the Lord, and said: Skin for skin, for all that a man has he will give for his life. But put forth Your hand now, and touch his bone and his flesh, and he will curse You to Your face. And the Lord said to the Satan: Behold, he is in your hand; only spare his life. So the Satan went forth from the presence of the Lord, and smote Job** with vile sores from the sole of his foot to his crown" (Job 2:4–7). **Rabbi Yitzḥak says: Satan's suffering was more difficult than that of Job.** This can be explained by means of **a parable involving a servant whose master said to him: Break the barrel but save its wine.** Here too, God told the Satan that he could do whatever he liked short of taking Job's life, and that limitation caused Satan to suffer.

אָמַר רֵישׁ לָקִישׁ: הוּא שָׂטָן, הוּא יֵצֶר הָרָע, הוּא מַלְאַךְ הַמָּוֶת. הוּא שָׂטָן – דִּכְתִיב: ״וַיֵּצֵא הַשָּׂטָן מֵאֵת פְּנֵי ה׳״; הוּא יֵצֶר הָרָע – כְּתִיב הָתָם: ״רַק רַע כָּל הַיּוֹם״, וּכְתִיב הָכָא: (״רַק אֶת נַפְשׁוֹ שְׁמֹר״) [״רַק אֵלָיו אַל תִּשְׁלַח יָדֶךָ״]; הוּא מַלְאַךְ הַמָּוֶת, דִּכְתִיב: ״(רַק) [אַךְ] אֶת נַפְשׁוֹ שְׁמֹר״, אַלְמָא בְּדִידֵיהּ קַיְימָא.

Reish Lakish says: Satan, the evil inclination, and the Angel of Death are one, that is, they are three aspects of the same essence. **He is the Satan** who seduces people and then accuses them, **as it is written: "So the Satan went forth from the presence of the Lord,** and smote Job with vile sores" (Job 2:7). **He is** also **the evil inclination,** as **it is written there:** "The impulse of the thoughts of his heart **was only evil continuously"** (Genesis 6:5); **and it is written here: "Only upon himself do not put forth your hand"** (Job 1:12). The verbal analogy between the various uses of the word "only" teaches that the evil inclination is to be identified with the Satan. **He is** also **the Angel of Death, as it is written: "Only spare his life"** (Job 2:6); **apparently** Job's life **depends upon him,** the Satan, and accordingly the Satan must also be the Angel of Death.

אָמַר רַבִּי לֵוִי: שָׂטָן וּפְנִינָּה לְשֵׁם שָׁמַיִם נִתְכַּוְּונוּ. שָׂטָן, כֵּיוָן דַּחֲזָיָא לְהַקָּדוֹשׁ בָּרוּךְ הוּא דְּנָטְיָה דַּעְתֵּיהּ בָּתַר אִיּוֹב, אֲמַר: חַס וְשָׁלוֹם, מִינְשֵׁי לֵיהּ לְרַחְמָנוּתֵיהּ דְּאַבְרָהָם; פְּנִינָּה, דִּכְתִיב: ״וְכִעֲסַתָּה צָרָתָהּ גַּם כַּעַס בַּעֲבוּר הַרְּעִמָהּ״. דְּרָשָׁהּ רַב אַחָא בַּר יַעֲקֹב בְּפַפּוּנְיָא, אֲתָא שָׂטָן נַשְׁקֵיהּ לְכַרְעֵיהּ.

Rabbi Levi says: Both **Satan,** who brought accusations against Job, **and Peninnah,** who tormented Hannah, mother of Samuel the prophet, acted with **intent** that was **for the sake of Heaven.** As for **Satan, when he saw that the Holy One, Blessed be He, inclined to** favor **Job** and praised him, **he said: Heaven forbid that He should forget the love of Abraham.** With regard to **Peninnah, as it is written: "And her rival wife also provoked her sore, to make her fret"** (I Samuel 1:6), i.e., Peninnah upset Hannah in order to motivate her to pray. **Rav Aḥa bar Ya'akov taught** this **in Paphunya,** and **Satan came and kissed his feet** in gratitude for speaking positively about him.

״בְּכָל זֹאת לֹא חָטָא אִיּוֹב בִּשְׂפָתָיו״ – אָמַר רָבָא: בִּשְׂפָתָיו לֹא חָטָא, בְּלִבּוֹ חָטָא. מַאי קָאָמַר? ״אֶרֶץ נִתְּנָה בְיַד רָשָׁע פְּנֵי שֹׁפְטֶיהָ יְכַסֶּה אִם לֹא אֵיפוֹ מִי הוּא״, אָמַר רָבָא: בִּקֵּשׁ אִיּוֹב לַהֲפוֹךְ קְעָרָה עַל פִּיהָ; אֲמַר לֵיהּ אַבַּיֵי: לֹא דִּבֵּר אִיּוֹב אֶלָּא כְּנֶגֶד הַשָּׂטָן.

The Gemara considers the character of Job. The verse states: **"In all this Job did not sin with his lips"** (Job 2:10). **Rava says:** A close reading of the verse indicates that **he did not sin with his lips,** but **he sinned in his heart. What did he say** that suggests that he had wicked thoughts? **"The earth is given into the hand of the wicked, he covers the faces of its judges; if not he, then who is it?"** (Job 9:24). **Rava says: Job sought to turn the bowl upside down,** that is to say, he alluded here to a heretical thought, as he said that the earth is given into the hand of the wicked, indicating that he had God in mind. **Abaye said to him: Job was referring** here **only to the Satan,** he being the wicked one into whose hands the land was given.

כְּתַנָּאֵי: ״אֶרֶץ נִתְּנָה בְיַד רָשָׁע״ – רַבִּי אֱלִיעֶזֶר אוֹמֵר: בִּקֵּשׁ אִיּוֹב לַהֲפוֹךְ קְעָרָה עַל פִּיהָ; אָמַר לוֹ רַבִּי יְהוֹשֻׁעַ: לֹא דִּבֵּר אִיּוֹב אֶלָּא כְּלַפֵּי שָׂטָן.

The Gemara comments: This is **parallel to** a dispute between ***tanna'im,*** as it was taught in a *baraita*: **"The earth is given into the hand of the wicked." Rabbi Eliezer says: Job sought to turn the bowl upside down; Rabbi Yehoshua said to him: Job was referring** here **only to the Satan.**

NOTES

It would be impossible to say this – אִי אֶפְשָׁר לְאוֹמְרוֹ: The Talmud and midrash use this expression in connection with biblical formulations that are either anthropomorphic or disrespectful to God's honor, and that one would otherwise have been prohibited from uttering.

NOTES

To exempt the whole world – לִפְטוֹר אֶת כָּל הָעוֹלָם כּוּלּוֹ: The phrase: "Although you know that I am not wicked" (Job 10:7), can be understood as follows: If You so desired, You could prevent me from sinning. Consequently, a person's desires and actions are dictated to him by God, and there is no room whatsoever for reward and punishment.

He used to steal a field from orphans – שֶׁהָיָה גּוֹזֵל שָׂדֶה מִיתוֹמִים: The Meiri raises the difficulty that one is prohibited from stealing under all circumstances, even if he intends to repay the victim. He suggests that since Job was known as a righteous person, nobody thought that he really meant to steal another person's property. Nevertheless, the Meiri holds that such behavior is inappropriate. The Ramah writes that such behavior is praiseworthy only in the case of gentiles, but Jews may not steal under any circumstance.

"עַל דַּעְתְּךָ כִּי לֹא אֶרְשָׁע וְאֵין מִיָּדְךָ מַצִּיל" – אָמַר רָבָא: בִּקֵּשׁ אִיּוֹב לִפְטוֹר אֶת כָּל הָעוֹלָם כּוּלּוֹ מִן הַדִּין, אָמַר לְפָנָיו: רִבּוֹנוֹ שֶׁל עוֹלָם, בָּרָאתָ שׁוֹר פַּרְסוֹתָיו סְדוּקוֹת, בָּרָאתָ חֲמוֹר פַּרְסוֹתָיו קְלוּטוֹת; בָּרָאתָ גַּן עֵדֶן, בָּרָאתָ גֵּיהִנָּם; בָּרָאתָ צַדִּיקִים, בָּרָאתָ רְשָׁעִים; מִי מְעַכֵּב עַל יָדְךָ!

The Gemara continues to discuss Job's statements: **"Although You know that I am not wicked, and there is none that can deliver out of Your hand"** (Job 10:7). **Rava says: Job sought to exempt the whole world**[N] **from judgment,** claiming that all of a person's actions are directed by God, and therefore one cannot be held culpable for his misdeeds. Job **said before** God: **Master of the Universe, You created the ox with split hooves,** making it kosher, and **You created the donkey with closed hooves,** making it forbidden; **You created the Garden of Eden,** and **You created Gehenna;** and similarly, **You created righteous people** and **You created wicked people; who can restrain You?** Seeing that You created people as either righteous or wicked, You cannot later complain about their actions.

וּמַאי אַהְדַרוּ לֵיהּ חַבְרֵיהּ [דְּאִיּוֹב]? "אַף אַתָּה תָּפֵר יִרְאָה וְתִגְרַע שִׂיחָה לִפְנֵי אֵל" – בָּרָא הַקָּדוֹשׁ בָּרוּךְ הוּא יֵצֶר הָרָע, בָּרָא לוֹ תּוֹרָה תַּבְלִין.

And how did Job's friends answer him? "You do away with fear, and impair devotion before God" (Job 15:4) with such statements. True, **the Holy One, Blessed be He, created the evil inclination,** but **He** also **created the Torah** as **an antidote** to counter its effects and prevent it from gaining control of a person.

דָּרַשׁ רָבָא, מַאי דִּכְתִיב: "בִּרְכַּת אֹבֵד עָלַי תָּבֹא וְלֵב אַלְמָנָה אַרְנִן"? "בִּרְכַּת אֹבֵד עָלַי תָּבֹא" – מְלַמֵּד שֶׁהָיָה גּוֹזֵל שָׂדֶה מִיתוֹמִים וּמַשְׁבִּיחָהּ וּמַחֲזִירָהּ לָהֶן; "וְלֵב אַלְמָנָה אַרְנִן" – דְּכָל הֵיכָא דַּהֲוָה אִיכָּא אַלְמָנָה דְּלָא הָווּ נָסְבִי לַהּ, הֲוָה אָזֵיל שָׁדֵי שְׁמֵיהּ עִילָּוָוהּ, וַהֲווּ אָתוּ נָסְבִי לַהּ.

Rava interpreted a verse **homiletically: What** is the meaning of that **which is written,** Job saying about himself: **"The blessing of him that was lost came upon me, and I caused the widow's heart to sing for joy"** (Job 29:13). **"The blessing of him that was lost came upon me" teaches that** Job **used to steal a field from orphans,**[N] cultivate it, **improve it, and** then **return it to them;** consequently, they would bless him for the field they had lost. **"I caused the widow's heart to sing for joy"** teaches that **anywhere that there was a widow whom no one would marry, he would go** and **cast his name upon her,** i.e., he would start a rumor that she was related to him, **and** then **somebody would** come forward and **marry her.**

"לוּ שָׁקוֹל יִשָּׁקֵל כַּעְשִׂי וְהַוָּתִי בְּמֹאזְנַיִם יִשְׂאוּ יָחַד" – אָמַר רַב: עַפְרָא לְפוּמֵּיהּ דְּאִיּוֹב, חַבְרוּתָא כְּלַפֵּי שְׁמַיָּא? "לוּ יֵשׁ בֵּינֵינוּ מוֹכִיחַ יָשֵׁת יָדוֹ עַל שְׁנֵינוּ" – אָמַר רַב: עַפְרָא לְפוּמֵּיהּ דְּאִיּוֹב, כְּלוּם יֵשׁ עֶבֶד שֶׁמּוֹכִיחַ אֶת רַבּוֹ? "בְּרִית כָּרַתִּי לְעֵינָי וּמָה אֶתְבּוֹנֵן עַל בְּתוּלָה" – אָמַר רָבָא: עַפְרָא לְפוּמֵּיהּ דְּאִיּוֹב, אִיהוּ – בְּאַחֲרָנִיתָא, אַבְרָהָם – אֲפִילּוּ בְּדִידֵיהּ לָא אִיסְתַּכַּל, דִּכְתִיב: "הִנֵּה נָא יָדַעְתִּי כִּי אִשָּׁה יְפַת מַרְאֶה אָתְּ", מִכְּלָל דְּמֵעִיקָּרָא לָא הֲוָה יָדַע לַהּ.

Job further said: **"O that my vexation were thoroughly weighed, and my calamity laid in the balances"** (Job 6:2). **Rav says: Dust** should be put **in the mouth of Job,** meaning, he should not have spoken in such a manner, as if he were weighing his deeds against those of God; may one act as if he is in **a friendship with Heaven?** And similarly, Job said: **"There is no arbiter between us, who may lay his hand upon us both"** (Job 9:33). **Rav says: Dust** should be put **in the mouth of Job** for saying this; **is there a servant who rebukes his master?** Job also said: **"I have made a covenant with my eyes; why then should I look upon a virgin?"** (Job 31:1). **Rava says: Dust** should be put **in the mouth of Job** for saying this; **he** did not look **at other** women, but **Abraham did not even look at his own** wife, **as it is written: "Now I know that you are a beautiful woman"** (Genesis 12:11). One may learn **by inference that initially he did not know** how beautiful she was because he had not gazed at her.

"כָּלָה עָנָן וַיֵּלַךְ כֵּן יוֹרֵד שְׁאוֹל לֹא יַעֲלֶה" – אָמַר רָבָא: מִכָּאן שֶׁכָּפַר אִיּוֹב בִּתְחִיַּית הַמֵּתִים. "אֲשֶׁר בִּשְׂעָרָה יְשׁוּפֵנִי וְהִרְבָּה פְצָעַי חִנָּם" – אָמַר רַבָּה: אִיּוֹב בִּסְעָרָה חֵרֵף וּבִסְעָרָה הֱשִׁיבוּהוּ;

Job further said: **"As the cloud is consumed and vanishes away, so he who goes down to the grave shall come up no more"** (Job 7:9). **Rava says: From here** it may be inferred **that Job denied the resurrection of the dead,** as he said that one who goes down to the grave will not come up and live again, just as a cloud that dissipates will not return. He also stated: **"He crushes me with a tempest, and multiplies my wounds without cause"** (Job 9:17). **Rabba says: Job blasphemed with** mention of **a tempest and he was answered with** mention of **a tempest.**

בִּסְעָרָה חֵרֵף, דִּכְתִיב: "אֲשֶׁר בִּשְׂעָרָה יְשׁוּפֵנִי", אָמַר לְפָנָיו: רִבּוֹנוֹ שֶׁל עוֹלָם, שֶׁמָּא רוּחַ סְעָרָה עָבְרָה לְפָנֶיךָ וְנִתְחַלֵּף לְךָ בֵּין אִיּוֹב לְאוֹיֵב! בִּסְעָרָה הֱשִׁיבוּהוּ, דִּכְתִיב: "וַיַּעַן ה' אֶת אִיּוֹב מִן הַסְּעָרָה וַיֹּאמַר [וגו'] אֱזָר נָא כְגֶבֶר חֲלָצֶיךָ אֶשְׁאָלְךָ וְהוֹדִיעֵנִי".

Rabba explains: **He blasphemed with** mention of **a tempest** [*bise'ara*], **as it is written: "He crushes me with a tempest."** Job **said before** God: **Master of the Universe, perhaps a tempest passed before You and You confused** *Iyov*, Job, with *oyev*, enemy. **He was answered with** mention of **a tempest, as it is written: "Then the Lord answered Job out of the tempest, and said:** Who is this that darkens counsel by words without knowledge? **Gird up now your loins like a man, for I will demand of you and let me know your answer"** (Job 38:1–3).

אָמַר לוֹ: הַרְבֵּה נִימִין בָּרָאתִי בָּאָדָם, וְכָל נִימָא וְנִימָא בָּרָאתִי לָהּ גּוּמָּא בִּפְנֵי עַצְמָהּ, שֶׁלֹּא יְהוּ שְׁתַּיִם יוֹנְקוֹת מִגּוּמָּא אַחַת, שֶׁאִלְמָלֵי שְׁתַּיִם יוֹנְקוֹת מִגּוּמָּא אַחַת – מַחְשִׁיכוֹת מְאוֹר עֵינָיו שֶׁל אָדָם; בֵּין גּוּמָּא לְגוּמָּא לֹא נִתְחַלֵּף לִי, בֵּין אִיּוֹב לְאוֹיֵב נִתְחַלֵּף לִי?

What is the meaning of "out of the tempest"? God **said to him: I have created many hairs** [*nimin*][L] **on a person, and for each hair I created its own follicle**[B] through which the hair is sustained, **so that two** hairs **should not draw from one follicle. As were two** hairs **to draw from one follicle, they would impair a man's vision.** Now, **if I do not confuse one follicle with another, would I confuse** ***Iyov*** **with** ***oyev*****?** The Hebrew word for tempest, *se'ara*, is phonetically identical to the Hebrew word for hair.

"מִי פִלַּג לַשֶּׁטֶף תְּעָלָה" [וגו'] – הַרְבֵּה טִיפִּין בָּרָאתִי בֶּעָבִים, וְכָל טִיפָּה וְטִיפָּה בָּרָאתִי לָהּ דְּפוּס בִּפְנֵי עַצְמָהּ, כְּדֵי שֶׁלֹּא יְהוּ שְׁתֵּי טִיפִּין יוֹצְאוֹת מִדְּפוּס אֶחָד, שֶׁאִלְמָלֵי שְׁתֵּי טִיפִּין יוֹצְאוֹת מִדְּפוּס אֶחָד – מְטַשְׁטְשׁוֹת אֶת הָאָרֶץ וְאֵינָהּ מוֹצִיאָה פֵּירוֹת; בֵּין טִיפָּה לְטִיפָּה לֹא נִתְחַלֵּף לִי, בֵּין אִיּוֹב לְאוֹיֵב נִתְחַלֵּף לִי? מַאי מַשְׁמַע דְּהַאי "תְּעָלָה" לִישָּׁנָא דִּדְפוּס הִיא? אָמַר רַבָּה בַּר שֵׁילָא, דִּכְתִיב: "וַיַּעַשׂ תְּעָלָה כְּבֵית סָאתַיִם זֶרַע".

God further said to Job: **"Who has divided a channel** [*te'ala*] **for the torrent** of rain, or a path for the lightning of thunder"? (Job 38:25). **I have created many drops** of water **in the clouds, and for each drop I created its own channel, so that two drops should not emerge from the same channel.**[B] **As were two drops to emerge from the same channel they would destroy the earth and it would not yield produce.** Now, **if I** do not **confuse one drop with another, would I confuse** ***Iyov*** **with** ***oyev*****?** Incidentally, the Gemara asks: **From where may** it be inferred **that this** term *te'ala* means **a channel? Rabba bar Sheila said: As it is written** with regard to Elijah the prophet: **"And he fashioned a channel** [*te'ala*] about the altar, **as great as would contain two** ***se'a*** **of seed"** (I Kings 18:32).

"וְדֶרֶךְ לַחֲזִיז קֹלוֹת" – הַרְבֵּה קוֹלוֹת בָּרָאתִי בֶּעָבִים, וְכָל קוֹל וְקוֹל בָּרָאתִי לוֹ שְׁבִיל בִּפְנֵי עַצְמוֹ, כְּדֵי שֶׁלֹּא יְהוּ שְׁתֵּי קוֹלוֹת יוֹצְאוֹת מִשְּׁבִיל אֶחָד, שֶׁאִלְמָלֵי שְׁתֵּי קוֹלוֹת יוֹצְאוֹת מִשְּׁבִיל אֶחָד – מַחֲרִיבִין אֶת כָּל הָעוֹלָם; בֵּין קוֹל לְקוֹל לֹא נִתְחַלֵּף לִי, בֵּין אִיּוֹב לְאוֹיֵב נִתְחַלֵּף לִי?

The second half of the aforementioned verse in Job states: **"Or a path for the lightning of thunder,"** which is interpreted as follows: God said: **I have created many thunderclaps in the clouds, and for each and every thunderclap I created its own path, so that two thunderclaps should not issue forth from the same path. As were two thunderclaps to issue from the same path, they would destroy the world.** Now, **if I** do not **confuse one thunderclap with another, would I confuse** ***Iyov*** **with** ***oyev*****?**

"הֲיָדַעְתָּ עֵת לֶדֶת יַעֲלֵי סָלַע חֹלֵל אַיָּלוֹת תִּשְׁמֹר" – יַעֲלָה זוֹ אַכְזָרִית עַל בָּנֶיהָ, בְּשָׁעָה שֶׁכּוֹרַעַת

It is further stated there: **"Do you know when the wild goats of the rock give birth? Can you mark when the hinds do calve?"** (Job 39:1). **This** goat **is cruel to her young** and shows them no pity; **when she squats**

Perek **I**
Daf **16** Amud **b**

לָלֶדֶת, עוֹלָה לְרֹאשׁ הָהָר כְּדֵי שֶׁיִּפּוֹל מִמֶּנָּה וְיָמוּת, וַאֲנִי מַזְמִין לָהּ נֶשֶׁר שֶׁמְּקַבְּלוֹ בִּכְנָפָיו וּמַנִּיחוֹ לְפָנֶיהָ, וְאִלְמָלֵי מַקְדִּים רֶגַע אֶחָד אוֹ מִתְאַחֵר רֶגַע אֶחָד מִיָּד מֵת; בֵּין רֶגַע לְרֶגַע לֹא נִתְחַלֵּף לִי, בֵּין אִיּוֹב לְאוֹיֵב נִתְחַלֵּף לִי?

to give birth she ascends to the top of a mountain so that the kid **should fall down from her and die. And I summon her an eagle that receives it with his wings and places it before her; and if** the eagle **reached** her **one moment early or was one moment late,** the kid **would immediately die.** Now, **if I** do not **confuse one moment with another moment, would I confuse** ***Iyov*** **with** ***oyev*****?**

"חֹלֵל אַיָּלוֹת תִּשְׁמֹר" – אַיָּלָה זוֹ רַחְמָהּ צַר, בְּשָׁעָה שֶׁכּוֹרַעַת לָלֶדֶת, אֲנִי מַזְמִין לָהּ דְּרָקוֹן שֶׁמַּכִּישָׁהּ בְּבֵית הָרֶחֶם וּמִתְרַפָּה מִמּוֹלַדְתָּהּ, וְאִלְמָלֵי מַקְדִּים רֶגַע אֶחָד אוֹ מְאַחֵר רֶגַע אֶחָד מִיָּד מֵתָה; בֵּין רֶגַע לְרֶגַע לֹא נִתְחַלֵּף לִי, בֵּין אִיּוֹב לְאוֹיֵב נִתְחַלֵּף לִי?

Similarly: **"Can you mark when the hinds do calve?"** (Job 39:1). **The womb of this hind is narrow,** which makes for a difficult delivery. **When she squats to give birth, I summon her a snake** [*derakon*][L] **that bites her at the opening of the womb,** which then **becomes loose, and she gives birth, and if** the snake **reached** her **one moment early or was one moment late,** she **would immediately die.** Now, **if I** do not **confuse one moment with another moment, would I confuse** ***Iyov*** **with** ***oyev*****?**

"[אִיּוֹב] לֹא בְדַעַת יְדַבֵּר וּדְבָרָיו לֹא בְהַשְׂכֵּל", וּכְתִיב: "כִּי לֹא דִבַּרְתֶּם אֵלַי נְכוֹנָה כְּעַבְדִּי אִיּוֹב"! אָמַר רָבָא: מִכָּאן שֶׁאֵין אָדָם נִתְפָּס בִּשְׁעַת צַעֲרוֹ.

The Gemara comments: On the one hand, the text states: **"Job has spoken without knowledge, and his words were without wisdom"** (Job 34:35). **But** on the other hand, **it is written** with regard to Job's friends: **"You have not spoken of Me the thing that is right, like my servant Job"** (Job 42:8). **Rava said: From here** it may be inferred **that a person is not held responsible** for what he says **when he is in distress.** Although Job uttered certain words that were wrong and inappropriate, he was not punished for them because he said them at a time of pain and hardship.

LANGUAGE

Hair [*nima*] – **נִימָא:** From the Greek νῆμα, *nēma*, meaning a thread.

BACKGROUND

Hair and follicle – **נִימָא וְגוּמָּא:**

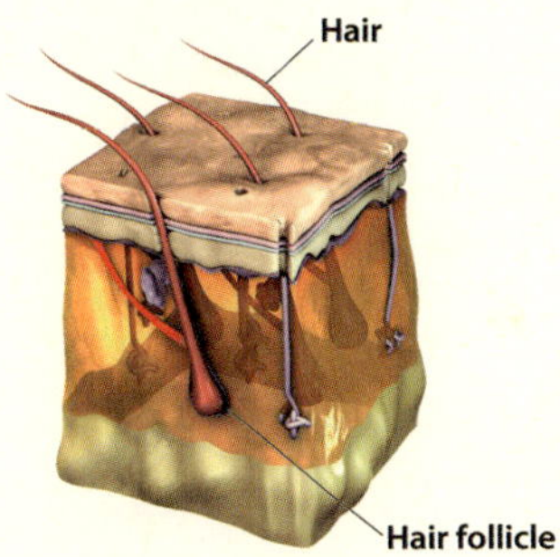

Anatomy of a hair follicle

Drop and channel – **טִיפָּה וּדְפוּס:** Drops of rain are formed from water vapor that condenses into drops. These drops remain distinct and do not join together into a single stream.

LANGUAGE

Snake [*derakon*] – **דְּרָקוֹן:** From the Greek δρακών, *drakon*, meaning a snake or large monster.

״וַיִּשְׁמְעוּ שְׁלֹשֶׁת רֵעֵי אִיּוֹב אֵת כׇּל הָרָעָה הַזֹּאת הַבָּאָה עָלָיו וַיָּבֹאוּ אִישׁ מִמְּקוֹמוֹ אֱלִיפַז הַתֵּימָנִי וּבִלְדַּד הַשּׁוּחִי וְצוֹפַר הַנַּעֲמָתִי וַיִּוָּעֲדוּ יַחְדָּו לָבוֹא לָנוּד לוֹ וּלְנַחֲמוֹ״ – מַאי ״וַיִּוָּעֲדוּ יַחְדָּו״? אָמַר רַב יְהוּדָה אָמַר רַב: מְלַמֵּד שֶׁנִּכְנְסוּ כּוּלָּן בְּשַׁעַר אֶחָד. וְתָנָא: בֵּין כׇּל אֶחָד וְאֶחָד שְׁלֹשׁ מֵאוֹת פַּרְסֵי.

The verse states: **"And Job's three friends heard of all this evil that was come upon him, they came every one from his own place, Eliphaz the Temanite, and Bildad the Shuhite, and Zophar the Naamathite; for they had made an appointment together to come to mourn with him and to comfort him"** (Job 2:11). **What does "they had made an appointment together" mean? Rav Yehuda says** that **Rav says: This** phrase **teaches that they all entered** through **one gate**[N] at the same time. **And** a Sage **taught** in a *baraita*: There were **three hundred parasangs between each and every one** of them, i.e., each one lived three hundred parasangs away from the other.

מְנָא הֲווּ יָדְעִי? אִיכָּא דְּאָמְרִי: כְּלִילָא הֲוָה לְהוּ, וְאִיכָּא דְּאָמְרִי: אִילָנֵי הֲוָה לְהוּ, וְכֵיוָן דְּכָמְשִׁי הָווּ יָדְעִי. אֲמַר רָבָא, הַיְינוּ דְּאָמְרִי אֱינָשֵׁי: אוֹ חַבְרָא כְּחַבְרֵי דְּאִיּוֹב, אוֹ מִיתוּתָא.

The Gemara asks: **How did they** all **know** at the same time what had happened to Job so that the three of them came together? **There are** those **who say** that **they** each **had a crown** which displayed certain signs when something happened to one of the others. **And there are** those **who say they** each **had trees and when** the trees **withered they knew** that sorrow had visited one of them. **Rava said** that **this** closeness between Job and his friends explains the adage **that people say: Either a friend like the friends of Job or death.** If a person lacks close friends, he is better off dead.

״וַיְהִי כִּי הֵחֵל הָאָדָם לָרֹב עַל פְּנֵי הָאֲדָמָה וּבָנוֹת יֻלְּדוּ לָהֶם״ – רַבִּי יוֹחָנָן אָמַר: רְבִיָּה בָּאָה לָעוֹלָם; רֵישׁ לָקִישׁ אָמַר: מְרִיבָה בָּאָה לָעוֹלָם. אֲמַר לֵיהּ רֵישׁ לָקִישׁ לְרַבִּי יוֹחָנָן: לְדִידָךְ דְּאָמְרַתְּ רְבִיָּה בָּאָה לָעוֹלָם, מִפְּנֵי מָה לֹא נִכְפְּלוּ בְּנוֹתָיו שֶׁל אִיּוֹב?

The Gemara cites another place where Job is mentioned. **"And it came to pass, when men began to multiply** [*larov*] **on the face of the earth, and daughters were born to them"** (Genesis 6:1). **Rabbi Yoḥanan says:** *Larov* means that **propagation** [*reviyya*] **came to the world**[N] through these daughters. **Reish Lakish says: Strife** [*meriva*] **came to the world.** Once daughters were born, the men began to fight among themselves over them. **Reish Lakish said to Rabbi Yoḥanan: According to you who say** that due to the daughters **propagation came to the world, for what** reason **were** the number of **Job's daughters not doubled,** when at the end of the story God doubled everything that Job had lost (see Job 1:3, 42:12)?

אֲמַר לוֹ: נְהִי דְּלֹא נִכְפְּלוּ בְּשֵׁמוֹת, אֲבָל נִכְפְּלוּ בְּיוֹפִי, דִּכְתִיב: ״וַיְהִי לוֹ שִׁבְעָנָה בָנִים וְשָׁלוֹשׁ בָּנוֹת. וַיִּקְרָא שֵׁם הָאַחַת יְמִימָה וְשֵׁם הַשֵּׁנִית קְצִיעָה וְשֵׁם הַשְּׁלִישִׁית קֶרֶן הַפּוּךְ״.

Rabbi Yoḥanan **said to him: Granted,** the numbers of Job's daughters **were not doubled in name,** meaning they did not become twice as many, **but they were doubled in beauty, as it is written: "He had also seven sons and three daughters. And he called the name of the first Jemimah, and the name of the second was Keziah, and the name of the third one was Keren-happuch"** (Job 42:13–14). All three names relate to the daughters' beauty.

יְמִימָה – שֶׁהָיְתָה דּוֹמָה לְיוֹם, קְצִיעָה – שֶׁהָיָה רֵיחָהּ נוֹדֵף כִּקְצִיעָה, קֶרֶן הַפּוּךְ – אָמְרִי דְּבֵי רַבִּי שֵׁילָא: שֶׁדּוֹמָה לְקַרְנָא דְּקֶרֶשׁ. מְחַיְּיכוּ עֲלַהּ בְּמַעַרְבָא, קַרְנָא דְּקֶרֶשׁ לְקוּתָא הִיא! אֶלָּא אֲמַר רַב חִסְדָּא: כְּכוּרְכְּמָא דְּרִישְׁקָא בְּמִינַהּ, שֶׁנֶּאֱמַר: ״כִּי תִקְרְעִי בַפּוּךְ״.

Jemimah [*Yemima*]; in her beauty **she was similar to the day** [*yom*]. **Keziah; her scent wafted like** the cassia [*ketzia*][B] tree. **Keren-happuch; in the school of Rav Sheila they say: She was similar to the horn** [*keren*] **of a *keresh*,**[L] an animal whose horns are particularly beautiful. **They laughed at this in the West,** Eretz Yisrael, since it is considered **a blemish** when a person resembles **the horn of a *keresh*. Rather, Rav Ḥisda said:** She was **like garden saffron** [***kekurkema derishka***],[L] which is the best **of its kind.** *Keren* refers to a garden, and *pukh* means ornament, **as it is stated: "Though you enlarge** your eyes **with paint** [***pukh***], you beautify yourself in vain" (Jeremiah 4:30).

NOTES

They all entered through one gate – שֶׁנִּכְנְסוּ כּוּלָּן בְּשַׁעַר אֶחָד: The Maharsha explains that the expression "they had made an appointment [*vayyiva'adu*]" indicates that they were in the usual gathering spot, which is the city gate, the place where the city elders sit and meet, and Job was sitting there as well. The word "together [*yahdav*]" indicates that they arrived at the same spot simultaneously.

Propagation came to the world – רְבִיָּה בָּאָה לָעוֹלָם: Rashi explains that daughters speed the process of population growth, because they marry and have children at a younger age than do sons. Rabbeinu Gershom explains the term *reviyya* as related to development and upbringing; i.e., that daughters help raise children. The Maharsha explains that population growth depends exclusively upon the number of women who give birth; an increase in the number of men in the world does not to lead to more children being born.

LANGUAGE

Keresh – **קֶרֶשׁ:** Apparently from the Greek κεράς, *keras*, meaning a horn. The Greek word μονοκεράς, *monokeras*, means a creature with a single horn. The term can also refer to a wild ox, especially in the Septuagint. It is unclear which creature is referred to here. Some commentaries suggest *keresh* refers to the rhinoceros, some species of which have only a single horn. Alternatively, it might be comparing her to a mythical beast, the unicorn.

Indian rhinoceros, a single-horned species

Garden saffron [*kurkema derishka*] – כּוּרְכְּמָא דְּרִישְׁקָא: The word *kurkema*, meaning saffron, seems to have originated in Sanskrit as *kunkuma*, from where it entered into many languages, e.g., as *karkom* in Hebrew; κρόκος, *krokos*, in Greek; and crocus in Latin. In modern Hebrew and Arabic, this word refers to turmeric. The word *rishka* is apparently derived from the Middle Iranian term rēsak, a fiber. As such, the phrase *kurkema derishka* may refer to saffron fibers.

Saffron flower

BACKGROUND

Cassia – קְצִיעָה: Some identify the specific species of cassia mentioned in the Gemara here as the Chinese cinnamon. It is cultivated in various regions of Asia and is widely used as a spice around the world.

Chinese cinnamon

רַבִּי שִׁמְעוֹן בְּרַבִּי אִיתְיְלִידָא לֵיהּ בְּרַתָּא, הֲוָה קָא חָלַשׁ דַּעְתֵּיהּ, אֲמַר לֵיהּ אֲבוּהּ: רְבִיָּה בָּאָה לָעוֹלָם. אֲמַר לֵיהּ בַּר קַפָּרָא: תַּנְחוּמִין שֶׁל הֶבֶל נִיחַמְךָ אֲבוּךְ; [דְּתַנְיָא:] אִי אֶפְשָׁר לָעוֹלָם בְּלֹא זְכָרִים וּבְלֹא נְקֵבוֹת, אֶלָּא אַשְׁרֵי לְמִי שֶׁבָּנָיו זְכָרִים, אוֹי לוֹ לְמִי שֶׁבָּנָיו נְקֵבוֹת; אִי אֶפְשָׁר לָעוֹלָם בְּלֹא בַּסָּם וּבְלֹא בּוּרְסִי, אַשְׁרֵי מִי שֶׁאוּמָּנוּתוֹ בּוּסְמִי, אוֹי לְמִי שֶׁאוּמָּנוּתוֹ בּוּרְסִי.

It is reported that a **daughter was born to Rabbi Shimon, son of Rabbi** Yehuda HaNasi, and **he was upset** that he did not have a son. **His father said to him: Propagation has come to the world** through the birth of a daughter. **Bar Kappara said to** Rabbi Shimon: **Your father has consoled you with meaningless consolation, as it is taught** in a ***baraita*****: The world cannot endure without males and females,** as both are needed for the perpetuation of humanity. **But fortunate is he whose children are males and woe to him whose children are females.** Similarly, **the world cannot endure without** either **a spice dealer** whose wares are sweet-smelling, **or a tanner** [***bursi***],[L] who is engaged in a foul-smelling occupation. **Fortunate is he whose occupation is a spice seller,** and **woe to him whose occupation is a tanner.**

כְּתַנָּאֵי: ״וַה׳ בֵּרַךְ אֶת אַבְרָהָם בַּכֹּל״ – מַאי ״בַּכֹּל״? רַבִּי מֵאִיר אוֹמֵר: שֶׁלֹּא הָיְתָה לוֹ בַּת; רַבִּי יְהוּדָה אוֹמֵר: שֶׁהָיְתָה לוֹ בַּת; אֲחֵרִים אוֹמְרִים: בַּת הָיְתָה לוֹ לְאַבְרָהָם וּ״בַכֹּל״ שְׁמָהּ; רַבִּי אֶלְעָזָר הַמּוֹדָעִי אוֹמֵר: אִיצְטַגְנִינוּת הָיְתָה בְּלִבּוֹ שֶׁל אַבְרָהָם אָבִינוּ, שֶׁכָּל מַלְכֵי מִזְרָח וּמַעֲרָב מַשְׁכִּימִין לְפִתְחוֹ; רַבִּי שִׁמְעוֹן בֶּן יוֹחַי אוֹמֵר: אֶבֶן טוֹבָה הָיְתָה תְּלוּיָה בְּצַוָּארוֹ שֶׁל אַבְרָהָם אָבִינוּ, שֶׁכָּל חוֹלֶה הָרוֹאֶה אוֹתוֹ מִיָּד מִתְרַפֵּא, וּבְשָׁעָה שֶׁנִּפְטַר אַבְרָהָם אָבִינוּ מִן הָעוֹלָם – תְּלָאָהּ הַקָּדוֹשׁ בָּרוּךְ הוּא בְּגַלְגַּל חַמָּה. אֲמַר אַבַּיֵי, הַיְינוּ דְּאָמְרִי אֱינָשֵׁי: אִידְלֵי יוֹמָא אִידְלֵי קְצִירָא.

The Gemara comments that this disagreement is **parallel to** a dispute between ***tanna'im***: The Torah states: **"And the Lord blessed Abraham with everything** [***bakkol***]**"** (Genesis 24:1), and the Sages disagree about **what *bakkol*** means. **Rabbi Meir says:** The blessing is **that he did not have a daughter. Rabbi Yehuda says:** On the contrary, the blessing was **that he had a daughter. Others say: Abraham had a daughter and her name was Bakkol. Rabbi Elazar HaModa'i says: Abraham our forefather was so knowledgeable in astrology** [***itztagninut***][L] **that all the kings of the East and the West would come early to his door** due to his wisdom. This is the blessing of *bakkol*, that he possessed knowledge that everybody needed. **Rabbi Shimon ben Yoḥai says: A precious stone hung around the neck of Abraham our forefather; any sick person who looked at it would immediately be healed. When Abraham our forefather died, the Holy One, Blessed be He, hung** this stone **from the sphere of the sun,** which from that point on brought healing to the sick. **Abaye said: This** explains the adage **that people say: As the day progresses, sickness is lifted.**

דָּבָר אַחֵר: שֶׁלֹּא מָרַד עֵשָׂו בְּיָמָיו. דָּבָר אַחֵר: שֶׁעָשָׂה יִשְׁמָעֵאל תְּשׁוּבָה בְּיָמָיו. שֶׁלֹּא מָרַד עֵשָׂו בְּיָמָיו, מְנָלַן? דִּכְתִיב: ״וַיָּבֹא עֵשָׂו מִן הַשָּׂדֶה וְהוּא עָיֵף״, וְתָנָא: אוֹתוֹ הַיּוֹם נִפְטַר אַבְרָהָם אָבִינוּ, וְעָשָׂה יַעֲקֹב אָבִינוּ תַּבְשִׁיל שֶׁל עֲדָשִׁים לְנַחֵם אֶת יִצְחָק אָבִיו.

Alternatively, what is the blessing of *bakkol*? **That Esau did not rebel in** Abraham's **lifetime,** that is to say, as long as Abraham lived Esau did not sin. **Alternatively,** the blessing of *bakkol* is **that Ishmael repented in** Abraham's **lifetime.** The Gemara explains: **From where do we** derive that **Esau did not rebel in** Abraham's **lifetime? As it is written:** "And Jacob was cooking a stew **and Esau came in from the field and he was faint"** (Genesis 25:29), **and a *baraita* taught: On that day Abraham our forefather passed away, and Jacob our forefather prepared a lentil stew to comfort Isaac, his father,** as it was customary to serve mourners lentil stew.

[וּמַאי שְׁנָא שֶׁל עֲדָשִׁים]? אָמְרִי בְּמַעַרְבָא מִשְּׁמֵיהּ דְּרַבָּה בַּר מָרִי: מָה עֲדָשָׁה זוֹ אֵין לָהּ פֶּה, אַף אָבֵל אֵין לוֹ פֶּה. דָּבָר אַחֵר: מָה עֲדָשָׁה זוֹ מְגוּלְגֶּלֶת, אַף אֲבֵילוּת מְגַלְגֶּלֶת וּמַחֲזֶרֶת עַל בָּאֵי הָעוֹלָם. מַאי בֵּינַיְיהוּ? אִיכָּא בֵּינַיְיהוּ לְנַחוּמֵי בְּבֵיעֵי.

The Gemara explains: **And what is different about lentils** that they in particular are the fare customarily offered to mourners? **They say in the West,** Eretz Yisrael, **in the name of Rabba bar Mari: Just as this lentil has no mouth,** i.e., it does not have a crack like other legumes, **so too a mourner has no mouth,** that is, his anguish prevents him from speaking. **Alternatively, just as this lentil is** completely **round, so too mourning comes around to the inhabitants of the world.** The Gemara asks: **What is** the practical difference **between** the two explanations? The Gemara answers: **There is** a practical difference **between them** with regard to whether it is appropriate **to console** a mourner **with eggs,**[H] which have no opening but are not completely round.

אָמַר רַבִּי יוֹחָנָן, חָמֵשׁ עֲבֵירוֹת עָבַר אוֹתוֹ רָשָׁע בְּאוֹתוֹ הַיּוֹם: בָּא עַל נַעֲרָה מְאוֹרָסָה, וְהָרַג אֶת הַנֶּפֶשׁ, וְכָפַר בָּעִיקָּר, וְכָפַר בִּתְחִיַּית הַמֵּתִים, וְשָׁט אֶת הַבְּכוֹרָה.

Rabbi Yoḥanan says: That wicked Esau **committed five transgressions on that day** that Abraham died: **He engaged in sexual intercourse with a betrothed maiden, he killed a person, he denied the principle** of God's existence, **he denied resurrection of the dead, and he despised the birthright.**

LANGUAGE

Tanner [*bursi*] – בּוּרְסִי: From the Greek βυρσεύς, *burseus*, meaning a tanner.

Astrology [*itztagninut*] – אִיצְטַגְנִינוּת: The origin of this word is uncertain, but it clearly refers to the science of stars and constellations. It can refer to either astronomy or astrology.

HALAKHA

To console with eggs – לְנַחוּמֵי בְּבֵיעֵי: The first food served to a mourner following a funeral consists of eggs or lentil stew, which are indications of mourning. Other foods may subsequently be offered (*Shulḥan Arukh*, *Yoreh De'a* 378:9).

NOTES

Gevia and *asifa* – גְּוִיעָה וַאֲסִיפָה: The Maharal explains that the term *gevia* connotes deterioration; the body ceases to function and becomes completely useless. The term *asifa* connotes survival of the soul. Taken together, the two terms aptly reflect the death of a righteous person; his body ceases to exist, but his soul achieves its full reward.

LANGUAGE

Children [*dardekei*] – דַּרְדְּקֵי: From the Aramaic word meaning youth. It appears in the Aramaic translation of the book of Job, where the word *tze'irim* is rendered as *dardakin*. From there it was incorporated into Hebrew and Arabic.

בָּא עַל נַעֲרָה מְאוֹרָסָה – כְּתִיב הָכָא: ״וַיָּבֹא עֵשָׂו מִן הַשָּׂדֶה״, וּכְתִיב הָתָם: ״כִּי בַשָּׂדֶה מְצָאָהּ״. הָרַג אֶת הַנֶּפֶשׁ – כְּתִיב הָכָא: ״עָיֵף״, וּכְתִיב הָתָם: ״אוֹי נָא לִי כִּי עָיְפָה נַפְשִׁי לְהֹרְגִים״. וְכָפַר בָּעִיקָּר – כְּתִיב הָכָא: ״לָמָּה זֶּה לִי״, וּכְתִיב הָתָם: ״זֶה אֵלִי וְאַנְוֵהוּ״. וְכָפַר בִּתְחִיַּית הַמֵּתִים – דִּכְתִיב: ״הִנֵּה אָנֹכִי הוֹלֵךְ לָמוּת״. וְשָׁט אֶת הַבְּכוֹרָה – דִּכְתִיב: ״וַיִּבֶז עֵשָׂו אֶת הַבְּכוֹרָה״.

The Gemara cites proofs to support these charges. **He engaged in sexual intercourse with a betrothed maiden, as it is written here: "And Esau came in from the field"; and it is written there** with regard to rape of a betrothed maiden: **"For he found her in a field"** (Deuteronomy 22:27). **He killed a person, as it is written here:** "And he was **faint"; and it is written there: "Woe is me, for my soul faints before the slayers"** (Jeremiah 4:31). **And he denied the principle** of God's existence, as **it is written here: "What profit is this to me"** (Genesis 25:32); **and it is written there: "This is my God and I will glorify Him"** (Exodus 15:2). When he questioned the profit of "this," he was challenging the assertion that "this is my God." **And he denied resurrection of the dead, as it is written: "Behold, I am at the point of death"** (Genesis 25:32), indicating that he did not believe in resurrection after death. **And he despised the birthright, as it is written: "And Esau despised the birthright"** (Genesis 25:34).

וְשֶׁעָשָׂה יִשְׁמָעֵאל תְּשׁוּבָה בְּיָמָיו, מְנָלַן? כִּי הָא דְּרָבִינָא וְרַב חָמָא בַּר בּוּזִי הֲווּ יָתְבִי קַמֵּיהּ דְּרָבָא וְקָא מְנַמְנֵם רָבָא; אֲמַר לֵיהּ רָבִינָא לְרַב חָמָא בַּר בּוּזִי: וַדַּאי דְּאָמְרִיתוּ: כׇּל מִיתָה שֶׁיֵּשׁ בָּהּ גְּוִיעָה – זוֹ הִיא מִיתָתָן שֶׁל צַדִּיקִים? אֲמַר לֵיהּ: אִין. וְהָא דּוֹר הַמַּבּוּל! אֲמַר לֵיהּ: אֲנַן גְּוִיעָה וַאֲסִיפָה קָאָמְרִינַן.

And from where do we derive **that Ishmael repented in** Abraham's **lifetime? From** the incident involving **Ravina and Rav Ḥama bar Buzi,** who **were sitting before Rava, and Rava was dozing** while they were talking. **Ravina said to Rav Ḥama bar Buzi: Is it true that you say** that **any death with regard to which** the word *gevia*, expire, is mentioned **is the death of the righteous?** Rav Ḥama bar Buzi **said to him: Yes.** For example: "And Isaac expired [*vayyigva*], and died" (Genesis 35:29). Ravina objected: **But** with regard to **the generation of the flood** it states: "And all flesh expired [*vayyigva*]" (Genesis 7:21), and there they died for their wickedness. Rav Ḥama bar Buzi **said to him: We say** this only when both ***gevia* and *asifa***, gathering, are used; when these two terms are mentioned together they indicate the death of a righteous person.

וְהָא יִשְׁמָעֵאל דִּכְתִיב בֵּיהּ גְּוִיעָה וַאֲסִיפָה! אַדְּהָכִי אִיתְּעַר בְּהוּ רָבָא, אֲמַר לְהוּ: דַּרְדְּקֵי, הָכִי אָמַר רַבִּי יוֹחָנָן: יִשְׁמָעֵאל עָשָׂה תְּשׁוּבָה בְּחַיֵּי אָבִיו, שֶׁנֶּאֱמַר: ״וַיִּקְבְּרוּ אֹתוֹ יִצְחָק וְיִשְׁמָעֵאל בָּנָיו״.

Ravina asked: **But isn't there Ishmael, about whom *gevia* and *asifa*[N] are written,** as it is stated: "And these are the years of the life of Yishmael … and he expired and died [*vayyigva vayyamot*]; and was gathered to his people" (Genesis 25:17)? **Meanwhile Rava,** who had heard the discussion in his dozed state, fully **awoke** and **said to them: Children [*dardekei*],**[L] **this is what Rabbi Yoḥanan says: Ishmael repented in the lifetime of his father, as it is stated: "And Isaac and Ishmael, his sons, buried him"** (Genesis 25:9). The fact that Ishmael allowed Isaac to precede him demonstrates that he had repented and accepted his authority.

וְדִילְמָא דֶּרֶךְ חׇכְמָתָן קָא חָשֵׁיב לְהוּ! אֶלָּא מֵעַתָּה ״וַיִּקְבְּרוּ אוֹתוֹ עֵשָׂו וְיַעֲקֹב בָּנָיו״, מַאי טַעֲמָא לָא חָשֵׁיב לְהוּ דֶּרֶךְ חׇכְמָתָן? אֶלָּא מִדְּאַקְדְּמֵיהּ – אַדְבּוּרֵי אַדְבְּרֵיהּ, וּמִדְּאַדְבְּרֵיהּ – שְׁמַע מִינַּהּ: תְּשׁוּבָה עֲבַד בְּיָמָיו.

The Gemara asks: **But perhaps** the verse **listed them in the order of their wisdom;** that is to say, perhaps in fact Ishmael preceded Isaac but the Torah did not list them in that order. The Gemara answers: **But if that is so,** consider that the verse states: **"And Esau and Jacob, his sons, buried him"** (Genesis 35:29). **What is the reason** that the verse there **did not list them in the order of their wisdom? Rather, since** Ishmael **allowed** Isaac **to precede him,** it is clear that he **made** Isaac **his leader, and since he made him his leader, learn from it that he repented in** Abraham's **lifetime.**

תָּנוּ רַבָּנַן: שְׁלֹשָׁה הִטְעִימָן הַקָּדוֹשׁ בָּרוּךְ הוּא בָּעוֹלָם הַזֶּה

Incidental to the discussion of the verse "And God blessed Abraham with everything" (Genesis 24:1), the Gemara states that **the Sages taught:** There were **three** people **to whom the Holy One, Blessed be He, gave** already **in this world**

Perek **I**
Daf **17** Amud **a**

מֵעֵין הָעוֹלָם הַבָּא, אֵלּוּ הֵן: אַבְרָהָם, יִצְחָק וְיַעֲקֹב. אַבְרָהָם – דִּכְתִיב בֵּיהּ ״בַּכֹּל״; יִצְחָק – דִּכְתִיב בֵּיהּ ״מִכֹּל״; יַעֲקֹב – דִּכְתִיב בֵּיהּ ״כֹּל״.

a taste of the World-to-Come. They are: Abraham, Isaac, and Jacob. Abraham, as it is written with regard to him: "And the Lord blessed Abraham **with everything"** (Genesis 24:1). **Isaac, as it is written with regard to him:** "And I have eaten **from everything"** (Genesis 27:33). **Jacob, as it is written with regard to him:** "Because I have **everything"** (Genesis 33:11). This teaches that already in their lifetimes they merited everything, i.e., perfection.

שְׁלֹשָׁה לֹא שָׁלַט בָּהֶן יֵצֶר הָרָע, אֵלּוּ הֵן: אַבְרָהָם, יִצְחָק וְיַעֲקֹב, דִּכְתִיב בְּהוּ: ״בַּכֹּל״, ״מִכֹּל״, ״כֹּל״. וְיֵשׁ אוֹמְרִים: אַף דָּוִד, דִּכְתִיב: ״וְלִבִּי חָלַל בְּקִרְבִּי״. וְאִידָךְ? צַעֲרֵיהּ הוּא דְּקָא מַדְכַּר.

There were **three** people **over whom the evil inclination had no sway.**[N] **They are: Abraham, Isaac, and Jacob, as it is written** with regard **to them,** respectively: **"With everything," "from everything," "everything."** The completeness of their blessings means that they did not have to contend with their evil inclinations. **And some say** that **even David** was not subject to his evil inclination, **as it is written: "And my heart has died within me"** (Psalms 109:22), meaning that the evil inclination in his heart was nullified as if his heart had died. **And** how does **the other** authority, who does not include David in his list, explain this verse? **He is mentioning his travails.** David means to say that his heart died within him owing to all the suffering that he endured, but he says nothing about his evil inclination.

תָּנוּ רַבָּנַן: שִׁשָּׁה לֹא שָׁלַט בָּהֶן מַלְאַךְ הַמָּוֶת, וְאֵלּוּ הֵן: אַבְרָהָם, יִצְחָק וְיַעֲקֹב, מֹשֶׁה, אַהֲרֹן וּמִרְיָם. אַבְרָהָם, יִצְחָק וְיַעֲקֹב – דִּכְתִיב בְּהוּ: ״בַּכֹּל״, ״מִכֹּל״ ״כֹּל״; מֹשֶׁה, אַהֲרֹן וּמִרְיָם – דִּכְתִיב בְּהוּ: ״עַל פִּי ה׳״.

The Sages taught: There were **six** people **over whom the Angel of Death had no sway** in their demise, **and they are: Abraham, Isaac, and Jacob, Moses, Aaron, and Miriam. Abraham, Isaac, and Jacob, as it is written** with regard **to them,** respectively: **"With everything," "from everything," "everything"**; since they were blessed with everything they were certainly spared the anguish of the Angel of Death. **Moses, Aaron, and Miriam, as it is written** with regard **to them** that they died **"by the mouth of the Lord"** (Numbers 33:38; Deuteronomy 34:5), which indicates that they died with a kiss, and not at the hand of the Angel of Death.

וְהָא מִרְיָם לָא כְּתִיב בָּהּ ״עַל פִּי ה׳״! אָמַר רַבִּי אֶלְעָזָר: מִרְיָם נַמִּי בִּנְשִׁיקָה מֵתָה, דְּאָתְיָא ״שָׁם״ ״שָׁם״ מִמֹּשֶׁה, וּמִפְּנֵי מָה לֹא נֶאֱמַר בָּהּ ״עַל פִּי ה׳״? שֶׁגְּנַאי הַדָּבָר לוֹמַר.

The Gemara asks: **But with regard to Miriam it is not written: "By the mouth of the Lord." Rabbi Elazar says: Miriam also died with a kiss, as this is learned** through a verbal analogy between the word **"there"** mentioned in regard to Miriam: "And Miriam died there" (Numbers 20:1), and the word **"there"** mentioned in regard **to Moses:** "And Moses died there" (Deuteronomy 34:5). **And for what** reason **is "by the mouth of the Lord" not stated with** regard to **her? It is unseemly to mention** death by a kiss with regard to a woman.

תָּנוּ רַבָּנַן: שִׁבְעָה לֹא שָׁלַט בָּהֶן רִמָּה וְתוֹלֵעָה, וְאֵלּוּ הֵן: אַבְרָהָם, יִצְחָק וְיַעֲקֹב, מֹשֶׁה, אַהֲרֹן וּמִרְיָם, וּבִנְיָמִין בֶּן יַעֲקֹב. אַבְרָהָם, יִצְחָק וְיַעֲקֹב – דִּכְתִיב [בְּהוּ]: ״בַּכֹּל״, ״מִכֹּל״, ״כֹּל״; מֹשֶׁה, אַהֲרֹן וּמִרְיָם – דִּכְתִיב [בְּהוּ]: ״עַל פִּי ה׳״, בִּנְיָמִין בֶּן יַעֲקֹב – דִּכְתִיב: ״וּלְבִנְיָמִין אָמַר יְדִיד ה׳ יִשְׁכֹּן לָבֶטַח עָלָיו״. וְיֵשׁ אוֹמְרִים: אַף דָּוִד, דִּכְתִיב: ״אַף בְּשָׂרִי יִשְׁכֹּן לָבֶטַח״. וְאִידָךְ? הַהוּא רַחֲמֵי הוּא דְּקָא בָּעֵי.

The Sages taught: There were **seven** people **over whom the worm and the maggot had no sway, and they are: Abraham, Isaac, and Jacob, Moses, Aaron and Miriam, and Benjamin, son of Jacob. Abraham, Isaac, and Jacob, as it is written with regard to them,** respectively: **"With everything," "from everything," "everything." Moses, Aaron, and Miriam, as it is written with regard to them: "By the mouth of the Lord"; Benjamin, son of Jacob, as it is written: "And to Benjamin he said: The beloved of the Lord, he shall dwell in safety by Him"** (Deuteronomy 33:12). Even in death, he rests securely, unbothered by worms. **And some say** that **even David** is included, **as it is written: "My flesh also dwells secure"** (Psalms 16:9). The Gemara asks: **And** how does **the other** authority, who does not include David, explain this? The Gemara answers: **He is asking for mercy,** that his flesh should dwell secure and not be subject to worms and maggots, but his request was denied.

תָּנוּ רַבָּנַן: אַרְבָּעָה מֵתוּ בְּעֶטְיוֹ שֶׁל נָחָשׁ, וְאֵלּוּ הֵן: בִּנְיָמִין בֶּן יַעֲקֹב, וְעַמְרָם אֲבִי מֹשֶׁה, וְיִשַׁי אֲבִי דָוִד, וְכִלְאָב בֶּן דָּוִד. וְכוּלְּהוּ גְּמָרָא, לְבַר מִיִּשַׁי אֲבִי דָוִד דִּמְפָרֵשׁ בֵּיהּ [קְרָא], דִּכְתִיב: ״וְאֶת עֲמָשָׂא שָׂם אַבְשָׁלֹם תַּחַת יוֹאָב עַל הַצָּבָא וַעֲמָשָׂא בֶן אִישׁ וּשְׁמוֹ יִתְרָא הַיִּשְׂרְאֵלִי אֲשֶׁר בָּא אֶל אֲבִיגַיִל בַּת נָחָשׁ אֲחוֹת צְרוּיָה אֵם יוֹאָב״, וְכִי בַּת נָחָשׁ הִיא? וַהֲלֹא בַּת יִשַׁי הִיא, דִּכְתִיב: ״וְאַחְיוֹתֵיהֶם צְרוּיָה וַאֲבִיגָיִל״! אֶלָּא, בַּת מִי שֶׁמֵּת בְּעֶטְיוֹ שֶׁל נָחָשׁ.

The Sages taught in a *baraita*: There were **four** people **who died** only **because of the counsel of the** primordial **snake,** in the wake of which all of humanity became mortal, and not on account of any personal sin. **And they are: Benjamin, son of Jacob; Amram, father of Moses; Yishai, father of David; and Chileab, son of David. And all of these are known through tradition except for Yishai, father of David, with regard to** whom **it is written explicitly: "And Absalom placed Amasa over the army instead of Joab, and Amasa was the son of a man whose name was Ithra the Israelite, who engaged in intercourse with Abigail, daughter of Nahash, the sister of Zeruiah, mother of Joab"** (II Samuel 17:25). **But was** Abigail **the daughter of Nahash? Was she not the daughter of Yishai, as it is written: "And their sisters were Zeruiah and Abigail"** (I Chronicles 2:16)? **Rather,** she was called "daughter of Nahash" to indicate that **she was the daughter of one who died** only **because of the counsel of the snake.**

הדרן עלך השותפין

NOTES

Over whom the evil inclination had no sway – לֹא שָׁלַט בָּהֶן יֵצֶר הָרָע: This does not mean that they were born without any desires at all, but rather that after years of proving they were capable of controlling their passions, God granted them a gift, that they would no longer need to combat their inclinations (*Tosafot*).

Summary of **Perek I**

This chapter established that with regard to walls that form partitions in a courtyard, regional custom dictates the materials out of which such walls must be constructed, as well as the thickness of those walls. When two neighbors agree to build a wall between their respective properties, each party contributes half of the space upon which the wall is to be constructed and pays half of the construction costs. If the wall later collapses, the space and the materials are divided equally between them. If one of the neighbors builds the wall on his own, he builds it wholly on his property and at his expense, and he fashions a border mark to indicate that he alone built the wall.

The Gemara also concluded that invasion of privacy resulting from exposure to the gaze of one's neighbor is considered damage, and therefore in a place where there is such an invasion of privacy one party can compel the other to build a barrier, which must be at least four cubits high.

One party can compel the other to build a partition in three other instances: Where there is an invasion of privacy in one's courtyard or in a garden where it is customary to erect a barrier; when a neighbor who initially opposed building a wall demonstrates that he is pleased that it was built, e.g., by completing a fence erected by his neighbor; or when the initially reluctant neighbor derives benefit from the barrier, such as by building another wall close to it in order to cover both walls with a roof.

Just as neighbors can compel each other to build a wall, so too, the residents of a courtyard or a city can compel each other to build whatever is necessary for their protection. Mention is therefore made in this chapter of various ordinances with regard to communal obligations that are cast upon all the residents of a city, such as charity and municipal improvements. The Gemara determined that responsibility for funding whatever brings benefit to all of the city's residents is imposed upon all of them, including minor orphans, whereas funds for that which is merely for protection are not collected from Torah scholars.

The Sages established that every property is subject to the *halakha* of division, provided that it is large enough that each of its co-owners will receive a portion that can still be used and the division will not interfere with the original use of the property. In such a case each party can compel the other to either buy his portion or sell him his.

The above applies to a division of property demanded by one of the co-owners. If both parties agree to divide their jointly owned property, every property can be divided, with the exception of books of the Bible contained in a single volume, which owing to the honor that must be shown them may not be divided.

Incidental to the discussion of these issues, the chapter addressed some of the *halakhot* governing charity, taxes, and the authorship of the books included in the Bible.

In addition to the halakhic discussions in this chapter, there were also two large sections of *aggada*, which were not directly connected to the subject matter of the chapter but were discussed incidentally to matters arising in the course of the halakhic discussion. The first dealt primarily with the mitzvot of charity, while the second discussed a Torah scroll in particular and the Bible in general. The latter section also explored the biblical character of Job, along with his era and character.

Introduction to **Perek II**

This chapter discusses those occasions in which one performs an activity on his own property and thereby causes damage to his neighbor.

Damage to one's neighbor comes in various forms and results from different types of actions. The problems discussed in the Gemara concern the limit of private activities: To what extent is an individual entitled to act within his own property, and when is the damage he inflicts considered so severe that he is barred from certain activities, notwithstanding the fact that they are performed in his private domain?

Some actions cause immediate damage to the property of another, in which case they can be compared to an act of direct harm, or, in the language of the Gemara, the shooting of one's arrows. In other situations the damage is not immediate, and its effects on the neighbor's property are apparent only at a later stage.

Likewise, there are certain types of damage that are tangible, while others are intangible, e.g., the ability to peer into another's house. Some types of damage cause only a slight loss or a sense of discomfort; others are unbearable, might lead to extensive financial loss, or might even entail physical danger.

An analysis of these issues raises several fundamental questions. Is it correct to say that in general, there is a principle that it is the responsibility of the one who has the potential to cause damage to distance himself from another's property or person in order to ensure that he avoids causing damage, or does an individual generally have the right to do as he pleases on his own property, and it is the neighbor's responsibility to distance himself if he is likely to sustain damage? This leads to a further issue: If one distances his activities from his neighbor so as not to cause damage, is he entitled to compensation, or is he simply fulfilling an obligation for which he does not receive payment? Yet another dilemma concerns a case where one took precautions to avoid causing damage to another, and nevertheless his activity damaged his neighbor's property. Do his efforts serve to exempt him from responsibility? Or must he still pay for the damage he caused, in which case the instructions of the Sages can be considered mere good advice that does not have legal ramifications in the event of damage?

Just as one's actions can damage the property of another individual, they can also damage public property. This chapter discusses the right of the public to prevent an individual from harming their collective interest, and the differences between one who causes damage to another individual and one who causes damage to the public.

The discussion and resolution of these matters and are the main topics of this chapter.

מתני׳ לֹא יַחְפּוֹר אָדָם בּוֹר סָמוּךְ לְבוֹרוֹ שֶׁל חֲבֵירוֹ, וְלֹא שִׁיחַ וְלֹא מְעָרָה, וְלֹא אַמַּת הַמַּיִם, וְלֹא נִבְרֶכֶת כּוֹבְסִין – אֶלָּא אִם כֵּן הִרְחִיק מִכּוֹתֶל חֲבֵירוֹ שְׁלֹשָׁה טְפָחִים וְסָד בַּסִּיד.

MISHNA **A person may not dig**[N] **a pit**[H] **close to the pit of another,** in order to avoid damaging the latter's pit. **And** similarly, one **may not** dig **a ditch, nor a cave,** i.e., a covered pit, **nor a water channel, nor a launderer's pond,**[B] which is a pit used for washing clothes, **unless he distanced** all of these **three handbreadths from the wall of another and he plasters lime** on the place where there is water.

וּמַרְחִיקִים אֶת הַגֶּפֶת וְאֶת הַזֶּבֶל, וְאֶת הַמֶּלַח, וְאֶת הַסִּיד, וְאֶת הַסְּלָעִים, מִכּוֹתְלוֹ שֶׁל חֲבֵירוֹ שְׁלֹשָׁה טְפָחִים אוֹ סָד בַּסִּיד. מַרְחִיקִין אֶת הַזְּרָעִים וְאֶת הַמַּחֲרֵישָׁה וְאֶת מֵי רַגְלַיִם מִן הַכּוֹתֶל שְׁלֹשָׁה טְפָחִים.

And one must distance the solid residue of produce that has been pressed free of its oil,[HB] e.g., the refuse of olives from which oil has been squeezed, **and** animal **manure, and salt, and lime, and rocks**[N] **three handbreadths from the wall of another,** as all these items produce heat and can damage the wall. **Or, alternatively, he** may **plaster** the wall **with lime** to prevent damage. **One must** likewise **distance seeds,**[H] i.e., one may not plant seeds, **and** one may not operate **the plow, and** one must eliminate **urine, three handbreadths from the wall** of another.

וּמַרְחִיקִין אֶת הָרֵיחַיִם שְׁלֹשָׁה מִן הַשֶּׁכֶב, שֶׁהֵן אַרְבָּעָה מִן הָרֶכֶב; וְאֶת הַתַּנּוּר – שְׁלֹשָׁה מִן הַכָּלְיָא, שֶׁהֵן אַרְבָּעָה מִן הַשָּׂפָה.

The mishna continues: **And one must distance a mill**[H] from a neighbor's wall by **three** handbreadths **from the lower stone** of the mill, **which is four** handbreadths **from the** smaller **upper stone** of the mill.[B] **And** there must be a distance of **three** handbreadths **from the** protruding **base** [***hakalya***][NL] **of an oven**[H] until the wall, **which is four** handbreadths **from the** narrow **upper rim** [***hassafa***] of the oven.

NOTES

May not dig – לֹא יַחְפּוֹר: The commentaries disagree with regard to the reason for this restriction. While the Gemara (19a) states that the concern is about the moisture that seeps from the various pits, on 17b the Gemara indicates that the construction of the pit itself weakens the ground. Some commentaries write that the digging weakens the walls of nearby structures (Rashba). *Tosafot* claim that the main damage to the neighbors' property is from the moisture, while the digging merely causes the first stage of the damage. Yet others contend that both reasons are correct, as each is a sufficient reason to mandate keeping a distance (Ritva; Ramah). Alternatively, some say that there is a difference in this regard between a ditch and a cave on the one hand, in which the construction is the problem, and a water channel or a launderer's pond on the other, where the issue is the inevitable moisture (Ramban).

Rocks – סְלָעִים: Rashi maintains that this refers to flint; consequently, these too produce heat similar to that produced by olive refuse. Alternatively, rocks tend to crumble, which damages the ground (Rabbeinu Ḥananel). Yet others claim that people will walk on rocks, which causes them to shift and thereby damage a nearby wall (Ramah).

Base [*kalya*] – כָּלְיָא: The commentaries disagree with regard to the meaning of the term *kalya*, translated here as base, and that of the term *safa*, translated here as upper rim. According to Rashi, the *kalya* is the base of the oven, which is designed to prevent the ground from cooling off the oven. The *safa* is its upper narrow part, which has the same circumference as the oven. Others say that the *kalya* is the belly of the oven, which is shaped like a pitcher and protrudes in the middle, while the *safa* is the upper, narrower part of the oven (Rabbeinu Ḥananel; Ri Migash; Ramah). Alternatively, the *kalya* is the cement covering, which is one handbreadth thick and serves to maintain the oven's heat. The *safa* is the body of the oven itself (see Ri Migash).

HALAKHA

May not dig a pit – לֹא יַחְפּוֹר...בּוֹר: One may not dig a pit, or pass a water channel, or prepare a launderer's pit near the wall of his neighbor's pit unless he distances it three handbreadths from that pit and plasters it with lime on the side facing the neighbor's property. Some claim that this is the *halakha* even where the presence of water is not constant, e.g., in the case of a pipe that is opened occasionally. One may not dig a pit very close to the wall of another even if it is not intended that the pit will hold water, and if one does so, he must prevent workers from using it (Rambam *Sefer Kinyan*, *Hilkhot Shekhenim* 9:1; *Shulḥan Arukh*, *Ḥoshen Mishpat* 155:10, and in the comment of Rema and *Beur HaGra* there).

And one must distance the solid residue of produce pressed of its oil – וּמַרְחִיקִים אֶת הַגֶּפֶת: Olive refuse, manure, salt, lime, rocks, and wet sand must all be kept at a distance of three handbreadths from the wall of a neighbor (Rambam *Sefer Kinyan*, *Hilkhot Shekhenim* 9:2; *Shulḥan Arukh*, *Ḥoshen Mishpat* 155:4).

One must distance seeds – מַרְחִיקִין אֶת הַזְּרָעִים: The planting of seeds, the use of a plow, and the placement of a pit for urine all must be done at a distance of three handbreadths from the wall of a neighbor, even if the wall is built of stone (*Sma*). Some add that a pit for urine must be plastered with lime (Rema). In the absence of such a pit, one may not urinate within three handbreadths of a neighbor's wall (Rambam *Sefer Kinyan*, *Hilkhot Shekhenim* 9:2; *Shulḥan Arukh*, *Ḥoshen Mishpat* 155:5).

And one must distance a mill – וּמַרְחִיקִין אֶת הָרֵיחַיִם: The bottom stone of a mill must be kept at a distance of three handbreadths from a neighbor's wall, or is four handbreadths from the upper stone. Some write that this *halakha* applies specifically to small hand mills, whereas more distance must be maintained in the case of large, animal-driven mills (Rambam *Sefer Kinyan*, *Hilkhot Shekhenim* 9:3; *Shulḥan Arukh*, *Ḥoshen Mishpat* 155:7, and in the comment of Rema).

Of an oven – וְאֶת הַתַּנּוּר: The bottom of an oven must be kept at a distance of three handbreadths from a neighbor's wall, i.e., the upper rim should be four handbreadths from the wall. The measurement of three handbreadths is from the inner rim of the oven (Rambam *Sefer Kinyan*, *Hilkhot Shekhenim* 9:4; *Shulḥan Arukh*, *Ḥoshen Mishpat* 155:8).

LANGUAGE

Base [*kalya*] – כָּלְיָא: From the Greek κοιλία, *koilia*, meaning space or belly. From here it came to mean the widest part of the inside of an oven. The oven of the time was essentially a large earthenware jug, which had a protruding section. The *safa*, upper rim, refers to the opening or mouth of the oven. The lower, wider section of the angled structure is called the *kalya*. The numbers in the image indicate the distance in handbreadths from the oven to the wall.

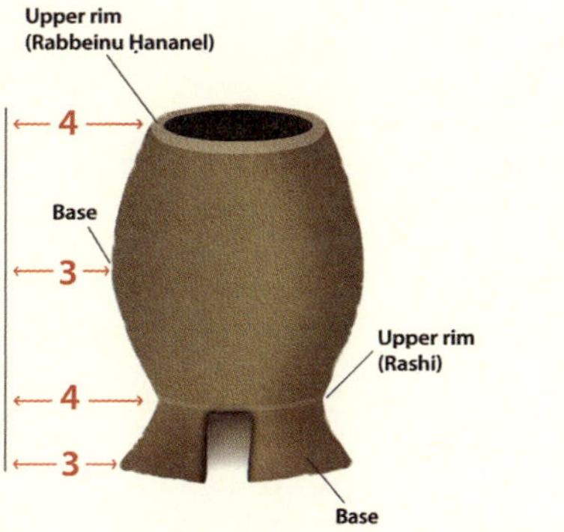

Position of base and upper rim of an oven according to two opinions

BACKGROUND

Launderer's pond – נִבְרֶכֶת כּוֹבְסִין:

Ancient laundry vat in Pompeii

The solid residue of produce that has been pressed free of its oil [*gefet*] – גֶּפֶת: *Gefet* refers to the refuse that remains once the oil has been pressed out of olives or sesame seeds. This refuse was usually fed to animals. The substance and moistness of the refuse can cause the refuse to ferment, which can generate heat in the absence of ventilation. At this stage it is even possible for the refuse to catch fire.

Millstones – רֶכֶב וְשֶׁכֶב:

Millstones

גמ׳ פָּתַח בְּבוֹר וּמְסַיֵּים בְּכוֹתֶל; לִיתְנֵי: אֶלָּא אִם כֵּן הִרְחִיק מִבּוֹרוֹ שֶׁל חֲבֵירוֹ שְׁלֹשָׁה טְפָחִים!

GEMARA The *tanna* of the mishna **opens by** speaking of **a pit:** A person may not dig a pit close to the pit of another, **and** yet **he ends with** a reference to **a wall:** Unless he distances it from the wall of another. **Let** the *tanna* **teach: Unless he distanced** his pit or ditch **three handbreadths from the pit of another,** just as he begins his statement by referring to a pit. Why does the mishna suddenly mention a wall here?

אֲמַר אַבַּיֵי, וְאִיתֵּימָא רַב יְהוּדָה: מִכּוֹתֶל בּוֹרוֹ שָׁנִינוּ.

Abaye said, and some say it was Rav Yehuda who said: **We learned** that the mishna means: **From the wall of his pit.**[B] In other words, one should read the mishna as follows: Unless he distanced his pit or ditch three handbreadths from the wall of another's pit. The neighbor also built his pit close to the border between the two properties, and the mishna is teaching that the one digging a pit must distance it three handbreadths from the wall of the pit of the other.

וְלִיתְנֵי: אֶלָּא אִם כֵּן הִרְחִיק מִבּוֹרוֹ שֶׁל חֲבֵירוֹ שְׁלֹשָׁה טְפָחִים! הָא קָא מַשְׁמַע לָן, דְּכוֹתֶל בּוֹר שְׁלֹשָׁה טְפָחִים, נָפְקָא מִינָּהּ – לְמִקָּח וּמִמְכָּר; כִּדְתַנְיָא: הָאוֹמֵר לַחֲבֵירוֹ ״בּוֹר וְכוֹתְלֶיהָ אֲנִי מוֹכֵר לְךָ״ – צָרִיךְ שֶׁיְּהֵא הַכּוֹתֶל שְׁלֹשָׁה טְפָחִים.

The Gemara challenges: **But** even so, **let it teach: Unless he distanced** his excavations **three handbreadths from the pit of another,** and one would understand that the term pit is referring to the wall of the other's pit. The Gemara responds: By using the phrase: From the wall of another, **this teaches us** incidentally **that the wall of a pit** must be at least **three handbreadths** thick, as the wall of the other's pit occupied the full three handbreadths between the cavity of his pit and the property of his neighbor. The practical **difference** of this observation is **with regard to buying and selling, as it is taught** in a *baraita*: With regard to **one who says to another: I am selling you a pit and its walls,**[H] **the wall** of the pit **must be** at least **three handbreadths** thick.

אִיתְּמַר: הַבָּא לִסְמוֹךְ בְּצַד הַמֶּצֶר – אַבַּיֵי אָמַר: סוֹמֵךְ, וְרָבָא אָמַר: אֵינוֹ סוֹמֵךְ. בְּשָׂדֶה הָעֲשׂוּיָה לְבוֹרוֹת – דִּבְרֵי הַכֹּל אֵינוֹ סוֹמֵךְ, כִּי פְּלִיגִי – בְּשָׂדֶה שֶׁאֵינָהּ עֲשׂוּיָה לְבוֹרוֹת;

§ **It was stated:** With regard to **one who comes to** dig any of these excavations or **place** any of the items listed in the mishna **close to the boundary**[H] of his field, where his neighbor currently has no pit, **Abaye says: He may** dig or **place** them **close**[N] to the boundary; **and Rava says: He may not** dig or **place** them **close** to the boundary. The Gemara explains: **All agree that he may not** dig or **place** them **close** to **a field** of his neighbor if **that field is designated for** digging **pits,**[N] as he will thereby restrict his neighbor from using his field in the manner it is expected to be used. **When they disagree** it is **with regard to a field that is not designated for** digging **pits.**

אַבַּיֵי אָמַר: סוֹמֵךְ, דְּהָא אֵינָהּ עֲשׂוּיָה לְבוֹרוֹת; רָבָא אָמַר: אֵינוֹ סוֹמֵךְ, דְּאָמַר לֵיהּ: כִּי הֵיכִי דְּאַתְּ אִימְּלַכְתְּ וְחָפְרַתְּ, אֲנָא נַמִי מִמְּלַכְנָא וְחָפַרְנָא.

The Gemara elaborates: **Abaye says: He may** dig these excavations or **place** these items **close** to the boundary, **as** the neighbor's field **is not designated for pits,** so he is not causing any damage by doing so. **Rava says: He may not** dig these excavations or **place** these items **close** to the boundary, **as** the neighbor can **say to him: Just as you changed your mind and dug** a pit, **I too** might **change my mind and dig** a pit, and I will no longer be able to dig near my border if you dig your pit close to the boundary.

אִיכָּא דְּאָמְרִי: בְּשָׂדֶה שֶׁאֵינָהּ עֲשׂוּיָה לְבוֹרוֹת – דִּבְרֵי הַכֹּל סוֹמֵךְ, כִּי פְּלִיגִי – בְּשָׂדֶה הָעֲשׂוּיָה לְבוֹרוֹת; אַבַּיֵי אָמַר: סוֹמֵךְ; אֲפִילּוּ לְרַבָּנַן דְּאָמְרִי: מַרְחִיקִין אֶת הָאִילָן מִן הַבּוֹר עֶשְׂרִים וְחָמֵשׁ אַמָּה, הָתָם הוּא דִּבְעִידָּנָא דְּקָא נָטַע אִיתָא לְבוֹר, אֲבָל הָכָא בְּעִידָּנָא דְּקָא חָפַר לֵיתָא לְבוֹר.

There are those **who say** a different version of this discussion: **All agree** that **one may** dig these excavations or **place** these items **close** to the boundary of **a field that is not designated for** digging **pits. When they disagree** it is **with regard to a field that is designated for** digging **pits. Abaye says: One may** dig these excavations or **place** these items **close** to the boundary; and this is the *halakha* **even according to** the opinion of **the Rabbis, who say** in the mishna (25b): **One must distance a tree twenty-five cubits from a cistern,** lest the roots of the tree grow and damage a neighbor's cistern in his field. The difference is that **there it** is prohibited, **as when he plants** the tree **there is** already **a cistern. But here,** at the time **when he digs** his cistern, **there is** as yet **no cistern** in his neighbor's field.

BACKGROUND

Wall of a pit – כּוֹתֶל בּוֹר: The discussion of the wall of a pit is referring to one digging in the ground, usually in rock. The wall of the pit is the thickness of the ground or the rock that is necessary to restrain the water. Occasionally a stone wall is built inside the pit when the soil is soft. In that situation, the expression: The wall of the pit, is referring to this additional stone, which must be three handbreadths thick.

HALAKHA

I am selling you a pit and its walls – בּוֹר וְכוֹתְלֶיהָ אֲנִי מוֹכֵר לְךָ: If one sells a pit and its walls, the walls must be at least three handbreadths thick (Rambam *Sefer Kinyan*, *Hilkhot Mekhira* 21:12; *Shulḥan Arukh*, *Ḥoshen Mishpat* 217:5).

One who comes to place the items close to the boundary – הַבָּא לִסְמוֹךְ בְּצַד הַמֶּצֶר: If one wishes to dig a pit next to the boundary of his neighbor's field, he may do so adjacent to the border, provided that the other field is not designated for digging pits. If the neighbor changes his mind and wants to dig a pit as well, this neighbor will have to distance it six handbreadths from the first pit. If one's neighbor's field was designated for digging pits, he must distance his pit three handbreadths from the boundary of his field. If the neighbor decides to dig a pit, he must also distance his pit three handbreadths from the boundary. The *halakha* is in accordance with the opinion of Rava, based on the second version of his dispute with Abaye. The Rema, citing the Ramah, adds that in addition to the distancing, the wall of the pit must be plastered with lime, while the Rosh disagrees with this ruling (Rambam *Sefer Kinyan*, *Hilkhot Shekhenim* 9:10; *Shulḥan Arukh*, *Ḥoshen Mishpat* 155:18).

NOTES

Abaye says he may place them close – אַבַּיֵי אָמַר סוֹמֵךְ: Some early commentaries claim that according to this opinion, if one digs his pit near the boundary, which is permitted, then when his neighbor subsequently digs his own pit he must distance it six handbreadths from the first pit, to ensure sufficient distance is kept between the two pits (Rambam; Ramban). Others contend that the neighbor is required to distance it only three handbreadths (Rabbeinu Yona).

Designated for pits – הָעֲשׂוּיָה לְבוֹרוֹת: The early commentaries write that this refers to an irrigated field, in which a pit is required for watering it.

וְרָבָא אָמַר: אֵינוֹ סוֹמֵךְ; וַאֲפִילּוּ לְרַבִּי יוֹסֵי דְּאָמַר: זֶה חוֹפֵר בְּתוֹךְ שֶׁלּוֹ וְזֶה נוֹטֵעַ בְּתוֹךְ שֶׁלּוֹ – הָנֵי מִילֵּי הָתָם, דִּבְעִידָּנָא דְּקָא נָטַע לֵיתְנְהוּ לְשָׁרָשָׁיו דְּמַזְּקִי לָהּ לַבּוֹר, אֲבָל הָכָא – אָמַר לֵיהּ: כָּל מָרָא וּמָרָא דְּקָא מָחְיַית קָא מְרַפֵּית לָהּ לְאַרְעַאי.

And Rava says: One **may not** dig these excavations or **place** these items **close** to the boundary; and this is the *halakha* **even according to** the opinion of **Rabbi Yosei, who says** in that same mishna: **This one may dig in his field and that one may plant in his** field, i.e., one need not distance his tree for fear of damaging his neighbor's field through expanding roots. The reason that Rava maintains that his ruling is correct even according to the opinion of Rabbi Yosei is that **this matter** applies only **there, as when he plants** the tree, **its roots, which** might **damage the cistern, are not** yet present. Consequently, when he plants he does not cause any damage. **But here,** the neighbor can **say to him: Each and every strike of yours with the hoe loosens my earth,** and therefore you are already causing damage as you dig your cistern.

תְּנַן: לֹא יַחְפּוֹר אָדָם בּוֹר סָמוּךְ לְבוֹרוֹ שֶׁל חֲבֵירוֹ; טַעֲמָא דְּאִיכָּא בּוֹר, הָא לֵיכָּא בּוֹר – סוֹמֵךְ. בִּשְׁלָמָא לְהַךְ לִישָּׁנָא דְּאָמְרַתְּ: בְּשָׂדֶה שֶׁאֵינָהּ עֲשׂוּיָה לְבוֹרוֹת דִּבְרֵי הַכֹּל סוֹמֵךְ, מַתְנִיתִין – בְּשָׂדֶה שֶׁאֵינָהּ עֲשׂוּיָה לְבוֹרוֹת,

The Gemara suggests a proof: **We learned** in the mishna that **a person may not dig a pit close to the pit of another,** unless he does so at a distance of three handbreadths from his neighbor's wall. The Gemara analyzes this statement: Apparently, the **reason** he may not dig close to the boundary of his neighbor's field **is that there is a pit** there, from which it may be inferred that if **there is no pit he** may dig his pit **close** to his neighbor's wall. **Granted, according to that** second **version** of the dispute, **in which you said: All agree** that **one may** dig these excavations or **place** these items **close** to the boundary of **a field that is not designated for** digging **pits,** one can explain that **the mishna** is referring **to a field that is not designated for** digging **pits.**

אֶלָּא לְהַךְ לִישָּׁנָא דְּאָמְרַתְּ: בְּשָׂדֶה שֶׁאֵינָהּ עֲשׂוּיָה לְבוֹרוֹת פְּלִיגִי, בִּשְׁלָמָא לְאַבָּיֵי נִיחָא, אֶלָּא לְרָבָא קַשְׁיָא!

But according **to that** first **version** of the dispute, **in which you said** that **they disagree with regard to a field that is not designated for** digging **pits,** there is a difficulty. **Granted,** this **works out well according to** the opinion of **Abaye,** who says that one may dig one's pit near the boundary when the neighbor has no pit. **But according to** the opinion of **Rava,** who maintains that it is prohibited to dig a pit near the boundary under any circumstances, the ruling of this mishna is **difficult.**

אָמַר לָךְ רָבָא: הָא אִיתְּמַר עֲלַהּ, אָמַר אַבָּיֵי וְאִיתֵּימָא רַב יְהוּדָה: מִכּוֹתֶל בּוֹרוֹ שָׁנִינוּ.

The Gemara explains: **Rava** could have **said to you: Wasn't it stated with regard to that** mishna that **Abaye says, and some say it was Rav Yehuda** who says: **We learned** that the mishna means: **From the wall of his pit?** This indicates that the neighbor must distance the edge of his pit from the boundary by the thickness of his wall, which is three handbreadths. Therefore, even according to the ruling of the mishna, one may not dig his pit directly adjacent to the boundary.

אִיכָּא דְּאָמְרִי: וְאִיתְּמַר עֲלַהּ, אָמַר אַבָּיֵי וְאִיתֵּימָא רַב יְהוּדָה: מִכּוֹתֶל בּוֹרוֹ שָׁנִינוּ; בִּשְׁלָמָא לְהַךְ לִישָּׁנָא דְּאָמְרַתְּ: בְּשָׂדֶה הָעֲשׂוּיָה לְבוֹרוֹת דִּבְרֵי הַכֹּל אֵינוֹ סוֹמֵךְ, מַתְנִיתִין – בְּשָׂדֶה הָעֲשׂוּיָה לְבוֹרוֹת,

There are those **who say** this discussion in the form of a challenge to the opinion of Abaye. The mishna teaches that one must distance his pit from that of his neighbor, **and it was stated with regard to that** ruling that **Abaye says, and some say it was Rav Yehuda** who says: **We learned** that it means: **From the wall of his pit.** In other words, the edge of the neighbor's pit must be three handbreadths away from the boundary. **Granted, according to that** first **version** of the dispute, **in which you said: All agree that he may not** dig or **place** them **close** to **a field** of his neighbor if **that** field **is designated for** digging **pits,** one can explain that **the mishna** is referring **to a field that is designated for** digging **pits.**

אֶלָּא לְהַךְ לִישָּׁנָא דְּאָמְרַתְּ: בְּשָׂדֶה הָעֲשׂוּיָה לְבוֹרוֹת פְּלִיגִי, בִּשְׁלָמָא לְרָבָא נִיחָא, אֶלָּא לְאַבָּיֵי קַשְׁיָא!

But according to that second **version** of the dispute, **in which you said** that **they disagree with regard to a field that is designated for** digging **pits,** there is a difficulty. **Granted,** this **works out well according to** the opinion of **Rava,** who says that it is prohibited to dig a pit near the boundary in this case. **But according to** the opinion of **Abaye,** the ruling of this mishna is **difficult,** as if the mishna is referring to the wall of the neighbor's pit, this indicates that the first pit was dug close to the boundary.

אָמַר לָךְ אַבָּיֵי: מַתְנִיתִין – שֶׁבָּאוּ לַחְפּוֹר בְּבַת אַחַת.

The Gemara explains: **Abaye** could have **said to you: The mishna** is referring to the specific case **where** both neighbors **came to** dig their **pits at the same time.** Consequently, they must both distance their pits from one another. If there is no pit as yet next to the boundary, and the neighbor is not digging at that point, one may dig his pit alongside the boundary.

BACKGROUND

Rock that crumbles in one's hands – סֶלַע הַבָּא בְּיָדַיִם: This is referring to soil that is so soft that it can be hewn by hand. It might mean sand-like rock that can be crumbled manually, or clumps of stones held together with a layer of earth that do not require any type of tool to break.

He who asked it, etc. – דְּקָאָרֵי לָהּ וכו׳: This expression is used in the Gemara when the answer to a question is self-evident. In this case, the Gemara will ask: And he who asked this question, why did he ask it, when its resolution is so obvious? Some commentaries claim that this and similar questions are not part of the original talmudic text, but were added by the *savora'im* when they redacted the Talmud (*Halikhot Olam*).

NOTES

Rock that crumbles in one's hands is different – בָּא בְּיָדַיִם שָׁאנֵי: This is Rashi's version of the text. Other early commentaries cite the version of the *ge'onim*, which reads: Abaye can say to you that here too it is referring to when they come to dig at the same time, and it is necessary to state this with regard to soil that crumbles in one's hands (see Ramban).

תָּא שְׁמַע: סֶלַע הַבָּא בְּיָדַיִם – זֶה חוֹפֵר בּוֹרוֹ מִכָּאן, וְזֶה חוֹפֵר בּוֹרוֹ מִכָּאן, זֶה מַרְחִיק שְׁלֹשָׁה טְפָחִים וְסָד בְּסִיד, וְזֶה מַרְחִיק שְׁלֹשָׁה טְפָחִים וְסָד בְּסִיד! בָּא בְּיָדַיִם שָׁאנֵי.

The Gemara suggests: **Come** and **hear** a proof from a *baraita*: In the case of **rock that** is so soft that it **crumbles in** one's **hands**,[B] and no tool is needed, **this one may dig his pit from here, and that one may dig his pit from there. This one distances** his pit **three handbreadths and plasters with lime, and that one distances** his pit **three handbreadths and plasters with lime.** This indicates that the first one who digs a pit must distance his pit even when the second one does not yet have a pit. The Gemara rejects this proof: Rock that **crumbles in** one's **hands is different.**[N] In this case, one must maintain a distance from the boundary due to the softness of the ground.

וּדְקָאָרֵי לָהּ מַאי קָאָרֵי לָהּ? בָּא בְּיָדַיִם אִיצְטְרִיכָא לֵיהּ; סָלְקָא דַּעְתָּךְ אָמִינָא: כֵּיוָן דְּבָא בְּיָדַיִם לִיבָעֵי נַמִי רַוְוחָא טְפֵי, קָא מַשְׁמַע לָן.

The Gemara is puzzled by this exchange: **And he who asked it,**[B] **why did he ask it?** The *baraita* is explicitly referring to rock that crumbles in one's hands, so this is clearly a unique case. The Gemara answers that the Sage who asked the question assumed that the *halakha* of the *baraita* includes all types of soil, and he thought that **it was necessary for** the *tanna* to mention the specific example of rock that **crumbles in** one's **hands,** as it could **enter your mind to say that since** this substance **crumbles in** one's **hands he is required** to keep his pit at an even **greater distance.** To counter this, the *baraita* **teaches us** that a distance of three handbreadths is sufficient.

תָּא שְׁמַע: מַרְחִיקִין אֶת הַגֶּפֶת, וְאֶת הַזֶּבֶל, וְאֶת

The Gemara suggests: **Come** and **hear** a proof from the mishna: **One must distance the solid residue** of produce that has been pressed free of its oil, **and** animal **manure, and**

Perek **II**
Daf **18** Amud **a**

LANGUAGE

Dampness [*metunta*] – מִתּוּנְתָּא: Some commentaries claim that this term is from the Greek νότιος, *notios*, meaning moisture, and it took on an Aramaic form.

הַמֶּלַח, וְאֶת הַסִּיד, וְאֶת הַסְּלָעִים מִכּוֹתְלוֹ שֶׁל חֲבֵירוֹ שְׁלֹשָׁה טְפָחִים אוֹ סָד בְּסִיד; טַעְמָא דְּאִיכָּא כּוֹתֶל, הָא לֵיכָּא כּוֹתֶל – סוֹמֵךְ!

salt, and lime, and rocks three handbreadths from the wall of another, or he can **plaster** the wall **with lime.** The Gemara analyzes this statement: The **reason** for this ruling **is that there is a wall** there belonging to his neighbor, from which it may be inferred that if **there is no wall** there, **one may place** these substances **close** to the boundary of his neighbor's courtyard. This presents a difficulty for the opinion of Rava according to the first version of the dispute, which states that one may not place these substances close to a boundary even in the case of a field that is not designated for pits.

לָא, כִּי לֵיכָּא כּוֹתֶל נַמִי לָא סָמֵיךְ. וְאֶלָּא מַאי קָא מַשְׁמַע לָן? הָא קָא מַשְׁמַע לָן, דְּהָנֵי קָשׁוּ לְכוֹתֶל.

The Gemara rejects this proof: **No,** even **if there is no wall one may also not place** these substances **close** to the boundary.[N] The Gemara asks: **Rather, what does** mentioning a wall here **teach us?** The Gemara answers: **This teaches us that** all **these** substances **are damaging to a wall.**

תָּא שְׁמַע: מַרְחִיקִים אֶת הַזְּרָעִים, וְאֶת הַמַּחֲרֵישָׁה, וְאֶת מֵי רַגְלַיִם מִן הַכּוֹתֶל שְׁלֹשָׁה טְפָחִים; טַעְמָא דְּאִיכָּא כּוֹתֶל, הָא לֵיכָּא כּוֹתֶל – סָמֵיךְ! לָא, כִּי לֵיכָּא כּוֹתֶל נַמִי לָא סָמֵיךְ. וְאֶלָּא מַאי קָא מַשְׁמַע לָן? הָא קָא מַשְׁמַע לָן, דְּמִתּוּנְתָּא קָשָׁה לְכוֹתֶל.

The Gemara suggests: **Come** and **hear** another proof from the mishna: **One must distance seeds, and the plow, and urine three handbreadths from the wall** of another. The Gemara analyzes this ruling: The **reason** for this ruling **is that there is a wall,** from which it may be inferred that if **there is no wall, one may place** these substances **close** to the boundary of the field. The Gemara rejects this proof as well: **No,** even **if there is no wall, one may also not place** these substances **close** by the boundary. The Gemara asks: **But rather, what does** this **teach us?** The Gemara answers: **This teaches us that dampness** [*dimtunta*][LN] **is damaging to a wall.**

NOTES

If there is no wall one may also not place them close to the boundary – כִּי לֵיכָּא כּוֹתֶל נַמִי לָא סָמֵיךְ: Even according to the opinion of Rava, why should it be prohibited to place these substances close to the boundary? After all, he causes no damage, and he can always remove the materials at a later stage. One answer is that since, if the neighbor did have a wall, these substances would cause damage and he would be required to remove the materials, the neighbor can prevent him from placing those substances close to his property even now by saying he wants to avoid potential future damage (Rashba). Alternatively, even now his actions cause damage to the neighbor's land. Furthermore, it will be difficult to remove at a later date materials he has already placed there (Ritva).

Dampness [*metunta*] – מִתּוּנְתָּא: Rashi explains that this means dampness or moisture. The later commentaries raise several problems with this interpretation, and suggest that *metunta* refers to rust that loosens the soil (*Torat Ḥayyim*).

תָּא שְׁמַע: וְאֶת הָרֵיחַיִם – שְׁלֹשָׁה מִן הַשֶּׁכֶב שֶׁהֵן אַרְבָּעָה מִן הָרֶכֶב; טַעְמָא דְּאִיכָּא כּוֹתֶל, הָא לֵיכָּא כּוֹתֶל – סָמֵיךְ! לָא, כִּי לֵיכָּא כּוֹתֶל נַמִי לָא סָמֵיךְ. וְאֶלָּא מַאי קָא מַשְׁמַע לָן? הָא קָא מַשְׁמַע לָן, דְּטִירְיָיא קָשָׁה לְכוֹתֶל.

The Gemara suggests: **Come** and **hear** another proof from the mishna: **And** one must distance **a mill** from a wall by **three** handbreadths **from the lower stone** of the mill, **which is four** handbreadths **from the upper stone.** The Gemara analyzes this statement: The **reason** for this ruling **is that there is a wall,** from which it may be inferred that if **there is no wall, one may place** a mill **close** by the boundary. The Gemara rejects this proof: **No,** even **if there is no wall, one may also not place** his mill **close** by the boundary. The Gemara asks: **But rather, what does** this **teach us?** The Gemara answers: **This teaches us that vibrations are damaging to a wall.**

תָּא שְׁמַע: וְאֶת הַתַּנּוּר – שְׁלֹשָׁה מִן הַכַּלְיָא שֶׁהֵן אַרְבָּעָה מִן הַשָּׂפָה; טַעְמָא דְּאִיכָּא כּוֹתֶל, הָא לֵיכָּא כּוֹתֶל – סָמֵיךְ! לָא, כִּי לֵיכָּא כּוֹתֶל נַמִי לָא סָמֵיךְ. אֶלָּא מַאי קָא מַשְׁמַע לָן? הָא קָא מַשְׁמַע לָן, דְּהַבְלָא קָשֶׁה לְכוֹתֶל.

The Gemara suggests: **Come** and **hear** another proof from the mishna: **And the oven** must be distanced **three** handbreadths **from the base, which is four** handbreadths **from the upper rim** of the oven. The Gemara analyzes this statement: The **reason** for this ruling **is that there is a wall,** from which it may be inferred that if **there is no wall, one may place** an oven **close** by the boundary. The Gemara rejects this proof as well: **No,** even **if there is no wall, one may also not place** his oven **close** by the boundary. The Gemara asks: **Rather, what does** this **teach us?** The Gemara answers: **This teaches us that heat is damaging to a wall.**

תָּא שְׁמַע: לֹא יִפְתַּח אָדָם חֲנוּת שֶׁל נַחְתּוֹמִין וְשֶׁל צַבָּעִין תַּחַת אוֹצָרוֹ שֶׁל חֲבֵירוֹ, וְלֹא רֶפֶת בָּקָר; טַעְמָא דְּאִיכָּא אוֹצָר, הָא לֵיכָּא אוֹצָר – עָבֵיד!

The Gemara suggests: **Come** and **hear** a proof from the mishna (20b): **A person may not open a bakery**[N] **or a dye shop beneath** the wine **storeroom of another, nor may one** open **a cattle barn** there. The Gemara analyzes this mishna: The **reason** for this ruling **is that there is a storeroom** already in place, from which it may be inferred that **if there is no storeroom one may do** so. If this is the case, then with regard to a pit as well, one may dig next to a boundary if there is as yet no pit.

דִּירָה שָׁאנֵי. דַּיְקָא נַמִי, דְּתָנֵי עֲלָהּ: אִם הָיְתָה רֶפֶת בָּקָר קוֹדֶמֶת לָאוֹצָר – מוּתָּר.

The Gemara answers: The case of **a residence is different,**[N] as in general one can use his domicile in any manner of his choosing unless he directly causes damage to another or his property. The Gemara adds: The language of the mishna **is also precise, as** an explicit *baraita* **is taught with regard to that** mishna: **If** the construction of **the cattle barn preceded the storeroom,** it **is permitted.** Nothing can be inferred from the case of the *baraita* with regard to the *halakha* of the mishna, which does not concern living quarters.

תָּא שְׁמַע: לֹא יִטַּע אָדָם אִילָן סָמוּךְ לְשָׂדֶה אֶלָּא אִם כֵּן הִרְחִיק מִמֶּנּוּ אַרְבַּע אַמּוֹת, וְתָנֵי עֲלָהּ: אַרְבַּע אַמּוֹת שֶׁאָמְרוּ, כְּדֵי עֲבוֹדַת הַכֶּרֶם;

The Gemara suggests: **Come** and **hear** a proof from a mishna (26a): **A person may not plant a tree close to** another's **field unless he distances it four cubits from** his neighbor. **And it is taught with regard to this** mishna: The **four cubits of** which the Sages **spoke** are **to** enable **the work of the vineyard,** i.e., a small space next to the trees is necessary to enable animals to plow between them.

טַעְמָא דְּמִשּׁוּם כְּדֵי עֲבוֹדַת הַכֶּרֶם, הָא לָאו מִשּׁוּם כְּדֵי עֲבוֹדַת הַכֶּרֶם – סָמֵיךְ, וְאַף עַל גַּב דְּאִיכָּא שָׁרָשִׁין דְּקָא מַזְּקִי! הָכָא בְּמַאי עָסְקִינַן – דְּמַפְסִיק צוּנְמָא.

The Gemara analyzes this ruling: The **reason** this distance is required **is due to the work of the vineyard,** from which it may be inferred that if **not** for the problem **due to the work of the vineyard,** it would be permitted for one to plant his tree **close** to the boundary, **and** apparently, this is the *halakha* **even though there are roots** of the tree **that damage** his neighbor's field. The Gemara answers: **With what are we dealing here?** We are dealing with a case **where** a hard **rock** [***tzunema***][L] **interrupts** between the two fields, preventing the roots from passing through to the other field.

דַּיְקָא נַמִי, דְּקָתָנֵי: הָיָה גָּדֵר בֵּינְתַיִם – זֶה סוֹמֵךְ לַגָּדֵר מִכָּאן, וְזֶה סוֹמֵךְ לַגָּדֵר מִכָּאן.

The Gemara continues: The language of the mishna **is also precise** with regard to this point, **as it teaches** further on: If there **was a fence between them, this one places,** i.e., plants a tree, **close** to **the fence from here, and that one places,** i.e., plants a tree, **close** to **the fence from here.** If the mishna were referring to a case where the roots could travel across, how could it be permitted for both neighbors to plant their trees alongside each other? Consequently, it must be referring to a situation where a rock separates between the two fields below, and therefore the neighbors may plant their trees near the fence.

NOTES

Bakery – **חֲנוּת שֶׁל נַחְתּוֹמִין**: According to Rashi, the reason for this prohibition is that a large amount of smoke is found in these places. Alternatively, a bakery and a dye shop produce a great deal of heat (*Tosafot*).

A residence is different – **דִּירָה שָׁאנֵי**: There are two main interpretations of this statement. Some commentaries explain that if one has a barn or a store in his permanent residence, no one can prevent him from doing what he wants to do there, provided that the construction does not directly damage his neighbor's property. By contrast, the use of a field lacks permanence (Rashi; Rabbeinu Gershom Meor HaGola; Ramban). Others explain that when the second story is being used as a residence, the individual below need not take into account the possibility that his upstairs neighbor will convert his space into a storeroom. This differs from the digging of a pit in a field (Ri Migash; Ramah). Some commentaries reject this explanation, claiming that such uses by a neighbor are disruptive whether the area above is a storeroom or a residence (Ramban, citing the Jerusalem Talmud).

LANGUAGE

Rock [*tzunema*] – **צוּנְמָא**: This root, which appears in the Bible (Genesis 41:22), means hard or dry. *Tzunema* therefore means a hard rock or hard soil.

אִי הָכִי, אֵימָא סֵיפָא: הָיוּ שָׁרָשָׁיו יוֹצְאִין בְּתוֹךְ שֶׁל חֲבֵירוֹ – מַעֲמִיק לָהֶן שְׁלֹשָׁה טְפָחִים כְּדֵי שֶׁלֹּא יְעַכֵּב הַמַּחֲרֵישָׁה; וְאִי דְּמַפְסִיק צוּנְמָא, מַאי בָּעוּ הָתָם? הָכִי קָאָמַר: וְאִי לָאו צוּנְמָא, וְהָיוּ שָׁרָשָׁיו יוֹצְאִין לְתוֹךְ שֶׁל חֲבֵירוֹ – מַעֲמִיק שְׁלֹשָׁה טְפָחִים כְּדֵי שֶׁלֹּא יְעַכֵּב הַמַּחֲרֵישָׁה.

The Gemara responds: **If so, say the last clause** of that mishna: **If the roots** of the tree **extended into** the field **of another,** the neighbor **may cut them off to a depth of three handbreadths, so that they do not impede the plow.** The Gemara asks: **But if a rock interrupts** between the two fields and forms a barrier, **what are** these roots **doing there,** i.e., how did they get there? The Gemara answers: **This** is what the *tanna* of the mishna **is saying: And if** there is **no rock, and the roots** of the tree **extended into** the field **of another,** the neighbor **may cut them off to a depth of three handbreadths so that they do not impede the plow.**

תָּא שְׁמַע: מַרְחִיקִין אֶת הָאִילָן מִן הַבּוֹר עֶשְׂרִים וְחָמֵשׁ אַמָּה; טַעֲמָא דְּאִיכָּא בּוֹר, הָא לֵיכָּא בּוֹר – סָמֵיךְ! לָא, כִּי לֵיכָּא בּוֹר נַמִי לָא סָמֵיךְ, וְהָא קָמַשְׁמַע לָן, דְּעַד עֶשְׂרִים וְחָמֵשׁ אַמָּה אָזְלִי שָׁרָשִׁים וּמַזְּקִי לַבּוֹר.

The Gemara suggests: **Come** and **hear** a proof from a mishna (25b): **One must distance a tree twenty-five cubits from a cistern.** The Gemara analyzes this *halakha*: The **reason** for this ruling **is that there is a cistern,** from which it may be inferred that **if there is no cistern, one may place,** i.e., plant, his tree **close** to the neighbor's field. The Gemara answers: **No,** even **when there is no cistern one may also not place** it **close** to the neighbor's field. **And** by mentioning a cistern, the *tanna* of the mishna **teaches us this: That the roots** of a tree **extend and damage the cistern up to** a distance of **twenty-five cubits** away.

אִי הָכִי, אֵימָא סֵיפָא: וְאִם אִילָן קָדַם – לֹא יָקוֹץ; וְאִי דְּלָא סָמֵיךְ, הֵיכִי מַשְׁכַּחַתְּ לָהּ? כִּדְאָמַר רַב פָּפָּא: בְּלוֹקֵחַ, הָכִי נַמִי בְּלוֹקֵחַ.

The Gemara asks: **If so, say the last clause** of that mishna: **And if the tree preceded** the cistern, **one is not** required to **cut down** the tree. **But if** one **may not place** the tree **close** to the boundary even if there is no cistern, **how can you find** a case where the tree preceded the cistern? Why would its owner not be required to cut it down? The Gemara answers: This is **as Rav Pappa says** with regard to a similar matter, that it is referring **to a buyer** who purchases part of a field. **So too** here, it is referring **to a buyer.** In other words, a field contained a cistern and tree alongside each other, and the owner sold the part of the field containing the cistern.

תָּא שְׁמַע: מַרְחִיקִין אֶת הַמִּשְׁרָה מִן הַיָּרָק, וְאֶת הַכְּרֵישִׁין מִן הַבְּצָלִין, וְאֶת הַחַרְדָּל מִן הַדְּבוֹרִים; טַעֲמָא דְּאִיכָּא יָרָק, הָא לֵיכָּא יָרָק – סָמֵיךְ! לָא, כִּי לֵיכָּא יָרָק נַמִי לָא סָמֵיךְ, וְהָא קָא מַשְׁמַע לָן, דְּהָנֵי קָשׁוּ אַהֲדָדֵי.

The Gemara cites yet another source: **Come** and **hear** a proof from a mishna (25a): **One must distance the water in which flax is steeped from vegetables** growing in a neighbor's field, **and** one must distance **leeks from onions**[B] growing in a neighbor's field, **and** one must likewise distance **mustard from bees** that are in a neighbor's field. The Gemara analyzes this statement: The **reason is that there are vegetables** present, from which it may be inferred that **if there are no vegetables, one may place** the water **close** to the neighbor's field. The Gemara rejects this opinion: **No,** even **if there are no vegetables one may also not place** the water **close** to the neighbor's field. **And** the *tanna* **teaches us that these** items mentioned in that mishna **are harmful to each other.**

אִי הָכִי, אֵימָא סֵיפָא: רַבִּי יוֹסֵי מַתִּיר בַּחַרְדָּל, מִפְּנֵי שֶׁיָּכוֹל לוֹמַר לוֹ: עַד שֶׁאַתָּה אוֹמֵר לִי הַרְחֵק חַרְדָּלְךָ מִן דְּבוֹרַאי, הַרְחֵק דְּבוֹרֶךָ מִן חַרְדָּלַאי, שֶׁבָּאוֹת וְאוֹכְלוֹת לִגְלוּגֵי חַרְדָּלַאי;

The Gemara responds: **If so, say the last clause** of that mishna: **Rabbi Yosei renders it permitted** to plant near the neighbor's bees **in the** case of **mustard.** As explained in a *baraita*, this is **because he can say to** the owner of the bees: **Just as you say to me: Keep your mustard away from my bees,** I can say to you: **Keep your bees away from my mustard, as they come and eat my mustard plants.**[B] In other words, you are damaging my property as well.

BACKGROUND

Leeks from onions – הַכְּרֵישִׁין מִן הַבְּצָלִין: The leek, *Allium porrum,* known as *kereisha* or *karti* in the Talmud, is related to the onion, *Allium cepa.* Not only are these two plants similar to each other in appearance, but they belong to the same botanical genus. For this reason there is a concern that if they are planted next to each other, insects might cross-pollinate them, which will cause them to produce sterile seeds. If this occurs, any onions and leeks grown for their seeds will be rendered useless.

Mustard plants – לִגְלוּגֵי חַרְדָּל:

Mustard plants

וְאִי דְּלָא סָמֵיךְ, הֵיכִי מַשְׁכַּחַתְּ לַהּ? אָמַר רַב פַּפָּא: בְּלוֹקֵחַ.

And if one **may not place** an item that might cause damage **close** to his neighbor's boundary,[N] **how can you find** a case where each neighbor is damaging the property of the other? **Rav Pappa says:** This is referring **to a buyer** who purchased part of his neighbor's field, and it contains a substance or items that might cause damage, e.g., the water in which flax is steeped or mustard. In the other section of the field the neighbor retained an item or substance that could be damaged. In this manner, it is possible for the item that causes damage to be found near the boundary of the neighbor without one having violated the ruling of the mishna.

אִי בְּלוֹקֵחַ, מַאי טַעְמָא דְּרַבָּנַן? וְעוֹד, מַאי טַעְמָא דְּרַבִּי יוֹסֵי? אֲפִילּוּ מִשְׁרָה וְיַרְקָא נַמִי!

The Gemara asks: **If** this is referring **to a buyer, what is the reason of the Rabbis,** who say that the neighbor can demand that the buyer distance that which causes damage? After all, he has not acted improperly. **And furthermore, what is the reason of Rabbi Yosei** for disagreeing only in the case of the mustard and the bees? **Even** the case of **water in which flax is steeped and vegetables** is **also** subject to the same reasoning: Why should he have to distance his water, considering that he did not act improperly?

אֲמַר רָבִינָא, קָא סָבְרִי רַבָּנַן: עַל הַמַּזִּיק לְהַרְחִיק אֶת עַצְמוֹ.

Ravina said[N] that the explanation is as follows: **The Rabbis hold** that the responsibility falls **on the one who causes damage to distance himself.** The one who has the potential to cause damage must act to prevent the damage from occurring. This is the *halakha* even if his initial placement was done in accordance with *halakha*, as in the case where one bought part of a field.

מִכְּלָל דְּרַבִּי יוֹסֵי סָבַר: עַל הַנִּיזָּק לְהַרְחִיק אֶת עַצְמוֹ; אִי עַל הַנִּיזָּק – אֲפִילּוּ מִשְׁרָה וְיַרְקָא נַמִי!

The Gemara asks: Does this prove **by inference** that **Rabbi Yosei,** who disagrees with the ruling of the Rabbis, **holds that** that the responsibility falls **on the** one whose property **was damaged to distance himself;** i.e., to avoid being damaged? But **if** the responsibility to distance oneself falls **on the** one whose property **was damaged,**[H] **even** in the case of **water in which flax is steeped and vegetables** the owner should **also** not have to distance himself. Why does Rabbi Yosei distinguish between that situation and the case of bees and mustard?

אֶלָּא, לְעוֹלָם רַבִּי יוֹסֵי נַמִי עַל הַמַּזִּיק סְבִירָא לֵיהּ, וְהָכִי קָאָמַר לְהוּ רַבִּי יוֹסֵי לְרַבָּנַן: תֵּינַח מִשְׁרָה וְיַרְקָא, דְּהָנֵי מַזְּקִי הָנֵי וְהָנֵי לָא מַזְּקִי הָנֵי, אֶלָּא חַרְדָּל וּדְבוֹרִים – תַּרְוַיְיהוּ מַזְּקִי אַהֲדָדֵי!

Rather, actually Rabbi Yosei also holds that the responsibility to distance oneself falls **on the one who causes damage,** even if he did not act improperly. **And this** is what **Rabbi Yosei is saying to the Rabbis:** Your explanation **works out well** with regard to **water in which flax is steeped and vegetables,** where the one who causes damage must distance himself, as **these damage those, but those do not damage these,** i.e., the water in which flax is steeped damages the vegetables, but the vegetables do not damage the water. **But** in the case of **mustard and bees,**[B] **they both damage one another.** In light of this factor, and since the initial planting of the mustard was permitted, the owner of the bees should distance them from the mustard.

וְרַבָּנַן? דְּבוֹרִים לְחַרְדָּל לָא מַזְּקִי לֵיהּ, אִי בְּבִינְתָּא – לָא מַשְׁכְּחָא לֵיהּ, אִי בְּטַרְפָּא – הָדַר פָּארֵי.

And as for **the Rabbis,** how do they respond to this claim? They maintain that **bees do not damage mustard.** Their reasoning is that **if** it is referring **to a seed,** the bees will **not find**[N] it. **If** it is referring **to a leaf, it will grow back,** and therefore no damage has been caused.

HALAKHA

The responsibility to distance oneself falls on the one whose property was damaged – עַל הַנִּיזָּק לְהַרְחִיק אֶת עַצְמוֹ: If one sets up water for steeping flax next to a field where a neighbor has vegetables, and it is likely that the water will leak and damage those plants, he must distance the water three handbreadths to avoid causing damage. The same applies if one plants leeks alongside a field of onions. He is not required to now move them more than three handbreadths to avoid potential damage at a later stage. The *halakha* is in accordance with the opinion of Rabbi Yosei. The *Tur*, citing the Rosh, rules that a distance of three handbreadths must be kept only when steeping flax, whereas it is not necessary to keep a distance of three handbreadths between leeks and onions, nor between mustard and bees (Rambam *Sefer Kinyan*, *Hilkhot Shekhenim* 10:5; *Shulḥan Arukh*, *Ḥoshen Mishpat* 155:31 and *Sma* there).

NOTES

And if one may not place it close to his neighbor's boundary – וְאִי דְּלָא סָמֵיךְ: If one accepts Rava's opinion that in all circumstances one must distance from the boundary of his neighbor's field the item that causes the damage, in accordance with the first version of the dispute, then the bees were originally at the appropriate distance from the neighbor's field. Accordingly, the Gemara is asking: How, then, does this discussion between the neighbors arise? (Rashi).

Ravina said – אֲמַר רָבִינָא: There are two versions of the text here, which differ by a single word and yet lead to two very different explanations. The issue is whether the mention of Ravina is preceded by the word: Rather. This is significant, as in the terminology of the Gemara the word: Rather, is a technical term that indicates a rejection of the previous opinion.

The first version, which reads simply: Ravina said, is accepted by Rashi and the *ge'onim*. According to this reading, Ravina's statement is a continuation and explanation of Rav Pappa's comment. If this is the case, Ravina agrees that according to Rava it is prohibited to place any substance or item that will cause damage alongside a neighbor's boundary, at least not when there is a chance that the neighbor will be damaged, in accordance with the second version of Rava's statement. His reason is in accordance with the opinion of the Rabbis, who say that one who causes damage must distance himself in all circumstances, even if his actions are permitted. This reasoning is maintained through the end of the discussion. Even Rabbi Yosei, who holds that the responsibility to distance oneself falls on the one whose property was damaged, concedes that if both parties cause damage to one another, neither of them need distance himself (see Rabbeinu Tam, *Sefer HaYashar*).

The other version of the text reads: Rather, Ravina said. This indicates that Ravina does not accept the explanations that have been suggested to explain the various *mishnayot* cited earlier in accordance with the opinion of Rava. Instead, Ravina maintains that Rava disagrees with Abaye only in the case of digging a pit, as the act of digging itself causes damage (Ri Migash; Rabbeinu Ḥananel). According to this explanation, the Rabbis hold that the one who causes damage must distance himself only if the damage is already present.

If it is referring to a seed the bees will not find – אִי בְּבִינְתָּא לָא מַשְׁכְּחָא: The commentaries write that the mustard seeds are very small, which is why bees are unable to find them (Rabbeinu Gershom Meor HaGola). Others explain that this refers to mustard seeds that have been planted in the ground and are therefore hidden from the bees (Ri Migash).

BACKGROUND

Mustard and bees – חַרְדָּל וּדְבוֹרִים: The mustard plant is a honey plant found throughout Eretz Yisrael. Its colorful flowers are attractive to bees. Honeybees can bite off parts of the mustard plant's leaves and flowers. Although bees might bite off parts of the mustard plant, they cause minimal damage to the leaves relative to the damage caused by birds and insects. As for the seeds, they are inaccessible to bees, as stated here.

Bee on a mustard plant

וסבר רבי יוסי על המזיק להרחיק את עצמו? והתנן, רבי יוסי אומר: אף על פי שהבור קודמת לאילן – לא יקוץ, שזה חופר בתוך שלו, וזה נוטע בתוך שלו! אלא, לעולם רבי יוסי על הניזק סבירא ליה, ולדבריהם דרבנן קאמר להו.

The Gemara asks: **And does Rabbi Yosei hold** that the responsibility falls **on the one who causes damage to distance himself? But didn't we learn** in a mishna (25b) that **Rabbi Yosei says: Even though the cistern preceded the tree,** the owner need **not cut down** the tree, **as this one digs a cistern in his** property, **and that one plants** the tree **in his** property? **Rather, actually Rabbi Yosei holds** that the responsibility falls **on the** one whose property **was damaged to distance himself. And** Rabbi Yosei **spoke to the Rabbis in accordance with their statement.**

לדידי על הניזק להרחיק את עצמו, ואפילו משרה וירקא לא בעי רחוקי. אלא לדידכו, דאמריתו על המזיק, תינח משרה וירקא, דהני מזקי הני והני לא מזקי הני, אלא חרדל ודבורים – תרווייהו מזקי אהדדי!

The Gemara elaborates: Rabbi Yosei was saying to the Rabbis: **In my** opinion, the responsibility falls **on the** one whose property **was damaged to distance himself, and** therefore **even** in the case of **water in which flax is steeped and vegetables,** the owner of the water **need not distance** himself. **But according to your** opinion, that the responsibility falls **on the one who causes damage** to distance himself, this **works out well** with regard to **water in which flax is steeped and vegetables, as these damage those and those do not damage these. But mustard and bees both damage one another,** and if the mustard owner acted properly, the owner of the bees should be required to move his bees.

ורבנן? דבורים לחרדל לא מזקי ליה, אי בבינתא

The Gemara continues: **And** how do **the Rabbis** respond to this claim? They hold that **bees do not damage mustard: If** this is referring **to a seed,**

Perek **II**
Daf **19** Amud **a**

לא משכחת ליה, אי בטרפא – הדר פארי.

the bees will **not find it; if** it is referring **to a leaf, it will grow back.**

"ולא נברכת הכובסין" וכו׳. אמר רב נחמן אמר רבה בר אבוה: לא שנו אלא מן המחמצן, אבל מן הנדיין – ארבע אמות. תניא נמי הכי: נברכת הכובסין – ארבע אמות; והא אנן תנן: שלשה טפחים! אלא לאו שמע מינה כדרב נחמן.

§ The mishna teaches: **Nor** may one set up **a launderer's pond** near his neighbor's wall unless he distances it three handbreadths from the wall. **Rav Naḥman says** that **Rabba bar Avuh says: They taught this only with regard to a soaking pond,**[H] in which soiled clothes are left to soak for several days. **But** in the case **of a washing pond** [*hanadyan*],[NBLH] where clothes are actively cleaned, **four cubits** are required. **That** opinion **is also taught** in a *baraita*: **A launderer's pond** must be kept **four cubits** from one's neighbor's wall. **But didn't we learn** in the mishna that one must keep a distance of only **three handbreadths? Rather,** must one **not conclude from** the *baraita* that the statement **of Rav Naḥman** is correct?

ואיכא דרמי להו מירמי; תנן: נברכת הכובסין – שלשה טפחים, והתניא: ארבע אמות! אמר רב נחמן אמר רבה בר אבוה, לא קשיא: כאן מן המחמצן, כאן מן הנדיין. רב חייא בריה דרב אויא מתני לה בהדיא: אלא אם כן הרחיק משפת מחמצן ולכותל שלשה טפחים.

And some raise this as **a contradiction,** and present the mishna and *baraita* as apparently conflicting sources. **We learned** in the mishna that **a launderer's pond** must be kept **three handbreadths** from his neighbor's property. **But isn't it taught** in a *baraita* that **four cubits** are required? **Rav Naḥman says** that **Rabba bar Avuh says:** This is **not difficult. Here,** the mishna is referring to **a soaking pond,** which requires three handbreadths; **there,** the *baraita* is referring to **a washing pond,** in which case four cubits are necessary. **Rav Ḥiyya, son of Rav Avya, teaches** the mishna **explicitly** as reading: **Unless he distanced three handbreadths from the rim of the soaking pond and the wall.**

NOTES

But in the case of a washing pond [*nadyan*] – אבל מן הנדיין: The commentaries explain that the act of laundering by rubbing and shaking clothes was performed in a separate pond. Water would likely spray out of this pond and cause damage beyond a distance of three handbreadths. The term *nadyan* is related to the term *niydei*, meaning movement or sprinkling. Some maintain that the *nadyan*, or *menadyan*, was not a separate pond, but the rock upon which the soaked clothes were pounded (Ri Migash; Rambam).

BACKGROUND

A soaking pond and a washing pond – מחמצן ונדיין: In the talmudic period, laundering was performed in stages, much like it is today. The first step involved soaking the soiled clothes in water, usually with cleansing materials that dissolved the oils that stained the clothes. Occasionally foul odors would be emitted by the soaking items. In the second stage, the clothes were transferred to a different container where they were rubbed, by hand or foot, and shaken until both the dirt and cleansing materials were released.

LANGUAGE

Washing pond [*nadyan*] – נדיין: Various explanations have been offered concerning the origin and meaning of this term. Some relate it to movement, *naydei*, as the clothes are moved from place to place. Alternatively, it is associated with an Aramaic word for sprinkling, *nidda*, because the water sprays to a distance.

HALAKHA

With regard to a soaking pond – מן המחמצן: One may not dig a pond used for soaking clothes near his neighbor's wall unless he distances it three handbreadths and plasters its walls with lime (Rambam *Sefer Kinyan*, *Hilkhot Shekhenim* 9:1; *Shulḥan Arukh*, *Ḥoshen Mishpat* 155:10).

In the case of a washing pond, etc. – מן הנדיין וכו׳: If a launderer has a rock that he uses to pound clothes in order to clean them, he must distance this rock four cubits from his neighbor's wall. The reason is that the water sprays up to that distance and would otherwise damage the wall (Rambam *Sefer Kinyan*, *Hilkhot Shekhenim* 9:5; *Shulḥan Arukh*, *Ḥoshen Mishpat* 155:11).

״וְסָד בַּסִּיד״. אִיבַּעְיָא לְהוּ: ״וְסָד בַּסִּיד״ תְּנַן, אוֹ דִּילְמָא ״אוֹ סָד בַּסִּיד״ תְּנַן?

§ The mishna teaches that one who digs a pit must distance it three handbreadths from another's property and **plaster it with lime. A dilemma was raised before** the Sages: What is the precise wording of the mishna? **Did we learn: And plasters with lime,** meaning that the walls must be plastered with lime in addition to distancing the pit three handbreadths, **or perhaps we learned: Or plasters with lime,** i.e., one may plaster the walls with lime instead of digging the pit at a distance of three handbreadths.

פְּשִׁיטָא דִּ״וְסָד בַּסִּיד״ תְּנַן, דְּאִי סָלְקָא דַּעְתָּךְ דְּ״אוֹ סָד בַּסִּיד״ תְּנַן, אִם כֵּן לִיעָרְבִינְהוּ וְלִיתְנִינְהוּ!

The Gemara answers: It is **obvious that we learned: And plasters with lime,**[NH] as, **if it enters your mind** that **we learned: Or plasters with lime,** which is the same as what is stated in the clause of the mishna discussing olive refuse, **if so, let the** *tanna* **combine them and teach them** together.[N] If the same *halakha* applied in all circumstances, all of the mishna's cases could be taught together.

דִּילְמָא מִשּׁוּם דְּלָא דָּמֵי הַאי הֶיזֵּיקָא לְהַאי הֶיזֵּיקָא, רֵישָׁא – הֶיזֵּיקָא דְּמִתּוּנָא, סֵיפָא – הֶיזֵּיקָא דְּהַבְלָא.

The Gemara answers: This is not proof, as **perhaps** these cases are taught separately **because this** type of **damage is not similar to that** type of **damage. The first clause** of the mishna addresses the issue of **damage** due **to moisture,** whereas **the last clause** addresses the issue of **damage** due **to heat.**

תָּא שְׁמַע, רַבִּי יְהוּדָה אוֹמֵר: סֶלַע הַבָּא בְּיָדַיִם – זֶה חוֹפֵר בּוֹרוֹ מִכָּאן, וְזֶה חוֹפֵר בּוֹרוֹ מִכָּאן, זֶה מַרְחִיק שְׁלֹשָׁה טְפָחִים וְסָד בַּסִּיד, וְזֶה מַרְחִיק שְׁלֹשָׁה טְפָחִים וְסָד בַּסִּיד; טַעְמָא דְּבָא בְּיָדַיִם, הָא לֹא בָּא בְּיָדַיִם – לָא!

The Gemara suggests: **Come** and **hear** a proof from a *baraita*. **Rabbi Yehuda says:** With regard to **rock that** is so soft it **crumbles in** one's **hands, this one digs his pit from here,** on his property, **and that one digs his pit from there. This one distances** his pit **three handbreadths and plasters with lime, and that one distances** his pit **three handbreadths and plasters with lime.** The Gemara analyzes this ruling: The specific **reason** one must also plaster with lime is that he is using rock that **crumbles in** one's **hands,** from which it may be inferred that if it is rock that **does not crumble in** one's **hands,** one would **not** be required to plaster with lime as well.

הוּא הַדִּין דְּאַף עַל גַּב דְּלֹא בָּא בְּיָדַיִם נַמִי סָד בַּסִּיד, וּבָא בְּיָדַיִם אִיצְטְרִיכָא לֵיהּ; סָלְקָא דַּעְתָּךְ אָמִינָא כֵּיוָן דְּבָא בְּיָדַיִם לִיבָּעֵי רַוְוחָא טְפֵי, קָא מַשְׁמַע לָן.

The Gemara answers: One could say that **the same is true,** i.e., **that even though** he is using rock **that does not crumble in** one's **hands,** he must **also plaster with lime. And it was necessary for** the *tanna* to mention the case of rock that **crumbles in** one's **hands,** as it might **enter your mind to say** that **since it crumbles in** one's **hands, let us require a greater distance.** Therefore, the *tanna* **teaches us** that this is not the case.

״מַרְחִיקִין אֶת הַגֶּפֶת וְאֶת הַזֶּבֶל וְאֶת הַמֶּלַח וְאֶת הַסְּלָעִים״ וכו׳. תְּנַן הָתָם: בַּמֶּה טוֹמְנִין וּבַמֶּה אֵין טוֹמְנִין?

§ The mishna teaches that **one must distance the solid residue** of produce that has been pressed free of its oil, **and** animal **manure, and salt, and lime, and rocks** three handbreadths from the wall of another, or plaster its receptacle with lime. The Gemara comments: **We learned** in a mishna **there** (*Shabbat* 47b): **With what** substances **may one insulate**[NH] a pot of cooked food on Shabbat eve, **and with what** substances **may one not insulate** it?

אֵין טוֹמְנִין לֹא בַּגֶּפֶת וְלֹא בַּזֶּבֶל וְלֹא בַּמֶּלַח, וְלֹא בַּסִּיד וְלֹא בַּחוֹל, בֵּין לַחִין בֵּין יְבֵשִׁין. מַאי שְׁנָא הָכָא דְּקָתָנֵי סְלָעִים וְלָא קָתָנֵי חוֹל, וּמַאי שְׁנָא הָתָם דְּקָתָנֵי חוֹל וְלָא קָתָנֵי סְלָעִים?

One may insulate the pot **neither with the solid residue** of produce that has been pressed free of its oil,[B] **nor with manure, nor with salt, nor with lime, nor with sand, whether** those materials are **moist** or **whether** they are **dry.** All of these materials spontaneously generate heat when piled up for an extended period of time. Therefore, they add heat to the pot they insulate. The Gemara asks: **What is different here that** the mishna **teaches** the *halakha* in the case of **rocks and it does not teach** the *halakha* in the case of **sand, and what is different there that it teaches** the *halakha* in the case of **sand and it does not teach** the *halakha* in the case of **rocks?**

BACKGROUND

Neither with the solid residue of produce that has been pressed free of its oil – לֹא בַּגֶּפֶת: Food may not be insulated on Shabbat with any of the heat-producing substances mentioned in the Gemara. The solid residue of produce that has been pressed free of its oil and manure cause fermentation over time, which can raise the temperature of its contents considerably. Wet lime is also subject to a chemical process that produces heat.

NOTES

We learned, and plasters [*vesad*] with lime – וְסָד בַּסִּיד תְּנַן: It is not uncommon for *amora'im* to be uncertain of the precise language of a mishna. In such cases they will attempt to verify the correct version. Some commentaries are surprised that a textual problem arises here, as there is a significant halakhic difference between the two possibilities. Therefore, they suggest that everyone agrees that the text reads *vesad*, and the uncertainty is concerning how to understand the conjunction *ve*, which can mean: And, but can also mean: Or (Ramban).

Let the *tanna* combine them and teach them together – לִיעָרְבִינְהוּ וְלִיתְנִינְהוּ: If the *halakha* of plastering applied in exactly the same manner to all the examples, there would be no need to distinguish between the clauses in the mishna. The *tanna* could simply have listed all the items that require distancing or plastering with lime.

With what may one insulate – בַּמֶּה טוֹמְנִין: It is permitted to leave cooked food or water on Shabbat while it is covered with a substance that preserves its heat. This is the *halakha* with regard to insulation. Nevertheless, the Sages distinguish between materials that merely preserve the heat of the food, and those that increase its heat. Materials that merely preserve heat may be used if the food is wrapped before Shabbat begins, whereas those that increase heat may not be used even if the food is wrapped before Shabbat begins. The reason for this prohibition is either due to a concern that one might stir coals on Shabbat, or because the food might cook, which is prohibited (see Meiri).

HALAKHA

And plasters with lime – וְסָד בַּסִּיד: When one digs any kind of cistern for water near his neighbor's wall, it is insufficient to merely distance the cistern from the wall by three handbreadths. He must also plaster with lime the walls of the cistern that face the neighbor's wall (Rambam). The Rosh rules that as it is left unresolved in the Gemara whether one must plaster to walls in addition to distancing the cistern, one may be lenient and choose either to distance the cistern or to plaster it (Rambam *Sefer Kinyan*, *Hilkhot Shekhenim* 9:1; *Shulḥan Arukh*, *Ḥoshen Mishpat* 155:10, 18, and in the comment of Rema).

With what may one insulate – בַּמֶּה טוֹמְנִין: Food cooked on Shabbat eve may not be insulated with materials that add heat to the food, e.g., the solid residue of produce that has been pressed free of its oil, manure, salt, lime, and sand. This is the case whether those materials are damp or dry. It is permitted to insulate food with substances that merely preserve heat, such as wool fleece (Rambam *Sefer Zemanim*, *Hilkhot Shabbat* 4:1–2; *Shulḥan Arukh*, *Oraḥ Ḥayyim* 257:1, 3).

אָמַר רַב יוֹסֵף: לְפִי שֶׁאֵין דַּרְכָּן שֶׁל בְּנֵי אָדָם לְהַטְמִין בִּסְלָעִים. אֲמַר לֵיהּ אַבַּיֵי: וְכִי דַּרְכָּן שֶׁל בְּנֵי אָדָם לְהַטְמִין בְּגִיזֵּי צֶמֶר וּלְשׁוֹנוֹת שֶׁל אַרְגָּמָן? דְּתַנְיָא: טוֹמְנִין בְּגִיזֵּי צֶמֶר וּבְצִיפֵּי צֶמֶר, וּבִלְשׁוֹנוֹת שֶׁל אַרְגָּמָן וּבְמוֹכִין, וְאֵין מְטַלְטְלִין אוֹתָן!

Rav Yosef says: There is a practical reason for this difference. Rocks are not mentioned there **because it is not customary for people to insulate food with rocks. Abaye said to him: And is it customary for people to insulate** food **with wool fleece and tabs of purple wool? As it is taught** in a *baraita*: **One may insulate** food **with wool fleece; with combed wool clumps,** which are unwoven; **with tabs of purple wool;**[B] **and with** swatches of **soft material; but** one **may not move them**[N] on Shabbat because they are set-aside [*muktze*].

אֶלָּא אֲמַר אַבַּיֵי: ״יַגִּיד עָלָיו רֵעוֹ״, תְּנָא הָכָא סְלָעִים וְהוּא הַדִּין לְחוֹל, תְּנָא הָתָם חוֹל וְהוּא הַדִּין לִסְלָעִים. אֲמַר לֵיהּ רָבָא: אִי ״יַגִּיד עָלָיו רֵעוֹ״, לִיתְנִינְהוּ לְכוּלְּהוּ בַּחֲדָא, וְלִיתְנֵי חֲדָא מִינַּיְיהוּ בְּאִידָךְ וְהוּא הַדִּין לְאִידָךְ!

Rather, Abaye said that the *tanna* follows the biblical aphorism in the verse that states: **"Its neighbor tells about him"** (Job 36:33), i.e., one example is mentioned and the same applies to the other case. **He taught** the *halakha* in the case of **rocks here and the same is true of sand; he taught** the *halakha* in the case of **sand there and the same is true of rocks. Rava said to** Abaye: **If** this is correct, that **"its neighbor tells about him," let him teach** the *halakha* of **all of** these examples **in one** case, **and let him teach** the *halakha* of just **one in the other** case, **and** it can be said that **the same is true** with regard **to the others.**

אֶלָּא אֲמַר רָבָא: הָתָם הַיְינוּ טַעֲמָא דְּלָא קָתָנֵי סְלָעִים – מִשּׁוּם דִּמְשַׁתְּכִי לָהּ לַקְּדֵרָה, הָכָא הַיְינוּ טַעֲמָא דְּלָא קָתָנֵי חוֹל – מִשּׁוּם דִּמְחַמְּמֵי חָמֵי וּמְקָרְרֵי קָרֵיר.

Rather, Rava said: There, this is the **reason that** the *tanna* **does not teach** the *halakha* in the case of **rocks: Because they break,** i.e., scratch, **the pot,**[NH] and consequently people do not use them for insulating food at all. **Here, this is** the **reason that** the *tanna* **does not teach** the *halakha* in the case of **sand: Because it heats hot** items[B] **and cools cold** items, and therefore it does not cause any damage to the wall.

וְהָא תָּנֵי רַבִּי אוֹשַׁעְיָא חוֹל! הָתָם בִּמְתוּנָא. תַּנָּא דִּידָן נַמִי לִיתְנֵי וְלוֹקְמֵיהּ בִּמְתוּנָא! הָא תְּנָא לֵיהּ אַמַּת הַמַּיִם.

The Gemara asks: **But Rabbi Oshaya taught** in a *baraita* that one must distance **sand** from his neighbor's wall. The Gemara answers: **There,** it is referring **to damp** sand,[H] which must be kept at a distance due to its moisture. The Gemara challenges: **Let the *tanna* of our** mishna **also teach** the *halakha* in the case of sand **and we will interpret it** as referring **to damp** sand. The Gemara answers: This *tanna* **already taught** the case of **a water channel,** which is a source of dampness, and therefore there was no need to mention damp sand as well.

אַטּוּ מִי לָא קָתָנֵי אַמַּת הַמַּיִם, וְקָתָנֵי נִבְרֶכֶת הַכּוֹבְסִין?

The Gemara rejects this answer: That is incorrect, as **is that to say** that the mishna includes only one example of a source of dampness? **Doesn't** the mishna **teach** the case of **a water channel? And yet it** also **teaches** the example of **a launderer's pond.** This demonstrates that the mishna teaches many cases, despite the similarity between them, and therefore it should have mentioned the *halakha* in the case of sand as well.

הָנְהוּ צְרִיכִי, דְּאִי תְּנָא אַמַּת הַמַּיִם – מִשּׁוּם דִּקְבִיעָא, אֲבָל נִבְרֶכֶת הַכּוֹבְסִין דְּלָא קְבִיעָא – אֵימָא לָא; וְאִי תְּנָא נִבְרֶכֶת הַכּוֹבְסִין – מִשּׁוּם דְּקָווּ וְקַיְימִי, אֲבָל אַמַּת הַמַּיִם – לָא, צְרִיכָא.

The Gemara answers: Both of **those** particular examples **are necessary, as, had** the *tanna* **taught** only the case of **a water channel,** one would have claimed that a distance must be kept **because it is fixed,** i.e., water constantly passes through it. **But** with regard to **a launderer's pond, which is not fixed,** as it sometimes holds water and sometimes does not, one might **say** that one need **not** distance it from his neighbor's property. **And** conversely, **had** the *tanna* **taught** only the case of **a launderer's pond,** one might have said that this must be distanced **because** its water **is fixed and standing** in one location and therefore leaks out. **But** with regard to **a water channel,** one might say distancing it is **not** required. Consequently, **it is necessary** to state both examples. By contrast, including the *halakha* in the case of sand would not add any novel understanding.

״מַרְחִיקִין אֶת הַזְּרָעִים וְאֶת הַמַּחֲרֵישָׁה״ וכו׳. זְרָעִים, תֵּיפּוֹק לֵיהּ מִשּׁוּם מַחֲרֵישָׁה! בְּמַפּוֹלֶת יָד.

§ The mishna teaches: **One must distance seeds,** i.e., one may not plant seeds, **and** one may not operate **the plow,** and one must eliminate urine, three handbreadths from the wall of another. The Gemara asks: Why is it necessary to mention **seeds?** Let him **derive this** requirement to distance the seeds **due to** the requirement to distance **a plow,** as in any event the ground must be plowed before it can be sown? The Gemara answers: This is referring to planting **with a single hand motion,** which is performed without plowing.

BACKGROUND

Tabs of purple wool – לְשׁוֹנוֹת שֶׁל אַרְגָּמָן: This refers to bunches of wool that were washed and combed into strips before being woven. These strips were then fashioned into fixed sizes and forms. Their high value was due to their purple coloring, which was derived by extracting mucus from the glands of certain snails using complex methods of extraction. For this reason purple dye was an expensive commodity available only to the rich and influential.

It heats hot items – דִּמְחַמְּמֵי חָמֵי: Sand is made principally from quartz, which is a poor conductor of heat. The space between the grains enables sand to serve as an insulator, which preserves the heat of items wrapped in it. By the same token, this space also helps keep cold items cool.

NOTES

But one may not move them – וְאֵין מְטַלְטְלִין אוֹתָן: The prohibition against moving articles on Shabbat is called set-aside [*muktze*]. Some of these materials are set aside because they are used for work, others because they are intended for sale, and yet others, e.g., the tabs of wool dyed purple, are highly valuable. These precious items are considered *muktze* due to the possibility of financial loss, and they are generally not used because of their high cost.

Because they break [*dimshatkhi*] the pot – מִשּׁוּם דִּמְשַׁתְּכִי לָהּ לַקְּדֵרָה: Rashi explains that the rocks might break an earthenware pot, which is why people are hesitant to insulate food with them, whereas softer materials will not break or otherwise damage the pot (see Ramah and *Arukh*). Nevertheless, Rashi himself points out that this verb generally refers to the formation of rust, and many commentaries explain that rocks ruin food (Ramban).

HALAKHA

Because they break the pot – מִשּׁוּם דִּמְשַׁתְּכִי לָהּ לַקְּדֵרָה: Some commentaries rule that it is permitted to insulate food using rocks on Shabbat eve, despite the fact that they add heat. The reason is that this practice is uncommon and the Sages did not apply their decree to uncommon practices (Rema; Mordekhai). They did issue their decree with regard to substances that are used for this purpose occasionally (*Shulḥan Arukh, Oraḥ Ḥayyim* 257:3, and in the comment of Rema, and *Magen Avraham* there).

There it is referring to damp sand – הָתָם בִּמְתוּנָא: If one desires to place damp sand in his courtyard, he must distance it from his neighbor's wall or plaster it with lime (*Shulḥan Arukh, Ḥoshen Mishpat* 155:4 and see *Shakh* there).

מַחֲרֵישָׁה, וְתֵיפּוֹק לֵיהּ מִשּׁוּם זְרָעִים! בְּחוֹרֵשׁ לָאִילָנוֹת. וְתֵיפּוֹק לֵיהּ מִשּׁוּם מַיָּא! תַּנָּא בְּאֶרֶץ יִשְׂרָאֵל קָאֵי, דִּכְתִיב: ״לִמְטַר הַשָּׁמַיִם תִּשְׁתֶּה מָּיִם״.

The Gemara further challenges: The mishna teaches that one must distance **a plow; but** let him **derive this** requirement to distance a plow **due to** the requirement to distance the **seeds,** as plowing is preparation for planting. The Gemara answers: This is referring **to one who plows** to prepare the ground **for trees.** The Gemara challenges: **But** if so, let him **derive this** requirement to distance a plow due to the requirement to distance the **water.** If there are trees, there must be a water channel to irrigate them, and arranging one's field in such a manner should be prohibited for that reason. The Gemara answers: **The** ***tanna*** **is referring to Eretz Yisrael,** concerning **which it is written: "And drinks water as the rain of heaven comes down"** (Deuteronomy 11:11). In Eretz Yisrael, water channels were not needed.

לְמֵימְרָא, דִּזְרָעִים

The Gemara asks: **Is this to say that seeds**

Perek **II**
Daf **19** Amud **b**

לִצְדָדִין קָא מִשְׁתָּרְשִׁי? וְהָא תְּנַן: הַמַּבְרִיךְ אֶת הַגֶּפֶן בָּאָרֶץ, אִם אֵין עַל גַּבָּהּ עָפָר שְׁלֹשָׁה טְפָחִים – לֹא יָבִיא זֶרַע עָלֶיהָ,

take root to the sides, i.e., the growing roots spread sideways and cause damage to walls? **But didn't we learn** in a mishna (*Kilayim* 7:1): With regard to **one who bends**[B] a branch of **a grapevine**[H] **into the ground** so that it strikes roots and produces a new vine, **if it does not have three handbreadths of earth over it he may not plant a seed above** it, as he would thereby transgress the prohibition of diverse kinds?

וְתָנֵי עֲלָהּ: אֲבָל זוֹרֵעַ אֶת הַצְּדָדִין אֵילָךְ וְאֵילָךְ! אָמַר רַבִּי חַגָּא בְּשֵׁם רַבִּי יוֹסֵי: מִפְּנֵי שֶׁמַּחֲלִידִין אֶת הַקַּרְקַע וּמַעֲלִין עָפָר תִּיחוֹחַ.

And it is taught with regard to this mishna: **But one may plant on either side**[N] of that bent branch. This indicates that there is no concern that the roots of the seeds will spread out sideways. **Rabbi Ḥagga says in the name of Rabbi Yosei:** The issue here is not that the roots will spread out sideways and reach the wall. Rather, it is prohibited to plant seeds near one's neighbor's property **because they break up the ground**[N] **and cause loose soil to rise up,** which damages the foundation of the wall.

״וְאֶת מֵי רַגְלַיִם מִן הַכּוֹתֶל – שְׁלֹשָׁה טְפָחִים״ וכו׳. אָמַר רַבָּה בַּר בַּר חָנָה: מוּתָּר לְאָדָם לְהַשְׁתִּין מַיִם בְּצַד כּוֹתְלוֹ שֶׁל חֲבֵירוֹ, דִּכְתִיב: ״וְהִכְרַתִּי לְאַחְאָב מַשְׁתִּין בְּקִיר וְעָצוּר וְעָזוּב בְּיִשְׂרָאֵל״. וְהָא אֲנַן תְּנַן: וְאֶת מֵי רַגְלַיִם מִן הַכּוֹתֶל – שְׁלֹשָׁה טְפָחִים! הָתָם בְּשׁוֹפְכִין.

§ The mishna teaches: **And urine** must be kept at a distance of **three handbreadths from the wall** of one's neighbor. **Rabba bar bar Ḥana says:** It **is permitted** for **a person to urinate alongside the wall of another, as it is written: "And I will cut off from Ahab those who urinate against the wall, and him that is shut up and him that is left at large in Israel"** (I Kings 21:21). As the verse employs the term "those who urinate against the wall" to mean males, it seems that urinating against a wall was a common practice. The Gemara asks: **But didn't we learn** in the mishna that **urine** must be kept a distance of **three handbreadths from the wall?** The Gemara answers: **There,** the mishna is referring to urine **that is poured**[H] from a chamber pot, as opposed to urine that is passed from the body.

תָּא שְׁמַע: לֹא יִשְׁפּוֹךְ אָדָם מַיִם בְּצַד כּוֹתְלוֹ שֶׁל חֲבֵירוֹ אֶלָּא אִם כֵּן הִרְחִיק מִמֶּנּוּ שְׁלֹשָׁה טְפָחִים! הָתָם נַמִי בְּשׁוֹפְכִין.

The Gemara suggests: **Come** and **hear** a *baraita*: **A person may not pour water**[N] **at the side of the wall of another unless he distances** the water **three handbreadths from it.** If pouring water is prohibited, then all the more so should urination be prohibited. The Gemara explains: **There too,** it is referring to urine **that is poured** from a chamber pot.

BACKGROUND

One who bends – הַמַּבְרִיךְ:

Bent branch

NOTES

But one may plant on either side – אֲבָל זוֹרֵעַ אֶת הַצְּדָדִין: The early commentaries question this ruling, as even if the seed's roots extend sideways, the roots of a grapevine also extend sideways, which means that the two will intermingle and produce diverse kinds. They explain that the roots of the grapevine typically descend lower than three handbreadths, thereby precluding the possibility of any problem of diverse kinds (Rabbeinu Yona).

They break up the ground – מַחֲלִידִין אֶת הַקַּרְקַע: The commentaries explain that the seeds create holes in the ground, like those dug by a mole (Rabbeinu Gershom Meor HaGola; Rashi).

A person may not pour [*yishpokh*] water, etc. – לֹא יִשְׁפּוֹךְ אָדָם מַיִם וכו׳: This exchange in the Gemara is puzzling, as it is not clear why one should assume that if pouring water at the side of a wall is prohibited, urinating, which involves a lesser quantity of liquid, would be prohibited there as well. The Maharshal writes that this question and answer represent a corrupted version of the text and should be deleted. The Baḥ suggests emending the text of the *baraita* to read: A person may not place [*yatil*] water, as this phrase can be understood as referring to urination. Accordingly, the Gemara initially understood that the *baraita* is stating a ruling concerning urination that would run counter to the ruling of Rabba bar bar Ḥana, and answers that in fact the *baraita* is referring not to urination but to pouring out the urine from a chamber pot.

HALAKHA

One who bends a branch of a grapevine – הַמַּבְרִיךְ אֶת הַגֶּפֶן: If one bends the branch of a grapevine into the ground, it is permitted to plant above it if it is covered by three handbreadths of soil. This is the case even if the vine is placed in a dried gourd or an earthenware pipe. If there are not three handbreadths of soil over it, it is prohibited to plant above it. One may plant to its side (Rambam *Sefer Zera'im*, *Hilkhot Kilayim* 6:7; *Shulḥan Arukh*, *Yoreh De'a* 295:4).

That is poured – בְּשׁוֹפְכִין: It is prohibited to pour urine next to one's neighbor's wall, even into a pit, unless he distances it three handbreadths from the wall (*Shulḥan Arukh*, *Ḥoshen Mishpat* 155:5, and in the comment of Rema).

תָּא שְׁמַע: לֹא יַשְׁתִּין אָדָם מַיִם בְּצַד כּוֹתְלוֹ שֶׁל חֲבֵירוֹ אֶלָּא אִם כֵּן הִרְחִיק מִמֶּנּוּ שְׁלֹשָׁה טְפָחִים; בַּמֶּה דְּבָרִים אֲמוּרִים – בְּכוֹתֶל לְבֵינִים, אֲבָל בְּכוֹתֶל אֲבָנִים – בִּכְדֵי שֶׁלֹּא יַזִּיק, וְכַמָּה? טֶפַח. וְשֶׁל צוּנְמָא – מוּתָּר; תְּיוּבְתָּא דְּרַבָּה בַּר בַּר חָנָה! תְּיוּבְתָּא.

The Gemara suggests: **Come and hear** another proof from a *baraita*: **A person may not urinate**[H] **alongside the wall of another unless he distances** himself **three handbreadths from it. In what** case **is this statement said?** It is said **in the case of a brick wall.**[N] **But in the** case of **a stone wall,** one must distance himself **enough so that it does not cause damage. And how far** must he distance himself? One **handbreadth. And** if there is **hard rock**[N] present, it is **permitted** to urinate there. The Gemara comments: **The refutation of** the opinion of **Rabba bar bar Ḥana is a conclusive refutation,**[B] and his ruling is rejected.

וְהָא רַבָּה בַּר בַּר חָנָה קְרָא קָאָמַר! הָתָם הָכִי קָאָמַר: אֲפִילּוּ מִידֵּי דְּדַרְכֵּיהּ לְאִישְׁתּוּנֵי בַּקִּיר לָא שָׁבֵיקְנָא לֵיהּ, וּמַאי נִיהוּ? כַּלְבָּא.

The Gemara asks: **But Rabba bar bar Ḥana stated a verse** in support of his opinion; how can the *baraita* rule counter to what is written in a verse? The Gemara answers: **This** is what it **is saying there,** i.e., this is the meaning of that verse: **I will not even leave** Ahab **something whose manner is to urinate against a wall. And what is that? A dog.** According to this interpretation, the verse is not referring to people at all.

אָמַר רַבִּי טוֹבִי בַּר קִיסְנָא אָמַר שְׁמוּאֵל: רָקִיק אֵינוֹ מְמַעֵט בְּחַלּוֹן. מַאי אִירְיָא רָקִיק? אֲפִילּוּ עָבֶה נַמִּי!

§ **Rabbi Tovi bar Kisna says**[N] that **Shmuel says: A wafer does not reduce** the dimensions **of a window.**[H] When a corpse, or a significant part thereof, is in one room, its impurity can spread to a room adjacent to it if there is a window of a certain size between the rooms. Shmuel states that when one puts a wafer in a window, the wafer is not considered an obstruction, so the size of the opening as relevant to this *halakha* remains the same. The Gemara asks: **Why** discuss **specifically** this case? Why does Shmuel teach this *halakha* with regard to **a wafer? Even a thick** chunk of bread **also** does not reduce the dimensions of a window.

לָא מִיבַּעְיָא קָאָמַר: לָא מִיבַּעְיָא עָבֶה כֵּיוָן דְּאִיחֲזֵי לֵיהּ לָא מְבַטֵּיל לֵיהּ, אֲבָל רָקִיק דִּמְמָאִיס – אֵימָא בַּטּוֹלֵי מְבַטֵּיל לֵיהּ, קָא מַשְׁמַע לָן.

The Gemara answers: Shmuel **is speaking** utilizing the style of: **It is not necessary,** as follows: **It is not necessary** to state this *halakha* with regard to **thick** bread. **Since it is fit for him** to consume, **he does not nullify it,** i.e., he does not plan to leave it in the window for an extended amount of time. **But** in the case of **a wafer, which** becomes **disgusting**[N] when placed in a window, **I might say** that **he does nullify it** and it becomes part of the house, thereby reducing the size of the window. To counter this, Shmuel **teaches us** that even a wafer is not nullified, as it can be used to feed animals, as one is not particular about their food. Therefore, the wafer does not become part of the window in which it is placed.

NOTES

In the case of a brick wall – בְּכוֹתֶל לְבֵינִים: Sometimes bricks are only sun dried, as they can be ruined if they get wet.

And if there is hard rock – וְשֶׁל צוּנְמָא: Rashi explains that if a stone wall is built on hard rock there is no concern that water will corrode it. Others state that the wall itself is comprised of very hard stones (Rambam).

Rabbi Tovi bar Kisna says – אָמַר רַבִּי טוֹבִי בַּר קִיסְנָא: This passage, which does not relate to the issue at hand, is mentioned only because at its conclusion it discusses the damage that seeds can cause to walls (*Tosafot*).

A wafer which becomes disgusting – רָקִיק דִּמְמָאִיס: Since the wafer is thin, once it becomes wet or dirty due to the window it has no further use as food. By contrast, in the case of a thick piece of bread, the affected area can be sliced off, leaving the remaining part fit for consumption (Ri Migash).

HALAKHA

A person may not urinate – לֹא יַשְׁתִּין אָדָם: One may not urinate next to his neighbor's wall unless he moves himself a distance of three handbreadths from the wall. This is in the case of a wall constructed from bricks. It is sufficient to move one handbreadth away from a stone wall. If the stones and ground were rock hard, or built on rock (*Tur*), one need not distance himself (Rambam *Sefer Kinyan, Hilkhot Shekhenim* 9:6; *Shulḥan Arukh, Ḥoshen Mishpat* 155:6).

A wafer does not reduce the dimensions of a window – רָקִיק אֵינוֹ מְמַעֵט בְּחַלּוֹן: If a house contains an olive-bulk-sized part of a corpse and the window of the house is blocked by an item that is not susceptible to ritual impurity, and the item is placed in such a manner that less than a handbreadth of space remains in the window, that item serves as a barrier against the spread of the impurity. This is the *halakha* only if the item placed in the window is not meant to be removed. If food is placed there it does not serve as a barrier against the spread of impurity, as it will likely be removed (Rambam *Sefer Tahara, Hilkhot Tumat Met* 15:1 and Ra'avad there, and 7:1).

BACKGROUND

Conclusive refutation [*teyuvta*] – תְּיוּבְתָּא: This term is usually employed when the Gemara presents a conclusive refutation of an amoraic statement on the basis of a tannaitic source that contradicts the statement of the *amora*. This is one of a number of expressions based on the Aramaic root *tav, vav, beit*, which connotes refutation. When an *amora* objects to the opinion of another *amora*, citing a tannaitic source, the expression used is *eitivei*, an objection, e.g., X raised an objection [*eitivei*] to the statement of Y. When an *amora* raises an objection to an unattributed amoraic opinion, citing a tannaitic source, the expression employed is *meitiv*, meaning: He raises an objection. When the Gemara itself raises an objection citing a tannaitic source, the term is *meitivei*, meaning: An objection is raised. When the refutation is conclusive, the expression *teyuvta* is often used, bringing the discussion to a close.

וְתֵיפּוֹק לֵיהּ דַּהֲוָה לֵיהּ דָּבָר שֶׁהוּא מְקַבֵּל טוּמְאָה, וְכׇל דָּבָר שֶׁהוּא מְקַבֵּל טוּמְאָה – אֵינוֹ חוֹצֵץ בִּפְנֵי הַטּוּמְאָה! שֶׁנִּילּוֹשׁ בְּמֵי פֵּירוֹת.

The Gemara challenges: **And** let him **derive this** *halakha* from the fact that a wafer is **an item that is susceptible to ritual impurity, and any item that is susceptible to impurity does not serve as a barrier against** the spread of **impurity.** The Gemara explains: This is referring to a wafer **that was kneaded in fruit juice,**[N] which is not one of the liquids that renders food susceptible to ritual impurity, and therefore the wafer is not susceptible to ritual impurity. Consequently, one might have thought that it serves as a barrier before ritual impurity and reduces the dimensions of the window.

מֵיתִיבֵי: קוּפָּה מְלֵאָה תֶּבֶן וְחָבִית מְלֵאָה גְּרוֹגָרוֹת, הַמּוּנָּחִים בַּחַלּוֹן – רוֹאִין, כׇּל שֶׁאִילּוּ יִנָּטְלוּ וִיכוֹלִין תֶּבֶן וּגְרוֹגָרוֹת לַעֲמוֹד בִּפְנֵי עַצְמָן – חוֹצְצִין, וְאִם לָאו – אֵין חוֹצְצִין; וְהָא תֶּבֶן חֲזֵי לִבְהֶמְתּוֹ!

The Gemara **raises an objection** to Shmuel's opinion from a mishna (*Oholot* 6:2): With regard to **a basket** that is **full of straw,**[H] **or** an earthenware **barrel full of dried figs, which are placed in a window,** one **considers: If the straw or dried figs would stand on their own were** the basket or barrel **removed,** then **they would serve as a barrier against** the spread of impurity. **But if** they would **not** stand on their own **they would not serve as a barrier.** The Gemara explains the objection: **But** why should the straw or dried figs serve as a barrier? Even **straw** that can stand on its own **is fit for** feeding to **one's animal** and will likely be removed from the opening, which means it should not be considered part of the window.

בְּסַרְיָא. חֲזֵי לְטִינָא! דְּאִית בֵּיהּ קוֹצֵי. חֲזֵי לְהַסָּקָה! בִּמְתוּנָא. חֲזֵי לְהֶסֵּק גָּדוֹל! הֶסֵּק גָּדוֹל לָא שְׁכִיחַ.

The Gemara answers: The ruling of the mishna is stated **with regard to rotted** straw, which is unfit for animal consumption. The Gemara asks: But **it is fit for** use in the making of **clay** for bricks. The Gemara answers: This is referring to straw **that has thorns in it**[N] and therefore is not fit for making bricks. The Gemara challenges: Even so, it is **fit for kindling** a fire. The Gemara answers that this is referring **to wet** straw. The Gemara responds: Nevertheless, it is **fit for kindling a large** fire. If one builds a large fire, wet straw will dry and become ignitable. The Gemara answers: **A large fire is not common,** and therefore, in all likelihood, the straw will remain in the window.

גְּרוֹגָרוֹת – הָא חֲזוּ לֵיהּ! אָמַר שְׁמוּאֵל: בְּשֶׁהִתְרִיפוּ. וְכֵן תָּנֵי רַבָּה בַּר אֲבוּהּ: בְּשֶׁהִתְרִיפוּ.

The Gemara further asks: But **dried figs are fit for him** to consume, and he will certainly remove them. Consequently, they should not be considered fixed in their place. **Shmuel says:** This is referring to a case **where** the figs **became worm infested** [***beshehitrifu***].[NL] **And so Rabba bar Avuh teaches:** This is referring to a case **where** the figs **became worm infested.**

הַאי חָבִית הֵיכִי דָּמְיָא? אִי דְּפוּמָּא לְבַר

The Gemara clarifies: **What are the** exact **circumstances of this barrel** that held the dried figs? **If** this is referring to a case **where** its **opening faced outward,** i.e., not toward the source of the ritual impurity,

Perek **II**
Daf **20** Amud **a**

הִיא גּוּפָהּ תֵּיחוֹץ, דְּהָא כְּלִי חֶרֶשׂ אֵינוֹ מִטַּמֵּא מִגַּבּוֹ! אֶלָּא דְּפוּמָּא לְגַאו. וְאִי בָּעֵית אֵימָא: לְעוֹלָם דְּפוּמָּא לְבַר, הָכָא בְּמַאי עָסְקִינַן – בְּחָבִית שֶׁל מַתֶּכֶת.

let the barrel **itself serve as a barrier.**[N] It should not be susceptible to impurity in this case, **as an earthenware vessel does not contract impurity if its exterior** is exposed to impurity. **Rather,** one must say **that its opening faces inward,** and it is rendered impure because the impurity enters through its opening. **And if you wish, say** instead that **actually its opening faces outward, and with what are we dealing here?** We are dealing **with a metal barrel,** which does contract impurity through its exterior.

NOTES

Let the barrel itself serve as a barrier – הִיא גּוּפָהּ תֵּיחוֹץ: The early commentaries ask: Perhaps the barrel does not serve as a barrier to impurity because it is not nullified relative to the window, as the owner will presumably move it. Some answer that as the barrel contains worm-ridden figs, it too has become ruined and will not be moved from the opening (*Tosafot*). Others suggest that as it has been designated for this use, it will not be taken for any other purpose (Ramah). Many early commentaries explain that the principle that an item is not nullified if it is subject to removal applies only where the item merely reduces the space in question. In a case where the item completely blocks the window, such as a barrel, it is viewed as reducing the space even if it will eventually be moved (Rabbeinu Tam; Rabbeinu Yitzḥak of Dampierre, cited in *Tosafot*; Rashba; and see Ramban).

NOTES

That was kneaded in fruit juice – שֶׁנִּילּוֹשׁ בְּמֵי פֵּירוֹת: Food items become susceptible to contracting ritual impurity only after water or any of six other liquids has fallen onto them (see *Makhshirin* 6:4). Should fruit juice touch flour, the latter does not become susceptible to contracting ritual impurity.

That has thorns in it – דְּאִית בֵּיהּ קוֹצֵי: In talmudic times, clay was prepared by stomping on straw with bare feet. This action cannot be performed if the straw contains thorns (Rabbeinu Gershom Meor HaGola; Rashi).

The figs became worm infested – שֶׁהִתְרִיפוּ: This translation follows Rashi's interpretation. Others maintain that it means the figs became moldy (Rabbeinu Ḥananel). In either case they are no longer fit for human or animal consumption, as animals do not eat dried figs (Ramah).

HALAKHA

A basket full of straw – קוּפָּה מְלֵאָה תֶּבֶן: If a basket is full of rotted straw that is unfit for animal consumption or for use as clay or fuel, and the opening of the basket faces the impurity, if the straw would stand on its own it serves as a barrier against the spread of impurity. The *halakha* is the same in the case of a barrel of dried figs that are rotten and cannot be eaten: If the figs can stand on their own they serve as a barrier against the spread of impurity. If the figs cannot stand on their own they do not serve as a barrier against the spread of impurity (Rambam *Sefer Tahara, Hilkhot Tumat Met* 15:2).

LANGUAGE

Became worm infested [*hitrifu*] – הִתְרִיפוּ: The commentaries have suggested various interpretations of this term. Apparently, it is related to the word *torfa*, meaning a place of ruin. The verb *hitrif* derives from this term, and it refers to any state of ruin.

BACKGROUND

A child born after eight months of pregnancy – בֶּן שְׁמֹנָה: In talmudic times, there was an assumption that a child born after only eight months of pregnancy would not live, whereas one born after seven months had a greater chance of survival. This claim is not supported by medical research. In practice, the Sages established that the number of months of gestation cannot be used as a determining factor in assessing the viability of the newborn. Rather, the physical growth of nails and hair is a more reliable sign of fetal development, and consequently, it is a more accurate indicator of the likelihood that the fetus will live.

Afrazta – אַפְרַזְתָּא: There are various opinions with regard to the correct spelling and meaning of this term. Some commentaries identify it with the oleander, which is indeed poisonous. Some say it might be yellow iris, *Iris pseudacorus*. Others suggest that it is a species of plant containing a high concentration of oxalic acid, such as *Oxalis pes-caprae*, or sour grass, which is very common in Eretz Yisrael. It is harmful and possibly deadly to animals.

Oleander

Yellow iris

Sour grass

מֵיתִיבֵי: עֲשָׂבִין שֶׁתְּלָשָׁן וְהִנִּיחָן בַּחַלּוֹן, אוֹ שֶׁעָלוּ מֵאֲלֵיהֶן בַּחַלּוֹנוֹת, וּמַטְלוֹנִיּוֹת שֶׁאֵין בָּהֶן שָׁלֹשׁ עַל שָׁלֹשׁ, וְהָאֵבֶר וְהַבָּשָׂר הַמְדוּלְדָּלִין בִּבְהֵמָה וּבְחַיָּה, וְעוֹף שֶׁשָּׁכַן בַּחַלּוֹן, וְגוֹי שֶׁיָּשַׁב בַּחַלּוֹן, וּבֶן שְׁמֹנָה הַמּוּנָּח בַּחַלּוֹן, וְהַמֶּלַח, וּכְלִי חֶרֶס, וְסֵפֶר תּוֹרָה – כּוּלָּם מְמַעֲטִין בַּחַלּוֹן; אֲבָל הַשֶּׁלֶג, וְהַבָּרָד, וְהַגְּלִיד, וְהַכְּפוֹר, וְהַמַּיִם – כּוּלָּן אֵין מְמַעֲטִין בַּחַלּוֹן;

The Gemara **raises** another **objection** to the assumption that an item for which there is a use does not reduce the dimensions of a window, even if is not susceptible to impurity, from a *baraita* (*Tosefta*, *Oholot* 14:6): With regard to **grass**[N] **that one plucked**[H] **and placed in a window or that grew on its own in windows; and scraps of fabric**[NH] **that do not measure three by three** fingerbreadths; **and a limb or flesh dangling**[H] **from an animal or a beast; and a bird resting in the window;**[H] **and a gentile sitting**[N] **in the window;**[H] **and a child born** after **eight** months of pregnancy,[BH] who is not expected to survive, **that is placed in the window; and salt;**[H] **and an earthenware vessel;**[H] **and a Torah scroll,**[NH] **all these reduce the dimensions of the window.** Consequently, impurity passes through only if there remains an open space of a square handbreadth. **But** with regard to **snow, hail,**[NH] **frost, ice,**[N] **and water, all these do not reduce the dimensions of a window.**

וְהָא עֲשָׂבִין חֲזוּ לִבְהֶמְתּוֹ! בְּאַפְרַזְתָּא.

The Gemara proceeds to challenge Shmuel's ruling from each of the cases of the *baraita*. The Gemara asks: **But** according to Shmuel, who says that an item that has a use is not considered part of the window and does not reduce the dimensions of the space, **grass is fit** for consumption by **one's animal,** so it will not remain in the window. Yet the *baraita* states that grass reduces the dimensions of the window. The Gemara answers: This is referring **to *afrazta*,**[B] which is poisonous grass that is unfit for an animal to consume.

NOTES

Grass – עֲשָׂבִין: Even if grass is suitable for use as animal food, it is not susceptible to ritual impurity as food, because it is not fit for human consumption (Ramah).

Scraps of fabric – מַטְלוֹנִיּוֹת: Three by three fingerbreadths is the smallest measure of fabric that is susceptible to impurity (see *Makhshirin* 1:4).

And a gentile sitting – וְגוֹי שֶׁיָּשַׁב: By Torah law a gentile is not susceptible to ritual impurity while he is alive. Although the Sages decreed that gentiles have the status of a *zav*, since this level of impurity is by rabbinic law, a gentile reduces the dimensions of the window (*Tosafot*; Ramban).

And a Torah scroll – וְסֵפֶר תּוֹרָה: A Torah scroll is not considered a vessel, and therefore it does not contract impurity. Although the Sages decreed that sacred writings impart impurity to one's hands and disqualify *teruma*, since this level of impurity is by rabbinic law, a Torah scroll reduces the dimensions of the window, as in the case of a gentile (Ramah).

But snow, hail, etc. – אֲבָל הַשֶּׁלֶג וְהַבָּרָד וכו׳: These items do not reduce the dimensions of a window because they will eventually melt of their own accord (Rashbam).

Frost [*gelid*], ice [*kefor*] – וְהַגְּלִיד וְהַכְּפוֹר: Some commentaries explain that these terms both refer to frozen water. The difference is that *gelid* refers to thick ice, whereas *kefor* means a thin layer of frozen water (Ramah; see Rashi).

HALAKHA

Grass that one plucked – עֲשָׂבִין שֶׁתְּלָשָׁן: Plucked grass that is positioned in a window serves as a barrier before impurity and reduces the dimension of the space, provided that the grass is bitter and unsuitable as food for animals (Rambam *Sefer Tahara*, *Hilkhot Tumat Met* 15:2).

Scraps of fabric – מַטְלוֹנִיּוֹת: Scraps of fabric that are smaller than three by three fingerbreadths and are also stiff, dirty, and unsuitable for wiping blood reduce the dimensions of a window (Rambam *Sefer Tahara*, *Hilkhot Tumat Met* 15:2).

And a limb or flesh dangling – וְהָאֵבֶר וְהַבָּשָׂר הַמְדוּלְדָּלִין: A limb or flesh dangling from a non-kosher animal reduces the dimensions of a window. This ruling refers to a situation where the animal is tied in place and is too lean to be sold to a gentile (Rambam *Sefer Tahara*, *Hilkhot Tumat Met* 15:2).

And a bird resting in the window – וְעוֹף שֶׁשָּׁכַן בַּחַלּוֹן: A non-kosher bird resting in a window reduces the dimensions of the window. This *halakha* applies if the bird is one that scratches people and is therefore not suited for playing with a child, and provided it is tied in place (Rambam *Sefer Tahara*, *Hilkhot Tumat Met* 15:2).

And a gentile sitting in the window – וְגוֹי שֶׁיָּשַׁב בַּחַלּוֹן: If a gentile is tied to a window as a prisoner of the monarchy and people are afraid to release him, he reduces the dimensions of that window (Rambam *Sefer Tahara*, *Hilkhot Tumat Met* 15:2).

And a child born after eight months of pregnancy – וּבֶן שְׁמֹנָה: If a child is born after eight months of gestation and is placed in the window on Shabbat, he reduces the dimensions of that space with regard to impurity (Rambam *Sefer Tahara*, *Hilkhot Tumat Met* 15:2).

And salt – וְהַמֶּלַח: Bitter salt that sits on a small earthenware shard in a window and that contains thorns reduces the dimensions of the window (Rambam *Sefer Tahara*, *Hilkhot Tumat Met* 15:2).

And an earthenware vessel – וּכְלִי חֶרֶס: If a window is blocked with an earthenware vessel facing outward, the vessel reduces the dimensions of the window and serves as a barrier to the spreading of impurity. This is the case provided that the vessel is cracked and repulsive and therefore has no use, which means that it is unlikely to be moved (Rambam *Sefer Tahara*, *Hilkhot Tumat Met* 15:4).

And a Torah scroll – וְסֵפֶר תּוֹרָה: If a worn-out Torah scroll is placed in a window with the intent that it be stored there, it reduces the dimensions of the window and serves as a barrier to the spreading of impurity (Rambam *Sefer Tahara*, *Hilkhot Tumat Met* 15:2).

Snow, hail – הַשֶּׁלֶג וְהַבָּרָד: Snow, hail, frost, ice, and water placed in a window do not reduce the dimensions of the window (Rambam *Sefer Tahara*, *Hilkhot Tumat Met* 15:2).

״אוֹ שֶׁעָלוּ מֵאֲלֵיהֶן״, כֵּיוָן דְּקָשׁוּ לְכוֹתֶל שָׁקֵיל לְהוּ! אָמַר רַבָּה: בְּכוֹתֶל חוּרְבָּה. רַב פַּפָּא אָמַר: אֲפִילּוּ בְּכוֹתֶל יִישּׁוּב – בְּבָאִין חוּץ לִשְׁלֹשָׁה לַחַלּוֹן.

The *baraita* teaches: **Or** grass **that grew on its own** also reduces the dimensions of the window. The Gemara asks: But **since** the grass **damages the wall,** the owner **will remove it.** Therefore, it should not serve as a barrier to impurity. **Rabba says:** This is referring **to a wall of a ruin,** whose structural integrity is insignificant, and therefore the owner will not trouble himself to remove the grass. **Rav Pappa says:** The *baraita* may even be referring **to a wall** in **a settled** house, and it is referring to a case **where** the grass **comes from three** handbreadths **beyond** the **window.** In other words, the grass does not grow on the window but takes root some distance away, and from there it reaches the window. The homeowner is not particular about this grass and will not uproot it.

״מַטְלוֹנִיּוֹת״, חֲזוּ לֵיהּ לִקְרִיעָה דִּלְבוּשָׁא. בִּסְמִיכָתָא. חֲזוּ לְאוּמָּנָא! בְּרִיסְקָא.

The Gemara further asks: Why do **scraps of fabric** reduce the dimensions of the window? After all, **they are fit for** patching **a tear**[N] **in a garment.** The Gemara answers: This is referring **to thick** scraps,[N] which are unsuitable for patching. The Gemara challenges: Nevertheless, they are **fit for a bloodletter** to wipe up the blood at the point of incision. The Gemara answers: It is referring **to sackcloth,** which scratches the skin, and would not be used for that purpose.

אִי בְּרִיסְקָא, שֶׁאֵין בָּהֶן שָׁלֹשׁ עַל שָׁלֹשׁ? שֶׁאֵין בָּהֶן אַרְבָּעָה עַל אַרְבָּעָה מִיבְּעֵי לֵיהּ! כְּעֵין רִיסְקָא.

The Gemara asks: **If** it is referring **to sackcloth,** why does the *baraita* state **that it is not three by three** fingerbreadths? It **should have** said that **it is not four by four** handbreadths. Rough woven material of the kind used for sacks rather than clothes is susceptible to impurity only if its area measures at least four by four handbreadths. The Gemara answers: It is not actual sackcloth; rather, it is **like sackcloth,** i.e., it is stiff, and will therefore not be used by a bloodletter, but is woven like regular clothing.

״וְהָאֵבֶר וְהַבָּשָׂר הַמְדוּלְדָּלִין בִּבְהֵמָה וּבְחַיָּה״, עָרְקָא וְאָזְלָא! בִּקְשׁוּרָה.

The *baraita* teaches: **And a limb or flesh dangling from an animal or a beast** reduces the dimensions of a window. The Gemara asks: According to the opinion of Shmuel, why should this be so? After all, the animal can **arise and escape,** and therefore it should not be considered as part of the window. The Gemara answers: This is referring **to** an animal that is **tied** in place.

שָׁחֵיט לַהּ! בִּטְמֵאָה. מְזַבֵּין לַהּ לְגוֹי! בִּכְחוּשָׁה. פָּסֵיק שָׁדֵי לַהּ לִכְלָבִים! כֵּיוָן דְּאִיכָּא צַעַר בַּעֲלֵי חַיִּים לָא עָבֵיד.

The Gemara challenges: But the owner of the animal will take it and **slaughter it.** The Gemara answers: It is referring **to** an animal that is **non-kosher** and will not be slaughtered. The Gemara challenges: Even so, **he** will take it and **sell it to a gentile.** The Gemara responds: It is referring **to a lean** animal, which no one will buy. The Gemara continues: Even if the animal does not move, there is a use for the part that is dangling, **since he** can **cut it off** and **throw it to the dogs.** The Gemara answers: **Since there is suffering to an animal**[N] if he cuts it off, **he will not do** that.

״וְעוֹף שֶׁשָּׁכַן בַּחַלּוֹן״, פָּרַח וְאָזֵיל! בְּקָשׁוּר. שָׁחֵיט לֵיהּ! בְּטָמֵא. מְזַבֵּין לֵיהּ לְגוֹי! בְּקַלָּנִיתָא.

The *baraita* further teaches: **And a bird resting in the window** reduces its dimensions. The Gemara challenges: But it will **fly away,** and therefore it should not be considered as part of the window. The Gemara answers: This is referring to a bird **that is tied** in place. The Gemara further challenges: But the owner will take it and **slaughter it.** The Gemara answers: This is referring **to a non-kosher bird,** which he will not slaughter. The Gemara continues: Even if it is non-kosher **he** will take it and **sell it to a gentile.** The Gemara responds: It is referring **to a *kelanita*,**[NB] a type of bird that is so bony that no one would purchase it to consume it.

יָהֵיב לֵיהּ לִינוּקָא! בִּמְסָרֵט. קַלָּנִיתָא לָא מְסָרְטָא! כְּעֵין קַלָּנִיתָא.

The Gemara asks: But even so, **he** can **give it to a child** to play with, so why does it reduce the dimensions of the window? The Gemara answers: It is referring to a bird **that scratches.** The Gemara challenges: But **a *kelanita* does not scratch.** The Gemara answers: The *baraita* is referring to a type of bird that is **like a *kelanita*** in that it is bony, but is inclined to scratch people.

NOTES

They are fit for patching a tear – חֲזוּ לֵיהּ לִקְרִיעָה: Although these materials have some use, they are not classified as clothing with regard to ritual impurity. With regard to the case at hand, they are not nullified with respect to the window because they will ultimately be removed from their current location (*Tosafot*).

To thick scraps – בִּסְמִיכָתָא: This refers to material that is too thick to be used as a patch (Rashi). Others explain that the fabric is dirty (Ri Migash; Rambam).

There is suffering to an animal – דְּאִיכָּא צַעַר בַּעֲלֵי חַיִּים: The commentaries ask why the Gemara does not suggest that he will kill the animal and feed it to the dogs. Some say that this refers to a pet, as pets are unlikely to be killed (*Tosafot*). Others write that it is not customary to feed an entire animal to the dogs (Ri Migash).

Kelanita – קַלָּנִיתָא: Rashi and most commentaries explain that a *kelanita* is a bony bird that is not sold even to gentiles because it has so little meat. Others write that people believe that this bird brings bad luck, and consequently they will not buy it (Ri Migash).

BACKGROUND

Kelanita – קַלָּנִיתָא: Various explanations have been offered for the origin of this term. It is possibly Greek for a swallow. Yet, swallows do not fit the descriptions given here. Some commentaries suggest that this refers to a seabird, e.g., the petrel, which is bony and whose meat is tough and virtually inedible.

״וְגוֹי שֶׁיָּשַׁב בַּחַלּוֹן״, קָאֵי וְאָזֵיל! בְּכָפוּת. אָתֵי חַבְרֵיהּ שָׁרֵי לֵיהּ! בִּמְצוֹרָע. אָתֵי מְצוֹרָע חַבְרֵיהּ שָׁרֵי לֵיהּ! אֶלָּא בַּחֲבוּשֵׁי מַלְכוּת.

The *baraita* further states: **And a gentile sitting in the window** reduces its dimensions. The Gemara asks: But the gentile will **arise and leave,** so why does he reduce the dimensions of the window? The Gemara answers: This is referring **to** someone **who is tied** in place. The Gemara continues: **Another** person **will come** and **release him.** The Gemara answers: This is referring **to a leper,** whom people are afraid to touch. The Gemara challenges: **Another leper will come** and **release him. Rather,** this is referring **to a prisoner of the monarchy.** Since he is confined as a punishment, others are afraid to release him.

״וּבֶן שְׁמֹנָה הַמּוּנָּח בַּחַלּוֹן״, אָתְיָא אִמֵּיהּ דָּרְיָא לֵיהּ! בְּשַׁבָּת; דְּתַנְיָא: בֶּן שְׁמֹנָה הֲרֵי הוּא כְּאֶבֶן, וְאָסוּר לְטַלְטְלוֹ בְּשַׁבָּת, אֲבָל אִמּוֹ שׁוֹחָה עָלָיו וּמֵנִיקָתוֹ מִפְּנֵי הַסַּכָּנָה.

The *baraita* teaches: **And** a child **born** after **eight** months of pregnancy **who is placed in the window** reduces its dimensions. The Gemara challenges: Perhaps **his mother will come and remove him** from there. The Gemara answers: This is referring **to Shabbat,** when it is prohibited to move this child, **as it is taught** in a *baraita*: A child **born** after **eight** months **is like a stone** with regard to the *halakhot* of set-aside [*muktze*], **and** therefore **it is prohibited to move him; but his mother may bend over** the child **and nurse him, due to the danger**[N] that failure to nurse will cause her to fall ill.

״מֶלַח״, חַזְיָא לֵיהּ! בִּמְרִירְתָּא. חַזְיָא לְעוֹרוֹת! דְּאִית בָּהּ קוֹצֵי.

The *baraita* teaches: **Salt** reduces the dimensions of a window. The Gemara challenges: **It is fit** for use and people will remove it from there. The Gemara answers: This is referring **to bitter** salt,[B] which is not used as a seasoning. The Gemara challenges: Nevertheless, **it is fit for** tanning **hides.** The Gemara responds: It is referring to salt **that has thorns** mixed with it, and therefore it will not be used for tanning.

כֵּיוָן דְּקַשְׁיָא לְכוֹתֶל שָׁקְלָא! דְּיָתְבָא אַחַסְפָּא. חַסְפָּא גּוּפָא תֵּיחוֹץ!

The Gemara challenges: Even so, **since** this salt **is damaging to the wall, he will remove it** from there. The Gemara answers: This is referring to a case **where it sits on a shard** of earthenware, and consequently it does not damage the wall. The Gemara states: If it is resting on earthenware, **let the shard itself serve as a barrier** against the spreading of the impurity. Why, then, is the salt mentioned?

NOTES

Due to the danger – מִפְּנֵי הַסַּכָּנָה: Most commentaries explain that this refers to the danger posed to the mother due to the buildup of milk. Others claim that although the child is not expected to survive, any immediate danger it faces is cause for concern (Ramah).

BACKGROUND

Bitter salt – מֶלַח מְרִירְתָּא: When salt is harvested from the sea, other minerals besides cooking salt are collected as well, e.g., magnesium chloride, $MgCl_2$, which has a bitter taste. Table salt will be unusable if it is not separated from this substance.

Perek **II**
Daf **20** Amud **b**

דְּלֵית בָּהּ שִׁיעוּרָא, כִּדְתְנַן: חֶרֶס – כְּדֵי לִיתֵּן בֵּין פַּצִּים לַחֲבֵירוֹ.

The Gemara answers: This is referring to a case **where** the shard **does not have** the sufficient **measure**[N] for ritual impurity, and is therefore considered insignificant. **As we learned** in a mishna (*Shabbat* 82a): One who carries a shard of **earthenware** on Shabbat is liable only if it is **equivalent** in size to that which is used **to place between one pillar and another** when they are piled on the ground, to strengthen the pillars.

״כְּלִי חֶרֶס״, חֲזִי לֵיהּ! דְּמִיטַּנַּף. חֲזִי לְאוּמָּנָא! דְּמִנְקַב.

The *baraita* teaches: **An earthenware vessel** reduces the dimensions of a window. The Gemara challenges: But it is **fit for one** to use; therefore, it is likely to be removed from the window. The Gemara answers: This is referring to a case **where** the earthenware **is dirty.** The Gemara challenges: Even so, **it is fit for a bloodletter** to collect the blood. It would not matter to him if the earthenware were dirty. The Gemara answers: It is referring to a case **where it is perforated** and therefore unfit for that use.

״סֵפֶר תּוֹרָה״, חֲזִי לְמִקְרָא! בְּבָלוּי. וְהָא בָּעֵי גְּנִיזָה! שָׁם תְּהֵא גְּנִיזָתָהּ.

The *baraita* teaches: **A Torah scroll** reduces the dimensions of a window. The Gemara challenges: But it **is fit for reading;** therefore, it might be removed. The Gemara answers: This is referring to a Torah scroll **that is worn out** and unfit for reading. The Gemara challenges: **But** one is **required** to place the Torah scroll in **a repository** for unusable sacred books;[H] therefore, he will certainly remove it to be stored away. The Gemara answers: This is referring to one who determines that **its repository will be there.** In other words, it was placed in the window with the intent of storing it there in its worn-out state.

NOTES

It does not have the sufficient measure – דְּלֵית בָּהּ שִׁיעוּרָא: Rashi explains that because the earthenware shard is small and insignificant it is considered as though it is completely absent, just as it is too small to have significance with regard to carrying on Shabbat. Others question this explanation, as, if the dimensions of the window are reduced, what need is there for a precise measurement (Ramban)? Some versions of the text omit this clause altogether (Ramah; Meiri). One explanation is that the Gemara is referring to a case where the earthenware shard is too small to reduce the window to less than the minimum size, but the salt together with the shard reduces the size of the window. The Gemara then explains that although there is a possibility that one will move the shard, a shard so small has no use and therefore one will not move it (*Tosafot*).

HALAKHA

But one is required to place it in a repository for books – וְהָא בָּעֵי גְּנִיזָה: A worn-out Torah scroll must be placed in an earthenware jar and stored in the grave of a Torah scholar. The same applies to other sacred writings (Rambam *Sefer Ahava, Hilkhot Tefillin UMezuza VeSefer Torah* 10:3; *Shulḥan Arukh, Oraḥ Ḥayyim* 154:5 and *Magen Avraham* there).

וְאָמַר רַב: בַּכֹּל עוֹשִׂין מְחִיצָה, חוּץ מִמֶּלַח וּרְבָב; וּשְׁמוּאֵל אָמַר: אֲפִילּוּ מֶלַח. אָמַר רַב פַּפָּא: וְלָא פְּלִיגִי, הָא בְּמֶלַח סְדוֹמִית, הָא בְּמֶלַח אִיסְתְּרוֹקָנִית.

§ With regard to the *halakha* of the *baraita* referring to salt, the Gemara cites that which **Rav says: One can construct a barrier** to delineate a private domain on Shabbat or to block the spreading of ritual impurity **with anything**[H] **except for salt and fat,** as salt crumbles and fat melts in the heat. **And Shmuel says: Even salt** can be used as a barrier. **Rav Pappa said: And they do not disagree,** as **this** ruling of Shmuel is referring **to Sodomite salt,** which is like stone and can be used as a barrier, and **that** ruling of Rav is referring **to *isterokanit* salt,**[L] which is taken from the sea and is composed of grains.

וְהָשְׁתָּא דְּאָמַר רַבָּה: עוֹשֶׂה אָדָם שְׁנֵי צִבּוּרֵי מֶלַח וּמַנִּיחַ עֲלֵיהֶם קוֹרָה, שֶׁהַמֶּלַח מַעֲמֶדֶת אֶת הַקּוֹרָה וְהַקּוֹרָה מַעֲמֶדֶת אֶת הַמֶּלַח – אֲפִילּוּ מֶלַח אִיסְתְּרוֹקָנִית, וְלָא פְּלִיגִי: הָא דְּאִיכָּא קוֹרָה, הָא דְּלֵיכָּא קוֹרָה.

The Gemara adds: **And now that Rabba said:** If **a person makes two piles of salt** at the opening to an alleyway **and places a** cross **beam on top of them,**[N] so **that the salt supports the** cross **beam and the** cross **beam supports the salt** by weighing it down and compressing it, he can use this beam to render it permitted to carry in the alleyway on Shabbat, one can say that **even *isterokanit* salt** can be used as a barrier. **And** even so, Rav and Shmuel **do not disagree: This** ruling of Shmuel is referring to a case **where there is** a cross **beam** to weigh the salt down, and **that** ruling of Rava is referring to a case where **there is no** cross **beam.**

״מַרְחִיקִין אֶת הָרֵיחַיִם שְׁלֹשָׁה מִן הַשֶּׁכֶב, שֶׁהֵן אַרְבָּעָה מִן הָרֶכֶב״ וכו׳. מַאי טַעֲמָא? מִשּׁוּם טִירְיָא. וְהָא תַּנְיָא: וְשֶׁל חֲמוֹר – שְׁלֹשָׁה מִן הָאִיסְטְרוֹבִיל שֶׁהֵן אַרְבָּעָה מִן הַקֶּלֶת; הָתָם מַאי טִירְיָא אִיכָּא? אֶלָּא מִשּׁוּם קָלָא.

§ The mishna teaches that **one must distance a mill**[H] from a neighbor's wall by a distance of **three** handbreadths **from the lower stone** of the mill, **which is four** handbreadths **from the upper stone** of the mill. The Gemara asks: **What is the reason** that one must distance a mill from the property of his neighbor? It is **due to the vibrations** it causes. The Gemara asks: **But isn't it taught** in a *baraita*: **And** the measure for distancing a mill **on a base**[B] is **three** handbreadths **from the lower millstone** [***ha'isterobil***],[L] **which is four** handbreadths **from the mouth** [***hakelet***],[N] where the wheat is fed in? But **there, what vibrations are there?**[N] **Rather,** the reason for the distancing is **due to the noise**[N] generated by the mill.

״וְאֶת הַתַּנּוּר – שְׁלֹשָׁה מִן הַכָּלְיָא שֶׁהֵן אַרְבָּעָה מִן הַשָּׂפָה״. אָמַר אַבַּיֵי, שְׁמַע מִינָּהּ: כָּלְיָא דְּתַנּוּר – טֶפַח. נָפְקָא מִינָּהּ – לְמִקָּח וּמִמְכָּר.

The mishna teaches: **And** there must be a distance of **three** handbreadths **from the** protruding **base** of **an oven** until the wall, **which is four** handbreadths **from the** narrow **upper rim** of the oven. **Abaye said: Learn from** the mishna that **the base of an oven is a handbreadth** wider than its rim. The practical **difference** of this observation is with respect **to buying and selling,** i.e., a buyer should know that this is the proper ratio for the dimensions of an oven.

HALAKHA

One can construct a barrier with anything – בַּכֹּל עוֹשִׂין מְחִיצָה: Any material may be used to construct a barrier to enable one to carry on Shabbat, including utensils, food, as well as people, even if they are not tied up (*Magen Avraham*). Animals may also be used, but they must be tied in place to prevent them from wandering off (Rambam *Sefer Zemanim, Hilkhot Shabbat* 16:21; *Shulḥan Arukh, Oraḥ Ḥayyim* 362:5).

One must distance a mill – מַרְחִיקִין אֶת הָרֵיחַיִם: Mills must be kept at a distance of three handbreadths from a neighbor's wall. This *halakha* is referring to the lower millstone, which means that the upper millstone is four handbreadths from the wall. The reason is to prevent vibration of the wall, and so that noise does not disturb the neighbor. Large millstones that are turned by animals must be kept at a greater distance from a neighbor's wall (Rambam *Sefer Kinyan, Hilkhot Shekhenim* 9:3; *Shulḥan Arukh, Ḥoshen Mishpat* 155:7, and in the comment of Rema).

LANGUAGE

***Isterokanit* salt** – מֶלַח אִיסְתְּרוֹקָנִית: Some commentaries maintain that this word comes from the name of the town Ostrakine, located on the border between Eretz Yisrael and Egypt, along the coastline. Apparently, salt was harvested there.

Lower millstone [*isterobil*] – אִיסְטְרוֹבִיל: From the Greek στρόβιλος, *strobilos*, which refers to several items of spherical shape. Here it means the lower millstone.

BACKGROUND

A mill on a base – רֵיחַיִם שֶׁל חֲמוֹר: This type of mill, which was found in various excavations, is comprised of a lower millstone, *isterobil*, beneath the *kelet*, the upper millstone, which resembles an hourglass. The seeds are poured into the funnel-shaped top. Poles are fixed into the *kelet*, which helps people or donkeys turn the mill. This mill was called *reihayim shel hamor*, literally, a donkey mill, due to the base upon which it sat or because donkeys were employed to work it. The base and structure of the mill prevented the ground from shaking, although it created a fair amount of noise.

Flour mills found in Pompeii

NOTES

And places a cross beam on top of them – וּמַנִּיחַ עֲלֵיהֶם קוֹרָה: The Sages rendered it prohibited to carry on Shabbat even in a place that is not a full-fledged public domain, e.g., an alleyway. An alleyway is a space into which courtyards open and that leads to a public domain. Nevertheless, the Sages established a method by which one may carry in an alleyway, by erecting two posts at the end of it and placing a cross beam above them. This creates a type of private domain.

The lower part of the mill [*isterobil*]…the mouth [*kelet*] – אִיסְטְרוֹבִיל...הַקֶּלֶת: There are several interpretations of these terms. Some claim that these are synonymous with the lower and upper millstones (*Ge'onim*). Others suggest that these are located underneath the mill, as the *kelet* is a kind of depression in which the mill sits, while the *isterobil* is the receptacle into which the flour falls. Yet others agree with Rashi that the *kelet* is a type of funnel through which the wheat is directed into the mill (Ri Migash; Ramah).

What vibrations are there – מַאי טִירְיָא אִיכָּא: Since the mill is positioned on a base, the vibrations of the mill do not affect the surrounding area, nor do they damage the wall.

Rather it is due to the noise – אֶלָּא מִשּׁוּם קָלָא: Many early commentaries omit the word: Rather, which indicates a change from the previous explanation. Their reasoning is that the vibrations do in fact cause damage to the wall, and the Gemara is simply stating that the noise is also a reason to distance the mill. Some add that it is not uncommon for sound to cause vibrations and thereby damage a wall (Rashba).

NOTES

And in the case of a stove, one handbreadth – וּבַכִּירָה טֶפַח: The commentaries dispute the requisite measurement above the stove, which is not mentioned in the mishna.

מתני׳ לֹא יַעֲמִיד אָדָם תַּנּוּר בְּתוֹךְ הַבַּיִת – אֶלָּא אִם כֵּן יֵשׁ עַל גַּבָּיו גּוֹבַהּ אַרְבַּע אַמּוֹת. הָיָה מַעֲמִידוֹ בַּעֲלִיָּיה, צָרִיךְ שֶׁיְּהֵא תַּחְתָּיו מַעֲזִיבָה שְׁלֹשָׁה טְפָחִים, וּבַכִּירָה – טֶפַח;

MISHNA A person may not set up an oven[H] inside a house unless there is a space four cubits high above it, i.e., between the top of the oven and the ceiling, to avoid burning the ceiling, which serves as the floor of the residence above. If **one was setting up** an oven **in the upper story, there must be a plaster floor beneath it,** which serves as the ceiling of the lower story, at least **three handbreadths** thick, so that the ceiling below does not burn. **And** in the case **of a stove** the plaster floor must be at least one **handbreadth**[N] thick.

וְאִם הִזִּיק – מְשַׁלֵּם מַה שֶּׁהִזִּיק. רַבִּי שִׁמְעוֹן אוֹמֵר: לֹא אָמְרוּ כָּל הַשִּׁיעוּרִין הָאֵלּוּ, אֶלָּא שֶׁאִם הִזִּיק – פָּטוּר מִלְּשַׁלֵּם.

And if he **causes damage** in any case, **he pays** compensation for that **which he damaged. Rabbi Shimon says: They said all of these measurements** to teach **only that if he causes damage he is exempt from paying,** as he took all reasonable precautions.

לֹא יִפְתַּח אָדָם חֲנוּת שֶׁל נַחְתּוֹמִין וְשֶׁל צַבָּעִין תַּחַת אוֹצָרוֹ שֶׁל חֲבֵירוֹ, וְלֹא רֶפֶת בָּקָר; בֶּאֱמֶת, בַּיַּיִן הִתִּירוּ, אֲבָל לֹא רֶפֶת בָּקָר.

The mishna continues: **A person may not open a bakery**[H] **or a dye shop beneath the storeroom of another, and** he **may not** establish **a cattle barn** there, as these produce heat, smoke, and odors, which rise and damage the items in the storeroom. The mishna comments: **In truth,** the *halakha* is that in the case **of** a storeroom of **wine** the Sages rendered it **permitted** to set up a bakery and a dye shop beneath, as the heat that rises does not damage the wine. **But** they did **not** render it permitted to establish **a cattle barn,** because its odor damages the wine.

גמ׳ וְהָתַנְיָא: בְּתַנּוּר – אַרְבָּעָה, וּבַכִּירָה – שְׁלֹשָׁה! אֲמַר אַבַּיֵי: כִּי תַּנְיָא הַהִיא – בִּדְנַחְתּוֹמִין, דְּתַנּוּר דִּידָן כִּי כִּירָה דְּנַחְתּוֹמִין.

GEMARA The Gemara asks: **But isn't it taught** in a *baraita* that in the case of **an oven** the plaster floor must be **four** handbreadths thick, **and with regard to a stove** it must be **three?** By contrast, the mishna says that the plaster floor beneath and oven and a stove must be three handbreadths and one handbreadth thick, respectively. **Abaye said: When that** *baraita* **is taught** it is **with regard to** ovens and stoves **of bakers.**[H] Since they bake all day long, their implements get very hot. The **oven** discussed **in our** mishna is similar to **a baker's stove,** which is why in both cases a distance of three handbreadths is required.

״לֹא יִפְתַּח חֲנוּת״ וכו׳. תָּנָא: אִם הָיְתָה רֶפֶת קוֹדֶמֶת לָאוֹצָר – מוּתָּר. בָּעֵי אַבַּיֵי: כִּיבֵּד וְרִיבֵּץ לָאוֹצָר, מַהוּ?

The mishna teaches that one **may not open a bakery** or a dye shop beneath the storeroom of another, and he may not establish a cattle barn there. A Sage **taught: If the cattle barn preceded**[H] **the storeroom it is permitted,** i.e., the barn owner is not required to move it. With regard to this point, **Abaye raises a dilemma: If he cleaned and sprinkled**[H] the area, i.e., he prepared it for use **as a storeroom** but he has not yet filled it, **what is the** *halakha*? Is it considered a storeroom already, and therefore others may no longer put a cattle barn beneath it, or perhaps the *halakha* is that as long as it is empty he cannot prevent others from establishing a cattle barn?

HALAKHA

A person may not set up an oven – לֹא יַעֲמִיד אָדָם תַּנּוּר: One may not set up an oven in his house unless there are four cubits of space between the oven and the ceiling that serves as the floor of a neighbor above. This is the *halakha* even if the opening of the oven is to its side. Similarly, one who lives on an upper floor may not set up an oven unless there is a plaster floor beneath it with a thickness of three handbreadths. A single handbreadth is sufficient beneath a stove if there are four cubits above it (*Sma*). Even when these precautions are observed, the owner of an oven or stove is liable for damage caused if a fire ensues (Rambam *Sefer Kinyan*, *Hilkhot Shekhenim* 9:11; *Shulḥan Arukh*, *Ḥoshen Mishpat* 155:1).

A person may not open a bakery – לֹא יִפְתַּח אָדָם חֲנוּת שֶׁל נַחְתּוֹמִין: If one has a store beneath another individual's storeroom of fruit, oil, or wine, he may not convert it to a bakery, a dye shop, or a cattle barn. Furthermore, he may not use it for any other business that generates heat or creates a stench. In Eretz Yisrael it is permitted to establish bakeries or dye shops beneath wine storerooms, but not barns, as the odor from a barn spoils the wine (Rambam *Sefer Kinyan*, *Hilkhot Shekhenim* 9:12; *Shulḥan Arukh*, *Ḥoshen Mishpat* 155:2).

With regard to ovens of bakers – בִּדְנַחְתּוֹמִין: One may not set up a baker's oven in an upper story unless there is a plaster floor beneath it with a thickness of four handbreadths. A baker's stove must be positioned on a floor three handbreadths thick (Rambam *Sefer Kinyan*, *Hilkhot Shekhenim* 9:11; *Shulḥan Arukh*, *Ḥoshen Mishpat* 155:1).

If the cattle barn preceded – אִם הָיְתָה רֶפֶת קוֹדֶמֶת: If a bakery or cattle barn already exists and the upstairs neighbor subsequently decides to use his space for a storeroom, he cannot force the barn owner to move his operation (Rambam *Sefer Kinyan*, *Hilkhot Shekhenim* 9:12; *Shulḥan Arukh*, *Ḥoshen Mishpat* 155:2).

Cleaned and sprinkled – כִּיבֵּד וְרִיבֵּץ: If the owner of an upper story indicates his desire to use his space for a storeroom by cleaning and sprinkling the floor or by adding windows to the walls, he can prevent his downstairs neighbor from setting up an enterprise that increases heat from below. Once the downstairs neighbor has already set it up, the upstairs neighbor cannot force him to move (Rambam *Sefer Kinyan*, *Hilkhot Shekhenim* 9:13; *Shulḥan Arukh*, *Ḥoshen Mishpat* 155:3 and *Beur HaGra* there).

רִיבָּה בְּחַלּוֹנוֹת, מַהוּ? אַכְסַדְרָה תַּחַת הָאוֹצָר, מַהוּ? בָּנָה עֲלִיָּיה עַל גַּבֵּי בֵּיתוֹ, מַהוּ? תֵּיקוּ. בָּעֵי רַב הוּנָא בְּרֵיהּ דְּרַב יְהוֹשֻׁעַ: תַּמְרֵי וְרִמּוֹנֵי, מַאי? תֵּיקוּ.

Similarly, if he **added windows**[N] for ventilation, which demonstrates his intention to use it as a storeroom, **what is the** *halakha*? Likewise, if he establishes **an enclosed veranda beneath the storeroom,**[N] **what is the** *halakha*? If he **built an upper room**[N] **on top of his house** for storage, **what is the** *halakha*? None of these questions are answered, and the Gemara declares that they **shall stand** unresolved. The Gemara cites a similar question: **Rav Huna, son of Rav Yehoshua, raises a dilemma:** If he placed **dates and pomegranates**[N] there, **what is the** *halakha*? Is this considered the start of its use as a storeroom or not? No answer was found to this question either, and the Gemara declares: The dilemma **shall stand** [*teiku*][L] unresolved.

"בֶּאֱמֶת, בְּיַיִן הִתִּירוּ" וכו׳. תָּנָא: בְּיַיִן הִתִּירוּ מִפְּנֵי שֶׁמַּשְׁבִּיחוֹ, וְלֹא רֶפֶת בָּקָר מִפְּנֵי שֶׁמַּסְרִיחוֹ. אֲמַר רַב יוֹסֵף: הַאי דִּידָן, אֲפִילּוּ קוּטְרָא דִּשְׁרָגָא נַמִּי קַשְׁיָא לֵיהּ. אֲמַר רַב שֵׁשֶׁת: וְאַסְפַּסְתָּא – כְּרֶפֶת בָּקָר דָּמְיָא.

§ The mishna teaches that **in truth, it is permitted** in the case **of wine** but not in the case of a cattle barn. The Gemara states that a Sage **taught: They permitted** it in the case **of wine**[H] **because** the heat and the smoke **improve** the wine. **But** they did **not** permit one to establish **a cattle barn, because** a barn **creates a bad odor. Rav Yosef said: This** wine **of ours** spoils quickly, and therefore **even the smoke of a candle also damages it. Rav Sheshet said: And alfalfa** [*ve'aspasta*][L] **is considered like a cattle barn** in this regard, because it rots over time and creates a foul odor.

מתני׳ חֲנוּת שֶׁבֶּחָצֵר – יָכוֹל לִמְחוֹת בְּיָדוֹ וְלוֹמַר לוֹ: אֵינִי יָכוֹל לִישַׁן מִקּוֹל הַנִּכְנָסִין וּמִקּוֹל הַיּוֹצְאִין; אֲבָל עוֹשֶׂה כֵּלִים, יוֹצֵא וּמוֹכֵר בְּתוֹךְ הַשּׁוּק; וְאֵינוֹ יָכוֹל לִמְחוֹת בְּיָדוֹ וְלוֹמַר לוֹ: אֵינִי יָכוֹל לִישַׁן, לֹא מִקּוֹל הַפַּטִּישׁ וְלֹא מִקּוֹל הָרֵיחַיִם וְלֹא מִקּוֹל הַתִּינוֹקוֹת.

MISHNA If a resident wants to open **a store in** his **courtyard,**[H] his neighbor **can protest** to prevent **him** from doing so **and say to him: I am unable to sleep due to the sound of people entering**[N] the store **and the sound of people exiting. But** one **may fashion utensils** in his house **and go out and sell** them **in the market,** despite the fact that he is not allowed to set up a store in the courtyard, **and the neighbor cannot protest** against **him** doing so **and say to him: I am unable to sleep due to the sound of the hammer** you use to fashion utensils, **nor** can he say: I cannot sleep **due to the sound of the mill** that you use to grind, **nor** can he say: I cannot sleep **due to the sound of the children.** It is permitted for one to make reasonable use of his own home.

גמ׳ מַאי שְׁנָא רֵישָׁא וּמַאי שְׁנָא סֵיפָא? אֲמַר אַבַּיֵי: סֵיפָא אֲתָאן לְחָצֵר אַחֶרֶת. אֲמַר לֵיהּ רָבָא: אִי הָכִי, לִיתְנֵי: חָצֵר אַחֶרֶת – מוּתָּר! אֶלָּא אֲמַר רָבָא:

GEMARA The Gemara asks: **What is different in the first clause** of the mishna, which states that one can prevent his neighbor from opening a store in the courtyard because the noise keeps him awake, **and what is different** in the **latter clause,** which states that one cannot protest when his neighbor performs labor that is noisy? **Abaye said: In the latter clause we arrive at** the case of one who operates in **another courtyard,** i.e., one cannot prevent activity in a separate courtyard that is connected to the alleyway in which he lives. **Rava said to him: If so, let it teach** that **in a different courtyard it is permitted.** Why does the mishna not specify that it is referring to a different courtyard? **Rather, Rava said:**

LANGUAGE

It shall stand [*teiku*] – תֵּיקוּ: Various explanations have been offered with regard to the etymology of this term. One explanation is that the word is an abbreviated form of the word *tikom*, meaning let it stand. Another explanation is that its source is the word *tik*, meaning a case or pouch. Just as upon seeing a case or pouch one is unsure of its contents, so too, the word *teiku* is used in a situation where a resolution is unknown to us, as if the solution were hidden in a case (*Arukh*). Although not the literal meaning, some suggest that the term *teiku* is an allusion to an acrostic for the Hebrew phrase: *Tishbi yetaretz kushyot va'abayyot*, or: The Tishbite, i.e., Elijah the prophet, will resolve questions and dilemmas (*Tosefot Yom Tov*). This is in reference to the tradition that when Elijah returns to announce the coming of the Messiah he will also reveal the solutions to outstanding halakhic difficulties.

Alfalfa [*aspasta*] – אַסְפַּסְתָּא: From the Pahlavi word *aspast*, meaning fodder for horses.

HALAKHA

They permitted it in the case of wine – בְּיַיִן הִתִּירוּ: It is permitted to engage in an activity that produces heat beneath a wine storeroom in Eretz Yisrael, where the wine is strong and will not be damaged by the heat. This is prohibited in Babylonia, where the wine is too weak to withstand contact with heat. Additionally, one may not set up a cattle barn beneath a wine storeroom even in Eretz Yisrael (Rambam *Sefer Kinyan, Hilkhot Shekhenim* 9:12; *Shulḥan Arukh, Ḥoshen Mishpat* 155:2).

A store in his courtyard – חֲנוּת שֶׁבֶּחָצֵר: If one opens up a store or factory in his courtyard, his neighbors can prevent him from selling his wares there by claiming that the traffic of customers is disruptive. Some commentaries rule that if the neighbors did not protest for three years, his position is established and they can no longer force him to move (*Shakh*, citing Rosh). It is permitted for him to engage in this work in his house, even if it is noisy, provided that the neighbors did not protest against his activities. He need not wait three years to establish the right to perform this work. Nevertheless, the neighbors can protest at the outset. The Rema claims that one may do whatever he wants in his house, even *ab initio*, while the Rivash contends that the neighbors can complain if his actions cause them to fall ill (Rambam *Sefer Kinyan, Hilkhot Shekhenim* 6:12; *Shulḥan Arukh, Ḥoshen Mishpat* 156:2).

NOTES

He added windows – רִיבָּה בְּחַלּוֹנוֹת: Most commentaries agree with Rashi that the added windows are in the upper story, indicating his intention to use the space as a storeroom. He seeks to ventilate the area to prevent the wheat he plans to keep there from spoiling. Others claim that the owner of the lower level adds windows to allow the smoke produced by the barn to escape. This will reduce the annoyance caused to the upstairs neighbor (Rabbeinu Ḥananel).

An enclosed veranda beneath the storeroom – אַכְסַדְרָה תַּחַת הָאוֹצָר: Some explain that there is a veranda between the store and the storeroom, and the question is whether this separation is sufficient to disperse any source of damage from the store. Others contend that the question refers to a bakery built like a veranda: Does the increased ventilation remove any concern for damage? (Rabbeinu Ḥananel).

Built an upper room – בָּנָה עֲלִיָּיה: Rashi states that generally speaking, an upper story is constructed for storage, and the question is whether, due to the construction of the building, it is considered as though there is a functioning storeroom there. Others maintain that it is unclear whether the new story is meant to be used as a storeroom or for some other purpose (Rabbeinu Gershom Meor HaGola). Alternatively, he built an upper story above the top floor with the intention of moving his utensils from the original top story and using that as a storeroom (Meiri). Yet others contend that this is a continuation of the question with regard to the veranda: What is the *halakha* if a floor was built on top of the veranda, in the event that the veranda itself does not provide enough space (Ramah)?

Dates and pomegranates – תַּמְרֵי וְרִמּוֹנֵי: The question here is whether the placing of these items in that space reveals his intention to use it as a storeroom for wheat at a later stage. Some commentaries claim that the store will not harm these fruits, and the question is whether he can maintain that he intends to put other items there (Rabbeinu Gershom Meor HaGola). Others hold that the question is whether the store harms the dates and pomegranates themselves (Ri Migash).

Due to the sound of people entering – מִקּוֹל הַנִּכְנָסִין: Some commentaries write that the mishna refers to the extra sound in addition to the other complaints, as the main problem is the increased volume of traffic in the courtyard (Ramban). Others add that there are several reasons for the neighbor's complaint, including infringement on his privacy and increased noise, and the *tanna* chose just one of several examples to illustrate the point (Ramah).

סֵיפָא אֲתָאן לְתִינוֹקוֹת שֶׁל בֵּית רַבָּן, וּמִתַּקָּנַת יְהוֹשֻׁעַ בֶּן גַּמְלָא וְאֵילָךְ.

In **the latter clause we arrive at** the case of **schoolchildren**[H] who come to learn Torah in his house, **and** this ruling applies **from** the time of **the ordinance of Yehoshua ben Gamla and onward.**

דְּאָמַר רַב יְהוּדָה אָמַר רַב: בְּרַם זָכוּר אוֹתוֹ הָאִישׁ לַטּוֹב וִיהוֹשֻׁעַ בֶּן גַּמְלָא שְׁמוֹ, שֶׁאִלְמָלֵא הוּא נִשְׁתַּכַּח תּוֹרָה מִיִּשְׂרָאֵל; שֶׁבַּתְּחִלָּה, מִי שֶׁיֵּשׁ לוֹ אָב – מְלַמְּדוֹ תּוֹרָה, מִי שֶׁאֵין לוֹ אָב – לֹא הָיָה לָמֵד תּוֹרָה; מַאי דְּרוּשׁ? ״וְלִמַּדְתֶּם אֹתָם״ – וְלִמַּדְתֶּם אַתֶּם.

What was this ordinance? **As Rav Yehuda says** that **Rav says: Truly, that man is remembered for the good, and his name is Yehoshua ben Gamla.**[P] **If not for him the Torah would have been forgotten from the Jewish people. Initially, whoever had a father** would have his father **teach him Torah,** and **whoever did not have a father would not learn Torah** at all. The Gemara explains: **What** verse **did they interpret homiletically** that allowed them to conduct themselves in this manner? They interpreted the verse that states: **"And you shall teach them [*otam*]** to your sons" (Deuteronomy 11:19), to mean: **And you yourselves [*atem*] shall teach,** i.e., you fathers shall teach your sons.

הִתְקִינוּ שֶׁיְּהוּ מוֹשִׁיבִין מְלַמְּדֵי תִינוֹקוֹת בִּירוּשָׁלַיִם; מַאי דְּרוּשׁ? ״כִּי מִצִּיּוֹן תֵּצֵא תוֹרָה״. וַעֲדַיִין מִי שֶׁיֵּשׁ לוֹ אָב – הָיָה מַעֲלוֹ וּמְלַמְּדוֹ, מִי שֶׁאֵין לוֹ אָב – לֹא הָיָה עוֹלֶה וְלָמֵד. הִתְקִינוּ שֶׁיְּהוּ מוֹשִׁיבִין בְּכָל פֶּלֶךְ וּפֶלֶךְ; וּמַכְנִיסִין אוֹתָן כְּבֶן שֵׁשׁ עֶשְׂרֵה כְּבֶן שְׁבַע עֶשְׂרֵה,

When the Sages saw that not everyone was capable of teaching their children and Torah study was declining, **they instituted** an ordinance **that teachers of children should be established in Jerusalem.** The Gemara explains: **What** verse **did they interpret homiletically** that enabled them to do this? They interpreted the verse: **"For Torah emerges from Zion"** (Isaiah 2:3). **But still, whoever had a father,** his father **ascended with him** to Jerusalem **and had him taught, but whoever did not have a father, he did not ascend and learn.** Therefore, the Sages **instituted** an ordinance **that** teachers of children **should be established** in one city **in each and every region [*pelekh*].**[L] **And they brought** the students **in at** the **age of sixteen**[N] and **at the age of seventeen.**

וּמִי שֶׁהָיָה רַבּוֹ כּוֹעֵס עָלָיו – מְבַעֵיט בּוֹ וְיָצָא, עַד שֶׁבָּא יְהוֹשֻׁעַ בֶּן גַּמְלָא וְתִיקֵּן, שֶׁיְּהוּ מוֹשִׁיבִין מְלַמְּדֵי תִינוֹקוֹת בְּכָל מְדִינָה וּמְדִינָה וּבְכָל עִיר וָעִיר, וּמַכְנִיסִין אוֹתָן כְּבֶן שֵׁשׁ כְּבֶן שֶׁבַע.

But as the students were old and had not yet had any formal education, a student **whose teacher grew angry at him** would **rebel against him and leave.** It was impossible to hold the youths there against their will. This state of affairs continued **until Yehoshua ben Gamla came and instituted** an ordinance **that teachers of children should be established**[H] **in each and every province and in each and every town, and they** would **bring** the children **in** to learn **at the age of six** and **at the age of seven.**[HN] With regard to the matter at hand, since this system was established for the masses, the neighbors cannot prevent a scholar from teaching Torah in the courtyard.

אֲמַר לֵיהּ רַב לְרַב שְׁמוּאֵל בַּר שֵׁילַת: עַד שִׁית לָא תְּקַבֵּיל, מִכָּאן וְאֵילָךְ קַבֵּיל וְאַסְפֵּי לֵיהּ כְּתוֹרָא. וַאֲמַר לֵיהּ רַב לְרַב שְׁמוּאֵל בַּר שֵׁילַת: כִּי מָחֵית לִינוּקָא, לָא תִּמְחֵי אֶלָּא בְּעַרְקְתָא דִּמְסָנָא, דְּקָארֵי – קָארֵי, דְּלָא קָארֵי – לֶיהֱוֵי צַוְותָא לְחַבְרֵיהּ.

Concerning that same issue, **Rav said to Rav Shmuel bar Sheilat,** a teacher of children: **Do not accept** a student **before** the age of **six,** as he is too young, and it is difficult for him to learn in a steady manner. **From this point forward, accept him and stuff him** with Torah **like an ox. And Rav** further **said to Rav Shmuel bar Sheilat: When you strike a child**[H] for educational purposes, **hit him only with the strap of a sandal,** which is small and does not cause pain. Rav further advised him: **He who reads,** let him **read** on his own; **whoever does not read, let him be a companion to his friends,**[N] which will encourage him to learn to read.

HALAKHA

Schoolchildren – לְתִינוֹקוֹת שֶׁל בֵּית רַבָּן: If a resident of a courtyard wishes to open a school to teach children Torah, his neighbors cannot protest by saying that the noise of the children will disturb them. The Ramban rules that they need not tolerate more than fifty students (Rambam *Sefer HaMadda, Hilkhot Talmud Torah* 2:7 and *Sefer Kinyan, Hilkhot Shekhenim* 6:12; *Shulḥan Arukh, Ḥoshen Mishpat* 156:3 and *Sma* there).

Teachers of children should be established – שֶׁיְּהוּ מוֹשִׁיבִין מְלַמְּדֵי תִינוֹקוֹת: Schoolteachers must be set up in every city. A city can be placed under a ban for refusing to establish educators (Rambam *Sefer HaMadda, Hilkhot Talmud Torah* 2:1; *Shulḥan Arukh, Yoreh De'a* 245:7).

And they bring them in at age six and at age seven – וּמַכְנִיסִין אוֹתָן כְּבֶן שֵׁשׁ כְּבֶן שֶׁבַע: Children are enrolled in school upon the completion of their fifth year, or at the end of their sixth year if they are less intellectually advanced. The commentaries add that in any event three-year-olds should be taught the Hebrew alphabet in order to train them to read from the Torah (Rambam *Sefer HaMadda, Hilkhot Talmud Torah* 1:6, 2:2; *Shulḥan Arukh, Yoreh De'a* 245:5, 245:8, and in the comment of Rema).

When you strike a child – כִּי מָחֵית לִינוּקָא: It is permitted for a teacher to strike a student when necessary, but he may not do so with cruelty. He should not use a whip or a stick, but a small strap (Rambam *Sefer HaMadda, Hilkhot Talmud Torah* 2:2; *Shulḥan Arukh, Yoreh De'a* 245:10).

LANGUAGE

Region [*pelekh*] – פֶּלֶךְ: This term, which is mentioned in the Bible (Nehemiah 3:9), refers to a district or a large area of land. Apparently, it was borrowed from the Assyrian word pelekh, which bears the same meaning.

NOTES

At the age of sixteen – כְּבֶן שֵׁשׁ עֶשְׂרֵה: Since the students had to travel a lengthy distance, children were not taken to study, whereas teens were capable of making the journey (Ritva; Rashba).

At age six and at age seven – כְּבֶן שֵׁשׁ כְּבֶן שֶׁבַע: The age at which a child begins his studies is entirely dependent on the abilities and intellect of the child. Healthy and bright children begin to learn at the age of six. Less advanced children commence their formal studies at the age of seven (Ramah).

Let him be a companion to his friends – לֶיהֱוֵי צַוְותָא לְחַבְרֵיהּ: In other words, he should not be punished or expelled, but left to the company of his friends who do read, and ultimately he too will want to read (Rashi). Alternatively, by listening to his friends read he will learn from them.

PERSONALITIES

Yehoshua ben Gamla – יְהוֹשֻׁעַ בֶּן גַּמְלָא: Yehoshua ben Gamla was one of the last High Priests during the Second Temple period. He is mentioned by Josephus as Yehoshua ben Gamliel. He was appointed as High Priest by King Agrippa II and was killed during the destruction of the Temple. Some authorities maintain that there were two individuals by this name, although this is probably incorrect. While the Sages disapproved of the way he attained his office, they nevertheless enumerated his achievements (see *Yoma* 37a). He is praised for having donated golden lottery cards to the Temple, as well as for his efforts to promote Jewish education by establishing a wide-ranging system of schools in every town and region, as described by the Gemara here.

מֵיתִיבֵי: אֶחָד מִבְּנֵי חָצֵר שֶׁבִּיקֵּשׁ לַעֲשׂוֹת רוֹפֵא, אוּמָּן, וְגַרְדִּי, וּמְלַמֵּד תִּינוֹקוֹת – בְּנֵי חָצֵר מְעַכְּבִין עָלָיו! הָכָא בְּמַאי עָסְקִינַן – בְּתִינוֹקוֹת דְּגוֹיִם.

With regard to a courtyard, the Gemara concluded that it is permitted for one to establish an elementary school to teach Torah and the neighbors cannot protest. The Gemara **raises an objection** to this ruling from a *baraita*: With regard to **one member of a courtyard who wishes to become a doctor,**[H] **a bloodletter, a weaver** [***vegardi***],[L] **or a teacher of children, the** other **members of the courtyard can prevent him** from doing so. This indicates that neighbors can protest the teaching of children in their shared courtyard. The Gemara answers: **With what are we dealing here,** i.e., when can they protest his teaching children? We are dealing **with** a case of **gentile children,**[N] as there is no mitzva to educate them. In this situation, the neighbors can protest about the noise.

תָּא שְׁמַע: שְׁנַיִם שֶׁיּוֹשְׁבִין בֶּחָצֵר, וּבִיקֵּשׁ אֶחָד מֵהֶן לַעֲשׂוֹת רוֹפֵא, וְאוּמָּן, וְגַרְדִּי, וּמְלַמֵּד תִּינוֹקוֹת – חֲבֵירוֹ מְעַכֵּב עָלָיו! הָכָא נַמִּי בְּתִינוֹקוֹת דְּגוֹיִם.

Come and **hear** another *baraita*: With regard to **two people who are residing in** one **courtyard, and one of them sought to become a doctor, a bloodletter, a weaver, or a teacher of children, the other can prevent him** from doing so. The Gemara answers: **Here too,** we are dealing **with** a case of **gentile children.**

תָּא שְׁמַע: מִי שֶׁיֵּשׁ לוֹ בַּיִת בַּחֲצַר הַשּׁוּתָּפִין – הֲרֵי זֶה לֹא יַשְׂכִּירֶנּוּ לֹא לְרוֹפֵא, וְלֹא לְאוּמָּן, וְלֹא לְגַרְדִּי, וְלֹא לְסוֹפֵר יְהוּדִי, וְלֹא לְסוֹפֵר אֲרַמַּאי! הָכָא בְּמַאי עָסְקִינַן – בְּסוֹפֵר מָתָא.

The Gemara suggests: **Come** and **hear** another *baraita*: **One who has a house in a jointly owned courtyard may not rent it**[H] **to a doctor, nor to a bloodletter, nor to a weaver, nor to a Jewish teacher** [***sofer***], **nor to a gentile teacher.** This indicates that one's neighbors can prevent him from teaching Jewish children. The Gemara answers: **With what are we dealing here?** We are dealing **with the scribe** [***sofer***] **of the town,**[N] who does not teach children but writes documents and letters for residents of the town. This type of work is not a mitzva, and since many people seek his services, the residents of the courtyard can prevent him from performing this job near their houses.

אָמַר רָבָא: מִתַּקָּנַת יְהוֹשֻׁעַ בֶּן גַּמְלָא וְאֵילָךְ, לָא מַמְטִינַן יָנוֹקָא מִמָּתָא לְמָתָא, אֲבָל מִבֵּי כְנִישְׁתָּא לְבֵי כְנִישְׁתָּא מַמְטֵינַן. וְאִי מַפְסֵק נַהֲרָא לָא מַמְטֵינַן, וְאִי אִיכָּא תִּיתוֹרָא מַמְטֵינַן, וְאִי אִיכָּא גַּמְלָא לָא מַמְטֵינַן.

§ With regard to the ordinance of Yehoshua ben Gamla, and concerning teaching children in general, **Rava says: From** the time of **the ordinance of Yehoshua ben Gamla,** that schoolteachers must be established in each town, **and onward, one does not bring a child**[HN] **from one town to another.** Rather, each child is educated where he resides. **But one does bring them from one synagogue** where they learn **to another synagogue. And if a river separates** the areas **one does not bring** the children across, lest they fall into the river. **And if there is a bridge** spanning the river **one may bring** them across the river. **But if there is** only **a narrow bridge** [***gamla***][L] **one does not bring** them.

HALAKHA

Who wishes to become a doctor – שֶׁבִּיקֵּשׁ לַעֲשׂוֹת רוֹפֵא: If a resident of an alley or a courtyard wishes to become a doctor and see patients, or a bloodletter, or a weaver whose wares customers come to see, or a teacher of gentile children (Rambam), or a teacher of subjects other than Torah (*Shulḥan Arukh*), or a scribe who writes documents for the townspeople, his neighbors can protest about the resulting traffic. Some commentaries write that residents of a courtyard can protest but those of an alleyway cannot, unless there is already someone of the same profession in that alley (*Tosafot*). Similarly, it is not permitted for one to rent his residence to someone who will use it for these occupations (Rambam *Sefer Kinyan, Hilkhot Shekhenim* 6:11; *Shulḥan Arukh, Ḥoshen Mishpat* 156:1).

May not rent it – לֹא יַשְׂכִּירֶנּוּ: A resident of a jointly owned courtyard may not rent his house to a doctor, a weaver, a bloodletter, or a scribe for their professional use (Rambam *Sefer Kinyan, Hilkhot Shekhenim* 6:11; *Shulḥan Arukh, Ḥoshen Mishpat* 156:1).

One does not bring a child – לָא מַמְטִינַן יָנוֹקָא: Children should not be transported from one town to another for their education. They may be moved from one school to another within the same city. This is permitted even if the child has to travel a great distance, unless doing so requires that he cross an unsafe river (Rambam *Sefer HaMadda, Hilkhot Talmud Torah* 2:6; *Shulḥan Arukh, Yoreh De'a* 245:16).

NOTES

With gentile children – בְּתִינוֹקוֹת דְּגוֹיִם: The early commentaries write that the same *halakha* applies in the case of Jewish children who are being taught subjects other than Torah (Rambam's Commentary on the Mishna; Rabbeinu Yona; Rashba).

Scribe [*sofer*] of the town – סוֹפֵר מָתָא: Most commentaries agree with Rabbeinu Ḥananel that this is referring to the town scribe, who writes documents for its citizenry. Since his occupation does not involve a mitzva, the neighbors can protest against the number of people entering the courtyard. They can have no complaint if he is writing a Torah scroll or other sacred writings (Ri Migash). According to Rashi, this refers to a teacher of the city's youth. Since he establishes a large school in this location, this creates a lot of noise due to the great number of children (see Ramban). One version of the clause reads *sappar*, i.e., the local barber (Rabbeinu Gershom Meor HaGola; see *Tosafot*).

One does not bring a child – לָא מַמְטִינַן יָנוֹקָא: One does not bring a child to learn in a neighboring town, even if there is a better teacher there (Rambam). Instead, the local community must hire a teacher for its town (Rashi). Some commentaries claim that this is the case only if there are at least twenty-five students, as Rava subsequently states (*Tosafot*). Most early commentaries disagree and maintain that one forces the local residents to hire a teacher even if there are fewer than twenty-five students (see Rabbeinu Yona, Rashba, and Ritva).

LANGUAGE

Weaver [*gardi*] – גַּרְדִּי: From the Greek γέρδιος, *guerdios*, meaning a weaver.

Narrow bridge [*gamla*] – גַּמְלָא: This refers to a specific type of bridge. A regular bridge is constructed out of stones or wood and can handle a normal amount of human or animal traffic. A *gamla* is comprised of one or several beams placed across the width of a narrow river.

Log bridge

וַאֲמַר רָבָא: סָךְ מַקְרֵי דַּרְדְּקֵי – עֶשְׂרִין וַחֲמִשָּׁה יָנוּקֵי, וְאִי אִיכָּא חַמְשִׁין – מוֹתְבִינַן תְּרֵי, וְאִי אִיכָּא אַרְבְּעִין – מוֹקְמִינַן רֵישׁ דּוּכְנָא, וּמְסַיְּיעִין לֵיהּ מִמָּתָא.

And Rava said: The maximum **number** of students for one **teacher**[NH] **of children is twenty-five children. And if there are fifty** children in a single place, **one establishes two** teachers, so that each one teaches twenty-five students. **And if there are forty**[N] children, **one establishes an assistant, and** the teacher **receives help from** the residents of **the town** to pay the salary of the assistant.

וַאֲמַר רָבָא: הַאי מַקְרֵי יָנוּקֵי דְּגָרֵיס, וְאִיכָּא אַחֲרִינָא דְּגָרֵיס טְפֵי מִינֵּיהּ – לָא מְסַלְּקִינַן לֵיהּ, דִּלְמָא אָתֵי לְאִיתְרַשּׁוּלֵי. רַב דִּימִי מִנְּהַרְדְּעָא אֲמַר: כׇּל שֶׁכֵּן דְּגָרֵיס טְפֵי, קִנְאַת סוֹפְרִים תַּרְבֶּה חׇכְמָה.

And Rava said: If there is **a teacher of children who teaches** a few subjects, **and there is another who teaches more** subjects **than him, one does not remove** the first teacher from his position to hire the second, as **perhaps** the other teacher **will come to be negligent**[N] due to the lack of competition. **Rav Dimi from Neharde'a said:** On the contrary, **all the more so** is it the case that he will **teach**[NH] in a **better** manner if he knows that he is the sole instructor in the place, as **jealousy among teachers increases wisdom.** The one who was dismissed will try to refine his skills so that he will be rehired, and this will prevent negligence on the part of the other teacher.

וַאֲמַר רָבָא: הָנֵי תְּרֵי מַקְרֵי דַּרְדְּקֵי, חַד גָּרֵיס וְלָא דָּיֵיק, וְחַד דָּיֵיק וְלָא גָּרֵיס – מוֹתְבִינַן הַהוּא דְּגָרֵיס וְלָא דָּיֵיק, שַׁבֶּשְׁתָּא מִמֵּילָא נָפְקָא. רַב דִּימִי מִנְּהַרְדְּעָא אֲמַר: מוֹתְבִינַן דְּדָיֵיק וְלָא גָּרֵיס, שַׁבֶּשְׁתָּא כֵּיוָן דְּעָל – עָל;

And Rava said: If there are **two teachers of children, one** who **teaches** a lot of material **but is not precise** in his statements, **and one** who **is precise but does not teach** a lot of material, **one hires the one who teaches** a lot of material **but is not precise.** Why is this? **Errors will be corrected by themselves,** and no lasting harm will be caused. By contrast, **Rav Dimi of Neharde'a said: One hires** the instructor **who is precise**[H] **and does not teach** a lot of material, **as once an error is taught, it is taught,** and cannot be easily corrected.

דִּכְתִיב: "כִּי שֵׁשֶׁת חֳדָשִׁים יָשַׁב שָׁם יוֹאָב וְכׇל יִשְׂרָאֵל עַד הִכְרִית כׇּל זָכָר בֶּאֱדוֹם", כִּי אֲתָא לְקַמֵּיהּ דְּדָוִד, אֲמַר לֵיהּ:

The Gemara cites a proof for the opinion of Rav Dimi of Neharde'a: This is **as it is written: "For Joab and all Israel remained there six months until he had cut off every male in Edom"** (1 Kings 11:16). **When** Joab **came before** King **David** after this episode, David **said to him:**

NOTES

The maximum number for one teacher – סָךְ מַקְרֵי: In other words, if there are fewer than twenty-five children, the townspeople are not compelled to hire a teacher (*Tosafot*). Most early commentaries disagree and say that this refers to the ideal number of students in a classroom, and that one cannot force a division into a smaller group (Ramban). Similarly, when there is a group of more than twenty-five students, a teacher cannot be forced to instruct it, and an additional teacher or aide must be hired (Rabbeinu Yona).

And if there are forty – וְאִי אִיכָּא אַרְבְּעִין: Some early commentaries state that if there are between twenty-five and forty students an assistant must be hired, whereas if there are more than forty students a new teacher is hired (Rabbeinu Yona; Rashba). Others claim that a solitary teacher can be expected to teach up to forty students. An assistant is hired if there are between forty and fifty students, and another teacher is hired if there are more than fifty (Rosh).

The teacher will come to be negligent – אָתֵי לְאִיתְרַשּׁוּלֵי: According to Rashi, the chosen educator will come to believe that he is so good that he need not make an effort, and he will become negligent. Others explain that if the first teacher is replaced, the new teacher will be negligent, as he will assume that he too will soon be replaced by a better teacher (*She'iltot deRav Aḥai Gaon*). Yet others suggest that the teacher who has been dismissed will be negligent, will forget his studies, and will no longer be able to teach (Ri Migash).

All the more so he will teach – כׇּל שֶׁכֵּן דְּגָרֵיס: Rashi states that the teacher who remains will fear that the one who was dismissed will, out of jealousy, try to find fault with his teaching, and consequently the former will exert himself to be a better teacher. Others explain that as the remaining teacher knows that an incompetent teacher can be fired, he will try to avoid being negligent (Rabbeinu Gershom Meor HaGola). Yet others suggest that the teacher who has been replaced will work harder to be rehired (Ri Migash).

HALAKHA

The maximum number for one teacher – סָךְ מַקְרֵי: The appropriate number of students for one class is twenty-five children. If there are between twenty-five and forty students, an assistant must be hired, paid for by the townspeople (Rema, citing *Nimmukei Yosef*). If there are more than forty students, a second teacher is hired. Some authorities claim that if a town lacks twenty-five students, a teacher is not hired (*Haggahot Maimoniyyot*; Rabbeinu Yeruḥam). The *Nimmukei Yosef* rules that a teacher must be employed even if there are fewer than twenty-five students (Rambam *Sefer HaMadda, Hilkhot Talmud Torah* 2:5; *Shulḥan Arukh, Yoreh De'a* 245:15, and in the comment of Rema).

All the more so he will teach – כׇּל שֶׁכֵּן דְּגָרֵיס: If a town has a teacher of children and a more competent one arrives, the first one can be dismissed in favor of the second teacher, as stated by Rav Dimi (*Shulḥan Arukh, Yoreh De'a* 245:18).

One hires the instructor who is precise – מוֹתְבִינַן דְּדָיֵיק: If there are two teachers, and one of them covers a lot of material but is imprecise, while the other is more exact in his teaching but does not cover as much material, the one who is more precise is hired, in accordance with the opinion of Rav Dimi (Rambam *Sefer HaMadda, Hilkhot Talmud Torah* 2:6 and *Kesef Mishne* and *Leḥem Mishne* there; *Shulḥan Arukh, Yoreh De'a* 245:19).

מַאי טַעְמָא עֲבַדְתְּ הָכִי? אֲמַר לֵיהּ, דִּכְתִיב: ״תִּמְחֶה אֶת זְכַר עֲמָלֵק״. אֲמַר לֵיהּ: וְהָא אֲנַן ״זֵכֶר״ קָרֵינַן! אֲמַר לֵיהּ: אֲנָא ״זְכַר״ אַקְרִיוּן. אֲזַל שַׁיְילֵיהּ לְרַבֵּיהּ, אֲמַר לֵיהּ: הֵיאַךְ אַקְרִיתָן? אֲמַר לֵיהּ: ״זֵכֶר״.

What is the reason that you did that? Why did you kill only the males? Joab **said to him: As it is written: You shall blot out the males** [*zakhar*] **of Amalek,** i.e., the male descendants of Amalek, who descend from Edom. David **said to him: But we read** the verse as stating: **"You shall blot out the remembrance** [*zekher*] **of Amalek"** (Deuteronomy 25:19). Joab **said to him: I was taught to read it as** *zakhar*. Joab **went and asked his** childhood Bible **teacher.** Joab **said to him: How did you read** this word **to us?**[N] The teacher **said to him:** I read it as *zekher*. The teacher had read it the proper way, but he failed to notice that his student had learned it incorrectly.

שְׁקַל סַפְסֵירָא לְמִיקְטְלֵיהּ. אֲמַר לֵיהּ: אַמַּאי? אֲמַר לֵיהּ, דִּכְתִיב: ״אָרוּר עֹשֶׂה מְלֶאכֶת ה׳ רְמִיָּה״. אֲמַר לֵיהּ: שְׁבַקֵיהּ לְהַהוּא גַּבְרָא דְּלֵיקוּם בְּ״אָרוּר״. אֲמַר לֵיהּ, כְּתִיב: ״וְאָרוּר מֹנֵעַ חַרְבּוֹ מִדָּם״! אִיכָּא דְּאָמְרִי: קַטְלֵיהּ, וְאִיכָּא דְּאָמְרִי: לָא קַטְלֵיהּ.

Joab **took a sword to kill him.** The teacher **said to him: Why** do you want to kill me? Joab **said to him: As it is written: "Cursed is he who does the work of the Lord with a slack hand"** (Jeremiah 48:10),[H] and you taught me incorrectly. The teacher **said to him: Leave that man to remain as cursed.** This is a sufficient punishment; there is no need to kill me. Joab **said to him: It is** also **written: "And cursed is he who keeps back his sword from blood"** (Jeremiah 48:10). **There are** those **who say** that Joab **killed him, and there are** those **who say** that **he did not kill him.** In any event, this episode demonstrates that an error learned in one's childhood stays with him his whole life.

וְאָמַר רָבָא: מַקְרֵי יָנוּקָא, שַׁתָּלָא, טַבָּחָא, וְאוּמָּנָא, וְסוֹפֵר מָתָא – כּוּלָּן כְּמוּתְרִין וְעוֹמְדִין נִינְהוּ. כְּלָלָא דְּמִילְּתָא: כָּל פְּסֵידָא דְּלָא הָדַר – מוּתְרֶה וְעוֹמֵד הוּא.

And Rava says: With regard to **a teacher of children,**[HN] a professional **tree planter,**[N] **a butcher,**[N] **a bloodletter, and a town scribe,**[N] **all these are considered forewarned.** In other words, they need not be exhorted to perform their jobs correctly, as if they err in the performance of their duties they can be dismissed immediately. The **principle of the matter** is: With regard to **any** case **where loss is irreversible,** the individual **is considered forewarned.**

HALAKHA

Cursed is he who does the work of the Lord with a slack hand – אָרוּר עֹשֶׂה מְלֶאכֶת ה׳ רְמִיָּה: A teacher of children is considered one who does the work of the Lord. If he is negligent and does not properly track his students' development, or if he busies himself with other matters, he is dismissed. Some write that a teacher should not minimize his sleep or otherwise afflict himself, as that will impair his work (Rambam *Sefer HaMadda, Hilkhot Talmud Torah* 2:3; *Shulḥan Arukh, Yoreh De'a* 245:17, and in the comment of Rema).

A teacher of children – מַקְרֵי יָנוּקָא: Teachers of children, planters of trees, butchers, scribes of documents, and any other craftsmen whose errors cannot be fixed are considered forewarned. If they cause damage they can be dismissed without further warning. Nevertheless, some commentaries write that in practice they are discharged only if they cause multiple losses and have been warned (Rambam *Sefer Mishpatim, Hilkhot Sekhirut* 10:7; *Shulḥan Arukh, Ḥoshen Mishpat* 306:8, and in the comment of Rema).

NOTES

How did you read this word to us – הֵיאַךְ אַקְרִיתָן: Most commentaries agree with Rabbeinu Ḥananel's explanation, that Joab's teacher taught him to read *zekher* correctly but the instructor was unaware that his student read it incorrectly, and therefore Joab retained this mistake his entire life. Others maintain that the teacher himself read the word as *zakhar*, out of ignorance (Ramah). This lack of diligence shows that one who is imprecise should not be a teacher (Maharal; Maharsha).

A teacher of children – מַקְרֵי יָנוּקָא: In his commentary to tractate *Bava Metzia* (109a) Rashi writes that a teacher of children harms his charges if he teaches them an error that is never corrected. The early commentaries point out that Rava, who issued that statement, is the one who said that errors would eventually be discovered and corrected. They explain that if a teacher does not teach properly, he wastes the students' time, and time is irretrievable (*Tosafot*).

A professional tree planter – שַׁתָּלָא: This does not refer to a planter who actually destroys trees, as it is clear that this individual must pay for the damage he caused. Rather, it means one who plants in such a manner that the trees do not grow properly. Although this is irretrievable damage, the owner has no legal claim against the planter (*Tosafot*).

Butcher – טַבָּחָא: It is clear that if a butcher renders the animal meat forbidden he must pay for the damage. There is an additional loss that might be incurred, e.g., if a host is unable to honor his guests properly by serving them meat, and this would be cause for the butcher's dismissal (Rabbeinu Yona).

Town scribe – סוֹפֵר מָתָא: Based on Rashi, this apparently refers to a scribe who transcribes sacred writings, e.g., those of a Torah scroll. *Tosafot* are surprised by this explanation, as if a scribe errs his mistake can be corrected. The early commentaries explain that it might refer to a case where there are too many errors to salvage the Torah scroll. Most commentaries agree with Rabbeinu Ḥananel that this refers to one who writes documents and whose imprecision might lead to considerable financial losses. According to the letter of the law the scribe would not be liable to pay in this case because he is only indirectly responsible for the loss (*Tosafot*; Rabbeinu Yona). Other commentaries suggest that this is referring to a town official, whose mistakes might cause a loss of public funds (*Ge'onim*).

אֲמַר רַב הוּנָא: הַאי בַּר מְבוֹאָה דְּאוֹקֵי רֵיחַיָּא, וְאָתָא בַּר מְבוֹאָה חַבְרֵיהּ וְקָמוֹקֵי גַּבֵּיהּ – דִּינָא הוּא דִּמְעַכֵּב עִילָּוֵיהּ, דְּאָמַר לֵיהּ: קָא פָּסְקַתְּ לֵיהּ לְחַיּוּתִי.

§ **Rav Huna said:** There was **a certain resident of an alleyway who set up a mill** in the alleyway and earned his living grinding grain for people. **And** subsequently **another resident of the alleyway came and set up** a mill **next to his. The *halakha* is that** the first one **may prevent him** from doing so if he wishes, **as he** can **say to him: You are disrupting my livelihood** by taking my customers.

לֵימָא מְסַיַּיע לֵיהּ: מַרְחִיקִים מְצוּדַת הַדָּג מִן הַדָּג כִּמְלֹא רִיצַת הַדָּג; וְכַמָּה? אָמַר רַבָּה בַּר רַב הוּנָא: עַד פַּרְסָה. שָׁאנֵי דָּגִים, דְּיָהֲבִי סַיָּיארָא.

The Gemara suggests: **Let us say** that a *baraita* **supports his** opinion: **One must distance fish traps from fish,**[N] i.e., from other fish traps, **as far as the fish travels,** i.e., the distance from which the fish will travel. The Gemara asks: **And how much is** this distance? **Rabba bar Rav Huna says: Up to a parasang** [***parsa***]. This indicates that one must distance himself from the place where another has established his business. The Gemara responds that this is no proof: Perhaps **fish are different, as they look around.**[N] One fish explores the area ahead of the others, indicating to them where to go. Once they encounter the first trap they will not approach the second.

אֲמַר לֵיהּ רָבִינָא לְרָבָא: לֵימָא, רַב הוּנָא דְּאָמַר כְּרַבִּי יְהוּדָה; דִּתְנַן, רַבִּי יְהוּדָה אוֹמֵר: לֹא יְחַלֵּק חֶנְוָנִי קְלָיוֹת וֶאֱגוֹזִין לַתִּינוֹקוֹת, מִפְּנֵי שֶׁמַּרְגִּילָן אֶצְלוֹ, וַחֲכָמִים מַתִּירִין?

Ravina said to Rava: Shall we say that **Rav Huna spoke in accordance with** the opinion of **Rabbi Yehuda? As we learned** in a mishna (*Bava Metzia* 60a): **Rabbi Yehuda says: A storekeeper may not hand out toasted grain and nuts**[H] **to children** who patronize his store, **due to** the fact **that he** thereby **accustoms them to come to him** at the expense of competing storekeepers. **And the Rabbis permit** doing so. This indicates that according to the opinion of Rabbi Yehuda, all forms of competition are prohibited, which would include the scenario concerning the mill.

אֲפִילּוּ תֵּימָא רַבָּנַן, עַד כָּאן לָא פְּלִיגִי רַבָּנַן עֲלֵיהּ דְּרַבִּי יְהוּדָה הָתָם – אֶלָּא דְּאָמַר לֵיהּ: אֲנָא קָמְפַלְגִינָא אַמְגוּזֵי, אַתְּ פְּלוֹג שִׁיוּסְקֵי, אֲבָל הָכָא אֲפִילּוּ רַבָּנַן מוֹדוּ, דְּאָמַר לֵיהּ: קָא פָּסְקַתְּ לֵיהּ לְחַיּוּתִי.

The Gemara rejects this suggestion: **You** may **even say** that Rav Huna holds in accordance with the opinion of **the Rabbis. The Rabbis disagree with Rabbi Yehuda only there,** as the storekeeper **can say to** his competitor: **If I distribute walnuts, you** can **distribute almonds** [***shiyuskei***].[L] **But here,** with regard to a resident of an alleyway who sets up a mill in that alleyway where another mill already exists, **even the Rabbis concede that** the owner of the first mill can **say to him: You are disrupting my livelihood,** as beforehand whoever required grinding came to me, and you have provided them with another option.

מֵיתִיבֵי: עוֹשֶׂה אָדָם חֲנוּת בְּצַד חֲנוּתוֹ שֶׁל חֲבֵירוֹ, וּמֶרְחָץ בְּצַד מֶרְחָצוֹ שֶׁל חֲבֵירוֹ, וְאֵינוֹ יָכוֹל לִמְחוֹת בְּיָדוֹ, מִפְּנֵי שֶׁיָּכוֹל לוֹמַר לוֹ: אַתָּה עוֹשֶׂה בְּתוֹךְ שֶׁלְּךָ וַאֲנִי עוֹשֶׂה בְּתוֹךְ שֶׁלִּי!

The Gemara **raises an objection** from a *baraita*: **A man may establish a shop alongside the shop of another, and a bathhouse alongside the bathhouse of another, and** the other **cannot protest, because** the newcomer **can say to him: You operate in your** space, **and I operate in my** space.

תַּנָּאֵי הִיא; דְּתַנְיָא: כּוֹפִין בְּנֵי מְבוֹאוֹת זֶה אֶת זֶה שֶׁלֹּא לְהוֹשִׁיב בֵּינֵיהֶן לֹא חַיָּיט וְלֹא בּוּרְסְקִי, וְלֹא מְלַמֵּד תִּינוֹקוֹת, וְלֹא אֶחָד מִבְּנֵי בַּעֲלֵי אוּמָּנִיּוֹת, וְלִשְׁכֵנוֹ אֵינוֹ כּוֹפֵיהוּ; רַבָּן שִׁמְעוֹן בֶּן גַּמְלִיאֵל אוֹמֵר: אַף לִשְׁכֵנוֹ כּוֹפֵיהוּ.

The Gemara answers: This entire matter **is a dispute between *tanna'im*, as it is taught** in a *baraita*: **The residents of an alleyway can compel one another**[H] to agree **not to allow among them**[N] in that alleyway **a tailor, a tanner, a teacher of children, nor any type of craftsman.** They can bar outside craftsmen from plying their trade in that alleyway. **But one cannot compel his neighbor,** i.e., one who already lives in the alleyway, to refrain from practicing a particular occupation there. **Rabban Shimon ben Gamliel says:** One can **even compel his neighbor** not to conduct such work in the alleyway. Rav Huna holds in accordance with the opinion of Rabban Shimon ben Gamliel.

NOTES

One must distance fish traps from fish – מַרְחִיקִים מְצוּדַת הַדָּג מִן הַדָּג: Rashi explains that if a fisherman intends to catch a particular fish, no one else may cast his net in the same place. Others explain that the phrase: From fish, means from a fish trap. The reason a trap would be referred to as: Fish, is that it was common practice to put one fish in the trap in order to attract other fish (Rabbeinu Ḥananel; see Rabbeinu Yona). Generally, one does not acquire an item that has not yet entered his possession, and one who seizes it beforehand is not considered wicked. Nevertheless, this principle refers only to an item that is available only on occasion, e.g., a found item. If one goes fishing near a place where another is already fishing, he is negatively affecting the other's steady livelihood.

As they look around – דְּיָהֲבִי סַיָּיארָא: There are different versions and interpretations of the text here. Rashi explains that a fish searches for food, and therefore one who puts food in his trap will certainly catch the fish. This is not the case with regard to a mill, where customers freely choose whom to patronize. Others state that fish can see other fish feeding from a distance of a parasang, which attracts them. For this reason they are considered caught in the net of the first fisherman (Rabbeinu Ḥananel). Alternatively, if the fish food is dispersed in one location, it can cause fish to migrate from the place where the second fisherman has cast his net to the area of the first fisherman (*Arukh*, citing Rabbeinu Gershom Meor HaGola). This is considered theft (Ramban). Yet others maintain that this refers to scouting fish who lead their school away from traps in general, including those of both fishermen mentioned here (Ri Migash).

Not to allow among them – שֶׁלֹּא לְהוֹשִׁיב בֵּינֵיהֶן: Some commentaries write that this refers to a place where there is already a craftsman of that type present, and therefore the residents of a courtyard can agree to bar another such craftsman from competing with the first (Rashi; *Tosafot*). Others explain that the residents of the courtyard can object to allowing these craftsmen to conduct business there because they attract many customers, who will increase the traffic and noise in the courtyard.

HALAKHA

Toasted grain and nuts – קְלָיוֹת וֶאֱגוֹזִין: It is permitted for a storekeeper to distribute toasted grain and nuts to children, or to reduce his prices in order to attract customers. Other storekeepers cannot protest this practice, in accordance with the opinion of the Rabbis (Rambam *Sefer Kinyan*, *Hilkhot Mekhira* 18:4; *Shulḥan Arukh*, *Ḥoshen Mishpat* 228:18).

The residents of an alleyway can compel one another – כּוֹפִין בְּנֵי מְבוֹאוֹת זֶה אֶת זֶה: Residents of an alleyway can prevent residents of other alleyways from setting up certain businesses in their alleyway. If a particular craftsman was operating in the alleyway without protest, another resident of the same alleyway may set up the same type of service there. Nevertheless, the residents may prevent someone from another city from doing so. If the outsider pays taxes in the town, they cannot prevent him from setting up his business. Some authorities write that although the first craftsman cannot prevent the outsider from working in the town, he can prevent him from working in the alleyway in which he is operating (Rambam *Sefer Kinyan*, *Hilkhot Shekhenim* 6:8; *Shulḥan Arukh*, *Ḥoshen Mishpat* 156:5, and in the comment of Rema and *Sma* there).

LANGUAGE

Almonds [*shiyuskei*] – שִׁיוּסְקֵי: The precise origin and meaning of this term are subject to dispute. Rashi explains that it means almonds, whereas elsewhere he says it means prunes. The *Arukh* identifies this fruit as the peach, while others maintain that it refers to the *Ziziphus jujuba*, i.e., the fruit of a leafy tree with a large stone.

אָמַר רַב הוּנָא בְּרֵיהּ דְּרַב יְהוֹשֻׁעַ: פְּשִׁיטָא לִי, בַּר מָתָא אַבַּר מָתָא אַחֲרִיתִי מָצֵי מְעַכֵּב, וְאִי שַׁיֵּיךְ בִּכְרָגָא דְּהָכָא – לָא מָצֵי מְעַכֵּב; בַּר מְבוֹאָה אַבַּר מְבוֹאָה דְּנַפְשֵׁיהּ – לָא מָצֵי מְעַכֵּב.

Rav Huna, son of Rav Yehoshua, says: It is **obvious to me** that **a resident of** one **town can prevent a resident of another town** from establishing a similar business in the locale of the first individual. **But if he pays the tax**[B] **of that** first town, **he cannot prevent him** from doing business there, as he too is considered a resident of the town. **The resident of an alleyway cannot prevent a resident of his alleyway** from practicing a particular trade there, in accordance with the opinion of the Rabbis in the *baraita*, and contrary to the opinion of Rabban Shimon ben Gamliel.

בָּעֵי רַב הוּנָא בְּרֵיהּ דְּרַב יְהוֹשֻׁעַ: בַּר מְבוֹאָה אַבַּר מְבוֹאָה אַחֲרִינָא, מַאי? תֵּיקוּ. אָמַר רַב יוֹסֵף: וּמוֹדֵי רַב הוּנָא בְּמַקְרֵי דַרְדְּקֵי דְּלָא מָצֵי מְעַכֵּב, דְּאָמַר מָר: עֶזְרָא תִּיקֵּן לָהֶן לְיִשְׂרָאֵל שֶׁיְּהוּ מוֹשִׁיבִין סוֹפֵר בְּצַד סוֹפֵר.

With these conclusions in mind, **Rav Huna, son of Rav Yehoshua, raises a dilemma:** With regard to **a resident of** one **alleyway** protesting about **a resident of another alleyway**[N] conducting business there, **what** is the *halakha*? No answer was found, and the Gemara states that the dilemma **shall stand** unresolved. **Rav Yosef said: And Rav Huna,** who said that a resident of an alleyway can prevent another from setting up an additional mill, **concedes with regard to those who teach children**[H] **that one cannot prevent** him from working, **as the Master said: Ezra instituted**[B] an ordinance **for the Jewish people** requiring **that they establish** one **teacher alongside** another **teacher,** to raise the standard of teaching.

וְנֵיחוּשׁ דִּילְמָא אָתֵי לְאִיתְרַשּׁוּלֵי! אֲמַר לֵיהּ:

The Gemara challenges: **And let us be concerned lest** the teachers **will** thereby **come to be negligent.** Rav Yosef **said to** the Sage who raised this objection:

NOTES

A resident of another alleyway – אַבַּר מְבוֹאָה אַחֲרִינָא: The question is as follows: According to the opinion of the Rabbis in the *baraita*, who maintain that one cannot prevent his neighbor from establishing his trade, is a citizen of the city who is a resident of a different alleyway considered a neighbor, whom one cannot prevent from performing his trade in the alleyway, or is he considered an outsider (Rashi)? Some commentaries explain that this refers to an individual who seeks to set up shop in a nearby alleyway, and the question is whether that is close enough to allow the neighbors to protest (Rabbeinu Yona; see Ramban).

BACKGROUND

He pays the tax – שַׁיֵּיךְ בִּכְרָגָא: Several sources in the Gemara suggest that this tax was collected in every town and district, and it went directly into the tax collectors' own pockets. For the purpose of this collection the country was divided into regions and each town was included in a specific region.

Ezra instituted – עֶזְרָא תִּיקֵּן: Ezra the Scribe moved to Eretz Yisrael in 457 BCE, where he served as a leader of the Jewish community that returned from the Babylonian exile. The Talmud (*Bava Kamma* 82a) lists ten ordinances that he instituted for a variety of purposes, including to improve the people's commitment to the Torah, to ensure modest behavior, and to enhance domestic harmony. This particular ordinance, allowing competition among teachers of schoolchildren, is not included in that list, although it may be a subcategory of the ordinance requiring the public reading of the Torah during the week. Both ordinances share the common denominator of spreading the knowledge of and dedication to Torah.

HALAKHA

With regard to those who teach children – בְּמַקְרֵי דַרְדְּקֵי: A teacher of children is permitted to work alongside another teacher (Rambam *Sefer Kinyan*, *Hilkhot Shekhenim* 6:12 and *Sefer HaMadda*, *Hilkhot Talmud Torah* 2:7; *Shulḥan Arukh*, *Ḥoshen Mishpat* 156:3 and *Beur HaGra* there).

Perek **II**
Daf **22** Amud **a**

קִנְאַת סוֹפְרִים תַּרְבֶּה חָכְמָה.

Jealousy among teachers increases wisdom.

אָמַר רַב נַחְמָן בַּר יִצְחָק: וּמוֹדֶה רַב הוּנָא בְּרֵיהּ דְּרַב יְהוֹשֻׁעַ בְּרוֹכְלִין הַמַּחֲזִירִין בָּעֲיָירוֹת דְּלָא מָצֵי מְעַכֵּב, דְּאָמַר מָר: עֶזְרָא תִּקֵּן לָהֶן לְיִשְׂרָאֵל שֶׁיְּהוּ רוֹכְלִין מַחֲזִירִין בָּעֲיָירוֹת, כְּדֵי שֶׁיְּהוּ תַּכְשִׁיטִין מְצוּיִין לִבְנוֹת יִשְׂרָאֵל.

Rav Naḥman bar Yitzḥak said: And Rav Huna, son of Rav Yehoshua, who said that townspeople can bar craftsmen who come from other cities, **concedes with regard to** perfume **salesmen who travel from** one **town** to another[H] **that** the townspeople **cannot prevent** them from entering their town. **As the Master said: Ezra instituted** an ordinance **for the Jewish people that** perfume **salesmen shall travel from town to town so that cosmetics will be available to Jewish women.** Since this ordinance was instituted on behalf of Jewish women, the Sages ruled that these peddlers could not be barred from entering a town.

וְהָנֵי מִילֵּי לְאַהֲדוּרֵי, אֲבָל לְאַקְבּוֹעֵי – לָא. וְאִי צוּרְבָא מֵרַבָּנַן הוּא – אֲפִילּוּ לְאַקְבּוֹעֵי נָמֵי, כִּי הָא דְּרָבָא שְׁרָא לְהוּ לְרַבִּי יֹאשִׁיָּה וּלְרַב עוֹבַדְיָה לְאַקְבּוֹעֵי, דְּלָא כְּהִלְכְתָא, מַאי טַעְמָא? כֵּיוָן דְּרַבָּנַן נִינְהוּ, אָתוּ לְטַרוּדֵי מִגִּירְסַיְיהוּ.

The Gemara continues: **And this matter** applies only to one who seeks **to travel** from town to town as a salesman. **But** if he wants **to establish** a shop, this ruling was **not** stated, and the townspeople can prevent him from doing so. **And if he is a Torah scholar**[N] **he may even establish** a shop as a perfume salesman. This is **like that** incident in **which Rava permitted Rabbi Yoshiya and Rav Ovadya to establish** a shop **not** in accordance **with the** *halakha*. **What is the reason** for this ruling? The reason is that **since they are rabbis, they are likely to be distracted from their studies** should they be required to travel from place to place.

HALAKHA

With regard to perfume salesmen who travel from one town to another – בְּרוֹכְלִין הַמַּחֲזִירִין בָּעֲיָירוֹת: Perfume salesmen who travel from town to town selling their wares to Jewish women cannot be prevented by local residents from doing so, despite the fact that other kinds of merchants can be barred (Rema). Even perfume salesmen cannot set up a permanent business, and instead must travel from town to town. Torah scholars and schoolteachers are permitted to operate wherever they want (Rambam *Sefer Kinyan*, *Hilkhot Shekhenim* 6:9; *Shulḥan Arukh*, *Ḥoshen Mishpat* 156:6, and in the comment of Rema).

NOTES

And if he is a Torah scholar – וְאִי צוּרְבָא מֵרַבָּנַן הוּא: It is permitted for a Torah scholar to set up shop to sell his perfumes in a place he is visiting, and he need not go door to door or from town to town. The commentaries note that this is permitted only in the case of perfume salesmen, as they serve Jewish women, but not in the case of other types of merchants (Rabbeinu Ḥananel; Ramah).

הָנְהוּ דִּיקוּלָאֵי דְּאַיְיתוּ דִּיקְלָאֵי לְבָבֶל, אֲתוּ בְּנֵי מָתָא קָא מְעַכְּבִי עִלָּוַיְיהוּ, אֲתוּ לְקַמֵּיהּ דְּרָבִינָא, אֲמַר לְהוּ: מֵעָלְמָא אָתוּ, וּלְעָלְמָא לִיזַבְּנוּ. וְהָנֵי מִילֵּי בְּיוֹמָא דְּשׁוּקָא, אֲבָל בְּלָא יוֹמָא דְּשׁוּקָא – לָא. וּבְיוֹמָא דְּשׁוּקָא נַמִי לָא אָמְרִינַן אֶלָּא לְזַבּוֹנֵי בְּשׁוּקָא, אֲבָל לְאַהֲדוּרֵי – לָא.

§ The Gemara relates: There were **these basket sellers**[N] **who brought baskets to Babylonia. The townspeople came** and **prevented them** from selling there. The two parties **came before Ravina** for a ruling. Ravina **said to them:** The basket sellers **came from outside**[H] the town, **and they sell to** those from **outside**[N] the town, i.e., to guests who are not residents of the town. The Gemara comments: **And this statement** applies only **on a market day,** when people from other towns come to shop, **but** they may **not** sell their wares **on non-market days. And even with regard to market days, we say** so **only** with regard **to selling in the market, but** this *halakha* does **not** apply **to circulating** around the town.

הָנְהוּ עָמוֹרָאֵי דְּאַיְיתוּ עַמְרָא לְפוּם נַהֲרָא, אֲתוּ בְּנֵי מָתָא קָא מְעַכְּבִי עִלָּוַיְיהוּ, אֲתוּ לְקַמֵּיהּ דְּרַב כָּהֲנָא, אֲמַר לְהוּ: דִּינָא הוּא דִּמְעַכְּבִי עֲלַייְכוּ. אֲמַרוּ לֵיהּ: אִית לָן אַשְׁרַאי. אֲמַר לְהוּ: זִילוּ זַבְּנוּ שִׁיעוּר חִיּוּתַיְיכוּ, עַד דְּעָקְרִיתוּ אַשְׁרַאי דִּידְכוּ וְאָזְלִיתוּ.

The Gemara further relates: There were **these wool sellers who brought wool to** the city of **Pum Nahara. The townsfolk came** and **prevented them** from selling it. The two parties **came before Rav Kahana** for a ruling. Rav Kahana **said to them: The *halakha* is that they may prevent you** from selling your wares. The wool sellers **said to him: We have debts** to collect in the city, and we must sell our wares in the meantime to sustain ourselves until we are paid. Rav Kahana **said to them: Go** and **sell the amount** needed **to sustain yourselves until you have collected your debts,** and then **leave.**

רַב דִּימִי מִנְּהַרְדְּעָא אַיְיתֵי גְּרוֹגָרוֹת בִּסְפִינָה, אֲמַר לֵיהּ רֵישׁ גָּלוּתָא לְרָבָא: פּוּק חֲזֵי, אִי צוּרְבָא מֵרַבָּנַן הוּא נְקֵיט לֵיהּ שׁוּקָא. אֲמַר לֵיהּ רָבָא לְרַב אַדָּא בַּר אַבָּא: פּוּק תְּהִי לֵיהּ בְּקַנְקַנֵּיהּ.

§ The Gemara relates: **Rav Dimi of Neharde'a**[P] **brought dried figs on a ship** to sell them. **The Exilarch said to Rava: Go** and **see; if he is a Torah scholar, reserve the market for him,**[H] i.e., declare that he has the exclusive right to sell dried figs. **Rava said to** his student **Rav Adda bar Abba:**[P] **Go** and **smell his jar,**[N] i.e., determine whether or not Rav Dimi is a Torah scholar.

נְפַק [אֲזַל], בְּעָא מִינֵּיהּ: פִּיל שֶׁבָּלַע כְּפִיפָה מִצְרִית וְהֵקִיאָהּ דֶּרֶךְ בֵּית הָרְעִי, מַהוּ? לָא הֲוָה בִּידֵיהּ. אֲמַר לֵיהּ: מָר נִיהוּ רָבָא? טְפַח לֵיהּ בְּסַנְדָּלֵיהּ, אֲמַר לֵיהּ: בֵּין דִּידִי לְרָבָא אִיכָּא טוּבָא, מִיהוּ עַל כָּרְחָךְ אֲנָא רַבָּךְ וְרָבָא רַבָּה דְּרַבָּךְ.

Rav Adda bar Abba **went** and **asked** Rav Dimi a question: With regard to **an elephant that swallowed**[N] **a wicker basket**[H] **and excreted it** intact along **with its waste, what is the** *halakha*? Is the vessel still susceptible to ritual impurity or is it considered digested and not susceptible to impurity? An answer **was not available to** Rav Dimi. Rav Dimi **said to** Rav Adda bar Abba: **Is the Master Rava,** i.e., are you Rava, as you have asked me such a difficult question? Rav Adda bar Abba **struck him on his shoe** in a disparaging way and **said to him: There is a great** difference **between me and Rava; but I am perforce your teacher, and Rava is your teacher's teacher.**

לָא נְקַטוּ לֵיהּ שׁוּקָא, פָּסֵיד גְּרוֹגָרוֹת דִּידֵיהּ. אֲתָא לְקַמֵּיהּ דְּרַב יוֹסֵף, אֲמַר לֵיהּ: חֲזֵי מָר מַאי עֲבַדוּ לִי! אֲמַר לֵיהּ: מַאן דְּלָא שָׁהְיָיהּ לְאוֹנִיתָא דְּמַלְכָּא דֶּאֱדוֹם – לָא נִשְׁהֲיָיהּ לְאוֹנִיתָךְ, דִּכְתִיב: "כֹּה אָמַר ה׳ עַל שְׁלֹשָׁה פִּשְׁעֵי מוֹאָב וְעַל אַרְבָּעָה לֹא אֲשִׁיבֶנּוּ עַל שָׂרְפוֹ עַצְמוֹת מֶלֶךְ אֱדוֹם לַסִּיד".

Based on this exchange, Rav Adda bar Abba decided that Rav Dimi was not a great Torah scholar, and therefore **he did not reserve the market for him, and** Rav Dimi **lost his dried figs,** as they rotted. Rav Dimi **came before Rav Yosef** to complain, and **said to him: The Master** should **see what they did to me.** Rav Yosef **said to him: He Who did not delay** retribution for **the humiliation of the King of Edom should not delay** His response to **your humiliation,** but should punish whoever distressed you, **as it is written: "So says the Lord: For three transgressions of Moab, indeed for four I will not reverse for him, because he burned the bones of the King of Edom into lime"** (Amos 2:1).

NOTES

Basket sellers – דִּיקוּלָאֵי: According to Rashi this refers to basket sellers, while others say it is referring to those who sell cauldrons. Some claim that the Gemara is referring to sellers of pots (Ramah).

And they sell to those from outside – וּלְעָלְמָא לִיזַבְּנוּ: Since people come from other towns on market days, the residents of that town do not have the right to prevent non-local merchants from selling to them. Such conduct on the part of visiting merchants should not be seen as competing with local salesmen.

Smell his jar – תְּהִי לֵיהּ בְּקַנְקַנֵּיהּ: This expression is derived from the practice of testing wine by smelling it in a jug. Here it means that Rava wants Rav Adda bar Abba to test Rav Dimi to determine whether or not he is a Torah scholar as Rav Dimi claimed.

An elephant that swallowed – פִּיל שֶׁבָּלַע: This question refers to ritual purity. According to the conclusion of the Gemara in tractate *Menaḥot* (69a), this does not refer to an impure basket that was swallowed, as it is clear from the discussion there that the item retains its impurity. Rather, it refers to an elephant that ate soft willow reeds that formed a sort of basket in its digestive tract. The question is whether this is now considered a utensil that is susceptible to impurity, or whether the reeds are considered like dung, which cannot become impure (see *Tosafot*).

HALAKHA

They came from outside – מֵעָלְמָא אָתוּ: If merchants arrive from another town, the local townspeople can prevent them from selling their wares. They cannot prevent them from doing so on market days, provided that they sell only in the market, as opposed to going from door to door. It is permitted for salesmen who are owed money to sell as much as they need to survive until they can collect the debts. Some commentaries write that the residents can prevent outsiders from selling their products only if the prices and quality of their wares are equal to those offered by the local salesmen (Rema). They cannot protest if the traveling salesmen offer lower prices or superior-quality goods (*Tur*, citing *Tosafot* and Rosh). This is also the *halakha* if the visitors are offering a slightly different product (Rambam *Sefer Kinyan*, *Hilkhot Shekhenim* 6:10; *Shulḥan Arukh*, *Ḥoshen Mishpat* 156:7).

Reserve the market for him – נְקֵיט לֵיהּ שׁוּקָא: If a Torah scholar wants to sell his merchandise, it is not permitted for other salesmen to sell their wares until he disposes of his entire stock (Rambam *Sefer HaMadda*, *Hilkhot Talmud Torah* 6:10; *Shulḥan Arukh*, *Yoreh De'a* 243:4 and *Ḥoshen Mishpat* 156:5, and in the comment of Rema).

An elephant that swallowed a wicker basket – פִּיל שֶׁבָּלַע כְּפִיפָה מִצְרִית: If an elephant swallows a wicker basket and excretes it, the vessel remains susceptible to ritual impurity (Rambam *Sefer Tahara*, *Hilkhot Kelim* 1:7).

PERSONALITIES

Rav Dimi of Neharde'a – רַב דִּימִי מִנְּהַרְדְּעָא: Rav Dimi was an *amora* from Babylonia who lived in the fourth and fifth generations of *amora'im*. Although he was apparently a younger contemporary, Rav Yosef considered him an important Torah scholar, as he engaged in disputes with Abaye and Rava. Rav Dimi was probably a merchant. Based on the many *halakhot* cited in his name, he was also the leader of the town where he lived. According to Rav Sherira Gaon, Rav Dimi enjoyed a long life and served as head of the yeshiva of Pumbedita between the years 385 and 388 CE.

Rav Adda bar Abba – רַב אַדָּא בַּר אַבָּא: This *amora* lived in Babylonia during the fourth and fifth generations of *amora'im*, during the period of Rav Yosef. He was the outstanding student of Rava, although he also studied with Abaye. Reports about him illustrate that he was particularly sharp and expressed himself pointedly in his disputes with the Sages. Little is known of Rav Adda bar Abba's life, although as indicated by the Gemara here, he apparently died young.

נָח נַפְשֵׁיהּ דְּרַב אַדָּא בַּר אַבָּא. רַב יוֹסֵף אָמַר: אֲנָא עֲנִישְׁתֵּיהּ, דַּאֲנָא לְטַיְיתֵיהּ. רַב דִּימִי מִנְּהַרְדְּעָא אָמַר: אֲנָא עֲנִישְׁתֵּיהּ, דְּאַפְסֵיד גְּרוֹגְרוֹת דִּידִי. אַבָּיֵי אָמַר: אֲנָא עֲנִישְׁתֵּיהּ, דְּאָמַר לְהוּ לְרַבָּנַן: אַדִּמְגָרְמִיתוּ גַּרְמֵי בֵּי אַבָּיֵי, תּוּ אִכְלוּ בִּישְׂרָא [שְׁמֵינָא] בֵּי רָבָא. וְרָבָא אָמַר: אֲנָא עֲנִישְׁתֵּיהּ, [דְּכִי הֲוָה אָזֵיל לְבֵי טַבָּחָא לְמִשְׁקַל אוּמְצָא], אָמַר לְהוּ לְטַבָּחֵי: אֲנָא שָׁקֵילְנָא בִּישְׂרָא מִיקַּמֵּי שַׁמָּעֵיהּ דְּרָבָא, דַּאֲנָא עֲדִיפְנָא מִינֵּיהּ.

The Gemara reports that **Rav Adda bar Abba died. Rav Yosef said: I punished him,**[N] i.e., I am to blame for his death, **as I cursed him. Rav Dimi from Neharde'a said: I punished him, as he caused my loss of dried figs. Abaye said: I punished him,** i.e., he was punished on my account because he did not exhibit the proper respect for me. As Rav Adda bar Abba **said to the Sages: Instead of gnawing the bones in the school of Abaye, you would** do **better to eat fatty meat in the school of Rava,** i.e., it is preferable to study with Rava than with Abaye. **And Rava said: I punished him, as when he would go to the butcher to buy a piece of meat, he would say to the butchers: I will take meat before Rava's servant, as I am greater than he is.**[N]

רַב נַחְמָן בַּר יִצְחָק אָמַר: אֲנָא עֲנִישְׁתֵּיהּ, דְּרַב נַחְמָן בַּר יִצְחָק רֵישׁ כַּלָּה הֲוָה, כָּל יוֹמָא מִיקַּמֵּי דְּנֵיעוּל לְכַלָּה, מְרַהֵיט בַּהֲדֵיהּ רַב אַדָּא בַּר אַבָּא לִשְׁמַעְתֵּיהּ וַהֲדַר עָיֵיל לְכַלָּה.

Rav Naḥman bar Yitzḥak said: I punished him, i.e., he was punished because of me, **as Rav Naḥman bar Yitzḥak was the head of the *kalla* lectures,** the gatherings for Torah study during Elul and Adar. Rav Naḥman bar Yitzḥak would teach the students immediately following the lesson taught by the head of the academy. **Every day, before he went in for the *kalla* lecture, he reviewed his lecture with Rav Adda bar Abba, and then he would enter** the study hall **for the *kalla*** lecture.

הָהוּא יוֹמָא נַקְטוּהּ רַב פָּפָּא וְרַב הוּנָא בְּרֵיהּ דְּרַב יְהוֹשֻׁעַ לְרַב אַדָּא בַּר אַבָּא מִשּׁוּם דְּלָא הֲווּ בְּסִיּוּמָא, אָמְרוּ לֵיהּ: אֵימָא לַן הָנֵי שְׁמַעְתָּתָא דְּמַעְשַׂר בְּהֵמָה הֵיכִי אָמְרִינְהוּ רָבָא. אָמַר לְהוּ: הָכִי אָמַר רָבָא וְהָכִי אָמַר רָבָא. אַדְּהָכִי נְגַהּ לֵיהּ [לְרַב נַחְמָן בַּר יִצְחָק], וְלָא אָתֵי רַב אַדָּא בַּר אַבָּא.

On that day Rav Pappa and Rav Huna, son of Rav Yehoshua, seized Rav Adda bar Abba, because they had not been present at the conclusion of Rava's lecture. **They said to him: Tell us how Rava stated these *halakhot* of animal tithe.**[B] Rav Adda bar Abba **said to them: Rava said this and Rava said that. Meanwhile, it grew late for Rav Naḥman bar Yitzḥak, and Rav Adda bar Abba** had **not** yet **arrived.**

אָמְרוּ לֵיהּ רַבָּנַן לְרַב נַחְמָן בַּר יִצְחָק: קוּם דִּנְגַהּ לַן, לָמָּה יָתֵיב מָר? אָמַר לְהוּ: יָתֵיבְנָא וְקָא מְנַטְרָא לְעַרְסֵיהּ דְּרַב אַדָּא בַּר אַבָּא. אַדְּהָכִי נְפַק קָלָא דְּנָח נַפְשֵׁיהּ דְּרַב אַדָּא בַּר אַבָּא. וּמִסְתַּבְּרָא, דְּרַב נַחְמָן בַּר יִצְחָק עַנְשֵׁיהּ.

The Sages said to Rav Naḥman bar Yitzḥak: Arise and teach us, **as it is late for us. Why does the Master sit** and wait? Rav Naḥman bar Yitzḥak **said to them: I am sitting and waiting for the bier of Rav Adda bar Abba,** who has presumably died. **Meanwhile, a rumor emerged that Rav Adda bar Abba had** indeed **died.** The Gemara comments: **And so too, it is reasonable** to conclude **that Rav Naḥman bar Yitzḥak punished him,** i.e., he died as a result of Rav Naḥman bar Yitzḥak's statement, as the unfortunate event occurred just as he announced that Rav Adda bar Abba's bier was on its way.

מתני׳ מִי שֶׁהָיָה כּוֹתְלוֹ סָמוּךְ לְכוֹתֶל חֲבֵירוֹ, לֹא יִסְמוֹךְ לוֹ כּוֹתֶל אַחֵר אֶלָּא אִם כֵּן הִרְחִיק מִמֶּנּוּ אַרְבַּע אַמּוֹת. הַחַלּוֹנוֹת, בֵּין מִלְמַעְלָן בֵּין מִלְּמַטָּן בֵּין כְּנֶגְדָּן – אַרְבַּע אַמּוֹת.

MISHNA **One whose wall was close**[H] **to the wall of another may not build another wall** close to the neighbor's wall **unless he distances it four cubits** from the wall of the neighbor. And one who desires to build a wall opposite **the windows** of a neighbor's house must distance the wall **four cubits** from the windows, **whether above,**[NH] **below, or opposite.**

גמ׳ וְקַמָּא הֵיכִי סָמֵיךְ? אָמַר רַב יְהוּדָה, הָכִי קָאָמַר:

GEMARA The Gemara comments: Before addressing the construction of the second wall, one could ask: **And** with regard to the **first** man, **how did he place** his wall **close** to the neighbor's wall in the first place? **Rav Yehuda said** that **this is what** the *tanna* **is saying:**

NOTES

I punished him – אֲנָא עֲנִישְׁתֵּיהּ: *Tosafot* explain that each of the Sages who said this feared that what Rav Adda bar Abba did to him caused his premature death. The Talmud states elsewhere (*Shabbat* 149b): With regard to anyone who causes another to be punished on his account, they do not bring him within the partition of the Holy One, Blessed be He.

As I am greater than he is – דַּאֲנָא עֲדִיפְנָא מִינֵּיהּ: The later commentaries are surprised at this comment. As Rav Adda bar Abba himself said earlier: Rava is your teacher's teacher, how could he say that he was greater than him? Some explain that Rav Adda bar Abba meant that he is greater than Rava's servant. He acted inappropriately because the servant represented Rava (Riaf).

Whether above – בֵּין מִלְמַעְלָן: According to Rashi, the terms above and below refer to the height of the wall relative to the windows. It means that one must build the wall either four cubits higher than or lower than the window, as he must take care that the top of the wall measures more than four cubits from the level of the window to preclude him from being able to look inside the window from the wall. Others write that the terms above and below refer to the position of the window in the neighbor's house, so that it is understood to mean: Whether the windows are built into the upper or lower part of the wall. In the former case, the new wall must be built to a maximum height of four cubits lower than the window, and in the latter case, to a minimum height of four cubits higher than the window (Rambam's Commentary on the Mishna; see *Tosefot Yom Tov*).

BACKGROUND

Animal tithe – מַעְשַׂר בְּהֵמָה: On three occasions each year, the owner of a herd of kosher animals was required to gather into an enclosure all the animals born during the preceding period, and to let them out one by one. These animals were passed "under the rod" of the shepherd (see Leviticus 27:32), and every tenth animal was marked with red paint to indicate that it was consecrated. These animals were consecrated as animal tithe. If the animal was fit to be sacrificed, it was brought to the Temple and sacrificed in a manner similar to that of a peace-offering. Its blood was sprinkled on the altar, and its meat was eaten by its owner, but not by the priests. The *halakhot* of animal tithe are enumerated in tractate *Bekhorot*.

HALAKHA

One whose wall was close – מִי שֶׁהָיָה כּוֹתְלוֹ סָמוּךְ: If one has a wall that is near a neighbor's wall, the neighbor may not build another wall parallel to the first wall unless he distances it from the neighbor's wall by four cubits (Rambam *Sefer Kinyan*, *Hilkhot Shekhenim* 9:9; *Shulḥan Arukh*, *Ḥoshen Mishpat* 155:12).

The windows…whether above – הַחַלּוֹנוֹת בֵּין מִלְמַעְלָן: If one has a window in his wall and a neighbor establishes a courtyard next to it (see *Sma*), the owner of the courtyard cannot compel the owner of the window to block the window. If the owner of the courtyard wants to build a wall opposite the window to prevent his neighbor from looking into his courtyard, he must keep it a distance of four cubits from the window so that the light entering the window is not blocked. With regard to the height of the wall, if the window is built into the lower part of the wall, its owner can force the owner of the courtyard to raise the wall to four cubits above the window. If the window is built into the upper part of the wall, the top of the wall must be at least four cubits above the top of the window or four cubits below the bottom of the window, respectively (Rambam *Sefer Kinyan*, *Hilkhot Shekhenim* 7:1–3; *Shulḥan Arukh*, *Ḥoshen Mishpat* 154:21).

הַבָּא לִסְמוֹךְ, לֹא יִסְמוֹךְ אֶלָּא אִם כֵּן הִרְחִיק מִמֶּנּוּ אַרְבַּע אַמּוֹת. מַתְקִיף לַהּ רָבָא: וְהָא ״מִי שֶׁהָיָה כּוֹתְלוֹ סָמוּךְ לְכוֹתֶל חֲבֵירוֹ״ קָתָנֵי!

One who comes to place a wall **close** to his neighbor's wall **may place** that wall **close** to the neighbor's wall **only if he distances** his wall **four cubits from the existing wall.** Accordingly, the mishna is discussing one constructing a wall close to his neighbor's wall the first time. **Rava objects to this** explanation: **But** the mishna **teaches: One whose wall was near the wall of another,**[N] which indicates that there had already been a wall there.

אֶלָּא אָמַר רָבָא, הָכִי קָתָנֵי: מִי שֶׁהָיָה כּוֹתְלוֹ סָמוּךְ לְכוֹתֶל חֲבֵירוֹ בְּרִחוּק אַרְבַּע אַמּוֹת וְנָפַל, לֹא יִסְמוֹךְ לוֹ כּוֹתֶל אַחֵר אֶלָּא אִם כֵּן הִרְחִיק מִמֶּנּוּ אַרְבַּע אַמּוֹת; מַאי טַעְמָא? דְּדַוְושָׁא דְּהָכָא מַעֲלֵי לְהָתָם.

Rather, Rava said that **this** is what the mishna **is teaching:** In a case of **one whose wall**[N] **was near the wall of another**[B] **at a distance of four cubits and it fell, he may not place another wall close** to his neighbor's wall **unless he distances** the wall **four cubits from it. What is the reason** that this distance must be observed? The reason is **that walking here benefits there,** i.e., the ground is strengthened by people walking on the land in the area between the walls.

אָמַר רַב: לֹא שָׁנוּ אֶלָּא כּוֹתֶל גִּינָּה, אֲבָל כּוֹתֶל חָצֵר – אִם בָּא לִסְמוֹךְ סוֹמֵךְ; רַבִּי אוֹשַׁעְיָא אוֹמֵר: אֶחָד כּוֹתֶל גִּינָּה וְאֶחָד כּוֹתֶל חָצֵר – אִם בָּא לִסְמוֹךְ אֵינוֹ סוֹמֵךְ.

Rav says: They taught that one must leave a space of four cubits between his wall and that of his neighbor **only** if he builds it alongside **the wall of** his neighbor's **garden,**[HN] where people do not usually walk due to the seeds. **But** with regard to **the wall of a courtyard,** where people walk, **if he comes to place** his wall **close** by, **he may place** it **close** by. By contrast, **Rabbi Oshaya says:** With regard to **both the wall of a garden and the wall of a courtyard, if one comes to place** his wall **close** by, **he may not place** his wall **close** by.

אָמַר רַבִּי יוֹסֵי בַּר חֲנִינָא: וְלָא פְּלִיגִי, הָא בְּעִיר יְשָׁנָה, הָא בְּעִיר חֲדָשָׁה.

Rabbi Yosei bar Ḥanina said: And the two *amora'im* **do not disagree,** as they are referring to different cases. **This** statement of Rav is referring **to an old city,** whose ground is well trodden and stable, and **that** statement of Rabbi Oshaya is referring **to a new city,** where even the wall of a courtyard requires walking on its adjacent ground to strengthen it.

BACKGROUND

One whose wall was near the wall of another – מִי שֶׁהָיָה כּוֹתְלוֹ סָמוּךְ לְכוֹתֶל חֲבֵירוֹ:

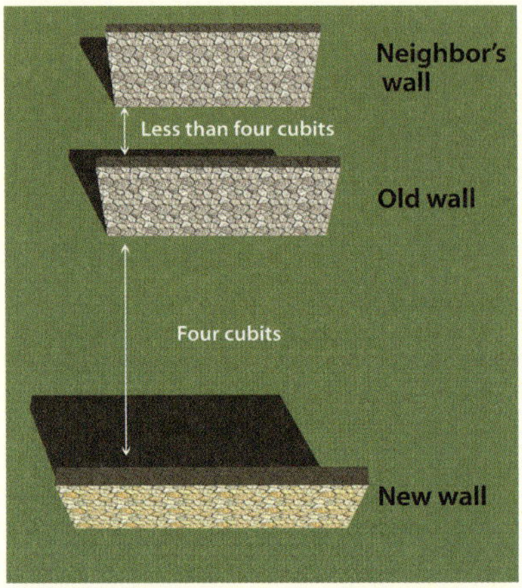

Wall juxtaposed to neighbor's wall according to the *ge'onim*

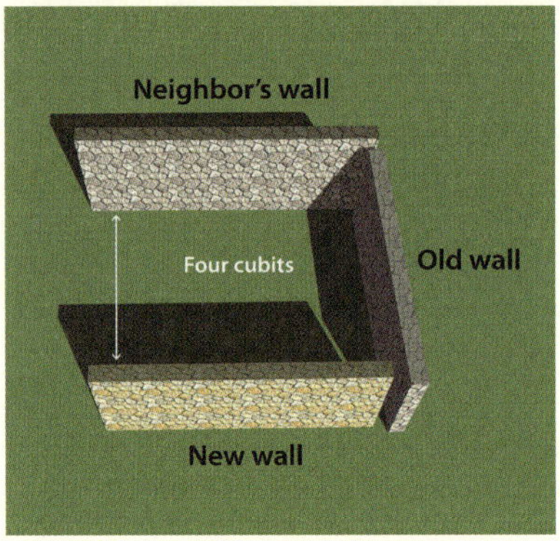

Wall juxtaposed to neighbor's wall according to the Rambam

HALAKHA

They taught this only if he builds alongside the wall of a garden – לֹא שָׁנוּ אֶלָּא כּוֹתֶל גִּינָּה: A wall may not be placed alongside a neighbor's wall of a garden or a courtyard in a new town, where the ground has not yet been strengthened by people walking on it. In a situation where the ground has been strengthened by people walking on it, e.g., next to the wall of a courtyard of an old town constructed at least sixty years ago, it is permitted to build a wall close by (Rambam *Sefer Kinyan, Hilkhot Shekhenim* 9:9; *Shulḥan Arukh, Ḥoshen Mishpat* 155:12–13, and in the comment of Rema, and *Shakh* and *Beur HaGra* there).

NOTES

But the mishna teaches, one whose wall was near the wall of another – וְהָא מִי שֶׁהָיָה כּוֹתְלוֹ סָמוּךְ לְכוֹתֶל חֲבֵירוֹ קָתָנֵי: Another version of the text here simply reads: What is another? In other words, the mishna states that one may not build another wall, which indicates that one was built there already.

This is what the mishna is teaching, one whose wall – הָכִי קָתָנֵי מִי שֶׁהָיָה כּוֹתְלוֹ: The early commentaries discuss at length the meaning of Rava's explanation of the mishna, as there are variant readings of the text. According to Rashi, this refers to one who has a wall situated four cubits from his neighbor's wall and it collapses. When the owner rebuilds his wall, he must distance it four cubits from his neighbor's wall and is not permitted to move it any closer. The commentaries explain that this is a novel ruling, as one might have thought that since a wall stood there previously, the ground has been sufficiently trampled on and requires no further strengthening. Nevertheless, the wall may not be built any closer to the neighbor's wall than the previous one was (Rabbeinu Tam, *Sefer HaYashar*).

Rabbeinu Ḥananel also cites this version of the text but suggests a different explanation: If one's neighbor's wall collapsed, one may not build his wall within four cubits of where the neighbor's wall stood, because if the neighbor later wishes to rebuild his wall, he will be forced to move it away from its original location.

The term: And it fell, does not appear in certain versions of the Gemara. That version of the text has also been explained in different ways. According to some commentaries, the Gemara is referring to a case where the wall was already built, with permission, at less than four cubits from one's neighbor's wall, and he now seeks to build an additional wall parallel to the first one. The mishna rules that the second wall must be placed at a distance of four cubits from the first wall, to allow people to walk easily between those walls, as the walking on the ground between these walls will strengthen the walls of the neighbor (Rav Hai Gaon; Ramah).

Alternatively, this refers to a case where a wall was positioned perpendicular to the neighbor's wall, and as the width of the wall takes up little space, there is no concern that people are unable to walk there. The owner of that wall now wishes to build an additional wall parallel to his neighbor's wall, in which case he is obligated to distance the new wall four cubits from his neighbor's wall (Rabbeinu Ḥananel; Ri Migash; Rambam's Commentary on the Mishna). The Ri Migash and the Meiri provide other interpretations based on this version of the text.

The wall of a garden – כּוֹתֶל גִּינָּה: Since seeds are planted there, the ground is not trampled down on the inner side but only on the outer side of the wall. Therefore, the neighbor may not build a wall that will prevent people from walking on that side (Rashi).

תְּנַן: הַחַלּוֹנוֹת, בֵּין מִלְמַעְלָן בֵּין מִלְמַטָּן בֵּין מִכְּנֶגְדָּן – אַרְבַּע אַמּוֹת, וְתָנֵי עֲלַהּ: מִלְמַעְלָן – כְּדֵי שֶׁלֹּא יָצִיץ וְיִרְאֶה, מִלְמַטָּן – שֶׁלֹּא יַעֲמוֹד וְיִרְאֶה, וּמִכְּנֶגְדָּן – שֶׁלֹּא יַאֲפִיל;

With regard to the claim that the *halakha* of the mishna is due to the need for space for people to walk on the ground between the walls, the Gemara asks: **We learned** in the mishna: And one who desires to build a wall opposite **the windows** of a neighbor's house must distance the wall **four cubits** from the windows, **whether above,**[B] **below,**[B] **or opposite. And it is taught** in a *baraita* **with regard to this**[N] ruling: Concerning the requirement of a distance **above,** the wall must be high **enough so that one cannot peer** into the window **and see** into the window; concerning the requirement of a distance **below,** the wall must be low **so that he will not** be able to **stand** on top of it **and see** into the window; **and** concerning the requirement of a distance **opposite,** one must distance the wall from the windows **so that it will not darken** his neighbor's house by blocking the light that enters the house through the window.

טַעְמָא שֶׁלֹּא יַאֲפִיל, אֲבָל מִשּׁוּם דַּוְושָׁא לָא! הָכָא בְּמַאי עָסְקִינַן – בְּבָבָא מִן הַצַּד.

The Gemara analyzes this statement: The **reason** that distance is required opposite the window is so **that he will not darken** his neighbor's house by blocking the light that enters the house through the window, **but** it is **not due to** the fact that **walking** will strengthen the ground. The Gemara answers: **With what are we dealing here?** We are dealing with a wall **that is positioned to the side,**[H] i.e., perpendicular to the wall with the window in it, and therefore it blocks the light from entering the house through the window but does not prevent walking along the length of the neighbor's wall.

וְכַמָּה? אָמַר יֵיבָא חֲמוּהּ דְּאַשְׁיָין בַּר נִדְבָּךְ מִשְּׁמֵיהּ דְּרַב: כִּמְלֹא רֹחַב חַלּוֹן. וְהָלֹא מֵצִיץ! אָמַר רַב זְבִיד: בְּמַדִּיר אֶת כּוֹתְלוֹ.

The Gemara asks: **And how far**[N] must one distance his wall if it is perpendicular to the other wall? **Yeiva, the father-in-law of Ashyan bar Nidbakh, says in the name of Rav:** As much **as the full width of the window.**[N] The Gemara asks: **But** why is this sufficient? **Can't he** still **peer into**[N] the window if he is that close? **Rav Zevid says:** This is referring **to one who slopes his wall,** i.e., he fashions an incline on the upper surface of the wall so that he will not be able to stand on top of it and look through the window.

וְהָא אֲנַן תְּנַן: אַרְבַּע אַמּוֹת! לָא קַשְׁיָא: כָּאן מֵרוּחַ אַחַת, כָּאן מִשְׁתֵּי רוּחוֹת.

The Gemara asks: **But didn't we learn** in the mishna that one must keep the wall **four cubits** away from the window? The Gemara answers: This is **not difficult; here,** he builds the wall **on one side** of the window, whereas **there,** in the mishna, he builds walls **on two sides**[NH] of the window. In the latter case, if he builds the walls any closer he will block the light from entering the house through the window even if they are perpendicular.

תָּא שְׁמַע: וְאֶת הַכּוֹתֶל מִן הַמַּזְחִילָה – אַרְבַּע אַמּוֹת, כְּדֵי שֶׁיְּהֵא זוֹקֵף אֶת הַסּוּלָּם; טַעְמָא מִשּׁוּם סוּלָּם, אֲבָל מִשּׁוּם דַּוְושָׁא לָא! הָכָא בְּמַאי עָסְקִינַן – בְּמַזְחִילָה מְשׁוּפַּעַת, דְּאִי מִשּׁוּם דַּוְושָׁא הוּא, הָא קָא אָזֵיל וְאָתֵי תּוּתֵיהּ.

The Gemara suggests: **Come** and **hear** a further difficulty from the mishna below with regard to the claim that the requisite gap between the walls is for the purpose of walking, as the mishna teaches: **And** one must distance his **wall four cubits from a roof gutter so that** his neighbor **can lean a ladder** in the empty space to clean and repair the gutter. The Gemara analyzes this statement: The **reason** this distance is required **is due to** the fact that he will be able to lean **a ladder, but** it is **not due to** the fact that **walking** will strengthen the ground. The Gemara answers: **With what are we dealing here?** We are dealing **with a sloping roof gutter,** which protrudes beyond the boundary of the wall. **As in this case, if** the reason for distancing the wall **is due to walking, one can walk back and forth beneath it.** Nevertheless, a distance of four cubits from the roof gutter is required so that repairs can be performed.

BACKGROUND

Above – מִלְמַעְלָן:

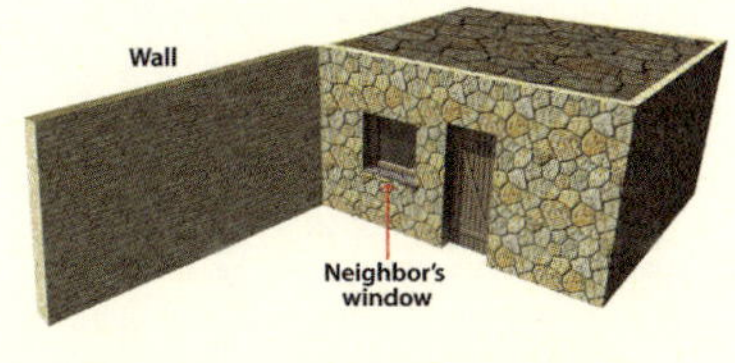

Wall obscuring one's view through the window

Below – מִלְמַטָּן:

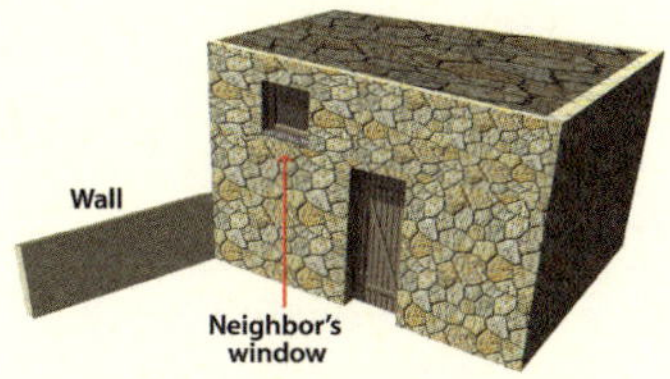

Wall low enough to prevent one standing on it from peering into the window

NOTES

And it is taught with regard to this – וְתָנֵי עֲלַהּ: It can be assumed that the *baraita* complements rather than disputes the mishna. In other words, it is teaching that there are cases where more than four cubits are necessary, or where fewer are required to prevent an invasion of privacy or the blockage of light (Rashi; Ramban).

And how far – וְכַמָּה: Some commentaries claim that this question and answer are not stated by the Gemara, as the measure of the width of the window is later challenged based on the mishna. Rather, Yeiva himself posed the question and provided the answer (*Tosafot*; Rabbeinu Yona).

As the full width of the window – כִּמְלֹא רֹחַב חַלּוֹן: An alternative version of the text reads: The full width of the window, a handbreadth (Rabbeinu Ḥananel). Other commentaries claim that any amount of distance is sufficient, provided that the sunlight is not blocked. Some say that this is a cubit (Ri Migash), while others maintain that he must distance the second wall from the first by an amount of space that is equal to the width of that particular window, whether that is a large or small amount (Meiri).

But can't he peer into – וְהָלֹא מֵצִיץ: Even though he raises the wall so that he cannot peer into the window from close up, he can still see into his neighbor's house from the top of his wall (see Rashi and Rabbeinu Yona).

There on two sides – כָּאן מִשְׁתֵּי רוּחוֹת: If he builds walls on either side of the window, he will greatly diminish the available light. With regard to the measure of four cubits, some commentaries write that one wall must be one handbreadth from one side of the window while the other wall must be four cubits from the other side of the window (Rabbeinu Yona). Rabbeinu Ḥananel explains that if he builds walls on two sides of the window, both walls must be four cubits from it. The Rambam understands that the wall-to-window distance for both walls combined must be four cubits.

HALAKHA

That is positioned to the side – בְּבָבָא מִן הַצַּד: One who builds a wall next to his neighbor's window must distance the structure one handbreadth from the actual window, not the frame. The top of the wall must be raised so that it is four cubits above the top of the window or altered to prevent anyone from standing atop it and peering into the window. The Rosh and *Tur* rule that both precautions must be observed (Rambam *Sefer Kinyan, Hilkhot Shekhenim* 7:4; *Shulḥan Arukh, Ḥoshen Mishpat* 154:22).

There he builds on two sides – כָּאן מִשְׁתֵּי רוּחוֹת: One who builds two walls perpendicular to a neighbor's window must allow four cubits of space between the walls, with the width of the window included in the four cubits of space (*Sma*; *Shakh*). Others claim that the width of the window is not included in the requisite four cubits (*Tur*). Should the owner of the walls wish to lay a cover over them, he must distance the cover four cubits from the wall with the window so that it does not block the sunlight (Rambam *Sefer Kinyan, Hilkhot Shekhenim* 7:5; *Shulḥan Arukh, Ḥoshen Mishpat* 154:24).

מתני׳ מַרְחִיקִין אֶת הַסּוּלָּם מִן הַשּׁוֹבָךְ אַרְבַּע אַמּוֹת, כְּדֵי שֶׁלֹּא תִּקְפּוֹץ הַנְּמִיָּיה; וְאֶת הַכּוֹתֶל מִן הַמַּזְחִילָה – אַרְבַּע אַמּוֹת, כְּדֵי שֶׁיְּהֵא זוֹקֵף אֶת הַסּוּלָּם.

MISHNA **One must distance** his **ladder**[H] **four cubits from** a neighbor's **dovecote so that a mongoose**[B] **will not** be able to **jump** from the ladder to the dovecote and devour the birds. **And** one must distance his **wall four cubits from a roof gutter,**[H] **so that** the neighbor **can lean**[N] **a ladder** in the empty space to clean and repair the gutter.

גמ׳ לֵימָא, מַתְנִיתִין דְּלָא כְּרַבִּי יוֹסֵי, דְּאִי רַבִּי יוֹסֵי, הָא אָמַר: זֶה חוֹפֵר בְּתוֹךְ שֶׁלּוֹ וְזֶה נוֹטֵעַ בְּתוֹךְ שֶׁלּוֹ?

GEMARA **Let us say that the mishna is not in accordance** with the opinion of **Rabbi Yosei, as,** if it were in accordance with the opinion of **Rabbi Yosei, doesn't** he **say** with regard to planting a tree next to a neighbor's cistern: **This one digs within his** land, **and that one plants within his** land, and neither individual need consider what is happening in the property of the other?

אֲפִילּוּ תֵּימָא רַבִּי יוֹסֵי, הָא אֲמַר רַב אַשִׁי: כִּי הָוֵינַן בֵּי רַב כָּהֲנָא הֲוָה אָמַר: מוֹדֵי רַבִּי יוֹסֵי בְּגִירֵי דִּידֵיהּ, הָכָא נַמִּי זִמְנִין דְּבַהֲדֵי דְּמַנַּח לֵיהּ יָתְבָא בְּחוֹר וְקָפְצָה. וְהָא גְּרָמָא הוּא! אֲמַר רַב טוֹבִי בַּר מַתָּנָה, זֹאת אוֹמֶרֶת: גְּרָמָא בְּנִיזָקִין אָסוּר.

The Gemara answers: **You** may **even say** that the mishna follows the opinion of **Rabbi Yosei,** as **didn't Rav Ashi say: When we** were studying **in the study hall of Rav Kahana, he would say** to us that **Rabbi Yosei concedes with regard to his arrows,**[H] i.e., he concedes that one must distance himself if his actions will cause damage to his neighbor. **Here too, sometimes when he places** the ladder, the mongoose might be **sitting in a hole and** will immediately **jump** up and climb the ladder to the dovecote. The Gemara challenges: **But that is indirect** damage, as he is not the immediate cause. **Rav Tovi bar Mattana said: That is to say** that it **is prohibited** to cause even **indirect damage.**[H]

רַב יוֹסֵף הֲוָה לֵיהּ הָנְהוּ תָּאלֵי דְּהָווּ

The Gemara relates: **Rav Yosef had certain small palm trees** [***talei***],[L] and

NOTES

So that he can lean – כְּדֵי שֶׁיְּהֵא זוֹקֵף: The early commentaries ask what right the owner of the gutter has to compel his neighbor to leave four cubits of empty space for his usage. Some claim that this is referring to a case where he bought or was granted the right to use the area from the neighbor. Consequently, the discussion focuses on the measure of the area that must be kept clear (*Tosafot*). Alternatively, the case involves two brothers who divide up a courtyard. Although the Gemara on 7b states that neither has the right to place a ladder, if they divide the courtyard according to value and one builds a wall, he will prevent the other from using the gutter (Ramban). Others contend that as the neighbor allowed him to construct a gutter through which water runs into his courtyard, he is obligated to grant him the necessary space for a ladder to service that gutter (Rabbeinu Gershom Meor HaGola; Ri Migash).

LANGUAGE

Small date trees [*talei*] – תָּאלֵי: The common name for date trees is *diklei*. The term *ta'aley* apparently refers to young date trees. It is likely from the Akkadian talu, palm tree.

BACKGROUND

Mongoose – נְמִיָּיה: A mongoose is a thin, short-legged animal with a pointed nose. Its body is roughly 65 cm long, and it has a long and hairy tail about 45 cm in length. The coat of the mongoose is grayish and its legs are black. A mongoose that enters a bird coop is likely to kill many birds. Its flexible body enables it to climb ladders and to jump long distances despite its short legs.

Egyptian mongoose

HALAKHA

One must distance his ladder – מַרְחִיקִין אֶת הַסּוּלָּם: One must distance his ladder from his neighbor's dovecote, in order to prevent a mongoose from climbing the ladder and entering the dovecote to eat the chicks (Rambam *Sefer Kinyan*, *Hilkhot Shekhenim* 9:7; *Shulḥan Arukh*, *Ḥoshen Mishpat* 155:16).

And one must distance his wall…from a roof gutter – וְאֶת הַכּוֹתֶל מִן הַמַּזְחִילָה: If one wishes to build a wall next to that of his neighbor's house, he must distance it four cubits from the gutter to allow the neighbor enough space to lean a ladder against the house so that he can repair the gutter (Rambam *Sefer Kinyan*, *Hilkhot Shekhenim* 9:8; *Shulḥan Arukh*, *Ḥoshen Mishpat* 155:17).

Rabbi Yosei concedes with regard to his arrows – מוֹדֵי רַבִּי יוֹסֵי בְּגִירֵי דִּידֵיהּ: If one's actions in his courtyard will cause immediate damage to his neighbor's property, he must distance himself to avoid causing damage. Even Rabbi Yosei accepts this principle (Rambam *Sefer Kinyan*, *Hilkhot Shekhenim* 10:5; *Shulḥan Arukh*, *Ḥoshen Mishpat* 155:31–32).

It is prohibited to cause indirect damage – גְּרָמָא בְּנִיזָקִין אָסוּר: One may not cause damage to another even if he will not be required to pay compensation for causing damage. The halakhic authorities dispute whether this prohibition applies by Torah law or by rabbinic law (Rambam *Sefer Nezikin*, *Hilkhot Nizkei Mamon* 5:1; *Tur*, *Ḥoshen Mishpat* 378, 397).

אָתוּ אוּמָּנֵי וְיָתְבִי תּוּתַיְיהוּ, וְאָתוּ עוֹרְבֵי אָכְלִי דָּמָא וְסָלְקִי אַבֵּי תָאלֵי וּמְפַסְדִי תַּמְרֵי. אֲמַר לְהוּ רַב יוֹסֵף: אַפִּיקוּ לִי קוּרְקוּר מֵהָכָא. אֲמַר לֵיהּ אַבָּיֵי: וְהָא גְּרָמָא הוּא! אֲמַר לֵיהּ: הָכִי אָמַר רַב טוֹבִי בַּר מַתָּנָה, זֹאת אוֹמֶרֶת: גְּרָמָא בְּנִיזָּקִין אָסוּר.

bloodletters would **come and sit beneath them** and perform their work there, **and crows** would **come, eat the blood, and fly up to the palm trees and damage the dates. Rav Yosef said to** the bloodletters: **Remove these crowing birds**[HN] **from here**, i.e., leave in order to avoid further damage. **Abaye said to him: But it is an indirect** action, as the bloodletters themselves are not damaging the dates. Rav Yosef **said to him** that **Rav Tovi bar Mattana said** as follows: **That is to say** that it **is prohibited** to cause even **indirect damage.**

וְהָא אַחְזִיק [לְהוּ]! הָא אָמַר רַב נַחְמָן אָמַר רַבָּה בַּר אֲבוּהּ: אֵין חֲזָקָה לְנִזָּקִין. וְלָאו אִיתְּמַר עֲלַהּ, רַב מָרִי אָמַר: בְּקוּטְרָא, וְרַב זְבִיד אָמַר: בְּבֵית הַכִּסֵּא? אֲמַר לֵיהּ: הָנֵי לְדִידִי, דַּאֲנִינָא דַּעְתַּאי, כִּי קוּטְרָא וּבֵית הַכִּסֵּא דָּמוּ לִי.

Abaye said to Rav Yosef: **But they have established an acquired privilege** to use that particular spot for their work. Rav Yosef replied: **Doesn't Rav Naḥman say** that **Rabba bar Avuh says: There is no acquired privilege** of use in cases of **damage,**[HN] i.e., an established situation may not be allowed to continue in the event that damage results. Abaye inquired further: **But wasn't it stated with regard to that** statement of Rav Naḥman that **Rav Mari said** it is referring specifically **to smoke, and Rav Zevid said** it is referring **to a bathroom?**[N] In other words, this principle was stated specifically in the context of damage caused by these substances. Rav Yosef **said to him: For me, as I am sensitive,**[N] **these are like smoke and a bathroom to me,** which is why I have the right to demand that the bloodletters leave.

מתני׳ מַרְחִיקִין אֶת הַשּׁוֹבָךְ מִן הָעִיר חֲמִשִּׁים אַמָּה. וְלֹא יַעֲשֶׂה אָדָם שׁוֹבָךְ בְּתוֹךְ שֶׁלּוֹ, אֶלָּא אִם כֵּן יֵשׁ לוֹ חֲמִשִּׁים אַמָּה לְכׇל רוּחַ; רַבִּי יְהוּדָה אוֹמֵר: בֵּית אַרְבַּעַת כּוֹרִין מְלֹא שֶׁגֶר הַיּוֹנָה. וְאִם לְקָחוֹ, אֲפִילּוּ בֵּית רוֹבַע – הֲרֵי הוּא בְּחֶזְקָתוֹ.

MISHNA **One must distance a dovecote**[H] **fifty cubits from the city**[N] to prevent doves from eating seeds in the town. **And a person should not establish a dovecote within his own** property **unless he has fifty cubits in each direction** between the dovecote and the edge of his property. **Rabbi Yehuda says** that one must have surrounding the dovecote the **area required for sowing four *kor*** of seed[B] on each side, which generally extends **as far as a dove flies** in a single flight. **And if one bought** the dovecote with the land, **he has the acquired privilege** of its use **even if** it has surrounding it only the **area required for sowing a quarter-*kav* of seed** [*beit rova*] around it, and he need not remove it from there.

HALAKHA

Remove these crowing birds – אַפִּיקוּ לִי קוּרְקוּר: If one's occupation involves blood or carcasses that attract crows, which disturb the neighbors with their noise, the neighbors can force him to relocate. This is the *halakha* if a neighbor is elderly or ill, if the crows sully the fruit on the courtyard trees with blood, or if a neighbor is sensitive. In this case one applies the principle that there is no acquired privilege of use if it causes damage (Rambam *Sefer Kinyan, Hilkhot Shekhenim* 11:5; *Shulḥan Arukh, Ḥoshen Mishpat* 155:39).

There is no acquired privilege in cases of damages – אֵין חֲזָקָה לְנִזָּקִין: In most cases where one causes damage to his neighbor, if the neighbor permits the activity to continue or if he assists him in performing that activity, he has legally waived his rights to protest. Nevertheless, there are certain situations in which this principle does not apply. Constant smoke that is blown into a courtyard by a typical wind, an exposed bathroom, dust, and shaking of the ground are examples in which the neighbor is not considered to have waived his rights, notwithstanding his apparent consent (Rambam *Sefer Kinyan, Hilkhot Shekhenim* 11:4; *Shulḥan Arukh, Ḥoshen Mishpat* 155:34–39).

One must distance a dovecote – מַרְחִיקִין אֶת הַשּׁוֹבָךְ: A dovecote must be kept a distance of fifty cubits from the city. Furthermore, one may set up a dovecote in his field only if it is fifty cubits away from settled areas in all directions. Nevertheless, if one bought a dovecote he need not move it even in the absence of this space, as he retains the privilege of use (Rambam *Sefer Nezikin, Hilkhot Gezeila VaAveda* 6:9; *Shulḥan Arukh, Ḥoshen Mishpat* 155:24).

BACKGROUND

Area…for sowing four *kor* of seed – בֵּית אַרְבַּעַת כּוֹרִין: A *beit kor* is the area of land in which one would sow one *kor*, or thirty *se'a*, of grain. The amount of land required for one *se'a* is fifty cubits by fifty cubits, i.e., 2,500 square cubits. A *beit kor* is therefore an area of 75,000 square cubits, which is approximately 18,750 sq m.

NOTES

Remove these crowing birds – אַפִּיקוּ לִי קוּרְקוּר: The commentaries note that Rav Yosef did not protest the bloodletters' use of the location for their activity. Rather, his complaint concerned the crows that came to his trees (*Tosafot*). Based on the context, he apparently did not protest the loss of the fruit to the crows, either through consumption or pecking, as an acquired privilege to use property is not negated even if the use causes monetary loss. Instead, Rav Yosef was expressing revulsion at the bloodied fruit and the noise of the crows (Ritva).

There is no acquired privilege in cases of damage – אֵין חֲזָקָה לְנִזָּקִין: Some commentaries claim that not only is there no right based on acquired privilege, but even if one has conclusive proof that the neighbor waived his rights, this is disregarded. The reason is even if the one using the property bought the rights to use it in this manner from the owner, the latter can later claim that he had thought he would be able to tolerate the damage, but now realizes that he cannot (*Tosafot*, citing Rabbeinu Tam). Others maintain that a conclusive proof is effective (Ramban). Some commentaries claim that if the neighbor performed an act of acquisition recorded in a document, he cannot renege. The early commentaries further dispute whether uninterrupted possession of three years is effective to establish an acquired privilege (see Ramah and Ri Migash).

To a bathroom – בְּבֵית הַכִּסֵּא: According to Rashi this refers to outhouses that were not fully enclosed and that were situated in fields (see *Tosafot*). Other commentaries claim that the issue is not dependent on whether or not it was enclosed, but on whether it produces an intolerable odor.

For me as I am sensitive – לְדִידִי, דַּאֲנִינָא דַּעְתַּאי: The commentaries infer from here that the principle that there is no acquired privilege of use in cases of damage does not apply exclusively to damage caused by smoke and bathrooms. Rather, these are merely examples of damage that people cannot tolerate (Rabbeinu Ḥananel). The Rambam apparently concurs. The early commentaries explain that while it is generally presumed that if one does not protest a matter he is considered to have consented to it, with regard to circumstances that induce suffering, there is no need to protest, as their unpleasantness is evident. It is assumed that one is merely waiting for an opportunity to complain (Rabbeinu Yona).

A dovecote fifty cubits from the city – שׁוֹבָךְ מִן הָעִיר חֲמִשִּׁים אַמָּה: Rashi explains that the doves eat garden seeds. Alternatively, the birds devour the grains and seeds that are laid out to dry on the town's rooftops (*Tosafot*).

גמ׳ חֲמִשִּׁים אַמָּה וְתוּ לָא? וּרְמִינְהִי: אֵין פּוֹרְסִין נִשְׁבִּין לְיוֹנִים, אֶלָּא אִם כֵּן הָיָה רָחוֹק מִן הַיִּשּׁוּב שְׁלֹשִׁים רִיס!

GEMARA The Gemara asks: Must one distance a dovecote only **fifty cubits** from the city **and no more?** Is that as far as one can expect a dove to fly? **And** the Gemara **raises a contradiction** from a mishna (*Bava Kamma* 79b): One **may spread out traps** [*neshavin*] **for doves only if** this was performed **at a distance**[H] of at least **thirty** *ris*,[L] or four *mil*, which is eight thousand cubits, **from** any **settled area,**[L] to avoid catching birds that belong to another. Apparently, doves fly a distance of thirty *ris*, whereas the mishna here states fifty cubits.

אָמַר אַבָּיֵי: מֵישָׁט שָׁיְיטִי טוּבָא, וְכַרְסַיְיהוּ בַּחֲמִשִּׁים אַמְּתָא מַלְיָא. וּמִשָּׁט שְׁלֹשִׁים רִיס וְתוּ לָא? וְהָתַנְיָא: וּבַיִּשּׁוּב – אֲפִילּוּ מֵאָה מִיל לֹא יִפְרוֹס! רַב יוֹסֵף אָמַר: בְּיִשּׁוּב כְּרָמִים,

Abaye said: Doves do **fly great distances,** which is why one must avoid catching others' birds by keeping traps thirty *ris* away from settled areas. **But** as they eat along their way, **their stomachs are filled** after a distance of **fifty cubits,** at which point they will do no more damage to seeds. The Gemara asks: **And do they fly** only **thirty** *ris* **and no more? But isn't it taught** in a *baraita*: **And in a settled area,** one **may not spread out** a trap **even** if the area under his control extends as far as **one hundred** *mil* in each direction? **Rav Yosef says:** That *baraita* is referring **to a settled area of vineyards,** i.e., a contiguous region of vineyards and gardens. In that case the doves pass from place to place even over a great distance.

רָבָא אָמַר: בְּיִשּׁוּב שׁוֹבָכִין. וְתֵיפּוֹק לֵיהּ מִשּׁוּם שׁוֹבָכִין גּוּפַיְיהוּ! אִיבָּעֵית אֵימָא: דִּידֵיהּ; וְאִיבָּעֵית אֵימָא: דְּגוֹי; וְאִיבָּעֵית אֵימָא: דְּהֶפְקֵר.

Rava said: The *baraita* is referring **to a settled area of dovecotes,** i.e., where many dovecotes are distributed. The Gemara asks: **And** according to Rava, **let** the *tanna* **derive** that one may not establish a new dovecote there **due to** the other **dovecotes themselves,** as he will trap doves belonging to others. The Gemara answers: **If you wish, say** that this is referring to **his own** dovecotes. **And if you wish, say** it is referring to the dovecotes of **a gentile,**[N] whose property one is not obligated to protect from harm. **And if you wish, say** it is referring **to ownerless** dovecotes.

״רַבִּי יְהוּדָה אוֹמֵר: בֵּית אַרְבַּעַת כּוֹרִין״ וכו׳. אָמַר רַב פַּפָּא, וְאִיתֵּימָא רַב זְבִיד, זֹאת אוֹמֶרֶת: טוֹעֲנִין לְלוֹקֵחַ וְטוֹעֲנִין לְיוֹרֵשׁ.

§ **Rabbi Yehuda says** that one must have surrounding the dovecote the **area required for sowing four** *kor* of seed on each side, which is as far as a dove flies in a single flight. And if one bought the dovecote with the land, he has the acquired privilege of its use. **Rav Pappa said, and some say** it was **Rav Zevid: That is to say** that a court **issues a claim** on behalf **of a buyer,**[H] **and issues a claim** on behalf **of an heir.** This is referring to the *halakha* of taking possession. If one has been physically in possession of an item for a period of time, generally three years, this serves as proof that he is in fact the legal owner. This possession must be accompanied by a claim of how one acquired the item; he cannot simply state that no one protested his possessing the item for three years. Rav Pappa is saying that the court will lodge a claim on behalf of a buyer or heir that they acquired the item from someone who was the owner, just as here the court assumes that the previous owner of the dovecote came to an agreement with his neighbors that he may use it.

יוֹרֵשׁ תְּנֵינָא: הַבָּא מִשּׁוּם יְרוּשָּׁה – אֵינוֹ צָרִיךְ טַעֲנָה! לוֹקֵחַ אִיצְטְרִיכָא לֵיהּ. לוֹקֵחַ נַמִי תְּנֵינָא: לָקַח חָצֵר וּבָהּ זִיזִין וּגְזוּזְטְרָאוֹת – הֲרֵי זֶה בְּחֶזְקָתָהּ!

The Gemara asks: Why is it necessary for Rav Pappa to state this *halakha*? **We** already **learn** this with regard to **an heir** (41a): In the case of land **that comes as an inheritance, one is not required to make a claim** as to how the land came into his benefactor's possession when one's ownership of the land is challenged. The Gemara answers: **It was necessary for him** to state this *halakha* with regard to **a buyer.** The Gemara asks: With regard to **a buyer as well, we learn** this in a mishna (60a): If one **bought a courtyard in which there are projections and balconies** [*ugzuztraot*][L] extending into the public domain, this courtyard **retains its presumptive status,** i.e., the owner has the acquired privilege of their use, and the court does not demand their removal.

HALAKHA

One may spread out traps for doves only if at a distance – אֵין פּוֹרְסִין נִשְׁבִּין לְיוֹנִים אֶלָּא אִם כֵּן הָיָה רָחוֹק: The Sages prohibited setting dove traps in a settled area because the birds that are there are assumed to belong to people. A trap may be set only if it is at least four *mil* from a town. Some commentaries write that dove traps must be placed four *mil* away from the settled area, but if there are vineyards in the vicinity no traps may be spread out even within a distance of one hundred *mil*, as doves will travel a great distance by stopping at the vineyards (*Tur*). Traps may not be spread out even near dovecotes that belong to gentiles, ones that are ownerless, or ones that belong to the one setting the traps, as birds belonging to others may be caught as well (Rambam *Sefer Nezikin*, *Hilkhot Gezeila VaAveda* 6:8; *Tur*, *Ḥoshen Mishpat* 370).

Issues a claim on behalf of a buyer – טוֹעֲנִין לְלוֹקֵחַ: If one bought an item that is located next to a neighbor and that item causes the neighbor damage, it is assumed that the neighbor had previously waived his rights, and one may use the item. It is even permitted for him to repair it in the event that it is broken (*Shulḥan Arukh*, *Ḥoshen Mishpat* 155:24).

LANGUAGE

Traps [*neshavin*] – נִשְׁבִּין: Similar to the Arabic term أنشب, *'anshaba*, which is used to indicate trapping in a net.

Ris – רִיס: A shortened form of the Persian asprēs, meaning stadium or place where horses are raced. The length of a *ris* is calculated in different sources as the distance an arrow can fly, 266 cubits or between 133 and 152 m (see *Arukh*). This is slightly more than one eighth of a *mil*, as a *mil* is two thousand cubits. A variation of this term is *rus*, whose Hebrew letters have the numerical value of 266, the number of cubits in a *ris*.

Balcony [*gezuztra*] – גְּזוּזְטְרָא: From the Greek ἐξώστρα, *exostra*, meaning a balcony or an area that protrudes from a building.

NOTES

And if you wish say it is referring to dovecotes of a gentile – וְאִיבָּעֵית אֵימָא דְּגוֹי: The early commentaries write that this answer is valid even according to those who maintain that it is prohibited to steal from gentiles. The reason is that in a case that does not involve outright theft, e.g., trapping doves, which are not associated exclusively with a single owner like other animals, taking the item is prohibited by a rabbinic ordinance, which the Sages did not apply in the case of a gentile. The reason is that gentiles themselves do not consider this theft, so there is no profanation of God's name involved in taking the item. According to those commentaries who claim that this kind of theft from a gentile is prohibited, the Gemara provides the alternative answer that the doves are ownerless (Ritva).

צְרִיכָא, דְּאִי אַשְׁמְעִינַן הָתָם גַּבֵּי רְשׁוּת הָרַבִּים – דְּאֵימוֹר כּוֹנֵס לְתוֹךְ שֶׁלּוֹ הוּא, אִי נַמִי אַחוּלֵי אַחוּל בְּנֵי רְשׁוּת הָרַבִּים גַּבֵּיהּ, אֲבָל הָכָא לָא;

The Gemara answers: It was **necessary** for the *tanna* of the mishna to state this *halakha* in both cases, **as, if he had taught us this** only **there,** in that mishna, one might have said that it applies specifically **with regard to** a protrusion or a balcony that extends into **the public domain, as** one can **say** that perhaps **it is** a case where the seller had **drawn back into his own** land before adding the projections and balconies, and they in fact do not extend into the public thoroughfare. **Alternatively,** perhaps **the public waived** their right **to him** and allowed him to place them over the common area, as otherwise they would have protested. **But here,** where he causes damage to private individuals, one might have thought that the buyer does **not** have a privilege of use, and therefore the mishna teaches us otherwise.

וְאִי אַשְׁמְעִינַן הָכָא, דְּכֵיוָן דְּיָחִיד הוּא – אֵימָא פַּיּוּסֵיהּ פַּיְּיסֵיהּ, אִי נַמִי אַחוּלֵי אַחֵיל גַּבֵּיהּ, אֲבָל רַבִּים – מַאן פַּיֵּיס וּמַאן שָׁבֵיק – אֵימָא לָא, צְרִיכָא.

And if he had taught this only in the mishna **here,** one might **say** that **since** the party potentially suffering damage **is an individual,** the owner of the dovecote **appeased** his neighbor by paying him to permit him to construct it. **Alternatively,** the neighbor might have **waived** his right **to him. But** in a case where damage is caused to **the public,** one might argue: **Whom did he appease,**[N] **and who yielded** to him? Consequently, one might **say** that the purchaser does **not** retain the privilege of use. Therefore, it is **necessary** for the *tanna* to state the *halakha* in this case as well.

״הֲרֵי הוּא בְּחֶזְקָתוֹ״. וְהָא אָמַר רַב נַחְמָן אָמַר רַבָּה בַּר אֲבוּהּ: אֵין חֲזָקָה לִנְזָקִין! רַב מָרִי אָמַר: בְּקוּטְרָא, רַב זְבִיד אָמַר: בְּבֵית הַכִּסֵּא.

§ The mishna teaches that if one bought the dovecote with the land, **he has the acquired privilege** of use. The Gemara asks: **But doesn't Rav Naḥman say** that **Rabba bar Avuh says: There is no acquired privilege** of use **for** cases of **damage?** Why should he retain his acquired privilege of use when his doves cause damage? **Rav Mari said:** Rav Naḥman's statement is referring specifically **to smoke,** which causes serious damage, and that is why it overrides an acquired privilege. **Rav Zevid said:** It is referring **to a bathroom,** whose odor is particularly strong.

NOTES

But the public, whom did he appease – אֲבָל רַבִּים מַאן פַּיֵּיס: He certainly is unable to compensate every individual member of the public (Rabbeinu Gershom Meor HaGola). Rashi writes that there is no one individual who can accept payment from him to allow him to build in the public domain, or who can waive the common rights to the space. Others claim that only the seven town Elders can sell or yield this right on behalf of the town, and these people gather together on rare occasions (*Tosafot*; see 60a).

Perek **II**
Daf **23** Amud **b**

מתני׳ נִיפּוּל הַנִּמְצָא בְּתוֹךְ חֲמִשִּׁים אַמָּה – הֲרֵי הוּא שֶׁל בַּעַל הַשּׁוֹבָךְ, חוּץ מֵחֲמִשִּׁים אַמָּה – הֲרֵי הוּא שֶׁל מוֹצְאוֹ; נִמְצָא בֵּין שְׁנֵי שׁוֹבָכוֹת, קָרוֹב לָזֶה – שֶׁלּוֹ, קָרוֹב לָזֶה – שֶׁלּוֹ, מֶחֱצָה עַל מֶחֱצָה – שְׁנֵיהֶם יַחֲלוֹקוּ.

MISHNA With regard to a dove **chick** [*nippul*][L] **that was found**[H] **within fifty cubits** of a dovecote, **it belongs to the owner of the dovecote.** If it was found **beyond fifty cubits** from a dovecote, **it belongs to its finder.** In a case where it **was found between two dovecotes,** if it was **close to this one,** it belongs **to** the owner of this dovecote; if it was **close to that one,** it belongs **to** the owner of that dovecote. If it was **half and half,** i.e., equidistant from the two dovecotes, **the two** owners **divide** the value of the chick.

LANGUAGE

A chick [*nippul*] – **נִיפּוּל:** According to Rashi this means a chick. Some commentaries claim that it refers specifically to a dove chick. In contrast to a chicken and a young duck, which are able to walk on their own soon after hatching, a dove chick is completely immobile and is like a *nefel*, a stillborn. Others suggest that the term derives from the fact that it fell [*nafal*] from its nest (*Arukh*).

HALAKHA

A dove chick that was found – **נִיפּוּל הַנִּמְצָא:** If a chick is found within fifty cubits of a dovecote, it belongs to the owner of that dovecote. If it is found beyond fifty cubits from a dovecote, it belongs to the finder. If it is found between two dovecotes it belongs to the owner of the closer one; if it is found exactly in the middle, its value is divided between them. These *halakhot* apply when the two dovecotes have roughly the same number of birds. If one dovecote contains many more doves than the other, the bird belongs to the owner of the larger dovecote, even if it is farther away (Rambam *Sefer Nezikin, Hilkhot Gezeila VaAveda* 15:18; *Shulḥan Arukh, Ḥoshen Mishpat* 260:8).

HALAKHA

Majority but proximate – **רוֹב וְקָרוֹב:** By Torah law one follows both proximity and the majority. When these considerations conflict, one follows the majority (Rambam *Sefer Nezikin, Hilkhot Rotze'aḥ UShmirat HaNefesh* 9:7; *Tur, Yoreh De'a* 129 and *Ḥoshen Mishpat* 259).

There might be another that is larger – **דְּאִיכָּא אַחֲרִיתִי דִּנְפִישָׁא:** Although the Torah states that in the case of a murder victim whose murderer is unknown the closest town must bring the heifer whose neck is broken, this obligation is imposed on a more distant town if its population is greater (Rambam *Sefer Nezikin, Hilkhot Rotze'aḥ UShmirat HaNefesh* 9:6).

גמ׳ אָמַר רַבִּי חֲנִינָא: רוֹב וְקָרוֹב – הוֹלְכִין אַחַר הָרוֹב; וְאַף עַל גַּב דְּרוּבָּא דְּאוֹרַיְיתָא וְקוּרְבָא דְּאוֹרַיְיתָא, אֲפִילּוּ הָכִי רוּבָּא עָדִיף.

GEMARA

Rabbi Ḥanina says: When resolving an uncertainty with regard to the halakhic status of an item, e.g., a found item, if the status of the **majority** of like items indicates that it has one status **but** the item in question is **proximate**[H] to a source that indicates otherwise, one **follows the majority.**[N] **And even though** the *halakha* of **majority** applies **by Torah law and** the *halakha* **of proximity** also applies **by Torah law, even so the majority is preferable.**

מְתִיב רַבִּי זֵירָא: ״וְהָיָה הָעִיר הַקְּרֹבָה אֶל הֶחָלָל״ – וְאַף עַל גַּב דְּאִיכָּא אַחֲרִיתִי דִּנְפִישָׁא מִינָּהּ!

Rabbi Zeira raises an objection from the Torah's statement with regard to a murder victim where the identity of the murderer is unknown. In a case of this kind, the court measures the distances between the corpse and the nearby towns, in order to determine which town is closest and must consequently perform the rite of the heifer whose neck is broken. The verse states: **"And it shall be, that the city that is nearest to the slain man,** the Elders of that city shall take a heifer of the herd… and shall break the heifer's neck" (Deuteronomy 21:3–4). **And** this town is chosen **even though there** might **be another** town **that is larger**[H] in population **than it.** According to Rabbi Ḥanina, in a case of this kind one should follow the majority.

בִּדְלֵיכָּא. וְלֵיזִיל בָּתַר רוּבָּא דְּעָלְמָא! בְּיוֹשֶׁבֶת בֵּין הֶהָרִים.

The Gemara answers: This verse is referring to a situation **where there is no** other[N] town that is larger than that one. The Gemara asks: **And** still, if one follows the majority, why should the court follow the closest city? **Let us follow the majority of the world,** as most people are found elsewhere. The Gemara answers: This is referring **to** a case where the city **sits** in isolation **between mountains,** and therefore it is unlikely that the murderer arrived from elsewhere.

תְּנַן: נִיפּוּל הַנִּמְצָא בְּתוֹךְ חֲמִשִּׁים אַמָּה – הֲרֵי הוּא שֶׁל בַּעַל הַשּׁוֹבָךְ; וְאַף עַל גַּב דְּאִיכָּא אַחֲרִינָא דְּנָפֵישׁ מִינֵּיהּ! בִּדְלֵיכָּא.

The Gemara continues to discuss the issue of majority as opposed to proximity. **We learned** in the mishna: With regard to a dove **chick that was found within fifty cubits** of a dovecote, **it belongs to the owner of the dovecote. And** as the mishna does not make a distinction between different cases, it indicates that this is the *halakha* **even though there is another** dovecote **that is larger than** the proximate one in terms of number of birds. This shows that closeness, not majority, is the determining factor. The Gemara answers: This is referring to a case **where there is no** other dovecote in the area.

אִי הָכִי, אֵימָא סֵיפָא: חוּץ מֵחֲמִשִּׁים אַמָּה – הֲרֵי הוּא שֶׁל מוֹצְאוֹ; וְאִי דְּלֵיכָּא, וַדַּאי מֵהַהוּא נָפַל! הָכָא בְּמַאי עָסְקִינַן – בִּמְדַדֶּה, דְּאָמַר רַב עוּקְבָא בַּר חָמָא: כׇּל הַמְדַדֶּה – אֵין מְדַדֶּה יוֹתֵר מֵחֲמִשִּׁים.

The Gemara asks: **If so, say the latter clause** of the mishna: If it was found **beyond fifty cubits** from a dovecote, **it belongs to its finder. And if there is no** other dovecote in the area, it **certainly fell from that** dovecote. How, then, can it be given to the finder? The Gemara answers: **With what are we dealing here?** We are dealing **with** a chick that **hops**[N] from place to place but does not yet fly. **As Rav Ukva bar Ḥama says:** With regard to **any** creature **that hops,** it **does not hop more than fifty**[N] cubits. Consequently, any bird found within fifty cubits of a dovecote is assumed to have come from there. If it is farther away than that, it likely came from elsewhere or was dropped by travelers.

NOTES

One follows the majority – **הוֹלְכִין אַחַר הָרוֹב:** Some early commentaries maintain that Rabbi Ḥanina is not teaching that one follows a majority rather than proximity, as this is stated later (24a) with regard to the nine stores. Rather, the novelty of his statement is that even in the presence of an obviously close determinant, one follows the majority, although it is ostensibly logical to rule based on proximity.

Where there is no other – **בִּדְלֵיכָּא:** In other words, none of the towns close to the corpse is larger than the closest one (Rashi). The commentaries discuss whether in a situation where there is a large town farther from the corpse than the closest town if the heifer is brought by the larger town (Rambam) or whether no heifer is brought, as the requirement of the closest town cannot be fulfilled (Rid).

With a chick that hops – **בִּמְדַדֶּה:** Once this answer has been accepted, the mishna can be explained as referring even to a case where there is a larger dovecote nearby, but beyond fifty cubits from where the chick was found. Since the chick would not hop that far, the bird belongs to the owner of the closer dovecote (Rashi).

Does not hop more than fifty – **אֵין מְדַדֶּה יוֹתֵר מֵחֲמִשִּׁים:** Rashi explains that if the chick is found beyond fifty cubits from a dovecote, it means that the bird is now capable of flight, in which case it might have come from anywhere. In this case one follows the majority of the world, and it belongs to the finder.

בָּעֵי רַבִּי יִרְמְיָה: רַגְלוֹ אַחַת בְּתוֹךְ חֲמִשִּׁים אַמָּה וְרַגְלוֹ אַחַת חוּץ מֵחֲמִשִּׁים אַמָּה, מַהוּ? וְעַל דָּא אַפְּקוּהוּ לְרַבִּי יִרְמְיָה מִבֵּי מִדְרְשָׁא.

Rabbi Yirmeya raises a dilemma: If **one leg** of the chick was **within fifty cubits** of the dovecote, **and one leg** was **beyond fifty cubits, what is** the *halakha*? The Gemara comments: **And it was for** his question about **this** far-fetched scenario **that they removed Rabbi Yirmeya from the study hall,**[N] as he was apparently wasting the Sages' time.

תָּא שְׁמַע: נִמְצָא בֵּין שְׁנֵי שׁוֹבָכוֹת, קָרוֹב לָזֶה – שֶׁלּוֹ, וְקָרוֹב לָזֶה – שֶׁלּוֹ; וְאַף עַל גַּב דְּחַד מִינַּיְיהוּ נָפִישׁ מֵחַבְרֵיהּ! הָכָא בְּמַאי עָסְקִינַן – שֶׁשְּׁנֵיהֶן שָׁוִין. וְלֵיזִיל בָּתַר רוּבָּא דְעָלְמָא! הָכָא בְּמַאי עָסְקִינַן

The Gemara further suggests: **Come** and **hear** the mishna: In a case where it **was found between two dovecotes,** if it was **close to this one,** it belongs **to** the owner of this dovecote; if it was **close to that one,** it belongs **to** the owner of that dovecote. The Gemara comments: **And** this is the *halakha* **even though one of them is greater** in number of birds **than the other one.** Apparently, one rules based on proximity, not majority. The Gemara explains: **With what are we dealing here?** We are dealing with a situation **where the two** dovecotes **are equal** in size. The Gemara asks: **But** even so, why should one follow the closer dovecote? **Let us follow the majority of the world,** as there are many other dovecotes besides these, and the number of doves they contain is greater. The Gemara responds: **With what are we dealing here?**

NOTES

They removed Rabbi Yirmeya from the study hall – **אַפְּקוּהוּ לְרַבִּי יִרְמְיָה מִבֵּי מִדְרְשָׁא**: *Tosafot* explain that it was not due to the unlikelihood of this scenario occurring that they removed Rabi Yirmeya from the study hall, as it is common for the Gemara to clarify the limitations of *halakhot* by discussing unlikely cases. In fact, the mishna itself addresses the case of a chick found precisely between two dovecotes. Rather, it was because there had been a definitive statement that a bird would not hop more than fifty cubits, according to which Rabbi Yirmeya should have understood that it would not go farther than that even with one foot. See 165b, where the Gemara relates the circumstance in which Rabbi Yirmeya was invited to return to the study hall.

Perek **II**
Daf **24** Amud **a**

בִּשְׁבִיל שֶׁל כְּרָמִים, דְּאִם אִיתָא דְּמֵעָלְמָא אָתֵי, כֵּיוָן דִּמְדַדֵּי לָא מָצֵי אָתֵי, דְּכָל דִּמְדַדֵּי וְהָדַר חָזֵי לֵיהּ לְקִינֵּיהּ – מְדַדֵּי, וְאִי לָא – לָא מְדַדֵּי.

We are dealing **with a path that** passes between **vineyards,** and these two dovecotes are situated there. **As, if it is so that** you claim the chick **came from** anywhere else in **the world, since it** only **hops, it could not have come** there. The reason is **that any** bird **that hops and turns** and **sees its nest** will continue **to hop; but if it does not** see its nest because it has gone too far, **it will not hop** farther. Consequently, this found chick that hops must have come from one of these two dovecotes.

אָמַר אַבָּיֵי, אַף אֲנַן נָמֵי תְּנֵינָא: דָּם שֶׁנִּמְצָא בַּפְּרוֹזְדוֹר – סְפֵיקוֹ טָמֵא, שֶׁחֶזְקָתוֹ מִן הַמָּקוֹר; וְאַף עַל גַּב דְּאִיכָּא עֲלִיָּיה דְּמִקָּרְבָא!

Abaye said: We learn in a mishna (*Nidda* 17b) **as well** that one follows the majority rather than proximity: With regard to **blood that is found in the corridor** [***baperozdor***],[HL] i.e., the cervical canal, and **it is uncertain** whether or not it is menstrual blood, it is **ritually impure** as menstrual blood, **as** there is **a presumption** that **it** came **from** the uterus, which is **the source** of menstrual blood. **And** this is the *halakha* **even though there is an upper chamber,**[B] which empties into the canal, **which is closer.**

אָמַר לֵיהּ רָבָא: רוֹב וּמָצוּי קָא אָמְרַתְּ? רוֹב וּמָצוּי לֵיכָּא לְמַאן דְּאָמַר,

Rava said to Abaye, in response to this claim: **You state** a proof from a case where the factors of **majority and frequency**[N] are both present. When there is **majority and frequency, there is no one who says** that one ignores the majority and follows proximity. Here, not only is the blood from the uterus greater in quantity, it also passes through the canal more frequently, as blood generally does not come from the upper chamber.

HALAKHA

Blood that is found in the corridor – **דָּם שֶׁנִּמְצָא בַּפְּרוֹזְדוֹר**: If blood was found in a woman's cervical canal, it is considered menstrual blood, and the woman is ritually impure. She would be liable for entering the Temple, and any *teruma* or sacrificial meat she touches must be burned. The commentaries state that as nowadays people no longer have the expertise necessary to distinguish between ritually pure and impure blood, all blood of a woman found in the cervical canal is impure (Rambam *Sefer Kedusha*, *Hilkhot Issurei Bia* 5:5 and *Maggid Mishne* there).

LANGUAGE

Corridor [***perozdor***] – **פְּרוֹזְדוֹר**: This word is Greek in origin, although the precise derivation is subject to debate. Some maintain it is related to the term **προστάδος**, *prostados*, meaning entrance or corridor. Here it is a euphemism for the cervical canal.

BACKGROUND

The corridor and the upper chamber – **פְּרוֹזְדוֹר וַעֲלִיָּיה**: The Sages employ euphemisms to describe genitalia and the reproductive system. These euphemisms can occasionally be a source of confusion. The mishna in tractate *Nidda* (17b) refers to three parts of the body: The chamber, referred to in this passage as the source; the corridor; and the upper chamber. While the first refers to the uterus and the second refers to the cervical canal, the identity of the upper chamber is not clear.

NOTES

You state a proof of majority and frequency – **רוֹב וּמָצוּי קָא אָמְרַתְּ**: Rashi explains that there are two relevant factors in this case. In terms of quantity, there is the majority of blood that comes from the uterus, and in terms of frequency, blood that emerges is usually menstrual, whereas blood from the upper chamber would be the result of injury or illness. Others write that the issue of frequency refers to the fact that blood from the uterus flows for a greater period of time, usually five to seven days, which is not true of blood from the upper chamber (Ritva). Yet others explain that majority and frequency are not two distinct issues; rather, the point here is that the larger quantity of blood emerging from the uterus is not a rare occurrence (Ri Migash).

דְּתָנֵי רַבִּי חִיָּיא: דָּם הַנִּמְצָא בַּפְּרוֹזְדוֹר – חַיָּיבִין עָלָיו עַל בִּיאַת מִקְדָּשׁ, וְשׂוֹרְפִין עָלָיו אֶת הַתְּרוּמָה.

Rava cites a proof for his statement. As **Rabbi Ḥiyya teaches: Blood that is found in the corridor** is considered definite menstrual blood, and therefore if she engages in sexual intercourse, both she and her partner would be **liable as a result of it**[N] to receive *karet* **for entering the Temple** intentionally when ritually impure or to bring an offering for entering unwittingly. **And one burns *teruma* due to it,** if the woman touches such produce. Evidently, the status of this blood is not considered uncertain.

וְאָמַר רָבָא, שְׁמַע מִינָּהּ מִדְּרַבִּי חִיָּיא תְּלָת: שְׁמַע מִינָּהּ רוֹב וְקָרוֹב – הַלֵּךְ אַחַר הָרוֹב; וּשְׁמַע מִינָּהּ רוּבָּא דְּאוֹרַיְיתָא; וּשְׁמַע מִינָּהּ אִיתָא לִדְרַבִּי זֵירָא,

And Rava says: Learn from that which **Rabbi Ḥiyya** said **three** conclusions: **Learn from** his statement that when the relevant factors are **majority and proximity, follow the majority; and learn from** his statement that the *halakha* that one follows **the majority** applies **by Torah law,**[N] as *teruma* is burned in this case on account of the blood and she is liable to receive *karet* if she enters the Temple in this state; **and learn from** his statement that **there is** a source **for that which Rabbi Zeira** said.

דְּאָמַר רַבִּי זֵירָא: אַף עַל פִּי שֶׁדַּלְתוֹת מְדִינָה נְעוּלוֹת.

This statement of Rabbi Zeira was issued in reference to a case discussed in tractate *Ketubot* (15a). If there are ten stores in a city, nine of which sell kosher meat and one of which sells non-kosher meat, and one found meat outside the stores and he does not know from which store it came, one follows the majority. The Gemara there suggests that perhaps one follows the majority only in a case where the gates of the city are unlocked, when the meat could have come to the city from the majority of kosher meat outside in a circumstance where the majority of the meat sold in the surrounding area was kosher. In this case there are two majorities, the majority of kosher meat stores inside the city, and the majority from outside. The Gemara there explains **that Rabbi Zeira says** that **even if the city gates are locked**[N] one follows the majority, and the meat is kosher, as there is a no need for a double majority.

דְּהָא אִשָּׁה דְּכִי דַּלְתוֹת מְדִינָה נְעוּלוֹת דָּמְיָא, וַאֲפִילּוּ הָכִי קָא אָזְלִינַן בָּתַר רוּבָּא.

The Gemara elaborates: The two cases are analogous, **as the woman** here **is considered like the locked gates of the city,** i.e., there is only a single majority, **and even so we follow the majority.**

וְהָא רָבָא הוּא דְּקָאָמַר: רוֹב וּמָצוּי לֵיכָּא לְמַאן דְּאָמַר! הֲדַר בֵּיהּ רָבָא מֵהַהִיא.

The Gemara asks: **But Rava is the one who says** with regard to the case of the blood that when there is **majority and frequency, there is no** one **who says** that one ignores the majority and follows the proximity. In other words, Rava rejected this case as proof of the principle that one follows the majority even when it is not frequent. Here, by contrast, Rava claims that one can learn from the ruling of Rabbi Ḥiyya that one follows the majority by Torah law. The Gemara answers: **Rava retracted that** claim in favor of the opinion that one follows the majority in all cases.

אִיתְּמַר: חָבִית שֶׁצָּפָה בְּנָהָר – אָמַר רַב: נִמְצֵאת כְּנֶגֶד עִיר שֶׁרוּבָּהּ יִשְׂרָאֵל – מוּתָּר, כְּנֶגֶד עִיר שֶׁרוּבָּהּ נׇכְרִים – אֲסִירָא; וּשְׁמוּאֵל אָמַר: אֲפִילּוּ נִמְצֵאת כְּנֶגֶד עִיר שֶׁרוּבָּהּ יִשְׂרָאֵל – אֲסִירָא, אֵימוּר מֵהַאי דְּקִירָא אֲתַאי.

§ **It was stated:** In the case of **a barrel** of wine **that** was found **floating in a river,**[H] and the status of the wine was unknown, **Rav says:** If it was **found opposite a town of which the majority** of residents **are Jews,** the wine is **permitted,** as it can be assumed that the wine belongs to a Jew. If it was **found opposite a town of which the majority are gentiles, it is forbidden,** as it presumably belongs to a gentile. **And Shmuel says: It is forbidden even** if it was **found opposite a town of which the majority are Jews.** Why? Regardless of where it was found, one can **say** that **it came from that** place called **Dekira,** where the majority of people are gentiles. In other words, there is a distinct possibility that a floating barrel came from far away.

לֵימָא, בִּדְרַבִּי חֲנִינָא קָא מִיפַּלְגִי, דְּמָר אִית לֵיהּ דְּרַבִּי חֲנִינָא, וּמָר לֵית לֵיהּ דְּרַבִּי חֲנִינָא?

The Gemara suggests: **Shall we say that** Rav and Shmuel **disagree with regard to** the statement **of Rabbi Ḥanina,** in **that** one **Sage,** Shmuel, **is of** the opinion that the ruling is in accordance with the opinion **of Rabbi Ḥanina,** and he rules based on the majority, which in this case includes even distant locales, **and** one **Sage,** Rav, **is of** the opinion that the ruling is **not** in accordance with the opinion **of Rabbi Ḥanina,** which is why he rules based on proximity.

NOTES

Liable as a result of it – **חַיָּיבִין עָלָיו**: If this woman entered the Temple area unwittingly she must bring an offering. In the event that she was actually ritually pure, the offering would in fact be a non-sacred animal, as it was consecrated assuming that she was impure, and the result would be a non-sacred animal being sacrificed in the Temple courtyard. The fact that this concern is not taken into account indicates that the woman's status as impure is definite. Similarly, the fact that *teruma* she touches is burned rather than held in suspension and neither burned nor eaten indicates that her status is considered definite rather than uncertain. In this regard the ruling of Rabbi Ḥiyya is brought as proof rather than the ruling of the mishna, as the mishna refers to the blood as uncertain, which might be interpreted as indicating an uncertain status of impurity.

The *halakha* that one follows the majority applies by Torah law – **רוּבָּא דְּאוֹרַיְיתָא**: The basic source of the principle that one follows the majority is the verse: "To follow the majority" (Exodus 23:2). Yet, that verse refers to a majority that can be easily counted, e.g., the judges stating their opinions. Therefore, it is necessary to state that even when the majority cannot be counted, i.e., a statistical likelihood, or in the terminology of the Gemara: A majority that is not before us, one still follows it (*Tosafot*). Other commentaries write that the novelty here is that one follows the majority even when it is opposed by other factors, e.g., proximity. This indicates that the factor of a majority is stronger than other determinants (Ri Migash).

The city gates are locked – **דַּלְתוֹת מְדִינָה נְעוּלוֹת**: There is no need for two majorities, i.e., the majority of the city itself and the majority of meat that enters the city. Although a double majority is required in certain cases, e.g., with regard to the *halakhot* of lineage, a single majority is sufficient for most biblical prohibitions (Rashi).

HALAKHA

A barrel that was floating in a river – **חָבִית שֶׁצָּפָה בְּנָהָר**: With regard to a barrel of wine that is found floating on a river, one may derive benefit from it if it is found opposite a town whose population is mostly Jewish and obstacles in the river preclude it having come from anywhere else. If the river is clear of obstacles or the majority of people in the town are gentiles, the wine is forbidden. If it is found opposite a town of gentiles, and the river lacks obstacles, and the majority of the people in the region are Jews, the wine is permitted. If there are obstacles, it is forbidden. This is in accordance with the opinion of Rav, as the *halakha* follows his opinion in his disputes with Shmuel with regard to ritual law (Rambam *Sefer Kedusha, Hilkhot Ma'akhalot Assurot* 12:28; *Shulḥan Arukh, Yoreh De'a* 129:17).

לָא, דְּכוּלֵּי עָלְמָא אִית לְהוּ דְּרַבִּי חֲנִינָא, וְהָכָא בְּהָא קָמִיפַּלְגִי, דְּמָר סָבַר: אִם אִיתָא דְּמֵהַאי דְּקִירָא אֲתַאי, עִקּוּלֵי וּפְשׁוּרֵי הֲוָה מַטְבְּעִי לָהּ; וּמָר סָבַר: חֲרִיפָא דְּנַהֲרָא נְקַט וְאַתַאי.

The Gemara rejects this suggestion: **No; everyone agrees with** the opinion **of Rabbi Ḥanina, and here they disagree about this:** As **one Sage,** Rav, **holds** that **if it is so, that** the barrel **came from that** place called **Dekira,** this cannot be, as **the currents and bays** of the river, where the river flow is weak, **would have sunk it.** Therefore, it is logical that the barrel came from a nearby town. **And one Sage,** Shmuel, **holds** that perhaps **the force of the river caught** the barrel **and brought it,** as it is evident that the flow of a river can bring items from far away.

הַהוּא חַצְבָּא דְּחַמְרָא דְּאִישְׁתַּכַּח בְּפַרְדֵּיסָא דְּעָרְלָה, שַׁרְיָא רָבִינָא. לֵימָא, מִשּׁוּם דְּסָבַר לָהּ דְּרַבִּי חֲנִינָא?

The Gemara relates that **Ravina** deemed **permitted a certain barrel of wine that was found** hidden **in a vineyard** where there were ***orla***[HB] grapes, and he was not concerned that the wine might be from the grapes of that vineyard. The Gemara asks: **Shall we say** that this is **because he holds** in accordance with the opinion **of Rabbi Ḥanina** that one follows the majority of vineyards, which are not *orla*, rather than proximity?

שָׁאנֵי הָתָם, דְּאִי מִיגְנִיב מִינָּהּ – אַצְנוּעֵי בְּגַוֵּיהּ לָא מַצְנְעִי. וְהָנֵי מִילֵּי חַמְרָא, אֲבָל עִינְבֵי מַצְנְעִי.

The Gemara answers: It **is different there,** as, **if** thieves **had stolen** the barrel **from** that very vineyard **they would not have hidden it there.**[N] Since the barrel was hidden there, it is reasonable to assume that it was stolen from somewhere else. The Gemara comments: **And this matter,** that thieves would not hide a stolen barrel in the same vineyard from which they stole it, **applies only to wine; but** they would **hide grapes** there, as grapes are not readily identifiable by the owner. Consequently, there is a concern that grapes found hidden there might be from that same vineyard.

הָנְהוּ זִיקֵי דְּחַמְרָא דְּאִשְׁתַּכְּחָן בֵּי קוּפָאֵי, שָׁרִנְהוּ רָבָא. לֵימָא, לָא סָבַר לָהּ לְדְרַבִּי חֲנִינָא? שָׁאנֵי הָתָם, דְּרוּבָּא

The Gemara further relates that **there were these jugs**[B] **of wine**[H] **that were found between vines** [*bei kofa'ei*][NL] of a Jew. **Rava** deemed the contents **permitted** and was unconcerned that they might be wine owned by a gentile. The Gemara asks: **Shall we say** that Rava **does not hold in accordance with** the opinion of **Rabbi Ḥanina,** who says that one follows the majority, in this case gentiles? The Gemara answers: **There it is different, as the majority**

BACKGROUND

Orla – עָרְלָה: It is prohibited to eat or to derive benefit from fruit that grows from a tree during the first three years after the tree has been planted (see Leviticus 19:23). This prohibition applies only to the fruit, and not to the other parts of the tree. The prohibition does not apply to trees planted as a fence for property delineation or as a wind buffer, rather than for their fruit.

Jugs – זִיקֵי: Jugs were generally made from whole hides taken from different types of animals. These jugs were used for many purposes and were especially useful for carrying objects and food items. When a jug was to be used for liquids, e.g., water, wine or oil, care was taken to remove the animal's hide intact, including the hide of the legs. A spout, usually fashioned from a hollow reed tube, was inserted into one of the legs.

Figurine dating from 750 BCE of a man holding a wineskin

HALAKHA

Barrel of wine that was found in a vineyard of *orla* – חַצְבָּא דְּחַמְרָא דְּאִישְׁתַּכַּח בְּפַרְדֵּיסָא דְּעָרְלָה: If a barrel of wine was found hidden in a vineyard of *orla* grapes, it is prohibited to drink the wine, but one may derive benefit from it. It is assumed that the barrel was not stolen from the same vineyard where it was hidden. If stolen grapes were found there, no benefit may be derived from them, as they were presumably taken from the place where they were found (*Taz*). Some maintain that one may derive benefit from such grapes, as the *halakha* is in accordance with the opinion of Rabbi Ḥanina (Rambam *Sefer Kedusha, Hilkhot Ma'akhalot Assurot* 10:13; *Shulḥan Arukh, Yoreh De'a* 129:18, 294:11 and *Beur HaGra* there).

These jugs of wine – הָנְהוּ זִיקֵי דְּחַמְרָא: In a place where most wine merchants are Jews, one may derive benefit from large vessels of wine, e.g., those used by merchants, which are found discarded. If the vessels are small and of the type that travelers use, it is prohibited to derive benefit from them, because it is assumed that travelers dropped them and most travelers are gentiles. If large and small vessels were found together, they are all permitted (Rambam *Sefer Kedusha, Hilkhot Ma'akhalot Assurot* 12:29; *Shulḥan Arukh, Yoreh De'a* 129:19).

NOTES

They would not have hidden it there – אַצְנוּעֵי בְּגַוֵּיהּ לָא מַצְנְעִי: The thieves would be afraid that the grape harvesters might come to the vineyard and find the stolen barrels (Rashi).

Between vines [*bei kofa'ei*] – בֵּי קוּפָאֵי: This translation follows Rashi's interpretation. Other commentaries claim that *Bei Kofa'ei* is the name of a place where the majority of people were Jews (Rabbeinu Ḥananel; *Arukh*; Rabbeinu Yona). It is possible that the place was named after its vineyards.

LANGUAGE

Vines [*kofa'ei*] – קוּפָאֵי: Some indicate that *kofa* means vineyard, vine, or the sprig from a grapevine. Other commentaries cite the Latin ceppa, meaning sprig or vine, as a possible source.

דִּשְׁפּוּכָאֵי יִשְׂרָאֵל נִינְהוּ. וְהָנֵי מִילֵּי בְּרַבְרְבֵי, אֲבָל זוּטָרֵי – אֵימוּר: מֵעוֹבְרֵי דְרָכִים נְפוּל. וְאִי אִיכָּא רַבְרְבֵי בַּהֲדַיְיהוּ – אֵימוּר: בְּאַבְרוּרֵי הֲוָה מַנְחִי.

of those who pour wine from barrels into jugs **are Jews,** and therefore it is reasonable that the wine belongs to a Jew. The Gemara comments: **And this matter** applies **only to large** jugs. **But** if they were **small** jugs, one can **say** that **they were dropped by travelers,** most of whom are gentiles, and therefore the jugs of wine are forbidden. **And if there are large jugs**[N] **among** the found jugs, **say** that they all belong to Jews, as travelers do not usually carry large jugs; it can be assumed that the small ones **were placed to balance** the donkey's load, and the jugs all fell together.

מתני׳ מַרְחִיקִין אֶת הָאִילָן מִן הָעִיר עֶשְׂרִים וְחָמֵשׁ אַמָּה, וּבֶחָרוּב וּבַשִּׁקְמָה – חֲמִשִּׁים אַמָּה. אַבָּא שָׁאוּל אוֹמֵר: כָּל אִילָן סְרָק – חֲמִשִּׁים אַמָּה. וְאִם הָעִיר קָדְמָה – קוֹצֵץ וְאֵינוֹ נוֹתֵן דָּמִים, וְאִם אִילָן קָדַם – קוֹצֵץ וְנוֹתֵן דָּמִים, סָפֵק זֶה קָדַם וְסָפֵק זֶה קָדַם – קוֹצֵץ וְאֵינוֹ נוֹתֵן דָּמִים.

MISHNA **One must distance a tree**[N] **twenty-five cubits from the city,**[H] **and** in the cases **of a carob tree**[B] **and of a sycamore tree,**[B] which have a great many branches, they must be distanced **fifty cubits. Abba Shaul says: Every barren tree**[N] must be distanced **fifty cubits. And if the city preceded** the tree, as one later planted the tree alongside the city, he **cuts down** the tree, **and** the city **does not give money** to the tree's owner in compensation. **And if the tree preceded** the city, which expanded after one planted the tree until it reached the tree, he **cuts down** the tree **and** the city **gives money** to its owner. If it is **uncertain whether this one was first or that one was first,** he **cuts down** the tree **and** the city **does not give money.**

גמ׳ מַאי טַעְמָא? אָמַר עוּלָּא: מִשּׁוּם נוֹיֵי הָעִיר. וְתֵיפּוֹק לֵיהּ דְּאֵין עוֹשִׂין שָׂדֶה מִגְרָשׁ וְלֹא מִגְרָשׁ שָׂדֶה!

GEMARA The Gemara asks: **What is the reason** that one must distance a tree from a city? **Ulla says:** It is **due to the beauty of the city,** as it is unattractive for a city's walls to be obscured by tree branches. The Gemara suggests: **And let him derive** this *halakha*[N] from the statement in tractate *Arakhin* (33b) **that one may neither convert a field** of a city into **an open area**[HN] surrounding the city, **nor may one** convert **an open area into a field,** as these have fixed places and measurements (see Numbers 35:1–8). If one plants trees in a city's open area, he thereby turns the open area into a field.

לָא צְרִיכָא, לְרַבִּי אֶלְעָזָר דְּאָמַר: עוֹשִׂין שָׂדֶה מִגְרָשׁ וּמִגְרָשׁ שָׂדֶה, הָכָא מִשּׁוּם נוֹיֵי הָעִיר לָא עָבְדִינַן.

The Gemara answers: **No,** it is **necessary** to supply the reason given by Ulla **according to** the opinion of **Rabbi Elazar, who says:** One **may convert a field** into **an open area, and an open area into a field. Here, we do not** plant trees, **due to the beauty of the city.**

HALAKHA

One must distance a tree…from the city – מַרְחִיקִין אֶת הָאִילָן מִן הָעִיר: When trees are planted in Eretz Yisrael, they must be at least twenty-five cubits away from cities that are under Jewish control (*Maggid Mishne*; see *Beit Yosef*), in order to preserve the city's beauty. Carobs and sycamore trees must be kept at a distance of fifty cubits. A tree that is closer than this must be cut down. If the trees were there before the city was built, the owners of the trees receive compensation when they are cut down. If it is unknown whether or not a tree preceded the city, no money is paid when the tree is cut down (Rambam *Sefer Kinyan*, *Hilkhot Shekhenim* 10:1; *Tur*, *Ḥoshen Mishpat* 155).

A field into an open area – שָׂדֶה מִגְרָשׁ: In the case of Levite cities, part of the city may not be converted into an open area nor an open area into part of the city. Likewise, the area of fields surrounding the open areas may not be converted into open areas, nor may the open areas be converted into fields. This *halakha* is in accordance with the opinion of the Rabbis (Rambam *Sefer Zera'im*, *Hilkhot Shemitta VeYovel* 13:4).

BACKGROUND

Carob tree – חָרוּב:

Leaves of the carob tree

Sycamore tree – שִׁקְמָה:

Leaves and fruit of the sycamore fig

NOTES

And if there are large jugs – וְאִי אִיכָּא רַבְרְבֵי: Some commentaries provide an opposite explanation of the Gemara: That all of the jugs are considered to belong to travelers and are therefore forbidden. The reason is that travelers sometimes take along large jugs to balance the smaller ones (Rabbeinu Gershom Meor HaGola).

One must distance a tree – מַרְחִיקִין אֶת הָאִילָן: In the Jerusalem Talmud it is discussed whether the reason for this prohibition is to preserve the beauty of the city or to prevent the tree from blocking the light.

Every barren tree – כָּל אִילָן סְרָק: Rashi explains that barren trees must be distanced from a city because they are a blight on it.

And let him derive this *halakha* – וְתֵיפּוֹק לֵיהּ: Some note that this difficulty apparently applies not only to Ulla's opinion, but to the mishna itself, as it is unclear why the mishna does not require that trees be planted at the far end of the open areas, which is one thousand cubits away from the edge of the city. The Ramban explains that nothing in the mishna itself indicates that it is dealing specifically with Eretz Yisrael, and the requirement of open areas applies only in Eretz Yisrael. Nevertheless, if one accepts Ulla's point about beauty, which is applicable only in Eretz Yisrael, the question arises as to why the issue of a city's open areas is not taken into account as well.

One may neither convert a field into an open area – אֵין עוֹשִׂין שָׂדֶה מִגְרָשׁ: In Numbers 35:1–8 the Torah describes Levite cities and mentions a city's open area and field. As explained by Rabbi Eliezer, son of Rabbi Yosei HaGelili, in tractate *Sota* (27b), an open area is the area of one thousand cubits around a city that is kept undeveloped, while a field is the two thousand cubits beyond that, which may be cultivated. Some commentaries maintain that the *halakha* that a field cannot be turned into an open area is a principle that applies to all cities, whether or not they are in Eretz Yisrael (Ramah). There are those who claim that even according to this opinion, the prohibition is restricted to cities that are populated mostly or entirely by Jews (*Mirkevet HaMishne*). Others maintain that these *halakhot* of open areas and the beauty of cities apply only to cities in Eretz Yisrael, whose appearance must be maintained by Jews. This requirement does not apply outside of Eretz Yisrael (Ramban).

וּלְרַבָּנַן נַמִי, דְּאָמְרִי: אֵין עוֹשִׂין שָׂדֶה מִגְרָשׁ וְלֹא מִגְרָשׁ שָׂדֶה, הָנֵי מִילֵּי זְרָעִים, אֲבָל אִילָנוֹת עָבְדִינַן, וְהָכָא מִשּׁוּם נוֹיֵי הָעִיר לָא.

And according to the opinion of **the Rabbis as well, who say** that **one may not convert a field** into **an open area, nor** convert **an open area** into **a field,** one can say that **this matter** applies only to **seeds,** i.e., one may not plant seeds in a city's open area and thereby turn it into a field. **But** with regard to **trees, we do** plant them in an open area. **But here** we do **not** plant trees, **due to the beauty of the city.**

וּמְנָא תֵּימְרָא דְּשָׁאנֵי בֵּין זְרָעִין לְאִילָנוֹת? דְּתַנְיָא: קַרְפֵּף יוֹתֵר מִבֵּית סָאתַיִם שֶׁהוּקַּף לְדִירָה,

And from where do you say, i.e., on what basis do you maintain, **that** there is **a difference between seeds and trees? As it is taught** in a *baraita* that discusses the *halakhot* of Shabbat: With regard to **an enclosure** [*karpef*][N] whose area is **greater than two** ***beit se'a***[H] but **that was enclosed** from the outset **for the purpose of residence,** it is permitted to carry within it on Shabbat regardless of its size, as it is considered a private domain.

נִזְרַע רוּבּוֹ – הֲרֵי הוּא כְּגִינָּה וְאָסוּר, נִיטַּע רוּבּוֹ – הֲרֵי הוּא כְּחָצֵר וּמוּתָּר.

If subsequently **the greater part of it was sown** with seed crops, **it is considered like a garden,** which is not a place of residence, **and it is prohibited** to carry anything within it on Shabbat. If **the greater part of it was planted** with trees, **it is considered like a courtyard,**[N] which is a place of dwelling, **and it is permitted** to carry there on Shabbat. This shows that planting trees in an enclosure does not transform the area into a field, as is the case when seeds are planted.

״וְאִם הָעִיר קָדְמָה – קוֹצֵץ וְאֵינוֹ נוֹתֵן דָּמִים״ וכו׳. מַאי שְׁנָא גַּבֵּי בּוֹר דְּקָתָנֵי: קוֹצֵץ וְנוֹתֵן דָּמִים, וּמַאי שְׁנָא הָכָא דְּקָתָנֵי: קוֹצֵץ וְאֵינוֹ נוֹתֵן דָּמִים?

§ The mishna teaches: **And if the city preceded** the tree he **cuts down** the tree, **and** the city **does not give money.** The Gemara asks: **What is different with regard to a cistern, that** the *tanna* of another mishna (25b) **teaches** that if one plants a tree next to a neighbor's existing cistern, the owner of the tree **cuts down** the tree **and** the owner of the cistern **gives money; and what is different here that** the mishna **teaches** that the owner of the tree **cuts down** the tree **and** the city **does not give money?**

אֲמַר רַב כָּהֲנָא: קִידְרָא דְּבֵי שׁוּתָּפֵי לָא חֲמִימָא וְלָא קְרִירָא.

Rav Kahana said, citing a popular aphorism: **A pot belonging to partners**[N] **is neither hot nor cold,** i.e., no one takes responsibility for an item that belongs to several people, as opposed to a single individual. Here too, there is no specific person who will pay for the tree.

וּמַאי קוּשְׁיָא? דִּלְמָא שָׁאנֵי הֶיזֵּיקָא דְּרַבִּים מֵהֶיזֵּיקָא דְּיָחִיד!

The Gemara asks: **And what is the difficulty** to begin with? **Perhaps damage** caused **to public** property **is different from damage** caused to the property **of an individual.** Consequently, when one's tree causes damage to the public he is not compensated for having to cut it down, whereas he does receive payment when his tree damages a private cistern.

אֶלָּא אִי אִיתְּמַר דְּרַב כָּהֲנָא – אַסֵּיפָא אִיתְּמַר: אִם הָאִילָן קָדַם – קוֹצֵץ וְנוֹתֵן דָּמִים. וְלֵימָא לְהוּ: הֲבוּ לִי בְּרֵישָׁא דָּמֵי וַהֲדַר אֵיקוֹץ! אֲמַר רַב כָּהֲנָא: קִידְרָא דְּבֵי שׁוּתָּפֵי לָא חֲמִימָא וְלָא קְרִירָא.

Rather, if Rav Kahana's comment **was stated** in this context, **it was stated about the latter clause: If the tree preceded** the city, he **cuts down** the tree **and** the city **gives money** to its owner. Concerning this *halakha* one could ask: **And let** the tree owner **say to** the city residents: **Give me money first and then I will cut down** the tree. In this context, **Rav Kahana said: A pot belonging to partners is neither hot nor cold.** If the owner of the tree is entitled to wait until he had first collects money, a good deal of time would pass before the tree would be cut down. Therefore, a community need not collect money and pay immediately, unlike an individual.

NOTES

Enclosure [*karpef*] – **קַרְפֵּף:** By Torah law, an area that is surrounded by a barrier ten handbreadths high has the status of a private domain. The Sages decreed that a large area, bigger than two *beit se'a*, that is surrounded by a barrier for purposes other than human residence is considered a *karmelit*. A *karmelit* is an intermediate domain defined by the Sages as neither a private nor a public domain. It is prohibited to carry in a *karmelit* on Shabbat, as in a public domain. Similarly, one may not carry from a *karmelit* to a public or to a private domain on Shabbat. Here the Gemara discusses the case of an area that was surrounded with a barrier for the purpose of residence but was later planted with seeds, an action that grants it the status of a *karmelit*.

If the greater part of it was planted with trees it is considered like a courtyard – נִיטַּע רוּבּוֹ הֲרֵי הוּא כְּחָצֵר: It is common for people to plant trees in their courtyards, and doing so does not turn the area into a field (Ri Migash).

A pot belonging to partners – קִידְרָא דְּבֵי שׁוּתָּפֵי: Since this matter is not dependent on a single individual, a good deal of time is likely to pass before money is collected for the tree's owner. If the owner of the tree has the right to wait to receive the money before cutting down the tree, the tree will not be cut down. One cannot claim that this is the residents' problem and if they do not deal with it they will simply suffer, as this issue reflects on the honor and beauty of Eretz Yisrael (Rashi; see Ramah). As for the option that the tree should first be cut down and then the owner paid, there is a concern that the owner of the tree might delay cutting down the tree until he gets his money (*Tosafot*).

HALAKHA

A *karpef* greater than two *beit se'a* – **קַרְפֵּף יוֹתֵר מִבֵּית סָאתַיִם:** If a *karpef* larger than two *beit se'a* was surrounded with a barrier for the purpose of residence, and later most of it is planted with trees, it remains a private domain. If most of it is planted with seeds, it ceases to be a private domain and one may not carry inside it on Shabbat. Even if a small part of it is planted with seeds, if that area is greater than two *beit se'a* the *karpef* is not considered a private domain, and one may not carry within it on Shabbat (Rambam *Sefer Zemanim*, *Hilkhot Shabbat* 16:6; *Shulḥan Arukh*, *Oraḥ Ḥayyim* 358:9).

HALAKHA

One must distance a permanent threshing floor – מַרְחִיקִין אֶת גּוֹרֶן קָבוּעַ: A permanent threshing floor must be distanced fifty cubits from a city. If the threshing floor preceded the city, its owner must still remove it, but once he has done so he is compensated for his loss. If it is uncertain which was there first, the owner is not paid (Rema). One may set up a threshing floor in his field only if he has open space of fifty cubits in all directions between the threshing floor and the property of his neighbors (Rambam *Sefer Kinyan, Hilkhot Shekhenim* 10:2; *Shulḥan Arukh, Ḥoshen Mishpat* 155:22).

BACKGROUND

Winnow – זוֹרֶה: Winnowing was often performed with a dedicated shovel or fork.

Man winnowing with a winnowing fork

״סָפֵק זֶה קָדַם וְסָפֵק זֶה קָדַם – קוֹצֵץ וְאֵינוֹ נוֹתֵן דָּמִים״. מַאי שְׁנָא מִבּוֹר דְּאָמְרַתְּ: לֹא יָקוֹץ?

§ The mishna teaches that if it is **uncertain whether this one was first or that one was first,** he **cuts down** the tree **and** the city **does not give money.** The Gemara asks: In **what** way **is** this case **different from** that of a tree alongside **a cistern,** concerning **which you said** in the mishna (25b) that in a case of uncertainty the owner of the tree need **not cut down** the tree?

הָתָם דְּוַדַּאי לָאו לְמֵיקַץ קָאֵי – סְפֵיקוֹ נַמִי לָא אָמְרִינַן לֵיהּ קוֹץ, הָכָא דְּוַדַּאי לְמֵיקַץ קָאֵי – סְפֵיקוֹ נַמִי אָמְרִינַן לֵיהּ קוֹץ, וְאִי מִשּׁוּם דְּמֵי – אָמְרִינַן לֵיהּ: אַיְיתֵי רְאָיָה וּשְׁקוֹל.

The Gemara answers: **There,** if it were a case **of certainty**[N] the tree would **not** be **subject to being cut down;** therefore, in a case **of uncertainty too, we do not say to** the owner of the tree: **Cut it down.** In that case, if the tree preceded the cistern, the owner of the tree would not be required to cut it down. **Here,** if it were a case **of certainty,** the tree would be **subject to being cut down** even if it preceded the city, and the only uncertainty is whether or not the owner of the tree would need to be compensated. Consequently, in a case **of uncertainty too, we say to** the owner of the tree: **Cut it down. And if** the owner of the tree lodges a claim **due** to the **value** of the tree, as he wants compensation for it, **we say to him: Bring proof** that your tree came first, **and take** your money. Since he has no proof, he does not receive any money.

מתני׳ מַרְחִיקִין אֶת גּוֹרֶן קָבוּעַ מִן הָעִיר חֲמִשִּׁים אַמָּה. לֹא יַעֲשֶׂה אָדָם גּוֹרֶן קָבוּעַ בְּתוֹךְ שֶׁלּוֹ – אֶלָּא אִם כֵּן יֵשׁ לוֹ חֲמִשִּׁים אַמָּה לְכָל רוּחַ, וּמַרְחִיק מִנְּטִיעוֹתָיו שֶׁל חֲבֵירוֹ וּמִנִּירוֹ בִּכְדֵי שֶׁלֹּא יַזִּיק.

MISHNA One must distance a permanent threshing floor[H] **fifty cubits from the city,** so that the chaff will not harm the city's residents. Furthermore, **a person should not establish a permanent threshing floor** even **on his own** property **unless he has fifty cubits** of open space **in every direction. And one must distance** a threshing floor **from the plantings of another and from** another's **plowed field** far **enough that it does not cause damage.**

גמ׳ מַאי שְׁנָא רֵישָׁא וּמַאי שְׁנָא סֵיפָא? אֲמַר אַבַּיֵי: סֵיפָא אֲתָאן לְגוֹרֶן שֶׁאֵינוֹ קָבוּעַ.

GEMARA The Gemara asks: **What is different** in **the first clause** of the mishna, which states a fixed measurement for the distance of a threshing floor from a city, **and what is different** in **the latter clause,** which does not provide a measurement but simply states in general terms: Enough that it does not cause damage? **Abaye said:** In **the latter clause we arrive at** the case of **a threshing floor that is not permanent.** This threshing floor must be far enough from a neighbor that it does not cause damage to his property.

הֵיכִי דָּמֵי גּוֹרֶן שֶׁאֵינוֹ קָבוּעַ? אָמַר רַבִּי יוֹסֵי בְּרַבִּי חֲנִינָא: כֹּל שֶׁאֵינוֹ זוֹרֶה בְּרַחַת.

The Gemara asks: **What are the circumstances** of **a threshing floor that is not permanent? Rabbi Yosei, son of Rabbi Ḥanina, says:** It refers to **any** threshing floor **where** one processes such a small quantity of grain that **he does not winnow**[B] **with a winnowing shovel,**[N] but employs some other method that does not scatter the chaff as far. This is one resolution of the contradiction.

רַב אַשִׁי אֲמַר: מַה טַּעַם קָאָמַר, מַאי טַעֲמָא מַרְחִיקִין גּוֹרֶן קָבוּעַ מִן הָעִיר חֲמִשִּׁים אַמָּה? כְּדֵי שֶׁלֹּא יַזִּיק.

Rav Ashi said that the phrase: Enough that it does not cause damage, is not referring to a distance but provides an explanation. In other words, the *tanna* **is saying: What is the reason** for the ruling of the first clause, as follows: **What is the reason** that **one must distance a permanent threshing floor fifty cubits from the city?** It must be far **enough** away **that it does not cause damage.**

NOTES

There, if it were a case of certainty – הָתָם דְּוַדַּאי: That is, it is not certain that the tree would be subject to being cut down, as it is allowed to stand if it preceded the cistern. This is not the case with regard to a city, where the tree is removed even if it preceded the city.

With a winnowing shovel – בְּרַחַת: To winnow, one casts the grain up high with a shovel and the wind blows the chaff away. Without the use of the shovel, the wind will not carry the chaff as far (Rashi). Some explain that when a shovel is used the chaff travels in a single direction based on the prevailing wind. Without a shovel, the chaff flies in all directions (Rabbeinu Ḥananel).

מֵיתִיבֵי: מַרְחִיקִין גּוֹרֶן קָבוּעַ מִן הָעִיר חֲמִשִּׁים אַמָּה; וּכְשֵׁם שֶׁמַּרְחִיקִין מִן הָעִיר חֲמִשִּׁים אַמָּה, כָּךְ מַרְחִיקִין מִדְּלוּעָיו וּמִקִּשּׁוּאָיו וּמִנְּטִיעוֹתָיו וּמִנִּירוֹ שֶׁל חֲבֵירוֹ חֲמִשִּׁים אַמָּה, כְּדֵי שֶׁלֹּא יַזִּיק; בִּשְׁלָמָא לְרַב אַשִׁי נִיחָא, אֶלָּא לְאַבָּיֵי קַשְׁיָא! קַשְׁיָא.

The Gemara **raises an objection** against the opinion of Abaye from a *baraita*: **One must distance a permanent threshing floor fifty cubits from the city; and just as one distances it fifty cubits from the city, so too does one distance it fifty cubits from the gourds, cucumbers, plantings, and plowed field of another, enough that it does not cause damage. Granted,** this **works out well according to** the opinion of **Rav Ashi,** as he claims that in both clauses the same distance is required: One must move a threshing floor fifty cubits from a plowed field and from those plantings. **But according to** the explanation of **Abaye,** it is **difficult.** The Gemara comments: Indeed, it is **difficult.**

בִּשְׁלָמָא מִמִּקְשׁוּאָיו וּמִדְּלוּעָיו, דְּאָזֵיל אֲבָקָא וְאָתֵי בְּלִיבֵּיהּ וּמְצַוֵּי לֵיהּ, אֶלָּא מִנִּירוֹ אַמַּאי? אָמַר רַבִּי אַבָּא בַּר זַבְדָּא, וְאִיתֵּימָא רַבִּי אַבָּא בַּר זוּטְרָא: מִפְּנֵי

The Gemara asks with regard to the *baraita*: **Granted,** one must distance his threshing floor **from his** neighbor's **cucumbers and gourds,**[B] **as the chaff** from the threshing floor **goes** and penetrates **into the heart** of the flower **and dries it out. But why** must one distance the threshing floor **from** another's **plowed field? Rabbi Abba bar Zavda said, and some say** it was **Rabbi Abba bar Zutra:** It is **because**

BACKGROUND

From his cucumbers and gourds – מִמִּקְשׁוּאָיו וּמִדְּלוּעָיו: This refers to plots of land where gourds and cucumbers are grown. These plants are mentioned because the chaff can enter their large flowers and harm them. This is not the case with other plants, whose smaller flowers are not vulnerable to such damage.

Flower of the bottle gourd

שֶׁעוֹשֶׂה אוֹתוֹ גָּלָל.

he turns it into **manure,** i.e., the chaff acts like manure, and an excessive amount of manure damages the seeds.

מתני׳ מַרְחִיקִין אֶת הַנְּבֵלוֹת וְאֶת הַקְּבָרוֹת וְאֶת הַבּוּרְסְקִי מִן הָעִיר חֲמִשִּׁים אַמָּה. אֵין עוֹשִׂין בּוּרְסְקִי אֶלָּא לְמִזְרַח הָעִיר; רַבִּי עֲקִיבָא אוֹמֵר: לְכָל רוּחַ הוּא עוֹשֶׂה, חוּץ מִמַּעֲרָבָהּ, וּמַרְחִיק חֲמִשִּׁים אַמָּה. וּמַרְחִיקִין אֶת הַמִּשְׁרָה מִן הַיָּרָק, וְאֶת הַכְּרֵישִׁין מִן הַבְּצָלִים, וְאֶת הַחַרְדָּל מִן הַדְּבוֹרִים, וְרַבִּי יוֹסֵי מַתִּיר בַּחַרְדָּל.

MISHNA **One must distance** animal **carcasses,**[H] **and graves, and a tannery** [*haburseki*],[L] a place where hides are processed, **fifty cubits from the city. One may establish a tannery only on the east side**[N] of the city,[H] because winds usually blow from the west and the foul smells would therefore be blown away from the residential area. **Rabbi Akiva says: One may establish** a tannery **on any side**[B] of a city **except for the west,** as the winds blowing from that direction will bring the odors into the city, **and one must distance** it **fifty cubits** from the city. **One must distance from vegetables water in which flax is steeped,**[HN] because this water ruins them; **and** likewise one must distance **leeks from onions,**[N] **and mustard from bees. And Rabbi Yosei permits** one not to do so in the case **of mustard.**

LANGUAGE

Tannery [*burseki*] – בּוּרְסְקִי: From the Greek βυρσικός, *bursikos*, which refers to matters relating to the tanning of hides and leather.

BACKGROUND

On any side – לְכָל רוּחַ: In Eretz Yisrael the most frequent wind comes from the west, off the sea. Throughout most of the country the wind blows even in the summer, at least in the evening hours. For this reason Rabbi Akiva prohibited the positioning of any nuisance on the western side of the city, as the wind is likely to carry its foul odors toward the populace.

HALAKHA

One must distance carcasses, etc. – מַרְחִיקִין אֶת הַנְּבֵלוֹת וכו׳: Carcasses, graves, and tanneries must be kept a distance of fifty cubits from the city. The same applies to public ovens and bees (Rambam *Sefer Kinyan, Hilkhot Shekhenim* 10:3; *Shulḥan Arukh, Ḥoshen Mishpat* 155:23).

One may establish a tannery only on the east side of a city – אֵין עוֹשִׂין בּוּרְסְקִי אֶלָּא לְמִזְרַח הָעִיר: A tannery may be set up only on the eastern side of city, to reduce the likelihood of foul odors bothering the populace. The *halakha* is in accordance with the opinion of the first *tanna* (Rambam *Sefer Kinyan, Hilkhot Shekhenim* 10:4; *Shulḥan Arukh, Ḥoshen Mishpat* 155:23).

Water in which flax is steeped – הַמִּשְׁרָה: If one wishes to steep flax in water near a neighbor's vegetables, or to plant leeks near his neighbor's onions, or to plant mustard near a beehive of another, he need not distance his enterprise. This is because the Gemara determines later (25b) that the *halakha* is in accordance with the opinion of Rabbi Yosei that one may do whatever he wants on his own property provided that he does not cause immediate damage to another. Nevertheless, water in which flax is steeped, leeks, and mustard should be distanced three handbreadths in these cases, to avoid immediate damage. Some commentaries maintain that this requirement applies specifically to the case of water in which flax is steeped near vegetables (Rambam *Sefer Kinyan, Hilkhot Shekhenim* 10:5; *Shulḥan Arukh, Ḥoshen Mishpat* 155:31 and *Sma* and *Beur HaGra* there).

NOTES

Only on the east side – אֶלָּא לְמִזְרַח: Generally speaking, eastern winds are not very strong (Rashi). Rambam, in his Commentary on the Mishna, adds that this is true in Eretz Yisrael and to the east of Eretz Yisrael. He further claims that the eastern wind mitigates the harmful effects of bad odors.

One must distance from vegetables water in which flax is steeped – וּמַרְחִיקִין אֶת הַמִּשְׁרָה מִן הַיָּרָק: The mishna does not mandate distances for each of the items that follow. The commentaries explain that in each particular case, the item must be moved enough to prevent harm (Ramban). Other commentaries maintain that according to the first *tanna*, the distance for each item is fifty cubits, the measurement stated earlier in the mishna (Rashba; Ritva).

Leeks from onions – הַכְּרֵישִׁין מִן הַבְּצָלִים: The commentaries explain that leeks that grow close to onions are less pungent (Rambam's Commentary on the Mishna).

BACKGROUND

The southern wind – רוּחַ דְּרוֹמִית: Southerly winds in the Middle East generally come from the desert and are dry and very hot. Consequently, they are detrimental to plants and people.

***Ben Netz* – בֶּן נֵץ:** Although these matters were stated in a homiletic vein, they do provide an accurate description of the world. The southern wind and the hot dry weather it brings cause severe damage, which is exacerbated over time. Following such an occurrence, a cold front usually appears that causes the wind to change direction. The subsequent cold winds break the hot spell.

גמ׳ אִיבַּעְיָא לְהוּ: רַבִּי עֲקִיבָא הֵיכִי קָאָמַר? לְכָל רוּחַ הוּא עוֹשֶׂה וְסוֹמֵךְ, חוּץ מִמַּעֲרָבָהּ דְּמַרְחִיק חֲמִשִּׁים אַמָּה וְעוֹשֶׂה. אוֹ דִּלְמָא: לְכָל רוּחַ הוּא עוֹשֶׂה וּמַרְחִיק חֲמִשִּׁים אַמָּה, חוּץ מִמַּעֲרָבָהּ דְּאֵינוֹ עוֹשֶׂה כְּלָל?

GEMARA **A dilemma was raised before** the Sages: With regard to **what** case **is Rabbi Akiva speaking?** Did he mean that **one may establish** a tannery **on any side** of a city, **and** one may even **place** the tannery **close** to the city, **except for the west side,** where **one must establish it at a distance of fifty cubits? Or perhaps** he meant that **one may establish** a tannery **on any side and distance it fifty cubits, except for the west side,** where one **may not establish** a tannery **at all.**

תָּא שְׁמַע: דְּתַנְיָא, רַבִּי עֲקִיבָא אוֹמֵר: לְכָל רוּחַ הוּא עוֹשֶׂה וּמַרְחִיק חֲמִשִּׁים אַמָּה, חוּץ מִמַּעֲרָבָהּ דְּאֵינוֹ עוֹשֶׂה כָּל עִיקָּר, מִפְּנֵי שֶׁהִיא תְּדִירָא.

The Gemara cites a proof: **Come** and **hear, as it is taught** in a *baraita*: **Rabbi Akiva says** that **one may establish** a tannery **on any side** of the city **and distance it fifty cubits, except for the west side,** where one **may not establish** a tannery **at all, because** the western wind is **frequent.**

אֲמַר לֵיהּ רָבָא לְרַב נַחְמָן: מַאי תְּדִירָא? אִילֵּימָא תְּדִירָא בְּרוּחוֹת; וְהָא אָמַר רַב חָנָן בַּר אַבָּא אָמַר רַב: אַרְבַּע רוּחוֹת מְנַשְּׁבוֹת בְּכָל יוֹם, וְרוּחַ צְפוֹנִית עִם כּוּלָּן, שֶׁאִילְמָלֵא כֵּן – אֵין הָעוֹלָם מִתְקַיֵּים אֲפִילּוּ שָׁעָה אַחַת. וְרוּחַ דְּרוֹמִית קָשָׁה מִכּוּלָּן, וְאִילְמָלֵא בֶּן נֵץ שֶׁמַּעֲמִידָהּ – מַחֲרֶבֶת אֶת הָעוֹלָם, שֶׁנֶּאֱמַר: ״הֲמִבִּינָתְךָ יַאֲבֶר נֵץ יִפְרֹשׂ כְּנָפָו לְתֵימָן״!

§ With regard to the last statement of the *baraita*, **Rava said to Rav Naḥman: What** does **frequent** mean in this context? **If we say** it means **frequent among the winds,** i.e., this wind blows all the time, that is difficult. **But doesn't Rav Ḥanan bar Abba say** that **Rav says: Four winds blow every day** from different directions, **and the northern wind** blows **with each of** the other three; **as, if this were not so,** i.e., if it did not blow, **the world would not exist for even one hour,** as the northern wind is pleasant and tempers the bitter effects of the other winds. **And the southern wind**[B] **is harsher than all of them, and were it not** for the angel named ***Ben Netz*,**[B] who **stops it** from blowing even harder, it would **destroy the** entire **world, as it is stated: "Does the hawk** [*netz*] **soar by your wisdom, and stretch her wings toward the south?"** (Job 39:26). This indicates that the northern wind is the most constant, not the western wind.

אֶלָּא מַאי תְּדִירָא? תְּדִירָא בַּשְּׁכִינָה, דְּאָמַר רַבִּי יְהוֹשֻׁעַ בֶּן לֵוִי: בּוֹאוּ וְנַחֲזִיק טוֹבָה לַאֲבוֹתֵינוּ שֶׁהוֹדִיעוּ מְקוֹם תְּפִלָּה, דִּכְתִיב: ״וּצְבָא הַשָּׁמַיִם לְךָ מִשְׁתַּחֲוִים״.

Rather, what is the meaning of **frequent?** It means **frequent with the Divine Presence,** i.e., the Divine Presence is found on the western side, and therefore it is inappropriate to set up a tannery there with its foul odors. **As Rabbi Yehoshua ben Levi says: Come and let us be grateful to our ancestors who revealed** to us **the place of prayer,**[N] **as it is written: "And the hosts of heaven bow down to You"** (Nehemiah 9:6). Since the celestial bodies move from east to west, they bow in that direction, which indicates that the Divine Presence is in the west.

מַתְקִיף לָהּ רַב אַחָא בַּר יַעֲקֹב: וְדִלְמָא כְּעֶבֶד שֶׁנּוֹטֵל פְּרָס מֵרַבּוֹ, וְחוֹזֵר לַאֲחוֹרָיו וּמִשְׁתַּחֲוֶה! קַשְׁיָא.

Rav Aḥa bar Ya'akov objects to this: But perhaps the celestial bodies are **like a servant who receives a gift from his master and walks backward** while **bowing.** If so, the Divine Presence is in the east and the celestial bodies are moving backward. The Gemara comments: Indeed, this is **difficult,** i.e., the verse does not provide a definitive proof.

וְרַבִּי אוֹשַׁעְיָא סָבַר: שְׁכִינָה בְּכָל מָקוֹם, דְּאָמַר רַבִּי אוֹשַׁעְיָא, מַאי דִּכְתִיב: ״אַתָּה הוּא ה׳ לְבַדֶּךָ אַתָּ עָשִׂיתָ אֶת הַשָּׁמַיִם״ וגו׳? שְׁלוּחֶיךָ לֹא כִּשְׁלוּחֵי בָּשָׂר וָדָם; שְׁלוּחֵי בָּשָׂר וָדָם – מִמָּקוֹם שֶׁמִּשְׁתַּלְּחִים לְשָׁם מַחֲזִירִים שְׁלִיחוּתָן, אֲבָל שְׁלוּחֶיךָ – לְמָקוֹם שֶׁמִּשְׁתַּלְּחִין מִשָּׁם מַחֲזִירִין שְׁלִיחוּתָן, שֶׁנֶּאֱמַר: ״הַתְשַׁלַּח בְּרָקִים וְיֵלֵכוּ וְיֹאמְרוּ לְךָ הִנֵּנוּ״; ״יָבוֹאוּ וְיֹאמְרוּ״ לֹא נֶאֱמַר, אֶלָּא: ״וְיֵלֵכוּ וְיֹאמְרוּ״, מְלַמֵּד שֶׁהַשְּׁכִינָה בְּכָל מָקוֹם.

The Gemara comments: **And Rabbi Oshaya holds** that **the Divine Presence** is found **in every place, as Rabbi Oshaya says: What** is the meaning of that **which is written: "You are the Lord, even You alone, You have made heaven…** You preserve them all alive and the hosts of heaven bow down to You" (Nehemiah 9:6)? This indicates that **Your messengers are not like the messengers of flesh and blood. The messengers of flesh and blood return to the place from where they were sent** to report on **their mission. But Your messengers return** and report on **their mission from the** very same **place to which they are sent, as it is stated "Can you send forth lightnings, that they may go out and say to you: Here we are?"** (Job 38:35). The verse **does not state: They will come and say,** i.e., they do not return to their point of departure, **but: "They may go out and say,"** which **teaches that the Divine Presence** is found **in every place.**

NOTES

Who revealed to us the place of prayer – שֶׁהוֹדִיעוּ מְקוֹם תְּפִלָּה: Some claim that the Gemara's opinion here differs from that in tractate *Berakhot* (27a), where it is stated that one should always face Jerusalem and the Temple in prayer, regardless of the direction of the compass (*Tosafot*). Others suggest that there is a difference between the contention that the Divine Presence is located in a particular direction and the determination of the appropriate direction for prayer, which is toward the Temple (Ramah; see *Tiferet Yisrael*).

וְאַף רַבִּי יִשְׁמָעֵאל סָבַר: שְׁכִינָה בְּכׇל מָקוֹם, דְּתָנָא דְּבֵי רַבִּי יִשְׁמָעֵאל: מִנַּיִן שֶׁשְּׁכִינָה בְּכׇל מָקוֹם? שֶׁנֶּאֱמַר: ״הִנֵּה הַמַּלְאָךְ הַדֹּבֵר בִּי יֹצֵא וּמַלְאָךְ אַחֵר יֹצֵא לִקְרָאתוֹ״; ״אַחֲרָיו״ לֹא נֶאֱמַר, אֶלָּא: ״לִקְרָאתוֹ״, מְלַמֵּד שֶׁשְּׁכִינָה בְּכׇל מָקוֹם.

The Gemara comments: **And Rabbi Yishmael, too, holds** that **the Divine Presence** is **in every place, as** one of the Sages of **the school of Rabbi Yishmael taught: From where** is it derived **that the Divine Presence** is **in every place? As it is stated: "And behold the angel who spoke with me went forth, and another angel went out to meet him"** (Zechariah 2:7). Although both angels were coming from the Divine Presence, the verse **does not state: After him, but: "To meet him,"** which **teaches that the Divine Presence** is **in every place,** and therefore the angels depart for their missions from every place.

וְאַף רַב שֵׁשֶׁת סָבַר: שְׁכִינָה בְּכׇל מָקוֹם, דַּאֲמַר לֵיהּ רַב שֵׁשֶׁת לְשַׁמָּעֵיהּ: לְכׇל רוּחָתָא אוֹקְמָן לְבַר מִמִּזְרָח, וְלָאו מִשּׁוּם דְּלֵית בֵּיהּ שְׁכִינָה, אֶלָּא מִשּׁוּם דְּמוֹרוּ בַּהּ מִינֵי.

And Rav Sheshet, too, holds that **the Divine Presence** is **in every place, as Rav Sheshet said to his servant: Set me facing any direction** to pray **except for the east.** Rav Sheshet, who was blind, required the assistance of his aide to prepare for prayer. He explained to his servant: **And** the reason I do not wish to face east is **not because it does not contain the Divine Presence, but because the heretics instruct** people to pray **in that** direction.[NHB]

וְרַבִּי אַבָּהוּ אָמַר: שְׁכִינָה בְּמַעֲרָב, דְּאָמַר רַבִּי אַבָּהוּ: מַאי אוֹרְיָה? אֲוִיר יָהּ.

But Rabbi Abbahu says: The Divine Presence is **in the west, as Rabbi Abbahu says: What** is the meaning of ***oriyya***,[N] which is a name for the west? It means **the air of God** [***avir Yah***], i.e., this is the place of the Divine Presence.

אָמַר רַב יְהוּדָה: מַאי דִּכְתִיב ״יַעֲרֹף כַּמָּטָר לִקְחִי״? זוֹ רוּחַ מַעֲרָבִית שֶׁבָּאָה מֵעׇרְפּוֹ שֶׁל עוֹלָם;

The Gemara cites a statement connected to the four winds. **Rav Yehuda said: What** is the meaning of that **which is written: "My doctrine shall drop as the rain,** my speech shall distill as the dew; as the small rain upon the tender growth, and as the showers upon the herb" (Deuteronomy 32:2)? "My doctrine shall drop [*ya'arof*] as the rain"; **this is the western wind, which comes from the back of** [***me'orpo***] **the world,**[N] as the west is also referred to as the back.

״תִּזַּל כַּטַּל אִמְרָתִי״ – זוֹ רוּחַ צְפוֹנִית שֶׁמַּזֶּלֶת אֶת הַזָּהָב, וְכֵן הוּא אוֹמֵר: ״הַזָּלִים זָהָב מִכִּיס״;

"My speech shall distill [***tizzal***] **as the dew"; this is the northern wind, which** brings dry air that reduces the rain and grain and thereby **devalues** [***mazzelet***] **gold.**[N] When grain crops are reduced their price appreciates, and consequently the value of gold decreases. **And in addition, it says: "You who lavish** [***hazzalim***] **gold out of the bag"** (Isaiah 46:6).

״כִּשְׂעִירִם עֲלֵי דֶשֶׁא״ – זוֹ רוּחַ מִזְרָחִית שֶׁמַּסְעֶרֶת אֶת כׇּל הָעוֹלָם כְּשָׂעִיר; ״וְכִרְבִיבִים עֲלֵי עֵשֶׂב״ – זוֹ רוּחַ דְּרוֹמִית שֶׁהִיא מַעֲלָה רְבִיבִים וּמְגַדֶּלֶת עֲשָׂבִים.

"As the small rain [***kisirim***][N] **upon the tender growth"; this is the eastern wind that rages through** [***maseret***] **the entire world like a demon** [***sa'ir***] when it blows strongly. **"And as the showers upon the herb"; this is the southern wind, which raises showers and causes herbs to grow.**

תַּנְיָא, רַבִּי אֱלִיעֶזֶר אוֹמֵר: עוֹלָם

It is taught in a *baraita* that **Rabbi Eliezer says: The world**

HALAKHA

Because the heretics instruct people to pray in that direction – מִשּׁוּם דְּמוֹרוּ בַּהּ מִינֵי: In synagogues that face east due to their location to the west of Eretz Yisrael, the ark and place of prayer are not situated due east because that is the direction to which heretics pray. Rather, the congregation turns slightly to the southeast (*Shulḥan Arukh, Oraḥ Ḥayyim* 94:2, and in the comment of Rema and *Levush* there).

BACKGROUND

The heretics instruct people to pray in that direction – מוֹרוּ בַּהּ מִינֵי: Heretical groups, which included Christians, were many and varied in talmudic times. The early Christians initially did not choose a particular direction for their prayers, but they built their structures either to face Jerusalem, or to face west or east. The Gemara here is apparently referring to heretical sects that were associated with the cult of the sun. These sects were widespread during Rav Sheshet's lifetime.

NOTES

The heretics instruct people to pray in that direction – דְּמוֹרוּ בַּהּ מִינֵי: The commentaries explain that the heretics pray to the sun, which rises in that direction (Rabbeinu Gershom Meor HaGola; see Ezekiel 8:16). The Jews in the Temple would deliberately act contrary to this practice (see *Sukka* 51b). Rashi claims that the term heretics refers to Christians, as is generally the case.

***Oriyya* – אוֹרְיָה:** Most commentaries maintain that *oriyya* is a name of the western wind (see Rabbeinu Gershom Meor HaGola, *Tosafot*, and Rabbeinu Ḥananel). Rashi cites an interpretation that *oriyya* refers to the eastern wind, although this has no bearing on the main idea that the Divine Presence is in the west.

From the back of [*me'orpo*] the world – מֵעׇרְפּוֹ שֶׁל עוֹלָם: The east is termed *kedem*, meaning forward, and accordingly the west is referred to as the back. Consequently, the western wind is said to come from the back of the world. Alternatively, *me'orpo* means from the strength of the world, as Rav Yehuda agrees with Rabbi Yehoshua ben Levi and Rabbi Abbahu that the Divine Presence is in the west (Rabbeinu Gershom Meor HaGola).

Which devalues [*mazzelet*] gold – שֶׁמַּזֶּלֶת אֶת הַזָּהָב: If this wind grows stronger, it clears the sky of clouds. Although the wind is relatively pleasant, it can also be accompanied by drought, which drives up the price of grain, which in turn leads to the depreciation of the price of gold (Rashi). Some commentaries interpret *mazzelet* in a positive manner and claim that this is a blessing, as the northern wind brings rain, which increases the grain crop. This enriches grain farmers, providing them with gold (*Torat Ḥayyim*; see Maharsha).

As the small rain [*kisirim*], etc. – כִּשְׂעִירִם וכו׳: The commentaries explain that one who studies Torah with ulterior motives is like a demon, as he draws storms across the world like an eastern wind. Conversely, one who learns Torah for its own sake brings showers of blessing and plenty (Rabbeinu Gershom Meor HaGola).

NOTES

Is similar to a partially enclosed veranda – **לְאַכְסַדְרָה הוּא דּוֹמֶה**: Some commentaries maintain that this entire passage should not be understood literally. Rather, it is a metaphor for the lack of perfection in the world due to its limitations (Maharal).

Out of the chamber…this is the southern side – **מִן הַחֶדֶר...זוֹ רוּחַ דְּרוֹמִית**: A verse in Job also refers to the south as a chamber: "The chambers of the south" (Job 9:9).

LANGUAGE

Veranda [*akhsadra*] – **אַכְסַדְרָה**: From the Greek ἐξέδρα, *exedra*, meaning an entrance room or sitting room.

Small tent [*kubba*] – **קוּבָּה**: The Mishna uses this term in reference to a small house. It is surmised that the term comes from the Latin cuppa, one of whose meanings is a very small niche.

לְאַכְסַדְרָה הוּא דּוֹמֶה, וְרוּחַ צְפוֹנִית אֵינָהּ מְסוּבֶּבֶת, וְכֵיוָן שֶׁהִגִּיעָה חַמָּה אֵצֶל קֶרֶן מַעֲרָבִית צְפוֹנִית – נִכְפֶּפֶת וְעוֹלָה לְמַעְלָה מִן הָרָקִיעַ; וְרַבִּי יְהוֹשֻׁעַ אוֹמֵר: עוֹלָם לְקוּבָּה הוּא דּוֹמֶה, וְרוּחַ צְפוֹנִית מְסוּבֶּבֶת, וְכֵיוָן שֶׁחַמָּה מַגַּעַת לְקֶרֶן מַעֲרָבִית צְפוֹנִית – מַקֶּפֶת וְחוֹזֶרֶת אֲחוֹרֵי כִּיפָּה,

is similar to a partially enclosed **veranda** [*le'akhsadra*],[NL] enclosed on three sides, **and the northern side** of the world **is not enclosed** with a partition like the other directions. The sun begins its revolution in the east and passes to the south and the west, **and once the sun reaches the northwestern corner it turns around and ascends** throughout the night **above the sky** to the east side and does not pass the north side. **And Rabbi Yehoshua says: The world is similar to a small tent** [*lekubba*],[L] **and the north side is enclosed** with a partition as well, **but once the sun reaches the northwestern corner** it emerges from this small tent, and **circles and passes behind the dome,** i.e., outside the northern partition, until it reaches the east.

שֶׁנֶּאֱמַר: ״הוֹלֵךְ אֶל דָּרוֹם וְסוֹבֵב אֶל צָפוֹן״ וגו׳, ״הוֹלֵךְ אֶל דָּרוֹם״ – בַּיּוֹם, ״וְסוֹבֵב אֶל צָפוֹן״ – בַּלַּיְלָה, ״סוֹבֵב סֹבֵב הוֹלֵךְ הָרוּחַ וְעַל סְבִיבֹתָיו שָׁב הָרוּחַ״ – אֵלּוּ פְּנֵי מִזְרָח וּפְנֵי מַעֲרָב, שֶׁפְּעָמִים מְסַבַּבְתָּן וּפְעָמִים מְהַלַּכְתָּן.

As it is stated: "The sun also rises and the sun goes down, and hastens to its place, where it rises again. **It goes toward the south,**[B] **and turns about to the north;** round and round goes the wind, and on its circuits the wind returns" (Ecclesiastes 1:5–6). The verse is understood as describing the sun's movements, as follows: **"It goes toward the south"** **during the day, "and turns about to the north,"** on the outside of the firmament, **at night. "Round and round goes the wind** [*ruaḥ*] **and the wind returns again to its circuits"**; as the word *ruaḥ* can also mean direction or side, Rabbi Yehoshua explains that **these are the face of the east and the face of the west. Sometimes,** in the short winter days, the sun **turns about them** without being seen, **and sometimes,** in the long summer days, **it traverses them** visibly.

הוּא הָיָה אוֹמֵר, אֲתָאן לְרַבִּי אֱלִיעֶזֶר: ״מִן הַחֶדֶר תָּבֹא סוּפָה״ – זוֹ רוּחַ דְּרוֹמִית, ״וּמִמְּזָרִים קָרָה״ – זוֹ רוּחַ צְפוֹנִית, ״מִנִּשְׁמַת אֵל יִתֶּן קָרַח״ – זוֹ רוּחַ מַעֲרָבִית, ״וְרֹחַב מַיִם בְּמוּצָק״ – זוֹ רוּחַ מִזְרָחִית.

The *baraita* continues: **He would say.** Before continuing its citation, the Gemara interjects: In this statement, **we arrive at** the opinion of **Rabbi Eliezer** that the world is like a partially enclosed veranda. The Gemara resumes its citation of the *baraita*: There is proof from a verse that the north side is open: **"Out of the chamber comes the storm"; this is the southern side**[N] that forms a room with the other two sides. **"And cold out of the dispersed parts"** (Job 37:9); **this is the northern side,** which is open, and from which a cold wind comes. **"By the breath of God ice is given"; this is the western side. "And the breadth of the waters is straitened"** (Job 37:10); **this is the eastern side,** from which the rains come.

BACKGROUND

It goes toward the south – **הוֹלֵךְ אֶל דָּרוֹם**: The path of the sun through the sky appears different to observers in different parts of the world. In countries north of the equator, the sun's zenith, the highest point it reaches in the sky, will always be to the south. As the sun rises in the east, its path will have a southward tilt, and when it descends to the west, its path will tend back northward. In general, sunrise does not occur directly in the east, but oscillates between the northeast in the summer and the southeast in the winter. Sunset likewise varies between the northwest in the summer and southwest in the winter. Therefore, in the summer the sun can be seen passing a point directly eastward as it rises and a point directly westward as it sets, but this will not occur in winter. Still the sun will never be seen further north than its northernmost point of rising and setting. Since the sun is never seen in the northern section of the sky, Rabbi Eliezer says that there is no enclosure there over which the sun is able to continue northward after sunset. Rather, at night the sun passes to the outer face of the firmament and doubles back over the southern side to its point of rising in the east. According to Rabbi Yehoshua, the southern side of the sky is enclosed as well, and when the sun passes to the firmament's outer face at night, it travels over the northern side of the outer face of the firmament until it reaches its point of rising in the east.

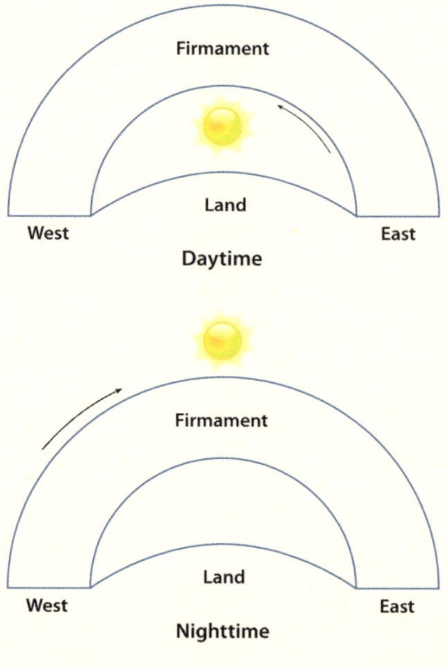

Top: Path of the sun during the day according to the opinion of the Sages
Bottom: Path of the sun at night according to the opinion of the Sages

והאמר מר: רוח דרומית מעלה רביבים ומגדלת עשבים! לא קשיא: הא דאתיא מטרא בניחותא, הא בשפיכותא.

The Gemara asks: **But doesn't the Master say** that **the southern wind raises showers and causes herbs to grow?** The Gemara answers that this is **not difficult: This** is referring to **rain that falls gently,** which waters plants and brings growth; **that** is referring to **a downpour** of rain that causes damage.

אמר רב חסדא, מאי דכתיב: "מצפון זהב יאתה" – זו רוח צפונית שמזלת את הזהב, וכן הוא אומר: "הזלים זהב מכיס".

Rav Ḥisda said: What is the meaning of that **which is written: "Out of the north comes gold"** (Job 37:22)? **This is the northern wind, which devalues gold** by causing a drought that raises the price of grain. **And, in addition, it says: "You who lavish gold out of the bag"** (Isaiah 46:6).

אמר רפרם בר פפא אמר רב חסדא: מיום שחרב בית המקדש – לא הוגשמה רוח דרומית, שנאמר: "ויגזר על ימין ורעב ויאכל על שמאל ולא שבעו", וכתיב: "צפון וימין אתה בראתם".

§ **Rafram bar Pappa says** that **Rav Ḥisda says: From the day the Temple was destroyed the southern wind has not brought rain, as it is stated** in the description of the destruction of the Temple: **"He decrees on the right and there is hunger, and consumes on the left and they are not satisfied"** (Isaiah 9:19). This means that God decreed that the southern wind, which is called right, shall bring famine with it. **And it is written: "North and right, You have created them"** (Psalms 89:13). This proves that the term right means south.

ואמר רפרם בר פפא אמר רב חסדא: מיום שחרב בית המקדש – אין הגשמים יורדין מאוצר טוב, שנאמר: "יפתח ה׳ לך את אוצרו הטוב", בזמן שישראל עושין רצונו של מקום וישראל שרויין על אדמתם – גשמים יורדין מאוצר טוב, בזמן שאין ישראל שרויין על אדמתם – אין גשמים יורדין מאוצר טוב.

And Rafram bar Pappa says that **Rav Ḥisda says: From the day the Temple was destroyed, the rains** no longer **descend from the good storehouse, as it is stated: "The Lord will open to you His good storehouse,** the skies, to give the rain of your land in its season" (Deuteronomy 28:12). **In a time when the Jewish people perform God's will, and the Jewish people are settled in their land, rain descends from the good storehouse. In a time when the Jewish people are not settled in their land, rain does not descend from the good storehouse.**

אמר רבי יצחק: הרוצה שיחכים – ידרים, ושיעשיר – יצפין, וסימניך: שלחן בצפון ומנורה בדרום; ורבי יהושע בן לוי אמר: לעולם ידרים, שמתוך שמתחכם מתעשר, שנאמר: "ארך ימים בימינה בשמאלה עשר וכבוד".

Rabbi Yitzḥak says: One who wishes to become wise should face south,[HN] **and** one who wishes **to become wealthy should face north. And your mnemonic** for this is that in the Temple the **Table,** which symbolized blessing and abundance, **was in the north, and the Candelabrum,** which symbolized the light of wisdom, **was in the south**[H] of the Sanctuary. **And Rabbi Yehoshua ben Levi says: One should always face south, as once he becomes wise he will** subsequently also **become wealthy, as it is stated** with regard to the Torah: **"Length of days is in her right hand; in her left hand are riches and honor"** (Proverbs 3:16).

והא רבי יהושע בן לוי אמר: שכינה במערב! דמצדד אצדודי. אמר ליה רבי חנינא לרב אשי: כגון אתון דיתביתו בצפונה דארץ ישראל – אדרימו אדרומי. ומנא לן דבבל לצפונה דארץ ישראל קיימא? דכתיב "מצפון תפתח הרעה על כל ישבי הארץ".

The Gemara asks: **But Rabbi Yehoshua ben Levi says** that **the Divine Presence is in the west.** How, then, can one pray facing south? The Gemara explains **that one should turn aside** slightly, so that he faces southwest. **Rabbi Ḥanina said to Rav Ashi:** An individual **such as you, who lives to the north of Eretz Yisrael, should face south** when you pray. **And from where do we derive that Babylonia is located to the north**[N] **of Eretz Yisrael? As it is written** in a prophecy concerning the destruction of Jerusalem by the Babylonians: **"Out of the north evil shall break forth upon all the inhabitants of the land"** (Jeremiah 1:14).

HALAKHA

One who wishes to become wise should face south – הרוצה שיחכים ידרים: Even one who wishes to fulfill the words of the Sages and face south or north in prayer should nevertheless face Jerusalem. The later commentaries write that one may face his body toward Jerusalem while turning his face to the south or to the north (*Shulḥan Arukh*, *Oraḥ Ḥayyim* 94:2, and in the comment of Rema).

The Table was in the north and the Candelabrum was in the south – שלחן בצפון ומנורה בדרום: The Candelabrum stood in the south of the Sanctuary, while the Table was in the north (Rambam *Sefer Avoda*, *Hilkhot Beit HaBeḥira* 1:7).

NOTES

One who wishes to become wise should face south – הרוצה שיחכים ידרים: This means that one should pray facing the south (Rashi; Rabbeinu Ḥananel). Rabbeinu Ḥananel also suggests an alternative explanation, that facing south means to go study from the Sages of the south of Eretz Yisrael. Some claim that south and north in this context refer to right and left, respectively. One who devotes himself entirely to Torah study with the strength of his right hand, while expending less effort on other matters, parallel to the weakness of one's left hand, will earn the rewards of wisdom and wealth (Riaf).

That Babylonia is…to the north – דבבל לצפונה: The commentaries note that the Talmud often refers to Eretz Yisrael as the West, as Babylonia was not due north of Eretz Yisrael, but northeast. Therefore, it can be called both north and east (Rid).

NOTES

If the cistern preceded the tree the owner of the tree cuts down the tree and the owner of the cistern pays money – אִם הַבּוֹר קָדְמָה קוֹצֵץ וְנוֹתֵן דָּמִים: Since a tree causes damage only after a long time and is therefore not considered to cause immediate (Rabbeinu Yona), the owner of the tree is entitled to compensation (Rashi). Some claim that the Sages were lenient with regard to the owner of the tree to maintain an incentive for people to plant trees (Ramban).

Even if the cistern preceded – אַף עַל פִּי שֶׁהַבּוֹר קוֹדֶמֶת: As explained earlier (18b), the Gemara maintains that according to Rabbi Yosei one need not distance an activity that he performs within his own property, even if he might thereby cause damage to his neighbor. The reason is that he is acting within the boundaries of *halakha*, while the one who is damaged can always relocate if he chooses. In the Jerusalem Talmud the dispute is explained slightly differently: According to the Rabbis, settlement of the land depends on digging cisterns, and therefore they take precedence over trees. By contrast, Rabbi Yosei maintains that trees are also crucial to the well-being of the world, which is why they are not cut down in favor of cisterns.

HALAKHA

Even if the cistern preceded the tree – אַף עַל פִּי שֶׁהַבּוֹר קוֹדֶמֶת לָאִילָן: If one has a tree in his field close to his neighbor's cistern, or if he wants to plant a tree there (*Tur*), the owner of the cistern cannot compel him to cut it down by arguing that the tree's roots damage his cistern. The reason is that this damage occurs only after a period of time, and if the damage is not immediate each of the neighbors is permitted to act within his own property. The *halakha* is in accordance with the opinion of Rabbi Yosei (Rambam *Sefer Kinyan*, *Hilkhot Shekhenim* 10:7; *Shulḥan Arukh*, *Ḥoshen Mishpat* 155:32).

״מַרְחִיקִין אֶת הַמִּשְׁרָה מִן הַיָּרָק״ וכו׳. תָּנָא: רַבִּי יוֹסֵי מַתִּיר בְּחַרְדָּל, שֶׁיָּכוֹל לוֹמַר לוֹ: עַד שֶׁאַתָּה אוֹמֵר לִי הַרְחֵק חַרְדָּלְךָ מִן דְּבוֹרַיי, הַרְחֵק דְּבוֹרֶךָ מִן חַרְדָּלַיי, שֶׁבָּאוֹת וְאוֹכְלוֹת לִגְלוּגֵי חַרְדָּלַיי.

§ The mishna teaches that **one must distance from vegetables the water in which flax is steeped,** and distance mustard from bees. A Sage **taught** that **Rabbi Yosei permits** one not to do so in the case **of mustard because he can say to** the beekeeper: **Before you tell me: Distance your mustard from my bees,** I can tell you: **Distance your bees from my mustard, as they come and eat my mustard plants.** In other words, you are also causing damage to my property. Since they each cause damage to the other, neither can force his neighbor to move.

מתני׳ מַרְחִיקִין אֶת הָאִילָן מִן הַבּוֹר עֶשְׂרִים וְחָמֵשׁ אַמָּה, וּבֶחָרוּב וּבַשִּׁקְמָה – חֲמִשִּׁים אַמָּה, בֵּין מִלְמַעְלָה בֵּין מִן הַצַּד. אִם הַבּוֹר קָדְמָה – קוֹצֵץ וְנוֹתֵן דָּמִים, וְאִם אִילָן קָדַם – לֹא יָקוֹץ. סָפֵק זֶה קָדַם וְסָפֵק זֶה קָדַם – לֹא יָקוֹץ; רַבִּי יוֹסֵי אוֹמֵר: אַף עַל פִּי שֶׁהַבּוֹר קוֹדֶמֶת לָאִילָן – לֹא יָקוֹץ, שֶׁזֶּה חוֹפֵר בְּתוֹךְ שֶׁלּוֹ וְזֶה נוֹטֵעַ בְּתוֹךְ שֶׁלּוֹ.

MISHNA **One must distance a tree twenty-five cubits from a cistern, and** in the case **of a carob and of a sycamore tree,** whose roots extend farther, one must distance the tree **fifty cubits.** This is the *halakha* **whether** the cistern or tree is located **above or to the side** of the other. **If** the digging of **the cistern preceded** the tree, the owner of the tree **cuts down** the tree[N] **and** the owner of the cistern **pays** him **money. And if the tree preceded** the cistern the owner of the tree need **not cut down** the tree. If it is **uncertain whether this came first or that came first,** the owner of the tree need **not cut down** the tree. **Rabbi Yosei says: Even if the cistern preceded**[N] **the tree,**[H] the owner of the tree need **not cut down** the tree. This is due to the fact **that this one digs in his own** property, **and that one plants in his own** property.

גמ׳ תָּנָא: בֵּין שֶׁהַבּוֹר לְמַטָּה וְאִילָן לְמַעְלָה, בֵּין שֶׁהַבּוֹר לְמַעְלָה וְאִילָן לְמַטָּה. בִּשְׁלָמָא בּוֹר לְמַטָּה וְאִילָן לְמַעְלָה – קָא אָזְלִין שָׁרָשִׁין מַזְּקִי לָהּ לַבּוֹר, אֶלָּא בּוֹר לְמַעְלָה וְאִילָן לְמַטָּה – אַמַּאי? אָמַר רַבִּי חַגָּא בְּשֵׁם רַבִּי יוֹסֵי: מִפְּנֵי שֶׁמַּחֲלִידִין אֶת הַקַּרְקַע וּמַלְקִין קַרְקָעִיתָהּ שֶׁל בּוֹר.

GEMARA The Gemara discusses the mishna's statement that a tree must be distanced if it is above a cistern. A Sage **taught:** This is the *halakha* **whether the cistern is below and the tree is above,**[B] or **whether the cistern is above and the tree is below.** The Gemara asks: **Granted,** if the **cistern is below and the tree is above,** it will cause damage, as **the roots extend and damage the cistern** when they breach its walls. **But if the cistern is above and the tree is below, why** should he have to distance the tree, considering that the roots extend downward? **Rabbi Ḥagga says in the name of Rabbi Yosei:** He must distance the tree **because** its roots **form holes in the ground and ruin the floor of the cistern.**

רַבִּי יוֹסֵי אוֹמֵר: אַף עַל פִּי שֶׁהַבּוֹר קוֹדֶמֶת לָאִילָן – לֹא יָקוֹץ, שֶׁזֶּה חוֹפֵר בְּתוֹךְ שֶׁלּוֹ וְזֶה נוֹטֵעַ בְּתוֹךְ שֶׁלּוֹ. אָמַר רַב יְהוּדָה אָמַר שְׁמוּאֵל: הֲלָכָה כְּרַבִּי יוֹסֵי. אֲמַר רַב אַשִׁי, כִּי הֲוָאן בֵּי רַב כָּהֲנָא הֲוָה אָמְרִינַן: מוֹדֵי רַבִּי יוֹסֵי בְּגִירֵי דִּידֵיהּ.

Rabbi Yosei says: Even if the cistern preceded the tree, the owner of the tree need **not cut down** the tree. This is due to the fact **that this one digs in his own** property, **and that one plants in his own** property. **Rav Yehuda says** that **Shmuel says:** The *halakha* **is in accordance with** the opinion of **Rabbi Yosei. Rav Ashi said: When we were studying in the study hall of Rav Kahana, we would say** that **Rabbi Yosei concedes with regard to one's arrows,** i.e., one must distance his activities from his neighbor if his actions will cause immediate damage to his neighbor, even if he is acting on his own property.

BACKGROUND

The cistern is below and the tree is above, etc. – בּוֹר לְמַטָּה וְאִילָן לְמַעְלָה וכו׳:

Cistern under a sycamore tree

Cistern above a sycamore's roots

פָּאפֵּי יוֹנָאָה עָנִי וְהֶעֱשִׁיר הֲוָה, בְּנָה אַפַּדְנָא, הָווּ הָנָךְ עָצוֹרֵי בְּשִׁיבָבוּתֵיהּ, דְּכִי הָווּ דָּיְיקִי שׁוּמְשְׁמֵי הֲוָה נַיְידָא אַפַּדְנֵיהּ; אֲתָא לְקַמֵּיהּ דְּרַב אַשִׁי, אֲמַר לֵיהּ, כִּי הֲוָאן בֵּי רַב כָּהֲנָא הֲוָה אָמְרִינַן: מוֹדֵי רַבִּי יוֹסֵי בְּגִירֵי דִּילֵיהּ.

The Gemara relates that a man called **Pappei Yona'a was poor and became wealthy.**[N] He **built a mansion** [*appadna*][L] on his land. **There were these** sesame seed **pressers**[H] **in his neighborhood** who would work, and **when they would press the sesame seeds** their activity **would shake his mansion. He came before** Rav **Ashi** to complain. Rav Ashi **said to him: When we were** studying **in the study hall of Rav Kahana, we would say** that **Rabbi Yosei concedes with regard to one's arrows.** Here too, because the sesame seed pressers cause immediate damage they must distance themselves.

וְכַמָּה?

The Gemara asks: **And how much** must the mansion shake for the owner to have the right to compel the sesame seed pressers to distance themselves?

HALAKHA

These sesame seed pressers – הָנָךְ עָצוֹרֵי: If one is grinding wheat or other grains on his property and the activity causes the ground to shake to such an extent that a lid of a jug resting on a neighbor's wall rattles, he must move his enterprise (see *Sma*). Some commentaries rule that it is sufficient if the wall itself vibrates. This is the *halakha* even if the neighbor constructs his courtyard after one is already operating. The Rivash notes that one causing damage must move even if his activity merely causes headaches and the like (Rambam *Sefer Kinyan, Hilkhot Shekhenim* 11:3; *Shulḥan Arukh, Ḥoshen Mishpat* 155:15, and in the comment of Rema).

NOTES

He was poor and became wealthy – עָנִי וְהֶעֱשִׁיר הֲוָה: This detail is necessary, as when Pappei Yona'a was poor it did not occur to him to build a house for himself on his land. This explains why he did not initially protest the activity of the sesame seed pressers. The effects of their activities became clear to him only after he had constructed his mansion. The commentaries cite this incident as proof that one who causes damage cannot claim an acquired privilege of use, even if he was there first. This *halakha* applies only in a case similar to this one, where the situation of the plaintiff changed. If the one suffering was rich from the outset, his lack of protest gives credence to the acquired privilege, even if the damage is significant (Rabbeinu Yona; Rashba).

LANGUAGE

Mansion [*appadna*] – אַפַּדְנָא: This term, which also appears in the Bible (Daniel 11:45), is from the Old Persian apādana. It was borrowed by other languages in ancient times, and it means a mansion, a fortified house, or an elegant structure.

Perek **II**
Daf **26** Amud **a**

כִּדְנָיֵיד נַכְתְּמָא אַפּוּמֵיהּ דְּחַצְבָּא.

It must shake enough **that the lid** [*nakhtema*][L] positioned **at the mouth of a jug shakes**[N] if it is placed on a wall.

דְּבֵי בַּר מָרְיוֹן בְּרֵיהּ דְּרָבִין כִּי הֲוָה נָפְצִי כִּיתָּנָא, הֲוָה אָזְלָא רַקְתָּא וּמַזְקָא אֱינָשֵׁי; אָתוּ לְקַמֵּיהּ דְּרָבִינָא, אֲמַר לְהוּ: כִּי אָמְרִינַן מוֹדֶה רַבִּי יוֹסֵי בְּגִירֵי דִּילֵיהּ – הָנֵי מִילֵּי דְּקָא אָזְלָא מִכֹּחוֹ, הָכָא זִיקָא הוּא דְּקָא מַמְטֵי לָהּ.

The Gemara relates: **When the** members of the **household of bar Maryon, son of Ravin, would beat their flax, the chaff** [*rakta*][L] **would fly off and harm people.** Those people **came before Ravina** to complain. Ravina **said to them: When we say** that **Rabbi Yosei concedes with regard to his arrows, this statement** applies only **when** the damaging item **moves by his direct force. Here,** by contrast, **it is the wind that carries** the chaff.

מַתְקִיף לָהּ מָר בַּר רַב אַשִׁי: מַאי שְׁנָא מִזּוֹרֶה וְרוּחַ מְסַיַּיעְתּוֹ? אֲמָרוּהָ קַמֵּיהּ דְּמָרֵימָר, אֲמַר לְהוּ: הַיְינוּ זוֹרֶה וְרוּחַ מְסַיַּיעְתּוֹ.

Mar bar Rav Ashi objects to this: In **what** way is this case **different from** one who **winnows**[N] on Shabbat by throwing the grain into the wind so that the chaff is blown away **and the wind assists him?**[H] That is considered a primary category of labor on Shabbat despite the fact that the act is performed partly with the aid of the wind. The Gemara relates that the Sages **stated** this objection with regard to beating flax **before Mareimar. Mareimar said to them: This** case **is** the same as **one who winnows and the wind assists him.** Just as this is considered his direct force for the purposes of the *halakhot* of Shabbat, it is likewise considered his direct force with regard to the *halakhot* of damages.

NOTES

That the lid positioned at the mouth of a jug shakes – כִּדְנָיֵיד נַכְתְּמָא אַפּוּמֵיהּ דְּחַצְבָּא: Rashi explains that a jug with its lid is hung on the wall of the house, and if the lid shakes due to the activity of the sesame seed pressers, it is considered a damaging activity. If there is less vibration than that, it is not necessary to halt the activity. Others say that a jug is placed on the floor, touching the wall, and one observes whether the lid moves (Ramah; Ramban). Alternatively, the Gemara means that the activity is considered harmful if the walls move as much as the lid of a jug does when it is carried normally (Rabbeinu Yitzḥak of Dampierre; *Tosafot*; Rabbeinu Yona; Rashba).

In what way is this case different from one who winnows – מַאי שְׁנָא מִזּוֹרֶה: Winnowing is one of the primary categories of labor prohibited on Shabbat. It can be performed with the assistance of the wind, which blows away the chaff when the grain is thrown into the air. Since this is a standard manner to perform this task, it is considered a complete act despite the fact that it requires the aid of the wind. Some commentaries explain that Ravina distinguishes between a prohibited act on Shabbat, where the determining factor is creative action, and cases of causing damage. With regard to causing damage, the scattering of the chaff is considered an indirect cause, and one is not liable for damage he causes indirectly, nor does he have to distance himself.

LANGUAGE

Lid [*nakhtema*] – נַכְתְּמָא: Some commentaries maintain that this word is related to the Akkadian *nakhamu*, which bears a similar meaning.

Chaff [*rakta*] – רַקְתָּא: Some versions of the text read *dakta*. Both words have the same meaning of a thin and small item. Therefore, the term is used for chaff, the tiny bits that emerge from beating wheat.

HALAKHA

One who winnows and the wind assists him – זוֹרֶה וְרוּחַ מְסַיַּיעְתּוֹ: With regard to one who works in his courtyard, or at a threshing floor, or performs any other labor that might create dust, dirt, or odor, he must distance his activity so that the unpleasant by-product of his work does not reach his neighbor's field. This is the *halakha* even if the by-product reaches his neighbor's field only due to the wind. Nevertheless, even if he does not distance his activity and it leads to damage, he is not liable, due to the significant contribution of the wind (Rambam *Sefer Kinyan, Hilkhot Shekhenim* 11:1; *Shulḥan Arukh, Ḥoshen Mishpat* 155:34).

NOTES

In Babylonia two cubits – בְּבָבֶל שְׁתֵּי אַמּוֹת: Rashi explains that plows in Babylonia were narrow, which is why two cubits of space sufficed. Other commentaries maintain that the soil in Eretz Yisrael is harder, and therefore people plow with oxen, which require four cubits of space. By contrast, in Babylonia, where the soil is softer, donkeys are used for plowing, or even one's hands. Consequently, less space is necessary (Rabbeinu Gershom Meor HaGola; Ramah).

וּלְרָבִינָא, מַאי שְׁנָא מִגֵּץ הַיּוֹצֵא מִתַּחַת הַפַּטִּישׁ וְהִזִּיק, דְּחַיָּיב לְשַׁלֵּם? הָתָם נִיחָא לֵיהּ דְּלֵיזִיל, הָכָא לָא נִיחָא לֵיהּ דְּלֵיזִיל.

The Gemara asks: **And according to** the opinion of **Ravina,** who rejects this comparison and claims that flying chaff is not considered one's arrow, in **what** way **is** this situation **different from** that **of a spark that flies from a hammer**[H] **and causes damage,** in which case all agree **that** the one wielding the hammer **is liable to pay?** The Gemara answers: **There,** it is **preferable for him that** the spark **go** as far as possible, rather than staying nearby. **Here** it is **not preferable for him,** i.e., it is immaterial to him, **that** the chaff **go** some distance.

מתני׳ לֹא יִטַּע אָדָם אִילָן סָמוּךְ לִשְׂדֵה חֲבֵירוֹ – אֶלָּא אִם כֵּן הִרְחִיק מִמֶּנּוּ אַרְבַּע אַמּוֹת, אֶחָד גְּפָנִים וְאֶחָד כׇּל אִילָן. הָיָה גָּדֵר בֵּינְתַיִם – זֶה סוֹמֵךְ לַגָּדֵר מִכָּאן וְזֶה סוֹמֵךְ לַגָּדֵר מִכָּאן.

MISHNA **A person may not plant a tree near the field of another**[H] **unless he distances** it **four cubits from** the field. This is the case **whether** he is planting **grapevines or** any kind **of tree.** If there **was a fence between** them, **this** one **may place,** i.e., plant, his grapevines or trees **close to the fence from here, and that** one **may place,** i.e., plant, his produce **close to the fence from there.**

הָיוּ שׇׁרָשִׁים יוֹצְאִים לְתוֹךְ שֶׁל חֲבֵירוֹ – מַעֲמִיק שְׁלֹשָׁה טְפָחִים כְּדֵי שֶׁלֹּא יְעַכֵּב אֶת הַמַּחֲרֵישָׁה. הָיָה חוֹפֵר בּוֹר, שִׁיחַ וּמְעָרָה – קוֹצֵץ וְיוֹרֵד, וְהָעֵצִים שֶׁלּוֹ.

If the **roots were spreading**[H] **into** the field **of another,** the owner of the field **may dig to a depth** of **three handbreadths** even if he severs those roots, **so that** they do **not impede** his **plow.** If he **was digging a cistern** in that spot, or **a ditch, or a cave,** and he came upon the roots of his neighbor's tree, **he may cut downward** normally, **and the wood** from the roots **is his.**

גמ׳ תָּנָא: אַרְבַּע אַמּוֹת שֶׁאָמְרוּ – כְּדֵי עֲבוֹדַת הַכֶּרֶם. אָמַר שְׁמוּאֵל: לֹא שָׁנוּ אֶלָּא בְּאֶרֶץ יִשְׂרָאֵל, אֲבָל בְּבָבֶל – שְׁתֵּי אַמּוֹת. תַּנְיָא נַמִי הָכִי: לֹא יִטַּע אָדָם אִילָן סָמוּךְ לִשְׂדֵה חֲבֵירוֹ, אֶלָּא אִם כֵּן הִרְחִיק מִמֶּנּוּ שְׁתֵּי אַמּוֹת; וְהָא אֲנַן תְּנַן: אַרְבַּע אַמּוֹת! אֶלָּא לָאו כִּדְשְׁמוּאֵל, שְׁמַע מִינַּהּ.

GEMARA A *tanna* **taught:** The **four cubits that** the Sages **stated** one must leave between a vineyard and a neighbor's field are **for the work of the vineyard,** so that the owner of the vineyard does not take oxen and a plow into his neighbor's field while working his vineyard. **Shmuel says: They taught** this *halakha* **only with regard to Eretz Yisrael, but in Babylonia two cubits**[N] are sufficient, as their plows are shorter. **This** opinion **is also taught** in a *baraita*: **A person may not plant a tree near the field of another unless he distances** the tree **two cubits from** the field. **But didn't we learn** in the mishna: **Four cubits? Rather, is it not** correct that there is a difference between Eretz Yisrael and Babylonia in this regard, **as** stated **by Shmuel?** The Gemara concludes: Indeed, **learn from it** that it is so.

וְאִיכָּא דְּרָמֵי לַהּ מִירְמָא; תְּנַן: לֹא יִטַּע אָדָם אִילָן סָמוּךְ לִשְׂדֵה חֲבֵירוֹ – אֶלָּא אִם כֵּן הִרְחִיק מִמֶּנּוּ אַרְבַּע אַמּוֹת; וְהָתַנְיָא: שְׁתֵּי אַמּוֹת! אָמַר שְׁמוּאֵל, לָא קַשְׁיָא: כָּאן בְּבָבֶל, כָּאן בְּאֶרֶץ יִשְׂרָאֵל.

And there are those **who raise** this matter in the form **of a contradiction. We learned** in the mishna that **a person may not plant a tree near the field of another unless he distances it four cubits from** the field. **But isn't it taught** in a *baraita* that **two cubits** are sufficient? **Shmuel said** that this is **not difficult: Here** it is referring **to Babylonia,** whereas **there** it is referring **to Eretz Yisrael.**

HALAKHA

From a spark that flies from a hammer – מִגֵּץ הַיּוֹצֵא מִתַּחַת הַפַּטִּישׁ: If a smith strikes a hammer and a spark flies out, he must pay for any damage it causes (Rambam *Sefer Nezikin, Hilkhot Ḥovel UMazik* 6:11; *Shulḥan Arukh, Ḥoshen Mishpat* 384:2).

A tree near the field of another – אִילָן סָמוּךְ לִשְׂדֵה חֲבֵירוֹ: One may not plant a tree near his neighbor's trees, or vines near his neighbor's vines, unless he leaves four cubits of space to allow for working the land around the trees. If both neighbors decide to plant at the same time, they divide the requisite amount of space (Rema, citing *Maggid Mishne*). This distance of four cubits applies in Eretz Yisrael, whereas only two cubits are necessary between trees and trees or vines and vines in Babylonia, as stated by Shmuel. Four cubits must be left between vines and trees, or between trees of the same type (Rambam) even in Babylonia. Some commentaries state that even more space must be preserved (Rema, citing *Tur*). If there is a fence between the fields, one may plant next to the fence without maintaining any distance (Rambam *Sefer Kinyan, Hilkhot Shekhenim* 10:8, *Shulḥan Arukh, Ḥoshen Mishpat* 155:25).

If the roots were spreading – הָיוּ שׇׁרָשִׁים יוֹצְאִים: If the roots of one's tree extend into a neighbor's field, the neighbor has the right to cut them out to a depth of three handbreadths so that they do not impede his plow. If the neighbor finds roots when digging a cistern, he may cut them. In both cases the neighbor may keep the wood of the roots if the trees are more than sixteen cubits from his field. If the trees are not that far away, the roots belong to the owner of the tree (Rambam *Sefer Kinyan, Hilkhot Shekhenim* 10:7, *Shulḥan Arukh, Ḥoshen Mishpat* 155:30).

רָבָא בַּר רַב חָנָן הָווּ לֵיהּ הָנְהוּ דִּיקְלֵי אַמֵּיצְרָא דְּפַרְדֵּיסָא דְּרַב יוֹסֵף, הָווּ אָתוּ צִפּוֹרֵי יָתְבִי בְּדִיקְלֵי וְנָחֲתִי בְּפַרְדֵּיסָא וּמַפְסְדִי לֵיהּ; אֲמַר לֵיהּ: זִיל קוֹץ, אֲמַר לֵיהּ: וְהָא אַרְחֵיקִי לִי! אֲמַר לֵיהּ: הָנֵי מִילֵּי לְאִילָנוֹת, אֲבָל לִגְפָנִים בָּעֵינַן טְפֵי.

The Gemara relates: **Rava bar Rav Ḥanan had these palm trees** that stood **adjacent to the boundary of Rav Yosef's vineyard. Birds would come and roost on the palm trees and** would subsequently **descend to the vineyard and damage it.** Rav Yosef **said to** Rava bar Rav Ḥanan: **Go and cut down**[N] your palm trees. Rava bar Rav Ḥanan **said to him: But I distanced** them the required amount. Rav Yosef **said to him: This matter,** i.e., this specific distance, applies only **to trees, but a greater** distance **is required for vines.**[N]

וְהָא אֲנַן תְּנַן: אֶחָד גְּפָנִים וְאֶחָד כָּל אִילָן! אֲמַר לֵיהּ: הָנֵי מִילֵּי אִילָן לְאִילָן וּגְפָנִים לִגְפָנִים, אֲבָל אִילָן לִגְפָנִים בָּעֵינַן טְפֵי.

Rava bar Rav Ḥanan protested: **But didn't we learn** in the mishna that this is the *halakha* **whether** he is planting **grapevines or any** kind of **tree?** Rav Yosef **said to him: This matter** applies only to the distance between one **tree and** another **tree, or** the distance between one **vine and** other **vines. But** with regard to the space between **a tree and vines, one requires a greater distance.**

אֲמַר לֵיהּ: אֲנָא לָא קָייְצְנָא, דַּאֲמַר רַב: הַאי דִּיקְלָא דְּטָעֵין קַבָּא – אָסוּר לְמִקְצְיֵיהּ, וְאָמַר רַבִּי חֲנִינָא: לָא שְׁכִיב שִׁכְחַת בְּרִי אֶלָּא דְּקַץ תְּאֵנְתָא בְּלָא זִימְנֵיהּ, מָר אִי נִיחָא לֵיהּ לִיקוֹץ.

Rava bar Rav Ḥanan **said to him:** I myself **will not cut them down,**[N] **as Rav said:** With regard to **this palm tree that produces one** ***kav***[H] of fruit, it is **prohibited to cut it down,** due to the verse: "You shall not destroy the trees" (Deuteronomy 20:19). **And Rabbi Ḥanina says: My son Shikhḥat died only because he cut down a fig tree before its time.** Rava bar Rav Ḥanan continued: **If the Master is amenable** to do so, he **may cut** them down, but I will not do it.

רַב פַּפָּא הָווּ לֵיהּ הָנְהוּ דִּיקְלֵי אַמֵּיצְרָא דְּרַב הוּנָא בְּרֵיהּ דְּרַב יְהוֹשֻׁעַ, אֲזַל אַשְׁכְּחֵיהּ דַּהֲוָה חָפַר וְקָא קָאֵיץ שָׁרָשָׁיו; אֲמַר לֵיהּ: מַאי הַאי? אֲמַר לֵיהּ, תְּנַן: הָיוּ שָׁרָשִׁים יוֹצְאִים לְתוֹךְ שֶׁל חֲבֵירוֹ – מַעֲמִיק שְׁלֹשָׁה כְּדֵי שֶׁלֹּא יְעַכֵּב הַמַּחֲרֵישָׁה.

The Gemara further relates that **Rav Pappa**[P] **had these palm trees** that stood **adjacent to the boundary of** the property of **Rav Huna, son of Rav Yehoshua. He went** and **found** Rav Huna **digging and cutting his roots.** Rav Pappa **said to him: What is this?** Rav Huna **said to him** that **we learned** in the mishna: If the **roots were spreading into** the field **of another,** the owner of the field **may dig to a depth** of **three handbreadths** even if he severs those roots, **so that** they do **not impede** his **plow.**

אֲמַר לֵיהּ: הָנֵי מִילֵּי שְׁלֹשָׁה, מָר קָא חָפַר טְפֵי! אֲמַר לֵיהּ: אֲנָא בּוֹרוֹת שִׁיחִין וּמְעָרוֹת קָא חָפַרְנָא, דִּתְנַן: הָיָה חוֹפֵר בּוֹר, שִׁיחַ וּמְעָרָה – קוֹצֵץ וְיוֹרֵד וְהָעֵצִים שֶׁלּוֹ. אֲמַר רַב פַּפָּא: אֲמַרִי לֵיהּ כּוּלְּהִי וְלָא יְכִילִי לֵיהּ,

Rav Pappa **said to him: This statement** applies only up to **three** handbreadths, whereas the **Master is digging** and cutting **more** than three. Rav Huna **said to him: I am** digging **cisterns, ditches, and caves, as we learned** in the mishna: If he **was digging a cistern, a ditch, or a cave, he may cut downward** normally **and the wood** from the roots **is his. Rav Pappa said: I told him all** the proofs I could find, **but I was unable to** convince **him** that I was correct,

HALAKHA

This palm tree that produces one ***kav*** – **דִּיקְלָא דְּטָעֵין קַבָּא**: Even in a situation where a fruit tree causes damage, it may be cut down only if it a produces a small enough amount of fruit that it is unworthy of tending. An olive tree that produces a quarter-*kav* of olives and a palm tree that produces one *kav* of dates may not be cut down (Rambam *Sefer Shofetim, Hilkhot Melakhim UMilḥemoteihem* 6:9).

NOTES

Go cut down – **זִיל קוֹץ**: The commentaries point out that the damage caused by the birds was not a direct result of Rava bar Rav Ḥanan's actions, and therefore one cannot claim that it is considered like his arrows. Why, then, should he have to cut down the trees? They answer that he might cause the birds to fly over to Rav Yosef's vineyard. The damage in this case would in fact be considered like his arrows (Rabbeinu Yona; Rashba; Ritva).

A greater distance is required for vines – **לִגְפָנִים בָּעֵינַן טְפֵי**: The halakhic authorities rule in accordance with the opinion of Rav Yosef, but they dispute the required measurement. Some state that one must distance his tree four cubits and that Rava bar Rav Ḥanan had distanced it only two cubits, which is the requirement in Babylonia. According to this opinion, the *halakha* does not mandate a greater distance for trees (Ri Migash, citing Rif). Other commentaries write that the required distance is fifty cubits (Ramah). There are also those who claim that there is no fixed distance and that the ruling depends on the judges' discretion (Rabbeinu Yona).

I will not cut them down – **אֲנָא לָא קָייְצְנָא**: Many commentaries point out that if Rava bar Rav Ḥanan were causing damage, he would certainly be required to cut down his trees. Some explain that one is permitted to cut down a fruit tree only if it causes a great loss (*Tosafot*). Others write that Rav Yosef did not claim that the tree had to be cut down according to the strict letter of the law; rather, he wanted Rava bar Rav Ḥanan to do so as an act of piety, to avoid being responsible for the damage. Rava bar Rav Ḥanan responded that if it is an appeal to piety, one should also take into consideration the problem of cutting down fruit trees (Rashba). Yet others contend that Rava bar Rav Ḥanan said that he does not maintain that this is the *halakha*, and that he could not follow the ruling of Rav Yosef, who was personally involved in the case. Therefore, he was unwilling to act, and he suggested that if Rav Yosef was certain of the *halakha* he should take action himself (Rabbeinu Yona).

PERSONALITIES

Rav Pappa – **רַב פַּפָּא**: Rav Pappa, a fifth-generation *amora* in Babylonia, was a student of both Abaye and Rava in Pumbedita. Rav Pappa established an academy in Neresh, where he was joined by his close friend Rav Huna, son of Rav Yehoshua, in teaching in the academy. After Rava's death, many of his students came to study under Rav Pappa, who had more than two hundred students attending his lectures.

Rav Pappa's father was a wealthy merchant who supported him in order to allow him to study. Rav Pappa later became a wealthy businessman in his own right, as a brewer of date beer as well as other business ventures. The Talmud records that he engaged in trade with both Jews and gentiles and had a reputation for fairness and generosity in his business dealings.

עַד דַּאֲמַרִי לֵיהּ הָא דְּאָמַר רַב יְהוּדָה: מֵצַר שֶׁהֶחְזִיקוּ בּוֹ רַבִּים – אָסוּר לְקַלְקְלוֹ. לְבָתַר דִּנְפַק, אֲמַר: אַמַּאי לָא אֲמַרִי לֵיהּ: כָּאן בְּתוֹךְ שֵׁשׁ עֶשְׂרֵה אַמָּה, כָּאן חוּץ לְשֵׁשׁ עֶשְׂרֵה אַמָּה.

until I told him that which **Rav Yehuda says:** With regard to a **strip** of land over **which the public has an acquired privilege** of use,[N] one **may not destroy it.** Here too, since I have an acquired privilege of use of this land, you are not permitted to destroy that which I possess. **After** Rav Pappa **left,** Rav Huna, son of Rav Yehoshua, **said: Why did I not say to him** that **there,** an acquired privilege of use is effective when it is **within sixteen cubits,**[N] as within that area the roots are considered part of the tree, whereas **here** I cut the roots of the palm trees **beyond sixteen cubits.**

״הָיָה חוֹפֵר בּוֹר, שִׁיחַ וּמְעָרָה – קוֹצֵץ וְיוֹרֵד וְהָעֵצִים שֶׁלּוֹ״ (וכו׳). בְּעָא מִינֵּיהּ יַעֲקֹב הַדְּיָיבָא מֵרַב חִסְדָּא: עֵצִים שֶׁל מִי?

§ The mishna teaches that if **he was digging a cistern, a ditch, or a cave, he may cut downward and the wood is his.** The Sage **Ya'akov of Hadeyyav raised a dilemma before Rav Ḥisda: To whom does the wood belong?** The mishna says that the wood is his, without specifying to which of the two individuals this refers, the owner of the tree or the owner of the land.

אֲמַר לֵיהּ, תְּנֵיתוּהָ: שָׁרְשֵׁי אִילָן שֶׁל הֶדְיוֹט הַבָּאִין בְּשֶׁל הֶקְדֵּשׁ – לֹא נֶהֱנִין וְלֹא מוֹעֲלִין;

Rav Ḥisda **said to him: You learned** the answer in a mishna in tractate *Me'ila* (13b). If **roots of a tree** belonging **to an ordinary person** [*hedyot*][HL] **extend into** a field belonging **to the Temple** treasury, **one may not derive benefit** from them, but if one derived benefit from them he is **not** liable for **misuse** of consecrated property.[B] That is, even if one does transgress the prohibition and benefit from them, it is not considered misuse and he is not liable to bring an offering.

אִי אָמְרַתְּ בִּשְׁלָמָא בָּתַר אִילָן אָזְלִינַן, מִשּׁוּם הָכִי לֹא מוֹעֲלִין, אֶלָּא אִי אָמְרַתְּ בָּתַר קַרְקַע אָזְלִינַן, אַמַּאי לֹא מוֹעֲלִין?

Granted, if you say that **we follow the tree,** and the roots are considered part of it, it is **due to that** reason that **one is not** liable for **misuse,** as the tree is not consecrated. **But if you say we follow the land,** i.e., the roots belong to the land's owner, **why** is he **not** liable for **misuse** of consecrated property?

אֶלָּא מַאי, בָּתַר אִילָן אָזְלִינַן? אֵימָא סֵיפָא: שֶׁל הֶקְדֵּשׁ הַבָּאִים בְּשֶׁל הֶדְיוֹט – לֹא נֶהֱנִין וְלֹא מוֹעֲלִין; וְאִי בָּתַר אִילָן אָזְלִינַן, אַמַּאי לֹא מוֹעֲלִין?

The Gemara asks: **Rather, what** will you say, that **we follow the tree?** If so, **say the last clause** of that mishna: If roots of a tree belonging **to the Temple** treasury **extend into** a field **of an ordinary person,**[H] **one may not derive benefit** from them, but if one derived benefit from them he is **not** liable for **misuse** of consecrated property. **But if we follow the tree, why** is he **not** liable for **misuse** of consecrated property?

מִידֵּי אִירְיָא? בְּגִידּוּלִין הַבָּאִין לְאַחַר מִכָּאן עָסְקִינַן, וְקָא סָבַר: אֵין מְעִילָה בְּגִידּוּלִין.

The Gemara responds: **Are the cases comparable?** In both clauses of the mishna **we are dealing with growths that came thereafter,** i.e., after the tree was consecrated, **and the** *tanna* of that mishna **holds** that **with regard to growths** that grew from a consecrated plant or tree, they are **not** subject to the *halakhot* of **misuse** of consecrated property. Only the original plant is. Consequently, there is no connection between that mishna and the question of whether roots are considered part of the tree or part of the land.

רָבִינָא אֲמַר, לָא קַשְׁיָא: כָּאן בְּתוֹךְ שֵׁשׁ עֶשְׂרֵה אַמָּה, כָּאן חוּץ לְשֵׁשׁ עֶשְׂרֵה אַמָּה.

Ravina said that it is **not difficult: Here,** in the first clause of the mishna in *Me'ila*, it is referring to **within sixteen cubits** of the tree. In this case the roots are considered part of the tree. **There,** in the second clause, it is referring to roots **beyond sixteen cubits,** in which case the roots are considered part of the ground where they are found.

NOTES

A strip of land over which the public has an acquired privilege of use – מֵצַר שֶׁהֶחְזִיקוּ בּוֹ רַבִּים: Rashi explains as follows: If the public has established the privilege of use of a strip of land, the rightful owner may not ruin that strip of land. Here too, Rav Pappa claimed: Since I have used the land for the palm trees, you are not permitted to ruin it. Others explain that Rav Pappa contended that his ancestors established an acquired privilege of use on this land long ago (Rabbeinu Gershom Meor HaGola).

Most commentaries reject these interpretations, as it is difficult to compare the public's right to land to an individual's right to land he does not own. Instead, they explain that the spot where Rav Huna, son of Rav Yehoshua, was digging, where the roots of Rav Pappa's trees were found, belonged to Rav Huna, but he had given the public the right to walk there. Rav Pappa maintained that Rav Huna had no right to dig a cistern there and ruin the public space (Rabbeinu Ḥananel; Ri Migash; Ra'avad; Rivam in *Tosafot*). Some commentaries maintain that Rav Pappa did not dispute Rav Huna's right to cut out the roots, but he claimed the wood for himself. His proof from the public strip of land is that although the land belongs to an individual, he cannot restrict the public's privilege of use. In an analogous manner, although the owner of the land can prevent usage, the privilege should at least entitle the tree owner to the roots (Rabbeinu Tam).

There it is within sixteen cubits – כָּאן בְּתוֹךְ שֵׁשׁ עֶשְׂרֵה אַמָּה: Some commentaries explain that Rav Huna maintained that the tree owner retains his rights only within sixteen cubits of the tree, as in that space the tree draws nourishment from the ground. Since Rav Huna dug beyond that limit, he was permitted to remove the roots (Rashi). Other early commentaries, who maintain that this refers to a strip of land appropriated by the public, explain that there is a limit even to how wide the public area is, specifically sixteen cubits, which is the width of a public domain in other contexts. Beyond sixteen cubits, the owner of the land is permitted to ruin the strip of land (Ramah). According to Rabbeinu Tam, who contends that the discussion concerns ownership of the roots, Rav Huna is claiming that beyond sixteen cubits the roots belong to the owner of the land.

HALAKHA

Roots of a tree belonging to an ordinary person – שָׁרְשֵׁי אִילָן שֶׁל הֶדְיוֹט: If roots of a tree of an ordinary person extend into a field belonging to the Temple treasury, no benefit may be derived from the roots if the tree is located within sixteen cubits of the field of the treasury. Nevertheless, if one does derive benefit he is not liable for misuse of consecrated property. If the tree is farther away than sixteen cubits, any benefit derived from the roots is considered misuse of consecrated property (Rambam *Sefer Avoda, Hilkhot Me'ila* 5:6).

Roots of a tree belonging to the Temple treasury… extend into a field of an ordinary person – שֶׁל הֶקְדֵּשׁ הַבָּאִים בְּשֶׁל הֶדְיוֹט: In a case where roots of a tree belonging to the Temple extend into a field of an ordinary person, one who derives benefit from them misuses consecrated property, provided that the tree stands within sixteen cubits of the person's field. In a case where the tree is beyond sixteen cubits, one may not benefit from the roots, but if he does so he has not misused consecrated property (Rambam *Sefer Avoda, Hilkhot Me'ila* 5:6).

LANGUAGE

Ordinary person [*hedyot*] – הֶדְיוֹט: From the Greek ἰδιώτης, idiotēs, meaning a simple person, one with no particular stature. The term is also used to distinguish between sacred property and items that belong to a regular person.

BACKGROUND

Misuse of consecrated property – מוֹעֲלִין: The *halakha* of misuse of consecrated property is mentioned briefly in the Torah (see Leviticus 5:14–16), while the many details of its *halakhot* are discussed extensively in tractate *Me'ila*. Misuse [*me'ila*] is defined as any unlawful benefit derived from consecrated property, as one may not use for personal gain any property that has been consecrated to God. The prohibition against misuse is severe in that even one who acts unwittingly or by unavoidable accident is guilty of misuse and is liable to bring an offering. Furthermore, although in most situations one is not held accountable for the actions of his agent, this principle does not apply to cases of misuse. Tractate *Me'ila* details those instances when different types of offerings and other consecrated property are subject to misuse and when this prohibition does not apply.

אֲמַר עוּלָּא: אִילָן הַסָּמוּךְ לְמֶצֶר בְּתוֹךְ שֵׁשׁ עֶשְׂרֵה אַמָּה – גַּזְלָן הוּא, וְאֵין מְבִיאִין מִמֶּנּוּ בִּכּוּרִים.

Ulla said: An individual who maintains **a tree that is within sixteen cubits of a boundary is a robber,** as it draws nourishment from the neighbor's land, **and one does not bring first fruits**[B] **from it,**[N] since that would be a mitzva that is fulfilled by means of a transgression.

מְנָא לֵיהּ לְעוּלָּא הָא? אִילֵימָא מִדִּתְנַן: עֶשֶׂר נְטִיעוֹת הַמְפוּזָּרוֹת בְּתוֹךְ בֵּית סְאָה, חוֹרְשִׁין כׇּל בֵּית סְאָה בִּשְׁבִילָן עַד רֹאשׁ הַשָּׁנָה;

The Gemara asks: **From where does Ulla** derive **that** measurement? **If we say** it is from that **which we learned** in a mishna (*Shevi'it* 1:6), this is problematic. That mishna teaches: If there were **ten saplings**[HN] **scattered in a *beit se'a*, one may plow the entire *beit se'a* for their** sake **until Rosh HaShana** of the Sabbatical Year. Although it is prohibited to plow other land in the time leading into the Sabbatical Year, to avoid the appearance of preparing to work the ground in that year, it is permitted to do so for the purpose of sustaining these young trees.

כַּמָּה הָווּ לְהוּ? תְּרֵי אַלְפִין וְחָמֵשׁ מֵאָה גַּרְמִידֵי. לְכׇל חַד וְחַד, כַּמָּה מָטֵי לֵיהּ? מָאתָן וְחַמְשִׁין, הָא לָא הָוֵי דְּעוּלָּא!

The Gemara calculates: **How much is** the area of a *beit se'a*? It is **2,500** square **cubits.**[L] **And how much** area is allocated **for each and every one** of the ten trees? It is **250** square cubits. **This is not** the distance **that Ulla** taught. An area of sixteen cubits to each side of the tree is a square of thirty-two by thirty-two cubits, or 1,024 square cubits, which is much larger than 250.

וְאֶלָּא מִדִּתְנַן: שְׁלֹשָׁה אִילָנוֹת שֶׁל שְׁלֹשָׁה בְּנֵי אָדָם – הֲרֵי אֵלּוּ מִצְטָרְפִין, וְחוֹרְשִׁין כׇּל

But rather, Ulla derived this measurement **from** that **which we learned** in the following mishna (*Shevi'it* 1:5): If there were **three** large **trees**[HN] belonging **to three** different **people** in one *beit se'a*, **these** trees **combine, and one may plow the entire**

HALAKHA

Ten saplings – **עֶשֶׂר נְטִיעוֹת:** If ten saplings are planted in one *beit se'a*, equal to 2,500 square cubits, the entire field may be plowed on account of the saplings until Rosh HaShana of the Sabbatical Year. This ruling is a *halakha* transmitted to Moses from Sinai (Rambam *Sefer Zera'im*, *Hilkhot Shemitta VeYovel* 3:5).

Three trees – **שְׁלֹשָׁה אִילָנוֹת:** If three trees, either fruit trees or non-fruit trees, are planted in one *beit se'a* of land, and they are large enough that if they were fig trees they would produce enough figs to form cakes weighing sixty *maneh*, the field may be plowed on their account until Rosh HaShana of the Sabbatical Year. This is the *halakha* whether the trees belong to a single individual or to multiple owners, provided the plowing oxen can maneuver between the trees with the plow (Rambam *Sefer Zera'im*, *Hilkhot Shemitta VeYovel* 3:2).

LANGUAGE

Cubits [*garmidei*] – **גַּרְמִידֵי:** *Garmida* is the Aramaic name for a forearm, the basis for the measurement of a cubit. This term appears in the Bible with a slightly different spelling, as *gamod* (Judges 3:16). In Aramaic it is extended with an added letter *reish*.

BACKGROUND

First fruits – **בִּכּוּרִים:** The obligation to bring first fruits to the Temple is stated in the Torah (Deuteronomy 26:1–11) and is discussed in great detail in tractate *Bikkurim*, in the mishna and in the Jerusalem Talmud. This mitzva applies to the seven types of fruit with which Eretz Yisrael is specially favored and involves the bringing of a small amount of first fruits, one-sixtieth of the harvest, before *teruma* is separated from the crop. The first fruits must be brought to the Temple in Jerusalem. A large, festive ceremony accompanied the procession of the first fruits to Jerusalem. The owner of the fruit would bring his basket up to the altar, where he would wave it and recite the prayers of praise and thanksgiving that appear in the Torah. At this stage of the ritual, the status of the first fruits becomes like that of *teruma*, and the fruits belong to the priests.

NOTES

One does not bring first fruits from it – **אֵין מְבִיאִין מִמֶּנּוּ בִּכּוּרִים:** Rashi explains that one is not obligated to bring first fruits from this tree because it does not fulfill the requirement of: "Which you shall bring in from your land" (Deuteronomy 26:2), as the land occupied by the tree does not belong entirely to him. Others maintain that it is actually prohibited to bring first fruits from this tree. The reasoning is that the tree draws nourishment from the land of another, which puts its fruit in a category similar to that of a stolen item, and it is prohibited to offer a stolen item as an offering because this is a mitzva that comes to be fulfilled by means of a transgression (Rabbeinu Ḥananel).

Some early commentaries point out that Ulla's statement apparently contradicts the mishna, which rules that one need distance a tree only four cubits from a boundary. They explain that the mishna is referring to a case where there is a rock in the ground that prevents the tree from drawing nourishment from the neighboring field. For this reason the mishna does not address the issue of nourishment but simply discusses distancing from above the ground, to enable work in the vineyard (Rabbeinu Ḥananel; *Tosafot*; Rashba).

Ten saplings – **עֶשֶׂר נְטִיעוֹת:** When the Temple stood it was prohibited to work the land in the period before the Sabbatical Year, as a supplement to the prohibitions of the Sabbatical Year and to avoid improving the land for that year. This prohibition included the plowing of grain fields from Passover of the sixth year and fruit orchards from *Shavuot*. Nevertheless, in the event that young trees have not grown sufficiently, there is a concern that if one does not plow the field they will die. In this case, the Torah permits plowing the field until Rosh HaShana of the Sabbatical Year, a *halakha* that was transmitted to Moses from Sinai. This leniency applies only if there are ten trees, as a field with fewer than ten trees does not require plowing (*Tosafot*). Alternatively, the reason is that an arrangement of fewer than ten trees is not classified as a field of trees but as a scattering, which is treated like a grain field (Ri Migash). This leniency applies only when there are precisely ten trees, but not more, as if there are more than ten trees it is assumed they will not be left to grow so crowded together, but are slated for removal. Some commentaries maintain that this *halakha* came into effect only following the destruction of the Temple (Ramah).

Three trees – **שְׁלֹשָׁה אִילָנוֹת:** This refers to large trees that may be owned by three separate people. The area around them may be plowed on their account because they are situated in a single plot of land. According to Rashi the mishna is referring to plowing the land until *Shavuot*. Others cite a version of the text that states that the land may be plowed until Rosh HaShana (Ra'avad; Rabbeinu Yona). This is in accordance with the statement (*Moed Katan* 3a) that at a later stage Rabban Gamliel and his court permitted plowing until Rosh HaShana in all fields.

HALAKHA

One who buys a tree and its land – הַקּוֹנֶה אִילָן וְקַרְקָעוֹ: If one buys a tree that is situated in the field of another, he does not bring first fruits, as this purchase does not include the land automatically. If he bought the tree and the land, he brings first fruits and recites the relevant verses (Rambam *Sefer Zera'im, Hilkhot Bikkurim* 2:13 and *Kesef Mishne* there).

בֵּית סְאָה בִּשְׁבִילָן; כַּמָּה הָווּ לְהוּ? תְּרֵי אַלְפֵי וַחֲמֵשׁ מְאָה גַּרְמִידֵי. לְכֹל חַד כַּמָּה מָטֵי לֵיהּ? תְּמָנֵי מְאָה וּתְלָתִין וּתְלָתָא וְתִילְתָּא, אַכַּתִּי נְפִישׁ לֵיהּ דְּעוּלָּא! לָא דַּק.

beit se'a for their sake. How much is that area in cubits? It is 2,500 square **cubits. And how much** area is that **for each** of the trees? It is 833⅓. **Still, Ulla's** amount **is greater than** this. The Gemara answers: Ulla **was not precise** in this matter.

אֵימוּר דְּאָמְרִינַן לָא דַּק – לְחוּמְרָא, לְקוּלָּא לָא דַּק מִי אָמְרִינַן?

The Gemara asks: One can **say that we say** that a Sage **was not precise** in his measurements when his ruling leads **to a stringency;** but **do we say** that he **was not precise** if his measurements lead **to a leniency?** According to the previous explanation, Ulla exempts the owner of a tree from first fruits even in a case where his tree does not in fact draw nourishment from his neighbor's field.

מִי סָבְרַתְּ בְּרִיבּוּעָא קָא אָמְרִינַן? בְּעִיגּוּלָּא קָא אָמְרִינַן.

The Gemara answers: **Do you maintain** that **we say** the roots extend that far **in a square,** i.e., one measures sixteen cubits to each side of the tree? Not so; **we say** this **with regard to a circle,** that is, the roots extend in a circle surrounding the tree, as the area of a circle is smaller than that of the square circumscribing it.

מִכְּדִי כַּמָּה מְרוּבָּע יוֹתֵר עַל הָעִיגּוּל? רְבִיעַ, פָּשׁוּ לְהוּ שְׁבַע מְאָה וְשִׁתִּין וּתְמַנְיָא, אַכַּתִּי פָּשׁ לֵיהּ פַּלְגָא דְּאַמְּתָא! הַיְינוּ דְּלָא דַּק, וּלְחוּמְרָא לָא דַּק.

The Gemara asks: **Now,** by **how much is** the area of **a square greater than the** area of a **circle** with a diameter the length of the side of that square? It is greater by **one-quarter**[N] of the area of the circle. If so, **768** square cubits, three-quarters of 1,024, **remain** for each tree, but **there still remains half a cubit**[N] more based on the mishna's calculation. In other words, the measurement would be more accurate if a tree is considered to draw nourishment from a distance of sixteen and a half cubits on each side. The Gemara answers: **This is** why we said that Ulla **was not precise, and** he was **not precise** in a manner that leads **to a stringency,** as one brings first fruits even from a tree that stands just sixteen cubits from the boundary, rather than 16½.

תָּא שְׁמַע: הַקּוֹנֶה אִילָן וְקַרְקָעוֹ – מֵבִיא וְקוֹרֵא; מַאי לָאו כׇּל שֶׁהוּא? לָא, שֵׁשׁ עֶשְׂרֵה אַמָּה.

The Gemara cites a proof against the opinion of Ulla. **Come** and **hear** the following mishna (*Bikkurim* 1:11): **One who buys a tree and its land**[H] **brings** first fruits **and recites** the requisite Torah verses (Deuteronomy 26:5–11) over them. **What, is it not** referring to a case where one buys **any amount** of land with the tree? The Gemara rejects this claim: **No;** it is referring to a case where one buys **sixteen cubits** of land around the tree.

NOTES

One-quarter – רְבִיעַ: This number is not precise, as it is predicated on the assumption that the ratio of the circumference of a circle to its diameter is precisely three to one, when in fact this number, known as pi, is closer to 3.14. Rambam's Commentary on the Mishna (*Eiruvin* 1:5) notes that since the true ratio can only be approximated, as it is an irrational number, the Sages expressed the ratio in terms of whole numbers. Others explain, based on a verse (see I Kings 7:23), that for halakhic purposes, the Sages had a tradition that the ratio should be considered three to one. See *Tashbetz*, who discusses whether this smaller ratio is applied only in cases where it results in a stringency, or even in cases where it results in a leniency.

There still remains half a cubit – אַכַּתִּי פָּשׁ לֵיהּ פַּלְגָא דְּאַמְּתָא: According to Rashi, if one calculates Ulla's measurement not as sixteen cubits but as 16½, each tree receives roughly 816 square cubits, which is about one-third of a *beit se'a*, 833⅓. Rashi points out that it would be more precise to say two-thirds of a square cubit, but the Gemara was inexact. He further adds that there are versions of the text that state that number (see Rabbeinu Tam in *Tosafot*). In defense of the standard version of the text, other commentaries write that one must take the area of the tree itself into consideration, which is roughly one square cubit. Consequently, the area is 16½ cubits on each side (Ra'avad; *Tosafot*; Rid). Others state that one-third of a square cubit should be added for the space of the tree itself, which brings the measurement closer to 833⅓, even if one initially adds only half a square cubit for a tree (*Tosafot*). Some commentaries suggest that the half of a square cubit does not count for each tree but is deducted from each end of the *beit se'a*. This yields close to 816 square cubits for each tree.

תָּא שְׁמַע: קָנָה שְׁנֵי אִילָנוֹת בְּתוֹךְ שֶׁל חֲבֵירוֹ – מֵבִיא וְאֵינוֹ קוֹרֵא; הָא שְׁלֹשָׁה – מֵבִיא וְקוֹרֵא; מַאי לָאו כׇּל שֶׁהוּא? לָא, הָכָא נַמִּי שֵׁשׁ עֶשְׂרֵה אַמָּה.

The Gemara suggests: **Come** and **hear** an additional proof from another mishna (*Bikkurim* 1:6): If one **bought two trees**[NH] **in the** field **of another, he brings** first fruits **and does not recite** the verses, because the land does not belong to him. It may be inferred from here that if he bought **three** trees **he does bring**[H] first fruits **and recite** the verses. **What, is it not** referring to a case where one buys **any amount** of land with the trees? The Gemara rejects this claim as well: **No; here too** it is referring to a case where he acquires **sixteen cubits** of land around the trees.

תָּא שְׁמַע, רַבִּי עֲקִיבָא אוֹמֵר: קַרְקַע כׇּל שֶׁהוּא חַיָּיב בְּפֵאָה וּבְבִכּוּרִים, וְכוֹתְבִין עָלָיו פְּרוֹזְבּוּל,

The Gemara suggests: **Come** and **hear** a proof from a mishna (*Pe'a* 3:6). **Rabbi Akiva says:** The owner of **land of any size is obligated in** ***pe'a***[BH] **and in first fruits, and** a lender **can write a document that prevents the Sabbatical Year from abrogating an outstanding debt [*prosbol*]**[L] **for** this **land,**[NH] so that loans he provided will not be canceled at the close of the Sabbatical Year,

BACKGROUND

Pe'a – פֵּאָה: The Torah states that it is prohibited for a farmer to harvest the produce in the corner of his field. He must allow the poor to collect this produce for themselves. The Sages issued a decree that the area of the corner must be at least one-sixtieth of the field. This mitzva appears in the Torah (Leviticus 19:9, 23:22), and tractate *Pe'a* is devoted to the details of this mitzva. By Torah law, fields, vineyards, and olive groves are included in this mitzva (*Tosafot*).

LANGUAGE

Prosbol – פְּרוֹזְבּוּל: This term is clearly of Greek origin; its precise source remains unclear. Some commentaries suggest it is related to the word προβολή, *probolē*, which refers to a declaration before a court or communal gathering. Some associate it with the Greek προσβολή, *prosbolē*, meaning the conclusion of a sale.

NOTES

Bought two trees – קָנָה שְׁנֵי אִילָנוֹת: The commentaries point out: This indicates that even if the buyer has no land, since one who purchases two trees does not automatically acquire the land upon which they are situated, he nevertheless brings first fruits. This presents a difficulty for the opinion of Ulla, who states that if a tree draws nourishment from another's field, no first fruits are brought (Rid). The Rid explains that when one buys a tree he acquires the right to draw nourishment from the land for as long as the tree grows there, and there is consequently no robbery in this case. Nevertheless, one does not recite the verses, because the land does not belong to him.

And a lender can write a *prosbol* for it – וְכוֹתְבִין עָלָיו פְּרוֹזְבּוּל: By Torah law, all debts are abrogated at the end of the seventh year of the Sabbatical cycle. The institution of a *prosbol* prevents debts from being abrogated at the end of the Sabbatical Year. In effect, the creditor gives permission to the court to collect his debt, and a debt owed to the court is not abrogated by the Sabbatical Year. This mechanism was instituted by Hillel the Elder, who observed that people were reluctant to lend money to the poor at the approach of the Sabbatical Year. He therefore established this mechanism to benefit both the lenders, as it enables debts to be collected, and the borrowers, since otherwise people would be discouraged from providing loans. Rashi explains that land is needed for a *prosbol* because this arrangement was instituted to protect standard debts, which typically include a lien on land. Other commentaries explain that when the borrower has land from which the debt can be collected, it is viewed is if the debt were already repaid. Since the requirement of land for a *prosbol* is a technicality, any amount of land suffices for this purpose (see *Tosafot*).

HALAKHA

If one bought two trees – קָנָה שְׁנֵי אִילָנוֹת: If one buys two trees that are located in the field of another, he brings first fruits by means of an agent and does not recite the verses, as it is uncertain whether or not he owns land (Rambam *Sefer Zera'im, Hilkhot Bikkurim* 4:4).

If he bought three trees, he does bring – הָא שְׁלֹשָׁה מֵבִיא: One who buys three trees must bring first fruits and recite the verses. It is considered as though he purchased the land occupied by the trees even if he did not actually do so (Rambam *Sefer Zera'im, Hilkhot Bikkurim* 2:13).

The owner of land of any size is obligated in *pe'a* – קַרְקַע כׇּל שֶׁהוּא חַיָּיב בְּפֵאָה: Land of any size is subject to *pe'a*, even if it is owned by partners (Rambam *Sefer Zera'im, Hilkhot Mattenot Aniyyim* 2:3).

And a lender can write a *prosbol* for it – וְכוֹתְבִין עָלָיו פְּרוֹזְבּוּל: A *prosbol* may be written only if the borrower owns land. Even a small plot of land qualifies for this purpose (Rambam *Sefer Zera'im, Hilkhot Shemitta VeYovel* 9:19; *Shulḥan Arukh, Ḥoshen Mishpat* 67:22).

HALAKHA

And he can acquire property that does not serve as a guarantee along with it – וְנִקְנִין עִמָּהּ נְכָסִים שֶׁאֵין לָהֶם אַחֲרָיוּת: A large amount of movable property can be acquired by means of the concurrent acquisition of even a small amount of land (Rambam *Sefer Kinyan, Hilkhot Mekhira* 3:8; *Shulḥan Arukh, Ḥoshen Mishpat* 202:7).

A tree part of which is in Eretz Yisrael – אִילָן מִקְצָתוֹ בָּאָרֶץ: If a tree's roots are partially inside Eretz Yisrael and partially outside it, its fruit is considered a mixture of untithed produce and non-sacred produce, as stated by Rabbi Yehuda HaNasi. This is the *halakha* even if a hard rock divides the roots that are inside Eretz Yisrael from those that are outside (Rambam *Sefer Zera'im, Hilkhot Terumot* 1:24).

BACKGROUND

Untithed produce [*tevel*] – טֶבֶל: *Tevel* refers to produce from which the priestly dues of *teruma* and other tithes have not been separated, or dough from which *ḥalla* has not been separated. The Torah prohibits the consumption of untithed produce. Once tithes or *ḥalla* have been separated, even if they have not yet been given to those for whom they are designated, the item is no longer classified as untithed, and it may be eaten.

וְנִקְנִין עִמָּהּ נְכָסִים שֶׁאֵין לָהֶם אַחֲרָיוּת! הָכָא בְּמַאי עָסְקִינַן – בְּחִיטֵּי.

and he can acquire property that does not serve as a guarantee, i.e., movable property, along **with it.**[H] There are specific modes of acquisition for movable property, but if one is acquiring any amount of land at the same time as the movable property, the mode of acquisition employed to acquire the land suffices for the acquisition of the movable property as well. Apparently, any amount of land is subject to first fruits, whereas according to Ulla a tree acquired with less than sixteen cubits of land surrounding it draws nourishment from the land surrounding it and is exempt from first fruits. The Gemara rejects this: **With what are we dealing here?** We are dealing **with wheat,** which is subject to the *halakhot* of first fruits and requires very little land to nourish it.

דַּיְקָא נָמֵי, דְּקָתָנֵי: כׇּל שֶׁהוּא, שְׁמַע מִינַּהּ.

The Gemara comments that the language of the mishna **is also precise,** as it teaches: Land of any size, which indicates even a miniscule amount, and all normal trees certainly require more land than that. The Gemara affirms: **Learn from it** that it is so.

תָּא שְׁמַע: אִילָן מִקְצָתוֹ בָּאָרֶץ וּמִקְצָתוֹ בְּחוּץ לָאָרֶץ – טֶבֶל וְחוּלִּין מְעוֹרָבִין זֶה בָּזֶה, דִּבְרֵי רַבִּי.

The Gemara further suggests: **Come** and **hear** a proof from a *baraita* (*Tosefta, Ma'asrot* 2:22): If there is **a tree, part of which is in Eretz** Yisrael[H] **and part of which is outside of Eretz** Yisrael, it is considered as though **untithed produce,**[B] i.e., produce that is subject to the *halakhot* of *terumot* and tithes, **and non-sacred produce,** i.e., produce that is exempt from the *halakhot* of *terumot* and tithes, **are mixed together** in each one of this tree's fruits. This is **the statement of Rabbi** Yehuda HaNasi.

רַבָּן שִׁמְעוֹן בֶּן גַּמְלִיאֵל אוֹמֵר: הַגָּדֵל בְּחִיּוּב – חַיָּיב, הַגָּדֵל בִּפְטוּר – פָּטוּר;

Rabban Shimon ben Gamliel says: With regard to the fruits in the part of the tree that is **growing in** a place where there is **an obligation** to separate tithes, i.e., in Eretz Yisrael, the owner is **obligated** to separate tithes. With regard to the fruits that are **growing in** a place where there is **an exemption** from separating tithes, i.e., outside of Eretz Yisrael, the owner is **exempt.**

עַד כָּאן לָא פְּלִיגִי אֶלָּא דְּמָר סָבַר: יֵשׁ בְּרֵירָה, וּמָר סָבַר: אֵין בְּרֵירָה,

The Gemara comments: **They disagree only in that** one **Sage,** Rabban Shimon ben Gamliel, **holds** that **there is** retroactive **designation,** and therefore it is assumed that the nourishment drawn from Eretz Yisrael sustained the fruit that grew on that side of the tree, and the nourishment drawn from outside Eretz Yisrael sustained the fruit that grew there. **And** one **Sage,** Rabbi Yehuda HaNasi, **holds** that **there is no** retroactive **designation,** and the fruit is considered mixed.

אֲבָל גָּדֵל בִּפְטוּר – דִּבְרֵי הַכֹּל פָּטוּר!

But if the tree **grew** entirely **in** a place where there is **an exemption** from separating tithes, i.e., outside Eretz Yisrael, **all agree** that the owner is **exempt,** even though the tree might have roots within sixteen cubits of Eretz Yisrael and draw nourishment from there. This presents a difficulty for the opinion of Ulla, as he claims that the place from where a tree draws its nourishment is decisive with regard to first fruits.

הָכָא בְּמַאי עָסְקִינַן – דְּמַפְסִיק צוּנְמָא. אִי הָכִי, מַאי טַעְמֵיהּ דְּרַבִּי? דְּהָדְרִי עָרְבִי;

The Gemara answers: **With what are we dealing here?** We are dealing with a case **where a rock divides** the roots up to the trunk, and therefore it is possible to distinguish between the parts of the tree that draw nutrients from Eretz Yisrael and the parts that draw nutrients from outside of Eretz Yisrael. The Gemara asks: **If so, what is the reasoning of Rabbi** Yehuda HaNasi? Why does he view the fruits as being a mixture? The Gemara answers: He holds that although there is a division between the roots, they cannot be distinguished from one another, **as they then become mixed** in the body of the tree.

וּבְמַאי קָא מִיפַּלְגִי – מָר סָבַר: אֲוִירָא מְבַלְבֵּל, וּמָר סָבַר: הַאי לְחוּדֵיהּ קָאֵי וְהַאי לְחוּדֵיהּ קָאֵי.

The Gemara asks: **And with regard to what** principle **do they disagree?** The Gemara answers: One **Sage,** Rabbi Yehuda HaNasi, **holds: The air** above the ground **mixes** the nutrients, **and** one **Sage,** Rabban Shimon ben Gamliel, **holds: This** part of the tree **stands alone and this** part of the tree **stands alone.** From the roots up to the branches, it is as if the tree were cut along the line of the border.

וְשֵׁשׁ עֶשְׂרֵה אַמָּה וְתוּ לָא? וְהָא תְּנַן: מַרְחִיקִין אֶת הָאִילָן מִן הַבּוֹר עֶשְׂרִים וְחָמֵשׁ אַמָּה! אָמַר אַבָּיֵי: מֵיזַל טוּבָא אָזְלִי, אַכְחוּשֵׁי לָא מַכְחֲשֵׁי אֶלָּא עַד שֵׁשׁ עֶשְׂרֵה אַמָּה, טְפֵי לָא מַכְחֲשֵׁי.

The Gemara raises a difficulty against Ulla's opinion from a different perspective: **And do roots extend sixteen cubits and no more? Didn't we learn** in a mishna (25b): **One must distance a tree twenty-five cubits from a cistern?** This indicates that tree roots reach more than sixteen cubits. **Abaye said:** The roots **extend farther, but they weaken the ground only up to sixteen cubits;** with regard to an area any **more** distant than that, **they do not weaken** the ground.

כִּי אֲתָא רַב דִּימִי אָמַר, בְּעָא מִינֵּיהּ רֵישׁ לָקִישׁ מֵרַבִּי יוֹחָנָן: אִילָן הַסָּמוּךְ לַמֵּיצַר בְּתוֹךְ שֵׁשׁ עֶשְׂרֵה אַמָּה, מַהוּ? אֲמַר לֵיהּ: גַּזְלָן הוּא, וְאֵין מְבִיאִין מִמֶּנּוּ בִּכּוּרִים.

Concerning this matter the Gemara relates that **when Rav Dimi came** from Eretz Yisrael **he said: Reish Lakish raised a dilemma before Rabbi Yoḥanan:** With regard to **a tree** that is **within sixteen cubits of a boundary,**[H] what is the *halakha*? Rabbi Yoḥanan **said to him:** The owner **is a robber, and one does not bring first fruits from it.**

כִּי אֲתָא רָבִין אָמַר רַבִּי יוֹחָנָן: אֶחָד אִילָן הַסָּמוּךְ לַמֵּיצַר, וְאֶחָד אִילָן הַנּוֹטֶה – מֵבִיא וְקוֹרֵא, שֶׁעַל מְנָת כֵּן הִנְחִיל יְהוֹשֻׁעַ לְיִשְׂרָאֵל אֶת הָאָרֶץ.

By contrast, **when Ravin came** from Eretz Yisrael, he related that **Rabbi Yoḥanan says: Both** in the case of **a tree that is close to a boundary and a tree that leans** into a neighbor's yard, **one brings** first fruits **and recites** the verses, **as it was on this condition**[N] **that Joshua apportioned Eretz** Yisrael **to the Jewish people,** i.e., that they would not be particular about such matters.

מתני׳ אִילָן שֶׁהוּא נוֹטֶה לִשְׂדֵה חֲבֵירוֹ – קוֹצֵץ מְלֹא הַמַּרְדֵּעַ עַל גַּבֵּי הַמַּחֲרֵישָׁה, וּבֶחָרוּב וּבְשִׁקְמָה – כְּנֶגֶד הַמִּשְׁקוֹלֶת, בֵּית הַשְּׁלָחִין – כׇּל הָאִילָן כְּנֶגֶד הַמִּשְׁקוֹלֶת; אַבָּא שָׁאוּל אוֹמֵר: כׇּל אִילַן סְרָק כְּנֶגֶד הַמִּשְׁקוֹלֶת.

MISHNA With regard to **a tree that leans into the field of another,**[H] the neighbor **may cut** the branches **to the height of an ox goad**[B] raised **over the plow,**[N] in places where the land is to be plowed, so that the branches do not impede the use of the plow. **And in the case of a carob tree and the case of a sycamore tree,**[N] whose abundance of branches cast shade that is harmful to plants, all the branches overhanging one's property may be removed **along the plumb line,**[NB] i.e., along a line perpendicular to the boundary separating the fields. And if the neighbor's field is **an irrigated field, all** branches of **the tree** are removed **along the plumb line. Abba Shaul says: All barren trees** are cut **along the plumb line.**

גמ׳ אִיבַּעְיָא לְהוּ: אַבָּא שָׁאוּל, אַרֵישָׁא קָאֵי אוֹ אַסֵּיפָא קָאֵי?

GEMARA A dilemma was raised before them: Is **Abba Shaul referring to the first clause** of the mishna, which states that a tree extending into a neighbor's field is cut only to the height of an ox goad, and Abba Shaul maintains that barren trees have the same *halakha* as carob and sycamore trees in that they are cut along the plumb line? **Or** is he **referring to the latter clause,** which discusses an irrigated field, and he permits cutting only barren trees along the plumb line, but not fruit trees?

HALAKHA

A tree within…a boundary – אִילָן הַסָּמוּךְ לַמֵּיצַר: If one owns a tree that stands close to a neighbor's boundary or that extends into a neighbor's field, then even though it should have been kept at a distance, fruit from that tree is brought as first fruits and the verses are recited (Rambam *Sefer Zera'im, Hilkhot Bikkurim* 2:11).

A tree that leans into the field of another – אִילָן שֶׁהוּא נוֹטֶה לִשְׂדֵה חֲבֵירוֹ: If the branches of one's neighbor's tree extend into his field, he may cut the branches to the height of an ox goad raised over a plow, to facilitate the plowing of his field. If the tree in question is a carob or sycamore tree, all of the branches overhanging his property may be removed up to the boundary. Similarly, if the branches of any tree extend into an irrigated field or into a copse of trees, they may be removed up to the boundary (Rambam *Sefer Kinyan, Hilkhot Shekhenim* 10:8; *Shulḥan Arukh, Ḥoshen Mishpat* 155:26).

NOTES

As it was on this condition – שֶׁעַל מְנָת כֵּן: Since people are not particular about such matters, one cannot say that the owner of the tree is a robber. This permission does not need to be stated explicitly by the neighbor, as it is part of Joshua's conditions. Evidently, Ulla disputes the claim that Joshua imposed this condition, and he maintains that people are particular in this regard. In fact, in tractate *Bava Kamma* (80b) this condition is not included in a list of conditions established by Joshua, which demonstrates that the matter is subject to dispute (Rashba).

Over the plow – עַל גַּבֵּי הַמַּחֲרֵישָׁה: In other words, the width of the area that is cut is the space taken up by the plow.

And in the case of a carob tree and of a sycamore tree – וּבֶחָרוּב וּבְשִׁקְמָה: According to Rashi, these trees have a great number of thick branches, and the shade they cast impedes the growth of the field's produce. Others state that as the fruits of these trees are insignificant, this is an additional allowance for cutting them along the plumb line, despite their fruit-bearing status (Rabbeinu Gershom Meor HaGola).

Along the plumb line [*mishkolet*] – כְּנֶגֶד הַמִּשְׁקוֹלֶת: To determine the path of this line one employs a string with a weight [*mishkal*] attached to it, as used by builders.

BACKGROUND

The height of an ox goad – מְלֹא הַמַּרְדֵּעַ: This was a staff used to prod and direct animals. It is likely that this implement was of a fixed length, slightly less than 1 m, as the farmer who walked behind the plow had to be able to reach the oxen to prod them.

Plowman with ox goad

Along the plumb line – כְּנֶגֶד הַמִּשְׁקוֹלֶת: This means a straight line perpendicular to the ground. In order to ensure that walls were straight, builders would hang a weight at the end of a rope to produce a straight line.

Plumb line

NOTES

An irrigated field – בֵּית הַשְּׁלָחִין: The commentaries explain that the trees prevent dew from forming on the field. Since this type of field is not watered naturally and needs to be irrigated, the damage is more extensive (Rambam).

He is referring to the first clause – אַרֵישָׁא קָאֵי: Abba Shaul permits one to cut any barren tree growing over a field that is watered by natural sources, in addition to carob and sycamore trees (Rashi). Some commentaries explain that Abba Shaul permits one to cut only barren trees but not carob trees or sycamores, because their fruit is eaten (Rabbeinu Gershom Meor HaGola; Rambam's Commentary on the Mishna).

HALAKHA

A tree that extends into the public domain – אִילָן שֶׁהוּא נוֹטֶה לִרְשׁוּת הָרַבִּים: If the branches of a tree extend into the public domain, they are cut so that a camel with its rider can pass underneath. The *halakha* is in accordance with the opinion of the first *tanna* (Rambam *Sefer Nezikin, Hilkhot Nizkei Mamon* 13:26; *Shulḥan Arukh, Ḥoshen Mishpat* 417:4).

תָּא שְׁמַע, דְּתַנְיָא: בֵּית הַשְּׁלָחִין – אַבָּא שָׁאוּל אוֹמֵר: כׇּל הָאִילָן כְּנֶגֶד הַמִּשְׁקוֹלֶת, מִפְּנֵי שֶׁהַצֵּל רַע לְבֵית הַשְּׁלָחִין; שְׁמַע מִינַּהּ אַרֵישָׁא קָאֵי, שְׁמַע מִינַּהּ.

The Gemara answers: **Come and hear** a resolution to this dilemma, **as it is taught** in a *baraita*: With regard to **an irrigated field, Abba Shaul says: All** types of **trees** are cut **along the plumb line, because the shade is harmful to an irrigated field.**[N] This shows that he does not dispute the *halakha* of the latter clause. **Learn from it** that **he is referring to the first clause**[N] of the mishna. The Gemara affirms: **Learn from it** that it is so.

אָמַר רַב אָשֵׁי: מַתְנִיתִין נַמִי דַּיְקָא, דְּקָתָנֵי: כׇּל אִילָן סְרָק; אִי אָמְרַתְּ בִּשְׁלָמָא אַרֵישָׁא קָאֵי, הַיְינוּ דְּקָתָנֵי כׇּל אִילָן, אֶלָּא אִי אָמְרַתְּ אַסֵּיפָא קָאֵי, אִילַן סְרָק מִיבְּעֵי לֵיהּ? אֶלָּא לָאו שְׁמַע מִינַּהּ אַרֵישָׁא קָאֵי, שְׁמַע מִינַּהּ.

Rav Ashi **said** that the wording of **the mishna is also precise, as it teaches: All barren trees. Granted, if you say** that Abba Shaul **is referring to the first clause** of the mishna, **this is the reason that** Abba Shaul **teaches: All** barren **trees. But if you say** that **he is referring to the latter clause, he should have** said simply: **Barren trees,** as the first *tanna* permits one to cut down any type of tree. **Rather, isn't it** correct to **conclude from it** that he is **referring to the first clause?** The Gemara affirms: **Learn from it** that it is so.

מתני׳ אִילָן שֶׁהוּא נוֹטֶה לִרְשׁוּת הָרַבִּים – קוֹצֵץ כְּדֵי שֶׁיְּהֵא גָּמָל עוֹבֵר וְרוֹכְבוֹ; רַבִּי יְהוּדָה אוֹמֵר: גָּמָל טָעוּן פִּשְׁתָּן אוֹ חֲבִילֵי זְמוֹרוֹת; רַבִּי שִׁמְעוֹן אוֹמֵר: כׇּל הָאִילָן כְּנֶגֶד הַמִּשְׁקוֹלֶת, מִפְּנֵי הַטּוּמְאָה.

MISHNA With regard to **a tree that extends into the public domain,**[H] **one cuts** its branches **so that a camel can pass** beneath the tree **with its rider** sitting on it. **Rabbi Yehuda says:** One cuts enough branches that **a camel loaded with flax or bundles of branches** can pass beneath it. **Rabbi Shimon says:** One cuts **all** branches of **the tree that** extend into the public domain **along the plumb line,** so that they do not hang over the public area at all, **due to ritual impurity.**

גמ׳ מַאן תַּנָּא דִּבְנִזָּקִין בָּתַר אוּמְדָּנָא דְּהַשְׁתָּא אָזְלִינַן?

GEMARA The Gemara asks: **Who is the** *tanna* who **taught** that **with regard to damage** one **follows the current assessment,** and future damage is not taken into account? The mishna states that the tree's branches are cut to the height of a camel and its rider or load but no more, despite the fact that they will certainly grow again.

אָמַר רֵישׁ לָקִישׁ: בְּמַחֲלוֹקֶת שְׁנוּיָה, וְרַבִּי אֱלִיעֶזֶר הִיא; דִּתְנַן: אֵין עוֹשִׂין חָלָל תַּחַת רְשׁוּת הָרַבִּים, בּוֹרוֹת, שִׁיחִין וּמְעָרוֹת; רַבִּי אֱלִיעֶזֶר מַתִּיר בִּכְדֵי שֶׁתְּהֵא עֲגָלָה מְהַלֶּכֶת וּטְעוּנָה אֲבָנִים.

Reish Lakish says: This *halakha* **is taught as a dispute, and it is** the opinion of **Rabbi Eliezer. As we learned** in a mishna (60a): One **may not make** an empty **space beneath the public domain** by digging **pits, ditches, or caves. Rabbi Eliezer permits** one to dig a pit if it is subsequently covered with material strong **enough that a wagon loaded with stones can travel on it** without it collapsing. If the cover can withstand such weight when the pit is dug, it is permitted, despite the fact that the cover might eventually rot.

רַבִּי יוֹחָנָן אָמַר: אֲפִילּוּ תֵּימָא רַבָּנַן, הָתָם – זִימְנִין דְּמִפְחִית וְלָאו אַדַּעְתֵּיהּ, אֲבָל הָכָא – קַמָּא קַמָּא קָא קָיֵיץ לֵיהּ.

Rabbi Yoḥanan said: You may **even say** that the mishna here represents the opinion of **the Rabbis,** who prohibit one from digging beneath the public domain under any circumstances. The difference is that **there,** the cover **will occasionally deteriorate, and** as this matter is **not on his mind** it will cause damage. **But here,** as **each** branch grows **he cuts it off.** Since the potential cause of damage is visible, there is no concern that it might be neglected.

״רַבִּי יְהוּדָה אוֹמֵר: גָּמָל טָעוּן פִּשְׁתָּן אוֹ חֲבִילֵי זְמוֹרוֹת״. אִיבַּעְיָא לְהוּ: שִׁיעוּרָא דְּרַבִּי יְהוּדָה נְפִישׁ, אוֹ דִּלְמָא שִׁיעוּרָא דְּרַבָּנַן נְפִישׁ?

§ The mishna teaches that if the branches of a tree extend into the public domain, one may cut them to allow a camel and its rider to pass underneath; **Rabbi Yehuda says:** One cuts enough branches that **a camel loaded with flax or bundles of branches** can pass beneath it. **A dilemma was raised before** the Sages: Is **Rabbi Yehuda's measure greater, or is perhaps the Rabbis' measure greater?** Which reaches a greater height, a camel and rider or a camel loaded with flax?

פְּשִׁיטָא דְּשִׁיעוּרָא דְּרַבָּנַן נְפִישׁ, דְּאִי סָלְקָא דַּעְתָּךְ שִׁיעוּרָא דְּרַבִּי יְהוּדָה נְפִישׁ, רַבָּנַן בְּשִׁיעוּרָא דְּרַבִּי יְהוּדָה הֵיכִי עָבְדִי? וְאֶלָּא מַאי? שִׁיעוּרָא דְּרַבָּנַן נְפִישׁ, רַבִּי יְהוּדָה בְּשִׁיעוּרָא דְּרַבָּנַן מַאי עָבֵיד? אֶפְשָׁר דְּגָחִין וְחָלֵיף תּוּתֵיהּ.

The Gemara answers: It is **obvious that the Rabbis' measure** is **greater,** as, **if it enters your mind** that **Rabbi Yehuda's measure** is **greater, how would the Rabbis act in** the circumstance of **Rabbi Yehuda's measure?** It is clear that a camel will have to pass beneath the tree with a burden, and it would not be able to do so. The Gemara expresses surprise at this claim: **Rather, what** then would you say? That **the Rabbis' measure** is **greater?** If so, **how would Rabbi Yehuda act in** the circumstance of **the Rabbis' measure?** It is also clear that a camel will have to pass there with its rider. The Gemara answers: **It is possible for** the rider **to bend over and to pass underneath** the branches.

״רַבִּי שִׁמְעוֹן אוֹמֵר: כָּל הָאִילָן כְּנֶגֶד הַמִּשְׁקוֹלֶת, מִפְּנֵי הַטּוּמְאָה״. תָּנָא: מִפְּנֵי אֹהֶל הַטּוּמְאָה. פְּשִׁיטָא, ״מִפְּנֵי הַטּוּמְאָה״ תְּנַן!

§ The mishna teaches that **Rabbi Shimon says:** One cuts **all** branches of **the tree** that extend into the public domain **along the plumb line, due to ritual impurity.** The Gemara explains: A *tanna* **taught** in a *baraita* that this is **due to ritual impurity** imparted in **a tent.** Branches over a corpse might create a tent, thereby transferring impurity to whatever is beneath the branches, rendering impure those passing under the tree in the public domain. The Gemara expresses surprise at this statement: It is **obvious** that this is the reason. **We** already **learned** that it is **due to ritual impurity.** How else could ritual impurity be transferred through branches other than by means of a tent?

אִי מִמַּתְנִיתִין, הֲוָה אָמִינָא: דִּלְמָא מַיְיתִי עוֹרֵב טוּמְאָה וְשָׁדֵי הָתָם, וְסַגְיָא בְּדַחְלוּלֵי בְּעָלְמָא, קָא מַשְׁמַע לַן.

The Gemara answers: **If** this is learned **from the mishna** alone, **I would say** that the concern is that **perhaps a crow might bring** a source of **impurity** and perch on the tree's branches **and throw it there. And** if that were the only concern, **a mere scarecrow** [***bedaḥlulei***][NL] **would be sufficient** to frighten the crows away and prevent that type of impurity. Therefore, the *tanna* of the *baraita* **teaches us** that the concern is due to impurity imparted in a tent.

הדרן עלך לא יחפור

NOTES

Scarecrow [*daḥlulei*] – דַּחְלוּלֵי: Some commentaries explain that this term refers to hollowness [*ḥalal*], i.e., one simply needs to cut some branches to form a space between them. This will prevent any item that imparts impurity from being stuck in the tree's branches (Rashi; Rabbeinu Gershom Meor HaGola). Most commentaries maintain that this refers to a scarecrow (*Tosafot*; Ri Migash; Ramban; Ramah).

LANGUAGE

Scarecrow [*daḥlulei*] – דַּחְלוּלֵי: From the Aramaic *daḥal*, meaning fear. In Modern Hebrew this term became *daḥlil*, meaning scarecrow.

Summary of **Perek II**

This chapter examined cases in which one performs an activity on his own property and thereby causes damage to his neighbor. With regard to damage inflicted upon a neighbor, the *halakha* is in accordance with the opinion of Rabbi Yosei that the responsibility to distance oneself is not on the one whose activities might cause damage to his neighbor. Consequently, one who performs an activity on his own property that might cause damage to another at a later stage is not required to take steps to avoid this scenario. This principle applies only if the damage he inflicts is indirect. If the damage occurs immediately, or it begins to take effect immediately and its effects gradually increase, it is considered as though he has shot his neighbor with his arrows, and the neighbor can object to his activity. This applies to damage that is caused by one's actions to the neighbor's property, e.g., his walls, pit, and various plantings on his property, as well as damage that is caused by noise or foul odors. Similarly, if one plants trees and the like whose roots or branches extend into his neighbor's property and potentially cause damage, that neighbor is entitled to chop them down as necessary.

The Sages established certain limits within which the damaged party may compel a neighbor to distance the source of the damage from his private or jointly owned property. If one did distance these activities from a neighbor, he is nevertheless still liable for any damage he may cause.

Neighbors who live in the same courtyard can prevent one another from performing an activity that will lead to an increase in visitors to the courtyard, whether their objection is due to the noise or simply because they do not want crowds passing through their property. This right to protest applies only to visitors who will enter the outdoor area of the courtyard. If one wishes to work within the confines of his own home, the neighbors cannot prevent him from doing so even if his activity is noisy.

As neighbors and residents of the same courtyard can prevent someone from causing them damage, this applies all the more so to residents of a town that are suffering from the acts of a private individual. The rights of the public in this regard include the removal of stumbling blocks, items that interfere with traffic, and articles that spread ritual impurity, and imposing restrictions on activities that discharge foul odors into the city. Likewise, the residents can prevent an individual from spoiling the city landscape. The community can cut down interfering trees and the like, even if the owner originally planted them in a permitted manner. Furthermore, in a case of uncertainty the public can remove such obstructions without having to pay compensation.

Incidental to these discussions, the Gemara discusses several *halakhot* concerning teachers of children, and it includes a short aggadic passage about the different effects of winds that come from various directions.

Image **Credits**

All images are copyright © Koren Publishers Jerusalem Ltd., except:

p37 top image © High Contrast; **p37** bottom image © Clara Amit, Yoram Lehman, Yael Yolovitch, Miki Koren, and Mariana Salzberger, courtesy of the Israel Antiquities Authority; **p50** © Superikonoskop, **p59** © Hanay; **p60** top left image © Carole Raddato; **p60** bottom right image © Rosser1954; **p74** bottom right image © Lawrie Cate; **p89** ©Blamb, www.shutterstock.com; **p90** top left image © Krish Dulal; **p90** bottom left image © Zeynel Cebeci; **p90** bottom right image © Andy Firk; **p99** middle image © Dave & Margie Hill / Kleerup; **p99** bottom image © Michel Royon; **p104** © Skrissh2013; **p105** © Avital Pinnick; **p112** top image © Challiyan; **p112** middle image © Donald Hobern; **p112** bottom image © Zachi Evenor and MathKnight; **p115** © Dennis G. Jarvis; **p119** © Volga, www.shutterstock.com; **p128** © Katya Rudnev; **p135** © Captmondo; **p136** top image © Fuad Moadi, Lehava Activity 2013; **p136** bottom image © Roger Culos; **p138** © Ryan Kilpatrick; **p139** © Christer Johansson; **p153** right image © P.W. Hatcher.

תלמוד בבלי

— מהדורת נאה —

בבא בתרא חלק א

Steinsaltz Center

KOREN

Please note that the number ranges that appear at the bottom of each daf of the Vilna pages indicate the corresponding pages of the Koren Talmud Bavli translation and commentary.

תלמוד בבלי

הוצאת קורן ירושלים

מהדורת נאה

מסכת בבא בתרא
דף ב. עד דף כז:

COMMENTARY BY

Rabbi Adin Even-Israel Steinsaltz

EDITOR-IN-CHIEF

Rabbi Dr Tzvi Hersh Weinreb

EXECUTIVE EDITOR

Rabbi Joshua Schreier

•

STEINSALTZ CENTER
KOREN PUBLISHERS JERUSALEM

הַשּׁוּתָּפִין

[א]שֶׁרָצוּ לַעֲשׂוֹת מְחִיצָה בֶּחָצֵר — בּוֹנִין אֶת הַכּוֹתֶל בָּאֶמְצַע. מָקוֹם שֶׁנָּהֲגוּ לִבְנוֹת גְּוִיל, גָּזִית, כְּפִיסִין, לְבֵינִין — בּוֹנִין, [ב]הַכֹּל כְּמִנְהַג הַמְּדִינָה. (א) גְּוִיל — [ג]זֶה נוֹתֵן ג' טְפָחִים וְזֶה נוֹתֵן ג' טְפָחִים; בְּגָזִית — זֶה נוֹתֵן טְפָחַיִים וּמֶחֱצָה וְזֶה נוֹתֵן טְפָחַיִים וּמֶחֱצָה; בִּכְפִיסִין — זֶה נוֹתֵן טְפָחַיִים וְזֶה נוֹתֵן טְפָחַיִים; בִּלְבֵינִין — זֶה נוֹתֵן טֶפַח וּמֶחֱצָה וְזֶה נוֹתֵן טֶפַח וּמֶחֱצָה. [ד]לְפִיכָךְ, אִם נָפַל הַכּוֹתֶל — הַמָּקוֹם וְהָאֲבָנִים שֶׁל שְׁנֵיהֶם. [ה]וְכֵן בַּגִּינָּה, מָקוֹם שֶׁנָּהֲגוּ לִגְדּוֹר — מְחַיְּיבִין אוֹתוֹ; [ו]אֲבָל בַּבִּקְעָה, [ז]מָקוֹם שֶׁנָּהֲגוּ שֶׁלֹּא לִגְדּוֹר — אֵין מְחַיְּיבִין אוֹתוֹ, אֶלָּא אִם רָצָה, כּוֹנֵס לְתוֹךְ שֶׁלּוֹ וּבוֹנֶה וְעוֹשֶׂה חֲזִית מִבַּחוּץ. [ח]לְפִיכָךְ, אִם נָפַל הַכּוֹתֶל — הַמָּקוֹם וְהָאֲבָנִים שֶׁלּוֹ. אִם עָשׂוּ מִדַּעַת שְׁנֵיהֶם — בּוֹנִין אֶת הַכּוֹתֶל בָּאֶמְצַע וְעוֹשִׂין חֲזִית מִכָּאן וּמִכָּאן. לְפִיכָךְ, אִם נָפַל הַכּוֹתֶל — הַמָּקוֹם וְהָאֲבָנִים שֶׁל שְׁנֵיהֶם.§ **גמ'** סַבְרוּהָ מַאי מְחִיצָה? גּוּדָא, [א]כִּדְתַנְיָא: [ט]מְחִיצַת הַכֶּרֶם שֶׁנִּפְרְצָה — אוֹמֵר לוֹ "גְּדוֹר", חָזְרָה וְנִפְרְצָה — אוֹמֵר לוֹ "גְּדוֹר",

נִתְיָאֵשׁ

הַשּׁוּתָּפִין. שֶׁיֵּשׁ לָהֶן חָצֵר בְּשׁוּתָּפוּת, וּבָתֵּי שְׁנֵיהֶן פְּתוּחִין לְתוֹכוֹ. וְכָל חֲצֵירוֹת שֶׁשָּׁנוּ חֲכָמִים לִפְנֵי הַבָּתִּים הֵן, וְרוֹב תַּשְׁמִישָׁן בֶּחָצֵר. **בָּאֶמְצַע.** זֶה נוֹתֵן מֵחֶלְקוֹ חֲצִי מְקוֹם עוֹבִי הַכּוֹתֶל, וְכֵן זֶה. **גְּוִיל גָּזִית כְּפִיסִין.** הַכֹּל מְפָרֵשׁ בַּגְּמָרָא. **הַכֹּל כְּמִנְהַג הַמְּדִינָה.** אִם מִנְהָג לִבְנוֹת בִּגְוִיל אֵין חֲבֵירוֹ יָכוֹל לוֹמַר "אֵינִי חָפֵץ אֶלָּא גָּזִית". **זֶה נוֹתֵן ג' טְפָחִים כו'.** שֶׁעוֹבִי כּוֹתֶל גְּוִיל ו' טְפָחִים, וְשֶׁל גָּזִית חֲמִשָּׁה, וְשֶׁל כְּפִיסִים ד', וְשֶׁל לְבֵינִים ג'. **לְפִיכָךְ.** הוֹאִיל וּבִתְחִלַּת הַבִּנְיָן חִיְּיבוּם חֲכָמִים לִבְנוֹת בֵּין שְׁנֵיהֶם, אִם נָפַל הַכּוֹתֶל לְאַחַר שָׁנִים רַבִּים אֵין הָאֶחָד יָכוֹל לוֹמַר "כָּל הַכּוֹתֶל נִבְנָה בְּחֶלְקִי וּמִשֶּׁלִּי הָיוּ הָאֲבָנִים", אַע"פ שֶׁהוּחְזַק יוֹתֵר מֵחֲבֵירוֹ, וּכְגוֹן שֶׁנָּפַל הַכּוֹתֶל בְּחֶלְקוֹ, כִּדְמְפָרֵשׁ בַּגְּמָ'. **וְכֵן בַּגִּינָּה.** מְחַיְּיבִין אֶת שְׁנֵיהֶן לִבְנוֹת, בְּמָקוֹם שֶׁנָּהֲגוּ לִגְדּוֹר בָּאֶמְצַע. **אֲבָל בַּבִּקְעָה.** שָׂדֶה הַלָּבָן. **מָקוֹם שֶׁנָּהֲגוּ כו'.** בַּגְּמָ' מְפָרֵשׁ מַאי קָאָמַר. **וְעוֹשֶׂה חָזִית מִבַּחוּץ.** מְפָרֵשׁ בַּגְּמָ'. **וְעוֹשִׂין חָזִית מִכָּאן וּמִכָּאן.** לְהוֹדִיעַ שֶׁשְּׁנֵיהֶם עֲשָׂאוּהוּ. **גמ' גּוּדָא.** כּוֹתֶל. (ב) (כִּדְתְנַן). דְּקָרֵי תַּנָּא לְגוּדָא מְחִיצָה. **מְחִיצַת הַכֶּרֶם.** שֶׁסָּמוּךְ לִשְׂדֵה הַלָּבָן שֶׁל חֲבֵירוֹ. **אוֹמֵר לוֹ.** לְבַעַל הַכֶּרֶם: גְּדוֹר אַתָּה, שֶׁלֹּא יֶאֶסְרוּ גְּפָנֶיךָ אֶת תְּבוּאַת הַשָּׂדֶה מִשּׁוּם כִּלְאַיִם. לְפִי שֶׁסָּמַךְ בַּעַל הַשָּׂדֶה אֶת זְרָעָיו סָמוּךְ לַגָּדֵר, כִּדְתְנַן בְּפֶרֶק שֵׁנִי (דף כו.): הָיָה גָּדֵר בֵּינְתַיִם — זֶה סוֹמֵךְ לַגָּדֵר מִכָּאן אֶת אִילָנוֹתָיו, וְזֶה סוֹמֵךְ לַגָּדֵר אֶת זְרָעָיו מִכָּאן. וּכְשֶׁאֵין שָׁם גָּדֵר — תְּנַן בְּפֶ' שֵׁנִי: לֹא יִטַּע אָדָם אִילָן סָמוּךְ לִשְׂדֵה חֲבֵירוֹ אֶלָּא אִם כֵּן הִרְחִיק מִמֶּנּוּ ד' אַמּוֹת כְּדֵי עֲבוֹדַת הַכֶּרֶם, דִּבְהָכִי הָוֵי כִּלְאַיִם. **חָזְרָה וְנִפְרְצָה אוֹמֵר לוֹ.** לִגְדּוֹר.

קִידֵּשׁ

השותפין. כולה נזיקין חדא מסכתא היא, כדאמרינן ב"הגוזל קמא" (ב"ק דף קב.) ובפ"ק דע"ז (דף ז.). ואפי' לא הוי חדא מסכתא, צריך לפרש למה נשנית מסכתא זו אחר ב"מ, כדאשכחן דדייק גמ' בריש מס' שבועות (דף ב:): מכדי תנא ממכות סליק, מ"ש דקתני שבועות. וכן בכמה מקומות. והא דאמר (ב"ק קב.): בתרי מסכתות אין סדר למשנה — היינו לענין מחלוקת ואח"כ סתם, משום דרבי לא שנה לתלמידיו כסדר המסכתות, ופעמים שנה האחרונה קודם הראשונה. ואור"י: דהיינו טעמא, משום דקאי אהך פירקא דלעיל (ב"מ דף קטז:): הבית והעלייה של ב' שנפלו חולקים בעצים וכו', וקרי להו התם בגמ' "שותפין". וקתני נמי (שם דף קיח:): ב' גנות זו ע"ג זו וירק בינתים, דהוי ענין שותפות.

כפיסין. מפרש בגמ': ארחי. וקשה לר"י: והכתיב (חבקוק ב) "וכפיס מעץ יעננה", משמע שהוא של עץ! ואור"י: דשמא היו מניחין עליס מלמעלה ומלמטה. **בגויל** זה נותן ג' טפחים כו'. והא דלא קאמר "בגויל ו' טפחים" משום דלא נטעי למימר ו' לכל אחד. וא"ת: אמאי אצטריך למיתני מדת גויל וגזית? כיון דתנן "הכל כמנהג המדינה" — כמו שנהגו כן יעשו! וי"ל: דאם נהגו יותר מו' בגויל — לא יעשה, וכן כולם, אלא כשיעור המפורש. ומיהו, אם נהגו לעשות פחות מו' — יעשה, דאפילו אם נהגו בהוצא ודפנא יעשה, כדמפרש בגמרא. וא"ת, ומאי בעי בגמ': "הכל כמנהג המדינה" לאתויי מאי? ומשני: לאתויי אתרא דנהיגי בהוצא ודפנא. לימא: לאתויי כמנהג כל המקומות, כמו שנהגו! ונראה לר"ת: דדוקא בהוצא ודפנא, אבל פחות מכאן, אפילו נהגו — מנהג הדיוט הוא. ומוכיח מכאן דיש מנהגים שאין לסמוך עליהם, אפילו היכא דתנן "הכל כמנהג המדינה".

לפיכך אם נפל הכותל וכו'. פי': לפי שבונים הכותל בעל כרחם, או משום דהקנו זה לזה לעשות גודא, ללישנא קמא, וכגון דידוע לנו עדיין וזוכרים שהקנו זה לזה. וללישנא בתרא — משום היזק ראיה. וא"ת: ומאי איריא משום דבונין הכותל בעל כרחם? בלאו הכי נמי הוי של שניהם, אפי' נפל לרשותא דחד מינייהו, כיון דאין חזית לא לזה ולא לזה. כדפריך בתלמוד גבי בקעה: לא יעשה חזית לא לזה ולא לזה. ואי הוה דהאיך דנפל לרשותו — מאי פריך? הא צריך לעשות חזית שלא יפול לרשות אחר ויאמר שלו הן! והא דאמרינן ב"השואל" (ב"מ דף ק.) גבי מחליף פרה בחמור, וכן בריש "הבית והעלייה" (שם דף קטז:): וליחזי ברשות דמאן קיימא, וליהוי איידך המוציא מחבירו עליו הראיה — היינו משום דהתם מתחילה מבורר היה הדבר, וברשות אחד מהן נולד הספק. אבל הכא — מעיקרא נולד הספק, ואם היו באין לחלוק בעוד שהכותל קיים — היו חולקין בשוה מספק. אפילו לרבנן דסומכוס, דלית להו ממון המוטל בספק חולקין — הכא מודו, כיון דליכא הכא חזקה לזה יותר מלזה. הילכך, אפילו נפל לרשותא דחד מינייהו — לא יפסיד האחר כחו. והא דלא אמר הכא: כל דאלים גבר, כמו ב"זה אומר של אבותי" (לקמן דף לד:) — התם הוא דליכא דררא דממונא, אבל הכא איכא דררא דממונא! ומתרץ ר"י: דהיינו הך דפריך בתלמוד: פשיטא, כדפירש בקונטרס, דאפילו לא פסיק לן דינא דמתניתין שמתחילה בין שניהם עשאוה — בעל כרחם היו חולקין בשוה, ואפילו דנפל לרשותא דחד מינייהו כדמוכח גבי בקעה! ומשני: לא צריכא, דנפל לרשותא דחד מינייהו. פירוש: ושהו ברשותו הרבה, מהו דתימא: כיון דשהו ברשותו הרבה — ניהמניה שעשאוה כולה, מיגו דאיבעי אמר "ממך לקחתיה", והיה נאמן, משום דשהו הרבה. ואף על גב דאמר בריש "הבית והעלייה" דשותפין לא קפדי אהדדי — הכא איירי דשהו יותר מכדי רגילות, דאטו משום דשותפין ניהו לא יקפידו עד עולם? ולא דמי לגודרות דאין להם חזקה (לקמן דף לו.), לפי שאין ידוע ביד מי הם, אבל הכא — לא היה לו להשהותו כל כך ברשותו. קמ"ל, כיון דמעיקרא על שניהם היה לעשות — לא מהימן לומר שהוא עשה הכל. דמיגו במקום עדים הוא, דאנן סהדי שלא עשאה לבדו, כיון שהיה יכול לדחוק את חבירו בדין שהיה עושה עמו. אבל בבקעה, אם שהו הרבה — היה נאמן לומר שעשאה, במיגו דאי בעי אמר "לקחתיה". והאי שינויא אינו אלא מאבנים, אבל מקום הכותל — לעולם פשיטא שחולקין אותו. ואיידי דנקט "אבנים" נקט "המקום".

סברוה מאי מחיצה גודא. אע"ג דלבסוף קאי — קאמר "סברוה", לפי שזה הלשון אינו עיקר מחמת פירכא דלקמן, ודיחוי בעלמא הוא האי דמשני, וכלשון שני הלכה, וכן פוסק ר"ת. ואגב דנקט בהאי לישנא "סברוה", נקט נמי בלישנא אחריתי. ועוד אור"י: דבפרק קמא דנדרים (דף יא.) איכא "סברוה" אע"ג דלבסוף קאי, ומסיק הכי. **כדתניא** מחיצת הכרם שנפרצה. יש ספרים דגרסי: "דתנן". ואומר ר"ת: שאינה משנה בשום מקום. [ג](וא"כ) היכי פשיט מינה ב"הגוזל קמא" (ב"ק דף ק. ושם) דר"מ דאין דינא דגרמי? ואם היתה משנה — הוה אתי שפיר, דסתם משנה ר"מ היא. ואומר ר"ת: דמשמע ליה דאתיא כר"מ מכח מתניתין דכלאים, דמייתי התם: המסכך [את] גפנו על גבי תבואתו של חבירו — [ה"ז] קידש וחייב באחריותו. והיא סתם משנה היא, הילכך ההיא נמי דקתני "קידש" — רבי מאיר היא. ואין להאריך כאן יותר. **אומר** לו גדור. פירוש: לבעל הכרם. (ב) והוא המזיק, דארבע אמות שאמרו להרחיק — הוא בשביל עבודת הכרם, כדאמרי' בפ' שני לקמן (דף כו.). ואפילו ר' יוסי דקאמר לקמן (דף יח: כה:): על הניזק להרחיק את עצמו — האמר רב אשי לקמן (דף כה:): מודי ר' יוסי בגירי דיליה. ואומר ר"י: דלהכי קתני אומר לו "גדור", ולא קתני "חייב לגדור" — לפי שצריך להתרות בו, ואם לא התרו בו לגדור — אינו חייב באחריותו. ולהכי נקט נמי תרי זימני "נפרצה אומר לו גדור" — אף פעם שניה כשנפרצה צריך להתרותו, שאינו סבור להיות חייב לגדור כל שעה. ונפרצה פעם שלישית מספקא לר"י אם צריך להתרותו כל שעה, או שמא סגי בתרי זימני ואין צריך להתרות בו יותר. ור"ת מפרש דלהכי נקט תרי זימני — לאשמועינן שאם יש תוספת מאתים בין מה שהוסיף בנפרצה ראשונה, ובין מה שהוסיף בנפרצה שניה — דאין מצטרפין לאסור, ומראשונה ראשונה בטלי. והארכתי ב"הגוזל קמא" (ב"ק דף ק: ושם) ובפרק "במה אשה" (שבת דף סה.).

נתיאש

פירוש רבינו גרשום מאור הגולה

השותפין דאית להו חצר בשותפות ונתרצו לחלוק ולעשות מחיצה: בונין את הכותל לאמצע: **גמ'** גודא. כותל: כדתנן א) מחיצת הכרם שנפרצה לזה היה לו שדה תבואה ולזה היה לו כרם והיתה כותל מחיצה מפסקת בין השדה לכרם. ועכשיו נפרצה מחיצת כרמו דיש לחוש שלא יתערבו הזרעים בכרם. אומרים לו בית דין לבעל הכרם גדור.

מסורת הש"ס

א) [לקמן ג.] ב"ק ק. [תוספתא כלאים פ"ג]: ב) [נ"ל כדתניא]: ג) כ"א וא"ת:

עין משפט נר מצוה

א א מיי' פ"ב מהל' שכנים הל' יד סמג עשין פב טוש"ע ח"מ סי' קנז סעיף א:
ב ב מיי' שם הלכה טו טוש"ע שם סעיף ד:
ג ג מיי' שם הלכה יח טור שם:
ד ד מיי' שם טוש"ע שם סעיף ה:
ה ה ו ז מיי' שם הלכה טז וסמג שם טוש"ע ח"מ סי' קנח סעיף א:
ו ח מיי' שם טוש"ע שם סעיף ד:
ז ט מיי' פ"ז מהל' כלאים הל' יז סמג לאוין רפ טוש"ע י"ד סי' רצו סעיף מז:

הגהות הב"ח

(א) במשנה בגויל זה נותן: (ב) תום' ד"ה אומר וכו' דהוא המזיק:

ח א מיי' פ"ג מהל' שכנים הלכה ו ועיין בהשגות סמג עשין פב טוש"ע ח"מ סי' קנז סעיף ב וסי' קס סעיף א:

נתיאש הימנה ולא גדרה — ה"ז קידש וחייב באחריות'. (א) טעמא דרצו, הא לא רצו — אין מחייבין אותו, אלמא: א) היזק ראיה לאו שמיה היזק. ואימא: (ב) מחיצה — פלוגתא, כדכתיב: °"ותהי מחצת העדה" (במדבר לא), וכיון דרצו — בונין את הכותל בעל כרחו, אלמא: ב) היזק ראיה שמיה היזק! אי הכי, האי "שרצו לעשות מחיצה", "שרצו לחצות" מבעי ליה! אלא מאי, גודא? "בונין את הכותל", "בונין אותו" מבעי ליה! אי תנא "אותו", הוה אמינא במסיפס בעלמא, קמ"ל: כותל. § "בונין את הכותל באמצע" וכו'. § פשיטא! לא צריכא, דקדים חד ורצייה לחבריה; מהו דתימא מצי א"ל: כי איתרצאי לך — באוירא, בתשמישתא לא איתרצאי לך, קמ"ל. והיזק ראיה לאו שמיה היזק? (סימן: גינה כותל כופין וחולקין חלונות דרב נחמן) ת"ש: וכן בגינה! גינה שאני, כדר' אבא, ג) דאמר ר' אבא אמר רב הונא אמר רב: אסור לאדם לעמוד בשדה חבירו בשעה שהיא עומדת בקמותיה. והא "וכן" קתני! אגויל וגזית. ת"ש: ד) כותל חצר שנפל — מחייבין אותו לבנות עד ד' אמות! נפל שאני. ודקארי לה מאי קארי לה? סיפא איצטריכא ליה: מד' אמות ולמעלה — אין מחייבין אותו. ת"ש: ה) כופין אותו לבנות בית שער ודלת לחצר; ש"מ: היזק ראיה שמיה היזק! היזקא דרבים שאני. ודיחיד לא? ת"ש: ו) אין חולקין את החצר עד שיהא בה ד' אמות לזה וד' אמות לזה; הא יש בה כדי לזה וכדי לזה — חולקין, מאי לאו בכותל? לא, במסיפס בעלמא. תא שמע: ז) החלונות, בין מלמעלה בין מלמטה ובין מכנגדן — ד' אמות; ותני עלה: ח) מלמעלן — כדי שלא יציץ ויראה, מלמטן — כדי שלא יעמוד ויראה, מכנגדן — כדי שלא יאפיל! היזקא דבית שאני. תא שמע, ט) דאמר רב נחמן אמר שמואל: גג א) הסמוך לחצר חבירו — עושין לו מעקה גבוה ד' אמות! שאני התם, דאמר ליה בעל החצר לבעל הגג: לדידי קביעה לי (ג) תשמישי, לדידך לא קביעה לך תשמישתך, ולא ידענא בהי עידנא סליקא ואתית

דאיצטנע

רש"י

קידש. התבואה, אם הוסיף מאתים. לישנא דקרא נקט, "פן תוקדש" (דברים כב). וטעמא דרצו. לבנות כותל, (ד) דמדעת שניהן הוא, דחייביה חכמים שיבנו בין שניהן. ולקמן פריך: כשרצו מאי הוי? ליהדרי בהו! אבל לא רצו שניהן, שהיה אחד אומר: דייה לחלקה במסיפס של יתדות עצים תקועים בארץ נמוכים — לא כייפינן ליה, ואין זה יכול לומר לו "איני חפץ שתראה עסקי". פלוגתא. חלוקת חצר, שהושוו דעתם לחולקה. וכגון שלא היה בה ח' אמות כדי לזה וכדי לזה, שאין האחד יכול לכוף את חבירו לחולקה. ולהכי תני "שרצו", שכיון שרצו לחולקה — בונין כותל אבנים על כרחם. ואם בא האחד לומר: אי אפשי בגיליה זו, אלא מסיפס בעלמא — אין שומעין לו, משום היזק ראייה. הוה אמינא במסיפס בעלמא. מיירי מתני', דאיהו נמי מחיצה איקרו. ו"רצו" דקתני — אחלוקה קאי, וכשאין בה דין חלוקה. קמ"ל כותל, ו"רצו" דקתני — משום כותל, דאי לא רצו — פלגי לה במסיפס. דרצייה חד מינייהו לחבריה. ביקש ממנו לחולקה במחילה. מהו דתימא א"ל כשנתרציתי לך. במחילה, מחילה דקה נתרציתי, ולמעוטי באוירא, כגון של נסרים שהיא דקה והיזק ראיה אין בה, או תמשוך עובי הכותל בחלקך חוץ מדבר מועט. אבל לבנות כותל אבנים עב, למעוטי נמי תשמישתי — לא נתרציתי. אסור לאדם שיעמוד כו'. שלא יזיקנו בעין רעה. והא וכן קתני. דמשמע תרוייהו חד טעמא הוא, גינה וחצר. מחייבין אותו. והכא לא קתני "רצו", אלא על כרחו. נפל שאני. שכבר נתרצו הראשונים בכותל. ודקארי לה מאי קארי לה. וכי לא ידע דנפל שאני? סיפא איצטריך ליה. כלומר, הוא הדין נמי מעיקרא, והאי דקתני "נפל" — משום סיפא, לאשמועינן דיותר מד' אמות אין מחייבין, ואע"פ שהראשון היה גבוה יותר — לא מחייבין ליה. כופין אותו. כל אחד מבני החצר לתת חלקו בבנין. בית השער. שבונים כותל נגד השער עגול סביב, ועושין באותו היקף פתח קטן מן הצד, משום היזק ראיות בני רה"ר, שלא יראו תוך החצר. היזקא דרבים. שכל בני רה"ר מסתכלין שם. אין חולקין. אין האחד כופה את חבירו לחלוק. החלונות. אחד מבני השותפין הבונה כותל בחצר כנגד חלונותיו של חבירו, בין מלמעלה וכו', אם הכותל גבוה יותר מן החלונות — צריך להגביה למעלה מהן ד"א, כדמפרש ואזיל, כדי שלא יסמוך על כותלו וישחה ויראה בחלונותיו של חבירו. בין מלמטה. אם הכותל נמוך מן החלונות — צריך להשפילו מהן ד"א, כדי שלא יעמוד על עובי כותלו ויראה. ומכנגדן. צריך להרחיק את הכותל מן החלונות ד' אמות, כדי שלא יאפיל. היזקא דבית שאני. שאדם עושה בביתו דברי הצנע. מעקה גבוה ארבע אמות. כדי שלא יראה בחצר חבירו כשהוא משתמש בגגו. ולא ידענא בהי עידנא דקא אתית. להשתמש בגגך.

תוספות

נתיאש הימנה ולא גדרה. דוקא נתיאש, אבל לא נתיאש ועוסק כל שעה לגדור, אע"פ שהוסיף מאתים — מותר. כדתנן במסכת כלאים (פ"ה מ"ו): הרואה ירק בכרם, ואמר "כשאגיע לשם אלקטנו", הוסיף מאתים — מותר. "לכשאחזור אלקטנו", הוסיף מאתים — אסור. אלמא, כשהוא מחזר אחר לקיטתו, אפילו הוסיף מאתים — מותר. והטעם יש לפרש: משום דכתיב (דברים כב) "לא תזרע כרמך כלאים" — דומיא דזריעה, דניחא ליה. וחייב באחריותו. אע"ג דהיזק שאינו ניכר לא שמיה היזק (גיטין נג.), נראה לר"י דהאי חשיב היזק ניכר, שהרי ניכר הוא שהוא כלאים, כשרואה הגפנים בשדה. ומטמא, אע"פ שרואין השרץ על הטהרות — לא חשיב היזק ניכר, דמי יודע אם הוכשרו? אבל אין לומר דה"נ הוי היזק שאינו ניכר וקנסוהו, כמו במטמא (שם) שלא יהא כל אחד הולך ומטמא טהרותיו של חבירו. דהכא ליכא למיחש להכי, שבעל הכרם נמי מפסיד, ועוד: אי קנס הוא — במזיד דוקא היה לו להתחייב. ואימא מאי מחיצה פלוגתא. מפרש ר"י: משום דעל לשון גודא יש כמה קושיות, כדפריך בסמוך, לפיכך דוחק לפרש מחילה פלוגתא, אע"ג דבכל מקום הוי מחילה גודא. וכיון דרצו בונין את הכותל בעל כרחו. לקמן מוקי לה כשאין בה דין חלוקה. ותימה לר"י: דאמאי נקט תנא דמתני' באין בה דין חלוקה, וקתני "רצו"? לא ליתני "רצו", ולאיירי בשיש בה דין חלוקה! ותי': דקמ"ל, דס"ד כשאין בה דין חלוקה דמצי למימר: כי (ה) איתרצאי לך לחלוק — ע"מ שלא לעשות גודא, אבל על מנת לעשות גודא — לא איתרצי לך. ויש ספרים דמקשין ומתרץ כן להדיא בשילהי שמעתין. הוה אמינא במסיפס בעלמא. פי': ו"רצו" דקתני — אמסיפס. ואע"ג דבלאו רצו נמי עושין מסיפס בעל כרחם, כדמוכח בסמוך, דקאמר: מאי לאו בכותל? לא, במסיפס — היינו מסיפס גרוע, אבל כי רצו — עושין מסיפס מגויל וגזית כמנהג המדינה. ומקרי מסיפס — לפי שהוא מלא חלונות, כדפי' בערוך, ואינו מגין מהיזק ראיה. א"נ, לפי שאינו גבוה י', כדמוכח לקמן גבי גג הסמוך *לחצר, [נ"ל לגג] דאמר ר"נ: עושה לו מעקה גבוה י'. ופריך: למאי? אי להיזק ראיה — ד"א בעינן, ואי לנתפס כגנב — במסיפס סגי. ובקונטרס פי': ד"רצו" דקתני — אחלוקה קאי. ותימה: דהא אסיק דמחילה היינו גודא, דאי פלוגתא — "לחצות" מיבעי ליה! ועוד: היכי מצי למימר דה"א במסיפס בעלמא? הא שמעינן ליה מסיפא, דקתני: אבל בזמן ששניהם רוצים — אפילו פחות מכאן יחלוקו. והיינו לכל הפחות במסיפס! ועוד: היכא המ"ל במסיפס בעלמא? הא בהדיא קתני במתני' גזית וגויל! בונין את הכותל באמצע פשיטא. למ"ד גודא פריך, כמו כל הנך פירכי דלקמן. דכשהקנו לעשות גודא — כך הקנה זה כמו זה, ופשיטא דבאמצע. אבל למ"ד פלוגתא — איצטריך למימר, סד"א דמשום היזק ראיה יש לו לסייע בבנין הכותל, אבל אין לו לבנות בחלקו בשביל כך. תא שמע וכן בגינה. לקמן מסקינן דה"ק: וכן בגינה סתם, כמקום שנהגו לגדור דמי. הלכך דייק שפיר דהיזק ראיה שמיה היזק. גינה שאני כדרבי אבא וכו'. וא"ת: ומהאי טעמא יתחייב נמי לגדור בבקעה! ויש לומר: דשאני גינה שמגדלין בה ירק לאכילה, וכל שעה היא עומדת בקמותיה. אבל בקעה אינה עומדת בקמותיה אלא חדש אחד בשנה, ולא מיחייב לגדור, אבל אסור לעמוד בשעה שעומדת בקמותיה. וא"ת: ולמ"ד פלוגתא, כיון דאשמועינן דאפילו בחצר שמיה היזק — כל שכן בגינה, ואמאי איצטריך תו למיתני "וכן בגינה"? וי"ל: דאיצטריך "וכן בגינה" למיתני משום גויל וגזית. נפל שאני. שהורגלו לעשות דבר הצנע בחצר, ולא למדו ליזהר זה מזה. ודקארי לה מאי קארי לה. כלומר, פשיטא דנפל שאני. ואדרבה, היה לו להוכיח מדקתני "ונפל" — מכלל דבעלמא לא שמיה היזק. היזקא דרבים שאני. ואע"ג דלקמן משמע דאיירי בחצר שאינה סמוכה לרה"ר — מ"מ איכא היזקא דרבים, דזימנין דדחקי רבים ועיילי להתם, כדאמרי' לקמן. ורשב"ג, אע"ג דלית ליה האי טעמא דזימנין דדחקי רבים, מ"מ מרחוק יכולין לראות לפנים, ולכך לא פליג אלא אבית שער, אבל בדלת — מודה דכופין אותו לבנות. מאי לאו בכותל. תימה: ויהא בכותל, דילמא הכי פי': אין חולקין את החצר, אפי' האחד רוצה לבנות את הכותל בתוך שלו, עד שיהא בה ד' אמות לכל אחד. הא אם יש בה ד' אמות לכל אחד — חולקין אם רצה לכנוס ולבנות בתוך שלו! וי"ל: ד"חולקין" משמע באמצע, דאי אשמועינן כדפי' — הוה ליה למיתני: אין עושין כותל בחצר עד שיהא כו'. שאני התם דאמר ליה בעל החצר לבעל הגג כו'. תימה: אמאי לא מייתי מדתניא לקמן (דף ו:): שתי אלירות זו למעלה מזו — לא יאמר העליון "הריני בונה מכנגדי ועולה" אלא מסייע מלמטה ובונה, אלמא: שמיה היזק.

מסורת הש"ס

א) [לקמן נט:] ב) [שם]: ג) ב"מ קז. ע"ש: ד) לקמן ה.: ה) לקמן ז: ו) לקמן יא.: ז) לקמן כב.: ח) [שם]: ט) לקמן ו::

רבינו גרשום

נתייאש מן הזמן שקבעו לו ב"ד ולא גדרה ונתערבו הזרעים בכרם הרי זה קידש וטעונין שריפה ככלאי הכרם כדכתיב פן תקדש המלאה ודרשי' לה (חולין קט"ו) פן תוקד אש. ואותו בעל מחיצה חייב באחריות זרעוני של זה שהופסדו וחייב לשלם דמיהן. השתא כיון דאשכחן דהאי מחיצה דמתני' כותל הוא דילפי' לה ממחיצת הכרם דייקא מתני' טעמא דרצו שניהן לעשות מחיצה משום הכי בונין אותו באמצע שניהן ביחד הא לא רצו שניהם לבנות ביחד אלא אחד רוצה ואחד אינו רוצה אין מחייבין אותו שאינו רוצה לבנות חלקו בעל כרחו. והואיל דאין כופין אותו לבנות ש"מ שזה שהמעכב רואה בחצר חבירו אותו היזק ראיה לא שמיה היזק: ומקשה מאן לימא לן דהאי מחיצה דמתני' גודא דאיכא למידק כדקאמרת דהיזק ראיה לאו שמיה היזק. אימא מאי מחיצה דמתני' פלוגתא. חלוקה שנתרצו לעשות חלוקה. והכי פריש למתני' השותפין שרצו לחלוק חצירן בונין את הכותל באמצע. ואידוק הכי כיון דנתרצו לחלוק אם זה מעכב שאינו רוצה לעשות עמו הכותל הואיל דמקפידין זה על זה שלא ישתמש הא' בחלק חבירו (היו) כופין אותו ובונין את הכותל באמצע בעל כרחו משום דהיזק ראיה [דיליה] שמסתכל בחצר חבירו הוי היזק. ומהדר ליה אי הכי דפלוגתא הוי אמאי קתני שרצו לעשות מחיצה שרצו לחצות מיבעי ליה: אלא מאי גודא. אמאי קתני תו בונין את הכותל. והא כל לשון משנה לשון קצרה הוא. וכיון דההיא שרצו לעשות מחיצה היינו כותל בונין אותו מיבעי ליה ולא איצטריך למיתני כותל. ואכתי היזק ראיה שמיה היזק: ומתרץ ליה לעולם מחיצה גודא. ודקשיא לך בונין אותו מיבעי ליה משום הכי איצטריך למתני כותל דאי תנא בונין אותו הוה אמינא במסיפס בעלמא סגי. מחיצת הקנים עראי שקורין בל"ע פלפי"ט. קמ"ל כותל. דצריכי למיעבד כותל של קיימא ולעולם כדאמינא דמחיצה גודא היא וכדדייקי דהיזק ראיה לאו שמיה היזק: בונין את הכותל באמצע פשיטא. אכתי מקשה למאן דאמר גודא כי האי גוונא א) בשלמא אי אמרי' מאי מחיצה פלוגתא מש"ה איצטריך למיתני בונין את הכותל דלא סגי בלאו הכי דאיצטריך לאדכר כותל. והאי דקתני באמצע ודאי לא איצטריך למיתנייה הואיל דקאמר פלוגתא. אלא אגב דאיצטריך למתני כותל קתני באמצע ולא משום דוקא אלא אי אמרת דהאי מחיצה גודא היא בשלמא כותל לא מיותר הוא משום דאתי למעוטי מסיפס ולא לגופיה איצטריך. אלא ודאי באמצע מיותר הוא דכיון דשותפין נינהו בהאי חצר ורצו לעשות גודא פשיטא דבאמצע בונין אותו והשתא לא מצית למימר אגב דאיצטריך למתני כותל קתני באמצע משום דכותל גופיה לא אתא אלא לאפוקי מסיפס בודאי לא איצטריך באמצע אלא לעולם כדאמר' מחיצה פלוגתא והיזק ראיה שמיה היזק. לעולם אימא לך מחיצה גודא ודקא קשיא לך באמצע למה לי (לא) צריכי דודאי לא מייתר הוא דהכא במאי עסקינן דאקדים חד מינייהו וארציה לחבריה שלא רצו שניהן מתחלה אלא אחד פייסו לחבירו עד שנתרצה לו שיעשה כותל. עכשיו אי לא תני דבונין באמצע בחלק שניהן הוה אמינא דיכול למימר ליה כי נתרציתי לעשות מחיצה בכך נתרציתי שלא אשתמש באוירא דידך אבל למעוטי בתשמיש שלי ליתן מקום חצי הכותל לא נתרציתי: קמ"ל. דכיון נתרצה בונין את הכותל באמצע חצי בחלק זה וחצי בחלק זה. ולהכי איצטריך למתני באמצע ולעולם מחיצה גודא הוא ואכתי היזק ראיה לאו שמיה היזק: ת"ש וכן בגינה מקום שנהגו לגדור. בגינה העומדת בעיר קא מיירי דאיכא היזק ראיה שרואה מה שבחצר חבירו. קתני וכן בגינה דמחייבין אותו לגדור. אלמא היזק ראיה שמיה היזק: לא לעולם אימא לך לאו שמיה היזק ושאני גינה לאו משום דטעמא דהיזק ראיה. אלא משום דמסתכלין בגינתו ומכניסין בו עין הרע [כדר'] אבא: א"כ כדקאמרת דמשום טעמא דעין הרעה מחייבין לגדור בגינה ולאו משום היזק ראיה מאי וכן בגינה כלומר דמשמע דאותו דין עצמו שנוהג בחצר אותו [דין] עצמו נוהג בגינה ולטעמיך אינו דין א'. בשלמא לדידי דאמינא אידי ואידי משום היזק ראיה להכי אתי שפיר וכן בגינה אלא לדידך מאי וכן: ומשני האי וכן לא מהדר כלל ארישא אבונין את הכותל דתידוק מינה כשם שמחייבין לבנות כותל בחצר משום היזק ראיה כן בגינה אלא האי דקתני וכן בגינה אגויל וגזית מה בחצר מקום שנהגו לבנות בגויל ובגזית בונין כן בגינה ולעולם לא קשיא לי: כותל חצר שבין שני חצירות שנפל אם א' מהן מעכב מלבנותו מחייבין אותו לבנותו בעל כרחו עד שיהא גבוה ד"א דלא מצי אינש לאסתכולי דרך הליכתו עד שיהא גבוה ד' אמות אלמא משום היזק ראיה הוא. ומשני דהיכא דנפל שאני הואיל דהוי מעיקרא הכותל בדין הוא דמחייבין אותו עד ד' אמות דפחות מכן לא מצי למיבניה דהכי שמה מחיצה אבל גבי מתני' שלא היה מעולם מחיצה אין מחייבין המעכב: ודקארי לה אמאי קארי לה כלו' המקשה שהיה מקשה קושי' זו אמאי מקשה לה. וכי לא היה יודע דהיכא דנפל שאני ומה ראה להקשותה. ומשני לעולם משום קושיא מייתינן לה משום דחזא בסיפא איצטריך ליה למיתניי' בלשון קושיא דקתני סיפא מד' אמות ולמעלה אין מחייבין אותו לבנות גבוה כדמעיקרא אלמא ש"מ משום היזק ראייה הוא ומש"ה אין מחייבין אותו אלא כשיעור שאינו יכול לראות. והמתרץ מתרץ [לעולם] כדמעיקרא נפל שאני. והאי דאמר עד ד' אמות דבהכי הוא דין מחיצה ולא משום היזק ראייה: ת"ש בתים הפתוחים לחצר וחצר פתוח לרה"ר ונפל בית שער החצר. וכל בני החצר נתרצו לבנות. [כופין לא' מבני החצר המעכב לבנות] בית שער ודלת עמהן משום היזק ראייה דבני רה"ר. אלמא היזק ראייה שמיה היזק: היזק דרבים שאני. אבל היכא דאיכא היזק ראייה דיחיד כגון האי חצר השותפין לאו שמיה היזק: ת"ש קתני מתני' אין חולקין את החצר. האחין שבאו לחלוק בנכסי אביהן אין חולקין את החצר עד שיהא בה ד' אמות לזה וד' אמות לזה דהכי חזי לדירה. וכשהן חולקין מאי לאו כותל מעליא בעו למיעבד בינתייהו משום היזק ראייה: לא במסיפס בעלמא. חולקין דאע"ג דזה יכול לראות בזה: ת"ש חלונות שיש להם חזקה כדאמר לקמן מלמעלן ומלמטן ומכנגדן ד' אמות כלומר אם רוצה זה בעל החצר שהחלון פתוח בחצירו לבנות כותל בצד חלון. מלמעלה שאם רצה להגביה כותל (מן) החצר יותר מן החלון צריך להגביהו ד' אמות על החלון. אי נמי למטה אם רוצה ב) נמוך (מן) הכותל מן (הצד) שצריך להנמיכו ד' אמות ואם בא לבנות כותלו ג) עד הכותל ולזה יש לו חזקת חלון בחצירו של זה צריך להרחיק ד' אמות ויבנה כדי שלא יאפיל חלונותי': ותני עלה מלמעלה להם צריך שיהא גבוה ד' אמות על החלון כדי שלא יעמוד ע"ג

א) פשיטא היא: ב) [נראה דל"ל אם רוצה להנמיך הכותל מן החלון צריך להנמיכו ד' אמות וכו']: ג) [נראה דל"ל ואם בא לבנות כותל מנגד כותל החצר ולזה יש לו חזקת וכו']:

הגהות הב"ח (א) גמ' וטעמא דרצו: (ב) שם ואימא מאי מחיצה פלוגתא: (ג) שם קביעא לי תשמישתי: (ד) רש"י ד"ה וטעמא וכו' מדעת שניהן הוא דחייבום חכמים: (ה) תום' ד"ה וכיון וכו' כי איתרצאי לך וכו' לא איתרצאי לך ויש ספרים דמקשה ומתרץ:

דאיצטנע מינך. לישנא אחרינא אמרי לה: סברוה, מאי מחיצה? פלוגתא, (א) דכתיב: °"ותהי מחצת העדה", אוכיון דרצו — בונין את הכותל בעל כורחן, אלמא: בהיזק ראיה שמיה היזק. (ב) אימא: מאי מחיצה? גודא, א)(דתנן:) ב)מחיצת הכרם שנפרצה — אומר לו "גדור", נפרצה — אומר לו "גדור". נתיאש הימנה ולא גדרה — הרי זה קידש וחייב באחריותה; וטעמא דרצו, הא לא רצו — אין מחייבין אותו, אלמא: היזק ראיה לאו שמיה היזק! אי הכי, "בונין את הכותל", "בונין אותו" מבעי ליה! אלא מאי, פלוגתא? אי הכי, "שרצו לעשות מחיצה", "שרצו לחצות" מבעי ליה! כדאמרי אינשי: "תא נעביד פלוגתא". ואי היזק ראיה שמיה היזק, מאי איריא רצו? אפי' לא רצו נמי! א"ר אסי א"ר יוחנן: משנתנו — גכשאין בה דין חלוקה, והוא דרצו. מאי קמ"ל? (ג) דכי לית ביה דין חלוקה כי רצו פליגי? תנינא: ג)אימתי — בזמן שאין שניהם רוצים, אבל בזמן ששניהם רוצים — אפילו פחות מכאן חולקין! אי מהתם, הוה אמינא: אפילו פחות מכאן — במסיפס בעלמא, קמ"ל הכא: כותל. וליתני הא ולא ליתני הך! סיפא איצטריכא ליה: ד)וכתבי הקדש, אע"פ ששניהם רוצים — לא יחלוקו. (ד) ה)(ל"א: וכי רצו מאי הוי? ליהדר ביה! אמר רב אסי א"ר יוחנן: בשקנו מידו כו'. אדאשמעינן בשאין בה דין חלוקה והוא דרצו, לישמעינן ביש בה דין חלוקה ואע"ג דלא רצו! אי אשמעינן ביש בה דין חלוקה ואע"ג דלא רצו, הוה אמינא: שאין בה דין חלוקה אפילו רצו נמי לא, קמ"ל. ומי מצית אמרת הכי? והא קתני סיפא: אימתי? בזמן שאין שניהם רוצים, אבל בזמן ששניהם רוצים — יחלוקו; מאי לאו אכותל? לא, אמסיפס בעלמא. ליתני האי ולא ליתני האי! סיפא אצטריכא ליה: ובכתבי הקדש, אע"פ ששניהם רוצים — לא יחלוקו).§ במאי אוקימתא למתני' — בשאין בה דין חלוקה, אי בשאין בה דין חלוקה, כי רצו מאי הוי? נהדרו בהו! א"ר אסי א"ר יוחנן: ו)שקנו מידן. דוכי קנו מידן מאי הוי? קנין דברים בעלמא הוא! הבשקנו מידן ברוחות. רב אשי אמר: וכגון שהלך זה בתוך שלו והחזיק, וזה בתוך שלו והחזיק.§ "מקום שנהגו לבנות" כו'.§ ז)"גויל" — אבני דלא משפיא; "גזית" — אבני דמשפיא, דכתיב: °"כל אלה אבנים יקרות כמדות גזית" ח)(וגו'); "כפיסין" — ארחי; "לבינין" — ליבני. אמר ליה רבה בריה דרבא לרב אשי: ממאי דגויל — אבני דלא משפיא נינהו, והאי טפח יתירא למורשא דקרנתא? דילמא פלגא דגזית הוא, והאי טפח יתירא לביני אורבי הוא, כדקאמרינן: כפיסין — ארחי, לבינין — ליבני, והאי טפח יתירא לביני אורבי! אמר ליה: ולטעמיך, כפיסין — ארחי מנלן? אלא גמרא גמירי לה, גויל נמי אבני דלא משפיא — גמרא גמירי לה. איכא דאמרי, אמר ליה רב אחא בריה דרב אויא לרב אשי: ממאי דהאי כפיסין — ארחי נינהו, והאי טפח יתירא לביני אורבי? דילמא מאי כפיסין — אבני דלא משפיין, והאי טפח יתירא למורשא דקרנתא, כדקאמרינן: גויל — אבני דלא משפיין, גזית — אבני דמשפיין, והאי טפח יתירא למורשא דקרנתא! אמר ליה: ולטעמיך, גויל — אבני דלא משפיין מנלן? אלא גמרא גמירי לה, הכא נמי גמרא גמירי לה. אמר אביי, שמע מינה: כל ביני אורבי — טפח. הני מילי בטינא, אבל בריכסא בעי טפי. ואיכא דאמרי: הני מילי בריכסא, אבל בטינא לא בעי כולי האי. למימרא, דבגזית (ה) דכל ד' אמות גובה, אי הוי פותיא חמשא — קאי, אי לא — לא קאי? והא אמה טרקסין דהואי גבוה תלתין אמהתא, ולא הוה פותיא אלא שית פושכי, וקם! כיון דאיכא טפח יתירא קאי. ובמקדש שני מ"ט לא עבוד אמה טרקסין? כי קאי — בתלתין קאי, טפי לא קאי. ומנלן דהוה גבוה טפי? דכתיב: °"גדול יהיה כבוד הבית הזה האחרון מן הראשון" — רב ושמואל, ואמרי לה ר' יוחנן ור"א, חד אמר: בבנין, וחד אמר: בשנים

במדבר לא / תורה אור

רש"י

דאיצטנע מינך. דברי הצנע אבל חצר השותפין — לתרווייהו קביעא תשמישתי', לכל אחד בחלקו כל שעה, ולא עבדי בה מילי דצנעא. כיון דרצו. לחלוק. ולקמן פריך: מאי איריא רצו? אפילו לא רצו, הרי הן יכולין לכוף זה את זה! בונין כותל. של אבנים. גודא. כותל אבנים, ובחצר שיש בה דין חלוקה, ועל כרחן חולקים. וטעמא דרצו. שהתנו לחולקה בכותל אבנים, הא לא רצו — אין מחייבין אותו אלא מסיפס בעלמא. כדאמרי אינשי כו'. פירוגא הוא. שאין בה דין חלוקה. ח' אמות לא יחלוקו. ובכתבי הקדש. ספר תורה שהוא בכרך אחד, וכן נביאים וכתובים הכתובים בגליון כס"ת. קנין דברים הוא. ואין חליפין קונין אלא דבר הנקנה, או (ו) מכר או מתנה או שעבוד קרקעות שהקנין חל עליו, או מטלטלין. ברוחות. זה בורר לו חלק מזרחי וזה בורר לו חלק מערבי, וקנו מידם, ומעתה נקנה חלק מזרחי לזה, ואין לזה חלק בו. וכן השני לחבירו. והחזיק. בחלקו, רפק ביה פורתא. וקרקע נקנה בחזקה אחרי אשר רצו בשעת חלוקה. אריח. חצי לבינה. והלבינה ג' טפחים, והאריח טפח ומחצה. ועובי הכותל אריח מכאן ואריח מכאן, וטפח באמצע שנותן שם טיט לחבירו. לבינים ליבני. שלימות, לבינה לעובי הכותל. למורשא דקרנתא'. ראשי האבנים בולטות לחוץ, שאינן חלקות, ולהכי בעי רוחב טפח יתירא. לביני אורבי. בין דימוס שמכאן ובין דימוס שמכאן, ונותן טיט באמצע. ה"ג: אימא לביני דלא משפיין. ש"מ כו'. ונפקא מינה למקבל עליו לבנות כותל לחבירו. בריכסא. אבנים דקות וטיט בין שני הדימוסות. למימרא דבגזית כו' כל ד' אמות גובה אי הוה פותיא ה' טפחים קאי ואי לא לא קאי. כדתנן במתני': בגזית — זה נותן טפחיים ומחצה וזה נותן טפחיים ומחצה, וקתני סיפא: ט) מחייבין אותן לבנותו עד ד' אמות. ולפי חשבון זה לגובה שמנה צריך י' טפחים רוחב. והא אמה טרקסין. דבנין שלמה, דגזית הוה, דכתיב "אבני גזית" (מלכים א ה), והוי שלשים אמה קומתה, ואין עוביו אלא אמה, להבדיל בין ההיכל לקדשי הקדשים. דאיכא טפח יתירא. ומשום האי טפח פותיא מלי לאגבוה טובא, ואין צריך לתת לכל ארבע אמות ה' טפחים רוחב. בבנין. שהיה גובהו (ז) י) מאה אמות, כדתנן במסכת "מדות" (פרק ד מ"ו).

תוספות

מאי קא משמע לן בשאין בה דין חלוקה. אע"ג דקא משמע לן דשמיה היזק, ה"פ: מאי קמ"ל במאי דאיירי באין בה דין חלוקה? לישמעינן בשיש בה דין חלוקה [אע"ג דלא רצו] (כשרצו) פלגי. כ) תימה: הא קמ"ל דאפילו באין בה דין חלוקה, דאיכא למימר "על מנת לעשות גודא לא איתרצאי", כדפירש לעיל! כי רצו מאי הוי ניהדרו בהו. למ"ד מחיצה גודא לא פריך, דאיכא למימר דקנו ושיעבדו נכסיהן לבנין הכותל. אלא למ"ד פלוגתא — לא מהני קנין, דקנין דברים בעלמא הוא, דלא מסיק אדעתיה שקנו ברוחות.

קנין דברים בעלמא הוא. בפרק "השוכר את הפועלים" (ב"מ דף לד.), דתנן: מתנה ש"ח להיות כשואל, ומוקי לה בקנו מידו — התם לאו קנין דברים הוא, אלא קנין גמור הוא, שמשעבד את עצמו שאם יאנס שישלם ל).

רב אשי אמר כגון שהלך כו'. תימה לר"י: מה בא רב אשי להוסיף? וכי איצטריך לאשמועינן דחזקה מועלת כמו קנין? ונראה לר"י דהא קמ"ל: דאע"ג דקאמר לקמן ב"חזקת הבתים" (דף נג.): שלא בפניו צריך למימר לו "לך חזק וקני", הכא, כיון שאמרו "אתה תקח רוח צפונית ואני רוח דרומית", והלך והחזיק לו כל אחד בשלו, זה שלא בפני זה — נעשה כמי שקנו מידם ברוחות, אע"פ שלא אמרו זה לזה "לך חזק וקני".

ארבע אמות גובה אפותיא דה' קאי טפי לא קאי. וקשיא לר"ת: הא לבינין דגריעי קאי בשלשה טפחים! ועוד: הא קא חזינן דקאי בגזית טפי אפורתא! ותירץ דהכי קאמר: טפי לא קאי כמשפט גזית, שרוצים בני אדם לבנותו שיעמוד ימים רבים כשבונים בגזית.

טרקסין. אומר ר"ת: ד"טרק" הוי כמו "טרוקי גלי", ברכות (דף כח.). ו"סין" הוי סיני, כלומר, שהיה מפסיק וסוגר את הלוחות שנתנו בסיני, שהיו מונחות בארון שהיה בבית קדשי הקדשים. וי"מ: טרקסין — פנים וחוץ, שאותה אמה היתה ספק אם מקודשת פנים או חוץ, ולכך היו שם שתי פרוכת, כדאמרינן ביומא (דף נא:).

שאני התם דאיכא טפח יתירא. ה"מ לשנוי דאגב תקרה ומעזיבה קאי טפי, כדאמרי' בסמוך.

אמר

רבינו גרשום

ע"ג הכותל ויגחין ויציץ ויראה בחלון ומלמטן צריך לנמוך ד' אמות שלא יעמוד זקוף על גבי הכותל ויראה בבית אלמא היזק ראיה שמיה היזק: היזקא דבית שני טפי מחצר. דאינש א) צניע דשמיש בבית טפי מבחצר: גג הסמוך לחצר חבירו. דחצר גבוה קרקעיתה ושוותה לגג חבירו צריך בעל הגג לעשות (מעשה) מעקה גבוה ד' אמות שלא יסתכל בתוך חצר חבירו אלמא היזק ראיה שמיה היזק: לא לעולם אימא בחצר של שנים לא אמרי' היזק ראיה שמיה היזק ושאני התם לגבי חצר וגג דאמר בעל החצר לבעל הגג לדידי קביעא תשמישתאי בכל שעה בחצרי לדידך לא קביעה תשמישתך בכל שעה לגג ולהכי בעי למיעבד מעקה:
ל"א [מפיך] כולה הלכה דכיון שרצו לחלוק אם מעכב א' מלעשות כותל בונין אותו בעל כרחו: ב) וטעמא דרצו לעשות [כותל] מש"ה בונין הא לא רצו בין שניהן אלא א' רוצה וא' מעכב אין מחייבין אותו אלמא היזק ראיה לאו שמיה היזק: שרצו לחצות מיבעי ליה. כלומר אם איתא דמחיצה דמתני' פלוגתא אמאי תני לעשות ליתני לחצות בשלמא אי אמרת גודא אמטא להכי תני לעשות דלא מיתני בלא לעשות. ומשני לעולם מחיצה פלוגתא ודקא קשיא לך שרצו לחצות מיבעי ליה לא קשיא דמתני' משתעי בלשון בני אדם דאמרי תא ונעביד פלוגתא ולעולם היזק ראיה שמיה היזק: מאי אריא דתני מתני' רצו לחלוק מש"ה בונין את הכותל באמצע בעל כרחו משום היזק ראיה דהואיל דנתרצו לחלוק בונין אפי' לא רצו שניהן לחלוק הואיל דנתרצה א' מהן לחלוק בדין הוא דבונין את הכותל לאמצע אע"ג דלא נתרצה אידך משום היזק ראיה: משנתנו בשאין בה דין חלוקה שאין בה ד' אמות לזה וד' אמות לזה מש"ה אם נתרצו שניהן לחלוק בונין את הכותל בעל כורחו הואיל דנתרצו לחלוק משום היזק ראיה ואם לא נתרצה א' מהן לחלוק אע"ג דמעכב אידך אין בונין הואיל דאין בה דין חלוקה: תנינא. בסיפא דמתני' אימתי אמרי' דאין חלוקה הואיל דלית בה דין חלוקה בזמן שאין שניהן רוצין: במסיפס בעלמא. חולקין הואיל ונתרצו קמ"ל רישא דמתני' דקתני כותל דלא סגי בלא כותל משום היזק ראיה: וליתני הא רישא דמתני' ולא בעי סיפא למיתני. ומשני סיפא איצטריכא לה למיתני דקתני וכתבי הקדש לא יחלוקו. משום דקא נהוג בהו מנהג בזיון ואגב סיפא דלא סגי דלא ליתני קתני רישא אימתי בזמן כו': בשקנו מידן. דלא מצי למיהדר בהו: קנין דברים בעלמא הוא (קנין זה) [איזה] קנין הוא עיקר כגון מתנה או מכירה או שום דבר שמראה לו החפץ שנותן לו ומקבל מידו על כך אבל הכא שאדם אומר לחבירו ניטול קנין שנחלוק כגון זה קנין דברים בעלמא הוא דלא נברר על מה נוטל קנין ואכתי ליהדרו בהו: שקנו מידן ברוחות. דזה הקנה לזה אותו חלק שבצד רוח מזרח ... לזה חלק שבצד רוח מערב דהיינו קנין גמור הואיל והוברר על מה קנו: רב אשי אומר מש"ה לא מצי למיהדר בהו הואיל דקני אע"ג דלית בה דין חלוקה כגון שהלך זה לאחר קנין להחזיק בחלקו דנעל גדר ופרץ כל שהוא ודאי בתר הכי לא מצי למיהדר: פיסקא גויל. אבנים שנחצבו מן ההר דעדיין אין משופין והם ו' טפחים: גזית. אבנים משופין והן של ה' טפחים. כפיסין ארחי חצי לבינה לבינה שלימה היא ג' טפחים. מקום שנהגו לבנות בגויל דמן ו' טפחים זה נותן ג' טפח מחלקו בקרקע וזה ג' טפח. בגזית של חמש טפחים זה נותן טפחיים ומחצה בקרקע וזה נותן טפחיים ומחצה. כפיסין שהן טפח ומחצה זה נותן טפחיים וזה נותן טפחיים לפי שכשיתן זה כפים אחד מטפח ומחצה וזה כפים אחד מטפח ומחצה דהיינו ג' טפחים עדיין צריך טינא ביני אורבי לפי שכשמניחין כפים מכאן וכפים מכאן ג) ובאמצע כשיעור טפח של סיד כדי שיהיו מדובקות בטינא יפה והיינו ב' טפחים מן הקרקע לכל אחד: לבינים. כותל של לבינים לא הוי אלא ג' טפחים שאין מניחין לבינה כנגד לבינה אלא זו על גב זו: דלא משפיין. שאין משופות ומסותתות: ארחי. חצי לבינה: לבינים ליבני. הכי קרו להו בלשון [המון]. (האי) ממאי דהאי טפח יתירא דמייתרי מתני' בגויל טפי משום דצריך ההוא טפח למורש' דקרנתא מן הכותל טפי מכותל של גזית משום דגזית משפייא וגויל לא משפייא דילמא האי גויל לאו מו' טפחים הוי כי אם פלגא דגזית דהיינו ב' טפחים ומחצה ומש"ה צריך ליתן לכל חד וחד ג' טפחים מן הקרקע משום דהאי יהיב גויל מב' טפחים ומחצה [וכן] אידך הכי (טפי) וטפח דמייתר מתני' [בגויל] על אבני גזית משום טינא שמניחין ביני ארבי כדאמרי' כפיסין ארחי כול' וממאי דהני כפיסין דקתני מתני' ארחי נינהו דהיינו חצי לבינה והאי טפח יתירא דמייתר בכפיסין טפי מליבנא משום (דביה) [דביני] ארבי דלמא האי כפיסין דקתני מתני' אבנים דלא משפיין נינהו ולא מתוקנות כשאר ליבני. והאי טפח יתירא דמייתר למורשא דקרנתא שבולט מן הכותל הוא מי לא קאמרת נמי הכי כול': אמר אביי ש"מ ממתני' דקתני בכפיסים זה נותן טפחיים וזה נותן טפחיים איכא למשמע מינה כל ביני ארבי טפח ליתן בלי סיד. והני מילי דסגי בטפח בטינא שמגובל מחול וסיד אבל בריכסא היינו טיט חוצות שמגובל במים ועפר הואיל ואינו מדובק יפה בעי ודאי טפי מטפח: למימרא דכל כותל (בוני) [שבונין] מגזית גבוה ד' כגון זה שהיא להיזק ראיה שאין צריך להגביהו אלא ד' אמות כדתנן כותל חצר שנפל וכו' והוא מאבני גזית שהם ה' טפחים וקמ"ל מתני' דאי פותיא ה' טפחים ההוא כותל דגבוה ד' אמות מצי קאי הכותל אבל אי גבוה טפי מד' לא קאי בה' טפחים רוחב: והא אמה טרקסין. הכותל שהיה מפסיק בין ההיכל לקודש הקדשים קרי ליה אמה טרקסין דעובי הכותל הוי אמה בת ו' טפחים ואי קשיא אמאי מקשה מגזית טפי מגויל וכפיסין וליבני תריץ משום דבעי לאקשויי ליה מאמה טרקסין (דביני) [דבנו] מאבני גזית ומקדש ראשון היה גבוה ל' וההוא אמה טרקסין לא הוי אלא י' פושכי ואפ"ה קם ההוא כותל והיכי אמרת עד ד' אמות בגובה קאי כותל דעבה ה' טפחים לא שאני התם הואיל ואיכא טפח יתירא על ה' טפחים מצי קאי עד גובה ל': במקדש שני מ"ט לא עביד אמה טרקסין. אלא פרוכת כדתנן בפ' הוציאו לו (יומא נא.) שתי פרוכות היו שם וכו': אתלתין קאי. כלומר מקדש ראשון שהיה גבוה ל' אמה בעובי אמה מצי קאי טפי אמר בבנין. שהיה גבוה יותר מן הראשון:

א) [אולי צ"ל דאיירי לגבי גגות בתשמיש דבית טפי מבחצר]: ב) [נראה דצ"ל בונין אותו בעל כרחו משום דהיזק ראיה שמיה היזק ואימא מאי מחיצה גודא וכו' וטעמא דרצו וכו']: ג) [צ"ל צריך להניח באמצע וכו']:

מסורת הש"ס

א) [נ"ל דתניא:] ב) [לעיל ב.] ג) [לקמן יא.:] ד) [שם:] ה) ס"ח כ"ו לאינו: ו) [כ"מ טו. וש"נ] ז) ח) [נ"ל מגררות במגרה וכן הגי' בערוך ערך קב ב'] ט) [לקמן ה.] י) [עי' תוי"ט ריש פ"ה דיומא ד"ה לבין שתי דגרס מ' אמות ונכתב דנתחלף בין מ' למתא ע"ש] כ) ס"א ותירך מהר"ם ופי גירסתו ג"ל כשרצו והגי' שלפנינו הוא גי' מהרש"א: ל) [וע"ע תוס' כתובות נב: ד"ה אע"פ].

עין משפט נר מצוה

ט א ב ג מיי' פ"ב מהל' שכנים הל' יד סמג עשין פב טוש"ע ח"מ סי' קנז סעיף א:
י ד ה ו מיי' שם הל' י טוש"ע שם סעיף ב:

הגהות הב"ח

(א) גמ' כדכתיב ותהי מחצת: (ב) שם ואימא מאי מחיצה גודא כדתנן מחיצת הכרם שנפרצה אומר לו גדור חזרה ונפרצה: (ג) שם מאי קמ"ל (דכי לית ביה דין חלוקה) תא"מ ונ"ב גי' תוס' כשאין בה דין חלוקה: (ד) שם לא יחלוקו וכי רצו מאי הוי ליהדר ביה וכו' בשקנו מידן כו' לישנא אחרינא אדאשמעינן בשאין בה: (ה) שם למימרא דבגזית כל כנ"ל ואות ד' נמחק: (ו) רש"י ד"ה קנין וכו' או במכר או במתנה: (ז) ד"ה בבנין שהיה גובהו ק' נ"ב נראה דזה הוא ... ראשון היה גבוה ק"כ אמה דהיינו ל' מעלייה ראשונה והבית גופיה ל' א"כ מקדש ראשון גבוה יותר וע"כ נ"ל מ' ותשיב עד העלייה דראשון לא הוה רק שלשים ושני מ' וע"ל דף נ"ח ע"ב:

יא א מיי' פ"ב מהלכות שכנים הלכה יח סמג עשין פב טוש"מ סי' קנז:
יב ב מיי' פ"ז מהל' שבת הל' יג סמג עשין מד סא טוש"ע א"ח סי' שסג סעיף יז:
יג ג ד מיי' פי"א מהל' תפלה הל' יב סמג עשין יט טוש"ע א"ח סי' קנב [וברב אלפס פרק בני העיר דף רסד]:
יד ה ו מיי' פ"ח מהל' מתנות עניים הל' יא סמג עשין קסב טוש"ע י"ד סי' רנב סעיף א:
טו ז מיי' פי"א מהל' תפלה הלכה יג סמג עשין יט טוש"ע א"ח סי' קנב [וברב אלפס פרק בני העיר דף רסד]:

בְּשָׁנִים, וְאִיתָא לְהָא וְאִיתָא לְהָא. וְנִיעַבְדוּ תְּלָתִין אַמִּין בְּבִנְיָן, וְאִידָךְ נִיעֲבֵיד פָּרוֹכֶת! כִּי קָאֵי תְּלָתִין אַמְּהָתָא נַמִּי — אַגַּב תִּקְרָה וּמַעֲזִיבָה (א) הֲוָה קָאֵי, בְּלָא תִּקְרָה וּמַעֲזִיבָה לָא הֲוָה קָאֵי. וְלִיעֲבִיד מַה דְּאֶפְשָׁר בְּבִנְיָן, וְלִיעֲבִיד אִידָךְ פָּרוֹכֶת! אֲמַר אַבַּיֵי, גְּמִירִי: אִי כּוּלְּהוּ בְּבִנְיָן אִי כּוּלְּהוּ בְּפָרוֹכֶת; אִי כּוּלְּהוּ בְּבִנְיָן — מִמִּקְדָּשׁ, אִי כּוּלְּהוּ בְּפָרוֹכֶת — מִמִּשְׁכָּן. אִיבַּעְיָא לְהוּ: הֵן וְסִידָן, אוֹ דִילְמָא הֵן בְּלֹא סִידָן? אֲמַר ר"נ בַּר יִצְחָק: [א]מִסְתַּבְּרָא הֵן וְסִידָן, דְּאִי ס"ד הֵן בְּלֹא סִידָן, לִיתְנְיֵיהּ לְשִׁיעוּרֵיהּ! אֶלָּא לָאו ש"מ: הֵן וְסִידָן. לָא, לְעוֹלָם אֵימָא לָךְ: הֵן בְּלֹא סִידָן, וְכֵיוָן דְּלָא הָוֵי טֶפַח לָא תָּנֵי. וְהָא קָתָנֵי: (ב) בִּלְבֵינִין — זֶה נוֹתֵן טֶפַח וּמֶחֱצָה וְזֶה נוֹתֵן טֶפַח וּמֶחֱצָה! הָתָם חֲזִי לְאִיצְטְרוֹפֵי. ת"ש: א)[ב]הַקּוֹרָה שֶׁאָמְרוּ — רְחָבָה כְּדֵי לְקַבֵּל אָרִיחַ, וְהָאָרִיחַ — חֲצִי לְבֵינָה שֶׁל ג' טְפָחִים! הָתָם בְּרַבְרְבָתָא. דַּיְקָא נַמִי, דְּקָתָנֵי: שֶׁל שְׁלֹשָׁה טְפָחִים, מִכְּלָל דְּאִיכָּא זוּטְרָא, ש"מ. § ב)אֲמַר רַב חִסְדָּא: [ג]לָא לִיסְתּוֹר אִינִישׁ בֵּי כְנִישְׁתָּא עַד דְּבָנֵי בֵּי כְנִישְׁתָּא אַחֲרִיתִי. אִיכָּא דְּאָמְרִי: [ד]מִשּׁוּם פְּשִׁיעוּתָא, וְאִיכָּא דְּאָמְרִי: מִשּׁוּם צַלּוּיֵי. מַאי בֵּינַיְיהוּ? אִיכָּא בֵּינַיְיהוּ, דְּאִיכָּא ג)(בֵּי כְנִישְׁתָּא אַחֲרִיתִי.) מָרֵימָר וּמָר זוּטְרָא סָתְרִי וּבָנוּ בֵּי קַיְיטָא בְּסִיתְוָוא, (ג) וּבָנוּ בֵּי סִיתְוָוא בְּקַיְיטָא. א"ל רָבִינָא לְרַב אַשִׁי: גְּבוּ זוּזֵי וּמַחְתִּי, מַאי? אֲמַר לֵיהּ: [ה]דִּילְמָא מִיתְרַמֵּי לְהוּ ד)פִּדְיוֹן שְׁבוּיִים וְיָהֲבִי לְהוּ. שְׁרִיגֵי לִיבְנֵי וְהָדְרֵי הוּדְרֵי וּמַחְתֵּי כָּשׁוּרֵי, מַאי? א"ל: [ו]זִמְנִין דְּמִתְרַמֵּי לְהוּ פִּדְיוֹן שְׁבוּיִים, מְזַבְּנֵי וְיָהֲבִי לְהוּ. א"ה, אֲפִי' בָּנוּ נַמִי! אֲמַר לֵיהּ: דִּירָתֵיהּ דֶּאֱנָשֵׁי לָא מְזַבְּנֵי. וְלָא אֲמַרַן [ז]אֶלָּא דְּלָא חָזֵי בָּהּ תִּיוּהָא, אֲבָל חָזֵי בָּהּ תִּיוּהָא סָתְרֵי וּבָנֵי; כִּי הָא דְּרַב אַשִׁי חֲזָא בָּהּ תִּיוּהָא בִּכְנִישְׁתָּא דְּמָתָא מְחַסְיָא, סַתְרֵיהּ וְעַיֵּיל לְפוּרְיֵיהּ לְהָתָם, וְלָא אַפְּקֵיהּ עַד דְּמַתְקִין לֵיהּ שְׁפִיכֵי. וּבָבָא בֶּן בּוּטָא הֵיכִי אַסְבֵּיהּ לֵיהּ עֵצָה לְהוֹרְדוֹס לְמִיסְתְּרֵיהּ לְבֵית הַמִּקְדָּשׁ? וְהָאָמַר רַב חִסְדָּא: לָא לִיסְתּוֹר אִינִישׁ בֵּי כְנִישְׁתָּא עַד דְּבָנֵי בֵּי כְנִישְׁתָּא אַחֲרִיתָא! אִי בָּעֵית אֵימָא: תִּיוּהָא חֲזָא בֵּיהּ; אִיבָּעֵית אֵימָא: ה)מַלְכוּתָא שָׁאנֵי, דְּלָא הָדְרָא בֵּיהּ. דְּאָמַר ו)שְׁמוּאֵל: אִי אָמַר מַלְכוּתָא "עָקַרְנָא טוּרֵי" — עָקַר טוּרֵי וְלָא הָדַר בֵּיהּ. הוֹרְדוֹס עַבְדָּא דְּבֵית חַשְׁמוֹנַאי הֲוָה, נָתַן עֵינָיו בְּאוֹתָהּ תִּינוֹקֶת. יוֹמָא חַד (ד) שְׁמַע הַהוּא גַּבְרָא בַּת קָלָא דְּאָמַר: כָּל עַבְדָּא דְּמָרֵיד הַשְׁתָּא מַצְלַח, קָם קַטְלִינְהוּ לְכוּלְּהוּ מָרְוָתֵיהּ וְשַׁיְּירָהּ לְהַהִיא יְנוּקְתָּא. כִּי חֲזַת הַהִיא יְנוּקְתָּא דְּקָא בָּעֵי לְמִינְסְבָהּ, סְלִיקָא לְאִיגָּרָא (ה) וּרְמָא קָלָא, אֲמַרָה: ז)כָּל מַאן דְּאָתֵי וְאָמַר מִבֵּית חַשְׁמוֹנַאי קָאָתֵינָא — עַבְדָּא הוּא, דְּלָא אִישְׁתַּיְּירָא מִינַּיְיהוּ אֶלָּא הַהִיא יְנוּקְתָּא, וְהַהִיא יְנוּקְתָּא נָפְלָה מֵאִיגְּרָא לְאַרְעָא. טְמָנָהּ שֶׁבַע שְׁנִין בִּדְוּבְשָׁא. אִיכָּא דְּאָמְרִי: בָּא עָלֶיהָ, אִיכָּא דְּאָמְרִי: לֹא בָּא עָלֶיהָ. דְּאָמְרִי לָהּ בָּא עָלֶיהָ, הָא דִּטְמָנָהּ — לְיַתּוֹבֵיהּ לְיִצְרֵיהּ; וּדְאָמְרִי לָהּ לֹא בָּא עָלֶיהָ, הַאי דִּטְמָנָהּ — כִּי הֵיכִי דְּנֵאמְרוּ: בַּת מֶלֶךְ נָסַב. אֲמַר: מַאן דָּרֵישׁ °"מִקֶּרֶב אַחֶיךָ תָּשִׂים עָלֶיךָ מֶלֶךְ"? (דברים יז) רַבָּנַן, קָם קַטְלִינְהוּ לְכוּלְּהוּ רַבָּנַן, שַׁבְקֵיהּ לְבָבָא בֶּן בּוּטָא לְמִשְׁקַל עֵצָה מִינֵּיהּ.

אַהֲדַר

בְּשָׁנִים. בַּיִת רִאשׁוֹן עָמַד ד' מֵאוֹת וָעֶשֶׂר, וּבַיִת שֵׁנִי ד' מֵאוֹת וְעֶשְׂרִים. אַגַּב תִּקְרָה וּמַעֲזִיבָה. שֶׁהָעֲלִיָּיה הָיְתָה נְתוּנָה עָלָיו, וּמַעֲזִיבָה שֶׁל טִיט טְרַכָּס עַל גַּגָּהּ, וְכוֹבֶד הַמַּשָּׂא מַעֲמִיד הַכּוֹתֶל שֶׁלֹּא יַטֶּה לַצְּדָדִין. הִלְכָּךְ, בְּמִקְדָּשׁ שֵׁנִי שֶׁלֹּא הָיָה כּוֹתֶל ל' מַגִּיעַ לָעֲלִיָּיה — לֹא יוּכַל לַעֲמוֹד. הֵן וְסִידָן אוֹ הֵן בְּלֹא סִידָן. הָנֵי שִׁיעוּרֵי דְּמַתְנִי' עִם עוֹבִי הַטִּיחַ קָא חָשֵׁיב לְהֶן, אוֹ דִּילְמָא מְקוֹם הָאֲבָנִים הָוֵי בְּפוּתְיָא, לְבַד טִיחַ הַסִּיד. וְהָא קָתָנֵי טְפָחַיִים וּמֶחֱצָה. אַלְמָא חֲלִי טֶפַח נַמִי חָשֵׁיב. חֲזִי לְאִיצְטְרוּפֵי. שֶׁל זֶה וְשֶׁל זֶה מִצְטָרְפִין לְטֶפַח. הַקּוֹרָה שֶׁאָמְרוּ. לְעִנְיַן הֶכְשֵׁר מָבוֹי. ג' טְפָחִים. אַלְמָא, ג' טְפָחִים דְּקָתָנֵי לְגַבֵּי מַתְנִי' גַּבֵּי לְבֵינִין, כִּדְקָתָנֵי: זֶה נוֹתֵן טֶפַח וּמֶחֱצָה וְזֶה נוֹתֵן טֶפַח וּמֶחֱצָה — הֵן בְּלֹא סִידָן קָאָמַר, דְּהָא לְבֵינָה לְחוּדָהּ שְׁלֹשָׁה טְפָחִים. הָתָם בְּרַבְרְבָתָא. וּמַתְנִי' בְּזוּטַרְתָּא, דְּעִם סִידָן לָא הָווּ אֶלָּא ג' טְפָחִים. מִשּׁוּם פְּשִׁיעוּתָא. דִּילְמָא מִתְרַמֵּי אוֹנֶס, וּפָשְׁעִי וְלֹא בָּנוּ אַחֲרִיתִי. מִשּׁוּם צַלּוּיֵי. כָּל זְמַן הַבִּנְיָן. בֵּי קַיְיטָא בְּסִיתְוָוא. בֵּית הַכְּנֶסֶת הָיָה לָהֶם לִימוֹת הַחוֹרֶף, נָמוּךְ, בִּכְתָלִים רְחָבִים וְחַלּוֹנוֹת מוּעָטִין, מִפְּנֵי הַצִּינָּה. וּבִימוֹת הַחַמָּה בֵּית הַכְּנֶסֶת אַחֵר, שֶׁאֲוִיר שׁוֹלֵט בּוֹ. זוּזֵי. לְצוֹרֶךְ בֵּית הַכְּנֶסֶת הֶחָדָשׁ, וּמוּנָּחִים בְּיַד הַגַּבַּאי, מִי אִיכָּא לְמֵיחַשׁ לִפְשִׁיעוּת אוֹ לֹא? שְׁרִיגֵי לִיבְנֵי. מְסוּדָּרִים הַלְּבֵינִים זֶה עַל גַּב זֶה, וּמְזוּמָּנִין לִתֵּן בַּבִּנְיָן. הָדְרֵי הוּדְרֵי. מְשׁוּפִּין וּמְתוּקָּנִין רְהִיטֵי הַגַּג, קיברונ"ש. כִּי בָּנוּ נַמִי. בֵּי כְנִישְׁתָּא חַדְתָּא, לָא נִסְתְּרוּהּ לְעַתִּיקָא, דְּדִילְמָא מִתְרַמֵּי פִּדְיוֹן שְׁבוּיִין וּמְזַבְּנֵי לֵיהּ. וְלָא אֲמַרַן. דְּלָא לִיסְתְּרוּהּ לְעַתִּיקָא. אֶלָּא דְּלָא חֲזוּ בֵּיהּ תִּיוּהָא. בִּיקּוּעַ, שֶׁיְּהֵא מְזוּמָּן לִיפּוֹל. עַיְילֵיהּ לְפוּרְיֵיהּ הָתָם. כְּדֵי שֶׁלֹּא יִתְיָיאֵשׁ בְּבִנְיָנוֹ, שֶׁהַחַמָּה וְהַגְּשָׁמִים מְצַעֲרִין אוֹתוֹ. שְׁפָכֵי = מַרְזְבִין. הֵיכִי אַסְבֵּיהּ עֵצָה לְהוֹרְדוֹס. כִּדְאָמְרִי' לְקַמָּן בִּשְׁמַעְתִּין. וּכְתוּבָה הִיא בְּיוֹסִיפוֹן בֶּן גּוֹרְיוֹן.

תורה אור הן בלא סידן.

אמר אביי גמירי. השתא לא צריך לשנויא קמא. **מכלל** דאיכא זוטרתי. וא"ת: ודילמא מכלל דאיכא רברבתא, ומה דיקא הוא זהו? ותירץ ר"י: דאם אין פחות משלשה אבל גדולות יש — א"כ בכדי נקט חצי לבינה של ג' טפחים, דלא הוה צריך למתני אלא: והאריח חצי לבינה, ותו לא, וממילא הייתי משער בקטנה, הואיל ולא מפרש שיעורא. **הג"ה:** בי קייטא ובי סיתווא הוי כמו איכא תיוהא, ושרי. ואם שתי בתי כנסיות היו בב' מקומות, של קייטא ושל סיתווא — איירי כגון דחזו בה תיוהא. ועוד נראה: כיון דיש שם בהכ"נ אחר — אין לחוש אם לא יבנו זאת. והא דקאמר דאיכא דוכתא לצלויי — היינו שאין בהכ"נ. ועוד, מחמת קור וחום אין לחוש שמא יפשעו, או בזמן גדול כל כך אין לחוש. ע"כ הגה"ה. **אי** הכי כי בנייה נמי. פירוש: עד שיתפללו בה.

ועייליה לפורייה להתם. ותימה: והא אמרת בתי כנסיות אין ישנים בהם לא שינת קבע ולא שינת עראי! ואין לתרץ משום דבבבל הוי, ואמר רב אסי בפ' בתרא דמגילה (דף כח: ושם ד"ה בתי): בתי כנסיות של בבל על תנאי הן עשויות, ופ"ה התם: נפקא מינה לענין הא דקתני לעיל, אין אוכלין בהן ואין שותים בהן ואין נכנסין בהן בחמה מפני החמה ובגשמים מפני הגשמים, ובשל בבל מותר. דהא קאמר התם בתר הכי: רבינא ורב אדא הוו קיימי ושיילי שמעתא מרבא, אתא זילחא דמטרא עלייהו ועיילי לבי כנישתא, ולא משום מטרא אלא משום דשמעתא בעי' צילותא. והשתא, והלא בהכ"נ של בבל היה והיו יכולין ליכנס בה מפני המטר! וי"ל: דלאו ממש לבהכ"נ עיילה לפוריי', אלא בסמוך לבהכ"נ, במקום שהאורחין רגילין לישן שם ולאכול, כדאמרינן ב"ע"פ" (פסחים דף קא. ושם ד"ה דאכלי): ושמואל למה לי' לקדושי בבי כנישתא — לאפוקי אורחים ידי חובתן, דאכלו ושתו וגנו בבי כנישתא. והא דאמר דעל תנאי הן עשויין — מפרש ר"י לענין שאם יחרבו, יעשו מהן מה שירצו, לבד מקלות ראש, כדאמרי' התם. **כל** דאמר מבית חשמונאי אתינא עבדא הוא. וכן הוא, דהכי נמי אמר שמואל בפרק "עשרה יוחסין" (קדושין דף ע:). ומכאן קשה על פ"ה ב"אלו נאמרים" (סוטה דף מא.), דאמר: אמרו לו לאגריפס "אחינו אתה", ופ"ה התם שאמרו לו "אחינו" לפי שהיתה אמו מישראל. דא"כ, כיון, דבני הורדוס נשאו ישראלית — אמאי עבדא הוה? הא שמואל גופיה אית ליה: גוי ועבד הבא על בת ישראל הולד כשר, ב"החולץ" (יבמות דף מה.)! וי"ל שלא נשאו ישראלית, וקראוהו "אחינו אתה" לפי שעבד אחינו [הוא] במצות. [וע"ע תוס' יבמות מה: ד"ה כיון דאמו]. **מאן** דריש מקרב אחיך רבנן. דפשטי' דקרא לא משמע למעוטי עבד שהוא אחיך במצות, אלא גוי. ורבנן דרשו (ב"ק פח.): ממובחר שבאחיך. **קטלינהו** לכולהו רבנן. לאו דוקא לכולהו, דהא הוו בני בתירא שהיו נשיאים כשעלה הלל מבבל, כדאמרינן בפסחים בפרק "אלו דברים" (דף סו.). והלל היה בפני הבית מאה שנה, כדאמרינן בפרק קמא דשבת (דף טו.), ומלכות הורדוס היה בפני הבית ק"ג שנה, כדאמרינן בפרק קמא דע"ז (דף ט.).

שכל

רבינו גרשום

איתא להא ואית' להא. דהא בין בבנין בין בשנים היה גדול: כי קאי נמי תלתין אמה בעובי אמה בבית ראשון משום דהתקרה והמעזיב' מונחת עליו וסומכתו שלא יפול הא לאו הכי לא קאי אפי' בתלתין: ונעבד כמה דאפשר. לעמוד בגובה בבנין כותל ומכאן ולמעלה עד התקרה ליעבד פרוכת: אי כוליה בפרוכת. ממשכן [כדכתיב] והבדילה הפרוכת וגו': הן וסידן. כלומר הא דתנינן בגויל זה נותן ג' טפחים וזה נותן ג' טפחים תני מקום אבנים בהדי סיד שמסידו מבחוץ צריך ג' טפחים (דאי לא הכי) [דליכא הכא] ו' טפחים שלימות דבצר שיעור מקום הסיד או הן בלא סידן כלומר דלמקום גויל גרידא בעי למיתן זה ג' טפחים וזה ג' טפחים חוץ ממקום הסיד: דאי ס"ד הן בלא סידן. ו' טפחים (ולמקום) [ולעולם] בעי למיתב תרוייהו א"כ ניתנייהו לשיעורא דסיד ולימא הכי זה נותן ג' טפחים ומשהו למקום הסיד והשני כמו כן וכן בכולהו אלא מדלא תני הכי ש"מ מקום הגויל ומקום הסיד לא הוי אלא ו' טפחים (אלא) [לא] לעולם אימא לך הן ולא סידן ואי אמרת אמאי לא תני שיעורא דסיד כיון דלא הוי טפח לא חשיב למתנייה: התם חזי לאצטרופי. ב' חצאי טפח לטפח אבל מקום הסיד לא חזי לאצטרופי לשום חשבון: קורה שאמרו. לגבי מבוי מדתני לבינה של ג' טפחים מכלל דג' טפחים שלימות הוי כל לבינה וש"מ דלמקום לבינה בעינן ג' טפחים שלימות לבד ממקום הסיד וה"ה לגויל וכפים וגזית: (מיהו) [ודחי דמהא] לא

לא תידוק דמקום לבינה ג' טפחים שלימות דאותן טפחים א) דתני גבי לבינות מבוי גדולים טפח בגודל אבל מתני' בטפחים בינונים הן ומש"ה הן וסידן ג' טפחים: משום פשיעותא. דדלמא מטריד בשאר מילי ולא בני ליה: משום לצלויי. דלא הוה להו דוכתא לצלויי עד שיעסוק בבנין: סתרו ובנו בי קייטא בסיתוא. שמעתי [דשתי] בתי כנסיות היו להם באחד היו מתפללין בימות הגשמים ובאחד בימות החמה אותו של ימות החמה היו מחזקין אותו בימות הגשמים ושל ימות הגשמים בימות החמה כדי שיהא להם מקום תפלה בכל שעה: גבו זוזי. מציבורא לצורך בית הכנסת: ומחתי. ומונחין הן במקום אחד [מי] אמרינן הואיל והמעות גבויין לא פשעי ומצי למיסתריה או דלמא ניחוש דלמא יהבינהו למצוה אחריתי. אם תמצא לומר דהמעות יתנו לפדיון שבוים. הדרי הודרי. מתוקנים הזיזין שריגי ליבני שמתוקנין וערוכין הלבינים ומחתי כשורי ומונחין הקורות והכל [שקנו] להתחיל הבנין מאי יכול לסתור הישן קודם שיתחילו החדש או לאו: אי הכי דאכתי איכא למיחש אפי' כי מיבני האי לא ליסתור אחרינא דאיכא למיחש דמתרמי להו פדיון שבוים ומזבני ליה ואיכא פשיעותא ומשני דירתא דאינשא לא מזדבן כ"ש בית הכנסת הואיל ומתוקן הוא וליכא למיחש: ולא אמרן דלא לסתור עד דבני אחרינא אלא דלא חזו ביה תיוהא רעוע או סדק אבל חזו ביה תיוהא סתר לאלתר: ועיילה לפורייה להתם. כדי שיהיו הגשמים יורדין ומנטפין עליו והוא ימהר במלאכת בהכ"נ יותר: שפיכי. מרובין: אי הכי דלא ליסתור עד דבני אחרינא. בבא בן בוטא היכי אסביה עצה כו'. מלכא שאני דכיון דאמר למיבנייה לא הדר ביה וליכא למיחש לפשיעות': כאותה תינוקת. דבית חשמונאי:

א) [ונראה דצ"ל דאותן לבינות דתני גבי מבוי לבינות גדולות של ג"ט אבל מתני' בלבינות בינונים הן וכו'.

א) עירובין יג: ב) מגילה כו: ג) נ"א דוכתא לצלויי. רש"א: ד) נ"א מלתא דמצוה ויהבי. רש"ל: ה) [ערכין ו.]: ו) [שם]: ז) קדושין ע::

הגהות הב"ח (א) גמ' ומעזיבה קאי בלא תקרה ומעזיבה לא קאי כצ"ל ותיבת הוה נמחק ב' פעמים: (ב) שם לא תני והא קתני בגזית זה נותן טפחים ומחצה וזה נותן טפחים ומחצה התם חזי לאצטרופי: (ג) שם בי קייטא בסיתווא וסתרי ובנו בי סיתווא: (ד) שם יומא חד שמעיה לבת קלא דאמר כצ"ל ותיבת ההוא גברא נמחק: (ה) שם ורמת קלא:

מסורת הש"ס

א) [יבמות כב: ב"ק לד: ב"מ מח: סב. סנהדרין מז. פה. מכות ח:] ב) סוכה נא: ע"ש: ג) [שם איתא רבא]: ד) נ"א דלא סגיא ליה בלא מלכא: ה) מגילה טו.: ו) ס"א ועביו: ז) [וכן בפירקי דר"א פ"ג]:

אַהֲדַר לֵיהּ כְּלִילָא דְיָילֵי, נַקְרִינְהוּ לְעֵינֵיהּ. יוֹמָא חַד אֲתָא וִיתֵיב קַמֵּיהּ, אֲמַר: חֲזֵי מָר הַאי עַבְדָּא בִּישָׁא מַאי קָא עָבֵיד! אֲמַר לֵיהּ: מַאי אַעֲבֵיד לֵיהּ? א"ל: נְלַטְיֵיהּ מָר! א) אֲמַר לֵיהּ, [כְּתִיב:] °"גַּם בְּמַדָּעֲךָ מֶלֶךְ אַל תְּקַלֵּל". אֲמַר לֵיהּ: הַאי לָאו מֶלֶךְ הוּא! א"ל: ב) וְלֶיהֱוֵי עָשִׁיר בְּעָלְמָא, וּכְתִיב: °"וּבְחַדְרֵי מִשְׁכָּבְךָ אַל תְּקַלֵּל עָשִׁיר". ג) וְלָא יְהֵא אֶלָּא נָשִׂיא, וּכְתִיב: °"וְנָשִׂיא בְעַמְּךָ לֹא תָאֹר". א"ל: א) בְּעוֹשֶׂה מַעֲשֵׂה עַמְּךָ, וְהַאי לָאו עוֹשֶׂה מַעֲשֵׂה עַמְּךָ! א"ל: מִסְתְּפֵינָא (א) מִינֵּיהּ. א"ל: לֵיכָּא אִינִישׁ דְּאָזֵיל דְּלֵימָא לֵיהּ, דַּאֲנָא וְאַתְּ יָתֵיבְנָא. א"ל: כְּתִיב: °"כִּי עוֹף הַשָּׁמַיִם יוֹלִיךְ אֶת הַקּוֹל וּבַעַל כְּנָפַיִם יַגֵּיד דָּבָר". א"ל: אֲנָא הוּא, אִי הֲוַאי יָדַעְנָא דְּזָהֲרִי רַבָּנַן כּוּלֵּי הַאי לָא הֲוָה קָטֵילְנָא לְהוּ, הַשְׁתָּא מַאי תַּקַּנְתֵּיהּ דְּהַהוּא גַּבְרָא? א"ל: הוּא כִּבָּה אוֹרוֹ שֶׁל עוֹלָם, דִּכְתִיב: °"כִּי נֵר מִצְוָה וְתוֹרָה אוֹר", יֵלֵךְ וְיַעֲסוֹק בְּאוֹרוֹ שֶׁל עוֹלָם, דִּכְתִיב: °"וְנָהֲרוּ אֵלָיו כָּל הַגּוֹיִם". אִיכָּא דְּאָמְרִי, הָכִי א"ל: הוּא סִימֵּא עֵינוֹ שֶׁל עוֹלָם, דִּכְתִיב: °"וְהָיָה אִם מֵעֵינֵי הָעֵדָה", יֵלֵךְ וְיִתְעַסֵּק בְּעֵינוֹ שֶׁל עוֹלָם, דִּכְתִיב: °"הִנְנִי מְחַלֵּל אֶת מִקְדָּשִׁי גְּאוֹן עֻזְּכֶם מַחְמַד עֵינֵיכֶם". א"ל: מִסְתְּפֵינָא מִמַּלְכוּתָא. א"ל: שְׁדַר שְׁלִיחָא, וְלֵיזִיל שַׁתָּא וְלִיעַכֵּב שַׁתָּא וְלִהְדַר שַׁתָּא, אַדְּהָכִי וְהָכִי סָתְרִית [לֵיהּ] וּבָנְיִית [לֵיהּ] עֲבַד הָכִי. שְׁלַחוּ לֵיהּ: אִם לֹא סָתַרְתָּה אַל תִּסְתּוֹר, וְאִם סָתַרְתָּה אַל תִּבְנֵי, וְאִם סָתַרְתָּה וּבָנִיתָ, עַבְדֵי בִּישָׁא בָּתַר דְּעָבְדִין מִתְמַלְּכִין, אִם זַיְינָךְ עֲלָךְ סִפְרָךְ כָּאן, לָא רֵכָא וְלָא בַּר רֵכָא, הוֹרְדוֹס [עַבְדָּא] קַלְנְיָא מִתְעֲבֵיד. מַאי רֵכָא? מַלְכוּתָא, דִּכְתִיב: °"אָנֹכִי הַיּוֹם רַךְ וּמָשׁוּחַ מֶלֶךְ". וְאִי בָּעֵית אֵימָא, מֵהָכָא: °"וַיִּקְרְאוּ לְפָנָיו אַבְרֵךְ". ב) אָמְרִי: מִי שֶׁלֹּא רָאָה בִּנְיַן הוֹרְדוֹס, לֹא רָאָה בִּנְיָן נָאֶה [מִיָּמָיו] בְּמַאי בְּנָיֵיהּ? אָמַר ג) רַבָּה: בְּאַבְנֵי שֵׁישָׁא וּמַרְמָרָא. אִיכָּא דְּאָמְרִי: בְּאַבְנֵי כּוּחְלָא, שֵׁישָׁא וּמַרְמָרָא. אַפֵּיק שָׁפָה וְעַיֵּיל שָׁפָה, כִּי הֵיכִי דְּנִקַבֵּיל סִידָא. סְבַר (ב) לְמִשְׁעֲיֵיהּ בְּדַהֲבָא, אָמְרוּ לֵיהּ רַבָּנַן: שְׁבַקֵיהּ, דְּהָכִי שַׁפִּיר טְפֵי, דְּמִיחֲזֵי כִּי אִידְווֹתָא דְיַמָּא. וּבָבָא בַּר בּוּטָא ד) הֵיכִי עֲבַד הָכִי? וְהָאָמַר רַב יְהוּדָה אָמַר רַב, וְאִיתֵּימָא ר' יְהוֹשֻׁעַ בֶּן לֵוִי: ה) מִפְּנֵי מָה נֶעֱנַשׁ דָּנִיֵּאל? מִפְּנֵי שֶׁהִשִּׂיא עֵצָה לִנְבוּכַדְנֶצַּר, שֶׁנֶּאֱמַר: °"לָהֵן מַלְכָּא מִלְכִּי יִשְׁפַּר עֲלָךְ וַחֲטָאָךְ בְּצִדְקָה פְרוּק וַעֲוָיָתָךְ בְּמִחַן עֲנָיִין הֵן תֶּהֱוֵי אַרְכָּא לִשְׁלֵוְתָךְ" וגו', וּכְתִיב: °"כֹּלָּא מְטָא עַל נְבוּכַדְנֶצַּר מַלְכָּא"; וּכְתִיב: "לִקְצָת יַרְחִין תְּרֵי עֲשַׂר" וגו'! אִיבָּעֵית אֵימָא: שָׁאנֵי עַבְדָּא, דְּאִיחַיַּיב בְּמִצְוֹת. וְאִיבָּעֵית אֵימָא: שָׁאנֵי בֵּית הַמִּקְדָּשׁ, ד) דְּאִי לָא מַלְכוּת לָא מִתְבְּנֵי. וְדָנִיֵּאל מְנָלַן דְּאִיעֲנַשׁ? אִילֵימָא מִשּׁוּם דִּכְתִיב: °"וַתִּקְרָא אֶסְתֵּר לַהֲתָךְ", ה) וְאָמַר רַב: הֲתָךְ — זֶה דָּנִיֵּאל? הָנִיחָא לְמ"ד: שֶׁחֲתָכוּהוּ מִגְּדוּלָּתוֹ, אֶלָּא לְמ"ד: שֶׁכָּל דִּבְרֵי מַלְכוּת נֶחְתָּכִין עַל פִּיו, מַאי אִיכָּא לְמֵימַר? דְּשַׁדְיוּהוּ לְגוֹבָא דְאַרְיָוָותָא.§ "הַכֹּל כְּמִנְהַג הַמְּדִינָה".§ "הַכֹּל" לְאֵתוֹיֵי מַאי? ו) לְאֵתוֹיֵי אַתְרָא דִּנְהִיגֵי בְּהוּצָא וְדַפְנָא.§ "לְפִיכָךְ, אִם נָפַל הַכּוֹתֶל — הַמָּקוֹם וְהָאֲבָנִים שֶׁל שְׁנֵיהֶם".§ פְּשִׁיטָא! לָא צְרִיכָא, ז) דִּנְפַל לִרְשׁוּתָא דְּחַד מִינַּיְיהוּ, אִי נַמִּי ח) דְּפַנִּינְהוּ חַד לִרְשׁוּתָא דִּידֵיהּ; מַהוּ דְּתֵימָא: נֶיהֱוֵי אִידָּךְ הַמּוֹצִיא מֵחֲבֵירוֹ עָלָיו הָרְאָיָה, קמ"ל.§ "וְכֵן בַּגִּינָּה, מָקוֹם שֶׁנָּהֲגוּ לִגְדּוֹר — מְחַיְּיבִין אוֹתוֹ".§ הָא גּוּפָא קַשְׁיָא, אָמְרַתְּ: וְכֵן בַּגִּינָּה, מָקוֹם שֶׁנָּהֲגוּ לִגְדּוֹר — מְחַיְּיבִין אוֹתוֹ, הָא סְתָמָא — אֵין מְחַיְּיבִין אוֹתוֹ; אֵימָא סֵיפָא: אֲבָל בַּבִּקְעָה, מָקוֹם שֶׁנָּהֲגוּ שֶׁלֹּא לִגְדּוֹר — אֵין מְחַיְּיבִין אוֹתוֹ, הָא סְתָמָא — מְחַיְּיבִין אוֹתוֹ; הַשְׁתָּא סְתָם גִּינָּה אָמְרַתְּ לָא, סְתָם בִּקְעָה מִיבַּעְיָא? אָמַר אַבַּיֵּי, ה"ק: וְכֵן סְתָם גִּינָּה, וּבְמָקוֹם שֶׁנָּהֲגוּ לִגְדּוֹר בַּבִּקְעָה — מְחַיְּיבִין אוֹתוֹ. אֲמַר לֵיהּ רָבָא: אִם כֵּן, מַאי "אֲבָל"? אֶלָּא אָמַר רָבָא, ט) הָכִי קָתָנֵי: וְכֵן סְתָם גִּינָּה כְּמָקוֹם שֶׁנָּהֲגוּ לִגְדּוֹר דָּמֵי, וּמְחַיְּיבִין אוֹתוֹ; אֲבָל סְתָם בִּקְעָה כְּמָקוֹם שֶׁלֹּא נָהֲגוּ דָּמֵי, וְאֵין מְחַיְּיבִין אוֹתוֹ.§ "אֶלָּא אִם רָצָה, כּוֹנֵס לְתוֹךְ שֶׁלּוֹ וּבוֹנֶה וְעוֹשֶׂה חָזִית".§ מַאי חָזִית? אָמַר רַב הוּנָא: אַכְפֵּיהּ לֵיהּ לְקַרְנָא לְבַר. וְנַעֲבֵיד מִלְּגָיו! עָבֵיד חַבְרֵיהּ נַמִּי מִלְּבַר, וְאָמַר: דִּידִי וְדִידֵיהּ הוּא. אִי הָכִי, הַשְׁתָּא נַמִּי גָּיֵיז לֵיהּ חַבְרֵיהּ, וְאָמַר: דִּידִי וְדִידֵיהּ הוּא! גִּיזּוּזָא מִידַע יְדִיעַ. אִיכָּא דְּאָמְרִי, אָמַר רַב הוּנָא: מִיכְפָּא לְקַרְנָא מִלְּגָיו. וְנַעֲבַד מִלְּבַר! גָּיֵיז לֵיהּ חַבְרֵיהּ, וְאָמַר: דִּידִי וְדִידֵיהּ הוּא. אִי הָכִי, הַשְׁתָּא נַמִּי לָיֵיף לֵיהּ חַבְרֵיהּ, וְאָמַר: דִּידִי וְדִידֵיהּ הוּא! לִיפּוּפָא מִידַע יְדִיעַ. וְהָא "מִבַּחוּץ" קָתָנֵי! קַשְׁיָא. רַבִּי יוֹחָנָן אָמַר:

נִשְׁעֲיֵיהּ

תורה אור

קהלת י (גם במדעך) · שם (ובחדרי משכבך) · שמות כב (ונשיא בעמך) · קהלת י (כי עוף השמים) · משלי ו · ישעיה ב · במדבר טו · יחזקאל כד · שמואל ב ג · בראשית מא · דניאל ד · שם · אסתר ד

תוספות

שכל דברי מלכות נחתכין על פיו. לפי תרגום [של] אחשורוש ז) נענש הרבה, שנהרג, דכתיב "ויגידו למרדכי את דברי אסתר" ולא כתב התם התך — לפי שהרגו המן, על שהיה משיב דברים בין אסתר למרדכי. ומיהו, גמ' שלנו אין תופס כן, דדרשינן במגילה (דף טו.): והתך להיכן הלך? ומפרש: לפי שאין משיבין על הקלקלה.

הכי קתני וכן בגינה סתם כו'. וסיפא נמי יש לפרש כן: אבל סתם בקעה, ומקום שלא נהגו לגדור בגינה — אין מחייבין אותו.

והא מבחוץ קתני קשיא. ותיובתא אינה, דמלינן למימר: היינו שבולט חוץ לחומה. מ"מ קשיא היא, דא"כ "מחוץ" הוה ליה למיתני.

***גייז** ליה חבריה ושדי ליה. אע"ג דלעיל אמר: גזוזא מידע ידיע, בהולא לא ידיע. (שייך לע"ב)

לאפוקי

רש"י

אהדר ליה כלילא דיילי. "הָאֲנָקָה" מְתַרְגְּמִינַן: יָלָא (ויקרא יא), וְהוּא שֶׁרֶץ שֶׁקּוֹרִין הרלו"ן, וּשְׂעָרוֹ קָשֶׁה כְּמַחְטִין. וְעָשָׂה לוֹ עֲטָרָה מֵעוֹרוֹ סְבִיבוֹת עֵינָיו. **השתא מיהא** [**דאנא ואת**]. אֲנָא וְאַתְּ שָׁנִינוּ כָּאן, וְאֵין שׁוֹמֵעַ. **הנני מחלל את מקדשי.** סֵיפֵיהּ דִּקְרָא "מַחְמַד עֵינֵיכֶם". **מסתפינא ממלכותא.** כְּפוּפִים הָיוּ לְמַלְכוּת רוֹמִיִּים. **מתמלכין** = נוֹטְלִין רְשׁוּת. **אי זיינך עלך ספרך כאן.** אִם נִתְגָּאִיתָ בִּכְלֵי מִלְחַמְתְּךָ, שֶׁהָרַגְתָּ בֵּית אֲדוֹנֶיךָ — סֵפֶר יוֹחֲסִין שֶׁלְּךָ בְּיָדֵינוּ הוּא, [יָדַעְנוּ] שֶׁאַתָּה עֶבֶד. **לא רכא כו'.** = לֹא מֶלֶךְ וְלֹא בֶּן מֶלֶךְ. **קלניא מתעביד.** נַעֲשָׂה בֶּן חוֹרִין מֵאֵלָיו. **שישא.** שַׁיִשׁ יָרוֹק, שֶׁקּוֹרִין ביי"ש. **ומרמרא.** שַׁיִשׁ לָבָן. **כוחלא.** שַׁיִשׁ צָבוּעַ כְּעֵין כָּחוֹל. **אידוותא דימא.** גַּלֵּי הַיָּם, [שֶׁהֵם נָעִים וְנָדִים וְהָעַיִן *מִתְעַשֶּׁשֶׁת בִּרְאִיָּתָן]. **נענש דניאל.** לְקַמֵּיהּ מְפָרֵשׁ עוֹנְשׁוֹ. **מלכי ישפר עלך.** = עֲצָתִי תֵּיטַב בְּעֵינֶיךָ. **במיחן עניין** = בַּחֲנִינַת עֲנִיִּים. **בכן תהא ארכא לשלותך** = [יְהֵא אוֹרֶךְ] לִשְׁלוֹמְךָ. **כולא מטא.** כָּל הַחֲלוֹם שֶׁל פּוּרְעָנוּת בָּא עָלָיו. **לקצת ירחין תרי עשר.** בִּשְׁבִיל עֲצָתוֹ שֶׁל דָּנִיֵּאל תָּלָה לוֹ שְׁנֵים עָשָׂר חֹדֶשׁ. **בהוצא.** לוּלְבֵי דְקָלִים. **ודפנא.** עַנְפֵי עֵץ עַרְמוֹנִים שֶׁקּוֹרִין לו"ר, וּפְרִי שֶׁלּוֹ קוֹרִין ביי"ש. **פשיטא.** דְּהָאֲבָנִים שֶׁל שְׁנֵיהֶם. דַּאֲפִי' לָא פָּסַק לָן דִּינָא דְּמַתְנִי', הַמְּלַמְּדֵנוּ שֶׁמִּתְּחִלָּה בֵּין שְׁנֵיהֶם עֲשָׂאוּהָ — עַל כָּרְחָם הָיוּ חוֹלְקִין בְּשָׁוֶה הָאֲבָנִים, שֶׁהֲרֵי בִּרְשׁוּת שְׁנֵיהֶם מוּנָּחִים, וְיַד מִי מֵהֶם תִּגְבַּר! (הג"ה: בְּפֵי' ר"ח: קמ"ל דְּלָא בָּעֵינַן רְאָיָה, אֶלָּא שׁוּתָּף מַפֵּיק מִינֵּיהּ בְּלֹא רְאָיָה, וְאִיהוּ דְּטָעֵין דְּדִילֵיהּ נִינְהוּ — עָלָיו הָרְאָיָה. וְכָל כה"ג הָכִי דָּיְינִינַן לֵיהּ. וְזֶה הַדִּין מְפוֹרָשׁ עוֹד כְּמוֹ כֵן בְּפֶרֶק "הַבַּיִת וְהָעֲלִיָּיה" בִּתְחִילָּתוֹ. אִיבָּעֵית אֵימָא: בְּשׁוּתָּפִין כִּי הַאי גַּוְונָא, אַנּוּחֵי אֲבָנִים בִּרְשׁוּת חֲבֵירוֹ לָא קָפְדִי, וַחֲזָקַת רְשׁוּת לָאו כְּלוּם הוּא. שָׁמְעִינַן מִינַּהּ דְּכָל כְּהַאי גַּוְונָא דְּמִילְּתָא דִּידִיעָא בְּשׁוּתָּפָא לְתַרְוַיְיהוּ, אע"ג דְּמַנְחֵי בִּרְשׁוּתָא דְּחַד מִינַּיְיהוּ — לָא יָכוֹל לְמִיטְעַן "דִּידִי נִינְהוּ דְּבִרְשׁוּתִי מַנְחֵי", דְּקיי"ל: שׁוּתָּפִין לָא קָפְדִי אַהֲדָדֵי. ע"כ). **השתא** סְתָם גִּינָּה **אמרת לא.** אע"פ שֶׁהֶיזֵּק רְאִיָּיה קָשֶׁה. **אמר אביי כו'.** הַאי "מָקוֹם שֶׁנָּהֲגוּ לִגְדּוֹר" דְּקָתָנֵי מַתְנִי' — אַבִּקְעָה קָאֵי. **א"כ מאי אבל** בַּבִּקְעָה. הָא מִינַּהּ סָלֵיק, וְהָכִי אִיבָּעֵי (ג) לְמִיתְנֵי: אֲבָל מָקוֹם שֶׁנָּהֲגוּ שֶׁלֹּא לִגְדּוֹר — אֵין מְחַיְּיבִין אוֹתוֹ! **מכפייה לקרנא** לְבַר. רָאשֵׁי הַכּוֹתֶל יָכוֹף לְצַד חֲבֵירוֹ. וְכָל חָזִית לְשׁוֹן קָצֶה הוּא, וְכֵן שָׁנִינוּ בְּ"תָמִיד" (פ"ב מ"ד) גַּבֵּי מַעֲרָכָה: וַחֲזִיתָהּ מִזְרָחָה — רָאשֵׁי הַגְּזִירִין, וְכֵן "מֶחֱזֶה מוּל מֶחֱזֶה" דִּמְלָכִים (א ז) — רָאשֵׁי הַנְּסָרִים מוּסָבִּין זֶה מוּל זֶה ו) וְעָבֵי' מֵהַבְרַאי כּוֹפֶה לְצַד רָאשֵׁי הַכּוֹתֶל, שֶׁמְּחַבֵּר בְּרֹאשׁוֹ אֲבָנִים וָטִיט וּמְעַבֵּהוּ. **דידי ודידיה הוא.** כִּדְקָתָנֵי מַתְנִיתִין: כְּשֶׁעוֹשִׂין אוֹתוֹ בֵּין שְׁנֵיהֶם עוֹשִׂין חָזִית מִכָּאן וּמִכָּאן. **השתא** נַמִּי גָּיֵיז לָהּ. לְהַהִיא כְּפוּפָה שֶׁהָיָה לְצִדּוֹ, וְאֵימָא: דִּידִי וְדִידֵיהּ הוּא, וְלֹא עָשִׂינוּ חָזִית! **מלגיו.** לְצַד שֶׁלּוֹ. **ולקמיה פריך:** הָא מִבַּחוּץ קָתָנֵי! **לייף ליה.** מְחַבֵּר חָזִית אַחֶרֶת לְצִדּוֹ.

נִשְׁעֲיֵיהּ

רבינו גרשום

כלילא דיילי. כתר של מיני האנקה שהן עלוקות נתן סביב ראשו וניקרו עיניו: כי נר מצוה ותורה אור. אלו תלמידי חכמים שעוסקין בתורה אלו סנהדרין: ממלכותא. זו מלכות רומאי שהיה משועבד להם: שלחו ליה. ממלכות רומיים אם זיינך עלך ספרך כאן כלומר אם מלחמתך עליך שאתה מתגבר לשם ייחוסך כאן שיודעין אנו מאיזה משפחה אתה לפי שהורקנוס אביו של הורדוס פעם אחת הלך על הרומים להלחם ונצח וראה בשביה שפחה אחת יפת תואר וחמדה ועשה לה כדין תורה ובא עליה והוליד ממנה אותו הורדוס ולפיכך היו מחרפין אותו מיחוסו: קלניא. בן חורין נעשה: שישא. שיש לבן: ומרמרא. מנומרין: כוחלא. שחורין: כאדוותא דימא. כגלי הים שזו יורדת וזו עולה: שאני עבד משום דהוי שייך במצות עשה (שהזמן) [שאין הזמן] גרמא והורדוס עבד היה: בהוצא ודפנא. שנוהגין לעשות גדר מכפות תמרים ודפנא עץ של (עור) [ערמון] שקורין לו"ר וכיון דנתרצו לעשות כותל על זה ועל זה לעכב שלא יעשו אלא כמנהג המדינה: קמ"ל. כיון דזה נותן מחצה וזה נותן מחצה אין צריך להביא ראיה: **פיסקא** וכן בגינה מקום שנהגו לגדור בגויל או בגזית וחבירו מעכב היו כופין אותו משום דאיכא היזק ראיה כדאוקימנא [לעיל ג:] בגינה הסמוכה לעיר אבל בבקעה של שדות כו': הא סתמא. דיש שגודרין ויש שאין גודרין: השתא סתם גינה. דאיכא היזק ראיה אמרת לא דאין מחייבין סתם בקעה דליכא היזק ראיה מחייב: אמר אביי ה"ק. כלומר כגון חסורא מיחסרא וכן גינה סתם משום דאיכא היזק ראיה ובמקום שנהגו לגדור בבקעה מחייבין אותו: א"ל רבא. לאביי אי הכי כדקא תרצת א"כ מאי אבל דקתני במתני' אבל בבקעה אי אמרת בשלמא דרישא לא איירי בדינא דבקעה כלל היינו דקתני בסיפא אבל בבקעה דעד השתא לא איירי בדינא דבקעה אלא לדעתך דתרצת דרישא איירי בבקעה מאי אבל בבקעה תו דתני בסיפא: אלא אמר רבא. אנא מתריצנא דלא תקשי אבל ולא תקשי סתמא דרישא לסתמא דסיפא וה"ק וכן בגינה סתם דינא דגינה סתם כדינא דמקום שנהגו לגדור בבקעה דמחייבין לגדור ועדיין לא שמעי' דינא דסתם בקעה ואמטו להכי צריך למתני בסיפא אבל בבקעה לאשמעינן דינא דסתם בקעה דכמקום שנהגו שלא לגדור דמי דאין מחייבין לגדור דהשתא מיתרצא כולה מתני': ועושה לכותל חזית. סימן היכרא שידעו בני אדם שזה בנאו כולו בקרקע שלו משלו לפיכך כיון דעשה חזית אם נפל הכותל כו': דכייף ליה קרנא מלבר. דלשקע בראש הכותל בסופו קנים בטיט ויכוף ראשם של קנים מבחוץ לצד הכותל לצד אויר חבירו: אזיל אידך חבירו וכייף ליה נמי מלבר לצד שלו ואמר הרי אית לי נמי חזית ודידי ודידך הוא הכותל ומקומו הלכך לא כייף אלא מלבר: אכתי אתי האי וגייז להחיא חזית שהוא (פצע) [לצד] שלו ואמר דידי ודידך הוא: השתא נמי לייף ליה. כלומר יחברם לכותל בטיט בלא שקיעה: מידע ידיע. יכולין להבין ולהבחין בין דבוקה לשקיעה: והא מבחוץ קתני. ועושה לו חזית מבחוץ קשיא להך לישנא דאיכא דאמרי: ור' יוחנן אמר. היינו חזית:

עין משפט נר מצוה

טז א ב ג מיי' פכ"ו מהל' סנהדרין הל' א סמג לאוין רט:

יז ד ה מיי' פי"ב מהל' רוצח הלכה טו:

יח ו מיי' פ"ב מהל' שכנים הל' טו סמג עשין פב טוש"ע ח"מ סי' קנז סעיף ד:

יט ז ח מיי' שם הלכה יח טוש"ע שם סעיף ה:

כ ט מיי' שם הלכ' יז סמג שם טוש"ע ח"מ סי' קנח סעיף א:

הגהות הב"ח

(א) גמ' א"ל מסתפינא איכא איניש דשמע מלתא ואזיל ומודע ליה א"ל השתא מיהא ליכא איניש גבן דאזיל ולימא ליה: (ב) שם סבר למחפייה בדהבא: (ג) רש"י ד"ה א"כ מאי וכו' איבעי ליה למיתנא:

כ א מיי' פ"ב מהל' שכנים הלכה טז טוש"ע ח"מ סי' קנז סעיף ז:

כא א ב ג ד מיי' פ"ג מהל' שכנים הל' ג סמג עשין פב טוש"ע ח"מ סי' קנח סעיף ו:

לאפוקי מדאביי. ואביי סבר דשפיר אית ליה למיתני תקנתא לרמאי. **אם** עמד וגדר את הרביעית. ל"ג "אם עמד ניקף", דהא לכולהו לישני דתלמוד קאי אמקיף, בר מלישנא בתרא דקאמר: מקיף וניקף איכא בינייהו. והא דדייק בפרק "כילד הרגל" (ב"ק דף כ: ושם): טעמא דניקף, הא מקיף פטור — היינו להאי לישנא. **דמי** קנים בזול. וא"ת: מאי שנא משדה שאינה עשויה ליטע, דאם נטעה חבירו שלא ברשות, אמר רב ושמואל ב"השואל" (ב"מ דף קא.): שמין לו וידו על התחתונה? ואור"י: דשאני הכא, דמצי א"ל: לדידי סגי לי בנטירא בר זוזא. ומ"מ, דמי קנים בזול יהיב ליה, דאנן סהדי דאם היה מוצא כ"כ בזול — היה גודר בהם. **שניה** ושלישית לא. אומר ר"י דהיינו טעמא: דאין לך אדם שלא היה מסייע לרביעית ע"מ שיהא גדור מד' רוחותיו. ובקונטרס פירש: לפי שכבר יצא מן השלשה מב"ד זכאי. הג"ה: וקצת קשה, דא"כ גם ברביעית יצא זכאי עד טפח אחרון. ע"כ. **ורבי** יוסי סבר אם עמד ניקף וגדר את הרביעית. אע"ג דעד השתא היה מחמיר, כדמשמע לישנא ד"מגלגלין עליו את הכל" — להך לישנא לא הוי הכי, דלשון "אם עמד" — משמע ניקף.

הגה"ה

נִשְׁעֲיֵיהּ בְּאַמְּתָא מִלְּבַר. יְהֵא טָח בְּטִיט אַמָּה בְּרֹאשׁ הַכּוֹתֶל מִבַּחוּץ. וּמְקַפֵּל לֵיהּ. (ד) מְקַפְּלוֹ. הוּצָא. אִם עָשׂוּ מְחִיצַת נְסָרִים, כֵּיצַד יַעֲשׂוּ חֲזִית? סִינוּפֵי ד) יְרִיכֵי לְבַר. רָאשֵׁי הַהוּצִים *יָשֵׁב לְצַד שְׂדֵה חֲבֵירוֹ, וּכְשֶׁיִּהְיֶה סוֹנֵף הַהוּצִים כְּשֶׁיִּכְלֶה הָאֶחָד וְיִתֵּן אֶת חֲבֵירוֹ — יְסַנְּפֶנּוּ מִבַּחוּץ. הג"ה: יְרִיכֵי — כִּדְאָמְרִי' לְעֵיל: טֶפַח יְתֵירָא לְבֵינֵי (ה) אוּרְבֵּי. תמ"ש. וְר"ח פֵּי': מוֹלִיא רָאשֵׁי הַקָּנִים, וְדַפְנָא (ו) שֶׁהוּא הַקָּנִים הָעוֹמְדִים לְחִיזּוּק הַמְּחִיצָּה, לַחוּץ. מִתּוֹךְ פֵּירוּשׁוֹ מַשְׁמַע שֶׁהַקָּנִים שֶׁמַּעֲמִידִין מִן הַצַּד לִסְמוֹךְ הַכּוֹתֶל, וְזֶהוּ לְשׁוֹן סְנִיפִין, ע"כ. **אֶלָּא בִּשְׁטָרָא.** אִם עָשָׂה הָאֶחָד — יָבִיא עֵדִים וְיַחְתְּמוּ לוֹ, וְאִם (ז) עָשָׂהוּ שְׁנֵיִם — יָעִידוּ עֵדִים וְיַחְתְּמוּ. דס"ל: קוּפְלָא דְּטִינָא מֵעִילּוּיֵהּ הוּצָא לָא יְדִיעַ. **וְלֹא יַעֲשׂוּ.** חֲזִית לֹא לָזֶה וְלֹא לָזֶה, וַהֲרֵי סִימָן שֶׁלֹּא עֲשָׂאָהּ הָאֶחָד בְּשֶׁלּוֹ, שֶׁאִילּוּ עֲשָׂאָהּ — הָיָה עוֹשֶׂה חֲזִית מִבַּחוּץ! **וְעָבֵיד דִּידֵיהּ.** עָשָׂה חֲזִית מִבַּחוּץ. **וְתַקַּנְתָּא לְרַמַּאי.** בִּתְמִיָּה: וְכִי מִפְּנֵי דַּאֲגַת רַמָּאִין אִיכְפַּל תַּנָּא לְמִיתְנֵי הָא מַתְנִי'? **וְרֵישָׁא.** דְּקָתָנֵי: וְעוֹשֶׂה חֲזִית מִבַּחוּץ — לָאו תַּקַּנְתָּא מִשּׁוּם רַמַּאי הוּא, דְּלָא לֵימָא חַבְרֵיהּ "שֶׁל שְׁנֵינוּ הוּא"? **תְּנָא דִּינָא.** הוֹאִיל וּבִקְעָה אֵין מִנְהָג לִגְדּוֹר — אֵין יָכוֹל לְכוֹפוֹ, אֶלָּא כּוֹנֵס לְתוֹךְ שֶׁלּוֹ וּבוֹנֶה. וְאַיְּידֵי דִּתְנָא דִּינָא — תְּנָא תַּקַּנְתָּא: וְעוֹשֶׂה חֲזִית מִשּׁוּם רַמַּאי. אֶלָּא סֵיפָא דִּינָא לָא תְּנָא, דְּהָא פְּשִׁיטָא דְּאִם עָשׂוּ מִדַּעַת שְׁנֵיהֶם — תֵּעָשֶׂה מִשֶּׁל שְׁנֵיהֶם, וְכוּלָּהּ מִשּׁוּם תַּקַּנְתָּא הוּא דְּתַנְיָיהּ. **מַתְנִי'** הַמַּקִּיף אֶת חֲבֵירוֹ מִשָּׁלֹשׁ רוּחוֹתָיו. שֶׁקָּנָה ג' שָׂדוֹת סְבִיב שְׂדֵה חֲבֵירוֹ לִשְׁלֹשֶׁת מְצָרֶיהָ, וְגָדַר אֶת שְׁלָשְׁתָּן, וְנִמְצָא שָׂדֵהוּ שֶׁל אֶמְצָעִי זֶה מוּקָּף מִשָּׁלֹשׁ רוּחוֹתָיו. אֵין מְחַיְּיבִין אוֹתוֹ. לָתֵת כְּלוּם, כִּדְאָמְרִי' דִּסְתַם בִּקְעָה מָקוֹם שֶׁנָּהֲגוּ שֶׁלֹּא לִגְדּוֹר הוּא. הג"ה, תמ"ש: וְל"נ טַעֲמָא — מִשּׁוּם דְּהַשְׁתָּא לָא מְהַנֵּי לֵיהּ מִידֵי, שֶׁהַכֹּל יְכוֹלִים לִיכָּנֵס מֵרוּחַ רְבִיעִית, אֲבָל אִם גָּדַר רְבִיעִית — מְחַיְּיבִין אוֹתוֹ, כִּדְאָמְרִינַן בַּגְּמָ'. וְאע"ג דְּאָמְרִינַן לְעֵיל דִּסְתַם בִּקְעָה מָקוֹם שֶׁנָּהֲגוּ שֶׁלֹּא לִגְדּוֹר הוּא — ה"מ בֵּין בִּקְעָה לְבִקְעָה, וְכוֹתֶל גָּבוֹהַּ ד' אַמּוֹת לְשֵׁם הוּא דְּלָא בָּעֵינַן. (ח) מ"ט — דְּלֵיכָּא הֶיזֵּק רְאִיָּה. אֲבָל בִּשְׁבִיל הֶיזֵּק בְּהֵמוֹת שֶׁלֹּא יִכָּנְסוּ לַשָּׂדֶה צָרִיךְ לִגְדּוֹר גָּדֵר שֶׁלּוֹ עֲשָׂרָה טְפָחִים, הַמּוֹנֵעַ מִלִּיכָּנֵס הַבְּהֵמוֹת. ה"ג: ר' יוֹסֵי אוֹמֵר אִם עָמַד וְגָדַר אֶת הָרְבִיעִית. ה) וְלָא גָּרְסִי' "נִיקָּף". הג"ה: וְכֵן בְּפֵירוּשׁ ר"ח. וּמִיהוּ אַנִּיקָּף מְפָרְשִׁינַן לַהּ לְקַמָּן. תּוֹסָ': וְהָכִי מוּכַח בְּפ"ב דְּב"ק, וְהַלָּשׁוֹן מוֹכִיחַ, דְּקָתָנֵי "אִם עָמַד", וְלָא קָתָנֵי "אִם גָּדַר" — מִכְּלָל דְּלָאו בְּהַהוּא

[א] נִשְׁעֲיֵיהּ בְּאַמְּתָא מִלְּבַר. וְנֶיעֱבַד מִלְּגָיו! עָבֵיד חַבְרֵיהּ מִלְּבַר, וְאָמַר: דִּידִי וְדִידֵיהּ הוּא. אִי הָכִי, הַשְׁתָּא נַמִּי דְּקָפֵיל לֵיהּ חַבְרֵיהּ, וְאָמַר: דִּידִי וְדִידֵיהּ הוּא! א) קִילּוּפָא מֵידַע יְדִיעַ. הוּצָא — אֲמַר רַב נַחְמָן: סִינוּפֵי ב) יְרִיכֵי מִלְּבַר. וְנֶיעֱבַד מִלְּגָיו! עָבֵיד נַמִּי חַבְרֵיהּ מִלְּבַר, וְאָמַר: דִּידִי וְדִידֵיהּ הוּא. אִי הָכִי, הַשְׁתָּא נַמִּי גָּיֵיז וְשָׁדֵי לֵיהּ, וְאָמַר: דִּידִי וְדִידֵיהּ הוּא! מַשְׁרִיק לֵיהּ טִינָא. הַשְׁתָּא נַמִּי אָתֵי חַבְרֵיהּ וְקָלֵיף לֵיהּ! קִילּוּפָא מֵידַע יְדִיעַ. אַבַּיֵּי אֲמַר: הוּצָא לֵית לֵיהּ תַּקַּנְתָּא אֶלָּא בִּשְׁטָרָא.§ "אֲבָל אִם עָשׂוּ מִדַּעַת שְׁנֵיהֶם". § אֲמַר לֵיהּ רָבָא מִפַּרְזִיקָא לְרַב אַשִׁי: לֹא יַעֲשׂוּ לֹא זֶה וְלֹא זֶה! א"ל: לָא צְרִיכָא, דְּקָדֵים חַד מִנַּיְיהוּ וַעֲבַד דִּידֵיהּ, וְאִי לָא עָבֵיד חַבְרֵיהּ — אָמַר: דִּידֵיהּ הוּא. (א) וְתָנָא, תַּקַּנְתָּא לְרַמַּאי קמ"ל? א"ל: וְרֵישָׁא לָאו תַּקַּנְתָּא לְרַמַּאי הוּא? א"ל: בִּשְׁלָמָא רֵישָׁא תְּנָא דִּינָא, וּמִשּׁוּם דִּינָא תְּנָא תַּקַּנְתָּא, אֶלָּא סֵיפָא דִּינָא קָתָנֵי, דְּקָתָנֵי תַּקַּנְתָּא? אֲמַר רָבִינָא: הָכָא בְּהוּצֵי עָסְקִינַן, לְאַפּוּקֵי מִדְּאַבַּיֵּי דַּאֲמַר: הוּצָא לֵית לֵיהּ תַּקַּנְתָּא אֶלָּא בִּשְׁטָרָא, קמ"ל דִּבְחָזִית סַגְיָא.§ **מתני'** ג)א הַמַּקִּיף אֶת חֲבֵירוֹ מִשְּׁלֹשׁ רוּחוֹתָיו, וְגָדַר אֶת הָרִאשׁוֹנָה וְאֶת הַשְּׁנִיָּה וְאֶת הַשְּׁלִישִׁית — אֵין מְחַיְּיבִין אוֹתוֹ; רַבִּי יוֹסֵי אוֹמֵר: באִם עָמַד וְגָדַר אֶת הָרְבִיעִית — מְגַלְגְּלִין עָלָיו אֶת הַכֹּל.§ **גמ'** אָמַר רַב יְהוּדָה אָמַר שְׁמוּאֵל: הֲלָכָה כְּר' יוֹסֵי, דְּאָמַר: אִם עָמַד וְגָדַר אֶת הָרְבִיעִית — מְגַלְגְּלִין עָלָיו אֶת הַכֹּל, גל"ש עָמַד נִיקָּף, ל"ש עָמַד מַקִּיף. אִיתְּמַר, רַב הוּנָא אָמַר: דהַכֹּל — לְפִי מַה שֶּׁגָּדַר; חִיָּיא בַּר רַב אָמַר: הַכֹּל — לְפִי דְּמֵי קָנִים בְּזוֹל. תְּנַן: הַמַּקִּיף אֶת חֲבֵירוֹ מִשְּׁלֹשׁ רוּחוֹתָיו, וְגָדַר אֶת הָרִאשׁוֹנָה וְאֶת הַשְּׁנִיָּה וְאֶת הַשְּׁלִישִׁית — אֵין מְחַיְּיבִין אוֹתוֹ; הָא רְבִיעִית — מְחַיְּיבִין אוֹתוֹ. אֵימָא סֵיפָא, רַבִּי יוֹסֵי אוֹמֵר: אִם עָמַד וְגָדַר אֶת הָרְבִיעִית — מְגַלְגְּלִין עָלָיו אֶת הַכֹּל; בִּשְׁלָמָא לְרַב הוּנָא דְּאָמַר: הַכֹּל לְפִי מַה שֶּׁגָּדַר בָּהּ, הַיְינוּ דְּאִיכָּא בֵּין ת"ק (ג) וְרַבִּי יוֹסֵי, ת"ק סָבַר: הַכֹּל לְפִי דְּמֵי קָנִים בְּזוֹל אִין, וּמַה שֶּׁגָּדַר לָא, וְרַבִּי יוֹסֵי סָבַר: הַכֹּל לְפִי מַה שֶּׁגָּדַר; אֶלָּא לְחִיָּיא בַּר רַב דְּאָמַר: הַכֹּל לְפִי דְּמֵי קָנִים בְּזוֹל, מַאי אִיכָּא בֵּין ת"ק לְר' יוֹסֵי? אִי דְּמֵי קָנִים בְּזוֹל לָא קָיָהֵיב לֵיהּ, מַאי קָיָהֵיב לֵיהּ? אִי בָּעֵית אֵימָא: אֲגַר נְטִירָא אִיכָּא בֵּינַיְיהוּ, תַּנָּא קַמָּא סָבַר: אֲגַר נְטִירָא אִין, דְּמֵי קָנִים בְּזוֹל לָא, וְרַבִּי יוֹסֵי סָבַר: דְּמֵי קָנִים בְּזוֹל. וְאִי בָּעֵית אֵימָא: רִאשׁוֹנָה שְׁנִיָּה וּשְׁלִישִׁית אִיכָּא בֵּינַיְיהוּ, ת"ק סָבַר: רְבִיעִית הוּא דְּיָהֵיב לֵיהּ, אֲבָל רִאשׁוֹנָה שְׁנִיָּה וּשְׁלִישִׁית — לָא יָהֵיב לֵיהּ, וְר' יוֹסֵי סָבַר: רִאשׁוֹנָה שְׁנִיָּה וּשְׁלִישִׁית נַמִּי יָהֵיב לֵיהּ. אִיבָּעֵית אֵימָא: מַקִּיף וְנִיקָּף אִיכָּא בֵּינַיְיהוּ, דְּת"ק סוֹבֵר: טַעְמָא דְּעָמַד נִיקָּף (ג) דִּמְגַלְגְּלִין עָלָיו אֶת הַכֹּל, אֲבָל עָמַד מַקִּיף — אֵינוֹ נוֹתֵן לוֹ אֶלָּא דְּמֵי רְבִיעִית; וְרַבִּי יוֹסֵי סָבַר: ל"ש נִיקָּף וְל"ש מַקִּיף, אִם עָמַד וְגָדַר — מְגַלְגְּלִין עָלָיו אֶת הַכֹּל. לִישָּׁנָא אַחֲרִינָא: מַקִּיף וְנִיקָּף אִיכָּא בֵּינַיְיהוּ, ת"ק סָבַר: אִם גָּדַר מַקִּיף אֶת הָרְבִיעִית נַמִּי יָהֵיב לֵיהּ, וְרַבִּי יוֹסֵי סָבַר: אִם עָמַד נִיקָּף וְגָדַר אֶת הָרְבִיעִית הוּא דְּיָהֵיב לֵיהּ, דְּגַלֵּי דַּעְתֵּיהּ דְּנִיחָא לֵיהּ, אֲבָל אִם גָּדַר מַקִּיף — לָא יָהֵיב לֵיהּ מִידֵי.
רוֹנְיָא

דְּגָדַר הַשָּׁלֹשׁ מַיְירֵי. ת' מו' שְׁמ', ע"כ. מְגַלְגְּלִין עָלָיו אֶת הַכֹּל. לָתֵת חֶלְקוֹ בִּשְׁלֹשֶׁת הָרִאשׁוֹנוֹת. דְּכֵיוָן דְּגָדַר אֶת הַצַּד הַפָּתוּחַ — גַּלֵּי דַּעְתֵּיהּ דְּנִיחָא לֵיהּ בְּמַאי דְּגָדַר חַבְרֵיהּ. **גמ'** לְפִי מַה שֶּׁגָּדַר. בְּכָל יְצִיאוֹת שֶׁהוֹצִיא בָּהֶן הָרִאשׁוֹן — יַחֲזִיר לוֹ מֶחֱצָה. דְּמֵי קָנִים. דְּאָמַר לֵיהּ: לְדִידִי סַגֵּי לִי בְּגֶדֶר קָנִים, וְאִי אֶפְשִׁי בְּהוֹצָאָה שֶׁל גֶּדֶר אֲבָנִים. ה"ג: תְּנַן הַמַּקִּיף אֶת חֲבֵירוֹ מג' רוּחוֹתָיו אֵין מְחַיְּיבִין אוֹתוֹ הָא רְבִיעִית מְחַיְּיבִין אוֹתוֹ אֵימָא סֵיפָא ר' יוֹסֵי אוֹמֵר כו' וְגָדַר אֶת הָרִאשׁוֹנָה כו' אֵין מְחַיְּיבִין אוֹתוֹ. דְּהָא לָא אַהֲנֵי לֵיהּ מִידֵי, שֶׁהֲרֵי גָּלוּי הוּא מִצַּד רְבִיעִית. הָא אִם גָּדַר עוֹד מַקִּיף אֶת הָרְבִיעִית — מְחַיְּיבִין אוֹתוֹ, דְּאַהֲנֵי לֵיהּ. **אֵימָא סֵיפָא** רַבִּי יוֹסֵי אוֹמֵר. בִּשְׁלָמָא לְרַב הוּנָא דְּאָמַר: "הַכֹּל" דְּר' יוֹסֵי כְּמָה שֶׁגָּדַר הוּא — הַיְינוּ דְּאִיכָּא בֵּין ת"ק לְר' יוֹסֵי; דְּת"ק דְּלָא נָקַט לִישָּׁנָא דְּ"הַכֹּל" סָבַר דְּמֵי קָנִים בְּזוֹל הוּא דִּמְחַיְּיבִין אוֹתוֹ, וְר' יוֹסֵי סָבַר כו'. דְּהָא לֵיכָּא לְמֵימַר דְּת"ק דַּוְקָא אִם גָּדַר מַקִּיף אֶת הָרְבִיעִית הוּא דִּמְחַיְּיבִין אוֹתוֹ, אֲבָל אִם גָּדַר נִיקָּף לֹא — דְּכ"ש הוּא: הַשְׁתָּא הֵיכָא דְּלָא גַּלֵּי דַּעְתֵּיהּ דְּנִיחָא לֵיהּ בְּהֶיקֵּיפָא קָא מְחַיֵּיב לֵיהּ, כ"ש הֵיכָא דְּגַלֵּי. וּלְר' יוֹסֵי נַמִּי, קס"ד הַשְׁתָּא דְּתָנָא נִיקָּף וְה"ה לְמַקִּיף, אֶלָּא בְּגִלְגּוּל דְּהַכֹּל הוּא דִּפְלִיגֵי. אֶלָּא לְת"ק דְּמֵי קָנִים נַמִּי לָא יָהֵיב לֵיהּ אֶלָּא מַאי יָהֵיב לֵיהּ. מַאי מְחַיְּיבִין אוֹתוֹ דְּדַיְיקִינַן מִמִּילְּתֵיהּ? יָהֵב לֵיהּ אֲגַר נְטִירָא. דָּבָר מוּעָט שֶׁהָיָה צָרִיךְ לִיתֵּן לַשּׁוֹמֵר בְּכָל שָׁנָה כְּשֶׁהִיא בְּקָמוֹתֶיהָ. דְּתַנָּא קַמָּא סָבַר. דְּמֵי רְבִיעִית יָהֵיב לֵיהּ אִם גְּדָרָהּ מַקִּיף. אֲבָל דְּמֵי הָרִאשׁוֹנוֹת לָא יָהֵיב לֵיהּ, שֶׁכְּבָר יָצָא מֵהֶם זַכַּאי בְּבֵית דִּין, שֶׁהָיוּ שָׁם יָמִים רַבִּים וְלֹא הוֹעִילוּ לוֹ. וְאִם גְּדָרָהּ נִיקָּף לָרְבִיעִית — לָא יָהֵיב לֵיהּ מִידֵי, כִּדְפֵירַ', שֶׁכְּבָר יָצָא יְדֵי בֵּית דִּין מֵהֶם. וּלְר' יוֹסֵי, לָא שְׁנָא גְּדָרָהּ נִיקָּף וְלָא שְׁנָא מַקִּיף — מְגַלְגְּלִין עָלָיו (ט) אֶת הַכֹּל בְּכוּלָּן דְּמֵי קָנִים. **וְאִיבָּעֵית אֵימָא מַקִּיף וְנִיקָּף אִיכָּא בֵּינַיְיהוּ.** דְּתַנָּא קַמָּא אִית לֵיהּ כְּרַבִּי יוֹסֵי הֵיכָא דִּגְדָרָהּ נִיקָּף, אֲבָל רַבִּי יוֹסֵי לֵית לֵיהּ דְּתַנָּא קַמָּא בְּגָדַר מַקִּיף. תַּנָּא קַמָּא סָבַר: לָא שְׁנָא נִיקָּף וְלָא שְׁנָא מַקִּיף, כִּי גָּדַר לָרְבִיעִית — מְחַיְּיבִין אוֹתוֹ, דְּהָא תַּנָּא קַמָּא בְּמַקִּיף אַיְירֵי, וְדַיְיקִינַן מִמִּילְּתֵיהּ: הָא רְבִיעִית — מְחַיְּיבִין אוֹתוֹ. וְכָל שֶׁכֵּן כְּשֶׁגְּדָרָהּ נִיקָּף, דְּגַלֵּי דַּעְתֵּיהּ. וְרַבִּי

רבינו גרשום

נשעייה עליה אמה מלבר. שאמה העליונה מייסד אותה בסיד על פני כולה לאורך הכותל מבחוץ לצד חבירו: קפיל ליה. שיבא חבירו בסתר ומקליף אותו הסיד: מידע ידיע. מקום הקילוף ולא יועיל לו: כל הני דאמרן היינו בכותל של אבנים אבל [אם] אותו כותל מקני הוצא הוא מאי חזית מצי למקבע ביה דסניף ליה ריבי מלבר דלכי גדיל להו להוצא ליכוון דליהוי רישייהו דהוצא כייפי לבר לאותו צד של חבירו (שדין) [ושריק] ליה טינא דלא מצי חבירו לגוזו להו (ולא למישדינהו) [ולמישדינהו] דאיכא היכרא ומקשינן אפ"ה אתי חבריה (ומקבל) [ומקפל] לההוא טינא ושדי ליה ואמר דידי ודידך הוא (וישנו) [ומשני] קילופא מידע ידיע: אביי אמר. בשום ענין לכותל הוצין אין לו תקנה לעשות שום היכר שיהא כולו שלו שחבירו לא יכול לרמותו אלא בשטרא אא"כ יכתבו לו שטר שכולו שלו ואין לחבירו בו כלום: ואם עשו מדעת שניהם. כותל בבקעה בונין אותו שניהן בשותפות ועושין חזית מכאן ומכאן להיכרא שהכותל של שניהם הוא: ולא יעשה חזית לא זה ולא זה. וממילא ידעינן דשל שניהם הוא דכיון דלאחד אין לו חזקה בו יותר מחבירו לא יוכל לטוענו דכולו שלו הוא: לא צריכא. דאקדים חד ועביד חזית מצד שלו להכי צריך למעבד אידך: אמר לו וכי תנא דמתני' לא אתי לאשמועינן בהא סיפא אלא תקנתא דרמאי. בשלמא רישא תנא דינא ותנא תקנתא. תנא אם רוצה כונס בתוך שלו דאף על גב דחבירו אינו רוצה שימעט לו באויר אינו יכול לעכב עליו היינו דינא ואגב דאיצטריך למיתני דינא תנא נמי תקנתא אבל סיפא לא אית ביה דינא כלל דהא דקתני מתני' אבל אם עשו מדעת שניהם בונין את הכותל באמצע לאו דינא הוא דמדעתייהו עבדי: רבינא אמר בהוצא עסקינן כו'. כלומר אפי' סיפא לא אתי לאורויי תקנתא כלל לרמאי אלא לאורויי אכותל דהוצא לאפוקי מדאביי דאמר לית ליה תקנתא אלא בשטרא קמ"ל דבחזית סגי בלא שטרא: **מתני'** המקיף את חבירו מג' רוחותיו.

כגון שהיו לו למקיף ד' שדות א' מכאן וא' מכאן לשדה של אדם אחר שהיה באמצעיתן של אותן שדות ורצה בעל אותן ד' שדות לגדור שדותיו וגדר את הא' ואת הב' ואת ג' ומאותן גדרים של אותן שדות לא היתה משתמרת שדהו של זה הואיל שלא גדר שדה רביעית אין מחייבין הניקף ליתן חלקו

א) [גי' הערוך ערך קפל ג' קיפולא]: ב) נ"א ריבי. רש"ל: ג) ב"ק כ: ד) נ"א ריכי. רש"ל: ה) כך ול"ג ניקף אינו מפירש"י רק שייך בהג"ה. רש"ל:

רבינו גרשום

המגיעו באותן ג' גדרים הואיל ועדיין אינו משומר שדהו שעדיין פתוח מרוח א': ר' יוסי אומר אם עמד מקיף וגדר שדה רביעית מגלגלין לו את הכל לניקף ליתן בכל אותן ג' גדרים לפי חלקו המגיעו דעכשיו שדהו משתמרת בכל צד: גמ' הכל כמה שגדר. כלומר אם זה המקיף גדר שדותיו בכותל יפה של אבנים חייב ליתן לו זה הניקף לפי חלקו במה שהוציא זה על אותן גדרים ואין יכול לטעון לדידי סגי לי בכותל רעוע של מחיצת קנים: הכל לפי דמי קנים. כלומר חייא בר רב אמר מצי לטעון ליה לא יהיב ליה אלא דמי קנים בזול כמו שאם שם היו גדרים של קנים: בשלמא לרב הונא דאמר במה שגדר היינו דאיכא בין ת"ק ור' יוסי. דדייק הכי הא רביעית לת"ק מחייבין אותו דמי קנים בזול ואתי ר' יוסי למימר לחלוק על ת"ק ואמר את אמרת דמי קנים בזול ואנא אמינא מחייבין אותו במה שגדר כעין שהוציא: אלא לחייא בר רב דאמר דר' יוסי דמחייב לניקף ליתן דמי קנים בזול מאי איכא בין ת"ק לר' יוסי כלומר מאי יהיב לת"ק בציר מדמי קנים בזול (ולטעמיה) אי האי פורתא לא יהיב ליה דמי קנים בזול מאי יהיב ליה. לעולם כדאמר חייא בר רב דלר' יוסי לא יהיב ליה אלא דמי קנים בזול והאי דמקשית מאי איכא בין ת"ק לר' יוסי איכא ביניהו ראשונה שנייה ושלישית דת"ק סבר אם עמד מקיף וגדר את הרביעית מחייבין ליה לניקף ליתן דמי קנים בזול מאותה רביעית אבל מאינך אחריני לא יהיב ליה כלל ור' יוסי סבר דראשונה שנייה ושלישית נמי יהיב ליה דמי קנים בזול: ואיבעית אימא מקיף וניקף איכא ביניהו. דת"ק סבר אם עמד מקיף וגדר את הרביעית מחייבין ליה לניקף ליתן דמי קנים בזול מאותה רביעית ולא יותר דמצי ליטען ניקף אנא הוינא יתיב ומנטר לשדה שלי. ור' יוסי אומר אם עמד ניקף וגדר את הרביעית יהיב ליה מכוליה גדרים דמי קנים בזול דהואיל והוא עצמו גדר את הרביעית גלי אדעתיה דניחא ליה באינך גדרים. אבל אם עמד מקיף וגדר את הרביעית לא יהיב ליה כלל דמצי למימר אנא קיהיב ליה אגר נטירא

הויתי מנטר שדה שלי: אגר נטירא איכא ביניהו. דהאי דקשיא ליה לעיל לת"ק מאי קיהיב ליה אגר נטירא מאי דהאי ניקף הוי יהיב לשומר שדהו דעכשיו לא צריך דהיינו בציר מדמי קנים בזול. ור' יוסי סבר מגלגלין עליו את הכל דיהיב ניקף דמי קנים בזול מכולהו גדרים:

הגהות הב"ח (א) גמ' דידיה הוא א"ל ותנא תקנתא לרמאי וכו' א"ל האי מאי בשלמא רישא: (ב) שם היינו דאיכא בין ת"ק לר' יוסי ת"ק סבר דמי קנים כצ"ל ותיבת הכל לפי נמחק: (ג) שם דעמד ניקף הוא דמגלגלין: (ד) רש"י ד"ה ומקפל ליה מקלפו הס"ד: (ה) ד"ה הג"ה יריכי וכו' יתירא לביני ירכי תמ"ש. נ"ב כך היה גורס בעל הג"ה וכך הוא גי' נימוקי יוסף: (ו) בא"ד ודפנא שהן הקנים: (ז) ד"ה אלא כו' ואם עשאוהו שנים: (ח) ד"ה הג"ה תמ"ש וכו' דלא בעינן דליכא כצ"ל ותיבת מ"ט נמחק: (ט) ד"ה דת"ק סבר וכו' מגלגלין עליו בכולן כצ"ל ותיבת את הכל נמחק:

רוניא, אקפיה רבינא מארבע רוחותיו. א"ל: "הב לי כמה דגדרי", לא יהיב ליה. "הב לי לפי (א) קנים בזול", לא יהיב ליה. "הב לי אגר נטירותא", לא יהיב ליה. יומא חד הוה קא גדר דיקלי, אמר ליה לאריסיה: זיל שקול מניה קיבורא דאהיני. אזל לאתויי, רמא ביה קלא. א"ל: גלית דעתך דמינח ניחא לך, לא יהא אלא עיזא בעלמא, מי לא בעי נטירותא? א"ל: עיזא בעלמא (ב) לאו לאכלויי בעיא? א"ל: ולא גברא בעית דמיכלי לה? אתא לקמיה דרבא, א"ל: זיל פייסיה במאי דאיפיים, ואי לא דאיננא לך דינא כר"ה אליבא דרבי יוסי. רוניא זבן ארעא אמיצרא דרבינא, סבר רבינא לסלוקי משום דינא דבר מצרא; א"ל: רב ספרא בריה דרב ייבא לרבינא, אמרי אינשי: ארבעה לצלא, ארבעה לצללא.§

מתני' א)אכותל חצר שנפל — מחייבין אותו לבנותו בעד ארבע אמות; בחזקת שנתן, עד שיביא ראיה שלא נתן. גמד' אמות ולמעלן — אין מחייבין אותו. דסמך לו כותל אחר, אע"פ שלא נתן עליו את התקרה — מגלגלין עליו את הכל; הבחזקת שלא נתן, עד שיביא ראיה שנתן.§

גמ' אמר ריש לקיש: הקובע זמן לחבירו, ב)ואמר לו "פרעתיך בתוך זמני" — אינו נאמן, ולואי שיפרע בזמנו. אביי ורבא דאמרי תרוייהו: עביד איניש דפרע בגו זימניה, זימנין דמתרמו ליה זוזי, אמר: איזיל איפרעיה,

---

ג) **ור' יוסי סבר.** דוקא גדרה ניקף, דגלי דעתיה. אבל גדרה מקיף – לא. **רוניא אקפיה רבינא.** ד' שדות היו לרבינא סביבות ארבעה מצריו של רוניא, וגדרן. **הב לי כמה דגדרי.** כרב הונא אליבא דר' יוסי, דאמר: הכל לפי מה שגדר. דהכי קי"ל, כדמוכח לקמן. **יומא חד הוה גדר.** רוניא היה גודר תמרים מדקל שבשדהו. **קיבורא דאהיני.** אשכול של תמרים משל רוניא ובפניו. **רמא ביה קלא.** גער בו רוניא, באריסיה דרבינא. **א"ל.** רבינא: גלית אדעתיך שחביבין הדקלין עליך, וניחא לך בשמירתן. **לא יהא אלא עיזי בעלמא מי לא בעית כו'.** כלומר, אפי' אינך ירא מן הגנבים – צריך אתה לשמרן מן העזים. **ולאו גברא בעית לאכלויי.** להזעיק ולגעור בהן. ד) *) "ויִרעס" מתרגמי': אכליי* (ת סז), וכן כל לשון הכרזה בתרגום יהונתן. **פייסיה במה דאיפיים.** טוב לך (ג) להתפיים באגר נטירא, הואיל ונתרצה לכך. הגה"ה: ואי לא דאיננא לך כר' יוסי כו' – מכלל דהכי הלכתא. וכן פסק ר"ת. תמ"ס. **ארבעה לצלא וד' לצללא.** אני שמעתי: צלא – רצען עני, וצללא – רצען עשיר. וכך אמר לו: ארבע ככרות צריכין לרצען עני למאכלות ביתו ליום, כמו שצריכין לעשיר. וזה עני הוא, וצריך לו השדה לפרנסה. וכשם שאתה אומר לו: הסתלק מעלי בדינא דבר מצרא, משום "ועשית הישר והטוב", כך אני אומר לך: עשה ישר וטוב לעני זה, ואל תסלקהו. ויש לגמגם, דהעור קרוי צלא ולא הרצען, כדאמרי' בעלמא (נדרים דף נו:): מאי דרגש – ערסא דצלא. ואומר אני: רוניא רצען היה, (ד) ונותן עורות לעבדנין לעשות מהן מנעלין למוכרן בשוק: וכך אמר לו רב ספרא לרבינא: העני זה שכרו מועט, שהוא צריך ליתן שכר הרבה לעבדנין, דאמרי אינשי: ארבעה זוזי לצורך מקח העור, וארבעה זוזי לשכר העבדנין, והיינו צללא. לפיכך עשה ישר וטוב, ותהי לו שדה זו לפרנסת ביתו. ה) ול"נ: ד' לצלא – ד' ככרות צריך לעבדן עני, וד' לצללא – כמו כן ד' לצורך עבדן עשיר. ומשל הוא כנגד רוניא שהיה לו שדה אחת בתוך שדות של רבינא, כדאמר לעיל דרבינא אקפיה מארבע רוחותיו, ועכשיו קנה לו שדה אצל מצר רבינא, ומפסיק שדה רבינא בין שדותיו. וא"ל רב ספרא לרבינא שיעשה הישר והטוב, להניח לרוניא אותה, (ה) דעכשיו יהיה לו שנים, שכמו שצריך שמירה לשני שדות [צריך] ג"כ לאחד, ומכמה דברים יציאת האחד מרובה כיציאת שנים, ונמצא רוניא משתכר. **מתני' מחייבין אותו לבנותו עד ד' אמות.** דבהכי סגי להיזק ראיה. **בחזקת שנתן.** אם אמר האחד לאחר שבנאו: "אני עשיתיו משלי, שלא רצה זה לסייעני", ותובעו חצי היציאה. וזה אומר: "נתתי חלקי" – נאמן. **עד שיביא התובע.** עדים שתבעו ולא נתן לו. דכיון דחובה עליו לסייעו, ומשפט זה לכל גלוי – לא היה בונה משלו, אלא היה צועק עליו בב"ד. **סמך לו כותל אחר.** לאחר שבנאו האחד למעלה מד' אמות הרבה, ולא רצה האחר לסייעו בהגבהתו – סמך השני כותל אחר כנגד כותל זה כדי לסכך ולתת עליו תקרה מכותל לכותל, אע"פ שלא נתן עליו עדיין התקרה. **מגלגלין עליו את הכל.** דגלי דעתיה דניחא ליה בהגבהה דהילך. **בחזקת שלא נתן.** אם בא הראשון ותבעו לדין לאחר שסמך את כותלו לכותל ראשון, ואומר לו: "תן לי חלקך במה שהגבהתי", וזה אומר: "נתתי חלקי" – אינו נאמן אלא בעדים. שאין משפט זה גלוי לכל, ועד שיחייבוהו בית דין – אינו עשוי ליתן. **גמ' הקובע זמן לחבירו.** במלוה שהלוהו. אילימא

*) נ"ל ירעס והוא בש"ב כב וכן הוא בס"י.

---

*הגה"ה כתב בספרים: אבל מקיף לא יהיב ליה אלא דמי רביעית. וקשה: דמנלן דיהיב ליה אפי' דמי רביעית? דילמא לא יהיב ליה כלל! וכן משמע בפ' "כילד הרגל" (ב"ק דף כ: ושם ד"ה טעמא) דקאמר: טעמא (ו) דניקף, הא מקיף — פטור. ש"מ: זה נהנה וזה לא חסר פטור. ודחי: שאני התם, דא"ל: לדידי סגי לי בנטירא בר זוזא. מיהו, יש לדחות דה"ק: לדידי סגי לי בנטירא בר זוזא, הלכך פטור מלסייע לד' רוחות. אבל רביעית יסייע, דאין לך אדם שלא יסייע לרביעית שיהיה גדור מארבע רוחותיו. **ואי לא דאיננא** לך כרב הונא אליבא דר' יוסי. קצת היה נראה שלא להפחידו היה אומר כן, מדלא קאמר: "ואי לא — מגבינא לאפדנא מינך", או: "מחינא לך בסילואה דלא מבע דמא". ואע"ג דב"לולב הגזול" (סוכה דף לד: ושם ד"ה ולדרוש) אמר שמואל להנהו דמזבני אסא: "אשוו זבינייכו, ואי לא — דרשינן לכו כר' טרפון", ובעי למימר התם דלהפחידם היה אומר כן, הכא נראה דהכי ס"ל, כדפירש רש"י. ועוד, מדקאמר ליה: "זיל פייסיה במאי דאיפיים" — משמע דמן הדין היה לו יותר, אם לא בשביל שכבר נתפיים. **ארבעה** לצלא כו'. לפירוש הקונטרס מקשה ר"ת: [הא] אין מרחמים בדין! ו)ועוד, דקאמר "סבר רבינא לסלוקי" — משמע שטעה רבינא. ועוד: מה שייך כאן האי מעשה? אי משום דאיירי ברבינא ורוניא — לייתי נמי מעשה ד"המקבל" (ב"מ דף קט.): רוניא שתלא דרבינא הוה, והנך תרי עובדי דשמעתין לייתי נמי התם! ועוד: דצלא הוא עור, כדאמרי' (מו"ק דף כז.): מאי דרגש — ערסא דצלא. ואומר ר"ת: דזבן ארעא אמיצרא דרבינא — היינו אמיצר אותם שדות דאקפיה רבינא מארבע רוחות, והיה רבינא מצרן מג' רוחות ורוניא מרוח אחת. ואף על גב דאמר ב"המקבל" (ב"מ דף קח:): הני ארבע בני מצרא דקדים חד מינייהו וזבן — מאי דזבן זבן, מ"מ סבר רבינא לסלוקי משום שהיה מצרן מג' צדדין, ורוניא רק מרוח אחת. א"ל רב ספרא: אמרי אינשי ארבעה לצלא — פירוש: לעור גדול, צריך ליתן לעבדן ד' זוזי, וד' לצללא — עור קטן, כלומר צריך ליתן מן הקטן כמו מן הגדול, שיש טורח בקטן כמו בגדול. ה"נ, מאי טעמא דינא דבר מצרא — משום שיהיו כל שדותיו סמוכין, שיוכל לחורשן בבת אחת, ולכך הוא מצרן מרוח אחת כמו אתה מג' רוחות. וה"ר אברהם פירש דהך ארעא דזבן רוניא אמיצרא דרבינא — היינו אמצרא דאותן שדות שהיה רוניא אריס בהן, כדאמרי': רוניא שתלא דרבינא הוה. וה"ק ליה רב ספרא לרבינא: אע"פ שאין לרוניא בגוף הקרקע כלום, מכל מקום הואיל שהוא עובדן הרי הוא מצרן, (ז) כמו דאמרי אינשי: ארבעה לצלא — נותנין ד' זוז על העור, וכמו כן צריך ליתן לצללא — לאומן המעבד את העור. **מארבע** אמות ולמעלה אין מחייבין אותו כו' בחזקת שלא נתן. איירי כגון דידעינן דקדם חד ואצליה לחבריה, והיה מסרהב, כדמשמע לישנא "אין מחייבין אותו". ולכך הוי בחזקת שלא נתן, וא"צ להעמיד בשעשה חזית. **אע"פ** שלא נתן (ח) תקרה מגלגלין עליו את הכל. אע"ג דזה נהנה וזה לא חסר פטור, מ"מ כיון דגלי דעתיה דניחא ליה בהגבהה — חייב. וכן משמע נמי ב"כילד הרגל" (ב"ק דף כ: ושם) דקאמר: טעמא — דניקף, הא מקיף — פטור. ש"מ: זה נהנה וזה לא חסר פטור. ואפ"ה, כשעמד ניקף חייב. כן נראה לי. אי נמי: הכא זה חסר הוא, שגורם לו שהגביה הכותל למעלה מד' אמות, כדי שלא יהיה לו היזק ראיה בשום ענין ממנו. **הקובע** זמן לחבירו. אור"י: דוקא קובע זמן, אבל בסתם הלואה — לא חשיב ליה תוך שלשים תוך זמנו. **ובא** בזמנו ואמר פרעתיך תוך זמני אינו נאמן. ונראה לי שיש עדים שחייב לו, וקבע לו זמן. דאי לאו הכי ניהמניה שפרעו תוך זמן, במיגו דאי בעי אמר "לא הלוית לי כלום", או "לא קבעת לי שום זמן". ולקמן מיבעי ליה אי

רבינו גרשום

הב לי כמה דגדרי. הואיל והוקפת שדך מד' רוחותיה ומשתמרת תן לי לפי חלקך המגיעך מהוצאותי: הב לי דמי קנים בזול. כלומר אם לא תרצה ליתן שיעור גדר טוב תן לי מיהו שיעור דמי קנים בזול: הוה קא גדר דיקלא. היה (ולקט) [לוקט] דיקלא: א"ל רבינא לאריסיה זיל אייתי לי קיבורא. כגון אשכול של ג' או ד' תמרים תלוים בקנה א' מאותו דקל: רמא קלא. גער בו באותו ארים שלא יגע בתמרים: דניחא לך. בהני גדרים דגדרי: אלא עיזא בעלמא. כלומר מי לא בעית למעביד נטירותא מחמת עיזי דלא ליפסדו בשדך והשתא לא צריכת: פסיקנא לך כרב הונא אליבא דר' יוסי. דאמר הכל כמה שגדר: ארבעה לצלא ארבעה לצללא. כלומר דהיכי דצריכי לאושכף עשיר שהוא (דלא) [צלא] ד' ככרות למזונותיו ואנשי ביתו כך צריכין לעבדן עני משל אמר לו כלומר מעשה זה דבר מיצרא אינו אלא משום ועשית הישר והטוב וכיון דזה רוניא עני הוא (אעפ"כ) אינו יכול לחיות בלא שדה (שאם) [ואם] לא יקח עכשיו יפסיד מעותיו ואין לו במה להתפרנס משום הכי לא תוכל לסלוקיה דאין לך ועשית הישר והטוב גדול מזה דתשביק ליה למיזבן: **פיסקא** כותל חצר שבין ב' חצירות שנפל מחייבין אותו למעכב שיסייע לבנות עד ד' אמות משום היזק ראיה והואיל דמחייבין ליה לסיועיה אם טוען הלה לא נתן לי כלום אלא אני לבדי בניתי לי משלי וזה אומר נתתי הרי הוא בחזקת שנתן עד שיביא ראיה עדים שלא נתן: מד' אמות ולמעלה אין מחייבין אותו. לסייעו לבנותו דהשתא ליכא היזק ראיה: סמך לו זה. שלא נתן מד' אמות ולמעלה ובנה זה בחלקו כותל אחר גבוה כמו זה שהגביה חבירו משלו שנתכוין לבנות שניהן ביחד ושיהיה כותל זה שהגביה חבירו אחד מכותלי הבית: אע"פ שלא נתן עליו את התקרה. על כותל זה שהגביה חבירו אלא כעין קונדסין ונתן עליהם את התקרה מצד אחד על כותליו אעפ"כ מגלגלין עליו את הכל מה שהוציא זה על אותו גובה יותר על ד' שאע"פ שלא נתן התקרה עליו נהנה הוא מן הכותל א) וההנאה היא בביתו מחמת אותו כותל: והואיל דמארבע אמות ולמעלה אין מחייבין אותו לבנות אם טוען הלה ואמר אני נתתי והגבהתי עמו והלה אומר לא נתת הרי הוא בחזקת שלא נתן עד שיביא ראיה שנתן: הקובע זמן לחבירו. לפרוע את חובו: כי

א) נראה דצ"ל והכנאה היא מחמת שהוא דר בביתו ע"י אותו כותל.

מסורת הש"ם

א) [לעיל ב:]: ב) נ"א ובא בזמנו. רש"ל: ג) שייך לעמוד הקודם: ד) [אכלויי לשון הרמת קול כצ"ל רש"ל]: ה) ס"א ל"ג ול"נ רק הוא הגה"ה עד הס"ד. רש"ל: ו) [כלאיתא בכתובות פד.]:

עין משפט נר מצוה

שייך לעמוד הקודם

כב א מיי' פ"ג מהל' שכנים הל' א סמג עשין פב טוש"ע ח"מ סי' קנז סעיף י:

כג ב מיי' שם הל' ב טוש"ע שם סעיף ח:

כד ג ד מיי' שם הל' א טוש"ע שם סעיף י:

כה ה מיי' שם הל' ב טוש"ע שם סעיף יא:

הגהות הב"ח

(א) גמ' הב לי לפי דמי קנים: (ב) שם בעלמא לאכלויי בעיא כצ"ל ותיבת לאו נמחק: (ג) רש"י ד"ה פייסיה וכו' טוב לך שניאות להתפיים: (ד) ד"ה ארבעה לצלא וכו' רצען היה ולוקח עורות ונותן עורות לעבדנין: (ה) בא"ד אותה שדה דעכשיו: (ו) תום' ד"ה הג"ה וכו' דקאמר טעמא לגדר ניקף: (ז) ד"ה ארבעה וכו' הרי הוא מצרן כמוך דאמרי אינשי: (ח) ד"ה אע"פ שלא נתן עליו את התקרה מגלגלין וכו' טעמא לגדר ניקף:

כו א ב מיי' פי"ד מהל' מלוה הל' א' סמג עשין פד טוש"ע ח"מ סי' עח סעיף א:

כז ג מיי' שם סמג עשין צד טוש"ע ח"מ סי' קח סעיף יז:

כח ד ה מיי' שם סמג שם טוש"ע ח"מ סי' עח סעיף א:

כִּי הֵיכִי דְּלָא לִיטַּרְדָן. תְּנַן: בְּחֶזְקַת שֶׁנָּתַן, עַד שֶׁיָּבִיא רְאָיָה שֶׁלֹּא נָתַן; הֵיכִי דָּמֵי? אִילֵימָא דְּאָמַר לֵיהּ: "פְּרַעְתִּיךְ בִּזְמַנִּי" — פְּשִׁיטָא בְּחֶזְקַת שֶׁנָּתַן! אֶלָּא לָאו דְּאָמַר לֵיהּ: "פְּרַעְתִּיךְ בְּתוֹךְ זְמַנִּי"; אַלְמָא עָבִיד אִינִישׁ דְּפָרְעֵיהּ בְּתוֹךְ זְמַנֵּיהּ! שָׁאנֵי הָכָא, דְּכָל א) שָׁפָא וְשָׁפָא זִימְנֵיהּ הוּא. ת"ש: בְּחֶזְקַת שֶׁלֹּא נָתַן, עַד שֶׁיָּבִיא רְאָיָה שֶׁנָּתַן; הֵיכִי דָּמֵי? אִילֵימָא דְּאָמַר לֵיהּ: "פְּרַעְתִּיךְ בִּזְמַנִּי", אַמַּאי לָא? אֶלָּא לָאו דְּאָמַר לֵיהּ: "פְּרַעְתִּיךְ בְּתוֹךְ זְמַנִּי"; אַלְמָא לָא עָבִיד אִינִישׁ דְּפָרַע בְּגוֹ זִימְנֵיהּ! שָׁאנֵי הָכָא, דְּאָמַר: מִי יֵימַר דִּמְחַיְּיבוּ לִי רַבָּנַן. רַב פַּפָּא וְרַב הוּנָא בְּרֵיהּ דְּרַב יְהוֹשֻׁעַ עָבְדִי כְּאַבַּיֵי וְרָבָא. מָר בַּר רַב אַשִׁי עָבַד כְּר"ל. אוְהִלְכְתָא כְּר"ל, בוַאֲפִילּוּ מִיַּתְמֵי; וְאע"ג ב) דְּאָמַר מָר: גהַבָּא לִיפָּרַע מִנִּכְסֵי יְתוֹמִים לֹא יִפָּרַע אֶלָּא בִּשְׁבוּעָה, דחֲזָקָה לָא עָבִיד אִינִישׁ דְּפָרַע בְּגוֹ זִימְנֵיהּ. האִיבַּעְיָא לְהוּ: תְּבָעוֹ לְאַחַר זְמַן, וְאָמַר לוֹ "פְּרַעְתִּיךְ בְּתוֹךְ זְמַנִּי", מַהוּ? ג) מִי אָמְרִינַן: בִּמְקוֹם חֲזָקָה (א) אָמְרִינַן ד)"מַה לִּי לְשַׁקֵּר" אוֹ

אילימא דא"ל פרעתיך בזמני. כשהשלמת את גובה ארבע אמות. פשיטא. דנאמן, שהרי זו טענת "מנה לי בידך", והלה אומר "אין לך בידי כלום". אלא לאו דאמר ליה פרעתיך בתוך זמני. קודם שהשלמת לארבע אמות. ת"ש. מסיפא: בחזקת שלא נתן כו'. אילימא דא"ל פרעתיך בזמני. כשגמרתי את כותלי, וידעתי כמה נתחייבתי לסייע כהגבהתך. מי יימר דמחייבו לי רבנן. הילכך, אפילו אמר "פרעתיך בזמני" — לא מהימן. ואפילו מיתמי. אם מת הלוה בתוך זמנו — גובה חובו מן היתומים בלא שבועה, ולא חיישינן דילמא פרעיה. מה לי לשקר. אי בעי אמר ליה "פרעתיך בזמני". הילכך, כי א"ל נמי "פרעתיך בתוך זמני" — נאמן בשבועה. או

אי אמרינן מיגו במקום חזקה. ומ"מ, אין להוכיח מכאן דקסבר ריש לקיש המלוה את חבירו בעדים אין צריך לפורעו בעדים. דאפשר דמיירי הכא שהלוהו שלא בעדים, אלא הודה לו בפני עדים. דאפילו למ"ד צריך לפורעו בעדים — ה"מ היכא דהלוהו בפני עדים מעיקרא, דלא הימניה אלא בפני עדים. ואם תאמר: מכל מקום ניפשוט מהכא דלא אמרינן מיגו דאי בעי אמר "פרעתיך עתה"! ואומר ר"י: דהא לא חשיב מיגו, כיון דמיירי דקיימי ביום אחרון של זמן. ואע"ג דמסקינן בשילהי ד"השואל" (ב"מ דף קב: ושם) דעביד איניש דפרע ביומא דמישלם זימניה — מ"מ אין זה מיגו, דלא חציף איניש למימר "פרעתיך היום", אבל רגיל הוא לומר "פרעתיך אתמול" ושכחת. **כי** היכי דלא ליטרדן. אע"ג דבפ' "יש בכור" (בכורות דף מט. ושם) תנן: בכור בתוך שלשים יום — בחזקת שלא נפדה. ואומר ר"י: דהתם לא שייך האי טעמא דלא ליטרדן, דהוי ממון שאין לו תובעין. מיהו קשיא לרבי מפרק "השואל" (ב"מ דף קב: ושם) דאמר: בעו מיניה מרבי ינאי: שוכר אומר "נתתי" ומשכיר אומר "לא נטלתי", על מי להביא ראיה? אימת, אי בתוך זמנו — תנינא: מת (ב) בתוך שלשים יום — בחזקת שלא נפדה. והשתא היכי מדמי לה לבכור? דהתם לא שייך למימר לא ליטרדן! ולכך צריך לומר דבכור נמי איכא טירדא דמלוה, שצריך מיד ליתן, דזריזין מקדימין. ומפרש ר"י טעם אחר: דהכא, כיון דחייב לו ואיתרמי ליה זוזי — פורע לו תוך הזמן, דלא ליטרדן. אבל גבי בכור, דאכתי לא איחייב כלל עד לאחר ל' יום — ושמא ימות בתוך ל' ויפטר. וכן שוכר — שמא יפול ביתו של משכיר, ויצטרך שוכר לצאת, דלא עדיף מיניה. ומיהו, קשיא: הא דפריך לר"ל מכותל חצר שנפל, ודייק מיניה דעביד איניש דפרע בגו זימניה — לאביי ורבא נמי תיקשי, דמודו התם דלא עביד דפרע, דשמא לא יבנה זה את הכותל! ומיהו, בכמה מקומות יכול לומר "וליטעמיך", ולא קאמר. **אילימא** דא"ל פרעתיך בזמני פשיטא. וא"ת: ואמאי פשיטא? הא כיון דאין אדם פורע תוך זמנו, ואנן סהדי שזה עשה כותל — איצטריך לאשמועינן דאין צריך לפורעו בעדים! וי"ל: דאפילו מ"ד גבי מלוה חבירו בעדים צריך לפורעו בעדים — התם משום דלא הימניה מעיקרא, אבל הכא ליכא שום הוכחה דלא הימניה. הילכך, פשיטא דאין צריך לפורעו בעדים. **ואפילו** מיתמי. ואע"ג דאמור רבנן הבא ליפרע כו'. נראה דביתומים גדולים איירי, אבל בקטנים — לא גבי אפי' תוך זמנו, (ג) לרב פפא דמפרש טעמא דאין נזקקין משום פריעת בעל חוב מצוה, ויתמי לאו בני מיעבד מצוה נינהו. ואפילו לרב הונא בריה דרב יהושע דמפרש טעמא משום צררי — לא גבי מיתמי קטנים אפילו תוך זמנו, דאין מקבלים עדים שלא בפני בעל דין, דקטנים חשוב שלא בפניו, כדמוכח בריש פרק "הגוזל בתרא" (ב"ק דף קיב.). ואפילו נתקבלה עדות בחיי האב (ד) — מצית למימר דחיישינן לצררי אפילו תוך הזמן בקטנים, כדאשכחן גבי אלמנה בפרק "השולח" (גיטין דף לד: ושם), דתנן: אין האלמנה נפרעת מנכסי יתומים אלא בשבועה, וטעמא — משום שמא התפיסה הבעל צררי, אע"פ שהוא תוך הזמן. ומיהו, מאלמנה אין ראיה, דהתם חיישינן לצררי אפילו בגדולים, משום דאית לה בתנאי בית דין, כדאמרינן ב"הנושא" (כתובות דף קב: ושם) דחיישינן טפי לצררי בבנותיו מבבת אשתו, משום כיון דאיתנהו בתנאי בית דין — אימור צררי אתפסינהו. ואין להביא ראיה מדלא קאמר הכא: אע"ג דאמור רבנן אין נזקקין לנכסי יתומים קטנים אא"כ רבית אוכלת בהן כו' — דלא איירי בקטנים אלא דוקא בגדולים. דשמא משום רב פפא נקט מילתיה בגדולים. אי נמי, נקט ההוא ד"הבא ליפרע" לאשמועינן דגבי אפילו בלא שבועה. ואין להביא ראיה משלהי דמכילתין (דף קעד:) דקאמר: מאי בינייהו דרב פפא ורב הונא בריה דרב יהושע, ולא קאמר איכא בינייהו כגון דמית לוה תוך הזמן, דלרב הונא גבי, דהא רב הונא ורב פפא אמר בשמעתין דלית להו חזקה דריש לקיש. ועוד, דבכמה מקומות יכול למצוא איכא בינייהו טובא, ואינו חושש לומר אלא דבר אחד או שנים, כדאמרינן ב"המניח" (ב"ק דף לג. ושם ד"ה הקדישו) גבי פלוגתא ד"יוסם השור". מיהו, יש להביא ראיה דאפילו רב הונא דמפרש טעמא משום צררי — לא גבי מיתומים קטנים אפילו תוך הזמן. דפריך עליה דרב אסי בפ' "שום היתומים" (ערכין דף כב. ושם), ודחיק עלה לשנויי בבעל חוב שקיבל עליו לזו ולא לזו, ולא משני: הכא במאי עסקינן — בשלא הגיע הזמן בחיי האב. ואין לומר דההיא סוגיא סברה כטעמא דרב פפא — דהא במסקנא משני: כשחייב מודה, והאי שינויא ליתא אליבא דטעמא דרב פפא. וכן יש להוכיח מגופיה דמילתיה דרב אסי, דקאמר: אלא אם כן רבית אוכלת בהן, ור' יוחנן אינו מוסיף כי אם כתובת אשה משום מזוני — משמע: בעל חוב לא משתכח בשום ענין דנפרעין. ומסתמא רב אסי ורבי יוחנן אית להו חזקה דריש לקיש, דהכי הלכתא, כדפסיק בשמעתין. ועוד: אי לית להו חזקה דריש לקיש — א"כ קי"ל כריש לקיש בארבעה דברים, ובריש "החולץ" (יבמות דף לו. ושם) לא פסיק רבא כוותיה אלא בתלת. אע"ג דרבא ודאי פליג אריש לקיש בשמעתין, מ"מ גם לדידן מוכח דלא קי"ל כריש לקיש אלא בתלת. ובפרק ד' וה' (ב"ק דף לט. ושם) דפריך לרבי יוחנן דאמר מעליית יתומים: והאמר רבי יוחנן אין נזקקין לנכסי יתומים אלא לכתובת אשה, אע"ג דקיימא לן דטעמא הוי משום צררי, והתם בשור שנגח לא שייך צררי — מ"מ פריך שפיר, דרבי יוחנן אית ליה אין נזקקין בכל ענין, אפילו במלוה הבא מחמת עצמו דלא שייך צררי, מטעם דאין מקבלין עדות שלא בפני בעל דין. **אע"ג** דאמור רבנן הבא ליפרע מנכסי יתומים כו'. ותניא נמי בפ' "הכותב" (כתובות דף פז. ושם): "אבל מה אעשה, שהרי אמרו חכמים הבא ליפרע" כו'. משמע שהיא משנה בשום מקום. ותימה: היכא אמרו חכמים? דמאלמנה ליכא למילף, דשאני אלמנה דאית לה בתנאי ב"ד, וחיישינן לצררי טפי! ואומר ר"י: מדתנן בפרק "הכותב" (שם דף פד.) גבי מי שמת והניח אשה ובעל חוב, והיה לו מלוה ופקדון ביד אחרים כו' — יתנו ליורשים, שכולם צריכים שבועה ואין היורשין צריכין שבועה. ועוד תנן בשבועות (דף מה.): וכן היתומים מן היתומים — לא יפרעו אלא בשבועה וכו' שלא מצינו בין שטרותיו של אבא שטר זה פרוע. אלמא, גם האב היה נשבע שאינו פרוע. מכאן משמע שאם הוציא שטר חוב על חבירו, וא"ל "אישתבע לי דלא פרעתיך בגו זימניה" — אין צריך לעשות שבועה. **מי** אמרי' במקום חזקה מה לי לשקר או לא. הקשה הר"י בר מרדכי: והא הך חזקה עדיפא משטר, דבשטר אינו גובה אלא בשבועה, ובהך חזקה גובה בלא שבועה, וא"כ מאי קא מיבעיא ליה? הא פשיטא דמיגו במקום עדים לא אמרינן, כ"ש במקום חזקה, דעדיפא טפי! ואור"י: דלא קשה כלל, דודאי עדים עדיפי מחזקה, דאי אמרי שפרעו אפי' בתוך הזמן — פטור, ואי אמרי אפילו אחר זמן "ידענו שלא פרעו" — היה גובה מן היתומים בלא שבועה. ומה שצריך שבועה ביש לו שטר — זהו לפי שאינו מוכיח מתוך השטר אם פרע ואם לאו, דזימנין דזייר ליה אפסיקי דספרא, כדאמרינן בפ"ק דב"מ (דף יז.). אך קשה: דמ"מ תפשוט דלא אמרי' מיגו במקום חזקה מדרמי בר חמא, דאמר בפרק "כל הנשבעין" (שבועות דף מה: ושם): המפקיד אצל חבירו בשטר — צריך להחזיר לו [ה](בשטר) ולא מהימן לומר "החזרתי לך" במיגו דאי בעי אמר דנאנסו, משום דמי א"ל "שטרך בידי מאי בעי". וכ"ש דלא אמר מיגו במקום חזקה, דחזקה עדיפא, דאין צריך שבועה, וטעמא ד"שטרך בידי מאי בעי" לא מהני לפוטרו משבועה! ושמא סוגיא דהכא לא סברה כרמי בר חמא. ולא דמי כלל לההוא *דפרק "האומר" (דף סד: ושם) דאמר: היכא דמוחזק לן דאית ליה אחים, ואמר "יש לי בנים" — דנאמן במיגו, דאי בעי פטר לה בגיטא. וכן ההיא ד"האשה שלום" (יבמות דף קטו. ושם) דבעי: החזיקה היא מלחמה בעולם, מי אמר מיגו דאי בעי אמרה "שלום בעולם", או דלמא כיון דהחזיקה היא ואמרה בדדמי — לא אתי "מה לי לשקר" ומרע לחזקה. ומייתי התם מעין ההיא בעיא — לא דמי כלל להך דהכא. ומיהו, קשה: מדתנן ביבמות בפרק "בית שמאי" (דף קיא:): יבמה שאמרה תוך שלשים יום "לא נבעלתי" — כופין אותו, אחר שלשים — מבקשים הימנו. ומפרש התם דעד שלשים יום מוקי איניש אנפשיה, טפי לא מוקי. ולכך, לאחר שלשים יום אין כופין, דלא מהימנה, אף על גב דאית לה מיגו, דאי בעיא אמרה "אינו יכול לבא עלי" דנאמנת, כדמוכח בסוף נדרים (דף צא.).

ואמר

רבינו גרשום

כי היכי דלא ליטרדן. שלא יתבעו בזמנו: אילימא בזמנו. בשעת השלמת ד' אמות פשיטא דנאמן דמי איכא למאן דאמר דבזמנו לא הוי נאמן: אלא בתוך זמנו. קודם השלמת ד' אמות ואפ"ה קתני דנאמן דבחזקת שנתן הוא אלמא עביד אינש דפרע בגו זימניה ותיובתא דריש לקיש. אמר לך ריש לקיש בעלמא אימא לך דלא עביד אינש דפרע בגו זימניה ושאני הכא גבי כותל אמאי נאמן דליכא תוך זמנו דכל שעה ושעה כל דימוס ודימוס שבנה זמנו הוא לסייע ומש"ה נאמן: ת"ש מסיפא. הא סיפא קשיא לאביי ורבא אמרי לך אביי ורבא בעלמא אימא לך דעביד אינש דפרע בגו זימניה ושאני הכא גבי סמך לו כותל דמש"ה אינו נאמן כי טעין דפרע חלקו קודם שסמך א) דאמרי' ליה אימר אמר סבר בדעתו הואיל ואינו חייב עכשיו לסייע בהגבהה למה ליה למיתן ליה מי יימר דמחייבי (ליה) [לי] רבנן למיתן כשאסמוך הכותל ומשום האי סברא לא יהיב ליה מידי ואי טעין דיהיב אינו נאמן: ואפי' מיתמי. שאם טען אחד לחבירו פרעתיך תוך זמנו ומת והניח יתומים חייבין היתומין לשלם דלא יכלי למטען שמענו מאבינו שאמר שפרע לו בתוך זמנו ואע"ג דאמרי' הבא ליפרע מנכסי יתומין אע"פ שיש לו שטר לא יפרע אלא בשבועה דאמרי' אלו הוה אבוהן קיים הוה מפיק שובר ומרע ליה לשטרא אפ"ה דמחמרינן כל כך בנכסי יתמי אפ"ה אי אמר אבוהן לבעל חובו פרעתיך בתוך זמנו ומת מגבי מיתמי: מה לי לשקר במקום חזקה. כלומר הואיל ויכול הוא לטעון לפטור עצמו ולומר שפרע בזמנו ב) בחזקה דאדם פורע בזמנו והואיל ויכול לפטור עצמו בזמנו ואמר תוך זמנו אמרי' מה לי לשקר:

א) [נראה דצ"ל דאמרי' ליה דודאי אמר וסבר בדעתו הואיל וכו'].

ב) [ואולי צ"ל שפרע בזמנו אמרינן מה לו לשקר ונאמן לטעון שפרע תוך זמנו ואף שהוא נגד החזקה דאדם פורע בזמנו והואיל ויכול לפטור עצמו ולומר שפרע בזמנו].

א) [גי' הערוך בערך סף ד' ספא וספא פי' כל נדבך ונדבך זמניה הוא] ב) [לקמן לג. גיטין לד:] כתובות פז: ג) [ועי' תוס' כתובות יט. ד"ה חזקה וכו' מה שכתבו בנ"ע] ד) [קדושין סד: וש"נ] ה) [נ"ל בעדים]

הגהות הב"ח

(א) גמ' במקום חזקה מה לי כצ"ל ותיבת אמרי' נמחק: (ב) תוס' ד"ה כי היכי וכו' בתוך זמנו תנינא מת בתוך: (ג) ד"ה ואפי' וכו' תוך זמנו (לרב פפא) וכו' ואפילו לרב הונא בריה דרב יהושע ולא מיבעיא לרב פפא דלא אלא אפי' לרב הונא בריה דרב יהושע וכו': (ד) בא"ד עדות בחיי האב נמי מצית למימר:

א) שבועות מא: ב) שם מח: כתובות פה. ג) [בערוך ערך לפת הלריך כפי' סוגיא זו] ד) לפי' מהרש"א הכ"ח

או דילמא. כיון דמוחזק לן דאין אדם פורע בתוך זמנו, לא אמרינן במקום דאיכא חזקה דמרעיא לדבוריה "מה לי לשקר", וליהמנוהו. אמר לו הין. ובפני עדים. אין לך בידי. מפרש ואזיל מאי היא. לא היו דברים מעולם. הלכך חייב לשלם, שהרי יש עדים שהודה לו בפניהם. וכיון דאמר "לא לויתי" — מודה הוא שלא פרע, שכל מי שאינו לוה — אינו פורע, הלכך כאומר "לא פרעתי" דמי. דאילו אמר "פרעתי" — נאמן, אפילו לוה בפני עדים, דקי"ל בשבועות (דף מא:): המלוה את חבירו בעדים — אין צריך לפורעו בעדים. סמך לפלגא. שלא היה כותל חדש ארוך ככותל הראשון אלא באחיו, או בגובהו לא הגיע לגובהו של ראשון. סמך לכולה. חייב ליתן לו חלקו בכותל הראשון, כאילו סמך כותל שני כנגד כל הראשון. דכיון דהתחיל — סופו לגמור, ויתן תקרה, ותנן: אע"פ שלא נתן עליו את התקרה — (ד) נותן מיד. תוס': ויעשה עליות ע"ג תקרה, ויצטרך לו כותל שהגביה חבירו. ע"כ. ומודה רב הונא בקרנא ולופתא. בחיבור שבקרן זוית. לופתא = חיבור. הרי שהיה סוף ביתו של ראובן דבוק לכותל זה שבין שתי חצרות, ולאחר זמן נמלך ראובן זה וחיבר בנין מועט בקרן זוית של סוף ביתו, ובליטת הבנין משוכה כנגד מקצת אורך הכותל המבדיל בין החצרות — מודה רב הונא דלמאי דלא סמך לא סמך, שאין בנין כזה עשוי לימשך (ה). ומודה רב נחמן באפריזא ובאקבועי כשורי. לענין גובה, דקאמר רב נחמן דלמאי דלא סמך לא סמך, מודה הוא שאם עשה בכותל שסמך מקום הנחת ראשי קורות עלייה על פני כולה — סופו להגביהו עוד כשיעור גובה עלייה, וניחא ליה בגובה דכותל ראשון, ונותן חלק בכל גובהו. אפריזא. עץ ארוך ועב שנותן על פני כל אורך הכותל להניח עליו ראשי קורות, ומגין עליהם שלא ירקבו מחמת ליחלוח הכותל. ובלשון משנה קרוי מלטיסין, ומי שאין לו (ו) עץ עב עושה חורים בכותל ונותן נסרים קטנים למעלה ולמטה ולצדדין, ומניח בתוכו ראשי קורות, והיינו אקבעתא דכשורי. בי כוי לא הוי חזקה. שמעון שהגביה כותל החולק בחצר למעלה מד' אמות, ועשה בו חלונות לצד ראובן להנחת ראשי קורות, כמו שפירשתי — לא הויא חזקה לגבי ראובן, לאמר: אני סייעתיך להגביהו, שאלולי שסייעתיך לא היית עושה לי הנחת קורות, שאם אבא לסמוך לו כותל אחר לאחר זמן שאתן עליה תקרה. ואף על גב דמתנח ביה הימלטי — הם נסרים עבים שנותנים בצדי החורים להגין על ראשי הקורות. ולא מצי למימר ראובן: אי לאו דסייעי בהדך — לא טרחית כל האי טירחא. דא"ל שמעון (ז) דכי מפייסת לי לא תתרע אשיתאי. אמרתי בלבי: שמא תמלך לסמוך לי כותל אחר ולתת תקרה, ותפייסני בממון במה שהגבהתי — לא אצטרך לקלקל כותלי לנקוב בו חורים להנחת ראשי קורותיך. תוס': אחזיק להורדי. כל חזקות הללו דשמעתין אינן חזקות שלש שנים, דלא שייך שלש שנים אלא גבי חזקת קרקע, שמחזיק בשדה חבירו ואומר: "לקחתיו ממך". אבל הכא — בחזקת תשמישין בעלמא מיירי, שמשתמש בשל חבירו, ובשעה אחת משתמש בפניו ושותק — הויא חזקה, כדמוכח לקמן, דאמרי': ואי חבריה בטינא — לאלתר הויא חזקה. וטעמא — משום דאמרינן: לא שביק איניש לאישתמושי בתוך שלו תשמיש של קביעות בלא רשותו. וכיון דמשתמש זה לפניו ושותק — י"ל דנטל רשות ממנו, או נתן לו ממון ומכר לו תשמיש זה. והני מילי דהויא חזקה — כגון שטוען: "הוא מכר לי", או "נתן לי במתנה". אבל אם טען: "נשתמשתי בפניו ושתק" — אינה חזקה. כדתנן לקמן ב"חזקת הבתים" (דף מא.): כל חזקה שאין עמה טענה — אינה חזקה. כיצד? אמר לו: "מה אתה עושה בתוך שלי"? והוא א"ל: "שלא אמר לי אדם דבר מעולם" — אינה חזקה כו'. ובכל חזקות מיירי, לא שנא חזקת שלש שנים, ל"ש חזקת יום אחד כי הני. ע"כ. אחזיק להורדי. להניח ראשי רהיטים דקים על כותל חבירו. לכשורי. להניח עלי קורות כבדות תחת אלו. הכי גרסינן: אחזיק לנטפי אחזיק לשפכי לא אחזיק לנטפי. היתה לו חזקה בחצר חבירו שיטפטף גגו מי גשמים לתוכו על פני כל אורך גגו, בלא מרזב. אחזיק לשפכי. אם רצה עושה מרזב ויקלח כל מי הגג במקום אחד, דהא עדיפא ליה לבעל החצר. א"ד אמר רב נחמן כו'. אבל לצריפא דאורבני לא = גג של צריף, שרדי"ל בלע"ז, שמכסין אותו בענפי ערבה, והיינו אורבני. ומתוך שהטיפין סמוכין מאד — אין בעל החצר יכול להשתמש תחתיהם.

או דילמא במקום חזקה לא אמרינן "מה לי לשקר"? ת"ש: בחזקת שנתן, עד שיביא ראיה שלא נתן; היכי דמי? אילימא שתבעו לאחר זמן, ואמר לו: "פרעתיך בזמני" — פשיטא! אלא לאו דאמר ליה: "פרעתיך בתוך זמני"; אלמא אפילו במקום חזקה אמרי' "מה לי לשקר"! שאני הכא, דכל שפא ושפא זמניה הוא. ת"ש: מד' אמות ולמעלה — אין מחייבין אותו; סמך לו כותל אחר כו' עד שיביא ראיה שנתן; ה"ד? אילימא שתבעו לאחר זמנו, ואמר לו: "פרעתיך בזמני", אמאי לא? אלא לאו דאמר: (א) "פרעתיך בתוך זמני", אלמא במקום חזקה לא אמרינן "מה לי לשקר". שאני הכא, דאמר: מי ייטר דמחייבי לי רבנן. א"ל רב אחא בריה דרבא לרב אשי, ת"ש: א)"מנה לי בידך", אמר לו: "הין". למחר אמר לו: "תנהו לי", אם אמר "נתתיו לך" — פטור, "אין לך בידי" — חייב; מאי לאו "נתתיו לך" — דא"ל: "פרעתיך בזמני", "אין לך בידי" — דא"ל: "פרעתיך בתוך זמני", וקתני: חייב; אלמא במקום חזקה לא אמרינן "מה לי לשקר". לא, מאי "אין לך בידי"? לא היו דברים מעולם, ב)דאמר מר: כל האומר "לא לויתי", כאומר "לא פרעתי" דמי.§ "סמך לו כותל אחר — מגלגלין עליו את הכל" כו'.§ א"ר הונא: סמך לפלגא סמך לכולה; ורב נחמן אמר: ג)למאי דסמך — סמך, למאי דלא סמך — לא סמך. ג) ומודה רב הונא בקרנא ולופתא. ד)ומודה ר"נ באפריזא (ג) ובקבעתא דכשורי. אמר רב הונא: ה)בי כוי לא הוי חזקה, ואע"ג דעבד ליה הימלטי, דא"ל: אמינא, לכי פייסת לי לא ליתרע אשיתאי. (ג) אמר ר"נ: אחזיק להורדי לא אחזיק לכשורי, לכשורי — אחזיק להורדי; רב יוסף אמר: אחזיק להורדי אחזיק לכשורי. א"ד אמר רב נחמן: ו)אחזיק להורדי אחזיק לכשורי, לכשורי — אחזיק להורדי. אמר רב נחמן: אחזיק לנטפי אחזיק לשפכי, אחזיק לשפכי לא אחזיק לנטפי; ורב יוסף אמר: אפילו אחזיק לשפכי אחזיק לנטפי. א"ד, אמר רב נחמן: ז)אחזיק לשפכי אחזיק לנטפי, לנטפי — אחזיק לשפכי, אבל לצריפא דאורבני לא; רב יוסף אמר: ח)אפי' צריפא דאורבני. עבד רב יוסף עובדא בצריפא דאורבני. אמר רב נחמן אמר רבה בר אבוה: המשכיר בית לחבירו

בבירה

ואמר לו פרעתיך בזמני אמאי לא כו'. הוה מצי לשנויי: הא דקתני "בחזקת שלא נתן" — היינו בתוך זמנו או בזמנו, ואמר "פרעתיך בתוך הזמן", דליכא מיגו, כדפרי' לעיל. אבל לאחר זמנו — הוי בחזקת שנתן, דבמקום חזקה אמרינן "מה לי לשקר". אך ניחא ליה לשנויי: התם מימר אמר "מי יימר דמחייבי לי רבנן", דלא תיקשי נמי לאביי ולרבא. כל האומר לא לויתי כאומר כו'. הקשה ה"ר יצחק: מה צריך כאן לטעם "כל האומר" כו'? הא ודאי, כיון שכבר הודה — תו לא מהימן לומר שלא לוה! דבשלמא בשבועות (דף מא: ושם ד"ה כל) צריך להאי טעמא, שאומר לו "מנה לי בידך" והלה אומר "להד"מ", ואתו עדים ואמרי "ראינו שלוה ופרע", השתא הא דקאמרי סהדי שלוה — מהימני, והא דקאמרי (ח) פרע — לא מהימני, דהא איהו קמכחיש להו, דאמר "לא לויתי", והאומר "לא לויתי" — כאומר "לא פרעתי" דמי. אבל הכא לא צריך כלל! ואומר ר"י: דאיצטריך לאשמועינן דלא מצי למימר: האומר "לא לויתי" — לא שלא לוה כלל, אלא כאילו לא לויתי לפי שפרעתי, קמ"ל דכאילו אומר "לא פרעתי" בהדיא. סמך לפלגא סמך לכולה. האי "לפלגא" איירי בין לאורך בין לגובה. ד)ומודה רב הונא בקרנא ולופתא. מפרש ר"ת: קרנא — היכר שלא יאריך החומה יותר, שבסוף אותו כותל שסמך (ט) כייפיה לקרנא כלפי כותלו של חבירו. ולופתא — הוי היכר שלא יגביה הכותל יותר, כגון שעשה היכר בראש החומה. לפי שרגילין לעשות החומה צרה למעלה, שיפלו הגשמים מחוץ לחומה ולא ישהו שם. ומודה רב נחמן באפריזא — היא היכר שיאריך עדיין הכותל. שבסוף אורך החומה אינו שוה, אלא אבן אחת בולטת ואחת שוקעת, דודאי עדיין יאריכנו. ואקבעתא דכשורי — היינו שעשה מקום הנחת ראשי קורות, דמוכח שסופו להגביה עד שיעור גובה עלייה.

האי

רבינו גרשום

והלה אומר לפני עדים הן. אין לך בידי מעולם חייב הואיל והודה לו מעיקרא: פרעתיך בזמנו. באותו [היום] שתבעו. אלמא דבמקום חזקה לא אמרי' מה לי לשקר. לא לעולם בעלמא אמרי' מה לי לשקר והכא כי אמר ליה אידך אין לך בידי משום מאי חייב לאו זמן ותוך זמן איכא הכא. אלא מש"ה חייב אתמול אמר לו הן בפני עדים ועכשיו אמר ליה אין לך בידי כמאן דכפר ליה בתר הודאתו דמי א) הכא אמר לויתי ויש עדים שלא יכול לומר לא פרעתי דמי וחייב לפרוע ולעולם מיהא ליכא למישמע מינה: פיסקא סמך לו כותל אחר. כדפרישית לעיל: סמך לפלגא סמך לכולה. שאם סמך זה כותל כנגד אותו כותל שהגביהו חבירו משלו ולא האריכו כשיעור אותו כותל כולו אלא כנגד חציו (משום דאמר סמך לכולה) אעפ"כ אמר רב הונא מגלגלין עליו את הכל ויתן חלקו המגיע בכל הכותל אע"פ שלא סמך אלא כנגד חציו משום דאמרי' היום או למחר ימלך בעצמו ויאריכנו כנגד כולו: מה דסמך סמך. שכנגד אותו שיעור שסמך יתן חלקו ותו לא דלא מחייבי ליה עכשיו משום היום ומחר: בקרנא ולופתא. קרנא שאם התחיל אותו כותל שסמך מרחוק שלא כנגד אותו כותל שהגביה חבירו אלא סופו של אותו כותל שסמך אותו כנגד זוית של אותו כותל שהגביה חבירו בהא מודה רב הונא שאין מגלגלין עליו ליתן אלא כנגד חלקו באותו קרן שאם היה דעתו לסומכו היום ומחר כולו כנגד אותו כותל לא היה בונה משך בנינו לצד אחר לופתא אנפנדי"ף בלע"ז כלומר שלא סמך האי כותל כנגד גובה של כותל חבירו אלא הגביהו כנגד מחצית כותלו של חבירו ולא משום בית אלא לקרות עליו מעט בהא מודה רב הונא שלא יתן אלא כנגד אותו גובה של אותו לופתא לפי שאין בדעתו להגביהו יותר: ומודה רב נחמן באפריזא. היינו מורפט"א בל"ע אע"ג דאמר רב נחמן למאי דסמך סמך דלא יתן אלא כנגד שיעורא דסמך מודה שאם סמך כותלו כנגד חציו גבוה כמו אותו כותל שהגביה חבירו וחציו האחר עשה נמוך והניח על הנמוך אפריזא ודאי גלי דעתיה דהיום ומחר יניח על אותו אפריזא קורות ויגביהו בשוה לאחר זמן ובהאי מודה רב נחמן דמגלגלין עליו את הכל ואית דאמרי אפריזא (נתר) [נסר] ארוך שמשקעין באורך הכותל ובונין עליו כדי שתקשר הכותל יפה וכן בקבעתא דכשורי שאם עשה באותו מחיצה הנמוך מקום חורין כדי לקבוע בהן לאחר זמן קורות אע"ג דהשתא לא קבע בהן מגלגלין עליו את הכל דגילה דעתו דלאחר זמן יעשה שם עלייה ויגביהו: בי כוי לא הוי חזקה. כגון סמך כותלו לחצר חבירו והוי בכותלו של זה חלונות חורין לצד חצר חבירו אין יכול חבירו להחזיק בזה הכותל ולומר שיש לו חלק בזה הכותל מחמת אלו החורין הפתוחין לרשותו ואע"ג דעביד ביה בהנהו כוי המלטה כעין שעושין בחלונות שקובעין שם הקורות מקיפין החור בלבנים כדי שלא ירקבו ראשי הקורות מלחלוח החומר ואע"פ שטוען בעל חצר אני עשיתי כל זה אין חזקה לחבירו לטעון שיש לו חלק בכותל מחמת אותן המלטות משום דמצי אמר בעל הכותל האי דעבדי הכי מצד שלך להכי עבדי דכי מפייסת לי ותקנה ממני שיהא לך רשות להשתמש בכותלי ולקבוע בו קורות שיהיו מזומנין החורין ולא תצטרך לחתור בכותל דלא מיתרע אשיתאי: אחזיק להורדי. שאם היה לאחד חזקה בכותל חבירו לקבוע בו זיזין לא יקבע בו קורות דיכול לעכב עליו ולומר אם הוחזקת לזיזין שהם דקין שאין מרעין את הכותל כל כך בקורות ודאי לא תחזיק בו לקבוע קורותיך שהם עבין: איכא דאמרי אחזיק להורדי אחזיק לכשורי. הואיל והחזיק בו בכותל קיבע מה שירצה: אחזיק לשפכי. שאם יש לא' חזקה שמרזיבו מקלח לחצר חבירו אם ירצה לסלק את מרזיבו ולהניח כל ב) תקרתו בניטוף יכול חבירו לעכב עליו ויכול לטעון טוב לי לקבל מימיך במקום א' יותר מכמה מקומות: איכא דאמרי. אחזיק נמי לנטיפי דיכול זה בעל הגג לטעון מאחר שהוחזקת לקבל מימיי מה לי בשפכי מה לי בנטפי: אבל לצריפא דאורבני. כלומר הני מילי דאמרין אחזיק לשפכי אחזיק לנטפי אם הגג מכוסה מן דפין שבולע המים אבל אם מכוסה בצריפא דאורבני באגודות של גמי או של קנים שמקלחת המים הרבה שאין שוהה בהן המים יכול לעכב עליו: ג) איכא דאמרי היינו צריפא דאורבני כלו' הני מילי דאין יכול לעכב על נטפי אם הגג עשוי כמות כל גגין שאין

א) [אולי צ"ל בתר הודאתו דמי וכהיכי דאומר לא לויתי ויש עדים שלוה דאינו יכול לומר לו דפרעתי דמי וחייב לפרוע וכו']: ב) [אולי צ"ל לסלק את מרזבו ולהניח שיזוב המים מכל תקרתו בניטוף וכו']: ג) [ר"ל דאיכא דמפרשי פירוש אחר בצריפא דאורבני: מנטף

כט א ... ל ב ... ג ... לא ... לב ... לג ... לד ...

הגהות הב"ח

עין משפט
נר מצוה

לה א ב ג מיי' פ"ו מהל' שכירות הל' א סמג עשין סט טוש"ע ח"מ סי' שיג סעיף א:

לו ד ה ו מיי' פ"ח מהל' שכנים הל' ז סמג עשין פב טוש"ע ח"מ סי' קנג סעיף יז:

לז ז ח מיי' שם פ"ג הלכה ה סמג שם טוש"ע ח"מ סי' קנט סעיף א:

לח ט מיי' שם הל' ו ועי' בהשגות סמג שם טוש"ע שם סעיף ב וסי' קס סעיף א.

לט י כ מיי' וסמג שם טוש"ע ח"מ סי' קנט סעיף ב:

מ ל מיי' שם הלכה ז ועי' בהשגות ובמ"מ ובכ"מ סמג שם טוש"ע ח"מ סי' קס סעיף ג:

מא מ מיי' שם טוש"ע שם סעיף א וסעיף ב:

אבְּבִירָה גְּדוֹלָה, מִשְׁתַּמֵּשׁ (א) בְּזִיזֶיהָ וּבִכְתָלֶיהָ עַד ד' אַמּוֹת, וּבְעוֹבִי הַכּוֹתֶל בְּמָקוֹם שֶׁנָּהֲגוּ, אֲבָל בְּתַרְבַּץ אַפַּדְנֵי לֹא; וְרַב נַחְמָן דִּידֵיהּ אָמַר: באֲפִילּוּ בְּתַרְבַּץ אַפַּדְנֵי, אֲבָל רְחָבָה שֶׁאֲחוֹרֵי הַבָּתִּים לֹא; וְרָבָא אָמַר: גאֲפִילּוּ רְחָבָה שֶׁאֲחוֹרֵי הַבָּתִּים. אָמַר רָבִינָא: דהַאי כְּשׁוּרָא דִּמְטַלַּלְתָּא – עַד תְּלָתִין יוֹמִין לָא הָוֵי חֲזָקָה, בָּתַר תְּלָתִין יוֹמִין הָוֵי חֲזָקָה; הוְאִי סוּכָּה דְּמִצְוָה הִיא – עַד שִׁבְעָה יוֹמִין לָא הָוֵי חֲזָקָה, בָּתַר שִׁבְעָה יוֹמִין הָוֵי חֲזָקָה; ווְאִי חַבְרֵיהּ בְּטִינָא – לְאַלְתַּר הָוֵי חֲזָקָה. אָמַר אַבַּיֵי: זשְׁנֵי בָתִּים בִּשְׁנֵי צִדֵּי רְשׁוּת הָרַבִּים – זֶה עוֹשֶׂה מַעֲקֶה לַחֲצִי גַּגּוֹ וְזֶה עוֹשֶׂה מַעֲקֶה לַחֲצִי גַּגּוֹ, זֶה שֶׁלֹּא כְּנֶגֶד זֶה, וּמַעֲדִיף. מַאי אִירְיָא בִּרְשׁוּת הָרַבִּים? חאֲפִילּוּ רְשׁוּת הַיָּחִיד נַמִי! רְשׁוּת הָרַבִּים אִיצְטְרִיכָא לֵיהּ; מַהוּ דְּתֵימָא נֵימָא לֵיהּ: סוֹף סוֹף הָא בָּעֵית לְאִצְטְנוּעֵי מִבְּנֵי רְשׁוּת הָרַבִּים, קמ"ל דְּא"ל: רַבִּים – בִּימָמָא חָזוּ לִי, בְּלֵילְיָא (ב) לָא חָזוּ לִי, אַתְּ – בֵּין בִּימָמָא בֵּין בְּלֵילְיָא חָזֵית לִי; א"נ, רַבִּים – כִּי קָאֵימְנָא חָזוּ לִי, כִּי יָתֵיבְנָא לָא חָזוּ לִי, אַתְּ חָזֵית לִי בֵּין כִּי קָאֵימְנָא בֵּין כִּי יָתֵיבְנָא; רַבִּים – כִּי מְעַיְּינוּ חָזוּ לִי, כִּי לָא מְעַיְּינוּ לָא חָזוּ לִי, אַתְּ מִמֵּילָא נַמִי חָזֵית לִי. אָמַר מָר: זֶה עוֹשֶׂה מַעֲקֶה לַחֲצִי גַּגּוֹ וְזֶה עוֹשֶׂה מַעֲקֶה לַחֲצִי גַּגּוֹ, זֶה שֶׁלֹּא כְּנֶגֶד זֶה וּמַעֲדִיף. פְּשִׁיטָא! לָא צְרִיכָא, דְּקָדֵים חַד מִנַּיְיהוּ וַעֲבַד; (ג) מַהוּ דְּתֵימָא, נֵימָא לֵיהּ אִידָךְ: שְׁקוֹל אוּזִינְקָא וַעֲבֵידֵיהּ אַתְּ כּוּלֵּיהּ, קמ"ל דְּא"ל: אַתְּ מ"ט לָא עֲבַדְתְּ? מִשּׁוּם דְּמִיתְרַע אֲשִׁיתָךְ, אֲנָא נַמִי מִיתְרַע לֵיהּ אֲשִׁיתַאי. א)אָמַר ר"נ אָמַר שְׁמוּאֵל: טגַּג הַסָּמוּךְ לַחֲצַר חֲבֵירוֹ – עוֹשֶׂה לוֹ מַעֲקֶה גָּבוֹהַּ ד' אַמּוֹת, אֲבָל בֵּין גַּג לְגַג לֹא; וְר"נ דִּידֵיהּ אָמַר: יאֵינוֹ זָקוּק לְד"א, אֲבָל זָקוּק לִמְחִיצַת עֲשָׂרָה. לְמַאי? אִי לְהֶיזֵּק רְאִיָּה – אַרְבַּע אַמּוֹת בָּעֵינַן, אִי לְנִתְפָּס עָלָיו כְּגַנָּב – בִּמְסִיפָס בְּעָלְמָא סַגְיָא, אִי לִגְדָיִים וּטְלָאִים – בִּכְדֵי שֶׁלֹּא יִזְדַּקֵּר בְּבַת רֹאשׁ סַגִּי! כלְעוֹלָם לְנִתְפָּס עָלָיו כְּגַנָּב; בִּמְסִיפָס מָצֵי מִשְׁתַּמֵּיט לֵיהּ, ב) [אָמַר: מִמְּצוּרֵי קָמְמַצֵּירְנָא,] בִּמְחִיצַת עֲשָׂרָה לָא מָצֵי מִשְׁתַּמֵּיט לֵיהּ. מֵיתִיבֵי: אִם הָיָה חֲצֵרוֹ לְמַעְלָה מִגַּגּוֹ שֶׁל חֲבֵירוֹ – אֵין נִזְקָקִין לוֹ; מַאי לָאו אֵין נִזְקָקִין לוֹ כְּלָל? לָא, אֵין נִזְקָקִין לְד' אַמּוֹת, אֲבָל נִזְקָקִין לִמְחִיצַת עֲשָׂרָה. אִיתְּמַר: שְׁתֵּי חֲצֵרוֹת זוֹ לְמַעְלָה מִזּוֹ – אָמַר רַב הוּנָא: תַּחְתּוֹן בּוֹנֶה מִכְּנֶגְדּוֹ וְעוֹלֶה, וְעֶלְיוֹן בּוֹנֶה מִכְּנֶגְדּוֹ וְעוֹלֶה; וְרַב חִסְדָּא אָמַר: עֶלְיוֹן מְסַיֵּיעַ מִלְּמַטָּה וּבוֹנֶה. תַּנְיָא כְּוָותֵיהּ דְּרַב חִסְדָּא: לשְׁתֵּי חֲצֵרוֹת זוֹ לְמַעְלָה מִזּוֹ, לֹא יֹאמַר הָעֶלְיוֹן: "הֲרֵינִי בּוֹנֶה מִכְּנֶגְדִּי וְעוֹלֶה", אֶלָּא מְסַיֵּיעַ מִלְּמַטָּה וּבוֹנֶה. מוְאִם הָיְתָה חֲצֵרוֹ לְמַעְלָה מִגַּגּוֹ שֶׁל חֲבֵירוֹ – אֵינוֹ זָקוּק לוֹ. הָנְהוּ בֵּי תְּרֵי דַּהֲווֹ דָּיְירִי, חַד הֲוָה דָּיֵיר עִילָּאֵי וְחַד הֲוָה דָּיֵיר תַּתָּאֵי. (ד) אִיתְּבַר תַּתָּאֵי, א"ל תַּתָּאֵי לְעִילָּאֵי: תָּא וְנִבְנְיֵיהּ, א"ל: אֲנָא שַׁפִּיר קָא דָּאֵירְנָא. אָמַר

רש"י

בִּירָה גְּדוֹלָה. בַּיִת אָרוֹךְ מְאֹד, וְחָלוּק מִתּוֹכוֹ לְהַרְבֵּה חֲדָרִים (ה) קְטַנּוֹת, וְהִשְׂכִּיר לָזֶה אֶחָד מֵהֶן. הֲרֵי זֶה מִשְׁתַּמֵּשׁ בִּכְתָלֶיהָ – בַּחוּרֵי הַכְּתָלִים עַל פְּנֵי אָרְכָּהּ מִבַּחוּץ עַד ד' אַמּוֹת, אַף שֶׁלֹּא כְּנֶגֶד בֵּיתוֹ, וּבַזִּיזִים הַיּוֹצְאִים מִכְּתָלִים. וּבְעוֹבִי הַכּוֹתֶל. בְּרֹאשׁוֹ, כְּגוֹן אִם הִשְׂכִּיר לוֹ בָּהּ עֲלִיָּיה. אֲבָל בְּתַרְבַּץ אַפַּדְנֵי לֹא. דֶּרֶךְ בּוֹנֵי בִּירָה חֲשׁוּבָה לְהַנִּיחַ לָהּ כְּנֶגֶד פֶּתַח הַטְּרַקְלִין הֶחָשׁוּב שֶׁבָּהּ כְּעֵין גִּינָּה קְטַנָּה לָאֲוִיר וְעוֹלִין בָּהּ דְּשָׁאִים, וְיָפֶה הַמַּרְאֶה לָעֵינַיִם, וְשָׁם אֵין רְשׁוּת לָזֶה לִתְלוֹת בַּכְּתָלִים כְּלוּם, שֶׁאֵינוֹ עָשׂוּי לִיכָּנֵס לְתוֹכוֹ. אֲבָל רְחָבָה שֶׁאֲחוֹרֵי הַבָּתִּים. כָּל הֶיקֵּף שֶׁאֲחוֹרֵי הַבָּתִּים קָרוּי רְחָבָה, וְשֶׁלִּפְנֵי הַבָּתִּים קָרוּי חָצֵר. (ו) אֵין הָרְחָבָה מוּשְׂכֶּרֶת לוֹ לְהִשְׁתַּמֵּשׁ. לָא הָוְיָא חֲזָקָה. אִם סְמָכָהּ עַל כּוֹתֶל חֲבֵירוֹ וְלֹא מִיחָה בְּתוֹךְ שְׁלֹשִׁים [יוֹם] – לֹא הָוְיָא חֲזָקָה לִטְעוֹן וְלוֹמַר "פִּיַּיסְתִּיךָ בְּמָעוֹת עַד עוֹלָם". דְּכָל תְּלָתִין יוֹמִין לָא קָפֵיד אִינִישׁ וְלָא מָחֵי, סָבוּר: חֲבֵרִי זֶה צָרִיךְ לְצֵל, וּלְיָמִים מוּעָטִים יִטְּלֶנּוּ מִשָּׁם. וְאִי סוּכָּה דְּמִצְוָה הִיא לְבָתַר ז' הָוְיָא חֲזָקָה. דְּכֵיוָן דְּשַׁבְקוּהָ עֲלָהּ יוֹתֵר מִן הַצּוֹרֶךְ – הֲוָה לֵיהּ לְמִחוּיֵי. תּוּם': וּמִדְּלָא מִיחָה אִיכָּא לְמֵימַר דְּזֶה פִּיְּיסוֹ בְּמָעוֹת עַד עוֹלָם, שֶׁכֵּן הָיָה דַּרְכָּם לִקְבּוֹעַ סוּכָּתָן לְצוֹרֶךְ כָּל הַשָּׁנִים. וְהִלְכָּךְ, מִיָּד לְאַחַר ז' הָוְיָא חֲזָקָה. דְּלָא דָּמֵי לְסוּכָּה דִּמְטַלַּלְתָּא דְּלָא הָוֵי חֲזָקָה עַד תְּלָתִין יוֹמִין, דְּהַהִיא לְצֵל בְּעָלְמָא הוּא דַּעֲבָדָהּ. אֲבָל סוּכָּה זוֹ – לְצוֹרֶךְ כָּל יְמוֹת הֶחָג שֶׁבְּכָל שָׁנָה עֲשָׂאָהּ. ע"כ. זֶה שֶׁלֹּא כְּנֶגֶד זֶה. זֶה סוֹתֵם גַּגּוֹ לְצַד צָפוֹן, וְזֶה לְצַד דָּרוֹם. וּמַעֲדִיף. מוֹשֵׁךְ הַמַּעֲקֶה יוֹתֵר מֵחֲצִי הַגַּג, כְּדֵי שֶׁיִּהְיֶה בְּמִקְלַט כְּנֶגֶד סְתִימָתוֹ שֶׁל זֶה, וּמִתּוֹךְ כָּךְ לֹא יִרְאֶה בְּהֶדְיָא לְגַגּוֹ שֶׁל חֲבֵירוֹ. פְּשִׁיטָא. דְּהַאי פַּלְגָא וְהַאי פַּלְגָא. לָא צְרִיכָא דְּקָדֵים חַד וַעֲבֵיד דִּידֵיהּ. מַעֲקֶה לַחֲצִי גַּגּוֹ קוֹדֶם שֶׁבָּא לְב"ד, וְאַחַ"כ תָּבַע אֶת חֲבֵירוֹ לַעֲשׂוֹת בְּשֶׁלּוֹ. מַהוּ דְּתֵימָא: הוֹאִיל וְהִתְחִיל לַעֲשׂוֹת – יִגְמוֹר הַמַּעֲקֶה בְּגַגּוֹ, וְזֶה יִתֵּן לוֹ חֲצִי הוֹצָאָה. אוּזִינְקָא = יְלִיאָה. תּוּם': (ז) דְּאִי לָא קָדֵים, אֶלָּא בָּא לְב"ד עַל עֵסֶק הַמַּעֲקֶה, וְלֹא זֶה רוֹצֶה לַעֲשׂוֹת בְּגַגּוֹ – ג) פְּשִׁיטָא דְּב"ד עוֹשֶׂה פְּשָׁרָה בֵּינֵיהֶם לַעֲשׂוֹת כָּל אֶחָד חֲצִי מַעֲקֶה, אוֹ הָאֶחָד יַעֲשֶׂה כּוּלּוֹ וַחֲבֵירוֹ יַחֲזִיר לוֹ שְׂכַר הוֹרָעַת אֲשִׁיּוּתָא. אֲבָל הַשְׁתָּא דְּקָדֵים, יָכוֹל לִטְעוֹן אִידָךְ: אִילּוּ לֹא קִדַּמְתָּ אוֹתִי – הָיִיתִי עוֹשֶׂה כּוּלּוֹ בְּגַגִּי, אֲבָל לַחֲצָאִין לָא עָבֵידְנָא, דִּטְרִיחָא לִי לַחֲזוֹר אַחַר פּוֹעֲלִין בִּשְׁבִיל דָּבָר מוּעָט. ע"כ. לָא תִּתְרַע אֲשִׁיתַאי. מְכוֹבֶד הַבִּנְיָן שֶׁמַּכְבִּידִין עַל חוֹמָה. טִיט מְמַהֶרֶת לְקַלְקֵל לְמַעְלָה. גָּבוֹהַּ אַרְבַּע אַמּוֹת. מִשּׁוּם הֶיזֵּק רְאִיָּה. אֲבָל בֵּין גַּג לְגַג. לֹא צָרִיךְ, כִּדְאָמְרִינַן בִּשְׁמַעְתִּין קַמַּיְיתָא: חָצֵר קְבִיעָא תַּשְׁמִישֵׁיהּ וְגַג לֹא קְבִיעָא תַּשְׁמִישֵׁיהּ, וְלָא יָדְעָנָא בְּהֵי עִדָּנָא (ח) דְּסָלְקַתְּ דְּאִיטַּשַּׁע מִמָּךְ. אֵין זָקוּק לוֹ. בֵּין גַּג לְגַג לְאַרְבַּע אַמּוֹת גּוֹבַהּ. אִם נִתְפָּס כְּגַנָּב. שֶׁאִם יִכָּנֵס לִפְנִים מִן הַמְּחִיצָּה – לְשֵׁם גְּנֵיבָה נִכְנַס. מָצֵי מִשְׁתַּמֵּיט לֵיהּ. וְלוֹמַר: חֵפֶץ נָפַל מִיָּדִי עַל גַּגְּךָ, וְנִכְנַסְתִּי אֵלֵךְ לִיטּוֹל. הָיְתָה חֲצֵירוֹ לְמַעְלָה מִגַּגּוֹ שֶׁל חֲבֵירוֹ. שֶׁהָיָה קַרְקַע הֶחָצֵר גָּבוֹהַּ מִקַּרְקַע הַבַּיִת. אֵין זָקוּק לוֹ. בַּעַל הֶחָצֵר לַעֲשׂוֹת לוֹ מְחִיצָּה בֵּין חָצֵר לְגַג, דְּכֵיוָן דְּגַג לָא קְבִיעַ תַּשְׁמִישֵׁיהּ – נוֹחַ לִיזָּהֵר מִשְּׁכֵנָיו שֶׁלֹּא יִרְאוּהוּ. זוֹ לְמַעְלָה מִזּוֹ. קַרְקָעִית הָאֶחָד גָּבוֹהַּ מֵחֲבֵירְתָּהּ. זֶה בּוֹנֶה מִכְּנֶגְדּוֹ וְעוֹלֶה. הַתַּחְתּוֹן בּוֹנֶה מִשֶּׁלּוֹ מִלְּמַטָּה עַד שֶׁמַּגִּיעַ לְגוֹבַהּ קַרְקָעִיתוֹ שֶׁל חֲבֵירוֹ, וְאַחַר כָּךְ מַתְחִיל זֶה לְסַיְּיעוֹ וְנוֹתֵן חֶלְקוֹ מִכְּנֶגְדּוֹ וּלְמַעְלָה, וְלֹא יְהֵא עֶלְיוֹן נִפְסָד בִּשְׁפָלוּת קַרְקָעִיתוֹ שֶׁל תַּחְתּוֹן. דַּהֲווֹ דָּיְירֵי חַד עִילָּאֵי וְחַד תַּתָּאֵי. כְּשֶׁחָלְקוּ הָאַחִין נָטַל זֶה בַּיִת וְזֶה עֲלִיָּיה. (ט)אִיתְּבַר תַּתָּאֵי. נִטְבְּעוּ הַכְּתָלִים הַתַּחְתּוֹנִים בָּאָרֶץ עַד שֶׁשָּׁפְלָה תִּקְרַת הָעֲלִיָּיה, וְאֵין הַתַּחְתּוֹן יָכוֹל לִיכָּנֵס בְּתוֹכוֹ אֶלָּא אִם כֵּן שׁוֹחֶה. תָּא וְנִבְנְיֵיהּ. בּוֹא וְנִסְתּוֹר אֶת כָּל הַבַּיִת וְנִבְנֶנּוּ. ד) אִיבְנְיֵיהּ אֲנָא. מִשֶּׁלִּי. אָמַר לֵיהּ. עֶלְיוֹן: לֵית לִי דּוּכְתָּא דְּדַיְירָנָא בֵּיהּ. לָא קָא מִתְּדַר לִי. אֵינִי יָכוֹל לָדוּר בְּבֵיתִי, מִפְּנֵי עֲלִיָּיתְךָ. שׁוּף

תוספות

האי כשורא דמטללתא. אומר ר"ת: דאמתני' קאי, דעד שלשים יום לא הוי חזקה, והוי בחזקת שלא נתן. מכאן ואילך – הוי בחזקת שנתן. ואתי שפיר דנקטיה הכא, ולא ב"חזקת הבתים". עד שבעה יומי. לאו דוקא שבעה, דבשמיני עצרת לא יוכל לסתור. ואי חבריה בטינא לאלתר הוי חזקה. ואומר רבינו שמואל: דחזקות דלעיל לאו דשלש שנים, אלא לאלתר, כדאמרינן הכא.

בשני צדי רשות הרבים. אומר ר"י: דוקא בשני צדי רשות הרבים, שאין האחד מרגיש בחבירו כשעולה בגגו שיזהר ממנו, מדאמרינן בסמוך: אבל בין גג לגג – לא.

מהו דתימא מצי א"ל שקול אוזינקא כו'. וא"ת: והיכי הוי ס"ד דמצי למימר ליה הכי? דאטו משום דקדם זה ועשה הורע כחו, ויכול לדוחקו זה לעשות כל הכותל? ויש לומר: דס"ד, כיון דאם לא קדם זה ועשה (י) זה הוה מצי למימר: שקול אוזינקא וזיל ועשה כל הכותל, או: הב לי אוזינקא ואעשה אני הכל וכרויא בין שנינו, שלא נצטרך להעדיף – השתא נמי מצי למימר ליה הכי. קמ"ל דלא מצי אמר ליה, כיון שכבר עשה זה ולא אמר לו קודם.

שתי חצרות זו למעלה מזו. וא"ת: ותחתון למה יסייע לעליון? דמכי מטי לארבע אמות ולא יוכל התחתון לראות בחצר העליון – יבנה העליון! ואומר ר"ת: כגון שחצר התחתון אינו נמוך אלא אצל חצרו של עליון ה)(אלא מצד א'), ומצד א' הוא גבוה כחצר העליון, שיוכל לראות שם. ור"י מפרש: דהתחתון מזיק לעליון כי קאי עליון, (כ) כדאמרי' לעיל: כי קאימנא חזו לי, ולכך צריך לסייע עד ד' אמות בחצר העליון.

רבינו גרשום

מנטף אלא משני עברי הבית אבל בנוי כעין צריף הוט"א בל"ע שהוא עגול ומנטף בכל סביבותיו לא [אחזיק] ויכול לעכב עליו: בבירה גדולה. כעין מגדל גדול ובונין בתוכה בתים הרבה סביבותיה ויש סביבותיה חצר וגנות ופרדסין הרי זה השוכר משתמש חוץ לביתו בכתליה דבירה הסמוכות א) לכותל אם יש בה חורין או זיזין שתולין בה חפציהן עד ד' אמות סמוך לבית דשייך בתר בית: ובעובי הכותל במקום שנהגו. לישתמש על גב ב) הבית משתמש חוץ לגג בעובי החומה ד' אמות: אבל בתרבץ אפדני. גינת ביתן שסמוך לפלטין אינו משתמש לבתים אלא לפלטין: אבל רחבה גדולה שאחורי הבתים. היא ודאי עשויה לצורך הפלטין עצמה: האי כשורא דמטללתא. אם נעץ אחד קורתו בכותל חבירו מדעתו של בעל הכותל לסכך עליה מפני החמה אם נעוצה בו הקורה יותר מל' יום ולא מיחה בעל הכותל הוי חזקה לזה שנעצה לקובעה שם לעולם שסתם שאלה משאיל כותלו לחבירו לנעוץ בו [מידי] ל' יום ותו לא: ואי סוכה דמצוה היא. כלומר אם הרשהו לנעוץ קורה לצורך סוכת החג דמצוה ודאי אם הניחה שם יותר על ז' ימים בפני בעל הכותל שלא מיחה יכול להחזיק בה לעולם: ואי חבריה לקורה בטינא. כלומר שקבעה לקורה בכותל בחומר ובלבנים בקביעות בפני בעל הכותל ולא מיחה הוה חזקה לאלתר דאיכא למימר דמחל לו: ב' בתים משני צדי רה"ר. אם מקום הוא שמשתמשין על הגגות זה עושה לחצי גגו מעקה גבוה ד' אמות משום היזק ראיה וכן השני זה שלא כנגד זה ומעדיף מעט זה כנגד זה כדי שלא יוכל א' להציץ בתוך גג חבירו ג) אלא ברה"ר מצי למימר חבריה דמעכב מאי [נפקא] לך מינה אי לא עבידנא מעקה כוותך סוף סוף אי לא הואי אנא הכא אפ"ה קביעית לאצטנועי מבני רה"ר קמ"ל דמצי אמר ליה אידך ד) אי לא מבני רה"ר יכילנא לאצטנועי דכי יתיבנא לא חזו לי קמ"ל ה) דאפ"ה יכול לכופו שיעשה חצי מעקה לגגו: דקדים חד מינייהו ועביד. מעקה לחצי גגו: אוזינקא. חצי הוצאתך שתוציא בכולו: משום דאיתרע אשיתך. שלא יכביד על הכותל ויפול הכותל אנא נמי מסתפינא הכי: גג הסמוך לחצר חבירו. דמקום החצר גבוה ושוה לגגו עושה מעקה ד' אמות לגג שלא יציץ לחצר חבירו. ואי קשיא למה אין מחייבין בעל חצר לעשות מחיצה לחצירו שלא יסתכל לגג חבירו. הא לא תיקשי דהיוקא דחצר עדיף מהיוקא דגג דחצר קביעא תשמישתא וגג לא קביעא תשמישתיה: אבל בין גג לגג דלא קביעא תשמישתייהו לא להאי ולא להאי לא: אי לנתפס עליו כגנב. כלומר אי לכך צריך מחיצה דלא יכנס חבירו לשם בלא רשות ויתפס כגנב דיכול לומר לו לגנוב באת: במסיפס בעלמא סגי. אפי' במחיצה כל שהוא אם יעבור עליו בלא רשות יתפס כגנב: במסיפס יכול לאשתמוטי. דטעין דכיון דלא הוי האי מחיצה גבוה י' טפחים לא הוה ידענא אי משום מחיצה הוי משום הכי עברנא ולא משום גניבה: למעלה מגגו של חבירו. שקרקעית החצר גבוה יותר על הגג: מאי לאו אין נזקקין לו כלל לעשות מחיצה וקשיא לעיל דהתרצת ו) זקוק למחיצה: שתי חצירות זו למעלה מזו. שהאחת גבוה יותר מן האחרת תחתון יחקוק מחיצה בקרקע עליון ובונה עד שיהיה הכותל שוה לחצר העליון ושוב יגביהו העליון עד ד' אמות: ורב חסדא אמר עליון מסייע מלמטה עם התחתון. לפי שהעליון יכול לראות התחתון ולא תחתון העליון לפיכך צריך העליון לעשות רוב הבנין כפי שלא יזיק לתחתון מראייתו: ואם היתה חצירו למעלה מגג של חבירו אין זקוק לו. משום דגג לא קביעא תשמישתיה: איתבר ביתא דתתאי. שנפלו קצת מכותלי התחתון וירד בית העליון ונח על אותו קצת כותל התחתון שנשתיירו: אמר ליה תתאי לעילאי תא נבניה. כלומר סייע לי לבנות הבית כבראשונה: שפיר דאירנא. כלומר איני צריך שאני יפה דר שלא נפלה עלייתי:

מסורת הש"ס

א) לעיל ב: ב) [ערוך ערך מצר]: ג) בדפוס ישן איתא ולא זה רוצה לעשות בגגו: ד) [שייך לדף ז.]: ה) ס"א ל"ג:

הגהות הב"ח

(א) גמ' משתמש בכתליה ובזיזיה עד ארבע אמות: (ב) שם לא חזו לי. נ"ב ע"ל דף ס': (ג) שם ועבד דידיה מהו דתימא: (ד) שם איתבר תתאי: (ה) רש"י ד"ה בירה וכו' חדרים קטנים והשכיר: (ו) ד"ה אבל רחבה אלר הס"ד ואח"כ מה"ד לא אין הרחבה: (ז) ד"ה תום' פשיטא ל"ל דקדים דאי לא קדים: (ח) ד"ה אבל וכו' בהי עדנא סלקת כצ"ל ואות ד' נמחק: (ט) ד"ה איתבר תתאי: (י) תום' ד"ה מהו כו' ועשה הוה מצי כצ"ל ותיבת זה נמחק: (כ) ד"ה שתי וכו' כי קאי עליון בשפת חצירו כדאמרי' לעיל:

א) [אולי צ"ל בכותליה דבירה הסמוכות לכותל ביתו אם יש בה חורין וכו']: ב) [נראה דצ"ל על גג הבית וכו']: ג) [נראה דצ"ל רה"ר איצטריכא ליה דמהו דתימא דמצי למימר ליה חבריה וכו']: ד) [נראה דצ"ל דמצי למימר ליה אידך אי לאו את מבני רה"ר וכו']: ה) [אולי צ"ל דכי יתיבנא לא חזו לי ומש"ה יכול לכופו שיעשה חצי מעקה לגגו]: ו) [אולי צ"ל דהרצת דזקוק למחיצה י']:

מסורת הש"ס

א) כ"א מצינן דאיטרח: ב) ס"א דרבא: ג) לקמן לח.: ד) ס"א רבא: ה) [לקמן קנא: ע"ז לז: חולין נ.]: ו) כ"א מצינן דאיטרח: ז) [עי' מ"ש בב"ק פה. על הגליון]: ח) ב"מ קד.:

עין משפט נר מצוה

מב א ב ג ד מיי' פ"ד מהל' שכנים הל' ו ז סמג עשין פב טוש"ע ח"מ סימן קסד סעיף ב ועיין בהג"ה:

מג ה ו מיי' שם פ"ז הלכה ט סמג עשין פב טוש"ע ח"מ סי' קנד סעיף יג:

מד ז טוש"ע שם וסימן קסד סעיף ב:

מה ח ט מיי' שם הל' י סמג שם טוש"ע ח"מ סי' קנד סעיף כז:

מו י מיי' פכ"ד מהל' מכירה הל' י סמג שם טוש"ע ח"מ סי' קעג סעיף ד:

מז כ מיי' פ"ז מהלכות שכנים הל' י סמג עשין פב טוש"ע ח"מ סי' קנד סעיף כז:

[אינדרונא וכן בסמוך]

מח ל מיי' פכ"ח מהל' מכירה הל' יד סמג עשין פב טוש"ע ח"מ סי' ריח סעיף יז:

מט מ נ מיי' שם הל' יד טוש"ע שם סעיף יח:

שוף אכריסך. שחה קומתך עד כריסך. **כשורי** = קורות העלייה. **אבל אתנו אהדדי.** כשחלקו, אם תשפל עלייה (ו) יסתרוהו הבית ויבנוהו. **עד כמה.** תשפיל העלייה ויכוף את העליון לסתור ולבנות. **כאותה ששנינו.** ב"המוכר פירות": המקבל עליו מחבירו לבנות לו בית – עושה רומו כחצי ארכו וחצי רחבו. **כבנין ההיכל,** שהיה ארכו ארבעים ורחבו עשרים וגבהו שלשים. **איסוריתא.** חבילות קנים ארוכין. **והדר.** מחזיר עצמו לכל צדדין. **סכרנא לך הכא.** אסתום לך חלונותיך באבנים וטיט, ואפתח לך למעלה מכותלי בגובה כתליך חלונות אחרים שיאירו (ז) בביתך. **קמרעת לאשיתאי.** כשתפתח בה חלונות תנוע החומה מחמת המכה. **סתרנא לך.** הכותל מראש גובהו עד שיגיע למקום החלונות שאעשה לך. **לא קיימא.** שאין טיט החדש נדבק יפה בטיט הישן שיבש כבר. **דאע"ג דקא משתמש בה בציבי ותיבני.** ואין הוא עצמו דר בתוכו, מצי א"ל: לא מצינא דאטרח להוציא העצים והתבן. **אספלידא** = טרקלין יפה. **תרביצא.** גינה שבצד הטרקלין, שהיתה מאירה לתוכו. **בדנפשאי אנא בנינא.** בשלי אני בונה, ואתה אין לך עלי חזקת אורה של שלש שנים, דהשתא הוא דפלגינוהו. **ד' אמות לעבודת הכרם.** שהיו חורשין אותה בשוורים. **דעלו אהדדי.** שנתן בעל הכרם לבעל השדה לבן דמים של עילוי הכרם, הילכך כרם בעי למשקל עם עבודתו. **בשופטני עסקינן.** וכי שוטה היה, שנטל גינה חלקה כנגד בית בנוי ולא נטל עילוי דמים? **והשתא** (ח) **אידרונא.** חדר אפל, ואני על כונת אספלידא נתתי עילוי דמים. **שמא בעלמא.** (ט) אם אספלידא שמה, ואע"פ שאינו כשאר אספלידא – לא בטיל שמו. **בית כור.** לפי חשבון (י) סאתים כחצר המשכן.

א"ל: (א) איסתריה אנא ואבנייה, אמר: לית לי דוכתא למידר בה. א"ל: אנא אוגר לך דוכתא, א"ל: לא [א]טרחנא. (ב) לא קא מתדר לי. שוף אכריסך ועול, ושוף אכריסך ופוק. אמר רב חמא: [א]בדינא קא מעכב. והני מילי דלא מטו כשורי למטה מעשרה, [ב]אבל מטו כשורי למטה מעשרה, מצי א"ל: למטה מי' רשותא דידי הוא ולא משעבד לך. וה"מ דלא אתנו גבי הדדי, [ג]אבל אתנו גבי הדדי – סתרי ובנו. וכי אתנו בהדי הדדי עד כמה? אמרו רבנן קמיה [ב]דרבה משמיה דמר זוטרא בריה דרב נחמן, דאמר משמיה דר"נ: כאותה ששנינו: [ג]רומו כחצי ארכו וכחצי רחבו. אמר להו [ד]רבה, [ה]לאו אמינא לכו: לא תיתלו ביה בוקי סריקי ברב נחמן? הכי אמר ר"נ: (ג) כי דדיירי אינשי. וכמה? אמר רב הונא בריה דרב יהושע: [ד]כי היכי דעיילי איסוריתא דמחוזא והדר. [ה]ההוא גברא דהוה בני אשיתא אחורי כווי דחבריה, אמר ליה: קא מאפלת עלי, א"ל: סכרנא לך הכא ועבידנא לך כווי לעיל מאשיתאי. א"ל: קא מרעת ליה לאשיתאי, א"ל: סתרנא לך לאשיתך עד דוכתא דכווי, ובנינא לה ועבידנא לך כווי בבנינא לעיל מאשיתאי. א"ל: אשיתא מתתאה עתיקא ומלעיל חדתא לא קיימא. אמר ליה: סתרנא לה עד לארעא, ובנינא לה ועבידנא לך כווי בגוה. א"ל: חדא אשיתא חדתא בכוליה ביתא עתיקא לא קיימא, א"ל: סתרנא לה לכוליה ביתא, ובנינא לך כווי בבנינא. א"ל: לית לי דוכתא למידר בה. א"ל: אגירנא לך דוכתא, א"ל: לא [ו]טרחנא. אמר רב חמא: [ו]בדין קא מעכב. היינו הך, והא תו למה לי? הא קמ"ל, דאע"ג דלא משתמש [ז]אלא תיבנא (ד) וביה ציבי בעלמא. [ח]הנהו בי תרי אחי דפלגי בהדי הדדי, חד מטייה אספלידא וחד מטייה תרביצא, אזל ההוא דמטייה תרביצא וקא בני אשיתא אפומא דאספלידא. א"ל: קא מאפלת עלי, א"ל: בדידי קא בנינא. אמר רב חמא: [ט]בדין קאמר ליה. א"ל רבינא לרב אשי, מאי שנא מהא דתניא: [י]שני אחין שחלקו, אחד מהן נטל שדה כרם ואחד מהן נטל שדה לבן – יש לו לבעל הכרם ד' אמות בשדה לבן, שעל מנת כן חלקו? א"ל: התם דעלו להדדי. אבל הכא מאי, דלא עלו להדדי? [ז]וכי בשופטני עסקינן, דהאי שקיל אספלידא והאי שקיל תרביצא ולא עלו להדדי? א"ל: [כ]נהי דעלו להדדי דמי ליבני כשורי והודרי, דמי אוירא לא עלו להדדי. ולימא ליה: מעיקרא אספלידא פלגת לי, השתא משוית לי (ה) אידרונא! אמר רב שימי בר אשי: שמא בעלמא פלג ליה; מי לא תניא: [ח]] [ל]האומר: "בית כור עפר אני מוכר לך", אע"פ שאינו אלא לתך – הגיעו, שלא מכר לו אלא שמא, והוא דמיתקרי בית כור; [מ]"פרדס אני מוכר לך", אע"פ שאין בו רמונים – הגיעו, שלא מכר לו אלא שמא, והוא דמיתקרי פרדס; [נ]"כרם אני מוכר לך", אע"פ שאין בו גפנים – הגיעו, שלא מכר לו אלא שמא, והוא דמיתקרי כרמא! מי דמי? התם מצי אמר ליה מוכר ללוקח: שמא זביני לך, הכא מצי א"ל: אדעתא דהכי פלגי, דדאירנא ביה כי היכי דדרו אבהתן. אמרו ליה

מר

נהרדעי

שוף אכריסך. פ"ה: שחה קומתך. ולר"י נראה: שוף – לשון שפשוף, שמתחכך בארץ. **בוקי** סריקי. "אנשים רקים" מתרגמינן: גוברין סריקין (שופטים יא). **היינו** הך. וא"ת: והא אשמעינן בהאי עובדא דחדתא אעתיקא לא קאי, דלא שמעינן מההיא דלעיל. ולעיל איצטריך, כדאמרינן: וה"מ דלא מטו כשורי למטה מי' וכו'! וי"ל: דמילתא דפשיטא היא דחדא חדתא וכולה עתיקא לא קאי, ומשום הא לא הוה צריך לאתויי האי עובדא. **אספלידא.** פרש"י: טרקלין יפה. ובערוך פירש: מערה, כדמתרגם (תהלים נז) "מפני שאול במערה" – באספלידא. ואור"י: דאספלידא דהכא א"א להיות מערה, מדקאמר *נמי: דעלו להדדי בכשורי והודרי, ובמערה ליכא כשורי והודרי. ועוד, מדקאמר: מעיקרא אספלידא והשתא *אידרונא, ובמערה ליכא אורה כלל. ומפרש ר"י: דאספלידא דהכא הוי אכסדרה שיש בה אורה גדולה, שפרוצה ברוח אחד, כדאמרינן ב"לא יחפור" (לקמן דף כה.): עולם דומה לאכסדרה וכו'. וכן מוכח ב"הקומץ רבה" (מנחות דף לג: ושם ד"ה אספלידא) דאמר אביי: חזינא להו לאספלידי דבי מר דאית להו פלימי ולית להו מזוזה. ופריך, מיתיבי: בית שער ואכסדרה ומרפסת חייבין במזוזה. **א"ל** בדידי קבנינא. פ"ה: אתה אין לך עלי חזקת אורה של שלש שנים. ותימה שהיה יכול להאפילו עליו שלא יהא לו בטרקלין אורה כלל! ועוד: דמאי קאמר באוירא לא עלו אהדדי – פשיטא דעלו נמי באוירא, דבית בלא אורה אינו שוה כלום! ומפרש ר"ת: שמאספלידא היה יכול לראות לשדותיו דרך החרדינא, ודקאמר: מאפלת עילוי – היינו שהיה מעכבו שלא היה יכול לראות שדותיו. וקרי לה נמי אידרונא – שלא היה יכול להביט למרחוק. וכן מפרש ההוא דלקמן אין להם חלונות זה על זה. ומיהו, קשיא לר"י: דמאי קפריך מאי שנא מהא דתניא כו'? התם ודאי יש לו ד' אמות – לפי שהם צורך לעבודת הכרם, אבל הכא זה לא היה צורך האספלידא, מש"ה בדין קאמר ליה! ונראה לר"י: דודאי היה מאפיל עליו האורה, שלא היה בו אורה גדולה כאשר צריך לאכסדרה, אבל עדיין היה בו אור גדול. והא דאמר: ומכנגדן מרחיק ד' אמות שלא יאפיל – היינו שלא יאפיל לגמרי, עד שלא יהא ראוי להשתמש בו יפה. ומש"ה קרי ליה אידרונא, משום דלגבי אכסדרה אידרונא היא. והשתא נמי אתי שפיר דלא עלו להדדי באוירא שהוא צורך האכסדרה. **והוא** דקרו ליה בית כור. וכגון שהלוקח יודע שיש לו קרקע שקרוי בית כור, דאל"כ – הרי הטעהו. ואפי' אם רואה בשעת מכירה שאין שם בית כור – יכול לומר: סבור הייתי שהיית משלים לי בית כור. ואם תאמר: וניחא דדמים מודיעים, ואם נתן לו דמי בית כור – אפילו קרו ליה בית כור ישלים לו בית כור שלם! ויש לומר: דמיירי כגון דאוזיל גביה, ואינו נותן לו אפילו דמי לתך. ואי קרו ליה בית כור, אפילו אין בו אלא לתך – הגיעו, ואי לא קרו ליה בית כור – חייב לתת לו בית כור שלם. אי נמי, דלא אוזיל גביה, וכגון דנתן לו דמי לתך. והשתא, אי לא קרו ליה בית כור – היה יכול לומר לוקח: אם תרצה לתת לי בית כור שלם, ולעמוד במקחך – עמוד, ואם לאו – תחזור לי מעותי. אבל אי קרו ליה בית כור – הגיעו, אע"פ שאין בו אלא לתך.

מר

הגהות הב"ח

(א) גמ' א"ל אבנייה אנא אמר ליה לית לי דוכתא כצ"ל ותיבת איסתריה נמחק: (ב) שם לא טרחנא א"ל לא קא מתדר לי א"ל שוף אכריסך ועול: (ג) שם אמר ר"נ כדדיירי כצ"ל ותיבת כי נמחק: (ד) שם אלא תיבנא וציבי בעלמא כצ"ל ותיבת ובי נמחק: (ה) שם משוית לי אינדרונא: (ו) רש"י ד"ה אבל וכו' יסתרו הבית: (ז) ד"ה סכרנא וכו' שיאירו לך בביתך: (ח) ד"ה והשת' אינדרונא: (ט) ד"ה שמא בעלמא אספלידא שמא כצ"ל ותיבת אם נמחק: (י) ד"ה בית כור לפי חשבון. נ"ב עיין לקמן בפי' רשב"ם ריש פ' בית כור:

רבינו גרשום

לא מצינא דאטרח (לבנות) [לפנות] ביתי: שוף אכריסך עול. כלומר הואיל וגרם מזלך א) חפור בארץ וכפוף בטנך וצא והכנס. דינא קאמר ליה דבתוך שלו יבנה: לא אמרן דדינא קאמר ליה אלא דלא מטו כשורי. שלא ירדה העליה למטה מי' אז יכול לטעון לו דור בדוחק בתוך עשרה: [דלא] אתנו בהדי הדדי. שלא התנו זה לזה לבנות אחר נפילה: עד כמה. גבוה יכול לכופו שיסייע לו: כאותה ששנינו. בפ' המוכר: רומו כחצי ארכו וכחצי רחבו. שאם היה הבית כ' אמה באורך ורוחב י' אמה עושה גבוה חצי כ' וחצי י' שהם ט"ו אמה וראיה לדבר מהיכל: לא תיתלו בוקי סריקי. כלומר לא תאמינו בדברים רקים הללו מעולם לא אמרן ר' נחמן שיבנהו גבוה כזה: שיעור אסורייתא דמחוזא כדי שיהא יכול לישא משאוי על גבו כמשאוי של אנשי מחוזא ויכול לחזור בריוח בהכי מצי לכופו טפי לא: אשיתא ב) אגב כוי דחברי'. שהיה בונה כותלו כנגד חלון חבירו שהיה לו חזקה לחלון ולא הרחיק ד' אמות: מרעית אשיתאי. שתחתור בו חלונות אחרות: סתרנא לך. עד חלונות אלו ובנינא לך מחדש: דינא אמר ליה. דלא מצי למיטרח לפנות ביתו: היינו הך. דקאמר רב חמא בהני בי תרי וכו' והא תו למה לי: הא איצטריך למיתני. שאפי' אלו חלונות שיש לו בהן חזקה: בי תבני וציבי. שאין צריך בהן לאורה כל כך אפ"ה לא מצי לכופו לפנות: אספלידא. חדר שלוויין קמערא: תרביצא. גינה שסמוך לה: אפומא דאספלידא. לפני הפתח: אחד של שדה לבן. שדה תבואה: יש לו לבעל הכרם ד' אמות בשדה לבן. כמלא צמד בקר וכליו כדי לחרוש גפנו עומדין על המיצר ששם היו עומדים פנותיהם בחרישה: שעל מנת כן חלקו השדות. והכי נמי לא יבנה כותלו לאספלידא שלו כדי שלא לאפיל עליו: א"ל התם. מש"ה יש לו לבעל הכרם ד' אמות בשדה לבן משום דעלו להדדי שמעלה זה בעל הכרם לבעל שדה משדה לבן יותר מחלק שדה כרם כדי שיהא לו ד' אמות אבל הכא גבי אספלידא לא העלהו יותר בתרביצא ומש"ה מצי למימר ליה בדידי קבנינא: א"ל וכי בשופטני עסקינן. דלא מעלו אהדדי כלומר וכי באנשים שוטים עסקינן דבלא עלוי קרקע נטל זה תרביצא תחת האספלידא הלא זה בנוי וזה [אינו] בנוי אלא בודאי עלו אהדדי בדמים: כשורי והודרי. ולא עלו באוירא ולא נתן לו בקרקע יותר ובדין קאמר בדידי קא בנינא: ולימא ליה. בעל האספלידא עד האידנא הויא לה אספלידא דהויא לה נהורא מעליא אבל השתא אי בנית אשיתא קא מאפלת עלי והוה לי אדרונא דחשיכה טפי ובהא טענה מצי מעכב עלויה: אמר רב שימי בר אשי שמא בעלמא פליג ליה. דהשתא נמי שם אספלידא קרי ליה אע"ג דמאפלא: מי לא תניא כו'. אע"פ שאין שם גפנים שתים כנגד שתים ואחת יוצא זנב (אילנות): דדיירנא ביה כדדרו ביה אבהתי. כלומר להכי איכוונא למיתב חלק אספלידא שאהי' דר כשדרו בה אבותי שהיה לה מאור גדול:

נהרדעי

א) [אולי צ"ל שוף בארץ ועי' תוס' ד"ה שוף]: ב) [לפנינו הגי' אחורי כוי דחבריה]: ג) [הלשון צריך תיקון ואולי דצ"ל דאז היו מעמידין גפניהם ע"י חרישה]:

מָר יְנוּקָא וּמָר קַשִּׁישָׁא בְּרֵיהּ דְּרַב חִסְדָּא לְרַב אַשִׁי: נְהַרְדְּעֵי לְטַעֲמַיְיהוּ, [א]דְּאָמַר ר"נ אָמַר שְׁמוּאֵל: [א]הָאַחִין שֶׁחָלְקוּ — אֵין לָהֶן לֹא דֶּרֶךְ זֶה עַל זֶה, וְלֹא חַלּוֹנוֹת זֶה עַל זֶה, וְלֹא סוּלָּמוֹת זֶה עַל זֶה, וְלֹא אַמַּת הַמַּיִם זֶה עַל זֶה, וְהִזָּהֲרוּ בָּהֶן שֶׁהֲלָכוֹת קְבוּעוֹת הֵן; (א) וְרָבָא אָמַר: יֵשׁ לָהֶן.§ הַהוּא שְׁטָרָא דְּיָתְמֵי דִּנְפַק עֲלֵיהּ תַּבְרָא, אֲמַר רַב חָמָא: [ב]אַגְבּוּיֵי לָא מַגְבִּינַן לֵיהּ וּמִיקְרַע לָא קָרְעִינַן לֵיהּ; אַגְבּוּיֵי לָא מַגְבִּינַן לֵיהּ — דִּנְפַק תַּבְרָא עֲלֵיהּ; מִיקְרַע לָא קָרְעִינַן לֵיהּ — דְּכִי גָּדְלִי יַתְמֵי דִּילְמָא מַיְיתוּ רְאָיָה וּמַרְעִי לֵיהּ. אֲמַר לֵיהּ רַב אַחָא בְּרֵיהּ דְּרָבָא לְרָבִינָא: הִלְכְתָא מַאי? א"ל: בְּכוּלְּהוּ הִלְכְתָא כְּרַב חָמָא, לְבַר מִתַּבְרָא, דְּסָהֲדֵי בְּשַׁקְרֵי לָא מַחְזְקִינַן. מָר זוּטְרָא בְּרֵיהּ דְּרַב מָרִי אָמַר: [ג]בְּהָא נַמִי הִלְכְתָא כְּרַב חָמָא, דְּאִם אִיתָא דְּתַבְרָא מְעַלְּיָא הוּא — אִיבָּעֵי לֵיהּ לְאַפּוּקֵי בְּחַיֵּי אֲבוּהוֹן, וּמִדְּלָא אַפְּקֵיהּ, שְׁמַע מִינָּהּ זַיּוּפֵי זַיְּיפֵיהּ.§ **מתני'** ב)[ד]כּוֹפִין אוֹתוֹ לִבְנוֹת בֵּית שַׁעַר וְדֶלֶת לֶחָצֵר; רַבָּן שִׁמְעוֹן בֶּן גַּמְלִיאֵל אוֹמֵר: לֹא כָּל הַחֲצֵרוֹת רְאוּיוֹת לְבֵית שַׁעַר. [ה]כּוֹפִין אוֹתוֹ לִבְנוֹת לָעִיר חוֹמָה וּדְלָתַיִם וּבְרִיחַ; רשב"ג אוֹמֵר: לֹא כָּל הָעֲיָירוֹת רְאוּיוֹת לְחוֹמָה. ג)[ו]כַּמָּה יְהֵא בָּעִיר וִיהֵא כְּאַנְשֵׁי הָעִיר? י"ב חֹדֶשׁ. [ז]קָנָה בָּהּ בֵּית דִּירָה — הֲרֵי הוּא כְּאַנְשֵׁי הָעִיר מִיָּד.§ **גמ'** לְמֵימְרָא דְּבֵית שַׁעַר מַעַלְּיוּתָא הִיא? וְהָא הַהוּא חֲסִידָא דַּהֲוָה רָגִיל אֵלִיָּהוּ דַּהֲוָה מִשְׁתָּעֵי בַּהֲדֵיהּ, עֲבַד בֵּית שַׁעַר וְתוּ לָא מִשְׁתָּעֵי בַּהֲדֵיהּ! לָא קַשְׁיָא: הָא מִגַּוַּאי, הָא (ב) מִבָּרַאי. וְאִי בָּעֵית אֵימָא: הָא וְהָא מִבָּרַאי, וְלָא קַשְׁיָא: הָא דְּאִית לֵיהּ דֶּלֶת, הָא דְּלֵית לֵיהּ דֶּלֶת. אבע"א: הָא וְהָא דְּאִית לֵיהּ דֶּלֶת, וְלָא קַשְׁיָא: הָא דְּאִית לֵיהּ פּוֹתַחַת, הָא דְּלֵית לֵיהּ פּוֹתַחַת. אִי בָּעֵית אֵימָא: הָא וְהָא דְּאִית לֵיהּ פּוֹתַחַת, וְלָא קַשְׁיָא: הָא דְּפוֹתַחַת דִּידֵיהּ מִגַּוַּאי, הָא דְּפוֹתַחַת דִּידֵיהּ (ג) מִבָּרַאי.§ "כּוֹפִין אוֹתוֹ לִבְנוֹת בֵּית שַׁעַר וְדֶלֶת לֶחָצֵר".§ תַּנְיָא, רַבָּן שִׁמְעוֹן בֶּן גַּמְלִיאֵל אוֹמֵר: לֹא כָּל חֲצֵרוֹת רְאוּיוֹת לְבֵית שַׁעַר, אֶלָּא, חָצֵר הַסְּמוּכָה לִרְשׁוּת הָרַבִּים — רְאוּיָה לְבֵית שַׁעַר, וְשֶׁאֵינָהּ סְמוּכָה לִרְשׁוּת הָרַבִּים — אֵינָהּ רְאוּיָה לְבֵית שַׁעַר. וְרַבָּנַן? זִימְנִין דְּדָחֲקִי בְּנֵי רְשׁוּת הָרַבִּים וְעָיְילוּ וְאָתוּ.§ "כּוֹפִין אוֹתוֹ לִבְנוֹת לָעִיר" כו'.§ ד)(ת"ר: כּוֹפִין אוֹתוֹ לַעֲשׂוֹת לָעִיר דְּלָתַיִם וּבְרִיחַ.) וְרַבָּן שִׁמְעוֹן בֶּן גַּמְלִיאֵל אוֹמֵר: לֹא כָּל הָעֲיָירוֹת רְאוּיוֹת לְחוֹמָה, אֶלָּא, עִיר הַסְּמוּכָה לַסְּפָר רְאוּיָה לְחוֹמָה, וְשֶׁאֵינָהּ סְמוּכָה לַסְּפָר — אֵינָהּ רְאוּיָה לְחוֹמָה. וְרַבָּנַן? זִימְנִין דְּמִקְרוּ וְאָתֵי גַּיְיסָא. בְּעָא מִינֵּיהּ רַבִּי אֶלְעָזָר מֵרַבִּי יוֹחָנָן: כְּשֶׁהֵן גּוֹבִין, לְפִי נְפָשׁוֹת גּוֹבִין, אוֹ דִּילְמָא לְפִי שֶׁבַח מָמוֹן גּוֹבִין? אֲמַר לֵיהּ: לְפִי מָמוֹן גּוֹבִין, וְאֶלְעָזָר בְּנִי, קְבַע בָּהּ מַסְמְרוֹת. אִיכָּא דְּאָמְרִי, בְּעָא מִינֵּיהּ רַבִּי אֶלְעָזָר מֵרַבִּי יוֹחָנָן: כְּשֶׁהֵן גּוֹבִין, לְפִי קֵירוּב בָּתִּים הֵן גּוֹבִין, אוֹ דִּילְמָא לְפִי ה)מָמוֹן גּוֹבִין? אֲמַר לֵיהּ: [ח]לְפִי קֵירוּב בָּתִּים הֵן גּוֹבִין, וְאֶלְעָזָר בְּנִי, קְבַע בָּהּ מַסְמְרוֹת. רַבִּי יְהוּדָה נְשִׂיאָה רְמָא דְּשׁוּרָא אַדְּרַבָּנַן, אֲמַר (ד) רֵישׁ לָקִישׁ: ו)[ט]רַבָּנַן לָא צְרִיכִי נְטִירוּתָא, דִּכְתִיב: °"אֶסְפְּרֵם מֵחוֹל יִרְבּוּן", אֶסְפְּרֵם לְמַאן? אִילֵימָא לְצַדִּיקִים דִּנְפִישִׁי מֵחָלָא, הַשְׁתָּא כּוּלְּהוּ יִשְׂרָאֵל כְּתִיב בְּהוּ: °"כַּחוֹל אֲשֶׁר עַל שְׂפַת הַיָּם", צַדִּיקִים עַצְמָם מֵחוֹל יִרְבּוּן?! אֶלָּא הָכִי קָאָמַר: אֶסְפְּרֵם לְמַעֲשֵׂיהֶם שֶׁל צַדִּיקִים — מֵחוֹל יִרְבּוּן, וְק"ו: וּמָה חוֹל שֶׁמּוּעָט — מֵגֵין עַל הַיָּם, מַעֲשֵׂיהֶם שֶׁל צַדִּיקִים שֶׁהֵם מְרוּבִּים — לֹא כָּל שֶׁכֵּן שֶׁמְּגִינִּים עֲלֵיהֶם. כִּי אֲתָא לְקַמֵּיהּ דְּרַבִּי יוֹחָנָן, אֲמַר לֵיהּ, מַאי טַעֲמָא לָא תֵּימָא לֵיהּ מֵהָא: ז)°"אֲנִי חוֹמָה וְשָׁדַי כַּמִּגְדָּלוֹת" — זוֹ תּוֹרָה, "וְשָׁדַי כַּמִּגְדָּלוֹת" —

אֵלּוּ

תהלים קלט; בראשית כב; שיר השירים ח

רש"י

נְהַרְדְּעֵי לְטַעֲמַיְיהוּ. רַב חָמָא דְּמִן נְהַרְדְּעָא הוּא, דְּלָא ס"ל הָא דְּאִידּוּר בָּהּ כִּדְדָרוּ אֲבָהָתַי, וּלְשֵׁם כָּךְ חִילַּקְנוּ — אָזֵיל לְטַעֲמַיְיהוּ דִּנְהַרְדְּעֵי, דְּאָמַר שְׁמוּאֵל דְּהוּא מִנְּהַרְדְּעָא. הָאַחִין שֶׁחָלְקוּ. וְנָטַל זֶה שָׂדֶה לַצָּפוֹן וְזֶה לַדָּרוֹם, וְהָיָה אָבִיו רָגִיל לִהְיוֹת לוֹ לִיכָּנֵס דֶּרֶךְ זוֹ לְתוֹךְ זוֹ — אֵין יָכוֹל לוֹמַר "דֶּרֶךְ לִי עָלֶיךָ". וְלֹא חַלּוֹנוֹת. לְעַרְעֵר עַל סְתִימַת אוֹרוֹ. וְלֹא סוּלָּמוֹת. אִם נָטַל זֶה בַּיִת וְחָצֵר, וְזֶה נָטַל עֲלִיָּיה — אֵין לוֹ לִקְבּוֹעַ סוּלָּם בַּחֲצֵירוֹ שֶׁל זֶה לַעֲלוֹת לַעֲלִיָּיתוֹ. וְלֹא אַמַּת הַמַּיִם. לַהֲבִיאָהּ מִן הַנָּהָר דֶּרֶךְ שָׂדֵהוּ שֶׁל זֶה לְתוֹךְ שֶׁלּוֹ. תַּבְרָא. שׁוֹבָר שֶׁהוּא פָּרוּעַ לַאֲבִיהֶם. וּמַרְעִי לֵיהּ. לַשּׁוֹבָר, שֶׁהֵן עֵדֵי שֶׁקֶר. **מתני'** כּוֹפִין אוֹתוֹ. אֶת בֶּן הֶחָצֵר שֶׁאֵינוֹ רוֹצֶה לְסַיֵּיעַ אֶת בְּנֵי הֶחָצֵר, לִבְנוֹת לָהֶן בֵּית שַׁעַר לִהְיוֹת שׁוֹמֵר הַפֶּתַח יוֹשֵׁב שָׁם בַּצֵּל וּמַרְחִיק אֶת בְּנֵי רְשׁוּת הָרַבִּים מִלְּהָלִין בֶּחָצֵר. וְדֶלֶת. לְשַׁעַר הֶחָצֵר לְנוֹעֲלוֹ. לֹא כָּל הַחֲצֵרוֹת רְאוּיוֹת לְבֵית שַׁעַר. בַּגְּמָ' מְפָרֵשׁ אֵיזוֹ הִיא הָרְאוּיָה. וִיהֵא כְּאַנְשֵׁי הָעִיר. לָשֵׂאת עִמָּהֶם בָּעוֹל. **גמ'** וְלָא אִישְׁתָּעֵי בַּהֲדֵיהּ. לְפִי שֶׁמַּפְסִיק בָּעֲנִיִּים הַצּוֹעֲקִין, וְאֵין קוֹלָם נִשְׁמָע. מִגַּוַּאי. לֶחָצֵר — גְּרִיעוּתָא הוּא, לְפִי שֶׁדֶּלֶת הֶחָצֵר נָעוּל, וְהֶעָנִי צוֹעֵק, וּבֵית שַׁעַר שֶׁבִּפְנִים מַפְסִיק הַקּוֹל. מִבָּרַאי. אֵינוֹ מַפְסִיק בְּפָנָיו, שֶׁהֲרֵי נִכְנָס לְתוֹכוֹ. וּכְשֶׁאֵין לוֹ דֶּלֶת עָסְקִינַן. פּוֹתַחַת דִּידֵיהּ מֵאַבָּרַאי. הֶעָנִי פּוֹתְחָהּ וְנִכְנָס. פּוֹתַחַת = שִׁירוּד"ר בְּלַעַ"ז, וְהוּא שֶׁל עֵץ, וְאָמִיד הַמַּפְתֵּחַ לְתוֹכוֹ. שֶׁאֵינָהּ סְמוּכָה. שֶׁמְּשׁוּכָה לְהַלָּן מֵרְשׁוּת הָרַבִּים. כְּשֶׁהֵם גּוֹבִים. לְחוֹמַת הָעִיר. קְבַע בָּהּ מַסְמְרוֹת. הִזָּהֵר לָדוּן כֵּן, וְלֹא תָּזוּז מִמֶּנָּה. קֵירוּב בָּתִּים. בַּיִת הַקָּרוֹב לַחוֹמָה צָרִיךְ לְחוֹמַת הָעִיר יוֹתֵר מִן הָרָחוֹק. רְמָא דְּשׁוּרָא אַדְּרַבָּנַן. הִטִּיל יְצִיאַת חוֹמַת הָעִיר עַל הַחֲכָמִים, כְּמוֹ עַל שְׁאָר בְּנֵי אָדָם. חוֹל. שֶׁהוּא מוּעָט מִמַּעֲשֵׂיהֶם שֶׁל צַדִּיקִים. מֵגֵין עַל הַיָּם. וְהוּא לוֹ לְחוֹמָה, כִּדְכְתִיב: "אֲשֶׁר שַׂמְתִּי חוֹל גְּבוּל לַיָּם" (ירמיהו ה).

אֵלּוּ

תוספות

מר ינוקא. הוא הגדול, ועל שם שנולד בינקותו של רב חסדא קרי ליה מר ינוקא. ומר קשישא הוא הצעיר, ונולד בקשישותו של רב חסדא. (ועיין רש"י כתובות פט: ד"ה מר). **נהרדעי** לטעמייהו. רב חמא נהרדעי הוא, כדאמרינן בפרק קמא דסנהדרין (דף יז:): "[אמוראי] דנהרדעי" — רב חמא. ושמואל נמי נהרדעי הוא, כדאמר שמואל (ברכות דף נח:): נהירין לי שבילי דרקיע כשבילי דנהרדעי. **אין** להם דרך זה על זה. טעמא, משום דפסיק שמואל בפרק "המוכר את הבית" (לקמן דף סד.) כר"ע, דאמר: מוכר בעין יפה מוכר, ולפיכך אין להם דרך זה על זה, שלא שייר לעצמו כלום כל אחד (ה) חלק בחלק חבירו, והוה לו כמוכר. ואף על גב דאמרינן: המוכר בית ושייר חצר — מכר לו עם הדרך, למ"ד מוכר בעין יפה מוכר — לא דמי, דהכא כולם מוכרין, וכל אחד מכר ולא שייר לעצמו כלום בחלק חבירו, וה"ל כמוכר חצר ושייר בית, דצריך ליקח לו דרך מבעל החצר. **ולא** סולמות זה על זה. פי' בקונט': אם נטל זה בית וחצר וזה נטל עלייה — אין לקבוע סולם בחצירו של זה לעלות לעלייתו. וקשה לר"י: דהיינו "ולא דרך זה על זה"! ונראה לר"י: כגון שלקח זה בית וזה עלייה וחצר — אין לו לסמוך הסולם בכותל של זה ולעלות בעלייתו.

ואי בעית אימא הא והא מבראי. ולא גרסינן "הא והא מגוואי". דמגוואי אין שייך לחלק בין אית ליה דלת ללית ליה, ובין אית ליה פותחת ללית ליה, דבכל ענין הוא רע, כיון שאין יכול לבא אלא עד פתח החצר. ואין לפרש "הא דאית ליה דלת" כו' — אחצר קאי, דהא במתני' בהדיא קתני: כופין אותו לבנות דלת לחצר. ולמאי דגרסי' "מבראי" קצת קשה: דלא הוי כשאר שינויי, דנקט צד דלא מעלי — הא והא דאית ליה דלת, והא והא דאית ליה פותחת, והכא נקיט ההוא דמעלי.

לפי שבח ממון הן גובין. כיון דאין (ו) סכנת נפשות — לא אזלינן אלא בתר ממון. והכי נמי אמר ב"הגוזל בתרא" (ב"ק דף קטז:): שיירא ההולכת במדבר ועמד עליה גיים — מחשבין לפי ממון, דליכא סכנת נפשות, כיון דאין הגיים בא רק בשביל ממון. ואף על גב דאמר בפ' "בן סורר" (סנהדרין דף עב.) דהבא במחתרת נידון על שם סופו, ומפרש רבא טעמא בגמ' משום חזקה דאין אדם מעמיד עצמו על ממונו כו' — ואפי' הכי אין מחשבין אלא לפי ממון, כיון דהגיים ברצונו אינו בא על הנפשות, דאם לא יעמדו נגדם לא יזיק לגופם — הילכך לא חשיב סכנת נפשות. לפיכך, אם יעמדו עליהם לסטים ונתפשרו עמהם — גובין לפי ממון. אבל היכי (ז) דטעו במדבר, אמר התם דמחשבינן אף לפי הנפשות, משום כיון דטעו איכא סכנת נפשות.

לפי קירוב בתים הן גובין. פירש ר"ח: ונותנין עניים קרובים יותר מרחוקים, וכן עשירים קרובים יותר מעשירים רחוקים. אבל עשירים רחוקים נותנין יותר מעניים קרובים, דלפי שבח ממון נמי הן גובין. **אילימא** לצדיקים כו'. דבהכי מיירי קרא, דלעיל מיניה כתיב: "ולי מה יקרו רעיך אל מה עצמו ראשיהם", וכתיב בתריה: "אספרם מחול ירבון".

לא

רבינו גרשום

נהרדעי לטעמייהו. דרב נחמן ושמואל ורב חמא מנהרדעי: האחין שחלקו אין להם דרך זה על זה. כגון בתחלה היו כל השדות בחיזוק א' של אביהם ולא הוה בכולהו אלא דרך אחד לילך מזה לזה והשתא כשחלקו אין להם דרך אם לא קנו זה מזה וחלונות שאם הגיע חצר לזה ולזה בית והיו חלונות הבית פתוחים לחצר יכול זה לבנות כנגדן ולסותמן וכן לאמת המים צריך ליקח דרך זה מזה. כה"ג יכול בעל תרביצא לבנות אשיתא נגד אספלידא: שהלכות קבועות הן לדון הכי: דנפיק עליה תברא. דפריע השטר של יתומין: דגדלי יתמי. (למייתי) [דלמא מייתו] ראיה דהאי תברא מזויף הוא שהוחזק בפני עדים לאחר מיתת אביהן שעדיין היה חייב לו: לבר מהא. דודאי קרעי' לשטר. דסהדי דחתימי על שובר בשקרי לא מחזקינן: א) לעולם לא קרעי' לשטרא כדרב חמא. דאם כן הוה מפיק ליה האי שובר בחיי האב מדלית עדים דאפקה בחיי האב משום הכי לא קרעי' לשטרא: בית שער. ב) מקום שהשומר ישן ששומר החצר כופין לא' מבני חצר המעכב: מעליותא הוא. בית שער: ולא אשתעי אליהו בהדיה. משום דכי אתי עני צועק על פתח שער מפסיק אותו בית שער קולו ואינו נשמע לבעל הבית: הא מגואי גריעותא הוא. כלומר אם נעשה בנין בית שער מבפנים לחצר מפסיק הקול שאין העני יכול ליכנס לתוכו אבל אם בנו מאבראי ברה"ר ודאי מעליותא היא והיו כופין אותו לבנות הואיל והחצר פתוח לרה"ר יכול העני ליכנס בתוך מחיצות בית שער עד השער וצועק ויכול לשומעו דאין מפסיק אלא שער לחודיה: אית ליה דלת לבית שער גריעותא. שהשער והדלת מעכבין קולו. אית ליה פותחת מנעול לדלת לאו מעליותא היא שאין העני יכול לפותחו מפני המנעול. הא דמשנתנו דכופין לבנות בית שער דלית ליה דלת לבית שער. ואי קשיא דהא תנא כופין לבנות בית שער ודלת הא לא תקשי דהא תני דלת [לחצר] במתני' ולחצר תנן לא לבית השער: חצר הסמוכה לרה"ר צריכה בית שער. כלומר אם מבוי שאינו מפולש ויש בו חצירות אותן שבפנים אין צריכות שער ולא היו כופין אבל אותה הסמוכה לרה"ר צריך והיו כופין: ורבנן דמתני' לא פליגי בין סמוכה לשאינה סמוכה דזימנין דדחקי רבים במבוי ועיילי ואתי וקא חזו לההוא ואיכא היזק ראיה מבני רה"ר: הסמוכה לספר. לצורך חומה ודלתים: לפי שבח ממון. מי שהוא עשיר נותן יותר או לפי נפשות שבעיר שכולן יתנו בשוה: משום גייסות: כשהן גובין מבני העיר. קבע בה מסמרות. קבע הלכה (שם) [יתד] הוא שלא תמוט: לפי קירוב בתים. כלומר אותן בתים חיצוניות שצריכין להם יותר לחיזוק החומה יותר מן הפנימית ויתנו יותר אי לא: דשורא אדרבנן. שפסק עליהם ליתן חלקם לבנות החומה: רבנן לא צריכי נטירותא. שתורה ומעשים טובים שלהם משמרים אותן: השתא כל ישראל עם הצדיקים כחול וצדיקים לבדם יותר מחול בתמיה. ומה חול שמועט ממעשיהם של צדיקים מגין על הים שאין עוברין אותו גלי ים. על אחת כמה וכמה שמגינין עליהם מעשיהם ולא צריכי נטירותא: כי אתא. ריש לקיש לקמיה דר' יוחנן: אני חומה. זו תורה שמגינה על לומדיה כחומה שמגינה על אנשי העיר: ושדי כמגדלות

אלו

א) נ"ל בהא נמי הלכתא כרב חמא ולעולם לא קרעינן וכו'. ב) נ"ל מקום ששומר החצר ישן כופין וכו'.

עין משפט נר מצוה

נ א מיי' פ"ב מהלכות שכנים הל' יב סמג עשין פב טוש"ע ח"מ סי' קעג סעיף ג:

נא ב ג מיי' פי"ז מהל' מלוה הל' ח סמג עשין צד טוש"ע ח"מ סי' קח סעיף טז:

נב ד מיי' פ"ה מהל' שכנים הל' א סמג עשין פ"ב טוש"ע ח"מ סי' קסא סעיף א:

נג ה מיי' שם פ"ו מהל' א סמג שם טוש"ע ח"מ סי' קסג סעיף א:

נד ו ז מיי' שם הל' ה טוש"ע שם סעיף ב:

נה ח מיי' שם הל' ד טוש"ע שם סעיף ג:

נו ט מיי' שם הלכה ו טוש"ע שם סעיף ד וטוש"ע יד סי' רמג סעיף ב:

מסורת הש"ס

א) [לקמן סה.]: ב) [לעיל ב:]: ג) [סנהדרין קיב.]: ד) רש"ל מ"ז וצ"ל תניא רשב"ג כו': ה) [שבח ממון וכן הוא ברא"ש]: ו) [לקמן ח. ב"מ קח.]: ז) [פסחים פז.]:

הגהות הב"ח

(א) גמ' ורב אמר יש להן: (ב) שם הא מאבראי וכו' הא והא מאבראי: (ג) שם דפותחת דידיה מאבראי רשב"ג אומר וכו' תניא רשב"ג אומר לא כל כצ"ל ופיסקא כופין אותו לבנות בית שער ודלת לחצר נמחק: (ד) שם אמר ליה ר"ל רבנן: (ה) תוס' ד"ה אין להם וכו' כל אחד בחלק חבירו כצ"ל ותיבת חלק נמחק: (ו) ד"ה לפי כו' דאין בה סכנת: (ז) בא"ד אבל היכא דתעו במדבר וכו' כיון דתעו איכא:

אֵלּוּ ת"ח? ור"ל סָבַר לָהּ א)כִּדְדָרֵשׁ רָבָא: °"אֲנִי חוֹמָה" — זוֹ כְּנֶסֶת יִשְׂרָאֵל, "וְשָׁדַי כַּמִּגְדָּלוֹת" — אֵלּוּ בָּתֵּי כְנֵסִיּוֹת וּבָתֵּי מִדְרָשׁוֹת. ב)רַב (א) נַחְמָן בַּר רַב חִסְדָּא רְמָא כַּרְגָּא אַרַבָּנַן, א"ל רַב נַחְמָן בַּר יִצְחָק: עֲבַרְתְּ אַדְּאוֹרַיְיתָא וְאַדִּנְבִיאֵי וְאַדִּכְתוּבֵי. אַדְּאוֹרַיְיתָא, דִּכְתִיב: °"אַף חֹבֵב עַמִּים כָּל קְדֹשָׁיו בְּיָדֶךָ", אָמַר מֹשֶׁה לִפְנֵי הקב"ה: רִבּוֹנוֹ שֶׁל עוֹלָם, אֲפִילּוּ בְּשָׁעָה שֶׁאַתָּה מְחַבֵּב עַמִּים — כָּל קְדוֹשָׁיו יִהְיוּ בְּיָדֶךָ. "וְהֵם תֻּכּוּ לְרַגְלֶךָ" — תָּנֵי רַב יוֹסֵף: אֵלּוּ תַּלְמִידֵי חֲכָמִים, שֶׁמְּכַתְּתִים רַגְלֵיהֶם מֵעִיר לְעִיר וּמִמְּדִינָה לִמְדִינָה לִלְמוֹד תּוֹרָה, "יִשָּׂא מִדַּבְּרֹתֶיךָ" — לִישָּׂא וְלִיתֵּן בְּדִבּוּרוֹתָיו שֶׁל מָקוֹם. אַדִּנְבִיאֵי, דִּכְתִיב: °"גַּם כִּי יִתְנוּ בַגּוֹיִם עַתָּה אֲקַבְּצֵם וַיָּחֵלּוּ מְּעָט מִמַּשָּׂא מֶלֶךְ וְשָׂרִים", אָמַר ג)עוּלָּא: פָּסוּק זֶה בִּלְשׁוֹן אֲרָמִית נֶאֱמַר; אִי תָּנוּ כּוּלְּהוּ — עַתָּה אֲקַבְּצֵם, וְאִם מְעַט מֵהֶם — יָחֵלּוּ מִמַּשָּׂא מֶלֶךְ וְשָׂרִים. אַדִּכְתוּבֵי, דִּכְתִיב: °"מִנְדָּה בְלוֹ וַהֲלָךְ לָא שַׁלִּיט לְמִרְמֵא עֲלֵיהֹם", ד)וְאָמַר רַב יְהוּדָה: "מִנְדָּה" — זוֹ מִנַּת הַמֶּלֶךְ, "בְּלוֹ" — זוֹ כֶּסֶף גּוּלְגַּלְתָּא, "וַהֲלָךְ" — זוֹ אַרְנוֹנָא. רַב פַּפָּא בְּרָמָא כַּרְיָא חֲדַתָּא אַיָּתְמֵי, א"ל רַב שֵׁישָׁא בְּרֵיהּ דְּרַב אִידִי לְרַב פַּפָּא: וְדִילְמָא לָא מִדְוִיל! א"ל: מִישְׁקַל שָׁקֵילְנָא מִנַּיְיהוּ, אִי מִדְוִיל — מִדְוִיל, וְאִי לָא — גמַהַדַּרְנָא לְהוּ נִיהֲלַיְיהוּ. ה)אֲמַר רַב יְהוּדָה: דהַכֹּל לְאַגְלֵי גַּפָּא, אֲפִילּוּ מִיָּתְמֵי, ו)האֲבָל רַבָּנַן לָא צְרִיכִי נְטִירוּתָא; והַכֹּל לְכַרְיָא פַּתְיָא, אֲפִי' מֵרַבָּנַן. זוְלָא אֲמָרַן אֶלָּא דְּלָא נָפְקִי בְּאַכְלוּזָא, אֲבָל נָפְקִי בְּאַכְלוּזָא, רַבָּנַן לָאו בְּנֵי מֵיפַּק בְּאַכְלוּזָא נִינְהוּ.§ רַבִּי פָּתַח אוֹצָרוֹת בִּשְׁנֵי בַצּוֹרֶת, אָמַר: יִכָּנְסוּ בַּעֲלֵי מִקְרָא, בַּעֲלֵי מִשְׁנָה, בַּעֲלֵי תַלְמוּד, בַּעֲלֵי הֲלָכָה, בַּעֲלֵי הַגָּדָה, אֲבָל עַמֵּי הָאָרֶץ אַל יִכָּנְסוּ. דָּחַק רַבִּי יוֹנָתָן בֶּן עַמְרָם וְנִכְנַס, אָמַר לוֹ: רַבִּי, פַּרְנְסֵנִי! אָמַר לוֹ: בְּנִי, קָרִיתָ? אָמַר לוֹ: לָאו. שָׁנִיתָ? א"ל: לָאו. אִם כֵּן, בַּמֶּה אֲפַרְנֶסְךָ? [א"ל:] פַּרְנְסֵנִי כְּכֶלֶב וּכְעוֹרֵב. פַּרְנְסֵיהּ. בָּתַר דִּנְפַק, חיָתֵיב רַבִּי וְקָא מִצְטַעֵר וְאָמַר: אוֹי לִי שֶׁנָּתַתִּי פִּתִּי לְעַם הָאָרֶץ! אָמַר לְפָנָיו ר' שִׁמְעוֹן בַּר רַבִּי: שֶׁמָּא יוֹנָתָן בֶּן עַמְרָם תַּלְמִידְךָ הוּא, שֶׁאֵינוֹ רוֹצֶה לֵיהָנוֹת מִכְּבוֹד תּוֹרָה מִיָּמָיו? בְּדַקוּ וְאַשְׁכַּח, אָמַר רַבִּי: יִכָּנְסוּ הַכֹּל. רַבִּי לְטַעֲמֵיהּ, דְּאָמַר רַבִּי: ז)אֵין פּוּרְעָנוּת בָּא לָעוֹלָם אֶלָּא בִּשְׁבִיל עַמֵּי הָאָרֶץ. כְּהַהוּא דְּמֵי ח)כְּלִילָא דְּשָׁדוּ אַטְּבֶרְיָא, אָתוּ לְקַמֵּיהּ דְּרַבִּי וַאֲמַרוּ לֵיהּ: לֵיתְבוּ רַבָּנַן בַּהֲדַן, אֲמַר לְהוּ: לָא. אֲמַרוּ לֵיהּ: עָרוֹקִינַן, [א"ל:] עֲרוֹקוּ. עֲרַקוּ פַּלְגֵיהוֹן, דַּלְיוּהּ פַּלְגָּא. אָתוּ הָנְהוּ פַּלְגָּא קַמֵּי דְּרַבִּי, א"ל: לֵיתְבוּ רַבָּנַן בַּהֲדַן, אֲמַר לְהוּ: לָא. עָרוֹקִינַן, עֲרוֹקוּ. עֲרַקוּ כּוּלְּהוּ, פַּשׁ הַהוּא כּוֹבֵס, שַׁדְיוּהּ אַכּוֹבֵס. עֲרַק כּוֹבֵס, פְּקַע כְּלִילָא. א"ר: רְאִיתֶם, שֶׁאֵין פּוּרְעָנוּת בָּא לָעוֹלָם אֶלָּא בִּשְׁבִיל עַמֵּי הָאָרֶץ.§ "וְכַמָּה יְהֵא בָּעִיר וִיהֵא כְּאַנְשֵׁי הָעִיר" וכו'.§ וּרְמִינְהִי: ט)טהַחַמֶּרֶת וְהַגַּמֶּלֶת הָעוֹבֶרֶת מִמָּקוֹם לְמָקוֹם, וְלָנָה בְּתוֹכָהּ וְהוּדְּחָה עִמָּהֶן — הֵן בִּסְקִילָה וּמָמוֹנָן פָּלֵט, וְאִם נִשְׁתַּהוּ שָׁם שְׁלֹשִׁים יוֹם — הֵן בְּסַיִיף וּמָמוֹנָן אָבֵד! אֲמַר רָבָא, לָא קַשְׁיָא: הָא לִבְנֵי מָתָא, הָא לְיָתוּבֵי מָתָא; כִּדְתַנְיָא: י)יהַמּוּדָּר הֲנָאָה מֵאַנְשֵׁי הָעִיר, כָּל שֶׁנִּשְׁתַּהָא שָׁם שְׁנֵים עָשָׂר חֹדֶשׁ — אָסוּר לֵיהָנוֹת מִמֶּנּוּ, פָּחוֹת מִכָּאן — מוּתָּר; מִיּוֹשְׁבֵי הָעִיר, כָּל שֶׁנִּשְׁתַּהָא שָׁם שְׁלֹשִׁים יוֹם — אָסוּר לֵיהָנוֹת מִמֶּנּוּ, פָּחוֹת מִכָּאן — מוּתָּר לֵיהָנוֹת מִמֶּנּוּ. וּלְכָל מִילֵּי מִי בָּעֵינַן י"ב חֹדֶשׁ? וְהָתַנְיָא: כ)כשְׁלֹשִׁים יוֹם — לְתַמְחוּי, שְׁלֹשָׁה חֳדָשִׁים — לְקוּפָּה, שִׁשָּׁה — לִכְסוּת, תִּשְׁעָה — לִקְבוּרָה, שְׁנֵים עָשָׂר — ל)לְפַסֵּי הָעִיר! אָמַר ר' אַסִּי אָמַר ר' יוֹחָנָן: לכִּי תְּנַן נַמִּי מַתְנִיתִין שְׁנֵים עָשָׂר חֹדֶשׁ — לְפַסֵּי הָעִיר תְּנַן.§ וא"ר אַסִּי אָמַר ר' יוֹחָנָן: מהַכֹּל לְפַסֵּי הָעִיר וַאֲפִי' מִיָּתְמֵי, נאֲבָל רַבָּנַן לָא, מ)דְּרַבָּנַן לָא צְרִיכִי נְטִירוּתָא. אֲמַר רַב פַּפָּא: סלְשׁוּרָא וּלְפָרָשָׁאָה וּלְטַרְזִינָא — אֲפִילּוּ מִיָּתְמֵי, עאֲבָל רַבָּנַן לָא צְרִיכִי נְטִירוּתָא. כְּלָלָא דְּמִילְּתָא: כָּל מִילְּתָא דְּאִית לְהוּ הֲנָאָה מִינֵּיהּ — אֲפִילּוּ מִיָּתְמֵי. רַבָּה רְמָא צְדָקָה אַיָּתְמֵי דְּבֵי בַּר מָרְיוֹן, א"ל אַבַּיֵי, וְהָתָנֵי רַב שְׁמוּאֵל בַּר יְהוּדָה: פאֵין פּוֹסְקִין צְדָקָה עַל הַיְתוֹמִים אֲפִילּוּ לְפִדְיוֹן שְׁבוּיִם! א"ל: אֲנָא צלְאַחְשׁוּבִינְהוּ קָא עָבֵידְנָא. נ)קאִיפְרָא הוּרְמִיז, אִימֵּיהּ דְּשָׁבוּר מַלְכָּא, שַׁדְרָה אַרְנְקָא דְּדִינָרֵי לְקַמֵּיהּ דְּרַב יוֹסֵף, אֲמַרָה: לֶיהֱוֵי לְמִצְוָה רַבָּה. יָתֵיב רַב יוֹסֵף וְקָא מְעַיֵּין בָּהּ: מַאי מִצְוָה רַבָּה? א"ל אַבַּיֵי, מִדְּתָנֵי רַב שְׁמוּאֵל בַּר יְהוּדָה: אֵין פּוֹסְקִין צְדָקָה עַל הַיְתוֹמִים אֲפִילּוּ לְפִדְיוֹן שְׁבוּיִם, רשְׁמַע מִינָּהּ:

פִּדְיוֹן

תורה אור: אני חומה — שיר ח; אף חובב עמים — דברים לג; גם כי יתנו בגוים — הושע ח; מנדה בלו — עזרא ז

אֵלּוּ תַּלְמִידֵי חֲכָמִים. אַלְמָא אֵין צְרִיכִין חוֹמָה. [זוֹ] כְּנֶסֶת יִשְׂרָאֵל. כּוּלָּם שָׁוִין לְעִנְיַן חוֹמָה, וְגוֹדְרִים עַצְמָן מִלְּהִטָּמֵא בַּגּוֹיִם. שֶׁאַתָּה מְחַבֵּב עַמִּים. שֶׁאַתָּה מַגְבִּיהַּ לָהֶם פָּנֶיךָ לְהַשְׁלִיטָן עַל בָּנֶיךָ. כָּל קְדוֹשָׁיו. שֶׁל יִשְׂרָאֵל, בְּיָדְךָ [הֵם] לְשׁוֹמְרָן. בִּלְשׁוֹן אֲרַמִּי נֶאֱמַר. "יִתְנוּ" תַּרְגּוּם שֶׁל יִשְׁנוּ, כְּמוֹ "וְשִׁנַּנְתָּם" = וּתְנֵינוּן (דברים ו). אִם תָּנוּ כּוּלָּם. וְכֵן רוּבָּן יִהְיוּ שׁוֹנִין וְעוֹסְקִים בַּתּוֹרָה כְּשֶׁיִּגְלוּ בָּעַמִּים. עַתָּה אֲקַבְּצֵם. בְּקָרוֹב אֲקַבְּצֵם. וַיָּחֵלּוּ מְעַט וגו'. וְאַף [אִם] מוּעָטִין הֵן הַשּׁוֹנִין בָּעַמִּים — "יָחֵלּוּ מִמַּשָּׂא מֶלֶךְ וְשָׂרִים", יִהְיוּ בְּטֵלִים מִלָּשֵׂאת מַשָּׂא מֶלֶךְ וְשָׂרִים. "יָחֵלּוּ" — כְּמוֹ "לֹא יַחֵל דְּבָרוֹ" (במדבר ל). מִנְדָּה בְלוֹ וַהֲלָךְ. דָּרְיָוֶשׁ צִוָּה אֶת פַּחַת עֵבֶר הַנָּהָר עַל אַנְשֵׁי כְּנֶסֶת הַגְּדוֹלָה. מִנַּת הַמֶּלֶךְ. מִגְבַּת מִסִּים שֶׁהֵן מַטִּילִין תָּמִיד עַל בְּנֵי הַמְּדִינָה. אַרְנוֹנָא. עִישּׂוּרֵי תְבוּאוֹת וּבְהֵמוֹת מִדֵּי שָׁנָה בְּשָׁנָה. כַּרְיָא חֲדַתָּא. יְלִיאַת כְּרִיַּית בְּאֵר מַיִם חַיִּים לִשְׁתּוֹת. לָא מִדְוִיל. לֹא יִמָּצְאוּ בּוֹ מַיִם, וְהִפְסַדְתֶּם חִנָּם, וְיָתְמֵי לָאו בְּנֵי מְחִילָה נִינְהוּ דְּלִיחֲלוּ. לְאַגְלֵי גַּפָּא. לְשַׁעֲרֵי חוֹמוֹת הָעִיר לְהַצִּיב בָּהֶן דְּלָתוֹת. אַגְלֵי = דְּלָתוֹת, כְּמוֹ: טְרוֹקוּ גַּלֵּי, בִּבְרָכוֹת (דף כח.) גַּפָּא = סְתִימָה, כְּמוֹ: מָלֵא אַחַר הַגַּפָּה, בְּ"אֵלּוּ מְצִיאוֹת" (ב"מ דף כה:). לְכַרְיָא פַּתְיָא. חֲפִירַת בּוֹר לִשְׁתּוֹת מַיִם. וְעַל שֵׁם הַכְּלִי הַמּוּנָּח שָׁם בַּבּוֹר תָּמִיד לִשְׁתּוֹת בּוֹ עוֹבְרֵי דְרָכִים, קוֹרֵהוּ פַּתְיָא. אֲפִילּוּ מֵרַבָּנַן. שֶׁהַכֹּל צְרִיכִין לַמַּיִם. דְּלָא נָפְקִי בְּאַכְלוּזָא. שֶׁאֵין הֵן עַצְמָם יוֹצְאִין בְּהַכְרָזָה לַחְפּוֹר, אֶלָּא שׂוֹכְרִים פּוֹעֲלִים. כְּכֶלֶב וּכְעוֹרֵב. שֶׁחָס הקב"ה עֲלֵיהֶם (שבת קנה:), שֶׁנֶּאֱמַר: "יוֹדֵעַ צַדִּיק דִּין דַּלִּים" (משלי כט), לְפִי שֶׁהַכֶּלֶב מְזוֹנוֹתָיו מוּעָטִין — לְפִיכָךְ שׁוֹהֶה אֲכִילָתוֹ בְּמֵעָיו שְׁלֹשֶׁת יָמִים. וְגַבֵּי עוֹרֵב כְּתִיב: "לִבְנֵי עֹרֵב אֲשֶׁר יִקְרָאוּ" (תהלים קמז), לְפִי שֶׁהָעוֹרֵב אַכְזָרִי עַל בָּנָיו, וְהקב"ה מְזַמֵּין לָהֶן יַתּוּשִׁין מִתּוֹךְ צוֹאָתָם, וְאוֹכְלִין. דְּמֵי כְּלִילָא. עֲטָרָה לַמֶּלֶךְ קֵיסָר. אָתוּ. עַמֵּי הָאָרֶץ לְקַמֵּיהּ דְּרַבִּי. דַּלְיוּהּ לְפַלְגָּא. מָחַל הַמֶּלֶךְ דְּמֵי הַחֵצִי, וְסִילְּקָהּ מֵעֲלֵיהֶן. שַׁדְיוּהּ אַכּוֹבֵס. הִטִּילוּהָ פַּחְתֵי הַמֶּלֶךְ עַל הַכּוֹבֵס. הַחַמֶּרֶת וְהַגַּמֶּלֶת. שַׁיָּירָא שֶׁל חַמָּרִים וְשֶׁל גַּמָּלִים. הֲרֵי אֵלּוּ בִּסְקִילָה. כְּדִין שְׁאָר יְחִידִים. יָתוּבֵי מָתָא. בִּשְׁלֹשִׁים יוֹם. וְגַבֵּי עִיר הַנִּדַּחַת כְּתִיב "יוֹשְׁבֵי הָעִיר" (דברים יג). וּלְכָל מִילֵּי. וּמִתְקַמֵּי הָכִי לָא יָהֵיב מִידֵּי עִם בְּנֵי הָעִיר. שְׁלֹשִׁים יוֹם לְתַמְחוּי. כֵּיוָן שֶׁשָּׁהָה שָׁם שְׁלֹשִׁים יוֹם — גּוֹבִין הֵימֶנּוּ [גַּבָּאֵי] תַמְחוּי מַאֲכָל לַעֲנִיִּים. לְקוּפָּה. לִצְדָקָה. לִכְסוּת. עֲנִיֵּי הָעִיר. לִקְבוּרָה. לִקְבּוֹר עֲנִיֵּי הָעִיר, שֶׁהִיא יְגִיעָה יְתֵירָה. לְשׁוּרָא. לְתִיקּוּן הַחוֹמָה. לְפָרָשָׁא. (ג) פָּרָשׁ שֶׁהוֹלֵךְ סְבִיבוֹת הָעִיר לְשׁוֹמְרָהּ, וְלֵידַע מַה הִיא צְרִיכָה. לְטַרְזִינָא. שׁוֹמֵר כְּלֵי זַיִן שֶׁל בְּנֵי הָעִיר, וְיוֹשֵׁב בַּבַּיִת אֵצֶל הַשַּׁעַר.

שֶׁבִּי

לא שליט למרמא עליהם. לפי שהיו עסוקים במלאכת שמים בבנין בית המקדש, ה"נ אין להטיל מס על לומדי תורה.

והלך זו ארנונא. פי' בקונטרס: עישור בהמות ותבואה כו'. ור"ת פי': ארוחת דורון לשלטון העובר ממקום למקום, שנותן לו כל עיר ועיר ארוחה, ופירושו מלשון "ויבא הלך לאיש העשיר" (שמואל ב יב).

כריא פתיא. פירש ר"ת: להסיר גבשושית מרחוב העיר.

איפרא הורמיז. פר"ת דמשמעות הלשון: חן מאת המקום. איפרא — כמו: אפריון נמטייה לר"ש (ב"מ דף קיט.). הורמיז — שם — שכינה, כי ההיא דס"פ "אחד דיני ממונות" (סנהדרין דף לט. ושם ד"ה דהורמיז): מפלגא דידך ולעיל דהורמיז בזיי"ן, מפלגא ולתחת דהורמין בנו"ן, כמו הורמין בר לילתא לקמן (דף עג.).

(לעיל) ככלב וכעורב. כמו שפי' הקונטרס. והיינו דכתיב "נותן לבהמה לחמה לבני עורב" וגו', "בהמה" בגימטריא כלב.

יתיב רב יוסף וקא מעיין בה. וא"ת: וכי לית ליה "ביבש קצירה תשברנה" וגו' (ישעיה כז) כדאמרי' בפירקין (דף י:)? וי"ל: דקבל' משום שלום מלכות, כדעבד רבא לקמן (שם). וכי היכי דפלגינהו רבא לעניי גוים — ה"נ פדה בהו רב יוסף שבויי גוים. ומיהו, לא צריכי להכי, אלא כדפירש הקונט', (ג) ס)דרבא דקבלה משום שלום מלכות, וכיון שאמר לו ליתן למצוה רבה — לא היה אפשר לחלקם לעניי גוים, דאסור לגנוב דעת הבריות, ואפי' דעתו של גוי (חולין צד.). אבל מעות המתחלקים לעניים — אין כאן גניבת דעת, דאינהו נמי ידעי שישראל רגילין לפרנסם, כדאמר ב"הנזקין" (גיטין דף סא.): מפרנסים עניי גוים עם עניי ישראל מפני דרכי שלום. והא דקבל מההוא טייעא דנדב שרגא לבי כנישתא בפ"ק דערכין (דף ו: ושם ד"ה עד) אע"ג דהתם לא היה שלום מלכות — התם טעמא משום דהוו כמו קרבן, ואמרינן (נזיר סב.): "איש איש" — לרבות גוים, שנודרים נדרים ונדבות כישראל.

רבינו גרשום

אלו ת"ח. שלומדין זה מזה כתינוק יונק משדי אמו: וריש לקיש דמפיק מאספרם מחול ירבון דריש האי אני חומה בכל ישראל ולא בצדיקים בלבד: כרגא. כסף גולגלתא: אע"פ שאתה מחבב אומות העולם. שאתה נותן להם על ישראל ממשלה בזמן שישראל בגלות אעפ"כ קדושיו של ישראל העוסקים בתורה יהיו מסורין בידך: לרגלך. משמע בשבילך ומשמע רגל ממש: יתנו בגוים. בלשון ארמי כמו ושננתם ותתנינון כלומר גם יתנון שעוסקים בתורה כולהו עתה אקבצם מגלותם ואם מעט מהם יעסקו ויחלו אותו מעט ויחלו כמו לא יחל דברו: מנת המלך. שנותנין מתנות למלך מסים: ארנונא. מס של קרקע: כריא חדתא. חפירה גדולה שחופרין ליכנס שם מים הרבה להשקות ממנה שדות ע"י דלייה ודרך נגרים ופסק א) ליתן ליתומין חלק בחפירה זו שהן נהנין ממנה כאחרים: לא מדויל. שלא ינבעו המים ונמצאת מוציא מעות יתומים בכדי: לאגלי גפא. זהו שעושין מחיצה או גדר סמוך לחומת העיר מבחוץ כדי להגן על החומה ועל שם כך קרי אגלי גפא לשון הגפת דלתות כלומר לנעול שערים שעושין לפני פינת העיר משום מצור העיר: לכריא פתיא. שחופרין למלאות ממנו מים לשתות ועל שם כך קרי ליה כריא פתיא שדולין בכלי חרס כמו (ברכות נ וש"מ) פתיא אוכמא: אפי' מרבנן. שהן שותין ממנו כאחרים: ואי קא נפקי באכלוזא. כלומר שיוצאין חבורות בני העיר הן עצמן (ואינן) [ואינהו] חופרין ואינן שוכרין רבנן לא עבדי הכי מפני כבוד תורה: פתח אוצר בשני בצורת. לפרנס עניים: בעל הלכות. זה ששונה ברייתות. אף על גב דבדוכתא אחרינא אמרי' בעלי הלכות אלו בעלי משנה הכא הואיל ותני בעלי משנה צריכין למימר דהלכות אלו ברייתות הן: ככלב וכעורב. דכתיב ורחמיו על כל מעשיו: רבי לטעמיה. שלא היה רוצה לפרנס עם הארץ דההוא דמי כלילא. שהשליך המלך מס על יושבי טבריא כדי שיקנו לו כתר: אמר להו. לא תסייען [לכו] רבנן: ערקינן. דלא מצינן למיתן כולי דמי כלילא אמר להו ערוקו: דלייה לדמי כלילא. על ההוא פלגא דאשתייר: פקע כלילא. בטל גזירת הכתר: הראיתם שאין פורעניות בא לעולם אלא בשביל עמי הארץ. דכיון דלא נשארו שם אלא רבנן לא גזרו עליהן ליתן דמי כתר שכל זמן שאחד מעמי הארץ היה שם גזרו ושוב לא גזרו: **פיסקא** ויהא כאנשי העיר. ליתן בכל מילי שנותנין בני העיר שנים עשר חדש: החמרת והגמלת. שיירא של חמרין וגמלין העוברים ממקום למקום ולנה בתוך עיר הנדחת והודחה עמה כדכתיב וידיחו את יושבי עירם הן בסייף וממונן אבד כאנשי עיר הנדחת כדכתיב הכה תכה את יושבי העיר וגו': הן נדונין בסקילה וממונן פלט. הואיל ולא נשתהו שם כלל אלא כדי לינה אלמא דל' יום הוי כיושבי העיר וקשיא למתני' דבעי י"ב חדש ב) למיקרייא מיתבא מתא לא בעינן אלא ל' יום ונידון כמותם משום דהכתוב מיירי בלשון יושבי כדכתיב הכה תכה את יושבי העיר וגו' אבל למיקרייא מבני מתא להיותן כאנשי העיר ליתן עמהם לכל דבר לא הוי עד י"ב חודש כדתניא המודר וכו': ולכל מילי כלומר דמשמע במתני' שלא יתן כלום בדבר עד י"ב חודש והא תניא נמי הבא לעיר ונשתהה שם ל' יום חייב ליתן לתמחוי היינו כלי שבו נותנין מאכל ומקבצין וגובין מבני העיר ליתן מנות ממאכלים בתמחוי להאכיל לעניי העולם העוברים עליהם ואם נשתהה שם ג' חדשים יתן חלקו לקופה של צדקה שגובין מע"ש לערב שבת לפרנס עניי אותה העיר ואם נשתהה ו' חדשים חייב ליתן ג) חלקו העיר שקורין שפיצ"א ותירות שעושין חוץ לחומה לחזוק העיר אלמא לכל מילי לא בעינן י"ב חדש: הכל לפסי. מן הכל גובין לצורך תקון פסי העיר: לשורא. לחזוק החומה: לפרשא. שקונים סוסים לפרשים (כפי) [כדי] שיצאו חוץ לעיר לעיין אם [באו] גייסות: לטורזינא. לצורך [כלי] זיין שנושאין אותן שומרי חומות העיר: בר מריון. איש א' היה עשיר גדול: אנא לאחשובינהו בעינא. שיהו חשובין בכל דבר מצוה כמו אביהן:

נהרג

א) נראה דצ"ל ופסק שיתנו היתומים חלק וכו'. ב) נ"ל הא למיקרייא מיתבא מתא וכו'. ג) נ"ל חייב ליתן חלקו בכסות: לפסי העיר שקורין שפילא וכו'.

מסורת הש"ס

א) [פסחים פז:] ב) ס"א רב הונא: ג) ס"א רבא: ד) נדרים סב: ה) ב"מ קח. ו) [שם ולעיל ז:] ז) [שבת קלט. ע"ש יבמות סג. ע"ש] ח) [פי' נגנב נזר המלך אמר המלך הואיל ופשעו היהודים בשמירת העיר ישלמו דמי הנזר. ערוך ערך כלל א'] ט) סנהדרין קיב. ע"ש: י) [סנהדרין שם תוספתא נדרים פ"ד] כ) [תוספתא פאה פ"ד] ל) פי' קרסי עץ לחזק שערי העיר. ערוך ערך פס א'] מ) [לעיל ז: וש"נ] נ) [ועי' פירש"י נדה כ: ובתענית כד:] ס) נ"ל לרב יוסף. רש"ל:

עין משפט נר מצוה

נז א מיי' פ"ו מהלכות ת"ת הלכה י סמג עשין יב טוש"ע ח"מ סי' קסג סעיף ה וטוש"ע י"ד סי' רמג סעיף ב:

נח ב ג ד מיי' פ"ו מהל' שכנים הל' ו ז סמג עשין פב טוש"ע ח"מ סי' קסג סעיף ד:

נט ה ו ז מיי' שם ופ"ז מהל' מ"ע הל' י סמג שם וסי' יב טוש"ע שם וטוש"ע י"ד סי' רמג סעיף א ב:

ס ח טוש"ע י"ד סי' רנג סעיף א:

סא ט מיי' פ"ט מהל' ע"ז הל' ט:

סב י מיי' פ"ט מהל' נדרים הל' יז סמג לאוין רמג טוש"ע י"ד סי' ריז סעיף לב:

סג כ מיי' פ"ט מהל' מתנות עניים הל' יב סמג עשין קסב טוש"ע י"ד סי' רנו סעיף ה:

סד ל מיי' פ"ו מהל' שכנים הל' ה סמג עשין פב טוש"ע ח"מ סי' קסג סעיף ב:

סה מ מיי' שם טוש"ע שם סעיף ז:

סו נ ס ע מיי' שם ופ"ז מהל' ת"ת הלכה י סמג שם טוש"ע שם וטוש"ע י"ד סי' רמג סעיף ב:

סז פ צ מיי' פ"ח מהל' מתנות עניים הלכה יב סמג עשין קסב טוש"ע י"ד סי' רמח סעיף ג:

סח ק מיי' שם פ"ח הל' יא סמג עשין קסב טוש"ע י"ד סי' רנב סעיף ט:

סט ר מיי' שם הל' י סמג שם טוש"ע י"ד סי' רנב סעיף א:

הגהות הב"ח

(א) גמ' רב חנן בר רב חסדא רמא כרגא וכו' עבר מר אדאורייתא: (ב) רש"י ד"ה לפרשא פרש הרוכב סביבות: (ג) תוס' ד"ה יתיב וכו' כדפי' הקונטרס דרב יוסף קבלה הכא משום שלום. נ"ב לקמן דף י"א ד"ה דלא סיימוה:

פִּדְיוֹן שְׁבוּיִם מִצְוָה רַבָּה הִיא. אֲמַר לֵיהּ רָבָא לְרַבָּה בַּר מָרִי: מְנָא הָא מִילְּתָא דַּאֲמוּר רַבָּנַן דְּפִדְיוֹן שְׁבוּיִם מִצְוָה רַבָּה הִיא? א"ל, דִּכְתִיב: °"וְהָיָה כִּי יֹאמְרוּ אֵלֶיךָ אָנָה נֵצֵא וְאָמַרְתָּ אֲלֵיהֶם ירמיה טו
כֹּה אָמַר ה' אֲשֶׁר לַמָּוֶת לַמָּוֶת וַאֲשֶׁר לַחֶרֶב לַחֶרֶב וַאֲשֶׁר לָרָעָב לָרָעָב וַאֲשֶׁר לַשְּׁבִי לַשֶּׁבִי", וְאָמַר רַבִּי יוֹחָנָן: כָּל הַמְּאוּחָר בְּפָסוּק זֶה קָשֶׁה מֵחֲבֵירוֹ. חֶרֶב קָשֶׁה מִמָּוֶת — א)אִי בָּעֵית אֵימָא קְרָא, וְאִי בָּעֵית אֵימָא סְבָרָא; אִי בָּעֵית אֵימָא סְבָרָא: הַאי קָא מִינַּוֵּול וְהַאי לָא קָא מִינַּוֵּול; וְאבע"א קְרָא: °"יָקָר בְּעֵינֵי ה' הַמָּוְתָה לַחֲסִידָיו". תהלים קטז
רָעָב קָשֶׁה מֵחֶרֶב — אִיבָּעֵית אֵימָא (א) סְבָרָא: הַאי קָא מִצְטַעֵר וְהַאי לָא קָא מִצְטַעֵר; אִיבָּעֵית אֵימָא קְרָא: °"טוֹבִים הָיוּ חַלְלֵי חֶרֶב מֵחַלְלֵי איכה ד
רָעָב". שֶׁבִי [קָשֶׁה מִכּוּלָּם] דְּכוּלְּהוּ אִיתְנְהוּ בֵּיהּ.§ תָּנוּ רַבָּנַן: ב)אקוּפָּה שֶׁל צְדָקָה נִגְבֵּית בִּשְׁנַיִם וּמִתְחַלֶּקֶת בִּשְׁלֹשָׁה, נִגְבֵּית בִּשְׁנַיִם — ג)בשֶׁאֵין עוֹשִׂים שְׂרָרוּת עַל הַצִּבּוּר פָּחוֹת מִשְּׁנַיִם, וּמִתְחַלֶּקֶת בִּשְׁלֹשָׁה — כְּדִינֵי מָמוֹנוֹת; גתַּמְחוּי נִגְבֵּית בִּשְׁלֹשָׁה וּמִתְחַלֶּקֶת בִּשְׁלֹשָׁה, שֶׁגִּבּוּיָהּ וְחִלּוּקָהּ שָׁוִים; דתַּמְחוּי — בְּכָל יוֹם, קוּפָּה — מֵעֶרֶב שַׁבָּת לְעֶרֶב שַׁבָּת, התַּמְחוּי — לַעֲנִיֵּי עוֹלָם, קוּפָּה — לַעֲנִיֵּי הָעִיר; ווְרַשָּׁאִים בְּנֵי הָעִיר לַעֲשׂוֹת קוּפָּה תַּמְחוּי וְתַמְחוּי קוּפָּה, וּלְשַׁנּוֹתָהּ לְכָל מַה שֶּׁיִּרְצוּ; זוְרַשָּׁאִין בְּנֵי הָעִיר לְהַתְנוֹת עַל הַמִּדּוֹת וְעַל הַשְּׁעָרִים, וְעַל שְׂכַר פּוֹעֲלִים, וּלְהַסִּיעַ עַל קִיצָתָן. אָמַר מָר: אֵין עוֹשִׂין שְׂרָרוּת עַל הַצִּבּוּר פָּחוֹת מִשְּׁנַיִם. מְנָא הָנֵי מִילֵּי? אָמַר רַב נַחְמָן, אָמַר קְרָא: °"וְהֵם יִקְחוּ אֶת הַזָּהָב" וגו'. שמות כח
שְׂרָרוּת הוּא דְּלָא עָבְדִי, חהָא הֵימוּנֵי מְהֵימַן; מְסַיֵּיעַ לֵיהּ לְרַבִּי חֲנִינָא, דְּאָמַר רַבִּי חֲנִינָא: מַעֲשֶׂה טוּמִינָּה רַבִּי שְׁנֵי אַחִין עַל הַקּוּפָּה. מַאי שְׂרָרוּתָא? דְּאָמַר רַב נַחְמָן אָמַר רַבָּה בַּר אֲבוּהָ: לְפִי ד)ישֶׁמְּמַשְׁכְּנִין עַל הַצְּדָקָה וַאֲפִילּוּ בְּעֶ"שׁ. אִינִי? וְהָא כְּתִיב: °"וּפָקַדְתִּי עַל כָּל לֹחֲצָיו", וְאָמַר ר' יִצְחָק בַּר שְׁמוּאֵל בַּר ירמיה ל
מָרְתָא מִשְּׁמֵיהּ דְּרַב: וַאֲפִי' עַל גַּבָּאֵי צְדָקָה! לָא קַשְׁיָא: כהָא דַּאֲמִיד, הָא דְּלָא אֲמִיד. ה)כִּי הָא דְּרָבָא אַכְפְּיֵהּ לְרַב נָתָן בַּר אַמִי, וְשָׁקֵיל מִינֵּיהּ אַרְבַּע מְאָה זוּזֵי לִצְדָקָה. °"וְהַמַּשְׂכִּלִים יַזְהִרוּ כְּזֹהַר הָרָקִיעַ" וגו'. ו)("הַמַּשְׂכִּילִים יַזְהִירוּ כְּזוֹהַר הָרָקִיעַ") — זֶה דניאל יב
דַּיָּין שֶׁדָּן דִּין אֱמֶת לַאֲמִתּוֹ, °"וּמַצְדִּיקֵי הָרַבִּים כַּכּוֹכָבִים לְעוֹלָם וָעֶד" — אֵלּוּ גַּבָּאֵי שם
צְדָקָה. בְּמַתְנִיתָא תָּנָא: "וְהַמַּשְׂכִּילִים יַזְהִירוּ כְּזוֹהַר הָרָקִיעַ" — זֶה דַּיָּין שֶׁדָּן דִּין אֱמֶת לַאֲמִתּוֹ וְגַבָּאֵי צְדָקָה, "וּמַצְדִּיקֵי הָרַבִּים כַּכּוֹכָבִים לְעוֹלָם וָעֶד" — אֵלּוּ מְלַמְּדֵי תִינוֹקוֹת. כְּגוֹן מַאן? אָמַר רַב: כְּגוֹן רַב שְׁמוּאֵל בַּר שִׁילַת. דְּרַב אַשְׁכְּחֵיהּ לְרַב שְׁמוּאֵל בַּר שִׁילַת דַּהֲוָה קָאֵי בְּגִינְתָא, א"ל: שְׁבַקְתֵּיהּ לְהֵימָנוּתָךְ? אֲמַר לֵיהּ: (ב) הָא תְּלֵיסַר שְׁנִין דְּלָא חַזְיָא לִי, וְהַשְׁתָּא נַמִּי דַּעְתַּאי ז)עִלָּוַיְהוּ. ח)וְרַבָּנַן מַאי? אָמַר רָבִינָא: °"וְאוֹהֲבָיו כְּצֵאת הַשֶּׁמֶשׁ בִּגְבֻרָתוֹ". ת"ר: ט)לגַּבָּאֵי צְדָקָה אֵינָן רַשָּׁאִין לִפְרוֹשׁ זֶה שופטים ה
מִזֶּה, אֲבָל פּוֹרֵשׁ זֶה לַשַּׁעַר וְזֶה לֶחָנוּת; ממָצָא מָעוֹת בַּשּׁוּק — לֹא יִתְּנֵם בְּתוֹךְ כִּיסוֹ, אֶלָּא נוֹתְנָן לְתוֹךְ אַרְנְקִי שֶׁל צְדָקָה, וְלִכְשֶׁיָּבֹא לְבֵיתוֹ יִטְּלֵם; כַּיּוֹצֵא בּוֹ, נהָיָה נוֹשֶׁה בַּחֲבֵירוֹ מָנֶה וּפְרָעוֹ בַּשּׁוּק — לֹא יִתְּנֶנּוּ לְתוֹךְ כִּיסוֹ, אֶלָּא נוֹתְנָן לְתוֹךְ אַרְנְקִי שֶׁל צְדָקָה, וְלִכְשֶׁיָּבֹא לְבֵיתוֹ יִטְּלֵם. י)תָּנוּ רַבָּנַן: סגַּבָּאֵי צְדָקָה שֶׁאֵין לָהֶם עֲנִיִּים לְחַלֵּק — פּוֹרְטִין לַאֲחֵרִים, וְאֵין פּוֹרְטִין לְעַצְמָן; עגַּבָּאֵי תַמְחוּי שֶׁאֵין לָהֶם עֲנִיִּים לְחַלֵּק — מוֹכְרִין לַאֲחֵרִים, וְאֵין מוֹכְרִין לְעַצְמָן; פמָעוֹת שֶׁל צְדָקָה אֵין מוֹנִין אוֹתָן שְׁתַּיִם, (ג) אֶלָּא אַחַת אַחַת. אָמַר אַבַּיֵי: מֵרֵישׁ לָא הֲוָה יָתֵיב מָר אַצִּיפֵי דְּבֵי כְנִישְׁתָּא, כֵּיוָן דִּשְׁמָעָהּ לְהָא דְּתַנְיָא: וּלְשַׁנּוֹתָהּ לְכָל מַה שֶּׁיִּרְצוּ, הֲוָה יָתֵיב. אָמַר אַבַּיֵי: מֵרֵישׁ הֲוָה עָבֵיד מָר תְּרֵי כִּיסֵי, חַד לַעֲנִיֵּי דְעָלְמָא וְחַד לַעֲנִיֵּי דְמָתָא, כֵּיוָן דִּשְׁמָעָהּ לְהָא דַּאֲמַר לֵיהּ שְׁמוּאֵל לְרַב תַּחְלִיפָא בַּר אַבְדִּימִי: עֲבֵיד חַד כִּיסָא וְאַתְנֵי

שבי כולהו איתנהו ביה. שהוא ביד הגויים לעשות בו כל חפצו אם למות [אם לחרב] אם לרעב. מפני שהוא כדיני ממונות. לעיין ולתת לכל אחד כפי טפלים התלויין בו. שגבויה וחלוקה שוה. בכל יום מדי יום ביום, כדקתני לקמיה. לפיכך אין גבויו בשנים, שלא יצטרכו לטרוח ולבקש את השלישי לחלק. לעשות קופה תמחוי. לחלק לעניי עולם, אם ירבו עליהן. להתנות על המדות. להגדיל סאת העיר או להקטין. ועל השערים. שער חטין והיין, שלא ימכרנה שנה זו יותר מכך וכך דמים. להסיע על קיצתם. לקנוס את העובר על קיצת דבריהם, להסיעם מדת דין תורה. הא הימוני מהימן. יחיד, להיות גזבר. שני אחים. לגבי המנותא, כחד דמו. מאי שררותיה. דקופה, דקאמרת עלה: לפי שאין עושין שררה על הצבור כו'? אפילו בע"ש. שיש פתחון פה לבעה"ב לומר טרוד אני. ופקדתי וגו'. אלמא אסור למשכן. אמיד. עשירכ). גבאי צדקה. המשכילים אל דל מהו צריך. מלמדי תינוקות. מצדיקי רבים הן, שמלמדין ומחנכין אותן בדרך טובה. שבקתיה להמנותיך. שהיית רגיל ללמדם באמונה, וללמד ולישב על גבם תמיד. דעתאי להתם. לתינוקות. ורבנן מאי. תלמידי חכמים העוסקים בתורה תמיד, מאי כתיב בהו? לפרוש זה מזה. מפני החשד, שלא יאמרו: זה הגובה יחידי — דעתו לגנוב. אבל זה פורש לחנות וזה לשער. זה לגבות מיושבי השער, וזה לגבות מיושבי החנות, ובלבד שיראו שניהן כאחד. לא יתנם לתוך כיסו. שלא יאמרו: מעות של צדקה הוא גונב. פורטין. פרוטות שגבו לוקחין דינרי כסף, לפי שהפרוטות של נחושת מחלידות. ואין פורטין לעצמם. פן יחשדום שפורטין בזול. אין מונין אותם שנים שנים. פן יאמרו: שנים הוא נוטל ואינו מונה אלא אחד. אציפי דבי כנישתא. מחצלות של בית הכנסת, משום דמזבני להו ממעות הקופה. ואתני

פדיון שבוים מצוה רבה. והא דאמר בפרק "בני העיר" (מגילה דף כז.): אין מוכרין ס"ת אלא ללמוד תורה ולישא אשה, ולא קתני פדיון שבוים — שמא מילתא דפשיטא היא, ולא איצטריך למיתני. ומתחלקת בג' מפני שהיא כדיני ממונות. וא"ת: מהאי טעמא נמי תהא נגבית בג'! ופר"ת לפי שהיה ידוע סכום של כל אחד ואחד כמה יתן. ולשנות' לכל מה שירצו. נראה לר"ת דיכולים לשנותו אף לדבר הרשות. אע"ג דאמרינן בערכין בפ"ק (דף ו: ושם): האי מאן דנדב שרגא לבי כנשתא — אסור לשנותה לדבר הרשות. ואמר נמי התם: האומר "פרוטה זו לצדקה", עד שלא באה ליד הגבאי — מותר לשנותה, משבאה ליד הגבאי — אסור לשנותה (ד) לדבר הרשות. הכא, שבני העיר משנים אותה — שאני. לפיכך מותר לשנותה אפילו לדבר הרשות, ואפילו באה ליד הגבאי. וכן היה ר"ת נוהג לתת מעות הקופה לשומרי העיר, לפי שעל דעת בני העיר נותנים אותם. כי הא דרבא אכפיה. אחר היה עמו. דאין עושין שררה על הצבור פחות מב', ולא חשיב ליה מפני כבודו של רבא. אכפיה לרב נתן. וא"ת: והא בפרק "כל הבשר" (חולין דף קי: ושם ד"ה כל) אמר: כל מ"ע שמתן שכרה [כתובה] בצדה — אין ב"ד של מטה מוזהרים עליה. וגבי צדקה כתיב "כי פתוח תפתח את ידך לו" וכתיב "כי בגלל הדבר הזה יברכך" (דברים טו)! ואר"ת: דהאי כפיה — בדברים, כמו: כפייה (ה) ועל, בפרק "נערה שנתפתתה" (כתובות דף נג.). ועוד תירץ: דהכא קבלו עליהם שיכופו אותן הגבאי. ולר"י נראה: דבצדקה כופין, משום דאית בה לאו, דכתיב בה "לא תאמץ את לבבך ולא תקפוץ" וגו'. ולריצב"א נראה: דהא דאין ב"ד מוזהרין על מצות עשה שמתן (ו) שכרן בצדה — היינו דאין נענשין. וכן משמע בירושלמי ד"המוכר את הספינה". והיא ד"כל הבשר" (שם) דלא הוה מוקיר אבוה וכפתוהו, ואמר להו שבקוהו — ה"פ: אינכם מוזהרין להכריחו עד שיעשה כשאר מצות עשה, דאם א"ל עשה סוכה ולולב ואינו עושה — מכין אותו עד שתצא נפשו, כדאמר ב"הכותב" (כתובות דף פו: ושם). [וע"ע תוס' כתובות מט: ד"ה אכפייה ותוס' חולין קי: ד"ה כל]. דין אמת לאמתו. "אמת" — לאפוקי דין מרומה, אע"ג שהעדים מעידין אותו [אין מתכוים אותו], כיון שיודעים שמשקרים. כדדרשינן (בסנהדרין דף ז.) [צ"ל: בשבועות ל:]: "לאמתו" — שלא יטו את הדין. [וע"ע תוס' מגילה טו: ד"ה זה]. ומצדיקי הרבים וגו' אלו מלמדי תינוקות. אומר ר"י: דצריך לומר דרקיע מזהיר טפי מכוכבים. דהא בס"פ "אלו עוברין" (פסחים מט: ושם ד"ה לא) משמע דגבאי צדקה עדיפי ממלמדי תינוקות, דאמר: לא מצא בת תלמיד חכם — ישא בת גבאי צדקה, לא מצא בת גבאי צדקה — ישא בת מלמדי תינוקות. ואריב"א כי מצא בפרקי דרבי אליעזר דרקיע דהאי קרא ד"המשכילים יזהירו כזוהר הרקיע" — היינו רקיע שעל ראשי החיות, שמזהירין מכוכבים, שאורו כאור החמה. והאי דקאמר: ורבנן מאי, אמר רבינא: "ואוהביו כצאת השמש" — היינו שמש של עתיד לבא, דהוא שבעתים כאור שבעת הימים, ואור שבעת ימי בראשית היה שבעתים מאור חמה של עכשיו, כדמפרש תרגום של "רני ושמחי" (זכריה ב). ואע"פ

רבינו גרשום

נהרג בחרב מינויל. דמתלכלך בדמו: נגבית בשנים. משום דמתחלקת לעניי העיר ודבר קצוב הוא שיודעין כמה כל אחד ואחד צריך ליתן בקצוב ונותנין בשוה וליכא א) אלא סידורי בעלמא דגובין אותו גבאי צדקה מהם: ומתחלקת בג'. מפני שהיא כדיני ממונות מה דיני ממונות נוטלין מזה ונותנין לזה אף מחלקי צדקה מרבין לא' וממעטין לא' לפי שיראו צרכי עניים: גיבויו וחילוקיו שוה. שגובין מכל א' לפי מה שידו משגת וכעין דין שמעיינין בדין על מי להרבות ועל מי למעט משא"כ בקופה שאין גובין מכל אחד אלא לפי מה שרוצה ליתן ב) וקרוב נותנין כולן בשוה: לעשות קופה תמחוי. שאם ניתותר בקופה יותר על צורך עניי העיר ונתמעט בתמחוי לעניי כל אדם שבאו עניים הרבה וכן תמחוי לקופה כמו כן: להתנות על המדות. להגדילן או למעטן מכמות שהיו: ועל השער. שאם היה השער ביוקר רשאין להתנות שילך בזול: ועל שכר הפועלין. שאם נשכרין פועלים בג' פשי' ביום רשאין להתנות שלא ישכרום אלא בב': ולהסיע על קיצתן. לקנום על מי שעובר על תנאי שקצבו אנשי העיר: והם יקחו. ואין הם פחות משנים: שררות הוא דלא עבדי פחות משנים. כלומר דמשמע טעמו דשררות הוא דבעינן ב' ולא לשום דין ולא לשום עדות הלכך (הא) המוני מהמני אפי' ב' קרובים למנות על הקופה והיינו ג) מאי שררות איכא בגבאי צדקה הואיל ודבר קצוב הוא ונותנין ברצון: ממשכנין. אם מעכב ליתן צדקה בקופה. ואפי' בע"ש דטרידי אינשי בתיקון מאכלם: הא דאמיד. אם אומדין אותו שהוא עשיר וממאן ליתן ממשכנין אותו בעל כרחו והא דלא אמיד שאין לו מה ליתן אם (לוה) [ליה] ממשכנין עליו נאמר ופקדתי על כל לוחציו. שקל מיניה [ד' מאה] זוזי לצדקה. דהוה אמיד שהיה עשיר גדול: זה דיין. שמשכיל לדין הדין לאמתו. ומצדיקי הרבים אלו גבאי צדקה שמעשין בני אדם ליתן צדקה ומצדיקין אותן: שבקת לאומנותך. שהיה מלמד תינוקות כלומר אם היית מלמד עדיין לא היית מבטל לעמוד בגינה: דעתי עליהו. על התינוקות שלא הסחתי דעתי מהם שלא לזוז ממקום זה שאני עומד: ורבנן מאי. כלומר כיון דלדיין נתת זוהר הרקיע לעתיד לבא [ולגבאי] צדקה נתת אור הכוכבים רבנן עצמן מאי לאיזה אור יזכו הן: כצאת השמש בגבורתו. דעדיף מכולהו: לפרוש זה מזה. בשוק משום חשדא שלא יחשדו זה לזה שא' מהם יתן לתוך כיסו ולא לכיס של צדקה אבל רשאי לפרוש זה לשער וזה לחנות משום דקרובין זה לזה: פורטין לאחרים. שאם יש בכיס של צדקה פרוטות ורוצה לחלפן בסלע כסף פורטין לאחרים חלפי לאחרים ולא לעצמן שלא יחשדום שמרויחים בצדקה: אין מונין אותן שתים שתים כשפורטין לאחרים אלא מונה אחת אחת שלא יטעה: לא יתיב מר. רבה: אציפי. אמחצלאות שפורסין על כותלי בית הכנסת והיו קנויות מצדקה: מחצלאות. ששוכבין עליהן עניים: עביד חד. ואתני

א) נראה דל"ל וליכא רק סדורי בעלמא. ב) נראה דל"ל [illegible] וקרוב שנותנין כולן בשוה כל"ל. ג) נראה דל"ל והיינו [illegible]

עין משפט נר מצוה

ע א ב ג מיי' פ"ט מהל' מתנות עניים הל' ה סמג עשין קסב טוש"ע י"ד סי' רנו סעיף ג:
עא ד ה ו מיי' שם הל' ו ז טוש"ע שם סעיף ד:
עב מיי' פי"ד מהל' מכירה הל' ט סמג לאוין קע טוש"ע ח"מ סי' רלא סעיף כח:
עג ח ט מיי' פ"ט מהל' מתנות עניים הל' ה סמג עשין קסב טוש"ע י"ד סי' רנו סעיף ג:
עד י מיי' שם פ"ז הל' י סמג שם טוש"ע י"ד סי' רמח סעיף ב:
עה כ מיי' שם הל' י והל' יא טוש"ע שם סעיף א וסעיף ז:
עו ל מ נ מיי' שם פ"ט הל' ח ט סמג שם טוש"ע י"ד סי' רנז סעיף א:
עז ס ע מיי' שם הל' יא טוש"ע שם סעיף ב:
עח פ מיי' שם הל' י טוש"ע שם סעיף ח:

מסורת הש"ס

א) [ברכות ז: וש"נ]: ב) [פאה פ"ח מ"ז סנהדרין יז:]: ג) שקלים פ"ה מ"ב: ד) [קדושין עו:]: ה) כתובות מט: ו) [בילקוט ליתא וכן בע"י ליתא]: ז) נ"א להתם: ח) [בשאלתות פרשת תשא איתא ורבנן אמרו מאי דכתיב ואוהביו כצאת השמש בגבורתו אלו גבאי צדקה ופרנסי העיר]: ט) [תוספתא פאה פ"ד]. י) פסחים יג. ב"מ לח.: כ) [מבואר היטב בפירש"י גיטין נב: ד"ה ולא אמיד]:

הגהות הב"ח

(א) גמ' רעב קשה מחרב איבעית אימא קרא ואיבעית אימא סברא אב"א סברא האי קא מצטער: (ב) שם א"ל לאו הא האידנא תליסר שנין דלא חזיא לי: (ג) שם אין מונין אותן שתים שתים אלא: (ד) תוס' ד"ה ולשנות' וכו' משבא' ליד הגבאי אסור לשנות' הכא כצ"ל ותיבות לדבר הרשות נמחק: (ה) ד"ה אכפיה וכו' כמו כפייה רב פפא לרב יהודה בפ' נערה: (ו) בא"ד שמתן שכרה כתובה בצדה:

וְאַתְנֵי עֲלָהּ, אִיהוּ נַמִּי עֲבַד חַד כִּיסָא וְאַתְנֵי עֲלָהּ. רַב אַשִׁי אֲמַר: אֲנָא אַתְנוּיֵי נַמִּי לָא צְרִיכְנָא, דְּכָל דְּקָא אָתֵי אַדַּעְתָּא דִּידִי אָתֵי, וּלְמַאן דְּבָעֵינָא יָהֵיבְנָא לֵיהּ. הָנְהוּ (א) בֵּי תְּרֵי טַבָּחֵי דַּעֲבַדִי עֲנְיָנָא בַּהֲדֵי הֲדָדֵי, דְּכָל מַאן דְּעָבֵיד בְּיוֹמָא דְּחַבְרֵיהּ נִקְרְעוּהּ לְמַשְׁכֵיהּ. אֲזַל חַד מִנַּיְיהוּ עֲבַד בְּיוֹמָא דְּחַבְרֵיהּ, קָרְעוּ לְמַשְׁכֵיהּ; אֲתוֹ לְקַמֵּיהּ דְּרָבָא, חַיְּיבִינְהוּ רָבָא לְשַׁלּוּמֵי. אֵיתִיבֵיהּ רַב יֵימַר בַּר שְׁלֶמְיָא לְרָבָא: וּלְהַסִּיעַ עַל קִיצָתָם! לָא אַהֲדַר לֵיהּ רָבָא. אֲמַר רַב פַּפָּא: שַׁפִּיר עֲבַד דְּלָא אַהֲדַר לֵיהּ מִידֵּי; אה"מ הֵיכָא דְּלֵיכָּא אָדָם חָשׁוּב, אֲבָל הֵיכָא דְּאִיכָּא אָדָם חָשׁוּב — לָאו כָּל כְּמִינַּיְיהוּ דְּמַתְנוּ. ת"ר: באֵין מְחַשְּׁבִין בִּצְדָקָה עִם גַּבָּאֵי צְדָקָה, וְלֹא בְּהֶקְדֵּשׁ עִם הַגִּזְבָּרִין, וְאַע"פ שֶׁאֵין רְאָיָה לַדָּבָר — זֵכֶר לַדָּבָר, שֶׁנֶּאֱמַר: °"וְלֹא יְחַשְּׁבוּ אֶת הָאֲנָשִׁים (מ"ב יב) אֲשֶׁר יִתְּנוּ אֶת הַכֶּסֶף עַל יָדָם לָתֵת לְעוֹשֵׂי הַמְּלָאכָה כִּי בֶאֱמוּנָה הֵם עוֹשִׂים". א"ר אֶלְעָזָר: אע"פ שֶׁיֵּשׁ לוֹ לְאָדָם גִּזְבָּר נֶאֱמָן בְּתוֹךְ בֵּיתוֹ — יָצוּר וְיִמְנֶה, שֶׁנֶּאֱמַר: °"וַיָּצוּרוּ וַיִּמְנוּ" (שם). אָמַר רַב הוּנָא: בּוֹדְקִין לִמְזוֹנוֹת וְאֵין בּוֹדְקִין לִכְסוּת; א)אִי בָּעֵית אֵימָא קְרָא, וְאִי בָּעֵית אֵימָא סְבָרָא; אב"א סְבָרָא: הַאי קָא מִבַּזֵּי וְהַאי לָא קָא מִבַּזֵּי; אִי בָּעֵית אֵימָא קְרָא: °"הֲלֹא ב)פָרֹשׂ לָרָעֵב לַחְמֶךָ" (ישעיה נח) בְּשִׁי"ן כְּתִיב — פְּרוֹשׂ וַהֲדַר הַב לֵיהּ, וְהָתָם כְּתִיב: °"כִּי תִרְאֶה עָרֹם וְכִסִּיתוֹ" (שם), "כִּי תִרְאֶה" — לְאַלְתַּר. וְרַב יְהוּדָה אָמַר: גבּוֹדְקִין לִכְסוּת וְאֵין בּוֹדְקִין לִמְזוֹנוֹת; אִי בָּעֵית אֵימָא סְבָרָא, וְאִי בָּעֵית אֵימָא קְרָא; אִי בָּעֵית אֵימָא סְבָרָא: הַאי קָמְצַעֲרָא לֵיהּ וְהַאי לָא קָמְצַעֲרָא לֵיהּ; אִי בָּעֵית אֵימָא קְרָא: הָכָא כְּתִיב: "הֲלֹא פָרוֹס לָרָעֵב לַחְמֶךָ" — פְּרוֹס לְאַלְתַּר, וְכִדְקָרֵינַן, וְהָתָם כְּתִיב: "כִּי תִרְאֶה עָרֹם וְכִסִּיתוֹ" — כְּשֶׁיֵּרָאֶה לְךָ. תַּנְיָא כְּוָותֵיהּ דְּרַב יְהוּדָה: אָמַר "כַּסּוּנִי" — בּוֹדְקִין אַחֲרָיו, "פַּרְנְסוּנִי" — אֵין בּוֹדְקִין. ג)תְּנַן הָתָם: דאֵין פּוֹחֲתִין לְעָנִי הָעוֹבֵר מִמָּקוֹם לְמָקוֹם מִכִּכָּר בְּפוּנְדְּיוֹן, מֵאַרְבַּע סְאִין בְּסֶלַע; לָן — נוֹתְנִין לוֹ פַּרְנָסַת לִינָה. מַאי פַּרְנָסַת לִינָה? אֲמַר רַב פַּפָּא: הפּוּרְיָא וּבֵי סַדְיָא. שַׁבָּת — נוֹתְנִין לוֹ מְזוֹן שָׁלֹשׁ סְעוּדוֹת. תָּנָא: ד)אִם הָיָה מַחֲזִיר עַל הַפְּתָחִים — אֵין נִזְקָקִין לוֹ. הַהוּא עַנְיָא דַּהֲוָה מַחֲזִיר עַל הַפְּתָחִים דַּאֲתָא לְקַמֵּיהּ דְּרַב פַּפָּא, לָא מִזְדַּקֵּיק לֵיהּ. א"ל רַב סַמָּא בְּרֵיהּ דְּרַב יֵיבָא לְרַב פַּפָּא: אִי מָר לָא מִזְדַּקֵּיק לֵיהּ, אֱינָשׁ אַחֲרִינָא לָא מִזְדַּקֵּיק לֵיהּ, לֵימוּת (ב) לֵיהּ? וְהָא תַּנְיָא: אִם הָיָה עָנִי הַמַּחֲזִיר עַל הַפְּתָחִים — אֵין נִזְקָקִין לוֹ! א"ל: ואֵין נִזְקָקִין לוֹ לְמַתָּנָה מְרוּבָּה, אֲבָל נִזְקָקִין לוֹ לְמַתָּנָה מוּעֶטֶת. אָמַר רַב אַסִי: זלְעוֹלָם אַל יִמְנַע אָדָם עַצְמוֹ [מִלָּתֵת] שְׁלִישִׁית הַשֶּׁקֶל בְּשָׁנָה, שֶׁנֶּאֱ': °"וְהֶעֱמַדְנוּ עָלֵינוּ מִצְוֹת לָתֵת עָלֵינוּ שְׁלִישִׁית הַשֶּׁקֶל בַּשָּׁנָה (נחמיה י) לַעֲבוֹדַת בֵּית אֱלֹהֵינוּ". וְאָמַר רַב אַסִי: שְׁקוּלָה צְדָקָה כְּנֶגֶד כָּל הַמִּצְוֹת, שֶׁנֶּאֱמַר: "וְהֶעֱמַדְנוּ עָלֵינוּ מִצְוֹת" וגו', "מִצְוָה" אֵין כְּתִיב כָּאן, אֶלָּא "מִצְוֹת". (סִימָן: גדול מקדש משה) א"ר אֶלְעָזָר: חגָּדוֹל הַמְעַשֶּׂה יוֹתֵר מִן הָעוֹשֶׂה, שֶׁנֶּאֱמַר: °"וְהָיָה (ישעיה לב) מַעֲשֵׂה הַצְּדָקָה שָׁלוֹם וַעֲבוֹדַת הַצְּדָקָה הַשְׁקֵט וָבֶטַח עַד עוֹלָם", זָכָה — "הֲלֹא פָרוֹשׂ לָרָעֵב לַחְמֶךָ", לֹא זָכָה — "וַעֲנִיִּים מְרוּדִים תָּבִיא בָיִת". אֲמַר לְהוּ רָבָא לִבְנֵי מְחוֹזָא: בְּמָטוּתָא מִנַּיְיכוּ, עוּשׂוּ בַּהֲדֵי הֲדָדֵי, כִּי הֵיכִי דְּלֶיהֱוֵי לְכוּ שְׁלָמָא בְּמַלְכוּתָא. וְא"ר אֶלְעָזָר: בִּזְמַן שֶׁבֵּהמ"ק קַיָּים, אָדָם שׁוֹקֵל שִׁקְלוֹ וּמִתְכַּפֵּר לוֹ, עַכְשָׁיו שֶׁאֵין בהמ"ק קַיָּים, אִם עוֹשִׂין צְדָקָה — מוּטָב, וְאִם לָאו — בָּאִין גּוֹיִם וְנוֹטְלִין בִּזְרוֹעַ. ה)וְאַעפ"כ נֶחְשָׁב לָהֶן לִצְדָקָה, שֶׁנֶּאֱ': °"וְנוֹגְשַׂיִךְ צְדָקָה" (שם ס). אֲמַר רָבָא: הַאי מִילְּתָא אִישְׁתַּעֵי לִי עוּלָּא

מְשַׁגֵּשׁ

ואתני. מתנה עם הצבור לחלקם לכל הבא. דכל דאתי. לתת מעות לקופה. ענייא. תנאי. למשכיה. עור הבהמה. לאו כל כמינייהו דמתנו. אלא בפניו. אין מחשבין. לומר: היכן נתתם מעות שגביתם. שאין ראיה לדבר. דלא בגבאי צדקה כתיב, אלא בגיזברי הקדש הנותנים (ג) לכס לעושי המלאכה, שהפועלים מרודין למלאכות הרבה: לגודרין, ולחוצבי האבן, לכתפים, ולחמרים, ולקנות עצים, ואבני מחצב, וא"א לעמוד על החשבון, כדאמרינן בעלמא (שבועות דף מה.): בעל הבית טרוד בפועליו הוא, ואינשי. יצור וימנה. הכסף שהוא מוסר בידו. ואע"פ שאינו בא עמו לחשבון לאחר מכאן — יצור וימנה, שנאמר: "ויצורו וימנו" וגו' והדר: "ונתנו את הכסף המתוכן" — המנוי, "על ידי עושי המלאכה" וגו'. בודקין למזונות. אם בא עני ואמר "פרנסוני" — בודקין שלא יהיה רמאי. ואין בודקין לכסות. בא ערום ואמר "כסוני" — לוקחין כסות מיד. פרוש. דרוש וחקור תחלה. לכשיראה לך. שאינו רמאי. מככר בפונדיון. ככר הלקוח בפונדיון כשלוקחין ארבע סאין חטין בסלע. ומגיע לפונדיון חצי קב, שהסלע מ"ח פונדיונין, וארבע סאין מ"ח חצאי קבין. והחנוני שהוא טוחן ואופה ומוכר בשוק משתכר מחצה, הרי שנותן ככר של רובע הקב בפונדיון. לן. בלילה. פרנסת לינה. צרכי לינה. בי סדיא. כר לתת מראשותיו. אין נזקקין לו. לתת מעות מן הקופה, אחרי שלמד לחזור על הפתחים — דיו בכך. ולא אזדקיק ליה. אפי' (ו) לפרנסה. מעשה הצדקה. טורח המעשים את חבריהם, מדלא כתיב: "והיתה הצדקה שלום". זכה. למזל טוב. עניים מרודים. זו ממשלת רומי, שצועקת תמיד: הבו הבו, שאנו צריכין. מרודים = קונפליינ"ט בלע"ז, כמו "אריד בשיחי" (תהלים נה). עולא משגש ארחתיה דאימיה. לרב ששת קרו ליה הכי, עולל המשגש דרכי אמו, שגרס (ד) להטותה מדרך שאר נשים, כדלקמן.

משגש

ואע"פ שאין ראיה לדבר זכר לדבר. ראיה גמורה אינה, דשאני התם, שהיו צדיקים גמורים. אין פוחתין לעני העובר ממקום למקום מככר בפונדיון כו'. הככר עולה ששה ביצים, דלא מהן מחצה לחנוני, והוא מזון שתי סעודות, כדתניא בפרק "כיצד משתתפין" (עירובין דף פב:). וקשה לר"י: דבפרק "כל כתבי" (שבת דף קיח. ושם) משמע שהוא רגילות דאיכא סעודה בהדיה, דקאמר התם: דכי אזיל — מלווינא ליה סעודה בהדיה, דכי אזיל לאו בריקן אזיל. וא"כ, למה נותנין לו שתי סעודות? די לו בסעודה אחת, ההיא סעודה דאיכא בהדיה יאכל מיד, וסעודה שנותנין לו עכשיו יוליכנו עמו! ונראה לר"י: דאין מחלקין תמחוי בלילה, לפי שאין יכולין להבחין למי נתנו ולמי לא נתנו. וכן משמע מדקאמר: לן, נותנים לו פרנסת לינה, ומפרש דהיינו פוריא ובי סדיא, אבל ככר אין נותנין לו. ולכך נותנין לו ב' סעודות, שיאכל אחת בלילה ואחת למחר, (ה) דכי אזיל — לאו בריקן אזיל. וטעמא דבעינן שלא ילך ריקס — דאינו דומה מי שיש לו פת בסלו למי שאין לו, ולא יהא רעב כל כך. אבל אין לפרש דהטעם שמא לא יגיע בין היהודים ויהא לו מה לאכול, דאי חיישינן להכי — היה ליתן לו שלש סעודות, כי גם בלילה לא יתנו אף כשיגיע בין היהודים, שאין מחלקין תמחוי בלילה. ואין לומר דלעולם מחלקין, ולכך נותנין שתים, דחיישינן שמא לא יגיע בין היהודים שתי פעמים. אי נמי לא חיישינן אלא לפעם אחת, והשניה נותנין לו כדי שיהא לו פת בסלו — דאם כן היכי קאמר התם דמלוינן ליה סעודה אחת בהדיה? ואם יש לחוש שמא לא יגיע בין היהודים — היה לו ליתן שתים. לכך נראה כדפרישית. **שבת** נותנין לו מזון שלש סעודות. פירוש: בשבת בצהרים. (ו) אותן שתי סעודות שנתן לו אתמול בערב שבת — אכל ליל שבת ושבת שחרית, ושלש סעודות שנותנים לו בשבת — יאכל אחת בשבת בסעודה שלישית, ואחת למוצאי שבת, ושלישית ישאר לו למחר בדרך, שלא ילך ריקס, ואין להאריך. וקשה לרשב"א: הא דתנן במסכת פאה (פ"ח מ"ז) ומייתי לה בפרק "כל כתבי" (שבת דף קיח. ושם): מי שיש לו מזון שתי סעודות בביתו לא יטול מן התמחוי. ואמאי? הא אחד יאכל מיד ואחד בלילה, וא"כ כי אזיל — ריקס אזיל! וצריך לפרש: דמזון שתי סעודות דקאמר — היינו בלא אותה שיש לו לאכול מיד. וא"ת: שבת אמאי נותנין לו שלש סעודות? והא הך מתני' ר"ע היא, דקתני רישא: כל מי שיש לו מזון י"ד סעודות לא יטול מן הקופה, ופריך בפרק "כל כתבי הקדש" (שם): מני? אי רבנן — חמיסר הוין, אי רבי חדקא — שיתסר הוין! ומשני: הא מני — ר"ע היא, דאמר: עשה שבתך חול! ונראה לרשב"א: דבשביל סעודת שבת אין לו להתחיל וליטול, אבל בשכבר צריך ליטול — נוטל גם כדי לסעודת שבת. **לא** אזדקיק ליה. רב פפא גבאי היה, ולא נתן לו מן הקופה, כדתניא: אין נותנין לו מן הקופה, כיון שמחזר על הפתחים. וא"ל רב סמא: אי מר לא אזדקיק ליה לתת לו מן הקופה, (ז) היינו כדי סעודה — כ"ש שגם אחרים לא יתנו לו. ומסיק: הא דתניא: אין נזקקין לו מן הקופה — היינו כדי סעודה, אבל דבר מועט יתנו לו. **שנאמר** והעמדנו עלינו מצות. ואע"ג דהאי קרא גבי "בית אלהינו" כתיב, דהיינו בדק הבית — כ"ש לצדקה.

מנין

עין משפט נר מצוה

עט א מיי' פי"ד מהל' מכירה הלכה יא סמג לאוין קע טוש"ע ח"מ סי' רלא סעיף כח וטוש"ע י"ד סי' רנו סעיף ד:

פ ב מיי' פ"ט מהלכות מתנות עניים הל' יא סמג עשין קסב טוש"ע י"ד סי' רנז סעיף ב:

פא ג מיי' שם פ"ז הל' ו סמג שם טוש"ע י"ד סי' רנא סעיף י:

פב ד ה מיי' שם הל' ח סמג שם טוש"ע י"ד סי' רנ סעיף ד:

פג ו מיי' שם הל' ז טוש"ע שם סעיף ג:

פד ז מיי' שם הל' ה סמג שם טוש"ע י"ד סי' רמט סעיף ב:

פה ח מיי' שם פ"י הל' ו סמג עשין קסב טוש"ע שם סעיף ה:

מסורת הש"ס

א) [ברכות ז:וש"נ]: ב) בכל הספרים מדויקים כתיב פרום ולכאורה היא פליאה וצריכין ליישב ע"פ מ"ש תוס' שבת נה: ד"ה מעבירים כתיב ועיין במהרש"א בח"א שעמד על פליאה זו ונכנס לשנות בדוחק בשינוי הגירסא קצת שלא במקומו ד"ה הלא פרוש בשי"ן כתיב]: ג) פאה פ"ח מ"ז שבת קיח.: ד) [תוספ' פאה פ"ד]: ה) נ"א אמר מר עוקבא כו': ו) ס"א לפרוסה. רש"ל:

רבינו גרשום

ואתני. אם יצטרכו לעניי העיר שיהיו לעניי העיר ואם לאו שיותירו על עניי העיר שיהיו לעניי כל אדם: דכל דאתי למיתן צדקה אדעתא דידי אתיא. כל מי שנותן לי על דעת כן נותן לי שאני אתנן לכל עני שארצה משום דרב אשי היה אדם גדול והיה יודע מה הוא עושה: [הנהו בי תרי טבחי]. התנו ביניהן שכל א' מהן ישחוט ביומו: קרעוה למשכיה. דחיותא: וחייביה רבא לשלם. דמי העור שקרע: ולהסיע על קיצתן. והלא רשאין לקנוס כל מי שעבר על תנאן: הני מילי. דיכולין להתנות ולהסיע על קיצתן: היכא דליכא אדם חשוב. להתנות לפניו: אבל אי איכא אדם חשוב. ולא אתנו קמיה לאו תנאיהו תנאה ואיכא דאמר היכא דליכא אדם חשוב עביד אינש דינא לנפשיה אבל אי איכא אדם חשוב נקיט ליה בדינא קמיה: אין מחשבין בצדקה עם הגבאין. מה גבו ומה נתנו דאין צריך לחשדן: אע"פ שאין ראיה לדבר זכר לדבר. גבי גבאי צדקה זכר לדבר ממקדש שנא' (מ"ב כב) אך לא יחשב וגו' אבל גבי גזברין של הקדש הוי ראיה גמורה: יצור. בעה"ב בקשר ובחותם וימנה דכתיב ויצורו וימנו כלומר אע"ג דהגזברין היו נאמנין אף על פי כן הגזברין עצמן היו צרין ומונין: בודקין למזונות. שאם אמר עני תנו לי מזונות בודקין אחריו קודם שיתנו לו אם רמאי הוא שאין צריך אם לאו: ואין בודקין לכסות. שאם בא עני ערום ואמר כסוני אין בודקין אחריו אלא נותנין מיד: פרוש כתיב. כלומר צריך אתה לידע בפירוש אם צריך ואם לאו: (פרוש) [פרום]. לאלתר (פרוש) [פרום] הלחם ותן לו: לכשיראה לך. שהוא צריך כשתבדוק אחריו: העובר ממקום למקום. שאין לן אלא דרך עברה עובר: ככר בפונדיון. ככר שקונין פונדיון כשנותנין ד' סאין בסלע דהוי ככר של חצי קב כיצד בסלע הם מ"ח פונדיונות דסלע ד' דינר ודינר שש מעות ומעה ב' פונדיונות נמצא מ"ח פונדיונות בסלע וכיצד הוי חצי קב בפונדיון דחצי קב אחד ממ"ח בד' [סאין] דסאה ו' קבים נמצא כ"ד קבין שהם מ"ח חצאי קבין בסלע שהוא מ"ח פונדיונות ושיערו חכמים דבהם אית ליה ב' סעודות א' לכאן וא' קודם שיגיע לישוב: פוריא ובי סדיא. כר וכסת: אין נזקקין לתת לו מכים של צדקה. דהואיל ומחזר על הפתח הכל נותנין לו וא"צ ליטול מכים של צדקה: משליש שקל. בצדקה: לעבודת אלהינו. דהיינו צדקה: מצות. הרבה משמע: א) ועבודת [הצדקה] מעשה הוא: עכשיו באין וכו'. ודאי יתן או לעובדי כוכבים או לצדקה. אם זכה הלא פרוש לרעב שיתנהו לעניים אם לא זכה ליתנהו לעניים אעפ"כ יתן לעובדי כוכבים בשביל שהיה חייב לעניים. באים [עניים] מרודים כלומר גוים הרודים לביתו ונטלוהו בזרוע: ונוגשיך צדקה. מה שתתן לנוגשיך: עולא. עלם אחד כמו עול [ימים] לא היה שמו עולא אלא (אחד בלי) [אחריו]:

משגש

א) [רבינו מפרש לגדול המעשה נלמד מסיפא דקרא דכתיב ועבודת הצדקה וגו' ודלא כפירש"י]

הגהות הב"ח

(א) גמ' הנהו טבחי כצ"ל ותיבת בי תרי נמחק: (ב) שם לימות אמר ליה והא תניא אם היה: (ג) רש"י ד"ה שאין ראיה וכו' הנותנים לעושי המלאכה כצ"ל ותיבת לכס נמחק: (ד) ד"ה עולא וכו' שגרס לה להטות וכו' נשים להתבזות כדלקמן: (ה) תום' ד"ה אין פוחתין וכו' ואחת למחר כשילך דכי אזיל לאו: (ו) ד"ה שבת וכו' בצהרים כי אותן: (ז) ד"ה לא וכו' לתת לו מן הקופה כ"ש שגם אחרים כצ"ל ותיבות היינו כדי סעודה נמחק:

עין משפט נר מצוה

פו א מיי' פי"א מהל' טומאת צרעת הל' ב:
פז ב מיי' פ"ד מהל' אבות הטומאה הל' ב:
פח ג מיי' שם פ"ה הלכה א:
פט ד מיי' פ"י מהל' מתנות עניים הלכה ד ה סמג עשין קסב טוש"ע י"ד סי' רמט סעיף ג וסעיף ד:

[גמרא]

משגש ארחתיה דאימיה, משמיה דר' אלעזר, מאי דכתיב: "וילבש צדקה כשריון"? (ישעיה נט) לומר לך, מה שריון זה — כל קליפה וקליפה מצטרפת לשריון גדול, אף צדקה — כל פרוטה ופרוטה מצטרפת לחשבון גדול. רבי חנינא אמר, מהכא: "וכבגד עדים כל צדקותינו", (שם סד) מה בגד זה — כל נימא ונימא מצטרפת לבגד גדול, אף צדקה — כל פרוטה ופרוטה מצטרפת לחשבון גדול. אמאי קרו ליה עולא משגש ארחתיה דאימיה? דבעא מיניה רב אחדבוי בר אמי מרב ששת: [א]מנין למצורע בימי ספורו שמטמא אדם? אמר לו: הואיל ומטמא בגדים מטמא אדם. א"ל: דילמא טומאה בחבורים שאני, דהא הסיט נבילה דמטמא בגדים ואינו מטמא אדם! אמר ליה: ואלא שרץ [ב]דמטמא אדם מנלן, לאו משום דמטמא בגדים? א"ל: שרץ בהדיא כתיב ביה: "או איש אשר יגע בכל שרץ" (ויקרא כב). אלא [ג]שכבת זרע דמטמא אדם מנלן, לאו משום דהואיל ומטמא בגדים מטמא אדם? א"ל: שכבת זרע נמי בהדיא כתיב ביה: "או איש" (שם) — לרבות את הנוגע. אהדר ליה בבדיחותא. חלש דעתיה דרב ששת, אישתיק רב אחדבוי בר אמי ואתיקר תלמודיה. אתיא אימיה וקא בכיא קמיה, צווחה צווחה ולא אשגח בה. אמרה ליה: חזי להני חדיי דמצית מינייהו! בעא רחמי עליה ואיתסי. ודאתאן עלה, מנא לן? כדתניא, ר"ש בן יוחי אומר: נאמר כבוס בגדים בימי ספורו, ונאמר כבוס בגדים בימי חלוטו — מה להלן מטמא אדם, אף כאן מטמא אדם. אמר רבי אלעזר: גדול העושה צדקה בסתר יותר ממשה רבינו, דאילו במשה רבינו כתיב: "כי יגורתי מפני האף והחמה" (דברים ט), ואילו בעושה צדקה כתיב: "מתן בסתר יכפה אף [ושחד בחיק חמה עזה]" (משלי כא) ופליגא דרבי יצחק, דאמר ר' יצחק: אף כופה, חמה אינו כופה, שנא': "ושחד בחיק חמה עזה", אע"פ ששוחד בחיק — חמה עזה. איכא דאמרי, א"ר יצחק: כל דיין שנוטל שחד — מביא חמה עזה לעולם, [שנאמר: "ושחד בחיק" וגו']. ואמר רבי יצחק: כל הנותן פרוטה לעני מתברך בשש ברכות, והמפייסו בדברים — מתברך בי"א ברכות. הנותן פרוטה לעני מתברך בשש ברכות, דכתיב: "הלא [א]פרוש וגו' ועניים מרודים תביא בית וגו' כי תראה ערום" וגו' (ישעיה נח); (א) [ד]והמפייסו בדברים מתברך באחת עשרה ברכות, שנאמר: "ותפק לרעב נפשך ונפש נענה תשביע (שם) וזרח בחשך אורך ואפלתך כצהרים. ונחך ה' תמיד והשביע בצחצחות נפשך (ב) וגו', ובנו ממך חרבות עולם מוסדי דור ודור תקומם" וגו'. ואמר רבי יצחק, מאי דכתיב: "רודף צדקה וחסד ימצא חיים צדקה וכבוד"? (משלי כא) משום דרודף צדקה ימצא צדקה? אלא לומר לך: כל הרודף אחר צדקה — הקדוש ברוך הוא ממציא לו מעות ועושה בהן צדקה. רב נחמן בר יצחק אמר: הקדוש ברוך הוא ממציא לו בני אדם המהוגנים לעשות להן צדקה, כדי לקבל עליהם (ג) שכרו. לאפוקי מאי? לאפוקי מדדרש רבה; [ב]דדרש רבה, מאי דכתיב: "ויהיו מוכשלים לפניך בעת אפך עשה בהם"? (ירמיה יח) אמר ירמיה לפני הקדוש ברוך הוא: רבונו של עולם, [אפילו] בשעה שכופין את יצרן ומבקשין לעשות צדקה לפניך, הכשילם בבני אדם שאינן מהוגנין, כדי שלא יקבלו עליהן שכר. רבי יהושע בן לוי אמר: כל הרגיל לעשות צדקה — (ד) זוכה, הויין לו בנים בעלי חכמה, בעלי עושר, בעלי אגדה. בעלי חכמה — דכתיב:

ימצא

[תוספות]

מנין למצורע בימי ספורו שמטמא אדם. פשיטא לן דמטמא, כדתנן בריש מס' כלים (פ"א מ"א): אבות הטומאות: השרץ, ושכבת זרע, (ה) ונבלה, וטמא מת, ומצורע בימי ספורו כו' — הרי אלו מטמאין אדם וכלים במגע, וכלי חרס באויר. ולכך בעי מנלן דמטמא, דהא כתיב "ורחץ במים וטהר" — משמע דבאותה טבילה נטהר. דהא הסיט נבלה מטמא בגדים ואינו מטמא אדם. (ו) לאו משום דטומאה בחבורין שאני? פ"ה: דאינו מטמא אלא בגדים שהוא לבוש. וקשה לריב"ס: דבתורת כהנים פ' "ויהי ביום השמיני" (ז) מרבה שמטמא אפילו כלים (בחבורים) אע"ג דלא שייך בהו לבישה, ואינו ממעט מ"בגדיו" אלא אדם וכלי חרס שנוגע בהן. אלא ודאי מטמא בגדים בשעה שמסיט, אפילו אין לבוש בהן. וכן משמע, מדקאמר: אלא מעתה שרץ דמטמא אדם מנלן, לאו משום דמטמא בגדים מטמא אדם נמי כו'? ואי קרי חבורים בגדים שהוא לבוש — מאי פריך משרץ דלא שייך ביה לבישה? התם ודאי ילפינן אדם מבגדים! ונראה לריב"ס: דלא גרס (ח) "בחבורים", אלא הכי גרס: ודילמא טומאת בגדים שאני, תדע דהא מסיט נבלה דמטמא בגדים ואינו מטמא אדם. ולא גרסינן "מ"ט לאו משום דטומאה בחבורים שאני", דלא מהדר אלא שיש חילוק בין טומאת בגדים לטומאת אדם. וכן משמע, דאיהו גופיה לא קא מיבעיא ליה אם מטמא בגדים וכלים במגע, אלא אאדם בעי.

אתיא אימיה וקא בכיא קמיה. פר"ח: דהיינו אימיה דרב אחדבוי. ולדידיה קרי "עולא משגש אורחא דאימיה", שגרם לאמו להתבזות לפני רב ששת. והיא היתה מניקתו של רב ששת, לכך *אמר "חזי הני חדיי דמלית מינייהו". (* אולי צ"ל אמרה)

מה כיבוס בגדים האמור בימי חלוטו כו'. בכמה דברים חמור ימי חלוטו מימי ספורו, ולא גמר מהיקשא. והיינו טעמא, משום דלגמרי לא מצי למגמר — דהא כתב "וטהר", דמשמע דנטהר מכמו שהיה מתחלה. אלא דוקא להך מילתא גמרי, לפי שהן שוין דאין אדם וכלים מקבלין טומאה אלא מאב הטומאה.

גדול העושה צדקה בסתר יותר ממשה רבינו. פירוש: יותר משכך חמה ממשה רבינו בתפלתו. ואע"ג דמשה נמי עשה צדקה בסתר — שמא אותה שעה כבר פסק אותו זכות.

חמה אינו כופה. תימה: דבפרק "ארבעה נדרים" (דף לב.) אמרינן דחמה משה הרגו (ט).

והמפייסו בדברים מתברך בי"א. יש מגיהין: והנותן פרוטה לעני והמפייסו, משום דמשמע להו דקראי איירי בנותן צדקה, דכתיב "ותפק לרעב נפשך ונפש נענה תשביע". ולאו מילתא היא, ד"נפש נענה תשביע" — היינו תשביע בדברים, שתפייסנו בדברים. וע"כ לא גרסי' ליה, דלההיא גיר' הוה ליה למימר מתברך בי"ז, הנך שש דלעיל והני אחת עשרה.

ואיזו

[פירוש]

משגש. לשון מהומה ושגעון. קליפה = מייל"א בלע"ז. וכבגד עדים כל צדקותינו. כלומר, אף כל צדקותינו נמאסו מחמת רשעינו כבגד עדים. כדמתרגמינן "ויסר" — ואעדי, וכן "מעדה בגד ביום קרה" (משלי כה). מ"מ מקיש צדקה לבגד, צדקת הצדיקים לבגד הגון. בימי ספורו. בשבעת ימים שבין טהרת הצפרים להבאת קרבנותיו. בשלמא בימי חלוטו איתקש למת, לטמא אף באהל. הואיל ומטמא בגדים. דהא ביום השביעי כתיב "וכבס בגדיו". טומאה בחבורין. כגון בגדי לבושו — הרי הן כמוהו. אבל שאר בגדים, הנוגע בהן, וכן אם יגע באדם — לא מטמא. תדע, שהרי המסיט נבילה כתיב ביה: "והנושא את נבלתה יכבס בגדיו" (ויקרא יא), ולא אשכחן דלהוי אב הטומאה לטמא אדם ושאר בגדים. שכבת זרע מטמא בגדים. "וכל בגד וכל עור אשר יהיה עליו שכבת זרע" וגו'. בהדיא כתיב ביה כו'. ה"ה נמי דהוה מצי למיפרך דהא טומאת בגדים לא דמיא לבגדים דבימי ספורו, דהא בגדים דהכא לאו בגדי לבוש שרץ הן, וטומאת מגע הוא. אלא דעדיפא מיניה קא מותיב ליה. או לרבות הנוגע. דהכי תניא במסכת נדה (דף מג:): מנין לרבות הנוגע בשכבת זרע — ת"ל "או איש". הוה קמהדר ליה. רב אחדבוי לרב ששת בבדיחותא, לפי שהיה רב ששת נכשל בתשובותיו. אישתתק רב אחדבוי. נעשה אלם. אתיא אימיה. דרב ששת. צווחה קמיה. שיתפלל עליו. להני חדיי = הדדים הללו. חדי תרגום של "חזה". דמצית מינייהו = שינקת מהן. ודאתאן עלה. ואחרי שבא לידינו שאלה זו לקובעה בגמ', מנלן דמטמא אדם? נאמר כיבוס בגדים בימי ספורו. "והיה ביום השביעי יגלח את כל שערו" וגו', ונאמר כיבוס בגדים למעלה — ביום טהרת הצפרים, כשיוצא מטומאת החלט "וכבס המטהר את בגדיו". אף וחימה. שני לגיונות קשים הם, ליפרע מן החוטאים. אע"פ ששוחד בחיק. שהוא עושה צדקה בסתר. חימה עזה. עדיין היא בתוקפה. ורבי אלעזר סבר דהאי "שוחד בחיק" ארישא קאי, "ושוחד בחיק יכפה חימה עזה". ותפק לרעב נפשך. הוא פיוס דברי נחומים. ימצא צדקה. משמע, יבא לידי עניות, וימצא בני אדם שיעשו לו צדקה. ויהיו מוכשלים לפניך. את אנשי ענתות היה מקלל, שהיו מבקשין נפשו.

מסורת הש"ס

א) [צ"ל פרוס]: ב) כ"ק טז: [ושם איתא רבא]:

הגהות הב"ח

(א) גמ' כי תראה ערום וגו' וכתיב אז יבקע כשחר אורך וארוכתך מהרה תצמח והלך לפניך צדקך וכבוד ה' יאספך וכתיב אז תקרא וה' יענה תשוע ויאמר הנני והמפייסו בדברים: (ב) שם והשביע בצחצחות נפשך ובנו כצ"ל ותיבת וגו' נמחק: (ג) שם עליהם שכר כצ"ל ואות ו' נמחק: (ד) שם כל הרגיל לעשות [צדקה] הוויין כצ"ל ותיבת זוכה נמחק: (ה) תוס' ד"ה מנין וכו' אבות הטומאות השרץ ושכבת זרע וטמא מת כצ"ל ותיבת ונבלה נמחק: (ו) ד"ה דהא הסיט כו' ואינו מטמא אדם מ"ט לאו משום: (ז) בא"ד פרשת ויהי ביום השמיני מוכח שמטמא אפי' כלים אע"ג דלא כצ"ל ותיבת בחיבורים נמחק: (ח) בא"ד ונראה לריב"ס דלא גרס ודלמא טומאה בחיבורים שאני וכו' ומאי אלא הכי: (ט) ד"ה חמה וכו' משה הרגו. נ"ב עיין ריש דף ד' בתוס':

רבינו גרשום

משגש. מבזה ארחתיה דאימיה שהצריכה להתבזות במה שדרכה להצניע שגלתה דדיה בשבילו כדאמר לקמן: וכבגד עדים. אלו אותן בגדים בלוים ונסחבים שמשימין שם התינוק כשהוא נולד ולפיכך נקרא עדים א) כמו ועדיאתו: בימי ספורו. היינו אותן ימים דכתיב וישב מחוץ לאהלו שבעת ימים דכבר עברו לימי חלוטו והזאתו: אמר ליה הואיל ומטמא בגדים בימי ספורו דכתיב והיה ביום השביעי יגלח שערו וגו' וכבס בגדיו והואיל דמטמא בגדים דטעונין כבוס הכי נמי מטמא אדם: אמר ליה. דלמא טומאה בחבורין שני דהני בגדים מחוברין עליו שלובש בהן אבל לעולם אימא לך אם יגע בבגדים אחרים אינו מטמאן וכי היכי דלא מטמא בגדים מעלמא אימא נמי דלא מטמא אדם תדע דהנה אשכחן דמטמא בגדים בחבורין ולא מטמא אדם: היסט נבלה. אדם שהסיט נבלה ומטמא בגדים דכתיב והנושא את נבלתה יכבס בגדיו וטמא עד הערב אלמא דבגדים טמאים הן ואינו [מטמא אדם] כדכתיב וטמא עד הערב הוא טמא ואינו מטמא אדם: היסט בכלל נושא. כדכתיב נישא וקרינן נושא (חולין קכד:): אמר ליה רב ששת. ולטעמיך דקא אמרת דטומאה בחבורין שאני מש"ה אין מטמא אדם אלא שרץ דמטמא אדם מנא לן לאו משום הואיל דמטמא בגדים דכתיב וכל אשר יפול עליו מהם במותם יטמא מכל כלי עץ או בגד או עור או שק והני לאו בחבורין נינהו: אמר ליה רב אחדבוי. שרץ דמטמא אדם בהדיא כתיב או איש אשר יגע בכל שרץ אלא פריך הכי ולטעמיך דאמרת טומאה בחבורין שני שכבת זרע דמטמא אדם מנלן משום דהואיל ומטמא בגדים דכתיב ואיש (אשר) [כי] תצא ממנו שכבת זרע וכתיב וכל בגד וכל עור אשר יהיה עליו שכבת זרע וכבס במים וטמא עד הערב ה"נ מטמא אדם ה"נ גבי מצורע: אמר ליה רב אחדבוי. שכבת זרע בהדיא כתיב ביה דמטמא כל אדם הנוגע בו דכתיב או דמייתר דמצי למכתב איש אשר תצא ממנו וגו' או ל"ל לרבות את הנוגע ואכתי מנין למצורע שמטמא בימי ספורו: הוה קא מהדר ליה בבדיחותא. כלומר שמח היה רב אחדבוי שנצחו לרב ששת שלא היה לו להשיב: אישתתק. נאלם: אתיא אימא. נ) דרב אחדבוי בכיא קמיה דרב ששת שהיתה מינקת שלו בשביל בנה דלימחל ליה ובעי רחמי עליה דרב אחדבוי ולא אשגח בה עד דמפקי דדיה לפניו כלומר עשה בשביל אלו דדין שינקת מהן ולהכי שהצריכה לכך קרי ליה עולא משגש ארחתיה דאימיה: ודאתאן עלה מיהא. הואיל ובאת לידינו שאילה זו דרב אחדבוי נעסוק בה: מנלן. דמצורע מטמא אדם בימי ספורו: כבוס בגדים בימי חלוטו. דכתיב וכבס המטהר את בגדיו דניטמו בימי חלוטו: מה להלן בימי חלוטו מטמא אדם. דכתיב כל ימי אשר הנגע בו יטמא וגו': מתן בסתר [יכפה] אף ושוחד בחיק. כלומר מי שנותן בחיק של עני בצנעה כופה נמי חימה עזה: אע"פ ששוחד בחיק. של עני אעפ"כ חימה עזה שאינה נכפית בשביל השוחד בחיק: והמפייסו בדברים. שמנחמו ומדבר על לבו דברי נחומין: דכתיב ותפק לרעב נפשך וגו'. כלומר משתוציא מנפשך דברים טובים לנחם הרעב ונפש נענה תשביע בדברים טובים אז תוכה לדברים הללו: משום דרודף צדקה. שעושה צדקה משלו בא לידי צדקה שיצטרך לבריות בתמיה:

צדקה

א) ולכאורה מסתבר דכוון לתרגום אונקלוס על ותהר ועדיאתה אבל צ"ע דמשם זה לא שייך לקרותם עדים וצ"ע: ב) [עי' בתוס' כאן ד"ה אתיא מה שכתב בשם ר"ח]:

"יִמְצָא חַיִּים", בַּעֲלֵי עוֹשֶׁר — דִּכְתִיב "צְדָקָה"; בַּעֲלֵי אֲגָדָה — דִּכְתִיב "וְכָבוֹד", כְּתִיב הָכָא "וְכָבוֹד", וּכְתִיב הָתָם: °"כָּבוֹד חֲכָמִים יִנְחָלוּ". תַּנְיָא: הָיָה רַבִּי מֵאִיר אוֹמֵר: יֵשׁ לוֹ לְבַעַל הַדִּין לְהָשִׁיבְךָ וְלוֹמַר לְךָ: אִם אֱלֹהֵיכֶם אוֹהֵב עֲנִיִּים הוּא, מִפְּנֵי מָה אֵינוֹ מְפַרְנְסָן? אֱמוֹר לוֹ: כְּדֵי שֶׁנִּיצּוֹל אָנוּ בָּהֶן מִדִּינָהּ שֶׁל גֵּיהִנָּם. וְזוֹ שְׁאֵלָה שָׁאַל טוּרְנוּסְרוּפּוּס הָרָשָׁע אֶת ר"ע: אִם אֱלֹהֵיכֶם אוֹהֵב עֲנִיִּים הוּא, מִפְּנֵי מָה אֵינוֹ מְפַרְנְסָם? א"ל: כְּדֵי שֶׁנִּיצּוֹל אָנוּ בָּהֶן מִדִּינָהּ שֶׁל גֵּיהִנָּם. א"ל: [אַדְּרַבָּה,] זוֹ שֶׁמְּחַיַּבְתָּן לְגֵיהִנָּם! אֶמְשׁוֹל לְךָ מָשָׁל, לְמָה הַדָּבָר דּוֹמֶה? לְמֶלֶךְ בָּשָׂר וָדָם שֶׁכָּעַס עַל עַבְדּוֹ וַחֲבָשׁוֹ בְּבֵית הָאֲסוּרִין, וְצִוָּה עָלָיו שֶׁלֹּא לְהַאֲכִילוֹ וְשֶׁלֹּא לְהַשְׁקוֹתוֹ, וְהָלַךְ אָדָם אֶחָד וְהֶאֱכִילוֹ וְהִשְׁקָהוּ, כְּשֶׁשָּׁמַע הַמֶּלֶךְ לֹא כּוֹעֵס עָלָיו? וְאַתֶּם קְרוּיִן עֲבָדִים, שֶׁנֶּאֱמַר: °"כִּי לִי בְנֵי יִשְׂרָאֵל עֲבָדִים"! אָמַר לוֹ ר"ע: אֶמְשׁוֹל לְךָ מָשָׁל, לְמָה הַדָּבָר דּוֹמֶה? לְמֶלֶךְ בָּשָׂר וָדָם שֶׁכָּעַס עַל בְּנוֹ וַחֲבָשׁוֹ בְּבֵית הָאֲסוּרִין, וְצִוָּה עָלָיו שֶׁלֹּא לְהַאֲכִילוֹ וְשֶׁלֹּא לְהַשְׁקוֹתוֹ, וְהָלַךְ אָדָם אֶחָד וְהֶאֱכִילוֹ וְהִשְׁקָהוּ, כְּשֶׁשָּׁמַע הַמֶּלֶךְ לֹא דּוֹרוֹן מְשַׁגֵּר לוֹ? וַאֲנַן קְרוּיִן בָּנִים, דִּכְתִיב: °"בָּנִים אַתֶּם לַה' אֱלֹהֵיכֶם"! אָמַר לוֹ: אַתֶּם קְרוּיִם בָּנִים וּקְרוּיִן עֲבָדִים, בִּזְמַן שֶׁאַתֶּם עוֹשִׂין רְצוֹנוֹ שֶׁל מָקוֹם אַתֶּם קְרוּיִן בָּנִים, וּבִזְמַן שֶׁאֵין אַתֶּם עוֹשִׂין רְצוֹנוֹ שֶׁל מָקוֹם אַתֶּם קְרוּיִן עֲבָדִים, וְעַכְשָׁיו אֵין אַתֶּם עוֹשִׂין רְצוֹנוֹ שֶׁל מָקוֹם! אָמַר לוֹ, הֲרֵי הוּא אוֹמֵר: °"הֲלֹא פָרֹס לָרָעֵב לַחְמֶךָ וַעֲנִיִּים מְרוּדִים תָּבִיא בָיִת", אֵימָתַי "עֲנִיִּים מְרוּדִים תָּבִיא בָיִת" — הָאִידָּנָא, וְקָאָמַר: "הֲלֹא פָרֹס לָרָעֵב לַחְמֶךָ".§ דָּרַשׁ ר"י בְּרַבִּי שָׁלוֹם: כְּשֵׁם שֶׁמְּזוֹנוֹתָיו שֶׁל אָדָם קְצוּבִין לוֹ מֵרֹאשׁ הַשָּׁנָה, כָּךְ חֶסְרוֹנוֹתָיו שֶׁל אָדָם קְצוּבִין לוֹ מֵרֹאשׁ הַשָּׁנָה, זָכָה — "הֲלֹא פָרֹס לָרָעֵב לַחְמֶךָ", לֹא זָכָה — "וַעֲנִיִּים מְרוּדִים תָּבִיא בָיִת". כִּי הָא דִּבְנֵי אַחְתֵּיהּ דְּרַבָּן יוֹחָנָן בֶּן זַכַּאי חֲזָא לְהוּ בְּחֶילְמָא דְּבָעוּ לְמֶיחְסַר שְׁבַע מְאָה דִּינָרֵי, עַשִּׂינְהוּ, שְׁקַל מִינַּיְהוּ לִצְדָקָה, (א) פּוּשׁ גַּבַּיְיהוּ שִׁיבְסַר דִּינָרֵי. כִּי מְטָא מַעֲלֵי יוֹמָא דְּכִיפּוּרֵי, שְׁדוּר דְּבֵי קֵיסָר נַקְטִינְהוּ. אֲמַר לְהוּ רַבָּן יוֹחָנָן בֶּן זַכַּאי: לָא תִּדְחֲלוּן, שִׁיבְסַר דִּינָרֵי גַּבַּיְיכוּ שַׁקְלִינְהוּ מִינַּיְיכוּ. אָמְרֵי לֵיהּ: מְנָא יָדְעַתְּ? אֲמַר לְהוּ: חֶלְמָא חֲזַאי לְכוּ. א"ל: וְאַמַּאי לָא אֲמַרְתְּ לָן [דְּנֵיתְבִינְהוּ]? אֲמַר לְהוּ: אָמִינָא, כִּי הֵיכִי דְּתַעַבְדוּ מִצְוָה לִשְׁמָהּ. רַב פָּפָּא הֲוָה סָלֵיק בְּדַרְגָּא, אִישְׁתְּמִיט כַּרְעֵיהּ בָּעֵי לְמִיפַּל, (ב) אֲמַר: הָשְׁתָּא כֵּן אִיחַיַּיב מַאן דְּסָנֵי לָן כִּמְחַלְּלֵי שַׁבָּתוֹת וּכְעוֹבְדֵי עֲבוֹדָה זָרָה?! א"ל חִיָּיא בַּר רַב מִדִּפְתִּי לְרַב פָּפָּא: שֶׁמָּא עָנִי בָּא לְיָדְךָ וְלֹא פִּרְנַסְתּוֹ. [א]דְּתַנְיָא, רַבִּי יְהוֹשֻׁעַ בֶּן קָרְחָה אוֹמֵר: [א]כָּל הַמַּעֲלִים עֵינָיו מִן הַצְּדָקָה — כְּאִילּוּ עוֹבֵד עֲבוֹדָה זָרָה; כְּתִיב הָכָא: °"הִשָּׁמֶר לְךָ פֶּן יִהְיֶה דָבָר עִם לְבָבְךָ בְלִיַּעַל", וּכְתִיב הָתָם: °"יָצְאוּ אֲנָשִׁים בְּנֵי בְלִיַּעַל", מָה לְהַלָּן עֲבוֹדָה זָרָה, אַף כָּאן עֲבוֹדָה זָרָה. תַּנְיָא, [ב]א"ר אֶלְעָזָר בְּר' יוֹסֵי: כָּל צְדָקָה וָחֶסֶד שֶׁיִּשְׂרָאֵל עוֹשִׂין בָּעוֹלָם הַזֶּה, שָׁלוֹם גָּדוֹל וּפְרַקְלִיטִין גְּדוֹלִין בֵּין יִשְׂרָאֵל לַאֲבִיהֶן שֶׁבַּשָּׁמַיִם, שֶׁנֶּאֱמַר: °"כֹּה אָמַר ה' אַל תָּבוֹא בֵּית מַרְזֵחַ וְאַל תֵּלֵךְ לִסְפּוֹד וְאַל תָּנֹד לָהֶם כִּי אָסַפְתִּי אֶת שְׁלוֹמִי מֵאֵת הָעָם הַזֶּה [וגו' אֶת] הַחֶסֶד וְאֶת הָרַחֲמִים", "חֶסֶד" — זוֹ גְּמִילוּת חֲסָדִים, "רַחֲמִים" — זוֹ צְדָקָה. תַּנְיָא, ר"י אוֹמֵר: גְּדוֹלָה צְדָקָה שֶׁמְּקָרֶבֶת אֶת הַגְּאוּלָּה, שֶׁנֶּאֱמַר: °"כֹּה אָמַר ה' שִׁמְרוּ מִשְׁפָּט וַעֲשׂוּ צְדָקָה כִּי קְרוֹבָה יְשׁוּעָתִי לָבוֹא וְצִדְקָתִי לְהִגָּלוֹת". הוּא הָיָה אוֹמֵר, עֲשָׂרָה דְּבָרִים קָשִׁים נִבְרְאוּ בָּעוֹלָם: הַר קָשֶׁה — בַּרְזֶל מְחַתְּכוֹ, בַּרְזֶל קָשֶׁה — (ג) אוּר מְפַעְפְּעוֹ, אוּר קָשֶׁה — מַיִם מְכַבִּין אוֹתוֹ, מַיִם קָשִׁים — עָבִים סוֹבְלִים אוֹתָן, עָבִים קָשִׁים — רוּחַ מְפַזַּרְתָּן, רוּחַ קָשֶׁה — גּוּף סוֹבְלוֹ, גּוּף קָשֶׁה — פַּחַד שׁוֹבְרוֹ, פַּחַד קָשֶׁה — יַיִן מְפִיגוֹ, יַיִן קָשֶׁה — שֵׁינָה מְפַכַּחְתּוֹ, וּמִיתָה — קָשָׁה (ד) מִכּוּלָּם, [וּצְדָקָה — מַצֶּלֶת מִן הַמִּיתָה], דִּכְתִיב: °"וּצְדָקָה תַּצִּיל מִמָּוֶת". דָּרַשׁ רַבִּי דּוֹסְתַּאי בְּרַבִּי יַנַּאי: בּוֹא וּרְאֵה, שֶׁלֹּא כְּמִדַּת הקב"ה מִדַּת בָּשָׂר וָדָם; מִדַּת בָּשָׂר וָדָם, אָדָם מֵבִיא דּוֹרוֹן גָּדוֹל לַמֶּלֶךְ — סָפֵק מְקַבְּלִין אוֹתוֹ הֵימֶנּוּ, סָפֵק אֵין מְקַבְּלִין אוֹתוֹ הֵימֶנּוּ; [וְאִם תִּמְצָא לוֹמַר מְקַבְּלִים אוֹתוֹ מִמֶּנּוּ] סָפֵק רוֹאֶה פְּנֵי הַמֶּלֶךְ, סָפֵק אֵינוֹ רוֹאֶה פְּנֵי הַמֶּלֶךְ. וְהַקָּדוֹשׁ בָּרוּךְ הוּא אֵינוֹ כֵּן, אָדָם נוֹתֵן פְּרוּטָה לֶעָנִי — זוֹכֶה וּמְקַבֵּל פְּנֵי שְׁכִינָה, שֶׁנֶּאֱמַר: °"אֲנִי בְּצֶדֶק אֶחֱזֶה פָנֶיךָ אֶשְׂבְּעָה בְהָקִיץ תְּמוּנָתֶךָ". רַבִּי אֶלְעָזָר [ג]יְהֵיב פְּרוּטָה לְעָנִי וַהֲדַר מְצַלֵּי, אֲמַר, (ה) דִּכְתִיב: "אֲנִי בְּצֶדֶק אֶחֱזֶה פָנֶיךָ". מַאי "אֶשְׂבְּעָה בְהָקִיץ תְּמוּנָתֶךָ"? אָמַר רַב נַחְמָן בַּר יִצְחָק: אֵלּוּ תַּלְמִידֵי חֲכָמִים שֶׁמְּנַדְּדִין שֵׁינָה מֵעֵינֵיהֶם בָּעוֹלָם הַזֶּה, וְהקב"ה מַשְׂבִּיעָן מִזִּיו הַשְּׁכִינָה לָעוֹלָם הַבָּא. א"ר יוֹחָנָן, מַאי דִּכְתִיב: °"מַלְוֵה ה' חוֹנֵן דָּל"? אִלְמָלֵא מִקְרָא כָּתוּב אִי אֶפְשָׁר לְאוֹמְרוֹ, כִּבְיָכוֹל "עֶבֶד לֹוֶה לְאִישׁ מַלְוֶה". א"ר חִיָּיא בַּר אַבָּא, רַבִּי יוֹחָנָן [ג](רָמֵי,) כְּתִיב: °"לֹא יוֹעִיל הוֹן בְּיוֹם עֶבְרָה וּצְדָקָה תַּצִּיל מִמָּוֶת", וּכְתִיב: °"לֹא יוֹעִילוּ אוֹצְרוֹת רֶשַׁע וּצְדָקָה תַּצִּיל מִמָּוֶת", שְׁתֵּי צְדָקוֹת הַלָּלוּ לָמָּה? אַחַת שֶׁמַּצִּילָתוֹ מִמִּיתָה מְשׁוּנָּה, וְאַחַת שֶׁמַּצִּילָתוֹ מִדִּינָהּ שֶׁל גֵּיהִנָּם; וְאֵי זוֹ הִיא שֶׁמַּצִּילָתוֹ מִדִּינָהּ שֶׁל גֵּיהִנָּם — הַהוּא דִּכְתִיב בֵּיהּ "עֶבְרָה", דִּכְתִיב: °"יוֹם עֶבְרָה הַיּוֹם הַהוּא"; וְאֵי זוֹ הִיא שֶׁמַּצִּילָתוֹ מִמִּיתָה מְשׁוּנָּה —
נוֹתְנָהּ

משלי ג | ויקרא כה | דברים יד | ישעיה נח | דברים טו | שם יג | ירמיה טז | ישעיה נו | משלי י | תהלים יז | משלי יט | שם יא | שם י | צפניה א

רש"י

יִמְצָא חַיִּים. וּכְתִיב גַּבֵּי חָכְמָה: "כִּי מוֹצְאִי מָצָא חַיִּים". בַּעֲלֵי אֲגָדָה. מִתּוֹךְ שֶׁהֵן דַּרְשָׁנִין וּמוֹשְׁכִין אֶת הַלֵּב — הַכֹּל מְכַבְּדִין אוֹתָם. לְבַעַל הַדִּין. רָשָׁע אוֹ גּוֹי. לְהִנָּצֵל אָנוּ בָּהֶן כו'. שֶׁהַצְּדָקָה מַצֶּלֶת מִגֵּיהִנָּם, כִּדְאָמְרִי' לְקַמָּן בִּשְׁמַעְתִּין. שֶׁמְּזוֹנוֹתָיו שֶׁל אָדָם. שָׂכָר שֶׁיִּתְפַּרְנֵס מִמֶּנּוּ. חֶסְרוֹנוֹתָיו. הֶפְסֵד שֶׁעָתִיד לְהַפְסִיד. זָכָה. לְמַזָּל טוֹב — יִתֵּן אוֹתוֹ חִסָּרוֹן לָעֲנִיִּים. חֲזָא [לְהוּ] בְּחֶלְמָא. בְּמוֹצָאֵי (ו) יוה"כ. דְּבָעוּ מֶחְסַר שְׁבַע מְאָה דִּינָרִין. בְּאוֹתָהּ שָׁנָה. שְׁקֵיל צְדָקָה מִינַּיְיהוּ. כָּל הַשָּׁנָה הָיָה כּוֹפָן בִּדְבָרִים, וְגוֹבֶה מֵהֶן לִצְדָקָה. פַּשׁ גַּבַּיְיהוּ. עֶרֶב רֹאשׁ הַשָּׁנָה שִׁיבְסַר דִּינָרֵי שֶׁלֹּא נָתְנוּ לִצְדָקָה, מִשְּׁבַע מֵאָה דִּינָרֵי. לָא תִּדְחֲלוּ. לְמִיפְסַד יוֹתֵר. אַמַּאי לָא אֲמַרְתְּ לָן. מִתְּחִלָּה, שֶׁכָּךְ חֲלַמְתָּ, וְהָיִינוּ נוֹתְנִין כּוּלָּן. הָשְׁתָּא כֵּן. אִם נָפַלְתִּי. אִיחַיַּיב מַאן דְּסָנֵי לָן. כְּאָדָם שֶׁתּוֹלֶה קִלְלָתוֹ בַּחֲבֵירוֹ. מְחַלְּלֵי שַׁבָּת וְעוֹבְדֵי עֲבוֹדָה זָרָה. בִּסְקִילָה, וְאָמַר מָר (כתובות דף ל:): מִי שֶׁנִּתְחַיֵּיב סְקִילָה — אוֹ נוֹפֵל מִן הַגַּג אוֹ חַיָּה דּוֹרַסְתּוֹ, דְּדָמֵי לִסְקִילָה, דִּתְנַן (סנהדרין דף מה.): בֵּית הַסְּקִילָה הָיָה גָּבוֹהַּ שְׁתֵּי קוֹמוֹת וכו'. פְּרַקְלִיטִין. מְלִיצֵי יוֹשֶׁר [שֶׁל מַלְאֲכֵי הַשָּׁרֵת]. כִּי אָסַפְתִּי אֶת שְׁלוֹמִי מֵאֵת הָעָם הַזֶּה. וּמַהוּ הַשָּׁלוֹם — "אֶת הַחֶסֶד וְאֶת הָרַחֲמִים" שֶׁהָיוּ רְגִילִין לַעֲשׂוֹת. מְפַעְפְּעוֹ. מְרַכְּכוֹ. הַגּוּף סוֹבְלוֹ. [כָּל הַגּוּף] מָלֵא רוּחַ. וַאֲנִי בְּצֶדֶק. בִּתְחִלָּה, וְאַחַ"כ "אֶחֱזֶה פָנֶיךָ" בִּתְפִלָּה. אֶשְׂבְּעָה בְהָקִיץ תְּמוּנָתֶךָ. בִּשְׂכַר הַקִּיצָה אֶשְׂבַּע תְּמוּנָתֶךָ. מַלְוֵה ה' חוֹנֵן דָּל. הַחוֹנֵן דַּלִּים נַעֲשֶׂה מַלְוֶה לְהקב"ה, וּכְתִיב: "וְעֶבֶד לֹוֶה לְאִישׁ מַלְוֶה" (משלי כב). וְאֵיזוֹ הִיא צְדָקָה הַמַּצֶּלֶת מִדִּינָהּ שֶׁל גֵּיהִנָּם. כְּלוֹמַר, אֵיזֶה מִן הַמִּקְרָאוֹת הַלָּלוּ מְדַבֵּר מִדִּין שֶׁל גֵּיהִנָּם — אוֹתוֹ שֶׁכָּתוּב: "לֹא יוֹעִיל הוֹן בְּיוֹם עֶבְרָה".
נוֹתְנָהּ

תוספות

ואיזו שמצלת ממיתה משונה נותנה ואינו יודע למי נותנה. וא"ת: אדרבה, זאת שהיא מצוה רבה היה לה להציל מדינה של גיהנם, שהוא רע ביותר! ואומר ר"י: דרוב דברים אין עומדין לאדם בעולם הזה, אלא לאחר מיתה. ובעולם הזה אין עומדין לאדם אלא מצות גדולות, כדתנן (קדושין דף לט:): אלו דברים שאדם אוכל מפירותיו בעולם הזה והקרן קיימת לעולם הבא, לכך קאמר דאפילו ממיתה משונה, דהוי בעולם הזה — מצלת.
אלא

מסורת הש"ס

א) [תוספ' פאה פ"ד] כתובות סח.: ב) [תוס' פאה פ"ד]: ג) [בילקוט ובע"י ליתא] והגי' אמר ר"ח ב"א אר"י:

רבינו גרשום

צדקה זו עושר שיהיו לו נכסים ועושר שיעשה מהם צדקה: כבוד. זו אגדה בשביל שיודע לדרוש באגדות מכבדין אותו: יש לו לבעל הדין. יצר הרע להשיבך ולהטעותך ולומר לך: ועכשיו אי אתם עושין רצונו של מקום. לפי שאתם בגלות ואי אתם יכולים לקיים כל התורה: עניים מרודים. שנרדים מבני אדם ששללום: איכי השתא נפלי. הייתי נידון בסקילה כדאמר בית הסקילה היה גבוה ב' קומות (סנהדרין מה). וכעובדי עבודה זרה דכתיב (דברי' יז) וסקלתם באבני' ומתו ופרקליטין. מלמדי סניגוריאה כי אספתי את שלומי בשביל שאינם עושים לא חסד ולא רחמים. הא עושין יהיה להם שלום גדול: מפעפעו. עושהו רך: אני בצדק. שאעשה צדקה מתחילה והדר אחזה פניך

עין משפט נר מצוה

צ א מיימוני פ"י מהל' מתנות עניים הל' ג סמג עשין קסב טוש"ע י"ד סי' רמז סעיף א:
צא ב מיי' שם הל' טו [טוש"ע א"ח סי' לב סעי' ז] וטוש"ע י"ד סי' רמט סעי' יד:

הגהות הב"ח

(א) גמרא פש גבייהו כצ"ל ואות ו' נמחק: (ב) שם בעי למיפל חלש דעתיה אמר השתא: (ג) שם ברזל קשה אש מפעפעו אש קשה מים: (ד) שם ומיתה קשה (מכולם) תז"מ ונ"ב ס"א משינה: (ה) שם והדר מצלי אמר כתיב כצ"ל ואות ד' נמחק: (ו) רש"י ד"ה חזא להו בחלמא במוצאי ראש השנה הס"ד:

צב א ב מיי' פ"י מהל' מתנות עניים הלכה ח סמג עשין קסב טוש"ע י"ד סי' רמט סעיף ז:
צג ג ד מיי' שם פ"ח הלכה ט סמג שם טוש"ע י"ד סימן רנד סעיף ב:

תורה אור

[א]נותנה, ואינו יודע למי נותנה נוטלה ואינו יודע ממי נוטלה. נותנה ואינו יודע למי נותנה — לאפוקי מדמר עוקבא; נוטלה ואינו יודע ממי נוטלה — לאפוקי מדרבי אבא. ואלא היכי ליעביד? ליתיב לארנקי של צדקה. מיתיבי: מה יעשה אדם ויהיו לו בנים זכרים? ר"א אומר: יפזר מעותיו לעניים; ר' יהושע אומר: ישמח אשתו לדבר מצוה; [א]ר' אליעזר בן יעקב אומר: [ב]לא יתן אדם פרוטה לארנקי של צדקה אלא א"כ ממונה עליה כר' חנניא בן תרדיון! כי קא אמרינן — דממני עלה כר' חנניא בן תרדיון. א"ר אבהו, אמר משה לפני הקב"ה: רבש"ע, במה תרום קרן ישראל? אמר לו: ב"כי תשא". וא"ר אבהו, שאלו את שלמה בן דוד: עד היכן כחה של צדקה? אמר להן, צאו וראו מה פירש דוד אבא: °"פזר נתן לאביונים צדקתו עומדת לעד קרנו תרום בכבוד" (תהלים קיב). [ב]רבי אבא אמר, מהכא: °"הוא מרומים ישכון מצדות סלעים משגבו לחמו נתן מימיו נאמנים" (ישעיה לג), מה טעם "מרומים ישכון מצדות סלעים משגבו"? משום ד"לחמו נתן" ו"מימיו נאמנים". וא"ר אבהו, שאלו את שלמה: איזהו בן העולם הבא? אמר להם: כל °ש"כנגד זקניו כבוד". [ג]כי הא (א) דיוסף בריה דר' (שם כד) יהושע חלש, אינגיד. א"ל אבוה: מאי חזית? א"ל: עולם הפוך ראיתי, עליונים למטה ותחתונים למעלה. א"ל: עולם ברור ראית. ואנן היכי חזיתינן? [א"ל:] כי היכי דחשבינן הכא חשבינן התם. ושמעתי שהיו אומרים: [ד]אשרי מי שבא לכאן ותלמודו בידו. ושמעתי שהיו אומרים: הרוגי מלכות — אין כל בריה יכולה לעמוד במחיצתן. מאן נינהו? אילימא ר"ע וחבריו — משום הרוגי מלכות ותו לא? פשיטא, [ה]בלאו הכי נמי! אלא הרוגי לוד. תניא, אמר להן רבן יוחנן בן זכאי לתלמידיו: בני, מהו שאמר הכתוב °"צדקה תרומם גוי וחסד לאומים חטאת"? (משלי יד) נענה רבי אליעזר ואמר: "צדקה תרומם גוי" — אלו ישראל, דכתיב: °"ומי כעמך ישראל (שמואל ב ז) גוי אחד בארץ", "וחסד לאומים חטאת" — כל צדקה וחסד שאומות העולם עושין, חטא הוא להן, [ו]שאינם עושין אלא להתגדל בו, כמו שנאמר: °"די (עזרא ו) להוון מהקרבין ניחוחין לאלהה שמיא ומצליין לחיי מלכא ובנוהי". ודעביד הכי לאו צדקה גמורה היא? [ז]והתניא: האומר "סלע (ב) זה לצדקה בשביל שיחיו בני, ובשביל שאזכה לעולם הבא" — הרי זה צדיק גמור! לא קשיא: כאן בישראל, כאן בגוי. נענה רבי יהושע ואמר: "צדקה תרומם גוי" — אלו ישראל, דכתיב: "ומי כעמך ישראל גוי אחד", "וחסד לאומים חטאת" — כל צדקה וחסד שאומות העולם עושין, חטא הוא להן, שאין עושין אלא כדי שתמשך מלכותן, שנאמר: °"להן מלכא מלכי ישפר עליך (דניאל ד) וחטיך בצדקה פרוק ועויתך במיחן ענין הן תהוי ארכא לשלותיך" וגו'. נענה רבן גמליאל ואמר: "צדקה תרומם גוי" — אלו ישראל, דכתיב: "ומי כעמך ישראל" [וגו'], "וחסד לאומים חטאת" — כל צדקה וחסד שגוים עושין, חטא הוא להן, שאין עושין אלא להתיהר בו, [ח]וכל המתיהר נופל בגיהנם, שנאמר: °"זד יהיר לץ שמו עושה (משלי כא) בעברת זדון", ואין עברה אלא גיהנם, שנאמר: °"יום עברה היום ההוא". (צפניה א) אמר רבן גמליאל: עדיין אנו צריכין למודעי. רבי אליעזר המודעי אומר: "צדקה תרומם גוי" — אלו ישראל, דכתיב: "ומי כעמך ישראל גוי אחד", "וחסד לאומים חטאת" — כל צדקה וחסד שאומות העולם עושין, חטא הוא להן, שאין עושין אלא לחרף אותנו בו, שנאמר: °"ויבא ויעש ה' כאשר דבר כי חטאתם לה' ולא שמעתם בקולו והיה לכם הדבר (ירמיה מ) הזה". נענה רבי נחוניא בן הקנה ואמר: "צדקה תרומם גוי וחסד" — לישראל, ו"לאומים" — חטאת. אמר להם רבן יוחנן בן זכאי לתלמידיו: נראין דברי רבי נחוניא בן הקנה מדברי ומדבריכם, לפי שהוא נותן צדקה וחסד לישראל, ולאומות העולם חטאת. מכלל דהוא נמי אמר, מאי היא? דתניא, אמר להם רבן יוחנן בן זכאי: כשם שהחטאת מכפרת על ישראל, כך צדקה מכפרת על אומות העולם.§ איפרא הורמיז, אימיה דשבור מלכא, שדרה ארבע מאה דינרי לקמיה דרבי אמי ולא קבלינהו; (ג) שדרינהו קמיה דרבא, [ג]וקבלינהו משום שלום מלכות. שמע רבי אמי איקפד, אמר: לית ליה °"ביבש קצירה תשברנה (ישעיה כז) נשים באות מאירות אותה"? ורבא, משום שלום מלכות. ורבי אמי נמי, משום שלום מלכות — [ד]דאיבעי ליה למפלגינהו לעניי גוים. ורבא נמי, לעניי גוים יהבינהו. ור' אמי דאיקפד הוא — דלא

אלא א"כ ממונה עליה כרבי חנניא בן תרדיון. פי': נאמן כמותו. אבל לדיק כמותו לא, דהא גבאים דימי אמוראים לא היו לדיקים כמותו. ולהכי נקט ר' חנניא בן תרדיון — משום מעשה שבא לידו, דאמר פ"ק דמסכת ע"ז (דף יז:): מעות פורים נתחלפו לי במעות של לדקה, וחלקתים לעניים. וכן בפרק "במה טומנין" (שבת דף מט. ושם) דאמר: תפילין לריכין גוף נקי כאלישע — לא לדיק כאלישע קאמר, אלא גוף נקי, שידע ליזהר שלא ישן בהם ושלא יפיח בהם קאמר. ולא נקט אלישע אלא משום דאיתרחיש ביה ניסא.

עליונים למטה ותחתונים למעלה. פי' ר"ת, דאמרו הגאונים שקבלה בידם רב מפי רב, דעולם הפוך — היינו שראה שמואל דהוה יתיב קמיה דרב יהודה תלמידיה, משום דמיחה בשמואל בפר' "במה בהמה" (שם דף נה.) גבי ההיא איתתא דאתיא וצווחא קמיה דשמואל ולא אשגח בה, א"ל רב יהודה: לית ליה למר "אוטם אזנו מזעקת דל" וגו'.

ויבא ויעש ה' כאשר דבר כי חטאתם וגו'. ואותה שעה עשה לדקה, שהיה (ד) מקנא להקב"ה. א"נ: שהיה מתיר את ירמיה מן הזיקים, כדכתיב התם.

ולא

נותנה ואינו יודע למי נותנה. כדמסיים בסיפיה: יתננה בכיס של גבאי לדקה. דרב עוקבא ור' אבא. במסכ' כתובות (דף סז:): מר עוקבא הוה שדי לעניא דשבבותיה כל יומא ארבעה זוזי בצינורא דדשא, הרי שהעני אינו יודע ממי נוטלה, והוא יודע למי נותנה. ור' אבא הוה צייר בסודריה ושדי לאחוריה ומפליא נפשיה לביני עניי, והעני נוטלה ויודע ממי נוטלה, ואינו יודע למי נותנה. לדבר מצוה. לפני תשמיש. אמר לו בכי תשא. אם באת לשאת ראשם בהגבהה — קח מהם כופר לצדקה. כנגד זקניו כבוד. אותם שחולקין להם כבוד בעולם הזה מחמת חכמת זקנתם. עליונים למטה. אותם שהם עליונים כאן מחמת עושרן — ראיתי שם שהם למטה. ותחתונים למעלה. ראיתי עניים שהם בינינו שפלים, שם ראיתים חשובים. ואנן. בעלי תורה, היאך אתינן, היאך יש חשיבותינו? כי היכי. דאתינן הכא, חשובים ונכבדים, הכי אתינן התם. הרוגי מלכות ותו לא. כלומר, הך מעלה לחודא הוא דהוי בהו, שנהרגו על קידוש השם, ותו לא הוה בהו? הרוגי לוד. לוליינוס ופפוס, אחים שהרגם (*טורנוסרופוס) הרשע בלודקיא, כדאמרינן במסכת תענית (דף יח:), על ידי גזירה שנגזרה על ישראל להשמיד, על שנמצאת בת מלך הרוגה וחשדו את ישראל עליה, ועמדו האחי' הללו ואמרו: מה לכם על ישראל, אנו הרגנוה. ה"ז צדיק גמור. על דבר זה ומחשבה זו. כאן בישראל וכאן בגוי. ישראל דעתן לשמים, בין יחיה בין לא יחיה אינו מהרהר אחר מדת הדין, אבל גוי אינו נותן אלא ע"מ כן, ואם לאו — מתחרט. יום עברה היום ההוא. ביום הדין משפטי, בנבואת צפניה. המודעי. מעיר המודעי היה. ויבא ויעש ה' כאשר דבר כי חטאתם לה' וגו'. נבוזראדן קאמר ליה לירמיה, כשהיה מגלה את ישראל לבבל. ביבש קצירה תשברנה. כשתכלה זכות שבידן, ויבש לחלוחית מעשה צדקה שלהן — אז ישברו.

דלא

[*] נ"ל טוריינוס

רבינו גרשום

בתפלה: ואינו יודע למי נותנה. לאפוקי ממר עוקבא דמנה לצדקה אצינורא דדשא של עני העני לא היה יודע מי נתנה שם ומר עוקבא יודע איזה עני נטלה. נוטלה העני ואינו יודע ממי נטלה. לאפוקי דר' אבא דצייר בסודריה ומפשילו לאחוריו ואתי עני ושרי ושקל. עני היה יודע ממי נוטל ור' אבא אינו יודע איזה עני נוטלה: יתן לארנקי של צדקה ולא ידע העני מי נתן והנותן לא ידע מי נטל: ישמח אשתו בדבר מצוה. שיפקדנה שלא בזמן עונה: אלא א"כ ממונה עליה כר' חנינא בן תרדיון שהיה אדם גדול והיה יודע לבדוק למי יתן אלמא (דלא) [דאי לא] מצינן למשכח ממונה כגון זה. הוא עצמו מפזרן ונותן. כי אמרינן נמי דיתן לארנקי בשיש ממונה עליה כר' חנינא בן תרדיון. אי לא יפוזרן הוא עצמו: אמר לו בכי תשא. משום דכתי' שם ונתנו איש כופר נפשו: אמר להן כל שכנגד זקניו כבוד. זה שקנה חכמה כלומר כל שחולקין לו כבוד בשביל חכמתו ולא משום עושרו: עליונים למטה. כלומר אותן שהן עליונים בעולם הזה בשביל עושרם ולא בגין חכמתם ושם בעולם הבא שרוין למטה: ותחתונים בעולם הזה שהם חכמים ומסכינין ובני מעשים טובים לא חשיבי הכא. לעולם הבא שרוין למעלה: ואנן מאי כלומר איך תלמידי חכמים (האיך) חושבין אותם שם: כי היכי דחשיבין הכא חשיבין התם והיינו נגד זקניו כבוד: ותלמודו בידו. בגירסא: ר' עקיבא ועשרה חביריו. פשיטא כלומר בלא זכותא דהריגה דהוו צדיקין גמורים: הרוגי לוד. שפעם אחת נמצאת בת מלך הרוגה ומושלכת ברחוב ולא נודע מי הרגה וחשדו לכל היהודים ורצה המלך לשלוח יד בכולן עד שבאו שנים ומסרו עצמן ואמרו שהן הרגוה והצילו את כולם על ידן: כאן בישראל. ודאי מעליותא היא דאעפ"כ לבו לשמים לשם מצוה אבל הרבה אומות אין עושין אלא לצורך עצמן ולא לשם שמים ומשום הכי דלא עבדיתו צדקה כו':
ויבא ויעש וגו' כי האי גונא מחרפין אותן. ור' נחוניא דריש הכי צדקה תרומם ישראל וחסד דמשים צדקה וחסד לישראל. וכל מה שאמרו הרבה אומות עושין חטאת הוא להן מכלל דהא ריב"ז דריש האי קרא כשם שחטאת קרבן חטאת מכפר על ישראל: לקמיה דר' אמי דהוי גבאי ליתנם לצדקה: איקפד על רבא דקבלינהו: אמר לית ליה לרבא ביבש קצירה תשברנה. כלומר כעין שהקציר מבושל יפה משברין אותו כך כשימלא ספקם ומגרש אותם מחטאתם תשבר זרועם נשים באות מאירות כגון אריתי מורי כלומר שאפי' הנשים (אין) יכולין למשול בם והיכי עביד רבא דקביל צדקה מהן להימשך מלכותן בזכות הצדקה: ור' אמי דאקפד לא

מסורת הש"ם

א) ע"ז דף יז: ב) [כע"י איתא רבא]: ג) פסחים נ. [ושם איתא כי הא דיוסף בריה דר' יהושע בן לוי חלש ואיתנגיד כי הדר א"ל כו']: ד) [מ"ק כח. כתובות עז:]: ה) ס"א דהא איכא מעשים טובים בלאו ה"נ אלא כו': ו) ס"א לפי שאין עושין כו' וכן בכולן: ז) פסחים ח. ר"ה ד.: ח) [לקמן עח: ע"ש] ע"ז יח:

הגהות הב"ח

(א) גמרא כי הא דרב יוסף בריה דר' יהושע: (ב) שם סלע זו לצדקה: (ג) שם שדרתינהו קמיה דרבא: (ד) תום' ד"ה ויבא וכו' עשה צדקה שהיה נראה כמקנא להקב"ה:

דְּלָא סִיימוּהָ קַמֵּיהּ. תַּנְיָא: אָמְרוּ עָלָיו עַל בִּנְיָמִין הַצַּדִּיק שֶׁהָיָה מְמוּנֶּה עַל קוּפָּה שֶׁל צְדָקָה, פַּעַם אַחַת בָּאתָה אִשָּׁה לְפָנָיו בִּשְׁנֵי בַצּוֹרֶת, אָמְרָה לוֹ: רַבִּי, פַּרְנְסֵנִי! אָמַר לָהּ: הָעֲבוֹדָה, שֶׁאֵין בְּקוּפָּה שֶׁל צְדָקָה כְּלוּם! אָמְרָה לוֹ: רַבִּי, אִם אֵין אַתָּה מְפַרְנְסֵנִי, הֲרֵי אִשָּׁה וְשִׁבְעָה בָנֶיהָ מֵתִים! עָמַד וּפִרְנְסָהּ מִשֶּׁלּוֹ. לְיָמִים חָלָה וְנָטָה לָמוּת, אָמְרוּ מַלְאֲכֵי הַשָּׁרֵת לִפְנֵי הקב"ה: רבש"ע, אַתָּה אָמַרְתָּ: א)אכָּל הַמְקַיֵּים נֶפֶשׁ אַחַת מִיִּשְׂרָאֵל כְּאִילּוּ קִיֵּים עוֹלָם מָלֵא, וּבִנְיָמִין הַצַּדִּיק שֶׁהֶחֱיָה אִשָּׁה וְשִׁבְעָה בָנֶיהָ יָמוּת בְּשָׁנִים מוּעָטוֹת הַלָּלוּ? מִיָּד קָרְעוּ לוֹ גְּזַר דִּינוֹ. תָּנָא: הוֹסִיפוּ לוֹ עֶשְׂרִים וּשְׁתַּיִם שָׁנָה עַל שְׁנוֹתָיו. ת"ר: ב)מַעֲשֶׂה בְּמוּנְבַּז הַמֶּלֶךְ שֶׁבִּזְבֵּז אוֹצְרוֹתָיו וְאוֹצְרוֹת אֲבוֹתָיו בִּשְׁנֵי בַצּוֹרֶת, וְחָבְרוּ עָלָיו אֶחָיו וּבֵית אָבִיו וְאָמְרוּ לוֹ: אֲבוֹתֶיךָ גָּנְזוּ וְהוֹסִיפוּ עַל שֶׁל אֲבוֹתָם, וְאַתָּה מְבַזְבְּזָם! אָמַר לָהֶם: אֲבוֹתַי גָּנְזוּ לְמַטָּה, וַאֲנִי גָּנַזְתִּי לְמַעְלָה, שֶׁנֶּאֱמַר: °"אֱמֶת מֵאֶרֶץ תִּצְמָח וְצֶדֶק מִשָּׁמַיִם נִשְׁקָף"; אֲבוֹתַי גָּנְזוּ בְּמָקוֹם שֶׁהַיָּד שׁוֹלֶטֶת בּוֹ, וַאֲנִי גָּנַזְתִּי בְּמָקוֹם שֶׁאֵין הַיָּד שׁוֹלֶטֶת בּוֹ, שֶׁנֶּאֱמַר: °"צֶדֶק וּמִשְׁפָּט מְכוֹן כִּסְאֶךָ"; אֲבוֹתַי גָּנְזוּ דָּבָר שֶׁאֵין עוֹשֶׂה פֵּירוֹת, וַאֲנִי גָּנַזְתִּי דָּבָר שֶׁעוֹשֶׂה פֵּירוֹת, שֶׁנֶּאֱמַר: °"אִמְרוּ צַדִּיק כִּי טוֹב כִּי פְּרִי מַעַלְלֵיהֶם יֹאכֵלוּ"; אֲבוֹתַי גָּנְזוּ [אוֹצְרוֹת] מָמוֹן וַאֲנִי גָּנַזְתִּי אוֹצְרוֹת נְפָשׁוֹת, שֶׁנֶּאֱמַר: °"פְּרִי צַדִּיק עֵץ חַיִּים וְלוֹקֵחַ נְפָשׁוֹת חָכָם"; אֲבוֹתַי גָּנְזוּ לַאֲחֵרִים, וַאֲנִי גָּנַזְתִּי לְעַצְמִי, שֶׁנֶּאֱמַר: °"וּלְךָ תִּהְיֶה צְדָקָה"; אֲבוֹתַי גָּנְזוּ לָעוֹלָם הַזֶּה, וַאֲנִי גָּנַזְתִּי לָעוֹלָם הַבָּא, שֶׁנֶּאֱמַר: °"וְהָלַךְ לְפָנֶיךָ צִדְקֶךָ כְּבוֹד ה' יַאַסְפֶךָ". § "וְאִם קָנָה בָּהּ בֵּית דִּירָה — הֲרֵי הוּא כְּאַנְשֵׁי הָעִיר". § מַתְנִיתִין דְּלָא כְּרשב"ג; דְּתַנְיָא, רַבָּן שִׁמְעוֹן ב"ג אוֹמֵר: אִם קָנָה בָּהּ קַרְקַע כָּל שֶׁהוּא — הֲרֵי הוּא כְּאַנְשֵׁי הָעִיר. וְהָא תַּנְיָא, רַבָּן שִׁמְעוֹן בֶּן גַּמְלִיאֵל אוֹמֵר: אִם קָנָה שָׁם קַרְקַע הָרְאוּיָה לְבֵית דִּירָה — הֲרֵי הוּא כְּאַנְשֵׁי הָעִיר! תְּרֵי תַּנָּאֵי וְאַלִּיבָּא דְּרַבָּן שִׁמְעוֹן בֶּן גַּמְלִיאֵל. §

מתני' ג)באֵין חוֹלְקִין אֶת הֶחָצֵר — עַד שֶׁיְּהֵא אַרְבַּע אַמּוֹת לָזֶה וְאַרְבַּע אַמּוֹת לָזֶה. גוְלֹא אֶת הַשָּׂדֶה — עַד שֶׁיְּהֵא בָּהּ ד)תִּשְׁעָה קַבִּין לָזֶה וְתִשְׁעָה קַבִּין לָזֶה; ר' יְהוּדָה אוֹמֵר: עַד שֶׁיְּהֵא בָּהּ תִּשְׁעַת חֲצָיֵי קַבִּין לָזֶה וְתִשְׁעַת חֲצָיֵי קַבִּין לָזֶה. דוְלֹא אֶת הַגִּינָּה — עַד שֶׁיְּהֵא בָּהּ חֲצִי קַב לָזֶה וַחֲצִי קַב לָזֶה; ר' עֲקִיבָא אוֹמֵר: בֵּית רוֹבַע. הוְלֹא אֶת הַטְּרַקְלִין, וְלֹא אֶת הַמּוֹרָן, וְלֹא אֶת הַשּׁוֹבָךְ, וְלֹא אֶת הַטַּלִּית, וְלֹא אֶת הַמֶּרְחָץ, וְלֹא אֶת בֵּית הַבַּד, וְלֹא אֶת בֵּית הַשְּׁלָחִין — עַד שֶׁיְּהֵא בָּהֶן כְּדֵי לָזֶה וּכְדֵי לָזֶה. וזֶה הַכְּלָל: כָּל שֶׁיֵּחָלֵק וּשְׁמוֹ עָלָיו — חוֹלְקִין, וְאִם לָאו — אֵין חוֹלְקִין. ה)אֵימָתַי? בִּזְמַן שֶׁאֵין שְׁנֵיהֶם רוֹצִים, זאֲבָל בִּזְמַן שֶׁשְּׁנֵיהֶם רוֹצִים — אֲפִי' פָּחוֹת מִכָּאן יַחֲלוֹקוּ. ו)חוְכִתְבֵי הַקֹּדֶשׁ, אע"פ שֶׁשְּׁנֵיהֶם רוֹצִים — לֹא יַחֲלוֹקוּ. §

גמ' א"ר אַסִי א"ר יוֹחָנָן: טאַרְבַּע אַמּוֹת שֶׁאָמְרוּ, חוּץ מִשֶּׁל פְּתָחִים. תַּנְיָא נַמִי הָכִי: אֵין חוֹלְקִים אֶת הֶחָצֵר — עַד שֶׁיְּהֵא בָּהּ שְׁמוֹנֶה אַמּוֹת לָזֶה וּשְׁמוֹנֶה אַמּוֹת לָזֶה; וְהָא אֲנַן תְּנַן: אַרְבַּע אַמּוֹת לָזֶה וְאַרְבַּע אַמּוֹת לָזֶה! אֶלָּא ש"מ כִּדְרַבִּי אַסִי, שְׁמַע מִינַּהּ. וְאִיכָּא דְּרָמֵי לְהוּ מִירְמָא; תְּנַן: אֵין חוֹלְקִין אֶת הֶחָצֵר — עַד שֶׁיְּהֵא בָּהּ אַרְבַּע אַמּוֹת לָזֶה וְאַרְבַּע אַמּוֹת לָזֶה; וְהָתַנְיָא: שְׁמוֹנֶה אַמּוֹת לָזֶה וּשְׁמוֹנֶה אַמּוֹת לָזֶה! א"ר אַסִי אָמַר ר' יוֹחָנָן: אַרְבַּע אַמּוֹת שֶׁאָמְרוּ, חוּץ מִשֶּׁל פְּתָחִים. ז)אָמַר רַב הוּנָא: חָצֵר מִתְחַלֶּקֶת לְפִי פִּתְחֶיהָ; וְרַב חִסְדָּא אָמַר: ינוֹתְנִין אַרְבַּע אַמּוֹת לְכָל פֶּתַח וּפֶתַח, וְהַשְּׁאָר חוֹלְקִין בְּשָׁוֶה. תַּנְיָא כְּוָותֵיהּ דְּרַב חִסְדָּא: כפְּתָחִים שֶׁבֶּחָצֵר יֵשׁ לָהֶן אַרְבַּע אַמּוֹת; הָיָה לָזֶה פֶּתַח אֶחָד וְלָזֶה שְׁנֵי פְּתָחִים — זֶה שֶׁיֵּשׁ לוֹ פֶּתַח אֶחָד נוֹטֵל אַרְבַּע אַמּוֹת, וְזֶה שֶׁיֵּשׁ לוֹ שְׁנֵי פְּתָחִים נוֹטֵל שְׁמוֹנֶה אַמּוֹת, וְהַשְּׁאָר חוֹלְקִין בְּשָׁוֶה; הָיָה לָזֶה פֶּתַח רָחָב שְׁמוֹנֶה אַמּוֹת — נוֹטֵל שְׁמוֹנֶה אַמּוֹת כְּנֶגֶד הַפֶּתַח וְאַרְבַּע אַמּוֹת בֶּחָצֵר. אַרְבַּע אַמּוֹת בֶּחָצֵר מַאי עֲבִידְתַּיְיהוּ? אֲמַר אַבָּיֵי, להָכִי קָאָמַר: נוֹטֵל שְׁמוֹנֶה אַמּוֹת בְּאוֹרֶךְ הֶחָצֵר וְאַרְבַּע אַמּוֹת בְּרוֹחַב הֶחָצֵר. אֲמַר אֲמֵימָר: מהַאי פֵּירָא דְּסוּפְלֵי — יֵשׁ לוֹ אַרְבַּע אַמּוֹת לְכָל רוּחַ וְרוּחַ. נוְלָא אֲמַרַן אֶלָּא דְּלָא מְיַיחֵד לֵיהּ פִּתְחָא, אֲבָל

רש"י

דְּלָא סִיימוּהָ קַמֵּיהּ. דְּר' אַמִי, דְּלַעֲנִיֵּי גוֹיִם חִלְּקָן רָבָא. וְהָנָךְ דַּאֲמַרַן לְעֵיל (דף ח.) דְּשַׁדְרָה נַמִי אִיפְרָא הוּרְמִיז לְמִצְוָה רַבָּה — מִשּׁוּם שָׁלוֹם מַלְכוּת נַמִי קַבְּלִינְהוּ, וְלֹא אֶפְשָׁר לֵיהּ לְחַלְּקָן לַעֲנִיֵּי גוֹיִם — דְּאָסוּר לִגְנוֹב דַּעַת הַבְּרִיּוֹת, וַאֲפִילּוּ דַּעְתּוֹ שֶׁל גּוֹי. אֲבָל בְּמָעוֹת הַמִּתְחַלְּקוֹת לַעֲנִיִּים — אֵין גְּנֵיבַת דַּעַת, דְּאִינְהוּ נַמִי יָדְעִי שֶׁיִּשְׂרָאֵל רְגִילִים לְפַרְנֵס עֲנִיֵּי גוֹיִם, כִּדְאָמְרִי' בְּמַסֶּ' גִּיטִּין (דף סא.): מְפַרְנְסִין עֲנִיֵּי גוֹיִם עִם עֲנִיֵּי יִשְׂרָאֵל, מִפְּנֵי דַּרְכֵי שָׁלוֹם. אַתָּה אָמַרְתָּ כו'. מִתּוֹרָתְךָ לָמַדְנוּ, לְפִיכָךְ נִבְרָא אָדָם יְחִידִי — לוֹמַר לְךָ: כָּל הַמְקַיֵּים נֶפֶשׁ אַחַת [מִיִּשְׂרָאֵל] כְּאִילּוּ קִיֵּים הָעוֹלָם מָלֵא, וּכְתִיב (בראשית ד): "קוֹל דְּמֵי אָחִיךָ" — דָּמוֹ וְדַם זַרְעִיּוֹתָיו. אַף כְּשֶׁאַתָּה מְקַיֵּים דְּמֵי אָחִיךָ עִמְּךָ — מַעֲלֶה עָלֶיךָ חַיָּיו וְחַיֵּי זַרְעִיּוֹתָיו, שֶׁמִּדָּה טוֹבָה מְרוּבָּה מִמִּדַּת פּוּרְעָנוּת. מוּנְבַּז הַמֶּלֶךְ. בְּנָהּ שֶׁל הֵילֶנִי הַמַּלְכָּה, מִזֶּרַע הַחַשְׁמוֹנָאִים. כְּשֶׁאֱמֶת מֵאֶרֶץ תִּצְמָח. אַף מִשָּׁמַיִם נִשְׁקָף הַצֶּדֶק, לְשַׁלֵּם גְּמוּל. נִשְׁקָף = מַבִּיט, כְּמוֹ "נִשְׁקְפָה וַתְּיַבֵּב" (שופטים ה). כְּלוֹמַר, זְכוּת הַצְּדָקָה מַבִּיט וּמִסְתַּכֵּל לְמַטָּה. מְכוֹן כִּסְאֶךָ. גְּנִיזָתָן תַּחַת מְכוֹן הַכִּסֵּא. (בְּמָקוֹם) [דָּבָר] שֶׁעוֹשֶׂה פֵּירוֹת. וְהַקֶּרֶן קַיָּים לָעוה"ב, וְהַפֵּירוֹת אוֹכֵל בְּחַיָּיו, שֶׁנֶּאֱמַר: "כִּי פְרִי מַעַלְלֵיהֶם יֹאכֵלוּ". אוֹצְרוֹת נְפָשׁוֹת. שֶׁנֶּאֱמַר: "וְלוֹקֵחַ נְפָשׁוֹת חָכָם" בְּהַאי קְרָא. **מתני'** טְרַקְלִין וּמוֹרָן. מִינֵי פַּלָּטִין. בֵּית הַשְּׁלָחִין. מִתּוֹךְ שֶׁיֵּשׁ לוֹ מַעְיָן, וּבְיָדוֹ לְהַשְׁקוֹתוֹ תָּדִיר, אִם אֵין בּוֹ ט' קַבִּין — זוֹרְעִין בּוֹ שְׁאָר זְרָעִים, לְפִיכָךְ אֲפִילּוּ בְּפָחוֹת מִכָּאן יֵשׁ בּוֹ דִּין חֲלוּקָה. אֲפִילּוּ בְּפָחוֹת מִכָּאן יַחֲלוֹקוּ. מִשּׁוּם דְּבָעֵי לְמִיתְנֵי: וּבְכִתְבֵי הַקֹּדֶשׁ אע"פ שֶׁשְּׁנֵיהֶם רוֹצִים לֹא יַחֲלוֹקוּ, תָּנֵי רֵישָׁא(א). כִּתְבֵי הַקֹּדֶשׁ. כ"ד סְפָרִים. וְהָיוּ רְגִילִים לְכוֹתְבָן בְּגִלָּיוֹן כְּס"ת שֶׁלָּנוּ, לְפִיכָךְ גְּנַאי הַדָּבָר לְחָתְכָן. **גמ'** חוּץ מִשֶּׁל פְּתָחִים. חָצֵר שֶׁל שְׁנֵיהֶם שְׁנֵי בָתִּים פְּתוּחִין לְתוֹכָהּ. וְלִפְנֵי הַפֶּתַח אַרְבַּע אַמּוֹת לְאוֹרֶךְ הַבַּיִת הֵן, לִפְרֵק מַשָּׂאוֹ מֵעַל חֲמוֹרוֹ. וְחוּץ מֵאוֹתָן ד' אַמּוֹת צָרִיךְ שֶׁיְּהֵא אַרְבַּע אַמּוֹת לִשְׁאָר תַּשְׁמִישִׁין. חָצֵר מִתְחַלֶּקֶת לְפִתְחֶי'. הָיְתָה לוֹ חָצֵר וּבָהּ שְׁנֵי בָתִּים, וְאֶחָד מֵהֶן פְּתוּחִין לוֹ שְׁנֵי פְתָחִים לֶחָצֵר, וְלַבַּיִת הַשֵּׁנִי אֵין פָּתוּחַ לֶחָצֵר אֶלָּא פֶּתַח אֶחָד, וְחוֹלֵק נְכָסָיו עַל פִּיו, וְנוֹתֵן הָאֶחָד לִרְאוּבֵן בְּנוֹ וְהַשֵּׁנִי לְשִׁמְעוֹן, וְחָצֵר לֹא חִילֵּק. אִם בָּאוּ לַחֲלוֹק אֶת הֶחָצֵר, זֶה שֶׁיֵּשׁ לוֹ שְׁנֵי פְתָחִים נוֹטֵל שְׁנֵי חֲלָקִים בֶּחָצֵר, וְאָחִיו נוֹטֵל חֵלֶק אֶחָד. נוֹתֵן לְכָל פֶּתַח (ב) ד' אַמּוֹת. בְּרוֹחַב הֶחָצֵר לְהַלָּן מִן הַפֶּתַח, כְּנֶגֶד הָרוֹחַב כְּפִי רוֹחַב הַפֶּתַח. נוֹטֵל שְׁמוֹנֶה אַמּוֹת. דְּהַיְינוּ כְּנֶגֶד רוֹחַב הַפֶּתַח, וְאַרְבַּע אַמּוֹת בְּרוֹחַב הֶחָצֵר לְהַלָּן מִן הַפֶּתַח. הַאי פֵּירָא דְּסוּפְלֵי. מִי שֶׁיֵּשׁ לוֹ חֲפִירָה בֶּחָצֵר שֶׁנּוֹתְנִין בָּהּ גַּרְעִינֵי תְמָרִים לְמַאֲכַל בְּהֵמָה — יֵשׁ לוֹ אַרְבַּע אַמּוֹת בֶּחָצֵר לְכָל סְבִיבוֹתֶיהָ. דְּלָא מְיַיחֵד לֵיהּ פִּיתְחָא. שֶׁלֹּא הָיָה לוֹ פֶּתַח אֵצֶל חֲפִירָה, אֶלָּא דֶּרֶךְ פֶּתַח בֵּיתוֹ שֶׁהוּא יוֹצֵא וְנִכְנָס בּוֹ הָיָה לוֹ דֶּרֶךְ לָצֵאת לֶחָצֵר וְלֵילֵךְ אַחַר הַחֲפִירָה שֶׁלִּפְנֵי סוֹף בֵּיתוֹ, וּמִשְׁתַּמֵּשׁ. אֲבָל

תוספות

ולא את השדה עד שיהיה בה ט' קבין וכו'. אף על גב דבכל דהו מקרי שדה, כדאמרינן בפרק "האומר" בקידושין (דף סא.): אין לי (ג) אלא בית כור זרע חומר שעורים, מנין לרבות סאה וחצי סאה תרקב וחצי תרקב — ת"ל "שדה", מ"מ אינו חשוב לטרוח לחרוש ולזרוע בפחות מט' קבין. והא דאמר בסוף כתובות (דף קיב.) אמר ההוא מינא לר' חנינא: יאות משבחיתו (ד) בארעייכו, בית סאה הניח לי אבא, ממנה משח, [ממנה חמר], ממנה עיבור, ממנה קטנית כו' — התם היה במקום שמתברך ביותר.

הכא

רבינו גרשום

לא סיימוה קמיה דחילקו לעניי גוים דאין להם זכות בכך: מונבז ממלכי חשמונים היה: במקום שאין עושין פירות. שהממון המונח באוצר אינו מייתר כלום: אם קנה בה קרקע הראוי לבית דירה אע"פ שלא עשה בה דירה: פיס': ארבע אמות לזה וד' אמות לזה שאמרו בחצר חוץ משל פתחים דלכל פתח יש לו בחצר ד' אמות לפרק משאו. ועכשיו אם יהיה חצר ט"ז אמה דמטי לפתחים ח' ולחלוק ח' (חלקים) והיינו ח' אמות לכל אחד עם הפתח שלו: אמר רב הונא חצר מתחלקת לפי פתחיה. שאם הניח להם אביהן לזה בית אחד של ב' פתחים ולזה בית אחד של פתח אחד ולפני בתים הללו היתה חצר מתחלקת אותה חצר לפי פתחיה וזה שיש לו ב' פתחים נוטל ב' ידות מן החצר וזה שאין לו אלא פתח אחד נוטל שליש דלפי שיש חזקה לזה טפי: ורב חסדא אמר ד' אמות לכל פתח ופתח. ולא כל שתי ידות החצר דאי מייתר מד' ד' נוטל ח' אמות באורך החצר כנגד ח' אמות של רוחב הפתח וד' אמות ברוחב החצר כנגד הפתח כלומר דלא שקיל אלא (על) ח' ברוחב ד': פירא דסופלי אם הגיעם חצר אחרת גדולה ובתוך אותה חצר היתה פירא דסופלי חפירה שמשימין גרעיני תמרים לצורך מאכל בהמה והגיע לירש אחד אותה פירא דסופלי. יש לו ד' אמות בחצר וזה הואיל דעדיין לא נעשה פתח ודרך לאותה חפירה אמרינן דיש לו ד' אמות לכל רוח ליכנס באיזה רוח שירצה ולהשתמש ד' אמות לכל רוח: אלא שלא ייחד אביהן פתח. לאותה חפירא דסופלי:

מסורת הש"ס

א) [סנהדרין לז.]: ב) [תוס' פאה פ"ד]: ג) [לעיל ב:] סוכה ג: ד) [לקמן קג: כתובות לח.]: ה) [לעיל ג.]: ו) [לקמן יג: לעיל ג.]: ז) [סוכה ג:]:

תורה אור: תהלים פה; שם פט; ישעיה ג; משלי יא; דברים כד; ישעיה נח

עין משפט נר מצוה

צד א מיי' פ"א מהל' רוצח ושמירת נפש הלכה טז:

צה ב ג ד מיי' פ"א מהל' שכנים הל' ד ופ"ב הלכה א סמג עשין פב טוש"ע ח"מ סי' קעא סעיף ג:

צו ה מיי' שם פ"א הל' ה סמג שם:

צז ו מיי' שם הל' ד סמג שם טוש"ע שם סעיף ג:

צח ז ח מיי' שם פ"ב הלכה ט סמג שם טוש"ע ח"מ סי' קעג סעיף א:

צט ט מיי' שם הל' א וסמג שם טוש"ע ח"מ סי' קעא סעיף ג:

ק י כ ל מיי' שם וסמג שם טוש"ע ח"מ סי' קעב סעיף א:

קא מ נ מיי' שם הל' ב טוש"ע שם ס"ג:

הגהות הב"ח

(א) רש"י ד"ה אפי' וכו' תני רישא יחלוקו הס"ד: (ב) ד"ה נותן לכל פתח ד' אמות להלן מן הפתח כנגדו והרוחב כפי רוחב הפתח כצ"ל ותיבת ברוחב החצר נמחק ואח"כ מ"ה הכי קאמר נוטל ח' אמות באורך החצר דהיינו וכו' מן הפתח כנגדו הס"ד: (ג) תוס' ד"ה ולא וכו' אין לי אלא זרע חומר שעורים בחמשים מנין לרבות לתך סאה תרקב כצ"ל ותיבת בית כור ותיבת וחצי סאה נמחק: (ד) בא"ד משבחיתו לארעייכו:

אֲבָל מְיַיחֵד לֵיהּ פִּיתְחָא — אֵין לוֹ אֶלָּא אַרְבַּע אַמּוֹת לִפְנֵי פִּתְחוֹ. אָמַר רַב הוּנָא: אאַכְסַדְרָה אֵין לָהּ ד' אַמּוֹת; טַעֲמָא מַאי? מִשּׁוּם פֵּירוּק מַשָּׂאוֹ, הָכָא אֶפְשָׁר דְּעָיֵיל לְגַוַּאי וּמְפָרֵק. מְתִיב רַב שֵׁשֶׁת: אֶחָד שַׁעֲרֵי בָתִּים וְאֶחָד שַׁעֲרֵי אַכְסַדְרָאוֹת — יֵשׁ לָהֶן ד' אַמּוֹת! כִּי תַּנְיָא הַהִיא — א)בְּאַכְסַדְרָה דְּבֵי רַב. אַכְסַדְרָה דְּבֵי רַב, פְּשִׁיטָא, ב)אִידְרוֹנָ' מְעַלְּיָא הוּא! באֶלָּא, בְּאַכְסַדְרָה רוֹמַיְיתָא. ת"ר: גבֵּית שַׁעַר, אַכְסַדְרָה וּמִרְפֶּסֶת יֵשׁ לָהֶן ד' אַמּוֹת; דהָיוּ (א) חֲמִשָּׁה בָתִּים פְּתוּחִין לְמִרְפֶּסֶת — אֵין לָהֶן אֶלָּא ד' אַמּוֹת בִּלְבַד. בְּעָא מִינֵּיהּ ר' יוֹחָנָן מר' יַנַּאי: לוּל שֶׁל תַּרְנְגוֹלִין, יֵשׁ לוֹ ד' אַמּוֹת אוֹ אֵין לוֹ ד' אַמּוֹת? הא"ל: טַעֲמָא מַאי? מִשּׁוּם פֵּירוּק מַשָּׂאוֹ, הָכָא מְטַפֵּס וְעוֹלֶה, מְטַפֵּס וְיוֹרֵד. בְּעָא מִינֵּיהּ רָבָא מֵרַב נַחְמָן: בַּיִת חֶצְיוֹ מְקוֹרֶה וְחֶצְיוֹ אֵינוֹ מְקוֹרֶה, יֵשׁ לוֹ ד' אַמּוֹת אוֹ אֵין לוֹ ד"א? א"ל: ואֵין לוֹ ד' אַמּוֹת; לָא מִבָּעֲיָא קֵירוּיוֹ מִלְּגָיו, דְּאֶפְשָׁר דְּעָיֵיל לְגַוַּאי וּמְפָרֵק, אֶלָּא אֲפִילּוּ קֵירוּיוֹ כְּלַפֵּי חוּץ, אֶפְשָׁר דְּעָיֵיל לְגַוַּאי וּמְפָרֵק. בְּעָא מִינֵּיהּ רַב הוּנָא (ב) מֵרַבִּי אַמִי: אֶחָד מִבְּנֵי מָבוֹי שֶׁבִּקֵּשׁ לְהַחֲזִיר פִּתְחוֹ לְמָבוֹי אַחֵר, בְּנֵי מָבוֹי מְעַכְּבִין עָלָיו אוֹ אֵין מְעַכְּבִין עָלָיו? א"ל: זבְּנֵי מָבוֹי מְעַכְּבִין עָלָיו. אַכְסַנְיָא, לְפִי בְּנֵי אָדָם מִתְחַלֶּקֶת אוֹ לְפִי פְּתָחִים מִתְחַלֶּקֶת? א"ל: חלְפִי בְּנֵי אָדָם מִתְחַלֶּקֶת. תַּנְיָא נַמִי הָכִי: טזֶבֶל שֶׁבֶּחָצֵר מִתְחַלֶּקֶת לְפִי פְּתָחִים, אַכְסַנְיָא — לְפִי בְּנֵי אָדָם. אָמַר רַב הוּנָא: אֶחָד מִבְּנֵי מָבוֹי שֶׁבִּקֵּשׁ לִסְתּוֹם כְּנֶגֶד פִּתְחוֹ — בְּנֵי מָבוֹי מְעַכְּבִין עָלָיו, שֶׁמַּרְבֶּה עֲלֵיהֶן אֶת הַדֶּרֶךְ. מֵיתִיבֵי: יחָמֵשׁ חֲצֵרוֹת פְּתוּחוֹת לְמָבוֹי — כּוּלָּן מִשְׁתַּמְּשׁוֹת עִם הַחִיצוֹנָה, וְהַחִיצוֹנָה מִשְׁתַּמֶּשֶׁת לְעַצְמָהּ. וְהַשְּׁאָר מִשְׁתַּמְּשׁוֹת עִם הַשְּׁנִיָּה, וְהַשְּׁנִיָּה מִשְׁתַּמֶּשֶׁת לְעַצְמָהּ וּמִשְׁתַּמֶּשֶׁת עִם הַחִיצוֹנָה. נִמְצֵאת פְּנִימִית מִשְׁתַּמֶּשֶׁת לְעַצְמָהּ וּמִשְׁתַּמֶּשֶׁת עִם כָּל אַחַת וְאַחַת! תַּנָּאֵי הִיא; דְּתַנְיָא: אֶחָד מִבְּנֵי מָבוֹי שֶׁבִּקֵּשׁ לְהַחֲזִיר פִּתְחוֹ לְמָבוֹי אַחֵר — בְּנֵי מָבוֹי מְעַכְּבִין עָלָיו. הָיָה סָתוּם וּבִקֵּשׁ לְפוֹתְחוֹ — אֵין בְּנֵי מָבוֹי מְעַכְּבִין עָלָיו, דִּבְרֵי רַבִּי; ר"ש בֶּן אֶלְעָזָר אוֹמֵר: חָמֵשׁ חֲצֵרוֹת הַפְּתוּחוֹת לְמָבוֹי — כּוּלָּן מִשְׁתַּמְּשׁוֹת בַּמָּבוֹי זוֹ עִם זוֹ. חֲצֵרוֹת מַאן דְּכַר שְׁמַיְיהוּ? חַסּוּרֵי מִחַסְּרָא וְהָכִי קָתָנֵי: וְכֵן חָמֵשׁ חֲצֵרוֹת הַפְּתוּחוֹת לְמָבוֹי — כּוּלָּן מִשְׁתַּמְּשׁוֹת עִם הַחִיצוֹנָה, וְהַחִיצוֹנָה מִשְׁתַּמֶּשֶׁת לְעַצְמָהּ וכו', דִּבְרֵי רַבִּי; ר' שִׁמְעוֹן בֶּן אֶלְעָזָר אוֹמֵר: חָמֵשׁ חֲצֵרוֹת הַפְּתוּחוֹת לְמָבוֹי — כּוּלָּן מִשְׁתַּמְּשׁוֹת בַּמָּבוֹי.§ אָמַר מָר: כהָיָה סָתוּם וּבִקֵּשׁ לְפוֹתְחוֹ — אֵין בְּנֵי מָבוֹי מְעַכְּבִין עָלָיו. אָמַר רָבָא: ללֹא שָׁנוּ אֶלָּא שֶׁלֹּא פָּרַץ אֶת פְּצִימָיו, אֲבָל פָּרַץ אֶת פְּצִימָיו — בְּנֵי מָבוֹי מְעַכְּבִין עָלָיו. א"ל אַבַּיֵי לְרָבָא, תַּנְיָא דִּמְסַיֵּיע לָךְ:

בַּיִת

רש"י

אֲבָל מְיַיחֵד לֵיהּ פִּיתְחָא. שֶׁהָיָה לוֹ פֶּתַח לְסוֹף בֵּיתוֹ אֵצֶל הַחֲפִירָה, וְדֶרֶךְ אוֹתוֹ פֶּתַח הָיָה רָגִיל לְהַשְׁלִיךְ הַגַּרְעִינִין וְלִיטְּלָן — אֵין לוֹ בֶּחָצֵר בִּשְׁבִיל הַחֲפִירָה אֶלָּא ד' אַמּוֹת שֶׁלִּפְנֵי אוֹתוֹ פֶּתַח. אַכְסַדְרָה. (ג) שֶׁיֵּשׁ לוֹ מִן הַפֶּתַח לֶחָצֵר. אֵין לוֹ ד' אַמּוֹת. בַּחֲלוּקַת הֶחָצֵר. טַעֲמָא מַאי. אָמוּר רַבָּנַן שֶׁיֵּשׁ לְפֶתַח בַּיִת ד' אַמּוֹת בֶּחָצֵר. מִשּׁוּם פֵּירוּק מַשָּׂאוֹ. שֶׁיְּפָרֵק שָׁם מַשָּׂאוֹ מֵעַל חֲמוֹרוֹ. לְפִי שֶׁפֶּתַח בַּיִת אֵינוֹ פָּנוּי מִכֵּלִים, וְאִי אֶפְשָׁר לְהַכְנִיס חֲמוֹר עִם מַשָּׂאוֹ בַּבַּיִת לְפָרֵק לְשָׁם. הָכָא. בָּאַכְסַדְרָה, כֵּיוָן ג) (דְּאִית) לָהּ דְּפָנוֹת — אֶפְשָׁר דִּמְעַיֵּיל לְגַוָּהּ וּמְפָרֵק. אַכְסַדְרָה דְּבֵי רַב. דְּפָנוֹת סָבִיב לָהּ, אֶלָּא שֶׁמּוּקָּפוֹת חַלּוֹנוֹת. אַכְסַדְרָה רוֹמַיְיתָא. מוּקָּפוֹת דְּפָנוֹת נְמוּכוֹת, שֶׁאֵין מַגִּיעוֹת לַתִּקְרָה. בֵּית שַׁעַר. בַּיִת קָטָן שֶׁלִּפְנֵי פֶּתַח טְרַקְלִין, וְקוֹרִין לוֹ פורק"א בְּלַעַ"ז. מִרְפֶּסֶת = אלוי"ר. וְהַרְבֵּה פִּתְחֵי עֲלִיָּיה פְּתוּחִין לוֹ, וְכוּלָּן עוֹלִין דֶּרֶךְ סוּלָּם אֶחָד, שֶׁקּוֹרִין דגרי"ד. אֵין לָהֶן אֶלָּא אַרְבַּע אַמּוֹת. בֵּין כּוּלָּן, אֵצֶל רַגְלֵי הַסּוּלָּם. לוּל שֶׁל תַּרְנְגוֹלִין. בַּיִת קָטָן שֶׁמְּגַדְּלִין בּוֹ תַּרְנְגוֹלִין, וְיֵשׁ לוֹ פֶּתַח לֶחָצֵר. יֵשׁ לוֹ ד' אַמּוֹת. בֶּחָצֵר אוֹ לֹא. מְטַפֵּס וְעוֹלֶה. הַתַּרְנְגוֹל מְטַפֵּס וְטוֹרֵחַ וְעוֹלֶה דֶּרֶךְ רֹאשׁ הַכּוֹתֶל לְתוֹךְ הַלּוּל. בַּיִת חֶצְיוֹ מְקוֹרֶה כו'. וּפָתוּחַ לֶחָצֵר, יֵשׁ לוֹ ד' אַמּוֹת בֶּחָצֵר אוֹ לֹא? לָא מִבָּעֲיָא קֵירוּיוֹ מִלְּגָיו. וְהַחֵצִי שֶׁאֵינוֹ מְקוֹרֶה לְצַד הֶחָצֵר, דְּאֵין לוֹ אַרְבַּע אַמּוֹת בֶּחָצֵר. דְּהָא אֶפְשָׁר דִּמְעַיֵּיל חֲמוֹר בְּמַשָּׂאוֹ וּמְפָרֵק שָׁם, שֶׁאֵין דֶּרֶךְ לָתֵת כֵּלִים *בֶּחָצֵר שֶׁאֵינוֹ מְקוֹרֶה. אֶלָּא אֲפִי' קֵירוּיוֹ לְצַד הַחוּץ. וְגִילּוּיָיו לְצַד פְּנִים, נַמִי אֵין לוֹ ד' אַמּוֹת דְּהָא אֶפְשָׁר דִּמְעַיֵּיל חֲמוֹר עַד הַגִּילּוּי וּמְפָרֵק. לְמָבוֹי אַחֵר. כְּגוֹן בַּיִת שֶׁבֵּין שְׁנֵי מְבוֹאוֹת. בְּנֵי מָבוֹי מְעַכְּבִין. אַבְּנֵי מָבוֹי (ד) אַחֵר, שֶׁאֵינוֹ רָגִיל אֶצְלָם. אַכְסַנְיָא. חַיִל שֶׁל מֶלֶךְ הַמּוּטָּל עַל בְּנֵי הָעִיר לָתֵת לָהֶן אַכְסַנְיָא בְּבָתֵּיהֶם. לְפִי בְּנֵי אָדָם. הַדָּרִים בַּבַּיִת. מִתְחַלֶּקֶת לְפִי פְּתָחִים. לְזֶבֶל שָׂדוֹת. לְפִי שֶׁדֶּרֶךְ הַפְּתָחִים הִשְׁלִיכוּ שָׁם, עַד שֶׁנַּעֲשֵׂית אַשְׁפָּה. שֶׁבִּקֵּשׁ לִסְתּוֹם כְּנֶגֶד פִּתְחוֹ. לְהַקִּיף מְחִיצָּה סְבִיבוֹת ד"א שֶׁיֵּשׁ לוֹ בַּמָּבוֹי כְּנֶגֶד פִּתְחוֹ. שֶׁמַּרְבֶּה עֲלֵיהֶם הַדֶּרֶךְ. שֶׁהַהוֹלֵךְ מֵרֹאשׁוֹ (ה) עַד צַד סוֹפוֹ צָרִיךְ לְהַקִּיף סָבִיב הַמְּחִיצָּה. חָמֵשׁ חֲצֵרוֹת הַפְּתוּחוֹת לְמָבוֹי. זוֹ אֵצֶל זוֹ לְאָרְכּוֹ. וּסְתָם מְבוֹאוֹת סְתוּמִין הֵן בְּסוֹפָן, וְאֶחָד מִקְּצוֹתָיו פָּתוּחַ לִרה"ר. כּוּלָּם מִשְׁתַּמְּשׁוֹת בַּמָּבוֹי עִם הַחִיצוֹנָה. כְּנֶגְדָּהּ, שֶׁהֲרֵי לְכוּלָּם יֵשׁ דֶּרֶךְ בַּמָּבוֹי לָצֵאת דֶּרֶךְ רֹאשׁוֹ לִרה"ר, וְכָל שֶׁיֵּשׁ לוֹ דֶּרֶךְ — יֵשׁ לוֹ תַּשְׁמִישׁ שֶׁאֵינוֹ מְעַכֵּב דֶּרֶךְ הַמָּבוֹי. וְהַחִיצוֹנָה מִשְׁתַּמֶּשֶׁת לְעַצְמָהּ. כְּנֶגְדָּהּ בְּרוֹחַב הַמָּבוֹי, אֲבָל לֹא כְּנֶגֶד חַבְרוֹתֶי', שֶׁאֵין לָהּ עֲלֵיהֶן דֶּרֶךְ. מִשְׁתַּמֶּשֶׁ' לְעַצְמָהּ. לְבַדָּהּ. וְקַשְׁיָא לְרַב הוּנָא, דְּאָמַר כּוּלָּן מְעַכְּבִין, וַאֲפִי' הַחִיצוֹנִים מְעַכְּבִין עַל הַפְּנִימִיִּים. הָיָה סָתוּם. שֶׁהָיָה לוֹ מִקּוֹדֶם פֶּתַח פָּתוּחַ לוֹ, וּסְתָמוֹ, וּלְאַחַר זְמַן נִמְלַךְ לְפוֹתְחוֹ. כּוּלָּם מִשְׁתַּמְּשִׁין בַּמָּבוֹי. בְּכָל הַמָּבוֹי, וַאֲפִי' חִיצוֹן עַל הַפְּנִימִי. שֶׁלֹּא פָּרַץ פְּצִימָיו. כְּשֶׁנִּסְתַּם פִּתְחוֹ לֹא סִלֵּק מְזוּזָתוֹ (ו) וּמַשְׁקוֹף וּמִפְתָּן, דְּגַלֵּי דַּעְתֵּיהּ דְּלָא סִילֵּק נַפְשֵׁיהּ, וְסוֹפוֹ לְפוֹתְחוֹ לְאַחַר זְמַן.

בַּיִת

תוספות

הכא אפשר דמעייל לגואי ומפרק. פרש"י: דסתם אכסדרה אין לה דפנות כלל. וגרס נמי בסוף פ' "כל גגות" (עירובין דף לד: ושם. ד"ה בשתי): כי לית ליה לשמואל פי תקרה — בד', אבל בג' — אית ליה. פירוש: באכסדרה שאין לה דפנות כלל לית ליה לשמואל פי תקרה יורד וסותם בכל ארבע מחיצות, ולכך קאמר שמואל באכסדרה בבקעה דאין מטלטלין בה אלא בד'. אבל בשלש אית ליה, דהיינו אם יש בו דופן אחד אמרי' בג' פי תקרה. ולר"י נראה דסתם אכסדרה יש לה שלש מחיצות, כדאמר ב"לא יחפור" (לקמן דף כה:) דעולם הזה לאכסדרה הוא דומה, דרוח צפונית אינה מסובבת. ובסוף פרק "כל גגות" (עירובין דף לד:) גרסי': כי לית ליה בג' אבל בארבע אית ליה. פי': בשלש, כשאין כי אם שלש מחיצות — לא אמרי' פי תקרה ברביעית. אבל בד', כשיש קצת גם ממחיצה רביעית — אמר פי תקרה. ואכסדרה דבי רב יש לה נמי שלש מחיצות גמורות, והרביעית גבוהה ד' אמות. ואכסדרה רומיתא — הרביעית אינה גבוהה רק עשרה טפחים. אי נמי, דבי רב גבוהה רביעית עשרה, ורומיתא פחות מעשרה טפחים. **בעא** רב הונא מרב אמי. והא דאמר בפרק "הניזקין" (גיטין דף נט: ושם) גבי רב הונא קרי בכהני: שאני רב הונא דאפי' ר' אמי ור' אסי כהני חשיבי דארעא דישראל מיכף כייפי לרב הונא, והכא היכי בעא מיניה? וי"ל: דרבי אמי לחוד ורב אמי לחוד. **אכסניא** לפי פתחים כו'. פירש רבינו חננאל: דמיבעיא ליה שיירא שחנתה במקום אחד, הזבל איך חולקין. **אחד** מבני מבוי שבקש לסתום כנגד פתחו. פירש הקונטרס: להקיף מחיצות סביבות הארבע אמות שיש לו במבוי כנגד פתחו. וקשה לרבינו יצחק: דלא מצינו שיהא לו ארבע אמות במבוי, אלא בחצר! ונראה לרבינו יצחק כפי' רבינו חננאל: כגון שיושב בסוף המבוי אצל צד הסתום, ורוצה לסתום כנגד פתחו כל רוחב המבוי, והשתא קאמר רב הונא שמעכבין עליו בני המבוי, אע"פ שהם חיצונים, לפי שמרבה עליהם את הדרך — פי': רגל בני אדם. שיכולין לומר בני המבוי: [אף] כשיש רבים במבוי יכולים ליכנס עד סוף המבוי, וע"י הסתימה תרבה עלינו את הדרך ע"י בני אדם הדורכים עלינו במבוי, ואף לאחרות יצטרכו ליכנס מרוב דוחק. ומצינו לשון "מרבה עליהם את הדרך" בענין זה, דתנן לקמן ב"חזקת הבתים" (דף נט:): לקח בית בחצר אחרת — לא יפתחנו לחצר השותפים. ומפר' טעמא בגמרא (דף ס.): מפני שמרבה עליהם את הדרך, דהיינו רגל בני אדם. ובתוספתא דפ"ק דמכילתין תניא: יש לו חנות ברשות הרבי' ומבקש לפותחו לחצר השותפים — יכולים לעכב על ידו, מפני שמרבה עליהם את הדרך. **והפנימית** משתמשת עם כולן ומשתמשת לעצמה. פי' "לעצמה" — שאין *)אחרונה משתמשת עמה. ו"חילונה משתמשת לעצמה" דלעיל — אין פירושו כמו זה, אלא "לעצמה" — שאינה משתמשת עם אחרות.

*) נ"ל אחרת ועי' רש"ש:

עין משפט נר מצוה

קב א ב ג ד מיי' פ"ב מהלכות שכנים הל' ג ד סמג עשין פב טוש"ע ח"מ סימן קעב סעיף ד:
קג ה מיי' שם הל' ה טוש"ע שם סעי' ה:
קד ו מיי' שם הל' ו טוש"ע שם סעיף ו:
קה ז מיי' שם פ"ה הלכה טו סמג שם טוש"ע ח"מ סי' קסב סעיף ו:
קו ח ט מיי' שם פ"ב הלכה ח סמג שם טוש"ע ח"מ סי' קעב סעיף ט:
קז י מיי' שם פ"ה הל' טז סמג שם טוש"ע ח"מ סי' קסב סעיף ז:
קח כ ל מיי' שם הל' טו טוש"ע שם סעי' ה:

מסורת הש"ס

א) [מנחות לג:]: ב) [תרגום של החדרה אידרון]: ג) [נ"ל לאין]:

רבינו גרשום

אבל וכו'. ל"א אם יש לאחד מן השותפים פירות דסופלי חריץ שמשימין בו תבן ומספוא לשוורים בהאי חצר נוטל ד' אמות לכל רוח של חריץ זו כלומר כשיעור תשמיש ועבודת טלטול החריץ לבד החלוקה שחולקין בשוות דיש לו ליטול לפי חזקה דאית ליה בתוך החצר. למורי הרב: אכסדרה גג מקורה הקבוע על ד' קונדסין ופתוחה מכל צדדיה ואינה עשויה אלא לצל בעלמא כשחולקין את החצר למי שיגיע לו האכסדרה אין נוטל ד' אמות חוץ לאכסדרה כמו לפתח דטעמא מאי אמרו דנוטל ד' אמות כנגד פתחו בחצר כדי עבודת הפתח לפרק משאו מעל גבי בהמתו בהני ד' אמות דאינו רוצה ללכלך ולטנף ביתו מזבל בהמתו אבל הכא באכסדרה זו הואיל שאין לה דפנות סביב אפשר לו דעייל באכסדרה זו (דבי בי רב שלומדין שם תלמידים שיש לה ג' דפנות) ומפרק דבלאו הכי נמי מטונפות מן הזבלים ומן הגשמים ולהכי אין צריכין ד' אמות: באכסדרה דבי רב שלומדין בה תלמידין שיש לה ג' דפנות עד הסכך (ופ') ודופן רביעית אינה מגעת לסכך משום שיהא אורה ופתח אותה אכסדרה יש לו ד' אמות ומקשינן אכסדרה דבי רב אידרונא חדר מעליא הוא ולא צריך למימר דיש לה ד' אמות: באכסדרה רומייתא דיש לה ג' מחיצות מגיעות לסכך ומחיצה רביעית נמוכה ובונין עליה על פני כולה חלונות גדולות על גבי פצימין כעין אותם שקורין קלושטי"ר ופתח באמצעיות אותה מחיצה נמוכה ולאותו פתח יש לו ד' אמות אף על גב דיש הרבה סביב חלונות גדולות אבל לא לאכסדר' העומדת על קונדסין. (כלומר) בית שער יש לו ד' אמות במבוי מרפסת היינו עלייה שיש לה ד' פתחים או יותר בשורה אחת ועושין לפניהם נסר ארוך שרופסין עליו ולסוף אותו נסר סולם שיורדין בו לארץ ולפני אותו סולם יש פתח שנועל בעד המרפסת כל אותן ד' פתחים של עלייה אין להם בחצר אלא ד' אמות שלפני פתח הסולם שכולם יוצאין באותו פתח: לול של תרנגולים. ארובה של עלייה שמשימין דרך אותה ארובה תרנגולין לעלייה כלומר אם אין לאותן היורשין שום פתח לשם אלא לול של תרנגולין משום חזקת אותו לול אינו נוטל ד' אמות בחצר כמו לפתח דליכא התם משום פריקת משוי שהתרנגול מטפס ועולה (ניסרין). יש לו לאחד מן היורשין בית שחציו מקורה וחציו אינו מקורה. מי אמרי' כיון דחציו אינו מקורה יכול לפרק משאו באותו צד שאינו מקורה ואין לו ד' אמות בחצר או דילמא כיון דיש לו ד' מחיצות ופתח כשאר בית אע"פ שחציו אינו מקורה יש לו ד' אמות: לא מיבעיא. היכא דהוה אותו חצי (קורה) [קירוי] כלפי פנים הבית כלומר לאחורי הבית והא דאינו מקורה סמוך לחצר דאע"ג דאיכא פתח בית הפתוח לחצר דאינו נוטל ד' אמות בחצר מתוך דהכא מצי לפרק משאו בהאי חצי דאינו מקורה שסמוך לחצר אלא אע"פ אי הוה אותו חצי קירוי לצד חוץ סמוך לחצר ושאינו מקורה לצד אחורי הבית אפי' הכי אינו נוטל ד' אמות בחצר כנגד פתח הבית משום דיכול להכניס באותו חצי שאחורי הכותל שאינו מקורה ומפרק שם לחצר: פתחו למבוי אחר. שאם היה פתחו פתוח למבוי זה ואחרי פתחו איכא מבוי אחר ורוצה לסתום פתחו מיכן ולפותחו למבוי שאחורי ביתו: בני מבוי. שעכשיו רוצה לפתוח

לפתוח פתחו לשם יכולין לעכבו לצאת ולבוא דרך מבואן הואיל ועד עתה לא הוחזק באותו מבוי או לא. ותו בעא מיניה אכסניא. אכסנאין של מלך שעוברין בעיר ומחלקין אותן בבתי העיר ליתן להם לינה ופרנסה השתא בעי לפי בני מבוי שיש להם בתים לכל בית מחלקים או לפי פתחיה מחלקים שאם יש בבית ב' פתחים שיתנו לו ב' חלקים מן האכסנאין שיעור שני בתים: זבל שבחצר לפי פתחים מתחלק שאם היו בבית ב' פתחים ולבית אחר פתח א' שמוציאין זבל ובאו לחלקן זה של שני פתחים נוטל פי שנים וחלק שלישי [נוטל האחר] לפי שיעור הפתחים היו מוציאים הזבל: לסתום כנגד פתחו. שכשם שיש לו לפתח ד' אמות בחצר כך יש לו לכל פתח חצר ד' אמות במבוי וזה בקש לסתום אותן ד' אמות שלו ולהקיפן בגדר בני מבוי שכניו מעכבין עליו שמרבה עליהן את הדרך להקיף אותו סתום (מבוי): ה' חצרות זו בצד זו הפתוחות למבוי אותה הסמוכה לרשות הרבים קרויה חיצונה ואותה שבסוף המבוי מצד אחר קרויה פנימית כולן הד' משתמשות עם חיצונית כלומר דיש לכולן רשות לעבור לפני פתח החיצונה והחיצונה משתמשת לעצמה שרשאה לסתום כנגד פתחה הד' אמות ולהשתמש בתוכן. והם הני השאר משתמשות עם השניה שעוברין לפני פתחיה ושניה משתמשת לעצמה שרשאה לסתום ד' אמות נגד פתחה ומשתמשת עם החיצונה שמקפת ד' אמות ויוצאת לחוץ. נמצאת הפנימית שבמבוי שהיא משתמש' עם כולן שעוברת עליהן ומשתמשת לעצמה קשיא לרב הונא: חסורי מיחסרא והכי קתני דתנא קמא מיירי [נמי] בחצירות נמצאת הפנימית משתמשת לעצמה ומשתמשת עם כולן דברי ר' דסבר אין מעכב עליו [בן] המבוי לסתום ד' אמות שלו ורבי שמעון אומר וכן כולם משתמשות במבוי כגון שהוא בהדיא שלא יסתום כנגד פתחו כדי שלא ירבה על האחרים את הדרך שיכולין בני מבוי לעכב עליו ורב הונא סבירא ליה כר"ש בן אלעזר. *) כפ"ה. ואית דאמרי חיצונה משתמשת לעצמה דיש לכולן רשות לעבור דרך עליה אבל היא משתמשת לעצמה דאין לה רשות לעבור דרך עליהן. ולהכי אם ביקשה החיצונה לסתום לפניהם מלעבור עליה אינה יכולה לסתום מתוך דרשות כולן יש (לו) לעבור עליה. אבל אם בקשו כולן לסתום לפני החיצונה כדי שלא תעבור עליהן. יכולין לסתום משום שאין דרכה של חיצונה לעבור עליהן. וכיון דסתמי לה הני שלא תעבור עליהן תהא החיצונה משמשת לעצמה וכן לשניה וכן לשלישית וכן לרביעית עד לחמישית שהיא פנימית דהשתא נמצא שיש לה רשות לעבור על כולן ואין לכולן רשות לעבור עליה להכי יכולה פנימית לישתמיש ולסתום בפני עצמה כדי שלא יעבור כולן עליה והן אין יכולין לסתום פנימית כדי שלא תעבור עליהן אלמא דהני יכולין לסתום זה על זה וקשיא למאן דאמר אחד מבני מבוי דהכי משמע ותני דמשום אחד מבני מבוי בין לחיצונה על כולן בין לכולן על החיצונה אין להם רשות זה על זה לסתום מפני שמרבה עליהן את הדרך לא תנאי היא וכן כו' עד החיצונה משתמשת לעצמה כדדייקינן לעיל דלכולם יש להן רשות לעבור ולסתום בפני החיצונה ואין לחיצונה רשות לעבור ולסתום בפניהם: ר' שמעון אומר כולם משתמשות במבוי אמטו להכי דאית לכולן תשמיש למבוי להכי יש רשות לכולן לעבור זו על זו בין לחיצונה על כולן בין לכולן על החיצונה וכי היכי דזו אינה יכולה לסתום בפני כולן כך כולן אינן יכולין לסתום בפניהם כ"ז **) למ"ה אבל מסתבר הכי: היה סתום ובקש לפותחו. כעין אמר מר שאם היה פתח פתוח לכתחילה לאותו מבוי שעכשיו רוצה לחזור פתחו שם וסתמו הואיל דהוה תמן מעיקרא אין יכולין לעכב עליו. אמר רבא לא שנו דאין מעכבין

*) הוא ר"ח כן פי' המורה. **) הוא ר"ח לא מפי המורה.

הגהות הב"ח (א) גמרא היו ארבעה או חמשה בתים פתוחים למרפסת: (ב) שם ר"ה מרב אמי כצ"ל: (ג) רש"י ד"ה אכסדרה שיש לה פתח לחצר כצ"ל ותי' מן ואות ה' נמחק: (ד) שם ד"ה בני מבוי מעכבין בני מבוי האחר כצ"ל: (ה) ד"ה שמרבה כו' ההולך מראשו לצד סופו כצ"ל ותי' עד נמחק: (ו) ד"ה שלא פרץ וכו' מזוזתו ומשקופו ומפתנו דגלי:

מסורת הש"ס

א) שבת קמו: ב) תוספתא דאהלות ספט"ז: ג) ב"ק כח. ע"ש לקמן כו: ע"ש [ודף ס: ע"ש ודף ק. ע"ש] ד) פסחים ג. וש"נ: ה) עירובין ס: בכורות מה. ו) [נ"ל בעינן לכל כו']:

עין משפט נר מצוה

קט א מיי' פ"ב מהל' שכנים הל' ז סמג עשין פב טוש"ע ח"מ סי' קעב סעיף ז:

קי ב מיי' פ"ז מהל' טומאת מת הל' א סמג עשין רלח:

קיא ג ד טוש"ע ח"מ סי' קסב סעיף ב:

קיב ה מיי' פי"ג מהל' נזקי ממון הל' כד סמג עשין סח טוש"ע ח"מ סי' שעז בהג"ה וסי' תיז סעיף ב:

קיג ו ז מיי' פ"ה מהל' שכנים הל' יג סמג עשין פב טוש"ע ח"מ סי' קסב סעי' א:

קיד ח ט מיי' פ"א מהל' שכני' הל' ד' סמג שם טוש"ע ח"מ סי' קעא סעיף ג:

גמרא

א)אבית סתום — יש לו ד' אמות, פרץ את פצימיו — אין לו ד' אמות; (קבר שפתחו סתום — אינו מטמא כל סביביו, פרץ את פצימיו וסתמו — מטמא כל סביביו;) ב)בבית סתום — אינו מטמא כל סביביו, פרץ פצימיו — מטמא כל סביביו. אמר רבה בר בר חנה א"ר יוחנן: גמבואות המפולשות לעיר אחרת ובקשו בני העיר לסותמן — בני אותה העיר מעכבין עליהן; דלא מיבעי כי ליכא דרכא אחרינא דמעכבי, אלא אפילו כי איכא דרכא אחרינא נמי מעכבי, משום דרב יהודה אמר רב, דאמר: (א) ג)המצר שהחזיקו בו רבים — אסור לקלקלו. (כדרב גידל, דא"ר גידל: רבים שבררו דרך לעצמן — מה שבררו בררו.) אמר רב ענן אמר שמואל: ומבואות המפולשין לרה"ר ובקשו בני מבואות להעמיד להן דלתות — בני רה"ר מעכבין עליהן. סבור מינה: הני מילי בד' אמות, כדר' זירא אמר רב נחמן, דאמר רבי זירא אמר רב נחמן: ד' אמות הסמוכות לרה"ר כרה"ר דמיין. ולא היא, התם — לענין טומאה, אבל הכא — זזימנין דדחקי בני רה"ר ועיילי טובא. § "ולא את השדה — עד שיהא בה תשעה קבין לזה ותשעה קבין לזה" כו'. § ולא פליגי, ד)מר כי אתריה ומר כי אתריה. בבבל מאי? אמר רב יוסף: חבי רדו יומא. מאי בי רדו יומא? אי יומא זרעא — תרי יומא כרבא לא הוי, אי יומא כרבא — יומא דזרעא לא הוי! אי בעית אימא: יומא דכרבא — דכריב ותני; ואי בעית אימא: יומא דזרעא — בהדורי. דוולא — אמר רב נחמן: בי דאלו יומא. פרדסא — אמר אבוה דשמואל: טבת שלשת קבין. תניא נמי הכי: האומר לחבירו "מנת בכרם אני מוכר לך" — סומכוס אומר: לא יפחות מג' קבין. א"ר יוסי: ה)אין אלו אלא דברי נביאות. בבבל מאי? אמר רבא בר קסנא: תלת אציאתה בני תריסר גופני, כי היכי דרפיק גברא ביומא. אמר רבי אבדימי דמן חיפה: מיום שחרב בית המקדש, ניטלה נבואה מן הנביאים וניתנה לחכמים. אטו חכם לאו נביא הוא? הכי קאמר: אע"פ שניטלה מן הנביאים, מן החכמים לא ניטלה. אמר אמימר: וחכם עדיף מנביא, שנאמר: °"ונביא לבב חכמה", מי נתלה במי? הוי אומר: קטן נתלה בגדול. אמר אביי: תדע, דאמר גברא רבה מילת', ומתאמר' משמיה דגברא רבה אחרינא כוותי'. אמר רבא: ומאי קושיא? ודילמא תרוייהו בני חד מזלא נינהו! אלא אמר רבא: תדע, דאמר גברא רבה מילתא, ומתאמרא

משמיה

תורה אור: °ונביא לבב חכמה — תהלים צ

רש"י

בית סתום. שהיה לו פתח לחצר, וסתמו. יש לו ד' אמות. בחלוקת החצר, אם בא לחלוק, כאילו הוא פתוח. אינו מטמא סביביו. אלא כנגד הפתח, אם מת בתוכו. פרץ את פצימיו. הרי הוא כקבר, וחכמים טימאו את סביבות הקבר ד' אמות, כדי שלא יקרבו עושי טהרות עד הקבר ויאהילו, ולאו אדעתייהו. לעיר אחרת. לדרך עיר אחרת. ובקשו בני העיר. שהמבואות בה, לסותמן מאחריהם. בני אותה העיר. האחרת, מעכבין עליהן, שכבר הוחזקו לקצר דרכן דרך אותן המבואות. בני רה"ר מעכבין עליהן. משום דכי דחקו בני רה"ר מסתלקי לתוך המבואות. הני מילי. תוך ד' אמות של (ב) ראש המבוי הסמוכות לרה"ר מעכבין מלהעמיד דלתות לשם. כרה"ר דמו. לענין ספק טומאה כרה"ר. ולא היא. שאפי' רצו להעמידם לפנים מד' אמות — מעכבין עליהן. בי רדו יומא = בית חרישת יום אחד, לזה וכן לזה. "לא תחרוש" — מתרגמינן: לא תרדי (דברים כב). ה"ג: בי רדו יומא מאי אי יומא זרעא תרי יומא כרבא לא הוי ואי יומא כרבא יומא דזרעא לא הוי. אי בעית אימא יומא דזרעא באתרא דכריב ותני ואי בעית אימא ביומא דכרבא ובאהדורי. אי יומא דזרעא. בשעת הזרע הוא נוח לחרוש, שכבר נחרשת בשעת (ג) הניר. תרי יומי כרבא לא הוי. כלומר בשעת הניר היאך ישכור שוורים? אין בו כדי מלאכת ב' ימים, ויש בו יותר מכדי מלאכת יום אחד. ואי ביומא כרבא. של שעת הניר קאמרת — לא הוי יומא דזרעא, והיאך ישכור שוורים בשעת הזרע? אי בעית אימא יומא דזרעא. ודקא קשיא לך: תרי יומי כרבא לא הוי — באתרא דכרבי ותנו בשעת הניר איכא ביומא דזרעא תרי יומי כרבא. ואי בעית אימא יומא כרבא. ודקאמרת: לא הוי יומא דזרעא — בהדורי עסקינן, שארץ קשה ויש בה מעלות ומורדות, ויש טורח בשעת הזרע כשעת הניר. לישנא אחרינא איכא גרסינן: ואי בעית אימא יומא דכרבא. ודקשי' לך: יומא דזרעא לא הוי — באתרא דכריב ותני בשעת הזרע, אחת קודם לזריעה ואחת לאחר הזריעה לכסות הזרעים'. ואי בעית אימא יומא זרעא, ודקאמר' תרי יומי כרבא לא הוי — בהדורי עסקינן, שיש טורח גדול בשעת הניר, ויומא זרעא הוי תרי יומי כרבא. ולשון זה הגון. דוולא. אם יש להן בור שממנו משקין שדה. בי דלו יומא. עד שיהא בו כדי להשקות שדה כדי פעולת יום לזה וכדי פעולת יום לזה, משום שכר פועל. פרדיסא. כרם. ג' קבין. לכל אחד, לפי חשבון סאתים כחצר המשכן. אין אלו אלא דברי נביאות. בלא טעם. אוציתא. כל י"ב גפנים קרי אוליא. דרפיק = עודר. ניטלה נבואה כו'. משום דאמר ליה לעיל "אין אלו אלא דברי נביאות" שקרא דברי חכמים נבואה, נקט לה להא מילתא. אטו חכם לאו נביא הוא. וכי אין חכם ראוי להיות נביא? דקאמר מר ניטלה מן הנביאים וניתנה לחכמים, מכלל דמעיקרא לא היתה נבואה לחכמים. הכי קאמר אע"פ שניטלה מן הנביאים. שאינם חכמים, מן חכמים לא ניטלה (ד) *)ונביאים יש להן לבב חכמה. תדע. שלא ניטלה מן חכמים.

משמיה

*) [וברש"י שבע"י איתא ונביא יש לו לבב חכמה].

תוספות

פרץ פצימיו מטמא כל סביביו. פי' הקונטר': כל סביביו — ד' אמות, כקבר. ואין נראה לר' שמשון, כיון דמסיימי מחילות, וליכא למיחש שמא יעלה על הבית ויאהיל עליו — לית לן למימר שיטמא ד' אמות סביביו, כדמוכח בפ' "משוח מלחמה" (סוטה דף מד.) גבי חצר הקבר, העומד בתוכה טהור — ה"מ חצר הקבר דמסיימי מחילו' אבל (ה) בעלמא תפיס. לכך נראה לו לפרש: כגון שיש זיזין הרבה בולטין מן הבית מכל צד, ויש בהן פותח טפח (ו) לכל אחד. ובשלא פרץ פצימיו, אף על פי שסתמו — אינו מטמא תחת השאר זיזין, שסתמו של מת עומד לצאת דרך פתח. אבל אם פרץ פצימיו וחזר ובנאו כשאר כותל, ואין כאן פתח כלל — מטמא כל סביביו, דכל זיז וזיז איכא לספוקי דשמא דרך תחת אותו זיז יצא מן הבית. ויש ליישב פי' הקונטרס: דבית נמי לא מסיימי מחילתא, דאע"ג דליכא למיחש שמא יעלה על הבית — מ"מ איכא למיחש שמא יגע בכתלי', דקבר מטמא במגע אפי' מן הצד, כדמוכח בספרי בפרשת פרה אדומה: (ז) "בקבר" — זה קבר סתום, או אינו אלא פתוח? אמרת ק"ו: ומה אהל שהוא מקבל טומאה — אינו מטמא מכל הצדדין כשהוא פתוח, הקבר שאינו מקבל טומאה — אינו דין שלא יטמא מכל הצדדין כשהוא פתוח? משמע דכשהוא סתום — מטמא אף בנוגע בו מן הצד.

מצר שהחזיקו בו רבים אסור לקלקלו. היינו כשהחזיקו ברשות. אבל אם באין להחזיק שלא ברשות — יש למחות בידם, ולנקוט פיזרא וליתיב, כדמוכח ב"המניח" (ב"ק דף כח. ושם). ולא פליגי מר כי אתריה ומר כי אתריה. פי' ר"י ב"ר מרדכי: דבאתריה דרבי יהודה היה קרקע חשוב וטוב, והיה חשוב לטרוח בתשעה חצאי קבין. (ח) אבל באתריה דתנא קמא לא היה קרקע טוב כל כך, שיהיה חשוב לטרוח בפחות מתשעה קבין. ואף על פי שלא היה בו כדי חרישת יום — ראוי היה לטרוח. והשתא בעי: בבבל מאי, שאין הקרקע טוב כל כך, ואינו ראוי כשיעור השנוי במשנתינו.

ה"ג ר"ח:(ט) ואי בעית אימא בכרבא וזרעא ובהדורי. פירוש: בית חרישת יום, ושפיר הוי יומא לזרעא, דכשיבא לזורעה — חורש, ובחזירתו עוד מושך המחרישה על הקרקע וזורע, וזה בהדורי. ואי בעית אימא יומא דזרעא. ודקאמרת לא הוי תרי יומי כרבא — כריב יומא ופלגא, והדר תני וכריב עד דשלים יומא.

דוולא. פר"ח: ארץ שמשקין אותה (י)בדלי, לכל אחד ארץ שדולין לה יום אחד. וקשה לר"י: דא"כ הוה ליה (י) למיתני "בבבל מאי", כדבעי באינך! ע"כ נראה כפ"ה.

א"ר יוסי אין אלו אלא דברי נביאות. לא לשבח קאמר, אלא כלומר שאומר בלא טעם. דכי האי גוונא בסוף (כ) "(אלו) מומין" (בכורות דף מה. ושם ד"ה עשו) גבי יתרת שאין בה ציפורן מטמא במגע ובמשא אבל לא באהל. וקאמר: עשו דבריהן כדברי נביאות; מה נפשך? אי אבר הוא — ליטמא באהל, ואי לא אבר הוא — לא ליטמא כלל! וכן י"ל בסוף פ' "כילד מעברין" (עירובין דף ס: ושם ד"ה אין).

אטו חכם לאו נביא הוא. וא"ת: בפ' "בן סורר" (סנהדרין דף עה.) דקאמר: משחרב בהמ"ק ניטל טעם ביאה וניתן לעוברי עבירה — תקשי ליה נמי: אטו קודם שנחרב לא הוה להו טעם ביאה לעוברי עבירה? הא מפיק ליה מדכתיב "מים גנובים ימתקו" (משלי ט), כדפריך הכא! וי"ל: דאיכא לשנויי התם כדמשני הכא: ניטל טעם ביאה, ומעוברי עבירה לא ניטלה. ולא חש להקשות בכל מקום. [וע"ע תוס' גיטין עב. ד"ה ומשום וכו'].

כל

רבינו גרשום

מעכבין אלא שלא פרץ את פצימיו הואיל שאין נפרצין חזקה יש לפותחו: אינו מטמא כל סביביו אם היה מת בבית אע"פ שסתום הוא הואיל ולא פרץ את פצימיו אינו מטמא כל סביביו דבית בד' אמות כקבר דאיכא למימר הואיל שלא עקר הפצימין ולא סתמו לגמרי באותו פתח יפתח ויוציאהו אבל פרץ את פצימיו וסתמו מהכל מטמא כל סביביו דיש לו דין קבר הואיל וסתום מכל צדדיו כקבר דטומאה בוקעת ויוצאה דליכא למימר מן הצד יוציאוהו: ענין אחר שלא פרץ את פצימיו כלומר היה סותם הפתח ולא היה סותר צורת הפתח המשקופין והמזוזות אלא בנה בנין סתימה עלייהו דמתוך שלא עקרן ודאי היה דעתו לפתוח להכי אין מעכבין בו מלפתוח. ודיקא נמי דתניא גבי בית דאע"ג דסתום פתחו יש לו ד' אמות והיינו נמי טעמא [כיון] דלא פרץ פצימיו והיה דעתו לפתוח: קבר שיש לאדם בחצירו ועשה מחיצה דפנות כל סביביו וסיכוך. והשתא אע"ג דאיכא מחיצה סביב הקבר ואיכא פתח בהנהו מחיצות. אם כשסתם אותו פתח לא פרץ פצימה כיון דנראה מקום הפתח. כמאן דאיתא לפתח דמי ובוקעת בו את הטומאה ומטמא סביביו. אבל אם פרץ והוי כשאר כותל לא. למ"ה: מבואות המפולשות פתוחין לעיר אחרת. כלומר דנהיגו בני העיר אחרת לעבור דרך האי מבוי וליכנס לעיר זו ולצאת ממנה דרך מבוי זה: [לקלקלו. לסותמו]. המפולשין לרשות הרבים. להעמיד להן דלתות לעכב בני רה"ר ליכנס במבוי כל שעה שירצו: סבור מינה הני מילי דמעכבין למיעבד דלתות ליסתם לבני רה"ר (הני מילי) בתוך ד' אמות של מבוי אותן ד' אמות הסמוכות לר"ה כדר' זירא: ולא היא דלענין טומאה אמרי' ד' אמות א] במבוי בר"ה דספיקו טהור באותן ד' אמות (מבוי דברשות הרבים) דגמרינן מסוטה. אבל הכא בכוליה מבוי מצו לעכב דלא מצו למיזל בני רה"ר אלא דרך אותו מבוי: **פיסקא.** ואין חולקין את השדה עד שתהא גדולה. דיכולין לזרוע בה ט' קבין לזה וט' קבין לזה דבציר מהכי לא חשיב שדה שהוא סאה וחצי שהוא ע"ה אמה אורך על רוחב ג' דגמרי לה מחצר המשכן דהוי ק' על נ' ואמרינן דהיינו בית זרע סאתים: מר כי אתריה דבהכי חשיב שדה בט' קבין בציר לא ובאתריה דר"י היו השדות ביוקר והוי חשיבי שדה בט' חצאי קבין: בבבל שלא היו שדות ביוקר כבא"י מאי בכמה חשוב התם שדה. א"ר יוסף בי רדו יומא. כלומר כי היכי דיש מלאכה לפועל לחרוש בה יום שלם לפי שלא ימצא פועל שישכיר עצמו כי אם ליום אחד שלם ואם יחלקו פחות מכדי ספוק יום פעולת יום אחד כל חד וחד נמצא הפועל משלים פעולתו בחצי היום או בט' שעות והיה מבקש הפועל שכירות יום שלם: היכי דמי. הא בי רדו יומא כלומר באיזה חריש אמרת שב' פעמים חורש את השדה אחת תיכף לקצירה ולאותה חרישה קרי כרבא ובאותה חרישה שתיכף לקצירה חורש הפועל כל היום עד לערב ושוב חורשין אותה ביום זריעה ואותו היום אין חורש הפועל אלא ט' שעות ובג' שעות זורע בעל הבית מה שהפועל חורש בט' שעות והכי מנהג ועכשיו בעי בעל גמרא באיזו חרישת פעולת יום יום זריעה דאינו אלא ט' שעות לא הוי יומא כרבא כלומר כשחוזר ומשכיר ביום קציר לא הוה פעולת יום שלם בחרישה דלאחר קצירה דבט' שעות תשלים פעולתו ונמצא יושב ובטל ג' שעות ונמצא מפסיד בעל הבית ואם בי רדו יומא כרבא כלומר אם מאותה חרישה אמרת דחורשין תיכף לקצירה כל היום לא הוי תרי יומא דזרעא כלומר אין שם פעולת חרישת ב' ימים של יום זריעה שביום חרישה תכף לקצירה חורש כל י"ב שעות ואם תאמר באותו יום חרישה אמרי דהיינו פעולת יום שלם כשיבא לאותה חרישה של זריעה לא ימצא שם פעולת ב' ימים כי ביום זריעה אינו חורש אלא ט' שעות ולא ישאר לפעולת מחרת אלא פעולת ג' שעות ונמצא פועל יושב ט' שעות ויפסיד בעה"ב שצריך לשוכרו ביום שלם שלא ירצה פועל להשכיר עצמו למחצית היום.

איבעית

א] נ"ל במבוי הסמוך לרה"ר כרה"ר דמי.

רבינו גרשום

איבעית אימ' יומא זרעא. ודקא קשיא לך לא הוי יומא כרבא: דכריב ותני. שחורש באותו יום שתיכף לקצירה פעמים מה שחורש בט' שעות חוזר ושונה בג' שעות והוה שוה בשוה: איבעית אימא יומא כרבא. ודקא קשיא לך לא הוי תרי יומא זרעא. לעולם איכא תרי יומי זרעא: בהדורי שהארץ קשה היא וארץ סלעים וטרשין היא ומה שפועל חורש ביום אחד תיכף לקצירה חוזרת ומתקשה וצריך לחרוש בה פעולת ב' ימים דזריעה מחמת הקשיות שמתקשה אחר חרישת קצירה. ול"א מוגה בספרים היכי דמי אי בי רדו יומי זריעה לא הוי תרי יומי כרבא. בהאי לישנא משמע דטפי חורש הפועל בהני ט' שעות דיום זריעה מבכולה יומא דכרבא דכבר רכיכא ארעא דחרושה כבר חדא זימנא והכי קאמר לא הוי [תרי] יומי כרבא דטפי מיומא הוי אבל לא הוי פעולת תרי יומי ואי בי רדו יומא כרבא להאי לישנא לא הוי יומא זרע דכל שחורש ביום כרבא יכול לחרוש ביום זריעה בפחות מט' שעות כדאמר בהאי לישנא דניחא לחרוש ביום זריעה מתיכף לקצירה. איבעית אימא בכרבא ודקא קשיא לך לא הוי יומא דזרעא לעולם הוי דאע"ג דניחא לחרוש חורשה באותו יום זריעה פעמים. ואיבעית אימא בזריעא ודקשיא לך לא הוי תרי יומי כרבא להאי לישנא. לעולם איכא תרי יומי בהדורי ארץ טרשים היא ובתחלה היא קשה הרבה דכל מה שחורש בב' ימים תיכף לקצירה יכול לחרוש ביום אחד דזריעא וכ"ך קבלת"י אנ"י מר' אב"ל חבירי"ו הבינו בזה הענין. היכא דמי אי בי רדו יומא בזרעא שבין זריעה ובין חרישה שחורשין את השדה פעם אחרת בימות הגשמים לבד מכריבה ראשונה שכורבין בימות החמה חורשין אותה בימות הגשמים סמוך [לזריע'] לפי שתהא נוחה לזרוע ואם צריך יום אחד למלאכה לפועל אחד בין חרישה בין זריעה אפילו הכי ליכא יומא כרבא יום חמה כי הימים הן ארוכין ומושכין ביותר ובט' שעות ביום יכול הפועל לחורשה ולתקנה כל הצורך ונמצא שמפסיד בעל השדה מט' שעות ולמעלה ואי בי רדו יומא כרבא שבכריבה ראשונה יש מלאכה לפועל אחד לחרוש בימות החמה כל היום כולו אפי' הכי לא הוי תרי יומי בזרעא כלומר בין זריעה ובין חרישה דבפחות מב' ימים בימות הגשמים יכול לחורשה פעם אחרת לזורעה נמצא שמפסיד זה בעל השדה מחצי יום ולמעלה לפי שאין פועל משכיר עצמו לחצאין. איבעית אימא דאיכא בי רדו יומא זרעא ודקא קשיא לך לא הוי יומא כרבא ודאי איכא יומא כרבא שלם ולא קא מפסיד ולא מידי דכרבא הוא דכריב זמנא חדא והדר תני זמנא אחריתא משום דבכריבא חדא לא קא הוי ארעא ניחא מחמת קשייתא דהשתא בין כריבות הללו איכא פעולה ליום אריכא ואיבעית אימא דאיכא בי רדו יומא כרבא ודקא קשיא לך לא הוי תרי יומי בזריעה ודאי איכא תרי יומי שלמין משום דההיא ארעא בהררי כלומר שדה קשה הוא וארץ הרים וטרשים היא ובימות החמה שהיום ארוך הוא צריך לחרוש יום אחד שלם מחמת קשיות שבה ועכשיו בימות הגשמים חוזרת לקשיותה וצריך לחורשה כדי שתהא נוחה לזורעה ובין חרישה וזריעה צריך שני ימים מפני כי הימים קטנים הן. ל"א מוג"ה בספרים וה"ג להא. בי רדו יומא בזריעה לא הוי תרי יומי בכרבא ואי בי רדו יומא בכרבא לא הוי חד יומא לזריעה והכי מפרש לה אם צריך יום אחד בין חרישה לזריעה בימות הגשמים לא צריך תרי יומא לכרבא דפחות מב' ימים יכול לכורבה פעם ראשונה ב] קשה קרקע וצריך ליום אחד של חרישה וזריעה יותר מיום אחד של

כרבא

ב] נ"ל כשהקרקע קשה.

הגהות הב"ח

(א) גמ' משום דרב יהודה אמר רב דאמר רב מצר: (ב) רש"י ד"ה הני מילי וכו' של ראשי המבואות הסמוכות לרה"ר: (ג) ד"ה אי יומא דזרעא וכו' בשעת הניר ואי האי בי רדו יומא דקאמרת ביומא דזרעא קאמרת תרי יומי כרבא לא הוי: (ד) ד"ה הכי קאמר וכו' לא ניטלה הס"ד ואח"כ מ"ה ונביא יש לו לבב חכמה: (ה) תוס' ד"ה פרץ וכו' אבל מת בעלמא תפיס: (ו) בא"ד טפח בכל אחד ובשלא פרץ: (ז) בא"ד פרה אדומה או בקבר: (ח) ד"ה ולא פליגי וכו' חשוב לטרות בט' חצאי קבין ואע"פ שלא היה בו כדי חרישת יום ראוי היה לטרות אבל באתריה דת"ק וכו' בפחות מט' קבין והשתא בעי בבבל כצ"ל: (ט) ד"ה ואי בעית אימא וד"ה ואי בעית אימא הס"א: (י) ד"ה דוולא וכו' הוה ליה למבעי בבבל מאי: (כ) ד"ה אמר וכו' בסוף מומין אלו גבי:

מִשְּׁמֵיהּ דְּר' עֲקִיבָא בַּר יוֹסֵף כְּוָותֵיהּ. אֲמַר רַב אַשִׁי: וּמַאי קוּשְׁיָא? דִּלְמָא לְהָא מִילְּתָא בַּר מַזְּלֵיהּ הוּא! אֶלָּא אֲמַר רַב אַשִׁי: תֵּדַע, דְּאָמַר גַּבְרָא רַבָּה מִילְּתָא, וּמִתְאַמְרָא הֲלָכָה לְמֹשֶׁה מִסִּינַי כְּוָותֵיהּ. א)וְדִלְמָא כְּסוּמָא בָּאֲרוּבָּה! וְלָאו טַעַם (א) יָהֵיב? א"ר יוֹחָנָן: מִיּוֹם שֶׁחָרַב בֵּית הַמִּקְדָּשׁ, נִיטְּלָה נְבוּאָה מִן הַנְּבִיאִים וְנִיתְּנָה לַשּׁוֹטִים וְלַתִּינוֹקוֹת. לַשּׁוֹטִים — מַאי הִיא? כִּי הָא דְּמָר בַּר רַב אַשִׁי דַּהֲוָה קָאֵי בְּרִסְתְּקָא דְּמָחוֹזָא, שְׁמָעֵיהּ לְהַהוּא שׁוֹטֶה דְּקָאָמַר: רֵישׁ מְתִיבְתָּא דְּמָלֵיךְ (ב) בְּמָתָא מְחַסְיָא — "טַבְיוֹמֵי" חָתִים. אֲמַר: מַאן חָתִים "טַבְיוֹמֵי" בְּרַבָּנַן? אֲנָא, שְׁמַע מִינַּהּ לְדִידִי קַיְימָא לִי שַׁעְתָּא. קָם אֲתָא. אַדַּאֲתָא אִימְנוּ רַבָּנַן לְאוֹתְבֵיהּ לְרַב אַחָא מִדִּפְתִּי בְּרֵישָׁא. כֵּיוָן דְּשָׁמְעִי דְּאָתָא, ב)שְׁדוּר זוּגָא דְּרַבָּנַן לְגַבֵּיהּ לְאִימְּלוּכֵי בֵּיהּ, (ג) עַכְּבֵיהּ. הֲדַר שְׁדוּר זוּגָא דְּרַבָּנַן אַחֲרִינָא, עַכְּבֵיהּ גַּבֵּיהּ, עַד דְּמָלוּ בֵּי עַשְׂרָה. כֵּיוָן דְּמָלוּ בֵּי עַשְׂרָה, פְּתַח הוּא וּתְנָא וּדְרַשׁ, לְפִי שֶׁאֵין פּוֹתְחִין בְּכַלָּה פָּחוֹת מֵעֲשָׂרָה. קָרֵי רַב אַחָא אַנַּפְשֵׁיהּ: ג)כָּל הַמְּרֵיעִין לוֹ — לֹא בִּמְהֵרָה מְטִיבִין לוֹ, וְכָל הַמְּטִיבִין לוֹ — לֹא בִּמְהֵרָה מְרִיעִין לוֹ. תִּינוֹקֶת — מַאי הִיא? כִּי הָא דְּבַת רַב חִסְדָּא הֲוָה יָתְבָה בְּכַנְפֵיהּ דַּאֲבוּהָ, הָווּ יָתְבִי קַמֵּיהּ רָבָא וְרָמִי בַּר חָמָא. אֲמַר לָהּ: מַאן מִינַּיְיהוּ בָּעֵית? אֲמַרָה לֵיהּ: תַּרְוַיְיהוּ, אֲמַר רָבָא: וַאֲנָא בַּתְרָא. (ד) א"ר אַבְדִּימִי דְּמִן חֵיפָה: קוֹדֶם ד)שֶׁיֹּאכַל אָדָם וְיִשְׁתֶּה יֵשׁ לוֹ שְׁתֵּי לְבָבוֹת, לְאַחַר שֶׁאוֹכֵל וְשׁוֹתֶה — אֵין לוֹ אֶלָּא לֵב אֶחָד, שֶׁנֶּאֱמַר: °"אִישׁ נָבוּב יִלָּבֵב", וּכְתִיב: °"נְבוּב לוּחוֹת", וּמְתַרְגְּמִינַן: חֲלִיל לוּחִין. אֲמַר רַב הוּנָא בְּרֵיהּ דְּרַב יְהוֹשֻׁעַ: הָרָגִיל בְּיַיִן, אֲפִי' לִבּוֹ אָטוּם כִּבְתוּלָה — יַיִן מְפַקְּחוֹ, שֶׁנֶּאֱמַר: °"וְתִירוֹשׁ יְנוֹבֵב בְּתֻלוֹת". § אֲמַר רַב הוּנָא בְּרֵי' דְּרַב יְהוֹשֻׁעַ: א)פְּשִׁיטָא, חֵלֶק בְּכוֹר וְחֵלֶק פָּשׁוּט — יָהֲבִינַן לֵיהּ ה)אַחַד מִצְרָא, יָבָם מַאי? אֲמַר אַבַּיֵי: הִיא הִיא; מ"ט? בְּכוֹר קָרְיֵיהּ רַחֲמָנָא. רָבָא אֲמַר, ב)אָמַר קְרָא: °"וְהָיָה הַבְּכוֹר", הֲוָיָיתוֹ כִּבְכוֹר וְאֵין חֲלוּקָתוֹ כִּבְכוֹר. הַהוּא דִּזְבַן אַרְעָא אַמִּצְרָא דְּבֵי ו)נָשְׁיֵהּ, כִּי קָא פָּלְגוּ א"ל: פְּלִיגוּ לִי אַמִּצְרַאי; ז)אֲמַר רַבָּה: ג)כְּגוֹן זֶה כּוֹפִין עַל מִדַּת סְדוֹם. מַתְקִיף לָהּ רַב יוֹסֵף: ד)אָמְרִי לֵיהּ אַחֵי: מַעֲלִינַן לֵיהּ עִלּוּיָא כִּי נִכְסֵי דְּבֵי בַּר מָרְיוֹן! וְהִלְכְתָא כְּרַב יוֹסֵף. תְּרֵי אַרְעָתָא אַתְּרֵי נִגְרֵי — אָמַר רַבָּה: כְּגוֹן זֶה כּוֹפִין עַל מִדַּת סְדוֹם. מַתְקִיף לָהּ רַב יוֹסֵף, זִמְנִין דְּהַאי מְדַוֵּיל וְהַאי לָא מְדַוֵּיל! וְהִלְכְתָא כְּרַב יוֹסֵף. תַּרְתֵּי (ה) אַחַד נִגְרָא — א"ר יוֹסֵף: ה)כְּגוֹן זֶה כּוֹפִין עַל מִדַּת סְדוֹם. מַתְקִיף לָהּ אַבַּיֵי, מָצֵי אָמַר: בָּעֵינָא דְּאַפֵּישׁ אֲרִיסֵי! וְהִלְכְתָא כְּרַב יוֹסֵף, אַפּוּשֵׁי (ו) לָאו מִילְּתָא הִיא.

חַד

רש"י

מִשְּׁמֵיהּ דְּרַבִּי עֲקִיבָא כְּוָותֵיהּ. וְלֵיכָּא לְמֵימַר בְּנֵי חַד מַזָּלָא נִינְהוּ, שֶׁהֲרֵי ר"ע חָכָם מִמֶּנּוּ הַרְבֵּה. וְלָאו טַעְמָא קָאָמַר. בְּמִילְּתֵיהּ? וְכֵיוָן דְּאָמַר טַעְמָא — אֵין זֶה כְּסוּמָא שֶׁמְּכַוֵּין לֵירֵד בָּאֲרוּבָּה בְּמִקְרֶה בְּעָלְמָא, אֶלָּא סְבָרַת הַלֵּב הִיא הַבָּאָה לוֹ בִּנְבוּאָה, וְזָכָה לְהַסְכִּים לַהֲלָכָה לְמֹשֶׁה מִסִּינַי. בְּרִיסְתְּקָא. שׁוּק רְשׁוּת הָרַבִּים. דְּמָלֵיךְ. הַשְׁתָּא בְּמָתָא מְחַסְיָא, שֶׁעָתִיד לִהְיוֹת רֹאשׁ הַיְשִׁיבָה עַכְשָׁיו. טַבְיוֹמֵי חָתִים. כְּשֶׁחוֹתֵם בְּאִיגֶּרֶת חוֹתֵם שְׁמוֹ טַבְיוֹמֵי. קַיְימָא לִי שַׁעְתָּא. מַזָּל. שְׁדַרוּ זוּגָא דְּרַבָּנַן לְגַבֵּיהּ. דְּמָר בַּר רַב אַשִׁי. לְאִימְּלוּכֵי בֵּיהּ. לִיטּוֹל עֵצָה וּרְשׁוּת לְהַמְלִיךְ אֶת רַב אַחָא. פְּתַח וּתְנָא. דְּרָשָׁה, וְנַעֲשָׂה רֹאשׁ הַיְשִׁיבָה. כָּל הַמְּרֵיעִין לוֹ כו'. כְּלוֹמַר, הוֹאִיל וְנִדְחָה הַשָּׁעָה לֹא יַמְלִיכוּנִי עוֹד. אִישׁ נָבוּב. כְּשֶׁהוּא חָלוּל, בְּלֹא כֶּרֶס מְלֵאָה. יִלָּבֵב. כַּמָּה לְבָבוֹת, שֶׁאֵינוֹ מַסְכִּים לָדַעַת שְׁלֵמָה. יְנוֹבֵב בְּתוּלוֹת. לֵב אָטוּם כִּבְתוּלוֹת עוֹשֶׂה נָבוּב וְחָלוּל. פְּשִׁיטָא חֵלֶק בְּכוֹר וְחֵלֶק פָּשׁוּט. שְׁנֵי חֲלָקִין שֶׁהַבְּכוֹר נוֹטֵל, אֶחָד מִשּׁוּם בְּכוֹרָה וְאֶחָד מִשּׁוּם פְּשִׁיטוּת, יָהֲבִינַן לֵיהּ אַחַד מִצְרָא זוֹ אֵצֶל זוֹ, שֶׁהֲרֵי שְׁנֵיהֶן חֶלְקוֹ הֵן, וַהֲרֵי הֵן כְּחֵלֶק אֶחָד. יָבָם מַאי. הַמְיַיבֵּם אֶת אֵשֶׁת אָחִיו, דְּקָם תַּחְתָּיו לְנַחֲלָה, וְנוֹטֵל שְׁנֵי חֲלָקִים, מַאי? מִי מָצוּ אָמְרֵי לֵיהּ: הוֹאִיל וּמִכֹּחַ אַחֲרִינָא קָאָתֵי — לָא יָהֲבִי לְהוּ (ז) נִיהֲלֵיהּ אַחַד מִצְרָא זוֹ אֵצֶל זוֹ, אִי לָאו מְעַלְּיָא גַּבָּן בְּדָמֵי. הַבְּכוֹר אֲשֶׁר תֵּלֵד. בְּיָבָם קָמִשְׁתָּעֵי, דְּמִצְוָה בַּגָּדוֹל לְיַיבֵּם, "אֲשֶׁר תֵּלֵד" — פְּרָט לָאַיְילוֹנִית. וְהָכִי מִדְרַשׁ קְרָא: "יְבָמָהּ יָבֹא עָלֶיהָ וגו' וְהָיָה הַבְּכוֹר", אֵיזֶה מִן הַיְּבָמִין יָבֹא עָלֶיהָ — "הַבְּכוֹר", "אֲשֶׁר תֵּלֵד" — וּכְגוֹן שֶׁהַיְּבָמָה בַּת וְוֹלָדוֹת הִיא, פְּרָט לָאַיְילוֹנִית. דִּזְבַן אַרְעָא אַמִּצְרָא דְּבֵי נָשָׁא. קָנָה קַרְקַע אֵצֶל שְׂדֵה אָבִיו. כִּי מְטָא לְמִיפְלַג. עִם אֶחָיו בְּנִכְסֵי אָבִיו. עַל מִדַּת סְדוֹם. זֶה נֶהֱנֶה וְזֶה לֹא חָסֵר. אָמְרוּ אַחֵי מַעֲלִינַן לֵיהּ עִילָּוָאי. לָנוּ הִיא מְשׁוּבַּחַת כְּקַרְקְעוֹתָיו שֶׁל בַּר מָרְיוֹן, שֶׁהָיוּ מְעוּלּוֹת. וּמִסְתַּבְּרָא הָא דְּרַב יוֹסֵף בִּשְׂדֵה (ח) בַּעַל, שֶׁיְּכוֹלִין לוֹמַר פְּעָמִים שֶׁזּוֹ מִתְבָּרֶכֶת מִשְּׁאָר הַשָּׂדוֹת. תְּרֵי אַרְעָתָא אַתְּרֵי נִגְרֵי. אִם בֵּית הַשְּׁלָחִין הִיא, וְיֵשׁ לִשְׁנֵי אַחִין לַחֲלוֹק שְׁתֵּי שָׂדוֹת, לְכָל אַחַת יֵשׁ לָהּ יְאוֹר לְהַשְׁקוֹת מִמֶּנּוּ, וְזֶה קָנָה שָׂדֶה אֵצֶל (ט) הָאֶחָד מֵהֶן, וְרוֹצֶה שֶׁיִּתֵּן אָחִיו זוֹ הַסְּמוּכָה לְשֶׁלּוֹ. כְּגוֹן זוֹ כּוֹפִין. דְּהָא לַקַּרְקַע הַשְּׁנִיָּה גַּם הִיא יֵשׁ לָהּ יְאוֹר לְהַשְׁקוֹת מִמֶּנּוּ. הַאי מְדַוֵּיל וְהַאי לָא מְדַוֵּיל. דֶּרֶךְ הַיְאוֹרִים לְיַיבֵּשׁ כְּשֶׁנָּהָר *)(שָׁם) נִמְשָׁכִין מִמֶּנּוּ מִתְמַעֵט, לִפְעָמִים שֶׁזֶּה יָבֵשׁ וְזֶה אֵינוֹ יָבֵשׁ. וְאוֹמֵר לוֹ: טוֹל חֶלְקְךָ בִּשְׁתֵּיהֶם, דְּלָאו מִדַּת סְדוֹם הִיא, אוֹ תֵּן לָנוּ עִילּוּי בְּדָמֵי. תַּרְתֵּי. אַרְעָתָא יֵשׁ לָהֶם לַחֲלוֹק עַל חַד נִגְרָא, וְאֶחָד מֵהֶן קָנָה קַרְקָעוֹ אֵצֶל הָאַחַת. כּוֹפִין עַל מִדַּת סְדוֹם. דְּכֵיוָן דְּאַחַד נִגְרָא נִינְהוּ — שְׁתֵּיהֶן שָׁווֹת. נִיחָא לִי לְאַפּוּשֵׁי אֲרִיסֵי. טוֹב לִי שֶׁיִּהְיוּ לְךָ שְׁתֵּי שָׂדוֹת, אַחַת מִכָּאן וְאַחַת מִכָּאן (י) וְאַחַת לִי בָּאֶמְצַע, כְּדֵי שֶׁתַּרְבֶּה לְךָ אֲרִיסִין, וּתְהֵא שָׂדֶה שֶׁלִּי מִשְׁתַּמֶּרֶת יָפֶה.

*) [ל"ל שהם]

תוספות

כל המריעין לו לא במהרה מטיבין לו. ובשילהי "מרובה" (ב"ק דף פ: ושם ד"ה לעולם) דקאמר רב אחא גופיה: לעולם אין מטיבין לו, איכא למימר דמתחל' אמר: לא במהרה מטיבין, שהיה מצפה שיחזירוהו לגדולתו, וכשראה שלא החזירוהו — שוב אמר: לעולם אין מטיבין לו. חלק בכור וחלק פשוט יהבינן ליה אחד מצרא. כדנפקא לן ב"יש נוחלין" (לקמן דף קכד.) מדכתיב "פי שנים" — מקיש חלק בכורה לחלק פשוט. אמיצרא דבי נשי. אית דגרס בתר הכי "אמרי אחוותא". א"כ "בי נשיה" — היינו חמיו, ולא היו לחמיו בנים כי אם בנות. ואית דגרס: "אמרי אחי", א"כ "בי נשיה" היינו אביו. [ועי' תוס' שבת כג: ד"ה דבי נשא].

כגון זה כופין על מדת סדום. תימה לר"י: לרבה, אמאי איצטריך קרא בבכור דיהבינן ליה אחד מצרא? ואומר ר"י: לפי שלא נתן לו (כ) כח הכתוב אלא כב' אחיו, ואילו היו שני אחיו רוצים להשתתף — לא כפינן לשלישי לתת להם חלק ביחד. ועוד: דבכור מתנה קרייה רחמנא, כדאמר ב"יש נוחלין" (שם) דכתיב "לתת לו פי שנים", ואין לכוף את הנותן. ולאביי נמי, אי לאו דקרייה רחמנא בכור — ה"א "יקום על שם אחיו" — כאילו הוא ואחיו קיימין. ורילב"א מפרש: דהא דאמר רבה כופין — לא מדין תורה קאמר, דבדין היה יכול למחות שכנגדו דאיכא קפידא ברוחות, כדאמר בכמה דוכתין. ועוד: הא דכופין על מדת סדום בזה נהנה וזה לא חסר — היינו בשכבר דר בחצר חבירו, שאינו מעלה לו שכר. אבל הא פשיטא שיכול למחות בו שלא יכנס לדור בביתו, אפי' בחצר דלא קיימא לאגרא, וגברא דלא עביד למיגר, דהוה זה *נהנה וזה לא חסר. אלא מתקנת חכמים קאמר הכא דכופין. והשתא אין להקשות כלל אמאי איצטריך קרא בבכור.

מעלינן ליה בנכסי דבר מריון. פירש הקונטרס: בשדה הבעל, (ל) שיכולים לומר שפעמים מתברכת משאר שדות. ובתרתי ארעתא אתרי נגרי לא שייך למימר מעלינן, כיון שצריך להשקות ואין מתברכת זו יותר מזו. ואין נראה, דגם אותם שצריך להשקות מתברכת אחת מהם פעמים יותר, שאחת לוקה בשידפון ואחת אינה לוקה. ופר"ת: מעלינן כנכסי דבר מריון — לא ניתן לך זכות שיש לנו בשדה זו אם לא בדמים יקרים, כמו בני מריון שהיו עשירים ולא היו מוכרים קרקעותיהם אלא בדמים יקרים. ותרתי ארעתא אתרי נגרי לא קאי אעובדא דההוא גברא, אלא מילתא באנפי נפשיה, כלומר, שתי שדות שיש לכל אחד נגר ורוצה האחד שיחלקו כל אחת לשתים, שיקח חצי שדה זו וחצי שדה זו, אמר רבה: כופין על מדת סדום ויטול כל (מ) שדה שלם, כדי שיהא לכל אחד חלק אחד מצרא. וכן יש לפרש תרתי ארעתא אחד נגרא — שהנגר מפסיק בין שתי השדות, ואם יחלקו כל שדה לשתים, לא יהיה חלקו אחד מצרא. והשתא בהני לא שייך למימר מעלינן כנכסי דבי בר מריון, דאטו אם האחד רצה לחלוק לעשרים נאמר שיחלקו משום מעלינן? ולשון "מעלינן" נמי אינו מתיישב לפ"ה.

א) חגיגה ב. פסחים פח. ערכין ב: עדיות פ"א מי"ג [גיטין מא.]: ב) לקמן קעב.: ג) [יבמות סו.]:

רבינו גרשום

דליהוו נפישי אריסין מיכן ומיכן וישמרו זה את זה ואמאי כופין. למ"ה. שנים שיש להם שדה אחת לחלוק ולצד מזרח של שדה היה מושך נהר ולצד דרום של שדה יש שם נגר משוך לאורך השדה שמשקין ממנו השדה ומצד צפון ומערב של שדה יבישה והשתא אין יכולין לחלוק בשום ענין שלא יהא חלק אחד יפה מחבירו אלא א"כ צריכין לחלוק בקרנא זול כעין אותו ציור בד' חלקים דמכל רוח יעשו ב' חלקין מן הנהר ב' ומן הנגר ב' ומן היבשה ב' ב' ויחלקו כי האי גונא כי היכי דלימטי לכל חד וחד שוה לחבירו מן הנהר ומן הנגר ומן צדי היבשה משום דנהר יפה מנגר ונגר יפה מיבשה ובחילוק ענין זה יחלוקו בקו השוה שלא יהא חלקו של אחד יפה משל חבירו ואין אחד מהם נוטל ב' חלקים בסמוך לו אלא כעין זה*). (הנהר המושך מצד מזרח): פיסקא אין חולקין את הטרקלין. פלטורין אא"כ יש בו כדי לזה וכדי לזה דהיינו י' על י' לזה וכן לזה דהיינו שיעור טרקלין. מורן הוא מגדל. ולא את הטלית אלא אם כן יכולין שניהן להתכסות בו זה בפני עצמו בטליתו ולא את המרחץ עד שיכולין לרחוץ כל אחד בחלקו המגיעו זה הכלל כל ששמו עליו כתחלה מקודם חלוקה שלאחר חלוקה אית לכל חלק שם אותו עצמו כמו שנקרא בתחלה חולקין. ואם לאו אין חולקין אלא מעלין זה לזה ברמים שיקנה אחד מהן חלק חבירו בדמים. ואי ליכא שיעור חלוקה מאי. רב יהודא אמר אית דינא דגוד או אגוד דאם אחד רוצה שישתמשו בו שניהם בשותפות זה שבוע אחד וזה שבוע אחד והאחד אינו רוצה יכול לומר האי דאינו רוצה נישום אותו בדמים ותקנה אתה חלקי או אני חלקך. גוד. משוך תרגו' א). ורב נחמן אמר לית דינא דגוד או אגוד כלומר אי האי אינו רוצה אינו יכול לכפותו ולומר לו כן אלא משתמשין בו בשותפות: בכור ופשוט והוא הדין לפשוט ופשוט אלא להכי בעי בכור ופשוט קשה טפי לחלק בג' חלקים. ולהכי נקיט בהמה טמאה. דאי אפשר לשוחטה ולחלוק הבשר אמר ליה עובד לפשוט יום אחד ולבכור ב' ימים וכן נמי בהמה טמאה זה ישתמש בה ב' ימים וזה יום אחד ואין כאן דין גוד או אגוד: וחציו בן חורין ששחררו אחד מן השותפין. לישא שפחה אינו יכול מפני צד חירות שבו וכותב שטר לרבו על חצי דמיו שיפרע לו ממה שירויח לאחר שיהיה כולו בן חורין מפני שכשהוא חצי עבד אין לו ממון כלום שכל מה שמרויח ביום שהוא עובד לעצמו סוף סוף למחר כשהוא עובד לרבו הרי הוא עבדו וכל מה שקנה עבד קנה רבו להכי צריך לכתוב שט"ח על חצי דמיו. וחזרו בית הילל כו' מפני תיקון העולם הא לאו מפני תיקון העולם אין כופין את רבו משום דאמרינן דלית דינא דגוד או אגוד דלא מצי עבד למימר לו שחררני ואתן לך דמי חציי או תן אתה לי דמי חציי ואהא מהכל עבדך ותיובתא דרב יהודה. לעולם אמר לך רב יהודה אית דינא דגוד או אגוד והכא גבי עבד שאני. דגוד איכא אגוד ליכא דעבד מצי למימר לרבו קצוב עלי דמים ואקנה חצי ממך אבל אינו יכול לומר לו אקצוב אני עליך דמי חציי ותקנה אותי מהכל דאינו יכול למכור צד שחרור שבו לישא שפחה. וא"ת דמפרש"י אגוד ליכא לא מצי עבד למימר לרבו קנה חלקי המשוחרר שאם נותן לו הרב דמים עכשיו כשהוא רבו מהכל חוזר ונוטלן הימנו דמה שקנה עבד קנה רבו ונמצא שאין גופו קנוי כשהוא חוזר ונוטלן. למ"ה: אם

*) עי' הציור בסוף המסכת א) [צ"ל תרגום משכו וענידו].

חַד גִּיסָא נִיגְרָא וְחַד גִּיסָא נַהֲרָא. שָׂדֶה שֶׁל שְׁנֵי אַחִים, שֶׁיֵּשׁ נָהָר עַל פְּנֵי מִזְרָח, וְנֶגֶר עַל פְּנֵי צְפוֹנָהּ. פָּלְגֵי לֵיהּ בְּקַרְנָא זוֹל. לְפִי שֶׁהַנָּהָר טוֹב מִן הַנֶּגֶר, וְהַסָּמוּךְ לַמַּיִם טוֹב מִן הָרָחוֹק. וְאִם תְּחַלְּקֶנָּה מִן הַצָּפוֹן – (ב) נִמְצָא (מִן) כָּל הַנָּהָר לְאֶחָד, וְהַשֵּׁנִי אֵין לוֹ אֶלָּא נֶגֶר בִּצְפוֹנוֹ, וּפְעָמִים שֶׁהוּא יָבֵשׁ. וְאִם תְּחַלְּקֶנָּה מִן הַמִּזְרָח לַמַּעֲרָב – יִהְיֶה לְאֶחָד הַנָּהָר עַל פְּנֵי מִזְרָחוֹ וְנֶגֶר עַל פְּנֵי צְפוֹנוֹ, וְלַשֵּׁנִי אֵין לוֹ אֶלָּא נָהָר בְּמִזְרָחוֹ. לְפִיכָךְ יַחֲלְקוּם לִשְׁמוֹנָה חֲלָקִים, שֶׁיְּהֵא לִשְׁנֵיהֶם בְּשָׁוֶה סָמוּךְ לַנָּהָר וְלַנֶּגֶר, וְכַאֲשֶׁר יִרְחַק מִזֶּה יִרְחַק מִזֶּה, כָּזֶה:

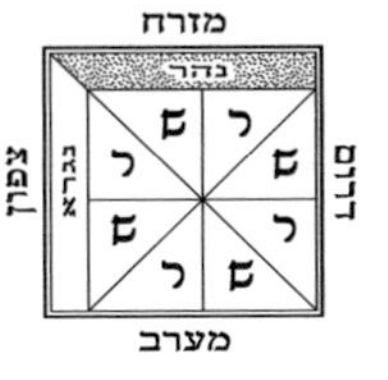

אִית דִּינָא דְּגוּד אוֹ אָגוּד. זֶה שֶׁרוֹצֶה לַחֲלוֹק אוֹמֵר לָזֶה שֶׁאֵינוֹ רוֹצֶה לַחֲלוֹק: אוֹ קוֹץ לִי דָּמִים וּקְנֵה לְךָ חֶלְקִי, אוֹ אֲנִי אֶקּוֹץ דָּמִים וְאֶתֵּן לְךָ בְּחֶלְקְךָ, שֶׁאִי אֶפְשִׁי בְּשׁוּתָּפוּתְךָ. לֵית דִּינָא. שֶׁזֶּה יָכוֹל לוֹמַר: לֹא שֶׁלְּךָ אֶקְנֶה וְלֹא שֶׁלִּי אֶמְכּוֹר, אֶלָּא שׁוּתָּפִין נִהְיֶה בָּהּ. עֶבֶד אוֹ בְּהֵמָה טְמֵאָה. שֶׁאִי אֶפְשָׁר לְחַלְּקָן, כֵּיצַד יַעֲשׂוּ? לְהָכִי נָקַט בְּכוֹר וּפָשׁוּט, דִּטְרִיחָא מִילְּתָא לִהְיוֹת שׁוּתָּפִין בָּהּ. וְחָזְרוּ בֵּית הִלֵּל לְהוֹרוֹת כו'. טַעֲמָא דְּמִפְּנֵי תִּיקּוּן הָעוֹלָם, הָא לָאו מִשּׁוּם פְּרִיָּה וּרְבִיָּה – לָא כָּיְיפִינַן לֵיהּ, וְלָא מָצֵי עֶבֶד לְמֵימַר לֵיהּ: אֶקּוֹץ בְּדָמִים וְאֶתֵּן לְךָ בְּחֶלְקְךָ. ה"ג: שָׁאנֵי הָכָא דְּאָגוּד אִיכָּא גּוּד לֵיכָּא. הָעֶבֶד יָכוֹל לִקְנוֹת, (ג) אֲבָל אֵינוֹ אוֹמֵר: קְנֵה חֶלְקִי, שֶׁאֵין דָּמִים לְבֶן חוֹרִין, שֶׁאֵין עֶבֶד עִבְרִי נִמְכָּר אֶלָּא לְשֵׁשׁ.

קח

אחַד גִּיסָא נִגְרָא וְחַד גִּיסָא נַהֲרָא – פָּלְגִין לָהּ בְּקַרְנָא זוֹל.§ "וְלֹא אֶת הַטְּרַקְלִין" כו'.§ אֵין בָּהֶן כְּדֵי לָזֶה וּכְדֵי לָזֶה, מַהוּ? רַב יְהוּדָה אָמַר: באִית דִּינָא דְּ"גוּד אוֹ אֲגוּד", רַב נַחְמָן אָמַר: לֵית דִּינָא דְּ"גוּד אוֹ אֲגוּד". א"ל רָבָא לְרַב נַחְמָן, לְדִידָךְ דְּאָמְרַתְּ: לֵית דִּינָא דְּ"גוּד אוֹ אֲגוּד", בְּכוֹר וּפָשׁוּט שֶׁהִנִּיחַ לָהֶן אֲבִיהֶן עֶבֶד וּבְהֵמָה טְמֵאָה, כֵּיצַד עוֹשִׂין? א"ל, שֶׁאֲנִי אוֹמֵר: עוֹבֵד לָזֶה יוֹם אֶחָד וְלָזֶה שְׁנֵי יָמִים. מֵיתִיבֵי: א)מִי שֶׁחֶצְיוֹ עֶבֶד וְחֶצְיוֹ בֶּן חוֹרִין, עוֹבֵד אֶת רַבּוֹ יוֹם אֶחָד וְאֶת עַצְמוֹ יוֹם אֶחָד, דִּבְרֵי ב"ה; ב"ש אוֹמְרִים: גתִּקַּנְתֶּם אֶת רַבּוֹ, אֶת עַצְמוֹ לֹא תִּקַּנְתֶּם, לִישָּׂא שִׁפְחָה אֵינוֹ יָכוֹל, לִישָּׂא בַּת חוֹרִין אֵינוֹ יָכוֹל, יִבָּטֵל? וַהֲלֹא לֹא נִבְרָא הָעוֹלָם אֶלָּא לִפְרִיָּה וּרְבִיָּה, שֶׁנֶּאֱמַר: °"לֹא תֹהוּ בְרָאָהּ לָשֶׁבֶת יְצָרָהּ"! אֶלָּא (א) דכּוֹפִין אֶת רַבּוֹ וְעוֹשִׂין אוֹתוֹ בֶּן חוֹרִין, וְכוֹתְבִין שְׁטָר עַל חֲצִי דָּמָיו. וְחָזְרוּ ב"ה לְהוֹרוֹת כְּדִבְרֵי ב"ש! שָׁאנֵי הָכָא, דְּ"אֲגוּד" אִיכָּא, "גּוּד" לֵיכָּא. ת"ש: ב)השְׁנֵי אַחִין, אֶחָד עָנִי וְאֶחָד עָשִׁיר, וְהִנִּיחַ לָהֶן אֲבִיהֶן מֶרְחָץ וּבֵית הַבַּד, עֲשָׂאָן לְשָׂכָר – הַשָּׂכָר לָאֶמְצַע, עֲשָׂאָן לְעַצְמוֹ – הֲרֵי עָשִׁיר אוֹמֵר לֶעָנִי:

ישעיה מה

קח

תוספות

חד גיסא ניגרא וחד גיסא נהרא. פירש רבינו חננאל: שדה אשר מזרחה ולפונה נהרא, ומערבה ודרומה מושך ניגרא — חולקין אותה בקרנא זול.

פירוש: חולקין אותה באלכסון, מקרן מזרחית לפונית לקרן מערבית דרומית, ויהיה לכל אחד לד אחד ניגרא וחד לד נהרא. וכל היכא דמשיך נהרא או ניגרא קרוי חד גיסא. **אית** דינא דגוד או אגוד. נראה לר"י דאפילו בדמים יקרים הרבה יותר משוויו יכול לומר לו: או גוד או אגוד. ואין נראה לריב"א, *דא"כ יוכל לסלק אחד את חבירו ע"י עילוי דמים (ד) בחצר שאין בה דין חלוקה. **בכור** ופשוט שהניח להן כו'. ותימה: דאמאי נקט בכור ופשוט, ולא נקט פשוט ופשוט? ואומר ר"ת: דפשוט ופשוט ניחא ליה שיעבוד לזה יום אחד ולזה יום אחד. אבל בכור ופשוט קשיא ליה, אם יעבוד לבכור ב' ימים — הרי נטל הבכור יותר מפי שנים, שאם יש עיר רחוקה מהלך יום אחד שמשתכרים בה הרבה, שיש שם סחורה בזול, ופשוט שאין לו שהות אלא יום אחד — לא יוכל לילך שם, והבכור שיש לו ב' ימים — יכול לילך שם, ומשתכר יותר הרבה מפשוט. ומשני, דמ"מ כך חולקין. ור"י מפרש: דלהכי נקט בכור ופשוט, משום דאמר ב"מי שהיה נשוי" (כתובות דף צג:) דשור לחרישה ועומד לחרישה — דכ"ע השכר לאמצע, אע"פ שאין לזה כי אם מנה ולזה מאתים. ולהכי פריך: כילד יעשו? דעכשיו אין הבכור נוטל פי שנים! ומשני: דעובד לזה יום אחד ולזה ב' ימים. ולא דמי לשור לחרישה ועומד לחרישה, דהתם הוי השכר לאמצע משום דמעיקרא אדעתא דהכי נשתתפו, אבל גבי בכור ופשוט דלא שייך האי טעמא — כל אחד נוטל כפי חלקו. **לישא** שפחה אינו יכול. ואע"ג דאמר ב"הבא על יבמתו" (יבמות דף סב. ושם ד"ה הכל) דהכל מודים בעבד שאין לו חייס, ולא קייס פריה ורביה, והכא נמי אם ישא שפחה — לא קייס, כיון שהולד מתייחס אחריה. ואפי' שבת לא קייס, כדמשמע התם דשבת תלוי בפריה ורביה — מ"מ אור"י (ד) לא כופין לרבו לעשותו בן חורין משום פריה ורביה, אם היה יכול לקייס אפי' שבת כל דהו, כיון שהוא אנוס. **שנאמר** לא תהו בראה וגו'. הא דלא מייתי קרא ד"פרו ורבו", אור"י בר מרדכי: משום ד"לשבת יצרה" שייך אפי' בלד עבדות. ואליה שפחה ואליה בת חורין ג)דלא כפו את רבה לשחררה אלא משום שנהגו בה מנהג הפקר, הא דלא כפו אותו משום שבת — דשמא אפילו כשתעשה בת חורין לא תקייס, משום דלא מפקדא אפריה ורביה, כדאמרינן ב"הבא על יבמתו" (שם דף סה: ושם) דאיתתא לא מפקדא אפריה ורביה. אבל עבד כשיהיה בן חורין — ע"כ יקייס. ור"י מפרש דלכך לא נקט קרא ד"פרו ורבו" — משום דפטור הוא מאותה מלוה, כיון שהוא אנוס, וכדי שיתחייב בה — לא כפינן לרבו לעשותו בן חורין, דא"כ בכל העבדים נכוף רבם לשחררם כדי שיתחייבו בכל המלות. ולכך נקט קרא "לא תהו בראה" — משום (ו) שהיא מלוה רבה, ומשום הכי כפינן. ובפ"ב דמגילה (דף כז.) נמי מייתי להאי קרא משום הכי, גבי אין מוכרין ספר תורה אלא ללמוד תורה ולישא אשה. ללמוד תורה, דאמר מר: גדול ת"ת שמביא לידי מעשה, לישא אשה נמי — "לא תהו בראה" אלא "לשבת יצרה". **כופין** את רבו. וא"ת: אמאי כופין? ליתי עשה ד"פרו ורבו" וידחה לא תעשה ד"לא יהיה קדש"! ואומר רבינו יצחק: חדא — דבעידנא דמיעקר לאו לא מקיים עשה, דמשעת הערארה קא עקר ללאו, ועשה ד"פרו ורבו" לא מקיים עד גמר ביאה. ועוד: דהיא אסורה לינשא לו, דלגבי דידה ליכא עשה. ועוד: אפי' מפקדא, (ז) דאפשר לה באחר. ועוד: כיון דאפשר לקיים שניהם ע"י כפיה — לא דחי. וא"ת: היכי כפינן לשחררו? והא אמרי' בפ' "השולח" (גיטין דף לח: ושם) דכל המשחרר עבדו עובר בעשה! וכי תימא מלוה שאני — וכי אומרים לו לאדם: חטא כדי שיזכה חבירך? כדאמרי' בריש שבת (דף ד. ושם ד"ה וכי). והא דשחרר ר"א עבדו ב"השולח" (גיטין שם) שנכנס לבית הכנסת ולא מלא שם י' — התם משום דר"א גופיה עשה מלוה בכך שהשלים המנין. והא דאמר נמי בפ' "בכל מערבין" (עירובין דף לב: ושם ד"ה ולא) דניחא ליה לחבר למיעבד איסורא זוטרא ולא ליעבד עם הארץ איסורא רבה — התם משום דקא עביד עם הארץ איסורא על ידו של חבר, דקא מאכיל ליה טבל. ואומר ר"י: דמשום מלוה רבה שרי, אע"ג דעובר בעשה, כדאמרי' ריש "תמיד נשחט" (פסחים דף נט. ושם ד"ה אתי): אין לך דבר שמתעכב אחר תמיד של בין הערבים אלא קטרת, ונרות, ופסח ומחוסר כפורים דערבי פסחים. ומפרש התם: משום דאתי עשה דפסח שיש בו כרת, ודחי עשה דהשלמה. אלמא קעבר כהן אעשה דהשלמה, כדי שיקיים מחוסר כפורים מלות פסח*. וא"ת: אמאי כופין? וימכור עלמו בעבד עברי, למ"ד בפ"ק דקדושין (דף יד: ושם): מוכר את עלמו רבו מוסר לו שפחה כנענית, ולמ"ד נמי דאפי' אין לו בנים (ח) רבו מוסר לו שפחה כנענית. ואע"ג דאין עבד עברי נוהג אלא בזמן שהיובל נוהג, כדאמרי' בפ' "האומר" בקדושין (דף סט. ושם) — הא בבית שני נהג יובל, כדפי' ר"ת ב"השולח" (גיטין דף לו. ד"ה בזמן) גבי הלל תקן פרוזבול! ואור"י: דאין זה תקנה, דאסור למכור עלמו בעבד עברי, כדאמרינן בפ"ק דקדושין (דף כב:): אוזן ששמעה על הר סיני "כי לי בני ישראל עבדים" וגו'. וא"ת: וישא אליה שפחה ואליה בת חורין! ונהי דאינו יכול לקדשה, דאתי לד עבדות ומשתמש בלד אשת איש (ט) — ישאנה בלא קדושין, כדאמר: לישא שפחה כו', משמע דאי הוה מותר בשפחה — לא כפינן לרבו. אע"ג דאין קידושין תופסין בשפחה, מ"מ היה נושאה בלא קידושין! וי"ל: דהשתא נמי אתי לד עבדות ומשתמש בלד חירות. ולא דמי לפרדה, דאמר בפרק "אותו ואת בנו" (חולין דף עט. ושם) דמרביעין עליה מינה, ולא אמר דאתי לד חמור ומשתמש בלד סוס. דהתם "כלאים" כתיב, דמשמע שני מינים דומיא דשור וחמור דחרישה, ופרדה מין אחד בפני עלמו, (י) ומטעם זה מותר לרכוב עליה. וא"ת: וישא ממזרת, דלד עבדות מותר בממזרת, כדתנן ב"האומר" בקדושין (דף סט.): יכולין ממזרין ליטהר, כילד? ממזר נושא שפחה. ובלד חירות נמי מותר, כדתנן בפרק "עשרה יוחסין" (שם דף סט.): ממזרים וחרורים מותרין לבא זה בזה! ואור"י: דאין זה תקנה להרבות ממזרים בישראל. וא"ת: וישא נתינה, דחרורי ונתיני מותרין לבא זה בזה, כדתנן בפ' "עשרה יוחסין" (שם). ולד עבדות נמי מותר בנתינה, דאמר בריש "יש מותרות" (יבמות דף פה:): ממזרת ונתינה לישראל איכא בינייהו, למ"ד מפני שמרגילה — הא [היא] מרגלה ליה, פי': שיכול להכשיר זרעו ע"י בנו, שישא שפחה! וי"ל: דלעולם אסור נתין בשפחה, מ"מ מרגלה ליה, כיון שיכול להכשיר אפי' ע"י איסור, דהאי גברא לא איכפת ליה באיסור, דהא נסיב ממזרת או נתינה. וא"ת: ומ"ש דאסור נתין בשפחה וממזר מותר? הא נתין נמי הוי מפסולי קהל כמו ממזר, דכתיב "לא תתחתן בם"! ואור"ת: משום דממזר קדש ועומד, לפי שנולד מאיסור חמור דלא תפסי קידושין, ולכך לא מיתסר בלאו ד"לא יהיה קדש". ומיהו, בזכור ובהמה אין להתירו, אפי' למאן דמפיק להו בפרק "ד' מיתות" (סנהדרין דף נד:) מ"ולא יהיה קדש". דאין להתירו בקדישות אלא באותן שהוא בא ממנו, ומקדישות דזכור ובהמה לא בא. וא"ת: ומ"ש דגירי וחרורי מותרים בנתינה ואסורים בשפחה, ואע"ג דתרווייהו חייבי לאוין? ואור"י: דנתיני דתפסי בהו קדושין גמרינן משאר פסולי קהל, כגון עמוני ומואבי מצרי ואדומי דמותרין בקהל גרים, דלא איקרי קהל. אבל שפחה, דלא תפסי בה קדושין — לא ילפא מינייהו.

שמע

עשאן

עין משפט נר מצוה

קיז א מיי' פי"ב מהל' שכנים הל' ג סמג עשין פב טוש"ע ח"מ סי' קעד סעיף ג:

קיח ב מיי' פ"א שם הלכה ב סמג שם טוש"ע ח"מ סי' קעא סעי' ו:

קיט ג ד מיי' פ"ז מהל' עבדים הל' ז סמג עשין פו טוש"ע י"ד סי' רסז סעי' סב:

קכ ה מיי' פ"א מהל' שכנים הל' ב ועיין בהשגות סמג עשין פב טוש"ע ח"מ סי קעא סעיף ו:

דא"כ כל עשיר יסלק עני שותפו בדבר שאין בה דין חלוקה כל"ל מהר"מ:

הגהות הב"ח

(א) גמ' לשבת יצרה אלא מפני תיקון העולם כופין את רבו: (ב) רש"י ד"ה פלגי לה בקרנזיל וכו' מן הצפון לדרום נמצא כל הנהר לאחד והשני אין לו אלא חצי נגר וכו' למערב יהיה לאחד חצי הנהר וכו' ולשני אין לו אלא חצי נהר במזרחו: (ג) ד"ה ה"ג וכו' העבד יכול לקנות עצמו ולילא לחרות אבל העבד אינו יכול לומר לרבו קנה חלקי שאין דמים: (ד) תום' ד"ה אית וכו' ע"י עילוי דחזה דדדר שאין בה דין חלוקה: (ה) ד"ה לישא וכו' אור"י דלא כופין: (ו) ד"ה שנאמר וכו' לא תוהו בראה משום שמשמע מלוה רבה: (ז) ד"ה כופין וכו' ועוד אפילו מפקדא אפרו ורבו אפשר לה באחר: (ח) בא"ד ולמ"ד נמי דאפי' אין לו בנים ואשה רבו: (ט) בא"ד בלד אשת איש מכל מקום ישאנה בלא קידושין וכו' מותר בשפחה לא הוה כפינן: (י) בא"ד בפני עלמו הוא ומטעם:

[וע"ע תוס' פסחים פח: ד"ה כופין]:

עין משפט נר מצוה

קכא א מיי' פ"א מהל' שכנים הל' ד סמג עשין פב טוש"ע ח"מ סי' קעא סעיף ג:
קכב ב ג מיי' שם הל' ה טוש"ע שם סעיף י:
קכג ד ה מיי' פ"ב שם הלכה ט סמג שם טוש"ע ח"מ סי' קעג סעיף א:
קכד ו ז טוש"ע ח"מ סי' קעא סעי' יג:
קכה ח ט מיי' פ"ז מהל' ס"ת הל' טו סמג עשין כה טוש"ע י"ד סי' רעג סעיף א וסי' רפג סעיף א:

תורה אור

"קַח לְךָ עֲבָדִים וְיִרְחֲצוּ בַּמֶּרְחָץ", "קַח לְךָ זֵיתִים וּבֹא וַעֲשֵׂה בְּבֵית הַבַּד"! הָתָם נַמִּי "גּוֹד" אִיכָּא, "אֲגוֹד" לֵיכָּא. ת"ש: (א) אכָּל שֶׁאִילּוּ יֵחָלֵק וּשְׁמוֹ עָלָיו – חוֹלְקִין, אִם לָאו – מַעֲלִין אוֹתוֹ בְּדָמִים! תַּנָּאֵי הִיא; דְּתַנְיָא: "טוֹל אַתָּה שִׁיעוּר וַאֲנִי פָּחוֹת" – שׁוֹמְעִין לוֹ. רַבָּן שִׁמְעוֹן בֶּן גַּמְלִיאֵל אוֹמֵר: באֵין שׁוֹמְעִין לוֹ; הֵיכִי דָּמֵי? אִילֵימָא כִּדְתָנֵי, מַאי טַעֲמָא דְּרשב"ג? אֶלָּא לָאו חַסּוּרֵי מִחַסְּרָא וְהָכִי קָאָמַר: "טוֹל אַתָּה שִׁיעוּר וַאֲנִי פָּחוֹת" – שׁוֹמְעִין לוֹ, וְ"גּוֹד אוֹ אֲגוֹד" – נַמִּי שׁוֹמְעִין לוֹ, וְאָתָא רשב"ג לְמֵימַר: אֵין שׁוֹמְעִין לוֹ! לָא, לְעוֹלָם כִּדְקָתָנֵי. וּדְקָאָמְרַתְּ: מ"ט דְּרשב"ג? מִשּׁוּם דְּאָמַר לֵיהּ: אִי בְּדָמֵי – לֵית לִי דָּמֵי לְמֵיתַן לָךְ, (ב) גבְּמַתָּנָה – לָא נִיחָא לִי, דִּכְתִיב: °"וְשׂוֹנֵא מַתָּנֹת יִחְיֶה". א"ל אַבָּיֵי לְרַב יוֹסֵף: הָא דְּרַב יְהוּדָה – דִּשְׁמוּאֵל הִיא, דִּתְנַן: *וְכִתְבֵי הַקֹּדֶשׁ, אע"פ שֶׁשְּׁנֵיהֶם רוֹצִים – לֹא יַחֲלוֹקוּ; וַאֲמַר שְׁמוּאֵל: דלֹא שָׁנוּ אֶלָּא בִּכְרָךְ אֶחָד, אֲבָל בִּשְׁנֵי כְּרִיכוֹת – חוֹלְקִין; וְאִי ס"ד לֵית דִּינָא דְּ"גוֹד אוֹ אֲגוֹד", מַאי אִירְיָא בִּכְרָךְ אֶחָד? אֲפִי' בִּשְׁנֵי כְּרִיכִין נַמִּי! תִּרְגְּמָא רַב שַׁלְמָן: הבְּשֶׁשְּׁנֵיהֶן רוֹצִין. אֲמַר אַמֵּימָר, הִלְכְתָא: אִית דִּינָא דְּ"גוֹד אוֹ אֲגוֹד". אֲמַר לֵיהּ רַב אַשִׁי לְאַמֵּימָר: הָא דְּרַב נַחְמָן מַאי? אֲמַר לֵיהּ: *לָא שְׁמִיעָא לִי, כְּלוֹמַר לָא סְבִירָא לִי. וְלָא? וְהָא רַבִּ' בַּר חִינָּנָא וְרַב דִּימִי בַּר חִינָּנָא שְׁבַק לְהוּ אֲבוּהּ תַּרְתֵּי אַמְהָתָא, חֲדָא יָדְעָא אָפְיָא וּבַשּׁוּלֵי, וַחֲדָא יָדְעָא פִּילְכָא וְנַוּוֹלָא, וַאֲתוֹ לְקַמֵּיהּ דְּרָבָא וַאֲמַר לְהוּ: ולֵית דִּינָא דְּ"גוֹד אוֹ אֲגוֹד"! שָׁאנֵי הָתָם, זדִּלְמָר מִיבָּעֵי לֵיהּ תַּרְוַיְיהוּ וּלְמָר מִיבָּעֵי לֵיהּ תַּרְוַיְיהוּ, כִּי קָאָמַר לֵיהּ: שְׁקוֹל אַתְּ חֲדָא וַאֲנָא חֲדָא – לָאו "גּוֹד אוֹ אֲגוֹד" הוּא. (וְכִי לָא מָצֵי לְמֵימַר הָכִי?) וְהָא כִּתְבֵי הַקֹּדֶשׁ דְּתַרְוַיְיהוּ מִיבָּעֵי לְהוּ, וְאָמַר שְׁמוּאֵל: לֹא שָׁנוּ אֶלָּא בִּכְרָךְ אֶחָד, אֲבָל בִּשְׁנֵי כְּרִיכִין – חוֹלְקִין! הָא תִּרְגְּמָא רַב שַׁלְמָן: (ג) בְּשֶׁרָצוּ. ת"ר: חמַדְבִּיק אָדָם תּוֹרָה נְבִיאִים וּכְתוּבִים כְּאֶחָד, דִּבְרֵי ר"מ; ר' יְהוּדָה אוֹמֵר: תּוֹרָה בִּפְנֵי עַצְמָהּ, נְבִיאִים בִּפְנֵי עַצְמָן, וּכְתוּבִים בִּפְנֵי עַצְמָן; וַחכ"א: כָּל אֶחָד וְאֶחָד בִּפְנֵי עַצְמוֹ. וְאָמַר רַב יְהוּדָה: מַעֲשֶׂה בְּבַיְתוֹס בֶּן זוֹנִין שֶׁהָיוּ לוֹ שְׁמוֹנָה נְבִיאִים מְדוּבָּקִין כְּאֶחָד, עַל פִּי ר"א בֶּן עֲזַרְיָה; (ד) וְי"א: לֹא הָיוּ לוֹ אֶלָּא אֶחָד אֶחָד בִּפְנֵי עַצְמוֹ. אָמַר רַבִּי: מַעֲשֶׂה וְהֵבִיאוּ לְפָנֵינוּ תּוֹרָה נְבִיאִים וּכְתוּבִים מְדוּבָּקִים כְּאֶחָד, וְהִכְשַׁרְנוּם. טבֵּין חוּמָּשׁ לְחוּמָּשׁ שֶׁל תּוֹרָה – אַרְבָּעָה שִׁיטִין, *וְכֵן בֵּין כָּל נָבִיא לְנָבִיא, וּבְנָבִיא שֶׁל שְׁנֵים עָשָׂר – ג' שִׁיטִין. וּמְסַיֵּים מִלְּמַטָּה וּמַתְחִיל מִלְמַעְלָה. ת"ר: הָרוֹצֶה לְדַבֵּק תּוֹרָה נְבִיאִים וּכְתוּבִים כְּאֶחָד – מְדַבֵּק, וְעוֹשֶׂה בְּרֹאשׁוֹ כְּדֵי לָגוֹל עַמּוּד וּבְסוֹפוֹ כְּדֵי לָגוֹל הֶיקֵּף. וּמְסַיֵּים מִלְּמַטָּה וּמַתְחִיל מִלְמַעְלָה, וְאִם

(משלי טו) (רס"ל מ"ז)

רש"י

קַח לְךָ עֲבָדִים. שֶׁיְּחַמְּמוּ אוֹתוֹ, וְרוֹחֵץ בּוֹ. וְלָא מָצֵי עָנִי לְמֵימַר לֵיהּ: קְנֵה חֶלְקִי. הָכָא נַמִּי גּוֹד אִיכָּא אֲגוֹד לֵיכָּא. שֶׁאֵין הֶעָנִי אוֹמֵר לוֹ: (ה) אַף אֲנִי אֶקְנֶה חֶלְקְךָ, שֶׁאֵין לוֹ בַּמֶּה לִקְנוֹת, לְפִיכָךְ אֵין יָכוֹל לְכוֹפוֹ. וּשְׁמוֹ עָלָיו. כָּל דָּבָר שֶׁיֵּשׁ בּוֹ שִׁיעוּר, שֶׁאִם תְּחַלְּקֶנּוּ – עֲדַיִין יְהֵא עָלָיו שְׁמוֹ הָרִאשׁוֹן. מַעֲלִין אוֹתוֹ בְּדָמִים. הַיְינוּ "גּוֹד אוֹ אֲגוֹד". טוֹל אַתָּה שִׁיעוּר וַאֲנִי פָּחוֹת. כְּגוֹן חָצֵר שֶׁאֵין בָּהּ שְׁמוֹנֶה אַמּוֹת, וְאָמַר זֶה: חֲלוֹק וְטוֹל לְךָ ד' אַמּוֹת, וַאֲנִי הַמּוֹתָר. וְגוֹד אוֹ אֲגוֹד נַמִּי. שֶׁלֹּא רָצָה לִמְחוֹל כְּלוּם, אֶלָּא: קְנֵה חֶלְקִי אוֹ אֶקְנֶה חֶלְקְךָ. הָא דְּרַב יְהוּדָה. דְּאָמַר: "גּוֹד אוֹ אֲגוֹד" – מִשְּׁמֵיהּ דְּרַבֵּיהּ קַבְּלָהּ. בִּכְרָךְ אֶחָד. כָּל סִפְרֵיהֶן עֲשׂוּיִין בְּגִלָּיוֹן, וְאִם יְבִיאֵהוּ לְבֵ"ד לְחַלְּקוֹ – בִּזָּיוֹן הוּא. אֲבָל בִּשְׁתֵּי כְּרִיכוֹת. כְּגוֹן תּוֹרָה בִּכְרָךְ אֶחָד, וּנְבִיאִים בִּכְרָךְ אֶחָד. חוֹלְקִין. קס"ד דַּאֲפִילּוּ אֵין שְׁנֵיהֶם רוֹצִים. וְע"כ אֵין דְּמֵיהֶן שָׁוִין. וְאִי לֵית דִּינָא דְּ"גוֹד אוֹ אֲגוֹד" הֵיאָךְ הוּא כּוֹפֵיהוּ? זֶה יֹאמַר: אֲנִי לֹא אֶתֵּן לְךָ עוֹדֶף הַדָּמִים, וְגַם לֹא אֶתֵּן לְךָ הַיָּפֶה שֶׁאֲקַבֵּל מִמְּךָ דָּמִים! וְלָא גָּרְסִי' "תַּרְוַיְיהוּ צְרִיכִין לְהַאי". בְּשֶׁשְּׁנֵיהֶם רוֹצִים. הָא דִּשְׁמוּאֵל – אַ"שְׁנֵיהֶם רוֹצִים" דְּמַתְנִיתִין קָאֵי, דְּקָתָנֵי: לֹא יַחֲלוֹקוּ, וְאָמַר שְׁמוּאֵל: בִּשְׁתֵּי כְּרִיכוֹת, אִם שְׁנֵיהֶם רוֹצִים – יַחֲלוֹקוּ. פִּילְכָא וְנַוּוֹלָא. לִטְווֹת וְלֶאֱרוֹג. ל"א: בִּיסְתַּרְקֵי – תַּכְשִׁיטֵי סַפְסָלִים, שֶׁקּוֹרִין טפי"ד. לֵית דִּינָא דְּגוֹד אוֹ אֲגוֹד. לְכוֹפוֹ לָתֵת דְּמֵי הָעוֹדְפִים בַּיָּפָה, וְלֹא לִמְכּוֹר חֶלְקוֹ. לָאו גּוֹד אוֹ אֲגוֹד הוּא. אִי לֹא אָמַר לֵיהּ: אוֹ קַח שְׁתֵּיהֶם אוֹ אֶקַּח שְׁתֵּיהֶם, דְּכָל אַחַת אֵין בָּהּ כְּדֵי לְאֶחָד. אֲבָל בְּב' כְּרִיכוֹת חוֹלְקִין. וְקס"ד: בְּע"כ שֶׁל אֶחָד מֵהֶן. אַלְמָא, כִּי אָמַר לֵיהּ: שְׁקוֹל חֲדָא וְגוֹד דְּמֵי הַיְּתֵירִים, אוֹ אֲגוֹד – כָּיְיפִינַן לֵיהּ! כָּל אֶחָד וְאֶחָד בִּפְנֵי עַצְמוֹ. כָּל סֵפֶר וְסֵפֶר שֶׁל נְבִיאִים וְשֶׁל כְּתוּבִים צָרִיךְ לִהְיוֹת כָּרֵךְ לְעַצְמוֹ. בְּבַיְתוֹס שְׁמוֹנָה נְבִיאִים. כָּל סִפְרֵי נְבִיאִים שְׁמוֹנָה הֵן. ה"ג: וְכֵן בֵּין כָּל נָבִיא וְנָבִיא וּבְנָבִיא שֶׁל שְׁנֵים עָשָׂר שָׁלֹשׁ שִׁיטִין וּמְסַיֵּים מִלְּמַטָּה וּמַתְחִיל מִלְמַעְלָה. אִם נִזְדַּמֵּן לוֹ סִיּוּם הַסֵּפֶר מִלְּמַטָּה, בְּסוֹף הַדַּף – מַתְחִיל סִפְרוֹ הָאַחֵר בְּרֹאשׁ הַדַּף, וְאֵינוֹ צָרִיךְ לְהַנִּיחַ רֵיוַח חָלָק בֵּינֵיהֶם. כְּדֵי לָגוֹל עַמּוּד. מַנִּיחַ קְלַף חָלָק לִגְלוֹל עַל גַּבֵּי עַמּוּד שֶׁל עֵץ שֶׁהַסֵּפֶר נִגְלָל עָלָיו. וְסוֹפוֹ כְּדֵי לָגוֹל הֶיקֵּף. בְּסוֹפוֹ מַנִּיחַ חֵלֶק גָּדוֹל כְּדֵי לָגוֹל בּוֹ כָּל הֶקֵּיפוֹ. שֶׁאֵין עוֹשֶׂה שְׁנֵי עַמּוּדִים לְגוֹלְלוֹ לְאֶמְצָעוֹ כְּמוֹ שֶׁאָנוּ עוֹשִׂין לְסֵפֶר תּוֹרָה, אֶלָּא גּוֹלְלוֹ מִתְּחִלָּתוֹ לְסוֹפוֹ, וְכוֹרֵךְ הַחֵלֶק עַל כָּל הַהֶיקֵּף. וְאִם

[לעיל יא.] [עירובין קב: וש"נ]

תוספות

(לעיל) **שמע** מינה דלית דינא דגוד או אגוד. וא"ת: שאני הכא, שאין העבד נותן לו דמים מיד, אלא כותב לו שטר על דמיו! וי"ל: דמשמע משום דלא יבטל הוא דכופין, הא לאו הכי אין כופין בכל ענין, אפי' יתן דמים. *__אם__ עשאן לשכר כו'. לאו דוקא עשאן לשכר, דהוא הדין אפילו עשאן לעצמו, אלא שמוצא להשכיר.

ואי ס"ד לית דינא דגוד או אגוד אפי' בשתי כריכות כו'. השתא ס"ד דחולקין כיון שאחד רוצה לחלוק, וב' כריכות דומיא דכרך אחד, שאין כתוב באחד מה שכתוב באחר, כגון יהושע ושמואל. ואמאי חולקין בע"כ? והא אינם שוין! אלא ודאי אית דינא ד"גוד או אגוד". וא"ת: אפילו אית דינא ד"גוד או אגוד", אמאי חולקין? כיון שכתוב בזה מה שאין בזה, ותרוייהו צריכי להאי ולהאי! וי"ל: דהוי מצי למימר "וליטעמיך". ולא גרס הכא מה שכתוב במיעוט ספרים: "ואי ס"ד לית ליה דינא דגוד או אגוד כי היכי דתרוייהו צריכי להאי תרוייהו צריכי להאי". דהא כל שכן דאי לא צריכי תרוייהו להאי ולהאי — פריך טפי שפיר: אי לית ליה דינא דגוד או אגוד אמאי חולקין? **מדביק** אדם תורה נביאים וכתובים כאחד. אע"פ שא"א שלא יתן נביאים וכתובים על גבי תורה, ובמגילה בפ"ב (דף כז.) משמע דאסור להניח — ה"מ בשתי כריכות, אבל כשהן מדובקין יחד — אינו גנאי. **רבי** יהודה אומר תורה בפני עצמה. לא מפני שאסור להניח זה על גב זה מצריך שיהא כל אחד בפני עצמו. דלא אשכחן שיהא אסור להניח אלא נביאים וכתובים על גבי תורה, אבל נביאים על גבי כתובים או איפכא — לא. אלא היינו טעמא: שלא יראה הכל כמו תורה או הכל נביאים. כי היכי דאמרי חכמים בתר הכי דבעו שיהא כל נביא ונביא בפני עצמו, וע"כ טעמא שלא יהא נראה הכל כמו נביא אחד. כן נראה לרשב"א. **ומסיים** מלמטה ומתחיל מלמעל'. פי' בקונטרס: ואינו צריך להניח ד' שיטין. ונראה לר"י: דבין חומש לחומש של תורה צריך להניח. ואנביאים דוקא קאמר דאין צריך, כדמפרש טעמא לקמן, שאם בא לחתוך — חותך, אבל בין חומש לחומש של תורה — לא. מידי דהוי אפרשה פתוחה, שאם היה מסיים מלמטה היה צריך להניח שיטה אחת — הכא נמי, דין הוא להניח בסוף כל חומש פרשה של ד' שיטין. ורילב"א מפרש: ומסיים מלמטה ומתחיל מלמעלה — ולעולם מניח ד' שיטין. ודוקא בין נביא לנביא, אבל בין חומש לחומש — לא יסיים מלמטה ומתחיל מלמעלה, אפי' בהנחת ד' שיטין. כדאמר בירושלמי בפ"ק דמגילה: וצריך שיהא גומר באמצע הדף ומתחיל באמצעיתו, ובנביא מסיים בסופו ומתחיל בראשו כו'. ונראה לי הטעם דאין לו לסיים בסוף הדף אפי' יניח ארבעה שיטין — משום שמא יבוא לחתוך. אבל בין נביא לנביא, שאם בא לחתוך חותך — מסיים מלמטה. **ועושה** בראשו כדי לגול עמוד ובסופו כדי היקף. כן כתוב בכל הספרים. וקשה לר"י, דתניא במס' סופרים: כל הספרים נגללין לתחלתן, ולקמן אמר נמי: ספר עזרה לתחלתו הוא נגלל. ומה שפי' הקונט': מתחלתו לסופו — אין הלשון משמע כן. וגבי מזוזה אמרינן נמי שכורכין אותה מ"אחד" כלפי "שמע", דהיינו לתחלתה. והדיא גרסי' בירושלמי בפ"ק דמגילה: עושה אדם עמוד לספר תורה בסופו. ע"כ נראה לר"י דגר': ועושה בראשו כדי היקף, ובסופו כדי לגול עמוד. ולרשב"א נראה לקיים גירסת הספרים. והכא שאני, דאיירי במדביק תורה נביאים וכתובים, ואז אין נכון לעשות עמוד בסופו כמו בעלמא, שגנאי הוא שתהא תורה נכרכת סביב נביאים וכתובים, *ונראה כאילו נעשית להם שומר מלכלוך. לכך עושה כאן עמוד בראשו, כדי שתהא תורה מבפנים ונביאים וכתובים מבחוץ. ולקמן דמשני: לגלדין קתני — לא גרס "תחלת הספר כדי לגול עמוד וסופו כדי לגול היקף", דהתם לא איירי במדביק תורה נביאים וכתובים, ואית לן למימר איפכא. (ו) וברוב ספרים לא גרס אלא: לגלדין קתני, ותו לא. ועוד אומר רשב"א: דאפי' לספרים דגרסי לה, לא קשיא כולי האי, דניחא ליה לשנויי דומיא דהך ברייתא דקאי עלה.

[ע' מג"א סי' כח ס"ק ד]

רבינו גרשום

עשאן אביהן לשכר שהיה רגיל להשכירן כדי שיהא משתכר בו הכי נמי ישכירום ויחלוקו השכר לאמצע: ואם לאו אינו יכול לומר עני לעשיר גוד והב לי דמי חלקי מן מרחץ ובית הבד דאין לי במה לישתמש בו כלום או תן לי דמים ממה שאתה משתמש בו יותר ממני דיכול העשיר לחזור ולומר לעני כו'. ומן שמיא קנסוהו לאותו עני ואין לו על העשיר כלום אלמא דלית דינא דגוד או אגוד. הכא נמי אגוד ליכא דאין לעני במה לפדות אבל בעלמא אמרינן אית דינא דגוד או אגוד: כל שאילו יחלק כל הני דאמרינן במתני' ואם לאו מעלי' אותו בדמים דהיינו גוד או אגוד אלמא אית דינא דגוד או אגוד וקשיא לרב נחמן. תנאי היא דתניא כו' דהיכא דיש לשותפין חצר של ז' אמות לחלוק דלאו ראויה לחלוקה אלא אם כן יש בה ח' אמות ואמר אחד לחבירו נחלוק חצר זה וחבירו מעכב ואמר ליה האי אמאי מעכבת טול אתה שיעור דין חלוקה הד' אמות ואני אטול פחות הג' אמות שומעין לו דאין יכול לעכב עליו הואיל דנותן לו שיעור חלוקה. אי נימ' כדקתני כלומר דליכא שום דברים בהדיהו אלא כדקתני. וגוד או אגוד נמי כלומר דהכי אמר ליה ברור לך אחד מב' דברים הללו או טול אתה שיעור ואני פחות או גוד או אגוד ואתא רשב"ג למימר מזה שומעין לו כשאמר לו טול אתה השיעור אבל מגוד או אגוד יכול לעכב עליו דקסבר דלית דינא דגוד או אגוד אלמא תנאי היא: ודקאמרת מאי טעמא דרשב"ג דבטול אתה שיעור נמי אין שומעין דמצי מעכב אידך משום דאמר ליה אותה אמה שאתה רוצה ליתן לי יותר איני מבקש אותה לא בדמים שאין לי דמים לקנותה וגם במתנה איני מבקשה ולא מצית מוקמת לה בתנאי: הא דר' יהודה דאמר לעיל אית דינא דגוד או אגוד דשמואל היא כלומר מינה דשמואל קבלה ולא מינה דרב דרב יהודה הוה תלמיד דרב ותלמיד דשמואל והא מילתא מינה דשמואל למדה ולא מינה דרב: אלא בכרך אחד היו נכרכין בראשית ואלה שמות משום הכי אין חולקין משום בזיון והיינו כרך שהיו רגילין לכתוב ספריהן כעין ספר תורה והפטרות שאנו כותבין ולהכי קרי כרך שכרוך כעין מגילה אבל בשתי כריכות בראשית בכרך אחד ואלה שמות בכרך אחד חולקין דליכא בזיון דספר ואי ס"ד דלגבי חצר היכא דליכא ד' לזה וד' לזה לית דינא דגוד או אגוד אלא תרווייהו ישתמשו ביה מאי אריא בכרך אחד דאין חולקין אפי' בב' כריכות נמי אין חולקין דשתיהן צריכי לתרווייהו כריכות והוי נמי שאין בחד כרך כדי לזה ולא יחלקו אפי' בב' כריכות אלא ליקום בשותפות אלא ש"מ מדחולקין להם משום דמצי למימר ליה חבריה או חלוק או גוד עלוי דמים ואסב תרווייהו או איגוד עליך ותיסב תרווייהו. תירגמא רב שלמן מהא ליכא למשמע מינה הא דינא דאגוד ודקא קשיא לך א"כ אפילו שתי כריכות אמאי חולקין משום כשרצו שניהן לחלוק ובשתי כריכות מצי לחלוק אבל בכרך אחד לא משום בזיון אבל אי חד מעכב וחד רוצה לא מצי למימר ליה גוד או אגוד. הא דרב נחמן מאי. דאמר לית דינא דגוד. מיפא פת. ובשולי מיני תבשיל. ביסתרקי בל"ע שפיע ואתו לקמיה דרבא אחד היה רוצה בשותפות השפחות ואחד לא היה רוצה דלא היה רוצה גוד לעצמך הני תרתי שפחות או אנא איגוד ואמר להו הלכה למעשה לית דינא דגוד או אגוד. דליכא דין חלוקה בהני שפחות דכל חד מניהו צריך לעבודת של הני תרתי שפחות אלא כדקיימי מעיקרא בשותפות לוקמו אלמא לית דינא דגוד כרב נחמן: לעולם אית דינא דגוד ושאני התם גבי הני שפחות לית דינא דגוד אלא לוקמי בשותפות משום דכל חד וחד צריך לעבודת דתרווייהו וכי אמר ליה חד לחבריה שקול את חדא ואנא חדא ואי לא גוד או איגוד לא מצי למימר הכי דמצי למימר ליה הכא לא גוד איכא ולא איגוד איכא דאת לא אפשר לך בלא תרווייהו ואנא לא אפשר לי בלא תרווייהו אבל בעלמא דאפשר בחלוקה אי מעכב חד מצי למימר אידך גוד או איגוד. והא כתבי הקדש דבשתי כריכות דהני תרי כריכות צריכי לכל חד ואפי' א) אוקמינן לה דלעולם אליבא דשמואל דסבר כר' יהודה דאית דינא דגוד כדדייקינן לעיל. ומתרגם כמתרגמינן דלעולם לית דינא דגוד ושאני הכא אמאי חולקין שתי כריכות כגון ששניהם רוצין: מדביק אדם כו' בחד כרך. תורה בפני עצמה משום דאי מדביקן אהדדי כי חזי הדפין של נביאים נמצא שעושין התורה שימוש לנביאים. כל אחד ואחד בפני עצמו. והכשרנום. ובלבד שיניח בין חומש לחומש כגון בין סיום בראשית לאלה שמות. של שנים עשר של ספר תרי עשר. ומסיים מלמטה כלומר כשיגיע לסיום ספרו מסיימו מלמטה מאותו דף ומתחיל הספר אחר מלמעלה מדף אחר שאע"פ שאין בסיום אותו ספר כדי השלמת כל אותו דף אפי' הכי מניח אותו דף

א) ואפילו הכי חלקין לה אליבא דשמואל דסבר כרב יהודה וכו'

הגהות הב"ח

(א) גמ' ת"ש זה הכלל כל שאילו יחלק: (ב) שם למיתן לך ואי במתנה: (ג) שם תרגמא רב שלמן בששניהם רוצים וכו': (ד) שם ר"א בן עזריה וחכמים אומרים לא היו לו אלא אחד: (ה) רש"י ד"ה הכא נמי וכו' (אף) תז"מ ונ"ב ס"א לו: (ו) תוס' ד"ה ועושה וכו' למימר איפכא כדי היקף ובסופו כדי לגול עמוד וכרוב ספרים:

[גיר' הרמב"ם והטור וכ"פ בש"ע סי' רפג סעיף א ובין כל נביא ונביא שלשה שיטין וכן בין כל נביא ונביא של תרי עשר וגם הוא מכוון במס' סופרים פ"ב ה"ד אבל ברב אלפס איתא כמו הכא]

תורה אור

וְאִם בָּא לַחְתּוֹךְ — חוֹתֵךְ. מַאי קָאָמַר? הָכִי קָאָמַר: [א]שֶׁאִם בָּא לַחְתּוֹךְ — חוֹתֵךְ. וּרְמִינְהִי: [ב]תְּחִלַּת סֵפֶר וְסוֹפוֹ — כְּדֵי לָגוֹל; כְּדֵי לָגוֹל מַאי? אִי כְּדֵי לָגוֹל עַמּוּד — קַשְׁיָא הֶקֵּף, אִי כְּדֵי לָגוֹל הֶקֵּף — קַשְׁיָ' עַמּוּד! א"ר נַחְמָן בַּר יִצְחָק: לִצְדָדִין קָתָנֵי. רַב אַשִׁי אָמַר: [ג]כִּי תַּנְיָא הַהִיא — בְּסֵפֶר תּוֹרָה; כִּדְתַנְיָא: [ד]כָּל הַסְּפָרִים נִגְלָלִים מִתְּחִלָּתָן לְסוֹפָן, וְס"ת נִגְלָל לְאֶמְצָעִיתוֹ, וְעוֹשֶׂה לוֹ עַמּוּד אֵילָךְ וְאֵילָךְ. א"ר אֱלִיעֶזֶר בר' צָדוֹק: כָּךְ הָיוּ כּוֹתְבֵי סְפָרִים שֶׁבִּירוּשָׁלַיִם עוֹשִׂין (א) סִפְרֵיהֶם. ת"ר: [ה]אֵין עוֹשִׂין סֵפֶר תּוֹרָה לֹא אָרְכּוֹ יוֹתֵר עַל הֶקֵּיפוֹ וְלֹא הֶקֵּיפוֹ יוֹתֵר עַל אָרְכּוֹ. שָׁאֲלוּ אֶת רַבִּי: שִׁיעוּר ס"ת בְּכַמָּה? אָמַר לָהֶן: [ו]בִּגְוִיל — שִׁשָּׁה. [ז]בִּקְלַף בְּכַמָּה? אֵינִי יוֹדֵעַ. רַב הוּנָא כְּתַב שִׁבְעִין סִפְרֵי דְּאוֹרַיְיתָא, וְלָא אִיתְרְמֵי לֵיהּ אֶלָּא חַד. רַב אַחָא בַּר יַעֲקֹב כְּתַב חַד אַמַּשְׁכֵיהּ דְּעִיגְלֵי וְאִיתְרְמֵי לֵיהּ, [א]יְהַבוּ בֵּיהּ רַבָּנַן עֵינַיְיהוּ וְנָח נַפְשֵׁיהּ. אֲמַרוּ לֵיהּ רַבָּנַן לְרַב הַמְנוּנָא: כְּתַב רַבִּי אַמִי ד' מֵאָה סִפְרֵי תוֹרָה. אֲמַר לְהוּ: דִּילְמָא °"תּוֹרָה צִוָּה לָנוּ מֹשֶׁה" כְּתַב. (דברים לג) א"ל רָבָא לְר' זֵירָא: נְטַע ר' יַנַּאי אַרְבַּע מֵאָה כַּרְמֵי. א"ל: דִּילְמָא שְׁתַּיִם כְּנֶגֶד שְׁתַּיִם וְאַחַת יוֹצֵא זָנָב. מֵיתִיבֵי: אָרוֹן שֶׁעָשָׂה מֹשֶׁה, אַמָּתַיִם וָחֵצִי אָרְכּוֹ וְאַמָּה וָחֵצִי רָחְבּוֹ וְאַמָּה וָחֵצִי קוֹמָתוֹ, בְּאַמָּה בַּת שִׁשָּׁה טְפָחִים. [ב]וְהַלּוּחוֹת, אָרְכָּן שִׁשָּׁה וְרָחְבָּן שִׁשָּׁה וְעָבְיָין שְׁלֹשָׁה, מוּנָּחוֹת כְּנֶגֶד אָרְכּוֹ שֶׁל אָרוֹן. כַּמָּה לוּחוֹת אוֹכְלוֹת בָּאָרוֹן? שְׁנֵים עָשָׂר טְפָחִים, נִשְׁתַּיְּירוּ שָׁם שְׁלֹשָׁה טְפָחִים; צֵא מֵהֶן טֶפַח, חֶצְיוֹ לְכוֹתֶל זֶה וְחֶצְיוֹ לְכוֹתֶל זֶה — נִשְׁתַּיְּירוּ שָׁם שְׁנֵי טְפָחִים שֶׁבָּהֶן סֵפֶר תּוֹרָה מוּנָּח, שֶׁנֶּאֱמַ': °"אֵין בָּאָרוֹן רַק שְׁנֵי לוּחוֹת הָאֲבָנִים אֲשֶׁר הִנִּיחַ שָׁם מֹשֶׁה" (מלכים א ח) [וגו'] מַאי "אֵין בָּאָרוֹן רַק"? מִיעוּט אַחַר מִיעוּט, [ג]וְאֵין מִיעוּט אַחַר מִיעוּט אֶלָּא לְרַבּוֹת ס"ת שֶׁמּוּנָּח בָּאָרוֹן. פִּירְנַסְתָּ אָרוֹן לְאָרְכּוֹ, צֵא וּפַרְנֵס אָרוֹן לְרָחְבּוֹ: כַּמָּה לוּחוֹת אוֹכְלוֹת בָּאָרוֹן? שִׁשָּׁה טְפָחִים, נִשְׁתַּיְּירוּ שָׁם שְׁלֹשָׁה טְפָחִים; צֵא מֵהֶן טֶפַח, חֶצְיוֹ לְכוֹתֶל זֶה וְחֶצְיוֹ לְכוֹתֶל זֶה — נִשְׁתַּיְּירוּ שָׁם שְׁנֵי טְפָחִים, שֶׁלֹּא יְהֵא סֵפֶר תּוֹרָה נִכְנָס וְיוֹצֵא כְּשֶׁהוּא דָּחוּק, דִּבְרֵי ר"מ. ר' יְהוּדָה אוֹמֵר: בְּאַמָּה בַּת חֲמִשָּׁה טְפָחִים. וְהַלּוּחוֹת, אָרְכָּן שִׁשָּׁה וְרָחְבָּן שִׁשָּׁה וְעָבְיָין שְׁלֹשָׁה, מוּנָּחוֹת בְּאוֹרְכּוֹ שֶׁל אָרוֹן. כַּמָּה לוּחוֹת אוֹכְלוֹת בָּאָרוֹן? שְׁנֵים עָשָׂר טְפָחִים; נִשְׁתַּיֵּיר שָׁם חֲצִי טֶפַח, אֶצְבַּע לְכוֹתֶל זֶה וְאֶצְבַּע לְכוֹתֶל זֶה. פִּירְנַסְתָּ אָרוֹן לְאָרְכּוֹ, צֵא וּפַרְנֵס אָרוֹן לְרָחְבּוֹ: כַּמָּה לוּחוֹת [ד]אוֹגְדוֹת בָּאָרוֹן? שִׁשָּׁה טְפָחִים, נִשְׁתַּיֵּיר שָׁם טֶפַח וּמֶחֱצָה; צֵא מֵהֶן חֲצִי טֶפַח, אֶצְבַּע (ב) וּמֶחֱצָה לְכוֹתֶל זֶה וְאֶצְבַּע וּמֶחֱצָה לְכוֹתֶל זֶה — נִשְׁתַּיֵּיר שָׁם טֶפַח שֶׁבּוֹ עַמּוּדִין עוֹמְדִין, שֶׁנֶּאֱמַר: °"אַפִּרְיוֹן עָשָׂה לוֹ הַמֶּלֶךְ שְׁלֹמֹה מֵעֲצֵי הַלְּבָנוֹן. עַמּוּדָיו עָשָׂה כֶסֶף רְפִידָתוֹ זָהָב מֶרְכָּבוֹ אַרְגָּמָן" וגו'; (שיר ג) (ג) וְאַרְגָּז שֶׁשִּׁיגְּרוּ בּוֹ פְּלִשְׁתִּים דּוֹרוֹן לֵאלֹהֵי יִשְׂרָאֵל מוּנָּח מִצִּדּוֹ, שֶׁנֶּאֱמַר: °"וְאֵת כְּלֵי הַזָּהָב אֲשֶׁר הֲשֵׁבוֹתֶם לוֹ אָשָׁם תָּשִׂימוּ בָאַרְגַּז מִצִּדּוֹ וְשִׁלַּחְתֶּם אוֹתוֹ וְהָלָךְ"; (שמואל א ו) וְעָלָיו ס"ת מוּנָּח, שֶׁנֶּאֱמַר: °"לָקוֹחַ אֵת סֵפֶר הַתּוֹרָה הַזֶּה וְשַׂמְתֶּם אוֹתוֹ מִצַּד אֲרוֹן בְּרִית ה'", (דברים לא) מִצַּד (ד) הוּא מוּנָּח וְלֹא בְתוֹכוֹ. וּמָה אֲנִי מְקַיֵּים "אֵין בָּאָרוֹן רַק"? לְרַבּוֹת

שִׁבְרֵי

רש"י

ואם בא לחתוך חותך מאי קאמר. מאי למימרא? הכל מודים דאם כל אחד ואחד בפני עצמו טפי עדיף. הכי קאמר. ומתחיל מלמעלה, ולא יניח חלק. שהרי אם בא לחתוך – חותך, ונמצא זה ראש הכרך, וגנאי הוא לו להיות דף זה משונה מחבירו על חנם. כדי לגול. קס"ד חד שיעורא יהיב ליה לתחילתו וסופו. לספריהן. לספרי תורה. לא ארכו יותר על הקיפו. צריך לצמצם הכתב לפי עובי הקלפי', לכשיגמור יהא חוט המקיף את עוביו כמדת ארכו. שיעור ספר תורה בכמה. ארכו מיבעיא להו. בגויל. שהוא עב והקיפו גדול – צריך ששה טפחים, זו היא מדה להיות נגמר בששה טפחים היקף בכתב בינוני. ולא איתרמי ליה. ארכו כהקיפו. איתרמי ליה. ארכו כהקיפו. דילמא תורה צוה לנו משה מורשה כתב. ארבע מאות פעמים. אבל ארבע מאה (ד) ספרים – אין פנאי לאדם אחד לכתוב. שתים כנגד שתים. שתי גפנים כנגד שתים וא' יוצא זנב, בכך קרוי כרם לגבי לחזור עליו מעורכי המלחמה, במסכת סוטה (דף מג.). באמה בת ששה טפחים. ר"מ לטעמיה, דאמר (סוכה ה:): כל האמות היו בינוניות. לארכו של ארון. זו אצל זו. אוכלות. תופסות. כך לשון המשנה (מדות פ"ג מ"א): אוכל בדרום אמה אחת, גבי יסוד המזבח. ואף בלשון מקרא: "כי יוכלו אפיקים מהנה" בספר יחזקאל (מז). צא מהם טפח. לעובי הכתלים, שהרי מבחוץ נמדד אמתי' וחצי ארכו. ס"ת. שכתב משה, כמו שנאמר: "ויכתוב משה את ה) (התורה)" וגו' (דברים לא). אין [מיעוט אחר מיעוט].ו) "אך" ו"רק" שני מיעוטין הן. שבהן ס"ת מונח. ארכו לרחבו של ארון. פירנסת ארון לארכו. כלומר, מלאת כל חללו לארכו, ופירשת צרכי מדתו. ששה טפחים. במדת רחבו. כדי שלא יהא ס"ת כו'. כלומר, לא היה צריך להיות רחבו כל כך אלא בשביל ס"ת המונח אורכו לרוחב הארון, שלא יהא נכנס ויוצא בדוחק. ר"י אומר. מדת הארון באמה של ה' טפחים היתה. רבי יהודה לטעמיה, דקאמר: אמת כלים באמה בת חמשה. מונחות לארכו של ארון. מוטלות על רוחבן, ולא על חודן. אצבע לכותל זה. שהטפח ארבע אצבעות ולמאן דגריס אצבע ומחצה – באצבע קטנה קאמר, שהטפח ד' בגודל, וחמש באצבע, ושש בקטנה. שבו עמודים עומדים. ב' עמודי כסף, כמין עמודי ספר תורה שוכבים לארכו, והלוחות ביניהן, שנאמר: "עמודיו עשה כסף". מונח שם בצדו. של ארון. ועליו ס"ת מונח. ולקמיה פריך: מעיקרא היכי הוה מונח?

שברי

תוספות

שאם בא לחתוך חותך. תימה לרשב"א: הא אמר לעיל: בשתי כריכות חולקין, ופ"ה: כגון תורה בכרך אחד, ונביאים בכרך א'. משמע: אבל תורה ונביאים בכרך א' — אין חולקין, אפי' שניהן רוצים. וא"כ היכי אמר הכא דחותך? ויש לומר: דלא הוי בזיון הספר אלא כשחותך מחמת מחלוקה. בגויל ששה טפחים בקלף בכמה. גויל הוא עור שלא ניתקן כלל, אלא שהשירו את השער וכותבין בו במקום שער. ולהכי קרי ליה גויל — שאינו מתוקן, כדאמר לעיל (דף ג.): גויל — אבני דלא משפיין. ופעמים חותכין אותו לשנים דרך עוביו, ואותו שכלפי שער קרוי קלף, ואותו שלצד בשר קרוי דוכסוסטוס. ולשון דוכסוסטוס הוי פירושו: מקום בשר, דבלשון *מדי קורין לבשר "סוסטוס", ו"דוך" היינו מקום, כמו: *דוך פלוני. וכותבין על הקלף לצד בשר, כדאמר בפ' "המוציא" (שבת דף עט:), ועל דוכסוסטוס לצד שער. ובשניהם במקום חתך, דשם הוא טוב לכתוב. ושלנו דין קלף יש להם ולא דין דוכסוסטוס, ולכך כותבין עליהם תפילין, שאין כשרים על דוכסוסטוס אלא על הקלף, כדאמר ב"המוציא יין" (שם). דילמא תורה צוה. ואומר ר"ת: דאותו פסוק קרוי תורה, כדאמר בפ' ג' דסוכה (דף מב.): קטן היודע לדבר, אביו מלמדו תורה. מאי תורה — "תורה צוה לנו משה". שלא יהא ספר תורה יוצא ונכנס כשהוא דחוק. וא"ת: והלא לא היו מוציאין אותו מן הארון, דהא אסור ליכנס בבית קדש הקדשים, וביום הכפורים לא אשכחן בסדר יומא שהיה מוציאו! וי"ל: דלצורך, כדי לתקן — שרי ליכנס בבית קדש הקדשים, כדאמרינן בעירובין (דף קה.). וה"נ יכולין ליכנס שם כדי לתקן ספר תורה כדי שלא יתעפש ויתקלקל. וגם משחרב משכן שילה עד שבנה שלמה בית המקדש היו יכולין להוציאו מן הארון ולעיין בו. אצבע ומחצה לכותל זה. נראה לר"ת דלא גרס "ומחצה", אלא: אצבע לכותל זה. דאי גרס "ומחצה" — תיקשי: שנים עשר (ו) היכי יתבי? כדפריך לקמן. אלא אצבע גרס, וזוטרתי, דהויין ששה בטפח. שבהן עמודים עומדין. נראה לר"ת דסימן להעמדת ישראל היה, ולא עשאום של זהב שלא להזכיר מעשה העגל, דאין קטיגור נעשה סניגור. וכן אמרינן [בר"ה] (דף כו.) דמשום הכי לא היה כהן משמש לפני ולפנים ביוה"כ בבגדי זהב, משום דאין קטיגור נעשה סניגור. והתם פריך: והא הוה ארון, שהיה של זהב, והיה לפנים! ומשני: מכפר קאמרי'. והני עמודים נמי היו כמו מכפר, שהם עשוים סימן להעמדת ישראל. והוא שיסד הפייט: *תבנית אות יוסף עמודיו עשה כסף. בשביל תבנית אות יוסף — סימן של יוסף, דהיינו עגל, דיוסף נקרא שור, שנאמר (דברים לג): "בכור שורו הדר לו" — לכך עמודיו עשה כסף ולא זהב, שלא להזכיר במעשה העגל.

תרי

[בשבת עט: ד"ה קלף כתבו דבלשון יון]

[ברכות יח:]

ביום ראשון דפסח

רבינו גרשום

דף פנוי מלמטה ומתחיל באחר מלמעלה שאם באו לחלוק שיכולין לחתוך ולחלק יפה כבשתי כריכות. שמונה נביאים ח' ספרים של נביאים. ועושה בראשו של ספר תורה חלק כשיעור לגול עמוד בתחלתו והאי תחלה הוי סוף הספר לפי כי בסוף מתחילין לגלגל המגילה ומגלגל והולך עד ראש לפי שכל ספריהם נכתבין כעין מגילה ולא בקונטרסים (והם) והכי נמי מניח מן הקלף חלק בסוף כל הכרך שהוא תחלת הספר כשיעור שיכול לגול את כל ההיקף על אותו חלק כדי שיהא משמש הקלף פנוי לכתבי הקדש: קשיא עמוד דלעיל קתני בראשו כדי לגול עמוד והכא קתני תחלת הספר וסופו כדי לגול עמוד. האי כדי לגול דברייתא נמי לצדדין קתני כדאמרן דתחלה כדי לגול עמוד ובסוף כדי לגול היקף רב אשי אמר לעולם לא קתני לצדדין אלא תחלתו וסופו כדי לגול עמוד ובספר תורה מיירי דלאמצעיתו נגלל על ב' עמודים אבל שאר ספרים היו נגללין הכל על עמוד אחד ואמטו להכי צריך להניח כדי היקף כדאמרן. ולא אורכו יותר על הקיפו שכשמושכין אותו בחוט של משיחה לאורכו של דף ומקיפין מן אותו חוט היקף הספר תורה שיהא שוים במדה. בגויל ו' טפחים אורך הדף שכך למד מגויל. אבל מן קלף לא אמר לפיכך אמר איני יודע. ולא איתרמי ליה שיהא אורכו שוה להקיפו. יהבי ביה עינייהו קינאו (אדון) בו שכך כיון. תורה צוה לנו כתב דדומה עליו גוזמא ורמינהו מקשה על מאי דאמר שיהא ס"ת הקיפו כאורכו. וארון שעשה משה היה דומה כמין תיבה שאין לה כיסוי שבכפרת היה מכוסה. באמת בת ו' טפחים. ואמתים וחצי אורכו עולין לט"ו טפחי': וכמה לוחות אוגדות בארון. כלומר כמה מחזיקות בארון י"ב טפחי' שהיו מונחין הלוחות זו בצד זו. ואין ורק תרי מיעוטי לרבות ספר תורה שמונח בארון באותן ב' טפח' שנשתיירו מאורך הארון והיה אורכו של ספר תורה כרוחבן של לוחות ו' טפחים נשתיירו ב' טפחים פנוי טפח לצד כותל זה וטפח לצד כותל זה שכל אותן ב' טפחים משימין ידיהן אחת מיכן ואחת מיכן ומגביהין ספר תורה בריוח ומוציאין אותו לחוץ כדי שלא יהא נכנס ויוצא בדוחק: שבו באותו טפח עמודיו של ארון עומדין שנאמר אפריון עשה לו זה ארון. המלך שלמה. המלך שהשלום שלו וכתב עמודיו עשה כסף של ארון. בצידו מבחוץ.

שברי

מסורת הש"ס

א) [ברכות נח:] ב) [נדרים לח.] ג) [יומא מג. וש"נ] ד) נ"א אוכלות: ה) [נ"ל הבירה:] ו) [אין ורק]:

עין משפט נר מצוה

קכו א מיי' פ"ז מהל' ס"ת הל' טו סמג עשין כה (טוש"ע שם):

קכז ב ג מיי' פ"ט מהל' ס"ת הלכה ב סמג עשין כה טוש"ע י"ד סי' רעג סעיף א:

קכח ד מיי' שם וסמג שם טוש"ע י"ד סי' רעח סעיף ב:

קכט ה ו ז מיי' שם פ"ט הלכה א וסמג שם טוש"ע י"ד סי' רעב סעיף א [וברב אלפס הלכות ספר תורה דף סו]:

הגהות הב"ח

(א) גמ' עושין לספריהם: (ב) שם צא מהן חצי טפח אצבע לכותל זה ואצבע לכותל זה כצ"ל ותיבת ומחצה נמחק ב' פעמים: (ג) שם מרכבו ארגמן וגו' תוכו רצוף אהבה וארגז: (ד) שם מצד היה מונח ולא: (ה) רש"י ד"ה דילמא וכו' ד' מאה ספרי תורות לא כתב דאין פנאי לאדם אחד לכתוב כולי האי הס"ד: (ו) תוס' ד"ה אצבע וכו' תקשה שנים עשר בי"ב היכי יתבי:

עין משפט נר מצוה

קל א ב מיי' פ"ז מהל' ס"ת הלכה טו סמג עשין כה טוש"ע י"ד סי' רפג סעיף ה:

גמרא

שברי לוחות שמונחים בארון; ואי ס"ד ס"ת הקיפו ו' טפחים, מכדי א)כל שיש בהקיפו שלשה טפחים יש בו רוחב טפח, וכיון דלאמצעיתו נגלל — ב)נפיש ליה מתרי טפחא רווחא דביני ביני, בתרי פושכי היכי יתיב? אמר רב אחא בר יעקב: ספר עזרה לתחלתו הוא נגלל. ואכתי ג)תרי בתרי היכי יתיב? אמר רב אשי: דכריך ביה פורתא וכרכיה לעיל. ור' יהודה, מקמי דליתי ארגז, ספר תורה היכי הוה יתיב? דפא הוה נפיק מיניה ויתיב עילויה ספר תורה. ור"מ, האי "מצד ארון" מאי עביד ליה? ההוא מיבעי ליה, דמתנח ליה מצד ולא מתנח בין לוחי, ולעולם בגויה מן הצד. ור"מ, עמודי' היכא הוו קיימי? מברא. ור"מ, שברי לוחות דמונחין בארון מנ"ל? נפקא ליה מדרב הונא; דאמר רב הונא, מאי דכתיב: "אשר נקרא שם שם ה' צבאות יושב הכרובים עליו"? (שמואל ב ו) מלמד, שלוחות ושברי לוחות מונחים בארון. ואידך? ההוא מבעי ליה לכדרבי יוחנן, דא"ר יוחנן א"ר שמעון בן יוחאי: מלמד, ד)שהשם וכל כינויו מונחין בארון. ואידך נמי מיבעי ליה להכי! אין הכי נמי. אלא שברי לוחות דמונחין בארון מנא ליה? נפקא ליה מדתני רב יוסף, ה)דתני רב יוסף: "אשר שברת ושמתם" (דברים י) — מלמד, שהלוחות ושברי לוחות מונחין בארון. ואידך? ההוא מיבעי ליה לכדריש לקיש, ו)דאמר ר"ל: "אשר שברת" — אמר לו הקב"ה למשה: יישר כחך ששברת. ת"ר, ח)סדרן של נביאים: יהושע ושופטים, שמואל ומלכים, ירמיה ויחזקאל, ישעיה ושנים עשר. מכדי הושע קדים, דכתיב: "תחלת דבר ה' בהושע", (הושע א) ז)וכי עם הושע דבר תחלה? והלא ממשה ועד הושע כמה נביאים היו! וא"ר יוחנן: שהיה תחלה לארבעה נביאים שנתנבאו באותו הפרק, ואלו הן: הושע וישעיה, עמוס ומיכה. וליקדמיה להושע ברישא! כיון דכתיב נבואתיה גבי חגי זכריה ומלאכי, וחגי זכריה ומלאכי סוף נביאים הוו, חשיב ליה בהדייהו. וליכתביה לחודיה וליקדמיה! איידי דזוטר מירכס. מכדי ישעיה קדים מירמיה ויחזקאל, ליקדמיה לישעיה ברישא! כיון דמלכים סופיה חורבנא, וירמיה כוליה חורבנא, ויחזקאל רישיה חורבנא וסיפיה נחמתא, וישעיה כוליה נחמתא, סמכינן חורבנא לחורבנא ונחמתא לנחמתא. ט)סדרן של כתובים: רות, וספר תהלים, ואיוב ומשלי, קהלת, שיר השירים וקינות, דניאל ומגילת אסתר, עזרא ודברי הימים. ולמ"ד: ח)איוב בימי משה היה, ליקדמיה לאיוב ברישא! מ)אתחולי בפורענותא לא מתחלינן. רות נמי פורענות היא! פורענות דאית ליה אחרית; י)דאמר רבי יוחנן: למה נקרא שמה רות? שיצא ממנה דוד שריווהו להקב"ה בשירות ותושבחות. ומי כתבן? משה כתב ספרו כ)ופרשת בלעם ואיוב; יהושע כתב ספרו ושמונה פסוקים שבתורה; שמואל כתב ספרו ושופטים ורות; דוד כתב ספר תהלים ע"י עשרה זקנים: ע"י אדם הראשון, על ידי מלכי צדק, ועל ידי אברהם, וע"י משה, ועל ידי הימן, וע"י ידותון, ועל ידי אסף, ועל

רש"י

תורה אור

שברי לוחות שמונחין. תחת הלוחות. יש בו רוחב טפח. וזה שהקיפו ששה — נמצא עובי רוחבו שני טפחים. רווחא דביני וביני. אויר שבין עמוד לעמוד. ובתרי פושכי היכי יתיב. דקתני: נשתיירו שם ב' טפחים שבהם ס"ת מונח. ספר עזרה. ספר שכתב משה ובו קורין בעזרה פרשת המלך ב"הקהל", וכהן גדול ביה"כ. לתחלתו הוא נגלל. אין לו אלא עמוד אחד, ונגלל מתחלתו לסופו ל). דכריך ביה פורתא. שאינו גוללו כולו, ומניח בו מקצת וכורכו לעצמו, ומניח אותו הכרך על הספר מלמעלה. וכרכיה לעיל. וכורכו למעלה על ההיקף. דמנח ליה מצד. אצל הכותל, ולא בין שני הלוחות. היכא הוי קיימי. כיון דמצריך טפח מכאן וטפח מכאן ברוחב הארון, שלא יהא ס"ת יוצא ונכנס בדוחק, העמודים היכא מנחי? הלא ימעטו את החלל! שם שם. תרי זימני כתיבי, ללוחות ולשברי לוחות. אשר שברת. קרא יתירה הוא, לאסמכיה ל"ושמתם" לדרשה. יישר כוחך. ללמדך שהוא מן הדברים שעשה משה רבינו ע"ה מדעתו, והסכימה דעתו לדעת המקום. שנתנבאו באותו הפרק. בימי אותם המלכים: עוזיה, יותם, אחז, יחזקיה. בארבעה נביאים הללו כתיב כן, חוץ ממיכה, שלא היה בימי עוזיהו אבל היה בימי יותם אחז יחזקיה. חגי זכריה ומלאכי סופן של נביאים. שהן היו בבית שני, בשנת שתים לדריוש האחרון. ישעיה קדים לירמיה ויחזקאל. שהרי ישעיה בימי עוזיה, וירמיה בימי יאשיה ובניו נתנבא בירושלים, ויחזקאל בגולה בימי צדקיה. רות תהלים איוב כו'. רות קדמה, "בימי שפוט השופטים". תהלים — דוד אמרן, והוא קדם לאיוב, כמ"ד: בימי מלכת שבא היה. ואחר כך שלשה ספרי שלמה. משלי קהלת. שניהם ספרי חכמה. שיר השירים. נראה בעיני שאמרו לעת זקנתו. קינות. ירמיה אמרן, שהיה אחר שלמה. דניאל. אחר ירמיה, בימי נבוכד נצר בגולה. אסתר. אחריו, בימי אחשורוש. עזרא. אחריו, בימי דריוש השני שעמד אחר אחשורוש. למ"ד איוב בימי משה היה. לקמן. רות נמי פורענותא היא. רעב וגלות ומיתת אלימלך ובניו. דאית ליה אחרית. סוף הפורענות נהפך לאחרית ותקוה, שיצא דוד משם. ופרשת בלעם. נבואתו ומשליו, אף על פי שאינן צורכי משה ותורתו וסדר מעשיו. ושמונה פסוקים. מן "וימת משה" עד סוף הספר. שמואל כתב ספרו וספר שופטים. שכולם קדמו לו, ועמד וכתב ספרן, ומה שעלתה לישראל בימיהם, וכן רות שהיתה בימי השופטים.

על ידי עשרה זקנים. כתב בו דברים שאמרו זקנים הללו שהיו לפניו, ויש שהיו בימיו, כגון: אסף והימן וידותון מן הלוים המשוררים. על ידי אדם הראשון. כגון "גלמי ראו עיניך", "ולי מה יקרו רעיך" (תהלים קלט) — אדם הראשון אמרן. על ידי מלכי צדק. "נאם ה' לאדוני [שב לימיני]" וכל המזמור (שם קי). ועל ידי אברהם. כדאמרינן לקמן: "איתן האזרחי" זה אברהם. ועל ידי משה. "תפלה למשה" (שם צ) וכל אחד עשר מזמורים כסדרן. ועל ידי הימן. "משכיל להימן". ועל ידי ידותון. "למנצח לידותון".

חזקיה

תוספות

תרי בתרי היכי יתיב. משמע שעם עמודין היה הקיפו ששה, שאם היה הקיפו בלא עמודין — אם כן נפיש ליה משני טפחים בהדי עמודים. ורבי מאיר עמודין היכא הוו קיימי. אע"פ שיש ריוח הרבה לר"מ בכל האורך, לבד מנגד ספר תורה — פשוט היו לו שהיו מונחים בצד ראש הארון שספר תורה מונח. ולמ"ד איוב בימי משה היה. וא"ת: מאי קאמר ולמ"ד? (א) והאי תנא גופיה סבר דבימי משה היה, דקתני סיפא: משה כתב ספר איוב! וי"ל: דהכתי לא ידע סיפא דברייתא. בפורענותא לא מתחילינן. וא"ת: ונכתביה מיד אחר רות! ואומר ר"י: משום שאחרית של רות היה אחרית שילא ממנה דוד שריוהו להקב"ה בשירות ותשבחות — לכך כתב אחר כך מיד אותן שירות, והוא אחרית שלה. וא"ת: ולמ"ד מעולי גולה היה — לכתביה לאיוב לבסוף! ואומר ר"י: דמשום הכי כתבו בהדי תהלים ומשלי — לפי שהוא מענין אחד: כתובין מעין שירה, ומקראות קצרים, וניגון אחד. דבימיהם היה ניגון, כדאמרינן (מגילה דף ג.): "ויקראו בספר תורת אלהים מפורש ושום שכל", מ) מאי "ושום שכל" — פסוקי טעמי. והא דלא כתבו אחר משלי — משום שלא להפסיק בדברי שלמה. ור"ת מפרש דלכן כתבו בהדי תהלים — משום דאמר לקמן: דוד כתב ספרו ע"י עשרה זקנים, ואיוב נמי נכתב ע"י ד' זקנים: צופר ובלדד ואליפז ואליהוא, והשתא אתי שפיר שלא כתבו אחר משלי. פורענות דאית ביה אחרית. וא"ת: איוב נמי אית ביה אחרית! וי"ל: דהאי אחרית דרות אחרית דכל ישראל. ועוד: דאיכא למ"ד ג) דלא כפל הקב"ה שכרו אלא לטורדו מן העולם.

רבינו גרשום

שברי לוחות מונחין בארון תחת השלימות. מיכדי הא א) (קרי) לכל דבר שיש בהקיפו ג' טפחים יש בו רוחב טפח וספר תורה ו' טפחים בהיקף וברוחב ב' טפחים. והני מילי כי נגלל כולו על עמוד אחד יש ברחבו ב' טפחים אבל כי הוי נגלל לאמצעיתו על ב' עמודין נפיש ליה שיעור בית מושבו יותר על ב' טפחים משום דאיכא ריוח ביני ביני של פתיחת חבור העמודין. והשתא אליבא דר' מאיר הואיל והוי רוחב הקיפו יותר מב' טפחים בתרי פושכי דפשו מארון על שיעור הלוחות היכי הוי יתיב ספר תורה. ספר עזרה היינו ספר תורה המונח בארון לתחלתו הוא נגלל הכל על עמוד אחד ולא הוי רוחב הקיפו אלא ב' טפחים. ואכתי אפי' הכי ספר תורה דהוי רוחב הקיפו ב' טפחים. בתרי טפח שבארון היכי יתיב אי לא הוי ביה רווחא פורתא אמר רב אשי דכריך בה בספר תורה פורתא לאחר שהיה כרוך כולו עמוד אחד היה חוזר וכורך מסופו לבדו כרך מעט כשיעור שיכנס האחד וישב בריוח באותן ב' טפחים ומנח ליה לאותו כרך קטן על הכרך הגדול וכי האי גוונא יתיב ברווחא. ואליבא דר' יהודה דספר תורה לא הוה יתיב בארון מיקמי דליתי ארגז וכו'. ור' מאיר דאמר דספר תורה בארון הוה יתיב האי מצד ארון מאי עביד ליה הא משמע מצדו ולא במתוכו: האי מצד כותל הארון ולעולם בתוכו. שהשם הקודש שאין מזכירין וכל כינויו כל שבעים שמות של הקב"ה מונחין בארון משמע כו'. והקשתי לר' מאי שנא דר' יהודה מרבה מאין רק שברי לוחות לידכר עמודין דקיימי לטעמיה באותו טפח הפנוי בארון כי היכי דמרבה ר' מאיר ספר תורה לטעמיה דקיימי בב' טפח פנוי והשיב לי משום הכי מרבה שברי לוחות הואיל וכתיבי בתורה ועמודיו לא כתיבי בתורה: חגי זכריה ומלאכי לסוף אינביאו וזוטר נביאותייהו כתבינן לה נמי גבייהו. ונכתביה באנפי נפשיה ונקדמיה מקמי [ישעיה] ומשני כיון דזוטר מירכס כלומר משום דכל הספרים נגללין מתחלתן אי כתבינן לה באפי נפשיה כשמגלגלין הספר מבליע נבואת הושע בהדי הספר ומירכס ומתעלם מן העין וליכא למיקם עלה היכא כתיבא משום הכי מוקמי' לה בהדי חגי זכריה דזוטר נבואתייהו: מכדי ישעיה הוה קדים לירמיה (דיחום) [ויחזקאל] דישעיה הוי בימי מנשה וירמיה הוה בחורבן הבית בתר הכא טובא ויחזקאל הוה בגלות: רות נמי פורענות. דהוה רעב ומתו מחלון וכליון: ומשני רות פורעניות דהוה ליה אחרית טוב שלקחה בועז ומשום הכי מתחילין ברות [ואח"כ] בתהלים שיצא ממנה דוד שתקנו: ופרשת בלעם. אע"ג דבלעם גופיה הוה נביא. שמונה פסוקים שבתורה מן וימת משה. על ידי עשרה זקנים ועל ידי אדם הראשון היינו מזמור שיר ליום

א) ואולי צ"ל הא קיי"ל דכל שיש וכו'.

מסורת הש"ס

א) [אהלות פי"ב מ"ו עירובין יג: עו. סוכה ז:]: ב) [עיין מה שמקשה תוס' על זה בעירובין יד. ד"ה והאיכא]: ג) [עיין תוס' עירובין שם]: ד) [סוטה מב:]: ה) [ברכות ח: מנחות לט:] ו) יבמות סב. שבת פז. [מנחות לט:]: ז) [פסחים פז.]: ח) [לקמן טו.]: ט) [לקמן קח.]: י) ברכות ז: ע"ש: כ) [עי' פי' הגון על זה בשל"ה דף שס"ב בפנים וגם בהג"ה ע"ש]: ל) [עי' תוס' לעיל יג: ד"ה ועושה בראשו]: מ) [במגילה שם ובנדרים לז: איתא ויבינו במקרא אלו פסקי טעמי']: נ) [לקמן טו:]:

הגהות הב"ח

(א) תוס' ד"ה ולמ"ד וכו' מאי קאמר ולמ"ד והא תנא:

גמרא

וְעַל יְדֵי שְׁלֹשָׁה בְּנֵי קֹרַח; יִרְמְיָה כָּתַב סִפְרוֹ וְסֵפֶר מְלָכִים וְקִינוֹת; חִזְקִיָּה וְסִיעָתוֹ כָּתְבוּ (ימש"ק סִימָן) יְשַׁעְיָה, מִשְׁלֵי, שִׁיר הַשִּׁירִים וְקֹהֶלֶת; אַנְשֵׁי כְנֶסֶת הַגְּדוֹלָה כָּתְבוּ (קנד"ג סִימָן) יְחֶזְקֵאל וּשְׁנֵים עָשָׂר, דָּנִיֵּאל וּמְגִילַּת אֶסְתֵּר; עֶזְרָא כָּתַב סִפְרוֹ וְיַחַס שֶׁל דִּבְרֵי הַיָּמִים עַד לוֹ. מְסַיְּיעָא לֵיהּ לְרַב, דְּאָמַר רַב יְהוּדָה אָמַר רַב: לֹא עָלָה עֶזְרָא מִבָּבֶל עַד שֶׁיִּחֵס עַצְמוֹ וְעָלָה. וּמַאן אַסְקֵיהּ? נְחֶמְיָה בֶּן חֲכַלְיָה. אָמַר מָר: יְהוֹשֻׁעַ כָּתַב סִפְרוֹ וּשְׁמוֹנָה פְּסוּקִים שֶׁבַּתּוֹרָה. תַּנְיָא כְּמַאן דְּאָמַר: שְׁמוֹנָה פְּסוּקִים שֶׁבַּתּוֹרָה יְהוֹשֻׁעַ כְּתָבָן, [א]דְּתַנְיָא: °"וַיָּמָת שָׁם מֹשֶׁה עֶבֶד ה'" — אֶפְשָׁר מֹשֶׁה [ב](מֵת) וְכָתַב "וַיָּמָת שָׁם מֹשֶׁה"? אֶלָּא, עַד כָּאן כָּתַב מֹשֶׁה, מִכָּאן וְאֵילָךְ כָּתַב יְהוֹשֻׁעַ, דִּבְרֵי ר"י, וְאָמְרִי לָהּ ר' נְחֶמְיָה. אָמַר לוֹ ר"ש: אֶפְשָׁר ס"ת חָסֵר אוֹת אַחַת? וּכְתִיב: °"לָקוֹחַ אֶת סֵפֶר הַתּוֹרָה הַזֶּה"! אֶלָּא, עַד כָּאן הקב"ה אוֹמֵר (א) וּמֹשֶׁה אוֹמֵר וְכוֹתֵב, מִכָּאן וְאֵילָךְ הקב"ה אוֹמֵר וּמֹשֶׁה כּוֹתֵב בְּדֶמַע, כְּמוֹ שֶׁנֶּאֱמַר לְהַלָּן: °"וַיֹּאמֶר לָהֶם בָּרוּךְ מִפִּיו יִקְרָא אֵלַי אֵת כָּל הַדְּבָרִים הָאֵלֶּה וַאֲנִי כּוֹתֵב עַל הַסֵּפֶר בַּדְּיוֹ". כְּמַאן אָזְלָא הָא דְּא"ר יְהוֹשֻׁעַ בַּר אַבָּא אָמַר רַב גִּידֵּל אָמַר רַב: [א]שְׁמוֹנָה פְּסוּקִים שֶׁבַּתּוֹרָה יָחִיד קוֹרֵא אוֹתָן? לֵימָא, [ג](ר"י הִיא) וּדְלָא כְּר"ש? אֲפִילּוּ תֵּימָא ר"ש, הוֹאִיל וְאִשְׁתַּנּוּ אִשְׁתַּנּוּ. § יְהוֹשֻׁעַ כָּתַב סִפְרוֹ. וְהָכְתִיב: °"וַיָּמָת יְהוֹשֻׁעַ בִּן נוּן עֶבֶד ה'"! דְּאַסְקֵיהּ אֶלְעָזָר. וְהָכְתִיב: °"וְאֶלְעָזָר בֶּן אַהֲרֹן מֵת"! דְּאַסְקֵיהּ פִּנְחָס. שְׁמוּאֵל כָּתַב סִפְרוֹ. וְהָכְתִיב: °"וּשְׁמוּאֵל מֵת"! דְּאַסְקֵיהּ גָּד הַחוֹזֶה וְנָתָן הַנָּבִיא. דָּוִד כָּתַב סֵפֶר תְּהִלִּים עַל יְדֵי עֲשָׂרָה זְקֵנִים. וְלִיחְשׁוֹב נַמִי אֵיתָן הָאֶזְרָחִי! אָמַר רַב: אֵיתָן הָאֶזְרָחִי זֶה הוּא אַבְרָהָם, כְּתִיב הָכָא: °"אֵיתָן הָאֶזְרָחִי", וּכְתִיב הָתָם: °"מִי הֵעִיר מִמִּזְרָח צֶדֶק" [וגו'] [ד]קָא חָשֵׁיב מֹשֶׁה וְקָא חָשֵׁיב הֵימָן; וְהָאָמַר רַב: הֵימָן זֶה מֹשֶׁה, כְּתִיב הָכָא: הֵימָן, וּכְתִיב הָתָם: °"בְּכָל בֵּיתִי נֶאֱמָן הוּא"! תְּרֵי הֵימָן הָווּ. מֹשֶׁה כָּתַב סִפְרוֹ וּפָרָשַׁת בִּלְעָם וְאִיּוֹב. מְסַיְּיעָא לֵיהּ לְר' לֵוִי בַּר לַחְמָא, דְּא"ר לֵוִי בַּר לַחְמָא: [ה]אִיּוֹב בִּימֵי מֹשֶׁה הָיָה, כְּתִיב הָכָא: °"מִי יִתֵּן אֵפוֹא וְיִכָּתְבוּן מִלָּי", וּכְתִיב הָתָם: °"וּבַמֶּה יִוָּדַע אֵפוֹא". וְאֵימָא: בִּימֵי יִצְחָק, דִּכְתִיב: °"מִי אֵפוֹא הוּא הַצָּד צַיִד"! וְאֵימָא: בִּימֵי יַעֲקֹב, דִּכְתִיב: °"אִם כֵּן אֵפוֹא זֹאת עֲשׂוּ"! וְאֵימָא: בִּימֵי יוֹסֵף, דִּכְתִיב: °"אֵיפֹה הֵם רוֹעִים"! לָא ס"ד, דִּכְתִיב: °"מִי יִתֵּן בַּסֵּפֶר וְיוּחָקוּ", וּמֹשֶׁה הוּא דְּאִיקְּרֵי מְחוֹקֵק, דִּכְתִיב: °"וַיַּרְא רֵאשִׁית לוֹ כִּי שָׁם חֶלְקַת מְחוֹקֵק סָפוּן". רָבָא אָמַר: אִיּוֹב בִּימֵי מְרַגְּלִים הָיָה, כְּתִיב הָכָא: °"אִישׁ הָיָה בְאֶרֶץ עוּץ אִיּוֹב שְׁמוֹ", וּכְתִיב הָתָם: °"הֲיֵשׁ בָּהּ עֵץ". מִי דָּמֵי? הָכָא "עוּץ", הָתָם "עֵץ"! הָכִי קָאָמַר לְהוּ מֹשֶׁה לְיִשְׂרָאֵל: יֶשְׁנוֹ לְאוֹתוֹ אָדָם, שֶׁשְּׁנוֹתָיו אֲרוּכוֹת כָּעֵץ וּמֵגֵין עַל דּוֹרוֹ כָּעֵץ? יָתֵיב הַהוּא מֵרַבָּנַן קַמֵּיהּ דְּר' שְׁמוּאֵל בַּר נַחְמָנִי, וְיָתֵיב וְקָאָמַר: אִיּוֹב לֹא הָיָה וְלֹא נִבְרָא, אֶלָּא מָשָׁל הָיָה. א"ל, עָלֶיךָ אָמַר קְרָא: "אִישׁ הָיָה בְאֶרֶץ עוּץ אִיּוֹב שְׁמוֹ". אֶלָּא מֵעַתָּה, °"וְלָרָשׁ אֵין כֹּל כִּי אִם כִּבְשָׂה אַחַת קְטַנָּה אֲשֶׁר קָנָה וַיְחַיֶּהָ" וגו', מִי הֲוָה? אֶלָּא מָשָׁל בְּעָלְמָא, הָכָא נַמִי מָשָׁל בְּעָלְמָא. א"כ, שְׁמוֹ וְשֵׁם עִירוֹ לָמָּה? רַבִּי יוֹחָנָן וְרַבִּי אֶלְעָזָר דְּאָמְרִי תַּרְוַיְיהוּ: אִיּוֹב מֵעוֹלֵי גוֹלָה הָיָה, וּבֵית מִדְרָשׁוֹ בִּטְבֶרְיָא הָיָה. מֵיתִיבֵי: יְמֵי שְׁנוֹתָיו שֶׁל אִיּוֹב, מִשָּׁעָה שֶׁנִּכְנְסוּ יִשְׂרָאֵל לְמִצְרַיִם וְעַד שֶׁיָּצְאוּ!

אֵימָא

רש"י

חִזְקִיָּה וְסִיעָתוֹ. בְּנֵי דּוֹרוֹ שֶׁהֶאֱרִיכוּ יָמִים אַחֲרָיו. כָּתְבוּ יְשַׁעְיָה. שֶׁהֲרָגוֹ מְנַשֶּׁה, וְלֹא כָּתַב סִפְרוֹ. שֶׁלֹּא הָיוּ הַנְּבִיאִים כּוֹתְבִים סִפְרֵיהֶן אֶלָּא לִפְנֵי מוֹתָן. מִשְׁלֵי קֹהֶלֶת. דִּכְתִיב בְּסֵפֶר מִשְׁלֵי (כה): "אֲשֶׁר הֶעְתִּיקוּ אַנְשֵׁי חִזְקִיָּה" וגו'. וְעַל שֶׁחִזְקִיָּה גָּרַם לָהֶן לַעֲסוֹק בַּתּוֹרָה, כִּדְאָמְרִינַן בְּ"חֵלֶק" (סנהדרין דף צד:): נָעַץ חֶרֶב עַל פֶּתַח בֵּית הַמִּדְרָשׁ כו' — נִקְרָא הַדָּבָר עַל שְׁמוֹ. אַנְשֵׁי כְּנֶסֶת הַגְּדוֹלָה. חַגַּי זְכַרְיָה וּמַלְאָכִי זְרוּבָּבֶל וּמָרְדְּכַי, וַחֲבֵרֵיהֶם. כָּתְבוּ יְחֶזְקֵאל. שֶׁנִּתְנַבֵּא בַּגּוֹלָה. וְאֵינִי יוֹדֵעַ לָמָּה לֹא כְּתָבוֹ יְחֶזְקֵאל בְּעַצְמוֹ, אִם לֹא מִפְּנֵי שֶׁלֹּא נִתְּנָה נְבוּאָה לִיכָּתֵב בְּחוּצָה לָאָרֶץ, וּכְתָבוּם אֵלּוּ לְאַחַר שֶׁבָּאוּ לָאָרֶץ. וְכֵן סֵפֶר דָּנִיֵּאל שֶׁהָיָה בַּגּוֹלָה. וְכֵן מְגִילַּת אֶסְתֵּר. וּשְׁנֵים עָשָׂר, מִתּוֹךְ שֶׁהָיוּ נְבוּאוֹתֵיהֶם קְטַנּוֹת לֹא כְּתָבוּם הַנְּבִיאִים עַצְמָם אִישׁ אִישׁ סִפְרוֹ, וּבָאוּ חַגַּי זְכַרְיָה וּמַלְאָכִי וְרָאוּ שֶׁרוּחַ הַקֹּדֶשׁ מִסְתַּלֶּקֶת, שֶׁהָיוּ הֵם נְבִיאִים אַחֲרוֹנִים, וְעָמְדוּ וְכָתְבוּ נְבוּאוֹתֵיהֶם, וְצֵרְפוּ נְבוּאוֹת קְטַנּוֹת עִמָּם, וַעֲשָׂאוּם סֵפֶר גָּדוֹל, שֶׁלֹּא יֹאבְדוּ מֵחֲמַת קָטְנָם. עַד לוֹ. עַד שֶׁיִּיחֵס עַצְמוֹ. מְסַיֵּיעַ לֵי' כו' עַד שֶׁיִּיחֵס עַצְמוֹ. שֶׁכָּתַב דִּבְרֵי הַיָּמִים עַד שֶׁיִּיחֵס בּוֹ אֶת עַצְמוֹ. וּמַאן אַסְקֵיהּ. מִי סִיְּימוֹ. תַּנְיָא כְּמַאן דְּאָמַר. כָּל הַךְ דְּקָתָנֵי לְעֵיל: יְהוֹשֻׁעַ כָּתַב סִפְרוֹ וּשְׁמוֹנָה פְּסוּקִים שֶׁבַּתּוֹרָה — אָתְיָא כִּי הַאי תַּנָּא דִּלְקַמֵּיהּ, דְּאָמַר נַמִי יְהוֹשֻׁעַ כְּתָבָן. דְּתַנְיָא. פְּלוּגְתָּא דְּתַנָּאֵי בְּהַאי "וַיָּמָת שָׁם מֹשֶׁה" כו'. כְּמוֹ שֶׁנֶּאֱמַר לְהַלָּן כו'. אַכּוּלֵּהּ מִילְּתָא קָאֵי, דְּקָאָמַר: הקב"ה אוֹמֵר וּמֹשֶׁה כּוֹתֵב, כְּמָה שֶׁמָּצִינוּ שֶׁהַנְּבִיאִים כּוֹתְבִים מִפִּי רַבָּם. יָחִיד קוֹרֵא אוֹתָן. כְּלוֹמַר, אֵין מַפְסִיקִין בָּהֶן. לֵימָא ר"י הִיא. דְּאָמַר: לֹא כְּתָבָם מֹשֶׁה, לְפִיכָךְ נִשְׁתַּנּוּ מִשְּׁאָר הַתּוֹרָה, וּדְלָא כְּר"ש? הוֹאִיל וְאִישְׁתַּנּוּ. לִכְתּוֹב בְּדֶמַע, אִישְׁתַּנּוּ. וְאֵימָא יַעֲקֹב כו'. לָא גָּרְסִינַן לָהּ. ל"א: (ב) גָּרְסִינַן [לְמַתְנִיתָא] דִּלְעֵיל בְּמִנְיָינָא דַּעֲשָׂרָה זְקֵנִים, דְּקָא חָשֵׁיב אַבְרָהָם וְאֵיתָן הָאֶזְרָחִי, וְלָא קָא חָשֵׁיב אָסָף, דְּקָסָבַר מִשְּׁלֹשָׁה בְּנֵי קֹרַח הוּא. וְהָא אָמַר רַב כו'. גַּבֵּי "וַיֶּחְכַּם מִכָּל הָאָדָם מֵאֵיתָן הָאֶזְרָחִי" וגו' (מלכים א ד) אִיתְּמַר. וְכֵן הַךְ דְּהֵימָן זֶה מֹשֶׁה — אַהֵימָן דְּהַהוּא קְרָא אִיתְּמַר, דִּכְתִיב בֵּיהּ: "וְהֵימָן וְכַלְכֹּל" וגו'. תְּרֵי הֵימָן הָווּ. "מַשְׂכִּיל לְהֵימָן הָאֶזְרָחִי" הֵימָן אַחֲרִינָא הֲוָה. שֶׁשְּׁנוֹתָיו כָּעֵץ. אִיּוֹב, שֶׁהֶאֱרִיךְ יָמִים רַבִּים. מָשָׁל הָיָה. לִלְמוֹד מִמֶּנּוּ תְּשׁוּבוֹת לַמְקַטְרְגִים עַל מִדַּת הַדִּין, וְשֶׁאֵין אָדָם נִתְפָּס עַל צַעֲרוֹ. אִישׁ הָיָה. אַלְמָא הֲוָה. אֶלָּא מֵעַתָּה וְלָרָשׁ אֵין כֹּל וכו'. וְסֵיפֵיהּ דִּקְרָא "וַתְּהִי לוֹ כְבַת". מִי הֲוָה. מִשּׁוּם דִּכְתִיב "וַתְּהִי"?

אֵימָא

תוספות

ועל ידי שלמה ועל ידי בני קרח. לפי הספרים דגרסי שלמה נ"ל דאסף הוה משלשה בני קרח, והוא אביאסף. ולספרים דל"ג שלמה — לא הוי אסף אביאסף, אלא אסף היה מן הלוים המשוררים. וא"ת: ולהנהו דלא גרסי ליה, אמאי לא חשיב ליה? הא כתיב (תהלים עב) "לשלמה אלהים משפטיך" וגו'! וי"ל: דדוד אמרו, והתפלל על שלמה. תדע, דכתיב בסוף המזמור "כלו תפלות דוד". וא"ת: לספרים דגרסי שלמה, הכתיב כלו תפלות דוד! וי"ל: לפי שסיימו דוד. והא דכתיב נמי "שיר המעלות לשלמה" — דוד כמו כן אמרו, דכל חמש עשרה מעלות דוד אמרן, ויש ספרים דקא חשיב אברהם ואיתן האזרחי. וגרים לקמן דקא חשיב אברהם וקא חשיב איתן, והאמר רב: איתן האזרחי הוא אברהם! ומשני: איתן האזרחי דקא חשיב הכא — יעקב. וקשה להאי גירסא: דמנא לן דדוד כתב ספרו על ידי אברהם? כיון דאיתן האזרחי לאו היינו אברהם. **ירמיה** כתב ספרו וספר מלכים. והא דלא כתב ישעיה, דהיה קודם ירמיה, ספר מלכים — לפי שנהרג, ולא היה בסוף מלכים ממנשה ואילך (לפי שנהרג), ואפילו ספרו לא כתב. **חזקיה** וסיעתו כתבו ישעיה. לפי שחזקיה גרם להם לעסוק בתורה נקרא הדבר על שמו, אבל הוא לא כתבו, שהרי מת קודם לישעיה, דמנשה *בן בתו הרג לישעיה*. **עד** לו. פירש ר"ח: עד פסוק "ולו אחים בני יהושפט" (דה"ב כא) ומסייע לרב, שייחס עצמו ועלה, שייחוס עצמו כתב לפני זה הפסוק. וקשה לפירושו דהל"ל עד "ולו", בוי"ו. **פ"ה** דיחזקאל לא כתב ספרו לפי שהיה בחוצה לארץ. וקשה: דהא ירמיה נמי בחוצה לארץ היה, שהלך למצרים ונתנבא שם כמה נבואות, ולא מצינו שחזר יותר לארץ ישראל. **שמונה** פסוקים שבתורה. ה"ר משולם היה מצריך מכאן לקרות לאחד אותן ח' פסוקים, שלא יקרא עמו שליח צבור. ואין נראה לר"ת, דהא כל התורה כולה נמי אחד קורא, כדתנן במגילה (דף כא:): קראוה שנים יצאו. ואמר בגמ': תנא, מה שאין כן בתורה. ואומר ר"ת: *דיחיד קורא — בלא הפסקה, שלא יקראו שנים זה ד' פסוקים וזה ד'. ומה שנוהגים עתה לקרוא שנים [בכל התורה] — אומר ר"ת: כדי שלא יתבייש מי שאינו יודע לקרות בעצמו. כענין שמצינו במסכת ביכורים (פ"ג מ"ז) דתנן: כל מי שיודע לקרות — קורא בעצמו, ושאינו יודע לקרות — מקרין לפניו. נמנעו מלהביא ביכורים, התקינו שיהיו מקרין את מי שיודע לקרות, ואת מי שאינו יודע לקרות. והא דאמר בירושלמי במגילה: רבי שמואל בר רב יצחק על לבי כנישתא וחזא חזנא דקאים וקורא, ולא קאי בר אינש תחתיו. א"ל: אסור, כשם שנתנה תורה על ידי סרסור — כך אנו צריכין לנהוג בה על ידי סרסור. אע"ג דמשמע שחזן עומד אצל הקורא — לא שיקרא עמו, אלא יעמוד ויקרא אותם שיש להם לקרות, כדי שתנתן תורה על ידי סרסור. ועוד אומר ר"י: דיכול להיות שקלת מסייע לו בנחת. והא דמשמע במגילה שלא יקראו שנים — היינו שניהם שוין בקול רם.

איוב לא היה ולא נברא. האי לא סבר כריש לקיש, דאמר בב"ר*: איוב לא היה שבאו עליו יסורין, ולא אמר הכתוב שבאו עליו — להודיעך כחו של איוב, שאילו באו עליו — היה יכול לעמוד בהן. דאי סבר האי אמורא דאיוב היה בעולם — א"כ מאי קאמר: שמו ושם עירו למה? טובא איצטריך, לאשמועינן מי הוא אותו צדיק שהיה יכול לעמוד באותן יסורין.

מסורת הש"ס

א) מנחות ל. ב) [שם איתא חזי] ג) [שם ליתא] ד) [שם א"ח ואימא יעקב דכתיב ביה ויזרח לו השמש ההוא מיבעי ליה שמש שבאה בעבורו וזרחה בעבורו קא כו'] ה) [לעיל יד:] ו) יבמות מט:

רבינו גרשום

ליום השבת שנאמר בשביל אדם הראשון ועל ידי [א] זקנים הני דקא חשיב א) לבר מאדם הראשון הוו י' והני י' כולהו קבוע בו מזמוריהן: וסיעתו. תלמידיו. ויחס דברי הימים עד לו. כלומר הוא חשב היחס בדברי הימים מאדם הראשון עד עצמו: הואיל ואשתני. משאר תורה שהללו כת' משה בדמע: אשתני. נמי משאר תורה דיחיד יקרא אותו ולא שנים. ולמאן דאמר יהושע כתבו להכי יחיד קורא אותו והיינו דלא כר' שמעון דאיהו אמר דמשה כתבו: תרי הימן הוו. בן בנו של שמואל: (עד שעשאה כבולת נקיה). רבא אתי לסיועי למאן דאמר איוב בימי משה הוה. שדומה לעץ נקי מחטא: אלא משל היה כמו שאמר שלמה יש צדיקים שמגיע אליהם כמעשה הרשעים ולא שמשמש הוה: שיצאו מכלל דבימי משה הוה ולא מעולי גולה: לעולם מעולי גולה

א) נראה דרבינו גרס גם ועי' שלמה וכמו שכתבו התוס' ולפיכך הוצרך לומר דקחשיב י' לבר מאדם הראשון.

הגהות הב"ח

(א) גמ' עד כאן הקב"ה אומר ומשה כותב כצ"ל ותיבת אומר נמחק: (ב) רש"י ד"ה לא הכי גרסינן למתניתא וכו' כבני קרח הוא. וגרסינן כאן קא חשיב אברהם וקא חשיב איתן והאמר רב כו' ומשני איתן האזרחי דקא חשיב הכא יעקב וכו' ביה ויזרח לו השמש כו':

עין משפט נר מצוה

קל א מיי' פי"ג מהל' תפלה הלכה ו ועיין בהשגות סמג עשין יט טוש"ע א"ח סי' קמא סעיף ז [וברב אלפס פרק ד' דמגילה דף רע:]

[נ"ל בנו וכ"א בס"י]

[כדאיתא יבמות מט:]

[וכך איתא ברש"י דהכא ובמנחות ל. אבל במגילה כא: ד"ה תנא כתבו דבר זה בשם רש"י]

[סוף פ' ויקרא]

אימא: כמשעה שנכנסו ישראל למצרים ועד [שעה] שיצאו. מיתיבי: שבעה נביאים נתנבאו לאומות העולם, ואלו הן: בלעם ואביו, ואיוב, אליפז התימני, ובלדד השוחי, וצופר הנעמתי, ואליהוא בן ברכאל הבוזי! א)(א"ל:) ולטעמיך, אליהוא בן ברכאל לאו מישראל הוה? והא כתי' "ממשפחת רם"! אלא אינבוי אינבי לאומות העולם, ה"נ איוב אינבוי אינבי [לאומות העולם]. אטו כולהו נביאי מי לא אינבוי לאומות העולם? התם עיקר נביאותייהו לישראל, הכא עיקר נביאותייהו לאומות העולם. מיתיבי: חסיד היה באומות העולם ואיוב שמו, ולא בא לעולם אלא כדי לקבל שכרו, הביא הקב"ה עליו יסורין, התחיל מחרף ומגדף, כפל לו הקב"ה שכרו בעוה"ז [כדי] לטרדו מן העולם הבא! תנאי היא; דתניא, רבי אלעזר אומר: איוב בימי שפוט השופטים היה, שנאמר: "הן אתם כולכם חזיתם ולמה זה הבל תהבלו", איזה דור שכולו הבל? הוי אומר: זה דורו של שפוט השופטים. רבי יהושע בן קרחה אומר: איוב בימי אחשורוש היה, שנאמר: "ולא נמצא נשים יפות כבנות איוב בכל הארץ", איזהו דור שנתבקשו בו נשים יפות? הוי אומר: זה דורו של אחשורוש. ואימא: בימי דוד, דכתיב: "ויבקשו נערה יפה"! התם בכל גבול ישראל, הכא בכל הארץ. רבי נתן אומר: איוב בימי מלכות שבא היה, שנאמר: "ותפל שבא ותקחם". וחכ"א: איוב בימי כשדים היה, שנאמר: "כשדים שמו שלשה ראשים". ויש אומרים: איוב בימי יעקב היה, ודינה בת יעקב נשא, כתיב הכא: "כדבר אחת הנבלות תדברי", וכתיב התם: "כי נבלה עשה בישראל". וכולהו (א) תנאי סבירא להו דאיוב מישראל הוה, לבר מ"יש אומרים", דאי ס"ד מאומות העולם הוה, בתר דשכיב משה מי ב)שריא שכינה על אומות העולם? והא ג)אמר מר: בקש משה שלא תשרה שכינה על אומות העולם, ונתן לו, שנאמר: "ונפלינו אני ועמך". א"ר יוחנן: דורו של איוב שטוף בזמה היה, שנאמר: "הן אתם כולכם חזיתם ולמה זה הבל תהבלו", וכתיב: "שובי שובי השולמית שובי שובי ונחזה בך". אימא: בנבואה, דכתיב: "חזון ישעיהו בן אמוץ"! א"כ, "למה זה הבל תהבלו" למה לי? וא"ר יוחנן, מאי דכתיב: "ויהי בימי שפוט השופטים"? דור ששופט את שופטיו; אומר לו: ד)טול קיסם מבין ה)(עיניך) — אומר לו: טול קורה מבין עיניך; אמר לו: "כספך היה לסיגים" — אמר לו: "סבאך מהול במים". א"ר שמואל בר נחמני א"ר יונתן: כל האומר מלכת שבא אשה היתה — אינו אלא טועה, מאי "מלכת שבא"? מלכותא דשבא. "ויהי היום ויבאו בני האלהים להתיצב על ה' ויבא גם השטן בתוכם. ויאמר ה' אל השטן מאין תבא ויען השטן" וגו' ו) אמר לפניו: רבש"ע, שטתי בכל העולם כולו ולא מצאתי נאמן כעבדך אברהם, שאמרת לו: "קום התהלך בארץ לארכה ולרחבה כי לך אתננה", ואפילו הכי בשעה שלא מצא מקום לקבור את שרה [עד שקנה בד' מאות שקל כסף] לא הרהר אחר מדותיך. "ויאמר ה' אל השטן השמת לבך אל עבדי איוב כי אין כמוהו בארץ" וגו', א"ר יוחנן: גדול הנאמר באיוב יותר ממה שנאמר באברהם, דאילו באברהם כתיב: "כי עתה ידעתי כי ירא אלהים אתה", ובאיוב כתיב: "איש תם וישר ירא אלהים [וסר מרע]" מאי "וסר מרע"? א"ר אבא בר שמואל: ז)איוב וותרן בממונו היה; מנהגו של עולם — נותן חצי פרוטה לחנוני, איוב ויתרה משלו. "ויען השטן את ה' ויאמר החנם ירא איוב אלהים. הלא אתה שכת בעדו ובעד ביתו" וגו' — ח)מאי "מעשה ידיו ברכת"? א"ר שמואל בר רב יצחק: כל הנוטל פרוטה מאיוב מתברך. מאי "ומקנהו פרץ בארץ"? א"ר יוסי בר חנינא: מקנהו של איוב פרצו גדרו של עולם; מנהגו של עולם — זאבים הורגים העזים, מקנהו של איוב — עזים הורגים את הזאבים. "ואולם שלח נא ידך וגע בכל אשר לו אם לא על פניך יברכך. ויאמר ה' אל השטן הנה כל אשר לו בידך רק אליו אל תשלח ידך" וגו'. "ויהי היום ובניו ובנותיו אוכלים ושותים יין בבית אחיהם הבכור. ומלאך בא אל איוב ויאמר הבקר היו חורשות" וגו' — מאי "הבקר היו חורשות והאתונות רועות על ידיהם"? א"ר יוחנן: מלמד, שהטעימו הקב"ה לאיוב מעין

אימא כמשעה שנכנסו כו'. מאתים ועשר, דכתיב (איוב מב): "ויוסף ה' את כל אשר לאיוב למשנה" — אף שנותיו הוכפלו, דכתיב: "ויחי איוב אחר זאת מאה וארבעים שנה" — למדנו שהיה בן שבעים כשבאו יסורין עליו, הרי מאתים ועשר. ולעולם מעולי גולה היה. **נתנבאו לאומות העולם.** אלמא גוי היה. **אליהוא.** על כרחך, מדייחסיה קרא בשמו [ושם אביו] ושם משפחתו — ישראל הוה. ואית דאמרי: ממשפחת רם היה — היינו אברהם. **שכולו הבל.** הטובים שבהן לא היו כלום, כדאמרינן לקמן: שהנשפט היה לו פתחון פה לשפוט את שופטו ומוכיחו. **בימי מלכות שבא היה.** ובא (ג) גדוד מכשדים עליו. **וחכ"א** בימי מלכות כשדים. בימי נבוכדנצר היה, ובא גם משבא גדוד עליו. **וכולהו הני תנאי כו'.** מסקנא דתירוצא הוא דתריץ לעיל: תנאי היא. ההוא מתניתא דלעיל ס"ל גוי הוה, והני תנאי דהך מתניתא כולהו סבירא להו דישראל הוה, בר מ"יש אומרים" דאמרי: בימי יעקב הוה. **והא אמר מר.** בפ"ק דברכות (דף ז.). **ונפלינו.** (ג) ונבדלנו, בלכתך עמנו מכל האומות. **ונחזה בך.** לשון זימה [הוא זה] להסתכל בנשים. שגוים אומרים לישראל: שובי לתורתנו ותזני עמנו. **ששופט את שופטיו.** שהיו השופטין עצמן מקולקלים, והיה פתחון פה לנשפט להוכיח את מוכיחו, שאם אמר לו השופט: טול קיסם מבין עיניך, הסתלק ופרוש מעבירה קטנה שבידך. יכול זה לומר: טול קורה מבין עיניך, פרוש מעבירה חמורה שבידך. **סבאך.** יינך, כמו "אל תהי בסבאי יין" (משלי כג). **מהול.** מעורב. וכן כל לשון הוללות שבתורה — לשון ערבוב. **קום התהלך.** היינו דקאמר "ומהתהלך בה", מאותו שאמרת לו "התהלך בארץ" אני בא. **ה"ג: מנהג עולם נותן חצי פרוטה לחנוני.** מי שיש לו מלאכה מועטת לעשות, אומר לפועל: חצי פרוטה אני נותן לך, ולך אצל חנוני וקנה בפרוטה ככר או בצלים, ונחלוק. ואיוב ויתרה לחצי השני משלו, ונותן לו כל הפרוטה, שהיה רע בעיניו לדקדק בדבר קל שאינו ממון. **והאתונות רועות [וגו'].** ע"י הבקר. דריש ליה לקרא שאוכלת חזיז מתלם המענה, שהזרע צומח בשעתו.

בלעם ואביו. כדאמר במגילה (דף טו.): כל ששמו ושם אביו בנביאות — בידוע שהוא נביא בן נביא.

ט)**אימא** כמשעה שנכנסו ישראל למצרים. וא"ת: ומאי קמ"ל? קרא כתיב "ויוסף ה' את כל אשר לאיוב למשנה" ואיוב אחרי אותו מעשה חיה ק"מ שנה, וא"כ היה בן שבעים קודם! וי"ל: דס"ד דלא כפל אלא בעושר ויופי של בנות, אבל בשנים לא. **אליהוא** לא מישראל הוה. משמע דפשיטא דאליהוא בן ברכאל מישראל הוה. לכך נראה דבפ"ק דע"ז (דף ג.), דאמר: יבא בלדד השוחי וצופר הנעמתי ויעידו בהן בישראל שקיימו כל התורה כולה — ל"ג התם ואליהוא בן ברכאל. ונראה דשמעתא דהתם סברה כמ"ד איוב בימי יעקב הוה, דהא אמר לקמן דממשה ואילך לא שרתה שכינה על גוים.

דור ששופט את שופטיו. תימה לר"י: דאמר *(בפ"ק) דתמורה (דף טו:): כל האשכולות שעמדו לישראל מימות משה עד שמת יוסף בן יועזר לא היה בהם שום דופי.

בפירוש רבינו חננאל גרס: כולהו תנאי ואמוראי מודו דאיוב ישראל היה. ולר"י נראה דל"ג "ואמוראי", דרבא ע"כ סבר לעיל דלאו מישראל הוה, דקאמר לעיל: הכי אמר להן משה למרגלים ישנו לאותו אדם ששנותיו כעץ כו'. **ויש** אומרים איוב בימי יעקב הוה. הני יש אומרים לאו היינו ר' נתן, דהא פליגי עליה י).

רבינו גרשום

אימא שהיה כשיעור שהיו ישראל במצרים והכי הוא חושבנא ישראל היו במצרים ר"י שנה ואיוב כשבאו עליו יסורין היה בן ע' שנה כדכתיב (איוב טו) גם שב גם ישיש בנו ואין שב פחות מע' שנה כדכתיב ימי שנותינו בהם שבעים שנה וכשהשיב הקב"ה שבותו נתן לו הכל למשנה ושנותיו הכפיל לו דכתיב ויחי איוב אחרי זאת ק"מ שנה והנהו ע' דמעיקרא הרי ר"י שנה: בלעם [ואביו] אינבויי אינבי לגוים על דור המבול ועל דור הפלגה בלעם אינבי לגוים לעמלק [ולכתיים] וקשיא לר' יוחנן ולר' אלעזר דאמרי מעולי גולה היה: כדי לטורדו מן העולם. אלמא דאיוב מגוים הוה: תנאי היא כו' וכולהו הני תנאי מהא ברייתא דר' אלעזר ואילך מודו דאיוב מישראל הוה מדקא מיירי טעמייהו ממשה ואילך איכא למשמע מינה הואיל ושרתה עליו שכינה ממשה ואילך: לבד מיש אומרים דאמר בימי יעקב הוה שעדיין לא בא משה לעולם: דאי ס"ד דלשאר תנאי מאומות העולם היה וכי ממשה ואילך כו'. א) ואמוראי קרי לר' יוחנן ולר' אלעזר דאמרי תרוייהו איוב מעולי גולה היה ורבא נמי אמורא: מה תחזו בשולמית דכי היכי דהאי קרא משתעי בנקבה דהיינו זימה הכי נמי הן אתם כולכם חזיתם: ששופט. מי שהיה שפוט על פי בית דין הוא שופט את שופטיו שאם אמר לו השופט טול קיסם שלך גזילה מתחת ידיך היה משיב הוא לשופט טול קורה כלומר אני גזלתי קיסם שהוא מעט אתה גזלת קורה שהוא גדול מזה: אדם נותן חצי פרוטה לחנוני שאם היה חייב לפועל חצי פרוטה היה נותן לו איוב פרוטה שלימה ולא היה הולך לחנווני לחלוף לו חצי ליתן לו חצי לפועל [כמנהגם] היינו וסר מרע שלא היתה מדתו כמדת רעיו בני אדם: שהטעימו הקב"ה

א) נראה מזה שרבינו היה גורס וכולהו תנאי ואמוראי

מסורת הש"ס

א) [בע"י ליתא]: ב) כ"א שרתה: ג) ברכות ז.: ד) [ערכין טז:]: ה) [גירסת הע"י והילקוט שיניך]: ו) [נ"ל משוט בארץ ומהתהלך בה]: ז) [מגילה כח.]: ח) [פסחים דף קיב.]: ט) [שייך קודם לד"ה בלעם]: י) [עי' תוס' סוטה יב. ד"ה אחרי' ותוס' ע"ז סד: ד"ה אחרים ותוס' לקמן לג: ד"ה מאן]:

הגהות הב"ח

(א) גמ' וכולהו הני תנאי סבירא: (ב) רש"י ד"ה בימי וכו' ובא גם גדוד: (ג) ד"ה ונפלינו נ"ב א"נ דבלכתך עמנו היא שאלה אחרת בקש שתשרה שכינה על ישראל מ"מ שאלת ונפלינו היא דבוקה עם בלכתך עמנו וכך אמר ועוד דבר אחר אני שואל ממך שנהיה נבדלים בלכתך עמנו מכל האומות:

מֵעֵין הָעוֹלָם הַבָּא. °"עוֹד זֶה מְדַבֵּר וְזֶה בָּא וַיֹּאמַר איוב א
אֵשׁ אֱלֹהִים" וגו'. "עוֹד זֶה מְדַבֵּר וְזֶה בָּא וַיֹּאמַר כַּשְׂדִּים
שָׂמוּ שְׁלֹשָׁה רָאשִׁים וַיִּפְשְׁטוּ עַל הַגְּמַלִּים וַיִּקָּחוּם" וגו'.
"עוֹד זֶה מְדַבֵּר וְזֶה בָּא וַיֹּאמַר בָּנֶיךָ וּבְנוֹתֶיךָ אוֹכְלִים
וְשׁוֹתִים יַיִן בְּבֵית אֲחִיהֶם הַבְּכוֹר. וְהִנֵּה רוּחַ גְּדוֹלָה
בָּאָה מֵעֵבֶר הַמִּדְבָּר וַיִּגַּע בְּאַרְבַּע פִּנּוֹת הַבַּיִת וַיִּפּוֹל
עַל הַנְּעָרִים" וגו'. "וַיָּקָם אִיּוֹב וַיִּקְרַע אֶת מְעִילוֹ וַיָּגָז אֶת
רֹאשׁוֹ" וגו', "וַיֹּאמֶר עָרֹם יָצָאתִי מִבֶּטֶן אִמִּי וְעָרֹם אָשׁוּב
שָׁמָּה ה' נָתַן וה' לָקָח יְהִי שֵׁם ה' מְבוֹרָךְ. בְּכָל זֹאת
לֹא חָטָא אִיּוֹב וְלֹא נָתַן תִּפְלָה לֵאלֹהִים". "וַיְהִי הַיּוֹם
וַיָּבוֹאוּ בְּנֵי הָאֱלֹהִים לְהִתְיַצֵּב" וגו'. "וַיֹּאמֶר ה' אֶל
הַשָּׂטָן אֵי מִזֶּה תָּבֹא וַיַּעַן הַשָּׂטָן אֶת ה' וַיֹּאמַר מִשּׁוּט
בָּאָרֶץ" [וגו'] אָמַר לְפָנָיו: רבש"ע, שַׁטְתִּי בְּכָל הָעוֹלָם וְלֹא
מָצָאתִי כְּעַבְדְּךָ אַבְרָהָם, שֶׁאָמַרְתָּ לוֹ: °"קוּם הִתְהַלֵּךְ בראשית יג

דִּרְקוֹן

בָּאָרֶץ לְאָרְכָּהּ וּלְרָחְבָּהּ כִּי לְךָ אֶתְּנֶנָּה", א)וּבְשָׁעָה שֶׁבִּקֵּשׁ לִקְבּוֹר שָׂרָה לֹא מָצָא מָקוֹם לְקָבְרָהּ, וְלֹא
הִרְהֵר אַחַר מִדּוֹתֶיךָ. °"וַיֹּאמֶר ה' אֶל הַשָּׂטָן הֲשַׂמְתָּ לִבְּךָ אֶל עַבְדִּי אִיּוֹב כִּי אֵין כָּמוֹהוּ בָּאָרֶץ" וגו', איוב ב
"וְעוֹדֶנּוּ מַחֲזִיק בְּתֻמָּתוֹ וַתְּסִיתֵנִי בוֹ לְבַלְּעוֹ חִנָּם" — אָמַר רַבִּי יוֹחָנָן: אִלְמָלֵא מִקְרָא כָּתוּב אִי אֶפְשָׁר לְאוֹמְרוֹ,
כְּאָדָם שֶׁמְּסִיתִין אוֹתוֹ וְנִיסָּת. בְּמַתְנִיתָא תָּנָא: יוֹרֵד וּמַתְעֶה וְעוֹלֶה וּמַרְגִּיז, נוֹטֵל רְשׁוּת וְנוֹטֵל נְשָׁמָה. °"וַיַּעַן הַשָּׂטָן שם
אֶת ה' וַיֹּאמַר עוֹר בְּעַד עוֹר וְכֹל אֲשֶׁר לָאִישׁ יִתֵּן בְּעַד נַפְשׁוֹ. אוּלָם שְׁלַח נָא יָדְךָ וְגַע אֶל עַצְמוֹ וְאֶל בְּשָׂרוֹ אִם
לֹא ב)(עַל) פָּנֶיךָ יְבָרְכֶךָּ. וַיֹּאמֶר ה' אֶל הַשָּׂטָן הִנּוֹ בְיָדֶךָ אַךְ אֶת נַפְשׁוֹ שְׁמוֹר. וַיֵּצֵא הַשָּׂטָן מֵאֵת פְּנֵי ה' וַיַּךְ אֶת אִיּוֹב"
וגו' — אָמַר רַבִּי יִצְחָק: קָשֶׁה צַעֲרוֹ שֶׁל שָׂטָן יוֹתֵר מִשֶּׁל אִיּוֹב; מָשָׁל לְעֶבֶד שֶׁאָמַר לוֹ רַבּוֹ: שְׁבוֹר חָבִית וּשְׁמוֹר אֶת
יֵינָהּ. אָמַר ר"ל: הוּא שָׂטָן, הוּא יֵצֶר הָרַע, הוּא מַלְאַךְ הַמָּוֶת. הוּא שָׂטָן — דִּכְתִיב: °"וַיֵּצֵא הַשָּׂטָן מֵאֵת פְּנֵי ה'"; הוּא שם
יֵצֶר הָרַע — כְּתִיב הָתָם: °"רַק רַע כָּל הַיּוֹם", וּכְתִיב הָכָא: ("רַק אֶת נַפְשׁוֹ שְׁמוֹר") [°"רַק אֵלָיו אַל תִּשְׁלַח יָדֶךָ"] הוּא בראשית ו איוב א
מַלְאַךְ הַמָּוֶת, דִּכְתִיב: (°רַק) [אַךְ] אֶת נַפְשׁוֹ שְׁמוֹר", אַלְמָא בִּדִידֵיהּ קַיְימָא. א"ר לֵוִי: שָׂטָן וּפְנִנָּה לְשֵׁם שָׁמַיִם שם ב
נִתְכַּוְּונוּ. שָׂטָן, כֵּיוָן דַּחֲזָיָא לְהַקָּדוֹשׁ בָּרוּךְ הוּא דְּנָטְיָה דַּעְתֵּיהּ בָּתַר אִיּוֹב, אָמַר: חַס וְשָׁלוֹם, מִינְשֵׁי לֵיהּ *לְרַחֲמָנוּתֵיהּ [וס"א לרחימותיה]
דְּאַבְרָהָם; פְּנִנָּה, דִּכְתִיב: °"וְכִעֲסַתָּה צָרָתָהּ גַּם כַּעַס בַּעֲבוּר הַרְעִמָהּ". דְּרָשָׁהּ רַב אַחָא בַּר יַעֲקֹב בְּפַפּוּנְיָא, אֲתָא שמואל א א
שָׂטָן נַשְׁקֵיהּ לְכַרְעֵיהּ. °"בְּכָל זֹאת לֹא חָטָא אִיּוֹב בִּשְׂפָתָיו" — אָמַר רָבָא: בִּשְׂפָתָיו לֹא חָטָא, בְּלִבּוֹ חָטָא. מַאי איוב ב
קָאָמַר? °"אֶרֶץ נִתְּנָה בְיַד רָשָׁע פְּנֵי שׁוֹפְטֶיהָ יְכַסֶּה אִם לֹא אֵיפוֹ מִי הוּא", אָמַר רָבָא: בִּקֵּשׁ אִיּוֹב לַהֲפוֹךְ קְעָרָה עַל שם ט
פִּיהָ; אָמַר לֵיהּ אַבַּיֵי: לֹא דִּבֵּר אִיּוֹב אֶלָּא כְּנֶגֶד הַשָּׂטָן. כְּתַנָּאֵי: "אֶרֶץ נִתְּנָה בְיַד רָשָׁע" — רַבִּי אֱלִיעֶזֶר אוֹמֵר:
בִּקֵּשׁ אִיּוֹב לַהֲפוֹךְ קְעָרָה עַל פִּיהָ; אָמַר לוֹ רַבִּי יְהוֹשֻׁעַ: לֹא דִּבֵּר אִיּוֹב אֶלָּא כְּלַפֵּי שָׂטָן. °"עַל דַּעְתְּךָ כִּי שם י
לֹא אֶרְשָׁע וְאֵין מִיָּדְךָ מַצִּיל" — אָמַר רָבָא: בִּקֵּשׁ אִיּוֹב לִפְטוֹר אֶת כָּל הָעוֹלָם כּוּלּוֹ מִן הַדִּין, אָמַר לְפָנָיו:
רִבּוֹנוֹ שֶׁל עוֹלָם, בָּרָאתָ שׁוֹר פַּרְסוֹתָיו סְדוּקוֹת, בָּרָאתָ חֲמוֹר פַּרְסוֹתָיו קְלוּטוֹת; בָּרָאתָ גַּן עֵדֶן, בָּרָאתָ גֵּיהִנָּם;
בָּרָאתָ צַדִּיקִים, בָּרָאתָ רְשָׁעִים; מִי מְעַכֵּב עַל יָדֶךָ! וּמַאי אַהֲדַרוּ לֵיהּ חַבְרֵיהּ [דְּאִיּוֹב] °"אַף אַתָּה תָּפֵר יִרְאָה שם טו
וְתִגְרַע שִׂיחָה לִפְנֵי אֵל" — בָּרָא הַקָּדוֹשׁ בָּרוּךְ הוּא יֵצֶר הָרַע, ג)בָּרָא לוֹ תּוֹרָה תַּבְלִין. דָּרַשׁ רָבָא, מַאי דִּכְתִיב:
°"בִּרְכַּת אוֹבֵד עָלַי תָּבֹא וְלֵב אַלְמָנָה אַרְנִין"? "בִּרְכַּת אוֹבֵד עָלַי תָּבֹא" — מְלַמֵּד שֶׁהָיָה גּוֹזֵל שָׂדֶה מִיתוֹמִים שם כט
וּמַשְׁבִּיחָהּ וּמַחֲזִירָהּ לָהֶן; "וְלֵב אַלְמָנָה אַרְנִין" — דְּכָל הֵיכָא דַּהֲוָה ד)(אִיכָּא) אַלְמָנָה דְּלָא הֲווּ נָסְבִי לָהּ, הֲוָה אָזֵיל שָׁדֵי
שְׁמֵיהּ עִלָּוַהּ, וַהֲווּ אָתוּ נָסְבִי לָהּ. °"לוּ שָׁקוֹל יִשָּׁקֵל כַּעְשִׂי וְהַוָּתִי בְּמֹאזְנַיִם יִשְׂאוּ יָחַד" — אָמַר ה)רַב: עַפְרָא לְפוּמֵּיהּ שם ו
דְּאִיּוֹב, חַבְרוּתָא כְּלַפֵּי שְׁמַיָּא? ו)°"לוּ יֵשׁ בֵּינֵינוּ מוֹכִיחַ יָשֵׁת יָדוֹ עַל שְׁנֵינוּ" — אָמַר ז)רַב: עַפְרָא לְפוּמֵּיהּ דְּאִיּוֹב, שם ט
כְּלוּם יֵשׁ עֶבֶד שֶׁמּוֹכִיחַ אֶת רַבּוֹ? °"בְּרִית כָּרַתִּי לְעֵינָי וּמָה אֶתְבּוֹנֵן עַל בְּתוּלָה" — אָמַר רָבָא: (א) עַפְרָא לְפוּמֵּיהּ שם לא
דְּאִיּוֹב, אִיהוּ — בְּאַחֲרָנִיתָא, אַבְרָהָם — אֲפִילּוּ בְּדִידֵיהּ לָא אִיסְתַּכַּל, דִּכְתִיב: °"הִנֵּה נָא יָדַעְתִּי כִּי אִשָּׁה יְפַת מַרְאֶה בראשית יב
אָתְּ", מִכְּלָל דְּמֵעִיקָּרָא לָא הֲוָה יָדַע לָהּ. °"כָּלָה עָנָן וַיֵּלַךְ כֵּן יוֹרֵד שְׁאוֹל לֹא יַעֲלֶה" — אָמַר רָבָא: מִכָּאן שֶׁכָּפַר איוב ז
אִיּוֹב בִּתְחִיַּית הַמֵּתִים. °"אֲשֶׁר בִּשְׂעָרָה יְשׁוּפֵנִי וְהִרְבָּה פְצָעַי חִנָּם" — ח)אָמַר רַבָּה: אִיּוֹב בִּסְעָרָה חֵרֵף וּבִסְעָרָה שם ט
הֱשִׁיבוּהוּ; בִּסְעָרָה חֵרֵף, דִּכְתִיב: "אֲשֶׁר בִּשְׂעָרָה יְשׁוּפֵנִי", אָמַר לְפָנָיו: רִבּוֹנוֹ שֶׁל עוֹלָם, שֶׁמָּא רוּחַ סְעָרָה
עָבְרָה לְפָנֶיךָ וְנִתְחַלֵּף לְךָ בֵּין אִיּוֹב לְאוֹיֵב! בִּסְעָרָה הֱשִׁיבוּהוּ, דִּכְתִיב: °"וַיַּעַן ה' אֶת אִיּוֹב מִן הַסְּעָרָה שם לח
וַיֹּאמַר [וגו'] אֱזָר נָא כְגֶבֶר חֲלָצֶיךָ אֶשְׁאָלְךָ וְהוֹדִיעֵנִי", אָמַר לוֹ: הַרְבֵּה נִימִין בָּרָאתִי בָּאָדָם, וְכָל נִימָא
וְנִימָא בָּרָאתִי לָהּ גּוּמָּא בִּפְנֵי עַצְמָהּ, שֶׁלֹּא יְהוּ שְׁתַּיִם יוֹנְקוֹת מִגּוּמָּא אַחַת, שֶׁאִלְמָלֵי שְׁתַּיִם יוֹנְקוֹת
מִגּוּמָּא אַחַת — מַחֲשִׁיכוֹת מְאוֹר עֵינָיו שֶׁל אָדָם; בֵּין גּוּמָּא לְגוּמָּא לֹא נִתְחַלֵּף לִי, בֵּין אִיּוֹב לְאוֹיֵב נִתְחַלֵּף
לִי? ט)°"מִי פִלַּג לַשֶּׁטֶף תְּעָלָה" [וגו'] — הַרְבֵּה טִיפִּין בָּרָאתִי בֶּעָבִים, וְכָל טִיפָּה וְטִיפָּה בָּרָאתִי לָהּ שם לח
דְּפוּס בִּפְנֵי עַצְמָהּ, כְּדֵי שֶׁלֹּא יְהוּ שְׁתֵּי טִיפִּין יוֹצְאוֹת מִדְּפוּס אֶחָד, שֶׁאִלְמָלֵי שְׁתֵּי טִיפִּין יוֹצְאוֹת
מִדְּפוּס אֶחָד — מְטַשְׁטְשׁוֹת אֶת הָאָרֶץ וְאֵינָהּ מוֹצִיאָה פֵּירוֹת; בֵּין טִיפָּה לְטִיפָּה לֹא נִתְחַלֵּף לִי,
בֵּין אִיּוֹב לְאוֹיֵב נִתְחַלֵּף לִי? מַאי מַשְׁמַע דְּהַאי "תְּעָלָה" לִישָּׁנָא דִּדְפוּס הִיא? אָמַר רַבָּה בַּר שֵׁילָא,
דִּכְתִיב: °"וַיַּעַשׂ תְּעָלָה כְּבֵית סָאתַיִם זֶרַע". °"וְדֶרֶךְ לַחֲזִיז קוֹלוֹת" — הַרְבֵּה קוֹלוֹת בָּרָאתִי בֶּעָבִים, וְכָל מלכים א יח שם
קוֹל וְקוֹל בָּרָאתִי לוֹ שְׁבִיל בִּפְנֵי עַצְמוֹ, כְּדֵי שֶׁלֹּא יְהוּ שְׁתֵּי קוֹלוֹת יוֹצְאוֹת מִשְּׁבִיל אֶחָד, שֶׁאִלְמָלֵי
שְׁתֵּי קוֹלוֹת יוֹצְאוֹת מִשְּׁבִיל אֶחָד — מַחֲרִיבִין אֶת כָּל הָעוֹלָם; בֵּין קוֹל לְקוֹל לֹא נִתְחַלֵּף לִי, בֵּין אִיּוֹב לְאוֹיֵב
נִתְחַלֵּף לִי? °"הֲיָדַעְתָּ עֵת לֶדֶת יַעֲלֵי סָלַע חוֹלֵל אַיָּלוֹת תִּשְׁמֹר" — יַעֲלָה זוֹ אַכְזָרִית עַל בָּנֶיהָ, בְּשָׁעָה שֶׁכּוֹרַעַת שם לט
לָלֶדֶת

מֵעֵין הָעוֹלָם הַבָּא. כִּדְכְתִיב (ירמיהו לא): "הָרָה וְיוֹלֶדֶת יַחְדָּו" – הֵרָיוֹן וְלֵידָה בְּיוֹם אֶחָד, הָכִי דָּרְשִׁינַן לֵיהּ בְּמַסֶּכֶת שַׁבָּת (דף ל:). הָכִי גָּרְסִינַן: בְּמַתְנִיתָא תָּנָא יוֹרֵד וּמַתְעֶה וְעוֹלֶה וּמַרְגִּיז נוֹטֵל רְשׁוּת וְנוֹטֵל נְשָׁמָה. [וְה"פ]: יוֹרֵד לְמַטָּה וּמַתְעֶה אֶת הַבְּרִיּוֹת לַחֲטוֹא, וְעוֹלֶה לְמַעְלָה וּמַרְגִּיז אֶת חֲמַת הַמֶּלֶךְ בְּהַשְׂטָנוֹתוֹ, נוֹטֵל מִמֶּנּוּ רְשׁוּת לַהֲרוֹג אֶת הַחוֹטֵא, מִכֵּיוָן שֶׁנָּתְנוּ רְשׁוּת דִּכְתִיב "וַתְּסִיתֵנִי בוֹ". צַעֲרוֹ שֶׁל שָׂטָן. שֶׁהוּזְקַק לִשְׁמוֹר אֶת נֶפֶשׁ אִיּוֹב שֶׁלֹּא תָּמֵת. אַלְמָא בִּדִידֵיהּ קַיְימָא. לִיטּוֹל אֶת הַנֶּפֶשׁ, וְהִזְהִירוֹ שֶׁלֹּא לִיטְּלָהּ. בַּעֲבוּר הַרְעִימָהּ. שֶׁמִּתְרָעֶמֶת עַל שֶׁהִיא עֲקָרָה, וְתִתְפַּלֵּל. לַהֲפוֹךְ קְעָרָה עַל פִּיהָ. (ב) לַעֲקוֹר כָּל כָּבוֹד, שֶׁחֵירֵף וְגִידֵּף. לִפְטוֹר אֶת כָּל הָעוֹלָם כּוּלּוֹ. מִדִּינוֹ שֶׁל הקב"ה, לוֹמַר שֶׁאֲנוּסִין הֵן ע"י הקב"ה, שֶׁבְּרָאָם (ג) יְלה"ר. וְהָכִי קָאָמַר: "עַל דַּעְתְּךָ כִּי לֹא אֶרְשָׁע" – אִם הָיִיתָ חָפֵץ לֹא הָיִיתִי רָשָׁע. בָּרָאתָ שׁוֹר בְּפַרְסוֹת סְדוּקוֹת וַחֲמוֹר בְּפַרְסוֹת קְלוּטוֹת. אֶת זֶה טִיהַרְתָּ וְאֶת זֶה טִימֵּאתָ, הַכֹּל בָּא עַל יָדְךָ, אַתָּה בָּרָאתָ בּוֹ סִימָנֵי הַטּוּמְאָה. בָּרָאתָ צַדִּיקִים. ע"י יֵצֶר טוֹב. בָּרָאתָ רְשָׁעִים. עַל יְדֵי יֵצֶר הָרַע. לְפִיכָךְ אֵין נִיצּוֹל מִיָּדְךָ, כִּי מִי יְעַכֵּב? אֲנוּסִין הֵן הַחוֹטְאִין. בָּרָא לוֹ תּוֹרָה. (ד) הֵן תַּבְלִין, שֶׁהִיא מְבַטֶּלֶת אֶת הִרְהוּרֵי עֲבֵירָה, כִּדְאָמַר בְּעָלְמָא (קדושין דף ל:): אִם פָּגַע בְּךָ מְנוּוָּל זֶה – מָשְׁכֵהוּ לְבֵית הַמִּדְרָשׁ, אִם אֶבֶן הוּא נִימּוֹחַ כּוּ'. הִלְכָּךְ לָאו אֲנוּסִין נִינְהוּ, שֶׁהֲרֵי יְכוֹלִין לְהַצִּיל עַצְמָן. בִּרְכַּת אוֹבֵד. שֶׁהָיָה סָבוּר שֶׁהָיָה אוֹבֵד אֶת שָׂדֵהוּ. שָׁדֵי שְׁמֵיהּ עִלָּוֵיהּ. אוֹמֵר שֶׁהִיא קְרוֹבָתוֹ, אוֹ מְדַבֵּר בָּהּ לְהַשִּׂיאָהּ. חַבְרוּתָא כְּלַפֵּי שְׁמַיָּא. מְדַבֵּר לִפְנֵי הַשְּׁכִינָה כְּאָדָם הַמִּתְוַוכֵּחַ לַחֲבֵירוֹ: בֹּא וְנִשְׁקוֹל מִי חַיָּיב לַחֲבֵירוֹ. מִן הַסְּעָרָה. לְשׁוֹן שֵׂעָר, כִּדְקָתָנֵי: הַרְבֵּה נִימִין בָּרָאתִי בָּאָדָם. מְטַשְׁטְשׁוֹת אֶת הָאָרֶץ. עוֹשׂוֹת אֶת הָאָרֶץ כְּטִיט.

מסורת הש"ס

א) [סנהדרין קיא.]: ב) [נ"ל אל]: ג) [קדושין ל:]: ד) [בע"י ליתא]: ה) כ"א רבא: ו) [בספרים שלפנינו כתיב לא בא"ף]: ז) כ"א רבא: ח) [נדה נב. ושם איתא רבא]: ט) עי' תוס' ע"ז יז: ד"ה מעות:

רבינו גרשום

מעין העולם הבא. שלאלתר תיכף לחרישה היו רועות על ידיהן מיד והיה עשב יוצא ורועות. וכן כתב לעולם הבא ונגש חורש בקוצר [עמו' ט]: כאדם שמסיתין אותו. אחרים וניסת על ידיהן: בעבור הרעימה. מה רעמים הללו לעולם אי אפשר בלא מטר כך היתה מתרעמת ומכעסת אותה כדי שתבקש רחמים עליה שיהיו לה ולדות: אלא בלבו חטא. שהיה מחשב בלבו על (פי) הבורא דברים אשר לא כן: להפוך קערה על פיה. להפוך יראת כל העולם. כלומר שאין דין אמת: על דעתך כי לא ארשע. כלומר בידך לבות בני אדם אם היה בדעתך להטותו לטובה לא היה רשע ובעבור שלא עשית כן אין מידך מציל: מי מעכב על ידך. שלא תתן לרשע לב צדיק: אף אתה תפר. כשתאמר כן תפר יראת חטא מבני אדם ותגרע תפלה מהם: ברא לו תבלין כנגדו. מכלל שהכל בידי אדם יעסוק בתורה ויהיה צדיק: כשמחזיר שדהו משובחת. שהוא היה סבור שגזלה לו: שדי שמיה עילויה. שהיה מוציא שם שהיא קרובתו: חברותא כלפי שמיא. דקאמר ישאו יחד: הנה נא ידעתי. כשראה בבואה במים: ויעש תעלה. דפום סילון לשטף המים:

הגהות הב"ח

(א) גמ' אמר רבא איהו באחרניתא לא אסתכל אברהם אפי' בדידיה כצ"ל ותיבות עפרא לפומיה דאיוב נמחק: (ב) רש"י ד"ה להפוך קערה על פיה כלומר לעקור: (ג) ד"ה לפטור וכו' שבראם להם יצה"ר: (ד) ד"ה בראת לו תורה תבלין כצ"ל ותיבת הן נמחק:

ללדת, עולה לראש ההר כדי שיפול ממנה
וימות, ואני מזמין לה נשר שמקבלו בכנפיו
ומניחו לפניה, ואלמלי מקדים רגע אחד או
(א) מתאחר רגע אחד מיד מת; בין רגע לרגע
לא נתחלף לי, בין איוב לאויב נתחלף לי?
"חולל אילות תשמור" — א) אילה זו רחמה צר, איוב לט
בשעה שכורעת ללדת, אני מזמין לה דרקון
שמכישה בבית הרחם (ב) ומתרפה ממולדה,
ואלמלי מקדים רגע אחד או מאחר רגע אחד
מיד מתה; בין רגע לרגע לא נתחלף לי, בין
איוב לאויב נתחלף לי? "[איוב] לא בדעת שם לד
ידבר ודבריו לא בהשכל", (וכתיב: "כי לא שם מב
דברתם אלי נכונה כעבדי איוב"!) אמר רבא:
מכאן שאין אדם נתפס בשעת צערו.
"וישמעו שלשת רעי איוב את כל הרעה שם ב
הזאת הבאה עליו ויבאו איש ממקומו
אליפז התימני ובלדד השוחי וצופר הנעמתי
ויועדו יחדו לבוא לנוד לו ולנחמו" — מאי
"ויועדו יחדו"? אמר רב יהודה אמר רב: מלמד
שנכנסו כולן בשער אחד. ותנא: בין כל אחד
ואחד שלש מאות פרסי. מנא הוו ידעי? איכא
דאמרי: כלילא הוה להו, ואיכא דאמרי: אילני
הוה להו, וכיון דכמשי הוו ידעי. אמר רבא,
היינו דאמרי אינשי: או חברא כחברי דאיוב,

בראשית ו או ב) מיתותא. "ויהי כי החל האדם לרוב על פני האדמה ובנות יולדו להם" — רבי יוחנן אמר: רביה
באה לעולם; ריש לקיש אמר: מריבה באה לעולם. אמר ליה ריש לקיש לרבי יוחנן: לדידך דאמרת
רביה באה לעולם, מפני מה לא נכפלו בנותיו של איוב? אמר לו: נהי דלא נכפלו בשמות, אבל נכפלו ביופי,
איוב מב דכתיב: "ויהי לו שבענה בנים ושלוש בנות. ויקרא שם האחת ימימה ושם השנית קציעה ושם השלישית
קרן הפוך". ימימה — שהיתה דומה ליום, קציעה — שהיה ריחה נודף כקציעה, קרן הפוך — אמרי דבי רבי שילא: שדומה
לקרנא דקרש. מחייכו עלה במערבא, קרנא דקרש לקותא היא! אלא אמר רב חסדא: ככורכמא דרישקא
ירמיה ד במיניה, שנאמר: "כי תקרעי בפוך". רבי שמעון ברבי איתילידא ליה ברתא, הוה קא חלש דעתיה, אמר
ליה אבוה: רביה באה לעולם. אמר ליה בר קפרא: תנחומין של הבל ניחמך אבוך; ג) דתניא: אי אפשר
לעולם בלא זכרים ובלא נקבות, אלא אשרי למי שבניו זכרים, אוי לו למי שבניו נקבות; אי אפשר לעולם
בראשית כד בלא בסם ובלא בורסי, אשרי מי שאומנותו בוסמי, אוי לו למי שאומנותו בורסי. כתנאי: "וה' ברך את
אברהם בכל" — ד) מאי "בכל"? רבי מאיר אומר: שלא היתה לו בת; רבי יהודה אומר: שהיתה לו בת;
ה) אחרים אומרים: בת היתה לו לאברהם ו"בכל" שמה; ר"א המודעי אומר: ו) איצטגנינות היתה בלבו של
אברהם אבינו, שכל מלכי מזרח ומערב משכימין לפתחו; רבי שמעון בן יוחי אומר: ז) אבן טובה היתה
תלויה בצוארו של אברהם אבינו, שכל חולה הרואה אותו מיד מתרפא, ובשעה שנפטר אברהם אבינו
מן העולם — תלאה הקדוש ברוך הוא בגלגל חמה. אמר אביי, היינו דאמרי אינשי: אידלי יומא אידלי קצירא.
דבר אחר: שלא מרד עשו בימיו. דבר אחר: שעשה ישמעאל תשובה בימיו. שלא מרד עשו בימיו,
שם כה מנלן? דכתיב: "ויבא עשו מן השדה והוא עיף", ותנא: אותו היום נפטר אברהם אבינו, ועשה יעקב אבינו
תבשיל של עדשים לנחם את יצחק אביו. [ומ"ש של עדשים]? אמרי במערבא משמיה דרבה בר מרי:
מה עדשה זו אין לה פה, אף אבל אין לו פה. דבר אחר: מה עדשה זו מגולגלת, אף אבילות מגולגלת
ומחזרת על באי העולם. מאי בינייהו? איכא בינייהו לנחומי בביעי. אמר רבי יוחנן, חמש עבירות עבר
אותו רשע באותו היום: בא על נערה מאורסה, והרג את הנפש, וכפר בעיקר, וכפר בתחיית המתים, ושט
דברים כב את הבכורה. בא על נערה מאורסה — כתיב הכא: "ויבא עשו מן השדה", וכתיב התם: "כי בשדה מצאה". בראשית כה
ירמיה ד הרג את הנפש — כתיב הכא: "עיף", וכתיב התם: "אוי נא לי כי עיפה נפשי להורגים". וכפר בעיקר — כתיב
שמות טו בראשית כה הכא: "למה זה לי", וכתיב התם: "זה אלי ואנוהו". וכפר בתחיית המתים — דכתיב: "הנה אנכי הולך למות". שם
ושט את הבכורה — דכתיב: "ויבז עשו את הבכורה". ושעשה ישמעאל תשובה בימיו, מנלן? כי הא דרבינא שם
ורב חמא בר בוזי הוו יתבי קמיה דרבא וקא מנמנם רבא. א"ל רבינא לרב חמא בר בוזי: ודאי דאמריתו:
(ג) ח) כל מיתה שיש בה גויעה — זו היא מיתתן של צדיקים? א"ל: אין. והא דור המבול! א"ל: אנן גויעה ואסיפה
קאמרינן. והא ישמעאל דכתיבה ביה גויעה ואסיפה! אדהכי איתער בהו רבא, אמר להו: ט) דרדקי, הכי א"ר יוחנן:
שם ישמעאל עשה תשובה בחיי אביו, שנאמר: "ויקברו אותו יצחק וישמעאל בניו". (ד) ודילמא י) דרך חכמתן קא
שם לה חשיב להו! אלא מעתה "ויקברו אותו עשו ויעקב בניו", מאי טעמא לא חשיב להו דרך חכמתן? אלא מדאקדמיה
— אדבורי אדבריה, ומדאדבריה — שמע מינה: תשובה עבד בימיו. ת"ר: שלשה הטעימן הקב"ה בעולם הזה
מעין

רש"י

דרקון. נחש. מכישה = נושכה. ומתרפה. לשון רפיון. שאין אדם נתפס. להתחייב על שהוא מדבר קשה מחמת צער ויסורין, דקאמר "לא בדעת ידבר" — לא אמר "לא ברשע ידבר", אלא: לא בדעת. כלילי הוו להו. כתרים, ובכל כתר שלשה פרצופים, ואיש את שמו מחוקק על פרצופו. וכשבאין יסורין על אחד מהן — פרצופו משתנה וכן אילני. דכמשי = פלטיי"א. או חברא כחברי דאיוב. אם אין לו לאדם אוהבים — נוח לו שימות. לרוב על פני האדמה. ובנות יולדו וגו'. רביה באה לעולם. כשנולדה בת, לפי שממהרת להיות לו זרע. הוכפלו ביופי. ואין לך כפל טוב ממנו. שדומה ליום. ברה כחמה. כקציעה. מין בושם הוא. קרנא דקרש. מין חיה, וקרניה משחירין כמו צבע. כורכמא דרישקא. כרכום של גן הגדל בגינה. במיניה. שהוא מעולה (ה) ממין אחר בשמים. איצטגנינות. חוזה בכוכבים. משכימים לפתחו. ליטול עצה ממנו. אידלי יומא. הוגבה שמש, כשהחמה זורחת. אידלי קצירא. מיקל החולי. אבל אין לו פה. שהוא יושב ודומם. עדשין אין להן פה. כמו שיש לפולין ולשאר מיני קטניות, כמין סדק. לנחומי בביעי. אין להם פה, אבל אינם מגולגלים כגלגל. ושט את הבכורה. ובזיה את העבודה שהיתה בבכורות. שט — תרגום של בזיון, "מדוע הקילתני" (שמואל ב יט) תרגום יונתן: אשטתני.

בכל

תורה אור

תוספות

ככוחלא דרישקא במינה. פע"ג דכחול הוא שחור, כדפירש בה"ג: פוכמא פוכמא [חולין מו:] היינו דמיא לכוחלא — ה"פ: כי היכי דכוחלא דרישקא מקרין ומאיר משאר כוחלא — כך היא היתה נאה משאר נשים. ו"קרן הפוך" לשון "כי קרן עור פני משה" (שמות לד). והשתא אתי שפיר הא דמייתי "ותקרעי בפוך עיניך", דכחול דומה לפוך, שנותנין כחול בעין. אבל לפירוש רש"י דגרס: כי כורכמא דרישקא — קשה לרשב"א: א"כ מאי מייתי "ותקרעי בפוך עיניך"? ויונתן תרגם "נרד וכרכום" — רשק *וכרכום, "כפרים עם נרדים" — עם רישקא (שיר ד). [נ"ל ותרגום, יעב"ץ]

שכל חולה שרואה אותה מיד מתרפא. וא"ת: והא בימי אברהם אכתי לא היה חולי בעולם, כדאמרי' ב"השוכר את הפועלים" (ב"מ דף פז.) דעד יעקב לא הוה חולשא, ועד אלישע לא הוה דאיחלש ואיתפח! ומצינן למימר דהכא בחולה של מכה איירי. ור"ת ור"י מפרשים: דעד יעקב לא הוה דאיחלש — היינו חולי של מיתה, מכאן ואילך הוה דאיחלש — חולי של מיתה, ולא הוה דאיתפח, עד אלישע.

בא על נערה המאורסה. ואם תאמר: והלא לא נלטוו בני נח על נערה המאורסה, כדאמרי' בפ' "ארבע מיתות" (סנהדרין דף נז: ושם ד"ה לנערה): בעולת בעל יש להן, נכנסת לחופה ולא נבעלה אין להן! ואומר ר"י: דלאו על פי שלא נלטוו — מכל מקום מכוער הדבר. כמו "ושט את הבכורה", אף על פי שאינו מצווה על כך.

שלשה

רבינו גרשום

ומתרפא. רחמה ומרויה: מכאן שאין אדם נתפס על צערו. על מה שמדבר מכובד צערו דכתיב לא בדעת ידבר כלומר שאין דעתו מיושבת עליו מחמת צער: כי לא דברתם אלי נכונה כעבדי איוב. דברים הגונים חשיב ושאינן הגונין לא חשיב [לא] תפסו מכל מה שדבר כנגדו: כלילא הוה להו. כתר וחקוקין עליו ג' פרצופין של ג' חביריו וכשרואין שאחת מהן נשתנה פניה מיד היו יודעין שחבירו אין שרוי בנחת ויש אומרים ג' אילנות היו נטועין בפרדס שכל אחד היה קורא לכל א' על שם חבירו ואם היה מייבש אחד מן האילנות שבו היו יודעין שאין שרוי בטובה אותו שנקרא (העירה) [האילן] על שמו: רבייה. כלומר פריה ורביה שהנקבה מגדלת בניה: ולדידך דאמרת רבייה. דדבר טוב הוא: שבענה. היינו ב' פעמים ז': קציעה. קדה: בושם. שקורין קו"ש: דקרש. חיה ששמה קרש: לקותא היא. ואינה יפה מפני שיש בה כמה גוונין: כי כוחלא. שהוא שחור הרבה מבהיק מאד: רישקא. בלע"ז אריינטי"ל: במיניה. שהוא משובח במינו: כורכמא דרישקא. קרוק"ו. איינטי"ל. מה אותו צבע יפה הרבה במינו כך היתה יפה בין שאר נשים: איצטגנינות גדולה. שהיה בקי (אותו צבע) הרבה במזלות והיו שואלין מה יארע להן: אידלי יומא. [בשחרית] כשהשמש זורח שם מונחת אותה אבן: אידלי קצירא. מיקל חולה מחליו ולערב מכביד לו: ד"א. מאי בכל: מה עדשה שאין לה פה. שאין לה שום ביקוע: לנחומי בביעי. דלמאן דאמר פה עדשה אין לה פה ביצים [נמי] אין להם פה ומנחמין בהן אבלים כמו בעדשים ולמאן דאמר מה עדשה זו מגולגלת בביצים אין מנחמין מפני שאינם מגולגלים כל כך כעדשים: לאלתר בשמת אברהם עבר אותו רשע ה' עבירות: היינו בכל. דלא מרד בימיו: ש"מ דעבד תשובה. דנהג ביה כבוד ליצחק ואדבריה מקמיה.

מסורת הש"ס

א) [עירובין נד: יומא כט.]: ב) [תענית כג. ע"ש ברש"י]: ג) סנהדרין ק: קדושין פב: ע"ש [פסחים סה. ע"ש]: ד) לקמן קמא. ע"ש [תוספתא דקדושין פ"ה]: ה) [לפמ"ש תוס' ברכות ט: ובסוטה יב. ובע"ז סל: ד"ה אחרים יתייצב גם הכא]: ו) [יומא כח:] ז) כ"א מרגלית: ח) כ"א משמיה דר' יוחנן: ט) [עי' פרש"י בשבת קמה:]: י) [סנהדרין סט:]

הגהות הב"ח

(א) גמ' או מאחר רגע אחד מיד נופל ומת בין: (ב) שם ומתרפא ויולדת ואלמלי מקדים רגע: (ג) שם ודאי דאמריתו משמיה דר' יוסי כל מיתה שיש בה גויעה: (ד) שם יצחק וישמעאל בניו מכדי ישמעאל קשיש מיצחק מ"ט דקחשיב ליה ליצחק מקמיה ש"מ תשובה עביד ואדבריה ליצחק מקמיה ודלמא דרך חכמתן. (ה) רש"י ד"ה במיניה שהוא מעולה משאר כרכומין כצ"ל:

מעין העולם הבא, אלו הן: אברהם, יצחק ויעקב. אברהם — דכתיב ביה "בכל"; יצחק — דכתיב ביה "מכל"; יעקב — דכתיב ביה "כל". שלשה לא שלט בהן יצר הרע, אלו הן: אברהם, יצחק ויעקב, דכתיב בהו: "בכל", "מכל", "כל". ויש אומרים: אף דוד, דכתיב: "ולבי חלל בקרבי". ואידך? צעריה הוא דקא מדכר. תנו רבנן: ששה לא שלט בהן מלאך המות, ואלו הן: אברהם, יצחק ויעקב, משה, אהרן ומרים. אברהם, יצחק ויעקב — דכתיב בהו: "בכל", "מכל", "כל"; משה, אהרן ומרים — דכתיב בהו: "על פי ה'". והא מרים לא כתיב בה "על פי ה'"! אמר ר"א: א) מרים נמי בנשיקה מתה, דאתיא "שם" "שם" ממשה, ומפני מה לא נאמר בה "על פי ה'"? שגנאי הדבר לומר. תנו רבנן: שבעה לא שלט בהן רמה ותולעה, ואלו הן: אברהם, יצחק ויעקב, משה, אהרן ומרים, ובנימין בן יעקב. ב) אברהם, יצחק ויעקב — דכתיב [בהו] "בכל", "מכל", "כל"; משה, אהרן ומרים — דכתיב [בהו] "ע"פ ה'", בנימין בן יעקב — דכתיב: "ולבנימין אמר ידיד ה' ישכון לבטח עליו". וי"א: אף דוד, דכתיב: "אף בשרי ישכון לבטח". ואידך? ההוא רחמי הוא דקא בעי. תנו רבנן: ג) ארבעה מתו בעטיו של נחש, ואלו הן: בנימין בן יעקב, ועמרם אבי משה, וישי אבי דוד, וכלאב בן דוד. וכולהו גמרא, לבר מישי אבי דוד דמפרש ביה [קרא] דכתיב: "ואת עמשא שם אבשלום תחת יואב על הצבא ועמשא בן איש ושמו יתרא הישראלי אשר בא אל אביגיל בת נחש אחות צרויה אם יואב", וכי בת נחש היא? והלא בת ישי היא, דכתיב: "ואחיותיהם צרויה ואביגיל"! אלא, בת מי שמת בעטיו של נחש.

הדרן עלך השותפין

לא א) יחפור אדם בור סמוך לבורו של חבירו, ולא שיח ולא מערה, ולא אמת המים, ולא נברכת כובסין — אא"כ הרחיק (א) מכותל חבירו שלשה טפחים וסד בסיד. ב) ומרחיקים את הגפת ואת הזבל, ואת המלח, ואת הסיד, ואת הסלעים, (ב) מכותלו של חבירו שלשה טפחים ד) (או) סד בסיד. ג) מרחיקין את הזרעים ואת המחרישה ואת מי רגלים מן הכותל שלשה טפחים. ד) ומרחיקין את הריחים שלשה מן השכב, שהן ארבעה מן הרכב; ה) ואת התנור — שלשה מן הכליא, שהן ארבעה מן השפה. **גמ'** פתח

רש"י

בכל מכל כל. באברהם כתיב (בראשית כד): "וה' ברך את אברהם בכל", ביצחק כתיב (שם כז): "ואוכל מכל", ביעקב כתיב (שם לג): "וכי יש לי כל" — כלומר, לא חסרו שום טובה. חלל בקרבי. יצר הרע מת בקרבי. צעריה קא מדכר. על לבו מתאבל, ואומר שמת בקרבו מרוב צרות. שלא שלט בהן מלאך המות. אלא מתו בנשיקה על פי שכינה. בכל מכל כל. לא חסרו שום כבוד. ומעינו כבוד זה במשה ואהרן, שנאמר בהן: "על פי ה'", ואם אלו מתו ע"י מלאך [המות], נמצא שחסרו כבוד. כדאמרן. שמתו ע"פ שכינה. ואין לאוה רמה לשלוט במי שנשק משכינה, שהרי אין הרמה באה אלא מטפה מרה המטפטפת מסכינו של מלאך המות, דאמר מר (ע"ז דף כ:): ממנה מת, ממנה מסריח, ממנה פניו מוריקות. ישכון לבטח עליו. הכי דריש: (ג) ישכון לבטח בנימין על סמיכות ידידות השכינה. בעטיו של נחש = בעצתו של נחש. כלומר, לא היו ראוין למות, אלא שנגזרה גזירת מיתה על כל תולדותיו של אדם הראשון בעצתו של נחש. בעטיו — תרגום של עצתו, כדכתיב (דניאל ו) "אתייעטו כל" וגו', וכן "התיב עטא וטעם" (שם ב). ואחיותיהם. בבני ישי כתיב.

הדרן עלך השותפין

לא יחפור. בור שיח ומערה. מפורשים בבבא קמא, בפרק "שור שנגח את הפרה" (דף נ:). בור. עגול. שיח. ארוך וקצר. מערה. מקורה בקירוי. נברכת הכובסים. חופר חפירה מרובעת בעומק אמה או יותר, ומי גשמים מתכנסים בה, לכבס בגדיהם. והיו להם שתים, אחת ששורים את הבגדים יום או יומים בצואת כלבים, והיא קרויה מתמצין בגמ', ואחת שמשפשפים בה, והיא קרויה נדיין. אא"כ כו'. מפני שהחפירה הסמוכה לבור מחלשת כותלי הבור, ומרפה אותן. וסד בסיד. את כותלי חפירתן. גפת. פסולת זיתים שנתעצרו בבית הבד. הסלעים. אבנים שהאור יוצא מהן, שקורין קוליי"ש. שכל אלו קשין לחומה, שמוציאין הבל. מן הכותל. כותל אבנים של טיט הבנוי על גבי קרקע. ואלו בבור קאי המשנה. זרעים. קשין לכותל, כדמפרש בגמ'. ומחרישה. מרפה את יסודו, ונופל. מי רגלים. ממסמסין את הלבנים שהן של טיט יבש. ריחים. קשין לכותל, שמנידין את הקרקע בגלגול חבטתו. מן השכב. היא הריחים התחתונה. הרכב. היא העליונה הרוכבת על זו, והיא קצרה טפח מן התחתונה. ואת התנור שלשה מן הכליא. תנור כלי חרס הוא שרוף בכבשן כשאר קדירות, ופיו למעלה, והבא לקובעו בארץ עושה בנין טיט ואבנים שיהיו לו לבסיס, ומושיבין אותו עליו שלא יתנגבו שוליו מחמת קרקע. ואותו בנין עשוי בשיפוע, רחב מלמטה וקצר מלמעלה כמדת התנור. התחתונה קרוי כליא ועליונה קרוי שפה, כלומר שפת הכליא — שפתה עליונה. ולפי שהבלו של תנור קשה לכותל, צריך להרחיק. **גמ'** פתח

תוספות

שלשה כו' מעין העולם הבא. תימה לרשב"א: אמאי לא חשיב נמי איוב, דאמר לעיל (דף טו:): "והאתונות רועות על ידיהם" — מלמד שהטעימו הקב"ה מעין עולם הבא! וי"ל: דאיוב לא היה אלא בחד מילתא, ואברהם ויצחק ויעקב נהנו מעין עוה"ב מכל וכל.

שבעה שלא שלטה בהן רמה. תימה לרשב"א: דכולהו צדיקי נמי, דאמר בשבת בפ' "שואל" (דף קנב:): "ורקב עצמות קנאה" מי שיש לו קנאה בלבו — עצמותיו נרקבין, ושאין קנאה בלבו — אין עצמותיו מרקיבין! וי"ל: דיכול להיות שלא ירקב וישלוט בו רמה, כדאמר במעשה דרבי (ד) אלעזר בן שמעון ב"השוכר את הפועלים" (ב"מ דף פד:) דנפיק ריחשא מאודניה.

שלשה לא שלט בהן יצר הרע. אין לפרש שלא שלט כלל — דא"כ היכי קבלו עליה אגרא? אלא כדאמר (יומא דף לח:): מאי דכתיב "רגלי חסידיו ישמור", כיון שעבר אדם רוב שנותיו ולא חטא שוב אינו חוטא. א"נ, כיון שראה הקב"ה שהיו דוחקין עצמן כל כך להתרחק מן העבירה — סייעם הקדוש ברוך הוא מכאן ואילך, שלא שלט בהן יצר הרע.

הדרן עלך השותפין

לא יחפור. כל הני איירי דאית בהו מיא. וטעמא משום מתונתא, כדאמרינן בתלמוד. ותימה לר"י: והא אמרי' בגמ': כל מרא ומרא דקא מחית כו'! ואומר ר"י: דלא קאמר אלא שמאותה שעה מתחיל ההיזק, וכיון דבתחילת ההיזק הוו גירי דיליה — מודה ר' יוסי. ומיהו, אי לאו משום מיא — לא היה צריך הרחקה ג' טפחים.

לא שיח ולא מערה. וה"ה חריצין ונעיצין, והני נקט אגב בור, דבכל מקום רגיל לשנות שיח ומערה בהדי בור. ואמת המים ונברכת הכובסין דאין רגיל לשנותן גבי בור — מפרש בגמ' דצריכי תרוייהו. ומיהו, הא לא מפרש אמאי לא הוה שמעינן להו מבור. דמצי למימר דבור ושיח דעמוקין טפי — בעי הרחקת שלשה, אבל הנך דלא עמיקי כולי האי — הוה אמינא דלא בעי הרחקת שלשה. ואי תנא הני — הוה אמינא דבור ושיח דעמיקי טפי בעי הרחקה יותר מג'. ובפרק "הפרה" (ב"ק דף נ:) דתנן: אחד החופר בור ושיח ומערות, ומצריך להו לכולהו בתלמוד — התם ניחא, דלא הוה ליה לתנא למינקטינהו אגב בור, כיון דכתיב בור בקרא, אלא הוה ליה למיתני בור לחודיה.

סלעים. אבנים שאש יוצא מהן. ולא סלעי נחושת, דאין דרך להניחן אצל הכתלים. והא דאמר בירושלמי: אית תנא תני טומנין בסלעים ואית (ה) תני דאין טומנין, כאן בסלעים של כסף, כאן בסלעים של נחושת — הוה מצי לשנויי: כאן בסלעים של אבנים כאן בשל כסף, אלא ניחא ליה לשנויי כולהו במתכת. **וסד** בסיד. נראה לר"י דבסיפא נמי גרס: וסד בסיד, ולא גרס "או", דאי גרסי' בסיפא "או סד בסיד" — אם כן תפשוט דברישא "וסד בסיד" תנן, מדלא קתני "או סד" ברישא כמו בסיפא. אלא ודאי בסיפא נמי גרס "וסד". והא דפשיטא ליה בגמרא (לקמן דף יט.) דבסיפא הוי "או סד בסיד" — היינו משום דאין הזיק כל כך מרובה, שלא יועיל לו סיד לחודיה.

כליא. פירש ר"ח: בנין דתנור, צר מלמטה ובאמצעיתו מרחיב ובולט ויוצא כשיעור טפח, ומאמצעיתו מיצר ועולה.

פתח

מסורת הש"ס

א) [מו"ק כח.] ב) נ"א אברהם יצחק יעקב משה אהרן ומרים בנימין בן יעקב וכו' וכזה תכון פירש"י דהכלל ל"ה כדאמרן וכו': ג) שבת נה: ד) נ"א וסד:

עין משפט נר מצוה

א א מיי' פ"ט מהלכות שכנים הלכה א סמג עשין פב טוש"ע ח"מ סי' קנה סעיף י:
ב ב מיי' שם הלכה ב טוש"ע שם סעיף ל:
ג ג מיי' שם טוש"ע שם סעיף ה:
ד ד מיי' שם הלכה ג טוש"ע שם סעיף ז:
ה ה מיי' שם הלכה ד טוש"ע שם סעיף ח:

רבינו גרשום

על פי ה'. דמי שמת ע"י מלאך המות שולט בו רמה ותולעה מפני כי ג' טיפין של מרה תלוין בו בסכינו ממנה מת ממנה מסריח ממנה פניו מוריקים ואותם שמתו על פי ה' לא שלט בהן רמה ותולעה: חלל בקרבי. שאין בו יצר הרע: צעריה המדבר. כלומר זה בקרבו מפחד מאותו מעשה שאירע לו: רחמי הוא דבעי: א) שוכן בו לבטח: בעטיו של נחש. בעצה שיעצה לחוה ולא מפני חטא אדם עטיו לשון עצה כמו (דניאל ב) עטא וטעם:

הדרן עלך השותפין

לא יחפור אדם בור כו'. משום דקא מרפיה ליה לארעיה ומקלקל לבורו: ולא שיח. זהו חפירה שחופרין להשקות שדותיהן ועשויה ארוך וקטן: לא מערה. שהיא מרובעת: נברכת הכובסים. ששם רוחצין וכובסין את בגדיהן:

א) [נראה דצ"ל רחמי הוא דבעי שיקבון בקברו לבטח.]

הגהות הב"ח

(א) במשנה ולא נברכת כובסין אא"כ הרחיק מכותלו של חבירו: (ב) שם ואת הסלעים מן הכותל של: (ג) רש"י ד"ה ישכון וכו' הכי דריש ליה ישכון בנימין לבטח על סמיכות: (ד) תוס' ד"ה שבעה וכו' כר' אלעזר בר"ש: (ה) שם ד"ה סלעים כו' ואית תנא תני דאין טומנין:

ו א מיי' פכ"א מהלכות מכירה הל' יב סמג עשין פב טוש"ע ח"מ סי' ריז סעיף ה:

ז ב ג מיי' פ"ט מהל' שכנים הל' י סמג עשין פב טוש"ע ח"מ סי' קנה סעיף יח:

א) [לקמן כה: כז: ב"מ קיז.]: ב) [לקמן כב: כה:]: ג) לקמן יט. ע"ש [תוספתא פ"א]: ד) נ"ל סותר וכ"ה בע"י:

פָּתַח בְּבוֹר וּמְסַיֵּים בְּכוֹתֶל; (לִיתְנֵי: אֶלָּא אִם כֵּן הִרְחִיק מִבּוֹרוֹ שֶׁל חֲבֵירוֹ ג"ט!) אֲמַר אַבַּיֵי, וְאִיתֵּימָא רַב יְהוּדָה: מִכּוֹתֶל בּוֹרוֹ שָׁנִינוּ. וְלִיתְנֵי: אא"כ הִרְחִיק מִבּוֹרוֹ שֶׁל חֲבֵירוֹ ג' טְפָחִים! הָא קמ"ל, דְּכוֹתֶל בּוֹר שְׁלֹשָׁה טְפָחִים, נָפְקָא מִינַּהּ – לְמִקָּח וּמִמְכָּר; כִּדְתַנְיָא: [א]הָאוֹמֵר לַחֲבֵירוֹ "בּוֹר וְכוֹתְלֶיהָ אֲנִי מוֹכֵר לְךָ" – צָרִיךְ שֶׁיְּהֵא הַכּוֹתֶל שְׁלֹשָׁה טְפָחִים. אִיתְּמַר: הַבָּא לִסְמוֹךְ בְּצַד הַמֶּצֶר – אַבַּיֵי אָמַר: סוֹמֵךְ, וְרָבָא אָמַר: אֵינוֹ סוֹמֵךְ. בְּשָׂדֶה הָעֲשׂוּיָה לְבוֹרוֹת – דִּבְרֵי הַכֹּל אֵינוֹ סוֹמֵךְ, כִּי פְּלִיגִי – בְּשָׂדֶה שֶׁאֵינָהּ עֲשׂוּיָה לְבוֹרוֹת; אַבַּיֵי אָמַר: סוֹמֵךְ, דְּהָא אֵינָהּ עֲשׂוּיָה לְבוֹרוֹת; רָבָא אָמַר: אֵינוֹ סוֹמֵךְ, דְּאָמַר לֵיהּ: כִּי הֵיכִי דְּאַתְּ אִימְּלַכְתְּ וְחָפַרְתְּ, אֲנָא נַמִי מִמְּלַכְנָא וְחָפַרְנָא. אִיכָּא דְּאָמְרִי: [ב]בְּשָׂדֶה שֶׁאֵינָהּ עֲשׂוּיָה לְבוֹרוֹת – דִּבְרֵי הַכֹּל סוֹמֵךְ, כִּי פְּלִיגִי – בְּשָׂדֶה הָעֲשׂוּיָה לְבוֹרוֹת; אַבַּיֵי אָמַר: סוֹמֵךְ; אֲפִילּוּ לְרַבָּנַן דְּאָמְרִי: [א)]מַרְחִיקִין אֶת הָאִילָן מִן הַבּוֹר עֶשְׂרִים וְחָמֵשׁ אַמָּה, הָתָם הוּא דִּבְעִידָּנָא דְּקָא נָטַע אִיתָא לְבוֹר, אֲבָל הָכָא בְּעִידָּנָא דְּקָא חָפַר לֵיתָא לְבוֹר. וְרָבָא אָמַר: [ג]אֵינוֹ סוֹמֵךְ; וַאֲפִילּוּ לְר' יוֹסֵי דְּאָמַר: [ב)]זֶה חוֹפֵר בְּתוֹךְ שֶׁלּוֹ וְזֶה נוֹטֵעַ בְּתוֹךְ שֶׁלּוֹ – הָנֵי מִילֵּי הָתָם, דִּבְעִידָּנָא דְּקָא נָטַע לֵיתְנְהוּ לְשָׁרָשָׁיו דְּמַזְּקִי לָהּ לַבּוֹר, אֲבָל הָכָא – אָמַר לֵיהּ: כָּל מָרָא וּמָרָא דְּקָא מָחְיַית קָא מְרַפֵּית לָהּ לְאַרְעַאי. תְּנַן: לֹא יַחְפּוֹר אָדָם בּוֹר סָמוּךְ לְבוֹרוֹ שֶׁל חֲבֵירוֹ; טַעְמָא דְּאִיכָּא בּוֹר, הָא לֵיכָּא בּוֹר – סוֹמֵךְ. בִּשְׁלָמָא לְהַךְ לִישָּׁנָא דְּאָמְרַתְּ: בְּשָׂדֶה שֶׁאֵינָהּ עֲשׂוּיָה לְבוֹרוֹת דִּבְרֵי הַכֹּל סוֹמֵךְ, מַתְנִיתִין – בְּשָׂדֶה שֶׁאֵינָהּ עֲשׂוּיָה לְבוֹרוֹת, אֶלָּא לְהַךְ לִישָּׁנָא דְּאָמְרַתְּ: בְּשָׂדֶה שֶׁאֵינָהּ עֲשׂוּיָה לְבוֹרוֹת פְּלִיגִי, בִּשְׁלָמָא לְאַבַּיֵי נִיחָא, אֶלָּא לְרָבָא קַשְׁיָא! אָמַר לָךְ רָבָא: הָא אִיתְּמַר עֲלַהּ, אָמַר אַבַּיֵי וְאִיתֵּימָא רַב יְהוּדָה: מִכּוֹתֶל בּוֹרוֹ שָׁנִינוּ. אִיכָּא דְּאָמְרִי: (א) וְאִיתְּמַר עֲלַהּ, אָמַר אַבַּיֵי וְאִיתֵּימָא רַב יְהוּדָה: מִכּוֹתֶל בּוֹרוֹ שָׁנִינוּ; בִּשְׁלָמָא לְהַךְ לִישָּׁנָא דְּאָמְרַתְּ: בְּשָׂדֶה הָעֲשׂוּיָה לְבוֹרוֹת דִּבְרֵי הַכֹּל אֵינוֹ סוֹמֵךְ, מַתְנִיתִין – בְּשָׂדֶה הָעֲשׂוּיָה לְבוֹרוֹת, אֶלָּא לְהַךְ לִישָּׁנָא דְּאָמְרַתְּ: בְּשָׂדֶה הָעֲשׂוּיָה לְבוֹרוֹת פְּלִיגִי, בִּשְׁלָמָא לְרָבָא נִיחָא, אֶלָּא לְאַבַּיֵי קַשְׁיָא! אָמַר לָךְ אַבַּיֵי: מַתְנִי' – שֶׁבָּאוּ לַחְפּוֹר בְּבַת אַחַת. תָּא שְׁמַע: [ג)]סֶלַע הַבָּא בְּיָדַיִם – זֶה חוֹפֵר בּוֹרוֹ מִכָּאן, וְזֶה חוֹפֵר בּוֹרוֹ מִכָּאן, זֶה מַרְחִיק שְׁלֹשָׁה טְפָחִים וְסָד בְּסִיד, וְזֶה מַרְחִיק שְׁלֹשָׁה טְפָחִים וְסָד בְּסִיד! בָּא בְּיָדַיִם שָׁאנֵי. וּדְקָאָרֵי לָהּ מַאי קָאָרֵי לָהּ? בָּא בְּיָדַיִם אִיצְטְרִיכָא לֵיהּ; ס"ד אָמִינָא: כֵּיוָן דְּבָא בְּיָדַיִם לִיבָּעֵי נַמִי רַוְוחָא טְפֵי, קָא מַשְׁמַע לָן. תָּא שְׁמַע: מַרְחִיקִין אֶת הַגֶּפֶת, וְאֶת הַזֶּבֶל, וְאֶת הַמֶּלַח

רש"י

פָּתַח בְּבוֹר. "סָמוּךְ לְבוֹרוֹ שֶׁל חֲבֵירוֹ", וַהֲדַר סַיֵּים: "אֶלָּא אִם כֵּן הִרְחִיק מִכּוֹתֶל". הֲוָה לֵיהּ לְמִיתְנֵי: אֶלָּא אִם כֵּן הִרְחִיק מִבּוֹרוֹ, דְּאִילּוּ "מִכּוֹתְלוֹ" – כּוֹתֶל הַבָּנוּי עַל גַּבֵּי קַרְקַע הוּא! מִכּוֹתֶל בּוֹרוֹ שָׁנִינוּ. כְּלוֹמַר, הַאי "כּוֹתֶל" דְּקָתָנֵי – מִכּוֹתֶל בּוֹרוֹ קָאָמַר, שֶׁאַף הוּא קָרוּי כּוֹתֶל. וְלִיתְנֵי מִבּוֹרוֹ שֶׁל חֲבֵירוֹ. וַאֲנָא יָדַעְנָא דְּמִכּוֹתֶל קָאָמַר. דְּאִי מֵחֲלַל בּוֹרוֹ קָאָמַר – אֵין זֶה כּוֹנֵס לְתוֹךְ שֶׁלּוֹ כְּלוּם, וּפְעָמִים שֶׁהוּא סוֹתֵר אַף כּוֹתֶל חֲבֵירוֹ, אִם הוּא רָחָב מִשְּׁלֹשָׁה. הָא קָא מַשְׁמַע לָן. בְּמַאי (ב) דְּתַנְיָא "מִכּוֹתֶל בּוֹרוֹ" לָמַדְנוּ בָּהּ שֶׁהַכּוֹתֶל בּוֹרוֹ שֶׁל רִאשׁוֹן מִילְּאָ כָּל שְׁלֹשָׁה טְפָחִים שֶׁהוּזְקַק גַּם הוּא לְהַרְחִיק מִן הַמֵּיצַר. וּמִמַּאי – מִדְּקָתָנֵי שֶׁהַחֲפִירוֹת חֲלָלוֹ שֶׁל זֶה אֵינָהּ מוּפְלֶגֶת מִכּוֹתְלוֹ שֶׁל זֶה אֶלָּא שְׁלֹשָׁה טְפָחִים שֶׁהוּא כּוֹנֵס לְתוֹךְ שֶׁלּוֹ, נִמְצָא שֶׁשְּׁלֹשֶׁת הַטְּפָחִים שֶׁכָּנַס גַּם זֶה לְתוֹךְ שֶׁלּוֹ – הַכּוֹתֶל מִילְּאָם. וְאַשְׁמוּעִינַן שִׁיעוּר רוֹחַב כּוֹתְלֵי בּוֹר. וְנָפְקָא מִינָּהּ לְמִקָּח וּמִמְכָּר. וְא"ת: מְנָלַן (ג) שֶׁהַכּוֹתֶל הָרִאשׁוֹן הוּא הָוֵי שִׁיעוּר הַרְחָקָה מִן הַמֵּיצַר? וַהֲלֹא לֹא הָיָה לַחֲבֵירוֹ בּוֹר סָמוּךְ לַמֵּיצַר, וּפְלִיגֵי בָּהּ אַבַּיֵי וְרָבָא, וְשָׁמְעִינַן לֵיהּ לְאַבַּיֵי דְּאָמַר: רִאשׁוֹן אֵינוֹ צָרִיךְ לְהַרְחִיק! תָּרֵיץ: הָא שָׁמְעִינַן לֵיהּ לְאַבַּיֵי גּוּפֵיהּ דְּאוֹקְמָהּ כְּשֶׁבָּאוּ לַחְפּוֹר בְּבַת אַחַת, שֶׁשְּׁנֵיהֶן הוּזְקְקוּ לְהַרְחִיק כָּל אֶחָד וְאֶחָד שְׁלֹשָׁה טְפָחִים. הַבָּא לִסְמוֹךְ. בּוֹרוֹ תְּחִילָּה בְּצַד הַמֵּיצַר, וְלַחֲבֵירוֹ אֵין שָׁם בּוֹר. הָעֲשׂוּיָה לְבוֹרוֹת. כְּגוֹן בֵּית הַשְּׁלָחִין, שֶׁצְּרִיכָה לְהַשְׁקוֹת תָּדִיר. אֲפִי' לְרַבָּנַן דְּאָמְרִי כו'. דְּשָׁמְעִינַן מִינַּהּ: אָדָם צָרִיךְ לִכְנוֹס לְתוֹךְ שֶׁלּוֹ כְּדֵי שֶׁלֹּא יַזִּיק אֶת חֲבֵירוֹ, וְלָא אָמְרִינַן: זֶה חוֹפֵר בְּתוֹךְ שֶׁלּוֹ וְזֶה נוֹטֵעַ בְּתוֹךְ שֶׁלּוֹ. לֵיתְנְהוּ לְשָׁרָשִׁים. אֶלָּא סוֹפָן שֶׁיִּתְפַּשְּׁטוּ עֶשְׂרִים וַחֲמִשָּׁה אַמָּה, וְיַזִּיקוּ אֶת כּוֹתְלֵי הַבּוֹר. מְרַפֵּית לִי. שֶׁהִיא מַרְעֶדֶת וְנָדָה מֵחֲמַת הַמַּכָּה. הָא אִיתְּמַר עֲלַהּ מִכּוֹתֶל בּוֹרוֹ שָׁנִינוּ. וְלָמַדְנוּ בָּהּ שֶׁאַף הָרִאשׁוֹן הוּזְקַק לְהַרְחִיק כְּדֵי כּוֹתֶל, שֶׁהוּא שְׁלֹשָׁה טְפָחִים, כִּדְאָמַרַן. אֶלָּא לְאַבַּיֵי קַשְׁיָא. דְּהוּא גּוּפֵיהּ אוֹקִים דְּמִכּוֹתֶל בּוֹרוֹ שָׁנִינוּ, וְעַל כָּרְחָךְ לֹא הוּזְכַּר שָׁם כּוֹתֶל אֶלָּא לְלַמְּדֵנוּ שֶׁשִּׁיעוּר כּוֹתֶל כְּדֵי הַרְחָקַת הַמֵּיצַר הוּא. אַלְמָא, אַף הָרִאשׁוֹן הוּזְקַק לְהַרְחִיק. הַבָּא בְּיָדַיִם. קַרְקַע רַךְ מִתְכַּתֵּשׁ מֵאֵלָיו. זֶה וְזֶה מַרְחִיק. אַלְמָא, אַף עַל הָרִאשׁוֹן לְהַרְחִיק. ה"ג: בָּא בְּיָדַיִם שָׁאנֵי וּדְקָאָרֵי לָהּ מַאי קָאָרֵי לָהּ בָּא בְּיָדַיִם אִיצְטְרִיךְ סד"א כו'. כְּלוֹמַר, הוּא הַדִּין אע"ג דְּלֹא בָּא בְּיָדַיִם. וְהַאי דְּנָקַט (ד) "בְּיָדַיִם" – רְבוּתָא אַשְׁמְעִינַן, דְּאַף עַל גַּב דְּבָא בְּיָדַיִם – אֵין צָרִיךְ לְהַרְחִיק אֶלָּא שְׁלֹשָׁה טְפָחִים.

מְתוּנְתָּא

תוספות

פתח בבור וסיים בכותל. בקונטרס גרס, בתר דשני מכותל בורו שנינו: וליתני אלא אם כן הרחיק מבורו. ואינו נראה, כמו שאפרש. ואי גרס לה — הכי גרס לה: פתח בבור וסיים בכותל, וליתני אלא אם כן הרחיק מבורו. וכן משמע מתוך פירוש ר' חננאל. ואע"ג דבריש "המניח" (בבא קמא דף כז.) כי פריך: פתח בכד וסיים בחבית, לא קא מסיים וליתני ואם הוזק בעל הכד כו' — אין לשון הגמרא שוה, אלא פעמים מאריך ופעמים מקצר.

מכותל בורו שנינו. כלומר, לא מחלל בורו קאמר, אלא מכותל שיש לבור, שהראשון הניח כשחפר בורו. ומהך מילתא דרב יהודה דייקא לקמן דאסור לסמוך, מדהוזקק הראשון להניח כותל. ופריך מינה לאביי. והשתא לא אפשר למיגרס: וליתני אלא אם כן הרחיק מבורו — דא"כ הוה משמע מחלל בורו. ומה שפירש הקונטרס דאי הוה תני "מבורו" הוה ידעינא דמכותל בורו קאמר, דאי מחלל בורו קאמר — אין [זה] כונס לתוך שלו כלום כו' — גרסת ספרו דחקתו. אבל אין נראה, דודאי אי תני "מבורו" הוה אמינא מחלל בורו קאמר, ושרי לסמוך, ואם הראשון הרחיק מאליו מן המיצר ג' טפחים או יותר — ה"א דהשני יכול לסמוך עד המיצר. ואם כן צריך לשנות מכותלו — לאשמועינן דאסור לסמוך לרבא, ולאביי צריך הרחקה בין שני הבורות ששה טפחים. ומיהו, יש ליישב הגירסא, ופריך אליבא דאביי, דאליבא דידיה קיימא, דליתני: אלא אם כן הרחיק מבורו ששה טפחים.

למאי נפקא מינה למקח וממכר. הך נפקותא לא איצטריך לרבא, דהא קא משמע לן דאסור לסמוך. אלא לאביי, דקא סבר מותר לסמוך. וקאמר למאי נפקא מינה? אי לאשמועינן דבעי הרחקה ו' טפחים — ליתני: אלא אם כן הרחיק מבורו ו' טפחים. **אביי** אמר סומך דהא אינה עשויה לבורות. והואיל וכן אינו מזיק לו אם הוא סומך. וקשה לרשב"א: דהא מפסיד הוא, שאם יטע אילן — יצטרך להרחיקו יותר, מחמת שסומך זה עד המיצר, דמרחיקין האילן מן הבור חמש ועשרים אמה! וי"ל: דמכל מקום אינו עושה לו היזק, דהא דמרחיק יותר — לא מפני שלא יזיקנו הבור, אלא מפני שלא יזיק הוא לבור. ולהכי אין לזה להניח מלסמוך בשביל כך, דאם לא כן — ירחיק כל כ"ה אמה את בורו.

אביי אמר סומך. אומר ר"י: דלשתי הלשונות, לאביי דאמר סומך, אם בא אחד לחפור בור לאחר מכאן — צריך הוא להרחיק כל ששה טפחים.

לאביי ניחא. השתא ס"ד ד"מכותל בורו" היינו מחלל בורו, ולא דקדק בלשון. **ה"ג** בספרים ישנים: סלע הבא בידים כו' וזה מרחיק ג' טפחים וסד בסיד(ה). וקשה לאביי. ה"ג שבאו לחפור שניהם בבת אחת. ובא בידים איצטריך ליה, סד"א: כיון דבא בידים ליבעי רווחא טפי, קמ"ל. והשתא לא היה צריך לאסוקי ובא בידים איצטריך ליה, שהרי לא הקשה כלום מבא בידים, אלא אגב דאייתי ברייתא מפרש לה. ויש ספרים דגרסי: טעמא דבא בידים הא לא בא בידים לא. ופריך לרבא. ומשני: ה"ה אפי' לא בא בידים, ובא בידים איצטריך ליה וכו'. ואין נראה לר"ת לחלק לענין היתר לסמוך בין בא בידים ובין לא בא בידים. ולר"י נראה לחלק שפיר, דאע"ג דלא בא בידים שרי לסמוך, בבא בידים — אסור לסמוך, לפי שהקרקע מתבקעת, ונופלת קרקע של שדה חבירו. **מרחיקין** את הגפת כו' טעמא דאיכא כותל כו'. פירוש: וקשה לרבא. ותימה: מאי קושיא? הכא ודאי מותר לסמוך בשאין כותל, שאין מזיק כלום, וכשיתפוך זה לעשות כותל יסיר את הגפת! וי"ל: דהני נמי מקלקלין את הקרקע, ויזיק לכותל לכשיבנה, אפי' שוב יסיר. ועוד אומר ר"י: דבכל אלו יש טורח בסילוקן, ולכך מעתה יכול לעכב עליו, כי יש לחוש שמא לא ימהר לסלקו כשירצה לעשות כותל. וא"ת: אכתי מאי פריך לרבא? הא מפרש טעמא לעיל: משום דכל מרא ומרא דקא מחית מרפית לארעאי! וי"ל: דההוא טעמא לא קאמר אלא אליבא דרבי יוסי, והכא לא פריך אלא אליבא דרבנן.

דטירייא

רבינו גרשום

ומקשינן פתח בבור לא יחפור בור וסיים בכותל דקתני אא"כ הרחיק מכותל חבירו ליתני מבורו של חבירו. והא אכתי לא פריש מילי דבור: א) וג' טפחים הוי במחיצה של לבנים כדקתני באידך פירקין דלעיל בלבנים זה נותן טפח ומחצה וזה נותן טפח ומחצה: אין ה"נ קתני מתני' אא"כ הרחיק מכותל בורו של חבירו ג' טפחים דהיינו בין בור זה לבור חבירו ו' טפחים והא אתא לאשמועינן דכותל בור ג' טפחים הוי דאי חפיר סמוך לכותל בור חבירו צריך להרחיק ג' ואי עביד כותל לבורו לא צריך הרחקה כלל: הבא לסמוך בצד המצר. כלומר שאם רוצה אחד לחפור בורו סמוך לשדה חבירו הפנויה מבורות: אביי אמר סומך. בצד ממש בלא הרחקה הואיל דאינו מזיק לחבירו דלית ליה לחבירו השתא בור: ורבא אמר אינו סומך. אא"כ ירחיק כדין דאע"ג דלית ליה האידנא אימור אימלוך וחפיר נמי חבירו ואי לא ירחיק האי אתי לאזוקי ליה: שדה העשויה לבורות. שצריכה לבורות דבית השלחין היא (לחבירו) ד"ה אינו סומך האידנא בור דהואיל ולא סגי בלא בור ודאי עביד בה בור ואתי לאזוקי אי לא ירחיק: כי פליגי בשדה שאינה עשויה לבורות. דבית הבעל היא: דבעידנא דקא נטע אילן איתא לבור. משום הכי מרחיק כ"ה אמות כי היכי דלא ליזלו שרשיו ומזקי לבור אבל הכא ב) דתני במצר כמצר סמיך משום דבעידנא דקא חפיר ליתיה לבור דהיאך: ליתנהו לשרשיו. בההיא שעתא: מרפיית לארעא. וכי בעינא למיחפר בור יפול העפר לתוכו: טעמא דאיכא בור. סמוך ליה מש"ה אינו סומך בלא הרחקה הא דוק מינה אי ליכא בור סמוך למצר חבירו בלא הרחקה: בשלמא להך לישנא. בתראה בשדה עשויה לבורות דברי הכל סומך (מש"ה) [שפיר] מתוקמ' מתני' דקתני הא ליכא בור סמוך בשדה שאינה עשויה לבורות מש"ה אי ליכא בור סמיך ואתיא מתני' כד"ה: אלא להאך לישנא דאמרת בשדה שאינה עשויה לבורות פליגי. אבל בשדה העשויה לבורות דברי הכל אינו סומך א"כ לא מיתוקמא מתני' אלא אליבא דאביי. אלא לרבא דאמר בין שדה העשויה לבורות בין שאינה עשויה לבורות אינו סומך מתני' קשיא ליה דמתני' דיקא הא ליכא בור סמיך: אמר [לך] רבא. לעולם אינו סומך לא בשדה העשויה לבורות ולא בשדה שאינה עשויה לבורות וממתני' לא מצי למידק הא וקשיא לרבא דלעיל פסיק ואמר לא סמיך. למ"ה: גפת. פסולת זיתים שמוציאין מבית הבד: ואם הוא המלח

רבינו גרשום

הא ליכא בור סמיך דהא איתמר עלה דמתני' לעיל אמר אביי ואי תימא רב יהודה מכותל בורו של חבירו שנינו. מדקתני מכותל בורו מכלל דההוא דחפר מעיקרא הרחיק בורו ג' טפחים כשיעור כותל ולא סמיך בצד ממש בלא הרחקה: ג) מתני' מתוקמ' לד"ה אלא להיאך לישנא דאמר בשדה העשויה לבורות פליגי בשלמא לרבא דאמר אינו סומך ניחא ומתוקמא מתני' דתני לא יחפור אא"כ הרחיק לדעתיה ד): אלא לאביי דאמר בין בשדה העשויה לבורות ובין שאינה עשויה לבורות סומך לדעתיה מתני' דקתני אינו סומך קשיא ליה: אמר לך אביי. לעולם אפי' בשדה העשויה לבורות מצי סמיך אי ליכא בור אלא מתני' דקתני לא יחפור אא"כ הרחיק מיתוקמא כשבא לחפור בבת אחת זה בורו מכאן וזה בורו מכאן ומש"ה צריך להרחיק זה מזה משום רפיות קרקע אבל היכא דאינו חופר אלא חד מינייהו כדקא משמע ותני דעשויה לבורות לחבירו נמי אבל עדיין לא עשאו ואתי זה אחר לחפור אהאי לעולם סמיך אמיצריה הואיל דעדיין לא נחפר בורו של חבירו: סלע הבא בידים. ארץ שהיא רכה שיכולין לחופרה ביד בלא חפירה אם בא זה בעצמו וזה בעצמו לחפור זה חופר בורו כו' וסד בסיד כדי שלא יפול אלמא דלא סמיך וקשיא לאביי אמר לך אביי לעולם לא קשיא לי בא בידים שאני דהואיל דסלע תיחוח הוא מש"ה צריך הרחקה זו דלא אתי למנפל אבל בעלמא סמיך: ודקארי לה. משום קשיא מאי קארי וכי לא היה יודע דהיכא דבא בידים צריך הרחקה טפי ומאי טעמא מקשה ליה. אמר לך המקשה לעולם משום קושיא קא מייתינא לה והאי דקתני מתני' בא בידים הוא הדין נמי בשאר קרקע שלא בא בידים דצריך הרחקה אבל מש"ה מתני' בא בידים טפי משאר קרקע דאיצטריך למיתנייהו דס"ד כו' קמ"ל דלא צריך ריחוק טפי משאר קרקע. ולעולם לא מצי סמיך ה) ותיובתא דאביי מתרץ לה ו) נפל שאני. כפ"ה: איכא דאמר סלע הבא בידים. כלומר סלעים המונחין בין מיצרי השדות לסימן והיכר מחיצה בין זה לזה השתא אם הוי מונחין הני סלעים בידים צריך להרחיק [שלשה טפחים] דלא סמך דכיון דמונחין בידי אדם מתפרצין הקרקע. הא לאו בידים אלא הכי הוי מששת ימי בראשית דקיימא האי סלע בין המצרים הללו מצי סמיך אמיצריה משום דלא אתיא להתפוצץ אלמא דסמיך

א) [מכאן ועד זה נותן טפח ומחצה נראה דשייך להלן בסמוך אחר תיבות לא צריך הרחקה כלל]: ב) [אבל הכא דרוצה לחפור סמוך למיצר סמיך וכו']: ג) [חסר כאן וצ"ל מתני' בשדה העשויה לבורות וד"ה אלא להיאך לישנא וכו']: ד) אא"כ הרחיק לדעתיה בשדה העשויה לבורות: ה) [נראה דצ"ל ולעולם לא מצי סמיך אפי' בשאר קרקע שלא בא בידים ותיובתא דאביי וכו']: ו) [נראה דצ"ל שבאו לחפור בבת אחת]:

הגהות הב"ח (א) גמ' איכא דאמרי תנן לא יחפור אדם בור סמוך לבורו של חבירו ואיתמר עלה אמר אביי: (ב) רש"י ד"ה הא קמ"ל במאי דקתני מכותל בורו למדנו בה שכותל בורו וכו' מדקתני שחפירות חללו של זה אינה מופלגת. נ"ב כלומר אין הכותל קרויה הפלגה אלא בג"ט לאפוקי בפחות מג': (ג) ד"ה ונפקא וכו' מנלן שכותל הראשון: (ד) ד"ה ה"ג בא וכו' והאי דנקט בא בידים: (ה) תום' ד"ה הכי גר' וכו' וסד בסיד פי' וקשה לאביי:

א) ב"ח וסוד: ב) ג"א דהני: ג) לקמן כ: ד) [שם]: ה) לקמן כ: ו) [ועיין פג.]: ז) ג"א ת"ש: ח) לקמן כו.: ט) ג"א ה"נ בצונמא: י) לקמן כה: כ) ג"ז שם: ל) ג"א ותני עלה [לקמן כה:]:

הַמֶּלַח, וְאֶת הַסִּיד, וְאֶת הַסְּלָעִים מִכּוֹתְלוֹ שֶׁל חֲבֵירוֹ ג' טְפָחִים א)אוֹ סָד בַּסִּיד; טַעֲמָא דְּאִיכָּא כּוֹתֶל, הָא לֵיכָּא כּוֹתֶל — סוֹמֵךְ! לָא, כִּי לֵיכָּא כּוֹתֶל נַמִי לָא סָמֵיךְ. וְאֶלָּא מַאי קָא מַשְׁמַע לָן? הָא קָא מַשְׁמַע לָן, דְּהָנֵי קָשׁוּ לְכוֹתֶל. תָּא שְׁמַע: מַרְחִיקִים אֶת הַזְּרָעִים, וְאֶת הַמַּחֲרֵישָׁה, וְאֶת מֵי רַגְלַיִם מִן הַכּוֹתֶל שְׁלֹשָׁה טְפָחִים; טַעֲמָא דְּאִיכָּא כּוֹתֶל, הָא לֵיכָּא כּוֹתֶל — סָמֵיךְ! לָא, כִּי לֵיכָּא כּוֹתֶל נַמִי לָא סָמֵיךְ. וְאֶלָּא מַאי קמ"ל? הָא קָא מַשְׁמַע לָן, דְּמִתּוּנְתָּא קָשָׁה לְכוֹתֶל. תָּא שְׁמַע: וְאֶת הָרֵיחַיִם — ג' מִן הַשֶּׁכֶב שֶׁהֵן ד' מִן הָרֶכֶב; טַעֲמָא דְּאִיכָּא כּוֹתֶל, הָא לֵיכָּא כּוֹתֶל — סָמֵיךְ! לָא, כִּי לֵיכָּא כּוֹתֶל נַמִי לָא סָמֵיךְ. וְאֶלָּא מַאי קָא מַשְׁמַע לָן? הָא קָא מַשְׁמַע לָן, דְּטִירָיָא קָשָׁה לְכוֹתֶל. תָּא שְׁמַע: וְאֶת הַתַּנּוּר — שְׁלֹשָׁה מִן הַכָּלְיָא שֶׁהֵן ד' מִן הַשָּׂפָה; טַעֲמָא דְּאִיכָּא כּוֹתֶל, הָא לֵיכָּא כּוֹתֶל — סָמֵיךְ! לָא, כִּי לֵיכָּא כּוֹתֶל נַמִי לָא סָמֵיךְ. אֶלָּא מַאי קָא מַשְׁמַע לָן? הָא קָא מַשְׁמַע לָן, ב)דְּהַבְלָא קָשֶׁה לְכוֹתֶל. תָּא שְׁמַע: ג)לֹא יִפְתַּח אָדָם חֲנוּת שֶׁל נַחְתּוֹמִין וְשֶׁל צַבָּעִין תַּחַת אוֹצָרוֹ שֶׁל חֲבֵירוֹ, וְלֹא רֶפֶת בָּקָר; טַעֲמָא דְּאִיכָּא אוֹצָר, הָא לֵיכָּא אוֹצָר — עָבֵיד! דִּירָה שָׁאנֵי. דַּיְקָא נַמִי, דְּתָנֵי עֲלָהּ: ד)אִם הָיְתָה רֶפֶת בָּקָר קוֹדֶמֶת לָאוֹצָר — מוּתָּר. ת"ש: ה)לֹא יִטַּע אָדָם אִילָן סָמוּךְ לְשָׂדֶה אֶלָּא אִם כֵּן הִרְחִיק מִמֶּנּוּ ד' אַמּוֹת, וְתָנֵי עֲלָהּ: ו)ד' אַמּוֹת שֶׁאָמְרוּ, כְּדֵי עֲבוֹדַת הַכֶּרֶם; טַעֲמָא דְּמִשּׁוּם כְּדֵי עֲבוֹדַת הַכֶּרֶם, הָא לָאו מִשּׁוּם כְּדֵי עֲבוֹדַת הַכֶּרֶם — סָמֵיךְ, וְאע"ג דְּאִיכָּא שָׁרָשִׁין דְּקָא מַזְּקִי! הָכָא בְּמַאי עָסְקִינַן — דְּמַפְסִיק צוּנְמָא. ז)(דַּיְקָא נַמִי, דְּקָתָנֵי:) ח)הָיָה גָּדֵר בֵּינְתַיִם — זֶה סוֹמֵךְ לַגָּדֵר מִכָּאן, וְזֶה סוֹמֵךְ לַגָּדֵר מִכָּאן. ט)אִי הָכִי, אֵימָא סֵיפָא: הָיוּ שָׁרָשָׁיו יוֹצְאִין בְּתוֹךְ שֶׁל חֲבֵירוֹ — מַעֲמִיק לָהֶן שְׁלֹשָׁה טְפָחִים כְּדֵי שֶׁלֹּא יְעַכֵּב הַמַּחֲרֵישָׁה; וְאִי דְּמַפְסִיק צוּנְמָא, מַאי בָּעוּ (א) הָתָם? ה"ק: וְאִי לָאו צוּנְמָא, וְהָיוּ שָׁרָשָׁיו יוֹצְאִין לְתוֹךְ שֶׁל חֲבֵירוֹ — מַעֲמִיק שְׁלֹשָׁה טְפָחִים כְּדֵי שֶׁלֹּא יְעַכֵּב הַמַּחֲרֵישָׁה. ת"ש: י)מַרְחִיקִין אֶת הָאִילָן מִן הַבּוֹר עֶשְׂרִים וְחָמֵשׁ אַמָּה; טַעֲמָא דְּאִיכָּא בּוֹר, הָא לֵיכָּא בּוֹר — סָמֵיךְ! לָא, כִּי לֵיכָּא בּוֹר נַמִי לָא סָמֵיךְ, וְהָא קמ"ל, דְּעַד כ"ה אַמָּה אָזְלִי שָׁרָשִׁים וּמַזְּקִי לַבּוֹר. אִי הָכִי, אֵימָא סֵיפָא: וְאִם אִילָן קָדַם — לֹא יָקוֹץ; וְאִי דְּלָא סָמֵיךְ, הֵיכִי מַשְׁכַּחַתְּ לָהּ? כִּדְא"ר פַּפָּא: בְּלוֹקֵחַ, ה"נ בְּלוֹקֵחַ. ת"ש: כ)מַרְחִיקִין אֶת הַמִּשְׁרָה מִן הַיָּרָק, וְאֶת הַכְּרֵישִׁין מִן הַבְּצָלִין, וְאֶת הַחַרְדָּל מִן הַדְּבוֹרִים; טַעֲמָא דְּאִיכָּא יָרָק, הָא לֵיכָּא יָרָק — סָמֵיךְ! לָא, כִּי לֵיכָּא יָרָק נַמִי לָא סָמֵיךְ, וְהָא קמ"ל, דְּהָנֵי קָשׁוּ אַהֲדָדֵי. א"ה, אֵימָא סֵיפָא: רַבִּי יוֹסֵי מַתִּיר בַּחַרְדָּל, ל)מִפְּנֵי שֶׁיָּכוֹל לוֹמַר לוֹ: עַד שֶׁאַתָּה אוֹמֵר לִי הַרְחֵק חַרְדָּלְךָ מִן דְּבוֹרַאי, הַרְחֵק דְּבוֹרֶךָ מִן חַרְדָּלַאי, שֶׁבָּאוֹת וְאוֹכְלוֹת לִגְלוּגֵי חַרְדָּלַאי; וְאִי

מִתּוּנְתָּא. דָּבָר לַח. **טִירָיָא** = איטוני"ר בְּלַעַ"ז. כְּמוֹ דְּטַרְיָא לְרֵישֵׁיהּ, בְּ"אֵלּוּ טְרֵיפוֹת" (חולין דף מה.). **חֲנוּת שֶׁל נַחְתּוֹמִין.** מוֹכְרֵי לֶחֶם, שֶׁמַּסִּיקִין שָׁם אוּר תָּמִיד. **אוֹצָר.** עֲלִיָּיה שֶׁאוֹצְרִין בָּהּ תְּבוּאָה וְשֶׁמֶן וְיַיִן, וְהֶעָשָׁן קָשֶׁה לָהֶן. **וְלֹא רֶפֶת בָּקָר.** הָרֵיחַ קָשֶׁה לָהֶן. **דִּירָה שָׁאנֵי.** חֲנוּת וְרֶפֶת בָּקָר דִּירָתָן שֶׁל אָדָם הֵן, וְאֵין לָנוּ לֶאֱסוֹר דִּירָתוֹ עָלָיו, אא"כ הֶהֱיזֵק מוּכָן. **דַּיְקָא נַמִי.** דְּדִירָה שָׁאנֵי. דְּקָתָנֵי עֲלָהּ דְּהַהִיא: אִם הָיְתָה הָרֶפֶת בָּקָר קוֹדֶמֶת לָאוֹצָר מוּתָּר, וּבְכוּלְּהוּ שְׁאָר הַרְחָקוֹת דְּמַתְנִי' לָא תָּנָא הָכִי — ש"מ: הָכָא מִשּׁוּם דְּדִירָה שָׁאנֵי, אֲבָל אִינָךְ — אַף הָרִאשׁוֹן צָרִיךְ לְהַרְחִיק. **אֶלָּא אִם כֵּן הִרְחִיק מִמֶּנּוּ אַרְבַּע אַמּוֹת.** כִּדְמְפָרֵשׁ טַעֲמָא: כְּדֵי עֲבוֹדַת הַכֶּרֶם, שֶׁהָיוּ חוֹרְשִׁים הַכֶּרֶם בְּמַחֲרֵישָׁה. וְכֵן בִּשְׁעַת הַבָּצִיר בּוֹצְרִין אוֹתָם בָּעֲגָלוֹת, וְצָרִיךְ לָהֶן מָקוֹם פָּנוּי אַרְבַּע אַמּוֹת, שֶׁלֹּא תִּיכָּנֵס עֶגְלַת מַחֲרֵישָׁתוֹ בְּקַרְקַע חֲבֵירוֹ. **טַעֲמָא מִשּׁוּם עֲבוֹדַת הַכֶּרֶם.** שֶׁהוּא מַזִּיקוֹ בְּיָדַיִם. הָא לָאו הָכִי — סָמֵיךְ, וְאע"ג (ב) שֶׁיִּתְפַּשְּׁטוּ שָׁרָשָׁיו וְיַזִּיקוּ בַּשָּׂדֶה, בֵּין לְעַכֵּב הַמַּחֲרֵישָׁה בֵּין לַחֲפִירַת הַבּוֹר. **צוּנְמָא.** סֶלַע חָזָק, שֶׁלֹּא יִתְפַּשְּׁטוּ שָׁרָשָׁיו לְשָׁם. **גָּדֵר בֵּינְתַיִם.** שֶׁאֵין מַזִּיקוֹ עוֹד לַעֲבוֹדַת הַכֶּרֶם — זֶה סוֹמֵךְ אִילָנוֹת לַגָּדֵר מִכָּאן, וְזֶה סוֹמֵךְ אִילָנוֹת לַגָּדֵר מִכָּאן. וְאִי נַמִי אֶחָד מֵהֶן שְׂדֵה לָבָן — אֵין כָּאן כִּלְאַיִם, כִּדְאָמַר בְּעֵירוּבִין (דף יא.): אִם גְּפָנִים מִכָּאן — מוּתָּר לִזְרוֹעַ כָּאן, גַּבֵּי נָעַץ אַרְבָּעָה קוּנְדֵּיסִין וּמָתַח זְמוֹרָה עַל גַּבֵּיהֶן, דְּדָמְיָא לְצוּרַת הַפֶּתַח. קָתָנֵי מִיהָא: זֶה סוֹמֵךְ, וְאע"ג דְּאָזְלִי שָׁרָשִׁים תַּחַת הַגָּדֵר וּמִתְפַּשְּׁטִין לְתוֹךְ הַשָּׂדֶה. **מַעֲמִיק לָהֶן.** בַּעַל הַשָּׂדֶה קוֹצֵץ אֶת הַשָּׁרָשִׁין שֶׁיֵּלְכוּ בְּשָׂדֵהוּ בְּעוֹמֶק שְׁלֹשָׁה טְפָחִים. **וְאִי לָאו צוּנְמָא.** וְזֶה נוֹטֵעַ שָׁם שֶׁלֹּא כַּדָּת — מַעֲמִיק לְהוּ זֶה (ג) כְּשֶׁיַּזִּיקוּ הֵן. **עֶשְׂרִים וַחֲמִשָּׁה אַמּוֹת.** כָּךְ שִׁיעֲרוּ שֶׁהַשָּׁרָשִׁין נִמְשָׁכִין וְהוֹלְכִין וּמְקַלְקְלִין אֶת כּוֹתְלֵי הַבּוֹר. **הוּא הַדִּין כו'.** וְהָא קמ"ל דְּעַד כ"ה אַמָּה אָזְלֵי שָׁרָשִׁין וּמַזְּקִי לַבּוֹר. ה"ג **אִי הָכִי אֵימָא סֵיפָא אִם הָאִילָן קָדַם לֹא יָקוֹץ אִי לָא סָמֵיךְ הֵיכִי מַשְׁכַּחַתְּ לְהוּ.** דְּהָאִילָן קָדַם? וְאִי שֶׁלֹּא כַּדִּין סָמַךְ — אַמַּאי לֹא יָקוֹץ? מַה לִּי בּוֹר קָדַם, דְּקָתָנֵי: קוֹצֵץ, וּמַאי שְׁנָא אִילָן קָדַם, דְּתָנָא: לֹא יָקוֹץ? **כִּדְאָמַר רַב פַּפָּא.** לְקַמָּן בְּשְׁמַעְתִּין. **הָכָא נַמִי בְּלוֹקֵחַ.** אָדָם שֶׁנָּטַע אִילָן בְּתוֹךְ שָׂדֵהוּ, וְאַחַר כָּךְ מָכַר חֲצִי שָׂדֵהוּ לְאִישׁ אַחֵר, וּבָא הַלּוֹקֵחַ וְחָפַר בּוֹר — אֵין זֶה צָרִיךְ לָקוֹץ אִילָן שֶׁנְּטָעוֹ בִּרְשׁוּתוֹ. **אֶת הַמִּשְׁרָה.** מַיִם שֶׁשּׁוֹרִין בּוֹ אֶת הַפִּשְׁתָּן. **מִן הַיָּרָק.** שֶׁל מִינֵי מַאֲכָל, כְּרוּב וְשׁוּמִין וּכְרֵישִׁין. **וְאֶת הַכְּרֵישִׁין** = כַּרְתֵּי, פוריל"ש. **וְאֶת הַחַרְדָּל מִן הַדְּבוֹרִים.** שֶׁאוֹכְלִין אֶת הַחַרְדָּל, וּמְחַדֵּד אֶת פִּיהֶם, וְאוֹכְלוֹת אֶת דְּבַשׁ שֶׁלָּהֶן. **כִּי לֵיכָּא** יָרָק נַמִי לָא סָמֵיךְ. וְהָא קמ"ל דְּהָנָךְ קָשׁוּ אַהֲדָדֵי. **עַד שֶׁאַתָּה אוֹמֵר הַרְחֵק אֶת חַרְדָּלְךָ מִדְּבוֹרַיי.** שֶׁעַל הַמַּזִּיק לְהַרְחִיק עַצְמוֹ, הַרְחֵק אַתָּה דְּבוֹרֶיךָ מִן חַרְדָּלַיי, שֶׁאַף אַתָּה נִקְרָא מַזִּיק. וְאִי

דטירייא קשה לכותל. אע"ג דלקמן (דף כ:) הדר ביה מטעמא דטירייא, ומפרש: אלא משום קלא — מכל מקום נקט ליה הכא, משום דמעיקרא הוה בעי לפרושי טעמא משום טירייא. ולספרים דלא גרסי "אלא" אתי שפיר הכא, דלהכיא גירסא — טירייא וקלא חד טעמא הוא. **לא** יפתח אדם חנות של נחתומין. פ"ה: משום שהעשן קשה לאוצר. וקשה לר"ת: דלקמן אמר: ביין התירו, שמשביחו. ועשן ודאי מזיק ליין, דהא יין מעושן פסול לנסכים! אלא נראה לר"ת: דהיזק עשן ליכא, כיון דאיכא שם תקרה ומעזיבה לא יכנס שם העשן. אלא טעמא שההבל מזיק את האוצר, אבל את היין משביח. וגרסי' לקמן: אמר רב יוסף: והאי דידן אפילו שרגא קשיא ליה. כלומר, הבלא דשרגא. ולא גרסי' "קוטרא דשרגא". **הא** ליכא אוצר עביד. הוי מצי לשנויי: ה"ה כי ליכא לא סמיך, והא קמ"ל דהבלא (ד) קשיא לאוצר. **דיקא** נמי דקתני אם היתה רפת בקר קודמת כו'. ובכולהו הרחקות דמתני' לא תני הכי, והוה ליה לאשמועינן בשאר, וכ"ש בדירה. ותימה: דלעולם בשאר הרחקות נמי מותר לסמוך, והא דנקטיה הכא — לאשמועינן רבותא, דאע"ג דהוי גירי דיליה, אם היתה קודמת לאוצר — מותר, דהשתא הוי חידוש אפילו לרבי יוסי. ואי אשמועינן בשאר — לא הוי חידוש אלא לרבנן, אבל לרבי יוסי דקסבר על הניזק להרחיק — לא הוי שום חידוש. **דיקא** נמי דקתני כו'. ולאביי לא קשיא האי דיקא, דלא משמע ליה שיהא חידוש בשאר טפי מבדירה. **ואם** היתה רפת בקר כו'. והוא הדין חנות של נחתומין ושל צבעין, וחדא מינייהו נקט. **ותני** עלה ד' אמות שאמרו כדי עבודת הכרם. הוה ליה למינקט "כדי עבודת האילן", אלא נקט "עבודת הכרם" לפי שנזכר לשון זה במסכת כלאים, גבי כרם שצריך הרחקה ד' אמות. **טעמא** משום עבודת הכרם כו'. בלאו האי דיוקא מצי למפרך בפשיטות: דסגי בהרחקת ארבע אמות, ואי אסור לסמוך — היה צריך להרחיק כ"ה אמות, כדתנן לקמן (דף כה:): שמרחיקין את האילן מן הבור. אלא ניחא ליה למידק, דאפילו תוך ארבע אמות מותר לסמוך. **דמפסיק** צונמא. וא"ת: אמאי צריך ד' אמות? פשיטא שחוץ לצונמא לא יחרוש, שלא יועיל כלום לאילן! וי"ל: כשיחרוש עד הצונמא, וירצה להפוך המחרישה לצד אחר — המחרישה יכנס לשדה חבירו. **היו** שרשיו יוצאין כו'. וא"ת: היאך סמך? אי שלא ברשות — א"כ יקוץ! וצריך לאוקמי בלוקח. ולריב"א אין נראה להעמיד בלוקח, מדלא מסיק לה כדבסמוך. אלא נראה דמיירי בסמך שלא ברשות, דאינו קוצץ האילן אלא בנתינת דמים. ובזה לא רצה להאריך ולהשמיענו. **הכא** נמי בלוקח. פ"ה: שהאילן ביד מוכר. ואין נראה לר"י בר' מרדכי, דא"כ הול"ל "במוכר". אלא נראה לו לפרש שהאילן ביד לוקח. ולשני הפירושים אלו אין להקשות: מאי איריא שהאילן קדם? אפילו קדם בור נמי, כגון שאדם אחד עשה הבור ואח"כ נטע האילן, ומכר הבור לפ"ה, או אילן לפי' ר"י ברבי מרדכי — לא יקוץ, שהרי בהיתר עשאן. דבכה"ג "אילן קדם" קרינא ביה, שקדמה נטיעת האילן לערעור בעל הבור, דערעור אינו בא אלא ע"י מכירת בור או מכירת האילן. אבל לפר"ת, שפי' בלוקח — שלקח מאדם אחד את אילן, וטוענין ללוקח, קשה לר"י: מאי איריא אילן קדם! אפילו קדם בור נמי! ועוד: כיון דהחזיק באילן ג' שנים איירי, דבחזקת ג' שנים טוענין ללוקח, לוקמה נמי בלא לוקח, ובחזקה שיש עמה טענה! לגלוגי

רבינו גרשום

המלח. שחופרין להכבנים לתוכן מים לעשות מלח ושיחות שעושין לשרוף בהן הסיד ואת הסלעים חפירה מלאה אבנים: וסד בסיד. החפירה דכל אלו מזיקין לכותל: הא ליכא כותל. הוי כשאר כותל וסמיך וקשיא לרבא דאמר גבי שדה דלא סמיך: דמתונתא דהני. זה לחלוחית המים שמשקין הזרעים בנגר ודאי קשין לכותל שמקלקלין המים יסוד הכותל: מרחיקין את הריחים. העשוין בקרקע מן הכותל חבירו: ג' טפחים מן השכב. זו אבן התחתונה שמו שכב. ורכב זו אבן עליונה שמורכבת עליה והתחתונה רחבה מן העליונה טפח לכל צד והיינו ג' מן השכב שהוא ד' מן הרכב מתוך דפחותה טפח: טעמא דאיכא כותל. וקשיא לרבא: טירא קשה לכותל אותו זיעוע שמזעזעין הקרקע בשעה שמתקינין שם הריחים איכא דאמר טירא קול הברה שעושין הריחים: מרחיקין את התנור מן הכותל. אע"ג דלא תני כותל אפ"ה משמע דירחיק מן הכותל ג' טפחים מן הכיליא איזהו כיליא שכשעושין התנור מחרס שכל תנוריהן היו של חרס ועשוין כעין דלי פתוח מלמעלה והחרס קלוש ומדביקין סביב התנור מן הטיט בעובי טפח סביב כדי לחזק התנור מפני שהוא של חרס שלא ישבר ולאותו הדבק קרי כילייא והיינו דאמרי' במס' (פסחים) [חולין קכג:] וגורר את הטפילה עד שמגיע לארץ ואותה דאמרי' התם היינו כילייא ושפה זו שפת התנור עצמו שהוא מרחיק מן הכותל ד' טפחים כפ"ה. איכא דאמרי כילייא זה יסוד התנור דכל סביב התנור סמוך לקרקע יוצא בנין התנור טפח לחוץ וכי מעלה בנינו מקצר ועולה עד לשפה שלמעלה דפוחתת טפח למ"ה: הבלא. חמימות התנור: לא יפתח אדם חנות של נחתומין. שאופה פתו למכור בכל עת תמיד אופה ומחמם התבואה או היין של חבירו שבאוצר שלמעלה הימנו בעלייה ומש"ה קרי לעלייה אוצר שכן דרך בני אדם שאוצרין פירותיהן בעליות. וכן של צבעים לא יפתח תחת האוצר מפני שתדיר עושה היסק גדול לצורך הצבע ומחמם התבואה: ולא רפת בקר נמי משום הבלא דזבל. וטעמא מאי לא יפתח דאיכא אוצר דקדם מעיקרא מש"ה אינו יכול לפתוח להפסידו. הא לא הוי אוצר מעיקרא אלא חנות קדם ברישא והשתא קא פתח (הוי) [האי] חנות של נחתומין אע"ג דיכול למימר האי בעל (האוצר) [המיצר] למחר אי עביד הכא לעיל אוצר שלי ומזקת לי כיון דעדיין לא מינכר היזקו עביד וסמיך הכי נמי סמיך א] למיצר וקשיא לרבא אמר לך רבא לעולם בעלמא לא סמיך [ודקא דייקי הא היכא] דליכא אוצר סמיך היינו טעמא דדירתו של אדם שאני שצריך לו לאדם לעשות צרכיו בדירתו מש"ה לא מצי מעכב ליה הואיל ואין לו שום אוצר עכשיו אבל גבי בור ושדה דעלמא דלא קבע תשמישתיהו כדירה לא סמיך משום דמזיק ליה בכך [דמרפי] ליה ארעיה ואי מימלך למיעבד בור לא מצי למיעבד בור: דיקא נמי. דדירה שאני: דקתני אם היה רפת בקר קודם לאוצר מותר. משום דדירה שאני: כדי עבודת הכרם. כדי איכר בקר וכליו דלא דייש ליה לשדהו דהתם היו חורשין את הכרמים בשוורים וכך נמי היו חורשין לשדה אילנות בשוורים: דקא מפסיק צונמא. בין שדה שלו לשל חבירו דלא קא עבדין בהני סלעים מש"ה מצי סמיך אי לאו מפני עבודת הכרם אבל בעלמא לא: היה גדר בינתים. בין הכרם לשדה זה סומך נטיעותיו לגדר [אע"ג] דעברין שרשין לשדה: מעמיק לשרשיו בקרקע ג' טפחים כדי שלא יעכב את המחרישה. הכי קאמר אי לאו צונמא והוה מרחיק ליה לאילנות כ"ה אמה כשיעור האילן. ולאחר כן הגדילו שרשין יותר מכ"ה והיו שרשין יוצאין לתוך של חבירו כנ"ל: אית דמפרשי האי שדה כרם הוא כדי להשתמש בהני ד' אמות עבודת תשמיש דצריך לכרם כגון בית הגת וגיגית שלועין טיני. היינו בור שתחת הגת. אלמא דסמיך (ליה אלא) הכא במאי עסקינן דאי לאו משום עבודת הכרם סמיך דמפסיק צונמא כלומר דאיכא סלע חזק בין האילן לשדה דאינן יכולין השרשין לעבור ולהפסיד בשדה אבל גבי בור ושדה דעלמא דמפסיד לעולם לא סמיך. זה סומך אילנו לגדר וזה בורו אלמא דסמיך אע"ג דעברי שרשים תותי גדר לשדה חבירו וקא מזקי. לא הכא נמי דאיכא צונמא: מעמיק שרשי האילן בקרקע ג' טפחים [כן] כי היכי דלא ליתזקו שרשין ואמאי צריך להעמיק בתמיה: כדי שלא תעכב את המחרישה ולא יפסיד. להכי צריך להעמיק וסמיך אבל גבי בור ושדה דעלמא דלעולם אי אפשר דליכא פסידא של רפיית הקרקע מבור לבור (אמאי) [אימא] לעולם לא סמיך. למ"ה: אי הכי. דכי ליכא בור [נמי] לא סמיך האילן אימא סיפא אם האילן קדם לבור דאם היה נטוע האילן קודם דנחפר הבור אע"ג דמזיק לה לא יקוץ ואי לא סמיך האילן על מצר שדה חבירו קודם חפירת הבור היכי מצי משכחת לה דמזיק לה השתא אלא לאו ש"מ דסמיך: לא לעולם לא סמיך. וכי תימא א"כ היכי הוה זה סומך אילנו אצל שדה חבירו: כדאמר רב פפא לקמן בלוקח. כגון דהוה מעיקרא האילן והשדה לאדם אחד ומכרו לשני בני אדם לא' מכר מקום האילן והאילן ולשני מכר כל שאר השדה משפת אילן ולהלן ובא זה שלקח שאר השדה וחפר בורו סמוך לאילן דהשתא קדם האילן לבור ולא סמכו זה לוקח אלא המוכר דברשות סמכו דהכל היה שלו ומש"ה לא יקוץ ולעולם בעלמא לא סמיך: מרחיקין את המשרה. מים סרוחין ששורין בהן פשתן וקשה הוא לירק. א"ד משרה שמכבסין ושורין בהן את הבגדים: מן הירק מתוך ג] דאתנייהו ירקות דלא צריכי כל כך למים וניתזין ניצוצות הכביסה על הירק כל שעה ומזיק להו. למ"ה: ולא כרתי אצל בצלים. משום דמכחשי כרישין לבצלים וכן לחרדל מתוך דאכלי דבורים לחרדל: דאכלי לגלוגי. כלומר ענפי חרדלי: ואי

א] נראה דצ"ל והכא נמי סמיך בור סמוך למיצר. ב] נראה דצ"ל ג"ט כדי שלא תעכב את המחרישה ולא יפסיד ואמאי צריך להעמיק בתמי': ה"ק ואי לאו צונמא וכו' והכי צריך להעמיק וכו'. ג] אולי צ"ל מתוך דהנהו ירקות לא צריכי כ"כ וכו'.

הגהות הב"ח (א) גמ' מאי בעו שרשין התם: (ב) רש"י ד"ה טעמא וכו' ואע"ג דסופו שיתפשטו: (ג) ד"ה ואי לאו צונמא וכו' להו זה (כשיזיקו הן) תא"מ ונ"ב ס"א כדי שלא יזיקו כשיזיקו הן: (ד) תוס' ד"ה הא ליכא וכו' דהבלא דהני קשה לאוצר:

עין משפט
נר מצוה

ח א ב מיי' פ"י מהל' שכנים הל' ה סמג עשין פב טוש"ע ח"מ סי' קנה סעיף לא:

וְאִי דְּלָא סָמֵיךְ, הֵיכִי מַשְׁכַּחַתְּ לָהּ? אָמַר רַב פַּפָּא: בְּלוֹקֵחַ. אִי בְּלוֹקֵחַ, מַאי טַעֲמָא דְּרַבָּנַן? וְעוֹד, מַאי טַעֲמָא דְּרַבִּי יוֹסֵי? אֲפִילּוּ מִשְׁרָה וְיַרְקָא נַמִי! אֲמַר רָבִינָא, קָא סָבְרִי רַבָּנַן: עַל הַמַּזִּיק לְהַרְחִיק אֶת עַצְמוֹ. מִכְּלַל דְּר' יוֹסֵי סָבַר: עַל הַנִּיזָּק לְהַרְחִיק אֶת עַצְמוֹ; אִי עַל הַנִּיזָּק — אֲפִי' מִשְׁרָה וְיַרְקָא נַמִי! אֶלָּא, לְעוֹלָם ר' יוֹסֵי נַמִי עַל הַמַּזִּיק סְבִירָא לֵיהּ, וְהָכִי קָאָמַר לְהוּ רַבִּי יוֹסֵי לְרַבָּנַן: תֵּינַח מִשְׁרָה וְיַרְקָא, דְּהָנֵי מַזְּקִי הָנֵי וְהָנֵי לָא מַזְּקִי הָנֵי, אֶלָּא חַרְדָּל וּדְבוֹרִים — תַּרְוַיְיהוּ מַזְּקִי אַהֲדָדֵי! וְרַבָּנַן? דְּבוֹרִים לַחַרְדָּל לָא מַזְּקִי לֵיהּ, אִי בְּבִינְתָּא — לָא מַשְׁכְּחָא לֵיהּ, אִי בְּטַרְפָּא — הָדַר פָּארֵי. וְסָבַר ר' יוֹסֵי עַל הַמַּזִּיק לְהַרְחִיק אֶת עַצְמוֹ? וְהָתְנַן, [א]רַבִּי יוֹסֵי אוֹמֵר: אע"פ שֶׁהַבּוֹר קוֹדֶמֶת לָאִילָן — לֹא יָקוֹץ, שֶׁזֶּה חוֹפֵר בְּתוֹךְ שֶׁלּוֹ, וְזֶה נוֹטֵעַ בְּתוֹךְ שֶׁלּוֹ! אֶלָּא, לְעוֹלָם ר' יוֹסֵי עַל הַנִּיזָּק ס"ל, וּלְדִבְרֵיהֶם דְּרַבָּנַן קָאָמַר לְהוּ: לְדִידִי [א]עַל הַנִּיזָּק לְהַרְחִיק אֶת עַצְמוֹ, [ב]וַאֲפִי' מִשְׁרָה וְיַרְקָא לָא בָּעֵי רְחוּקֵי. אֶלָּא לְדִידְכוּ, דְּאָמְרִיתוּ עַל הַמַּזִּיק, תֵּינַח מִשְׁרָה וְיַרְקָא, דְּהָנֵי מַזְּקִי הָנֵי וְהָנֵי לָא מַזְּקִי הָנֵי, אֶלָּא חַרְדָּל וּדְבוֹרִים — תַּרְוַיְיהוּ מַזְּקִי אַהֲדָדֵי! וְרַבָּנַן? דְּבוֹרִים לַחַרְדָּל לָא מַזְּקִי לֵיהּ, אִי בְּבִינְתָּא —
לָא

וְאִי לָא סָמֵיךְ. אִינִישׁ הֶיזֵּק לְמֵילַר חֲבֵירוֹ אֲפִילּוּ בְּשֶׁאֵין שָׁם דְּבַר הַנִּיזּוֹק, אִית לֵיהּ לְר' יוֹסֵי, דְּאִלּוּ שְׁנֵיהֶן מַזִּיקִין הֵן, הֵיכִי מַשְׁכַּחַתְּ לֵיהּ דְּלִיסְמוֹךְ חַד מִינַּיְיהוּ בְּרֵישָׁא? הֲרֵי חֲבֵירוֹ מְעַכֵּב עָלָיו! **בְּלוֹקֵחַ.** אַחַר שֶׁעָשָׂה זֶה מִשְׁרָה בְּתוֹךְ שָׂדֵהוּ, אוֹ זָרַע שָׁם חַרְדָּל – מָכַר מֶחֱצָה שָׂדֵהוּ לְאַחֵר, וְהַלּוֹקֵחַ זָרַע שָׁם יָרָק אוֹ הֶעֱמִיד דְּבוֹרִים. **אַמַּאי** מַרְחִיק. הֲרֵי בִּרְשׁוּת עָשָׂה! **וְעוֹד** מַאי טַעֲמָא דְּרַבִּי יוֹסֵי. דְּלָא פָּלֵיג אֶלָּא בְּחַרְדָּל, וְטַעֲמָא מִשּׁוּם דְּתַרְוַיְיהוּ מַזִּיקִין הֵן? וְלִיפְלוֹג נַמִי בְּמִשְׁרָה וְיָרָק! **עַל הַמַּזִּיק לְהַרְחִיק אֶת עַצְמוֹ.** וְאַף עַל פִּי שֶׁמִּתְּחִלָּה עָשָׂה בִּרְשׁוּת. **אִי בְּבִינְתָּא.** גַּרְעִין הַזֶּרַע.
לָא

[ב]**לגלוגי** חרדל. פי' הקונטרס: פרחים. ובערוך פירש: גרעין. ותרוייהו אין נראה לר"י, דהא קאמרי רבנן: דבורים לחרדל לא מזקי אי בבינתא כו' אי בטרפא כו'. משמע דלא פירש רבי יוסי בדבריו מה הן מזיקין, ולכך היו מסתפקין אי בבינתא כו'. ונראה לר"י דלגלוגי הם ענפים. והשתא לא פירש רבי יוסי מה הם מזיקות, לכך אמרו ליה רבנן: אי בבינתא כו'. וא"ת: מכל מקום, הרי הן מזיקין לחרדל, שיאכלו הפרחים! ויש לומר: שהפרחים אינן כ"א מעט, וביום או יומים שיעמדו אין יכולין להזיק. **ואי** לא סמיך היכי משכחת לה. פר"י: בשלמא לאביי דאמר סמיך — אתי שפיר, דמיירי שסמך בעל דבורים תחילה. ואע"ג דהשתא קס"ד דדבורים נמי מזקי לחרדל לכ"ע, מכל מקום סברי רבנן דעל המזיק שני, דהיינו בעל חרדל, להרחיק את (א) כל ההרחקה, כמו גבי בור דאם סמך הראשון על המילר — השני מרחיק כל ששה טפחים. ורבי יוסי סבר: כיון דדבורים מזקי חרדל, ועשה קלת שלא כהוגן שסמך על המילר, שזה עתיד לסוף לזרוע חרדל, אע"פ שבדין אינו יכול למונעו שלא יסמוך — מ"מ קלת שלא כהוגן עושה, וגם בעל חרדל יכול לסמוך. ולא דמי לבור, דהתם משום דמרפי ליה לארעיה ומזיק השני בידים לכותל בורו של ראשון — לכך על השני להרחיק כל ההרחקה, אבל הכא לא. אלא לרבא דאמר לא סמיך — היכי משכחת לה דבעל החרדל ירחיק כל ההרחקה לרבנן, ולרבי יוסי לא ירחיק כלל? דכיון דתרוייהו מזקי אהדדי — על כל אחד ואחד להרחיק חצי ההרחקה. ואפילו סמך בעל דבורים תחלה — יש לו לסלקם, הואיל ושלא כדין סמכם! אמר רב פפא: בלוקח — שזרע חרדל ומכר חצי שדהו, והלוקח העמיד דבורים. וסברי רבנן כדמסיק דדבורים לא מזקי לחרדל, ועל המזיק להרחיק את עצמו אף על פי שסמך בהיתר. אע"ג דגבי אילן כשסמכו בהיתר אמרי דלא יקוץ — הני מילי אילן, שעשוי לעמוד שנים רבות ואיכא הפסד מרובה, אבל משרה כרישין וחרדל — לא. דהכי נמי אמרינן גבי אילן: אם הבור קדם — קולץ ונותן דמים, אע"ג דסמך אילנו באיסור, ובשאר דברים הנסמכים באיסור אינו נראה שיתנו דמים. אלא טעמא — להפסד מרובה חששו. ורבי יוסי סבר דדבורים מזקי לחרדל, וצריך בעל דבורים להרחיק כל ההרחקה, כיון דבעל חרדל לא עשה כלל שלא כהוגן. ומשום הכי נמי לא בעי לאוקמי כשסמך בעל דבורים תחלה ובלוקח, ולא היה צריך לדחוק ולומר דלרבנן על המזיק להרחיק אע"פ שעשה בהיתר, מה שאינו גבי אילן ובור, וגם לא יצטרך לומר דלרבנן דבורים לא מזקי לחרדל, ופליגי ארבי יוסי. דא"כ, כיון דבעל דבורים סמך בהיתר ולא עשה שלא כהוגן — לא היה מתיר רבי יוסי לבעל חרדל לסמוך. ואם תאמר: נוקי פלוגתייהו בלא לוקח, דלרבנן, דדבורים לא מזקי לחרדל — צריך בעל חרדל להסיר ולהרחיק כל ההרחקה, אע"פ שסמך תחלה. ולרבי יוסי, כיון דתרוייהו מזקי אהדדי — אין לבעל החרדל להרחיק כל ההרחקה, אלא החצי! וי"ל: דמתיר בחרדל — משמע דמתיר לגמרי לסמוך. אי הכי מאי טעמא דרבנן? כיון דבהיתר נסמכו משרה וכרישין — למה צריך להרחיקן כשבאו ירק ובצלים? וכ"ש חרדל, למה ירחיקוהו כשבאו דבורים, כיון שגם הם מזיקי? דס"ד דדבורים נמי מזקי לחרדל לכ"ע. ועוד: מ"ט דרבי יוסי דלא פליג אלא בחרדל, משום דדבורים נמי מזקי לחרדל? אפילו משרה וירק, כיון שנעשה המשרה בהיתר — לא יצטרך להרחיקה, כמו גבי אילן ובור! ומשני רבינא: לעולם בלוקח, וקא סברי רבנן על המזיק להרחיק את עצמו, אע"פ שעשה בהיתר. ולהכי על בעל החרדל להרחיק, שהוא [ג]הזיק. ופריך: כיון דשמעינן ממילתא דרבינא שהדבורים אינם מזיקים לחרדל, דלכך נתנו רבנן הרחקה על בעל החרדל — מכלל דרבי יוסי סבר על הניזק להרחיק עלמו, מדשרי סמיכת חרדל אע"פ שהוא מזיק ולא ניזק — א"כ אפילו משרה וירק נמי! וה"ה דה"מ לאקשויי (ב) דברייתא בהדיא משמע שהדבורים מזקי נמי לחרדל, דקתני: ואוכלות לגלוגי חרדלי. אלא ניחא ליה למינקט קושיא דאפי' משרה וירק נמי, משום דהתחיל כבר להקשות(ג). **מכלל** דסבר רבי יוסי על הניזק להרחיק וכו'. נ"ל לפירוש זה, דזה המקשה אינו אותו שהקשה בתחלה: ואי לא סמיך היכי משכחת לה. דהא לדידיה הוה ניחא ליה לאביי דאמר סמיך, ולא הוה קשה ליה מידי, וסבר רבי יוסי על הניזק כו'. וצ"ל שהמקשה הראשון הוה ידע שפיר המסקנא, דדבורים לחרדל לא מזקי לרבנן. אבל המקשה הזה לא ידע, להכי פריך: מכלל דסבר רבי יוסי כו', והקשה: כיון דלרבנן חשיב בעל דבורים ניזק ולא מזיק, שמצריכין לבעל חרדל להרחיק, אף על גב שהם מזיקין לחרדל, מכל מקום כיון דסמך בהיתר לא חשיב מזיק, ועל בעל חרדל להרחיק — א"כ גם לרבי יוסי חשיב ניזק, ואפ"ה מותר לסמוך לבעל החרדל — א"כ סבר דעל הניזק להרחיק את עלמו, אי הכי אפילו משרה וירק נמי כן! דאין סברא דלרבי יוסי חשיב בעל דבורים מזיק אע"פ שסמך בהיתר משום שעשה קלת שלא כהוגן, ולרבנן לית להו האי סברא, דאין סברא כלל דלפלוגינהו בהכי. ומשני: לעולם רבי יוסי על המזיק ס"ל, וחשיב בעל דבורים מזיק אע"ג שסמך בהיתר, כיון שעשה קלת שלא כהוגן בסמיכתו. ורבנן נמי הוו מודו ליה בהך סברא אי הוו סברי דדבורים מזקי לחרדל, אלא דס"ל דדבורים לא מזקי לחרדל, ולכך מרחיק בעל החרדל. וכמסקנא זו יש לפרש תחלת הסוגיא לדברי המקשה, דפריך: ואי לא סמיך היכי משכחת לה, דבשלמא אי סמיך, (ד)כדמסקינן השתא. ולא כמו שפי' לפ"ה שיחלקו, (ה) דלרבנן הוו דבורים כמו ירק, כיון שנסמכו בהיתר, אע"ג שגם הם מזיקין לחרדל כשיבא. ור' יוסי מתיר לסמוך החרדל, מפני שבעל הדבורים עשה קלת שלא כהוגן. (לעיל) **וסבר** ר' יוסי על המזיק כו'. לקמן על מקומה הוה ליה לאקשויי, אלא משום דאיצטריך ליה לפרש הכא דסבר רבי יוסי דעל המזיק להרחיק את עלמו, אסקוה לכולה מילתא הכא. ובלוקח דהכא אי אפשר לפרשו כפירוש רבינו חננאל, דפי' באדם שלוקח משרה וטוענין ללוקח — דא"כ למה ירחיק המשרה כשיבא שם ירק? כיון שטוענין לו שהמוכר קנה סמיכה זו! אלא צריך לפרש בלוקח כמו שפירש בקונטרס, או כר"י בר' מרדכי. כך פי' ר"י כל הסוגיא לפי שיטת רש"י. וקשה לו: מה הולרך לחלק בדוחק בין לוקח דאילן ללוקח דמשרה? ועוד: דלמה המתין להביא משנה זו דמשרה וירק באחרונה, המוקדמין במשנתנו? ועוד דקתני בתוספתא (פ"א): רבי יוסי מתיר בחרדל, שאומר לו: כדרך שעשית בתוך שלך — כך אני עושה בתוך שלי. משמע דבעל דבורים סמך תחלה. ומפרש רבינו תם ורבינו חננאל דהכי גרסינן: אלא אמר רבינא קסברי רבנן על המזיק להרחיק את עלמו. והשתא הדר ביה מכל שינויי דלעיל, דודאי בכולהו מודה רבא דכי ליכא כותל או ירק — דסמיך, משום דקא סברי רבנן דדוקא על המזיק להרחיק את עלמו, דהיינו כי איכא דבר הניזוק. אבל כי ליכא דבר הניזוק — לא מקרי הסומך מזיק, ולא אסר רבא לסמוך אפי' לרבנן, אלא דוקא בור, משום טעמא דכל מרא ומרא דקא מחית מרפית לארעאי, ולהכי חשוב הסומך מזיק, אפילו כי ליכא בור. וכיון דלרבנן נמי סמיך — אתי שפיר פלוגתייהו, כדפרישית לעיל אליבא דאביי. ולכך הדר ביה ולא מוקי בלוקח, וכגון שסמך בעל דבורים תחלה, משום דא"כ לא היה מתיר ר"י לסמוך לבעל החרדל, כיון דבעל הדבורים לא עשה כלל שלא כהוגן. ודוקא בדסמיך בלא לוקח, שעשה קלת שלא כהוגן בעל הדבורים, מתיר רבי יוסי לבעל החרדל לסמוך, כדפרישית לעיל. ולפי זה אתי שפיר, דלמסקנא זו לא נלטרך לחלק בין לוקח האילן ללוקח משרה. ולהכי המתין נמי כדי להביא מתניתין דמשרה, משום דמינה לריך לחזור מכל שינויי דלעיל. ואתי נמי שפיר דמיירי שסמך נמי בעל דבורים תחלה, כמו שמוכח בתוספתא.
ה"ג

רבינו גרשום

ואי לא סמיך. היכי משכחת לה דיכולין אלו לטעון הכי זה כנגד זה אנא סמיכנא ואת הרחק והלא אין סומכין אפי' כי ליכא עדיין היזקא לחבריה אלא מדיכולין לטעון הכי ש"מ דסמיך. לא לעולם בעלמא לא סמיך והכא מאי טעמא סמיך בלוקח שלקח מן אחד מקום חרדל ושני לקח שאר מקום השדה והכנים שם דבורים ומש"ה לא מצי מעכבי זה לזה לטעמיה דר' יוסי דבעל חרדל טעין אנא לא מרחקנא דאתינא מכח דמוכר הסמך ברשות בתוך שלו. אבל את הרחק את דבורך דמזקי לחרדלאי. ובעל דבורים טעין את מזקת לי טפי מדאנא מזיקנא לך: אי הכי כדתרצת בלוקח מאי טעמא דפליגי רבנן עליה דר' יוסי דמחייבי להרחיק החרדל הואיל ולוקח הוא וברשות סמך. ועוד קושיא אחריתי כיון דאוקמת לה בלוקח מאי טעמא מתיר ר' יוסי בחרדל לחודיה ומודה לרבנן במשרה וירק ליפלוג נמי עלייהו במשרה וירק דלא צריך להרחיק הואיל דלוקח הוא וברשות סמך המוכר המשרה והירק והשומין. לעולם בלוקח ומאי דאמרת מאי טעמא דרבנן דאמרי מרחיקין חרדל ולא סמיך משום דסבירא להו דעל המזיק רמי להרחיק עצמו שלא יזיק אע"ג דברשות סמך דמתוך ששורין פיהם מחריפות החרדל חוזרות ואוכלות את דובשן. ומקשי' מכלל דר' יוסי דפליג עלייהו סבר על הניזק להרחיק דיכול לומר מזיק לניזק הרחק עצמך ממני שלא תזוק ולהכי מתיר בחרדל ודבורים א"כ מאי שנא ממשרה וירק דלא פליג על רבנן כי היכי דפליג בחרדל. אלא ודאי מסתברא ר' יוסי סבר דעל המזיק רמי להרחיק דלא סמיך כרבנן וכי תימא א"כ מאי טעמא דר' יוסי דמתיר גבי חרדל לחודיה לסמוך ופליג עלייהו אמשרה וירק משום דהכי קאמר להו ר' יוסי לרבנן בשלמא להנך תרתי במשרה ושומין מודינא לכו דעל המזיק להרחיק משום דהן מזיקין את הירק ואת הבצלים והם לא מזקי למשרה ושומין אבל גבי חרדל ודבורים דזה מזיק זה וזה מזיק זה פליגנא עלייכו דלא צריך חד מינייהו להרחיק טפי מחבריה ואמרי ליה רבנן לר' יוסי ל"ש בין חרדל למשרה וירק דכולן מזיקין ולא ניזוקין דהחרדל מזיק החרדל דאכלי דבורים

מכחשו הדבש אבל דבורים לא מזקי לחרדל אמאי אמרת אי משום בינתא (בעתא בצתא) גרעינין דהחרדל ליכא למיחש דאכלי ליה דבורים דכיון דהן דקין מאד לא משכחי להו דבורים ואי בטרפא כלומר אם תאמר שאוכלין העלין של חרדל מאי איכפת ליה הדר פארי. חוזר וגדל ולהכי סבירא להו גבי חרדל ודבורין כגון משרה וירק: וזה נוטע בתוך שלו. אע"ג דמזיק לבור של חבירו דאי בעי בעל הבור דהוי ניזק להרחיק ירחיק דהאי לא יניח שלא יטע בתוך שלו אע"ג דמזיק ליה אלמא דסבר ר' יוסי דעל הניזק רמי להרחיק את עצמו: אלא לעולם ר' יוסי ודאי [ס"ל] על הניזק להרחיק וכי תימא א"כ מאי טעמא דמודה לרבנן במשרה וירק דמסברי דעל המזיק רמי לא תימא דמודה להו אלא לדבריהן דרבנן קאמר לדידי אפי' משרה וירק נמי לא צריך להרחיק משום דסבירא לי דעל הניזק להרחיק אלא לדידכו וכו':

מסורת הש"ס

א) לקמן כה.: ב) שייך לע"א: ג) מזיק:

הגהות הב"ח

(א) תום' ד"ה ואי לא וכו' להרחיק את עלמו כל הרחקות: (ב) בא"ד לאקשויי דברייתא: (ג) אחר ד"ה ואי לא נ"ל ד"ה וסבר ואח"כ ד"ה מכלל וכו' וג' דבורים אלו הד"א ואח"כ נ"ל ד"ה לגלוגי: (ד) בא"ד אי סמיך פליגי כדמסקינן וכו': (ה) בא"ד שיחלקו בזה דלרבנן כנ"ל:

לָא מַשְׁכַּחַת לֵיהּ, אִי בְּטַרְפָּא — הָדַר פָּאַרֵי.§ "וְלֹא נִבְרֶכֶת הַכּוֹבְסִין" וכו'.§ אָמַר רַב נַחְמָן אָמַר רַבָּה בַּר אֲבוּהּ: [א]לֹא שָׁנוּ אֶלָּא מִן הַמַּחְמְצָן, [ב]אֲבָל מִן הַנַּדְיָין — ד' אַמּוֹת. תַּנְיָא נַמִּי הָכִי: נִבְרֶכֶת הַכּוֹבְסִין — ד' אַמּוֹת; וְהָא אֲנַן תְּנַן: ג' טְפָחִים! אֶלָּא לָאו שְׁמַע מִינָּהּ כִּדְרַב נַחְמָן. וְאִיכָּא דְּרָמֵי לְהוּ מִירְמֵי; תְּנַן: נִבְרֶכֶת הַכּוֹבְסִין — ג' טְפָחִים, וְהָתַנְיָא: אַרְבַּע אַמּוֹת! אָמַר רַב נַחְמָן אָמַר רַבָּה בַּר אֲבוּהּ, לָא קַשְׁיָא: כָּאן מִן הַמַּחְמְצָן, כָּאן מִן הַנַּדְיָין. רַב חִיָּיא בְּרֵיהּ דְּרַב אָוְיָא מַתְנֵי לָהּ בְּהֶדְיָא: אֶלָּא אִם כֵּן הִרְחִיק מִשְׁפַּת מַחְמְצָן וְלַכּוֹתֶל ג' טְפָחִים.§ "וְסָד בַּסִּיד".§ אִיבַּעְיָא לְהוּ: "וְסָד בַּסִּיד" תְּנַן, אוֹ דִּילְמָא "אוֹ סָד בַּסִּיד" תְּנַן? [ג]פְּשִׁיטָא דִּ"וְסָד בַּסִּיד" תְּנַן, דְּאִי סָלְקָא דַּעְתָּךְ דְּ"אוֹ סָד בַּסִּיד" תְּנַן, אִם כֵּן לִיעָרְבִינְהוּ וְלִיתְנִינְהוּ! דִּילְמָא מִשּׁוּם דְּלָא דָּמֵי הַאי הֶיזֵּיקָא לְהַאי הֶיזֵּיקָא, רֵישָׁא — הֶיזֵּיקָא (א) דִּמְתוּנָא, סֵיפָא — הֶיזֵּיקָא דְּהַבְלָא. ת"ש, [א]רַבִּי יְהוּדָה אוֹמֵר: סֶלַע הַבָּא בְּיָדַיִם — זֶה חוֹפֵר בּוֹרוֹ מִכָּאן, וְזֶה חוֹפֵר בּוֹרוֹ מִכָּאן, זֶה מַרְחִיק ג' טְפָחִים וְסָד בַּסִּיד, וְזֶה מַרְחִיק ג' טְפָחִים וְסָד בַּסִּיד; טַעְמָא דְּבָא בְּיָדַיִם, הָא לֹא בָּא בְּיָדַיִם — לָא! ה"ה דְּאַף עַל גַּב דְּלֹא בָּא בְּיָדַיִם נַמִּי סָד בַּסִּיד, וּבָא בְּיָדַיִם אִיצְטְרִיכָא לֵיהּ; סד"א כֵּיוָן דְּבָא בְּיָדַיִם לִיבָּעֵי רַוְוחָא טְפֵי, קמ"ל.§ "מַרְחִיקִין אֶת הַגֶּפֶת וְאֶת הַזֶּבֶל וְאֶת הַמֶּלַח וְאֶת (ב) הַסְּלָעִים" וכו'.§ תְּנַן הָתָם: [ב][ד]בַּמֶּה טוֹמְנִין וּבַמֶּה אֵין טוֹמְנִין? אֵין טוֹמְנִין לֹא בַּגֶּפֶת וְלֹא בַּזֶּבֶל וְלֹא בַּמֶּלַח, וְלֹא בַּסִּיד וְלֹא בַּחוֹל, בֵּין לַחִין בֵּין יְבֵשִׁין. מַאי שְׁנָא הָכָא דְּקָתָנֵי סְלָעִים וְלָא קָתָנֵי חוֹל, וּמַאי שְׁנָא הָתָם דְּקָתָנֵי חוֹל וְלָא קָתָנֵי סְלָעִים? אָמַר רַב יוֹסֵף: לְפִי שֶׁאֵין דַּרְכָּן שֶׁל בְּנֵי אָדָם לְהַטְמִין בִּסְלָעִים. אֲמַר לֵיהּ אַבָּיֵי: וְכִי דַּרְכָּן שֶׁל בְּנֵי אָדָם לְהַטְמִין בְּגִיזֵּי צֶמֶר וּלְשׁוֹנוֹת שֶׁל אַרְגָּמָן? דְּתַנְיָא: [ג][ה]טוֹמְנִין בְּגִיזֵּי צֶמֶר וּבְצִיפֵּי צֶמֶר, וּבִלְשׁוֹנוֹת שֶׁל אַרְגָּמָן וּבְמוֹכִין, וְאֵין מְטַלְטְלִין אוֹתָן! [ד]אֶלָּא אָמַר אַבָּיֵי: ◦"יַגִּיד עָלָיו רֵיעוֹ", תְּנָא הָכָא סְלָעִים וְה"ה לְחוֹל, תְּנָא הָתָם חוֹל וְהוּא הַדִּין לִסְלָעִים. א"ל רָבָא: אִי "יַגִּיד עָלָיו רֵיעוֹ", לִיתְנִינְהוּ לְכוּלְּהוּ בַּחֲדָא, וְלִיתְנֵי חֲדָא מִנַּיְיהוּ בְּאִידָךְ (ג) וְה"ה לְאִידָךְ! אֶלָּא אֲמַר רָבָא: הָתָם הַיְינוּ טַעֲמָא דְּלָא קָתָנֵי סְלָעִים — מִשּׁוּם דְּמִשְׁתַּכֵּי לָהּ לַקְּדֵרָה, הָכָא הַיְינוּ טַעֲמָא דְּלָא קָתָנֵי חוֹל — מִשּׁוּם דִּמְחַמְּמֵי חַיֵּים וּמַקְרִירֵי קָרִיר. וְהָא תָּנֵי רַבִּי אוֹשַׁעְיָא חוֹל! הָתָם בִּמְתוּנָא. תָּנָא דִּידָן נַמִּי לִיתְנֵי וְלוֹקְמֵיהּ בִּמְתוּנָא! הָא תְּנָא לֵיהּ אַמַּת הַמַּיִם. אַטּוּ מִי לָא קָתָנֵי אַמַּת הַמַּיִם, וְקָתָנֵי נִבְרֶכֶת הַכּוֹבְסִין? הָנְהוּ צְרִיכִי, דְּאִי תְּנָא אַמַּת הַמַּיִם — מִשּׁוּם דִּקְבִיעָא, אֲבָל נִבְרֶכֶת הַכּוֹבְסִין דְּלָא קְבִיעָא — אֵימָא לָא; וְאִי תְּנָא נִבְרֶכֶת הַכּוֹבְסִין — מִשּׁוּם דְּקָווּ וְקַיְימִי, אֲבָל אַמַּת הַמַּיִם — לָא, צְרִיכָא.§ "מַרְחִיקִין אֶת הַזְּרָעִים וְאֶת הַמַּחֲרֵישָׁה" וכו'.§ זְרָעִים, תֵּיפּוֹק לֵיהּ מִשּׁוּם מַחֲרֵישָׁה! בְּמַפּוֹלֶת יָד. מַחֲרֵישָׁה, וְתֵיפּוֹק לֵיהּ מִשּׁוּם זְרָעִים! בְּחוֹרֵשׁ לָאִילָנוֹת. וְתֵיפּוֹק לֵיהּ מִשּׁוּם מַיָּא! [ה]תָּנָא בְּאֶרֶץ יִשְׂרָאֵל קָאֵי, דִּכְתִיב: ◦"לִמְטַר הַשָּׁמַיִם תִּשְׁתֶּה מָּיִם". לְמֵימְרָא, דִּזְרָעִים לִצְדָדִין

תורה אור — איוב לו | דברים יא

רש"י

לֹא מַשְׁכַּחַתְּ לֵיהּ. הַדְּבוֹרָה, לְפִי שֶׁהוּא טָמוּן בְּשַׁרְבִיטוֹ. וְאִי בְּטַרְפָּא. וְאִם יֹאכַל הֶעָלֶה. הָדַר פָּאַרֵי. חוֹזֵר וְצוֹמֵחַ. מִן הַמַּחְמְצָן. נִבְרֶכֶת שֶׁשּׁוֹרִין בּוֹ אֶת הַבְּגָדִים יוֹם אוֹ יוֹמַיִם בְּצוֹאַת כְּלָבִים, עַד שֶׁמַּחְמִילִין וּמַסְרִיחִין. אֲבָל מִן הַנַּדְיָין. נִבְרֶכֶת שֶׁכּוֹבְסִין וּמְשַׁפְשְׁפִין בָּהּ, מִתּוֹךְ שֶׁהַמַּיִם נִתָּזִין לְמֵרָחוֹק – צָרִיךְ לְהַרְחִיק ד' אַמּוֹת. ה"ג: אוֹ סָד בְּסִיד תְּנַן. כְּלוֹמַר: אוֹ יַרְחִיק אוֹ סָד. לִיעָרְבִינְהוּ. לְתַרְתֵּי בָּבֵי רֵישָׁא וּמְצִיעֲתָא, דְּהָתָם "אוֹ סָד בְּסִיד" תְּנַן! אֶלָּא מִדְּלָא עָרְבִינְהוּ – ש"מ דִּבְרֵישָׁא "וְסָד בְּסִיד" תְּנַן, דְּבָעִינַן תַּרְוַיְיהוּ, הַרְחָקָה וְסִיד. בָּא בְּיָדַיִם אִצְטְרִיךְ. לְמִנְקַט לֵיהּ לְתַנָּא. וְאַע"ג דְּה"ה לְלֹא בָּא בְּיָדַיִם. בַּמֶּה טוֹמְנִין. אֶת הַחַמִּין בְּשַׁבָּת, דְּאָמוּר רַבָּנַן דְּאָסוּר לְהַטְמִין בְּדָבָר הַמּוֹסִיף הֶבֶל. וְהָתָם מְפָרֵשׁ טַעְמָא: גְּזֵירָה שֶׁמָּא יַטְמִין בְּרֶמֶץ. לְשׁוֹנוֹת שֶׁל אַרְגָּמָן. צֶמֶר צָבוּעַ וְאַחַר כָּךְ חָזְרוּ וְהֶחֱלִיקוּהוּ בְּמַסְרֵק, וְעָשׂוּי לְשׁוֹנוֹת. וְכִי דַּרְכָּן לְהַטְמִין בָּהֶן. וְאַפ"ה אַיְירֵי בְּהוּ רַבָּנַן. צִיפֵּי צֶמֶר. לְאַחַר שֶׁסְּרָקוֹ וְנִפְּצוֹ בְּמַסְרֵק. וּבְמוֹכִין. שֶׁל שְׁחָקֵי בְּגָדִים, שֶׁהַסּוֹרֵק מוֹצִיא מִבִּגְדֵי הַצֶּמֶר בְּקוֹצִים. וְאֵין מְטַלְטְלִין אוֹתָם. שֶׁהֵן מוּקְצִים לִמְלֶאכֶת בְּגָדִים. ה"ג: אִי יַגִּיד עָלָיו רֵיעוֹ לִיתְנִינְהוּ לְכוּלְּהוּ בַּחֲדָא וְלִיתְנֵי חֲדָא מִינַּיְיהוּ בְּאִידָךְ וְלֵימָא כו'. לִיתְנִינְהוּ לְכוּלְּהוּ. כָּל הָנָךְ מִשּׁוּם הֶבְלָא בַּחֲדָא, אוֹ כָּאן אוֹ אֵצֶל שַׁבָּת. הָנָךְ מִשּׁוּם דְּמִשְׁתַּכֵּי לָהּ לַקְּדֵירָה. שֶׁמְּשַׁבְּרִין אֶת הַקְּדֵירָה. כָּךְ שָׁמַעְתִּי כָּאן. וּבְכָל מָקוֹם שָׁמַעְתִּיו: שֶׁמַּעֲלָה חֲלוּדָה. דִּמְחַמְּמֵי חַיֵּים. כְּשֶׁטּוֹמְנִין בּוֹ דָּבָר חַם – הוּא מִתְחַמֵּם. וְגַבֵּי הַטְמָנָה מְחַמְּמֵי הוּא, אֲבָל גַּבֵּי כּוֹתֶל – קָרִיר. וְהָתָנָא רַבִּי אוֹשַׁעְיָא. לְהַרְחָקוֹת דְּמַתְנִי' בַּתּוֹסֶפְתָּא שֶׁלּוֹ, (ד) וְקָאָמַר חוֹל בַּגַּוַּיְיהוּ. בִּמְתוּנָא. אֵצֶל הֶיזֵּק לִחְלוּחַ שֶׁנַּתָּה, וּבְחוֹל לַח, וְלֹא אֵצֶל הֶיזֵּק הֶבֶל. נִבְרֶכֶת כּוֹבְסִין. לֹא קְבִיעָא כְּאַמַּת הַמַּיִם. שֶׁאַמַּת הַמַּיִם (ה) עֲשׂוּיִין לִהְיוֹת שָׁם עוֹלָמִית, אֲבָל זוֹ – הַכּוֹבֵס פְּעָמִים שֶׁמִּשְׁתַּנֶּה לְאוּמָּנוּת אַחֶרֶת. דְּקָווּ וְקַיְימֵי. וְלִיחְלוּחָן קָשֶׁה יוֹתֵר מִשֶּׁל מַיִם חַיִּים. תֵּיפּוֹק לֵיהּ מִשּׁוּם מַחֲרֵישָׁה. שֶׁהֲרֵי חָרְשׁוּ תְּחִילָּה, וַאֲפִי' לֹא זָרַע (ו) לֵיהּ תָּנָא לֵי' מַרְחִיקִין. בְּמַפּוֹלֶת יָד. שֶׁזְּרָעוֹ בְּלֹא חֲרִישָׁה, חוֹפֵר בְּמָרָה וְאֵינוֹ מַעֲמִיק כְּעוֹמֶק הַמַּחֲרֵישָׁה. וְתֵיפּוֹק לֵיהּ מִשּׁוּם זְרָעִים. שֶׁסּוֹפָם חוֹרְשִׁין סוֹפָן לִזְרוֹעַ, וְהָא קָתָנֵי זְרָעִים! בְּחוֹרֵשׁ לָאִילָנוֹת. שֶׁיֵּשׁ שָׁם אִילָנוֹת מְיָמִים רַבִּים, וּבָא לַחֲרוֹשׁ תַּחְתֵּיהֶם לְהַשְׁבִּיחָן. וְתֵיפּוֹק לֵיהּ מִשּׁוּם מַיָּא. שֶׁצָּרִיךְ לְהַשְׁקוֹתָן תָּמִיד, וְכֵיוָן דְּאִי אֶפְשָׁר לִזְרָעִים בְּלֹא מַיִם – לָמָּה לֵיהּ לְמִתְנִינְהוּ? הָא תָּנָא הֶזֵּיק דְּלִיחְלוּחַ אֵצֶל כּוֹתֶל!

תוספות

ה"ג ר"ח: **בא** בידים אין לא בא בידים לא. אלמא "או סד בסיד" תנן, דלודקא בא בידים בעי הרחקה וסיד. ומשני: הוא הדין לא בא, ובא בידים איצטריך ליה כו'. ויש ספרים דלא גרסי האי דיוקא, אלא משני: בא בידים שאני, ודקארי לה מאי קארי כו'. ואין נראה, דהיכי בעי למיפשט "וסד בסיד" תנן? הא איכא למיבעי ההיא דרבי יהודה גופיה אי תרווייהו בעי אי לאו, כיון דהשתא סבר דאין חילוק בין בא בידים ללא בא.

משום דמשתכי. פי' הקונטרס: (ז)דמשברין הקדירה אין דרך להטמין בהן. ואם תאמר: אכתי תיקשי, וכי דרך להטמין בגיזי צמר, כדפריך לעיל? וי"ל: דלעיל הוה בעי למימר דאין דרך להטמין בסלעים לפי שההבל יוצא מבין הסלעים ואינו מתקיים, ואעפ"כ לפעמים טומנין בהן. להכי פריך שפיר מגיזי צמר, דתני לה, משום דלפעמים טומנין בהן. אבל הכא קאמר דאין דרך להטמין כלל בהן, לפי שמשברין הקדירה, והואיל ומילתא דלא שכיחא היא כלל — לא חש למיתנייה. ועוד יש לפרש: דכיון דלא שכיחא היא כלל — שרי להטמין בהן, דבמילתא דלא שכיחא לא גזרו בהו רבנן. וכן מנהג שלנו, שאנו נוהגין להטמין בסלעים שהאש יוצא מהן שקורין קיילו"ש. אבל מ"מ קשיא מה שהקשה בקונטר', דבכל מקום הוי שיתוך לשון חלודה, כמו ב"אלו מציאות" (ב"מ דף כו.): דשתיך טפי, ובפ' "הבונה" (שבת דף קג:): דכיון דמשתכי לא עבדי הכי, ובפרק קמא דתענית (דף ח.): אם ראית דור שהשמים משתכין עליו כנחושת. ומפרש ר"ת בענין אחר: דמשתכי — דהבל שלהן מקלקל המאכל. ולר"י נראה כפירוש רבינו חננאל, דמה שאמר להרחיקם משום דמשתכי — שמלקין את הארץ ומחלידים אותה, ומעלין עפר תיחוח, כדאמרינן לקמן גבי זרעים. ולא משום הבל, דאין מוסיפין שום הבל, וטומנין בהן. ואפילו לפי הספרים דגרסי "סלעים היינו טעמא דלא קתני להו התם" — יש לפרש דהכי קאמר: דלהכי לא קתני להו התם, משום דטעמא דהכא שצריך להרחיקם — לא משום הבל, אלא משום דמשתכי. וה"ר מרדכי הביא ראיה מירושלמי, דגרסי' [ו]התם איתמר(ח) שהסלעים מרתיחין [ז]והכא איתמר שאין הסלעים מרתיחין! א"ר יוסי: כאן וכאן אין הסלעים מרתיחין, אלא מפני שעושים עפר תיחוח ומלקין ארעית הכותל.

דמחממי חיים. והא דאמר בפ' "כירה" (שבת דף לח: ושם ד"ה ולא): ביצה אין טומנין אותה לא בחול ולא באבק דרכים! התם בחול שהוחם (ט) מחמת השמש, דומיא דאבק דרכים.

(סיין לע"ב) **המבריך** את הגפן. פירוש: גפן יחידי שהוא מושרש בארץ, וכופף את הגפן באמצעיתו, ומכסהו בקרקע ונשרש שם. וקאמר: מותר לזרוע את הצדדין. דאף על גב שאינו רחוק שלשה טפחים, ויונק עם הגפן מתחת הקרקע, כיון דמעל הקרקע ליכא עירובי' — שרי, כדמוכח בעירובין (דף לג.) ובמסכת כלאים (פ"ד), דזה סומך לגדר מכאן וזה מכאן. וא"ת: והיכי דמי שזורע לצדדין? אי כשהרחיק ג' טפחים מן הצדדין — אפילו על גביו נמי, ואי בלא הרחיק — מן הצדדין נמי לא! ואומר ר"י: דמיירי כשזורע הצדדין ברחוק ג' (י) טפחים מגפן היוצא מן הקרקע מכל צד, דליכא ערבוביא למעלה מן הקרקע. ומכל מקום אסור לזרוע על גביו מפני שהשרשין נכנסין בתוך הגפן, והוי כמרכיב זרעים באילן, דאסור. ואם תאמר: ומאי איריא דנקט גפן? אפי' שאר אילן נמי אסור! ואומר ר"י: דשאר אילנות שהן קשין — מותר לזרוע על גביו כנגד השורש, דלא חיישינן שיכנס שורש הזרע בתוך האילן, שהוא קשה. אבל גפן שהוא רך — חיישינן. והאי [ח](פירוקא) מלא ר"י בירושלמי בגמרא דהך משנה.

התם

מסורת הש"ס

א) לעיל יז: ע"ש [תוספתא פ"א]: ב) שבת מז: ג) שם מח.: ד) [יבמות לא: וש"נ]: ה) [שבת עג: וש"נ]: ו) מהר"ם התם הכא: ז) מהר"ם והתם: ח) ס"י פירכא:

עין משפט נר מצוה

ט א מיי' פ"ט מהלכות שכנים הל' א סמג עשין פב טוש"ע ח"מ סי' קנה סעיף י:

י ב מיי' שם הלכה ה ועי' פי' במ"מ טוש"ע שם סעיף יא:

יא ג מיי' שם הל' א טוש"ע שם סעיף י:

יב ד מיי' פ"ד מהל' שבת הל' א סמג לאוין סה טוש"ע או"ח סי' רנז סעיף ג:

יג ה מיי' וסמג שם טוש"ע א"ח סי' רנט סעיף א:

רבינו גרשום

פיסקא לא שנו דבג' טפחים סגי אלא מן המחמצן אותו מקום ששורין בה בגדי כביסה עם צואת כלבים להכי קרי ליה מחמצן דכי היכי דמניחין את העיסה עד שתתחמץ דלא נגעי בה כך מניחין אלו בגדים דלא נגעו בהו עד שישורו יפה ולהכי סגי ברחוק ג' טפחים דלא אזלי טפי ולא מנתזו מן הכותל: אבל מן הנדיין. מקום שמכבסין הבגדים עצמן בתוך המים ומכין אותם ומנתזין על הכתלים מש"ה צריך להרחיק ד' אמות: איבעיא להו וסד בסיד תנן. דמשמע לבר מג' טפחים כלומר דתרווייהו צריך למיעבד להרחיק ג' טפחים ולסייד שוב החפירה בסיד או דלמא או סד בסיד תנן דמשמע או ג' טפחים א) אמר ליה פשיטא דאו סד בסיד תנן דא"כ דס"ד דוסד בסיד תנן הא בבא אחריתי דקתני מרחיקין את הגפת ב) (כלומר) סד בסיד אי אתרווייהו בבי דסד בסיד ליערבינהו להנהו תרי בבי כחדא לא יחפור אדם כו' ומרחיקין את הגפת כו' וליתנינהו בתרווייהו חד וסד בסיד דמשמע אכולהו ותרי זמני וחד רחיד ל"ל דילמא לעולם אימא לך דתרווייהו וסד בסיד נינהו והאי דלא עירב להו משום דתרווייהו צריכי דלא דמי היזקא דרישא להיזקא דסיפא דהיזק דרישא משום מתונא מחמת לחלוח מים דשיח ובורות. והאי היזקא דסיפא דהבלא הוא דגפת וזבל ומלח כולהו מסקי הבלא נינהו וקשי טפי ומש"ה צריך למיתנינהו תרווייהו דמחדא לא נפקא אידך ומיהא לא תפשוט. ת"ש זה מרחיק ג' טפחים מכאן כשיעור כותל בורו וסד בסיד הבור וכן נמי אידך וטעמא מאי בעי להרחיק ג' טפחים כל חד וחד ולסוד משום דבא בידים דארעא רפיא היא. אבל לאו בא בידים דהוה צונמא חזקה לעולם לא צריך לסוד בסיד אם ירחיק ג' טפחים אלמא תפשוט מהכא דאו סד בסיד תנן לא לעולם מהא לא תפשוט ה"ה דאפי' לא בא בידים בעי ג' טפחים וסד בסיד ובא בידים איצטריכא ליה כו'. רווחא טפי מג' טפחים ילסוד בסיד קמ"ל דלא: מ"ש גבי מתני' דקתני סלעים משום הבלא ומ"ש גבי הטמנה דמשום הבלא נמי היא וקתני חול ולא סלעים: וא"ל אביי וכי דרכן של בני אדם להטמין בלשונות של ארגמן ואפ"ה קתני להו סלעים נמי אע"ג דאין דרכן להטמין ליתנייהו: גיזי צמר והוא צמר הגדל מן הבהמה כמו שהוא. ציפי צמר זהו צמר סרוק ומלובן לצורך צביעה. וי"א ציפי צמר כריכות צמר גדול כדרך שמביאין הסוחרין ממדינתן. ולשונות של ארגמן צמר שאינו טווי שצובעין בארגמן כדי לנסות ורוב צביעתו היה ארגמן. ובמוכין צמר שמסרקין מן הבגדים לאחר שמכבסין אותן: ויגיד עליו רעו. יוכיח עליו כלומר תנא הכי במתני' [סלעים] דמסקא הבלא וה"ה לחול דמסיק הבלא טפי

רבינו גרשום

תנא התם גבי שבת חול דאין טומנין משום דקא מבשל בשבת ה"ה לסלעים דמבשלין טפי. ואי יגיד עליו רעו דמשמע תרוייהו ליתנינהו תרוייהו סלעים וחול גבי בור או בחדא מתני' ודיניהן שוין אע"ג דלא כתיבי באידך אלא בחד' מינייהו ודאי אמרי' יגיד עליו [רעו] ויוכיח על משנה זו דה"ה לתרווייהו אלא לאו ש"מ מדלא קתני לה הכי דלא אמרי' תני סלע וה"ה לחול תנא התם חול וה"ה לסלע ואכתי הדר קושין לדוכתא: דמשתבר לה לקדרה. שמשתברין בסלעים הקדרה ולהכי לא תנא אין טומנין בסלעין דלא אתי לאטמוני בגווייהו. וחול אמאי לא תנא הכא גבי כותל משום דזהו מנהג חול דמחמם חמים. כלומר אם מניחין אותם במקום שמתחמם מחמת דבר אחר או מחמת חמה או מחמת אור הכירה מתחמם ומוסיף הבלא להכי אין טומנין שמתחמם מחמת כן: אבל מקרירי קריר. כשהוא מונח במקום קור בגומא מתקרר יותר ולא מזיק כלל לכותל להכי לא תנא ליה והא קתני ר' הושעיא בתוספתא דידיה הדר הני מתני' וקתני חול. דתני בהדי הני דרישא דמזיק משום מתונתא דמזיק לחלוח. ולא קתני לה בהדי הנך דסיפא דגפת וזבל דהנהו משום הבלא. ומקשי' מי לא תנן אמת המים וקתני נברכת הכובסין אע"ג דלא צריך הכא נמי ליתני חול ומשני אמת המים ונברכת הכובסין תרווייהו צריכי דאי תנא אמת המים דמרחיקין ג' טפחים הוה אמינא משום דקביעי כל הימים מרחיקין דמקלקל לכותל אבל נברכת הכובסין דלא קביעי דמים מכונסין נינהו אימא אין מרחיקין: דקוו וקיימי ומחלידין בקרקע ואתיין עד היסוד מש"ה מרחיקין אבל אמת המים דלא קוו וקיימי דדרך הליכתן קא אזלי ואין מחלידין אימא דלא צריך לרחוקי קמ"ל דודאי צריך:

פיסקא מרחיקין את הזרעים ואת המחרישה. משום דנכנסים שרשים של זרעים בכותל כדאמ' לקמן ומרעי לי'. הואיל דתני מחרישה למה לי למיתני זרעים פשיטא דאין זרעים באים אלא ע"י מחרישה ומשני דאפי' בלא מחרישה מצי לזרוע במפולת יד דא"צ מחרישה בזרעים משום כשזורעין בשוורים תולין שם שק מלא תבואה ומנקבין השק נקבים נקבים כשזורעין בכמה מקומות נופלת התבואה יותר ממקום אחד ולאחר כן חורשין כדי לכסות את התבואה ולהשוות את התבואה בשדה. אבל כשזורעין ביד משוה התבואה בשדה ואי"צ מחרישה מש"ה איצטריך למתני במתני' זרעים ומחרישה ג) דמזרעים לא מפקינן מחרישה ומקשה ומחרישה מ"ט איצטריך למתני

א) [ג' טפחים או סד בסיד]. ב) [מרחיקין את הגפת וכו' וסד בסיד ואי בתרוייהו בכי בעינן דוסד בסיד וכו']. ג) [נ"ל דזרעים לא מפקינן ממחרישה ומקשה מחרישה מ"ט וכו'].

הגהות הב"ח (א) גמ' רישא הזיקא דמתונתא כצ"ל וכן בסמוך: (ב) שם ואת המלח ואת הסיד ואת הסלעים: (ג) שם וליתני חדא מינייהו באידך ולימא יגיד עליו ריעו אלא אמר רבא: (ד) רש"י ד"ה והתנא ר' אושעיא וכו' שלו וקתני חול בגווייהו: (ה) ד"ה נברכת וכו' שאמת המים עשוי להיות: (ו) ד"ה תיפוק וכו' לא זרע תנא כצ"ל ותיבת ליה נמחק: (ז) תוס' ד"ה משום וכו' הקונטרס כאן דמשברין את הקדרה ואין: (ח) בא"ד איתמר מפני שהסלעים: (ט) ד"ה דמחממי וכו' שהוחם מחום השמש: (י) ד"ה המבריך וכו' ברחוק ג'. נ"ב עי' בפי' הר"ש מס' כלאים פ"ז:

לצדדין קא משתרשי? והא א)תנן: אהמבריך את הגפן בארץ, אם אין על גבה עפר שלשה טפחים — לא יביא זרע עליה, ותני עלה: באבל זורע את הצדדין אילך ואילך! אמר רבי חגא בשם רבי יוסי: מפני שמחלידין ב)את הקרקע ומעלין עפר תיחוח.§ "ואת מי רגלים מן הכותל — ג' טפחים" וכו'.§ אמר רבה בר בר חנה: מותר לאדם להשתין מים בצד כותלו של חבירו, דכתיב: °"והכרתי לאחאב משתין בקיר ועצור ועזוב בישראל". (מלכים א כא) והא אנן תנן: ואת מי רגלים מן הכותל — שלשה טפחים! התם בשופכין. (א) (ת"ש: לא ישפוך אדם מים בצד כותלו של חבירו אלא אם כן הרחיק ממנו ג' טפחים! התם נמי בשופכין.) ת"ש: ג)גלא ישתין אדם מים בצד כותלו של חבירו אלא אם כן הרחיק ממנו ג' טפחים; בד"א — בכותל לבינים, אבל בכותל אבנים — בכדי שלא יזיק, וכמה? טפח. ושל צונמא — מותר; תיובתא דרבה בר בר חנה! תיובתא. והא רבה בר בר חנה קרא קאמר! התם הכי קאמר: אפילו מידי דדרכיה לאישתוני בקיר לא שביקנא ליה, ומאי ניהו? כלבא. אמר ר' טובי בר קיסנא אמר שמואל: דרקיק אינו ממעט בחלון. מאי איריא רקיק? אפי' עבה נמי! לא מיבעיא קאמר: לא מיבעיא עבה (ב) כיון דאיחזי ליה לא מבטיל ליה, אבל רקיק דממאיס — אימא בטולי מבטיל ליה, קמ"ל. ותיפוק ליה דהוה ליה דבר שהוא מקבל טומאה, וכל דבר שהוא מקבל טומאה — אינו חוצץ בפני הטומאה! השנילוש במי פירות. מיתיבי: ד)וקופה מלאה תבן וחבית מלאה גרוגרות, המונחים בחלון — רואין, כל שאילו ינטלו ויכולין תבן וגרוגרות לעמוד בפני עצמן — חוצצין, ואם לאו — אין חוצצין; והא תבן חזי לבהמתו! זבסריא. חזי לטינא! חדאית ביה קוצי. חזי להסקה! (ג) טבמתונא. חזי להסק גדול! הסק גדול לא שכיח. גרוגרות — הא חזו ליה! אמר שמואל: יבשהתריפו. וכן תני רבה בר אבוה: בשהתריפו. האי חבית היכי דמיא? אי דפומא לבר —

היא

רש"י

לצדדין קא משתרשי. ומחלידין מתחת לכותל, ומקלקלים יסודו. המבריך את הגפן. גפן יחידי, שאין בזרעים ה) שאצלם משום עירבוב. דאין כרם בפחות מחמש גפנים, שתים כנגד שתים ואחת יוצאה זנב. אלא שלא ינק הזרע מן הגפן. מבריך. כמו "ויברך הגמלים" (בראשית כד) — כופף זמורת גפן מחוברת, ומבריכה בקרקע בצידיה לכאן ולכאן, וקורין בלע"ז פרובני"ר. שמחלידין את הקרקע. אצל הכותל במקומן, ומעלין עפר תיחוח, ומתמוטט (ד) קרקע יסוד הכותל לצדדין. משתין בקיר. אלמא דרך בני אדם כן. בשופכין. עביט מלא, ושופכו שם. לא ישתין. ליכא לאוקמי אלא במשתין ממש. בכותל לבינים. שהם של טיט, שנתייבשו בחמה, והם נימוקים מחמת המים. וכמה טפח. מפני שמטשטש את הקרקע סמוך ליסוד הכותל. ובצונמא. אם כותל זה בנוי בסלע, דליכא למיחש (ה) בטישטוש קרקע. מותר. סמוך ממש, ואסיפא קאי — בכותל אבנים. רקיק. סופגנין, חררה דקה ורכה. אינו ממעט בחלון. שבין בית לבית, ויש בו פותח טפח, ומת מונח באחת מהן וטומאה בוקעת לצד שני — אין רקיק (ו) ממעט שיעורן מלהוציא טומאה. דכיון דראוי לאכילה — לא מבטיל להתם דנהוי כמחיצה. אבל רקיק דמאים. מתוך שהוא דק, ולחלוח הכותל מרטבו — נמאס. שנילוש במי פירות. שאינן מכשירין. ואין אוכל מקבל טומאה בלא הכשר משקה הקרוי משקה, כגון מים ויין וחלב. וחבית מלא גרוגרות. תאנים יבשים, וכגון שלא הוכשרו. כל שאילו ינטלו. הקופה וחבית. ויכולין. התבן או הגרוגרות לעמוד בפני עצמן — חוצצין בפני הטומאה. ואם לאו אין חוצצין. שהחבית והקופה אין חוצצין, לפי שהן מקבלין טומאה. סריא = נרקב. והא חזי לטינא. ולא מבטל ליה. דאית ביה קוצי. (ז) והן היו רומסין ברגליהן בטיט. הא חזו. לאכילה. כולהו הנך תיובתא דשמואל, דאמר: מידי דחזי ליטלו משם לאחר זמן — אין ממעט בחלון. בשהתריפו = התליעו. אי פומיה לבר. לצד הבית שאין המת בתוכו.

שאין

תוספות

התם בשופכין. וא"ת: בשלמא אי איירי במשתין, אע"ג דתנא ליה אמת המים — תנא ליה נמי האי, דס"ד משום צניעותא לישתרי. אבל אי איירי בשופכין — מאי קמ"ל? הא תנא ליה אמת המים, דמהאי טעמא אמר לעיל דלא תני חול! י"ל: דשאני חול, שהוא כל שעה אצל הכותל, אבל הנך מי רגלים כלים כרגע.

ותיובתא דרבה בר בר חנה. ולא מצי לשנויי דכי קאמר רבה בר בר חנה — בצונמא. חדא, דהוה ליה לפרושי בהדיא, ועוד: דדריש מקרא, ש"מ דלא מפליג.

אמר רב טובי רקיק אינו ממעט. הך שמעתתא מייתי הכא אגב דפריך לקמן: (ח) זרעים כיון דקשו לכותל שקיל להו.

רקיק אינו ממעט בחלון. דיני חלון פי' ר"י ב"ר מרדכי על פי המשניות: דאם הוא חלון העשוי לתשמיש — שיעורו להביא טומאה בפותח טפח, וכשיתמעט מטפח אפילו במשהו — אינו מביא. ואם הוא חלון שעשוי לאורה, ועשוי בידי אדם — שיעורו כמלא מקדח גדול של לשכה, שהוא כמלא פונדיון האיטלקי, שהוא סלע נירונית. והיא יתירה על סלע סתם, דסלע סתם הוא פחות ממלא מקדח סתם, וכל שכן ממקדח גדול, כדאמרינן בבכורות (דף לז:). ואותו חלון שעשוי לאורה אינו מתמעט מסתימת משהו, כיון שהיה בו כשיעור, אלא עד שיתמעט שלא יהא בשיריים (ט) רום אצבעים על רוחב גודל. ומאור שאינו עשוי בידי אדם אלא מעצמו, כגון חררוהו מים או שרצים — שיעורו מלא אגרוף. חישב עליו לתשמיש — שיעורו פותח טפח, למאור — שיעורו מלא מקדח. ו"מלא אגרוף" מפרש התם — באגרופו של בן אבטיח, ורבי יוסי אומר: כראש כל אדם. ושאינו עשוי (י) לאורה ולא לתשמיש אלא לאויר ולשמור גגות ופרדסים — אותו שיעורו כמלא מקדח בינוני.

מאי איריא רקיק כו'. השתא ס"ד דנקט רקיק דוקא, משום דאית ביה תרתי: חדא (כ) — דלא סתימה מעלייתא, לפי שהוא רך ועשוי ליפול. ועוד, שאינו מבטלו. משום הכי פריך: אפי' עבה נמי, שמתקיים, הואיל ואינו מבטלו — אינו ממעט.

ותיפוק ליה. (ל) אפי' אם יבטלו דאינו חוצץ, משום דמקבל טומאה. ותימה: אם יבטל ליה — תו לא מקבל טומאה, וטהור. כדמוכח בפרק "העור והרוטב" (חולין דף קכט. ושם) דאמר: כיפת שאור שייחדה לישיבה — בטלה, ובית שסיככו בזרעים — טהורים. אלמא, כיון דבטליה לא מקבל טומאה! וי"ל: דהתם איירי כגון דעבד בהו שינוי מעשה, דהא אמרי' (שבת דף נב:): כל הכלים יורדין לידי טומאה במחשבה, ואין עולין מטומאה אלא ע"י שינוי מעשה. וה"ה באוכלין, דבעינן שינוי מעשה. דאפילו בידות האוכלין מוכח בפרק קמא דסוכה (דף יד. ושם) דאיכא תנא דאית ליה דבעינן בהו שינוי מעשה.

שנילושה במי פירות. הו"מ לשנויי: כגון שאין בו כביצה, ובמסכת אהלות (פי"ג מ"ה) חשיב פחות מכביצה אוכלין בהדי הנך (מ) שאמר שממעטים את הטפח.

מי פירות. פי' ר"ת: כגון שמן. ולא דק, דשמן מכשיר הוא, כדמוכח בפרק קמא דשבת (דף ה:) ובריש פרק "חבית" (שם קמד.) דשמן חשיב משקה. אלא דוקא מוהל היוצא מתחילה.

בתיבנא סריא. תימה: אכתי חזיא לבהמתו ע"י פירוק, כדמוכח בפרק בתרא דשבת (דף קנה:) דאמרינן, תא שמע: מפרכין את התבן כו', אלמא מיטרח באוכלא שרי! ומשני: בתיבנא סריא! וי"ל: דהכא איירי שהוא מוסרח כל כך, דאפי' ע"י שום תקון לא חזיא.

רואין כל שאילו ינטלו. אין לפרש דטעם משום דסופו ליטול חבית וקופה, ולהכי בעינן שיהו גרוגרות ותבן יכולין לעמוד בפני עצמן. דא"כ, למאי דפריך: תבן הא קא חזי ליה, ורוצה להוכיח מכאן דאפילו סופו ליטלו חוצץ — תיקשי ליה: אמאי צריך שיכולין לעמוד בפני עצמן? אלא אומר ר"י: דכך הוא הדין, דכל דבר החוצץ — בעינן שיוכל לעמוד בפני עצמו. דקתני לעיל מהך משנה במסכת אהלות (פ"ו מ"ב): קוברי המת שהיו עוברין באכסדרה, ובא אחד מהן והגיף את הדלת וסמכו במפתח, אם יכולה דלת לעמוד בפני עצמה — טהור, ואם לאו — טמא. וכן חבית של גרוגרות וקופה של תבן שהן נתונין בחלון. משמע דהכל חד טעמא הוא, והיינו טעמא — דסתימת עראי הוא, דכיון שאינו יכול לעמוד בפני עצמו. אי נמי, משום דבעינן דבר החוצץ עומד על ידי דבר שאינו מקבל טומאה. ומיהו בפירוש משניות מצא ר"י דמפרש אפילו במפתח שאינו מקבל טומאה איירי, *ומטמא [ומטמאת כל"ל ועי' רש"ש] — דלא חשיב אהל לחוץ בפני הטומאה, כיון שעמד על ידי כלי, אף על פי שאינו מקבל טומאה. ורבי אליעזר פליג עלה בתוספתא, וקאמר דטהור, כיון שהמפתח אינו מקבל טומאה. ואזלי לטעמייהו, דפליגי במסכת אהלות (בפ"ו מ"א) בנדבך שהוא נתון על גבי כלים, אפילו כלי גללים כלי אבנים כלי אדמה, דלרבי אליעזר נעשה אהל לטהר, ולרבנן אינו נעשה אהל אלא כשהוא נתון על גבי אבנים.

היא

עין משפט נר מצוה

יד א ב מיי' פ"ו מהל' כלאים הל' ז טוש"ע י"ד סי' רצה סעיף ז:
טו ג מיי' פ"ט מהל' שכנים הל' ו סמג עשין פב טוש"ע ח"מ סי' קנה סעיף ו:
טז ד ה מיי' פט"ו מהל' טומאת מת הלכה א:
יז ו ז ח ט י מיי' שם הלכה ב:

רבינו גרשום

למתני מאחר דתנא זרעים לא צריך למתני מחרישה דוודאי אין חרישה בלי זרעים ומשני לחרוש לאילנות לצורך נטיעת אילנות דהכא ליכא זרעים ומש"ה איצטריך למתני מחרישה דמזרעים לא מפיק מחרישה: ותיפוק ליה מינה דמרחיקין. דמאחר דקתני מתני' מרחיקין אמת המים וכל הני ממילא איכא למשמע דמרחיקין זרעי' ומחרישה דהיינו משום מתונתא ותרתי זימני למה לי משום מתונתא והא מש"ה מרחיקין זרעים ומחרישה משום דמשקין הזרעים מן המים וקשה לכותל: תנא בא"י קאי. דלא משקי זרעים אלא מטר אבל בבבל דצריכי להן מים להשקות שדותיהן מתוך שהיא יושבת במים אם יבשו מים צריך להביא לשם מים כדי להשקות השדה שמתוך שהיא רגילה בכך צריך להשקות בכל שעה: מדקתני מתני' מרחיקין את הזרעים ג' טפחים. מכלל דזרעים לצדדין מעקמי ומשתרשי ואזלי ומש"ה מרחיקין כי היכי דלא ליזקו בכותל ורמינהו המבריך את הגפן בארץ שנועץ ראש הגפן בקרקע ולאמצעיתו נמי כפהו ונועצו בקרקע כדי שישתרש ויגדל הכרם אם אין על גבי הגפן הכפוף ונעוץ עפר גבוה ג' טפחים ה"ז לא יביא זרעים לשם ויזרע על גבו משום דקא ינקי הדדי ואיכא כלאים בכרם אבל אי איכא עפר ג' טפחים זורע על גבו דלא אזלי שרשין דזרעין טפי מעומק ג' טפחים ולא מסתבכי בשרשי הגפן. אי ליכא על גבו עפר ג' טפחים אין זורע על גבו דגפן אבל זורע את הצדדין של גפן אילך ואילך מכאן ומכאן ומש"ה מצי לזרוע בסמוך מכאן ומכאן דלא קא אזלי הזרעין לצדדין אלא יורדין כנגדן בקרקע וליכא למיחש דלישתרשי לצדדין וליערבו בשרשי הגפן ואם כן אמאי מרחיקין אותן מן הכותל ג' טפחים: שמחלידין. ונוקבין בקרקע ריבוי השרשין ומעלין עפר תיחוח ומרפין יסוד הכותל: **פיסקא** והכרתי לאחאב משתין בקיר. במילי דאסורא לא משתעי קרא אלא במילי דהיתרא: בשופכין מכלי: ת"ש לא ישתין. בפירוש: בכותל לבנים דרכין נינהו מש"ה מרחיקין ג' טפחים וצונמא שחוקה היא מותר להשתין כרבה בר בר חנה דאמר לעיל מותר להשתין: רקיק אינו ממעט בחלון. דקי"ל אם יש מת בבית ויש בו חלון טפח על טפח ואותו חלון פתוח לבית אחד וחלון שהוא טפח על טפח מכנים ומוציא את הטומאה ואם יש באותו חלון פת רקיק אחד אינו ממעט בחלון ומיטמא בית האחר דלא מיבטל ליה ודעתיה עליה למיכליה וכמו כמאן דליתא מש"ה אין ממעט: אבל רקיק דממאס שמלוכלך מכאן ומכאן ודק הוא אינו יכול לקלופיה אימא מבטיל ליה ולמעט קמ"ל דלא: ותיפוק ליה דרקיק אינו ממעט משום דהוה ליה דבר המקבל טומאה משום דנילוש מעיקרא במים והוי מוכשר מחמת מים וכל דבר המקבל טומאה אינו חוצץ בפני הטומאה לסתום בו חלון שהוא טפח על טפח שלא תצא הטומאה או למעט ואיצטריך לאשמועינן דאינו ממעט. במי פירות ומי פירות אין מכשירין: לעמוד בפני עצמן בחלון. דחוצצת משום דחבית וקופה שהן כלי ומקבלין טומאה אינו חוצץ בפני הטומאה. והא תבן חזיא לבהמתו ולא מבטל ליה וחוצץ וקשיא לשמואל דאמר לעיל דכל מידי דחזיא ליה לא מבטל ליה ואינו חוצץ ומשני משום הכי חוצץ דודאי בטוליה בטליה ולא חזי ליה דתבנא סריא הוא. והא חזי לטינא ואמאי חוצץ הא לא מבטל ליה ומשני דאית ביה קוצים ולא חזי לטינא משום שגובלין הטיט ברגלים ואי הוי ביה קוצי היו נכנסין ברגליהן ומש"ה לא חזיא: היסק גדול לא שכיח. לא מיבעי ליה: בשהתריפו. שהתליעו: אי פומה של חבית מבחוץ:

היא

מסורת הש"ס

א) כלאים פ"ז מ"א: ב) [פי' רבינו חננאל יונקין כח הקרקע כחולדה שדרה בעיקרי הבתים. ערוך ערך חלד א']: ג) [תוספתא פ"א]: ד) אהלות פ"ו מ"ב ע"ש: ה) נ"א שאצלה:

הגהות הב"ח

(א) גמ' התם בשופכין ת"ש לא יטיל אדם: (ב) שם לא מיבעיא עבה דכיון דחזי ליה: (ג) שם במתונתא: (ד) רש"י ד"ה שמחלידין וכו' ומתמוטט הקרקע שתחת יסוד: (ה) ד"ה ובצונמא וכו' לטישטוש הקרקע: (ו) ד"ה אינו ממעט וכו' אין רקיק זה ממעט שיעורו וכו' לא מבטל ליה להתם: (ז) ד"ה דאית וכו' והם היו: (ח) תוס' ד"ה אמר וכו' לקמן אזרעים: (ט) ד"ה רקיק וכו' שלא יהא בשיריים כ"א אצבע על רוחב גודל: (י) בא"ד ושאינו עשוי לא לאורה: (כ) ד"ה מאי וכו' חדא דלאו סתימה מעלייתא היא לפי: (ל) ד"ה ותיפוק ליה פירוש אפי': (מ) ד"ה שנילושה וכו' בהדי הנך שממעטין כצ"ל ותיבת שאמר נמחק:

הִיא גּוּפָהּ תֵּיחוּץ, דְּהָא א)כְּלִי חֶרֶשׂ אֵינוֹ מְטַמֵּא מִגַּבּוֹ! (א) אאֶלָּא דְּפוּמָא לְגָאו. וְאִי בָּעֵית אֵימָא: לְעוֹלָם דְּפוּמָא לְבַר, הָכָא בְּמַאי עָסְקִינַן — בְּחָבִית שֶׁל מַתֶּכֶת. מֵיתִיבֵי: ב)בעֲשָׂבִין שֶׁתְּלָשָׁן וְהִנִּיחָן בַּחַלּוֹן, אוֹ שֶׁעָלוּ מֵאֲלֵיהֶן בַּחַלּוֹנוֹת, וּמַטְלוֹנִיּוֹת שֶׁאֵין בָּהֶן שָׁלֹשׁ עַל שָׁלֹשׁ, וְהָאֵבֶר וְהַבָּשָׂר הַמְּדוּלְדָּלִין בִּבְהֵמָה וּבְחַיָּה, וְעוֹף שֶׁשָּׁכַן בַּחַלּוֹן, וְגוֹי שֶׁיָּשַׁב בַּחַלּוֹן, וּבֶן שְׁמוֹנָה הַמּוּנָּח בַּחַלּוֹן, וְהַמֶּלַח, וּכְלִי חֶרֶס, וְסֵפֶר תּוֹרָה — כּוּלָּם מְמַעֲטִין בַּחַלּוֹן; אֲבָל הַשֶּׁלֶג, וְהַבָּרָד, וְהַגְּלִיד, וְהַכְּפוֹר, וְהַמַּיִם — כּוּלָּן אֵין מְמַעֲטִין בַּחַלּוֹן; וְהָא עֲשָׂבִין חֲזוּ לִבְהֶמְתּוֹ! גבְּאַפְרַזְתָּא. (ב) "אוֹ שֶׁעָלוּ מֵאֲלֵיהֶן", כֵּיוָן דְּקָשׁוּ לְכוֹתֶל שָׁקֵיל לְהוּ! אָמַר רַבָּה: דבְּכוֹתֶל חוּרְבָּה. רַב פַּפָּא אָמַר: אֲפִילּוּ בְּכוֹתֶל יִישׁוּב — בְּבָאִין חוּץ (ג) לִשְׁלֹשָׁה לַחַלּוֹן. "מַטְלוֹנִיּוֹת", חֲזוּ לֵיהּ לִקְרִיעָה דִּלְבוּשָׁא. הבִּסְמִיכָתָא. חֲזוּ לְאוּמָנָא! ובְּרִיסְקָא. אִי בְּרִיסְקָא, שֶׁאֵין בָּהֶן שָׁלֹשׁ עַל שָׁלֹשׁ? שֶׁאֵין בָּהֶן אַרְבָּעָה עַל אַרְבָּעָה מִיבְּעֵי לֵיהּ! ג)כְּעֵין רִיסְקָא. "וְהָאֵבֶר וְהַבָּשָׂר הַמְּדוּלְדָּלִין בִּבְהֵמָה וּבְחַיָּה", עָרְקָא וְאָזְלָא! זבִּקְשׁוּרָה. שָׁחֵיט לָהּ! בִּטְמֵאָה. מְזַבֵּין לָהּ לְגוֹי! בִּכְחוּשָׁה. פָּסֵיק שָׁדֵי לָהּ לִכְלָבִים! כֵּיוָן דְּאִיכָּא צַעַר בַּעֲלֵי חַיִּים לָא עָבֵיד. "וְעוֹף שֶׁשָּׁכַן בַּחַלּוֹן", פָּרַח וְאָזֵיל! חבְּקָשׁוּר. שָׁחֵיט לֵיהּ! בְּטָמֵא. מְזַבֵּין לֵיהּ לְגוֹי! בְּקַלָּנִיתָא. יָהֵיב לֵיהּ לְיָנוּקָא! בִּמְסָרֵט. קַלָּנִיתָא לָא מְסָרְטָא! כְּעֵין קַלָּנִיתָא. "וְגוֹי שֶׁיָּשַׁב בַּחַלּוֹן", קָאֵי וְאָזֵיל! בִּכְפוּת. אָתֵי חַבְרֵיהּ שָׁרֵי לֵיהּ! בִּמְצוֹרָע. אָתֵי מְצוֹרָע חַבְרֵיהּ שָׁרֵי לֵיהּ! טאֶלָּא בַּחֲבוּשֵׁי מַלְכוּת. "וּבֶן שְׁמוֹנָה הַמּוּנָּח בַּחַלּוֹן", אָתְיָא אִמֵּיהּ דָּרְיָא לֵיהּ! יבְּשַׁבָּת; ד)דְּתַנְיָא: כבֶּן שְׁמוֹנָה הֲרֵי הוּא כְּאֶבֶן, וְאָסוּר לְטַלְטְלוֹ בְּשַׁבָּת, אֲבָל אִמּוֹ שׁוֹחָה עָלָיו וּמֵנִיקַתּוֹ מִפְּנֵי הַסַּכָּנָה. "מֶלַח", חַזְיָא לֵיהּ! לבִּמְרִירְתָּא. חַזְיָא לְעוֹרוֹת! מדְּאִית בַּהּ קוֹצֵי. כֵּיוָן דְּקַשְׁיָא לְכוֹתֶל שָׁקְלָא! נדְּיָתְבָא אַחַסְפָּא. חַסְפָּא גּוּפָא תֵּיחוּץ! דְּלֵית

רש"י

שֶׁאֵין בָּהּ שָׁלֹשׁ עַל שָׁלֹשׁ. שֶׁאֵין מְקַבְּלִין טוּמְאָה. הַמְּדוּלְדָּלִין. שֶׁתְּלוּיִין וּמְעוּרִין בְּמִקְצָת, וְהַבְּהֵמָה עוֹמֶדֶת אֵצֶל הַחַלּוֹן וְהָאֵבֶר מוּנָּח עַל הַחַלּוֹן. וּתְנַן בְּ"הָעוֹר וְהָרוֹטֶב" (חולין קכט.): מְטַמְּאִין טוּמְאַת אוֹכָלִין בִּמְקוֹמָן, וּצְרִיכִין הֶכְשֵׁר, וְאֵלּוּ לֹא הוּכְשְׁרוּ. גּוֹי. אֵינוֹ מְקַבֵּל טוּמְאָה. וְכֵן בֶּן שְׁמוֹנָה, שֶׁהֲרֵי הוּא כְּאֶבֶן, לֹא חַי וְלֹא מֵת. הַמֶּלַח. לֹא מְקַבֵּל טוּמְאָה, דְּלָאו אוֹכֶל הוּא בְּאַנְפֵּי נַפְשֵׁיהּ. וּכְלִי חֶרֶס. שֶׁאֲחוֹרָיו לְצַד אֹהֶל הַטּוּמְאָה. וְהַשֶּׁלֶג וְהַבָּרָד כו'. הוֹאִיל וְנִימּוֹקִים מֵאֲלֵיהֶם — אֵין מְמַעֲטִים. וְכֵן מַיִם שֶׁבַּכְּלִי, הוֹאִיל וְאִם יִנָּטֵל הַכְּלִי אֵין עוֹמְדִים בִּפְנֵי עַצְמָן — אֵין מְמַעֲטִין בַּחַלּוֹן. הַבָּרָד = גלש"א. הַכְּפוֹר = גרייסל"ן. הַגְּלִיד. קֶרַח לָבָן, שֶׁאֵינוֹ שֶׁלֶג. ה"ג: וְהָא עֲשָׂבִים חֲזוּ לִבְהֶמְתּוֹ. וְסוֹפוֹ לִיטְּלָן, וְאַפ"ה כָּל כַּמָּה דְּאִיתְנְהוּ הָתָם מְמַעֲטֵי, וּתְיוּבְתָּא דִּשְׁמוּאֵל. בְּאַפְרַזְתָּא. (ד) וְהוּא סַם הַמָּוֶת לַבְּהֵמָה. וּמַאן דְּגָרֵיס "בְּאַרְזַפְתָּא" טוֹעֶה, ה) שֶׁהוּא קוֹרְנָס שֶׁל נַפָּחִים. כֵּיוָן דְּקָשׁוּ לְכוֹתֶל. שֶׁמַּחֲלִידִין אוֹתוֹ, כִּדְאָמְרִי' בְּמַתְנִי', שָׁקֵיל לְהוּ. וְאַפ"ה מְמַעֵט, וְקָשֶׁה לִשְׁמוּאֵל. בְּבָאִין חוּץ לִשְׁלֹשָׁה. טְפָחִים רָחוֹק מִן הַכּוֹתֶל, וְעוֹלִין לְתוֹךְ הַחַלּוֹן רָאשֵׁיהֶן. חֲזִי לִקְרִיעָה. לַעֲשׂוֹת טְלָאִי. בִּסְמִיכָתָא. עָב יוֹתֵר מִדַּאי. לְאוּמָנָא. לְמַקִּיז דָּם, לְקַנֵּחַ פִּי הַמַּכָּה. בְּרִיסְקָא. שֶׁהוּא מְסָרֵט. אֵין בָּהֶן אַרְבָּעָה עַל אַרְבָּעָה מִבָּעֵי לֵיהּ. שֶׁזּוֹ הִיא שִׁיעוּר שֶׁל שַׂק. קַלָּנִיתָא. עוֹף כָּחוּשׁ מְאֹד, וְאֵין רָאוּי לְשׁוּם אָדָם. כְּעֵין קַלָּנִיתָא. כָּחוּשׁ כְּקַלָּנִיתָא, וְהוּא מְסָרֵט. דְּאִית בֵּיהּ קוֹצֵי. וִיסָרְטוּ אֶת יָדָיו. כֵּיוָן דְּקָשֶׁה לַכּוֹתֶל. כִּדְתְנַן בְּמַתְנִיתִין.

תוספות

היא גופה תיחוץ. ותימה: היכי תיחוץ? הא לא מבטל ליה התם! ותירץ ר"י ב"ר מרדכי: דכיון שהתריפו הגרוגרות — גם החבית נתקלקל, ומבטלו. אבל קשה לר"י: דבפ"ב דשבת (דף קנז. ושם) דאמר: שפקקו את המאור בטפיח — כי פקקו מאי הוי? הא לא מבטל ליה, ואינו חוצץ! וליכא למימר דביטלו הטפיח — דא"כ היה בונה בשבת! ונראה לר"ת ולר"י: דכלי חרס לא בעי ביטול, אלא שפיר חוצץ, אע"ג דלא מבטל ליה. והא דקתני לקמן דכלי חרס ממעט בחלון, ופריך: כלי חרס הא חזי ליה! התם מיירי בממעט חלון מכשיעור, אבל אינו סותם כל החלון — להכי בעי ביטול. אבל היכא דסותם כל החלון, כי הכא דקתני "חוצצין", דמשמע דסותם לגמרי, וכן ההוא דפקקו את המאור — התם ודאי [לא] בעי ביטול בכלי חרס. ועוד אמר הר"ר שמואל: דכלי עץ נמי שאינו מקבל טומאה, כגון העשוי לנחת — לא בעי ביטול. דבפ"ב דמגילה (דף כו:) גבי ההוא בי כנישתא דיהודאי דהות פתיחא לההוא אינדרונא דהוה בה מיתנא ובעו כהני לעלויי בה (ה) עד דאמר להו: דלו תיבותא ואותבוה אבבא. ואי צריך ביטול — מאי מהני האי תיבה? דמסתמא לא ביטלוה שם. ועוד: שלא היו יכולים לבטלה — שהיה ספר תורה מונח בה, ואסור לשנותה בדבר אחר — דמעלין בקודש ולא מורידין. **בחבית** של מתכת. הקשה ר"ת: דחבית גופה תביא טומאה לבית אחר, דע"י אהל נעשית המתכת כחלל להיות אבי אבות הטומאה, כדמוכח במסכת אהלות, והוי כחלל נמי לטמא אחרים באהל. דכוליה קרא ד"וכל אשר יגע על פני השדה בחלל חרב" וגו' דריש לה בנזיר פרק "כ"ג" (דף נד. ושם) לענין אהל! ונראה לרבינו תם: דהכא מיירי כגון שהגרוגרות בולטות חוץ לפי חבית כל סביבותיו ומכסות אותו לגמרי, שאין נראה כלל. ודייק ר"ת מדנקט גרוגרות ולא נקט פירות, לפי שהם מדובקות יחד אע"פ שיוצאות חוץ לחבית אין נופלות. וכי האי גוונא דייק בפרק "חבית" (שבת דף קמו.). ועוד אומר ר' יצחק: דהכא מיירי בשאין חבית יוצאה חוץ לכותל, דהשתא דרך החלון לא יצא טומאה לבית, דטומאה רצוצה בוקעת ועולה, ואינה מתפשטת לצדדין, שהרי אין בו פותח טפח. **שעלו** מאיליהן. תימה: היאך ממעטין הטפח? הא תנן במס' אהלות (פ"ח מ"ה): אלו לא מביאין ולא חוצצין: הזרעים, והירקות המחוברין לקרקע, חוץ מן הירקות שמנו. פירוש: הנהו דמנו לעיל, דמביאין וחוצצין: האירוס והקיסוס וירקות חמור ודלעת יוונית. וא"כ, היכי קתני דעשבין שעלו מאליהן דחוצצין? ותירץ רבינו תם: דהתם איירי לענין אהל, דאין נעשין אהל לחוץ בפני הטומאה על מה שתחתיהם או שעליהם, או להביא טומאה — מפני שהרוח מנשבו, ואינו עומד במקום אחד, והוי דומיא דעוף הפורח שאינו לא חוצץ ולא מביא. הקשה ר"י: דהכא בכולה שמעתין לא בעינן מירוח לא בעשבים ולא בחבית, דפריך לעיל: היא גופה תיחוץ. וב"הגוזל קמא" (ב"ק דף קה.) אמר רבא: הרי ו)חבית שניקבה וסתמוה שמרים — הצילוה, פקקה בזמורה — עד שימרח מן הצדדין! וי"ל: דהתם (ו) בכלי בעינן מוקף צמיד פתיל, להכי צריך מירוח. אבל הכא — לא בעי צמיד פתיל. **ועוף** ששכן בחלון. נראה דאתי אפילו לר"מ דאמר (עירובין דף טו:): כל דבר שיש בו רוח חיים אין עושין אותו לא דופן לסוכה, ולא לחי למבוי כו' — דהיינו לענין מחילת עשרה טפחים דוקא, אבל הכא לענין ממעט בחלון — ממעטו בכל דבר שיבטלנו. **וגוי** שישב בחלון. דגוי אינו מקבל טומאה, כדנפקא לן מקרא בפ"ב דנזיר (דף סא: ושם) דכתיב "ואיש אשר יטמא וגו' מתוך הקהל" — יצא גוי שאין לו קהל. ואע"ג דחכמים עשאום כזבים לכל דבריהם (שבת דף פג. נדה דף לד.), כיון דמדאורייתא לא מקבלי טומאה — חוצצין מפני הטומאה. וא"ת: דבפרק "יוצא דופן" (נדה דף מג:) אמר: חומר בשרץ מבשכבת זרע, שהשרץ אין לו חלוקת טומאה. ומסיק: שכבת זרע דחלוקה טומאה מה היא? אילימא בין ישראלים לגוים — ה"נ הא איכא עכבר דים ועכבר דיבשה. משמע דשרץ אין חלוקה טומאתו בין ישראל לגוי! לאו פירכא היא, דאע"ג דאין גוים טמאים בשרץ — אין לו חלוקת טומאה דומיא דשכבת זרע. דבשכבת זרע גופה איכא חילוק, אבל בשרץ גופיה אין חילוק אלא בהנהו דמקבלי ממנו טומאה, הילכך צריך למינקט עכבר דים ועכבר דיבשה. והא דאיצטריך מיעוטא (שבת פג. נדה לד.), דגוי אינו מטמא בזיבה — משום דטומאת זיבה לאו טומאת מגע היא, ומטומאה זו לא אשכחן דאימעטו. ובן שמונה אינו מקבל טומאה כשהוא חי, דלא איקרי אדם. **והמלח**. משמע מהכא דאין מלח מקבל טומאה. אבל השלג מיירי שלא חישב עליו לאכילה, דלא מקבל טומאה. דאי חשב עליו — תיפוק ליה דהוי דבר המקבל טומאה, כדמוכח במסכת נדה [דף יז. וע"ש ולע"ג ואולי צ"ל אבל השלג מיירי שלא חישב עליו למשקה דלא מקבל טומאה וכו' וע"פ הג"ה זו מובנים דברי התוספות על נכון]. **כולן** אין ממעטין בחלון. וטעמא, משום דאין מתקיימין, (ח) ונימסין במים. דליכא למימר דטעמא משום דקשו לכותל ושקיל להו — דהא מלח נמי קשה לכותל, וקתני דממעט, ומיירי כגון דמנחי בחספא, והנך נמי ליתני דממעטי ודמנחי בחספא! אלא אפילו דמנחי בחספא דלא קשו לכותל — לא ממעטי. **חזי** לקריעה דלבושא. ואע"ג דאמר בפ"ק דסוכה (דף טז. ושם) ובשבת פרק "כל הכלים" (דף קכה.) דפחות משלש על שלש לא חזי לא לעניים ולא לעשירים — ודאי לא מקבל טומאה, כיון דלא מקבל טומאה. אבל מ"מ לא ממעט, דלא מבטל ליה, דקא שקיל ליה כי ז)מצטרך לקריעה דלבושא. **כיון** דאיכא צער בעלי חיים כו'. וא"ת: כולה בהמה שקיל ושדי לכלבים? וי"ל: דמיירי בקוף וכל דדמי ליה, דמנח התם לטיולי ביה. ויניחא דנקט אבר ובשר, ולא נקט בהמה גופה, דאי חזיא לטיולי — שקיל לה לטיולי בה, ואי לא חזיא שדי לה לכלבים. **אתיא** אמיה ודריא ליה בשבת. ואיירי בגוסס, שימות קודם שילא השבת, ואמר דשם תהא קבורתו.

רבינו גרשום

היא גופה תיחוץ בפני הטומאה. דהא קי"ל כלי חרס אינו מטמא מגבו: איבעית אימא דפומא לבר. (ומש"ה) אפ"ה אינה חוצצת: בחבית של מתכת. דמטמאה מגבה: או שעלו. שגדלו: ומטלניות שאין בהם ג' על ג'. דלא מקבלי טומאה. והאבר והבשר המדולדלין בבהמה ובחיה אבל עדיין סריכי בבהמה והן בחלון וכל הני מפרש לקמן למה ממעטין בחלון משום דלא הוי דבר חשוב ומבטלי להו אבל השלג וכול' אין ממעטין דמים הן: עשבים חזו לבהמה. ואמאי ממעטין הא לא מבטיל להו: באפרזתא. כלומר סם המות דבהמה דלא חזי לבהמה מש"ה מבטל ליה: כיון דקשי לכותל שקיל להו ולא מבטל להו ואמאי ממעטי בחלון. אמר רבא מש"ה ממעט דלא איכפת ליה מלקיית אותו כותל דחורבה היא ולא תליש להו בעוד שהטומאה בבית: בבאין חוץ מג' טפחים. חוץ מחלון דלא מזיק לכותל כלל וראשי ענפים מגיעין לכותל ליכא למיחש דילמא שקיל להו מש"ה ממעטין: ומטלניות. אמאי ממעט הא חזי לקריעה דלבושא לתקוני ומשני בסמיכתא דעב הוא ביותר ולא חזי: לאומנא. למקיז כלומר לקנח מן הדם ומשני ברשק דלא חזי לאומנא. אי הכי דמוקמת לה ברשק הא דתני שאין בהם ג' על ג' מש"ה לא מקבלי טומאה שאין בהן ד' על ד' מיבעי ליה דהכי דינא של שק. דעבה כעין שק ולא חזי שמחלדת כלי האומן כמו השק: בקלניתא. עוף הוא שכחש ביותר ואין ליה בשר וקא מבטל ליה ומקשא הא חזי לינוקא לשחק בו ולא מבטל ליה ואמאי ממעט ומשני במסרט דלא חזי לינוקא והא קי"ל דקלניתא לא מסרט. ואמאי לא קמבטל ליה דחזיא לינוקא ומשני כעין קלניתא דכחוש הוא ביותר ומסרט: וגוי ששכן בחלון. ה"ה נמי ישראל אלא מש"ה נקט גוי א) לא שרי ליה דגוים נמי מבדלו מן המצורע מפני הסכנה שלא ימות קודם שעתו: במרריתא. שאין ראוי למאכל: דאית בה קוצי. וכשמתקנו בו העור יכנסו הקוצים בידים ולהכי מבטל ליה. ומקשי: כיון דקשי מלח לכותל כדתני במתני' אמאי ממעט הא שקיל ליה שלא ילקה הכותל ומשני דמיתבא ההוא מלח בחספא דלא קשי לכותל. ומקשינן חספא גופא תיחוץ בלא מלח ואמאי נקט מלח: ומשני

א) [נראה דצ"ל עובד כוכבים לרבותא דאפילו עובד כוכבים לא שרי ליה דשבדי כוכבים נמי וכו']

מסורת הש"ס

א) [חולין כה.] ב) [תוספתא דאהלות פי"ד] ג) [ועי' תוס' לקמן קיז. ד"ה דין] ד) שבת קכח: יבמות פ. [תוספתא שבת פט"ז] ה) [עי' רש"י ברכות לה. ובמגילה כה. ד"ה ארזפתא ובגיטין נו: ד"ה ארזפתא ומגוה לייבש וע"ע רש"י ב"ק מז: ד"ה באפרזתא] ו) [צ"ל הרי אמרו] ז) [צ"ל מצטריך]

עין משפט נר מצוה

יח א ב ג ד ה ו ז ח מיי' פט"ו מהלכות טומאת מת הלכה ב:
יט ט מיי' פ"ב מהל' מילה הל' יג ועיין בכ"מ ופכ"ה מהל' שבת הל' ו וטוש"ע א"ח סי' של סעיף ח וטוש"ע י"ד סי' רסו סעיף יא בהג"ה:
כ ל מ נ מיי' פט"ו מהלכות טומאת מת הלכה ב:

הגהות הב"ח

(א) גמ' אינו מטמא מגבו לא לצריכה דפומא: (ב) שם באפרזתא חזיא להסקה בלחים או שעלו: (ג) שם חוץ משלשה לחלון: (ד) רש"י ד"ה באפרזתא וכו' גרסי' והוא סם: (ה) תוס' ד"ה היא וכו' ללוויי בה כו' עד דאמר להו וכו' לשנותה לדבר: (ו) ד"ה שעלו וכו' וי"ל דהתם בעינן כל"ל ותיבת בכלי נמחק: (ז) ד"ה וגוי וכו' וניימוסין וליכא כל"ל ותיבת במים נמחק:

דלית בה שיעורא, א) כדתנן: חרס — כדי ליתן בין פצים לחבירו. "כלי חרס", חזי ליה! אדמיטנף. חזי לאומנא! בדמנקב. "ספר תורה", חזי למקרא! גבבלוי. והא בעי גניזה! דשם תהא גניזתה. ב)(ואמר) רב: הבכל עושין מחיצה, חוץ ממלח ורבב; ושמואל אמר: אפילו מלח. אמר רב פפא: ולא פליגי, הא במלח סדומית, הא במלח איסתרוקנית. והשתא דאמר רבה: עושה אדם שני צבורי מלח ומניח עליהם קורה, שהמלח מעמדת את הקורה והקורה מעמדת את המלח — אפי' מלח איסתרוקנית, ולא פליגי: הא דאיכא קורה, הא דליכא קורה.§ "מרחיקין את הריחים ג' מן השכב, שהן ארבעה מן הרכב" וכו'.§ מאי טעמא? ימשום טיריא. והא תניא: ושל חמור — שלשה מן האיסטרוביל שהן ארבעה מן הקלת; התם מאי טיריא איכא? יאלא משום קלא.§ "ואת התנור — שלשה מן הכליא שהן ארבעה מן השפה".§ אמר אביי, שמע מינה: כליא דתנור — טפח. נפקא מינה — למקח וממכר.§

מתני' ג)חלא יעמיד אדם תנור בתוך הבית — אלא אם כן יש על גביו גובה ארבע אמות. היה מעמידו בעלייה, צריך שיהא תחתיו מעזיבה שלשה טפחים, ובכירה — טפח; טואם הזיק — משלם מה שהזיק. ר' שמעון אומר: לא אמרו כל השיעורין האלו, אלא שאם הזיק — פטור מלשלם. ד)ילא יפתח אדם חנות של נחתומין ושל צבעין תחת אוצרו של חבירו, ולא רפת בקר; ה)באמת, ביין התירו, אבל לא רפת בקר.§

גמ' והתניא: בתנור — ארבעה, ובכירה — שלשה! אמר אביי: כי תניא ההיא — כבדנחתומין, ו)דתנור דידן כי כירה דנחתומין.(א)§ "לא יפתח חנות" וכו'.§ ז)תנא: לאם היתה רפת (ב) קודמת לאוצר — מותר. מבעי אביי: כיבד וריבץ לאוצר, מהו? ריבה בחלונות, מהו? (ג) אכסדרה תחת האוצר, מהו? בנה עלייה על גבי ביתו, מהו? נתיקו. בעי רב הונא בריה דרב יהושע: תמרי ורמוני, מאי? סתיקו.§ "באמת, ביין התירו" וכו'.§ תנא: עביין התירו מפני שמשביחו, ולא רפת בקר מפני שמסריחו. אמר רב יוסף: פהאי דידן, אפילו קוטרא דשרגא נמי קשיא ליה. א"ר ששת: צואספסתא — כרפת בקר דמיא.§

מתני' קחנות שבחצר — יכול למחות בידו ולומר לו: איני יכול לישן מקול הנכנסין ומקול היוצאין; ח)אבל עושה כלים, יוצא ומוכר בתוך השוק; ט)ואינו יכול למחות בידו ולומר לו: איני יכול לישן, לא מקול הפטיש ולא מקול הריחים ולא מקול התינוקות.§

גמ' מ"ש רישא ומ"ש סיפא? אמר אביי: סיפא אתאן לחצר אחרת. א"ל רבא: אי הכי, ליתני: חצר אחרת — מותר! אלא אמר רבא: סיפא

רש"י

דלית בה שיעורא. והוי כמאן דליתא. חרס. לענין הוצאת שבת. כדי ליתן בין פצים לחבירו. פלימי חלונות שבכותל מרחיקין זה מזה ברוחב החלון ליכנס האורה בין כל אחד ואחד, ונותן בחומה למטה ולמעלה חרס רחב בין זה לזה, וטח בטיט, והחרס עב, והוי שם כאבן. והא בעי גניזה. ומסלקו לגנזו. חוץ ממלח ורבב. מפני שהמלח מתפזר, והרבב ניתך כשמתחמם. מלח סדומית. עבה וקשה כאבן. שני צבורי מלח. גבוהים עשרה אצל כותלי מבוי, ומניח שני ראשי קורות המבוי עליהן, שכובד הקורה מעמיד את המלח. ושל חמור. ריחים של חמור. איצטרובלא. הוא מושב הריחים שבתוך קליפת העץ, שקורין לרק"א. קלת. היא אפרכסת, שקורין טרויימוריי"ר. מאי טיריא איכא. ריחים קטנים וקלים הן, ואין הקרקע מרעיד בגילגולו. משום קלא. י"מ: קול הנהגת החמור, וי"מ: קול הריחים.

מתני' אלא אם כן יש על גביו. חלל גובה ארבע אמות מפי התנור עד התקרה, כדי שלא יאחוז האור בתקרה. עד שיהא תחתיו מעזיבה = אשטרי"ך בלע"ז, טיח קרקע ג' טפחי', שלא תבער תקרה התחתונה של עלייה. ועל גביו ד' אמות. ובכירה מעזיבה טפח. אף היא כלי חרס, ששופתים קדירה על חללה, ואין עושין בתוכה היסק גדול כמו שעושין בתנור. ואם הזיק. אחר (ד) שיהא שם כל השיעורין הללו — משלם מה שהזיק. ואעפ"כ מעכבין עליו השכנים להרחיק בכל השיעורים הללו, שמא ידליק בתיהם ואין לו מה לשלם. ביין התירו. אם היה אוצר של יין — התירו לפתוח תחתיו חנות של נחתומין ולצבעין, שאין העשן קשה ליין. אבל לא רפת בקר. שהריח קשה ליין.

גמ' והתניא. לענין מעמידה בעלייה, בתנור — ארבעה מעזיבה מתחתיו, ובכירה שלשה! בדנחתומין. שמסיקין אותו תמיד. וכן הכירה — בכירת נחתומין. תנור דידן. דיהב ביה תנא דמתני' שיעור ג"ט — ככירה דנחתומין דמי. כיבד וריבץ. גגו לצורך האוצר, ולא הספיק להכניס לו תבואה עד שפתח זה חנות תחתיו, מי הוי כקודם לאוצר, או דילמא דכיון דכיבד וריבץ — הוי כקידם האוצר? ריבה בחלונות. בעלייתו, דגלי דעתיה שלאוצר הוא עשוי, שיכנס לו אויר, שלא ירקב התבואה. בנה עלייה על גבי ביתו. על גגו, ורגילין היו לבנות שם לאוצר, מהו? את"ל ריבה בחלונות לאו הקדמה הוא, היכי דכולי בניינא להכי עביד, מאי? תמרי ורמוני. הכניס שם תמרים ורמונים, מי הויא התחלת אוצר, או דילמא אין אוצר אלא בתבואה ויין ושמן? והאי דידן. יין שלנו, אפילו עשן העולה מן הנר קשה לו. אספסתא. שחת של תבואה. כרפת בקר דמיא. מחמת שהוא לח (ה) ומתחמם ומעלה סרחון.

תוספות

דלית בה שיעורא. פירוש: דאין שיעור לחספא למעט מפותח טפח. ולא גרסינן "כדתנן", דמה ענין זה לשיעורי שבת? אלא "וכדתנן", בוי"ו. וה"פ: ואמאי מלח ממעט? הא כי שקיל חספא, כשילטרך לו, יסיר גם המלח כדי שלא יזיק את הכותל! ואהא מייתי "וכדתנן", כלומר, דמיירי נמי דלית ביה כדי ליתן בין פצים לחבירו, דאין ראוי לכלום ולא שקיל ליה. ואית ספרים דלא גרסי "חספא גופיה תיהוך", אלא גרסינן: "ותיפוק ליה משום חספא". כלומר, ותיפוק ליה שיסיר המלח כשיסיר חספא! ומשני: דלית בה שיעורא כדתנן כו', ולא שקיל ליה.

ושל חמור שלש מן האיצטרובלא. פי' רבינו חננאל: דשל חמור ליכא טיריא, דאין חמור טוחן בה. אלא "חמור" קורא לבנין העצים הנושאים את הריחים. כמו שמצינו דעצים הנושאים נקראים "חמור", כמו העץ שהמטה מוטלת עליו, כדתנן (כלים פי"ח מ"ג): נקליטי המטה וחמור טהורים. וכן העץ הסובל שידה תיבה ומגדל נקרא "חמור", דתנן: חמור שתחת המלבן, וספסלים שתחת הרגלים — טהור. וכן עץ שהנפח סומך עליו נקרא "חמור", דתנן (שם פי"ד מ"ג): חמור של נפחים (ו) טמאים. וכן הריחים — הבנין עשוי כמין כסא ועליה ריחים וזהו איצטרובל, ואדם יושב כנגד' במקום גבוה ורגליו (ז) מרווחת למטה, ומסבב הגלגל ברגליו וטוחן. ולית ביה טיריא אלא קול בעלמא. אבל בריחים שאדם טוחן בידיו או בגופו — אית ביה נדנוד, והיא טיריא. ולר"י נראה דשל חמור נמי טוחן ביד, אלא (ח) כשהוא על גבי בנין, כדתנן במס' זבים בפרק רביעי: חמור של ריחים ושל יד. והא דתניא בתוספת' בפ' קמא דמכילתין: מרחיקין הריחים של יד שלשה מן השכב שהן ארבע מן הרכב, ושל חמור שלשה מן האיצטרובל שהן ארבע מן הקלת — לא משום דבשל חמור אין טוחנין ביד, אלא סתם של יד אין בהן חמור אלא ע"ג קרקע, ולכך קתני בתר הכי "ושל חמור", אבל תרוייהו טוחנין ביד.

שמע מינה כליא דתנור טפח. הא דלא קאמר נמי לעיל: ש"מ שכב דריחים נמי טפח, לפי שהיה פשוט להם איך היה.

תנור דידן ככירה דנחתומין דמי. כל אחד היה עושה תנור שלו כפי מה שהיה רוצה, גדול או קטן. אבל כירות של נחתומין היו כולן שוות, והיו בקיאין בהן, ונפקא מינה למקח וממכר.

מאי שנא רישא ומאי שנא סיפא. השתא ס"ד ד"תינוקות" דסיפא היינו שבאין לקנות בחנות, ומשום הכי פריך: מ"ש? אבל מפטיש וריחים לא פריך, דאין שם נכנסין ויוצאין, דמי שיש לו חטין לטחון נותן לבעל הריחים, (ט) וכן פטיש.

רבינו גרשום

ומשני דלית ביה שיעור. מש"ה לא חייך: בין פצים לחבירו. כעין שסומכין את הקורות המוצעות על הקרקע כדי שלא יעקלו ומשימין תחת הקורה חתיכה של חרס לסומכן כמו שאנו רגילין לעשות באבנים: וכלי חרס נמי חזי ליה ושקל ליה ואמאי ממעט בחלון דאגב דצריכי לכלי נקט ליה עם המלח. ומשני דמיטנף דלא חזי: חזי לאומנא. לקבל בו דם: שם תהא גניזתו ומבטל ליה ולא שקל ליה: רבב. שומן: מחיצה. אי לענין שבת אי בפני הטומאה: מלח נמי א) מפשר כמים. מלח סדומית שעב הוא ואינו יפה ודאי עושין בו מחיצה לענין שבת משום דקא מבטל ליה ולא חזי אבל מלח אסתרוקנית שדק הוא לא מבטל ליה ואין עושין בו מחיצה: עושה אדם. לגבי מבוי. וקורה מעמדת את המלח שמכבשתו ומגנת עליו מן הגשמים. הא דאיכא קורה עושין בו מחיצה מפני שהקורה מעמידתו: **פיסקא** משום טיריא. שמזועז הכותל מחמת בנין הרחיים הקבועין סמוך לכותל וי"א טיריא המיית הרחיים קשה לכותל. והני רחיים ב) שמחזיר מחזיר ג"ט מן האצטרוביל קרי התחתון שכב הרחיים של חמור ורכב קרי קלת: מאי טריא איכא הא לא קביע בנינו בקרקע ולא מזועז הקרקע ואמאי מרחיקין אלא משום קלא של רחיים שקשה לכותל מרחיקין הכא נמי משום קלא: לא יעמיד אדם תנור בתוך הבית. אם העליה שעל גבי בית היא של חבירו אא"כ יש על גביו של תנור ועד העליה ד' אמות מפני הלהב שלא ידליק העליה: היה מעמיד. התנור בעליה שלו ותחת העליה בית של חבירו לא יעמידנו עד שיהא תחתיו מעזיבה ג' טפחים כדי שלא יזיק לבית של חבירו. ואפ"ה אם הזיק משלם מה שהזיק דפחות מן השיעור הזה ג) אין יכול לדוחקו אבל מן השיעור הזה יכול חבירו לעכב עליו אבל מן השיעור הזה אין יכול לדוחקו: והתניא בתנור. בעינן ד' טפחים ובכירה ג' והיכי קתני מתני' היה מעמיד בעליה עד שיהא תחתיו ג' ובכירה טפח כי תניא ההיא שיעור גדול בכירה ותנור של נחתומין משום דאיכא היסק גדול לא סגי אלא באותו שיעור דתנור דידן לא בעי אלא ג' טפחים ככירה של נחתומין: **פיסקא** בעי אביי כיבד וריבץ לאוצר. שהיה בדעתו לשום שם תבואה ולא הספיק לשום שם תבואה עד שבנה אידך רפת בקר שלו מהו. מי אמרי' הא שכיבד וריבץ כמאן דכבר אצר שם תבואתו דמי ולא היה רפת קודם. ומאחר שכיבד וריבץ זה לא יפתח אידך רפת שלו ואם ת"ל הואיל דכיבד וריבץ זה לא יפתח אידך רפת בקר הא קמיבעיא לן ריבה חלונות באוצר כדי שיכנס הרוח באותן חלונות כדי לייבש תבואתו מהו. מי אמרי' הואיל דריבה לא יפתח אידך רפת בקר או דילמא הואיל דעדיין לא אצר בו כמו דלא עביד ולא כלום הוא ומצי למפתח דהוי ליה קדים: בנה עליה על גבי בית. סתם דלא ידעי אי לצורך אוצר בנאו או לא מאי: תמרי ורמוני. דלא מזיק להו הבלא אצר זה באוצרו מהו. מי אמרי' הואיל וכבר אצר בה תמרי ורמוני עדיין דעתו לאצור שם תבואה ולא יפתח או דילמא הואיל ועדיין לא אצר דבר דמזיק ליה הבלא מצי למפתח דהוה ליה קדים תיקו: באמת ביין התירו. לפתח חנותו תחת אוצר של חבירו מפני שמשביח הבלא והעשן: האי יין דידן אפי' קוטרא [דשרגא]. עשן הנר קשה ליה: ואספסתא. חזיז למיתן תחת אוצר יין של חבירו שהוא מתחמם מחמת שהוא לח ומסריח וכרפת בקר דמי: **פיסקא** חנות שבחצר השותפין. אם רוצה חבירו לפתוח שם חנות יכול חבירו לעכב עליו ולומר ליה איני יכול לישן מקול הנכנסין ויוצאין בחנות לקנות אבל רשאי לעשות כלים בתוך החצר ויוצא ומוכרן: ולא מקול התינוקות. משמע ליה עכשיו תינוקות שבאין לקנות ממנו חפצים כעין שרגילין בני אדם לשלוח תינוקות בשליחותן מש"ה מקשה ליה בגמ' מ"ש רישא דקתני יכול חבירו למחות ולומר לו איני יכול לישן מפני הנכנסין והיוצאין ומ"ש סיפא דקתני אין יכול למחות בידו לא מפני

מתני' ולא מקול התינוקות. קא סלקא דעתך תינוקות הבאים לקנות יין ושמן וכל דבר הנמכר בחנות. **גמ'** מאי שנא רישא. דקתני: יכול לומר "איני יכול לישן מקול הנכנסין והיוצאין", וסיפא קתני: אינו יכול לומר לו "איני יכול לישן מקול התינוקות".

סיפא

מסורת הש"ס

א) שבת פב. ביצה לב.: ב) [נ"ל אמר]: ג) ב"ק סא: ב"מ קיח:: ד) לעיל יח.: ה) [בכלאים פ"ב מ"ב ובתרומות פ"ב מ"א ובב"מ נט: במשנה איתא באמת אמרו]: ו) גי' ת"ח [לפי פי' תוס'] ותנור: ז) [לעיל יח.]: ח) [בשהמ"ש ל"ג תי' אבל]: ט) [בשהמ"ש אבל אינו יכול]:

הגהות הב"ח

(א) גמ' כי כירה דנחתומין דמי לא: (ב) שם רפת בקר קודמת: (ג) שם ריבה בחלונות מהו בנה כצ"ל ותיבות אכסדרה תחת אוצר מהו נמחק: (ד) רש"י ד"ה ואם הזיק אחר שהיו שם: (ה) ד"ה כרפת וכו' שהוא לח מתחמם כצ"ל ואות ו' נמחק: (ו) תוס' ד"ה ושל וכו' של נפחים טמא וכו': (ז) בא"ד ורגליו מתוחות למטה ומסבב: (ח) בא"ד טוחן ביד אלא שהוא כצ"ל ואות כ' נמחק: (ט) ד"ה מאי וכו' לבעל הריחים וטוחן וכן פטיש:

עין משפט נר מצוה

כא א ב מיי' פט"ו מהל' טומאת מת הלכה ד:
כב ג ד מיי' שם הל' ב:
כג ה מיי' פט"ו מהל' שבת הל' כב סמג לאוין סה טוש"ע א"ח סי' שסג סעיף ה בהגה"ה ובכב ע"ש:
כד ו ז מיי' פ"ט מהל' שכנים הל' ג סמג עשין פב טוש"ע ח"מ סי' קנה סעיף ז:
כה ח מיי' שם הל' יג סמג שם טוש"ע ח"מ סי' קנה סעיף ז:
כו י מיי' שם הל' יב טוש"ע שם סעיף ב:
כז כ מיי' שם הל' יא טוש"ע שם סעיף א:
כח ל מיי' שם הל' יב טוש"ע שם סעיף ב:
כט מ נ ס מיי' שם הל' יג ועוש"ע שם סעיף ג:
ל ע פ צ מיי' שם הל' יב ועוש"ע שם סעיף ג:
לא ק מיי' שם פ"ו הל' יב סמג שם טוש"ע ח"מ סי' קנו סעיף ב:

א) [נראה דצ"ל חוץ מרבב ומלח רבב משום שניתך כשמתחמם מלח נמי מפשר כמים]. ב) [אולי צ"ל והני ריחים של חמור מרחיק ג' טפחים מן האצטרוביל וד' מן הקלת והתחתון שנקרא שכב קרי אצטרוביל ולרכב קרי קלת]. ג) [ונראה דצ"ל דפחות מן השיעור הזה יכול חברו לדחקו ולעכב עליו אבל כשמרחיק כשיעור זה אינו יכול לדוחקו ולעכב עליו]

א סֵיפָא אֲתָאן לְתִינוֹקוֹת שֶׁל בֵּית רַבָּן, וּמִתַּקָּנַת יְהוֹשֻׁעַ בֶּן גַּמְלָא וְאֵילָךְ. דְּאָמַר רַב יְהוּדָה אָמַר רַב: בְּרַם זָכוּר אוֹתוֹ הָאִישׁ לַטּוֹב וִיהוֹשֻׁעַ בֶּן גַּמְלָא שְׁמוֹ, שֶׁאִלְמָלֵא הוּא נִשְׁתַּכַּח תּוֹרָה מִיִּשְׂרָאֵל; שֶׁבַּתְּחִלָּה, מִי שֶׁיֵּשׁ לוֹ אָב — מְלַמְּדוֹ תּוֹרָה, מִי שֶׁאֵין לוֹ אָב — לֹא הָיָה לָמֵד תּוֹרָה; מַאי דְּרוּשׁ? °"וְלִמַּדְתֶּם אוֹתָם" — וְלִמַּדְתֶּם אַתֶּם. (דברים יא) הִתְקִינוּ שֶׁיְּהוּ מוֹשִׁיבִין מְלַמְּדֵי תִינוֹקוֹת בִּירוּשָׁלַיִם; מַאי דְּרוּשׁ? °"כִּי מִצִּיּוֹן תֵּצֵא תוֹרָה". (ישעיה ב) (א) וַעֲדַיִין מִי שֶׁיֵּשׁ לוֹ אָב — הָיָה מַעֲלוֹ וּמְלַמְּדוֹ, מִי שֶׁאֵין לוֹ אָב — לֹא הָיָה עוֹלֶה וְלָמֵד. הִתְקִינוּ שֶׁיְּהוּ מוֹשִׁיבִין בְּכָל פֶּלֶךְ וּפֶלֶךְ; וּמַכְנִיסִין אוֹתָן כְּבֶן ט"ז כְּבֶן י"ז, וּמִי שֶׁהָיָה רַבּוֹ כּוֹעֵס עָלָיו — (ב) מְבַעֵיט בּוֹ וְיָצָא, עַד שֶׁבָּא יְהוֹשֻׁעַ בֶּן גַּמְלָא וְתִיקֵּן, ב שֶׁיְּהוּ מוֹשִׁיבִין מְלַמְּדֵי תִינוֹקוֹת בְּכָל מְדִינָה וּמְדִינָה וּבְכָל עִיר וָעִיר, ג וּמַכְנִיסִין אוֹתָן כְּבֶן שֵׁשׁ כְּבֶן שֶׁבַע. א) אֲמַר לֵיהּ רַב לְרַב שְׁמוּאֵל בַּר שֵׁילַת: ד עַד שִׁית לָא תְּקַבֵּיל, מִכָּאן וְאֵילָךְ קַבֵּיל וְאַסְפֵּי לֵיהּ כְּתוֹרָא. וַא"ל רַב לְרַב שְׁמוּאֵל בַּר שֵׁילַת: ה כִּי מָחֵית לִינוּקָא, לָא תִּימְחֵי אֶלָּא בְּעַרְקְתָא דִּמְסָנָא, דְּקָארֵי — קָארֵי, דְּלָא קָארֵי — ו לֶיהֱוֵי צַוְותָא לְחַבְרֵיהּ. מֵיתִיבֵי: ז אֶחָד מִבְּנֵי חָצֵר שֶׁבִּיקֵּשׁ לַעֲשׂוֹת רוֹפֵא, אוּמָּן, וְגַרְדִּי, וּמְלַמֵּד תִּינוֹקוֹת — בְּנֵי חָצֵר מְעַכְּבִין עָלָיו! הָכָא בְּמַאי עָסְקִינַן — ח בְּתִינוֹקוֹת דְּגוֹיִם. ת"ש: ט שְׁנַיִם שֶׁיּוֹשְׁבִין בְּחָצֵר, וּבִיקֵּשׁ אֶחָד מֵהֶן לַעֲשׂוֹת רוֹפֵא, וְאוּמָּן, וְגַרְדִּי, וּמְלַמֵּד תִּינוֹקוֹת — חֲבֵירוֹ מְעַכֵּב עָלָיו! י ה"נ בְּתִינוֹקוֹת דְּגוֹיִם. ת"ש: כ מִי שֶׁיֵּשׁ לוֹ בַּיִת בַּחֲצַר הַשּׁוּתָּפִין — ה"ז לֹא יַשְׂכִּירֶנּוּ לֹא לְרוֹפֵא, וְלֹא לְאוּמָּן, וְלֹא לְגַרְדִּי, וְלֹא לְסוֹפֵר יְהוּדִי, וְלֹא לְסוֹפֵר אֲרַמַּאי! ל הָכָא בְּמַאי עָסְקִינַן — בְּסוֹפֵר מָתָא. אָמַר רָבָא: מִתַּקָּנַת יְהוֹשֻׁעַ בֶּן גַּמְלָא וָאֵילָךְ, מ לָא מַמְטִינַן יָנוּקָא מִמָּתָא לְמָתָא, נ אֲבָל מִבֵּי כְנִישְׁתָּא לְבֵי כְנִישְׁתָּא מַמְטִינַן. ס וְאִי מַפְסֵק נַהֲרָא לָא מַמְטִינַן, וְאִי ע אִיכָּא תִּיתוֹרָא מַמְטִינַן, פ וְאִי אִיכָּא גַּמְלָא לָא מַמְטִינַן. ב) וַאֲמַר רָבָא: צ סָךְ מַקְרֵי דַרְדְּקֵי — עֶשְׂרִין וַחֲמִשָּׁה יָנוּקֵי, וְאִי אִיכָּא חַמְשִׁין — מוֹתְבִינַן תְּרֵי, ק וְאִי אִיכָּא אַרְבְּעִין — מוֹקְמִינַן רֵישׁ ג) דּוּכָנָא, ר וּמְסַיְּיעִין לֵיהּ מִמָּתָא. וַאֲמַר רָבָא: הַאי מַקְרֵי יָנוּקֵי דְּגָרֵיס, וְאִיכָּא אַחֲרִינָא דְּגָרֵיס טְפֵי מִינֵּיהּ — לָא מְסַלְּקִינַן לֵיהּ, דִּלְמָא אָתֵי לְאִיתְרַשּׁוּלֵי. רַב דִּימִי מִנְּהַרְדְּעָא אָמַר: ש כ"ש דְּגָרֵיס טְפֵי, ד) קִנְאַת סוֹפְרִים תַּרְבֶּה חָכְמָה. וַאֲמַר רָבָא: הָנֵי תְּרֵי מַקְרֵי דַרְדְּקֵי, חַד גָּרֵיס וְלָא דָּיֵיק, וְחַד דָּיֵיק וְלָא גָּרֵיס — מוֹתְבִינַן הַהוּא דְּגָרֵיס וְלָא דָּיֵיק, שַׁבְּשְׁתָּא מִמֵּילָא נָפְקָא. רַב דִּימִי מִנְּהַרְדְּעָא אָמַר: ת מוֹתְבִינַן דְּדָיֵיק וְלָא גָּרֵיס, ה) שַׁבְּשְׁתָּא כֵּיוָן דְּעָל — עָל; דִּכְתִיב: °"כִּי שֵׁשֶׁת חֳדָשִׁים יָשַׁב שָׁם יוֹאָב וְכָל יִשְׂרָאֵל עַד הִכְרִית כָּל זָכָר בֶּאֱדוֹם", (מ"א יא) כִּי אֲתָא לְקַמֵּיהּ דְּדָוִד, אֲמַר לֵיהּ: מַאי

רש"י

סיפא אתאן לתינוקות של בית רבן. ואע"ג דקול הבא מחמת אחרים — לא מצי מחויי. משום תקנת יהושע בן גמלא. אחד מן הכהנים הגדולים שעמדו בבית שני, כדאמר ביבמות (דף סא.). ולמדתם (ו) אותם. האב עצמו מלוה ללמדו. פלך. הרבה מדינות בפלך אחד, והוא לשון אפרכיא. רב שמואל בר שילת. מלמד תינוקות היה (לעיל דף ח:). ואספי ליה. האכילהו והשקהו תורה בעל כרחו, כשור שנותנין (ג) עליו עול על צוארו. לא תמחייה אלא בערקתא דמסנא. ברצועות של מנעלים. כלומר, מכה קלה שלא יוזק. ליהוי צוותא לחבריה. אינך זקוק לייסרו יותר מדאי, ולא לסלקו מלפניך, אלא ישב עם האחרים בלוותא, וסופו לתת לב. רופא = מוהל. אומן = מקיז דם. מעכבין עליו. מפני שמרבה עליהן קול נכנסין ויוצאין. לסופר יהודי. מלמד תינוקות. בסופר מתא. מלמד תינוקות העיר, ומושיב מלמדים תחתיו, והוא מורה את כולם איך יעשו, ויש שם קול גדול. מתקנת יהושע בן גמלא ואילך. שישבו מלמדי תינוקות בכל עיר. לא ממטינן ינוקא ממתא למתא. ללמוד, מיום ליום, שמא יוזק בדרכים, שהשטן מקטרג בשעת הסכנה, שנאמר: "פן יקראנו אסון" (בראשית מב). אלא יוכל לכוף בני אותו מתא להושיב מלמדי תינוקות. תיתורא. גשר רחב. וחבירו במנחות (דף לה.): תיתורא דתפילין — מקום מושבם, שדומה לגשר. גמלא. לוח קצרה. סך מקרי דרדקי. מנין תינוקות הראויין למלמד אחד. ריש דוכנא. שומע עם התינוקות מפי המלמד, וחוזר ומשגירו בפי התינוקות. ואותו ריש דוכנא נוטל שכר. ומסייעין ליה ממתא. לשכור לו אותו ריש דוכנא. דילמא אתי לאיתרשולי. יתפאר בלבו שאין כמותו, ויתרשל מן התינוקות, ולא יירא שמא יסלקוהו. כל שכן. כשתשבנוהו, יתן לב להיות למד יפה, שדואג מקנאת חבירו שסלקוהו מפניו, שיביישנו בבני העיר. דגריס ולא דייק. שלומד הרבה, ולא דייק בלימוד התינוקות שלא ישתבשו.

תוספות

זכור אותו האיש לטוב ויהושע בן גמלא שמו. הוא אותו(ד) האיש דאמר רב יוסף (יבמות דף סא.): תרקבא דדינרי עיילא ליה מרתא בת בייתוס לינאי המלך עד דאוקים ליהושע בן גמלא בכהני רברבי. וצדיק גמור היה, כדאשכחן הכא. והא דקאמר התם (שם): "קטיר קא חזינא הכא" — לפי שהיו אחרים חשובים ממנו.

ולמדתם אותם ולמדתם אתם. יש ספרים דלא גרסי "ולמדתם אתם", ודריש מדכתיב "ולמדתם" — משמע (ה) מעצמכם. כי מציון תצא תורה. לפי שהיה רואה קדושה גדולה, וכהנים עוסקים בעבודה — היה מכוון לבו יותר ליראת שמים וללמוד תורה. כדדרשי' בספרי: "למען תלמד ליראה" וגו' — גדול מעשר שני שמביא לידי תלמוד, לפי שהיה עומד בירושלים עד שיאכל מעשר שני שלו, והיה רואה שכולם עוסקים במלאכת שמים ובעבודה — היה גם הוא מכוון ליראת שמים ועוסק בתורה. כבן שש כבן שבע. כבן שש בבריא, כבן שבע בכחוש. בבציר מבר שית לא תקבל. והא דתנן במסכת אבות (פ"ה מכ"א): בן חמש שנים למקרא — בבריא לגמרי, כדאמר בכתובות (דף נ. ושם): הלומד בנו פחות מבן שש — רץ אחריו ואינו מגיעו. ואיכא דאמרי: חבריו רצין אחריו ואין מגיעין אותו. ותרוייהו איתנהו, דחליש וגמיר. ואיבעית אימא: הא בכחוש והא בבריא. אחד מבני מבוי כו' פי' רשב"א: דלא גרס "מבוי", אלא: חצר. דאי גרס מבוי — תיקשי לאביי דשרי בחצר אחרת. והיא דעושה אדם חנות בצד חנות של חבירו שרי (ו) לכל הפחות בחצר אחר. ורבא נמי לא פליג עליה, אלא דמוקי מתני' דשריא אף באותה חצר, והכא אסר אפילו בחצר אחרת. אלא "אחד מבני חצר" גרס.

וגרדי. וא"ת: ומאי שנא גרדי מבעל ריחים, דתנן במתני' דאין יכול למחות בידו ולומר "איני יכול לישן מקול הריחים ומקול הפטיש"? וי"ל: דמתני' בעושה לעצמו, והכא בגרדי העושה לאחרים, דאיכא נכנסין ויוצאין. וא"ת: הא אמרי' בסמוך: האי בר מבואה דאוקי ריחייא כו' — דינא הוא דמעכב עליה, משום דאמר ליה "קא פסקת לחיותי". משמע דאי לאו משום ד"קא פסקת לחיותי" — היה יכול להעמיד שם הריחים, אע"ג דעושה לאחרים. ולקמן נמי תניא: עושה אדם חנות בצד חנותו של חבירו כו', דאף על גב דאיכא נכנסין ויוצאין טובא! ודוחק לחלק דהתם כבר יש יוצאין ונכנסין לריחים הראשון או לחנות הראשון. וי"ל: דהתם בחצר אחרת שרי. א"נ: מתני' נמי: בעושה לאחרים, ובריחים ובקול הפטיש — אין נכנסין ויוצאין כל כך, שנותנין לו פעם אחת וטוחן. אבל בגרדי יש הרבה יוצאין ונכנסין, שהרבה מביאין לו מטוה. ולא לסופר ארמאי. משמע דאם לא (ז) סופר הוה שרי להשכיר לארמאי. וא"ת: דאמרי' ב"הגוזל בתרא" (ב"ק דף קיד.): האי בר ישראל דזבין ליה ארעא לגוי אמיצרא דבר ישראל חבריה — משמתינן ליה, דא"ל: אריא ארבעת אמיצראי! ודוחק לחלק בין מכר לשכירות. ונראה לר"י: דהתם כשישראל רצה לקנות, אבל אם אין ישראל רוצה לקנות — מותר.

ז) בסופר מתא. אין נראה לפרש כפ"ה דסופר מתא היינו מלמד תינוקות של כל העיר, דאיכא קול גדול. דהא לקמן אמר רבא: מקרי דרדקי וסופר מתא — כמותרין ועומדין. כיון דאשמועינן דמקרי דרדקי הוי פסידא דלא הדר — ה"ה מלמד כל תינוקות העיר, ואמאי איצטריך תו למינקט סופר מתא? ואין לפרש נמי כפ"ה ח) ב"המקבל" (ב"מ דף קט:): סופר מתא — מספר אנשי העיר, דהא קרי (ח) הכא בברייתא סופר. אלא נראה כמו שפי' ר"ח: סופר מתא — כותב שטרות העיר, ולהכי חשיב ליה לקמן פסידא דלא הדר אם נכתב השטר שלא כדין.

מתקנת יהושע בן גמלא ואילך לא ממטינן ינוקא ממתא למתא. וכגון שיש כאן כ"ה ינוקי שראויין להשכיר להם מלמד. ואם תאמר: הא אי הוה ממטינן להו למתא אחריתי — יצטרכו מלמד בפני עצמן, כיון דאיכא כ"ה ינוקי, וא"כ מאי נפקא מינה? וי"ל: דנפקא מינה, דאי הוו ב' מלמדי תינוקות באידך מתא — היו יכולין להושיב חציים בפני זה וחציים בפני זה.

סך מקרי דרדקי כ"ה ינוקי. אבל פחות מכאן אין בני העיר יכולין לכוף זה את זה להשכיר להם מלמד. פר"ח דרביה אקרייה זֵכר כדין, והיינו "רמייה" — דלא אשגח למידע היכי הוה קרי תלמידיה, וכ"נ. אבל אין נראה לפרש שגם רבו טעה ולימדו זָכָר, דא"כ לאו רמייה הוא.

סופר

רבינו גרשום

מפני התינוקות של בית רבן שבאין ללמוד תורה זה אינו יכול לעכב עליו אפי' בחצר השותפין: מי שיש לו אב. שהיה חייב בלימודו מעלן: עד שית שנין לא תקבל ללומדו שאינו יכול לסבול עדיין טורח הלימוד: ואספי ליה כי תורא. כלומר תן עליו עול תורה כמו לשור זה שאובסין אותו בעל כרחו ומכניסין בו המאכל כדי שיהא שמן כך הכנס בו תורה: בערקתא דמסנא. ברצוע' של מנעל הכהו ואל תכהו יותר מדאי שבשביל רוב הכאות אין מתפקח אא"כ קרי מנפשי' קרי ואי לא ליהוי צוותא לחבריה דקרי ואל תחוש להכותו יותר מדאי: בתינוקות דגוים. אם רוצה ללמוד ספר רפואה או מקרא יכול לעכב עליו דלא מצי עביד: ולא לסופר יהודי. מלמד תינוקות אלמא דמצי מעכב. הכא במאי עסקינן בסופר מתא שהוא סופר העיר שכותב שטרות וספרים לכל מצי מעכב מחמת הנכנסין אצלו ואית דמפרשי בספר מתא שמגלח כל בני העיר: לא ממטינן ינוקא ממתא למתא. מפני כן התקינו להושיב מלמדי תינוקות בכל פלך ופלך: ואי מפסיק נהרא לא ממטינן. דאיכא למיחש דלמא יהא רגיל למיזל לחודיה ונפיל לנהרא: תיתורא. גשר מרוחב: גמלא. גשר עשוי מנסר צר ומשני צדי הנהר קבועין ב' יתדות וקשור חבל א' מזה לזה ואותן העוברין על אותו נסר צר סומכין ידיהן בחבל ועוברין אבל התינוקות שאין בהן דעת לסמוך לא ממטינן דילמא אזיל לחודיה ונפיל: סך מקרי דרדקי. עד כ"ה תלמידים יכול ללמוד אחד: ריש דוכנא. ממונה תחתיו עד שיסייע לו ללמוד הנער. ואין מנכין לו לרב משכירותו כדי לשכור אותו ריש דוכנא אלא מסייעין ליה ממתא הצבור שוכרין אותו ריש דוכנא. מאי טעמא לא מסלקי' ליה לההוא דלא גרים כל כך דאי מסלקינן ליה ומותבינן להו קמיה ההוא דגרים טפי אתי לרשולי למימר הואיל דליכא דגרים כוותי לא מסלקי לי ואתי לרשולי. כל שכן דמותבינן להו קמיה ההוא דגרם טפי מימר אמר אי מרשילנא מסלקו להו מקמאי כי היכי דסלקי להו מקמיה דאידך ומעיין בהו שלא יבא אחר דגרם טפי מיניה ויסלקו ממנו. ומתעסק בהן הרבה משום קנאת סופרים תרבה חכמה שזה מקנא לזה: חד דגרים הרבה ולא דייק כל כך: מאי

מסורת הש"ס

א) כתובות נ.: ב) [דיומינן דנפלי שאלתות ריש ואתחנן]: ג) פי' אילטבא נקרא לוכן ראש אילטבא ששם יושבין. ערוך ערך דכן]: ד) [לקמן כב.]: ה) פסחים קיב.: ו) צ"ל אתם: ז) בדפוס הישן דפוס ונציא בכל התוס' ספר בלא וי"ו רק האחרון הכא בברייתא סופר הוא בוי"ו: ח) [לפנינו שם לא נמצא שום פי' ברש"י]:

עין משפט נר מצוה

לב א מיי' פ"ו מהל' שכנים הל' יב ופ"ב מהל' ת"ת הל' ז סמג עשין פב טוש"ע ח"מ סי' קנו סעיף ג וטוש"ע י"ד סי' רמה סעיף כב:

לג ב מיי' פ"ב מהלכות ת"ת הלכה א סמג עשין יב טוש"ע י"ד סי' רמה סעיף ה:

לד ג ד מיי' שם הל' ב טוש"ע י"ד שם סעיף ה וסעיף ח:

לה ה מיי' שם טוש"ע י"ד שם סעיף ט:

לו ו טוש"ע שם סעיף טו:

לז ז ח ט י כ ל מיי' פ"ו מהל' שכנים הל' יא סמג עשין פב טוש"ע ח"מ סי' קנו סעיף א:

לח מ נ ס ע פ מיי' פ"ב מהל' ת"ת הל' ו סמג עשין יב טוש"ע י"ד סי' רמה סעיף טז:

לט צ ק מיי' שם הל' ה טוש"ע י"ד שם סעיף טו:

מ ר מיי' שם טוש"ע שם סעיף יח:

מא ש טוש"ע שם סעיף יח:

מב ת מיי' שם הל' ו טוש"ע י"ד שם סעיף יט:

הגהות הב"ח

(א) גמ' תלה תורה וגו' ועדיין: (ב) שם מבעט כצ"ל ואות ו' נמחק: (ג) רש"י ד"ה ואספי וכו' שנותנין על עול: (ד) תום' ד"ה זכור וכו' הוא אותו האיש דאמר כצ"ל ותיבת האיש נמחק: (ה) ד"ה ולמדתם וכו' משמע אתם מעצמכם: (ו) ד"ה אחד וכו' שרי נמי לכל הפחות: (ז) ד"ה ולא וכו' דאם לא הוה סופר וכו' וא"ת לא אמרי': (ח) ד"ה בסופר וכו' דהא קרי ליה הכא:

מַאי טַעֲמָא עֲבַדְתְּ הָכִי? אֲמַר לֵיהּ, דִּכְתִיב: °"תִּמְחֶה אֶת זָכָר עֲמָלֵק". (דברים כה) אֲמַר לֵיהּ: וְהָא אֲנַן (א) "זֵכֶר" קָרֵינַן! א"ל: אֲנָא "זָכָר" אַקְרִיוּן. אֲזַל שַׁיְילֵיהּ לְרַבֵּיהּ, אֲמַר לֵיהּ: הֵיאָךְ אַקְרִיתָן? אֲמַר לֵיהּ: "זָכָר". שְׁקַל סַפְסֵירָא לְמִיקְטְלֵיהּ. אֲמַר לֵיהּ: אַמַּאי? א"ל, א)דִּכְתִיב: °"אָרוּר עוֹשֶׂה מְלֶאכֶת ה' רְמִיָּה". (ירמיה מח) א"ל: אשְׁבַקֵיהּ לְהַהוּא גַּבְרָא דְּלֵיקוּם בְּ"אָרוּר". א"ל, כְּתִיב: °"וְאָרוּר מוֹנֵעַ חַרְבּוֹ מִדָּם"! (שם) אִיכָּא דְּאָמְרִי: קַטְלֵיהּ, וְאִיכָּא דְּאָמְרִי: לָא קַטְלֵיהּ. ב)וְאָמַר רָבָא: במַקְרֵי יְנוּקָא, שַׁתָּלָא, טַבָּחָא, וְאוּמָּנָא, וְסוֹפֵר מָתָא — כּוּלָּן כְּמוּתְרִין וְעוֹמְדִין נִינְהוּ. גכְּלָלָא דְּמִילְּתָא: כָּל פְּסֵידָא דְּלָא הָדַר — מוּתְרֶה וְעוֹמֵד הוּא. אֲמַר רַב הוּנָא: הַאי בַּר מְבוֹאָה דְּאוֹקֵי רֵיחַיָּא, וְאָתָא בַּר מְבוֹאָה חַבְרֵיהּ וְקָמוֹקֵי גַּבֵּיהּ — דִּינָא הוּא דִּמְעַכֵּב עִילָּוֵיהּ, דְּא"ל: קָא פָּסְקַתְּ לֵיהּ לְחַיּוּתִי. לֵימָא מְסַיַּיע לֵיהּ: מַרְחִיקִים מְצוּדַת הַדָּג מִן הַדָּג כִּמְלֹא רִיצַת הַדָּג; וְכַמָּה? אֲמַר רַבָּה בַּר רַב הוּנָא: עַד פַּרְסָה. שָׁאנֵי דָּגִים, דְּיָהֲבִי סַיְּירָא. א"ל רָבִינָא לְרָבָא: לֵימָא, רַב הוּנָא דְּאָמַר כְּרַבִּי יְהוּדָה; ג)דְּתְנַן, רַבִּי יְהוּדָה אוֹמֵר: לֹא יְחַלֵּק חֶנְוָנִי קְלָיוֹת וֶאֱגוֹזִין לַתִּינוֹקוֹת, מִפְּנֵי שֶׁמַּרְגִּילָן (ב) אֶצְלוֹ, וַחֲכָמִים דמַתִּירִין? אֲפִי' תֵּימָא רַבָּנַן, עַד כָּאן לָא פְּלִיגִי רַבָּנַן עֲלֵיהּ דְּרַבִּי יְהוּדָה הָתָם — אֶלָּא דְּאָמַר לֵיהּ: ד)אֲנָא קָמְפַלְגִינָא אַמְגוּזֵי, אַתְּ פְּלוֹג שִׁיוּסְקֵי, אֲבָל הָכָא אֲפִילּוּ רַבָּנַן מוֹדוּ, דְּא"ל: קָא פָּסְקַתְּ לֵיהּ לְחַיּוּתִי. מֵיתִיבֵי: עוֹשֶׂה אָדָם חֲנוּת בְּצַד חֲנוּתוֹ שֶׁל חֲבֵירוֹ, וּמֶרְחָץ בְּצַד מֶרְחָצוֹ שֶׁל חֲבֵירוֹ, וְאֵינוֹ יָכוֹל לִמְחוֹת בְּיָדוֹ, מִפְּנֵי שֶׁיָּכוֹל לוֹמַר לוֹ: אַתָּה עוֹשֶׂה בְּתוֹךְ שֶׁלְּךָ וַאֲנִי עוֹשֶׂה בְּתוֹךְ שֶׁלִּי! תַּנָּאֵי הִיא; דְּתַנְיָא: הכּוֹפִין בְּנֵי מְבוֹאוֹת זֶה אֶת זֶה שֶׁלֹּא לְהוֹשִׁיב בֵּינֵיהֶן לֹא חַיָּיט וְלֹא בּוּרְסְקִי, וְלֹא מְלַמֵּד תִּינוֹקוֹת, וְלֹא אֶחָד ה)מִבְּנֵי בַּעֲלֵי אוּמָּנִיּוֹת, ו)וְלִשְׁכֵנוֹ אֵינוֹ כּוֹפֵיהוּ; רשב"ג אוֹמֵר: אַף לִשְׁכֵנוֹ כּוֹפֵיהוּ. אֲמַר רַב הוּנָא בְּרֵיהּ דְּרַב יְהוֹשֻׁעַ: זפְּשִׁיטָא לִי, בַּר מָתָא אַבַּר מָתָא אַחֲרִיתִי מָצֵי מְעַכֵּב, חוְאִי שַׁיֵּיךְ בְּכַרְגָּא דְּהָכָא — לָא מָצֵי מְעַכֵּב; בַּר מְבוֹאָה אַבַּר מְבוֹאָה דְּנַפְשֵׁיהּ — לָא מָצֵי מְעַכֵּב. טבָּעֵי רַב הוּנָא בְּרֵיהּ דְּרַב יְהוֹשֻׁעַ: בַּר מְבוֹאָה אַבַּר מְבוֹאָה אַחֲרִינָא, מַאי? תֵּיקוּ. אֲמַר רַב יוֹסֵף: יוּמוֹדֵי רַב הוּנָא בְּמַקְרֵי דַּרְדְּקֵי דְּלָא מָצֵי מְעַכֵּב, דְּאָמַר מָר: ז)כעֶזְרָא תִּיקֵּן לָהֶן לְיִשְׂרָאֵל שֶׁיְּהוּ מוֹשִׁיבִין סוֹפֵר בְּצַד סוֹפֵר. וְנֵיחוּשׁ דִּילְמָא אָתֵי לְאִיתְרַשּׁוּלֵי! א"ל:

קִנְאַת

מַאי טַעֲמָא עֲבַדְתְּ הָכִי. שֶׁלֹּא הָרַגְתָּ אֶת הַנְּקֵיבוֹת. **אֶת זֵכֶר עֲמָלֵק.** **אָרוּר מוֹנֵעַ חַרְבּוֹ.** סֵיפֵיהּ דְּהַאי קְרָא הוּא. **שַׁתָּלָא.** נוֹטֵעַ כַּרְמוֹ לְמֶחֱצָה. **אוּמָּנָא** = מַקִּיז דָּם. **סוֹפֵר מָתָא** = לַבְלָר. **כְּמוּתְרִין וְעוֹמְדִין** דָּמוּ. שֶׁלֹּא יְקַלְקְלוּ, וְאִם קִלְקְלוּ – מְסַלֵּק לְהוּ בְּלָא אַתְרָיְיתָא, אע"פ שֶׁלֹּא הִתְרוּ בּוֹ קוֹדֶם לָכֵן. **פְּסֵידָא דְּלָא הָדַר.** כְּגוֹן אֵלּוּ, שֶׁמְּשֶׁנִּתְנַבְּלָה הַבְּהֵמָה, אוֹ הָרַג הַמַּקִּיז, וְהַסּוֹפֵר כָּתַב סֵפֶר תּוֹרָה בְּטָעוּת. **דְּאוֹקֵי רֵיחַיָּא.** לִטְחוֹן וְלִשְׂכּוֹר. **מַרְחִיקִין מְצוּדַת הַדָּג מִן הַדָּג.** צַיָּיד שֶׁנָּתַן עֵינָיו בְּדָג עַד שֶׁהִכִּיר חוֹרוֹ – מַרְחִיקִין שְׁאָר צַיָּידִין מְצוּדָתָם מִשָּׁם. אַלְמָא, אע"ג דְּלָא זָכָה בֵּיהּ וְלָא מְטָא לִידֵיהּ – מַרְחִיקִין מִשָּׁם, דְּא"ל: קָא פָּסְקַתְּ לְחִיּוּתִי. **שָׁאנֵי דָּגִים דְּיָהֲבִי סַיְּירָא.** נוֹתְנִין עַיִן בְּהַבָּטָתָם לִהְיוֹת (ג) נוֹהֲגִים לָרוּץ לְמָקוֹם שֶׁרָאוּ שָׁם מְזוֹנוֹת. הִילְכָּךְ, כֵּיוָן שֶׁהִכִּיר זֶה חוֹרוֹ, וְנָתַן מְזוֹנוֹת בְּתוֹךְ מְלֹא רִיצָתוֹ – בָּטוּחַ הוּא שֶׁיִּלְכְּדֶנּוּ, דה"ל כְּמַאן דִּמְטָא לִידֵיהּ, וְנִמְצָא חֲבֵירוֹ מַזִּיקוֹ. אֲבָל הָכָא – מִי שֶׁבָּא אֶצְלִי יָבֹא, וּמִי שֶׁבָּא אֶצְלְךָ יָבֹא. **שֶׁמַּרְגִּילָם.** לָבֹא אֶצְלוֹ, כְּשֶׁאֲבוֹתֵיהֶם שׁוֹלְחִין אוֹתָן אֶל הַחֲנוּיוֹת לִקְנוֹת מִן הַחֶנְוָנִים. **שִׁיוּסְקֵי** = שְׁקֵדִים. **אֲבָל הָכָא.** שֶׁזֶּה הֶעֱמִיד תְּחִילָּה, וְהִרְגִּיל לְהִשְׂתַּכֵּר בְּכָךְ, וְזֶה בָּא לֵירֵד אֶצְלוֹ לְאוּמָּנוּתוֹ – אוֹמֵר לוֹ: פָּסַקְתָּ לְחַיּוּתָאִי. **שֶׁלֹּא לְהוֹשִׁיב בֵּינֵיהֶן חַיָּיט וּבוּרְסְקִי.** מִמָּקוֹם אַחֵר, לְהַשְׂכִּיר לוֹ בַּיִת בַּמָּבוֹי, (ד) וְיֵשׁ כָּאן בְּנֵי אוֹתָהּ אוּמָּנוּת. **וְלִשְׁכֵינוֹ.** הַדָּר בַּמָּבוֹי כָּמוֹהוּ. **אֵינוֹ כּוֹפֵהוּ.** מִלֵּירֵד לְאוֹתוֹ אוּמָּנוּת. **רשב"ג אוֹמֵר כו'.** וְרַב הוּנָא הוּא דְּאָמַר כְּרשב"ג. **מָצֵי לְעַכֵּב.** מִלַּעֲשׂוֹת כָּאן אוּמָּנוּתָם, וּלְהָבִיא כָּאן לִמְכּוֹר. וַאֲפִילּוּ לְרַבָּנַן, דְּאָמְרִי: לִשְׁכֵינוֹ אֵינוֹ כּוֹפֵהוּ. **וְאִי שַׁיֵּיךְ בְּכַרְגָּא דְּהָכָא.** שֶׁנּוֹתֵן מַס גּוּלְגָּלְתּוֹ לְמוֹשֵׁל הָעִיר הַזֹּאת, כְּבַר מָתָא – (ה) לָא מָצֵי בַּר מָתָא לְעַכֵּב עָלָיו כָּל הָעִיר. וּפְשִׁיטָא לִי דְּבַר מָבוֹי אַבַּר מָבוֹי דְּנַפְשֵׁיהּ – לָא מָצֵי מְעַכֵּב אֶת הַמָּבוֹי מִלֵּירֵד לְאוּמָּנוּתוֹ, כְּרַבָּנַן וְלָא כְּרַב הוּנָא. מִיהוּ, אִיבַּעְיָא לִי: בַּר מְבוֹאָה אַבַּר מְבוֹאָה אַחֲרִינָא מַאי? מִי מָצֵי מְעַכֵּב (ו) בֶּן הַמָּבוֹי הַזֶּה אוֹ לָא? מִי הָוֵי שְׁכֵינוֹ וְאֵינוֹ כּוֹפֵיהוּ. אוֹ דִּילְמָא: שְׁכֵינוֹ דַּאֲמוּר רַבָּנַן – בְּבַר מְבוֹאָה דְּהַהוּא מָבוֹי קָאָמְרִי, אֲבָל בַּר מְבוֹאָה אַחֲרִינָא – לָאו שְׁכֵינוֹ הוּא. **וּמוֹדֶה רַב הוּנָא.** דְּאָמַר לְעֵיל: בַּר מְבוֹאָה דְּאוֹקֵי רֵיחַיָּא כו', דְּאִית לֵיהּ כְּרשב"ג – מוֹדֵי הוּא בְּמַקְרֵי דַּרְדְּקֵי, דְּלָא מָצֵי מְעַכֵּב לְבַר מְבוֹאָה מְלַמֵּד גַּם הוּא הַתִּינוֹקוֹת. שֶׁמִּתּוֹךְ כָּךְ יִזָּהֲרוּ בְּאוּמָּנוּתָן, שֶׁיִּירְאוּ זֶה מִזֶּה, דְּאָמַר מָר: קִנְאַת סוֹפְרִים תַּרְבֶּה חָכְמָה.

וּמוֹדֶה

תורה אור

סופר מתא. לא כמו שפירש בקונטרס: כותב ספר תורה בטעות. דאין זה פסידא דלא הדר, דיכולין להגיהו. אלא כדפרישית לעיל: כותב שטרות. **ומקרי** דרדקי. פי' בקונטרס ב"המקבל" (ב"מ דף קט. ושם) דהוי פסידא דלא הדרא משום דשבשתא כיון דעל על. וקשה לר"י: דהא רבא גופיה אית ליה לעיל דשבשתא ממילא נפקא! ואומר ר"י: דהוה פסידא דלא הדר, דאותה שעה שמלמד להם טעות הם מתבטלים, ואותה שעה אין יכולין להחזיר לעולם. **שתלא.** וא"ת: מאי פסידא איכא? אי יפסיד ישלם! וי"ל: דאינו מפסיד, אלא שפושע, שאין הנטיעו' גדילות כמו שהיו ראויות ליגדל. **מרחיקין** מצודת הדג כו'. אע"ג דר"ת מפרש דבדבר של הפקר אפי' רשע לא מיקרי, כדתנן (פאה פ"ד מ"ג) גבי פאה: פירס טליתו עליה — מעבירין אותו ממנה. וכן תנן בפ"ק דב"מ (דף י.): ראה את המציאה ונפל עליה, ובא אחר והחזיק בה — זה שהחזיק בה זכה. ולא מיקרי רשע אלא בעני המהפך בחררה ובא אחר ונטלה, משום שאם לא ישתכר במקום זה — ימצא להשתכר במקום אחר. והך דשמעתא לא קשיא, דאע"ג דהוי דבר של הפקר — מ"מ בכמה מקומות ימצא שיוכל לפרוש מצודתו. ועוד: דהכא אומנותו בכך. והא דאמרינן בפרק "חזקת הבתים" (לקמן דף נד:): נכסי גוים הרי הן כמדבר, כל המחזיק בהן — זכה בהן. מאי טעמא? גוי מכי מטא זוזי לידיה איסתלק ליה, וישראל לא קני עד דמטי שטרא לידיה. ופי' רשב"ם התם דישראל המחזיק רשע מיהא מיקרי. ולפי' ר"ת אפי' רשע לא הוי, כיון שלא ימצא במקום אחר. וקשה לרשב"א, מהא דאמר ב"איזהו נשך" (ב"מ דף עג:): רב מרי בר רחל משכן ליה ההוא נכרי ביתא, אזל רבא זבניה, נטר תריסר ירחי שתא שקל אגר ביתא אמטייה לרבא. א"ל: האי דלא מטאי לה למר אגר ביתא עד השתא, דאמר מר: סתם משכנתא שתא, ולא מצי נכרי לסלוקי. והשתא, כיון שקדמה חזקת רב מרי לחזקת רבא — א"כ זכה בה רב מרי, דנכסי הגוי הרי הן כמדבר. ואי מקרי רשע — אתי שפיר, דלא היה רוצה לזכות בה, אבל לפירוש ר"ת, דאפילו רשע לא מיקרי — אמאי לא זכה בה רב מרי, כיון דהיתר גמור הוא? ושמא לפנים משורת הדין עבד. ולריב"א נראה דחזקת רב מרי לא היתה אלא בתורת משכון, ורבא קנה ממנו בשטר, וזכה בה ואחר כך נתן מעות. [וע"ע תוספות קדושין נט. ד"ה עני המהפך וכו' ותוס' ב"מ עג: סוף ד"ה נטר]. **תנאי** היא דתניא כו'. תימה לרשב"א: דאמאי לא מייתי ח)(הברייתא) דלעיל? דממה נפשך, רבי יהודה דאמר: לא יחלק חנוני קליות ואגוזים לתינוקות — פליג אהך ברייתא! ושמא ניחא לאתויי תנאי דפליגי בהדיא בהכי. **כופין** בני מבוי זה את זה כו' ולא מלמד תינוקות. נראה לר"י דבמלמד תינוקות נכרים איירי. ולא יתכן אי גרס לעיל "אחד מבני מבוי", דהא מוקמינן ליה (ח) בתינוקות נכרים, ומעכבין עליו בני מבוי, והכא קאמר דלשכינו אינו כופהו. ואפילו רשב"ג לא פליג אלא משום דפסיק לחיותיה — אבל משום קול תינוקות לא חייש. ומיהו, לפי מה שפירשתי [לעיל] דגרסינן "אחד מבני חצר" — אתי שפיר. ולר' שמשון בן אברהם נראה דהכא בתינוקות ישראל, ואפילו אחר תקנת יהושע בן גמלא. ושאני הכא, דכבר יש שם מלמד תינוקות אחר. ובסמוך דקאמר דמודה רב הונא במקרי דרדקי דלא מצי מעכב, ואף על גב דאיהו סבר כרבן שמעון בן גמליאל — צריך לומר דרבן שמעון בן גמליאל לא פליג אמלמד תינוקות, אלא אשארא. **פשיטא** לי דבר מתא אבר מתא [אחריתי מצי] מעכב. רב הונא בריה דרב יהושע כרבנן ס"ל, ומיבעי ליה בר מבואה אבר מבואה דעלמא אי מצי מעכב, אי הוי בכלל שכינו אי לאו, כדפירש הקונטרס. וכוותיה קיימא לן לגבי רב הונא, דבתרא הוא. **ואי** שייך בכרגא דהכא לא מצי מעכב. פירוש: בני העיר. אבל בני מבוי מצי מעכבי שלא יכנס במבואם.

קנאת

עין משפט נר מצוה

מג א מיי' פ"ב מהל' ת"ת הל' ג סמג שם טוש"ע י"ד סי' רמה סעיף יז:

מד ב ג מיי' פ"י מהל' שכירות הל' ז ועי' בהשגות ובמ"מ סמג עשין פח טוש"ע ח"מ סי' שו סעיף ח:

מה ד מיי' פי"ח מהל' מכירה הלכה ד סמג לאוין קע טוש"ע ח"מ סי' רכח סעיף יח:

מו ה ו ז ח ט מיי' פ"ו מהל' שכנים הל' ח סמג עשין פב טוש"ע ח"מ סי' קנו סעיף ה ועי"ש בהג"ה:

מז י כ מיי' שם הל' יב ופ"ב מהל' ת"ת הל' ז סמג שם וסי' יב טוש"ע שם סעיף ג וטוש"ע י"ד סי' רמה סעיף כב:

רבינו גרשום

מאי טעמא עבדת הכי דמשיירת נשים: האי בר מבואה א) מההוא מבוי (בני אדם) ולא היה רגיל לכך וקא מוקים ריחים שלו סמוך לריחים של חבירו: דינא הוא כו'. מרחיקין מצודת הדג מן הדג שאם היה רגיל אחד לפרוש מצודתו בַּשֶּׁכֶר שתיקן במים ובא חבירו ורצה לעשות מצודתו כמו כן מרחיקין אותה מן מצודת חבירו כמלוא ריצת הדג דמצי למימר ליה קא פסקת חיותאי ותסייע לרב הונא. מהא לא תסייע ליה דשאני דגים דיהבי סיירא דמשום הכי מרחיקין מפני כי מסיר לו דבר שבא כבר למצודתו במאכל שמשים במצודתו לפי שכשמעיינין ורואין מאכל במקום אחר בורחין ממצודתו של זה והולכין לשם וגזלו בידים דבר שכבר [בא] במצודתו אבל ברחוק פרסה אינו יכול להביט המאכל. אבל גבי ריחים דליכא למימר הכי דבר הבא לידי הסיר ממני שעדיין לא בא לידו כלום מודה דמצי לאוקמינהו במבוי: לימא דאמר כר' יהודה ולא כרבנן. מפני שמרגיל התינוקות לבוא אצלו ומצי למימר ליה שאר בעלי חנויות קא פסקת לחיותי: שיוסקי. שקדים: ומרחץ. שהיו רגילין לשכור מרחץ כדי לרחוץ: אתה עושה בתוך שלך ואני עושה בתוך שלי. וקשיא לרב הונא: כופין בני מבוי זה את זה שלא להושיב ביניהן לא חייט. כלומר אומנין של מבוי אחר אינן רשאין להושיב במבוי זה שלא לדעת כולן ולשכינו שבמבוי שלו אינו כופהו שלא יזקק מן אומנותו משום דאמר ליה אתה עושה בתוך שלך ואני בתוך שלי: רשב"ג אומר אף לשכינו כופהו. ורב הונא ס"ל כרשב"ג: בר מתא אבר מתא אחריתי מצי מעכב שאם היה אומן א' בעיר ובא אומן אחר מעיר אחרת כאותו ורצה לקבוע באותה מדינה יכול לעכב על ידו ולומר קא פסקת לחיותא ואי שייך אכרגא להתם שפורעין מס גולגלותם לאדון אחד דמי כמאן דהוה תרווייהו מאותה העיר ולא מצי מעכב ליה: דנפשיה. כלומר לשכינו לא מצי מעכב ורב הונא בריה דר"י לא ס"ל הא דרב הונא דלעיל. ב) לא צריכא דלא שייך מאי. מי אמרי' הואיל דממתא חדא תרוייהו אע"ג דלא שייך כרגייהו בחדא לא מצי מעכב ליה. או דלמא כיון דלמבוי דידיה הוא מצי מעכב דלא ליקבע במבוי דידיה תיקו: ברוכלין

מסורת הש"ס

א) [עי' תוס' גיטין סח. ד"ה וכתיב]: ב) [ב"מ קט.]: ג) שם ס.: ד) [שם]: ה) [גי' רב אלפס והרא"ש מבעלי]: ו) [תוספתא פ"א]: ז) [מפי' רש"י סד"ה ומודה רב הונא נראה דלא גריס לכל זה וכ"כ תוס' ג"כ להדיא בסמוך ד"ה קנאת סופרים]: ח) [צ"ל המשנה]:

הגהות הב"ח

(א) גמ' זכר קרינן א"ל לדידי זכר אקריון: (ב) שם מפני שמרגילן לבוא אצלו: (ג) רש"י ד"ה שאני דגים וכו' להיות רגילין לרוץ וכו' ונתן מלודה ומזונות וכו' וה"ל כמאן: (ד) ד"ה שלא וכו' במבוי זה ויש כאן: (ה) ד"ה ואי שייך וכו' כבר מתא הוא ולא וכו' לא מצי מעכב מלירד כצ"ל ותיבות את המבוי נמחק: (ו) בא"ד מעכב עליה בן המבוי הזה או לא: (ז) תוס' ד"ה כופין וכו' מוקמינן ליה לעיל בתינוקות:

א) נראה דצ"ל בר מבואה דאוקי ריחיא ואתא בר מבואה חבריה מההוא מבוי ולא היה כו': ב) [מד' רבינו ז"ל אלו נראה שהיה גורס בכאן ואי שייך בכרגא דהכא הא אמרת דלא מצי לעכב לא צריכא דלא שייך מאי עד כאן וכ"נ מדברי הרמב"ם ז"ל בפ"ו מהל' שכנים שגרס כן ע"ש].

א)קְנָאַת סוֹפְרִים תַּרְבֶּה חָכְמָה. אֲמַר רַב נַחְמָן בַּר יִצְחָק: וּמוֹדֶה רַב הוּנָא בְּרֵיהּ דְּרַב יְהוֹשֻׁעַ אבְּרוֹכְלִין הַמַּחֲזִירִין בָּעֲיָרוֹת דְּלָא מָצֵי מְעַכֵּב, ב)דְּאָמַר מָר: בעֶזְרָא תִּקֵּן לָהֶן לְיִשְׂרָאֵל שֶׁיְּהוּ רוֹכְלִין מַחֲזִירִין בָּעֲיָרוֹת, כְּדֵי שֶׁיְּהוּ תַּכְשִׁיטִין מְצוּיִין לִבְנוֹת יִשְׂרָאֵל. גוְהָנֵי מִילֵּי לְאַהֲדוּרֵי, אֲבָל לְאַקְבּוֹעֵי — לָא. דוְאִי צוּרְבָא מֵרַבָּנַן הוּא — אֲפִילּוּ לְאַקְבּוֹעֵי נַמִי, כִּי הָא דְּרָבָא שְׁרָא לְהוּ לְר' יֹאשִׁיָּה וּלְרַב עוֹבַדְיָה לְאַקְבּוֹעֵי, דְּלָא כְּהִלְכְתָא, מַאי טַעֲמָא? כֵּיוָן דְּרַבָּנַן נִינְהוּ, אָתוּ לְטַרְדוּ מִגִּירְסַיְיהוּ. הָנְהוּ דִּיקוּלָאֵי דְּאַיְיתוּ דִּיקְלָאֵי לְבָבֶל, אֲתוּ בְּנֵי מָתָא קָא מְעַכְּבִי עִלָּוַיְיהוּ, אֲתוּ לְקַמֵּיהּ דְּרָבִינָא, אֲמַר לְהוּ: המֵעָלְמָא אָתוּ, וּלְעָלְמָא לִיזַבְּנוּ. ווְהָנֵי מִילֵּי בְּיוֹמָא דְּשׁוּקָא, אֲבָל בְּלָא יוֹמָא דְּשׁוּקָא — לָא. וּבְיוֹמָא דְּשׁוּקָא נַמִי לָא אָמְרִינַן זאֶלָּא לְזַבּוֹנֵי בְּשׁוּקָא, אֲבָל לְאַהֲדוּרֵי — (א) לָא. הָנְהוּ עָמוֹרָאֵי דְּאַיְיתוּ עַמְרָא לְפוּם נַהֲרָא, אֲתוּ בְּנֵי מָתָא קָא מְעַכְּבִי עִלָּוַיְיהוּ, אֲתוּ לְקַמֵּיהּ דְּרַב כָּהֲנָא, אֲמַר לְהוּ: דִּינָא הוּא דִּמְעַכְּבִי עֲלַיְיכוּ. אֲמַרוּ לֵיהּ: אִית לָן אַשְׁרָאֵי. (ב) אֲמַר לְהוּ: חזִילוּ זַבְּנוּ שִׁיעוּר חִיּוּתַיְיכוּ, עַד דְּעָקְרִיתוּ אַשְׁרָאֵי דִּידְכוּ וְאָזְלִיתוּ. רַב דִּימִי מִנְּהַרְדְּעָא אַיְיתִי גְּרוֹגָרוֹת בִּסְפִינָה, א"ל רֵישׁ גָּלוּתָא לְרָבָא: פּוּק חֲזִי, אִי צוּרְבָא מֵרַבָּנַן הוּא נְקִיט לֵיהּ שׁוּקָא. א"ל רָבָא לְרַב אַדָּא בַּר אַבָּא: פּוּק תְּהִי לֵיהּ בְּקַנְקַנֵּיהּ. נְפַק [אֲזַל] בְּעָא מִינֵּיהּ: גפִּיל שֶׁבָּלַע כְּפִיפָה מִצְרִית וְהֵקִיאָהּ דֶּרֶךְ בֵּית הָרְעִי, מַהוּ? לָא הֲוָה בִּידֵיהּ. א"ל: מָר נִיהוּ רָבָא? דטְפַח לֵיהּ בְּסַנְדְּלֵיהּ, א"ל: בֵּין דִּידִי לְרָבָא אִיכָּא טוּבָא, מִיהוּ עַל כָּרְחָךְ אֲנָא רַבָּךְ וְרָבָא רַבֵּהּ דְּרַבָּךְ. לָא נַקְטוּ לֵיהּ שׁוּקָא, פְּסֵיד גְּרוֹגָרוֹת דִּידֵיהּ. אֲתָא לְקַמֵּיהּ דְּרַב יוֹסֵף, א"ל: חֲזֵי מָר מַאי עֲבַדוּ לִי! א"ל: מַאן דְּלָא שַׁהְיֵיהּ לְאוֹנִיתָא דְּמַלְכָּא דֶּאֱדוֹם — לָא נִשְׁהְיֵיהּ לְאוֹנִיתָךְ, דִּכְתִיב: עמוס ב"כֹּה אָמַר ה' עַל שְׁלֹשָׁה פִּשְׁעֵי מוֹאָב וְעַל אַרְבָּעָה לֹא אֲשִׁיבֶנּוּ עַל שָׂרְפוֹ עַצְמוֹת מֶלֶךְ אֱדוֹם הלַסִּיד". נָח נַפְשֵׁיהּ דְּרַב אַדָּא בַּר אַבָּא. רַב יוֹסֵף אֲמַר: אֲנָא עֲנַשְׁתֵּיהּ, דַּאֲנָא לְטַיְיתֵיהּ. רַב דִּימִי מִנְּהַרְדְּעָא אֲמַר: אֲנָא עֲנַשְׁתֵּיהּ, דְּאַפְסֵיד גְּרוֹגָרוֹת דִּידִי. אַבָּיֵי אֲמַר: אֲנָא עֲנַשְׁתֵּיהּ, דְּאָמַר לְהוּ לְרַבָּנַן: ואַדִּמְגָרְמִיתוּ גַּרְמֵי בֵּי אַבָּיֵי, תּוּ אִכְלוּ בִּישְׂרָא [שְׁמֵינָא] בֵּי רָבָא. וְרָבָא אֲמַר: אֲנָא עֲנִישְׁתֵּיהּ, [דְּכִי הֲוָה אָזֵיל לְבֵי טַבָּחָא לְמִשְׁקַל אוּמְצָא] אָמַר לְהוּ לְטַבָּחֵי: אֲנָא שָׁקֵילְנָא בִּישְׂרָא מִיקַּמֵּי שַׁמָּעֵיהּ דְּרָבָא, דַּאֲנָא עֲדִיפְנָא מִינֵּיהּ. רַב נַחְמָן בַּר יִצְחָק אֲמַר: אֲנָא עֲנִישְׁתֵּיהּ, דְּרַב נַחְמָן בַּר יִצְחָק רֵישׁ כַּלָּה הֲוָה, כָּל יוֹמָא מִיקַּמֵּי דְּנֵיעוּל לְכַלָּה, מַרְהֵיט בַּהֲדֵיהּ רַב אַדָּא בַּר אַבָּא לִשְׁמַעְתֵּיהּ וַהֲדַר עָיֵיל לְכַלָּה. הַהוּא יוֹמָא נַקְטוּהּ רַב פָּפָּא וְרַב הוּנָא בְּרֵיהּ דְּרַב יְהוֹשֻׁעַ לְרַב אַדָּא בַּר אַבָּא מִשּׁוּם דְּלָא הָווּ בְּסִיּוּמָא, אֲמַרוּ לֵיהּ: אֵימָא לָן הָנֵי שְׁמַעְתָּתָא דְּמַעֲשַׂר בְּהֵמָה הֵיכִי אָמְרִינְהוּ רָבָא. אֲמַר לְהוּ: הָכִי אֲמַר רָבָא וְהָכִי אֲמַר רָבָא. אַדְּהָכִי נְגַהּ לֵיהּ [לְרַב נַחְמָן בַּר יִצְחָק] ז)(וְלָא אָתֵי רַב אַדָּא בַּר אַבָּא,) אֲמַרוּ לֵיהּ רַבָּנַן לְרַב נַחְמָן בַּר יִצְחָק: קוּם דִּנְגַהּ לָן, לָמָּה יָתֵיב מָר? אֲמַר לְהוּ: יָתֵיבְנָא וְקָא (ג) מְנַטְרָא לְעַרְסֵיהּ דְּרַב אַדָּא בַּר אַבָּא. אַדְּהָכִי נְפַק קָלָא דְּנָח נַפְשֵׁיהּ דְּרַב אַדָּא בַּר אַבָּא. וּמִסְתַּבְּרָא, דְּרַב נַחְמָן בַּר יִצְחָק עֲנָשֵׁיהּ.§

מתני' טמִי שֶׁהָיָה כּוֹתְלוֹ סָמוּךְ לְכוֹתֶל חֲבֵירוֹ, לֹא יִסְמוֹךְ לוֹ כּוֹתֶל אַחֵר אא"כ הִרְחִיק מִמֶּנּוּ אַרְבַּע אַמּוֹת. ח)יהַחַלּוֹנוֹת, בֵּין מִלְמַעְלָן בֵּין מִלְמַטָּן בֵּין כְּנֶגְדָּן — אַרְבַּע אַמּוֹת.§ **גמ'** וְקַמָּא הֵיכִי סָמֵיךְ? אֲמַר רַב יְהוּדָה, הָכִי קָאָמַר: הַבָּא

תורה אור

רש"י

ומודה רב הונא בריה דרב יהושע. אע"ג דְּאָמַר: בַּר מָתָא אַבַּר מָתָא אַחֲרִיתֵי מָצֵי מְעַכֵּב מִלְּהָבִיא כָּאן וְלִמְכּוֹר, מוֹדֶה הוּא בְּרוֹכְלִין מוֹכְרֵי בְּשָׂמִים הַמַּחֲזִירִין בָּעֲיָירוֹת לְהָבִיא בְּשָׂמִים לַנָּשִׁים לְהִתְקַשֵּׁט בָּהֶן, דְּלָא מָצוּ לְעַכֵּב עֲלַיְיהוּ רוֹכְלֵי הָעִיר. לְאַהֲדוּרֵי. לַחֲזוֹר וּלְסַבֵּב בִּמְבוֹאוֹת הָעִיר וּבַבָּתִּים עַל כָּל הָרוֹצֶה לִקְנוֹת, וְאַחַר כֵּן יָשׁוּב לְעִירוֹ. וְאִי צוּרְבָא מֵרַבָּנַן הוּא. דְּטָרִיד בְּגִירְסָא, וְלָא אוֹרְחֵיהּ — לְאַהֲדוּרֵי אֲפִי' לְאַקְבּוּעֵי נַמִּי. דְּלָא כְּהִלְכְתָא. אֶלָּא לִפְנִים מִשּׁוּרַת הַדִּין. דִּיקוּלָאֵי = מוֹכְרֵי סַלִּים. וְיֵשׁ אוֹמְרִים מוֹכְרֵי יוֹרוֹת. וּלְעָלְמָא לִיזַבְּנָן. יוֹמָא דְּשׁוּקָא הֲוָה, וְהַרְבֵּה בָּאִין מִמָּקוֹם אַחֵר לִקְנוֹת מִן הַשּׁוּק, לְפִיכָךְ אֵין בְּנֵי הָעִיר מְעַכְּבִין גַּם עַל הַמּוֹכְרִים לְהָבִיא אוּמָנוּתָם וְלִמְכּוֹר לַמְּקַבְּלִים לַשּׁוּק. עָמוֹרָאֵי = מוֹכְרֵי צֶמֶר. אִית לָן אַשְׁרָאֵי בְּמָתָא. מָכַרְנוּ בַּאֲמָנָה, וּצְרִיכִים אָנוּ לִשְׁהוֹת כָּאן עַד שֶׁנִּגְבֶּה חוֹבוֹת שֶׁלָּנוּ. וְאִם אֵין אָנוּ מוֹכְרִין סְחוֹרוֹתֵינוּ — בַּמֶּה נִתְפַּרְנֵס? עַד דְּעָקְרִיתוּ. שֶׁתַּעַקְרוּ חוֹבוֹתֵיכֶם מִן הַלּוֹקְחִים מִכֶּם בְּאַשְׁרַאי. נְקִיט לֵיהּ שׁוּקָא. הַכְרֵז שֶׁלֹּא יִמְכּוֹר אִישׁ בָּעִיר גְּרוֹגָרוֹת אֶלָּא הוּא. תְּהִי לֵיהּ בְּקַנְקַנֵּיהּ = הָרִיחַ לוֹ בְּקַנְקַנּוֹ, אִם יַיִן הוּא אִם חוֹמֶץ. כְּלוֹמַר, בָּדְקֵהוּ בַּהֲלָכוֹת, אִם תַּלְמִיד חָכָם הוּא אִם לָאו. רֵיחַ הַיַּיִן כְּשֶׁמְּרִיחִין אוֹתוֹ אִם טוֹב הוּא קָרֵי תְּהִי, כִּדְאָמְרִינַן "בַּת תְּיָהָא" בְּמַסֶּכֶת ע"ז (דף סו.). וְכֵן בִּכְתוּבּוֹת (דף קה.): קַרְנָא הֲוָה תְּהִי בְּאַמְבַּרָא דַּחֲמְרָא. כְּפִיפָה מִצְרִית. סַל נְצָרִים שֶׁל עֲרָבָה. מַהוּ. מִי חָשׁוּב כִּמְעוּכָּל, וַהֲוָה לֵיהּ כִּכְלֵי גְּלָלִים, וְאֵין מְקַבֵּל טוּמְאָה עוֹד. א"ל. רַב דִּימִי לְרַב אַדָּא. מָר נִיהוּ רָבָא. אַתָּה הוּא רָבָא? לְפִי שֶׁשָּׁמַע עַל רָבָא שֶׁהוּא גָּדוֹל הָעִיר, וְסָבוּר שֶׁהוּא זֶה. טְפַח לֵיהּ בְּסַנְדְּלֵיהּ. הִכָּהוּ עַל סַנְדָּלוֹ בְּמַקֵּל דֶּרֶךְ שְׂחוֹק, כְּאָדָם שֶׁמַּכֶּה לְמִי שֶׁאֵינוֹ חָשׁוּב. דְּלָא שַׁהְיֵיהּ. שֶׁלֹּא נִמְנַע מִלְּהִפָּרַע. לְאוֹנִיתָא. אוֹנָאַת בּוֹשְׁתּוֹ. דְּמַלְכָּא דֶּאֱדוֹם. אע"פ שֶׁהוּא אֱדוֹמִי. עַל שָׂרְפוֹ. מֵחֲמַת בִּזָּיוֹן. דְּאָמַר לְהוּ לְרַבָּנַן אַדִּמְגָרְמִיתוּ גַּרְמֵי בֵּי אַבָּיֵי. שֶׁהָיָה רָגִיל לוֹמַר לְתַלְמִידִים: עַד שֶׁאַתֶּם הוֹלְכִים אֵצֶל אַבָּיֵי לִגְרֵס עֲצָמוֹת, כְּלוֹמַר לִלְמוֹד שֶׁלֹּא לָשׂוֹבַע. תּוּ אִכְלוּ כו'. בּוֹאוּ וְלִמְדוּ הֲלָכוֹת נְהוּבּוֹת מְרוּוָּחוֹת אֵצֶל רָבָא. שַׁמָּעֵיהּ דְּרָבָא. שְׁלוּחוֹ לִקְנוֹת בָּשָׂר. רֵישׁ כַּלָּה. דּוֹרֵשׁ בָּרַבִּים בַּשַּׁבָּתוֹת. דְּלָא הָווּ בְּסִיּוּמָא. יֵשׁ אוֹמְרִים: שֶׁלֹּא הָיוּ בְּעֵלָה כְּשֶׁנַּעֲשָׂה רַב נַחְמָן רֵישׁ כַּלָּה. וְיֵשׁ אוֹמְרִים: דְּלָא הָווּ בְּסִיּוּמָא דְּפִירְקָא, דְּרָבָא דְּדָרֵישׁ בְּשַׁבַּת הָרֶגֶל הֲלָכוֹת הָאֲמוּרוֹת בְּפֶרֶק אַחֲרוֹן שֶׁל בְּכוֹרוֹת. שְׁמַעְתָּתָא דְּמַעֲשַׂר בְּהֵמָה. בְּפֶרֶק אַחֲרוֹן דִּבְכוֹרוֹת, וְרָבָא אֲמָרִינְהוּ בְּסוֹפָא דְּפִירְקָא. אָתוּ רַבָּנַן. תַּלְמִידֵי הַיְשִׁיבָה הַבָּאִים לִשְׁמוֹעַ. נָטְרָנָא עַרְסֵיהּ דְּרַב אַדָּא. אֲנִי מְצַפֶּה כָּאן שֶׁיָּבִיאוּ אֶת מִטַּת רַב אַדָּא שֶׁמֵּת. **מתני'** לֹא יִסְמוֹךְ לְכוֹתֶל חֲבֵירוֹ כּוֹתֶל אַחֵר אֶלָּא אִם כֵּן כו'. מְפָרֵשׁ בַּגְּמָ'. וְהַחַלּוֹנוֹת. מִי שֶׁהָיוּ לוֹ חַלּוֹנוֹת פְּתוּחִים לַחֲצַר חֲבֵירוֹ, וְהוּחְזַק בְּדָבָר זֶה שָׁלֹשׁ שָׁנִים, וּבָא בַּעַל הֶחָצֵר לִבְנוֹת שָׁם כּוֹתֶל — צָרִיךְ לְשַׁעֵר ד' אַמּוֹת. בֵּין מִלְמַעְלָן. אִם בָּא לְהַגְבִּיהַּ — יַגְבִּיהַּ כּוֹתְלוֹ ד' אַמּוֹת מִן הַחַלּוֹנוֹת. בֵּין מִלְמַטָּן. אִם בָּא לִבְנוֹתוֹ נָמוּךְ — צָרִיךְ לְהַשְׁפִּילוֹ מִן הַחַלּוֹנוֹת ד' אַמּוֹת. וְטַעֲמָא מְפָרֵשׁ בַּגְּמָ'. בֵּין מִכְּנֶגְדָּן. צָרִיךְ לְהַרְחִיקוֹ מֵהֶן ד' אַמּוֹת. **גמ'** הַבָּא

תוספות

קנאת סופרים תרבה חכמה. ולא גרסי' כמו שיש בספרים: דאמר מר עזרא תיקן להם לישראל שיהו מושיבין סופר בצד סופר. דהא לא חשיב ליה ב"מרובה" (ב"ק דף פב.) גבי עשר תקנות שתיקן. **מעלמא** אתו ולעלמא ליזבנן. מכאן משמע דביומא דשוקא היה מותר להלוות לבני אדם הבאים ממקומות שם לשוק לנכרים דאתו מעלמא, אבל לבני המקום — לא. ודוקא בשוקא, אבל לאהדורי — לא. **אמר** ליה רבא לרב אדא בר אבא. כן גריס רבינו חננאל. ולא גרסי' "בר אהבה", דאותו היה בימי רבי, כדאמרינן בקדושין (דף עב: ושם):ט) היום ישב רב אדא בר אהבה בחיקו של אברהם אבינו. **פיל** שבלע כפיפה מצרית. בפ' "ר' ישמעאל" (מנחות דף סט. ושם ד"ה פיל) איתא להך בעיא דהכא, ומסיק התם: למאי? אי למבטל טומאתו — תנינא: כל הכלים יורדין לידי טומאה במחשבה ואין עולין מטומאה אלא בשינוי מעשה! וקאמר: לא צריכא, דבלע הוצין ועבדינהו כפיפה, אי הוי עיכול והוי ככלי גללים, או לא. והכא בלע הוצין בעא מיניה, דאי כפיפה שלימה — אמאי לא הוה בידיה? מתני' היא! וקשיא לר"ת: א"כ אמאי לא נקיטו ליה שוקא? הא בעיא זו לא איפשיטא התם! וי"ל: דמ"מ הוה ליה לאיתויי הנך ראיות דמייתי התם ודחי להו. **אנא** ענישתיה. כל אחד מהן היה מתאונן שעל ידו מת רב אדא, משום דאמרינן בשבת בפ' "שואל" (דף קמט:): כל מי שחבירו נענש על ידו — אין מכניסין אותו במחיצתו של הקב"ה, שנאמר (משלי יז) "גם ענוש לצדיק לא טוב" אלא רע, וכתיב (תהלים ה) "לא יגורך רע". ר"י. **וקמא** היכי סמיך. ס"ד דנפל איירי, שכן משמע הלשון, דקתני: מי שהיה כותלו סמוך לכותל חבירו. ומשני רב יהודה, הכי קאמר: הבא לסמוך כו'. ומתני' הכי פירוש': מי שהיה גבול כותלו סמוך לכותל חבירו. ורבא פריך: דכותל קתני, ולא גבול. וא"ת: לרבא, דאמר בריש פירקין דאסור לסמוך, קמא היכי סמך? ואפילו לפי' ר"ת דלמסקנא שרי רבא לכולהו לסמוך, לבד מבור — מ"מ אמאי לא פריך מהכא דהוי רישא, אלא ממשרה וירק דהוי סיפא? וי"ל: דלא אסר רבא לסמוך אלא מילתא דמגופיה אתי היזק, אבל הכא הכותל אינו מזיק כלום, אלא שגורם למעט הדוושא. אלא

רבינו גרשום

ברוכלין. שמוכרין תכשיטי נשים שרק וכחל אע"ג דלא שייכי בחד כרגא דלא מצי מעכב עליה האי רוכל דמתא: והני מילי דלא מצי מעכב לאהדורי לחזר ולילך משוק לשוק וממבוי למבוי ולמכור ולשוב לעירו אבל לקבוע חנותו בהני רוכלין למזבן תכשיטין לא: דלא כהלכתא. כלומר שלא ילמדו ממנו אחרים הלכה דלפנים משורת הדין עבד להו משום דרבנן נינהו דלא ליבטלו מגירסייהו לילך ולחזור בכל העיר ומשוק לשוק: הנהו דקולאי. שמוכרין סלים. אתו דקולאי דמתא ומעכבי להו אמר להו לא מציתו מעכבי עלייהו דמעלמא אתי ולהנהו דאתי מעלמא לשוק לזבני אבל לאהדורי בבתים לזבונינהו לא דודאי מצי למיעכב עלייהו: אית לן אשראי במתא. חוב שחייבין לנו ממון וצריכין לנו לעכובי הכא עד דפרעי לן והב לן רשותא דניזבין עד כפי חיותן עד דפרעי לן: נקיט ליה שוקא. שלא ימכור אדם עד שימכור כל גרוגרות שלו: תהי ליה. הוי מריח מה יש בו: מצרית. מצורי דקל מהו מי אמרי' הואיל דהוות במעיו והקיאה [דרך] בית הרעי כמאכל שנתעכל דמי ונתבטל ואין מקבלת טומאה או דלמא הואיל ואכתי קיימת היא דבר חשוב הוי ואינה מבוטלת ומקבלת טומא': אמר ליה. רב דימי לרב אדא מאן נינהו מר רבא את הוא רבא: טפח ליה. רב אדא לרב דימי בסנדליה כלומר שלא היה חשוב בעיניו: ורבא רביה דרבך. שהוא רבי ואנא רבך: מאן דלא שבקיה. לאוניתא (דעמון) דמואב למלכא דאדום: אדמגרמיתו גרמי בי אביי. שהיה רגיל לומר לתלמידי אביי כל זמן שאתם מגררין עצמות שאין בהן לחלוח בי אביי יכולין אתם ללמוד תורה כשורה וכהלכתא בי רבא לפי שאביי לא למד כל כך ולפיכך אמר אביי אנא ענישתיה שהיה מבזיני: ריש כלה הוה. שהיה רגיל לדרוש בשבת שלפני החג ורב נחמן היה דורש אותן שבתות והיו מתקבצין שם מהרבה מקומו' תלמידין לשמוע: עכביהו רב פפא ורב הונא לרב אדא בר אהבה משום דלא הוי בסיומא במס' בכורו' קמיה דרבא: קום והכנס לדרוש דנגה לן שכבר עבר מן היום הרבה: קא נטרנא לערסיה. כלומר שמת לפי שהיה מצערו כל כך שלא בא אליו לעיין עמו הדרשה: **פיסקא** מי שהיה כותלו סמוך לכותל חבירו ונפל לא יסמוך כותל אחר. שלא יבנה שם כותל אחר אלא אם כן הרחיק ממנו מכותל חבירו ד' אמות משום דוושא כדמפרש בגמ'. החלונות מלמעלן ומלמטן ומכנגדן ד' אמות כדמפרש בריש פ"ק: ומקשי' וכותל קמא דנפל דהוה מעיקרא היכי סמיך בקרוב מד' אמות: אמר רב יהודה. הכי תריץ מתני' הבא לסמוך תחלה לא יסמוך לכותל וכו': והא

מסורת הש"ס

א) [לעיל כח.]: ב) ב"ק פב.: ג) מנחות סט.: ד) [מו"ק כה. ב"ק לב:]: ה) [נ"ל לשיד]: ו) [נ"ל אדמגרסיתו. ערוך ערך גרס א']: ז) [רש"ל מ"ז וגרס רנב"י אתו רבנן א"ל לרב נב"י]: ח) [לעיל ב:]: ט) [ע"ש ד"ה היום וברש"י שם וע"ע תוס' תענית כ: ד"ה א"ל]:

עין משפט נר מצוה

מח א ב ג ד מיי' פ"ו מהל' שכנים הל' ט סמג עשין פב טוש"ע ח"מ סי' קנו סעיף ו:

מט ה ו ז ח מיי' שם הלכה י טוש"ע שם סעיף ז:

נ ט מיי' פ"ט שם הל' ט סמג שם טוש"ע ח"מ סי' קנה סעיף יב:

נא י מיי' שם פ"ז הל' א ב ג סמג שם טוש"ע ח"מ סי' קנד סעיף ג וסעיף כב:

הגהות הב"ח

(א) גמ' אבל לאהדורי במתא לא: (ב) שם אית לן אשראי במתא אמר: (ג) שם וקא נטרנא לערסיה:

נב א מיי' פ"ט מהל' שכנים הל' ט סמג עשין פב טוש"ע ח"מ סי' קנה סעיף יב ובהג"ה ועיין בטור:
נג ב ג מיי' שם הל' שם ועי' בהשגות וכמ"מ טוש"ע שם סעיף יג:
נד ד מיי' שם פ"ז הל' א ב ג סמג שם טוש"ע ח"מ סי' קנד סעיף כב:
נה ה מיי' שם הל' ד וסמג שם טוש"ע שם סעיף כג וסי' קנה סעיף יד בהג"ה:
נו ו ז מיי' שם הל' ד וסמג שם טוש"ע ח"מ סי' קנד סעיף כב:
נז ח מיי' שם טוש"ע שם סעיף כג:
נח ט מיי' פ"ט שם הל' ז סמג שם טוש"ע ח"מ סי' קנה סעיף טז:
נט י מיי' שם טוש"ע שם סעיף יז:
ס כ מיי' פ"ט שם הל' ח וסמג שם טוש"ע שם סעיף לג:

הַבָּא לִסְמוֹךְ, לֹא יִסְמוֹךְ אֶלָּא אִם כֵּן הִרְחִיק מִמֶּנּוּ אַרְבַּע אַמּוֹת. מַתְקִיף לָהּ רָבָא: וְהָא "מִי שֶׁהָיָה כּוֹתְלוֹ סָמוּךְ לְכוֹתֶל חֲבֵירוֹ" קָתָנֵי! אֶלָּא אֲמַר רָבָא, הָכִי קָתָנֵי: מִי שֶׁהָיָה כּוֹתְלוֹ סָמוּךְ לְכוֹתֶל חֲבֵירוֹ בְּרִחוּק אַרְבַּע אַמּוֹת וְנָפַל, לֹא יִסְמוֹךְ לוֹ כּוֹתֶל אַחֵר אֶלָּא אִם כֵּן הִרְחִיק מִמֶּנּוּ ד' אַמּוֹת; מ"ט? דְּדַוְושָׁא דְּהָכָא מַעֲלֵי לְהָתָם. אָמַר רַב: לֹא שָׁנוּ אֶלָּא כּוֹתֶל גִּינָּה, אֲבָל כּוֹתֶל חָצֵר — אִם בָּא לִסְמוֹךְ סוֹמֵךְ; רַבִּי אוֹשַׁעְיָא אוֹמֵר: אֶחָד כּוֹתֶל גִּינָּה וְאֶחָד כּוֹתֶל חָצֵר — אִם בָּא לִסְמוֹךְ אֵינוֹ סוֹמֵךְ. אֲמַר רַבִּי יוֹסֵי בַּר חֲנִינָא: וְלָא פְּלִיגִי, הָא בְּעִיר יְשָׁנָה, הָא בְּעִיר חֲדָשָׁה. תְּנַן: א)הַחַלּוֹנוֹת, בֵּין מִלְמַעְלָן בֵּין מִלְּמַטָּן בֵּין מִכְּנֶגְדָּן — אַרְבַּע אַמּוֹת, וְתָנֵי עֲלָהּ: מִלְמַעְלָן — כְּדֵי שֶׁלֹּא יָצִיץ וְיִרְאֶה, מִלְּמַטָּן — שֶׁלֹּא יַעֲמוֹד וְיִרְאֶה, וּמִכְּנֶגְדָּן — שֶׁלֹּא יַאֲפִיל; טַעְמָא שֶׁלֹּא יַאֲפִיל, אֲבָל מִשּׁוּם דַּוְושָׁא לָא! הָכָא בְּמַאי עָסְקִינַן — בְּבָא מִן הַצַּד. ב)וְכַמָּה? אָמַר (א) יֵיבָא חֲמוּהּ דְּאַשְׁיָין בַּר נִדְבָּךְ מִשְּׁמֵיהּ דְּרַב: כִּמְלֹא רֹחַב חַלּוֹן. וַהֲלֹא מֵצִיץ! א"ר זְבִיד: ג)בְּמַדִּיר אֶת כּוֹתְלוֹ. וְהָא אֲנַן תְּנַן: אַרְבַּע אַמּוֹת! לָא קַשְׁיָא: כָּאן מֵרוּחַ אַחַת, כָּאן מִשְׁתֵּי רוּחוֹת. ת"ש: וְאֶת הַכּוֹתֶל מִן הַמַּזְחִילָה — ד' אַמּוֹת, כְּדֵי שֶׁיְּהֵא זוֹקֵף אֶת הַסּוּלָּם; טַעְמָא מִשּׁוּם סוּלָּם, אֲבָל מִשּׁוּם דַּוְושָׁא לָא! הָכָא בְּמַאי עָסְקִינַן — בְּמַזְחִילָה מְשׁוּפַּעַת, דְּאִי מִשּׁוּם דַּוְושָׁא הוּא, הָא קָא אָזֵיל וְאָתֵי תּוּתֵיהּ.§

מתני' מַרְחִיקִין אֶת הַסּוּלָּם מִן הַשּׁוֹבָךְ אַרְבַּע אַמּוֹת, כְּדֵי שֶׁלֹּא תִּקְפּוֹץ הַנְּמִיָּיה; וְאֶת הַכּוֹתֶל מִן הַמַּזְחִילָה — ד' אַמּוֹת, כְּדֵי שֶׁיְּהֵא זוֹקֵף אֶת הַסּוּלָּם.§

גמ' לֵימָא, מַתְנִיתִין דְּלָא כְּר' יוֹסֵי, דְּאִי ר"י הָא אָמַר: ד)זֶה חוֹפֵר בְּתוֹךְ שֶׁלּוֹ וְזֶה נוֹטֵעַ בְּתוֹךְ שֶׁלּוֹ? אֲפִילּוּ תֵּימָא ר' יוֹסֵי, הָא ה)אָמַר רַב אַשִׁי: כִּי הֲוֵינַן בֵּי רַב כָּהֲנָא הֲוָה אָמַר: מוֹדֵי רַבִּי יוֹסֵי בְּגִירֵי דִּידֵיהּ, ה"נ זִמְנִין דְּבַהֲדֵי דְּמַנַּח לֵיהּ (ב) יָתְבָא בְּחוֹר וְקָפְצָה. וְהָא גְּרָמָא הוּא! א"ר טוֹבִי בַּר מַתָּנָה, זֹאת אוֹמֶרֶת: גְּרָמָא בְּנִיזָּקִין אָסוּר. רַב יוֹסֵף הֲוָה לֵיהּ הָנְהוּ תָּאלֵי דַּהֲווּ

אתו

רש"י

הַבָּא לִסְמוֹךְ. מִתְּחִילָּה כּוֹתֶל אֵצֶל כּוֹתֶל חֲבֵירוֹ. וְהָא מִי שֶׁהָיָה קָתָנֵי. אַלְמָא כְּבָר הָיָה! וְנָפַל לֹא יִסְמוֹךְ. לֹא יְקָרְבֶנּוּ לְצַד כּוֹתֶל חֲבֵירוֹ. דַּוְושָׁא דְּהָכָא מַעֲלֵי לְהָתָם. מַה שֶּׁדָּשִׁין בָּרֶגֶל בֵּין שְׁנֵי הַכְּתָלִים תָּמִיד מוֹעִיל לִשְׁנֵי הַכְּתָלִים, לְהַקְשׁוֹת קַרְקָעִית יְסוֹדוֹת הַכְּתָלִים וְלֹא יִמּוֹטוּ. אֶלָּא כּוֹתֶל גִּינָּה. מִתּוֹךְ שֶׁאֵין דָּשִׁין אוֹתָהּ מִבִּפְנִים צְרִיכָה דִּישָׁה מִבַּחוּץ. עִיר חֲדָשָׁה. שֶׁעֲדַיִין לֹא נִידוֹשָׁה, אַף כּוֹתֶל חָצֵר צְרִיכָה דַּוְושָׁא. מִלְמַעְלָן. צָרִיךְ לְהַגְבִּיהַּ שִׁיעוּר שֶׁלֹּא יָצִיץ בְּהִשָּׁעֲנוֹ עַל כּוֹתְלוֹ, וְיַשְׁפִּיל רֹאשׁוֹ וְיִרְאֶה דֶּרֶךְ חַלּוֹנוֹת, וְיִרְאֶה בְּבֵית חֲבֵירוֹ. שֶׁלֹּא יַעֲמוֹד. עַל רֹאשׁ עוֹבִי כּוֹתְלוֹ, וְיִרְאֶה. וּמִכְּנֶגְדָּן. צָרִיךְ לְהַרְחִיק כְּדֵי שֶׁלֹּא יַאֲפִיל, וְלָא יָהֵיב תַּנָּא דְּבָרַיְיתָא שִׁיעוּרָא. טַעְמָא שֶׁלֹּא יַאֲפִיל. בְּשֶׁיֵּשׁ חַלּוֹנוֹת, אֲבָל מִשּׁוּם דַּוְושָׁא, כְּשֶׁאֵין שָׁם חַלּוֹנוֹת — לָא, אַלְמָא לָא חָיְישִׁינַן לְדַוְושָׁא! מִן הַצַּד. שֶׁאֵין הַכּוֹתֶל (ג) הָאַחֲרוֹן מְהַלֵּךְ לְאוֹרֶךְ כּוֹתֶל רִאשׁוֹן, אֶלָּא מִן הַצַּד הוּא בָּא, אִם זֶה מִמִּזְרָח לְמַעֲרָב — זֶה בָּא מִצָּפוֹן לְדָרוֹם, וְרֹאשׁ עוֹבְיוֹ כְּנֶגֶד הַחַלּוֹן וּמַאֲפִיל. דְּהָכָא לֵיכָּא לְמֵיחַשׁ לְדַוְושָׁא דְּהַהוּא פּוּרְתָּא. וְכַמָּה. כְּדֵי שֶׁלֹּא יַאֲפִיל, לְתַנָּא דְּבָרַיְיתָא דְּלָא יָהֵיב שִׁיעוּרָא. וַהֲלֹא מֵצִיץ. כֵּיוָן דְּסָמוּךְ הוּא, אע"פ שֶׁהוּא מַגְבִּיהוֹ — יָכוֹל לְהָצִיץ. בְּמַדִּיר אֶת כּוֹתְלוֹ. עוֹשֶׂה רֹאשׁ כּוֹתְלוֹ מִדְרוֹן, וּמַשְׁפִּעוֹ לְצַד הַחַלּוֹנוֹת, עַד שֶׁאֵינוֹ רָאוּי לֹא לַעֲמוֹד עָלָיו וְלֹא לְהִשָּׁעֵן עָלָיו. מִשְׁתֵּי רוּחוֹת. שְׁנֵי כְתָלִים זֶה כְּנֶגֶד זֶה מִשְּׁנֵי צִדֵּי הַחַלּוֹן. אֶת הַכּוֹתֶל מִן הַמַּזְחִילָה ד' אַמּוֹת. מַזְחִילָה הוּא צִינּוֹר גָּדוֹל, כְּעֵין קנעל"א שֶׁלָּנוּ, וּמוּנַּחַת לְאוֹרֶךְ הַכּוֹתֶל עַל הַכּוֹתֶל, וּמֵי הַגַּג זָבִין לְתוֹכָהּ וְהִיא מְקַלַּחְתָּם לָאָרֶץ. וְאִם אוֹרֶךְ כּוֹתְלוֹ מְהַלֵּךְ עַל פְּנֵי חֲצַר חֲבֵירוֹ וּמַזְחֵילָה עָלָיו — צָרִיךְ זֶה לְהַרְחִיק מִמֶּנָּה אִם בָּא לִבְנוֹת כּוֹתֶל בְּגַדָּהּ, אַרְבַּע אַמּוֹת עַל פְּנֵי אָרְכָּהּ כו', כְּדֵי שֶׁיְּהֵא זוֹקֵף שָׁם סוּלָּם בְּשִׁיפּוּעַ לַעֲלוֹת בּוֹ לְתַקֵּן מַזְחֵילָתוֹ, לְנַקּוֹתָהּ מֵעָפָר וּצְרוֹרוֹת הַנּוֹפְלִין בָּהּ וּמְעַכְּבִין קִילּוּחַ הַמַּיִם. בְּמַזְחִילָה מְשׁוּפַּעַת. שֶׁתִּקְרַת הַגַּג מְשׁוּפַּעַת וְיוֹצֵאת לְהַלָּן מִן הַכּוֹתֶל לְתוֹךְ הֶחָצֵר, וְהַמַּזְחֵילָה בְּסוֹף הַתִּקְרָה מְשׁוּכָה לְהַלָּן מִן הַכּוֹתֶל לְתוֹךְ הֶחָצֵר. הִלְכָּךְ, אִי לָאו מִשּׁוּם זְקִיפַת סוּלָּם — לֹא הָיָה צָרִיךְ לְהִתְרַחֵק מֵרָאשֵׁי הַתִּקְרָה. דְּאִי מִשּׁוּם דַּוְושָׁא הָא אָזֵיל וְאָתֵי תּוּתֵיהּ. תַּחַת הַשִּׁיפּוּעַ. **מתני'** מַרְחִיקִין אֶת הַסּוּלָּם מִן הַשּׁוֹבָךְ. אִם יֵשׁ לָזֶה שׁוֹבָךְ בַּחֲצֵירוֹ סָמוּךְ לַכּוֹתֶל שֶׁבֵּין שְׁתֵּי הַחֲצֵירוֹת, וַחֲבֵירוֹ בָּא לְהַעֲמִיד סוּלָּם בַּחֲצֵירוֹ אֵצֶל הַכּוֹתֶל — יַרְחִיקֶנּוּ מִן הַשּׁוֹבָךְ אַרְבַּע אַמּוֹת. כְּדֵי שֶׁלֹּא תִּקְפּוֹץ הַנְּמִיָּיה. מִן הַסּוּלָּם לַשּׁוֹבָךְ, וְתַהֲרוֹג אֶת הַיּוֹנִים. וְהִיא חַיָּה קְטַנָּה ו). **גמ'** לֵימָא מַתְנִי' דְּלָא כְּרַבִּי יוֹסֵי. דִּפְלֵיג בְּסֵיפָא דְּפִירְקִין בְּנוֹטֵעַ אִילָן סָמוּךְ לַבּוֹר. וְטוּבָא מִילֵּי אִיכָּא בְּמַתְנִיתִין דְּוַדַּאי לָאו כְּרַבִּי יוֹסֵי, אֶלָּא לֵימָא אַף זוֹ דְּסוּלָּם וְשׁוֹבָךְ דְּלָא כְּרַבִּי יוֹסֵי. בְּגִירֵי דִּילֵיהּ. בְּחִצִּים הַבָּאִים לוֹ מִיַּד גּוּפוֹ שֶׁל בַּעַל הַבַּיִת מַמָּשׁ. דְּבַהֲדֵי דְּמַנַּח לֵיהּ. בְּעוֹד שֶׁאוֹחֵז בַּסּוּלָּם קָפְצָה. גְּרָמָא בְּנִיזָּקִין אָסוּר. וַאֲפִי' (ד) לְמ"ד (ב"ק דף נה. ק.) דְּלָא דָּאֵין דִּינָא דְּגַרְמֵי, וּפָטוּר מִלְּשַׁלֵּם — אָסוּר לִגְרוֹם, וּכְשֶׁבָּא לְהַעֲמִיד גְּרָמָא לְהַזִּיק — חֲבֵירוֹ מְעַכֵּב(ד). תָּאלֵי. דְּקָלִים קְטַנִּים.

אוּמָּנֵי

תוספות

אלא אמר רבא ה"ק מי שהיה כותלו כו'. הקשה ריב"ס: דלמה ליה למינקט בכי האי גוונא, שהיה לו כותל ברחוק ארבע אמות ונפל? ליתני שלא יסמוך כותלו לכותל חבירו אא"כ הרחיק ארבע אמות! וליכא למימר דדוקא בכי האי גוונא, שהיה רחוק כבר ארבע אמות והרחיק הראשון, קאמר דלא יסמוך — א"כ מאי פריך בסמוך: טעמא שלא יאפיל, אי משום סולם אבל משום דוושא לא? **אבל** משום דוושא לא. וא"ת: ולימא דאיירי בעיר ישנה! ואומר ר"ת: דבית הוי כגינה, לפי שנותנין מטה וכלים אצל הכותל. ועוד י"ל: דבחצר איכא דוושא דרבים, מה שאין כן בבית. ולר"י נראה: דניחא ליה לשנויי בעיר חדשה דומיא דרישא. וכן ההיא ד"מרחיקין את הכותל מן המזחילה", אע"ג דמפסקת בינתים ההיא ד"מרחיקין את הסולם מן השובך".

וכמה אמר רב ייבא כו'. ותימה: דהשתא בעי: וכמה, ובתר הכי פריך: והתנן ארבע אמות! וי"ל: דרב ייבא גופיה בעי וכמה, ולא גמר'. וכענין זה יש ב"אלו מציאות" (ב"מ דף כא. ושם ד"ה וכמה)[ז].

במדיר את כותלו. ולא מצי לשנויי במגביה כותלו ד' אמות, דכיון דקאי מן הצד, ואורך הכותל לרחבו של חלון — יכול לעמוד בסוף הכותל ולשחות ולהציץ.

והא אנן תנן ארבע אמות. דמתני' איירי נמי מן הצד, כיון דלא חייש לדוושא, אלא משום חלונות.

לימא תנן סתמא דלא כרבי יוסי. פר"ח: מדקאמר הכא טפי לימא דלא כרבי יוסי, ולא קאמר אמשניות דלעיל — משמע דכולהו אתי כר"י, והוי כולהו גירי דיליה, דמההיא שעתא משתכחא היזיקא, ולא פליג רבי יוסי אלא באילן. וצ"ל לפי' דמתניתין דלעיל הוי נמי גירי דיליה, דמיד כשסומך הכותל — מונע הדוושא.

כדי שיהא זוקף את הסולם. כשמכר ונתן לו זקיפת הסולם בחצירו איירי, וקמ"ל דבעי ארבע אמות.

והא גרמא הוא. תימה דלא פריך הכי לעיל גבי דוושא.

זאת אומרת גרמא בנזקין אסור. ומעיקרא ס"ד: כי היכי (ה) דמעיקרא פטור — ה"נ דמותר. הכא משמע דגרמא בנזקין דפטור, וכן בפ' "כילד הרגל" (ב"ק דף כו:): זרק כלי מראש הגג והיו תחתיו כרים וכסתות וקדם וסילקן, אפילו הוא — פטור. ובפרק "הפרה" (שם דף מז:): הכניס פירות לחצר בעל הבית שלא ברשות כו'. וקאמר בגמרא דאם אכלה והוזקה — פטור. ונתן סם המות לפני בהמת חבירו דפטור (שם), ושולח ח)בעירו ביד חרש שוטה וקטן (שם נט:), ופורץ גדר בפני בהמת חבירו, וכופף קמת חבירו בפני הדליקה, ועושה מלאכה במי חטאת (שם נה: נו.), וליבה וליבתו הרוח — דפטור בכל הנך, כדאמר בפרק "הכונס" (שם דף נט:), ומבעית חבירו דהוי נמי גרמא, כדאמר בפרק קמא דקדושין (דף כד:) דאיהו הוא דאבעית אנפשיה, וב"כילד הרגל" (ב"ק דף כג:): שיסה בו כלב שיסה בו נחש — פטור. ויש ליתן טעם, מאי שנא כל הני מדינא דגרמי, כגון אחויי אחוי ד"הגוזל בתרא" (שם דף קטז: ושם), ומראה דינר לשולחני ונמצא רע, ונפרלה אומר לו גדור, ודן את הדין דחייב לר"מ אפילו לא נשא ונתן בידו, והשורף שטרותיו של חבירו, ומוכר שטר חוב לחבירו וחזר ומחלו? וחילק רבינו יצחק לשון אח': דדינא דגרמי חייב — היינו שעושה הוא עצמו היזק לממון חבירו. ועוד חילק דדינא דגרמי דחייב — היינו (ו) משעת מעשה שבא ההיזק. ועל הכל קשה טיהר את הטמא, ובעה"ב עצמו עירבן עם פירותיו, ואמאי חייב? דהוא עצמו אינו עושה היזק בממון חבירו, וגם באותה שעה שמטהר אינו בא ההיזק! ונראה לרי"צב"א: דדינא דגרמי הוי מטעם קנס, כדמוכח בירושלמי. ולכך, כל היזק המצוי ורגיל לבא — קנסו חכמים. וטעם דקנסו — שלא יהא כל אחד הולך ומזיק לחבירו בעין. והיינו טעמא דמאן דמחייב בהיזק שאינו ניכר. ואפשר דבשוגג נמי קניס רבי מאיר, כי היכי דקניס במטמא ומדמע אחד שוגג ואחד מזיד.

אתו

רבינו גרשום

והא מי שהיה כותלו סמוך לכותל חבירו קתני. כלומר להוסיף על המשנה ולתרצה את יכול אבל לחסר מינה אין אתה יכול: אלא אמר רבא הכי קאמר מי שהיה וכו'. מאי טעמא דוושא דהכא מהני התם כלומר מש"ה צריכה להרחיק ד' אמות כדי שיהיו דשין שם בני אדם העוברין בינתים ומעלי ההיא דישה לכותל שניהם שמתחזקין היסודות: אמר רב לא שנו. דצריך להרחיק ד' אמות אלא מכותל גינה שאין דשין שם בני אדם בשדה מחמת הירקות אבל בכותל חצר שנידושה היא מעיקרא שאינה צריכה חזוק הבא לסמוך סומך בפחות מד': בעיר ישנה. שנידושה היא מכמה שנים אם בא לסמוך סומך אבל בעיר חדשה אינו סומך בלא הרחקה מפני שצריכה דישה לחזק: מלמעלן. אם בנה כותלו מן הצד סמוך לחלון חבירו צריך להגביה הכותל ד' אמות יותר מן החלון: כדי שלא יעמוד על כותלו וישוח ויציץ בחלון. ואם מנמיכו כותלו מן החלון צריך להנמיכו מן החלון ד' אמות: שלא יעמוד. על כותלו זקוף ויראה בחלון ואם בנהו כנגדו צריך להרחיק ד' אמות שלא יאפיל חלונו: הכא במאי עסקינן. דקתני שלא יאפיל בבונהו מן הצד של חלון ולא כנגדו וצריך להרחיק מן החלון כדי שלא יאפיל דהשתא לא מצי למידק דטעמא שלא יאפיל אבל משום דוושא לא דהא איכא מקום דוושא טובא אלא דוק מיניה הכי ומכנגדן כלומר אם בונהו מכנגד חלון צריך להרחיק ד' אמות כדי שלא יאפיל אבל אם בונהו מן הצד סמוך לחלון אין צריך להרחיק כולי האי ד' אמות דבבציר מהכי סגי דמן צדי חלון לא מאפיל עליה כולי האי כמו מכנגדו ובבציר הרחקה סגי: וכמה. שיעור צריך להרחיק כותלו מן צד החלון: כמלוא רוחב חלון. צריך להרחיק ולא מאפיל. ומקשי' הואיל ולא מרחיק כותלו משום היזק אורה אלא מלא רוחב החלון לא מגבי ליה נמי משום היזק ראיה למעלה מן החלון אלא כמלא רוחב חלון הא מציץ א"כ יכול להציץ בחלון: במדיר את כותלו. שעושהו חד למעלה כמדרון מכאן ומכאן שאינו יכול לעמוד עליו ולהציץ: והא אנן תנן ד' אמות צריך להרחיק. והיכי מצית למימר כמלא רוחב חלון. לא קשיא כאן מרוח אחת כלומר אם בנה כותל מרוח אחת מצידו אחד של חלון אינו צריך להרחיק אלא מלא רוחב חלון והא דקתני מתני' ד' אמות מן הצד נמי איירי וכגון שבנה ב' כתלים מב' רוחות של חלון הואיל ואלו ב' כתלים מאפילים הרבה מש"ה צריך להרחיק כל כותל וכותל מצד החלון ד' אמות. תנן ואת הכותל מרחיקין מן המזחילה של חבירו ד' אמות. שאם יש לחבירו חזקה בחצירו שהמזחילה של גגו שופכת בחצרו הואיל ויש לו כך חזקה יכול לזקוף סולם בחצר חבירו בעל כורחו ולעלות על גגו ואם רצה זה לבנות כותל סמוך לגגו צריך להרחיק ד' אמות ממנו כדי זקיפת סולם: הכא במאי עסקינן. דקתני זקיפת סולם ולאו משום דוושא צריך למיתני: דמצי אזלי תותי. ההיא שפוע היוצא חוץ לכותל ומצי למעביד דוושא אבל משום זקיפת סולם צריך להרחיק מן המזחילה ואילך ד' אמות: **פיסקא** כדי שלא תקפוץ הנמייה. חיה בסולם של שובך ואוכלת בשובך מיירי. דאם יש לזה שובך בצד כותלו של חבירו ולאידך סולם בצד כותלו מרחיקו מן השובך: מודה ר' יוסי בגיריה. כלומר הכא שאני דהוי כעין שזורק אדם חץ ומזיק באותה זריקה דחייב בו כך אם מזיק אדם לחבירו בידים ודאי חייב אע"ג דעביד בתוך שלו ומ"ט הוי הכא גיריה דזימנין דבהדי דמנח ליה לסולם בתוך ד' אמות שלו זימנין דיתבא ההיא נמייה בחור וקפצה לשובך והיינו גיריה דידיה והכא מודה דמרחיקין ד' אמות: והא גרמא היא. דבאותה גרמא שלו קפצה ולאו דעביד איהו בידיה דלא קא מאכיל היונים לנמייה והא דמודה ר' יוסי דבגיריה דידיה חייב היכא דעביד איהו בידים כדגרסי' בב"מ דף קי"ז דהנהו בי תרי דהוו דיירי חד בעליונה וחד בתחתונה כו' דהכא מודה ר' יוסי בגיריה דידיה משום דעילאי משי ידיה ונפל על תתאה דעבד בידים אבל הכא הא גרמא היא ואמאי חייב: תאלי. אילנות בחורים:

אתו

מסורת הש"ס

א) לעיל כ: ב) נ"א וכמה טפח: ג) נ"א במהדרד. רש"ל: ד) [לעיל יז: לקמן כה:] ה) [לקמן כו: ב"מ קיז.] ו) [בחולין נב: כתב רש"י ד"ה שכות מרטריכ"ו בלע"ז] ז) [וע"ע תוס' יומא עו. ד"ה הכי חתמה ותוס' פסחים לג. ד"ה תתן ותוס' בכורות כט. סד"ה היכי אזיל ותוס' נזיר ל. ד"ה פשיטא] ח) נ"ל הכבעירה.

הגהות הב"ח

(א) גמ' אמר רב ייבא: (ב) שם דמנח ליה ויתבא בחור) תא"מ ונ"ב רש"י ל"ג ליה: (ג) רש"י ד"ה מן הצד שאין הכותל האחר מהלך: (ד) ד"ה גרמא וכו' ואפי' למאן דלא דאין וכו' מעכב עליו הס"ד: (ה) תוס' ד"ה זאת וכו' כי היכי דפטור ה"נ כצ"ל ותיבת דמעיקרא נמחק: (ו) בא"ד היינו דבשעת מעשה בא ההיזק:

א) לקמן נ:: ב) [עס]. ג) כ"ק פג.: ד) [עס עג:]. ה) [עס פג.] ו) גיטין נח:. ז) לקמן מא.: ח) לקמן ס.: ט) כס"י אין זה: י) נ"ל לאחיק חזקה בנכסי אשתו וכו' כרא"ש: ז) ס"א ההא קשה ריקא לאסוף דריכא קתני ל' ריס מן השוב פורכין ובפועה קתני אפי' מאה מיל לא יפרוס.

סא א ב ג ד מיי' פי"א מהל' שכנים הל' ד ה סמג עשין פב טוש"ע ח"מ סי' קנה סעיף לו לט:

סב ה מיי' שם הל' ה טוש"ע שם סעיף לט:

סג ו ז מיי' פ"ו מהל' גזילה הל' ע סמג עשין עג טוש"ע ח"מ סי' קנה סעיף כד:

סד ח ט י כ ל מיי' שם הל' ח סמג שם טוש"ע ח"מ סי' שע:

סה מ נ טוש"ע ח"מ סי' קנה סעיף כד:

אָתוּ אוּמָּנֵי וְיָתְבֵי תּוּתַיְיהוּ, וְאָתוּ עוֹרְבֵי אָכְלֵי דָּמָא וְסָלְקִי (א) אַבֵּי תָאלֵי וּמַפְסְדִי תַּמְרֵי. אֲמַר לְהוּ רַב יוֹסֵף: אאַפִּיקוּ לִי קוּרְקוּר מֵהָכָא. א"ל אַבַּיֵי: וְהָא גְּרָמָא הוּא! א"ל: הָכִי אָמַר רַב טוֹבִי בַּר מַתָּנָה, זֹאת אוֹמֶרֶת: גְּרָמָא בְּנִיזָּקִין אָסוּר. וְהָא אַחֲזִיק [לְהוּ]! א)הָא אָמַר רַב נַחְמָן אָמַר רַבָּה בַּר אֲבוּהּ: באֵין חֲזָקָה לִנְזָקִין. וְלָאו אִיתְּמַר עֲלַהּ, ב)רַב מָרִי אֲמַר: גבְּקוּטְרָא, וְרַב זְבִיד אֲמַר: דבְּבֵית הַכִּסֵּא? אֲמַר לֵיהּ: הָנֵי הלְדִידִי, דַּאֲנִינָא דַּעֲתַאי, כִּי קוּטְרָא וּבֵית הַכִּסֵּא דָּמוּ לִי.§

מתני' ג)ומַרְחִיקִין אֶת הַשּׁוֹבָךְ מִן הָעִיר חֲמִשִּׁים אַמָּה. וְלֹא יַעֲשֶׂה אָדָם שׁוֹבָךְ בְּתוֹךְ שֶׁלּוֹ, אֶלָּא אִם כֵּן יֵשׁ לוֹ חֲמִשִּׁים אַמָּה לְכָל רוּחַ; רַבִּי יְהוּדָה אוֹמֵר: בֵּית אַרְבַּעַת כּוֹרִין מְלֹא שֶׁגֶר הַיּוֹנָה. זוְאִם לְקָחוֹ, אֲפִילּוּ בֵּית רוֹבַע — הֲרֵי הוּא בְּחֶזְקָתוֹ.§

גמ' חֲמִשִּׁים אַמָּה וְתוּ לָא? וּרְמִינְהִי: ד)חאֵין פּוֹרְסִין נִשְׁבִּין לְיוֹנִים, אֶלָּא אִם כֵּן הָיָה רָחוֹק מִן הַיִּשּׁוּב שְׁלֹשִׁים רִיס! ה)אֲמַר אַבַּיֵי: מֵישָׁט שָׁיְיטִי טוּבָא, וּכְרֵסַיְיהוּ בַּחֲמִשִּׁים אַמְּתָא מַלְיָא. וּמֵישָׁט שְׁלֹשִׁים רִיס וְתוּ לָא? וְהָתַנְיָא: טוּבַיִּשּׁוּב — אֲפִילּוּ מֵאָה מִיל לֹא יִפְרוֹס! רַב יוֹסֵף אָמַר: יבְּיִשּׁוּב כְּרָמִים, (ב) רָבָא אָמַר: כבְּיִשּׁוּב שׁוֹבָכִין. וְתֵיפּוֹק לֵיהּ מִשּׁוּם שׁוֹבָכִין גּוּפַיְיהוּ! לאִיבָּעֵית אֵימָא: דִּידֵיהּ; וְאִיבָּעֵית אֵימָא: דְּגוֹי; וְאִיבָּעֵית אֵימָא: דְּהֶפְקֵר.§ "רַבִּי יְהוּדָה אוֹמֵר: בֵּית אַרְבַּעַת כּוֹרִין" וכו'.§ אֲמַר רַב פַּפָּא, וְאִיתֵּימָא רַב זְבִיד, מזֹאת אוֹמֶרֶת: ו)טוֹעֲנִין לְלוֹקֵחַ וְטוֹעֲנִין לְיוֹרֵשׁ. יוֹרֵשׁ תְּנֵינָא: ז)הַבָּא מִשּׁוּם יְרוּשָּׁה — אֵינוֹ צָרִיךְ טַעֲנָה! לוֹקֵחַ אִיצְטְרִיכָא לֵיהּ. לוֹקֵחַ נַמִי תְּנֵינָא: ח)לָקַח חָצֵר וּבָהּ זִיזִין וּגְזוּזְטְרָאוֹת — הֲרֵי (ג) זֶה בְּחֶזְקָתָהּ! צְרִיכָא, דְּאִי אַשְׁמְעִינַן הָתָם גַּבֵּי רְשׁוּת הָרַבִּים — (ד) דְּאֵימוֹר כּוֹנֵס לְתוֹךְ שֶׁלּוֹ הוּא, אִי נַמִי אַחוּלֵי אַחוּל בְּנֵי רְשׁוּת הָרַבִּים גַּבֵּיהּ, אֲבָל הָכָא לָא; וְאִי אַשְׁמְעִינַן הָכָא, דְּכֵיוָן דְּיָחִיד הוּא — אֵימָא פַּיּוֹסֵיהּ פַּיְּיסֵיהּ, (ה) אִי נַמִי אַחוּלֵי אַחֵיל גַּבֵּיהּ, אֲבָל רַבִּים — מַאן פַּיֵּים וּמַאן שָׁבֵיק — אֵימָא לָא, נצְרִיכָא.§ "הֲרֵי הוּא בְּחֶזְקָתוֹ".§ וְהָא אָמַר רַב נַחְמָן אָמַר רַבָּה בַּר אֲבוּהּ: אֵין חֲזָקָה לִנְזָקִין! רַב מָרִי אֲמַר: בְּקוּטְרָא, רַב זְבִיד אֲמַר: בְּבֵית הַכִּסֵּא.§

מתני'

רשב"ם

אוּמָּנֵי = מַקִּיזֵי דָּם. קוּרְקוּר. עוֹרְבִים, שֶׁדּוֹמִים בְּצַעֲקָתָן כְּקוֹרִין "קוּרְקוּר". **אַפִּיקוּ** לִי. כְּלוֹמַר, אַל יַקִּיזוּ לִי עוֹד כָּאן, שֶׁעַל כֵּן הָעוֹרְבִים בָּאִין. **בְּקוּטְרָא** = עָשָׁן. **בְּבֵית הַכִּסֵּא.** שֶׁעַל גַּבֵּי קַרְקַע, וְנִרְאֶה לָעֵינַיִם. שֶׁכָּךְ הָיוּ בָּתֵּי כִסְאוֹת שֶׁלָּהֶן. **מתני'** מַרְחִיקִין הַשּׁוֹבָךְ מִן הָעִיר. שֶׁהַיּוֹנִים מַפְסִידִין זֵרְעוֹנֵי גִּנּוֹת. **אא"כ** יֵשׁ לוֹ כו'. שֶׁלֹּא יַפְסִידוּ הַיּוֹנִים בִּשְׂדֵה חֲבֵירוֹ. **מְלֹא** שֶׁגֶר הַיּוֹנָה. מְרוּצַת פְּרִיחָתָהּ פַּעַם אַחַת. **וְאִם** לְקָחוֹ. כְּמוֹ שֶׁהוּא, עִם הַקַּרְקַע, אֲפִילּוּ אֵין לוֹ כָּל סְבִיבָיו אֶלָּא בֵּית רוֹבַע הַקַּב — הֲרֵי הוּא בְּחֶזְקָתוֹ, שֶׁהֲרֵי הוּחְזַק בּוֹ הָרִאשׁוֹן כֵּן. **גמ'** אֵין פּוֹרְסִין נִשְׁבִּין. שֶׁלֹּא יִלָּכְדוּ בָּהֶם יוֹנֵי הַיִּשּׁוּב. שְׁלֹשִׁים רִיס. אַרְבַּע מִילִין. וּכְרֵסַיְיהוּ בַּחֲמִשִּׁים אַמָּה קָמַלְיָיא. בְּמַה שֶּׁהֵן מְלַקְּטִין בְּתוֹךְ חֲמִשִּׁים אַמָּה מִתְמַלֵּא כְּרֵיסָן, וְאֵין מַפְסִידִים בַּזְּרָעִים מִכָּאן וּלְהַלָּן. **לֹא** יִפְרוֹס. נְשָׁבִין. בְּיִשּׁוּב כְּרָמִים. שֶׁפּוֹרְחִין מִכֶּרֶם לְכֶרֶם, וְשָׁטִים הַרְבֵּה. בְּיִשּׁוּב שׁוֹבָכִין. שֶׁמְּדַלֵּג מִשּׁוֹבָךְ לְשׁוֹבָךְ. וְתֵיפּוֹק לֵיהּ מִשּׁוּם שׁוֹבָכִין גּוּפַיְיהוּ. מַאי מֵאָה מִיל דְּקָאָמַר, דְּמַשְׁמַע דְּבִשְׁבִיל יוֹנֵי הָעִיר מִתְרַחֵק, שֶׁבָּאִין כָּאן דֶּרֶךְ שׁוֹבָכִין? בְּלָאו יוֹנֵי הָעִיר נַמִי לֹא יִפְרוֹס, שֶׁהֲרֵי לוֹכֵד יוֹנֵי שׁוֹבָכוֹת שֶׁל אֲחֵרִים! טוֹעֲנִין לְיוֹרֵשׁ וְטוֹעֲנִין לְלוֹקֵחַ. בֵּית דִּין פּוֹתְחִים פֶּה וְטַעֲנָה לְיוֹרֵשׁ וּלְלוֹקֵחַ, שֶׁעִרְעֵר אָדָם עֲלֵיהֶן וְיֵשׁ לוֹ עֵדִים שֶׁהָיְתָה שֶׁלּוֹ אוֹ שֶׁל אֲבוֹתָיו, וְזֶה אוֹמֵר: יְרַשְׁתִּיו מֵאַבָּא, אוֹ: לְקַחְתִּיו מִפְּלוֹנִי שֶׁהוּחְזַק בּוֹ יָמִים רַבִּים. וְהֵבִיא עֵדִים שֶׁהוּחְזַק בּוֹ אָבִיו אוֹ הַמּוֹכֵר לוֹ שָׁלֹשׁ שָׁנִים, אע"פ שֶׁלֹּא טָעַן: וְהֵן לְקָחוּהָ מִמְּךָ אוֹ מֵאֲבוֹתֶיךָ — טוֹעֲנִין לוֹ בֵּית דִּין, (ו) וּפוֹתְחִים לוֹ פֶּה. וְאִילּוּ לְמִי שֶׁלֹּא יְרָשָׁהּ וְלֹא לְקָחָהּ מֵאַחֵר, כְּשֶׁאָמַר לוֹ הַמְעוֹרֵר: מָה אַתָּה עוֹשֶׂה בְּתוֹךְ שֶׁלִּי? וְהוּא אוֹמֵר: הֶחֱזַקְתִּי בָּהּ ג' שָׁנִים וְלֹא אָמְרוּ לִי דָּבָר — תְּנָא בְּמַתְנִי' (לקמן דף מא.) דְּאֵין לוֹ חֲזָקָה. וּמַתְנִי' דְּקָתָנֵי: הֲרֵי הוּא בְּחֶזְקָתוֹ — אַשְׁמוֹעִינַן דְּהֵיכָא דִּלְקָחָהּ מֵאַחֵר, וּבָאוּ וְעִרְעֲרוּ עָלָיו — אֵין צָרִיךְ לְהַרְחִיק. אַלְמָא: טָעֲנִינַן לֵיהּ *בִּשְׁבִילוֹ שֶׁאוֹתוֹ שֶׁלְּקָחָהּ מִמֶּנּוּ ט) (וְנֵימָא) נִתְפַּיֵּיס עִם סְבִיבָיו בְּמָעוֹת עַד שֶׁנְּאוֹתוּ. **אֵינוֹ** צָרִיךְ טַעֲנָה. אֵינוֹ צָרִיךְ לוֹמַר: אַתָּה מָכַרְתָּ לְאָבִי, אֶלָּא: רָאִיתִי לְאָבִי שֶׁהֶחֱזִיק בָּהּ וְלֹא עִרְעֵר אָדָם עָלָיו. **לָקַח** חָצֵר וּבָהּ זִיזִין. (ז) בְּמַתְנִי' בְּ"חֶזְקַת הַבָּתִּים" תְּנַן: אֵין מוֹלִיאִין זִיזִין וּגְזוּזְטְרָאוֹת לִרְשׁוּת הָרַבִּים. אָדָם הַבּוֹנֶה בַּיִת לֹא יוֹצִיא רָאשֵׁי קוֹרוֹת תִּקְרָתוֹ לִרה"ר, אֲבָל אִם רוֹצֶה — כּוֹנֵס בִּנְיָנוֹ לְתוֹךְ שֶׁלּוֹ, וּבוֹנֶה וּמוֹצִיא רָאשֵׁי קוֹרוֹתָיו לַחוּץ. וְאִם לָקַח חָצֵר וּבָהּ זִיזִין וּגְזוּזְטְרָאוֹת יוֹצְאִים לִרה"ר — הֲרֵי הוּא בְּחֶזְקָתָהּ, שֶׁבֵּית דִּין טוֹעֲנִין לוֹ שֶׁהָרִאשׁוֹן כָּנַס לְתוֹךְ שֶׁלּוֹ, אוֹ נִתְפַּיֵּיס עִם הָרַבִּים. (ח) **אֵימָא** לְתוֹךְ שֶׁלּוֹ הוּא כּוֹנֵס. שֶׁאִילְמָלֵא כֵּן הָיוּ הָרַבִּים מְעַכְּבִין עָלָיו, וְלֹא הָיָה יָכוֹל לַעֲשׂוֹת בִּזְרוֹעַ. אֲבָל כְּנֶגֶד הַיָּחִיד — אֵימָא בִּזְרוֹעַ עָשָׂה, שֶׁהָיָה חָזָק מִמֶּנּוּ. **מַאן** פַּיֵּים. מִי הָיָה רַשַּׁאי לְקַבֵּל מָעוֹת? **וּמַאן** שָׁבֵיק. מִי הוּא שֶׁבְּיָדוֹ לִמְחוֹל וְלִסְלוֹחַ?

מתני'

תוספות

אתו אומני ויתבי תותייהו. בקרקע שלהן היו יושבין, ולא בקרקע של רב יוסף, מדפריך בתר הכי: והא גרמא הוא. **והא** אחזיקו להו. פי' ר"י ב"ר מרדכי: כיון שלא בא להחזיק בקרקע של חבירו ולומר שלו הוא, אלא לתשמיש בעלמא, שנהנה ממנה — מועלת חזקה שלא בטענה. דמסתמא לא היו אומרים שמכר להם רב יוסף תשמיש זה. והוו כי הנהו דלעיל (דף ו.) דאחזוק להורדי, דמועלת חזקה שלא בטענה, דמדלא מיחה ג' שנים מחל לו. ואין נראה, דאם לא הקנה לו, כי החזיק להורדי אמאי החזיק לכשורי? אלא על כרחך התם שטוען שהקנה לו, ולהכי אחזיק לכשורי, דאין אדם עושה קנין למחצה(ט). **אין** חזקה לנזקין. אומר ר"ת: דאפי' הקנה(י) יכול לחזור בו, דקנין בטעות הוא, דסבור היה שיכול לקבל, ועכשיו אין יכול לקבל. ואין נראה, דמדקאמר אין חזקה לנזקין, איכא למידק: הא ראיה — יש, כדדייקינן ב"חזקת הבתים" (לקמן דף מט:) גבי הא דתנן: ולא י)(לאשה חזקה בנכסי בעלה).

בקוטרא. נראה לר"י: דדוקא בקוטרא דכבשן, שהוא גדול ומזיק ביותר אין חזקה, כדאמר ב"מרובה" (ב"ק דף פב:): אין עושין כבשונות בירושלים, מ"ט — משום קוטרא. ודוקא נמי בית הכסא שלהן, (כ) שהיה למעלה מן הקרקע והיה מסריח ביותר. אבל בשלנו, שהוא מכוסה — יש חזקה. **לדידי** דאנינא דעתאי. פי': שהיה איסטניס, כדאמרינן ב"ערבי פסחים" (פסחים דף קיג: ושם): שלשה חייהם אינן חיים: הרחמנים והרתחנים ואניני הדעת. אמר רב יוסף: וכולהו איתנהו בי.

בקוטרא ובית הכסא דמו. והא דקאמר "אפיקו קורקור מהכא", משמע דמשום עורבים היה אומר — ודאי, אם לא היו עורבים היה סובל, אף על גב דאנינא דעתיה. אי נמי, העורבים היו אוכלים הדם, ופורחים ומקנחים בפירות.

מרחיקין השובך מן העיר חמשים אמה. מפני התבואה הנשטחת בגגות העיר כדי לייבש. אבל לתבואה שבשדות — ליכא למיחש בקרוב לעיר, לפי שהשדות רחוקין מן העיר אלף אמה, כדתנן (ערכין דף לג:): אין עושין מגרש שדה ולא שדה מגרש. **ולא** יעשה שובך תוך שלו. ברחוק מן העיר בין השדות. ואצטריך למיתני תרוייהו, דאי תנא רישא להרחיק מן העיר — התם דוקא מרחיק, מפני שתבואות העיר מגולות, הן בחצר הן בגג. אבל תבואה הנזרעת בשדה ומכוסה — אין צריך להרחיק. ואי תנא סיפא — משום דבשדות שכיחא תבואה, אבל בעיר דלא שכיח כולי האי — אימא לא. **בית** ארבעת כורין כמלא שגר היונה. ור' יהודה ורבנן לא פליגי בשגר היונה כמה הוי, דמודו רבנן דבית ארבעה כורין הוי שגר היונה. אלא רבנן סברי: כיון דבחמשים אמה מליא כריסייהו, כדאמרינן בגמ' — תו לא מזקי טפי. ור' יהודה סבר: דכמלא שגר מזקי. **אלא** אם כן הרחיק שלשים ריס. היינו ד' מיל, דהמיל ז' ריס ומחצה. ופעמים שהגמרא נותן שיעור בריסין, ופעמים במילין, ופעמים בפרסה. **והתניא** ביישוב אפילו מאה מיל(ל). תימה: דמאי ס"ד דהוי פי' "וביישוב"? אי קרי העיר יישוב, א"כ אפילו מאה מיל לאו דוקא, כמו שמשמע, אלא אפילו אלף מיל או יותר — א"כ בשום מקום לא יפרוס, אפילו במדבר ורחוק לאין סוף מן העיר! ואפילו אם נאמר דמאה מיל דוקא — מכל מקום היאך יפרש את הברייתא? כ) דהכי תניא בתוספתא ד"מרובה": אין פורסין נשבין ליונים אא"כ הרחיק מן היישוב שלשים ריס. בד"א — במדבר, אבל ביישוב — אפי' מאה מיל לא יפרוס, כיון דעיר קרי "יישוב"! ואי ס"ד דהכי פירושו: בד"א — במדבר, פי': שאין זרעים. אבל ביישוב, פי': ביישוב זרעים — אפילו מאה מיל לא יפרוס, אם כן מאי קשיא ליה? ואומר ריב"א: דודאי ס"ד דאיירי ביישוב זרעים, ולהכי פריך: ומישט שייטי שלשים ריס ותו לא, אפי' ביישוב זרעים? והא מוכח דביישוב זרעים שייטי טובא, ואין זה אלא משום אכילה — אלמא דלא מליא כריסייהו בחמשים אמה! ומשני: דלא איירי ביישוב זרעים, אלא ביישוב שובכין ויישוב כרמים, וקרי מדבר היכא דליכא שובכים וכרמים. **יורש** תנינא. וס"ד המקשה דמתני' אשמעינן ביורש וה"ה בלוקח. ומיהו רב זביד דנקט נמי יורש — אמתני' דלקמן סמיך, אבל מתני' דהכא לא שמעינן מינה יורש, מדאיצטריך מתני' דלקמן. **וצריכי**. וא"ת: ביורש נמי ליתני תרתי! וי"ל: דאשמעינן בלוקח, וה"ה ביורש. **אחולי** אחילו גביה. פי': ז' טובי העיר במעמד אנשי העיר, שהרשות בידם, כדאמר בפרק בתרא דמגילה (דף כו.). וכיון דליכא לכל חד בדרך אלא פורתא — מחלי טפי מיחיד.

חוץ

רבינו גרשום

אתו אומני. שהיו מקיזין והיו רגילין אנשים הרוצין להקיז באין שם להקיז ואגב שמתקבצין שם עורבים מחמת הדם עולין ומפסידין פירות האילנות: אפיקו לי קורקור מהכא. כלומר הוציאו עורבים הללו שקורין קורקור ומנקרין באילנות כלומר הוציאו האומנין משם ויכלו העורבין ולא יפסידו האילנות: והא אחזיקו להו. האומנין שרגילין להקיז תחת האילנות: לא איתמר עלה. היכא אמרי' אין חזקה לניזקין בקוטרא שאם היה חלון פתוחה לביתו של חבירו והיה עולה עשן ומזיק לו ודאי אין חזקה לניזקין דהאי נזקא גופא מחמת העשן הוא וכן הכי נמי אם היה בית הכסא סמוך לביתו של חבירו והסרחון הולך אין חזקה משום אנינות גופא אבל שאר היזיקות אם החזיק יש חזקה: דמו לי. האי דמא: **פיסקא** מן העיר נ' אמה. כדי שלא יאכלו היונים זרעוני גינת העיר וכן נמי צריך להעמיד בתוך שלו א) שהיא לו נ' אמה לכל רוח שלא יאכלו זרעוני חבירו: כמלא שגר היונה. כמו שיכולה היונה לפרוח בבת אחת: ואם לקחו. שנים מאחד והגיע לחלק אחד מקום השובך ולשני מקום הפנוי ואפי' אין בין שובך לגינת זה אלא הרחקת בית רובע הרי הוא השובך בחזקתו [שלא] להרחיק יותר הואיל ומתחלה היה השובך והגינה של א': נשבין. מצודות: אלא אם כן הרחיק הנשבין מן הישוב ל' ריס. דאתו יוני הישוב ונכנסין לתוך הנשבין ותפים להו אלמא דשייטי טפי מן נ' אמה והיכי קתני דבנ' אמה סגי: רב יוסף אמר. הא דתני בישוב אפי' ק' מיל לא יפרום ג) אפי' יהא ק' מיל לעיר משום דקאזלן יוני של עיר מכרם לכרם ואתו התם. והא דקתני אא"כ הרחיק ל' ריס דליכא ישוב כרמים בינתים. ורבא אמר בישוב שובכין דבהני ק' מיל איכא ישוב שובכין מש"ה לא יפרום דהא אזלי יוני העיר משובך לשובך כעין שעושין היונים שאלו באין בשביל אלו: ותיפוק ליה משום יוני שובכין גופן. הללו אין פורסין: איבעית אימא. דהנהו שובכין שלהן ומש"ה לא יפרום משום יוני העיר שבאין דרך שובכין הללו אבל משום יוני שובכין ליכא למיחש הואיל ושלו הן: ואם לקחו. שקנה (חצר מן) השובך אפי' בית רובע הרי הוא בחזקתו ולא צריך נ' אמה לכל רוח: זאת אומרת. דקתני ה"ז בחזקתו דטוענין ליורש וללוקח שאם אמר אדם לחבירו שדה זו גזלת ממני ג) והלה אמר אני קניתיה ממך ושני חזקה אכלתיה אין זו ראיה אבל אם אמר אבא הניחה לי כלומר יורש הבא מחמת ירושה א"צ טענה שכשאמר אבא הניחה לי א"צ לו יותר לטעון שלא יכול הלה לחזור ולומר לו הראני שטר מכירה שקנאה אביך ודאי א"צ לטעון לו יותר דב"ד טוענין בשבילו ויאמרו שמא אבד שטרו ואי אתה יכול להוציאה מתחת ידו וכן ה"נ לוקח שאם אמר ד) לקחתיה וכבר החזקתי בה שני חזקה אם טוען הלה ואמר הראה השטר א"צ ללוקח לטעון יותר שב"ד טוענין בשבילו שמא אבד השטר הכי נמי בשחלקו הרי הוא בחזקתו וא"צ להרחיק יותר: הא נמי תנינא. באידך פירקי חזקת הבתים אין מוציאין זיזין וגזוזטראות הרי הן בחזקתן: משום דכנס לתוך שלו וכו' אחולי אחילו גבה בני רה"ר. אבל גבי שובך לא אמרי' הרי הוא בחזקתו קמ"ל דאפ"ה הרי הוא בחזקתו: (דלא) הרי הוא בחזקתו שדה שלו ולא אמרי' דלא מחיל ליה שיכנוס יונים לתוך שדהו ולאו אמרי' הכי. אבל גבי שובך לא אמרי' הרי הוא בחזקתו משום דיחיד לא מחיל אבל רבים פיים ומאן שביק. דלא מצי למיחל ממון לכל העולם צריכא דאפי' הכא אמרי' הרי הוא בחזקתו: אין חזקה לניזקין. הא מזיק בחזקתו הא מזיק לשדות דאחרים: רב מרי אמר. היכא אמרי' אין חזקה בקוטרא כדפרישית לעיל אבל בשאר מילי יש חזקה:

פיסקא

הגהות הב"ח

(א) גמ' וסלקי ויתבי באחלי ומפסדי: (ב) שם רבה אמר ביישוב שובכין: (ג) שם הרי זו בחזקתה: (ד) שם גבי רה"ר אימור כונס לתוך שלו הוא אי נמי אחולי אחלי בני רה"ר גביה אבל יחיד אימא לא: (ה) שם פיוסיה פייסיה בממוניה אי נמי: (ו) רשב"ם ד"ה טוענין וכו' ב"ד טוען ופותחין: (ז) ד"ה לקח חצר ובה זיזין בח"ה דף ס. תנן כצ"ל ותיבת במתני' נמחק: (ח) ד"ה אימור לתוך שלו: (ט) תוס' ד"ה והא וכו' דאין אדם עושה קנין למחצה והכא נמי מיירי שהיו טוענים שהקנה להם והוי חזקה שיש עמה טענה הס"ד: (י) ד"ה אין וכו' דאפילו הקנה לו אפ"ה יכול לחזור: (כ) ד"ה בקוטרא וכו' בית הכסא שלהן שהיו למעלה: (ל) ד"ה והתניא ביישוב אפי' מאה מיל לא יפרוס תימה וכו' א"כ אם אפי' מאה מיל:

א) נ"ל אם יש לו נ' אמה וכו'. ב) נ"ל לא יפרום מיירי דבהכי מיל איכא ישוב כרמים משום דקאזלן וכו'. ג) נראה דצ"ל והלה אומר שלא קנית ממני ולכך קנייה אכלתיה וכו'. ד) נראה דצ"ל לוקח שאם אמר לקחתיה מפלוני ובכבר החזקתי בה.

מתני' אניִפּוּל הַנִּמְצָא בְּתוֹךְ חֲמִשִּׁים אַמָּה — הֲרֵי הוּא שֶׁל בַּעַל הַשּׁוֹבָךְ, חוּץ מֵחֲמִשִּׁים אַמָּה — הֲרֵי הוּא שֶׁל מוֹצְאוֹ; נִמְצָא בֵּין שְׁנֵי שׁוֹבָכוֹת, קָרוֹב לָזֶה — שֶׁלּוֹ, קָרוֹב לָזֶה — שֶׁלּוֹ, מֶחֱצָה עַל מֶחֱצָה — שְׁנֵיהֶם יַחֲלוֹקוּ.§ גמ' א)אָמַר רַבִּי חֲנִינָא: ברוֹב וְקָרוֹב — הוֹלְכִין אַחַר הָרוֹב; וְאע"ג דְּרוּבָּא דְּאוֹרַיְיתָא וְקוּרְבָא דְּאוֹרַיְיתָא, אֲפִילּוּ הָכִי רוּבָּא עָדִיף. מְתִיב רַבִּי זֵירָא: °"וְהָיָה הָעִיר הַקְּרוֹבָה אֶל הֶחָלָל" — וְאע"ג דְּאִיכָּא אַחֲרִיתִי דִּנְפִישָׁא מִינַּהּ! גבִּדְלֵיכָּא. וְלֵיזִיל בָּתַר רוּבָּא דְּעָלְמָא! דבְּיוֹשֶׁבֶת בֵּין הֶהָרִים. תְּנַן: נִיפּוּל הַנִּמְצָא בְּתוֹךְ חֲמִשִּׁים אַמָּה — הֲרֵי הוּא שֶׁל בַּעַל הַשּׁוֹבָךְ; וְאַף עַל גַּב דְּאִיכָּא אַחֲרִינָא דִּנְפִישׁ מִינֵּיהּ! הבִּדְלֵיכָּא. אִי הָכִי, אֵימָא סֵיפָא: חוּץ מֵחֲמִשִּׁים אַמָּה — הֲרֵי הוּא שֶׁל מוֹצְאוֹ; וְאִי (א) דְּלֵיכָּא, וַדַּאי מֵהַהוּא נָפַל! הָכָא בְּמַאי עָסְקִינַן — ובִּמְדַדֶּה, ב)דְּאָמַר רַב עוּקְבָא בַּר חָמָא: זכָּל הַמְדַדֶּה — אֵין מְדַדֶּה יוֹתֵר מִנ'. (ב) בָּעֵי ר' יִרְמְיָה: רַגְלוֹ אַחַת בְּתוֹךְ נ' אַמָּה וְרַגְלוֹ אַחַת חוּץ מֵחֲמִשִּׁים אַמָּה, מַהוּ? (ג) וְעַל דָּא אַפְּקוּהוּ לְרַבִּי יִרְמְיָה מִבֵּי מִדְרָשָׁא. תָּא שְׁמַע: נִמְצָא בֵּין שְׁנֵי שׁוֹבָכוֹת, קָרוֹב לָזֶה — שֶׁלּוֹ, וְקָרוֹב לָזֶה — שֶׁלּוֹ; וְאַף עַל גַּב דְּחַד מִינַּיְיהוּ נָפֵישׁ מֵחַבְרֵיהּ! חהָכָא בְּמַאי עָסְקִינַן — שֶׁשְּׁנֵיהֶן שָׁוִין. וְלֵיזִיל בָּתַר רוּבָּא דְּעָלְמָא! טהָכָא בְּמַאי עָסְקִינַן — בִּשְׁבִיל

דברים כא

מתני' נִיפּוּל = גּוֹזָל. הַנִּמְצָא בְּתוֹךְ חֲמִשִּׁים אַמָּה. שֶׁל שׁוֹבָךְ. נִמְצָא בֵּין שְׁנֵי שׁוֹבָכוֹת. בְּתוֹךְ חֲמִשִּׁים לִשְׁנֵיהֶן. גמ' רוֹב וְקָרוֹב. אִם בָּא דָּבָר לְפָנֵינוּ, וְיֵשׁ בּוֹ לְהַלֵּךְ אַחַר הָרוֹב וְהוּא כָּךְ, וְאִם תֵּלֵךְ בּוֹ אַחַר הַקָּרוֹב אֵינוֹ כָּךְ — הָלַךְ בּוֹ אַחַר הָרוֹב. וְאע"ג דְּתַרְוַיְיהוּ דְּאוֹרַיְיתָא. רוּבָּא דְּאוֹרַיְיתָא — דִּכְתִיב: "אַחֲרֵי רַבִּים לְהַטּוֹת" (שמות כג), וְקוּרְבָא דְּאוֹרַיְיתָא — דִּכְתִיב: "וְהָיָה הָעִיר הַקְּרוֹבָה" וגו'. וְאע"ג דְּאִיכָּא אַחֲרִיתִי. שֶׁרְחוֹקָה מִמֶּנּוּ, שֶׁגְּדוֹלָה מִמֶּנָּה בְּרוֹב עַם. בִּדְלֵיכָּא. רְחוֹקָה מִזּוֹ שֶׁגְּדוֹלָה מִמֶּנָּה, אֶלָּא כּוּלָּן שָׁווֹת. בֵּין הֶהָרִים. שֶׁאֵין דֶּרֶךְ רוֹצְחִים לָבֹא מִמְּקוֹמוֹ' אֲחֵרִים לְכָאן. לָאו אע"ג דְּאִיכָּא אַחֲרִינָא. חוּץ לַחֲמִשִּׁים אַמָּה, דִּנְפִישִׁי מֵהַאי? אֵימָא סֵיפָא כו'. הוּא הַדִּין דַּהֲוָה מָצֵי לְמִיפְרַךְ נַמִי: לֵיזִיל בָּתַר רוּבָּא דְּעָלְמָא, אֶלָּא דְּאִית לֵיהּ פִּירְכָא דַּעֲדִיפָא(ד). הָכָא בְּמַאי עָסְקִינַן. כּוּלָּהּ מַתְנִיתִין מִתָּרְצָא בִּמְדַדֶּה — בְּגוֹזָל שֶׁאֵינוֹ יָכוֹל לָעוּף אֶלָּא בְּדִידּוּי מְעַט מְעַט. הִלְכָּךְ, תּוֹךְ חֲמִשִּׁים אַמָּה — שֶׁל בַּעַל הַשּׁוֹבָךְ, וְאַף עַל גַּב דְּאִיכָּא אַחֲרִינֵי(ה) דִּנְפִישׁ, דְּכָל הַמְדַדֶּה אֵינוֹ מְדַדֶּה יוֹתֵר מֵחֲמִשִּׁים, וְחוּץ שֶׁל חֲמִשִּׁים — שֶׁל מוֹצְאוֹ, דְּכֵיוָן דְּאֵין מְדַדֶּה יוֹתֵר מֵחֲמִשִּׁים, וְזֶה יָצָא חוּץ לְנ' — נְפַק לֵיהּ מִתּוֹרַת מְדַדֶּה, וְקָם לֵיהּ בְּתוֹרַת מַפְרִיחַ, וְאִיכָּא לְמֵיזַל בֵּיהּ בָּתַר רוּבָּא דְּעָלְמָא. וְעַל דָּא אַפְּקוּהוּ. שֶׁהָיָה מַטְרִיחַ עֲלֵיהֶם. וְלֵיזִיל בָּתַר רוּבָּא דְּעָלְמָא. וְלֶיהֱוֵי שֶׁל מוֹצְאוֹ! דְּקָא ס"ד דְּנִמְצָא בֵּין שְׁתֵּי שׁוֹבָכוֹת אַחוּץ לַחֲמִשִּׁים אַמָּה נַמִי קָאֵי, דְּנָפֵיק לֵיהּ מִתּוֹרַת מְדַדֶּה.

תורה אור

חוץ לחמשים אמה הרי הוא של מוצאו. דאזלינן בתר רובא דעלמא. ואפי' למ"ד אין הולכין בממון אחר הרוב — היינו במקום (ו) שהוא מוחזק, אבל הכא, דליכא חזקה דממונא — אזלינן בתר רובא. וא"ת: בפרק "אלו מציאות" (ב"מ דף כד. ושם) לרבנן דרבי שמעון בן אלעזר דאמרי: אפילו בעיר שרובה גויים חייב להכריז בדבר שיש בו סימן, ואמאי לא אזלינן בתר רובא, כיון דליכא חזקה דממונא? וי"ל: דתקנת חכמים היא, כדי לקיים מצות השבת אבידה, כיון דיכול להתברר ע"י הכרזה אם היא של ישראל. וישראל נמי לא מייאש, דמסיק אדעתיה דלמא משכח ישראל ויכריז. רוב וקרוב הלך אחר הרוב. וא"ת: מאי קא משמע לן? מתניתא היא (כתובות דף טו.): ט' חנויות, כולן מוכרות בשר שחוטה ואחת מוכרת בשר נבילה [וכו'], ובנמצא הלך אחר הרוב. משמע אפי' נמצא קרוב לחנות המוכרת נבילה! ותירץ ר"י בר מרדכי: דאי ממתניתא הוה אמינא: כגון דאין דלתות מדינה נעולות, דאיכא תרי רובי — קמ"ל רבי חנינא דאפילו דלתות מדינה נעולות, דליכא אלא חד רובא. ור' זירא דפריך ליה בסמוך, אע"ג דר' זירא נמי אית ליה לקמן אפילו דלתות מדינה נעולות — היינו בתר דשני ליה, דקיבלה מרבי חנינא. ואין נראה לריצב"א, דאם כן, מאי פריך ליה מקרא? תיקשי ליה אמתניתא דתשע חנויות! ואפילו תוקמה כשאין דלתות מדינה נעולות — הא טעמא דבעינן תרי רובי אינו אלא מדרבנן, משום גזירה, כדאמר בסוף פ"ק דכתובות (דף טו.)! ונראה לר"י: דאי ממתני' ה"א בנמצא באמצע. ועוד נראה לר"י: דרבי חנינא אתא לאשמועינן דאפילו בקורבא דמוכח — דאזלינן בתר רובא. וכן משמע בסמוך גבי חבית שצפה בנהר, דבעי למימר דרב, דאמר: כנגד עיר שרובה ישראל מותרת — לית ליה דרבי חנינא. והיכי מתוקמא? דהא משמע דמותרת אפילו נמצאת סמוך לבית נכרי, וזהו מטעם דאזיל בתר רוב העיר ישראל, וכרבי חנינא! אלא ודאי לגבי קורבא דביתו של נכרי — הוי קורבא דלא מוכח, כיון שדרים רוב ישראל באותה העיר, ורב אזיל בתר רובא היכא דהקורבא לא מוכחא, ודלא כרבי חנינא. אבל אותה עיר כנגד האי דקירא — הוי קורבא דמוכח, ולכך אזיל בתרה. וכל ההלכה תתיישב כמו שאפרש. ולהכי לא מייתי בכוליה גמרא דרבי חנינא אלא לקמן גבי אגבא דאישתכח בפרדיסא של ערלה, דקורבא דמוכח הוא, שנמצא בפרדיסא דערלה גופיה. ובפ"ק דבילה (דף י:) מייתי ליה נמי גבי הא דתנן: זימן שחורים ומצא לבנים לבנים ומצא שחורים אסורים, ומפרש בגמ': כגון שזימן שחורים ולבנים ומצא שחורים במקום לבנים ולבנים במקום שחורים; מהו דתימא: אינהו נינהו, ואיתהפוכי איתהפיך — קמ"ל דהנך אזול לעלמא והני אחריני נינהו, ומעלמא אתו. ומסיק עלה: לימא מסייע ליה לרבי חנינא כו'. והתם קורבא דמוכח הוא, דהא שחורים ולבנים היו שם, ומוכח דאינהו נינהו. מתיב רבי זירא והיה העיר הקרובה כו' מאי לאו דאיכא אחריתי דנפישא מינה. אמתניתא דתשע חנויות נמי הוה ליה לאקשויי. אלא אמתניתא איכא לשנויי: בדליכא, ותו ליכא לאקשויי: ניזיל בתר רובא דעלמא, דלגבי רובא דעלמא הוה קורבת זו העיר קורבא דמוכח. אבל לר' חנינא, דאפילו בקורבא דמוכח הלך אחר הרוב — פריך שפיר, דכי נמי משנינן: בדליכא — אכתי תיקשי: ניזל בתר רובא דעלמא[ג]. בדליכא. תימה: דהכא משמע דטעמא דהעיר הקרובה מביאה עגלה ערופה, משום דמתוך הקורבא מוכח שמשם בא ההורג. ובסוטה (דף מה:) תניא: מנין שאם נמצא סמוך לעיר שאין בה בית דין, שמניחין אותה שאין בה בית דין והולכין לעיר אחרת שיש בה בית דין. ואמאי? והלא מתוך הקורבא נראה שמאותה שאין בה בית דין היה! ביושבת בין ההרים. ואם תאמר: ואמאי איצטריך קרא בסוף פרק "מרובה" (ב"ק דף פב:) דאין ירושלים מביאה עגלה ערופה? ואע"ג דכתיב (תהלים קכה) "ירושלים הרים סביב לה" מ"מ כל ישראל היו באין לרגל, וגם בשאר ימות השנה להביא נדרים ונדבות, וגם אומות העולם היו באין שם בסחורה, שקרויה "רוכלת עמים"! וי"ל: שהיו מקומות שלא היו רגילים לבא, רק בני ירושלים. אי נמי, בימי חזקיה, שכל ישראל היו שם ולא היו באין לסחורה. ניפול הנמצא בתוך חמשים אמה כו'. ואמתניתא דתשע חנויות לא מצי למיפרך, דהכא הוי קורבא דמוכח דהוי משובך זה, דהוי תוך חמשים, והנך דנפישי הוי חוץ לנ'. ולעיל אמרינן דכרסייהו בחמשים אמה מליין. בדליכא. לא מצי למיפרך דניזל בתר רובא דעלמא, דמיירי דליכא שום שובך תוך שלשים ריס, ואמר לעיל דלא שייטי אלא שלשים ריס, ותו לא. ואי דליכא אחריני ודאי מההוא נפל. דבשלמא אי איכא דנפיש מיניה — אתי שפיר דהוי של מוצאו, כגון דהוי ההוא דנפיש של הפקר או של גויים, אבל השתא, דליכא — ודאי מההוא נפל. ולא מצי לשנויי: כגון דליכא דנפיש, אלא שוין — דמכל מקום אמאי הוי של מוצאו, כיון שקרוב לזה? דהכי משמע דחוץ לחמשים אמה הרי הוא של מוצאו אע"פ שקרוב לזה מזה, דהא תנן: מצאו בין שני שובכין, קרוב לזה — שלו, דכשהן שוין אזלינן בתר קרוב. ודאי מההוא נפל. ואם תאמר: ודלמא מעוברי דרכים נפל, כדאמרינן לקמן גבי זיקי דחמרא דאישתכחן בי קופאי! וי"ל: דהיכא דודאי נפל ולא ידעינן ממי — תלינן בעוברי דרכים. אבל הכא דמצי למימר דמשובך בא — לית לן למיתלי ולאחזוקי בנפילה, דבני אדם נזהרין שלא יפלו מהם היונים. ועל דא אפקוהו לרבי ירמיה מבי מדרשא. אין לפרש משום דבעי מילתא דלא שכיחא כלל, דהיכי איתרמי דרגלו אחת תוך חמשים ורגלו אחת חוץ לחמשים בצמצום — דהא אשכחנא דמתניתין נמי בכהאי גוונא איירי, דקתני: מחצה על מחצה — יחלוקו. ונראה לרבינו תם: דמשום הכי אפקוהו, משום דמדדה אינו מדדה כלל יותר מחמשים אמה אפילו רגלו אחת, דכל מדות חכמים כן הוא. מצאו בין שני שובכין. ואע"ג דחד מינייהו נפיש. אומר ר"י: דהך פירכא הוי מצי למיפרך אמתניתא דתשע חנויות, דהאי קורבא דלא מוכח הוא, דאי הוי תוך חמשים לזה — הוי נמי תוך חמשים לזה, ואי הוי חוץ חמשים לזה — הוי נמי חוץ חמשים לזה, אפילו הכי אזלינן בתר קורבא. ומיהו, מלינן למימר דעיקר לא פריך אלא משום דבעי למיפרך: וניזל בתר רובא דעלמא. אבל קשיא לרשב"א: דהיכי מצי למימר אף על גב דחד מינייהו נפיש? הא קתני: מחצה על מחצה — שניהם יחלוקו, ואי חד מינייהו נפיש — ניזל בתר רובא! ואומר ר"י: דהוי מצי למימר "וליטעמיך". וליזיל בתר רובא דעלמא. הוי מצי לשנויי דאין כי אם שני שובכין תוך ל' ריס. אלא בעי לשנויי דומיא דרישא, דיש שובכין הרבה. אע"ג דהשתא דמוקי לה בשביל של כרמים לא הוי דומיא דרישא, דהא רישא לא מיירי בשביל של כרמים — בהא לא קפיד במאי דלא הוי דומיא דרישא, כיון שאין מזכיר במשנתינו שביל של כרמים בשום מקום. ועוד הוה מצי לשנויי קרוב לזה שלו — תוך חמשים אמה, ובמדדה. דכל

סו א מיי' פט"ו מהל' אבידה הל' יח סמג עשין עד טוש"ע ח"מ סי' רס סעיף ח:
סז ב מיי' שם ופ"ט מהל' רוצח הלכה ז סמג שם טוש"ע שם:
סח ג מיי' פ"ט מהל' רוצח הלכה ו:
סט ד הרמב"ם השמיט זה וע"ש בכ"מ:
ע ה ו ז ח ט מיי' פט"ו מהל' אבידה הל' יח סמג עשין עג טוש"ע ח"מ סי' רס סעיף ח:

רבינו גרשום

פיסקא ניפול הנמצא. גוזל שנפל מן השובך: חוץ מנ' אמה ה"ז של מוצאו. דאיכא למימר מעוברי דרכים נפל: אמר ר' חנינא. להיכא דאיכא רובא ואיכא קרוב הולכין אחר הרוב אע"ג דרובא דאורייתא דכתיב אחרי רבים להטות וקרוב דאורייתא דכתיב והיה העיר הקרובה אל החלל א) דאי איכא שובך ויש בו רוב הולכין אחריו דמיניה נפל: ואע"ג דאיכא. עיר רחוקה מינה דנפישי מינה דאיכא רובא דאינשי אלמא בתר קרוב אזלינן. ומשני בדליכא נפיש מינייהו מש"ה אזלינן בתר קרוב אבל היכא דהוי רוב וקרוב אזלינן בתר הרוב: וליזל בתר רובא דעלמא. דאיכא למימר דקטליה עוברין ושבין: ביושבת בין ההרים. דלא קא עברי ואזלי אינשי להתם וליכא למימר לזיל בתר רובא דעלמא הואיל דליכא אינשי מש"ה אזלינן בתר קרוב אבל בעלמא לא אזלי' בתר קרוב: הכא במאי עסקינן. דהוי של מוצאו: במדדה. שאין יכול לברוח אלא מדדה עצמו מעט מעט: דאמר רב עוקבא כל המדדה אינו מדדה יותר מנ' אמה. והואיל דהאי נמצא חוץ מנ' אמה ודאי מעלמא נפל ומש"ה הרי הוא של מוצאו: רגלו אחת בתוך נ' אמה ורגלו אחת חוץ מנ'. מי אזלינן בתר שובך או בתר רובא דעלמא: ועל דא אפקוהו לר' ירמי' מבי מדרשא. משום דמטריד להו בשאלות שאין בהן ממש:

א) נראה דל"ל ואם איכא שובך אחר רחוק מזה ויש בו הרבה יותר מזה הולכין אחריו וכו'.

א) ביצה י: ב) [שם יא.]: ג) [ועי' תוס' נדה יח. ד"ה הלך]:

הגהות הב"ח

(א) גמ' ואי בדליכא ודאי: (ב) שם יותר מנ' אמה בעי ר': (ג) שם על דא אפקוהו לר' ירמיה. נ"ב עי' בפ' גט פשוט סוף דף קס"ה דעל ידי מעשה עיילוהו לר' ירמיה: (ד) רש"י ד"ה אימא וכו' דעדיפא מינה הס"ד: (ה) ד"ה הכא במאי וכו' ואע"ג דאיכא אחריני חוץ לחמשים אמה דנפיש: (ו) תום' ד"ה חוץ וכו' היינו במקום שהאחר מוחזק:

א) נדה יז: ב) [שם], ג) כתובות טו: ד) צ"ל מדלה. יעב"ץ: ה) [ערך קף ע"ז ע"ש שכתב בריש גמ' דף אין עומדין (לא.) רב מרדכי וכו'].

בשביל של כרמים, דאם איתא דמעלמא אתי, כיון דמידדי לא מצי אתי, דכל דמידדי והדר חזי ליה לקיניה — מידדי, ואי לא — לא מידדי. אמר אביי, אף אנן נמי תנינא: א)אדם שנמצא בפרוזדור — ספיקו טמא, שחזקתו מן המקור; ואע"ג דאיכא עלייה דמקרבא! א"ל רבא: רוב ומצוי קא אמרת? רוב ומצוי ליכא למאן דאמר, דתני ר' חייא: ב)בדם הנמצא בפרוזדור — חייבין עליו על ביאת מקדש, ושורפין עליו את התרומה. (א) ואמר רבא, ש"מ מדרבי חייא תלת: שמע מינה רוב וקרוב — הלך אחר הרוב; ושמע מינה רובא דאורייתא; וש"מ איתא לדר' זירא, ג)דאמר רבי זירא: אע"פ שדלתות מדינה נעולות. דהא אשה דכי דלתות מדינה נעולות דמיא, ואפי' הכי קא אזלינן בתר רובא. והא רבא הוא דקאמר: רוב ומצוי ליכא למ"ד! הדר ביה רבא מההיא. איתמר: חבית שצפה בנהר — אמר רב: ג נמצאת כנגד עיר שרובה ישראל — מותר, כנגד עיר שרובה גוים — אסירא; ושמואל אמר: אפי' נמצאת כנגד עיר שרובה ישראל — אסירא, אימור (ב) מהאי דקרא אתאי. לימא, בדרבי חנינא קא מיפלגי, דמר אית ליה דרבי חנינא, ומר לית ליה דרבי חנינא? לא, דכולי עלמא אית להו דר' חנינא, והכא בהא קמיפלגי, דמ"ס: אם איתא (ג) דמהאי דקרא אתאי, ד עקולי ופשורי הוה מטבעי לה; ומר סבר: חריפא דנהרא נקט ואתאי. ה ההוא חצבא דחמרא דאישתכח בפרדיסא דערלה, שריא רבינא. לימא, משום דסבר לה (ד) דרבי חנינא? ו שאני התם, דאי מיגניב מינה — אצנועי בגויה לא מצנעי. והני מילי חמרא, אבל עינבי מצנעי. ז הנהו זיקי דחמרא דאשתכחן בי קופאי, שרנהו רבא. לימא, לא סבר לה לדרבי חנינא? ח שאני התם, דרובא דשפוכאי

רש"י

בשביל של כרמים. דע"י כרמים ד) נדדה חוץ לחמשים. (ה) ומיהו, בתר רובא דעלמא ליכא למיזל, דכל המדדה וחזי לקיניה כשמחזיר ראשו – מדדה, אי לא – לא מדדה. והאי, אי מעלמא אתא – לא מצי חזי לקיניה, דכרמים מפסיקין לפניו. אף אנן נמי תנינא. כר' חנינא, דרוב וקרוב הלך אחר הרוב. נמצא בפרוזדור. נמשל דם לאשה בין כותלי רחם מבחוץ, הקרוי בית החיצון. ספיקו טמא. ספק זה (ו) טומאה ודאית, מדקתני שחזקתו מן המקור. ומה ספיקא יש כאן? רישא דמתניתין במסכת נדה: משל משלו באשה; החדר והפרוזדור והעלייה. דם החדר טמא, והוא המקור. ומפרש בגמרא: החדר מבפנים בעובי גופה לצד אחוריה, והפרוזדור מבחוץ לצד פניה, והעלייה בנויה על גבי שניהם, ודם העלייה טהור, ולול פתוח מעלייה לפרוזדור. וקתני: נמצא בפרוזדור – חזקתו מן המקור זב, ויצא אל החוץ, הואיל ורוב דמים מצויים בו. ולא אמר מן העלייה נטף דרך הלול, ואע"ג דעלייה קרוב לפרוזדור, שעל גבו. רוב ומצוי. (ז) דמיו רבים יותר משל עלייה, ועוד שהן תדירין לזוב משם, ודמי העלייה אין תדירין לצאת – בהא ליכא מאן דפליג על רבי חנינא. חייבין עליו על ביאת מקדש. דלא מספקינן לה כמביא חולין לעזרה, דודאי דם נדה הוא. ושורפין עליו תרומה. ולא אמרי' ספק הוא, ותולין, לא אוכלין ולא שורפין. שמע מינה. מדאחזיק ליה כדם נדה ודאי, תלת. איתא לדר' זירא. דאמר גבי תשע חנויות, בשילהי פ"ק דכתובות: ובנמצא הלך אחר הרוב, ומותר. דאע"פ שדלתות מדינה נעולות, דליכא אלא חד רובא להכשירה – רוב העיר, שתשע חנויות שבה מוכרות בשר שחוטה, ואחת מוכרת נבלה. דאיכא מילתא דבעינן ביה (ח) תרתי רובי, כדאמרי' התם: כגון דלתות מדינות פתוחות, ורוב טבחים סביבות המדינה ישראל, דאיכא למיזל בתר תרי רובי להכשירה – רוב העיר ורוב הבאין מחוצה לה. דהא אשה כדלתות המדינה נעולות (ט). כלומר, דליכא למימר בה תרתי רובי אלא חד רובא, שרוב דמים מן המקור, וקא אזלי בה בתר רובא להביא קרבן לעזרה, ולשרוף תרומה, דמידי דאסור לעשותו מספק הוא. והא רבא הוא דאמר. לעיל: רוב ומצוי ליכא למאן דאמר, ולא תסייעין לר' חנינא מהא. והכא מסייע ליה מינה, דקאמר: ש"מ תלת! חבית. של יין. (י) מההיא דקרא. שם מחוז הוא על נהר פרת, כדאמר בקדושין (דף עא.) לענין יוחסין, ובגיטין. ואין ישראל מצויין שם, והוא למעלה מפרת, ויכולה חבית לבוא משם אללנו. רב לית ליה דרבי חנינא. ואזיל בתר קורבא, ושמואל אזל בתר רובא, דאית ליה לדרבי חנינא. עקולי ופשורי הוו טבעי ליה. הרבה מקומות יש משם ועד כאן, שהמים מתעקלין ומתגלגלין כגלגל במקום אחד, מחמת כיפי סלעים ערוכים הבאים אל תוך הנהר, והמים מכסין עליהם, והספינות מתגלגלות שם וטובעות. ופשורי. הפשרות שלגים הנקוים אצל הנהר, והוו וקיימי. ואם תבא החבית שם – תעמוד, שאין הנהר מוליכה. חריפותא דנהרא נקט ואתאי. שמא מתחלה נפלה באמצעית הנהר, במקום חוזקו, ומרוצת המים הביאתה, ולא הניחתה לנטות ימין ושמאל. בפרדיסא דערלה. בכרם של ערלה. שרי רבינא. ולא חש שמא מכרם זה גנב היין זה. (כ) אי גניב מיניה אצנועי בגויה לא מצנעי. אין דרך גנבים להצניע היין במקום שגנבוהו משם, משום דמתיירא שמא ימלאהו דורך הענבים. זיקי = נודות. בי קופאי. טמונים בין גפנים שבכרם, והיא של ישראל. לימא לא סבר לה לדרבי חנינא. לילך אחר הרוב, אלא אחר הקרוב. וכאן ישראל מצויים יותר מגוים, ולא אזלינן בתר רובא דעלמא.

תוספות

דכל דמידדי אי הדר חזי לקיניה מידדי. לא היה צריך למאי דקאמר "אי הדר חזי לקיניה מידדי", כיון דשובכין דעלמא יותר מחמשים מן הכרמים — [אז] ליכא למיחש לרובא דעלמא, דכל המדדה אינו מדדה יותר מחמשים. אבל הנך שני שובכין, שהכרמים בתוך חמשים אמה שלהם — אתי שפיר, דקרוב לזה שלו אפילו נמצא חוץ לחמשים אמה, דלא נפק מתורת מדדה, דע"י כרמים מידדי יותר מחמשים. אלא איירי דאפילו אם יהו שובכין דעלמא בין הכרמים. ועוד: מדנקט שביל — משמע שאלו ב' השובכין בתוך השביל, והניפול כמו כן נמצא בתוך השביל, דליכא למיחש שהן משובכין דעלמא אפי' אינם רחוקים כלל, כיון דלא מצי חזי לקיניה, אבל מאלו השובכין הוא, דאין דבר מפסיק בינו לבין השובך. **אמר** אביי אף אנן נמי תנינא דם הנמצא בפרוזדור טמא כו'. בנמצא בגג פרוזדור מן הלול ולפנים איירי, כדמוכח בפרק "כל היד" (נדה דף יז: ושם ד"ה מן), וסוגיא דהתם מפרש במקומה. **ואף** על גב דאיכא עלייה דמקרבא. וקרוב דמוכח הוא, דקרוב לעלייה הוא, ומן החדר אינו יכול לבא אא"כ שחתה ביותר, כמו (ל) שפירש במסכת נדה (שם). **דתני** רבי חייא. אי גרסינן "תני" — אתי שפיר, אבל אי גרסינן "דתני" — תימה: היכי מייתי מהכא דרוב ומצוי הוא? דלמא לאו משום דרוב ומצוי קאמר רבי חייא דשורפין עליו את התרומה, אלא משום דרוב וקרוב הלך אחר הרוב כרבי חנינא! (מ) וי"ל: דאפילו גרסי' "דתני" — לא מדברי רבא הוא, אלא גמרא הוא דמייתי לה. דשפיר הוה מוכח אביי ממתני' דנדה דרוב וקרוב הלך אחר הרוב. דאף על גב דקתני "ספיקו טמא" — על כרחך לאו ספיקא הוא, מדתני רבי חייא דחייבין עליו על ביאת מקדש ושורפין עליו תרומה. (הג"ה) ומהר"ם אומר: דרבא מייתי לה, דרוב ומצוי הוא, דאי אינו מצוי — א"כ מאי קמ"ל רבי חנינא, כיון דשמעינן לה מדתני רבי חייא? אבל ממתני' דנדה לא היה יכול להוכיח, דאפילו אם אינו רוב ומצוי — הוצרך רבי חנינא לאשמועינן דלא נימא "ספיקו טמא" הוה ספק ממש. ולמאי דהדר ביה רבא, וקאמר דלא הוי רוב ומצוי — אילטריך רבי חנינא לאשמועינן, דאי מדתני רבי חייא ה"א דרוב ומצוי הוא, קמ"ל ר' חנינא דלאו רוב ומצוי הוא (ע"כ הג"ה). **ושמע** מינה איתא לדר' זירא. נראה לריצב"א: דאע"ג דטעמא דבעינן תרי רובי הוי משום דגזרינן רוב סיעה אטו רוב העיר, מ"מ איצטריך ליה למימר גבי חנות דלא בעינן תרי רובי. דאע"ג דליכא למימר הכי — מ"מ איכא למיגזר שמא יקח מן הקבוע, אי לאו דאיכא רובא דעלמא. וגבי אשה נמי, אי גזרינן בעלמא — הוה לן להחמיר שלא לשרוף מן הלול ולפנים אטו מן הלול ולחוץ. (נ) ונראה לו דהלכה כרבי חנינא. *הג"ה וש"מ רובא דאורייתא. חשיב ליה רובא דליתיה קמן, דברובא דאיתיה קמן לא צריך למידק ש"מ, דקרא כתיב "אחרי רבים להטות", כדפריך פרק קמא דחולין (דף יא. ושם) גבי הא דבעי: מנ"ל הא דאמרינן זיל בתר רובא? ופריך: מנ"ל — דכתיב "אחרי רבים להטות". **אימור** (ס) מהאי דקרא אתאי. ולאו דוקא נמצאת כנגד עיר שרובה ישראל אסר שמואל, אלא אפי' עיר שכולה ישראל איכא למיחש להכי. **לימא** משום דסבר לה כר' חנינא. וליכא למימר דשריא משום דספק ערלה בחוצה לארץ מותרת, דהא אי לית ליה כרבי חנינא, אלא רוב וקרוב אזלינן בתר קרוב — א"כ הויא ודאי ערלה. **ואצנועי** בגויה. ואם תאמר: מכ"מ יהא אסור, דרובא דעלמא גויים נינהו, והוי יין נסך! וי"ל: דרוב גנבי ישראל, כדאמר בפרק בתרא דע"ז (דף ע.). **בי** קופאי. פי' בערוך: ה)מקום, כדאמרי' (סוטה דף מו:): רב מרדכי אלויה לרב שימי בר אשי לבי קופאי, ובכהאי גוונא היה, דהוה קורבא דמוכח. **לימא** רבא לית ליה דר' חנינא. פי': והא רבא אית ליה לעיל דר' חנינא! מרחיקין

רבינו גרשום

הכא במאי עסקינן דיחלוקו כגון דהוו הנהו שובכין במאה אמה ואותן ק' אמה הן שביל שבין ב' כרמים ונמצא באמצע הדרך שבין הללו שובכין דהשתא ליכא למיחש לרובא דעלמא וכיון דמדדה הוא ודאי מהנך שובכין נפל דאי מעלמא לא מצי אתי דקי"ל כל המדדה והדר חזי לקיניה מדדה ואי לא לא מדדי והאי הואיל דהוי שביל של כרמים מפסיק ומחיצות של שביל מפסקי לא הוי חזי לקיניה ולא מצי אתי מעלמא משום הכי יחלוקו דמהנהו שובכין נפלי: אמר אביי אף אנן נמי תנינא. דרוב וקרוב אזלי בתר רוב דתנן דם הנמצא בפרוזדור ספיקו טמא שחזקתו מן המקור בא שממנו רוב הדמים באין והמקור הוא פנימי מכולן והחדר סמוך למקור והפרוזדור הוא החיצוני ועליה בנויה על גבי שניהם על גבי החדר והפרוזדור ולול פתוח בין עליה ופרוזדור נמצא הדם מן הלול ולפנים ספיקו טמא מן הלול ולחוץ ספיקו טהור ודם הבא מן החדר טמא דמן המקור בא ומן העליה טהור מן הפרוזדור ספיקו טמא שחזקתו מן המקור בא ואע"ג דאיכא עלייה דדמה טהורה דמקרבא לגבי פרוזדור ממקור אזלינן בתר רוב דרוב דמים מן המקור באין: אמר רבא. מהא לא תסייע דרוב ומצוי שאני דדם המקור רוב הוא לכולהו ומצוי בו דם תדיר דתני ר' חייא דם הנמצא בפרוזדור חייבין עליו חטאת על ביאת מקדש אם נכנסה במקדש ואם נגעה בתרומה שורפין עליו את התרומה דלא אמרי' הכא כבשאר ספק טומאו' אם נגעו בתרומ' דתולין לא אוכלין ולא שורפין אבל הכא ודאי שורפין דספיקו ודאי טמא הוא דדם מקור רוב ומצוי ודאי מן המקור בא וטמא: ש"מ מדקתני ושורפין עליו את התרומה מכלל דרובא דאורייתא דרוב דמים מן המקור וש"מ מדקאזיל בתר רוב אע"ג דאתרע רוב במקצת דהא יש דם עלייה דטהור הוא דמקרבא ואפ"ה אזיל בתר רוב ש"מ דאיתא לדר' זירא דאמר בפ"ק דכתובות בהנהו דאמר ר' יוסי מעשה בתינוקת שירדה מן המעיין ונאנסה ואמר ר"ע אם רוב העיר משיאין לכהונה ורוב סיעה של כשרין עוברין לשם הרי זו תינשא לכהונה. ור' זירא אמר אע"ג שדלתות מדינה נעולות דאיתרע לה רובא דליכא אלא חד רובא דלא קא עוברת סיעה של כשרין לשם אפ"ה משיאין לכהונה הואיל דרוב העיר משיאין לכהונה דהא אשה כיון דלית בה אלא חד רובא דרוב דמים מן המקור בא [illegible] בדלתות מדינה נעולות דמיין ואפ"ה אזלינן בתר רובא: והא רבא הוא דאמר רוב ומצוי [illegible]

היכא דליכא אלא רוב וקרוב לא אזלינן בתר רוב והיכי אמר הכא ש"מ מדר' חייא דאזלינן בתר רוב דמשמע בכל דוכתא אזלי בתר רוב. הדר ביה רבא מההיא דלעיל דלא בעינן רוב ומצוי אלא דאזלינן בתר כל רוב: חבית של יין שצפה בנהר. ואין ידוע אם יין נכרים הוא אם יין ישראל: אימור מההיא דקירא באה כלומר מאותו עבר הקרייה של מעלה ממנה באה דרובא עיירות דנכרים נינהו. דשמואל אית ליה דר' חנינא ורב לית ליה דר' חנינא: עקולי. כעין שרגילין המים לעקול ולעקול סביב ובאותן מים שהתהום תחתיהן והולכין ומעגלין עד שמטביעין מה שצף על גבן. וכן הני פשורי לאותו מקום שהמים רפין ועומדין שאם היתה חבית זו צפה לשם הואיל שהמים רפין ואינן חריפין היתה נטבעת שם ומש"ה ליכא למיחש דמההיא דקירא אתאי: ושמואל אמר ודאי אסור דאיכא למיחש דמההיא דקירא אתאי והאי דלא טבעי עקולי ופשורי דחריפות' דנהרא שכבר לקחה החבית המרוץ קודם שהגיעה לעקולי ופשורי ונקט ואתאי בשבולת המים והלכך אסירא. לימא. דמש"ה שריא דקסבר כר' חנינא דאמר רוב וקרוב הולכין אחר הרוב והכא האי פרדס דערלה מיעוט הוא לגבי שאר פרדסים דלא הוי ערלה וקרוב דבגויה אשתכח: שאני התם. דמש"ה שריא דליכא למימר דמיניה הוא ההיא הצבא דאי מיגנב מיניה לעולם בגויה לא הוי מצנעי אינשי ומש"ה איכא למימר דמשאר פרדסים דהיתרא הוי ולא משום דס"ל כר' חנינא: והני מילי. דשרי. חמרא. משום דלא מצנעי אינשי חמרא בפרדיסא דגנובי מיניה: אבל ענבי מצנעי. ואסורין: זקי. נודות יין: בי קופאי. בין הגפנים: שרינהו רבא. משום דהנהו גפנים דישראל נינהו: לימא. מש"ה שרינהו דלית ליה לר' חנינא דאע"ג דרוב שאר גפנים דגוים נינהו אזיל בתר קרוב הואיל דמשתכחן ביני גופני דישראל דהוה קרוב

להנהו זיקי וקסבר רוב וקרוב הלך אחר קרוב: שאני התם. לעולם רבא סבר לה כר' חנינא דודאי אזלינן בתר רוב והתם נמי איכא רוב ישראל ומש"ה שרינהו דרובא דשפוכאי [illegible] ישראל נינהו ועל ידן הולך הכל ואישתכח נמי בי גופני ישראל ודאי ישראל אצנעינהו ומותרין והני

עין משפט נר מצוה

עא א ב מיי' פ"ט מהל' איסורי ביאה הל' ה סמג לאוין קיא ועשין רמג:
עב ג ד מיי' פ"ב מהל' מאכלות אסורות הל' כח סמג לאוין קמח טוש"ע י"ד סי' קכט סעיף יז:
עג ה ו מיי' שם פי"א הל' יג סמג לאוין קמח טוש"ע י"ד סי' קלב סעיף יא וסי' קכט סעיף יח:
עד ז ח מיי' שם פי"א הל' כט סמג לאוין קמח טוש"ע י"ד סי' קכט סעיף יט:

הגהות הב"ח

(א) גמ' אמר רבא ש"מ כו' ואות נ' נמחק: (ב) שם אימור מהאי דקרא אתאי: (ג) שם אם איתא דמהאי דקרא אתאי: (ד) שם דסבר לה כר' חנינא: (ה) רש"י ד"ה בשביל וכו' חוץ לחמשים אמה ומיהו וכו' [illegible] (ו) ד"ה ספיקו טמא ספק זה טומאה: (ז) ד"ה רוב ומצוי [illegible] (ח) ד"ה [illegible] (ט) ד"ה דהא אשה וכו' נעולות [illegible] (י) ד"ה מהאי דקרא [illegible] (כ) ד"ה דאי מגניב מיניה וכו' [illegible] (ל) תוס' ד"ה ואע"ג וכו' כמו שפירשנו: (מ) ד"ה דתני וכו' [illegible] (נ) ד"ה ושמע מינה וכו' [illegible] (ס) ד"ה אימור מהאי דקרא אתאי:

עה א ב מיי' פ"י מהל' מאכלות אסורות הל' כט סמג לאוין קמח טוש"ע יו"ד סי' קכט סעיף יט:

עו ג מיי' פ"י מהלכות שכנים הל' א סמג עשין פב טוש"ע חו"מ סי' קנה סעיף כו:

עז ד מיי' שם וסמג שם טוש"ע ח"מ סי' קנה סעיף כח בהג"ה:

עח ה מיי' שם הל' ב סמג שם:

עט ו מיי' פ"י מהל' שמיטה הל' ד סמג לאוין רעט ועשין קמט:

פ ז מיי' פ"י מהלכות שבת הלכה ו סמג עשין מד"ס א טוש"ע א"ח סי' שנח סעיף א:

פא ח ט מיי' פ"י מהל' שכנים הל' ב סמג עשין פב טוש"ע חו"מ סי' קנה סעיף כב:

דִּשְׁפּוּכָאֵי יִשְׂרָאֵל נִינְהוּ. א)וה"מ בְּרַבְרְבֵי, אֲבָל זוּטָרֵי — אֵימוּר: מֵעוֹבְרֵי דְרָכִים נְפוּל. ב)וְאִי אִיכָּא רַבְרְבֵי בַּהֲדַיְיהוּ — אֵימוּר: בְּאַבְרוּרֵי הֲוָה מַנְחִי.§

מתני' א)גמַרְחִיקִין אֶת הָאִילָן מִן הָעִיר עֶשְׂרִים וְחָמֵשׁ אַמָּה, וּבֶחָרוּב וּבַשִּׁקְמָה — חֲמִשִּׁים אַמָּה. אַבָּא שָׁאוּל אוֹמֵר: כָּל אִילָן סְרָק — חֲמִשִּׁים אַמָּה. (א) דוְאִם הָעִיר קָדְמָה — קוֹצֵץ וְאֵינוֹ נוֹתֵן דָּמִים, וְאִם אִילָן קָדַם — קוֹצֵץ וְנוֹתֵן דָּמִים, ב)סָפֵק זֶה קָדַם וְסָפֵק זֶה קָדַם — קוֹצֵץ וְאֵינוֹ נוֹתֵן דָּמִים.§ **גמ'** מַאי טַעֲמָא? אָמַר עוּלָּא: המִשּׁוּם נוֹיֵי הָעִיר. ג)וְתֵיפּוֹק לֵיהּ דְּאֵין עוֹשִׂין שָׂדֶה מִגְרָשׁ וְלֹא מִגְרָשׁ שָׂדֶה! לָא צְרִיכָא, לְר"א דְּאָמַר: ד)ועוֹשִׂין שָׂדֶה מִגְרָשׁ וּמִגְרָשׁ שָׂדֶה, הָכָא מִשּׁוּם נוֹיֵי הָעִיר לָא עָבְדִינַן. וּלְרַבָּנַן נַמִי, דְּאָמְרִי: אֵין עוֹשִׂין שָׂדֶה מִגְרָשׁ וְלֹא מִגְרָשׁ שָׂדֶה, ה"מ זְרָעִים, אֲבָל אִילָנוֹת עָבְדִינַן, וְהָכָא מִשּׁוּם נוֹיֵי הָעִיר לָא. (ב) וּמְנָא תֵּימְרָא דְּשָׁאנֵי בֵּין זְרָעִין לְאִילָנוֹת? ה)דְּתַנְיָא: זקַרְפֵּף יוֹתֵר מִבֵּית סָאתַיִם שֶׁהוּקַּף לְדִירָה, נִזְרַע רוּבּוֹ — הֲרֵי הוּא כְּגִינָּה וְאָסוּר, נִיטַּע רוּבּוֹ — הֲרֵי הוּא כְּחָצֵר וּמוּתָּר.§ "וְאִם הָעִיר קָדְמָה — קוֹצֵץ וְאֵינוֹ נוֹתֵן דָּמִים" וכו'.§ מ"ש גַּבֵּי בּוֹר דְּקָתָנֵי: ו)קוֹצֵץ וְנוֹתֵן דָּמִים, וּמַאי שְׁנָא הָכָא דְּקָתָנֵי: קוֹצֵץ וְאֵינוֹ נוֹתֵן דָּמִים? אָמַר רַב כָּהֲנָא: (ג) ז)קִידְרָא דְּבֵי שׁוּתָּפֵי לָא חֲמִימָא וְלָא קְרִירָא. וּמַאי קוּשְׁיָא? דִּלְמָא שָׁאנֵי הֶיזֵּיקָא דְּרַבִּים מֵהֶיזֵּיקָא דְּיָחִיד! אֶלָּא אִי אִיתְּמַר דְּרַב כָּהֲנָא — אַסֵּיפָא אִיתְּמַר: אִם הָאִילָן קָדַם — קוֹצֵץ וְנוֹתֵן דָּמִים. וְלֵימָא לְהוּ: הָבוּ לִי בְּרֵישָׁא דָּמֵי וַהֲדַר אֵיקוֹץ! אֲמַר רַב כָּהֲנָא: קִידְרָא דְּבֵי שׁוּתָּפֵי לָא חֲמִימָא וְלָא קְרִירָא.§ "סָפֵק זֶה קָדַם וְסָפֵק זֶה קָדַם — קוֹצֵץ וְאֵינוֹ נוֹתֵן דָּמִים".§ מַאי שְׁנָא מִבּוֹר דְּאָמְרַתְּ: לֹא יָקוֹץ? הָתָם דְּוַדַּאי לָאו לְמֵיקַץ קָאֵי — סְפֵיקוֹ נַמִי לָא אָמְרִינַן לֵיהּ קוֹץ, הָכָא דְּוַדַּאי לְמֵיקַץ קָאֵי — סְפֵיקוֹ נַמִי אָמְרִינַן לֵיהּ קוֹץ, וְאִי מִשּׁוּם דָּמֵי — אָמְרִינַן לֵיהּ: אַיְיתֵי רְאָיָה וּשְׁקוֹל.§ **מתני'** חמַרְחִיקִין אֶת גּוֹרֶן קָבוּעַ מִן הָעִיר חֲמִשִּׁים אַמָּה. טלֹא יַעֲשֶׂה אָדָם גּוֹרֶן קָבוּעַ בְּתוֹךְ שֶׁלּוֹ — אא"כ יֵשׁ לוֹ חֲמִשִּׁים אַמָּה לְכָל רוּחַ, וּמַרְחִיק מִנְּטִיעוֹתָיו שֶׁל חֲבֵירוֹ וּמִנִּירוֹ בִּכְדֵי שֶׁלֹּא יַזִּיק.§ **גמ'** מ"ש רֵישָׁא וּמַאי שְׁנָא סֵיפָא? אֲמַר אַבַּיֵי: סֵיפָא אֲתָאן לְגוֹרֶן שֶׁאֵינוֹ קָבוּעַ. הֵיכִי דָּמֵי גּוֹרֶן שֶׁאֵינוֹ קָבוּעַ? א"ר יוֹסֵי בְּר' חֲנִינָא: כָּל שֶׁאֵינוֹ זוֹרֶה בְּרַחַת. רַב אַשִׁי אֲמַר: ימַה טַּעַם קָאָמַר, מַאי טַעֲמָא מַרְחִיקִין גּוֹרֶן קָבוּעַ מִן הָעִיר חֲמִשִּׁים אַמָּה? כְּדֵי שֶׁלֹּא יַזִּיק. מֵיתִיבֵי: מַרְחִיקִין גּוֹרֶן קָבוּעַ מִן הָעִיר חֲמִשִּׁים אַמָּה; וּכְשֵׁם שֶׁמַּרְחִיקִין מִן הָעִיר חֲמִשִּׁים אַמָּה, כָּךְ מַרְחִיקִין מִדְּלוּעָיו וּמִקִּשּׁוּאָיו וּמִנְּטִיעוֹתָיו וּמִנִּירוֹ שֶׁל חֲבֵירוֹ חֲמִשִּׁים אַמָּה, כְּדֵי שֶׁלֹּא יַזִּיק; בִּשְׁלָמָא לְרַב אַשִׁי נִיחָא, אֶלָּא לְאַבַּיֵי קַשְׁיָא! קַשְׁיָא. בִּשְׁלָמָא מִמַּקְשׁוּאָיו וּמִדְּלוּעָיו, דְּאָזֵיל אֲבָקָא וְאָתֵי בְּלִיבֵּיהּ ח)וּמְצַוֵּי לֵיהּ, אֶלָּא מִנִּירוֹ אַמַּאי? א"ר אַבָּא בַּר זַבְדָּא, וְאִיתֵּימָא ר' אַבָּא בַּר זוּטְרָא: מִפְּנֵי

שֶׁעוֹשֶׂה

דִּשְׁפּוּכָאֵי. שׁוֹפְכֵי יַיִן מִן הֶחָבִית לַנּוֹדוֹת לִמְכּוֹר לְעוֹבְרֵי דְרָכִים בַּמְּדִינָה זֹאת, כְּדִמְסַיֵּים וְאָזֵיל. **בְּרַבְרְבֵי.** דְּלֵיכָּא לְמֵיחַשׁ לְרוּבָּא דְעָלְמָא, לְמֵימַר מֵעוֹבְרֵי דְרָכִים נְפוּל. **וְאִי אִיכָּא רַבְרְבֵי בַּהֲדַיְיהוּ.** אַף הַקְּטַנִּים מוּתָּרִין, דִּבְרַבְרְבֵי לָאו אוֹרְחַיְיהוּ דְּעוֹבְרֵי דְרָכִים, אֶלָּא כּוּלְּהוּ (ד) מְלוּקַּח יַיִן שֶׁל מְדִינָה זוֹ נִינְהוּ, וְיִשְׂרָאֵל הֵן, וּקְטַנִּים שֶׁאֵין דֶּרֶךְ לְלוֹקֵחַ יַיִן לַהֲבִיאָם. **אֵימוּר בְּאַבְרוּרֵי הֲוָה מַנְחִי.** לְהַשְׁווֹת מַשָּׂא הַחֲמוֹר, כְּשֶׁיֵּשׁ שְׁתֵּי נוֹדוֹת זֶה גָּדוֹל מִזֶּה מְעַט וּמַכְבִּיד הַמַּשָּׂא לְצַד אֶחָד — מַנִּיחִין נוֹד קָטָן אֶצְלוֹ, לְהַשְׁווֹת הַמַּשָּׂא. **מתני' מַרְחִיקִין אֶת הָאִילָן מִן הָעִיר.** בַּגְּמָרָא מְפָרֵשׁ: מִשּׁוּם נוֹיֵי הָעִיר, לְפִי שֶׁנּוֹי לָעִיר כְּשֶׁיֵּשׁ מֶרְחָב פָּנוּי לְפָנֶיהָ. **חָרוּב וְשִׁקְמָה.** עַנְפֵיהֶם רַבִּים. **וְאִילָן סְרָק.** גְּנַאי הוּא לָעִיר. **וְנוֹתֵן דָּמִים.** מִי שֶׁהָעִיר שֶׁלּוֹ. **גמ' וְתֵיפּוֹק לֵיהּ דְּאֵין עוֹשִׂין מִגְרָשׁ שָׂדֶה.** מִשְׁנָה הִיא בְּפֶ' אַחֲרוֹן שֶׁל עֲרָכִין (דף לג.). וּמִגְרָשׁ אֶלֶף אַמָּה הוּא, וְכָל אֶלֶף אַמָּה אָסוּר לַעֲשׂוֹתוֹ שָׂדֶה. וְקס"ד — לֹא שְׂדֵה לָבָן וְלֹא שְׂדֵה אִילָן. **לָא צְרִיכָא לְר' אֶלְעָזָר.** דִּפְלֵיג הָתָם, וְאָמַר: בד"א — בְּעָרֵי הַלְוִיִּם אֲבָל בְּעָרֵי יִשְׂרָאֵל כו'. ה"ג: **וּלְרַבָּנַן דְּאָמְרִי** אֵין עוֹשִׂין הָנֵי מִילֵּי בִּזְרָעִים אֲבָל בְּאִילָנוֹת עוֹשִׂין. בְּתוֹךְ אֶלֶף אַמָּה. **וְהָכָא.** בְּתוֹךְ עֶשְׂרִים וְחָמֵשׁ אַמָּה מִשּׁוּם נוֹיֵי הָעִיר אֵין עוֹשִׂין. **קַרְפֵּף יוֹתֵר מִבֵּית סָאתַיִם שֶׁהוּקַּף לְדִירָה.** סָאתַיִם הוּא שִׁיעוּר חֲצַר הַמִּשְׁכָּן, וּנְתָנוּהוּ חֲכָמִים שִׁיעוּר לְכָל הֶיקֵּף שֶׁלֹּא הוּקַּף לָדוּר בְּתוֹכוֹ אוֹ לְהִשְׁתַּמֵּשׁ מִן הַבַּיִת לְתוֹכוֹ, כְּגוֹן קַרְפֵּף שֶׁבַּבִּקְעָה. אֲבָל הַמּוּקָּף לְדִירָה — אֲפִי' בֵּית עֲשָׂרָה כּוֹרִין מְטַלְטְלִין בּוֹ. וְקָאָמַר הָכָא: יֶתֶר מִבֵּית סָאתַיִם שֶׁהוּקַּף לְדִירָה, הוּא מוּתָּר לְטַלְטֵל בְּכוּלּוֹ. **נִזְרַע רוּבּוֹ.** בָּטְלוּ הַזְּרָעִים שֵׁם דִּירָה מִמֶּנּוּ, וַהֲרֵי הוּא כְּגִינָּה שֶׁאֵין הַקָּפָה לְדִירָה, הוֹאִיל וְיָתֵר מִבֵּית סָאתַיִם הוּא — אֵין מְטַלְטְלִין בּוֹ עוֹד. **אֲבָל נִיטַּע רוּבּוֹ.** בָּאִילָנוֹת — אֵין הָאִילָנוֹת מְבַטְּלִין תּוֹרַת דִּירָתוֹ מִמֶּנּוּ, וַהֲרֵי הוּא כְּחָצֵר שֶׁלִּפְנֵי הַבָּתִּים שֶׁהִקִּיפוּהָ לְדִירָה, וּמוּתָּר. **מַאי שְׁנָא** (ה) **בּוֹר.** דְּבָעֵינַן נַמִי הַרְחָקָה, וְקָתָנֵי נַמִי אִם הַבּוֹר קָדְמָה — קוֹצֵץ וְנוֹתֵן בַּעַל הַבּוֹר דְּמֵי הָאִילָן לְבַעַל הָאִילָן. **לָא חֲמִימָא וְלָא קְרִירָא.** שֶׁזֶּה סוֹמֵךְ עַל זֶה. אַף כָּאן, דְּמֵי הָאִילָן מִי יִתְּנֵם? אִם בָּאתָ לְהַטִּילָם עַל בְּנֵי הָעִיר — כָּל אֶחָד אוֹמֵר: מִמֶּנִּי לֹא יַתְחִילוּ. וְנִמְצָא הָאִילָן עוֹמֵד, וְהָעִיר מְגוּנָּה, וְאֵין זוֹ תִּפְאֶרֶת אֶרֶץ יִשְׂרָאֵל. **וּמַאי קוּשְׁיָא.** מִבּוֹר לָעִיר, דְּאִיצְטְרִיךְ לְשַׁנּוּיֵי הָכִי? דִּלְמָא שָׁאנֵי הֶיזֵּק דְּרַבִּים מֵהֶיזֵּיקָא דְּיָחִיד; לֹא חִיְּיבוּ חֲכָמִים לָקוֹץ אִילָנוֹ בִּשְׁבִיל בּוֹר הַיָּחִיד בְּלֹא דָּמִים, אֲבָל בִּשְׁבִיל הֶיזֵּק רַבִּים חִיְּיבוּהוּ לָקוֹץ! **לָא חֲמִימָא כו'.** אִם בָּאתָ לְהַמְתִּין עַד מַתַּן מָעוֹת — יַעֲמוֹד (ו) זֶה לְאוֹרֶךְ יָמִים. בְּנֵי הָעִיר סוֹמְכִין זֶה עַל זֶה, וּבַעַל הָאִילָן רוֹצֶה בְּכָךְ. לְפִיכָךְ יָקוֹץ, וְאַחַר כֵּן יִגְבֶּה מְעוֹתָיו מֵהֶן בב"ד. **הָתָם.** גַּבֵּי בּוֹר, דְּוַדַּאי שֶׁל אִילָן, אִם וַדַּאי קָדַם — לָאו לְמֵיקַץ קָאֵי, כִּדְקָתָנֵי: אִם הָאִילָן קָדַם לֹא יָקוֹץ — סְפֵיקוֹ נַמִי לֹא אָמַר לֵיהּ קוֹץ, שֶׁעַל הַמַּזִּיק לְהָבִיא רְאָיָה. **הָכָא דְּוַדַּאי.** נַמִי לְמֵיקַץ קָאֵי, אֶלָּא שֶׁנּוֹטֵל דָּמִים, כִּדְקָתָנֵי: אִם הָאִילָן קָדַם קוֹצֵץ וְנוֹתֵן דָּמִים — סְפֵיקוֹ נַמִי אָמַר לֵיהּ: קוֹץ מִמ"נ עַל כָּרְחָךְ. וּכְשֶׁבָּא לִגְבּוֹת דָּמִים אָמַר לֵיהּ: אַיְיתֵי רְאָיָה דְּאַתְּ קָדַמְתְּ וּשְׁקוֹל. **מתני'** גּוֹרֶן קָבוּעַ. בַּגְּמָ' מְפָרֵשׁ מַאי קְבִיעוּתָא. **חֲמִשִּׁים אַמָּה.** מִפְּנֵי הַמּוֹץ הַמַּזִּיק אֶת בְּנֵי הָעִיר כְּשֶׁהוּא זוֹרֶה, וְגַם הַזְּרָעִים הוּא מְיַיבֵּשׁ. **וּמִנִּירוֹ שֶׁל חֲבֵירוֹ.** וּבַגְּמָרָא מְפָרֵשׁ מַאי הֶיזֵּק דְּמוֹץ לַנִּיר. נִיר הִיא חֲרִישָׁה שֶׁחוֹרְשִׁין בִּימֵי הַקַּיִץ, וְאֵין זוֹרְעִין בּוֹ עַד יְמוֹת הַחוֹרֶף כְּדֵי שֶׁיָּמוּתוּ שָׁרְשֵׁי הַקּוֹצִים וְהָעֲשָׂבִים, כְּדִכְתִיב: "נִירוּ לָכֶם נִיר וְאַל תִּזְרְעוּ אֶל קוֹצִים" (ירמיהו ד). **בִּכְדֵי שֶׁלֹּא יַזִּיק.** הַאי שִׁיעוּרָא מַשְׁמַע בָּצִיר מֵחֲמִשִּׁים אַמָּה. וּבַגְּמָרָא פָּרֵיךְ: מ"ש מֵרֵישָׁא, דְּאָמְרַתְּ: אֶלָּא אִם כֵּן יֵשׁ לוֹ חֲמִשִּׁים אַמָּה לְכָל רוּחַ? **גמ'** שֶׁאֵינוֹ זוֹרֶה בְּרַחַת. שֶׁאֵין הַכְּרִי גָּדוֹל, וְא"צ לִזְרוֹת בְּרַחַת, אֶלָּא הָרוּחַ מְנַשֶּׁבֶת בַּכְּרִי וְהַמּוֹץ נִדָּף מֵאֵלָיו. רַחַת = פל"ה בְּלַעַ"ז, כְּשֶׁהַכְּרִי גָּדוֹל צָרִיךְ לְהַגְבִּיהַּ הַתְּבוּאָה בְּרַחַת, וְזוֹרֵק כְּלַפֵּי מַעְלָה, וְהָרוּחַ מְנַשֶּׁבֶת וְדוֹחֶפֶת הַמּוֹץ לְמֶרְחוֹק. **רַב אַשִׁי אָמַר.** שִׁיעוּרָא דְּסֵיפָא כְּרֵישָׁא, וּמַה טַּעַם קָאָמַר. **מִקִּשּׁוּאָיו וּמִדְּלוּעָיו.** נְטִיעָה שֶׁהַקִּשּׁוּאִין וְהַדְּלוּעִין גְּדֵלִין בָּהּ. **בִּשְׁלָמָא לְרַב אַשִׁי נִיחָא.** דְּקָתָנֵי בְּכוּלְּהוּ חֲמִשִּׁים אַמָּה. **אֶלָּא לְאַבַּיֵי קַשְׁיָא קַשְׁיָא.** [הָכִי] גָּרְסִינַן.

שֶׁעוֹשֶׂה

מרחיקין את האילן [מן העיר] כ"ה אמה. וזרעים צריך להרחיק מן העיר עד אלף אמה, דאין עושין מגרש שדה.

מ"ש מבור דקוצץ ונותן דמים אמר רב כהנא קידרא דבי שותפי כו'. תימה לרשב"א: א"כ, כשהאילן קדם נמי, אמאי נותן דמים מהאי טעמא? וי"ל: דכשהאילן קדם, כיון דסמך בהיתר — אין לחוש אם יתעצלו וישאר האילן עומד. אבל עוד קשה לו: דמאי שייך הכא קידרא דבי שותפי? והלא קוצץ תחלה קודם שיתנו דמים! ואומר ר"י, דה"פ: דמשום קידרא דבי שותפי לא חיימא ולא קרירא — לא רצו לתקן שיתנו דמים. דאע"ג דקוצץ תחלה — פעמים שלא ישמע להם לקוץ תחלה אם לא ידע מי יתן לו הדמים, וכל אחד ואחד יתרשל ולא יקוץ כדי שלא ליתן דמים, כי בעל האילן ידרוש מעמו.

ולימא להו הבו לי ברישא והדר איקוץ. גבי בור לא שייך למיפרך הכי, דניחא, (ז) כיון שסמך באיסור — שיקוץ תחלה.

קשיא לאביי. תימה: מאי קשיא ליה? הא ברייתא איירי בגורן קבוע, ומתניתין בגורן שאינו קבוע! ויש לומר: דאביי גופיה הוה משני דמה טעם קאמר, אי לאו משום דקשיא ליה מה צריך לפרש טעמא כדי שלא יזיק. והשתא דבברייתא מפרש טעמא כדי שלא יזיק — מתני' נמי איכא לפרושי הכי.

שעושה

רבינו גרשום

והני מילי. דמותרין: היכא דהנהו זיקי ברברבי נינהו אבל אי משתכחו זוטרי ודאי אסור דאימר מעוברי דרכים נפלו: ואי איכא רברבי ואשכח זוטרי בהדייהו אסירי. דחיישי' דמעוברי דרכים נפל דאימור מאברורי קא מנחי על גבי החמור בעין שקושרין עוברי דרכים נודות על גבי חמוריהן וקושרין מצד החמור נוד גדול ומצד השני כמותו ומשימין בין שתי נודות הללו נוד אחד קטן ואם נמצאו גדולים כה"ג וקטנים עמהן ודאי מעוברי דרכים נפל ומשואי חמור ואסירי. ל"מ. ואי איכא רברבי בנייהו. אפי' דזוטרי מותרין דאימור מאברוראי נחתו שפוכי ישראל אנחנהו להתם בעין שתילין לעשות כדפרישית לעיל באידך לישנא והכי עיקר: **פיסקא** מרחיקין את האילן מן העיר כ"ה [אמה]. מפרש בגמ' טעמ' מאי: בחרוב ובשקמה נ' אמה. משום דאיכא תרתי לריעותא חדא דאין פירותיהן שוין כלום ועוד שענפיהן מרובין משאר אילנות. מ"ש. מרחיקין: אמר עולא משום נויי העיר. שיהיה משייר מישור פה סמוך לעיר בלא שום עיכוב. ועולא למה ליה למימר משום נויי העיר מרחיקין תיפוק ליה דאין עושין שדה שיש בו זרע או אילנות אין עושין מגרש ולא מגרש שדה כדרסי' במס' א) מכות לגבי ערים [דכתיב] ומדותם מחוץ לעיר וגו' משום דהוי ב) להם לוים דכתיב ומגרשיהם יהיו לבהמתם וגו' להכי ג) צריכי אלפים אמה מגרש אבל שאר הערים בכ"ה אמה מגרש סגא: לא צריכא לר"א דאמר עושין שדה מגרש ד) להיכא דזורע או נטע אילן בתוך כ"ה אמה סמוך לעיר: הני מילי דאין עושין להיכ' דזורע [דא"א] למיזל תחותיה בזרעים משום דקא מזיק זרעים

לבני העיר דלא מצי למדרם בזרעים אבל אילן דמצי למיזל תחותיה ה) דאפי' אילנות אין נוטעין משום נויי העיר: קרפף שהוא יותר מבית סאתים. כחצר המשכן שהוקף לשום דירה אם נזרע רובו הרי הוא כגינה דזריעה היא ואסור לילך בה בשבת משום דמדרסי זרעים ואיכא חלול שבת: נטע רובו מאילנות הרי הוא כחצר ומותר. משום דמצי למיזל בין אילן לאילן. ואיכא דאמרי כשדה אסור לטלטל בו כחצר מותר לטלטל בו: מ"ש גבי עיר דקתני: אם העיר קדמה קוצצין ואין נותן דמים ומ"ש גבי בור דקתני אם הבור קדמה קוצץ ונותן דמים אמר רב (הונא) [כהנא] מש"ה גבי עיר אינו נותן דמים משום דליכא למיקם עלה דמלתא. למאן שאיל דמים הואיל ורבים אתי למגבי סמכי אהדדי ולא יהבי כלום דקדירה דבי שותפי לא חמימא ולא קרירא שזה סומך על זה וזה על זה אבל גבי בור כיון דמיחיד אתי למגבי לא סמך אלא חד וידע למאן שאיל דמים ומש"ה קוצצין ונותן דמים ודלמא משום האי טעמא לא מצית למימר גבי עיר אם קדמה דאין נותן דמים דהא קתני גבי סיפא דמתני' אם האילן קדם קוצץ ונותן דמים אלמא דלא משום האי טעם הוא. אלא היינו טעם הוא דמתני' דשאני בין קדמה העיר לקדם הבור דשני היזק דיחיד מהיזק דרבים ולהכי גבי עיר דאיכא היזק דרבים קוצץ ואינו נותן דמים אבל גבי בור דליכא היזק דרבים קוצץ ונותן דמים: אמאי קוצץ והדר נותן דמים הא מעיקרא מצי למימר להו לבעל האילן הב לי דמי ברישא והדר איקוץ הואיל דאילני קדם אמר רב כהנא מש"ה קוצץ מעיקרא והדר נותנין דמים דמצו למימר ליה בני העיר קוץ דרמיא עלך מעיקרא משום דקידרא דבי שותפי לא חמימא ולא קרירא דכל מאי דבעי למגבי מכמה אינשי איכא טירחא יתירא דסמכי הני אהני אבל את קוץ הואיל דאת יחיד ומזקת לרבים ורמיא עלך והדר מגבי מבני העיר. ו) אבל לגבי בור הואיל דלית ליה מלתא אלא גבי חד לא מצי למימר ליה הב לי ברישא והדר איקוץ דודאי יהיב ליה מש"ה קוצץ ונותן דמים: ומ"ש מבור דאמר ספק זה קדם לא יקוץ. התם באילן דבור כיון דודאי דהיכא דידע' דודאי דהאילן קדם לא יקוץ ספיקו נמי לא יקוץ. קאי ז) זיל אייתי ראיה דאילנך קדם ושקול דמיך: **פיסקא** מרחיקין גורן קבוע מן העיר חמשים אמה. משום דקא מזיק התבן שזורין מן התבואה לבני העיר: מ"ש דגורן מרחיק נ' אמה. ולגבי נטיעות מרחיקין בכדי שלא יזיקו דהיינו בציר מחמשים אמה: רב אשי אמר. סיפא ורישא חדא טעמא הוא דמה טעם מרחיק נ' אמה מן העיר כדי שלא יזיק נטיעות ולנירו: בשלמא לרב אשי. דמפרש טעמא דמתני' ניחא דכן הכי נמי קתני בברייתא אלא לאביי קשיא דמתרץ סיפא לגורן שאינו קבוע והא קתני רישא דברייתא מרחיקין מן מקשואין ומדלועין דהיינו נטיעות נ' אמה: קשיא. בשלמא מקשואין ומדלועין מש"ה צריך להרחיק חמשים אמה דאזיל התבן ונפיל על פרח. בליבה. פרח. כמו ויצא פרח שתרגומו ואפיק לבלבין: מצוי ליה. ומנפחו ומיבשו: מפני שעושין אותו אויר גלל. התבואה הזריעה בקרקע תיעשה זבל ותירקב:

פיסקא

הגהות הב"ח

(א) במשנה סרק נ' אמה אם כל"ל ואות ו' נמחק: (ב) גמ' לא עבדינן ומנא תימרא דשאני בין זרעים לאילנות: (ג) שם אמר רב כהנא היינו דאמרי אינשי קידרא דבי שותפי: (ד) רש"י ד"ה ואי איכא וכו' מלוקחי יין וכו' וישראל הן הקטנים וכו' מניחין נוד קטן כל"ל והד"א: (ה) ד"ה מ"ש גבי בור וכו' וקתני נמי היה הבור: (ו) ד"ה לא חמימא וכו' יעמוד לאורך כל"ל ותיבת זה נמחק: (ז) תוס' ד"ה ולימא וכו' דניחא ליה כיון:

א) [ב"מ קיז:] ב) [שם קיז:] ג) מכות יב. [ערכין לג:] ד) [ערכין שם:] ה) עירובין כג: ו) [לקמן כה:] ז) עירובין ג: ח) [פי' שורף ומייבש לתלותיות. ערוך]

א) נ"ל במס' ערכין דף לג. ב) אולי צ"ל משום דהוי לצרך לוים וכו'. ג) עי' סוטה כז במשנה ועירובין דף נו ע"ב ונ"ע. ד) נראה דצ"ל ומגרש שדה מ"ש לתורה וכו' סמוך לעיר אסור. ה) נ"ל עבדינן אבל בתוך כ"ה אפי' אילנות וכו'. ו) עי' תד"ה ולימא ודו"ק. ז) נ"ל הכא דוודאי למיקץ קאי ספיקו נמי אמרינן ליה קוץ.

שֶׁעוֹשֶׂה אוֹתוֹ גָּלָל.§ **מתני'** א) מַרְחִיקִין אֶת הַנְּבֵלוֹת וְאֶת הַקְּבָרוֹת וְאֶת הַבּוּרְסְקִי מִן הָעִיר חֲמִשִּׁים אַמָּה. ב) אֵין עוֹשִׂין בּוּרְסְקִי אֶלָּא לְמִזְרַח הָעִיר; רַבִּי עֲקִיבָא אוֹמֵר: לְכָל רוּחַ הוּא עוֹשֶׂה, חוּץ מִמַּעֲרָבָהּ, וּמַרְחִיק חֲמִשִּׁים אַמָּה. א) וּמַרְחִיקִין אֶת הַמִּשְׁרָה מִן הַיָּרָק, וְאֶת הַכְּרֵישִׁין מִן הַבְּצָלִים, וְאֶת הַחַרְדָּל מִן הַדְּבוֹרִים, ג) וְרַבִּי יוֹסֵי מַתִּיר בַּחַרְדָּל.§ **גמ'** אִיבַּעְיָא לְהוּ: ר' עֲקִיבָא הֵיכִי קָאָמַר? לְכָל רוּחַ הוּא עוֹשֶׂה וְסוֹמֵךְ, חוּץ מִמַּעֲרָבָהּ דְּמַרְחִיק נ' אַמָּה וְעוֹשֶׂה. אוֹ דִּלְמָא: לְכָל רוּחַ הוּא עוֹשֶׂה וּמַרְחִיק חֲמִשִּׁים אַמָּה, חוּץ מִמַּעֲרָבָהּ דְּאֵינוֹ עוֹשֶׂה כְּלָל? ת"ש: דְּתַנְיָא, ר"ע אוֹמֵר: לְכָל רוּחַ הוּא עוֹשֶׂה וּמַרְחִיק חֲמִשִּׁים אַמָּה, חוּץ מִמַּעֲרָבָהּ דְּאֵינוֹ עוֹשֶׂה כָּל עִיקָּר, מִפְּנֵי שֶׁהִיא תְּדִירָא. א"ל רָבָא לְרַב נַחְמָן: מַאי תְּדִירָא? אִילֵימָא תְּדִירָא בְּרוּחוֹת? וְהָא ב) אָמַר רַב חָנָן בַּר אַבָּא אָמַר רַב: ד' רוּחוֹת מְנַשְּׁבוֹת בְּכָל יוֹם, וְרוּחַ צְפוֹנִית עִם כּוּלָּן, שֶׁאִילְמָלֵא כֵּן — אֵין הָעוֹלָם מִתְקַיֵּים אֲפִילּוּ שָׁעָה אַחַת. וְרוּחַ דְּרוֹמִית קָשָׁה מִכּוּלָּן, וְאִילְמָלֵא בֶּן נֵץ שֶׁמַּעֲמִידָהּ — מַחֲרֶבֶת אֶת הָעוֹלָם, שֶׁנֶּאֱמַר: (איוב לט) °"הֲמִבִּינָתְךָ יַאֲבֶר נֵץ יִפְרוֹשׂ כְּנָפָיו לְתֵימָן"! אֶלָּא מַאי תְּדִירָא? תְּדִירָא בִּשְׁכִינָה, דְּאָרִיב"ל: בּוֹאוּ וְנַחֲזִיק טוֹבָה לַאֲבוֹתֵינוּ (א) שֶׁהוֹדִיעוּ מְקוֹם תְּפִלָּה, דִּכְתִיב: (נחמיה ט) °"וּצְבָא הַשָּׁמַיִם לְךָ מִשְׁתַּחֲוִים". מַתְקִיף לָהּ רַב אַחָא בַּר יַעֲקֹב: וְדִלְמָא כְּעֶבֶד שֶׁנּוֹטֵל פְּרָס מֵרַבּוֹ, וְחוֹזֵר לַאֲחוֹרָיו וּמִשְׁתַּחֲוֶה! קַשְׁיָא. וְרַבִּי אוֹשַׁעְיָא סָבַר: שְׁכִינָה בְּכָל מָקוֹם, דְּאָמַר רַבִּי אוֹשַׁעְיָא, מַאי דִּכְתִיב: (שם) °"אַתָּה הוּא ה' לְבַדֶּךָ אַתָּה עָשִׂיתָ אֶת הַשָּׁמַיִם" וגו'? שְׁלוּחֶיךָ לֹא כִּשְׁלוּחֵי בָּשָׂר וָדָם; שְׁלוּחֵי בָּשָׂר וָדָם — מִמָּקוֹם שֶׁמִּשְׁתַּלְּחִים לְשָׁם מַחֲזִירִים שְׁלִיחוּתָן, אֲבָל שְׁלוּחֶיךָ — לְמָקוֹם שֶׁמִּשְׁתַּלְּחִין ג) מִשָּׁם מַחֲזִירִין שְׁלִיחוּתָן, שֶׁנֶּאֱמַר: (איוב לח) °"הַתְשַׁלַּח בְּרָקִים וְיֵלֵכוּ וְיֹאמְרוּ לְךָ הִנֵּנוּ"; "יָבוֹאוּ וְיֹאמְרוּ" לֹא נֶאֱמַר, אֶלָּא: "וְיֵלֵכוּ וְיֹאמְרוּ", מְלַמֵּד שֶׁהַשְּׁכִינָה בְּכָל מָקוֹם. וְאַף רַבִּי יִשְׁמָעֵאל סָבַר: שְׁכִינָה בְּכָל מָקוֹם, דְּתָנָא דְּבֵי רַבִּי יִשְׁמָעֵאל: מִנַּיִן שֶׁשְּׁכִינָה בְּכָל מָקוֹם? שֶׁנֶּאֱמַר: (זכריה ב) °"הִנֵּה הַמַּלְאָךְ הַדּוֹבֵר בִּי יוֹצֵא וּמַלְאָךְ אַחֵר יוֹצֵא לִקְרָאתוֹ"; "אַחֲרָיו" לֹא נֶאֱמַר, אֶלָּא: "לִקְרָאתוֹ", מְלַמֵּד שֶׁשְּׁכִינָה בְּכָל מָקוֹם. וְאַף רַב שֵׁשֶׁת סָבַר: שְׁכִינָה בְּכָל מָקוֹם, דְּא"ל רַב שֵׁשֶׁת לְשַׁמָּעֵיהּ: לְכָל רוּחָתָא אוֹקְמַן לְבַר מִמִּזְרָח, וְלָאו מִשּׁוּם דְּלֵית בֵּיהּ שְׁכִינָה, אֶלָּא ד) מִשּׁוּם דְּמוֹרוּ בָּהּ מִינֵי. וְרַבִּי אַבָּהוּ אָמַר: שְׁכִינָה בְּמַעֲרָב, דְּא"ר אַבָּהוּ: מַאי אוּרְיָה? אֲוִיר יָהּ. אָמַר רַב יְהוּדָה: (ב) מַאי דִּכְתִיב (דברים לב) °"יַעֲרֹף כַּמָּטָר לִקְחִי"? זוֹ רוּחַ מַעֲרָבִית שֶׁבָּאָה ד) מֵעָרְפּוֹ שֶׁל עוֹלָם; "תִּזַּל כַּטַּל אִמְרָתִי" — זוֹ רוּחַ צְפוֹנִית שֶׁמַּזֶּלֶת אֶת הַזָּהָב, וְכֵן הוּא אוֹמֵר: (ישעיה מו) °"הַזָּלִים זָהָב מִכִּיס"; "כִּשְׂעִירִם עֲלֵי דֶשֶׁא" — זוֹ רוּחַ מִזְרָחִית שֶׁמְּסַעֶרֶת אֶת כָּל הָעוֹלָם כְּשָׂעִיר; "וְכִרְבִיבִים עֲלֵי עֵשֶׂב" — זוֹ רוּחַ דְּרוֹמִית שֶׁהִיא מַעֲלָה רְבִיבִים וּמְגַדֶּלֶת עֲשָׂבִים. תַּנְיָא, ר"א אוֹמֵר: עוֹלָם לְאַכְסַדְרָה

רש"י

שֶׁעוֹשֶׂה אוֹתוֹ גָּלָל. מַרְבֶּה לוֹ זֶבֶל, וְשׂוֹרֵף אֶת הַזְּרָעִים שֶׁנִּזְרְעוּ בּוֹ. **מתני'** אֶת הַנְּבֵלוֹת וְאֶת הַקְּבָרוֹת כו'. מִשּׁוּם רֵיחַ רָע. **אֶלָּא לְמִזְרַח** הָעִיר. שֶׁאֵין הָרוּחַ מִזְרָחִית קָשָׁה (ג) תָּדִיר אא"כ בָּאָה לְפוּרְעָנוּת, אֲבָל כְּדַרְכָּהּ הִיא חַמָּה וּמְנַשֶּׁבֶת בְּנַחַת, דִּכְתִיב (יונה ד): "רוּחַ קָדִים חֲרִישִׁית וַתַּךְ הַשֶּׁמֶשׁ" וגו' — לְפִיכָךְ אֵינָהּ מְבִיאָה הָרוּחַ לָעִיר. חוּץ מִן מַעֲרָבָהּ. בַּגְּמָ' מְפָרֵשׁ טַעֲמָא. **גמ'** וְסוֹמֵךְ. אֵינוֹ צָרִיךְ לְהַרְחִיק נ' אַמָּה. שֶׁאֵינוֹ עוֹשֶׂה כְּלָל. וּמַרְחִיק נ' אַמָּה דְּקָאָמַר ר"ע — אַשְּׁאָר רוּחוֹת דְּרֵישָׁא קָאֵי. **תְּדִירָא** בְּרוּחוֹת. אוֹתוֹ צַד תָּדִיר בְּרוּחַ, שֶׁרוּחַ מַעֲרָבִית מְנַשֶּׁבֶת תָּדִיר מִשְּׁאָר רוּחוֹת. רוּחַ צְפוֹנִית מְנַשֶּׁבֶת עִם כָּל אַחַת. מֵהָרוּחוֹת, לְפִי שֶׁהִיא רַכָּה וּמְתוּקָה וּצְלוּלָה, כִּדְאָמַר בִּיבָמוֹת (דף עב.), וּמְמַתְּקָתָן. בֶּן נֵץ. מַלְאָךְ הֶעָשׂוּי בִּדְמוּת נֵץ. מַעֲמִידָהּ. בִּכְנָפָיו. **תְּדִירָא** בִּשְׁכִינָה. בַּמַּעֲרָב הִיא שׁוֹכֶנֶת. לַאֲבוֹתֵינוּ. אַנְשֵׁי כנה"ג, שֶׁאָמְרוּ מִקְרָא זֶה בְּסֵפֶר עֶזְרָא. **וּצְבָא** הַשָּׁמַיִם. הַשֶּׁמֶשׁ וְהַיָּרֵחַ הָעוֹמְדִים בַּמִּזְרָח. לְךָ מִשְׁתַּחֲוִים. לַמַּעֲרָב. **וְדִלְמָא**. הֵם לַמִּזְרָח מִשְׁתַּחֲוִים! וְכִי תֵּימָא אֵין דֶּרֶךְ לְהִשְׁתַּחֲווֹת סָמוּךְ לָרַב — הֵם עוֹשִׂין כְּעֶבֶד שֶׁנָּטַל פְּרָס מֵרַבּוֹ וְחוֹזֵר לַאֲחוֹרָיו וּמִשְׁתַּחֲוֶה כְּשֶׁהוּא הוֹלֵךְ לַאֲחוֹרָיו, מִשֶּׁנָּטַל פְּרָס מִתְרַחֵק תָּמִיד בְּהִשְׁתַּחֲוָיָה. פְּרָס = מַתָּן. **אַתָּה הוּא ה' לְבַדֶּךָ**. בָּתַר "וּצְבָא הַשָּׁמַיִם" כְּתִיב, וְעַל עִסְקֵי שְׁלִיחוּת צְבָא הַשָּׁמַיִם הוּא מְשַׁבֵּחַ וְאוֹמֵר: אַתָּה הוּא לְבַדְּךָ בְּמִדָּה זוֹ. **לְשָׁם** מַחֲזִירִין שְׁלִיחוּתָן. כְּשֶׁבָּאִין לוֹמַר עָשִׂינוּ שְׁלִיחוּתְךָ — צְרִיכִין לָשׁוּב אֶל מָקוֹם שֶׁהַשּׁוֹלְחָם עוֹמֵד שָׁם. **לְמָקוֹם** שֶׁמִּשְׁתַּלְּחִין. פֵּי': בְּאוֹתוֹ מָקוֹם שֶׁנִּשְׁתַּלְּחוּ שָׁם — אַף שָׁם הַשְּׁכִינָה מְצוּיָה, וְאוֹמְרִים לוֹ עָשִׂינוּ שְׁלִיחוּתְךָ. **וְהִנֵּה הַמַּלְאָךְ** הַדּוֹבֵר בִּי יוֹצֵא. בִּנְבוּאַת זְכַרְיָה, לָמוֹד אֶת יְרוּשָׁלַיִם כַּמָּה אָרְכָּהּ וגו', וּמַלְאָךְ אַחֵר יוֹצֵא לִסְתּוֹר שְׁלִיחוּתוֹ שֶׁל רִאשׁוֹן, שֶׁחָזַר בּוֹ הַמָּקוֹם (ד) וְלֹא יִתֵּן בָּהּ מִדָּה, וְאוֹמֵר "פְּרָזוֹת תֵּשֵׁב יְרוּשָׁלַיִם" וַהֲרֵי שְׁנֵיהֶם מֵאֵת הַשְּׁכִינָה בָּאִים, וְ"אַחֲרָיו" לֹא נֶאֱמַר, אֶלָּא "לִקְרָאתוֹ", זֶה בָּא מִכָּאן וְזֶה בָּא מִכָּאן. **רַב שֵׁשֶׁת**. מְאוֹר עֵינַיִם הֲוָה. **לְכָל רוּחָתָא אוֹקְמַן**. הַעֲמִידֵנִי לְהִתְפַּלֵּל. **דְּמוֹרוּ בָּהּ מִינֵי**. תַּלְמִידֵי יֵשׁוּ מוֹרִים הוֹרָאָה לְהִתְפַּלֵּל בַּמִּזְרָח. **אוּרְיָה**. אֲנִי שָׁמַעְתִּי כָּךְ קוֹרִין לַמַּעֲרָב בִּלְשׁוֹן פַּרְסִי. ול"נ שֶׁכָּךְ קוֹרִין לַמִּזְרָח בִּלְשׁוֹן לַעַז, וְהַיְינוּ דְּקָאָמַר אֲוִיר יָהּ, שֶׁהַשְּׁכִינָה בַּמַּעֲרָב וּפָנָיו לַמִּזְרָח, נִמְצָא הַמִּזְרָח אֲוִירוֹ. **יַעֲרֹף כַּמָּטָר לִקְחִי**. מֹשֶׁה רַבֵּינוּ דִּימָּה אֶת הַתּוֹרָה לְאַרְבַּע רוּחוֹת, כְּשֵׁם שֶׁאִי אֶפְשָׁר בְּלֹא הֵם — כָּךְ אִי אֶפְשָׁר לָעוֹלָם בְּלֹא תּוֹרָה. **מֵעָרְפּוֹ שֶׁל עוֹלָם**. אֲנִי שָׁמַעְתִּי: מֵחָזְקוֹ שֶׁל עוֹלָם, עַל שֵׁם שֶׁהַשְּׁכִינָה בַּמַּעֲרָב, ס"ל. וַאֲנִי אוֹמֵר: מֵאֲחוֹרָיו שֶׁל עוֹלָם — שֶׁהַמַּעֲרָב קָרוּי אָחוֹר, שֶׁנֶּאֱמַר: "הֵן קֶדֶם אֶהֱלֹךְ וְאֵינֶנּוּ וְאָחוֹר וְלֹא אָבִין" וגו' (איוב כג). **שֶׁמַּזֶּלֶת אֶת הַזָּהָב**. שֶׁמְּחַמֶּמֶת וּמְבִיאָה שָׁרָב, וְרַעֲבוֹן בָּא, וְהַזָּהָב זָל. וְכֵן הוּא אוֹמֵר. דִּכְתִיב זִילוּתָא גַּבֵּי זָהָב. **כִּשְׂעִיר** = שֵׁד.

תוספות

שעושה אותו גלל. אע"ג דגלל משביח הקרקע, כשהיא כולה גלל — מזיק. **אין** עושין בורסקי אלא למזרח העיר. משום דרוח מערבי שהוא קשה ירחיק ויוליך הריח מן העיר, כדאמרי' (ברכות מ.): היכן למזרח גרנו — דמו בראשו, מפני שרוח מערבית מביא הקש בחוטמו. **מפני** שהיא תדירה. לא גרסי' "מ"ע", דמן הברייתא היא, דהכי איתא בתוספתא. (פ"א ע"ש). **וצבא** השמים לך משתחוים. וא"ת: בלילה נמי במזרח משתחוים! וי"ל: דאין לנו ללמוד אלא ממה שאנו רואין. וא"ת: ואמאי לא נדע מקום תפלה מבית המקדש, שהיתה שם שכינה במערב? וי"ל: דמשם אין ללמוד, דאע"ג דשכינה בכל מקום — אי אפשר להשים ארון וכפורת אלא בצד אחד. וריב"א אומר: דמשם אין ללמוד דשכינה במערב, דנהי דבית קדשי הקדשים היה במערב המקדש, מ"מ הארון שהשכינה שם, כדכתיב (שמות כה) "ונועדתי לך שם" היה במזרח בית קדשי הקדשים[ה]. **לכל** רוחתא אוקמן. כל הני אמוראי לית להו הא דתניא בברכות (דף ל.) שחייב אדם להתפלל נגד ירושלים, משום דכתיב "והתפללו אליך דרך ארצם". אלא סברי כר' ישמעאל דאמר: (ה) בכ"מ שכינה. ומאן דאמר שכינה במערב — סבר כר"ע דאמר: מפני שהיא תדירה. ור' חנינא דשמעתין, דאמר: כגון אתון דיתבון לצפונא דארעא דישראל אדרימו סבר לה כברייתא דברכות.

אוריה. לשון פרסי, דאוריה מערב, נראה לר"ת ולר"ח עיקר.

רוח מערבית שבא מערפו של עולם. כדפי' בקונט': מאחורו של עולם, דמערב קרוי אחור, דכתיב "אחור וקדם צרתני", ודרשינן [בחגיגה] (דף יב.) לענין מזרח ומערב. וכתיב נמי "ארם מקדם ופלשתים מאחור" (ישעיה ט) וקרי נמי דרום "ימין", ולצפון "שמאל", כדאמרי' בשמעתין. והיינו משום דשכינה במערב, ופני השכינה למזרח, לכך קרוי מערב אחור ומזרח קדם, ודרום ימין, ולצפון שמאל. ולמ"ד שכינה בכל מקום — צ"ל דהאי דקרי מזרח "קדם", ומערב "אחור", ודרום "ימין", ולצפון "שמאל" — משום שכינה בבית המקדש שהיה במערב, ופני השכינה כלפי ישראל שהיו במזרח, ומשתחוים שם.

הגה"ה ורבינו יצחק בר יהודה פירש דכשעמד אדם הראשון כשנברא היו פניו למזרח. ואין נראה, שהיה ערפו כלפי השכינה — למאן דאמר שכינה במערב. ע"כ הגה"ה.

רוח מזרחית שמסערת כל העולם כולו. והא דמשמע במתניתין שהיא נוחה מכל הרוחות — היינו כשהיא באה כדרכה. אבל כשבאה לפורענות — היא מסערת, כדפי' הקונט' במתניתין.

ומזורים

רבינו גרשום

פיסקא בורסקי. מקום שמעבדין בו העורות ומסריח: אלא למזרח העי'. מפני שרוח מערבי שהיא תדירא מנשבת בו ודוחה הסריחה שאינה באה לעיר: חוץ ממערבה. שהיא תדירא ודוחה את הסריחה לעיר א) מש"ה אין עושין: שאלמלא כן. שרוח צפונית מבלבלתן אין העולם מתקיים: יפרוש כנפיו לתימן. משום דמעמידה לאותו רוח תדיר: בתפלה. שהשכינ' במערב ומש"ה צריך להרחיק משם: לך משתחוים. [צבא] השמים היינו השמש והירח כשיוצאים במזרח לך משתחוים למערב ושם צריך להחזיר בשעת תפלה: ואימא. שהשכינה במזרח ודקאמר לך משתחוים עושים כעבד שנוטל פרס מרבו ומשתחוה וחוזר לאחוריו. כך בשעה שיוצאין ממזרח חוזרין פניהם לשכינה במזרח ומשתחוים ושוב יוצאין וזורחין. קשיא: לבדך משליחותך ומשנה מבשר ודם: ויאמרו לך הננו. בכ"מ שהן. [מלמד] שהשכינה בכל מקום: והנה המלאך הדובר בי יוצא מאת השכינה ומלאך אחר יוצא לקראתו. מן צד אחר יוצא ולפני שכינה: דמודי בה מיני. שמשתחוין לצבא השמים היוצאין מן המזרח: אוריה. קורין בלשונן לרוח מערבי: יערוף כמטר לקחי. זה העוסק בתורה לשמה ומרכין אזניו לשמוע לקחי עושה טובה לעולם כמטר זה שבא מן מערב: שבאה מערפו של עולם. מרוח מערבי ערפו של שכינה הוא. דכתיב צפון וימין אתה בראתם דמשמע דימינו של שכינה בדרום ושמאלו לצד צפון ופניו למזרח וערפו למערב אלמא דשכינה במערב: ותזל כטל אמרתי. היינו שמזלזל תורה שעוסק שלא לשמה מביא רעה לעולם כרוח צפוני שמנשב ומביא רעה לעולם: עד שמזלת את הזהב. שנותנין בני אדם כספם וזהבם בזול בשביל התבואה: כשעירים עלי דשא. זהו העוסק בתורה שלא לשמה: כשעירים. כשד: וכל העוסק בתורה לשמה מביא טובה לעולם כרביבים הללו שיורדין בנחת

א) נראה דצ"ל מש"ה אין עושין כל עיקר.

מסורת הש"ס

א) לעיל יח.: ב) גיטין לא:: ג) [בילקוט ובע"י איתא שם]: ד) [עי' בערוך ערך ערף שכתב בשם רבינו גרשום פירוש נכון על זה]: ה) [ועי' תי"ט דהלכה סוף מ"ע ומ"ש עוד ביומא פ"ה מ"ב ע"ש]: ו) וכ"פ הערוך ערך אסטנא עי' תוס' גיטין לא: ד"ה שליא נשיב:

עין משפט נר מצוה

פב א ב מיי' פ"י מהל' שכנים הל' ג סמג עשין פב טוש"ע ח"מ סי' קנב סעיף כג:
פג ג מיי' שם הלכה ה סמג שם טוש"ע שם סעיף לא:
פד ד טוש"ע א"ח סי' צד סעיף ב בהג"ה:

הגהות הב"ח

(א) גמ' שהודיעונו מקום תפלה: (ב) שם אמר רב יהודה אמר רב מאי דכתיב יערוף: (ג) רש"י ד"ה אלא וכו' קשה תמיד אא"כ: (ד) ד"ה והנה המלאך וכו' שחזר בו המקום מליתן בה מדה: (ה) תום' ד"ה לכל וכו' דאמר שכינה בכ"מ ומאן דאמר:

לְאַכְסַדְרָה הוּא דּוֹמֶה, וְרוּחַ צְפוֹנִית אֵינָהּ מְסוּבֶּבֶת, וְכֵיוָן שֶׁהִגִּיעָה חַמָּה אֵצֶל קֶרֶן מַעֲרָבִית צְפוֹנִית — נִכְפֶּפֶת וְעוֹלָה לְמַעְלָה מִן הָרָקִיעַ; וְרַבִּי יְהוֹשֻׁעַ אוֹמֵר: עוֹלָם לְקוּבָּה הוּא דּוֹמֶה, וְרוּחַ צְפוֹנִית מְסוּבֶּבֶת, וְכֵיוָן שֶׁחַמָּה מַגַּעַת לְקֶרֶן מַעֲרָבִית צְפוֹנִית — מַקֶּפֶת וְחוֹזֶרֶת אֲחוֹרֵי כִּיפָּה, שֶׁנֶּאֱמַר: °"הוֹלֵךְ אֶל דָּרוֹם וְסוֹבֵב אֶל צָפוֹן" וגו', א)"הוֹלֵךְ אֶל דָּרוֹם" — בַּיּוֹם, "וְסוֹבֵב אֶל צָפוֹן" — בַּלַּיְלָה, "סוֹבֵב סוֹבֵב הוֹלֵךְ הָרוּחַ וְעַל סְבִיבוֹתָיו שָׁב הָרוּחַ" — אֵלּוּ פְּנֵי מִזְרָח וּפְנֵי מַעֲרָב, שֶׁפְּעָמִים מְסַבַּבְתָּן וּפְעָמִים מְהַלַּכְתָּן. הוּא הָיָה אוֹמֵר, אֲתָאן לְר' אֱלִיעֶזֶר: °"מִן הַחֶדֶר תָּבֹא סוּפָה" — זוֹ רוּחַ דְּרוֹמִית, "וּמִמְּזָרִים קָרָה" — זוֹ רוּחַ צְפוֹנִית, "מִנִּשְׁמַת אֵל יִתֶּן קָרַח" — זוֹ רוּחַ מַעֲרָבִית, "וְרֹחַב מַיִם בְּמוּצָק" — זוֹ רוּחַ מִזְרָחִית. וְהָאָמַר מָר: רוּחַ דְּרוֹמִית מַעֲלָה רְבִיבִים וּמְגַדֶּלֶת עֲשָׂבִים! לָא קַשְׁיָא: הָא דְּאָתְיָא מִטְרָא בְּנִיחוּתָא, הָא בְּשַׁפִּיכוּתָא. אֲמַר רַב חִסְדָּא, מַאי דִּכְתִיב: °"מִצָּפוֹן זָהָב יֶאֱתֶה" — זוֹ רוּחַ צְפוֹנִית שֶׁמַּזֶּלֶת אֶת הַזָּהָב, וְכֵן הוּא אוֹמֵר: °"הַזָּלִים זָהָב מִכִּיס". אָמַר רַפְרָם בַּר פַּפָּא אָמַר רַב חִסְדָּא: מִיּוֹם שֶׁחָרַב בֵּית הַמִּקְדָּשׁ — לֹא הוּגְשְׁמָה רוּחַ דְּרוֹמִית, שֶׁנֶּאֱמַר: °"וַיִּגְזֹר עַל יָמִין וְרָעֵב וַיֹּאכַל עַל שְׂמֹאל וְלֹא שָׂבֵעוּ", וּכְתִיב: °"צָפוֹן וְיָמִין אַתָּה בְרָאתָם". וְאָמַר רַפְרָם בַּר פַּפָּא אָמַר רַב חִסְדָּא: מִיּוֹם שֶׁחָרַב בֵּית הַמִּקְדָּשׁ — אֵין הַגְּשָׁמִים יוֹרְדִין מֵאוֹצָר טוֹב, שֶׁנֶּאֱמַר: °"יִפְתַּח ה' לְךָ אֶת אוֹצָרוֹ הַטּוֹב", בִּזְמַן שֶׁיִּשְׂרָאֵל (א) עוֹשִׂין רְצוֹנוֹ שֶׁל מָקוֹם וְיִשְׂרָאֵל שְׁרוּיִין עַל אַדְמָתָם — גְּשָׁמִים יוֹרְדִין מֵאוֹצָר טוֹב, בִּזְמַן שֶׁאֵין יִשְׂרָאֵל שְׁרוּיִין עַל אַדְמָתָם — אֵין גְּשָׁמִים יוֹרְדִין מֵאוֹצָר טוֹב. אָמַר רַבִּי יִצְחָק: אהָרוֹצֶה שֶׁיַּחְכִּים — יַדְרִים, וְשֶׁיַּעֲשִׁיר — יַצְפִּין, ב)בוְסִימָנָיךְ: שֻׁלְחָן בַּצָּפוֹן וּמְנוֹרָה בַּדָּרוֹם; וְרַבִּי יְהוֹשֻׁעַ בֶּן לֵוִי אָמַר: לְעוֹלָם יַדְרִים, שֶׁמִּתּוֹךְ שֶׁמִּתְחַכֵּם מִתְעַשֵּׁר, שֶׁנֶּאֱמַר: °"אֹרֶךְ יָמִים בִּימִינָהּ בִּשְׂמֹאלָהּ עֹשֶׁר וְכָבוֹד". וְהָא רַבִּי יְהוֹשֻׁעַ בֶּן לֵוִי אָמַר: שְׁכִינָה בַּמַּעֲרָב! דִּמְצַדֵּד אַצְדּוּדֵי. אֲמַר לֵיהּ רַבִּי חֲנִינָא לְרַב ג)אַשִׁי: כְּגוֹן אַתּוּן דְּיָתְבִיתוּ בִּצְפוֹנָהּ דא"י — אַדְרִימוּ אַדְרוּמֵי. וּמְנָא לָן ד)דְּבָבֶל לִצְפוֹנָהּ דְּאֶרֶץ יִשְׂרָאֵל קַיְימָא? דִּכְתִיב °"מִצָּפוֹן תִּפָּתַח הָרָעָה עַל כָּל יֹשְׁבֵי הָאָרֶץ".§ "מַרְחִיקִין אֶת הַמִּשְׁרָה מִן הַיָּרָק" וכו'.§ תָּנָא: רַבִּי יוֹסֵי מַתִּיר בַּחַרְדָּל, ה)שֶׁיָּכוֹל לוֹמַר לוֹ: עַד שֶׁאַתָּה אוֹמֵר לִי הַרְחֵק חַרְדָּלְךָ מִן דְּבוֹרַיי, הַרְחֵק דְּבוֹרְךָ מִן חַרְדָּלַיי, שֶׁבָּאוֹת וְאוֹכְלוֹת לְגִלּוּגֵי חַרְדָּלַיי.§

מתני' ו)מַרְחִיקִין אֶת הָאִילָן מִן הַבּוֹר עֶשְׂרִים וְחָמֵשׁ אַמָּה, וּבֶחָרוּב וּבַשִּׁקְמָה — חֲמִשִּׁים אַמָּה, בֵּין מִלְמַעְלָה בֵּין מִן הַצַּד. אִם הַבּוֹר קָדְמָה — ז)קוֹצֵץ וְנוֹתֵן דָּמִים, וְאִם אִילָן קָדַם — לֹא יָקוֹץ. ח)סָפֵק זֶה קָדַם וְסָפֵק זֶה קָדַם — לֹא יָקוֹץ; ט)ר' יוֹסֵי אוֹמֵר: גאע"פ שֶׁהַבּוֹר קוֹדֶמֶת לָאִילָן — לֹא יָקוֹץ, י)שֶׁזֶּה חוֹפֵר בְּתוֹךְ שֶׁלּוֹ וְזֶה נוֹטֵעַ בְּתוֹךְ שֶׁלּוֹ.§

גמ' תָּנָא: בֵּין שֶׁהַבּוֹר לְמַטָּה וְאִילָן לְמַעְלָה, בֵּין שֶׁהַבּוֹר לְמַעְלָה וְאִילָן לְמַטָּה. בִּשְׁלָמָא בּוֹר לְמַטָּה וְאִילָן לְמַעְלָה — קָא אָזְלִין שָׁרָשִׁין מַזְּקִי לָהּ לַבּוֹר, אֶלָּא בּוֹר לְמַעְלָה וְאִילָן לְמַטָּה — אַמַּאי? אָמַר רַבִּי חַגָּא בְּשֵׁם רַבִּי יוֹסֵי: מִפְּנֵי שֶׁמַּחֲלִידִין אֶת הַקַּרְקַע וּמְקַלְקְלִין קַרְקָעִיתָהּ שֶׁל בּוֹר.§ רַבִּי יוֹסֵי אוֹמֵר: אע"פ שֶׁהַבּוֹר קוֹדֶמֶת לָאִילָן — לֹא יָקוֹץ, שֶׁזֶּה חוֹפֵר בְּתוֹךְ שֶׁלּוֹ וְזֶה נוֹטֵעַ בְּתוֹךְ שֶׁלּוֹ.§ אָמַר רַב יְהוּדָה אָמַר שְׁמוּאֵל: הֲלָכָה כְּרַבִּי יוֹסֵי. כ)אָמַר רַב אַשִׁי, כִּי הֲוָאן בֵּי רַב כָּהֲנָא הֲוָה אָמְרִינַן: דמוֹדֵי ר' יוֹסֵי בְּגִירֵי דִידֵיהּ. פָּאפֵּי יוֹנָאָה עָנִי וְהֶעֱשִׁיר הֲוָה, בְּנָה אַפַּדְנָא, ההֲווּ הָנָךְ עֲצוּרֵי בְּשִׁיבָבוּתֵיהּ, דְּכִי הֲווּ דָּיְיקִי שׁוּמְשְׁמֵי הֲוָה נָיְידָא אַפַּדְנֵיהּ; אֲתָא לְקַמֵּיהּ דְּרַב אַשִׁי, א"ל, כִּי הֲוָאן בֵּי רַב כָּהֲנָא הֲוָה אָמְרִינַן: מוֹדֵי רַבִּי יוֹסֵי בְּגִירֵי דִילֵיהּ. וְכַמָּה?

כִּדְנַיְיד

רש"י

לְאַכְסַדְרָה. שֶׁאֵין לָהּ דּוֹפֶן רְבִיעִית. אֵינָהּ מְסוּבֶּבֶת. בִּמְחִילָה. לְמַעְלָה מִן הָרָקִיעַ. וּמְהַלֶּכֶת אֶת רוּחַ צָפוֹן בְּגַגּוֹ שֶׁל רָקִיעַ. לְקוּבָּה. אֹהֶל שֶׁכּוּלּוֹ מוּקָּף. לְקֶרֶן מַעֲרָבִית צְפוֹנִית. בַּלַּיְלָה, שֶׁהַחַמָּה לְעוֹלָם מְהַלֶּכֶת רוּחַ צְפוֹנִית בַּלַּיְלָה, וּמִן הַמַּעֲרָב הִיא פּוֹנָה לַצָּפוֹן. שֶׁכָּךְ הִילּוּכָהּ: מִן הַמִּזְרָח לַדָּרוֹם, מִן הַדָּרוֹם לַמַּעֲרָב, וּמִמַּעֲרָב לַצָּפוֹן. וּמַחֲזֶרֶת אֲחוֹרֵי כִּיפָּה. דֶּרֶךְ חַלּוֹן. הוֹלֵךְ אֶל דָּרוֹם. הֶיקֵּף הַיּוֹם קָרוּי הִילּוּךְ, שֶׁהוּא בְּתוֹךְ הֶחָלָל. וְאֶת הֶיקֵּף הַלַּיְלָה קָרוּי סִיבּוּב, שֶׁהוּא מַקִּיף בַּחוּץ. וּבַיּוֹם לְעוֹלָם מְהַלֶּכֶת בַּדָּרוֹם, אֲפִילּוּ בַּיּוֹם קָצָר אֵינוֹ מְהַלֵּךְ פָּחוֹת מֵרוּחַ דְּרוֹמִית. וְסוֹבֵב אֶל צָפוֹן בַּלַּיְלָה. אַף בַּלַּיְלָה קְצָרָה שֶׁל תְּקוּפַת תַּמּוּז אֵינוֹ סוֹבֵב פָּחוֹת מֵרוּחַ צְפוֹנִית. פְּעָמִים מְהַלַּכְתָּן. בַּיּוֹם אָרוֹךְ שֶׁל תְּקוּפַת תַּמּוּז, שֶׁהִיא יוֹצְאָה בְּקֶרֶן צְפוֹנִית מִזְרָחִית וְשׁוֹקַעַת בְּקֶרֶן מַעֲרָבִית צְפוֹנִית. פְּעָמִים סוֹבַבְתָּן. בַּיּוֹם קָצָר, שֶׁהִיא יוֹצְאָה בְּקֶרֶן מִזְרָחִית דְּרוֹמִית וְשׁוֹקַעַת בְּקֶרֶן מַעֲרָבִית דְּרוֹמִית, וּמְהַלֶּכֶת בַּלַּיְלָה ג' רוּחוֹת. אֲתָאן לְר' אֱלִיעֶזֶר. שֶׁאָמַר לְאַכְסַדְרָה דּוֹמֶה. וּמִמְּזָרִים קָרָה זוֹ רוּחַ צְפוֹנִית. שֶׁהַדּוֹפֶן מוּזֶּרֶת וּפְרוּצָה. וְהָאָמְרַתְּ רוּחַ דְּרוֹמִית מַעֲלָה רְבִיבִים. וְכָאן אַתָּה אוֹמֵר רוּחַ מִזְרָחִית מְבִיאָה מַיִם! הָא דְּאָתְיָא מִטְרָא בְּנִיחוּתָא. בָּא מִן הַדָּרוֹם, וְכִי אָתְיָא בְּשַׁפִּיכוּתָא — בָּא מִן הַמִּזְרָח, כִּדִכְתִיב: "מַיִם בְּמוּצָק". לֹא הוּגְשְׁמָה רוּחַ דְּרוֹמִית. שֶׁהָיְתָה רְגִילָה לְהָבִיא רְבִיבִים טוֹבִים. וּכְתִיב צָפוֹן וְיָמִין. אַלְמָא יָמִין הוּא דָּרוֹם, וּכְתִיב בֵּיהּ רָעָב. אֶת אוֹצָרוֹ הַטּוֹב. וְסֵיפָא "לָתֵת מְטַר אַרְצְךָ". יַדְרִים. בִּתְפִלָּתוֹ, יַחֲזִיר פָּנָיו לַדָּרוֹם. וְסִימָנָיךְ. שֶׁלֹּא תַּחֲלִיף. דִּמְצַדֵּד אַצְדּוּדֵי. (ב) מְעַט לְצַד דָּרוֹם. אַדְרִימוּ. שֶׁתִּהְיוּ פּוֹנִים לְצַד יְרוּשָׁלַיִם, מִשּׁוּם דִּכְתִיב: "וְהִתְפַּלְלוּ אֵלֶיךָ דֶּרֶךְ אַרְצָם" וגו' (מלכים א ח). עַד שֶׁאַתָּה אוֹמֵר לִי. שֶׁאֲנִי מַזִּיק, וְעָלַי לְהַרְחִיק אֶת עַצְמִי, אֲנִי אוֹמֵר לְךָ שֶׁאַתָּה מַזִּיק. לְגִלּוּגֵי חַרְדָּלַיי = פִּרְחֵי חַרְדָּלַיי. **מתני'** חָרוּב וְשִׁקְמָה. שֶׁשָּׁרְשֵׁיהֶם מְרוּבִּים. בֵּין מִלְמַעְלָה. שֶׁאֶחָד מֵהֶן מִלְמַעְלָן בְּגוֹבַהּ שִׁיפּוּעַ הַר, וְהַשֵּׁנִי בְּשִׁפּוּלוֹ. בֵּין מִן הַצַּד. בְּקַרְקַע שָׁוֶה. וְנוֹתֵן דָּמִים. דְּכֵיוָן דִּבִרְשׁוּת נָטַע, שֶׁאֵינוֹ מַזִּיק עַד זְמַן גָּדוֹל — לֹא חִייְבוּהוּ חֲכָמִים לָקוֹץ בְּלֹא דָּמִים, בְּשֶׁבִיל הֶיזֵּקָא דְּיָחִיד. **גמ'** שֶׁמַּחֲלִידִין. לְשׁוֹן חֻלְדָּה דְּהִלְכוֹת שְׁחִיטָה (חולין דף לג.), *שֶׁמְּהַלֶּכֶת מִתַּחַת לְקַרְקָעִית הַבּוֹר. הֲלָכָה כְּר' יוֹסֵי. שֶׁעַל הַנִּיזָּק לְהַרְחִיק אֶת עַצְמוֹ. בְּגִירֵי דִילֵיהּ. הֵיכָא דְּמָטֵי לֵיהּ הֶיזֵּיקָא מִתּוֹךְ יָדָיו שֶׁל מַזִּיק, כְּהַהִיא דְּאָמְרִי' בְּ"הַבַּיִת וְהָעֲלִיָּיה" (ב"מ דף קיז.): הָנְהוּ בֵּי תְּרֵי חַד דָּיֵיר עִילָּאֵי וְחַד דָּיֵיר תַּתָּאֵי, אִיפַּחִית מַעֲזִיבָה, וְכָל אֵימַת דְּמָשֵׁי יְדֵיהּ נָפְלֵי עֲלֵיהּ דְּתַתָּאֵי. דִּכְשֶׁנּוֹפְלִין מִיָּדוֹ מַמָּשׁ עַל הַתַּחְתּוֹן — קָרֵי לֵיהּ גִּירֵי דִילֵיהּ, וְכִי פָּסְקִי וַהֲדַר נָפְלֵי — (ג) לָא קָרֵי לֵיהּ גִּירֵי דִילֵיהּ. פָּאפֵּי יוֹנָאָה. כָּךְ שְׁמוֹ, עַל שֵׁם מְקוֹמוֹ. עֲצוּרֵי. עוֹצְרֵי שׁוּמְשְׁמִין לַעֲשׂוֹת שֶׁמֶן. בְּגִירֵי דִילֵיהּ. וְהָכָא נַמִּי מִידֵיהֶם הוּא בָּא לוֹ, שֶׁמַּכָּה מַכּוֹתֵיהֶם הוּא מַרְעִיד. וְכַמָּה. תָּנוּד אַפַּדְנָא, דְּבָעֵי אַרְחוֹקֵי.

כִּדְנַיְיד

תוספות

וממזרים(ד). פי': רוח לפונית שכותל שלה מושלך, כלומר שאינה מסובבת לרבי אליעזר. **וכתיב** צפון וימין וכו'. ד"ויגזור על ימין" (ה) איכא למימר דימין ושמאל של אדם מיירי (הג"ה. ועוד נראה: שמא (ו) מקרא קמא אין להוכיח שבדרום ימין, ולא נאמר אלא איפכא. ע"כ הג"ה). **תנא** בין שהבור למעלה ואילן למטה כו'. אילטריך לאיתויי הך, אע"ג דבמתני' נמי תנן "בין מלמעלן בין מלמטן" מ"מ, דאי ממתני' הוה אמינא דאחרוב ושקמה קאי, דעלה קאי, קמ"ל ברייתא בכל אילן. (הגה"ה. ולספרים דלא גרסינן במתני' "בין מלמטן" אתי שפיר, דאי ממתני' הוה אמינא: "בין מלמעלן" — אאילן קאי ולא אבור, משום דלא תקשי: אלא בור מלמעלה ואילן מלמטה אמאי? כדפריך אברייתא. עד כאן הג"ה). **עני** והעשיר הוה. רבותא נקט, שהיה עני, ולא איבעי(ז) לאסוקי אדעתייהו שיבנה האפדנא — אפי' הכי הוזקקו להרחיק, משום דהוו גירי דידהו. אף על גב דסמך בהיתר אין לריך להרחיק אפי' בגירי דיליה, כדתניא (לעיל דף כ:): אם היה רפת בקר קודמת לאולר — מותר, וה"ה חנות של נחתומים ולבעין, ואין חילוק בין דירה לשאר, לפי המסקנא — אומר ר"ת: דהכא היינו טעמא, משום דלא קביעא תשמישייהו כל כך כי הנך דלעיל. (הג"ה. ועוד: דהכא (ח) משום דבאיסור סמך, דכל מרא דמחי — מרפי לארעא. ע"כ הג"ה).

אפומא

עין משפט נר מצוה

פה א טוש"ע א"ח סי' לד סעיף ב בהג"ה:

פו ב מיי' פ"א מהל' בית הבחירה הל' ז סמג עשין קסז:

פז ג מיי' פ"י מהלכות שכנים הל' ז סמג עשין פב טוש"ע ח"מ סי' קנה סעיף לב:

פח ד מיי' שם הל' ה טוש"ע שם סעיף לא:

פט ה מיי' שם פי"א הלכה ג סמג שם טוש"ע שם סעיף טו:

מסורת הש"ס

א) עירובין ט.: ב) [לקמן קמז. יומא כח: מנחות פו:]: ג) כ"א ר' יאשיה: ד) [גיטין ו.]: ה) [לעיל יח.]: ו) ב"מ קיז. [לעיל יח. לקמן כז:]: ז) [לעיל כד:]: ח) (ב"מ קי:): ט) (לעיל יח:]: י) [לעיל יז: כב:]: כ) [לעיל כב: ב"מ קיז.]:

רבינו גרשום

עולם לאכסדרה הוא דומה. מה אכסדרה זו שיש לה ג' דפנות ולא יותר ומסוככת כך העולם: ורוח צפונית. אין לה דופן ואינה מסוככת: וכשחמה מגעת. שהלכה כל היום ועכשיו כשמגעת בלילה בקרן מערבית צפונית נכפפת באותו רוח צפוני שאינו מסוכך ועולה למעלה מרקיע: ור' יהושע אומר עולם דומה לקובה. כאהל הוא דומה. מה אהל זה מסוככת לכל דפנותיה אף עולם מכל וכל מסוכך וכשחמה זורחת ביום ארוך זורחת ברוח צפונית מזרחית והולכת במזרח דרום עד שמגעת לקרן מערבית צפונית סמוך לחשיכה לקרן צפוני נכנסת בחלון א' בלילה ומקפת וחוזרת אחורי כיפה של עולם וסובב רוח צפונית כל הלילה שנאמר הולך אל דרום ביום בין בימות החמה בין בימות הגשמים. וכן הכי נמי וסובב אל צפון בלילה בין בימות החמה בין בימות הגשמים: סובב סובב הולך אלו פני מזרח ומערב. שפעמים מסבבתן ביום קצר ששוקעת החמה בקרן מזרחית דרומית והולך כל היום על פני דרום ולא יותר ובלילה נכנסת בקרן דרומית מערבית בחלון אחד וסובבת כל הלילה פני המערב ופני הצפון ופני המזרח עד קרן מזרחית דרומית. ופעמים מהלכתן ביום ארוך שזורחת חמה בקרן צפונית מזרחית והולכת כל המזרח ופני הדרום ופני המערב עד הלילה ובלילה נכנסת בקרן מערבית צפונית וסובבת כל הלילה פני הצפון עד קרן צפונית. מהלכתן ביום ומסבבתן בלילה: הוא היה אומר ר' אליעזר דהא ברייתא אתאן לטעמא דר"א דאמר עולם לאכסדרה הוא דומה: מן החדר תבוא סופה זו רוח דרומית. שדופן שלה אמצעי ופנימי ודומה לחדר: סופה. סערה: וממזרים קרה זו רוח צפונית. שכל העולם ממזורים זרם מים לשם לפי שאין שם דופן והוא תהו ובהו ומים ואינה מסוככת: קרה. חורף אבל אינו קריר כל כך. קרח חורף ממש: זו רוח מזרחית. שמרחיבין שם הגשמים להציק. רוח של ניחותא מעלי. בשפיכותא שבא בקשיות ודאי קשה כסופה: לא הוגשמה רוח צפונית. שלא ירדו גשמים לשם: על ימין. זו רוח דרומית: ורעב. משמע פעמים רעב פעמים שבע: ויאכל ולא שבעו. משמע לא שבעו לפי שלא הוגשמה: צפון. הוא שמאל כדפרישית לעיל: ידרים. כלומר לרוח דרומית: יצפין. יתפלל לרוח צפון: שולחן בצפון. היינו עושר שיעריך שולחנו מחמת עושרו: ומנורה בדרום. היינו חכמה כדכתיב כי נר מצוה ותורה אור: שנאמר ארך ימים וגו'. האי קרא לא אתי לאשמועינן אלא דתורה שהיא חכמה יש בה נמי עושר וכבוד: דמצדד אצדודי. לא מכל וכל לרוח דרומית ולא מהכל לרוח מערבית: אדרימו. כלומר כשתתפללו חזרו פניכם לצד דרום שנאמר והתפללו [אליך] דרך ארצם: **פיסקא** והחרוב והשקמה נ' אמה. ששרשיהן הולכין הרבה: בין מלמעלה. שאם האילן עומד סמוך לבור והבור עמוק עד המים נ' אמה אינו מרחיק ואם לאו מרחיק ובין מן הצד שאם הבור אין עמוק צריך להרחיק האילן מן הבור נ' אמה ותנא בין שהבור מלמעלה של אילן שהבור עומד במקום גבוה והאילן במקום נמוך ובין שהבור כמקום נמוך והאילן במקום גבוה אם אין כ"ה אמה הרחקה מרחיק. והא לא קא מזיק ליה לבור כלל: ומלקין קרקעית של בור. ונעשה טיט: מודה ר' יוסי בגירי. כדפריש לעיל אע"פ שעושה בתוך שלו חייב: יונאה. שם מקום: הנך עצורי. שמכתשין ומעצרין את השומשמין כדי להוציא שמן: וכמה

הגהות הב"ח

(א) גמ' את אוצרו הטוב בזמן שישראל שרוין על אדמתם כצ"ל ותיבות עושים רצונו של מקום וישראל נמחק: (ב) רש"י ד"ה דמצדד אצדודי מטה לצד דרום: (ג) ד"ה בגירי דיליה וכו' והדר נפלי כגון דמגנדרי לא קרי ליה: (ד) תום' ד"ה וממזרים קרה זו רוח צפונית פי' שכותל שלה כצ"ל: (ה) ד"ה וכתיב וכו' על ימין ליכא להוכיח דאיכא למימר דבימין: (ו) בא"ד שמא דממקרא קמא אין להוכיח שדרום ימין: (ז) ד"ה עני וכו' ולא איבעי להו לאסוקי וכו' אע"ג דבסמך וכו' נחתומין ושל צבעין: (ח) בא"ד דהכא שאני משום דבאיסור וכו' מרא ומרא דמחי מרפי לארעא והוא דומיא דבור ע"כ הג"ה:

אכְּדְנֵייד נַכְתְּמָא אַפּוּמֵיהּ דְּחַצְבָּא. דְּבֵי בַּר מָרְיוֹן בְּרֵיהּ דְּרָבִין כִּי הֲוָה נָפְצֵי כִּיתָּנָא, הֲוָה אָזְלָא רַקְתָּא וּמַזְּקָא אֱינָשֵׁי; אֲתוּ לְקַמֵּיהּ דְּרָבִינָא, אֲמַר לְהוּ: כִּי אָמְרִינַן מוֹדֶה ר' יוֹסֵי בְּגִירֵי דִילֵיהּ — הָנֵי מִילֵּי דְּקָא אָזְלָא מִכֹּחוֹ, הָכָא זִיקָא הוּא דְּקָא מַמְטֵי לָהּ. מַתְקִיף לָהּ מָר בַּר רַב אַשִׁי: מַאי שְׁנָא א)מִזּוֹרֶה וְרוּחַ מְסַיַּיעְתּוֹ? אֲמַרוּהָ קַמֵּיהּ דְּמָרֵימָר, אֲמַר לְהוּ: בהַיְינוּ זוֹרֶה וְרוּחַ מְסַיַּיעְתּוֹ. וּלְרָבִינָא, מַאי שְׁנָא ב)מִגֵּץ הַיּוֹצֵא מִתַּחַת הַפַּטִּישׁ וְהִזִּיק, גדְּחַיָּיב לְשַׁלֵּם? הָתָם נִיחָא לֵיהּ דְּלֵיזַל, הָכָא לָא נִיחָא לֵיהּ דְּלֵיזַל.§ **מתני'** ג)דלֹא יִטַּע אָדָם אִילָן סָמוּךְ לִשְׂדֵה חֲבֵירוֹ — אֶלָּא אִם כֵּן הִרְחִיק מִמֶּנּוּ אַרְבַּע אַמּוֹת, אֶחָד גְּפָנִים וְאֶחָד כָּל אִילָן. ד)ההָיָה גָּדֵר בֵּינְתַיִם — (א) זֶה סוֹמֵךְ לַגָּדֵר מִכָּאן וְזֶה סוֹמֵךְ לַגָּדֵר מִכָּאן. והָיוּ שָׁרָשִׁים יוֹצְאִים לְתוֹךְ שֶׁל חֲבֵירוֹ — מַעֲמִיק ג' טְפָחִים כְּדֵי שֶׁלֹּא יְעַכֵּב אֶת הַמַּחֲרֵישָׁה. זהָיָה חוֹפֵר בּוֹר, שִׁיחַ וּמְעָרָה — קוֹצֵץ וְיוֹרֵד, וְהָעֵצִים שֶׁלּוֹ.§ **גמ'** תָּנָא: ה)אַרְבַּע אַמּוֹת שֶׁאָמְרוּ — כְּדֵי עֲבוֹדַת הַכֶּרֶם. אָמַר שְׁמוּאֵל: לֹא שָׁנוּ חאֶלָּא בְּאֶרֶץ יִשְׂרָאֵל, טאֲבָל בְּבָבֶל — שְׁתֵּי אַמּוֹת. תַּנְיָא נַמִי הָכִי: לֹא יִטַּע אָדָם אִילָן סָמוּךְ לִשְׂדֵה חֲבֵירוֹ, אֶלָּא אִם כֵּן הִרְחִיק מִמֶּנּוּ שְׁתֵּי אַמּוֹת; וְהָא אֲנַן תְּנַן: אַרְבַּע אַמּוֹת! אֶלָּא לָאו כִּדְשְׁמוּאֵל, שְׁמַע מִינַּהּ. וְאִיכָּא דְּרָמֵי לָהּ מִירְמָא; תְּנַן: לֹא יִטַּע אָדָם אִילָן סָמוּךְ לִשְׂדֵה חֲבֵירוֹ — אֶלָּא אִם כֵּן הִרְחִיק מִמֶּנּוּ אַרְבַּע אַמּוֹת; וְהַתַנְיָא: שְׁתֵּי אַמּוֹת! אֲמַר שְׁמוּאֵל, לָא קַשְׁיָא: כָּאן בְּבָבֶל, כָּאן בְּאֶרֶץ יִשְׂרָאֵל. רָבָא בַּר רַב חָנָן הָווּ לֵיהּ הָנְהוּ דִּיקְלֵי אַמֵּיצְרָא דְּפַרְדֵּיסָא דְּרַב יוֹסֵף, הָווּ אָתוּ צִפּוֹרֵי יָתְבִי בְּדִיקְלֵי וְנָחְתִי בְּפַרְדֵּיסָא וּמַפְסְדִי לֵיהּ; א"ל: (ב) זִיל קוֹץ, א"ל: וְהָא אַרְחִיקִי לִי! א"ל: ה"מ לְאִילָנוֹת, אֲבָל לִגְפָנִים בָּעֵינַן טְפֵי. וְהָא אֲנַן תְּנַן: אֶחָד גְּפָנִים וְאֶחָד כָּל אִילָן! א"ל: ה"מ אִילָן לְאִילָן וּגְפָנִים לִגְפָנִים, יאֲבָל אִילָן לִגְפָנִים בָּעֵינַן טְפֵי. א"ל: אֲנָא לָא קָיְיצְנָא, ו)דַּאֲמַר רַב: כהַאי דִּיקְלָא דְּטָעֵין קַבָּא — אָסוּר לְמִקְצְיֵיהּ, וְאָמַר ר' חֲנִינָא: ז)לָא שְׁכִיב שִׁכְחַת בְּרִי אֶלָּא דְּקַץ תְּאֵנְתָּא בְּלָא זִימְנֵיהּ, מָר אִי נִיחָא לֵיהּ לֵיקוֹץ. רַב פַּפָּא הוּ"ל הָנְהוּ דִּיקְלֵי אַמֵּיצְרָא דְּרַב הוּנָא בְּרֵיהּ דְּרַב יְהוֹשֻׁעַ, אֲזַל אַשְׁכְּחֵיהּ דַּהֲוָה חָפַר וְקָא קָאֵיץ שָׁרָשָׁיו; אֲמַר לֵיהּ: מַאי הַאי? אֲמַר לֵיהּ, תְּנַן: הָיוּ שָׁרָשִׁים יוֹצְאִים לְתוֹךְ שֶׁל חֲבֵירוֹ — מַעֲמִיק שְׁלֹשָׁה כְּדֵי שֶׁלֹּא יְעַכֵּב הַמַּחֲרֵישָׁה. אֲמַר לֵיהּ: הָנֵי מִילֵּי שְׁלֹשָׁה, מָר קָא חָפַר טְפֵי! אֲמַר לֵיהּ: אֲנָא בּוֹרוֹת שִׁיחִין וּמְעָרוֹת קָא חָפַרְנָא, דִּתְנַן: הָיָה חוֹפֵר בּוֹר, שִׁיחַ וּמְעָרָה — קוֹצֵץ וְיוֹרֵד וְהָעֵצִים שֶׁלּוֹ. אֲמַר רַב פַּפָּא: אֲמַרִי לֵיהּ (ג) כּוּלְּהִי וְלָא יְכִילִי לֵיהּ,

עַד

רש"י

כְּדְנֵייד נַכְתְּמָא **אַפּוּמָא דְּחַצְבָּא.** שֶׁאִם יָנִיחוּ כַּד עַל הַחוֹמָה וְכִיסּוּיָהּ עָלֶיהָ – יָנוּעַ הַכִּיסּוּי מֵחֲמַת הָרְעָדָה. רַקְתָּא. מַה שֶּׁמְּנַעֲרִין מִן הַפִּשְׁתָּן. **מַאי שְׁנָא** מִזּוֹרֶה. בְּשַׁבָּת דְּחַיָּיב, וְאַע"פ שֶׁהָרוּחַ מְסַיַּיעְתּוֹ חָשִׁיב לֵיהּ עוֹשֶׂה מְלָאכָה. אַלְמָא גִּירֵי דִּילֵיהּ נִינְהוּ! הַיְינוּ זוֹרֶה וְרוּחַ מְסַיַּיעְתּוֹ. כִּי הֵיכִי דִּלְעִנְיַן שַׁבָּת הָוֵי כֹּחוֹ – לְעִנְיַן נְזָקִין נַמִי כֹּחוֹ חָשִׁיב לֵיהּ. **וּלְרָבִינָא מַאי שְׁנָא** כו'. בִּשְׁלָמָא זוֹרֶה וְרוּחַ מְסַיַּיעְתּוֹ – לָא הָוְיָא לֵיהּ פִּירְכָא, דְּקָסָבַר: מְמוֹנָא מֵאִיסּוּר שַׁבָּת לָא יָלְפִינַן, דְּהָתָם מְלֶאכֶת מַחֲשֶׁבֶת אָסְרָה תּוֹרָה. וּכְה"ג מְתָרְצִינַן לֵיהּ לְהָא פִּירְכָא בְּבַ"ק בְּ"הַכּוֹנֵס צֹאן לַדִּיר" (דף ס.). **גֵּץ** = אֶטִינְצֵייל"א, הַיּוֹצֵאת מִן הַבַּרְזֶל כְּשֶׁהַפַּטִּישׁ מַכֶּה עָלָיו. חַיָּיב. וַהֲרֵי הוֹלִיכָן הָרוּחַ. **נִיחָא** לֵיהּ דְּלֵיזִיל. לַחוּץ, שֶׁלֹּא יַדְלִיק אֶת בֵּיתוֹ. **מתני'** סָמוּךְ לִשְׂדֵה חֲבֵירוֹ. בֵּין שְׂדֵה הַלָּבָן בֵּין שְׂדֵה הָאִילָן. וְטַעֲמָא – כְּדֵי עֲבוֹדַת הַכֶּרֶם, שֶׁכְּשֶׁיַּחֲרוֹשׁ אֶת אִילָנוֹתָיו לֹא יְהֵא צָרִיךְ לְהַכְנִיס מַחֲרֵישָׁתוֹ לְתוֹךְ שְׂדֵה חֲבֵירוֹ. מַעֲמִיק. לָהֶן בַּעַל הַשָּׂדֶה שֶׁיָּצְאוּ לְתוֹכוֹ. קוֹצֵץ. בְּעוֹמֶק ג' טְפָחִים. וְהָעֵצִים שֶׁלּוֹ. בַּגְּמָרָא מְפָרֵשׁ שֶׁל מִי. **גמ'** אֲבָל בְּבָבֶל שְׁתֵּי אַמּוֹת. שֶׁמַּחֲרֵישָׁתָן קַלָּה. **פַּרְדֵּיסָא** = כֶּרֶם. וְהָא אַרְחִיקִי לִי. ד' אַמּוֹת. שִׁכְחַת בְּרִי. כָּךְ שְׁמוֹ. אַשְׁכְּחֵיהּ. רַב פַּפָּא לְרַב הוּנָא דְּקָא חָפַר וְקָיֵיץ שָׁרָשִׁין. מַאי הַאי. אַמַּאי קַיְיצַתְּ? אֲמַרִי לֵיהּ כּוּלְּהִי. הֵבֵאתִי לוֹ רְאָיוֹת הַרְבֵּה שֶׁלֹּא יָקוֹץ.

שֶׁהֶחֱזִיקוּ

תוספות

אפומא דחצבא. על פי' הקונט' קשיא לר"י: דאיך יהא האפדנא נייד כולי האי עד שתתנדנד הנכתמא? דא"כ הבית קרוב ליפול! ולפי הענין משמע שהיה בנין חזק, שהרי מתוך העושר בנאה. ובמס' שבת (דף עז:) נמי אמר: מאי אפדנא — אפיתחא דין, שמאספין שם לדין. משמע דבירה גדולה היא! ונראה לר"י: דכד ניידא נכתמא — כשאדם אוחז הכד בידו, שזהו דבר מועט הרבה, א"כ מתנדנד האפדנא — חייב להרחיק. ולריב"א נראה שאין פ"ה דחוק, דבדבר מועט מתנדנד הנכתמא, שהוא דבר קל, אף על פי שהאפדנא אינו מתנדנד כל כך.

זיקא הוא דקא ממטי לה. קשיא לר"י: דליחייב משום אש, מידי דהוה אאבנו וסכינו ומשאו שהניחן בראש גגו ונפלו ברוח מצויה והזיקו, דחייב משום אש, כדאמר בפ"ק דב"ק (דף ו.)! והכא דאמטי ליה ברוח מצויה איירי, מדפריך עלה מזורה ורוח (ד) מסייעו, דאיירי ברוח מצויה, כדמשמע ב"הכונס" (שם דף ס. ושם) גבי ליבה וליבתו הרוח. ומדפריך מגץ היוצא מתחת הפטיש — דהיינו ברוח מצויה, דחייב משום אש, דגבי אש קתני לה ב"הכונס". ואומר ר"י: דלא דמי לאש, דאין חייב משום אש אלא כשעשה האדם את האש לבדו, כדכתיב "המבעיר את הבעירה" בלא סיוע הרוח, ואח"כ הולכת על ידי רוח מצויה. אבל הכא — אין עושה לבדו כל עיקר אלא ע"י הרוח, דאי לאו רוח — לא הוה רקתא אזלא כל עיקר, ודמי לליבה וליבתו הרוח דפטור. והיינו דמשני, כי פריך בסמוך: מ"ש מגץ? דהוה סלקא דעתך דדמי ממש לגץ. ומשני: התם ניחא ליה דליזל, ומתכוין להכות בכח עד שילא הגץ, (ה) ומתרחק בלא שום זיקא, וחייב משום אש על מה שגומר והולך על ידי רוח מצויה. אבל הכא — לא ניחא ליה דתיזל. כלומר, ואינו מכה בכח, ואי לאו (ו) רוח — אין הרקתא הולכת כלל. וא"ת: מ"מ יהא חייב להרחיק, מידי דהוה אגורן דמתניתין, דחייב להרחיק אע"ג דזיקא ממטי ליה! וי"ל: דמתני' כרבנן, והכא איירי אליבא דר' יוסי דלא מחייב אלא בגירי דיליה. והא דפריך מגן ולא מצי לאוקמי ההיא דגן כרבנן — משום דלא פליגי רבי יוסי ורבנן לענין חיוב תשלומין, אלא לענין הרחקה. וא"ת: מאי שנא מנמייה, דאפילו לר' יוסי מרחיקין, אע"ג דהיא גופה ממטיא נפשה (ז) כמר בר רב אשי! ומיהו, התם משום דזימנין דבהדי דנח כו' כדקאמר לעיל. אבל קשה מעורבין לעיל (דף כג.) דאמר רב יוסף: אפיקו לי קורקור מהכא! וי"ל: דגמרא לא סבר לה כרבינא. דר"ת פוסק כמר בר רב אשי וכאמימר. ועוד אומר ר"י: דבעלי חיים שאני, דחמירי טפי מרוח, דכח אחר מעורב בהן, כדאמרינן בבבא קמא (דף ו.).

מאי שנא מזורה ורוח מסייעתו. ורבינא לא חשיב לה פירכא, דסבר: כי היכי דלא גמרינן משבת לענין תשלומין, כדמפרש רב אשי ב"הכונס" (ב"ק דף ס. ושם) דגבי שבת מלאכת מחשבת אסרה תורה, אבל הכא גרמא הוא, וגרמא בנזקין פטור — הכי נמי לא גמרינן מהתם שיהא חייב להרחיק. ומר בר רב אשי סבר: נהי דחיוב תשלומין לא גמרי' לענין הרחקה דליחשב גירי דיליה — גמרינן שפיר, כיון דגרמא בנזקין אסור. **ורבינא** מאי שנא מגץ. וא"ת: ואמאי קאמר ורבינא? לאמימר נמי תיקשי לענין חיוב תשלומין, מאי שנא מגץ? וי"ל: משום הכי נקט רבינא, דאמימר הוי מצי לדחויי דה"נ (ח) חייב לדידיה בתשלומין, דלגמרי מדמה לה לזורה ורוח מסייעתו.

אחד גפנים ואחד כל אילן. מתוך פ"ה לעיל (דף יח.) משמע דנקט אחד גפנים — משום דשייך בהו כלאים, דהביא ראיה מכאן דכשיש גדר ליכא איסור כלאים, וזה סומך לגדר מכאן וזה מכאן. ואין נראה, ד"שדה חבירו" דקתני הכא על כרחך לאו בשל זרעים איירי, דהא מוקמי' בגמ' דמתני' אילנות לאילנות וגפנים לגפנים, אבל אילנות לגפנים — בעי טפי משום ליפרי, ומהאי טעמא גפנים לזרעים בעי טפי. אלא דנראה דנקט "אחד גפנים ואחד כל אילן", דלא תיסוק אדעתי' למימר דשיעור ד' אמות דמתני' דוקא בגפנים, שמצינו בהם שיעור זה במקום אחר, לענין כלאים. **אבל** בבבל ב' אמות. תימה: דבפרק "המוכר את הספינה" (לקמן דף פב: ושם דף פג.) גבי קנה ג' קנה קרקע, דאמר רב יוסף: עובדא הוה בדורא דרעותא כו'. משמע מהתם דבבבל נמי בעינן ד' אמות, דבבבל הוה מעשה! ול"ל: דההיא דורא דרעותא היה להם מחרישה גדולה כמו בארץ ישראל. **אבל** בגפנים בעי טפי. והוא כשנטע דקלים, כשהם גבוהים. אבל אם נטע גרעין — לא, דממילא קא גדל, ולא גירי דיליה הוא. **אנא** לא קייצנא דאמר רב כו'. וא"ת: והתנן במתניתא דקוצץ ונותן דמים! וי"ל: דאיכא לאוקמי באילן סרק. אבל קשה: דאמרינן ב"החובל" (ב"ק דף צב.) גבי הנהו דיקלי דמכחשי בגופני הוו, דקאמר: למחר אייתי לי מקורייהו, אלמא משום היזק גפנים מותר לקוץ דקלים! ויש לפרש: דשאני התם, שיותר מדאי היו מכחישים בגפנים, עד דהוה טעים בהו טעמא דחמרא.

עד

רבינו גרשום

וכמה נייד. דאמרי' דליהוו הני עצירי חייבין: כי היכי דנייד נכתמא אפומיה דחצבא. כלומר א) היכסה שמכסין ממנו הקיקל: רקתא. שלועזין ארישת"א. אבל הכא גבי הנהו רקתא אינו חייב משום דהוי ליה גירי דידיה דזיקא הוא דקא ממטי ליה ואינו חייב: מ"ש. מהא דתנן גבי שבת באבות מלאכות דהיכא דזורה תבואתו והרוח מסייעתו לדחות התבן דהוי חייב הכא נמי היכא דרוח ממטי לה אמאי אינו חייב. אמר ליה מרימר ודאי ברקתא חייב דהיינו כזורה ורוח מסייעתו דחייב לענין שבת. ולרבינא מייתי תו קושיא מ"ש מגץ היוצא כו'. דלעולם אין דליקה בלא רוח ואפ"ה חייב הכא נמי מאי שנא (ומאי שנא). התם גבי גץ מש"ה חייב דניחא ליה דליזל מביתו אבל הכא גבי רקתא לא ניחא ליה דליזל דהוא צריך נמי לרקתא לצורך שום דבר מש"ה הואיל דלא קא אזיל מכוחו דזיקא קא ממטי ליה פטור: **פיסקא** כדי עבודת הכרם. כדי כלי בקר וצמדו שלא ידוש שדה חבירו. לא שנו דבעינן ד' אמות אלא בארץ ישראל שרגילין לחרוש שדה אילן בשוורים ומפני חוזק הקרקע אבל בבבל שחורשין בחמורים או חופרין בב' אמות הרחקה סגי: דפרדיסא. גפנים: והא רחיקי ליה. ד' אמות: הני מילי באילנות. משדה אילנות: אחד שדה גפנים ואחד שדה אילן. אין מרחיקין אלא ד' אמות: אסור למקצייה. דכתיב כי ממנו תאכל ואותו לא תכרות: שכחת. הכי שמיה דבריה: תאלי. אילנות: אזל רב פפא אשכחיה לרב הונא אמר ליה מאי האי. דקצצת שרשי: שמעכבין לי. חרישתי: מר קא חפר טובא. וקא קציץ שרשין למטה מג' טפחים: אמרי ליה מכולהו. שהבאתי לו ראיות מכמה מקומות ולא יכלי ליה:

א) [נ"ל הכיסוי שמכסין בו וכו']

מסורת הש"ס

א) [ב"ק ס.]: ב) [שם סב: וש"נ]: ג) [לעיל יח.] לקמן פג.: ד) [לעיל יח.]: ה) [שם]: ו) ב"ק לא.: ז) [שם ע"ש]:

עין משפט נר מצוה

צ א מיי' פי"א מהל' שכנים הלכה ג סמג עשין פב טוש"ע ח"מ סי' קנה סעיף טו:

צא ב מיי' שם הל' א וסמג שם טוש"ע שם סעיף לד:

צב ג מיי' פ"ו מהל' חובל ומזיק הל' יא סמג עשין סח טוש"ע ח"מ סי' שפד סעיף ב:

צג ד ה מיי' פ"י מהל' שכנים הל' ח סמג עשין פב טוש"ע ח"מ סי' קנה סעיף כה:

צד ו ז מיי' שם הל' ז טוש"ע שם סעיף לג:

צה ח ט מיי' שם הל' ח טוש"ע שם סעי' כה:

צו י מיי' שם טוש"ע שם ועיין בהג"ה ובמ"מ:

צז כ מיי' פ"ו מהלכות מלכים הל' ט סמג לאוין רכט [וברב אלפס ב"ק סמוך לסוף פרק החובל דף לד: ועי' ע"ז בי"ד סי' קטז ס"ק ו]:

הגהות הב"ח

(א) במשנה זה סומך לגדר. נ"ב ע"ל דף י"ח דהיינו דוקא באפסוקי נונמא: (ב) גמ' א"ל רב יוסף זיל קוץ: (ג) שם אמרי ליה מכולהו ולא יכילנא ליה: (ד) תום' ד"ה זיקא וכו' ורוח מסייעתו: (ה) בא"ד שילא הגץ ויתרחק: (ו) בא"ד ואי לאו הרוח: (ז) בא"ד אע"ג דהיא גופא ממטיא נפשה ונניהו התם משום דזימנין דבהדי דמנח כו' כצ"ל ותיבות כמר בר רב אשי נמחק: (ח) ד"ה ורבינא וכו' דה"נ דחייב:

עין משפט
נר מצוה

צח א ב מיי' פ"ה מהל' מעילה הלכה ו:
צט ג מיי' שם ופ"י מהל' שכנים הל' ז סמג עשין פב טוש"ע ח"מ סי' קנה סעיף ל:
ק ד מיי' פ"ג מהלכות שמיטין הל' ה סמג לאוין רסז:
קא ה מיי' שם הל' ב:

עד דאמרי ליה הא [א]דאמר רב יהודה: מצר שהחזיקו בו רבים — אסור לקלקלו. לבתר דנפק, אמר: אמאי לא אמרי ליה: כאן בתוך שש עשרה אמה, כאן חוץ לשש עשרה אמה.§ "היה חופר בור, שיח ומערה — קוצץ ויורד והעצים שלו" (וכו').§ בעא מיניה יעקב [ב]הדייבא מרב חסדא: עצים של מי? אמר ליה, תניתוה: [ג][א]שרשי אילן של הדיוט הבאין בשל הקדש — לא נהנין ולא מועלין; אי אמרת בשלמא בתר אילן אזלינן, משום הכי לא מועלין, אלא אי אמרת בתר קרקע אזלינן, אמאי לא מועלין? אלא מאי, בתר אילן אזלינן? אימא סיפא: [ב]של הקדש הבאים בשל הדיוט — לא נהנין ולא מועלין; ואי בתר אילן אזלינן, אמאי לא מועלין? מידי איריא? בגידולין הבאין לאחר מכאן עסקינן, וקא סבר: אין מעילה בגידולין. רבינא אמר, לא קשיא: [ג]כאן בתוך שש עשרה אמה, כאן חוץ לשש עשרה אמה.§ אמר עולא: אילן הסמוך למצר בתוך שש עשרה אמה — גזלן הוא, ואין מביאין ממנו בכורים. מנא ליה לעולא הא? אילימא [ד]מדתנן: [ד]עשר נטיעות המפוזרות בתוך בית סאה, חורשין כל בית סאה בשבילן עד ראש השנה; כמה הוו להו? תרי אלפין וחמש מאה גרמידי. לכל חד וחד, כמה מטי ליה? מאתן וחמשין, הא לא הוי דעולא! ואלא [ה]מדתנן: [ה]שלשה אילנות של ג' בני אדם — הרי אלו מצטרפין, וחורשין כל בית

בית

רש"י

שהחזיקו בו רבים. לעשותו להן דרך, אסור לקלקלו, אע"פ שהוא של יחיד. ואנא נמי, הא אחזיקי ליה. לבתר דנפק. רב פפא. אמר. רב הונא: אמאי לא אמרי ליה. בתוך שש עשרה אמה. לאילן, הויא חזקה דאילן. אבל חוץ לשש עשרה אמה אין חזקתו חזקה. שאע"פ ששרשיו מתפשטין כ"ה אמה, אינן יונקין אלא בתוך ט"ז אמה סמוך לאילן, וכדאמרינן לקמן, ואנא (א) הוא חוץ לט"ז אמה קיימנא. ו) הדייבא = דמן הדייב. לא נהנין. מדרבנן. ולא מועלין. אם נהנה לא מעל. אלמא לא קדשי. מידי איריא. מסקנא דקושיא הוא: כלומר, מכולה לאו איריא היא, לא למשמע מינה בתר אילן, ולא למשמע מינה בתר קרקע. דטעמא, משום דהנך שרשים גידולים הבאים לאחר שהוקדש האילן הוא, ואיכא למ"ד במס' מעילה: אין מועלין בגידולין, אפי' שרשי הקדש בשדה הקדש. לא נהנין איצטריכא ליה. רבינא אמר ל"ק. רישא דקתני בתר אילן אזלינן — היינו בתוך ט"ז אמה, וסיפא דקתני של הקדש באין בתוך של הדיוט לא מועלין — היינו חוץ לט"ז. גזלן הוא. שיונק משדה חבירו. ואין מביאין ממנו בכורים. אין צריך להביא ממנו בכורים, דבעינן "אשר תביא מארצך" (דברים כו). עשר נטיעות מפוזרות בבית סאה. לארכו ולרחבו, כולן בשוה, יונקות מכל בית סאה, וכולם צריך להם. ומותר לחורשו ערב שביעית עד ראש השנה, שהלכה למשה מסיני הוא, ובית סאה — חמשים אמה על חמשים אמה, שחצר המשכן קרוי בית סאתים, והוא מאה על חמשים. כמה הוי להו. בית סאה, כי עבדת (ב) להו רצועה של אמה רוחב. תרי אלפים וחמש מאה גרמידי. שהרי יש כאן נ' רצועות של חמשים אמה ועולות לאלפים וחמש מאות אמה. חלוק אותן לעשר אילנות — תמצא צירוף קרקע יניקת כל אילן ואילן בין הכל מאתן וחמשין אמה אורך באמה רוחב. הא לא הוי כדעולא. דשיעור עולא נפיש, דאמר דאילן יונק שש עשרה (ג) לכל צד הרי ל"ב על ל"ב, עשה מהן רצועה אחת של אמה רוחב, כאשר עשית מבית סאה — תמצאנה של אלף וכ"ד אמה, שהרי יש כאן שלשים ושתים רצועות כל אחת ואחת ל"ב אמה. ואלא מדתנן שלשה אילנות. גדולים, שיונקים יותר מן הנטיעות ומפוזרין בבית סאה לארכו ולרחבו בשוה, אע"פ *שאינו של אדם אחד אלא של שלשה בני אדם — מצטרפין להיות שדה אילן, ולחרוש כל בית סאה בשבילן ערב שביעית עד עצרת, כדין שדה אילן. ואם לאו — אין חורשין אלא כל אחד כדי צרכו, דהיינו תחתיו וחוצה לו כמלא אורה וסלו, והשאר הוי שדה הלבן, ואין חורשין אותו אלא עד הפסח.

בית

נ"ל שאינו

תוספות

עד דאמרי ליה הא דאמר רב יהודה מיצר שהחזיקו כו'. תימה: מאי מייתי מרב יהודה? דרבים שאני, דאי לאו הכי — קשיא מתני', דקתני "קוצץ ויורד"! ופירש ר"ח וריב"ם: דרבים החזיקו במצריה דרב הונא וברשותו, דאי לאו הכי — אין חזקתו מועלת, כדמשמע ב"המניח" (ב"ק דף כח. ושם), ואתא רב הונא וקא חפר ברשות הרבים וקצץ שרשים דרב פפא, ומשום הכי פריך מדרב יהודה, דכיון שהחזיקו בו רבים — אינו רשאי לחפור. והא דקאמר: אמאי לא אמרי ליה כאן בתוך שש עשרה אמה וכו' — ה"פ: כלומר כי קאמר רב יהודה מצר שהחזיקו בו רבים אסור לקלקלו — ה"מ תוך ט"ז אמה, אבל חוץ לט"ז אמה — מותר לקלקלו, כיון שמניח ט"ז אמה כדין רשות הרבים. ובסוף "חזקת הבתים" (לקמן דף ס:) דאסר רבי יוחנן לאדם שכנס תוך שלו להחזיר כתלים במקומן, אע"ג דאיכא רווחא, כדמשמע התם אליבא דר"ל: הכא איכא רווחא. רווחא דקאמר התם (ד) — שאינו סותם כל רשות הרבים, אבל ליכא רווחא ט"ז אמה. אבל אי איכא רווחא ט"ז אמה — מודה רבי יוחנן דמותר לקלקלו ומחזיר כתלים למקומן, כדאמר הכא. ומיהו קשה: מאי קאמר רב פפא "אמרי ליה מכולהי", מאי "כולהי"? ומפרש ה"ר מנחם: ד"מכולהי" — היינו מכל הני דתנן: אם האילן קדם לא יקוץ, ספק כו'. "ולא יכלי ליה" — שהיה דוחה אותו דמיירי באילן עצמו, אבל השרשים יקוץ. ור"ת מפרש: דרב הונא היה קוצץ ולוקח השרשים לעצמו. וא"ל רב פפא: מאי האי? כלומר, למה אתה לוקח השרשים לעצמך? א"ל: דתנן קוצץ ויורד, וכיון שבדין אני קוצץ — כמו כן יהו העצים שלי. ו"אמרי ליה מכולהי" היינו הנהו דמייתי הכא, והיא דמייתי לקמן: שרשי אילן הדיוט הבאים כו', דמינה מוכח לקמן דהעצים שלו, דקתני במתני' היינו של בעל האילן. "ולא יכלי ליה" — שדחה לו כדדחי ליה לקמן, עד דא"ל מרב יהודה כו', דנהי שלא תועיל חזקתי כחזקת רבים לענין שלא תהא רשאי לקוצצו, לענין זה מיהא תועיל — שיהו העצים שלי. ומסיק: אמאי לא אמרי ליה חוץ לשש עשרה יש להיות העצים שלי, כדאמר רבינא לקמן: כאן תוך שש עשרה כו'.

אלא הכא בגידולין הבאין לאחר מכאן. ויש ספרים דגרסי: מידי איריא, הא בגידולין. וכל זה מדברי המקשה. כלומר, על כרחך לא תוכל לפשוט מכאן, דבגידולין הבאין לאחר מכאן איירי. ואי בתר אילן אזלינן — רישא אשמועינן דאין נהנין, וסיפא אשמועינן דאין מועלין. ואי בתר קרקע אזלינן — רישא אשמועינן דאין מועלין, וסיפא דאין נהנין בגידולין. וא"ת: ההיא בבא דאשמועינן דאין מעילה בגידולין — לשמעינן של הקדש הבאין בשל הקדש, דהוי רבותא טפי! וי"ל: דנקט הכי משום אידך בבא, דאשמועינן דאין נהנין, דהוי רבותא טפי, שאין הכל של הקדש. ור"ת לא גריס "אלא", והמתרץ הוא דקאמר הכי, דמוקי סיפא דאין מעילה — בגידולין. והא דלא נקט דשל הקדש בשל הקדש — משום דבעי למינקט דומיא דרישא, דאין הכל דהקדש אלא חד דהקדש וחד דהדיוט. אבל אי בתר קרקע אזלינן, ורישא אשמועינן דאין מעילה בגידולין — ליתני רישא של הקדש בשל הקדש, דאין מיושב כל כך לומר תנא רישא אגב סיפא, כמו תנא סיפא אגב רישא. רבינא אמר לא קשיא כאן תוך ט"ז כו'. רישא בתוך ט"ז אמה, דבתר אילן אזלינן. וסיפא חוץ לט"ז אמה, דבתר קרקע אזלינן. ואם תאמר: וליתני אידי ואידי תוך ט"ז, וליתני סיפא מועלין. אי נמי: אידי ואידי אחר ט"ז, וליתני ברישא מועלין! וי"ל: דתנא הכי לאשמועינן דבתרוייהו — בין בתוך ט"ז אמה בין חוץ לט"ז אמה — לא נהנין ולא מועלין. גזלן הוא ואין מביאין ממנו בכורים. פי' ר"ת: משום דאין מביאין גזל על גבי המזבח, שנאמר "אני ה' שונא גזל בעולה" (ישעיה סא) וכתיב "והבאתם גזול" וגו' (מלאכי א). ולית לן דעולא, דהא בהדיא פסקינן כרבי יוסי, דאמר: זה נוטע בתוך שלו כו'. וא"ת: לפירושו, עולא כמאן סבר? דכרבנן נמי לא הוי, דרבנן לא בעו הרחקה אלא ד' אמות, ולעולא שש עשרה אמה! וי"ל: דעולא הוי מוקי מתניתין בלגנמא, כדמוקי לה בריש פירקין, ולהכי לא בעי אלא ד' אמות. ומיהו קשיא לרבי יצחק, דפריך לקמן לעולא מהקונה אילן וקרקעו, מביא וקורא: מאי לאו כל שהוא! ומאי קושיא? שאני התם שקנאו, ולא הוה גזלן! ונראה כפי' הקונטרס: דאע"ג דמותר לסמוך — אין מביאין ממנו בכורים, דבעינן "אשר תביא מארצך". ולקמן דאמר: אילן הסמוך מביא וקורא, שעל מנת כן הנחיל יהושע את הארץ — לא קאמר שעל מנת כן הנחיל, שיהא מותר לסמוך — דבלאו הכי שרי. אלא על מנת כן הנחיל — שיהא חשוב כמו מארצך, ויכול לומר (ה) "אשר נתת לי". עשר נטיעות המפוזרות כו'. בסוכה (דף לד.) אמר: עשר נטיעות וערבה וניסוך המים הלכה למשה מסיני. ודוקא עשר לתוך בית סאה אבל פחות אין צריכין חרישה כל כך. וכן נמי אם היו בבית סאה יותר מעשר נטיעות אין חורשין, לפי שעומדין ליעקר.

כמה

רבינו גרשום

מצר שהחזיקו בו רבים אסור לקלקלו. ואבותי ואבות אבותי החזיקו בו מכמה שנים: לבתר דנפק רב פפא אמר רב הונא אמאי לא אמרי ליה כאן בתוך שש עשרה. סמוך למיצר אם נטוע ויוצאין שרשין מתחת ונכנסין לשדה חבירו קוצץ ויורד וכאן חוץ לט"ז אמה שהרחיקו כדין ושוב נכנסין שרשיו מתחת לשדה חבירו אמר רב יהודה דאסור לקלקלו:

פיסקא הבאין בשל הקדש בשדה הקדש לא נהנין מהן מן השרשין לכתחלה א) אבל הנהנה מהן כדין הקדש היינו דלא מועלין דבתר אילן אזלי דשל הדיוט הוא מש"ה מה שקוצצין מן השרשים יתן לבעל האילן: ושל הקדש: לעולם בתר אילן אזלי שרשים. ואמאי אין מועלין בסיפא משום דאותן השרשים של הקדש שבאין בשדה הדיוט בגדולין של הקדש באין בגדולין של הדיוט לאחר שהוקדש עסקינן ומש"ה אין מועלין דסבר אין מועלין בגדולין [ו]אבותי הקדישו קורות ואנו נתיד גמזיות [?]: ורבינא אמר. לעולם בתר אילן אזלינן ומש"ה לא מועלין ודקא קשיא לך בסיפא אמאי לא אזלינן בתר אילן ומועלין בתר אילן דרישא היה לא קשיא דרישא משום הכי אין מועלין דנטוע הוא בפחות מט"ז אמה סמוך למיצר אע"ג דאיכא למימר דינק הוא משל הקדש לא מועלין דשדהו עיקרו בתר אילן אבל סיפא דקתני אילן של הקדש לא מועלין משום דהחוץ מט"ז אמות הוא נטוע דליכא למימר דמשרשי הקדש הן דהואיל שהוא רחוק כל כך מי שקוצץ אותן שרשים שהן לסוף ט"ז אמה אין מכחיש כלום באילן מש"ה אין מועלין. ומתני' דקתני העצים של מי אם בתוך ט"ז אמה חופר וקוצץ הן של בעל האילן ואם חוץ לט"ז אמה חופר וקוצץ הן של בעל [הקרקע]: אמר עולא אילן הסמוך למצר של שדה חבירו בתוך לט"ז אמה. שרשיו יונקין משדה חבירו ואין מביא מפירותיו ביכורין דאין יכול לקרות את ראשית פרי האדמה אשר נתתה לפי שיונק משדה אחרים: מנא ליה לעולא הא. דאילן יונק מכל צידיו עד שש עשרה אמה אילימא מדתנן במס' שביעית עשר נטיעות המפוזרין בתוך בית סאה לפי שהנטיעות הן בחורות צריך לתקן ערב ששית הנכנסת לשביעית כדי שלא יתקלקלו לפי שאין חורשין בשביעית והיו חורשין כל בית סאה (שהן נטיעותיהן) בשבילן ל' יום קודם לראש השנה ועד ראש השנה דהכי קי"ל ערב שביעית דהיינו שנה ששית הנכנסת בשביעית לא חורשין כלל כי אם שדה לבן עד הפסח ושדה אילן עד העצרת אבל נטיעות שבחורות נינהו היו חורשין שלשים יום לפני ראש השנה כדכתיב בחריש ובקציר תשבות אם אינו ענין לשביעית עצמה שכבר נאמר והשביעית תשמטנה ונטשתה וכו' שדך לא תזרע וכרמך לא תזמור תנהו ענין לחריש ולקציר של שנה ששית הנכנסת לשביעית שאינו רשאי לקצור ולחרוש לצורך שביעית ולא בשביעית לצורך שמינית אבל הני נטיעות כדי שלא יתקלקלו היו חורשין עד ראש השנה שנכנסת שביעית:

כמה

א) נ"ל לכתחילה כדין הקדש אבל הנהנה מהן לא מועלין דבתר אילן אזלי: ב) כ"ה לשון הגמ' בפסחים דף ו ע"ב.

מסורת הש"ס

א) ב"ק כח. לעיל יב. ע"ש ולקמן ס. ודף ק.: ב) בס"י איתא חדייבא: ג) מעילה יג.: ד) שביעית פ"א מ"ו: ה) ג"ז שם מ"ה: ו) בס"י חדייבא:

הגהות הב"ח

(א) רש"י ד"ה בתוך שש וכו' ואנא חוץ כנ"ל ותיבת הוא נמחק: (ב) ד"ה כמה וכו' כי עבדת ליה רצועה אחת של אמה: (ג) ד"ה הא לא כו' שש עשרה אמה לכל: (ד) תום' ד"ה עד דאמרי ליה הא דאמר רב יהודה וכו' דקאמר התם היינו שאינו סותם: (ה) ד"ה גזלן וכו' ויכול לומר מן האדמה אשר נתת לי:

בית סאה בשבילן; (א) כמה הוו להו? תרי אלפי וה' מאה גרמידי. לכל חד כמה מטי ליה? תמני מאה ותלתין ותלתא ותילתא, אכתי נפישי ליה דעולא! לא דק. אימור דאמרינן לא דק — לחומרא, לקולא לא דק מי אמרינן? מי סברת בריבועא קא אמרינן? בעיגולא קא אמרינן. מכדי [א]כמה מרובע יותר על העיגול? רביע, (ב) פשו להו ז' מאה ושתין ותמניא, אכתי פש ליה פלגא דאמתא! היינו דלא דק, ולחומרא לא דק. תא שמע: [ב][א]הקונה אילן וקרקעו — מביא וקורא; מאי לאו [ב]כל שהוא? לא, י"ו אמה. תא שמע: [ג][ג]קנה שני אילנות בתוך של חבירו — מביא ואינו קורא; הא [ד]שלשה — מביא וקורא; מאי לאו כל שהוא? לא, הכא נמי י"ו אמה. ת"ש: [ד]ר"ע אומר: [ה]הקרקע כל שהוא חייב בפאה ובבכורים, [ו]וכותבין עליו פרוזבול, ונקנין

רש"י

בית סאה כמה הוו להו תרי אלפי ות"ק גרמידי. על אמה רוחב. כמה מטי. לכל חד מהנך אילנות — תתל"ג ותילתא. אכתי נפישין להו שש עשרה אמה דעולא, דהוי אלף וכ"ד. לא דק. עולא לא דקדק כל כך, הואיל וקרוב לשיעור זה קאמר, ולא איכפת ליה. אימור דאמרינן לא דק. היכא דאזיל לחומרא, הכא קא אזיל לקולא, דאינו יונק כל כך וקאמר איהו דיונק, ופטר ליה מביכורים! מי סברת. שש עשרה אמה דעולא בריבועא קאמר, דליהוי שלשים ושתים על ל"ב כדקאמרינן? בעיגולא קאמר. שכל סביביו יונק שש עשרה, והיינו בעיגולא. דאילו ברבוע — נמצא כנגד האלכסון יותר משש עשרה אמה. וכמה מרובע יתר על העיגול רביע. דל רביע מאלף וכ"ד, פשו להו תשס"ח אמות ברוחב אמה. אכתי לא שוו שיעורי, דהשתא (ג) פשו להו שיעורי דמתני' אדעולא פלגא דאמתא, ונמצא אילן יונק י"ו אמה ומחצה לכל צד, דהיינו ל"ג על ל"ג. דשיעורא דעולא תשס"ח, ושיעורא דמתני' תתל"ג, ונפיש שיעורא דמתניתין אדעולא ס"ה אמות באמה רוחב. חלוק הרצועה לרוחב — הרי ק"ל אמה אורך ברוחב חצי אמה, הקף מהם האילן ל"ב אמה לצפון וכנגדו לדרום — נמצא מהצפון לדרום ל"ג, שהרי הוספת עליו חצי אמה לכאן וחצי אמה לכאן, וילך נשארו ה) ס"ו ברוחב חצי אמה. תן חציין למזרח וחציין למערב — נמצא מוקף ברבוע. ולא דקדק הגמרא כל כך דנקט פלגא אמתא, דהא עולא בעיגול קאמר, ואילו בעיגול הייתי יכול להוסיף עליו שני שלישי אמה לכל צד, אלא משום האי פורתא לא דק כולי האי. ואית דגרסי: פש ליה תרי תילתי דאמתא. היינו דלא דק. עולא, דהוה מצי למימר שיתסרי ופלגא, ולחומרא לא דק, ואזיל לחומרא ולא נמלא שיעורו. מאי לאו כל שהוא. חוץ לעביו של אילן לכל צד. הקונה שני אילנות בתוך של חבירו מביא ואינו קורא כו'. לקמן תנן ב"המוכר את הספינה": המוכר שתי אילנות לחבירו ולא פירש לו קרקע — לא קנה קרקע, אבל קנה שלשה — קנה קרקע, ואף על פי שלא פירש. הלכך, גבי ביכורים נמי, שתי אילנות — מביא ואינו קורא, דלא מצי למימר "פרי האדמה אשר נתתה לי" (דברים כו). הא ג'. דקנה קרקע, מביא וקורא. מאי לאו. משום דקנה קרקע מיניה סביבם? לא. משום דקנה שש עשרה אמה סביב כל אחד. ובוידוי. לא גרסינן ליה במתני' במסכת פאה, דאין וידוי אלא במעשר, והוא אינו תלוי בקרקע. פרוזבול. תנן במסכת גיטין (דף לו.): הלל תיקן פרוזבול, שראה שנמנעו העם מלהלוות מפני השביעית המשמטת, ועוברים על מה שכתוב: "השמר לך פן יהיה דבר" וגו' — עמד והתקין תקנה שלא תשמט, שיהא מוסר שטרותיו לבית דין וכותב עליהן פרוזבול. וזה גופו של פרוזבול: מוסר אני לכם פלוני ופלוני הדיינים שבמקום פלוני, שכל חוב שיש לי אצל פלוני שאגבנו כל זמן שארצה. ותו לא משמטת ליה שביעית, דלא קרינא ביה "לא יגוש" שאין תובע חובו אלא ו) מב"ד. והתם מוקמינן לה בשביעית בזמן הזה דרבנן, ואמרינן התם: אין כותבין פרוזבול אלא על הקרקע, אבל אין לו קרקע ללוה — לא כתבינן ליה, דהלואה דלא שכיחא היא, דמסתמא אין אדם סומך אלא על קרקע הלוה, וכשאין לו — לא תיקן הלל פרוזבול. ונקנין

תוספות

כמה מרובע יתר על העיגול רביע. הכי איתא בברייתא דמסכת מדות, וכן בעירובין. הכי גרס ר"ת: פש להו תרי תילתא אמתא. פי': כשתקיף אילן דעולא רצועה רחבה שני שלישי אמה, יהא גדול כאילן המשנה, שהרי יותר ס"ה אמות ושליש ברוחב אמה. שהרי אם תקיף ל"ב על ל"ב מרובעים יצטרך קכ"ח, ולד' קרנות ח' שלישים — הרי ק"ל ושני שלישים אורך על שני שלישים רוחב. תחסר הרביע שהעיגול פחות — ישאר ל"ח. וכן ס"ה אמה ושליש תחתוך לג' חלקים לאורך — תהיה רצועה אחת של קצ"ו ברוחב שליש, תחתוך לשנים ותשים זה בצד זה — תהיה רצועה ארכה צ"ח על רוחב שני שלישי אמה. עוד מצא ר"י בספר (ד) אחר מפורש בגמרת הספר: להקיף בחוטים אילן דעולא, שהוא ל"ב על ל"ב, עד שיהא שני שלישי אמה סביב, תחתוך החוטין ותפשטם — יהיה העליון ארכו ק', שהוא מקיף ל"ג ושליש, וכל שיש ברחבו טפח — יש בהיקפו ג'. והתחתון ל"ו שהוא מקיף ל"ב, הרי(ה) התחתון פחות מן העליון מכל צד ב' אמות. ותחתוך העודף מצד אחד, ותמלא צד אחד האורך לצד הקצר — תהיה רצועה ל"ח, וכן הוא ס"ה ושליש. דרך אחרת: ל"ג ושליש על ל"ג ושליש מרובעים — עולה אלף ומאה וי"א אמות ושליש של שליש שהיא תשיעית אמה. תחסר הרביעית — ישאר תתל"ג ושליש — הרי אילן המשנה ל"ג ושליש על ל"ג ושליש (הג"ה. או כעין זה: שליש סאה הוי י"ו וב' שלישים על חמשים, תחתוך באמצע ושים זה על זה — יהיה עשרים וחמש על שלשים ושלש ושליש). דרך אחרת: בית סאה היא מאה על כ"ה, תקח השליש לאילן אחד — יהיה ל"ג ושליש על כ"ה, והם ל"ג ושליש על ל"ג ושליש עגולים, שהרי מוסיף הרביע מלבד שהיא שליש מלגיו, דהיינו ח' אמה ושליש באורך ל"ג ושליש — יהיו ל"ג ושליש על ל"ג ושליש מרובעים. (ולספרים דגרסינן פש להו פלגא דאמתא) ועשה אותו עגול, שיחסר הרביע שהוספת — ויהיה עגול ל"ג ושליש על ל"ג ושליש. ולספרים דגרסי "פש ליה פלגא דאמתא" יש לפרש דחשיב עולא י"ו לכל צד, לבד מקום האילן ומקום אילן שליש על שליש, נמצא אילן דעולא ל"ב ושליש על ל"ב ושליש, כשתקיף מכל צד פלגא דאמתא יהיה ל"ג ושליש על ל"ג ושליש. ורבינו משולם מפרש: דעולא לא חשיב מקום האילן, ומקום האילן הוי אמה על אמה. נמצא דהוי אילן דעולא ל"ג על ל"ג, ואם היו מרובעים — היה עולה אלף ופ"ט. תחסר הרביע ישאר תתי"ו ושלשה רבעי אמה. ול"ג (והוו) "[פשו] להו ז' מאה ושתין ותמניא". נמצא דאילן המשנה יתר על של עולא י"ו אמה ושליש ורביע. ופלגא דאמתא קאי אבית סאה, שהיא חמשים על חמשים, כשתסיר פלגא דאמתא לאורך וכן לרוחב — יעלה החסרון חמשים אמה חסר רביע, דהיינו לג' אילנות — ולאילן אחד יעלה י"ו אמה ושליש ורביע, וישאר כאילן דעולא.

לחומרא לא דק. וא"ת: והא נמי קולא הוא הא דמייתי ביכורים, דמפקע להו מתרומה ומעשר, כדאמרינן ב"המוכר את הספינה" (לקמן דף פא: ושם)! ויש לומר: דעולא לא איירי אלא במאי דאינו מביא בתוך י"ו, אבל חוץ לי"ו — פעמים מביא, ופעמים אינו מביא. אילן וקרקעו כו' למאי דמוקי לה בי"ו אמה צריך לפרש מאי אתא לאשמועינן. ונראה לרשב"א: דאתא לאשמועינן ולמידק: הא קנה אילן סתם — אינו מביא וקורא. ואם קנה ב', אפילו סתם — מביא וקורא, דקנה קרקע. וכר"מ דאמר (לקמן פא.): הקונה ב' אילנות — קנה קרקע. הא שלשה מביא וקורא. הוה מצי למיפרך מסיפא, דקתני בהדיא במסכת ביכורים, בסיפא דהך דמייתי הכא: הקונה ג' אילנות תוך של חבירו — מביא וקורא. אלא דאורחא דגמ' בכמה מקומות שמדקדק מרישא מה שיכול. [ועי' תוס' שבת לט: ד"ה אלא פניו].

לא שש עשרה אמה. וא"ת: והא אמרינן ב"המוכר את הספינה" (לקמן דף פג. ושם) גבי שלשה קנה קרקע, וכמה? תחתיהן, וביניהן, וחוצה להן כמלא אורה וסלו! וי"ל: דהתם כשענפי האילן גדולים הרבה, ויוצאין חוץ לשש עשרה אמה. ואם תאמר: קונה אילן אחד אמאי אינו מביא וקורא, למ"ד קנין פירות כקנין הגוף דמי, ומ"ש ממוכר שדהו לפירות דמביא וקורא לדידיה, כדאמרינן בפרק "השולח" (גיטין דף מז: ושם)? וליכא למימר דהאי תנא סבר דקנין פירות לאו כקנין הגוף דמי — דהא ר"מ אית ליה דקנין הגוף דמי ב"השולח" (שם דף מח.), וב"החובל" (ב"ק דף ל. ושם), ואית ליה לקמן (דף פא.) דקונה אילן אחד [ז](אינו מביא וקורא) וי"ל: דשאני התם, שהקרקע קנוי לו עד זמן קבוע, אבל הכא אם יתייבש מיד האילן — אין לו בקרקע כלום. אי נמי, התם קרקע קנויה לו לכל דבר, למשטח בה פירי ולמיזרע בה סילקא וירקא, אבל גבי אילן — אין לו אלא יניקה לבדה. ובוידוי. פי' בקונטרס דלא גרסינן "ובוידוי", דלא כתיב במעשר שני (שיש) שום וידוי, לא "מארלך" ולא "מאדמה אשר נתת לי". אע"ג דכתיב ביה "וברך את עמך את ישראל ואת האדמה אשר נתתה לנו" (דברים כו) — לא שיהא לו לחלק, אלא לכל ישראל. ומיהו, על כרחך אין וידוי בלא קרקע, דתני עלה בירושלמי: אף בוידוי, ומכל מקום לא גרסינן ליה, מדתני עלה בירושלמי — מכלל דבמשנה ליתיה[ח].

ולכתוב עליה פרוזבול. אבל אמטלטלין אין כותבין פרוזבול, מפני שיכול לכלותן, והיא הלואה דלא שכיחא. ועליך נקוב, אע"פ שיכול לכלותו — כותבין עליו פרוזבול, דלא פלוג רבנן במקרקעי. והא דכותבין אפילו על קרקע כל שהוא פי' רשב"ם ב"השולח" (גיטין דף לז. ד"ה אלא) — משום דאין אונאה לקרקעות, והוי כאילו יש לו משכון בכל. ואין נראה, דנהי דאין להן אונאה — ביטול מקח ביתר מפלגא יש להן. אלא היינו טעמא — משום דגבי והדר גבי, כמעשה דקטינא דאביי (כתובות דף נא:), דע"י כך ראוי לגבות כל חובו. וכענין זה איכא סוף פרק "כל הגט" (גיטין דף ל:) גבי המלוה מעות את הכהן כו': הניח מלא מחט — גובה מלא קורדוס. [ועי' תוס' גיטין לז. ד"ה אלא ותוספות קדושין כו: ד"ה ולכתוב].

רבינו גרשום

כמה הוו להו. כלומר עשר נטיעות הללו המפוזרות בכל בית סאה כשתחלק הבית סאה בשוה לאלו נטיעות כמה הוי בין נטיעה לנטיעה: תרין אלפין וחמש מאה אמין. דקי"ל בית סאה הוי נ' על נ' אמה כדגמרי' מחצר המשכן והני נטיעות מפוזרות בנ' על נ' ועכשיו חלק נ' [על] חמשים לרצועות שכל רצועה מבת נ' אמה אורך ואמה רוחב הויין נ' רצועות ועכשיו חבר הני רצועות ראשה של זו בצד ראשה של זו שתהא הכל רצועה אחת תמצא ארכה אלפים ות"ק אמה וברוחב רצועה אמה ועכשיו מדה אותן י' נטיעות בשוה בארכה של רצועה זו תמצא בין כל נטיעה ונטיעה ר"ן אמה אויר ומש"ה צריך לחרוש כל בית סאה דלא מהני כלל חרישה של אילן זה לאילן זה אם לא יחרשו לכולן מפני שמרוחקות הן כל כך זו מזו כדאמרן ומקשי הא לא הוו להו כלומר אכתי חשבון של י' נטיעות הללו אינו מגיע כלל לחשבון של אילן עולא אפי' למחצית חשבונו לפי שעולא לאילן א' היה נותן ט"ז אמה לכל ד' רוחות שיונק היינו ל"ב אמה על ל"ב אמה צא ופרום ועשה מהן רצועות ל"ב שכל אחת ל"ב אורך ואמה רוחב וצרפם לרצועה אחת תמצא שעולות ל' רצועות שכל אחת ל"ב אורך ועולה חשבונם ט' מאות וס' אמה ועדיין נשתיירו בידך ב' רצועות שכל אחת ל"ב אורך ואמה רוחב הרי חשבונם ס"ד אמות צרוף אלו ס"ד על תשע מאות וס' ובא החשבון אלף וכ"ד שכך עולה חשבון אילן אחד שאמר עולא באורך. וחשבון אורך של אחד מעשר נטיעות לא הוי אלא ר"ן ואכתי מנא ליה לעולא דמצריך כל כך. אלא מרישא מדתנן כו' כלומר אל תתמה מחשבון של י' נטיעות שאינו בא לחשבונו של עולא לפי שהנטיעות קטנות ובחורות לא צריך להו הרחקה כולי האי מש"ה סגי להו בר"ן הרחקה אבל באילן שאמר עולא בזקן שגדל כל צרכו קאמר דמינק ט"ז אמה מכל רוחותיו שעולה חשבונו בפישוט תתרכ"ד כדפרישית אלא מרישא ג' אילנות שכבר גדלו כל צרכן אפי' הן של ג' בני אדם ונטוען בתוך בית סאה הרי אלו מצטרפין כמו שאם היו של אדם אחד וחורשין כל בית סאה בשבילן שלא יקלקלו עד ר"ה שנכנס שביעית: כמה הוו להו לכל א' מהללו ג' אילנות ברצועות פשוטות תמני מאה ותלתין ותלתא ותילתא אמין שזהו השליש של חשבון בית סאה שחשבנו למעלה כ"ה מאות מישתכח דבין אילן לאילן תמני מאה ותלתין ותלתא ותילתא ואכתי נפיש ליה חשבון של עולא על האי חושבנא מאתן פחות ט'. ומשני עולא לא דק כלומר לא דקדק בדבר כל כך שהעמיד חשבון האילן על זה. ומקשי' אימור דאמרי' לא דק היכא דאיכא חומרא שאם היה מחמיר והיה מצריכו בפחות משיעור זה להביא ביכורין אמרי' ליה אימור לא דק א) אבל לחומרא אי לא דק ומי אמרי' דצריך ט"ז אמה לכל רוח כדפרישית אית ליה קולא דפחות מט"ז אמה שעולה חשבון לאלף וכ"ד אם נטוע הוא אין מביאין ממנו ביכורין מרבעת לה להוסיפה על רצועות של חצי אמה לא היתה אפי' כחוט השער מש"ה לא חשיב ליה: מביא וקורא. מן הארץ אשר נתת לי: מאי לאו. דקני קרקע כל שהוא וקשיא לעולא דאמר דאילן הסמוך לתוך ט"ז אמה גזלן הוא: מביא ואינו קורא. משום דקי"ל דקנה [שני] אילנות בתוך שדה חבירו לא קנה קרקע אבל ג' אילנות דקנה קרקע מביא וקורא. מאי קנה קרקע לאו דקנה כל שהוא וקשיא לעולא. לא ט"ז אמה קנה מן האחרון ועד חבירו: ולכתוב עליה פרוזבול. היינו תקנת עשירים שהיו מלוים על משכון קרקע דלאו שמיטה משמט לא מלוה בשטר ולא מלוה על המשכון וכתוב הכי מוסרני לכם אגב קרקע ב"ד פלוני ופלוני חוב שיש לי על פלוני שאגבנו בכל שעה שארצה ותותמין עליו ב"ד אלמא דקרקע כל שהוא חייב בביכורים אע"ג דסמיך האי קרקע למצר אחר וקשיא לעולא:

רבינו גרשום (המשך מן העמוד שמנגד): משום דקא יניק משדה חבירו והיינו קולא והוה ליה לעולא לעיין ולדקדק שלא יפטרנו מביכורין אלא כדינו ומאי לקולא לא דק: מי סברת. דהא דקחשיב עולא ט"ז אמה לכל רוח דאמות מרובעות קא בעי דאית להו מורשא דקרנתא בעגולא קא אמרי' דחשיב סביבות האילן ט"ז אמה בלא מורשא דקרנתא. ואכתי מקשה ליה למאי דבעי לתרוצי באמות עגולות מכדי כמה מרובע יותר על העיגול רביע וכשתוציא הרביע מן אלף וכ"ד אמות לא משתייר לך אלא תשס"ח כיצד מח' מאות תשליך מאתים נשתיירו שש מאות וממאתים תוציא נ' הרי הן ז' מאות ונ' אמות עגולות ומכ"ד תשליך הרביע נשתיירו י"ח ואותן י"ח מוסיף על ז' מאות ונ' הרי תשס"ח ואכתי אין מגיע חשבון של עולא לתמני מאה ותלתין ותלתא ותילתא לפי שחשבון של עולא שכשחושב בעיגול הוא פוחת חצי אמה מכלל ד' ב) אמות האילן מחשבון של תמני מאה ותלתין ותלתא ותילתא וכשתרצה להשוות חשבונו של עולא לחשבון זה צריך אתה להביא ד' רצועות של רוחב חצי אמה ואורך כל אחת ל"ב אמה שהן ס"ד ותשימם מבחוץ לאלו תשס"ח אמה עגולות תשים אותן ד' רצועות בריבוע ולא בעיגול ויבא החשבון שוה ומהיכן אתה נוטל אותן ס"ד אמה שאתה מחלק לד' רצועות של אורך ל"ב (אורך ל"ב) אמה ורוחב חצי אמה שאתה משים בריבוע מחוץ לעיגול זה מכאן אתה נוטלן לפי שחשבון תמני מאה ותלתין ותלתא ותילתא הוא עודף על ז' מאות וס"ח ששים וה' אמות ושליש אמה ומחשבון זה אינו חושב אותו שליש אמה שאינו דבר חשוב אלא ס"ה אמות חושב מס"ד אמות נעשה אותן ד' רצועות שארכן ל"ב ורחבן חצי אמה ואותה אמה חמישית הנשארת חלוק אותה לד' רביעי אמה ויהיה כל רביע חצי אמה אורך וחצי אמה רוחב ותן אלו ד' רבעין לד' הקרנות של רצועות למלאות הזויות והיינו דקאמר אכתי פש ליה לעולא פלגא דאמתא דבציר חשבונו מחשבון ג' אילנות והיינו דלא דק עולא ולחומרא לא דק שמחייב להביא ביכורים בפחות משיעור ברייתא של ג' אילנות. והא דלא חשבינן ההוא שליש אמה משום דאי

א) נראה דל"ל אבל לקולא לא דק מי אמרינן כיון דמגדיל וכו'. ב) אולי צ"ל מכל ד' צידי האילן:

מסורת הש"ס

א) [לקמן קא:] עירובין יד: ולקמן עו: נז. עט: סוכה ח. [אהלות פי"ב מ"ו]: ב) בכורים פ"א מי"א גיטין מח.: ג) לקמן פא. בכורים פ"א מ"ו [גיטין מח.]: ד) קדושין כו. פאה פ"ג מ"ו לקמן קנ.: ה) נ"ל ס"ה: ו) נ"ל ב"ד: ז) [נ"ל מביא ואינו קורא]: ח) [עי' תוס' קדושין כו. ועי' תי"ט ד"ה ובבכורים וכו' סתירת תוס' ע"ש]:

עין משפט נר מצוה

קב א ב מיי' פ"ב מהל' ביכורים הל' יג:

קג ג מיי' שם פ"ד הלכה ז:

קד ד מיי' שם פ"ב הלכה יג:

קה ה מיי' פ"ב מהל' מתנות עניים הל' ג:

קו ו מיי' פ"ט מהל' שמיטין הל' יט סמג לאוין רעא טוש"ע ח"מ סי' סז סעיף כב:

הגהות הב"ח

(א) גמ' בית סאה בשבילן עד עלגת כמה הוו: (ב) שם על העיגול רביע (פשו להו ז' מאה ושיתין ותמניא) תא"מ ונ"ב ר' משולם לא גרס לה: (ג) רש"י ד"ה וכמה מרובע וכו' דהשתא פשה ליה שיעורא דמתני': (ד) תוס' ד"ה הכי גרס ר"ת וכו' בספר אחר מפורש בגליון הספר וכו' עד שיהא רוחב החוט שני שלישי אמה: (ה) בא"ד הרי אורך התחתון פחות מן העליון:

ונקנין עמה נכסים שאין להם אחריות! הכא במאי עסקינן — בחיטי. דיקא נמי, דקתני: כל שהוא, ש"מ. ת"ש: א)באילן מקצתו בארץ ומקצתו בחו"ל — טבל וחולין מעורבין זה בזה, דברי רבי. ב)רבן שמעון בן גמליאל אומר: הגדל בחיוב — חייב, הגדל בפטור — פטור; ע"כ לא פליגי אלא דמר סבר: ג)יש ברירה, ומר סבר: אין ברירה, אבל גדל בפטור — דברי הכל פטור! (א) הכא במאי עסקינן — דמפסיק צונמא. אי הכי, מאי טעמיה דרבי? דהדרי ערבי; (ב) ובמאי קא מיפלגי — מר סבר: אוירא מבלבל, ומר סבר: האי לחודיה קאי והאי לחודיה קאי. ושש עשרה אמה ותו לא? והא תנן: ד)מרחיקין את האילן מן הבור כ"ה אמה! אמר אביי: מיזל טובא אזלי, אכחושי לא מכחשי אלא עד שש עשרה אמה, טפי לא מכחשי. כי אתא רב דימי אמר, בעא מיניה ריש לקיש מרבי יוחנן: אילן הסמוך למיצר בתוך י"ו אמה, מהו? אמר ליה: גזלן הוא, ואין מביאין ממנו בכורים. ה)כי אתא רבין אמר רבי יוחנן: גאחד אילן הסמוך למיצר, ואחד אילן הנוטה — מביא וקורא, שעל מנת כן הנחיל יהושע לישראל את הארץ.§ **מתני'** ו)דאילן שהוא נוטה לשדה חבירו — קוצץ מלא ז)המרדע על גבי המחרישה, ובחרוב ובשקמה — כנגד המשקולת, הבית השלחין — כל האילן כנגד המשקולת; אבא שאול אומר: כל אילן סרק כנגד המשקולת.§ **גמ'** איבעיא להו: אבא שאול, ארישא קאי או אסיפא קאי? תא שמע, דתניא: בית השלחין — אבא שאול אומר: כל האילן כנגד המשקולת, מפני שהצל רע לבית השלחין; שמע מינה ארישא קאי, שמע מינה. אמר רב אשי: מתניתין נמי דיקא, דקתני: כל אילן סרק; אי אמרת בשלמא ארישא קאי, היינו דקתני כל אילן, אלא אי אמרת אסיפא קאי, אילן סרק מיבעי ליה? אלא לאו שמע מינה ארישא קאי, שמע מינה.§ **מתני'** יאילן שהוא נוטה לרה"ר — קוצץ כדי שיהא גמל עובר ורוכבו; רבי יהודה אומר: גמל טעון פשתן או חבילי זמורות; רבי שמעון אומר: כל האילן כנגד המשקולת, מפני הטומאה.§ **גמ'** מאן תנא דבנזקין בתר אומדנא דהשתא אזלינן? אמר ר"ל: במחלוקת שנויה, ורבי אליעזר היא; דתנן: ח)אין עושין חלל תחת רשות הרבים, בורות, שיחין ומערות; רבי אליעזר מתיר בכדי שתהא עגלה מהלכת וטעונה אבנים. רבי יוחנן אמר: אפילו תימא רבנן, התם — ט)זימנין דמפחית ולאו אדעתיה, אבל הכא — קמא קמא קא קייץ ליה.§ ר' יהודה אומר: גמל טעון פשתן או חבילי זמורות".§ איבעיא להו: שיעורא דרבי יהודה נפיש, או דלמא שיעורא דרבנן נפיש? פשיטא דשיעורא דרבנן נפיש, דאי ס"ד שיעורא דרבי יהודה נפיש, רבנן בשיעורא דרבי יהודה היכי עבדי? ואלא מאי? שיעורא דרבנן נפיש, רבי יהודה בשיעורא דרבנן מאי עביד? אפשר דגחין וחליף תותיה.§ "רבי שמעון אומר: כל האילן כנגד המשקולת, מפני הטומאה".§ תנא: מפני אהל הטומאה. פשיטא, "מפני הטומאה" תנן! אי ממתניתין, הוה אמינא: דלמא מייתי עורב טומאה ושדי התם, (ג) וסגיא בדחלולי בעלמא, קא משמע לן.§

הדרן עלך לא יחפור

ונקנין עמה נכסים שאין להם אחריות. דתנן בקדושין (דף כו.): נכסים שאין להם אחריות נקנין עם נכסים שיש להם אחריות בכסף בשטר ובחזקה. שהמטלטלין אין נקנין אלא במשיכה, וקרקע נקנה בכסף. ואם מכר לו קרקע ומטלטלין יחד, כיון שנתן דמי הקרקע, או מסר לו שטר מכירת קרקע, או החזיק בקרקע מדעת מוכר – נקנו המטלטלין בלא משיכה, קתני מיהא: קרקע כל שהוא חייב בביכורים, וקס"ד ביכורי אילן קאמר. הכא במאי עסקינן בחטין. שכל ז' המינים חייבים בביכורים. מעורבין זה בזה. שאין סומכין על הברירה, לחלקו לחלאים ולומר שגדל הארץ חייבין ושגדל החוץ פטורין. אבל דכ"ע הגדל בפטור פטור. שאם היו כל שרשיו בחו"ל – פטור, ואפילו עומד האילן בתוך שש עשרה אמה לארץ, ולא אמרינן מן הארץ ינק. דמפסיק צונמא. באמצע שרשים, י) שאין שני לדדין יכולין לינק זה מזה. דהדרי וערבי. האילן נעשה אחד למעלה בעדיו. אוירא מבלבל. אע"פ שבתוך הקרקע (ד) כשני אילנות, הואיל ולמעלה באויר העולם נעשה אחד – מתערבין יונקותיו. כ"ה אמה. קשה לעולא, דאמר: י"ו אמה ותו לא. אכחושי לא מכחשי. בשדה חבירו אלא עד שיתסרי, הלכך טפי מהכי לאו גזלן הוא. הנוטה. נופו לתוך שדה של חבירו. שעל מנת כן הנחיל יהושע. התנה עמהם שלא יקפידו על כך. **מתני'** מרדע. מלמד בקר. קוצץ. הענפים עד גובה מלא מרדע, שלא יעכבוהו מלהוליך מחרשתו שם. החרוב והשקמה. שצילם מרובה וקשה לשדה. כנגד המשקולת. כל מה שנוטה לתוך שדהו. משקולת. חוט (ה) האמרכולין שבונין חומה, ותולין בה משקולת של אבר. ואם בית השלחין היא כל האילן. אפי' אינו חרוב ושקמה קוצץ כנגד המשקולת, שהצל רע לבית השלחין. אבא שאול אומר כו'. בגמ' מפרש אהייא קאי. **גמ'** ארישא קאי. דקאמר ת"ק: קוצץ מלא מרדע, ואפי' אילן סרק, חוץ מחרוב ושקמה. ואמר ליה אבא שאול: כל אילן סרק נמי כנגד המשקולת. או אסיפא קאי. דקאמר ת"ק: (ו) כל האילן כנגד המשקולת, ואפילו אילן העושה פירות. ואמר ליה אבא שאול: כל אילן סרק הוא דכנגד המשקולת, אבל אילן העושה פירות נמי – מלא מרדע ותו לא. כל האילן. כל האילנות. אי אמרת בשלמא ארישא קאי. ולטפויי אתא [מחרוב ושקמה דקאמר ת"ק] היינו דקאמר "כל". אלא אי אמרת אסיפא קאי. מאי "כל"? הא לגרועי אתא! **מתני'** אילן הנוטה לרשות הרבים קוצץ. מן הענפים התחתונות, כדי שיהא גמל עובר תחת העליונות. מפני הטומאה. מפרש בגמ'. **גמ'** בתר [אומדנא] דהשתא אזלינן. דקתני: קוצץ מן הענפים כדי שיהא גמל עובר ורוכבו. והרי חוזרין וגדלים לאחר זמן. כדי שתהא עגלה מהלכת. אם תקרתה חזקה כל כך – מותר, ואע"ג שסופה שתתליע ותפחת. קמא קמא קייץ ליה. כל ענף וענף שיקדים ויצמח יקצצנו. בשיעורא דרבי יהודה מאי עבדי ליה. כשילא גמל טעון פשתן היאך יעבור? מפני אהל הטומאה. שמא יפול כזית מת אצל האילן, והרי הענפים (ז) חרובים מאהילין עליו ועל עוברי הדרכים ומביאים עליהם את הטומאה. ושדי התם. על האילן, ומתוך שענפיו רבים הטומאה עומדת שם ואינה נופלת לארץ, ובני אדם עוברים תחתיה. ואי לא חיישינן אלא להכי – בדחלולי בעלמא סגי ליה, לקוץ אחד אחד מבינתים, כדי להרחיק אויר ביניהם ולא תעמוד שם טומאה. קמ"ל מתניתא, דאפילו לא נותר בו אלא ענף אחד – מזיק הוא את הרבים. **הדרן עלך לא יחפור**

בחטה. וא"ת: והא חטה יניקתה ג' טפחים, כדמוכח בשבת פרק "אמר ר"ע" בשמעתין דערוגה (דף פה.)! ואין לומר ד"כל שהוא" דהכא לאו דוקא, דהא בפ"ק דקדושין (דף כו.) קא מייתי לה בשמעתא דאי בעי לצורין בה או לאו, וקאמר: כל שהוא למאי חזי? ומשני: כגון שנעץ בה מחט. וקאמר: איכפל תנא לאשמועינן מחט? מי לא עסקינן דתלי ביה מרגניתא — משמע ד"כל שהוא" דוקא! וי"ל: דנהי דיניקתה ג', מ"מ עיקר יניקתה אינו אלא כנגדה. ואילן נמי, יניקתו כ"ה — אפ"ה עיקר יניקתו י"ו כ). **ואחד** אילן הנוטה מביא וקורא. בפרק "המקבל" (ב"מ דף קז. ושם) פליגי רב ושמואל באילן הנוטה על המיצר, רב אמר: הנוטה לכאן — לכאן, והנוטה לכאן — לכאן. ושמואל אמר: חולקין. ופירש בקונט' התם דבנטיית שרשים איירי, ולפיכך שמעתין הלכה כרב, דאזיל בתר שרשין. ורשב"א פירש שם בענין אחר. **שעל** מנת כן הנחיל יהושע וכו'. ב"מרובה" (ב"ק דף פב.) פריך: אמאי לא חשיב לה בהדי עשרה תנאין של יהושע? ומשני לה. **בדחלולי** סגי. פי' ר"ח: דחלולי — לשון יראה, שעושים צורה של עץ, ונראין כבני אדם, ואין העוף רשאי לישאר שם. קמ"ל, דאע"פ שברח העוף — פעמים שמשאיר שם בשר המת שמביא בפיו ונשאר שם בענף, הלכך אין לו תקנה אלא בקציצת ענפים כולם (ח).

הדרן עלך לא יחפור

קז א מיי' פ"ג מהל' מכירה הל' ח טוש"ע ח"מ סי' רב סעיף ז:
קח ב מיי' פ"ב מהל' תרומות הל' כב:
קט ג מיי' פ"ב מהל' ביכורים הל' יח:
קי ד ה מיי' פ"י מהל' שכנים הל' ח סמג עשין פב טוש"ע ח"מ סי' קנה סעיף כו:
קיא ו מיי' פי"ג מהל' נזקי ממון הל' כו סמג עשין סח טוש"ע ח"מ סי' תיז סעיף ד:

א) גיטין כב: ב) נדרים נט: ג) [עירובין ל: וש"נ], ד) [לעיל כה:] ה) כ"ק סב. ו) [לקמן פב:] ופי' כשיכול לחרוש ומרים המרדע להכות הבהמה שחורש בה לא יהיו ענפי האילן מעכבין אותו. ערוך ערך מרדע, ח) [לקמן ס:] [וש"נ], ט) ס"י שהלגרגין אין יכולין, כ) [וע"ע תוס' קדושין כו. ד"ה קרקע].

רבינו גרשום

בחטה. זרוע בתוכו וממנה מביא בכורים דלא אזלי שרשין כלום וליכא למימר דקא ינקי ממצר אחר: דיקא נמי. דבחטה עסקי' דקתני קרקע כל שהוא דאי באילן עסקינן לא סגיא בקרקע כל שהוא כלל ש"מ: אילן הנטוע על (שפת) [ספר] של ארץ ישראל מקצתו נוטה בארץ ומקצתו נוטה בחו"ל טבל וחולין מעורבין זה בזה דאותו הנוטה בארץ הוה ליה טבל ואותו הנוטה בחו"ל הוה ליה חולין ולאו בר עישורי נינהו ולהכי טבל וחולין מעורבין זה בזה ואסורין רשב"ג סבר א) משה"ה אמר הגדל בחיוב חייב משום דיש ברירה דיכול לברור איזה ענף נוטה בחו"ל ואיזה בארץ ורבי סבר אין ברירה מש"ה טבל וחולין מעורבין זה בזה ואסור אבל גדל בחיוב דכולה אילן היה בא"י אע"ג דאזלי שרשין בחו"ל וקא ינקי מחו"ל דברי הכל חייב דשדיין עיקרו בתר נופו וקשיא לעולא: דמפסיק צונמא. דלא קאזלי שרשין כלל בחוצה לארץ מפני הצונמא דמפסיק מש"ה דברי הכל חייב אבל אי לא מפסיק צונמא פטור מפני השרשין דקא ינקי מחוץ לארץ: אי הכי. דמפסיק צונמא בהא לימא רבי טבל וחולין מעורבין זה בזה ב) דאותו הנוטה בארץ הוי ליה טבל ואותו הנוטה בחו"ל הוי ליה חולין ולאו בר עישורי אינן (והא גדל כולו בארץ) ומשני דהדרי ערבי נופין ולמעלה מקצתן בארץ ומקצתן בחו"ל רבי סבר אויר ארץ ואויר חו"ל מבלבלן ולהכי טבל וחולין מעורבין זה בזה: מרחיקין את האילן ט"ז אמה ותו לא ורמינהו וכו'. מינק ינקי עד ט"ז אמה ואין מביא ממנו בכורים. ג) ור' יוחנן ס"ל בעולא אחד אילן הסמוך למצר חבירו וא' אילן הנוטה לתוך של חבירו מביא וקורא שעל מנת כן הנחיל יהושע לישראל את הארץ שזה חופר בתוך שלו וזה נוטע בתוך שלו: **פיסקא** קוצץ מלא מרדע על גבי המחרישה. שכשהוא עובר על גבי המחרישה והמרדע על כתיפו כל אותן הענפים שמעכבין לו קוצצין אותן שכנגד המחרישה: בחרוב ובשקמה. דאיכא תרתי לריעותא חדא דענפיו מרובים ומזיק לשדה ואין (שוין) פירותיהן חשובין: קוצץ כולו כנגד המשקולת. כל הענפים הנוטים לשדהו וקוצץ ממטה ועד למעלה כעין שיכול להוריד מלמעלה מן האילן ועד למטה קו המשקולת והולך שוה שאין שם עיכוב ענף: ואם בית השלחין היא. השדה דצריך לה מטר כל שעה להשקותה והצל רע לה קוצץ כל האילן בין עושה פרי בין אינו עושה כנגד המשקולת: אבא שאול אומר כל אילן סרק שאין בו פרי קוצץ כנגד המשקולת: איבעא להו. הא דקתני אבא שאול כל אילן סרק כנגד המשקולת ארישא דמתני' קאי דקתני בחרוב ובשקמה כנגד המשקולת ואמר אבא שאול כל אילן סרק קוצץ כנגד המשקולת ולא חרוב ושקמה משום דקא טעני פירות כל שהוא או אסיפא קאי דקתני בית השלחין כל האילן כנגד המשקולת בין אילן סרק ובין אילן פירות ואתא אבא שאול למימר כל אילן סרק כנגד המשקולת אפי' חרוב ושקמה דדמי לאילן סרק משום דאיכא תרתי לריעותא אבל אילן פרי אינו קוצץ כל עיקר אפי' בבי' השלחין: ת"ש אבא שאול אומר כל האילן כנגד המשקולת מפני שהצל רע לבית השלחין דמזקי ענפיו שאין יכול המטר לירד מש"ה קוצץ ש"מ הא דקתני במתני' כל אילן סרק כנגד המשקולת ארישא קאי דאתי לאפוקי חרוב ושקמה דאינו קוצץ משום דקא טעין פירא: אי אמרת בשלמא ארישא קאי היינו דקתני כל אילן סרק ולא חרוב ושקמה אלא אי אמרת אסיפא קאי וקאמר אילן סרק קוצץ ולא אילן פירות א"כ ל"ל למיתני כל אילן סרק אילן סרק מיבעי ליה למיתני (הכי) אבא שאול אומר אילן סרק כנגד המשקולת ולא כל האילן שעושה פרי אלא ש"מ מדקתני כל אילן סרק ארישא קאי ולחומרא דאתי לאפוקי חרוב ושקמה דאינו קוצץ דהיינו חומרא: **פיסקא** אילן הנוטה (לשדה חבירו) [לרשות הרבים] כו'. מאן תנא דלהיכא דאיכא נזק בתר אומדנא דהשתא אזלינן בתר נזק דשכיח ולא בתר נזק דעתיד למיתי: אמר ר"ל מחלוקת שנויה. במתני' אילן הנוטה ברה"ר קוצץ כדי שיהא הגמל עובר ברוכבו דאזלינן בתר היזק דהשתא ולא בתר דעתיד למיתי דאי אזלינן בתר העתיד מכל וכל צריך לקצצו דדלמא מגדלו וקא מזיק לרבים. ואליבא דר"א דאמר כדי שתהא עגלה מהלכת עליה וטעונה אבנים כלומר שתהא התקרה חזקה כדי שתהא יכולה לסבול עגלה טעונה אבנים אלמא דבנזקין אזלינן בתר אומדנא דהשתא ולא חייש דלמא היום או מחר מרקבת התקרה ונפלי בגווה אינשי דאזלי עלה. דזימנין דמפחית ולאו אדעתיה דלא מצי חזי ליה להכי קאמר אין עושין חלל. אבל הכא באילן דמתני' קמא קמא דמגדיל ומזיק חזי ליה וקוצץ ליה ולא צריך למיקציה קודם לכן: שיעור דרבנן נפיש. דמחייבי לקוץ כפי שיהא גמל ורוכבו עובר דאי שיעור דר' יהודה נפיש רבנן דלא בעו אלא שיעור גמל ורוכבו אותו שיעור דר' יהודה דנפיש היכי מצי עבר תותיה אלא ש"מ דרבנן נפיש ור' יהודה שיעור דרבנן דנפיש מאי עביד ליה. ומשני לעולם שיעור דרבנן נפיש ודקא קשיא לך ר' יהודה שיעור דרבנן מאי עביד ליה אפשר דגחין הרוכב מעל גמלו וחליף תותי אילן משא"כ בזמורות: מפני אהל טומאה. דזימנין דחליף להחתם מת תחת האילן וקא מאהיל עליה האילן וחליף כהן או מי שאוכל חולין בטהרה וקאי ליה באהל המת משו"ה קוצץ: פשיטא מפני טומאה תנן ומאי קא מוסיף תוספתא ומשני [דשפיר] מוסיף דאי ממתני' דאמר מפני טומאה אמינא היינו מפני טומאה דקתני זימנין דשדי עורב טומאה דמת להתם על גבי האילן ולא קא נפל לארעא ומש"ה צריך לקצוץ שלא יניח שם הטומאה על גבן (למד"א) ואין צריך לקצוץ האילן כנגד המשקולת אלא בדחלולי בעלמא סגי. כלומר שיקצוץ סביב הענפים ויקלוש אותם כדי שיהא חלול באויר כדי שלא יהא בכל האילן מקום עבה שיכול לעכב עליו הטומאה וכשתפול לארץ שלא תהא כנגדה על גבה שום סכך ובכך סגי קמ"ל תוספתא מפני אהל טומאה דזימנין שישאו תחתיו וקא מאהיל מש"ה קוצץ הכל כנגד המשקולת: **הדרן עלך לא יחפור**

א) נראה לחסר וצ"ל רשב"ג סבר הגדל בחיוב חייב והגדל בפטור פטור ומשו"ה אמר וכו'. ב) נראה דצ"ל טבל וחולין מעורבין זה בזה כיון דמפסיק צונמא אותו הנוטה וכו'. ג) לכאורה נראה דצ"ל ורבין אמר ר"י דלא ס"ל כעולא אלא אחד וכו':

הגהות הב"ח (א) גמ' הכא במאי עסקינן. נ"ב תימה הס"ל להקשות ממשנה ד' פ"ג דמעשרות לאילן העומד עיקרו בחו"ל פטור ממעשר וק"ל: (ב) שם דהדרי ערבי ובהא קא מיפלגי: (ג) שם ושדי התם ובדחלולי בעלמא סגיא קמ"ל: (ד) רש"י ד"ה אוירא וכו' הקרקע הם כשני: (ה) ד"ה משקולת חוט האמרכלין שבונין: (ו) ד"ה או אסיפא וכו' ת"ק כל האילן: (ז) ד"ה מפני אהל וכו' הענפים החרובים מאהילין: (ח) תוס' ד"ה ובדחלולי וכו' ענפים כולם כנגד המשקולת הס"ד: